WHY IS *JOY OF COOKING* THE BESTSELLING COOKBOOK OF ALL TIME?

Because it is the all-purpose cookbook that includes a complete range of recipes in every category: everyday, classic, foreign, and de luxe. JOY OF COOKING is the one indispensable cookbook, the foundation of many a happy kitchen and many a happy home.

Because everything needed for the success of the recipe is clearly explained and the information can be found at the point of use.

"For anyone with a limited knowledge of pots and pans but with an earnest desire to cook for pleasure I would recommend JOY OF COOKING by Irma S. Rombauer and Marion Rombauer Becker. It is a masterpiece of clarity...."

—*Craig Claiborne, Author,*
NEW YORK TIMES COOKBOOK

"JOY OF COOKING is a textbook for the new homemakers and a good old standby for those who have been building their culinary reputation on it since the first edition."

—*Joan Nilson,*
CHRISTIAN SCIENCE MONITOR

"JOY OF COOKING is fast becoming an institution almost as essential as the kitchen range."

—*Clementine Paddleford,*
THIS WEEK FOOD EDITOR

JOY OF COOKING

Irma S. Rombauer
Marion Rombauer Becker

Illustrated by Ginnie Hofmann and Beverly Warner

A PLUME BOOK

NEW AMERICAN LIBRARY

NEW YORK AND SCARBOROUGH, ONTARIO

DEDICATION

In revising and reorganizing "The Joy of Cooking" we have missed the help of my mother, Irma S. Rombauer. How grateful I am for her buoyant example, for the strong feeling of roots she gave me, for her conviction that, well-grounded, you can make the most of life, no matter what it brings! In an earlier away-from-home kitchen I acted as tester and production manager for the privately printed first edition of "The Joy." Working with Mother on its development has been for my husband, John, and for me the culmination of a very happy personal relationship. John has always contributed verve to this undertaking, but during the past ten years he has, through his constant support and crisp creative editing, become an integral part of the book. We look forward to a time when our two boys— and their wives—will continue to keep "The Joy" a family affair, as well as an enterprise in which the authors owe no obligation to anyone but themselves—and you.

MARION ROMBAUER BECKER

*"That which thy fathers have bequeathed to thee,
earn it anew if thou wouldst possess it."*

Goethe: Faust

FOREWORD AND GUIDE

"The cook," said Saki, "was a good cook, as cooks go; and as cooks go, she went." Indeed she did go, leaving us, whether in charge of established or of fledgling families, to fend for ourselves. We are confident that after you have used this book steadily for a few months, paying due attention to our symbols *, ▲, ( ), ☺, ⅄, ▤, ★, and to our "pointers to success" ♦—as identified at the end of the Foreword—you will master the skills the cook walked off with. What is more, we believe that you will go on to unexpected triumphs, based on the sound principles which underlie our recipes, and actually revel in a sense of new-found freedom. You will eat at the hour of your choice. The food will be cooked and seasoned to your discriminating taste. And you will regain the priceless private joy of family living, dining and sharing.

For a number of years, manuscript in hand, I have lunched with friends to whom the preparation and presentation of food is a major interest. At these meetings this text, as it grew, came in for lively critical evaluation. I wish you could have been part of the proceedings, as the chefs, food chemists, processors and artists piled in on the problems which arose, searching for the simplest, the most practical and the most comprehensive approaches to this fresh version of "The Joy," and pored over our new illustrations.

The nucleus of this group included Chef James E. Gregory, American-trained and French-finished, with his flair for making food as appetizing to look at as it is delicious, and Chef Pierre Adrian, at whose restaurant we gathered. Pierre grew up in the Vosges, and has a down-to-earth understanding of food as it comes from the land, coupled with a mastery of the *haute cuisine*.

Other "regulars" were Lolita Harper who, as chief home economist for Cincinnati's utility company, has made a career of rescuing frantic housewives from one dilemma after another; and Luella Schierland, a well-traveled, knowledgeable and skilled hostess. Always present through their handiwork, and sometimes in person, were Ginnie Hofmann and Beverly Warner, whose sensitive response to our layouts resulted in the spirited drawings which make our cooking techniques come alive.

What fun we have had talking out and resolving culinary questions—which I brought back for further scrutiny to the staff at home: to Jane Brueggeman who headed it, and whose unerring common sense and devotion have been invaluable; to Dorothy Wartenberg, our consultant for the English edition; and to Odessa Whitehead, who kept the stove warm and the kitchen bright.

As you can guess, we are also indebted to uncounted friends and "fans" of "The Joy," and to any number of technical consultants, both private and governmental, who have given generously of their time, experience and special competence. Of course, any expression of indebtedness does not discharge us from responsibility for the entire contents of the book—a responsibility which rests with Mother and me as its sole authors.

We have assumed that in buying this book you intend to use it daily. For this reason every effort has been made, space permitting, to provide information at the point of use. Whenever emphasis is needed, when an important principle is involved, we have inserted a "pointer." "Pointers" are vital, friendly reminders which guide you through more exacting processes—beating egg whites, heating delicate food over—not in—hot water, the proper temperatures for holding and storage.

There are also the seven other graphic symbols mentioned in the first paragraph. Among these we have retained from the previous edition the parentheses to indicate that an ingredient is optional: its use may enhance, but its omission will not prejudice, the success of a recipe.

You will notice too that we have attached to certain words, phrases and categories special meanings. For example, any meat, fish, or cereal, unless otherwise specified, is *raw*, not cooked. Again, eggs are the 2-ounce size; milk means fresh whole milk; butter means sweet, unsalted butter; chocolate means bitter baking chocolate; flour denotes the all-purpose variety; spices are ground, not whole; condensed canned soup or milk is to be used undiluted. Recipes which have the word "BLENDER" in their title are only successful when an electric blender is used. Many dishes made with cooked, canned and frozen cooked food are grouped in the chapter BRUNCH, LUNCH AND SUPPER DISHES.

Also, for greater clarity, we define culinary terms for which there are no generally accepted meanings: see the Index for "parboil," "simmer," and "casserole." Finally, in response to many requests from users of "The Joy" who ask "What are your favorites?", we have added to some of our recipes the word "Cockaigne", which signified in medieval times "a mythical land of peace and plenty," and also happens to be the name of our country home.

There are two other parts of the book with which we hope you will quickly acquaint yourself: KNOW YOUR INGREDIENTS, and THE FOODS WE HEAT. Both are brand new. INGREDIENTS will tell you in detail about the properties of the materials you commonly combine in cooking, how and why they react as they do and, when feasible, how to substitute for them. To us, the chapter on HEAT is one of the most important. When you become familiar with its contents you will understand why we assign a high priority to it. And do read the ABOUTS for special information.

We have tried to correlate the entire text so that you can readily find your way around in it. But, as in the past, we have kept in mind the tremendous importance of a detailed Index. Not the least of its virtues is the stimulus it gives to the cook's aspiring eye.

New, too, in this edition is a far more conscious emphasis on interpreting the classic cuisine—those dishes whose circulation is worldwide, and whose traditional language, like that of love and diplomacy, is French. We propose clearing up once and for all the distinctions between terms like *printanière, bonne femme, bordelaise, allemande,* and *polonaise,* while giving at the same time authentic descriptions of such national culinary enthusiasms as *couscous,* Devonshire cream, *strudel, zabaglione* and *rijsttafel.* Actually, the experienced cook will recognize many of these exotics as intimates whom she has known for years in her own kitchen under other names.

Ever since the last revision, a decade ago, we have been refashioning "The Joy" into a handbook which will more faithfully and flexibly meet your needs. How do we know these needs? From the hundreds and hundreds of heart-warming letters which have set out in detail your own experiences with our book, and reflected new tastes and trends in American living. Many of your messages reflected not only the revolution in transport which has made available distant and previously unobtainable foods, but showed a reawakened interest in the cookery of far-off lands.

Most important to us are all of you, both at home and abroad, who are pre-occupied every day with that old yet ever-new question, "What shall we have for dinner?" This revision, we hope, is the inclusive and effective answer.

WATCH FOR THESE SYMBOLS

▶ POINTERS TO SUCCESS

❄ FROZEN FOODS

( ) OPTIONAL

✪ PRESSURE COOKING

⅄ BLENDER

▤ OUTDOOR COOKING

★ CHRISTMAS

▲ ALTITUDE COOKING

CONTENTS

THE FOODS WE EAT

We enjoy the cynical story of the old-fashioned doctor who insisted first on going straight to the kitchen of the afflicted household. Not until he had effusively thanked the cook for giving him a new patient did he dash upstairs to see how he could relieve the cook's victim. The fact is that everyone who runs a kitchen can, in the choice and preparation of food, decisively influence family health and happiness.

Nutrition is concerned not with food as such but with the substances that food contains. To present these essential nutrients in the very best state for the body's absorption is the cook's first and foremost job. Usually taste, flavor and color, at their best, reflect a job well done. Read The Foods We Heat, and follow our pointers ◗ for effective ways to preserve nutrients during cooking.

To live we must eat. To live in health we must eat intelligently. By whose intelligence? How directed? The intuitions and impulses of the present generation seem, alas, not to be the kind that led our forebears to search for greens each spring. The sensational press releases which follow the discovery of fascinating fresh bits and pieces about human nutrition confuse the layman. And the oversimplified and frequently ill-founded dicta of food faddists can lure us into downright harm.

On the positive, scientific side we may turn to the helpful information contained in the United States Handbook on the Composition of Foods. For further guidance we print later in this book the daily allowances recommended by the Food and Nutrition Board of the National Research Council as well as calorie values based on the edible portion of common foods. All three are extremely helpful in alerting us to the source-material of a sound dietary. But no one chart or group of charts is the definitive answer for most of us, who are simply not equipped to evaluate the complex relationships of these elements, or to adapt them to the practicalities of daily living. Such studies are built up as averages, and thus have greater value in presenting an overall picture than in solving the nutrition problem of the individual.

Nevertheless, by applying plain common sense to available mass data, we, as well as the experts, are inclined to agree that most Americans are privileged to enjoy superabundance ◗ and that our nutritional difficulties have to do generally not with under- but overeating. Statistics on consumption also bear out other trends: first, that we eat too much of certain kinds of food; and, second, that many of us over-consume drugs as well as foods. Medication, often a lifesaver, may, when used habitually, induce an adverse effect on the body's ability to profit fully from even the best dietary intake.

We must consider, too, that while great strides have been made in the keeping of foods, page 744, many of today's additives and preserving processes have a devitalizing effect on them. ◗ If fresh foods are available, and in their prime, start with fresh foods every time. For the relative nutritive values in frozen, canned and dried vegetables, see page 251.

ABOUT CALORIES

With these thoughts in mind, let's review other changing attitudes that underlie today's thinking about nutrition. A too naive theory used to prevail for explaining regeneration through food. The human system was thought of as an engine, and you kept it stoked with foods to produce energy. Food can be and still is measured in units of heat, or calories, a Calorie being the amount of heat needed to raise one kilogram of water one degree Centigrade. Thus translated into food values, each gram of protein—egg, milk, meat, fish—is worth four calories; each gram of carbohydrate—starches and sugars—four calories; and each gram of fat—butters, vegetable oils, drippings, etc.—about nine. The mere stoking of the body's engine with energy-producing foods may keep life going in emergencies. But food, to maintain health, must also have, besides its energy values, the proper proportions of biologic values. Proteins, vitamins, enzymes, hormones, minerals and their regulatory functions are still too complicated to be fully understood. But fortunately for us the body is able to respond to them intuitively and instantly.

What we really possess, then, is not just a simple stoking mechanism, but a computing setup far more elaborate and knowledgeable than anything that man has been able to devise. The body sorts and routes nutrients on their way as soon as they are ingested. Our job is to help it along as much as possible, neither stinting it nor overloading it. Depending on age, weight and activity the following is a rough guide to the favorable division of daily caloric intake: about 15% for proteins, under 25% for fats and about 60% for carbohydrates.

ABOUT PROTEINS

A greater and greater emphasis has been placed in recent years on the need for protein at all ages—for proteins contain a great many of the essential elements the body must have to rebuild itself. Proteins are complexly constructed of amino acids, some of which the body can and some of which it cannot manufacture from other substances. So to make food really useful to the body we must include in every meal or snack some of those protein foods that have the non-manufacturable amino acids already built into them. These are present in the most favorable proportions in eggs, milk, meat and fish. They are also present in nuts, seeds, whole grains and legumes. But in such vegetable foods some of the essential aminos are either lacking entirely or are not available in satisfactory proportions. This is why pork is often served with beans, and why pastas are reenforced with cheese, meat or fish—to provide those essential aminos in which the vegetable content of the dish is deficient. Again, complete reliance on grain protein combinations is not nearly as satisfactory as one based on egg, milk, meat and fish; partly because such large quantities of the grain must be consumed to amass enough proteins whose biologic values approach animal-derived proteins in strength. Climate and age also change protein requirements. The colder the climate the greater the need. ♦ And no matter what the climate, growing children, pregnant women and nursing mothers need a larger proportion of protein than the average adult.

The need in everyone, from birth to death, to establish a kind of "endless chain" of protein intake persists. ♦ Since the vegetable proteins are incomplete, it is wise to draw two-thirds of the daily protein intake from animal sources. Meats should preferably be fresh, not pickled, salted or highly processed. Protein foods should also be very carefully cooked at not too high heat, so that their values are not impaired. Familiar danger signals are curdling in milk, "stringiness" in cheese, dryness in meat and fish.

ABOUT FATS

While fats have fallen into disrepute of late, we must not forget how essential they are. As parts of our body fabric ♦ they act as fuel and insulation against cold, as cushioning for the internal organs, and as lubricants. Without fats there is no way to utilize fat-soluble vitamins. Furthermore the fats we eat which are of vegetable origin contain unsaturated fatty acids which harbor necessary growth factors, and help with the digestion of other fats. For more about the character of fats and their use, see page 508.

♦ We suggest, again, the consumption of a variety of fats from animal and vegetable sources; but remind you that the fat consumption of the United States has climbed in twenty years from the recommended minimum of 20 per cent to over 40 per cent today. Check your diet for the percentage you are getting, taking into account that ♦ there are hidden fats in food —as discussed in greater detail on page 508.

All fats are sensitive to high temperatures, light and air. For best nutritive values store them carefully; and when cooking with them be sure that you do not let them reach the smoking point. If properly handled they have no adverse effect on normal digestion. Favorable temperatures are indicated in individual recipes. Fats are popular for their flavor, and for the fact that, being slow to leave the stomach, they give a feeling of satiety.

ABOUT CARBOHYDRATES

Vegetables and fruits are included in the carbohydrate category, as well as flour, cereals and sugars. The caloric value of fruits and vegetables is frequently lower than that of cereals; while that of all concentrated sweets is high. It is possible for children and athletes to consume larger amounts of sugars and starches with less harm than more inactive people; but most of us tend to eat a greater amount of carbohydrates than we can handle. Our consumption of sweet and starchy foods, to say nothing of highly sweetened beverages, is frequently excessive. The imbalance that results is acknowledged to be one of the major causes of malnutrition, for the demands excess carbohydrates make on the system may cause a deficiency in its supply of the vitamin B complex.

ABOUT ACCESSORY FACTORS IN FOOD

There are some forty-odd important known minerals, vitamins, enzymes, hormones and other accessory factors which the body needs from the diet. A few it can store; but many must constantly be replaced. These latter, like vitamin C, often occur in those fragile food constituents that are lost through indifferent handling, excessive processing, and poor cooking. To retain as many of them as possible please follow the cooking suggestions given in the chapters on vegetables, meats, fish, eggs and cereals.

While we have printed below the average daily caloric needs, and we have discussed their approximate distribution, we have still to assure ourselves a practical way of including optimal amounts of accessory factors. If you check prime sources of minerals and vitamins you will find that foods rich in one vitamin or mineral may also be rich in others. It happens too that some foods heavily weighted with biologic values yield the best quality proteins. Many of the foods rich in accessory values also have bulk, a factor to be considered in planning the daily intake so as to include more high- than low-residue foods. A few accessory factors the body can store—

such as the fat soluble vitamins A, D, E and K. Some, like the water-soluble C and B-complex, must be replenished constantly.

Here is a shopping guide for accessory factors. ▶ Fill your market basket so that it holds a minimum of 2 fruits and 3 vegetables daily. Concentrate on salad materials, especially the lively green ones, and on green and yellow vegetables. Cultivate the cabbage family, root vegetables, potatoes and especially sweet potatoes, tomatoes, peppers and avocados. Include in the fruits apricots, peaches and melons, as well as plenty of citrus types. Be on your guard in distinguishing genuine fruit juices from the so-called "juice drinks," for many of the latter are higher in carbohydrate values than anything else, and their C-vitamin values are frequently low. Prime choices in the protein budget are milk, cheese and eggs, fish and fish roe, organ meats such as liver, kidneys, heart and brains, lean-muscle cuts of beef, pork and lamb, dried peas and beans, especially soybeans and peanuts. See triple-rich Cornell Flour Formula, page 556. Include also 1 tablespoon daily of butter or fortified fat or oil, and 1 pint of milk or equivalent milk products. Bake with whole grains and flavor with brown sugar, molasses, wheat germ and butter. Don't forget the cheapest of all accessory factors, outdoor exercise, to whet your appetite, tone your muscles and get you out where you absorb the sunlight vitamin D.

Other incidentals to bear in mind are to drink seven or eight glasses of fluid a day, see About Water, page 493, and to use iodized salt, see About Salt, page 524, if you live in a region that calls for it.

The schedule outlined above is not necessarily a costly one. It is nearly always possible to substitute cheaper but equally nutritious items from the same food groups. Vegetables of similar accessory value, for example, may be differently priced. Seasonal foods, which automatically give us menu variations, are usually higher in food value and lower in cost. Whole-grain cereals are no more costly than highly processed ones. Fresh fruits are frequently less expensive than canned fruits loaded with sugar.

If you are willing to cut down on refined starch and sugar items, especially fancy baked goods, bottled drinks and candies, a higher percentage of the diet dollar will be released for dairy products, vegetables and fruits. Do not buy more perishable foods than you can properly store. Use leftovers cold, preferably. To reheat them with minimal loss, see page 139.

Summing up, our fundamental effort always must be to provide this highly versatile body of ours with those elements it needs for efficient functioning, and to provide them in such proportions as to subject it to the least possible strain.

Well-grown minimally processed foods are usually our best sources for complete nourishment; and a well-considered choice of them should in most cases meet our needs without the use of synthetic vitamin preparations.

You will find in this book, along with the classic recipes, a number which remain interesting and palatable although they lack some usual ingredient, like eggs, flour or fat, and which may be used by those who may be allergic. But we do not prescribe corrective diets, feeling that such situations demand special procedures in consultation with one's physician. As to the all-too-prevalent condition of overweight, it is now generally recognized that the on and off use of crash reducing diets is dangerous, and that a re-education in moderate eating habits is the only safe and permanent solution to this problem.

We stress again that the housewife who has the responsibility for supplying her family with food do well to keep alert to advances in the field of nutrition and to the individual needs of herself and her family.

CALORIE VALUES

"Personal size and mental sorrow have certainly no necessary proportions. A large, bulky figure has as good a right to be in deep affliction as the most graceful set of limbs in the world. But, fair or not fair, there are unbecoming conjunctions, which reason will patronize in vain—which taste cannot tolerate—which ridicule will seize." —Jane Austen.

The following calorie list is given hopefully to offset those "unbecoming conjunctions." We have tried, from data furnished by the U.S. Department of Agriculture and other authoritative sources, to give you as accurate a calorie count as possible for an average individual serving of food as it comes to you at table. In each instance, the number of calories is based on the total edible portion. These are not diet portions. Smaller servings of the foods mentioned will mean a proportionate reduction in their calorie count. Our soup figures are for canned soups diluted with the same amount of water—or whole milk, in the case of cream soups—unless we specify them as home-made. A cup is the standard 8 oz. measure, and a tablespoon or teaspoon is always a level one. Since we do not expect you to weigh your food at table, this chart should give you a fairly accurate guide for normal servings to a healthy adult. Remember, however, that two martinis before dinner count as much as a generous slice of pie for dessert and, if you are trying to keep your weight constant, second thoughts are better than second helpings. In addition, "Let your contours be your guide."

Food	Calories
Almonds, 12 to 14 shelled	100
Apple, 1 medium-sized, baked with 2 tablespoons sugar	200
Apple, 1 large fresh, 3″ diam.	117
Apple butter, 1 tablespoon	37
Apple dumpling, 1 medium-sized	235
Apple juice, 1 cup	126
Apple pie, ⅙ of 9″ pie	377
Applesauce, sweetened, ½ cup	92
Applesauce, unsweetened, ½ cup	50
Apricots, canned, sweetened, 4 halves, 2 tablespoons juice	80
Apricots, dried, stewed, sweetened, 4 halves, 2 tablespoons juice	123
Apricots, 3 whole fresh	60
Artichoke, globe, 1 large, cooked	51
Artichoke, Jerusalem, 4 small	70
Asparagus, 8 stalks	25
Asparagus soup, cream of, 1 cup	160
Avocado, ½ medium-sized	275
Bacon, 1 crisp 6″ strip	48
Banana, 1 medium-sized	130
Banana cream pie, ⅙ of 9″ pie	300
Batter cakes, 2	150
Beans, baked, canned, ½ cup	162
Beans, green or snap, ½ cup cooked	13
Beans, kidney, ½ cup cooked	115
Beans, Lima, ½ cup cooked or canned	80
Beans, navy pea, ½ cup cooked	118
Bean soup, 1 cup, home-made	260
Bean sprouts, Mung, ½ cup cooked	13
Bean sprouts, ½ cup raw	10
Beef, corned, 3 oz., 3 slices 3″ x 2½″ x ¼″	216
Beef, corned, hash, ½ cup	145
Beef, dried, 2 thin slices 4″ x 5″	61
Beef, 1 filet mignon, 4 oz.	400
Beef, hamburger, 1 large patty	300
Beef heart, 3 oz.	118
Beef loaf, 1 slice 2½″ x 2¼″ x ⅝″	115
Beef, rib roast, 3″ x 2½″ x ¼″ slice	96
Beef soup, 1 cup	113
Beefsteak, sirloin, 3 oz.	300
Beef stew, 1 cup	260
Beef tongue, 3 slices, 3″ x 2″ x ⅛″	160
Beer, 12 oz. can or bottle	173
Beer, 1 glass, 8 oz.	115
Beet greens, ½ cup cooked	30
Beets, ½ cup	40
Berry pies, ⅙ of 9″ pie, average	365
Biscuit, baking powder, 2½″ diam.	130
Blackberries, fresh, ¾ cup	62
Blueberries, fresh, ¾ cup	64
Bologna sausage, 1 slice, 4½″ diam. x ⅛″	66
Bouillon, 1 cup	32
Bouillon cube, 1	2
Brazil nut, 1 shelled	50
Bread, commercial, rye, 1 slice, ½″ thick	55
Bread, commercial, white, 1 slice, ½″ thick	60-65
Bread, commercial, whole wheat, 1 slice, ½″ thick	55

Food	Calories
Bread, gluten, 1 slice, 4″ x 4″ x ⅜″	64
Bread pudding, ½ cup	200
Broccoli, 1 large stalk or ⅔ cup, cooked	29
Brown Betty, ½ cup	254
Brussels sprouts, ½ cup, approx. 5	30
Butter, 1 square, ¼″ thick	50
Butter, 1 tablespoon	100
Buttermilk, 1 glass, 8 oz.	85
Cabbage, ½ cup chopped, raw	10
Cabbage, ½ cup, cooked	20
Cake, angel, plain, 3″ slice	150
Cake, cheese, 2″ wedge	250
Cake, chocolate layer, 2″ square	356
Cake, coffee, 1 piece 3″ x 2½″ x 2″	133
Cake, cup, 1 medium-sized, frosted	229
Cake, fruit, dark, 1 small slice ½″ thick	142
Cake, sponge, 2″ slice	145
Cantaloupe, ½ of a 4½″ melon	30
Caramels, 1 medium	42
Carbonated water	0
Carrots, ½ cup cooked	30
Carrot, 1 whole raw, small	20
Cashew nuts, 6 to 8	88
Catsup, 1 tablespoon	17
Cauliflower, cooked, 1 cup	30
Caviar, granular sturgeon, 1 tablespoon	66
Celeriac, 1 medium-sized	40
Celery, raw, 3 small inner stalks	9
Charlotte Russe, 1 serving	265
Cheese, American, 1″ cube	79
Cheese, Camembert, 2″ wedge	220
Cheese, cottage, ½ cup	100
Cheese, cream, ½ 3 oz. cake	159
Cheese, Edam, 1″ cube	51
Cheese, Liederkranz, 1 oz.	85
Cheese, Parmesan, 1 tablespoon, grated	20
Cheese, Roquefort, 1″ cube	39
Cheese, Swiss, 1 oz.	105
Cheese soufflé, 1 cup	238
Cheese straws, 3	100
Chef salad without dressing, ¾ cup	90
Cherries, canned, sweetened, ½ cup	100
Cherries, fresh, sweet, 15 large	61
Chicken, broiler, ½ medium	125
Chicken, canned, ½ cup boned meat	200
Chicken, fried, ½ breast	232
Chicken, fried, drumstick	64
Chicken livers, 1 medium-large liver	74
Chicken pie, 1 individual pie 3¾″ diameter	460
Chicken, roasted, 4″ x 4″ x ¾″ slice, dark meat	170
Chicken, roasted, 4″ x 4″ x ¾″ slice, light meat	166
Chicken salad, ½ cup	200
Chicory, or Curly Endive, 15 to 20 inner leaves	10
Chocolate, 1 cup made with milk	277
Chocolate bar, milk, 1 oz.	154
Chocolate creams, 1 small	51
Chocolate éclair, custard filling, 1 average-size	316

Food	Calories
Chocolate fudge, 1″ square	100
Chocolate ice cream, ½ cup	180
Chocolate malted milk, made with 8 oz. milk	502
Chocolate milk shake, made with 8 oz. milk	421
Chocolate soda	255
Cinnamon bun, 1 average	200
Clam chowder, Manhattan, 1 cup	87
Cocoa, made with milk and water, 1 cup	150
Cocoa, made with whole milk, 1 cup	232
Coconut, shredded, dried, 2 tablespoons	83
Coconut custard pie, ⅙ of 9″ pie	311
Codfish, creamed, ½ cup	200
Codfish balls, 2 of 2″ diameter	200
Cod liver oil, 1 tablespoon	100
Coffee, clear, 1 cup	0
Coffee, with 1 tablespoon cream, 1 cup	30
Coffee with 1 lump sugar, 1 cup	27
Cola beverages, 1 glass, 8 oz.	105
Consommé, canned, 1 cup	35
Cookies, sugar, 1 3″ diameter	64
Corn bread, 1 square 2″ x 2″ x 1″	139
Corn, canned, ½ cup drained solids	70
Corn flakes, ¾ cup	62
Corn meal, cooked, ⅔ cup	80
Corn on cob, 1 medium	92
Corn sirup, 1 tablespoon	57
Corn soup, cream, ½ cup	100
Cornstarch blancmange, ½ cup	152
Crab meat, canned, ½ cup	91
Crab meat fresh, ½ cup	54
Cracker, graham, 1 2½″ square	14
Crackers, oyster, 12 1″	50
Cracker, saltine, 1 2″ square	17
Cracker, soda, 1 2½″ square	24
Cracker, butter, 1	16
Cranberry jelly, 2 tablespoons	47
Cream, coffee, 18.5% fat, 2 tablespoons	60
Cream, cultured, sour, 1 tablespoon	45
Cream soups, canned	250
Cream, whipping, 36%-40% fat, 2 tablespoons	98
Cream of wheat, cooked, ¾ cup	100
Cream sauce, white, ¼ cup	180
Cucumber, 12 slices	10
Custard, ½ cup	164
Custard pie, ⅙ of 9″ pie	266
Daiquiri cocktail, 3 oz.	130
Dates, 3 or 4	85
Divinity, 1½″ cube	102
Doughnut, cake type, plain, 1	135
Doughnut, sugared, 1	151
Doughnut, yeast, plain, 1	121
Duck, roast, 1 medium piece	300
Dumpling, 1 small	100
Egg, 1 fried with 1 teaspoon butter	105
Egg, 1 scrambled with 2 tablespoons milk and 1 teaspoon butter	130
Egg, 1 whole, boiled or poached	75
Eggnog, ½ cup	196

Food	Calories
Eggplant, 2 slices ½″ thick, breaded and fried	210
Egg yolk, 1 raw	61
Farina, ¾ cup cooked	100
Fig, 1 large dried	55
Figs, 3 small fresh	79
Flounder, baked, average serving	204
Frankfurters, 1	125
French dressing, commercial, 1 tablespoon	59
French dressing, home-made, no sugar, 1 tablespoon	86
French toast, 1 piece	170
Frog legs, 2 large, fried	140
Fruit cocktail, fresh, ½ cup	50
Fruit cocktail, canned, drained, ½ cup	50
Fruit cocktail, fresh, with 1 tablespoon dressing	150
Gelatin, dry, 1 tablespoon	34
Gelatin dessert, ½ cup	103
Gin, 1 oz.	70
Ginger ale, 1 cup	80
Gingerbread, 1 2″ square	200
Ginger snap, 1	20
Goose, roast, 3½ oz. serving	354
Gooseberries, cooked, sweetened, ½ cup	100
Grapefruit, ½ medium	70
Grapefruit juice, unsweetened, 1 cup	92
Grape juice, 1 glass, 8 oz.	178
Grapes, green seedless, 60	66
Grapes, Malaga or Tokay, 22	66
Gravy, thick, 3 tablespoons	180
Green pepper, 1 whole	20
Griddle cakes, 2 of 4″ diam.	150
Grits, hominy, cooked, ¾ cup	90
Guavas, 1 medium	70
Gum drop, 1 large	35
Haddock, 1 fillet 3″ x 3″ x ½″, fried	214
Halibut steak, 3″ x ½″ x 1″, sautéed	125
Ham, baked, medium fat, 4¼″ x 4″ x ½″ slice	400
Ham, boiled, 4¼″ x 4″ x ¼″ slice	200
Hamburger—see Beef	
Hard Sauce, 1 tablespoon	50
Herring, fresh, 3 oz.	128
Herring, pickled Bismarck, 3½″ x 1½″ x 1¼″	218
Herring, smoked, 3 oz.	200
Hickory nuts, about 12	100
Hollandaise sauce, 1 tablespoon	65
Honey, 1 tablespoon	62
Honeydew melon, ¼ medium-sized	32
Horseradish, grated, 1 tablespoon	12
Ice cream, commercial, plain, ½ cup	100-150
Jam or jelly, 1 tablespoon	60
Kale, 1 cup, cooked	50
Kidneys, beef, braised, 3 ½ oz.	159

Food	Calories
Kohlrabi, ½ cup, cooked	23
Kumquats, 3	35
Lady fingers, 1	37
Lamb, roast leg, 2 slices	
3″ x 3¼″ x ⅛″	206
Lamb chop, broiled, 1 ¾″ thick	175
Lamb stew with vegetables, 1 cup	250
Lard, 1 tablespoon	126
Leek, 1	10
Lemon, 1 medium-sized	30
Lemonade, 1 cup	100
Lemon gelatin, ½ cup	100
Lemon ice, ½ cup	116
Lemon juice, 1 tablespoon	4
Lemon meringue pie, ⅙ of 9″ pie	280
Lentil soup, 1 cup, home-made	606
Lettuce, iceberg, ¼ large head	18
Lettuce, 6 large leaves	18
Lime juice, 1 tablespoon	4
Liver, beef, fried, 2 slices	
3″ x 2¼″ x ⅜″	175
Liver, calf, fried, 2 slices	
3″ x 2¼″ x ⅜″	147
Liverwurst or liver sausage, 2 slices	
3″ diam. x ¼″	160
Lobster, canned, 1 cup	108
Lobster, fresh, 1 cup	105
Lobster, whole, small, baked or	
broiled with 2 tablespoons butter	308
Loganberries, canned, ½ cup	55
Macaroni, cooked, plain, ½ cup	110
Macaroni and cheese, ½ cup	300
Mackerel, broiled, 3 oz.	200
Malted milk, 8 oz.	270
Mangoes, tropical, 1 large	85
Manhattan cocktail, 3 oz.	160
Maple sirup, 1 tablespoon	50
Margarine, 1 tablespoon	100
Marmalade, 2 tablespoons	120
Marshmallows, 5	125
Martini cocktail, 3 oz. 3:1	145
Mayonnaise, 1 tablespoon	109
Meat loaf, beef and pork, 1 slice	
4″ x 3″ x ⅜″	264
Melba toast, 1 slice 4″ x 4″	39
Milk, condensed, sweetened, ½ cup	490
Milk, evaporated, ½ cup	173
Milk, half and half, ½ cup	165
Milk, powdered, skim, 1 tablespoon	28
Milk, powdered, whole, 1 tablespoon	40
Milk, skimmed, 1 cup	88
Milk, whole fresh, 1 cup	166
Mincemeat pie, ⅙ of 9″ pie	398
Mints, chocolate cream, 3 small	100
Molasses, 1 tablespoon	55
Muffin, 2″ diameter	120
Muffin, English, 1 large	280
Mushrooms, canned, ½ cup	14
Mushrooms, fresh, 10 small	16
Mushrooms, sautéed, 7 small	78
Mustard greens, cooked, 1 cup	60
Mutton—see Lamb	
Nectarine, 1	40
Noodles, egg, cooked, ½ cup	100

Food	Calories
Oatmeal, cooked, ½ cup	75
Okra, 10 pods	38
Old-fashioned cocktail, 1 glass	185
Olive oil, 1 tablespoon	124
Olives, green, 2 small or 1 large	20
Olives, ripe, 2 small or 1 large	25
Onion soup, 1 cup	100
Onions, 4 small	100
Onions, creamed, ⅓ cup	100
Onions, raw green, 5 medium	23
Orange, 1 average-sized	75
Orange ice, ½ cup	110
Orange juice, 1 cup	110
Oxtail soup, 1 cup	100
Oysters, raw, 6 medium	75
Oyster stew, with milk, 1 cup	275
Pancake, 1 4″ dia.	75
Papaya, ½ medium	72
Parsley, chopped, 2 tablespoons	2
Parsnips, cooked, ½ cup	65
Peaches, canned, 2 halves with	
2 tablespoons juice	85
Peach, fresh, 1 large	50
Peanut butter, 2 tablespoons	180
Peanuts, 20 to 24 nuts	100
Pears, canned, 2 halves with	
2 tablespoons juice	85
Pear, fresh, 1 medium-sized	60
Peas, canned, ½ cup	73
Peas, dried, cooked, ½ cup	103
Peas, fresh, cooked, ½ cup	56
Pea soup, cream, 1 cup	270
Pecans, 6 halves or 2 tablespoons	
chopped	52
Pepper, green, 1 medium-sized	25
Perch, breaded and fried, 3 oz.	195
Persimmons, 1 medium-sized	78
Pickles, cucumber, 1 large dill	15
Pickles, cucumber, 1 sweet-sour	20
Pigs' feet, pickled, ½ foot	125
Pineapple, canned, 1 slice with juice	78
Pineapple, fresh, ½ cup sliced	52
Pineapple ice, ½ cup	120
Pineapple juice, 1 cup	120
Plums, fresh, 3 or 4	100
Plums, canned, 3 or 4 with juice	150
Pimiento, canned, 1 medium	10
Popcorn, 1½ cups, no butter	100
Popover, 1	100
Pork chop, rib, broiled, 3″ x 5″ x 1″	290
Pork roast, 4 oz.	450
Pork tenderloin, 2 oz.	200
Potato, baked, 1 medium-sized	90
Potato, boiled, 1 medium-sized	90
Potato chips, 8 to 10 large	100
Potato salad, ½ cup	167
Potato, sweet, baked,	
1 medium-sized	155
Potatoes, French-fried, 10 pieces	155
Potatoes, mashed, 1 cup, milk and	
butter added	230
Praline, 1	300
Preserves, 1 tablespoon	75
Pretzels, 5 small sticks	20
Prune juice, 1 cup	170
Prunes, dried, 1 large	25

Food	Calories
Prunes, stewed, 4 medium with 2 tablespoons juice	120
Pumpkin, 1 cup	76
Pumpkin pie, ⅙ of 9″ pie	300
Rabbit, baked, 3½ oz.	177
Radishes, 5 medium	10
Raisins, seedless, ¼ cup	107
Raspberries, red, fresh, ½ cup	42
Raspberries, red, frozen, sweetened, ½ cup	120
Red snapper, baked, 3″ x ½″ x 4″	183
Rhubarb, fresh, 1 cup diced	20
Rhubarb, stewed, sweetened, ½ cup	137
Rice, brown, cooked, ½ cup	100
Rice, white, cooked, ½ cup	100
Rice, wild, cooked, ⅔ cup	103
Roll, hard, white, 1 average-sized	95
Roll, Parker House, 1	81
Rum, 1 oz.	73
Rutabagas, cooked, ½ cup	25
Salmon, canned, ½ cup	206
Salmon, fresh, poached, 3½ oz.	200
Sardines, canned, 4 large	100
Sauerkraut, ⅔ cup	27
Sauerkraut juice, ½ cup	4
Sausage, pork link, 3″ x ½″	94
Scallops, fried, 5 to 6 medium-sized pieces	427
Shad roe, sautéed, average serving	175
Sherbets, ½ cup	135
Sherry, dry, 3 oz.	110
Sherry, sweet, 3 oz.	150
Shortcake with ½ cup berries and cream, 1 medium-sized biscuit	350
Shredded wheat biscuit, 1 large	100
Shrimp, boiled, 5 large	70
Shrimp, fried, 4 large	259
Shrimp cocktail with sauce, ½ cup	100
Sirup, corn, 1 tablespoon	57
Smelts, baked or broiled, 4 or 5 medium-sized	91
Smelts, fried, 4 to 5 medium-sized	448
Snow pudding, ⅔ cup	114
Sole, Dover, fried, 3½ oz.	241
Sole, Dover, steamed, 3½ oz.	84
Sole, fillet—see Flounder	
Soybeans, dried, cooked, ½ cup	120
Spaghetti, plain, cooked, 1 cup	218
Spareribs, meat from 6 average-sized ribs	246
Spinach, cooked and chopped, ½ cup	23
Spinach soup, cream, 1 cup	240
Split pea soup, 1 cup	268
Squab, 1 whole, unstuffed, 2½ oz. meat	149
Squash, Hubbard or winter, cooked, ½ cup	50
Squash, summer, cooked, ½ cup	19
Starch, cornstarch, etc., 1 tablespoon	29
Strawberries, fresh, ½ cup	30
Strawberries, frozen, sweetened, ½ cup	120
Strawberry shortcake with cream, average serving	350
Succotash, canned, ½ cup	85

Food	Calories
Sugar, brown, 1 tablespoon	50
Sugar, confectioners', 1 tablespoon	42
Sugar, granulated, 1 tablespoon	50
Sweetbreads, broiled, ½ pair medium	185
Swordfish, average serving	180
Tangerine, 1	35
Tangerine juice, ½ cup	50
Tapioca pudding, ½ cup	133
Tartar sauce, 1 tablespoon	100
Tea, clear, unsweetened, 1 cup	0
Tomatoes, canned, 1 cup	50
Tomato catsup, 1 tablespoon	17
Tomato, fresh, 1 medium-sized	25
Tomato juice, 1 cup	50
Tomato purée, 1 tablespoon	6
Tomato soup, clear, 1 cup	100
Tomato soup, cream, home-made, 1 cup	250
Tripe, cooked in milk, average serving	150
Trout, brook, broiled, 3 oz.	216
Trout, lake, broiled, 3 oz.	290
Tuna fish, canned, water packed, ½ cup	165
Tuna fish, canned in oil, ½ cup	300
Turkey, roast, dark meat, 4″ x 4″ x ¾″	205
Turkey, roast, light meat, 4″ x 4″ x ¾″	183
Turnip greens, cooked, 1 cup	45
Turnips, cooked, 1 cup	40
Veal chop, loin, fried, 1 medium-sized	186
Veal cutlet, breaded, average serving	217
Veal roast, 2 slices 3″ x 2″ x ⅛″	186
Veal stew, 1 cup	242
Vegetable cooking fats, 1 tablespoon	110
Vegetable juice, 1 cup	48
Vegetable soup, 1 cup	100
Venison, baked, 3 slices 3½″ x 2½″ x ¼″	200
Waffles, 1, 5½″ diameter	232
Waldorf salad, average serving	137
Walnuts, English, 4 to 8 halves	50
Water cress, 1 bunch	20
Watermelon, 1 slice, ¾″ thick, 6″ diameter	90
Welsh rarebit, 4 tablespoons on 1 slice toast	200
Whisky, bourbon, 1 oz.	83
Whisky, Scotch, 1 oz.	73
Whitefish, average serving	100
White sauce, ¼ cup	106
Wines, dry, 3 oz.	65-95
Wines, sweet or fortified, 3 oz.	120-160
Yams—see Potatoes, sweet	
Yeast, brewers, 2 teaspoons	18
Yeast, compressed, 1 cake	10
Yogurt, whole milk, ½ cup	83
Zucchini, cooked, 1 cup	40
Zwieback, 1 slice	35

RECOMMENDED DAILY DIETARY ALLOWANCES (ABRIDGED)[1]

[DESIGNED FOR THE MAINTENANCE OF GOOD NUTRITION OF HEALTHY PERSONS IN THE U.S.A.]

Persons	Age in years[3] From up to	Weight in pounds	Height in inches	Food energy	Protein	Calcium	Iron	Vitamin A	Thiamin	Riboflavin	Niacin equivalent[2]	Ascorbic acid
				Calories	*Grams*	*Grams*	*Milligrams*	*International units*	*Milligrams*	*Milligrams*	*Milligrams*	*Milligrams*
Infants	0–1/6	9	22	lb. x 54.5	lb. x 1.0	0.4	6	1,500	0.2	0.4	5	35
	1/6–1/2	15	25	lb. x 50.0	lb. x .9	0.5	10	1,500	0.4	0.5	7	35
	1/2–1	20	28	lb. x 45.5	lb. x .8	0.6	15	1,500	0.5	0.6	8	35
Children	1–2	26	32	1,100	25	0.7	15	2,000	0.6	0.6	8	40
	2–3	31	36	1,250	25	0.8	15	2,000	0.6	0.7	8	40
	3–4	35	39	1,400	30	0.8	10	2,500	0.7	0.8	9	40
	4–6	42	43	1,600	30	0.8	10	2,500	0.8	0.9	11	40
	6–8	51	48	2,000	35	0.9	10	3,500	1.0	1.1	13	40
	8–10	62	52	2,200	40	1.0	10	3,500	1.1	1.2	15	40
Boys	10–12	77	55	2,500	45	1.2	10	4,500	1.3	1.3	17	40
	12–14	95	59	2,700	50	1.4	18	5,000	1.4	1.4	18	45
	14–18	130	67	3,000	60	1.4	18	5,000	1.5	1.5	20	55
Men	18–22	147	69	2,800	60	0.8	10	5,000	1.4	1.6	18	60
	22–35	154	69	2,800	65	0.8	10	5,000	1.4	1.7	18	60
	35–55	154	68	2,600	65	0.8	10	5,000	1.3	1.7	17	60
	55–75+	154	67	2,400	65	0.8	10	5,000	1.2	1.7	14	60
Girls	10–12	77	56	2,250	50	1.2	18	4,500	1.1	1.3	15	40
	12–14	97	61	2,300	50	1.3	18	5,000	1.2	1.4	15	45
	14–16	114	62	2,400	55	1.3	18	5,000	1.2	1.4	16	50
	16–18	119	63	2,300	55	1.3	18	5,000	1.2	1.5	15	50
Women	18–22	128	64	2,000	55	0.8	18	5,000	1.0	1.5	13	55
	22–35	128	64	2,000	55	0.8	18	5,000	1.0	1.5	13	55
	35–55	128	63	1,850	55	0.8	18	5,000	1.0	1.5	13	55
	55–75+	128	62	1,700	55	0.8	10	5,000	1.0	1.5	13	55
Pregnant				+200	65	+0.4	18	6,000	+0.1	1.8	15	60
Lactating				+1,000	75	+0.5	18	8,000	+0.5	2.0	20	60

[1]Source: Adapted from Recommended Dietary Allowances, Seventh Edition 1968, Publication 1694, 169 pages. Published by National Academy of Sciences—National Research Council, Washington, D.C. 20418. Also available in libraries. This publication includes discussion of allowances, eight additional nutrients, and adjustments needed for age, body size, and physical activity.

[2]Niacin equivalents include dietary sources of the vitamin itself plus 1 milligram equivalent for each 60 milligrams of dietary tryptophan.

[3] . . . . age 22 to 35 year progress; the reference man and woman at age 22 . . .

Minimum Daily Requirements. The Recommended Dietary Allowances are amounts of nutrients recommended by the Food and Nutrition Board of National Research Council and are considered adequate for maintenance of good nutrition in healthy persons in the United States. The allowances are revised from time to time in accordance with newer knowledge of nutritional needs.

The Minimum Daily Requirements are the amounts of selected nutrients that have been established by the Food and Drug Administration as standards for labeling purposes of foods and pharmaceutical preparations for special dietary uses. These are the amounts

ENTERTAINING

When you are entertaining, try not to feel that something unusual is expected of you as a hostess. It isn't. Just be yourself. Even eminent and distinguished persons are only human. Like the rest of us, they shrink from ostentation; and nothing is more disconcerting to a guest than the impression that his coming is causing a household commotion. Confine all noticeable efforts for his comfort and entertainment to the period that precedes his arrival. Satisfy yourself that you have anticipated every known emergency—the howling child, the last-minute search for cuff links, your husband's exuberance, your helper's ineptness, your own ill humor. Then relax and enjoy your guests.

If, at the last minute, something does happen to upset your well-laid plans, rise to the occasion. The mishap may be the making of your party. Capitalize on it, but not too heavily.

The procedures below present simple, dignified, current practice in table service. If you plan to serve cocktails before a meal, have glasses for drinks and nonalcoholic beverages ready on a tray. With these, you may pass some form of cracker, canapé or hors d'oeuvre. If you and your guests are discriminating diners, you will keep this pick-up light. Too generous quantities of food and drink beforehand will bring jaded palates to the dinner on which you have expended such effort. Should you have the kind of guests who enjoy a long cocktail period and varied hors d'oeuvre, be sure to season your dinner food more highly than usual. Cocktail preliminaries, which have a bad habit these days of going on indefinitely, may be politely shortened by serving a delicious hot or cold consommé or soup, either near the bar area or from a tureen on a cart. Your guests are apt to welcome this transition heartily.

No matter for whom your preparations are being made, careful forethought and arrangement contribute greatly to the pleasure that results. Never forget that ◗ your family is really the most important assembly you ever entertain. Whether for them or for friends ◗ always check the freshness of the air, the temperature of the dining area and the proper heat or chill for plates, food and drinks—especially hot ones. If warming oven space is limited, use the heat cycle of your dishwasher or, if you entertain often, you may wish to install an infrared heating unit which can be raised or lowered above a heatproof counter. Be sure that each diner has plenty of elbow room, about 30 inches from the center of one plate service to the center of the next.

Formal meals, given in beautifully appointed homes, served by competent, well-trained servants—who can be artists in their own right—are a great treat. We cannot expect to have ideal conditions at all times in the average home. However, no matter what the degree of informality, always be sure that the table is attractive and immaculately clean—and always maintain an even rhythm of service.

ABOUT TABLE DÉCOR

As to the table itself, a top that is heat- and stain-resistant lends itself to the greatest ease of service and upkeep. You can expose as much or as little of its surface as you like. If you have a tabletop of natural hardwood, you must protect it against heat at all times with pads.

For versatility and effective contrast, keep your basic flatware and dishes simple in form and not too pronounced in pattern or color. Then you can combine them, without fear of clashing, with varied linens, fruits and flowers and—most importantly—varied foods. You will find that changes in décor and accessories stimulate the appetite, as much as do changes in seasoning.

Serve soups sometimes in covered soup bowls, and other times from a tureen or in cups. Serve salads on plates, in bowls or on crescent-shaped "bone plates" which are made to fit at the side of dinner plates—giving a less crowded feeling to the table. For variety, replace vegetable dishes with an outsize platter holding several vegetables attractively garnished. Also, small raw vegetables and fruits may substitute for garnishes of parsley and cress to give a meat platter a festive air. Instead of using pairs of matching dessert dishes, try contrasting bowls of glass or bright pottery. For a rustic effect, serve a hearty menu on your everyday dishes and use bright linens and wooden salad bowls with a centerpiece of wooden scoops filled with pears and hazelnuts in the husk.

For a more elegant effect, serve a dainty meal on the same dishes, against a polished board decorated with fragile glasses and flowers. See sketch.

Whatever your decorative scheme, flower arrangements should be low or lacy. Tall arrangements that obstruct the view discourage across-the-table conversation. There is nothing more distracting than dodging a floral centerpiece while trying to establish an intimate relationship among your guests. For the same reason, candles should be placed strategically. On a formal buffet or tea table, which is viewed from above, the decorations may be as tall as you wish. In fact, food or flower accents that are elevated on epergnes or stemmed dishes add a note of drama.

Table decorations need not be costly, and they can always express your own personality. Ingenious hostesses can confect stunning arrangements of vegetables, fruits, flowers—alone or in combination—or can use handsome man-made objects and leaves. Several harmonious small containers of flowers or fruit—similar or varied—can be effectively grouped around a central element or placed along the length of a table to replace a single focal point. Use one of these small units of long-needled pine tufts and snowdrops, or clematis, illustrated in the semiformal luncheon service, above.

A piece of sculpture of a suitable size for your table makes a charming base for a centerpiece. Surround it with an ivy ring and vary the décor from time to time with other greenery or any elements that suggest borders or garlands. If the sculpture is slightly raised on a base, it can be enjoyed to great advantage. Whatever you use, don't overcrowd the table. One of the most important things to remember is that ◗ no matter what the decoration, it should be suitable in color and scale with the foods served to enhance it. Don't make your effects so stagey that your guests' reactions will be, "She went to a lot of trouble." Make them say, rather, "She had a lot of fun doing it!"

ABOUT PLACING SILVER AND DISHES

There are certain time-honored positions for silver and equipment that result from the way food is eaten and served. So keep in mind these basic placements. ◗ Forks to the left except the very small fish fork, which goes to the right. ◗ Spoons, including iced-tea spoons, and knives to the right, with the sharp blade of the knife toward the plate. There is, of course, a practical reason for placing the knife at the diner's right, since right-handed persons, who predominate, commonly wield the knife with their favored hand, and do so early in the meal. Generally, having cut his food, the diner lays down his knife and transfers his fork to the right hand. Formal dining makes an exception to this rule; and with left-handed or ambidextrous persons the transfer seems to us, on any occasion, superfluous. ◗ Place silver that is to be used first farthest from the plate. It is also better form never to have more than three pieces of silver at either side. Bring in any other needed silver on a small tray as the course is served. The server is always careful to handle silver by the handles only, including carving and serving spoons and forks, which are placed to the right of the serving dish.

If you look at some of the place settings illustrated, you can, with a few exceptions, practically predict the menu. Let's consider the semiformal luncheon setting above. Line the base of the handles up about one inch from the edge of the table. Some people still consider it important to serve a knife at luncheon, even if that knife is not needed for the actual cutting of meat. Others omit the knife if a typical luncheon casserole is passed—or served in individual containers. For a formal luncheon, a butter plate is placed to the left on a level with the water glass. The butter knife is usually placed as shown and a butter ball or curl, page 56, is already in place before the guests are seated. Later, the butter plate is removed simultaneously with the salad plate. Both are taken from the left side. The butter plate is picked up with the left hand, the salad plate with the right.

At semiformal luncheons, you may have the dessert spoon and fork in place above the plate, as sketched. This indicates that no finger bowl will be served. Or you may, as in the dinner service, bring the dessert silver to the table with the finger bowl, as sketched on page 13.

Water and wine glasses are in place as sketched above. The water is poured in the former to about ¾ capacity; the wine glasses are left empty. ◗ Glasses, filled from the right, are never lifted by the server when pouring. Goblet types are always handled by the stem by the diner and by the server when he replaces or removes them. Tumbler types are always held well below the rim.

When it is time to serve coffee, empty cups and saucers are placed to the right. There is a spoon on the saucer, behind the cup and parallel to the cup handle, which is turned to the diner's right. After all the cups are placed, they are filled by the server and afterward sugar and cream are offered from a small tray from the left. But the entire coffee service may be served, even for luncheon, in the living room, after the dessert.

Individual ash trays and cigarettes may be placed on the table. Although smoking between courses is frowned on by all epicures because it lessens the sensitivity of the palate, guests must be permitted to do what pleases them. If you are a strong-willed hostess, you may prefer to have the ash trays and cigarettes placed on the table just after the dessert is served.

If your party is not formal, place cards may be omitted. If the party is to be for six, ten or fourteen, the host is at one end of the table, the hostess at the other. If the guests number eight or twelve, the host is at one end and the hostess just to the left at the other end.

The honor guest, if a woman, is seated to the right of the host; if a man, to the left of the hostess. At a formal meal, food is presented, but ◗ not served, to the hostess first. Food is actually offered first to the woman guest of honor. The other women are then all served. Finally, the men are served, beginning with the guest of honor. If there is no special guest of honor, you may want to reverse the direction of service every other course, so that the same people are not always served last.

While it is not the best form, some people prefer to have the hostess served first. She knows the menu and by the way she serves herself sets the pace for the other guests. This is a special help if the guest of honor is from another country. In America, it is customary for guests to wait until everyone is served and the hostess begins to eat. In Europe, however, where each individual service is usually complete in itself, it is permissible to start eating as soon as one is served.

◗ Plates are usually removed from the right and placed or passed from the left. Service and dinner plates are frequently of different patterns. For the purpose of clarity in the illustrations following, service plates, as a rule, are sketched with a solid banding, hot plates or plates on which cold food is being served are shown with a thin double-banded edge.

ABOUT FORMAL ENTERTAINMENT

Most of us moderns look with amazement, not to say dismay, at the menus of traditionally formal dinners. Such meals are a vanishing breed, like the bison—but, like the bison, they manage here and there to survive. They begin with both clear and thick soups. Then comes an alternation of relevés and removes, each with its accompanying vegetables. The relevés are lighter in quality than the hefty joints and whole fish which make up the removes. Any one of the rather ironically titled removes could count as the equivalent of what, in current parlance, is called an entrée, or main dish.

However, in the classic formal menu, the term entrée has a quite different significance. Classic entrées occur immediately after a final remove and consist of timbales, sea foods and variety meats, served in rich pastes and with delicate sauces—trifles distinguished for their elegance.

A salad takes next place in this stately procession, and is usually made of a seasoned cooked vegetable, such as asparagus, with greens doing garnish duty only. After this, the diner may choose from a variety of cheeses.

Entremets—hot or cold sweets—succeed the cheese course and these are topped off, in turn, by both hot and cold fruits. We now have completed the major framework of a classic formal menu, in which, it goes without saying, each course is accompanied by a sympathetic wine.

We marvel at the degree of gastronomic sophistication required to appreciate so studied and complex a service—to say nothing of the culinary skills needed to present the menu in proper style. But, more critically, we ask, "Where do the guests stow away all that food?" Granted that a truly formal dinner lasts for hours and that each portion may be a dainty one, the total intake is still bound to be formidable. Such an array is seldom encountered in this casual and girth-conscious era. But a semiformal dinner with traces of classic service still graces the privileged household.

When the guests come into the dining room, the table is all in readiness. ◗ The setting forecasts the menu through the first three courses. Should more silver be required, it is always brought in separately later. The water glasses are about ⅔ full; the wine glasses, though empty, stand in place, see illustrations, page 12.

At formal and semiformal dinners, butter plates are seldom used. Melba toast or crackers are served with the appetizer or soup, and hard rolls later, with the roast. The next setting sketched indicates a seafood cocktail, a soup, a meat course, a salad course, water and two wines. Water and wine are poured from the right. The glasses may stay in place throughout the meal, but it is preferable to remove each wine glass after use. A third wine glass may be strung out on a line with the others or placed to form a triangle slightly forward toward the guest and just above the soup spoon. However, if more than three wines are to be served, fresh glasses replace the used glasses as the latter are removed.

Once the guests are seated, the server's steady but unobtrusive labor begins. ◗ There is a plate, filled or unfilled, before each guest throughout the meal. The server usually removes a plate from the right and replaces it immediately with another from the left, so that the courses follow one another in unbroken rhythm. At such a dinner, second helpings are seldom offered.

When a platter is presented, it is offered from the left to the guest by the server who holds it on a folded napkin, on the palm of his left hand and may steady it with the right. The server should always make sure that the handles of the serving tools are directed toward the diner.

The passing of crackers, breads, relishes, the refilling of water glasses and the pouring of wines take place during, not between, the appropriate courses. When the party is less formal, the host may prefer to pour the wines himself from a decanter or from a bottle. If the wine is chilled, he will wrap it in a napkin and hold a napkin in the left hand to catch any drip from the bottle. The hostess on such occasions may pass relishes to the guest at her right and the guests may continue to pass them on to one another. Also, relishes may be arranged at strategic places on the table, but must be removed with the soup. However, even with these slight assists, the work of the server is one that calls for nicely calculated timing. It is easy to see why ◗ one server should not be called on to take care of more than six or eight guests—at the most—if smooth going is expected.

Let us go back to our dinner, which begins—as forecast by the setting sketched below—with a sea-food cocktail and goes on to the soup. For this dinner, the sea food, served in a specially iced glass, is in place when the guests are seated.

When the sea food has been eaten, the empty cocktail glasses are removed—leaving the service plate intact. The soup plate is now placed on it—served from the left. Crackers, melba toast and relishes are now presented.

The service plate is removed along with the empty soup plate, from the right. Now, if a platter of hot food is to be passed, an

empty hot plate is placed before the guest —from the left.

However, if the meat course is to be carved and served in the dining room, the soup plate only is removed, leaving the service plate before the guest. The meat platter has been put before the host and he carves enough meat for all the guests before any further serving takes place. The server, who has replaced the host's service plate with a hot one, stands to the left of the host, holding an extra hot plate on a napkin. When the host has filled the one before him, the server removes it and replaces it with the empty hot plate he has been holding. Then, after taking the service plate before the guest of honor from the right, the server gives him the filled hot plate from the left. He then returns to the host, and waits to replace the hot plate being filled by the host for another guest.

When all guests have been attended to, the server passes the gravy and then the vegetables—with a serving spoon and fork face down on the platter and the handles directed toward the guest. The hot breads come next. During this course, the server replenishes water and wine.

The menu we have been serving has consisted of three courses: sea-food cocktail, soup, meat-and-vegetable. A salad and dessert course will follow; but first let us consider a different menu—one that omits the cocktail and introduces a fish course.

Obviously, a different setting of silver is in order for this alternate menu. The illustration will show you that it consists of soup, first. After that, there is a fish course, followed by meat, salad and so on. You will notice that there are one water

and two wine glasses. Because no sea-food cocktail is included, the napkin is placed on the service plate, with a place card on top. For this setting, cigarettes, matches and an ash tray, as well as individual salt are placed on the right, with pepper on the left. No food is on the table when the guests are seated.

The meat course follows—either carved by the host, or previously arranged in the pantry. A separately served vegetable or the salad course, as sketched, may follow. With such vegetables as asparagus and artichokes or salads with vinegar dressings no wines are served.

A handsomely arranged fruit compote, passed during the meat course, can be used as an alternate to a salad. Crescent-shaped plates suit either of these courses. If a compote is substituted for a salad, a spoon is put on the right of the setting, instead of a salad fork on the left, as illustrated.

For this second menu, plates of soup are passed from the left and placed directly on the service plates—after guests have removed napkins and place cards. Should sherry be served with the soup course, both glass and plate are removed, along with service plate. Now the fish course arrives. It has been arranged on individual plates in the pantry. This is given from the left— just as the soup and service plates have been taken from the right.

After the salad course is removed, the table is denuded for a short time. Any unused silver, salts and peppers and relishes are taken away. The table is crumbed. The server uses a folded napkin and brushes the crumbs lightly onto a plate.

Now, the dessert setting is placed in front of each guest.

After the server has removed the empty fish plate from the right, a hot plate is put before the guest from the left, as shown next.

The finger bowl, partially filled with water, may have a scented geranium leaf, a fragrant herb or flower or a thin slice of lemon floating in it. Each guest places the fork and spoon to each side of the plate and then puts the doily, with finger bowl on it, to the upper left side of his place setting—opposite the water glass.

An exception to this finger bowl rule is made when fruit is to be served after dessert. In this case, the dessert plate complete with silver is placed in front of each guest. After the dessert has been passed and eaten, the dessert plate is removed. Next comes a fruit plate with doily, finger bowl, fruit knife and fork.

Now, if coffee is to be served at the table, empty demitasse cups and saucers are placed to the right of the diners. Demitasse spoons are on the saucers, behind the cup and parallel to the handle. Coffee is poured from the right and cream and sugar are passed on a small tray from the left. Liqueur may be served with the coffee or passed on a tray later, in the living room.

Men often like to loiter at the table, for strictly male conversation, over a glass of port or brandy. In England, before the port, a savory, page 708, is served. The hostess may retire to the drawing room with the women guests and later, pour coffee for her reassembled guests there. By this time, good food, wine and conviviality have usually broken down the minor social inhibitions, and the serving of coffee may be completely informal.

ABOUT INFORMAL ENTERTAINMENT

Your chances for a successful party are much greater if you key your efforts to your own belongings and service rather than struggle to meet the exacting demands of the kind of dinner which has just been described. Your standards need not be lowered in the least. ◗ Plan a menu which will simplify last-minute preparation and subsequent serving. Offer fewer courses and put several kinds of food on one platter. But please do not let your guests sit, trying to make conversation, with a gradually congealing slice of meat before them, while waiting longingly for the vegetables and the reluctant gravy boat to follow.

If you must rely on indifferent service, or if your harassed cook is trying to pinch-hit as a waitress, plan to serve the main course yourself from an attractive.y arranged platter. For informal meals, when the hostess may be both waitress and cook, it pays to spend lots of time planning menus that can be prepared in advance and served with little fuss. Here again, in order that food will reach the table at the right temperature, it is wise to choose co-operative equipment such as covered dishes —but do remember to allow a place to put hot lids—double dishes with provision underneath for ice or hot water, and a samovar arrangement for hot drinks.

For both service and removal, a cart may facilitate matters, especially if there are no children trained to help unobtrusively. Deputizing your guests invites chaos, and should, except in extreme emergencies, be avoided.

When service is completely lacking, it is sensible to decide well in advance what concessions will achieve the most peaceful and satisfying conditions for everyone. Plates, already prepared and garnished, can be brought into the dining area on a tray or cart. If the meal is a hot one, we find this scheme impractical for more than four people. For a larger number of guests, attractive platters and casseroles of food may be placed at each end of the table, so that serving responsibilities are divided ◗ but whatever the meal, be sure to serve hot foods hot and cold foods cold.

There are many devices for keeping foods hot during a meal and while it is true that food is always best when served just as it comes from the stove, the informal hostess should not scorn such heating aids as electric trays, candle warmers, chafing dishes or electric skillets. Be sure, though, that none of these devices allows the food to boil or permits steam to form. If it does, crusty foods go limp and sauces may become either too thick or too thin.

Try iced platters or an ice tray, page 46, for chilled foods. For a buffet, serve dramatic-looking meats en croûte, page 387, and chaud-froid, page 341. Both are "insulators" which will keep foods from drying out.

ABOUT BUFFET SERVICE

This is the most satisfactory service for large groups. However, plan your table placement so the guests are routed from tables to buffet without crowding.

For a buffet, plan a menu of foods that hold well—and the best way to keep an attractive buffet looking that way is to concentrate on individual portions. These can be replenished easily, thus keeping the table always intact. For instance, rather than a large aspic, use individual fancy molds—even paper cups. Use sea shells or vegetable cups, page 82, as individual containers for sea food or other mixtures. And cut turkey, ham and salmon in individual portions. Also see About Stuffed Vegetables, page 255 and Cases for Food, page 223. For garnishes see page 82 and 83.

If the servings are not individual, cater generously, as guests are apt to take larger portions at buffets. The following layouts show typical buffet settings. The first one represents a dinner at which the host or hostess serves the guests, who then pro-

ceed to tables which are already set. The menu includes duck with orange cups, wild rice, podded peas and a green salad. The serving platters are later removed and replaced by the dessert; or individual desserts may be served at table.

The drawing above shows a buffet at which the guests serve themselves and proceed to sit at small tables. If there are no tables, individual trays may be used. For tray service, plan food that does not call for the use of a knife.

Note also that height in candles and flowers is often a dramatic asset in buffet service as is the use of tiered dishes.

Shown below are a meat or fish casserole dish, artichokes vinaigrette filled with devilled eggs, relishes and rolls. A dessert may be on the table at the beginning of the service. If the serving table seems too crowded, place the water and hot drinks on another serving surface.

ABOUT TEA SERVICE

What is more hospitable than afternoon coffee or tea, whether served on a tray in the living room or on a lavish table in the dining room? For an informal tea, the hostess pours and serves. However, when the tea is formal, friends of the hostess sit at each end of the table and consider it an honor to pour.

The drawing on next page shows a large, formal tea table, with a coffee service at one end. Tea may be served at the other. It is wise to instruct a supplier to keep in frequent touch with the pourers to anticipate their need for additional hot water, coffee or cups. It is also canny to have additional platters ready to replace those at the table that have become rather ragged-looking. Medium-size rather than large platters are easier to keep in trim.

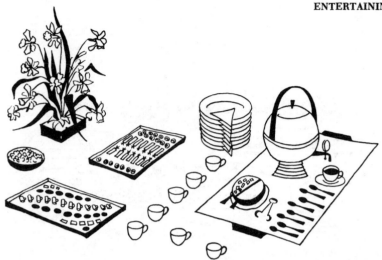

ABOUT CASUAL ENTERTAINING FOR ONE OR FOR MANY

Tray meals can be a delightful stimulant if they include a surprise element in the form of a lovely pitcher, a small flower arrangement or some seasonal delicacy. Make sure, especially if the recipient is an invalid, that all needed utensils are present, that the food is hot or cold as required, sufficient in amount and fresh and dainty looking.

A cookout, whether a mere wienie roast or a luau, can be—although it seldom is anymore—one of the least complicated ways to entertain. We suggest, unless your equipment is equal to that of a well-appointed kitchen and you can ensure your guests of comparably controlled cooking, that you choose menus which are really enhanced by outdoor cooking procedures, page 18.

Have enough covered dishes on hand to protect food from flies. Give your guests a tray or a traylike plate if there are no regular place sets or normal seating arrangements. And prepare an alternate plan of accommodation, in case of bad weather.

We remember a successful informal party that was really too big for our quarters and whose pattern might provide a substitute in case of a weather-beleaguered barbecue. The guests arrived to find no evidence of entertaining, only the most gorgeous arrangements of colchicum—those vibrant, large fall blooms which resemble vast, reticulated crocus. After drinks were served and hors d'oeuvre passed, a cart with soup tureen and cups circulated. This was followed by tray baskets containing white paper bags, each completely packaged with individual chicken salad, olives, endive filled with avocado, cocktail tomatoes, cress and cheese sandwiches, bunches of luscious grapes and foil-wrapped brownies. Coffee was served, again from the circulating cart.

In order to get an informal after-supper party rolling, young hostesses are often so eager to present the fruits of their labors that solid food is served too early for the comfort of the guests, most of whom have rather recently dined. If the party gets off to an early start, it sometimes seems too soon to start drinking alcoholic or carbonated drinks or punches. Why not suggest a tisane, page 30, to engender sociability at the take-off of an evening. Tisanes can also prove a pleasant variation for older people, who frequently refuse coffee when food is to be served later.

Here are a few parting shots—as we close this chapter on entertaining. In cooking for more people than you are normally accustomed to, allow yourself enough extra time for both food preparation and heating or cooling of food. Please read the comments on the enlarging of recipes, page 546. Be sure that your mixing and cooking equipment is scaled to take care of your group, and, ◆ most important of all, that you have the refrigerator space to protect chilled dishes and the heat surface to maintain the temperature of the hot ones. Don't hesitate to improvise steam tables or iced trays. Utilize insulated picnic boxes or buckets either way, and wheelbarrows or tubs for the cracked ice, on which to keep platters chilled.

If you entertain this way frequently, it may be worthwhile to make—as one of our friends did—a large rectangular galvanized deep tray, on which the dishes of a whole cold buffet can be kept chilled. Or try confecting an epergne-like form, such as that shown on page 46, for chilling sea foods, hors d'oeuvre or fruit.

For camping trips or boating parties, consider the safety factor in choosing the menu. No matter what the outing ♦ don't transport perishable foods in hot weather in the even hotter trunk of a car.

Not all types of entertaining—formal or casual or in between—can be detailed here. But, whatever the occasion, assemble your tried skills in menu planning so as to reflect the distinctive character of your home. Flavor the occasion with your own personality. And keep handy somewhere, for emergency use, that cool dictum attributed to Col. Chiswell Langhorne of Virginia: "Etiquette is for people who have no breeding; fashion for those who have no taste."

ABOUT COOKING FOR LARGE PARTIES

Most of the recipes in this book are for from 4 to 6 servings and will double satisfactorily for 8 to 12. But all of us are called on, at times, to produce meals for larger groups and this is when we must be on our guard. For unexpected surprises are apt to pop up just when we want everything to go particularly well. No matter how rich or how simple the menu, remember, first, that it is preferable to cook recipes with which you are familiar for special occasions. Secondly, cook in several moderate-sized batches, rather than in one big chunk. Because, mysterious as it sounds—but true, even for the experts—quantity cooking is not just a matter of indefinite multiplication, page 546. If you overexpand, too, you may run into a number of other problems.

Take into account the longer time needed in preparation—not only for paring and washing of vegetables or drying salad greens, but for heating up large quantities. Even more important, you may be confronted with a sudden pinch of refrigerator space—discovering that the shelves are needed for properly chilling large aspics or puddings just when they should be doubling to keep other sizable quantities of food at safe temperatures. ♦ This warning is of great importance if you are serving stuffed fowl, creamed foods, ground meat, mayonnaise, cream puffs, custards or custard pies. These foods spoil readily without showing any evidence of hazard. Before planning the menu for larger groups, assess equipment for mixing, cooking, refrigerating and serving.

Plan, if the meal is a hot one, to use recipes involving both the oven and top burners. Increase your limited heating surfaces with the use of electric skillets, steam tables or hot trays to hold food in good serving condition. Make sure, if you plan individual casseroles, that you have enough oven space; or if the casseroles are large, that they will fit. In fact, stage a dress rehearsal—from the cooking equipment requirements right through to the way the service dishes and table gear will be placed. Then, satisfied that the mechanical requirements are met, plan the actual work on the menu so enough can be done in advance to relieve the sink and work surface of last-minute crowding and mess.

Stick not only to those dishes you are confident you can handle without worry, but to those that make sense for the time you can spare for them. If one dish is going to require much last-minute hand work and fiddling, balance it against others that can be preassembled or are easy to serve: casseroles, baked or scalloped dishes, gelatins or frozen foods. See Menus for further suggestions, page 22.

One of the hardest things in mass cooking is to give the food that personalized and cherished look that is achieved in intimate dinners. Do not hesitate to serve simple foods for company. Choose seasonal ingredients and cook them skillfully. Then wind up with a home-baked cake or pastry —nothing is more delicious or more appreciated. Guests are really captives, so build a menu, in any case, that is not too restrictive. If you decide on Octopus Pasta, be sure you know the guests are adventurous enough or have sophisticated enough palates to enjoy it—or that they know you well enough to be able to ask for an egg instead.

MENUS

ABOUT MENU MAKING

When to eat what is a matter of ever-changing habit and custom. Think of an epicure's diet in pre-Communist China: the constant nibbling of small rich confections, interspersed with light, irregularly spaced meals. Think of the enormous breakfast, dinner and bedtime repasts of early 19th Century England, with a little sherry and biscuit served at lunch-time to guarantee survival. And, if you imagine for a moment that we have triumphantly freed ourselves from the excesses of the Groaning Board, think of the multitude of strange hors d'oeuvre that are downed during a typical big cocktail party in the Age of Anxiety.

Present-day nutritionists are divided. One group advises us that at least ⅓ of our daily intake should be consumed at breakfast, and that breakfast proteins are more completely utilized by the body than those eaten at any other time of the day or night. Another school, meanwhile, advocates something like a return to the traditional Chinese dietary—that is, scrapping our 3-square-meal schedule altogether in favor of intermittent snacks. ◗ For the sheer amounts of food that will suffice to hold the average American body and soul together, see page 744.

Whichever menu practice we decide to follow, there is in the combining of foods a perennial fascination; and we can still on all occasions respond sympathetically to Brillat-Savarin's dictum: "Menu mal-fait, diner perdu." Below are some suggestions for assembling successful meals. They are suggestions only. Your tastes, your girth, your circumstances, your market—and, we hope, your imagination—will considerably modify them. ◗ For service suggestions please read the chapter on Entertaining, page 9. ◗ Note also that individual recipes nearly always carry recommendations for suitable accompaniments.

BREAKFAST MENUS

Banana Slices and Orange Sections, p. 116
Eggs Baked in Bacon Rings, p. 201
Hot Biscuits, p. 583

Chilled Canned Pears with
Jelly Sauce, p. 710
French Omelet, p. 198
Bacon in Muffins, p. 580

Orange and Grapefruit Sections, p. 115, 116
Smoked Salmon with
Scrambled Eggs, p. 200
Brioches, p. 566
Apple Butter, p. 777

Orange and Lime Juice, p. 33
Pecan Waffles, p. 217, with
Brown Sugar Butter Sauce, p. 712

Poached Plums, p. 107
A hot cereal, p. 175-176
Soft-cooked Egg, p. 195

Stewed Rhubarb and
Pineapple Compote, p. 121
Sautéed Bacon, p. 412
Fluffy or Soufflé Omelet with
Cheese, p. 199
Toast

Pork Scrapple or Goetta, p. 438
Hot Applesauce, p. 112, or
Rhubarb, p. 121
Corn Sticks, p. 578

Dry cereal of wheat or bran biscuit type
covered with Baked Custard, p. 684
and garnished with
Sugared Strawberries, p. 113

Baked Eggs, p. 201, with
Sautéed Sausage Meat Patties, p. 437
Croissants, p. 567
Black Cherry Conserve, p. 780

Broiled Grapefruit Cups, p. 115
Chipped Beef in Sauce, p. 232
Squares of Corn Bread, p. 578
Guava Jelly, p. 776

Fresh Fruit Compôte Composée, p. 105
French Toast Waffles, p. 218
Blueberry Jam, p. 776

Blueberries and Cream, p. 113
Sautéed Ham or
Canadian Bacon, p. 411, and
Eggs, p. 412
Whole Grain Muffins, p. 581
Paradise Jelly, p. 775

Fresh Pineapple, p. 119
Broiled Fresh Mackerel, p. 358
Vienna Rolls, p. 568
Currant Jelly, p. 774

Sliced Rounds of Honeydew
Melon filled with Raspberries, p. 118
Ham and Potato Cakes, p. 230, with
Eggs, p. 195

Sliced Peaches
Broiled Kidneys, p. 444
Whole-Grain Toast
Lime Marmalade, p. 780

Ripe or Stewed Cherries, p. 107
Baked Brains and Eggs, p. 443
No-Knead Yeast Coffee Cake or
Panettone, p. 570

LUNCHEON MENUS
Below are listed some complete luncheon
menus. But if you turn to Brunch, Lunch
and Supper Dishes, page 223, Pastas, page
175, and Eggs, page 195, you will find
many combination dishes that need only a
simple salad or a bread to form a complete
menu. If speed is your object ▶ remember,
too, that many fish and ground meat dishes
are very quickly prepared.

LUNCHEON MENUS
Pilaf, p. 183
Tossed Green Salad, p. 79
Chutney Dressing, p. 313
Melba Toast, p. 587
Banana Pineapple Sherbet, p. 724

Jellied Ham Mousse, p. 97
Fresh Corn Pudding Cockaigne, p. 274
Sliced Fresh Cucumbers and Basil, p. 530
No-Knead Refrigerator Rolls, p. 569
Fruit Soup Cockaigne, p. 109

Eggs in Aspic Cockaigne on
Water Cress, p. 99
Brioche Loaf Cockaigne, p. 557
Macedoine of Fresh Fruits, p. 105
Molasses Crisps Cockaigne, p. 660

Tomato Aspic Ring II, p. 101, filled with
Chicken Salad, p. 91, with
Curry Mayonnaise, p. 315
Corn Dodgers, p. 579
Chocolate Bombe, p. 719

Frog Legs in Mushroom Sauce, p. 380
Melon Salad, p. 94
Biscuit Sticks, p. 584
Cream Meringue Tart Cockaigne, p. 641

Chicken Soufflé, p. 206, with
Mushroom Sauce and Cress Garnish, p. 327
Deep Fried Okra, p. 256
Filled Pineapple III, p. 119
Pecan Drop Cookies, p. 668

Turkey Divan, p. 236
Popovers, p. 582
Flambéed Peaches, p. 108
Curled Cookies, p. 666, with
Chocolate Cream Cheese Filling, p. 679

Garnished English Mixed Grill, p. 406
Tomato Pudding Cockaigne, p. 307
Asparagus Salad, p. 84
Hard Rolls, p. 568
Baked Fruit Compote I, p. 107

Cold Sliced Roast Beef, p. 398, or
Smoked Tongue, p. 446
Tomato Stuffed, p. 89, with
Russian Salad, p. 83
Sour Dough Rye Bread and
Cheese, p. 560
Flan with Fruit, p. 609

ONE PLATE LUNCHEON MENUS
Plate service is awkward at best for anyone in a crowded room, but it's the most
convenient way to serve food easily to a
large number of people, especially if the
food is of the type that requires no knife.
▶ Be sure if hot and cold things are to
be on the same plate that the hot food is in
ramekins or the cold food in a container
that will not be affected by the heated
plate.

Beef Stroganoff I, p. 401
Rice Ring or Mold, p. 180
Grilled Tomato, p. 306
Water Cress Garnish, p. 77

Eggplant Stuffed with Lamb or
Ham, p. 278
Garlic Bread, p. 586
Molded Vegetable Salad, p. 99, with
Boiled Salad Dressing II, p. 317

Ham Timbales, p. 208, or
Croquettes, p. 218, with
Mushroom Sauce, p. 327
Molded Pineapple Ring, p. 103
Hot Buttered Muffins, p. 581

Quick Chicken Pot Pie, p. 225
Romaine or Cos Salad, p. 76
Lorenzo Dressing I, p. 311

Molded Filled Fillets of Fish, p. 352, with
Hollandaise Sauce, p. 329
Fresh Asparagus, p. 257
Hard Rolls, p. 568

Blanquette of Veal, p. 419, on
Noodles, p. 188
Panned or Sicilian Spinach, p. 301

Creamed Eggs and Asparagus
Cockaigne II, p. 202
French Tomato Salad with
Bibb Lettuce, p. 88
Biscuit Sticks, p. 584

Honeydew Melon or Cantaloupe filled with
Creamed Cottage Cheese garnished with
Seedless Green Grapes, p. 94
Nut Bread, p. 574

VEGETABLE PLATTERS
Spinach Ring Mold, p. 209, filled with
Buttered Parsley Carrots, p. 270
Baked Winter Squash II, p. 304

Creamed Onions au Gratin in
Casserole, p. 284, surrounded by
Dauphine Potatoes, p. 296, and
Carrots in Bunches, p. 270

Celery Root Ring Mold filled with
Peas, p. 209, surrounded by
New Potatoes with Parsley, p. 290

Cauliflower with Buttered Crumbs, p. 271
surrounded by Snap Beans, p. 258

Wild Rice Ring, p. 179, filled with
Brussels Sprouts Hollandaise, p. 266
surrounded by Broiled Mushrooms, p. 281

Baked Macaroni, p. 186, or
Baked Noodle Ring, p. 188, filled with a
vegetable of your choice

MEATLESS MENUS
Vegetable Soup or Soup Paysanne, p. 150
Cheese Soufflé Cockaigne, p. 205
French Bread, p. 557
Avocado Fruit Salad, p. 93, with
French Dressing, p. 311

Cold Bulgarian Cucumber Soup, p. 158
Curried Eggs, p. 202
Cracked Wheat Bread Toast, p. 559
Fresh Cherry Pie, p. 602

Quiche Lorraine, p. 227
Tomato Aspic, p. 100
Strawberries with Kirsch, p. 114, on
Meringues, p. 600

Creamed Eggs and Asparagus
Cockaigne, p. 202
Cheese Bread, p. 556
Ambrosia, p. 105
Anise Drop Cookies, p. 656

Shrimp in
Seafood Curry, p. 238, in a
Rice Ring, p. 180, with
Chutney, p. 786
Spinach Salad, p. 78, with
French Dressing, p. 311
Chocolate Custard or
Pot-de-Creme I, p. 687

Jellied Beet Consommé, p. 149
Cold Stuffed Tomatoes II, p. 89
Swedish Rye, p. 560
Angel Pie, p. 613

Crab Louis, p. 90, garnished with
Avocado Slices, p. 92
Parkerhouse Rolls, p. 563
Lemon and Orange Ice, p. 722, with
Cherry Heering

Clam Broth, p. 369
Cheese Popovers, p. 582
Butterfly Shrimp, p. 376
Celery Salad, p. 78, with
Boiled Salad Dressing I, p. 316
Chocolate Charlotte, p. 644

Jambalaya with Fish, p. 182
Oakleaf Lettuce, p. 77, with
Chutney Dressing, p. 313
Melba Toast, p. 587
Orange Cream Pie, p. 611

Leek Potato Soup, p. 159
Fillets of Sole Florentine, p. 361
Corn Sticks I, p. 578
Spiked Honeydew Melon, p. 118

Cheese Casserole I, p. 243
Waldorf Salad, p. 92
Bread Sticks, p. 558
Raspberry Parfait, p. 721

Tomato Bouillon, p. 147
Fish Fillets Baked in
Sea Food Sauce Marguery, p. 351
Baked Green Rice, p. 178
Crêpes, p. 231, with
Tutti Frutti Cockaigne, p. 780

Quick Onion Soup, p. 167
Deviled Eggs in Sauce, p. 203
Snap Bean Salad, p. 85, with
Vinaigrette Sauce, p. 311
Rye Rolls, p. 566
Florentines, p. 670

Hot Double Consommé, p. 146
Stuffed French Pancakes I, p. 212, with
Creamed Oysters, p. 365
Celery and Olives, p. 69, 70
Fruit Brûlé, p. 108

Waffles, p. 216, with
Seafood à la King, p. 237
French Tomato Salad, p. 88
Lemon Ice with Rum, p. 723
Pecan Puffs, p. 669

Broiled Stuffed Mushrooms
Cockaigne, p. 281, on
Puréed Peas, p. 288
Bibb Lettuce Salad, p. 76, with
Green Goddess Dressing, p. 315
Overnight Rolls, p. 564
Lime Sherbet, p. 723

Sautéed Shad Roe, p. 360, with
Braised Endive, p. 278
Podded Peas, p. 288
Corn Zephyrs Cockaigne, p. 579
Frozen Orange Surprise, p. 723, with
Marzipan Leaf Decoration, p. 729

Melon Baskets, p. 117
Artichokes Stuffed with Crab Meat, p. 84
Buttermilk Corn Bread, p. 578
Pineapple Snow, p. 697

Quick Tomato Corn Chowder, p. 167
Cucumbers Stuffed with Tuna Fish, Shrimp
or Shad Roe Salad, p. 91
Sour Dough Rye Bread, p. 560
Cream Meringue Tart Cockaigne, p. 641

Smelts III, p. 361
Buttered Peas and Carrots, p. 288
New Potatoes with Dill, p. 290
Poached Apricots, p. 107
Sand Tarts, p. 662

Scalloped Scallops or Mornay, p. 370
Corn Creole, p. 274
Quick Blender Slaw, p. 81, with
Mayonnaise, p. 313
Bran Muffins, p. 581
Coffee Tarts, p. 610

Sea Food à la King, p. 237
Grilled Tomatoes II, p. 306
Water Cress, p. 77, with
Sour Cream Dressing, p. 317
Rhubarb Pie, p. 603

Poached Quenelles, p. 194, with
Sea Food Spaghetti Sauce, p. 335
Green Peas and Mushrooms, p. 288
Clover Leaf Rolls, p. 562
Wilted Cucumbers I, p. 86
Velvet Spice Cake, p. 628

Chilled Spinach Soup, p. 160
Made-in-Advance Cheese Soufflé, p. 204
Avocado and Fruit Salad, p. 93, with
Curry Dressing, p. 318
Rich Roll Cookies, p. 661

Tomatoes Stuffed with Crab Meat VI, p. 89
Pepper Slices with Cream Cheese
Filling, p. 87
Whole Grain Bread Plus, p. 559
Orange Fruit Soup, p. 109

SUGGESTIONS FOR AN AFTERNOON TEA

Serve tea, coffee or chocolate accompanied by cinnamon toast or a light sandwich: marmalade, pecan, water cress, etc., or nut, prune, fig or orange bread spread with cream cheese. You may follow this with a cup cake or other small cake or cookie.

Serve a sandwich without nut meats if you plan to have a nutty cake, and vice versa. See Tea Sandwiches, page 52, Cup Cakes, page 632. ◗ For more formal teas, see menus below, which begin with a very formal tea indeed!

AFTERNOON TEA MENUS

Spiced Tea, p. 29
Coffee, p. 27
Dry Sherry
Mixed Seafood Newburg, p. 238, in
Timbale Cases, p. 224
Puffed Roquefort Sticks, p. 58
Homemade White Bread Plus, p. 556
spread with Seasoned Butters, p. 57 and 338
Orange Tea Rolls, p. 568
Tortelettes, p. 655
Small Babas au Rhum, p. 640

Sweet Tea Spreads I on
Assorted Breads, p. 59
Deviled Eggs, p. 203
Canapé Snails, p. 56
Stuffed Choux or Puff Paste Shells, p. 55,
filled with Chicken Salad, p. 91
Orange or Lemon Ice, page 722
Glazed Fruits, p. 741
Hazelnut Torte, p. 638
Peppermint Cream Wafers, p. 729
Molasses Crisps Cockaigne, p. 660

Flower Canapés, p. 53
Pineapple Biscuits with
Cream Cheese, p. 584
Small Choux Paste Shell II filled with a
Large Strawberry, p. 55
Orange Marmalade Drops, p. 658
Caramel Curled Cookies, p. 668, filled with
Cream Cheese Icing, p. 678
Toasted Seeds, p. 66

Mushroom Canapes, p. 60
Bouchées filled with
Sea Food à la King, p. 596
Cucumber Lilies, p. 69
Toasted Cheese Logs, p. 59
Filled Cookies, p. 664
Coconut Macaroons, p. 658
Bourbon Balls, p. 737
Rolled Sandwiches, p. 53
Small Chicken and Cream Cheese
Sandwiches, p. 248
Cheese Puff Canapés, p. 58
Thin Ham on Beaten Biscuits, p. 585
Peach, p. 716, or
Strawberry Ice Cream, p. 717
German Honey Bars, p. 653
Small Mohrenkoepfe, p. 640
Candied Citrus Peel, p. 742
Salted Nuts, p. 521

COCKTAIL PARTY SUGGESTIONS

Cocktail parties, the favored mode of entertaining today, are of different kinds. In large metropolitan areas, when you are

invited for cocktails, this may be strictly
a prelude to dinner and the party does not
last through the night. In the "provinces,"
you have to have the assurance that there
will be adequate heavier foods to sustain
you if you are going on to the theatre. In
the first type of party, choose rich delicate
small tidbits which are drink-inducers and
appetite-stimulators, see Hors d'Oeuvre,
pages 63-75, and Canapés, pages 52-62.
The other kind of party calls for some
blander types of food which may include
large joints or fowl and even salads, and
turns into a light buffet. See Buffet Suggestions, below. In choosing your cocktail
menu, be sure to include something that is
rich enough to cut the impact of the alcohol—something heavy in cheese, butter
or oils.

BUFFET SUGGESTIONS
Cold Fillet of Beef, p. 399
Cold Baked Ham, p. 410
Tongue in Aspic, p. 447
Cold Glazed Salmon, p. 359
Mousseline of Shellfish, p. 98
Standing Rib Roast of Beef, p. 398
Cold Fried Chicken, p. 466
Jelled Chicken or Veal Mousse, p. 97
Sliced Turkey, p. 465
Terrines, p. 435

HOT BUFFET ENTRÉES
Seafood in Creole Sauce, p. 237
Lobster or Seafood Curry, p. 238
Spiced Beef, p. 416
Lasagne, p. 190
Mushroom Ring Mold with
Sweetbreads or Chicken, p. 210
Chicken or Turkey à la Campagne, p. 472
Gaston Beef Stew, p. 414
Beef Kabobs, p. 402
Welsh Rarebit in Chafing Dish, p. 242

PARTY MENUS
That, somehow, when we go to a dinner
party, the excitement lies most in the
unusual was demonstrated to us years ago
by our younger child. His brother was sick
and unable to attend a Thanksgiving feast
to which our family had been invited by a
great gastronome. We made our way
through an impressive sequence of delicacies—from oysters Rockefeller, served
at just the right temperature on their bed of
hot salt, to a fabulous mince pie. Ques-
tioned on his return by the drooling invalid, the five-year-old ecstatically ticked
off the highlights: "Ice water"—which we
seldom serve at home, since we regard our
well water as having just the right degree
of coolness, "salt crackers," and "candles"
—two other accessories which rarely grace
our table. These, to him, summed up the
only really memorable items on that Lucul-
lan menu. Try, then, serving as a dish for

occasions a true "spécialité de la maison"
—something you do particularly well, or
something your guests are not so likely to
prepare themselves, or find at the homes
of their more convention-bound friends.
Below we list a few more menus—this time
for company dinners.

PARTY DINNER MENUS
Stuffed Veal Roast, p. 403
Casserole Green Beans, p. 259
Cold Beet Cups, p. 85
Rice Flour Muffins, p. 581
Profiteroles, p. 598

Prosciutto and Fruit, p. 71
Olives, Fennel, and
Marinated Carrots, p. 70, 278, 69
Lasagne, p. 190
Tossed Salad, p. 78, with
French Dressing, p. 311
Zabaglione, p. 686
Bel Paese Cheese with Crackers, p. 707
Dry Red Wine, p. 41

Marinated Herring with Sour Cream, p. 73
German Meat Balls, p. 428
Noodles au Gratin II, p. 188
Carrots Vichy, p. 270
Tomato Aspic, p. 100
Linzertorte, p. 604

Fruit Cup, p. 105
Braised Sweetbreads, p. 442
Caesar Salad, p. 80
English Muffins, p. 568
Sour Cream Apple Cake Cockaigne, p. 691

Chicken Bouillon with Egg, p. 146
Small Tomatoes filled with
Cole Slaw de Luxe, VI, p. 89
Squab, p. 475, stuffed with
Dressing for Cornish Hen, p. 458
Purée of Green Beans, p. 259
Hard Rolls, p. 568
Strawberry Bombe, p. 719
Dry White Wine, p. 43

Lobster Parfait, p. 239, and thin salt wafers
Crown Roast of Lamb, p. 405, with
Bread Dressing, p. 456
Asparagus II, p. 258
Belgian Endive, p. 77, with
Sauce Vinaigrette, p. 311
Fruit Soup Cockaigne, p. 109

Tomatoes Stuffed with
Crab Meat Salad, p. 89
Fillet of Beef, p. 399, with
Marchand de Vin Sauce, p. 327
Franconia or Browned Potatoes, p. 293
Stuffed Baked Artichokes, p. 257
Ricotta Cheese Pie or Cake, p. 612

MENUS

Bouillabaisse, p. 163
Mixed Salad Greens, p. 78, with
French Dressing, p. 311
French Bread, p. 557
Assorted Fruit, p. 105

Shrimp, p. 377, in
Hot Snail Butter, p. 339
Pheasant in Game Sauce, p. 478
Wild Rice, p. 179
French Bread, p. 557
Gooseberry Preserves, p. 779
Strawberries Romanoff, p. 114
Dry Red Wine, p. 41

Onion Soup, p. 148
Roast Wild Duck, p. 477
Poached Oranges, p. 116
Kasha, p. 177
Creamed Lettuce, p. 279
Almond Tart Cockaigne, p. 637
Dry Red Wine, p. 41

EVERYDAY DINNER MENUS
Braised Lamb Shanks with
Vegetables, p. 422
Boiled Noodles, p. 188
Cucumber Salad, p. 85
Jelly Tot Cookies, p. 665

Pork Roast, p. 407
Celery and Carrot Stick Garnish
Sauerkraut Baked in Casserole, p. 269
Mashed Potatoes, p. 290
Sour Cream Apple Cake Cockaigne, p. 691

Veal Pot Roast, p. 420
Kohlrabi, p. 279
Wilted Greens, p. 80
Riced Potatoes, p. 290
Mocha Gelatin, p. 696

Beef Pot Roast, p. 414
Spatzen or Spaetzle, p. 192
Glazed Turnips, p. 309
Glazed Onions, p. 285
Pickled Beet Salad, p. 85
Brown Betty, 700

Leg of Lamb Roast, p. 405
Lemon Sherbet, p. 723
Grilled Tomatoes, p. 306, on
Broiled Eggplant Slices, p. 277
Individual Shortcakes, p. 644, with
Strawberries, p. 113

Sauerbraten, p. 415
Potato Dumplings, p. 192
Green Bean Casserole I, p. 259
Apple Pie, p. 600

Roast Chicken, p. 465, Stuffed with
Apricot Dressing, p. 459
Creamed Spinach, p. 300
Escarole, p. 77, with
Roquefort Dressing, p. 312
French Chocolate Mousse, p. 687

Chicken Braised in Wine or
Coq Au Vin, p. 468
Rice Cooked in Chicken Stock, p. 179
Molded Cranberry Salad, p. 102
Angel Cup Cakes, p. 633, with
Sauce Cockaigne, Whipped Cream, p. 709

Chicken Stew, p. 467, and
Dumplings, p. 191
Asparagus, p. 257, with
Polonaise Sauce, p. 340
Mixed Green Salad, p. 78, with
Green Goddess Dressing, p. 315
French Apple Cake, p. 607

Raw Smoked Ham Loaf, p. 432
Canned Baked Beans with Fruit, p. 261
Cole Slaw, p. 80
Rombauer Jam Cake, p. 636

Baked Ham, p. 410
Snap Beans with Butter, p. 258
Crusty or Soft Center Spoon Bread, p. 579
Pear and Grape Salad, p. 94
Angelica Parfait, p. 721

Rice Ring, p. 180, filled with
Creamed Oysters, p. 365
Belgian Endive, p. 77, with
French Dressing, p. 311
Pineapple Sponge Custard, p. 687
Pecan or Benne Wafers, p. 669

Steak Au Poivre, p. 401
Grilled Tomatoes, p. 306
Boston Lettuce, p. 76, with
Roquefort Dressing, p. 312
Refrigerator Potato Rolls, p. 569
Fresh Fruit Soufflé, p. 690

Roast Beef, p. 398
Franconia or Browned Potatoes, p. 293
Quick Creamed Broccoli, p. 265
Marinated Carrots, p. 69
No-Knead Refrigerator Rolls, p. 569
Chocolate Soufflé, p. 690

Lentil Soup, p. 153
Broiled Steak, p. 400, with
Sauce, p. 327
Never-Fail French Fries, p. 295
Sautéed Cauliflower, p. 271
Applesauce Cake, p. 629

Shrimp Bisque, p. 162
Chicken Tarragon with Wine, p. 469
Green Peas and Lettuce, p. 287
Beaten Biscuits, p. 585
Grape Jelly, p. 775
Pecan Pie, p. 605

Broiled Sausage Patties, p. 437, with
Sautéed Mushrooms, p. 281
Summer Squash Casserole
Cockaigne, p. 304
Boiled Noodles with Poppy Seeds, p. 188
Prunes in Wine, p. 120
Molasses Nut Wafers, p. 669

Sweetbreads on Skewers with
Mushrooms, p. 442
Boiled New Potatoes, p. 290
Grilled Tomatoes, p. 306
Cheese Straws, p. 174
Coffee Chocolate Custard, p. 685

Liver Lyonnaise, p. 439
Shoe String Potatoes, p. 295
Sweet Sour Beans, p. 259
Tomato and Onion Salad, p. 89
Fresh Fruit, p. 105

FORMAL LUNCHEON MENU
Quick Clam and Chicken Broth, p. 168
Refrigerator Cheese Wafers or
Straws, p. 174
Cooked Fish Soufflé with Lobster, p. 206
Broiled Lamb Chops, p. 406,
garnished with
Stuffed Baked Artichokes, p. 257
Tomato Olive Casserole, p. 306
Bibb, Water Cress and
Endive Salad, p. 76, 77, with
Avocado Dressing, p. 311
Assorted Cheeses, p. 707
French Bread, p. 557
Sweet Butter, p. 509
Cabinet Pudding, p. 693
Coffee, p. 27
Dry Champagne served
throughout, p. 43, 44

FORMAL DINNER MENU
Aperitifs, p. 36
Bread Sticks or Grissini, p. 558
Lobster Parfait, p. 239; Dry Sherry, 43
Consommé, p. 146, with
Royale, p. 170
Peach or Mango Chutney, p. 785
Seeded Crackers, p. 174
Chicken Kiev, p. 470; Dry White
Wine, p. 43
Raspberry Sherbet, p. 724
Filet Mignon, p. 400, with
Béarnaise Sauce, p. 329; Red Bordeaux or
Burgundy, p. 43
Soufflé or Puffed Potatoes, p. 294
Creamed Spinach, p. 300
Belgian Endive, p. 77, with
Vinaigrette, p. 311

Hard Rolls, p. 568
Assorted Cheeses, p. 707
French Bread, p. 557
Fruit Mousse, p. 720; Dessert Wine or
Champagne, 43
Madeleines, p. 633
Fresh Fruits, p. 105
Coffee, p. 27; Liqueur, p. 43

**THANKSGIVING OR CHRISTMAS
DINNER MENUS**
Christmas Canapés, p. 54
Clear Soup, p. 146, with
Marrow Balls, p. 173
Celery, p. 69
Goose, p. 474, Stuffed with
Sweet Potatoes and Fruit, p. 299
Turnip Cups filled with Peas II, p. 309
Parkerhouse Rolls, p. 563
Fruit Cake Cockaigne, p. 631
German Cherry Pie, p. 602

Oysters Rockefeller, p. 366
Chicken Broth, p. 146
Roast Stuffed Turkey, p. 465, with
Chestnut Dressing, p. 457
Glazed Onions, p. 285
Brussels Sprouts with
Hollandaise, p. 266
Celery, Radishes, Olives, p. 69, 83
Filled Pimientos or
Christmas Salad, p. 87, on
Water Cress, p. 77
Mince Pie Flambé, p. 603, or
Pumpkin Pie, p. 605
Dark Fruit Cake II, p. 632

Mushroom Broth with Sherry, p. 148
Roast Suckling Pig, p. 407, with
Onion Dressing, p. 457
Duchess Potatoes I, p. 296
Red Cabbage, p. 268
Escarole and Romaine, p. 77, 76, with
Thousand Island Dressing, p. 316
Hazelnut Soufflé, p. 691

NEW YEAR'S EVE BUFFET MENU
Champagne, p. 43, 44
Pâté De Foie De Volaille, p. 433
Boned Chicken, p. 472
French Bread, p. 557
Hot Consommé, p. 146
Hot Standing Rib Roast of Beef, p. 398
Casserole of Green Beans, p. 259
Tossed Salad, p. 79, with
Roquefort Dressing, p. 312
White Fruit Cake, p. 631
Brandy Snaps, p. 668
Pulled Mints, p. 734

WEDDING BUFFET MENU
Dry Champagne, p. 43, 44
Mushrooms in Batter, p. 281

Rolled Sandwiches, Cress and
Cucumber, p. 53
Pastry Cheese Balls, p. 68
Hot Consommé Brunoise, p. 146
Galatine of Turkey, p. 436
Hard Rolls, p. 568
Lobster Newburg, p. 238, in
Patty Shells, p. 596
Bibb and Water Cress Salad, p. 76, 77, with
Sour Cream Dressing, p. 317
Stuffed Endive and Olives, p. 69, 70
Macedoine of Fruits with Kirsch, p. 106
Wedding Cake, p. 624
Petits Fours, p. 634
Spiced Nuts and Mint Wafers, p. 737-729

HUNT BREAKFAST MENU
Bloody Marys, p. 40
Hot Buttered Rum, p. 51
Café Brûlot or Diable, p. 28
Blended Fruit Juice, p. 33
Baked Fresh Fruit, p. 107
Steak and Kidney Pie, p. 418, or
Pheasant in Game Sauce, p. 478
Broiled Bacon, p. 411
Pan Broiled Sausage, p. 437
Scrambled Eggs, p. 200
Grilled Tomatoes, p. 306
Chestnuts and Prunes in Wine, p. 120
Toasted English Muffins, p. 568
Croissants, p. 567
Red Strawberry Jam, p. 776
Orange Marmalade, p. 779
Scandinavian Pastry, p. 572

ABOUT PICNIC MEALS

Picnics are fun; but picnic food is subject
to hazards, and they are not all ants.
Transport perishables in the coolest part
of your car, covering them against the sun.
If you have no cold box or insulated
plastic bags carry frozen juices. Use them
en route to cool your mayonnaise and
deviled eggs. Or fill a plastic bag with
ice cubes and put it in a coffee can to improvise a chilling unit that will last out
transportation time. Or insulate the sandwich boxes with damp newspapers.
◗ Should you use dry ice be sure the
container and the car windows are partially open to allow the gas to escape.
◗ To wrap sandwiches for easy identification, see page 652. ◗ To mix picnic salads
conveniently, see page 79.
   Most important of all, if it's a basket
picnic ◗ plan the kind of food which holds
well and is easily served, so everyone can
enjoy every minute of the outing. If it's

to be a ◗ cookout, please read About Outdoor Cooking, page 133, and check your
menu against recipes marked ▤ which
are suitable for outdoor preparation. Check
also Clam Bake, page 368.
   Sandwiches, salads, fruits and cookies
are naturals for picnics. Consult these
sections; or for slightly fancier combinations, see the menus below.

PICNIC MENUS
Barbecued Frankfurters, p. 231
Bread and Butter Pickles, p. 782
Versatile Rolls, p. 565
Cheddar Cheese, p. 512
Gingerbread, p. 636 ◟
Pears and Grapes, p. 118, 117

Beef Kebabs, p. 402, with
Canned Potato Sticks
Tossed Salad, p. 79, with
Thousand Island Dressing, p. 316
Pickled Watermelon Rind, p. 785
Parkerhouse Rolls, p. 563
Pound Cake, p. 626

Beef Hamburger or Lamb Patties, 427, 428
Potato Salad Niçoise, p. 88
Corn Relish, p. 784
Health Bread, p. 561
Marble Cake, p. 625

Fried Fish, p. 349, or
Barbecued Chicken, p. 466
Campfire Potatoes, p. 253
Grilled or Roasted Corn, p. 273
Cole Slaw, p. 80
Quick Oatmeal Cookies, p. 657
Peaches, p. 118

Sautéed Eggs, p. 195, with
Bacon or Sausages, p. 411, 436
Baked Beans, p. 261
Pickles, p. 782
Toasted Buttered French
Bread Loaf, p. 586
Apples, p. 110
Gold Layer Cake, p. 625, with
Caramel Icing, p. 676

Baked Ham, p. 410
Picnic Tossed Salad, 79
Rye Rolls, p. 56
Nut Creams Rolled in Chives, p. 67
Chilled Melon, p. 118

BEVERAGES

As our friend, Edgar Anderson, points out in his stimulating book, "Plants, Man and Life," primitive man located the only sources of caffeine known to this day: in tea, coffee, cola, cocoa and yerba maté and its relatives. Other less brisk brews have been made from leaves, roots, bark, blossoms and seeds. In France, for example, the tisane mentioned so lovingly by Colette is frequently served as a comforting after-dinner drink, page 30. If you don't grow and dry your own herbs, the drugstore will do very well as a source.

The recipes in this chapter, except for a few variations under Coffee and Tea, are nonalcoholic. For alcoholic liquors of all kinds, their preparation and use, see **Drinks**, page 36. Remember that, in any beverage you may brew, the quality of the water greatly affects results.

ABOUT COFFEE

Coffee has always thrived on adversity—just as people in adversity have thrived on it. When this beverage began its highly successful career, the Mohammedan priesthood identified it with wine—a new kind of wine which was all the more offensive to Koranic teaching because it did not merely loosen men's tongues, but sharpened their critical faculties.

Thanks especially to vacuum-packed cans, making good coffee at home has become a surefire delight. Of the several ways of preparing this beverage, we prefer the drip method. Vacuum preparation and the percolator have their advocates, too; but we regard them as, respectively, more troublesome and less apt to produce fresh flavor. The steeped-coffee recipe which follows is suggested for campers or others who happen to lack any equipment more specialized than a saucepan. Illustrated are two devices for making filtered coffee: the first employs a metal filter, the second, which is made of chemical glass, uses a paper filter folded into conical shape. The latter gives a pure essence, with no sediment—which a coffee connoisseur demands in a perfect brew. Also sketched is the proper equipment for Caffè Espresso and Turkish coffee.

Whatever device you choose ◖ follow the directions of its manufacturer carefully, especially as to the grind recommended—regular, drip or fine. In each case, to assure a full-bodied brew, ◖ use not less than 2 level tablespoons of coffee to each ¾ cup of freshly drawn water. Other things to remember are: use soft, not softened or hard, water; when brewing coffee keep the coffeemaker almost full; time your method consistently; keep the coffeemaker scrupulously clean, rinsing it with water in which a few teaspoons of baking soda have been dissolved and always scalding it before re-use. If cloth filters are required, do not allow them to become dry, but keep them immersed in cold water. ◖ Never boil coffee, since boiling brings out the tannic acid in the bean and makes for a bitter as well as a cloudy brew. Remember that any moisture activates coffee and that water between $200°$-$205°$ is ideal for extracting flavor without drawing acids. Never, of course, re-use coffee grounds.

If coffee is ground in the household, it should be done in small quantities, in a meticulously clean grinder. Open only one can at a time. Store ground coffee in a tightly closed jar in the refrigerator.

For those who love coffee but are highly sensitive to caffeine or in whom it induces insomnia, we suggest the use of a decaffeinized product rather than a coffee substitute. It may be helpful to remember also, that certain varieties of coffee—such

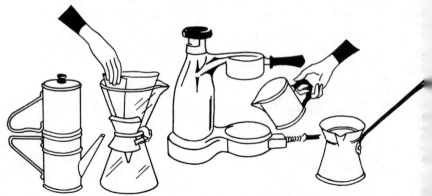

as those grown in Puerto Rico—have a substantially lower caffeine content than the typical Brazilian or Colombian bean.

For those who hanker after coffee such as the kind their German grandmother used to make or a brew which reminds them of that little brasserie on the Left Bank, the answer may be to add an ounce of ground chicory to a cup of ground coffee before brewing. ♦ When cream is used in coffee, allow it to reach room temperature beforehand, so as to cool the drink as little as possible. For coffee-chocolate combinations, see About Chocolate, page 30, and Brazilian Chocolate, page 31.

DRIP COFFEE OR CAFÉ FILTRÉ
Place finely ground coffee in drip filter. Allow:

> 2 tablespoons coffee for each ¾
> to 1 cup water

Pour freshly boiled water over the coffee. When the dripping process is complete, serve coffee at once. Dripping coffee more than once, contrary to popular belief, does not strengthen the brew. Serve with a:

> Twist of lemon peel

VACUUM-METHOD COFFEE
Allow:

> 2 tablespoons regular or fine-grind
> coffee for every
> ¾ to 1 cup water

Measure water into lower bowl. Place on heat. Place a wet filter in upper bowl and add the ground coffee. Insert upper bowl into lower one with a light twist to insure a tight seal. Insert it at this time or not, depending on your equipment. If your equipment has a vented stem, you may place it on the heat already assembled. If it does not have this small hole on the side of the tube above the hot-water line, wait until the water is actively boiling before putting the upper bowl in place. When nearly all the water has risen into the upper bowl—some of it will always remain below—stir the water and coffee thoroughly. In 1 to 3 minutes, the shorter time for the finer grinds, remove from heat.

PERCOLATED COFFEE
Place in the percolator:

> ¾ to 1 cup cold water for every
> 2 tablespoons coffee you have
> measured into the percolator basket

When water boils, remove percolator from heat. Put in the basket. Cover percolator, return to heat and allow to percolate slowly 6 to 8 minutes. Remove the coffee basket and serve. ♦ Over-percolating does not make coffee stronger. It impairs its flavor.

STEEPED COFFEE
Place in a pot:

> 2 tablespoons regular or fine grind
> coffee to each ¾ to 1 cup
> freshly boiling water

Stir the coffee for at least ½ minute. Let it stand covered in a pan of boiling water from 5 to 10 minutes, depending on the grind and the strength of brew desired. Pour the coffee off the grounds through a strainer; or, if preferred, settle the grounds by stirring into the pot before draining:

> (1 slightly beaten egg)

The egg merely serves to clarify the coffee. If anything, it detracts from rather than adds to its flavor.

COFFEE IN QUANTITY
40 to 50 Servings
Put in a cheesecloth bag large enough to allow for double expansion:

> 1 lb. medium-grind coffee

Shortly before serving, have ready a kettle holding:

> 5 to 7 quarts water

Bring the water to a boil. Place the coffee-filled bag in it. Permit to stand in a warm place from 7 to 10 minutes. Agitate the bag several times during this period. Remove bag, cover kettle, serve at once.

INSTANT COFFEE
The polls are against us, but we really can't yet regard the jiffy product as in any way comparable to the one that takes a few minutes longer to prepare. If you insist, use for each serving:

> 1 teaspoon instant coffee
> 5½ oz. boiling water

For 6 servings:

> 6 teaspoons instant coffee
> 1 quart boiling water

Add the water to the instant coffee to avoid foaming. A better flavor is obtained by simmering gently for about 2 minutes.

ESPRESSO COFFEE
This Italian specialty, which, of course, is called Caffè Espresso on its home grounds, must be carefully distinguished from any brew made by filtering, no matter how concentrated. The Espresso machine works by an entirely different "steam pressure" principle, uses a very dark, very powdery grind identified as "Espresso" on the package and delivers a powerful drink with the consistency of light cream. Use the recipe for Espresso which comes with your equipment and serve it after dinner, in a demitasse or Espresso glass, with or without lemon peel. Vary the brew with a dash of Tía Maria or a dash of Strega and a dollop of whipped cream.

COFFEE CAPUCCINO
Combine equal parts of:

> Espresso Coffee
> Hot Milk
> Dash of Cinnamon or
> Grating of Nutmeg

TURKISH COFFEE

As Turkish coffee settles very rapidly, it is made at the table, over an alcohol lamp. The average content of the long-handled metal pot is about 10 ounces of liquid, and it should never be filled to more than ⅔ capacity. The pot is narrowed before it flares at the top, to allow the swishing and swinging of its contents between "frothings"—a procedure which keeps the very finely divided grains in suspension, until the liquid is sipped from tiny stemmed cups holding about a tablespoon of fluid. In the Near East it is not considered polite to drink more than three of these—although more may be served in the United States. The glass of ice water and the Rahat Loukoum candy, page 739, served on the side for "non-habitués" are often welcome additions. The connoisseur adds no sweetening to the brew itself. Serve the coffee so that a little of the lighter frothy top goes into each cup first and is followed on the next round by some of the heavier liquid on the bottom. No commercial grind available in America proves fine enough for Turkish coffee; so take the finest you can get and pulverize it further in an electric blender. For each serving, bring to a boil in a Turkish coffeemaker:

    ⅓ cup water
    1 teaspoon to 1 tablespoon finely
      pulverized coffee
    (2 teaspoons sugar)

Place the pot over heat and allow the coffee to rise. Remove pot from heat, momentarily. Repeat this process a second and third time. ◗ Never allow the coffee to boil. Serve it at once, as described above.

CAFÉ AU LAIT

The famous milk coffee of France. Combine equal parts of:

    Strong coffee
    Hot milk
    (Sugar to taste)

CAFÉ BRÛLOT, DIABLE OR ROYAL

                    8 Servings

This festive coffee bowl requires a darkened room. Prepare:

    1 small orange

by studding it with:

    20 whole cloves

Place in a deep silver bowl the thinly sliced:

    Peel of 1 orange
    Peel of 1 lemon and
    2 sticks cinnamon
    10 small cubes sugar

Heat ◗ do not boil, and pour over these ingredients:

    ¾ cup brandy or ¼ cup Cointreau

Place bowl on a tray and bring bowl, orange and a ladle to the table. Ignite the brandy and ladle the mixture repeatedly over the spices until the sugar melts. Pour into the bowl:

    4 cups freshly made coffee

Now fill the ladle with:

    ¼ cup warm brandy or
    ¼ cup Cointreau

Tip the orange carefully into it, ignite liquid, and lower the flaming ladle into the bowl, floating the orange. Ladle the café brûlot into demitasse cups.

Here are 2 easier versions:

For individual servings put a small cube of sugar in a coffee spoon, saturate it with brandy, ignite. When sugar is melted, lower spoon into a partially filled demitasse of hot coffee. Add a lemon twist, 1 or 2 cloves and stir mixture with a cinnamon stick. Also, you may simply stir a teaspoonful of warmed light rum or whisky into a small cup of hot coffee—adding a twist of lemon peel and sweetening to taste.

IRISH COFFEE

                 Individual Serving

Some people hold that Irish coffee can only be made "proper" with Demarara sugar, page 506. It does make a difference. Try it sometime.

Heat ◗ but do not boil and place in a prewarmed 7-ounce goblet or coffee cup:

    1 jigger Irish whisky
    1 or 2 teaspoons sugar

Fill to within ½ inch of top with:

    Freshly made hot coffee

Stir until sugar is dissolved. Float on top of liquid:

    Chilled whipped cream

ICED COFFEE

Prepare any way you wish, using:

    2½ to 3 tablespoons to ¾ cup water,
    Coffee, page 27

Chill it or pour it hot over cubed ice in tall glasses. You may sweeten the drink with:

(Sugar or Sugar Sirup to taste)

Stir in:

(Cream)

or top with:

(Whipped Cream or
Vanilla Ice Cream)

ICED COFFEE VIENNOISE
Individual Serving
Prepare:

Iced Coffee

in a tall glass. Add:

1 small jigger light rum

Top with:

Whipped cream

⅄ BLENDER FROZEN COFFEE
Place in electric blender for each drink:

¼ cup coffee

prepared as for Iced Coffee, above.

1 tablespoon sugar
¹⁄₁₆ teaspoon ground cloves
(1 small jigger medium rum)

Add not less than:

2 cups crushed ice

Blend thoroughly and serve in chilled, tall glasses.

ABOUT TEA

In one of Lin Yutang's books, he tells of the infinite care with which a certain sage living in the second or Classical period of Chinese teamaking procured from a famous spring, in just the proper sort of earthen pot, sufficient water for a brew with which he intended regaling an honored guest; how, on a clear, calm evening, taking pains to keep the water undisturbed, he sailed with it cautiously across an arm of the sea to his home; and how, before steeping the choice leaves, he brought the water to precisely the critical boil. There were other refinements, too, most of them equally unthinkable in our less leisurely age.

However, no matter how we abridge the teamaking ritual today, it is well to keep in mind the importance of the water we use and its temperature. It should be freshly drawn, soft—not softened and not hard—and heated, if possible, in a glass or enameled vessel. When the leaves are dropped into it, the water should only just have arrived at a brisk rolling boil—so the tea will not have a flat flavor and the leaves will describe a deep wheel-like movement, each one opening up for fullest infusion. If you doubt the effectiveness of this step, test it for yourself, adding tea leaves to underboiled, just boiling and overboiled water. Then watch the difference.

Tea brewers who do not wish to trouble with a strainer and are willing to compromise may use a tea ball. In any case

⧫ stirring the brew just before serving in a scalded, preheated pot is imperative, since it circulates through the liquid the essential oils which contribute so much to tea's characteristic flavor.

There is only one tea plant; but there are many commercial varieties of tea, depending upon soil, locality, age of leaf, manufacture, grading, blending and the addition of blossoms, zests or spices. The two chief basic types are green and black. The former is dried immediately after plucking, the latter—by all odds the more favored—is allowed to ferment before further processing. Oolong, a semi-fermented leaf, is in a class by itself.

Chinese teas which, less than a century ago, dominated the world market, have now largely yielded to the more robustly aromatic varieties of India, Ceylon and Southeastern Asia. Unfortunately, tea producers have not yet followed the example of coffee manufacturers, by putting up tea in vacuum packages. Therefore, when it reaches your kitchen, we suggest you place it at once into a tightly sealed jar.

TEA
Place tea leaves in a preheated pot. Allow:

1 teaspoon tea leaves

for each:

5 to 6 oz. water

Proceed as indicated above, permitting the leaves to steep not less than 3 and not more than 5 minutes. Serve the tea promptly, stirring and straining. Sugar or lemon? Yes, if you wish—the earliest teamakers, curiously enough, added salt! On a chilly afternoon we sometimes like to put a small decanter of rum or brandy on the tea tray for the cup that cheers. But we draw the line at tea bags and cream. The bag container or the fat in the cream will adulterate the flavor of this subtle beverage. Milk, of course, is frequently added in England. Never steep tea leaves more than once.

SPICED TEA
8 Servings
Prepare an infusion by bringing to a boil:

½ cup water
¾ cup sugar

Remove from heat and add:

¼ cup strained orange juice
½ cup strained lemon juice
6 cloves
1 stick cinnamon

Meanwhile, prepare:

Tea, above

Use, in all, 10 teaspoons tea and 5 cups water—in a regular measuring cup. Put the hot, spiced infusion in a heavy crystal bowl. Pour the steeped tea over the mixture and serve at once in punch or tea cups.

ICED TEA
We swell with patriotic pride when we recall that this beverage originated in our

native town, St. Louis—even though the inventor was actually an Englishman who arrived at the concoction as an act of desperation. The year was 1904; the place, the St. Louis World's Fair; the provocation, the indifference of the general public, in the sweltering midwestern heat, to Richard Blechynden's tea concession. In brewing iced tea, avoid China teas—they lack the requisite "body." Hard water produces murky iced tea due to a precipitate.
Prepare:

Tea, page 29

Use twice the quantity of leaves indicated for making the hot beverage. Stir, strain and pour over cubed ice. Serve with:

Lemon slices
(Sprigs of mint)
(Sugar to taste)

FLAVORINGS FOR ICED TEA
I. Pour hot, steeped tea over:
Bruised mint leaves
Lemon rind
Chill the tea. Remove leaves and rind. Pour the tea into tall glasses. Add ice cubes and:
(Sprigs of mint)
Sugar to taste

II. Add to each serving of iced tea:
1 teaspoon rum
Garnish the glasses with:
Slices of lemon or lime
(Sprigs of lemon thyme)

ABOUT TISANES AND OTHER INFUSIONS
From time immemorial various plants, less stimulating than tea or coffee, have been used the world over as restoratives. They range all the way from such homely makings as rose hips and sassafras bark to that Paraguayan tea shrub, maté, the leaves of which are still commercially obtainable in some North American localities.

Some of the homegrown herbs which, singly or in combination, may become interesting beverages are the fresh or dried leaves of alfalfa, angelica, bergamot, hyssop, lemon verbena, mints, sages, thymes; the blossoms of camomile, clover, linden, orange, lemon, wintergreen and elderberry; also, the seeds of anise and fennel. There is a good general rule for quantity per cup of water in preparing these infusions.
For strong herbs, allow:
½ to 1 tablespoon fresh material
¼ to ½ teaspoon dried material
For mild herbs, allow:
Twice the above amounts
♦ Never use a metal pot. Steep for 3 to 10 minutes in water brought to a rolling boil before straining and serving. Serve with:
(Honey or lemon)
Habitués say "never use cream."
Try one of the following dried herbs, allowing for each cup:

1 star anise cluster
6 camomile flowers
⅛ teaspoon powdered mint
¼ teaspoon powdered fennel
½ teaspoon linden blossom
½ teaspoon verbena
Steep for 5 minutes before serving.

ABOUT CHOCOLATE AND COCOA BEVERAGES
Chocolate, an Aztec drink, comes to us via Spain with the addition of sugar and spice. ♦ It really pains us to speak evil of so distinctively delicious a drink. But chocolate, with its high fat and sugar content, if habitually substituted for milk, may create an imbalance in the diet. In some places, unless you ask for French chocolate, the base will be water and the drink garnished with whipped cream. In France, you can count on a milk base and cream incorporated into the drink. In Vienna, they add a generous topping of whipped cream. In America, you may have to face a marshmallow or a piece of cinnamon-stick candy; in Russia and Brazil, coffee is added; and in modern Mexico, we find in it cinnamon and even orange rind and sherry. For more information about chocolates and cocoas, see page 522.

Cocoa does not always combine easily with liquid. To remove any lumps before cooking, combine it with the sugar or mix it in the blender with a small quantity of the water called for in the recipe. You may want to keep on hand homemade cocoa or chocolate sirups, see page 31. ♦ Both cocoa and chocolate scorch easily, so brew them over hot water as suggested below. In Mexico, a special wooden stirrer or whipper called molinillo is used to fluff chocolate drinks just before serving. This also inhibits the formation of the cream "skin" which often forms on top. If you want this aerated effect, try a wire whisk or a rotary beater. Serve the hot beverage in a deep narrow chocolate cup so as to retain the heat.

COCOA
About 4 Servings
Combine, stir and boil for 2 minutes—in the top of a double boiler over direct but low heat:
1 cup boiling water
¼ cup cocoa
⅛ teaspoon salt
2 to 4 tablespoons sugar
Then add:
½ teaspoon cinnamon
¹⁄₁₆ teaspoon cloves and/or nutmeg
Place the top of the boiler ♦ over boiling water. Add:
3 cups scalded milk
Stir and heat the cocoa. Cover and keep over hot water for 10 more minutes. Beat with a wire whisk before serving.

CHOCOLATE

About 4 Servings

Melt ◗ in the top of a double boiler:

  1½ to 2 oz. chocolate

with:

  1 cup boiling water

Now, over direct heat, bring this mixture in the top of the double boiler to the point where it begins to foam up. Quickly lift it from the heat. Let the liquid recede, then repeat the foaming and receding process 3 or 4 times in all. Scald:

  3 cups milk

with:

  1 vanilla bean

Dissolve in the hot milk:

  ¼ cup sugar

  ⅛ teaspoon salt

Remove the vanilla bean. Pour these ingredients while hot over the smooth chocolate mixture and beat well with a wire whisk. In each cup, place:

  (A stick of whole cinnamon)

Before serving, fold into the mixture or top it with:

  (¼ cup whipped cream at room temperature)

BRAZILIAN CHOCOLATE

About 4 Servings

Melt in a double boiler ◗ over hot water:

  1 oz. chocolate

  ¼ cup sugar

  ⅛ teaspoon salt

Add and stir in:

  1 cup boiling water

Continue to heat 3 to 5 minutes. Add:

  ½ cup hot milk

  ½ cup hot cream

  1½ cups freshly made hot coffee

Beat mixture well and add:

  1 teaspoon vanilla

  (A grating of cinnamon)

ICED CHOCOLATE

Prepare and then chill:

  Chocolate, or

  Brazilian Chocolate, above

Serve over crushed ice. Top with:

  Whipped cream or coffee ice cream

Garnish with:

  Grated sweet chocolate

CHOCOLATE OR CHOCOLATE MALT SHAKE SIRUP

20 Servings

First, make the following sirup which you may keep on hand in the refrigerator about 10 days.

Melt in the top of a double boiler over hot water:

  7 oz. chocolate

Stir slowly into the melted chocolate:

  15 oz. sweetened condensed milk

  1 cup boiling water

Stir in, until dissolved:

  ½ cup sugar

Cool the sirup.

To make up an individual shake, use:

  2 tablespoons chocolate sirup

  1 cup chilled milk

Beat the mixture well or blend it. For increased food value, add:

  (½ cup milk solids or malt)

  (2 teaspoons debittered brewers' yeast)

Serve at once blended with:

  A dip of vanilla, chocolate, or mint ice cream

or over:

  Cracked ice

COCOA SHAKE SIRUP

About 8 servings

In the top of a double boiler make a lumpless paste of:

  1 cup sugar

  ½ cup cocoa

  ¼ cup cold water

  (½ cup malt)

Bring this mixture just to a boil over low direct heat, stirring constantly. Then continue to heat over hot water from 3 to 5 minutes. Cool mixture. You may store it covered and refrigerated for 2 to 3 weeks.

HANDY HOT CHOCOLATE OR COCOA

About 1 Serving

Prepare:

  Chocolate Shake Sirup or

  Cocoa Shake Sirup, above

For each 8 oz. cup of cocoa desired, use:

  2 tablespoons sirup

Stir in slowly:

  ¾ cup scalding milk

and heat thoroughly without boiling before serving.

MILK AND EGG BEVERAGES

Some of the formulas given in this section are nutritious enough to serve as complete meals for dieters or invalids.

MILK EGGNOG

4 Servings

Combine in a shaker:

  4 cups chilled milk

  4 eggs

  4 tablespoons confectioners' sugar or honey

  1 teaspoon vanilla, grated orange or lemon rind

  (½ cup orange juice)

  ½ cup cracked ice

Shake the eggnog well. Sprinkle the top with:

  Freshly grated nutmeg

Of course, it will do no harm to add a jigger or two of whisky, cognac or rum.

FRUIT MILK SHAKE

4 Servings

Combine in a shaker or blender:

  1⅓ cups chilled sweetened apricot, prune, strawberry or raspberry juice

  2⅔ cups cold milk

Serve over cracked ice.

ABOUT JUICES AND FRUIT BEVERAGES

Fresh herbs and fruits, when available, make attractive garnishes for cold fruit beverages. Try a sprig of common mint or velvety, frosty-looking apple mint. A few leaves of borage or its bright, starry blossoms are pretty additions or the wheel-like foliage of sweet woodruff—the German Waldmeister, see page 537. Use also garnishes of lemon balm, lemon thyme, pineapple sage and scented geranium.

Charming decorations for beverages are strawberries and cherries. So are pineapple slices or citrus fruits, cut into attractive shapes. For winter concoctions, put a few cloves into the citrus slices and use them to garnish the glasses, adding one or two thin twisted citrus rind shavings to the drink itself. Another way to heighten the charm of cold beverages is to spruce them up with decorative ice cubes. Fill a refrigerator tray with water. Place in each section one of the following: a maraschino cherry, a preserved strawberry, a piece of lemon or pineapple, a sprig of mint, etc.

You may flavor the cubes, before freezing, with sherry or whisky—using not more than 2 tablespoons per tray. The short recipes which immediately follow are designed mainly to whet the appetite. They are dedicated to two kinds of people—those who cannot take cocktails because of their alcoholic content and those who like to appear convivial but who are convinced that a stiff alcoholic drink before dinner blunts the flavor of good food. Their basic liquid ingredients may, of course, be served without our suggested modifiers.

To make rich vegetable juices, blend vegetables, but be sure to cook first any fibrous ones such as celery. Don't forget the convenience of frozen concentrates, especially for strongly flavored, quick-chilling drinks.

FRESH TOMATO JUICE
4 Servings

Simmer for ½ hour:
  12 medium-sized, raw, ripe tomatoes
with:
  ½ cup water
  1 slice onion
  2 ribs celery with leaves
  ½ bay leaf
  3 sprigs parsley
Strain these ingredients. Season with:
  1 teaspoon salt
  ¼ teaspoon paprika
  ¼ teaspoon sugar
Serve thoroughly chilled.

CANNED TOMATO JUICE
4 Servings

Combine in shaker:
  2½ cups tomato juice
  ½ teaspoon grated onion

  1 teaspoon grated celery
  ½ teaspoon horseradish
  1½ tablespoons lemon juice
    A dash of Worcestershire or hot pepper sauce
  ⅛ teaspoon paprika
  ¾ teaspoon salt
  ¼ teaspoon sugar
This juice may be served hot or chilled. Curry powder, a few cloves, a stick of cinnamon, tarragon, parsley or some other herb may be steeped in the cocktail and strained out before it is served.

CHILLED TOMATO CREAM
4 Servings

Combine in a shaker:
  1½ cups chilled tomato juice
  ¾ cup chilled cream
  1 teaspoon grated onion
  ⅛ teaspoon salt
  ⅛ teaspoon celery salt
    A few drops hot pepper sauce
    A few grains cayenne
  ¼ cup finely cracked ice

TOMATO AND CUCUMBER JUICE
4 Servings

Combine in a shaker:
  2 cups tomato juice
  2 tablespoons salad oil
  1 tablespoon vinegar
  ½ teaspoon salt
  ⅛ teaspoon paprika
  (¼ teaspoon basil)
Peel, seed, grate and add:
  1 cucumber
  ½ cup cracked ice

ORANGE AND TOMATO JUICE
4 Servings

Combine in a shaker:
  1½ cups tomato juice
  1 cup orange juice
  1 teaspoon sugar
  1 tablespoon lemon or lime juice
  ½ teaspoon salt
  ½ cup crushed ice

SAUERKRAUT JUICE
4 Servings

This is also called Lumpensuppe and is recommended by some people for a hangover.
I. Combine:
  1 teaspoon lemon juice
  ⅛ teaspoon paprika
  2 cups sauerkraut juice

II. Chill, then combine:
  1 cup sauerkraut juice
  1 cup tomato juice
  (½ teaspoon prepared horseradish)

CLAM JUICE
4 Servings

Combine:
  2 tablespoons lemon juice
  1½ tablespoons tomato catsup
  2 cups clam juice

A drop hot pepper sauce
Salt if needed
(½ teaspoon grated onion)
¼ teaspoon celery salt

Chill these ingredients. Strain before serving. This is a good combination, but there are many others. Horseradish may be added, so may Worcestershire sauce. The cocktail may be part clam juice and part tomato juice. Serve sprinkled with:

Freshly ground pepper

ORANGE AND LIME JUICE
4 Servings

Combine in a shaker:
2 cups orange juice
1 tablespoon lime juice or
2 tablespoons lemon juice
⅛ teaspoon salt
½ cup cracked ice

FRESH PINEAPPLE JUICE
About 1½ Cups of Juice

A very refreshing drink.
Peel a:
Pineapple

Cut it into cubes. Extract the juice by putting the pineapple through a food grinder or a ⅃ blender. There will be very little pulp. Strain the juice and serve it iced with:
Sprigs of mint

PINEAPPLE AND TOMATO JUICE
4 Servings

Combine in a shaker:
1 cup pineapple juice
1 cup tomato juice
¼ teaspoon salt
½ cup crushed ice

PINEAPPLE AND GRAPEFRUIT JUICE
4 Servings

Boil for 3 minutes:
⅛ cup sugar
⅛ cup water

Chill the sirup. Add:
1¼ cups grapefruit juice
⅔ cup pineapple juice
¼ cup lemon juice

Serve chilled.

FRUIT SHRUBS OR VINEGARS

These are most refreshing in hot weather. Try adding rum in the winter.
Prepare:
Fruit juice

Depending on the sweetness of the juice, simmer until the sugar is dissolved:
1 cup juice
1 to 1½ cups sugar

For every cup of juice, add:
¼ cup white wine vinegar

Bottle in sterile jars. Serve the shrub over shaved ice.

CITRUS-FRUIT JUICE MEDLEY
4 Servings

Combine in a shaker:
¾ cup grapefruit juice
¼ cup lemon juice
½ cup orange juice
⅓ to ½ cup sugar
1 cup cracked ice

Pour into glasses and serve garnished with:
Sprigs of mint

★ HOT OR MULLED CIDER

Good on a cold night, with canapés or sandwiches. Heat well, but do not boil:
Apple cider
A few cloves
A stick of cinnamon

CRANBERRY JUICE
4 Servings

Cook until skins pop open, about 5 minutes:
1 pint cranberries
2 cups water

Strain through cheesecloth. Bring the juice to a boil and add:
¼ to ⅓ cup sugar
(3 cloves)

Cook for 2 minutes. Cool. Add:
¼ cup orange juice or
1 tablespoon lemon juice

Serve thoroughly chilled. Garnish with:
A slice of lime

FRUIT JUICE TWOSOMES

Good combinations are equal parts of:
Orange juice and pineapple juice
or:
Loganberry juice and pineapple juice
or:
White grape juice and orange juice
or:
Cranberry juice and sweetened lime juice
or:
Grapefruit juice and cranberry juice

★ HOT CRANBERRY JUICE

Heat well, but do not boil:
Cranberry juice
A thinly sliced lemon
A few cloves
A cracked nutmeg
(Honey to taste)

Serve in mugs, with cinnamon stick stirrers.

⅃ ABOUT BLENDED JUICES

The blender transforms many kinds of fruit and vegetables into rich and delicious liquid food. The only trouble in using it is that the enthusiast often gets drunk with power and whirls up more and more weird and intricate combinations—some of them quite undrinkable. Resist the temptation to become a sorcerer's apprentice.

Sometimes too, a gray color results. If so, gradually stir in lemon juice, a little at a time. Serve immediately after adding the lemon juice, as the clear color may not last long. A few suggestions follow. Each recipe yields about 3 cups.

I. Combine in blender:
    1½ cups chilled, seeded orange pulp
    1 cup chilled melon meat
      (cantaloupe or honeydew)
    2 tablespoons lemon juice
    ⅛ teaspoon salt
    ½ cup finely crushed ice

II. This is almost like a sherbet.
Combine in blender:
    1½ cups chilled apricot or peach pulp
    ½ cup milk
    ½ cup cream
    2 tablespoons sugar
    ½ cup finely crushed ice
    (1 tablespoon lemon juice)

III. Combine in blender:
    1 cup chilled, unsweetened
      pineapple juice
    1 cup peeled, seeded, chilled cucumber
    ½ cup watercress
    2 sprigs parsley
    ½ cup finely crushed ice

IV. Combine in a blender:
    1½ cups chilled, unsweetened
      pineapple juice
    1 ripe banana
    2 teaspoons honey
    Juice of ½ lime
    ½ cup finely crushed ice
    (4 maraschino cherries)
Garnish with:
    (Sprigs of mint)

PINEAPPLE OR ORANGE EGGNOG
4 Servings

Combine in a shaker or blender:
    2 cups chilled pineapple or
      orange juice
    1 tablespoon confectioners' sugar
      or honey
    1½ tablespoons lemon juice
    1 egg or 2 egg yolks
    A pinch of salt
    ¼ cup cracked ice
Shake or blend well.

ABOUT PARTY BEVERAGES

As with Party Drinks, each of the following recipes, unless otherwise indicated, will yield about 5 quarts and accommodate approximately 20 people. For "ice-bowl" containers and other suggestions for attractively serving large groups of people, see Party Drinks, page 48.

GALA TOMATO PUNCH

For a summer brunch in a shady corner of the veranda.

Combine:
    4 quarts tomato juice, page 751
    1 quart canned beef consommé
Season to taste with:
    Garlic salt
    (A chiffonade of herbs)
Chill, pour into bowl and decorate with:
    Decorative ice ring, page 48
in which has been set:
    An herb bouquet

LEMONADE
For each cup of water, add:
    1½ tablespoons lemon juice
    3 to 4 tablespoons sugar
    ⅛ teaspoon salt
The sugar and water need not be boiled, but the quality of the lemonade is improved if they are. Boil the sugar and water for 2 minutes. Chill the sirup and add the lemon juice. Orange, pineapple, raspberry, loganberry, white grape juice and other fruit juices may be combined with lemonade. Chilled tea, added to these fruit combinations, about ⅓ cup for every cup of juice, gives lemonades an invigorating lift.

LEMONADE FOR 100 PEOPLE
Boil for 10 minutes:
    4 cups water
    8 cups sugar
Cool the sirup. Add:
    7½ cups lemon juice
Stir in the contents of:
    2 No. 2½ cans crushed pineapple or
      6 to 8 cans frozen juice concentrate
Add:
    8 sliced seeded oranges
    4 gallons water
Chill. Serve over ice.

LEMONADE SIRUP
About 4½ cups

I. Boil for 5 minutes:
    2 cups sugar
    1 cup water
    Rind of 2 lemons, cut into thin strips
    ⅛ teaspoon salt
Cool and add:
    Juice of 6 lemons
Strain the sirup. Store in a covered jar.
Add:
    2 tablespoons sirup
to:
    1 glass ice water or carbonated water

II. Add:
    1 tablespoon sirup
    2 tablespoons orange, apricot or
      pineapple juice
to:
    1 glass ice water or carbonated water

ORANGEADE
Serve undiluted:
    Orange juice
over:
    Crushed ice

or add to the orange juice, to taste:
    (Water, lemon juice and sugar)

PINEAPPLE PUNCH
Place in a large bowl:
    2 cups strong tea
Add and stir well:
    ¾ cup lemon juice
    2 cups orange juice
    2 tablespoons lime juice
    1 cup sugar
    Leaves from 12 sprigs mint
Place these ingredients on ice for 2 hours.
Shortly before serving, strain the punch
and add:
    8 slices pineapple and juice from can
    5 pints chilled ginger ale
    4 pints chilled carbonated water
    Crushed ice

FRUIT PUNCH
Boil for 10 minutes:
    1¼ cups sugar
    1¼ cups water
Add:
    2½ cups strong, hot tea
Cool the mixture. Add:
    1 cup crushed pineapple
    2½ cups strawberry juice or
        other fruit juice
    Juice of 6 lemons
    Juice of 7 oranges
Chill these ingredients for 1 hour. Add
sufficient water to make 4 quarts of liquid.
Immediately before serving, add:
    1 cup maraschino cherries
    1 quart carbonated water
Pour over large pieces of ice in punch
bowl.

FRUIT PUNCH FOR 50 PEOPLE
Make a sirup, by boiling for 10 minutes:
    1¼ cups water
    2½ cups sugar
Reserve ½ cup of this. Add to the remainder, stir, cover and permit to stand for
30 minutes or more:
    1 cup lemon juice
    2 cups orange juice
    1 cup strong tea
    2 cups white grape juice, grapefruit
        juice, pineapple juice or crushed
        pineapple
    1 cup maraschino cherries with juice
    2 cups fruit sirup

The fruit sirup, we find, is the main ingredient. Your punch is apt to be just as
good as this touch. Strawberry jam may be
diluted, canned raspberry or loganberry
juice may be sweetened and boiled until
heavy. Strain these ingredients. Add ice
water to make about 1½ gallons of liquid.
Add at the last minute:
    1 quart carbonated water
If you find the punch lacking in sugar, add
part or all of the reserved sugar sirup.

STRAWBERRY FRUIT PUNCH
Boil for 5 minutes:
    4 cups water
    4 cups sugar
Cool the sirup. Combine:
    2 quarts hulled strawberries
    1 cup sliced canned or
        fresh pineapple
    1 cup mixed fruit juice—
        pineapple, apricot, raspberry, etc.
    Juice of 5 large oranges
    Juice of 5 large lemons
    (3 sliced bananas)
Add the chilled sirup or as much of it as is
palatable. Chill these ingredients. Imme-
diately before serving, add:
    2 quarts carbonated water
    3 cups or more crushed ice
This is a strong punch. It is purposely pre-
pared this way, as the ice will thin it.
Water also may be added if desired.

MOCHA PUNCH
Prepare, then chill well:
    7 cups freshly made coffee
Whip until stiff:
    2 cups whipping cream
You may whip an additional ½ cup heavy
cream and then reserve about a cup to
garnish the tops. Have in readiness:
    2 quarts chocolate ice cream
Pour the chilled coffee into a large chilled
bowl. Add ½ the ice cream. Beat until the
cream is partly melted. Add:
    ¼ cup rum or 1 teaspoon
        almond extract
    ¼ teaspoon salt
Fold in the remainder of the ice cream and
all but a cup of the whipped cream.
Pour the punch into tall glasses. Garnish
the tops with the reserved cream. Sprinkle
with:
        Freshly grated nutmeg or grated
        sweet chocolate

DRINKS

Now and then we look into the work of our fellow cookbook authors and are usually surprised to discover how little attention they pay to liquor. In past editions we, too, have approached this subject rather apologetically—after all, there was a time when selling or serving alcoholic refreshment was considered disreputable in America. But here and now we drop all subterfuge, frankly concede that "something to drink" is becoming with us an almost invariable concomitant of at least the company dinner, and have boldly enlarged this section of the book. Always in the back of our minds, spurring us on, is the memory of a cartoon which depicted a group of guests sitting around a living room, strickenly regarding their cocktail glasses, while the hostess, one of those inimitable Hokinson types, all embonpoint, cheer, and fluttering organdy, announces, "A very dear friend gave me some wonderful old Scotch and I just happened to find a bottle of papaya juice in the refrigerator!"

COCKTAILS AND OTHER BEFORE-DINNER DRINKS

The cocktail is probably an American invention, and most certainly a typically American kind of drink. Whatever mixtures you put together—and part of the fascination of cocktail making is the degree of inventiveness it seems to encourage—hold fast to a few general principles. ◆ The most important of these is to keep the quantity of the basic ingredients—gin, whisky, rum, etc.—up to about 60% of the total drink, never below half. ◆ Remember, as a corollary, that cocktails are before-meal drinks—appetizers. For this reason they should be neither oversweet nor overloaded with cream and egg, in order to avoid spoiling the appetite instead of stimulating it.

If you mix drinks in your kitchen, your equipment probably includes the essential strainer, squeezer, bottle opener, ice pick, and sharp knife. Basic bar equipment also includes a heavy glass cocktail shaker; a martini pitcher; an ice bucket and tongs; a bar spoon; a strainer; a jigger; a muddler; a bitters bottle with the dropper type top; and—for converting cubes to crushed ice—a heavy canvas bag and wood mallet. We also show a lemon peeler guaranteed to get only the colored unbitter part of the rind, and the only corkscrew that doesn't induce complete frustration.

A simple syrup is a useful ingredient when making drinks. Boil for 5 minutes 1 part water to 2 parts sugar, or half as much water as sugar. Keep the syrup in a bottle, refrigerated, and use it as needed.

In addition to various liquors, it is advisable for the home bartender to have on hand a stock of: bitters, carbonated water; lemons, oranges, limes, olives, cherries. For Garnishes see page 35. See also the chapters on Canapés and Hors d'Oeuvre for suitable accompaniments for cocktails —besides a steady head.

Note the two types of cocktail glasses illustrated on page 37. Both are so designed that the heat of the hand is not transferred to the contents of the glass. These hold about 3 ounces each. The old-fashioned glass featured next holds about 6 ounces and retains its chill by reason of a heavy base. The next two drawings show typical sour and daiquiri glasses. Each holds about 4 ounces. Champagne cocktails, also about 4 ounces each, are often served in the saucer-bowl footed glass used for daiquiris. The small glass shown last is for straight whisky.

◆ Mix only one round at a time. Your

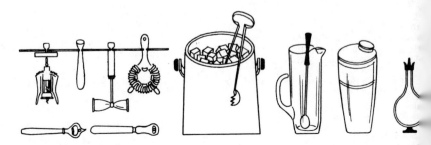

ock as a bartender will never go up on
e strength of your "dividend" drinks.
he cocktails which follow are some fun-
amental ones, listed according to their
asic ingredients. ♦ Each recipe, unless
herwise noted, makes about 4 drinks.
/hen cracked—not crushed—ice is indi-
ted, use about ¾ cup. ♦ All "shaken"
ocktails should be strained into the
asses just before serving.

ABOUT MEASUREMENTS
FOR DRINKS

dash	= 6 drops
teaspoons	= ½ ounce
pony	= 1 ounce
jigger	= 1½ ounces
large jigger	= 2 ounces
standard whisky glass	= 2 ounces
pint	= 16 fluid ounces
fifth	= 25.6 fluid ounces
quart	= 32 fluid ounces

ABOUT GIN AND GIN COCKTAILS

n is a spirit—that is, a distilled liquor.
uch of its distinctive flavor comes from
e juniper berry. Victorian novelists
nded to assume that only the lower
sses—footmen, scullery maids and the
e—had a taste for gin; just as they im-
ed that rum was an equally vulgar tip-
· and might be relegated to the common
man. The "bathtub" concoctions of the
aring Twenties did nothing to enhance
's repute. Recent generations, however,
ve recognized the fact that this liquor,
gardless of its shady past and its possi-
ities as a straight drink, is probably the
st mixing base ever invented.
Of the three general gin types, Geneva
d Holland are somewhat bitter and
ghly aromatic. They appeal to a small
nority and should be taken "neat." By
the most popular kind of gin is the
/ London type, which can be found in
liquor dispensaries. More perhaps than
the case with most other liquors, the
ality of commercial gin varies: its cost is
rough measure of its worth. Certain
nds of gin, which we happen to prefer,
aged for a time in sherry casks, a proc-
which imparts a golden color.

ALEXANDER
ake with ¾ cup cracked ice:
 1 jigger sweet cream
 ½ jiggers crème de cacao
 5 jiggers gin
ain into chilled glasses.

BRONX
Shake, using ¾ cup cracked ice:
 1 jigger dry vermouth
 1 jigger sweet vermouth
 1 jigger orange juice
 5 jiggers gin
Strain into chilled glasses. Add a twist of
orange peel to each glass.

GIMLET
Shake, using ¾ cup cracked ice:
 1 tablespoon sugar syrup
 2 large jiggers lime juice
 5 jiggers gin
Strain into chilled glasses.
Substituting orange juice for ½ the lime
juice changes a Gimlet into an **Orange
Blossom**. Vodka is becoming increasingly
popular as a base for both.

GIN BITTER
1 Serving
With bourbon or rye whisky this becomes a
Whisky Bitter.
Half fill an old-fashioned glass with
cracked ice. Shake, using ¾ cup cracked
ice:
 2 jiggers gin
 2 dashes angostura or orange bitters
Pour into glass. Top with twist of orange
peel.

GIN OR WHISKY SOUR
This recipe becomes a **Whisky, Rum** or
Brandy Sour if the base is changed.
Shake, using ¾ cup cracked ice:
 1 jigger sugar syrup
 2 jiggers lemon or lime juice
 5 jiggers gin or whisky
Strain into chilled glasses.

PERFECT MARTINI
Stir well, using ¾ cup cracked ice:
 1 jigger dry vermouth
 1 jigger sweet vermouth
 6 jiggers gin
Add to each drink:
 1 dash orange bitters
Serve with olive in bottom of glass.

MARTINI
With a small onion in each glass, this cocktail becomes a **Gibson**. Try also a hazelnut
and name it yourself. Changing the base
makes a **Vodka Martini**.
 In the last edition of The Joy we told
the story of a bartender who was proffered
so much advice on how to make a mint

julep that he retired in complete frustration. Purism still seems to run rampant in drinking circles; and this time we should like to substitute the experience of still another hapless barkeep who just couldn't seem to produce a martini dry enough for his customer. Finally, after the vermouth content had been reduced to what the bartender regarded as absolute minimum, the customer snarled: "Try it again! This time only a whisper." The barkeep tried again; the customer took a wary sip, set down his glass, glared furiously at him and shouted, "Loudmouth!"

Stir well, using ¾ cup cracked ice:
    1 to 2 jiggers dry vermouth
    6 to 7 jiggers gin
Twist over the top:
    Lemon peel
or add:
    A small seeded olive

PINK LADY
Shake, using ¾ cup cracked ice:
    ½ jigger grenadine
    1 jigger lemon or lime juice
    1 jigger apple brandy
    2 egg whites
    4½ jiggers gin
Strain into chilled glasses.

WHITE LADY
Shake, using ¾ cup cracked ice:
    1½ jiggers lemon juice
    1 jigger Cointreau
    2 egg whites
    4½ jiggers gin
Strain into chilled glasses.

ABOUT WHISKY AND WHISKY COCKTAILS

There are, as everyone knows, several kinds of whisky; but two in particular, bourbon and Scotch, far outrank all others in popularity. Bourbon is chiefly—and we believe preferably—of American, and by American we mean United States, manufacture, distilled from corn. Scotch is made, as might be expected, in Scotland, of barley. Its distinctive taste is achieved by smoking the barley malt before distillation on a porous floor, over peat fires.

Bourbon and Scotch differ again in that Scotch is always sold blended, several varieties being combined before bottling; whereas only bourbon of lower quality is blended. It is important to note in this connection that Scotch blends are invariably blends of whisky alone, but that bourbon blends may be either combinations of straight whiskies or of whisky and so-called neutral spirits, i.e., alcohol. The nature of the contents is always indicated on the label. Even if you must economize, we recommend buying only straight blends.

High quality or bonded bourbon, again always so labeled, is a straight whisky with **certain** important guarantees of quality:

first, as we have said, it is straight liquo[r] second, it is all of the same age, never le[ss] than 4 years; third, it contains no add[i]tives, except for the amount of water ne[c]essary to bring it down to 100 proof, th[e] legally required minimum. A word abo[ut] proof, which simply means the alcohol content, by volume, of a given spirit: 10[0] proof liquor is one which has an alcohol content of 50%; 90-proof of 45%; and [so] on. Age in whisky is important. Remem[...]ber, however, that aging takes place on[ly] in the cask to which whisky is transferr[ed] after distillation—never subsequently [in] the bottle. Moreover, bourbon whisky matured in charred casks; and since, aft[er] 10 or 12 years, the spirit penetrates t[he] char and is adversely affected by the r[aw] wood underneath, bourbon older than [a] decade or so becomes increasingly le[ss] acceptable.

Which is "better," bourbon or Scotc[h]? This is a little like asking whether a pea[ch] or a pear is better. It depends, like t[he] appreciation of a good many other kin[ds] of liquor, on one's personal taste. It c[an] certainly be said, however, that in co[n]cocting mixed drinks—cocktails, o[ld-] fashioneds, sours, etc.—bourbon, or if y[ou] happen to prefer it, rye, is immeasurab[ly] superior to Scotch, the smoky taste which tends to inhibit successful merge[r.] This situation is reflected in the formul[as] which follow.

Incidentally, a fourth kind of whisk[y,] Irish, which makes a rather off-beat choi[ce] —except in Irish Coffee, see page 28— now being manufactured in both smo[ky] and non-smoky types. If you are inclin[ed] to use Irish in cocktails, the same kind [of] discrimination as with Scotch should app[ly.]

PERFECT MANHATTAN
Scotch may replace the bourbon or rye [in] this formula and the one following; [in] which case the cocktail is called a **R[ob]** **Roy**. When a dash of Drambuie is add[ed] a **Rob Roy** becomes a **Bobbie Burns**. [By] substituting Peychaud bitters as a var[ia]tion.
Stir well with ice cubes:
    1 jigger dry vermouth
    1 jigger sweet vermouth
    6 jiggers bourbon or rye
Add to each drink:
    1 dash angostura bitters
    (maraschino cherry)

MANHATTAN
Stir well with ice cubes:
    1 to 2 jiggers dry vermouth
    6 to 7 jiggers bourbon or rye
Add to each drink:
    1 dash angostura bitters
    A twist of lemon peel

OLD-FASHIONED
                       1 Serv[ing]
Put into an old-fashioned glass and stir

½ teaspoon sugar syrup
2 dashes angostura bitters
1 teaspoon water
Add:
2 ice cubes
Fill glass to within ½ inch of top with:
  Bourbon or rye
Stir. Decorate with a twist of lemon peel,
a thin slice of orange and a maraschino
cherry. Serve with a muddler.
  The above formula, like that for the
Julep, which follows, page 46, is a rock-
bottom affair. Some like their old-fash-
ioneds on the fancy side, adding a squeeze
of lemon juice, a dash of curaçao, kirsch or
maraschino liqueur or a spear of fresh
pineapple; or substituting a fresh ripe
strawberry for the time-honored cherry.
Try also, if you care to, a Scotch old-
fashioned.

SAZERAC
Stir with ice cubes:
  4 teaspoons sugar syrup
  4 dashes Peychaud bitters
  4 dashes anisette or Pernod
  7 jiggers bourbon or rye
Pour into chilled glasses. Add a twist of
lemon peel to each glass.

ABOUT RUM AND RUM COCKTAILS

Another spirit, this, as blithe and potent as
whisky and gin and, next to gin, perhaps
the most versatile of "mixers." Rum is distilled from sugar cane—or, rather, molasses. Generally the rum available to the
American consumer is of two fairly sharply
differentiated types: Puerto Rican, or light-
bodied, and Jamaican, a heavier-bodied,
darker and quite dissimilar tasting product.
Only the light type and of the highest
quality should be used for cocktails: that
marked "white label" for dry drinks, "gold
label" for sweeter ones. Save the heavier,
more pungent types of rum for long drinks,
punches, nogs, colas and shakes.
  Some people like the taste and look of a
frosted glass and consider it the final fine
touch to cocktails of the rum type.
  To frost a cocktail glass: cool the glass
and swab the rim with a section of lemon
from which the juice is flowing freely or
dip it in grenadine. Swirl the glass to remove excess moisture, then dip the rim
to a depth of ¼ inch in powdered or confectioners' sugar. Lift the glass and tap it
gently to remove any excess sugar.

BENEDICTINE
Shake with ¾ cup cracked ice:
  1½ jiggers lime juice
  1½ jiggers Benedictine
  5½ jiggers rum
Strain into chilled glasses.

CUBANA
Shake with ¾ cup cracked ice:
  ½ jigger sugar syrup

  1½ jiggers lime juice
  2 jiggers apricot brandy
  4 jiggers rum
Strain into chilled glasses.

DAIQUIRI
With grenadine substituted for sugar
syrup, this cocktail becomes a **Pink Daiquiri** or **Daiquiri Grenadine.**
Shake well with ¾ cup cracked ice:
  ½ jigger sugar syrup
  1½ jiggers lime juice
  6 jiggers rum
Strain into chilled glasses.

⅄ BLENDER FROZEN DAIQUIRI
Spectacular and delicious frozen cocktails
may be made by using an electric blender.
In the Daiquiri recipe, for instance, by increasing the amount of crushed ice to between 2 and 3 cups, substituting 2 tablespoons confectioners' sugar for each jigger
of syrup and blending the ingredients until
they reach a snowy consistency, you will
achieve a hot weather triumph. Serve it in
champagne glasses. This is a formula
which can be interestingly varied. For a
group, try using more ice, more rum and
instead of the lime juice and sugar, a chunk
of frozen concentrated limeade, fresh out
of the can.

EL PRESIDENTE
Shake with ¾ cup cracked ice:
  1½ jiggers dry vermouth
  1½ jiggers lemon juice
  2 dashes grenadine
  2 dashes curaçao
  5 jiggers rum
Strain into chilled glasses and decorate
with a twist of orange peel.

KNICKERBOCKER
Shake well with ¾ cup of cracked ice:
  ½ jigger raspberry syrup
  ½ jigger pineapple syrup
  1½ jiggers lemon juice
  5½ jiggers rum
Strain into chilled glasses and serve with a
twist of orange peel.

ABOUT BRANDY AND BRANDY
COCKTAILS

Here is a spirit distilled from fruit, most
commonly from grapes. Except for apple
brandy, known in America as applejack
and in France as calvados, brandy is a
scarce commodity on these shores. Most
other alleged fruit brandies in this country
are cordials, not true distillates or true
brandies. In the formulas which follow,
references always apply to grape brandy,
although experimentation with a superior
grade of applejack is encouraged. Incidentally, the name "cognac" does not by
any means apply to all grape brandies—
only to the best.
  Aging is of great importance in the

quality of this liquor but, due to a variety of circumstances, most brandies sold over American counters neither boast of nor confess to their true age. The only sure signs, in order of increasing seniority, are these: Three-Star, V.O., V.S.O., V.S.O.P., and V.V.S.O.P. While we firmly adhere to the belief that "the better the liquor, the better the drink," no one in his right mind and of sound palate should use brandies more venerable than V.O. for any purpose other than reverential sipping.

Brandy cocktails, too, may be served in frosted glasses, see page 39, with grenadine substituted for the lemon juice in preparing the glass for frosting.

CHAMPAGNE COCKTAIL
                                          1 Serving
Pour into large champagne glass:
   ½ teaspoon sugar syrup
   ½ jigger chilled brandy
Fill glass almost to top with:
   Chilled dry champagne
Add:
   2 dashes yellow Chartreuse
   2 dashes orange bitters

CURAÇAO COCKTAIL
Shake well with ¾ cup cracked ice:
   1½ jiggers curaçao
   ½ jigger lemon juice
   6 jiggers brandy
Add to each drink:
   1 dash angostura bitters
Strain into chilled glasses and add a twist of lemon peel.

SIDECAR
Sometimes this drink is served in a frosted glass, page 39. The use of apple brandy changes a Sidecar into a **Jack Rose.**
Shake with ¾ cup cracked ice:
   ½ jigger Cointreau
   1½ jiggers lemon juice
   6 jiggers brandy
Strain into chilled glasses and serve with a twist of lemon peel.

STINGER
Shake with ¾ cup finely crushed ice:
   1½ jiggers white crème de menthe
   6 jiggers brandy
   (½ jigger lime juice)
Strain into chilled glasses.

ABOUT VODKA, AQUAVIT, TEQUILA AND THEIR COCKTAILS
The spirits mentioned above just about complete the roster of those normally obtainable in the American market. They are strikingly different in character. Vodka and aquavit look—deceptively, we hasten to add—like branch water. But whereas vodka is almost tasteless while going down and almost odorless afterwards, aquavit has a strong aroma of caraway. It follows that while vodka is often used instead of

gin or whisky in mixed drinks—particularly sours—aquavit is almost invariably drunk straight and very cold. Occasionally, it is combined with tomato juice as a cocktail. Tequila, which a friend of ours has dubbed "the Gulp of Mexico," appeals to a very limited number of aficionados. Try it before you buy it.

BLOODY MARY
Shake well or blend with ¾ cup crushed ice:
   3 jiggers vodka or aquavit
   6 jiggers or 1 cup chilled
      tomato juice
   1 teaspoon lemon juice
   1 teaspoon Worcestershire sauce
   2 drops hot pepper sauce
   ¼ teaspoon celery salt
   ¼ teaspoon salt
   Pinch garlic salt
Serve without straining in whisky sour glasses.

MARGARITA
Stir well with ¾ cup cracked ice:
   5 jiggers tequila
   2½ jiggers lime or lemon juice
   ½ jigger triple sec
Pour into glasses, the rims of which have been rubbed with citrus rind and then spun in salt.

ABOUT SHERRY AND OTHER FORTIFIED WINES
True sherry—the "sack" so esteemed by Falstaff—comes from a relatively small area around the town of Jerez in Spain. Its extraordinary qualities are the result of a continuous, elaborate and unique method of blending, called the "solera" system. Like port and Madeira, sherry is a fortified wine, bolstered, so to speak, with brandy. It is interesting to know that sherry, the Spanish kind—with its so-called domestic counterpart—is the most popular American wine.

Sherries fall into two basic types: "fino," or dry and "oloroso," more or less sweet. The imported product appears under these further subclassifications: for the finos, manzanilla—very dry, very pale, light body; fino—very dry, very pale, medium body; amontillado—dry, pale, full-bodied; for the olorosos, amoroso—medium sweet, golden, full-bodied; oloroso—sweeter, golden-brown, full-bodied; cream—sweet, deep gold, full-bodied; brown—very sweet, dark brown, full-bodied. Most Spanish sherries, except the very dry ones, are distinguished by an elusive and delightful "nutty" taste.

Sherry, in its drier manifestations, is a pleasant substitute for the more insistent cocktail, as well as a favorite wine for cooking. Along with the less frequently encountered port and Madeira, it makes an excellent late-afternoon tranquillizer or an after-dinner drink. Never, we counsel, serve any of these three fortified wines as accompaniments to a meal—at least not later than the soup—for they are simply too substantial for the symphonic effects required of table wines.

A good deal of dispute, it seems, can be sparked over whether or not to serve sherry at room temperature. On this, as in several other similar controversies, we are latitudinarians rather than fundamentalists and happen to prefer sherry cooled to about 50°. Extreme chilling often results in temporary but unattractive cloudiness.

Sometimes, for a preprandial pickup, a host or hostess will prefer to switch from sherry to other types of aperitif wines: a medium-dry vermouth, for example, Cinzano, Byrrh, Pernod, Positano, or Dubonnet of either the dark imported or the blond domestic variety. The temperature of these, again, we like lowered to about 20° below that of the room.

ABOUT WINES

A French general is reputed to have ordered his troops to present arms every time they marched past his favorite vineyard. Alexander Dumas père, himself a famous cook, declared that certain wines should only be drunk kneeling, with head bared. In this exceedingly complex and mystique-haunted preserve we can only, like the fools of the aphorism, rush good-naturedly in, make what points we regard as basic and rush even more quickly out again, before the sticklers take us apart.

First—to clear the air of a few widely held misconceptions—wine does not improve invariably or indefinitely with age. It is true that no wine whatever should be drunk until a year or so after it is made. White wines, except sweet ones which can live for a generation, should be drunk before they are ten years old, preferably earlier. Red wines, if properly stored, may go on getting better and better for many years. We say "may" because whether they do or not depends on the superiority of the original product and on the amount of alcohol and certain organic acids it contains—the more alcohol, by and large, the better maturation. Again, while it is true that red wines seem to consort well with certain kinds of food and white with others, it is pretty absurd to deprive yourself of wine with a meal just because the kind you have on hand does not traditionally match the entrée.

We should state categorically, however, that wine is ♦ never served with courses that include asparagus, artichokes, salads made with vinegar, vinaigretted foods, curries or oranges. We might also warn that fish with a fishy flavor, strongly flavored sauces like Diable, Remoulade, Poivrade, Chasseur, Provençale and mayonnaise, do much to destroy the subtleties of the wine which is served with them.

There is also this matter of temperature. We grant that, by and large, whites, including rosés, should be served chilled, 45° to 50°, and reds at room temperature. We confess, however, that we have known occasions when, like Kurt Stein's German-American concert-goer, "Wir haben uns by mistake entchoyed" a supper claret or an equally humble chianti served at 55° or so. Remember, too, if you like dry wine, to buy varieties that are naturally dry. Don't look for dryness in such wines as sauterne, Barsac, or Vouvray, which are inherently and characteristically sweet. See Wine Chart for usage and temperature, page 43. All wines should be stored in a dark, cool place, 55° to 60°, with the liquid contacting the cork.

For a quarter of a century, the French Government, to bring order out of what had been a chaotic situation, has rigorously defined which vineyards had the rights to which names. As a corollary, they induced the growers of the Burgundy region to bottle their own wines, label them accurately, and personally vouch for their authenticity—a practice which before 1930 had been systematically followed only in the other chief center of French viniculture, Bordeaux. As a result, it is possible to buy the world's greatest wines with considerable confidence.

If you pick up a bottle of French wine at your vintner's, you may be sure that it comes to you, without admixture or adulteration, directly from the vineyards whose name it bears, if you read any of the following: "Mise en bouteilles au chateau," "Mise en bouteilles par le propriétaire," "Mise à—or de—la propriété," "Mise au—or du—domaine," "Mise en bouteilles au domaine" or the name of the vineyard followed by "propriétaire," "propriétaire-récoltant," "vigneron" or "viticulteur."

Among French vintners another reform is a century past due—that of reclassification. Many of the traditionally great vineyards have gathered to themselves over the years lesser "crus" unworthy of their names. And a number of first-rate vineyards have been developed which are not yet listed even among the "honorable" ones. When these injustices are corrected—and there is increasing support for reclassification—we shall indeed be living in the Golden Age of Wine.

We have, of course, been speaking of the more important French wines—the "estate" wines. But these are not by any means the only palatable ones. Many lesser French wines are well worth enjoying. Nor, of course, is France the only country from which good wines come. Surprisingly enough, more white wines of German than of French origin are today being sold in the United States. And entirely acceptable imports are available from Italy and Spain—to say nothing of the domestic varieties produced in California, New York and Ohio.

Only a few of the comments which apply to still white wines apply also to champagne. Like other whites, it should be drunk before it rounds out its first decade, or as soon after as possible. Unlike them, except for rosés, champagne is usually considered fit to drink with any sort of food, as well as before and after a meal. Types range from dry to sweet, in the following order: brut, extra dry, sec, demi-sec and doux. A good many experts prefer the first, because its low sugar content permits the taste of the original wine to come through.

◗ Never open a bottle of champagne until it has been thoroughly chilled. In opening it, hold it away from you or anyone else in the room, at an angle of about 30° from the vertical. Then untwist the wires and gently ease out the cork.

To dispose of one more misconception about wine: sparkling Burgundy is definitely not a substitute for champagne. It is an inferior product.

A word of caution about purchasing wine. We have implied that you will deal best with an established vintner; not necessarily because he alone carries superior merchandise, but because he is likely to know more about it and consequently to handle and store it with greater care. It is amazing, in some sections of the country, how much fine wine has found its way into the corner grocery store and neighborhood delicatessen. But considering its preciousness and fragility, it is even more amazing to discover that the proprietors of these establishments, almost to a man, know absolutely nothing about the wines they sell, except their price, and that they are perfectly content to hustle them about as if they were so many cans of pork and beans.

It would take a bold connoisseur, indeed—and a foolish one—to undertake a listing of the world's wines in order of their excellence. As a matter of fact, many are excellent—inimitably so. Familiarity with acquaintances often breeds contempt; never with wines. To become discriminating, it is necessary to taste many varieties; and discrimination brings greater and greater enjoyment.

ABOUT SERVING WINES

Here are a few suggestions to guide the inexperienced host.

All wines respond favorably to a "resting period" of 24 hours or so before being brought to the table. With few exceptions, wines are served at 45° to 60°. Champagne is always served cold—35° to 40°. It should be cooled gradually in a refrigerator and placed in ice shortly before being used. The younger vintages of champagne call for 35°, the older for 40°. ◗ If champagne is not chilled, you may get an explosion instead of the characteristic "pop."

Except for bottles of sparkling wine, which must be drunk at one sitting, partly filled bottles of table wine may be "held over" for another occasion—as long as that occasion occurs within a week or so and provided the wine, if chilled, remains chilled.

We are aware that wrapping the wine bottle in a napkin, as it makes its rounds, is regarded by restaurateurs as poor practice—apparently because it may be used to disguise a poor-vintage label. We contend that different standards prevail at home. After all, you don't suspect your host of serving an inferior soup if he ladles it from a tureen! We still much prefer the napkin to the serving basket—it is simpler and provides better insulation.

Below are shown various types of glasses for wine. From left to right: a tall tulip glass for champagne, which is preferable to the rather outmoded saucer type, as it keeps the drink colder and preserves the fizz; a traditional Rhine wine römer; an all-purpose tulip glass, suitable for red and white wines generally; a bubble glass for sparkling Burgundy; a pipe-stem sherry glass; a balloon brandy snifter; a glass for liqueurs. All are shown filled to the proper levels at the initial pouring. All, except the brandy glass, are held by the stem when drinking. The brandy glass is held cradled in the hand, both before and during drinking, to warm the liquor and release its aroma.

Remember, in handling wine, to disturb the contents of the bottle as little as possible. At table, wine is poured from the right, since the glass occupies a top right location in table setting.

DINING WITH WINE

COURSE	WINE	HOW TO SERVE
SHELLFISH OR HORS	Chablis Graves Rhine Moselle	Cold— 40° to 45°
SOUP	Sauterne	Cold— 40° to 45°
	Dry Sherry	Room Temp.
	Madeira	Cool—50°
FISH	White Bordeaux White Burgundy Rhine, Moselle Other Whites	Cool—50°
ENTREES	White Wine Champagne	Cold— 40° to 45°
	Red Wine	Room Temp.
ROASTS Red Meats	Red Burgundy Red Bordeaux Other Reds	Room Temp.
	Sparkling Burgundy	Cold— 40° to 45°
ROASTS White Meats	White Bordeaux	Cold— 40° to 45°
	White Burgundy	Cool—50°
	Champagne	Cold— 40° to 45°
FOWL OR GAME	Red Burgundy Red Bordeaux Rhone Other Reds	Room Temp.
CHEESE	Red Burgundy Red Bordeaux Other Reds Port Sherry Madeira	Room Temp.
DESSERT	Madeira Sherry	Room Temp.
	Champagne	Cold— 40° to 45°
COFFEE	Cognac Port Sherry Madeira Liqueur Red Wine	Room Temp.

Note: Champagne—cold—may be served with any course.

The average serving of dinner wine or champagne is 3 to 3½ fluid ounces; of cocktail or dessert wine, 2 to 2½ ounces. The chart below gives volumes and servings:

SIZE	OUNCES	DINNER WINE— CHAMPAGNE SERVINGS	COCKTAIL— DESSERT WINE SERVINGS
Fifth ⅘ qt.	25.6	8	8-12
Tenth ⅘ pt.	12.8	4	4-6
Split	6.4	2	
Quart	32	10	10-14
Pint	16	5	5-7
½ Gallon	64	20	20-30
Gallon	128	40	40-60

ABOUT VINTAGES

Domestic wines and those produced abroad in similar mild or temperate climates do not vary greatly in quality. Differences between them, however, are due chiefly to predictable and more or less constant differences in selectivity and manufacture.

None of these fair-weather wines can approach French and German wines at their best. But climatic extremes and certain other individual factors introduce into the production of the vintages of France and of the Rhine a strong element of chance. As a consequence, they are not by any means always at their peak. Yet, even in a so-called poor vintage year, some of the many North European wines may be exceptional.

In view of this rather complicated situation we have resisted the temptation to draw up a detailed vintage guide for French and German wines. We do venture to note that, during the past couple of decades, the following years are generally regarded as having produced, in these regions, excellent wines: '59, '61, '62, '66, '69, '70, '71. Average or better were '64 and '67. '60, '63, '65, and '68 were poor.

There are events in life which should be celebrated with a gala! A single pouring from a jeroboam takes care of 34 glasses placed in fountain form. Whether you pour champagne or punch, the effect is memorable. Better practice first, though, with tap water! See next page.

modern beer demands, in its long, slow and intricately controlled processing.

Beers vary greatly in alcoholic and sugar content, depending on how they are brewed. Bock, which appears at Easter-time, is frequently advertised by a picture of a monk—for Shrove Tuesday was the traditional tasting and testing day in the old monasteries. This brew is dark and is usually higher in alcoholic content than beer set in the spring. Beer is light and tart, or dark and sweet—depending on whether the barley is processed with low, slow heat or with high, swift heat. Which to serve is a matter of personal taste.

Here are the traditional beer and ale glasses and mugs.

Steins, heirloom and everyday, the Pil-sener glass for light beer and an ale glass and mug are shown below. The true con-noisseur is probably happiest drinking beer from an opaque container. It does not allow him to see the small imperfections in the appearance of the beer, which are visi-ble when it is served in improperly washed glasses. Grease is the natural enemy of beer, for it kills the foam. So wash glasses with soda, not with soap. The glasses should never be dried, but should be al-lowed to drain on a soft cloth washed with a detergent.

Glasses may be chilled before using, but, in any case, they should be rinsed in cold water just before using and the beer should be poured into a tilted, wet glass.

You may like a high or a low collar, but the usual size is one-fourth the height of the glass or mug. A bottle of beer, despite popular superstition, is not so caloric as the average cocktail, but since it lacks the disembodied quality of table wines it is usually served with snacks and suppers.

ABOUT SERVING BEER AND ALE

The beer connoisseur, like the wine fan-cier, never forgets the living quality of his brew. Even today's pasteurized beer is still full of living organisms, subject to de-terioration and shock. So, if he wants to savor beer at its height, he looks at the date to make sure it won't be over 2 months old when it is served. He keeps it stored in a dark place. He chills it slowly before serving and once cold he does not allow it to warm up again and be re-chilled, nor does he ever allow it to freeze.

Like the wine connoisseur, the beer ex-pert is most particular about the tempera-tures at which he serves his brew. Forty degrees is favored as producing the fullest flavor, a not too great contrast between the temperature of the drink and that of the taste buds.

A slightly higher serving temperature is suggested for ale. This drink is made from the same ingredients as beer, except for the strain of the yeast. It is fermented rapidly and at room temperature rather than at the almost freezing temperatures

ABOUT LIQUEURS AND CORDIALS

A common characteristic of almost all liqueurs and cordials is their sweetness. This quality relegates them as straight drinks to the after-dinner hour, along with a second demitasse. With some, such as kümmel, curaçao, Cointreau, Grand Mar-nier, anisette, crème de menthe or crème de cacao, a single flavor predominates. In

others—Chartreuse, Benedictine, Vieille Curé, Drambuie, for example—the flavor is more intricate. Still a third class of liqueurs of which falernum and orgeat—almond, kirsch—wild cherry, crème de cassis—currant, grenadine—pomegranate, and maraschino—cherry are perhaps the best known, are used almost entirely as components of mixed drinks. However, do not overlook this potentiality with all other liqueurs: a few drops, experimentally added, have touched off many a brave new cocktail. By themselves, serve liqueurs at room temperature or a little below, and in small quantities.

ABOUT MIXED DRINKS

In the foregoing pages of this chapter we have dealt with our material on the "basic ingredient" principle and have attempted a chronological resumé of the drinks, simple or compound, which are likely to precede, go along with or follow meals—from the ceremonious to the completely informal. The following sections describe a number of between-meal or special-occasion drinks such variety as to defy systematic listing—at least as far as their components are concerned.

Glasses and cups for mixed drinks vary greatly in size and shape. Collins glasses, lemonade and highball glasses, shown at the left, are similar in shape and vary in content from 8 to 16 ounces.

Silver cups with a handle, so that the frost remains undisturbed, are highly favored for such drinks as mint juleps. Some persons dislike drinks served in metal, but if straws are used no metallic taste is noticeable. Juleps without straws should be served in very thin glassware. To frost the glasses, see page 46.

Tom and Jerry mugs, shown next, hold about 8 ounces; punch glasses or cups, 3 to 4 ounces. These are frequently made of porcelain, an advantage when serving mulled or flaming drinks.

ABOUT TALL DRINKS

King-size drinks are commonly served in glasses holding 8 ounces or more. When mixers such as carbonated water—seltzer, club soda, Vichy, etc.—or ginger ale are

used, refrigerate them if possible before adding them to the drink. To make decorative ice cubes for tall drinks, see page 32.

HIGHBALLS AND RICKEYS
Individual Servings
Use bourbon, Scotch, rye, or gin.
Into a 6-oz. glass, put 2 large ice cubes and add:
    1 jigger of liquor chosen
Fill the glass with:
    Carbonated water
Stir lightly with bar spoon and serve.
    For a rickey, add, before the carbonated water:
        Juice of ½ large lime
With dry liquors, you may add:
        ½ teaspoon sugar syrup
Interesting effects in the two drink categories above are possible by further varying the basic ingredient. Try an applejack highball or one made with Dubonnet. The three following drinks are classic results of using one's imagination freely in this area: **Vermouth Cassis,** with a base consisting of 1 pony crème de cassis and 1 jigger dry vermouth; **Horse's Neck or Cooler,** with a long spiral of lemon peel draped over the edge of the glass and ginger ale substituted for carbonated water; and **Spritzer,** with half Rhine wine and half carbonated water. A luxurious rickey can be concocted by adding a teaspoon or so of liqueur to the lime juice.

TOM COLLINS
1 Serving
Collinses, like rickeys, are a large family. But this one is the granddaddy of all the rest.
Combine in a 14- or 16-oz. glass, with 4 ice cubes:
    1 tablespoon sugar syrup
    Juice of medium-size lemon
    2 jiggers gin
Fill glass with:
    Carbonated water
Stir and serve immediately.

GIN FIZZ
1 Serving
Combine in a bar glass:
    1 tablespoon sugar syrup
    Juice of medium-size lemon or lime
    1½ jiggers gin
Shake well with ½ cup crushed ice and

strain into prechilled 8-oz. glass. Fill with:
    Carbonated water
Stir and serve.
A **Silver Fizz** is made by beating into the
above Gin Fizz ingredients:
    1 egg white
Fizzes may be made with whisky, rum or
brandy as a base.

MINT JULEP
              1 Serving
This drink can be superlative. And it is
well, at this point, to remember that, as
the French say, "The good is the enemy of
the best." Use only bonded bourbon,
tender, terminal mint leaves for bruising
and very finely crushed or shaved ice.
Chill a 14- or 16-oz. glass or silver mug in
refrigerator. Wash and partially dry:
    A long sprig of fresh mint
and dip it in:
    Powdered sugar
Combine in a bar glass:
    2 teaspoons sugar syrup
    6 medium-sized mint leaves
    (**1 dash angostura bitters**)
Bruise leaves gently with muddler and
blend all ingredients by stirring together.
Pour into bar glass:
    1 large jigger bourbon whisky
Stir again. Remove serving glass from refrigerator, pack it with ice and strain into
it the above mixture. With a bar spoon,
churn ice up and down. Add more ice to
within ¾ inch of top. Add:
    1 pony whisky
Repeat churning process until glass begins
to frost. Decorate glass with:
    Sprig of mint
Insert long straws and serve.
    When making a number of mint juleps,
a less nerve-racking way to frost the glasses
is to omit prechilling them. After churn-

ing, instead of waiting for them to frost in
the open, place them in the refrigerator
for 30 minutes. ◗ Be careful throughout
this whole process not to grasp glasses
with bare hands.
    The stand illustrated, with its tiers of
ice and carrying ring, makes a julep server
par excellence. If the number of glasses
required is not enough to fill all the shelf
space, use the ones at the top for hors
d'oeuvre. A deep tray, packed with finely
crushed ice, will make an acceptable substitute for the julep stand.

CUBA LIBRE
              1 Serving
Combine in bar glass:
    Juice of 1 lime
    ½ squeezed lime
    1 large jigger rum
Put ingredients into 12- or 14-oz. glass.
Fill glass with 3 large ice cubes. Add:
    Cola
Stir and serve.

RUM PUNCH
              1 Serving
Combine in 10-oz. glass:
    Juice of 1 lemon or lime
    1 tablespoon pure maple syrup
    1 jigger rum
    2 dashes grenadine
Fill glass with finely crushed ice and churn
up and down with bar spoon. Have ice
within ¾ inch of top. Add:
    1 pony rum
Churn again, insert straws and decorate
before serving with:
    Pineapple stick
    Slice of orange
    Cherry

ZOMBIE
              1 Serving
Combine in bar glass:
    1 teaspoon sugar syrup or falernum
    1 pony lemon juice
    1 pony pineapple juice
    1 large jigger light rum
    1 large jigger dark rum
    2 teaspoons apricot liqueur
    (**1 pony papaya juice**)
Shake with ¾ cup crushed ice and pour
into a 14- or 16-oz. glass. Float on top:
    1 teaspoon Demerara rum
Decorate with:
    Orange slices
    Pineapple stick
    Green and red cherries
    Sprig of mint
Sprinkle over top:
    Powdered sugar
Insert straws and serve.

PLANTER'S PUNCH
              1 Serving
Combine in bar glass:

2 teaspoons sugar syrup
Juice of ½ lemon
2 jiggers dark rum
2 dashes angostura bitters
1 dash grenadine

Shake well. Pour into a 12- or 14-oz. glass. Pack glass to top with crushed ice and fill to within ½ inch of top with:

Carbonated water

Churn contents with bar spoon until glass begins to frost. Insert straws and decorate before serving with:

Orange slice
Cherry
(Sprig of mint)

TONIC

1 Serving

Into a 12-oz. glass place 3 ice cubes and add:

1 large jigger gin or vodka

Fill glass with:

Quinine water
(Lime or lemon juice to taste)

ABOUT PLUGGED FRUIT

We had no luck when, much younger, we plugged a watermelon and cautiously tried to impregnate it with rum. We never quite solved the problem of distribution. Later we discovered we had been too impatient. Time does the trick—about 8 hours. For those fortunate ones who can easily come by an abundance of other kinds of fruit, we give the following formulas for a couple of picturesque and delightfully refreshing drinks.

COCONUT EXTRAVAGANZA

1 Serving

To hold a coconut upright, see page 524. Cut or saw off the top of:

A coconut

This should produce a hole about 1 inch in diameter. Drain and reserve the milk and add to it that of a second coconut. Pour into the hollow:

1 large jigger light rum
3 teaspoons apricot liqueur
or Cointreau
3 teaspoons coconut cream
The coconut milk

Add ¾ cup finely crushed ice, shake, insert straws and serve.

PINEAPPLE TROPIC

1 Serving

Slice off the top of:

A ripe pineapple

Hollow out a cavity about the size of a highball glass. Pour into it:

1 large jigger light rum
3 teaspoons Benedictine

Fill cavity with finely crushed ice; stir

well, bruising the inside of the pineapple and decorate with:

Fresh fruit

Insert straws and serve.

SHORT DRINKS

"Some like it hot, some like it cold." The drinks which follow are of both varieties, in that order.

TODDY

1 Serving

In an 8-oz. mug, place:

1 teaspoon sugar syrup
1 stick cinnamon
1 jigger whisky, rum or brandy

Fill mug with:

Very hot water

Impale over edge of mug:

½ lemon slice

studded with:

3 cloves

To serve cold, add cold water instead of hot with an ice cube.

GROG

1 Serving

In an 8 oz. mug, stir together:

1 teaspoon sugar syrup
1 tablespoon strained lemon juice
1 jigger dark rum

Fill mug with:

Very hot tea or water

Garnish with a twist of:

Lemon peel

Try this drink using molasses instead of sugar syrup. Dust top with a little:

Ground nutmeg or cinnamon

★ HOT TOM AND JERRY

4 Servings

Beat to a stiff froth:

3 egg whites

Beat separately until light in color:

3 egg yolks

Beat into yolks gradually:

3 tablespoons powdered sugar
½ teaspoon each ground allspice,
cinnamon and cloves

Fold yolks into whites and pour 2 tablespoons of this mixture into each of four 8-oz. china mugs. Add to each mug:

½ jigger lukewarm brandy
1 jigger lukewarm, dark rum

Fill mugs with very hot water, milk, or coffee. Stir well and sprinkle the tops with:

Grated nutmeg

SYLLABUB OR MILK PUNCH

4 Servings

Beat together in bar glass:

1 tablespoon sugar syrup

1 jigger top milk
1 large jigger heavy cream
½ cup sherry, port, Madeira or
   bourbon whisky
Serve at once in punch glasses.

POSSET OR HOT MILK PUNCH
                                6 Servings
Blanch and pound in a mortar:
   5 or 6 bitter almonds
Heat:
   1 quart milk
   1 teaspoon grated lemon rind
   ½ cup sugar
Add the almonds and when the milk begins to scald, page 487, remove the mixture from the heat. Beat and add:
   2 egg whites
Add and combine lightly, until the whole
drink is frothy:
   ½ cup dark rum
   1 cup brandy
Serve in punch cups.

FLIP
                                1 Serving
Shake in bar glass with cracked ice:
   1 whole egg
   1 teaspoon sugar
   1 jigger sherry, brandy or port
Strain into 6-oz. glass. Sprinkle over top:
   Grated nutmeg

★ EGGNOG
                                1 Serving
If you are preparing this drink for an invalid, see note on uncooked eggs on page
695.
In a small bowl, beat until light:
   1 egg yolk
Beat in slowly:
   1 tablespoon sugar
   ¼ cup cream
   ⅛ to ¼ cup rum, brandy or whisky
   A few grains salt
Whip separately until stiff:
   1 egg white
Fold white lightly into other ingredients.
Transfer mixture to punch glass. For eggnog in quantity, see About Party Drinks,
following.

ABOUT PARTY DRINKS
Most of the formulas in this section are of
the punchbowl variety. In each instance,
the ♦ quantity of liquid will amount to approximately 5 quarts and will serve about
20 persons—each one having two 4-oz.
cups. When the word "bottle" is used, it
means a fifth of a gallon or 25 oz.
   Fruit juices used in the concoction of
party drinks should preferably be fresh;
but frozen, unsweetened concentrates are
quite acceptable, as long as you dilute
them only about half as much as the directions on the container prescribe. Canned
and bottled juices vary in quality—the
best, in our opinion, being pineapple, apri-

cot, cranberry, raspberry and grape.
Ideally, punch mixes should be allowed to
blend for an hour or so and, if served cold,
chilled in the refrigerator before carbonated water or ice are added. With cold
punches, be on the alert for dilution. Ice
only ⅔ of the liquid at the outset and add
the remainder just before the guests come
back for seconds. Speaking of ice, avoid
small pieces. At the very least, remove the
cube grid from your ice trays and freeze a
full unit. However, the two chilling devices illustrated are a lot more fun.

DECORATIVE ICE MOLDS
Set aside in a bowl the amount of water to
be frozen. Stir it well 4 or 5 times during
a 10 or 15 minute period to break up and
expel the air bubbles with which newly
drawn tap water is impregnated. Otherwise, the ice mold you build will be cloudy
instead of crystal clear.
   Have at hand such decorative ingredients as: whole limes, lemons, oranges
slices of citrus fruit, large fresh cherries or
strawberries, clusters of grapes, sprigs of
mint, sweet woodruff, lemon thyme or
other herbs and a few handsome fresh
grape or bay leaves, etc.
   Select a decorative metal mold of the
tubular or ring type. Avoid vessels which
are so deep as to induce top-heaviness in
your final product and risk its turning turtle, later.
   Begin operations by partially freezing a
layer of water in the container—proceeding much as you would in making a fancy
gelatin salad, see page 517. In this case, of
course, successive hardenings are frozen
instead of being chilled. On the first slush-
like layer, arrange a wreath of fruit and
greenery. Cover the decoration carefully

with a second layer of very cold water, returning the mold to the freezer, so that
with renewed freezing the decoration is
completely surrounded by clear ice. Repeat this procedure if the depth of the
mold permits. Allow the contents to become thoroughly frozen. When the refrigerated drink has been transferred to
the punch bowl, reverse the ice mold container, wrap a hot wet towel around the
metal until the ice is disengaged, and float
it in this position on the drink.
   To make decorative ice cubes for individual drinks, see page 32.

ICE PUNCH BOWLS

Next, we show a punch bowl which is ice itself—particularly useful if you wish to dilute a cold drink as little as possible. Place in the kitchen sink a 50 lb. cube of ice. Choose a round metal bowl of at least 3 qt. capacity. Chip out a small depression in the center of the ice block and set the bowl over it. Fill the bowl with boiling water, being careful not to spill any on the ice beneath. As the heat of the bowl melts the ice, stir the water. As the water cools, empty and refill the bowl each time, bailing out the depression in the ice, until the desired volume is displaced. Now, move the ice block onto a square "tray" of aluminum foil. Set it where you wish to dispense the drink. The tray should be a couple of inches larger than the block, constructed of heavy-duty material in leak-proof fashion, the edges turned up about 1½ inches all around to form a gutter. Any crudities can be masked by greenery or flowers. The "ice bowl" may, of course, be utilized equally well for serving sherbets and mixing cocktails.

However you serve party drinks, go easy on solid fruit trimmings; launching too much of this sort of thing makes for a very ramshackle-looking bowl. Work for larger decorative effects. A subtle flavor can be imparted to punches by steeping in the basic mix, during the lagering period, pieces of peeled seeded cucumber, then removing them before the drink is further processed. Sometimes a few dashes of bitters will confer "the old one-two" on an otherwise flabby punch.

FISH HOUSE PUNCH

Mix in punch bowl:
> 1 cup sugar syrup
> 1 cup lemon juice
> 1 bottle dark rum
> 1 bottle light rum
> 1 bottle brandy
> 7 cups water
> ½ cup peach brandy

If peach liqueur is used instead of peach brandy, the amount of syrup should be reduced to taste. Some recipes for this famous punch use strong tea instead of water.

BOWLE

A German favorite, which may be made with any of a variety of fruits.
Slice and place in a large bowl one of the following fruits:
> 6 ripe unpeeled peaches or 8 ripe
> unpeeled apricots or 1 sliced
> pineapple or
> 1 quart strawberries

Sprinkle over the fruit:
> 1 cup powdered sugar

Pour over mixture:
> 1½ cups Madeira or sherry

Allow to stand 4 hours or longer. Stir, pour over a block of ice in a bowl. Add:
> 4 bottles dry white wine

CHAMPAGNE PUNCH

Most punches are traditionally mixed with plain, rather than carbonated water. When carbonated water is a component, the drink becomes a **cup**. Champagne Punch, sacred to weddings, occupies middle ground.
Peel, slice, crush and place in a large bowl:
> 3 ripe pineapples

Cover pineapple and juice with:
> 1 lb. powdered sugar

Let mixture stand, covered, for 1 hour. Add:
> 2 cups lemon juice
> ½ cup curaçao
> ½ cup maraschino
> 2 cups brandy
> 2 cups light rum

Stir and let stand for 4 hours. Place in a punch bowl with a block of ice. Stir to blend and chill. Just before serving, add:
> 4 bottles chilled champagne

WHISKY OR BRANDY CUP

Slice, place in a large bowl and crush:
> 2 cups fresh pineapple

Add:
> 1 quart fresh strawberries

Sprinkle over the fruit:
> ¾ lb. powdered sugar

Pour over mixture:
> 2 cups dark rum

Allow mixture to stand, covered, for 4 hours. Add:
> 2 cups lemon juice
> 1½ cups orange juice

1 cup grenadine
2 bottles bourbon or brandy
Place in punch bowl with block of ice.
Stir to blend and chill. Just before serving, add:
    2 quarts chilled carbonated water or
      dry ginger ale
If you like a predominant rum flavor, substitute for the fruit-steeping ingredient
above:
    1½ cups brandy
and for the basic ingredient:
    2 bottles light rum
In this, as in other punch bowl drinks, it is
wise to test the mix for flavor and sweetness before adding the diluent.

RUM CASSIS CUP
Mix in a punch bowl:
    2½ bottles light rum
    2½ cups dry vermouth
    2½ cups crème de cassis
Add block of ice. Pour over the ice:
    2 quarts carbonated water

CLARET CUP
Slice, place in large bowl and crush:
    1 cup fresh pineapple
Peel, halve and add:
    4 ripe peaches
    4 peach stones
    ½ cup brandy
Sprinkle over mixture:
    1 cup powdered sugar
Let stand for 4 hours. Add:
    1 cup lemon juice
    2 cups orange juice
    ½ cup maraschino
    ½ cup curaçao
    2 bottles claret or other red wine
Chill the mixture for 1 hour; remove
peaches and stones and pour over a block
of ice in a punch bowl. Stir and add:
    2 quarts carbonated water

RHINE WINE CUP
Mix in punch bowl:
    1 cup sugar syrup
    2 cups lemon juice
    1 cup brandy
    2 cups dry sherry
    1 cup strong tea
    3 bottles Rhine wine or other
      dry white wine
    2 cups thinly sliced, peeled,
      seeded cucumbers
After 20 minutes, remove cucumber. Add
a large block of ice and pour over it:
    1 quart carbonated water

MAY WINE
Another German drink, dedicated to
springtime and featuring fresh Waldmeister or sweet woodruff. This highly decorative plant may be grown in a shady corner
of your herb garden.
Place in a bowl:
    12 sprigs young Waldmeister

1¼ cups powdered sugar
1 bottle Moselle or other
   dry white wine
(1 cup brandy)
Cover this mixture for 30 minutes, ♦ no
longer. Remove the Waldmeister. Stir contents of bowl thoroughly and pour over
a block of ice in a punch bowl. Add:
    3 bottles Moselle
    1 quart carbonated water
      or champagne
Thinly sliced oranges, sticks of pineapple
and, most appropriately of all, sprigs of
Waldmeister, may be used to decorate the
"Maitrank."

★ EGGNOG IN QUANTITY
I. A rich and extravagant version that is
correspondingly good. Some people like
to add a little more spirit to the following
recipes, remembering Mark Twain's observation that "too much of anything is
bad, but too much whisky is just enough."
Beat separately until light in color:
    12 egg yolks
Beat in gradually:
    1 lb. confectioners' sugar
Add very slowly, beating constantly:
    2 cups dark rum, brandy,
      bourbon or rye
These liquors may each form the basic ingredient of the nog or may be combined to
taste.
    Let mixture stand covered for 1 hour
to dispel the "eggy" taste.
Add, beating constantly:
    2 to 4 cups of liquor chosen
    2 quarts whipping cream
    (1 cup peach brandy)
Refrigerate covered for 3 hours. Beat un-
til stiff ♦ but not dry:
    8 to 12 egg whites
Fold them lightly into the other ingredients. Serve the eggnog sprinkled with:
    Freshly grated nutmeg

II. Less powerful, less fluffy than the preceding nog, and a boon to the creamless
householder.
Beat until light in color:
    12 eggs
Beat in gradually:
    1 lb. confectioners' sugar
    ½ teaspoon salt
    ¼ cup vanilla
Stir in:
    8 cups evaporated milk
diluted with:
    3 cups water
Stir in:
    4 cups dark rum, brandy, bourbon
      or rye
Cover the nog closely and permit it to
ripen in the refrigerator for 24 hours. Stir
it again and serve it sprinkled with:
    Freshly grated nutmeg

Before taking leave of cold party drinks
we want to remind you that any of the

"sour" type cocktails—those made of an alcoholic base plus fruit juice—may serve as the foundation for delectable punches and cups. See Cocktails, pages 36-40.

In preparing the following hot drinks, bring the liquid almost to a boil ◢ but not to the boiling point.

★ TOM AND JERRY IN QUANTITY

Beat until stiff ◢ but not dry, cover and set aside:

    1 dozen egg whites

Beat separately until light in color:

    1 dozen egg yolks

Into the yolks, beat gradually:

    ¾ cup powdered sugar
    2 teaspoons each ground allspice,
      cinnamon and cloves

Fold seasoned yolks into whites. Into each of twenty 8-ounce china mugs, place 2 tablespoons egg mixture and:

    ½ jigger lukewarm brandy
    1 jigger lukewarm dark rum

Fill each mug with:

    Very hot water, milk or coffee

Stir vigorously until drink foams. Dust top with:

    Grated nutmeg

★ MULLED WINE OR NEGUS
  IN QUANTITY

Make a syrup by boiling for 5 minutes:

    2½ cups sugar
    1¼ cups water
    4 dozen whole cloves
    6 sticks cinnamon
    3 crushed nutmegs
    Peel of 3 lemons, 2 oranges

Strain syrup. Add to it:

    4 cups hot lemon or lime juice

Heat well and add:

    4 bottles red wine

Serve very hot with slices of:

    Lemon and pineapple

These proportions may be varied to taste. Sometimes Madeira, port or sherry is used in this formula.

★ WASSAIL

The best time to "come a-wassailing" is, of course, Christmas week.

Core and bake, see page 111:

    1 dozen apples

Combine in a saucepan and boil for 5 minutes:

    1 cup water
    4 cups sugar
    1 tablespoon grated nutmeg
    2 teaspoons ground ginger
    ½ teaspoon ground mace
    6 whole cloves
    6 allspice berries
    1 stick cinnamon

Beat until stiff ◢ but not dry:

    1 dozen egg whites

Beat separately until light in color:

    1 dozen egg yolks

Fold whites into yolks, using large bowl. Strain sugar and spice mixture into eggs, combining quickly. Bring almost to boiling point separately:

    4 bottles sherry or Madeira
    2 cups brandy

Incorporate the hot wine with the spice and egg mixture, beginning slowly and stirring briskly with each addition. Toward the end of this process, add the brandy. Now, just before serving and while the mixture is still foaming, add the baked apples.

Wassail can also be made with a combination of beer and wine, preferably sherry; in which case the proportion should be roughly 4 of beer to 1 of sherry.

HOT BUTTERED RUM
Individual Serving

Place in a hot tumbler:

    1 teaspoon powdered sugar

Add:

    ¼ cup boiling water
    ¼ cup rum
    1 tablespoon butter

Fill glass with boiling water. Stir well. Sprinkle on top:

    Freshly grated nutmeg

This is an old-time New England conception of an individual portion. It may be modified. Curious, isn't it, that the Pilgrims made rum—especially a drink like this one, which has been said to make a man see double and feel single.

CANAPÉS
AND TEA SANDWICHES

Canapés and hors d'oeuvre are appetizers offered with drinks. ♦ The canapé has a built-in bread or pastry. The hors d'oeuvre is served alone and may be accompanied by, but not served on, a pastry or bread base. For more details, see page 54. Canapés often resemble very small tea sandwiches and since the making of both of these is so similar they are discussed together. Additional fillings for sandwiches served as luncheon entrées and heartier, larger sandwiches will be found on page 244.

Since gay and festive presentation of canapés and tea sandwiches is so essential, we suggest ways in which breads and pastries can be made to look their best, either by fast and furious or by more leisurely and amusing methods.

It is often easier to make small sandwiches in quantity ♦ by working with a whole loaf rather than with individual slices. A number of ways to cut and combine different breads are illustrated. In several instances the crusts have been removed and the bread cut horizontally. It is possible to get six or seven long slices from the loaf and then spread the entire surface before stacking and shaping. A variation of forms that is economical of area is sketched below. Parti-colored sandwiches can be produced by combining white and whole wheat or white and brown bread. Rolled sandwiches can be made quickly by rolling long horizontal slices. A number of other shapes are illustrated on the next page. On the upper left are two-layer sandwiches, in which the top layer is doughnut-shaped to allow the color of the filling to show through. On the lower right, successive bread or sausage slices are shown bound with a filling and cut in pie-wedge ribbon slices.

In making sandwiches of any kind in quantity ♦ time is saved by setting up an assembly line and using mass-production techniques. Place bread slices in rows. Place dabs of seasoned butters or mayonnaise on one row, filling on the next. Then do the final spreading by bringing the fillings and butters well out to the edges. Put hard butter or mayonnaise twice through a grinder with other ingredients and use a coarse blade. For closed sandwiches, do all the assembling, stacking, cutting and packaging in turn. For open-faced sandwiches, have garnishes cut shortly in advance and keep them from drying out by placing them in foil, damp wrung-out towels or plastic bags—then refrigerate. After the base is spread, do all the garnishing of one type, then of another, before arranging for serving.

ABOUT BREAD FOR SANDWICHES

The number of sandwiches to a loaf of bread is hard to gauge because of shape variations, but from a 1-lb. loaf of sandwich bread you can expect at least 20 slices. Allow about 1 lb. butter for 3 to 4 lbs. of sandwich loaf. Do not have the loaf presliced, but slice it thin yourself. The number of sandwiches to allow for each guest is even harder to judge, although 8 to 10 small snacks, either sandwiches or hors d'oeuvre, are not too much to count per person, if drinking is protracted.

♦ To avoid raggedy sandwiches, use a finely textured bread. If not available, try chilling or freezing ordinary bread before cutting. Freezing before cutting and then spreading makes for easier handling throughout, and is a particularly good technique in preparing rolled shapes, which should be very thin and made of very fresh bread. Other sandwiches are easier to make if the bread is one day old. Cut fresh or frozen bread with a very sharp hot knife. Remember, though, that all bread

ich has been frozen dries out very
ckly after thawing and that precautions
uld be taken to keep the sandwiches as
st as possible. Have spreads at about
to protect bread from pulling or tear-

OUT KEEPING SANDWICHES

parations should be made ahead of time
rder to serve sandwiches in prime con-
on. Have ready foil or wax paper and
stened, wrung-out cloths, transparent
-sealing tissue or plastic bags. Refriger-
double sandwiches, wrapped, without
y. Open-faced sandwiches, if made
uitable materials, page 768, are often
k-frozen and can then be wrapped
out damage to their decorations or sur-
s. Store them wrapped and in boxes
eep them free from the weight of other
ls. Also place them away from the coils
the freezer, page 757. ♦ It is often
erable to freeze the fillings alone and
e up these fancy sandwiches shortly
re serving.
e sure that any moist or juicy filling is
on bread well spread with a firm
r of butter or of heavy mayonnaise, so
the bread will not get soggy. If to-
o or cucumber slices are used, see that
are cut and allowed to drain well on
ck before putting them in the sand-
es.
is sometimes suggested that bread be
d with a rolling pin to compress it, so
ill not be too absorptive when the but-
s put on, but we find that this rolling
s the bread a dense and rather horrid
ire.
Toasted canapés, if served immedi-
/ after their preparation, should be on
d that is toasted on one side only—
spread and heated. If serving is to be
yed, the bread should be toasted on
sides—or use Melba toast or crou-
Then reheat when the filling is ap-
.

UT SANDWICH SHAPES

surprising how a few fancy sand-
es with attractive garnishes, page 83,

will help to perk up a platter. If the platters are kept small, they are easier to replenish. A combination of open and closed
sandwiches gives variety to the tray. But
sometimes medium oblong trays, filled
with alternating rows of similarly cut but
contrastingly spread open-faced sandwiches—placed closely together—make a
quick and pleasant change from the large
platters more sparsely filled with fancy
sandwiches. To give variety to your tray,
plan both open and closed types.
Rolled sandwiches, especially with a
sprig of cress or parsley protruding, make
a charming intercepted wreath around the
edge of the platter—if they are placed like
spokes on a round tray. For other garnishes
for platters, see illustrations on page 83.

ROLLED SANDWICHES
Freeze:
   Fresh sandwich bread
Remove crusts and slice as thin as possible
with a sharp hot knife. Spread the bread
with:
   A softened filling
We particularly enjoy as a filling:
   **(Cream cheese mixed with cucumber
   and onion juice with cress)**
Be sure the filling goes out to the edge, so
the roll will be well sealed. When the
bread is well thawed, roll the sandwiches.
Tuck into the ends, but allow to protrude:
   Cress or parsley sprigs
♦ Wrap firmly and refrigerate, so they will
hold their cylindrical shape when served.

RIBBON SANDWICHES
Cut the crust from:
   White bread
   Dark bread
Spread the slices with:
   **Butter or Cream Cheese
   Spreads, page 58**
Place 3 to 5 slices of bread alternately in
stacks. Cut them into bars, squares or tri-
angles, see illustration, page 52.

FLOWER CANAPÉS
If you have an herb garden, many en-

chanting sandwiches can be made from the small-scaled leaves and blossoms. Or in winter try cutting:

Small rounds or squares of bread

Spread them with:

Soft cream cheese

Place across each sandwich a very narrow:

Strip of green pepper or a stem of chive or parsley

This represents a stem. Place at the top of the strip to form the flower:

A slice of stuffed olive or a fancy cut of carrot or radish

Cut into lengthwise slices to form leaves:

Small sour-sweet pickles

Place the pickle slices opposite each other on the green pepper stem.

★ **CHRISTMAS CANAPÉS**

I. Cut into 2-inch rounds:

Thin bread slices

Spread the rounds with:

A cream cheese mixture, page 58

Cut into tiny rounds, about ⅛-inch:

Maraschino cherries, pimiento, cranberries or use tiny red decorettes

Chop until fine:

Parsley

Make a narrow ring of the parsley around each piece of bread. Dot it at intervals with the red rounds to make it look like a holly wreath.

II. Or, use:

A sprig of parsley

shaped like a tree and dot it with the small red "balls" described above.

ZOO SANDWICHES

For very young children's parties, make closed double or triple sandwiches in animal shapes using fancy cookie cutters. Triple-layered sandwiches can be made to stand upright on the plate.

SANDWICH LOAVES

These can even be a meal by themselves— an excellent luncheon dish with coffee and a dessert, and—when made in individual size—real charmers. If you want a decorative sandwich center for a birthday buffet, make an individual loaf for each guest and group the loaves around a pile of gaily wrapped gifts.

I. Cut the crusts from:

A loaf of white or whole wheat bre

Cut the loaf into 3 or 4 lengthwise slic Butter the inner sides of the slices a spread them with a layer of:

Chicken, shrimp, egg or salmon sal

a layer of:

Drained crushed pineapple and cream cheese

a layer of:

Drained sliced tomatoes, lettuce o watercress

or with any good combination of salad sandwich ingredients. If it fits with y filling, add some:

Anchovy paste

to the cream cheese. Be sure to cut bread thin enough and spread the filli thick enough, see illustration, to keep bread from dominating. Wrap the firmly in a moist towel, chill well, unw and place on a platter. Cover with:

Softened cream cheese, smooth cottage cheese, or Mayonnaise Collée, page 341

An individual slice, cut from the finis loaf, is shown.

II. This holds well if prepared in adva Cut the top and bottom from:

A large round rye loaf

and reserve them as the base and lid f crust container. Carefully cut out in piece a straight-sided cylinder from soft center. Then slice this cylinder bread horizontally into 6 thin sl Spread the upper surfaces of the third and fifth slices with not too mois

Seasoned fillings

Cover the spread slices with the sec fourth and sixth slices. Keeping the sh of the large cylinder orderly, cut it narrow wedges. Now, carefully place cut cylinder on the bottom crust. I toothpicks around the edge of the bottom and impale the crust ring on picks to form a container for the sand wedges. Cover with the top crust as a Wrap and refrigerate until ready to s

ABOUT BREAD BASES FOR CANAPÉS

Use coarse ryes, whole wheats, ch breads from the Yeast and Quick B Chapter, page 553, and suggestions the Uses for Ready-Baked Breads, 586. There are good cracker suggestio Soups, page 173, and various pastrie the Pie Chapter, pages 591-592. Or use small versions of Luncheon S wiches, page 244; Ravioli, page 191; chées, page 596, or Tarts or Barque below.

TARTS AND TARTLETS FOR CANAPÉS

I. Prepare:

Biscuit Dough, page 583, or

Pie Dough, page 588
l or pat it until it is about ⅛-inch
:k. Cut it into 3-inch squares. Place in
center of each square one of the fill-
s listed under:
Fillings for Pastry Canapés, page 56
isten the corners of the dough lightly
h water. Fold up the sides of the dough
pinch the corners to make a tart
pe. Bake the tarts in a 425° oven for
ut 10 minutes.

Or, fill the tart with:
A thin slice of cheese, 1½ x 2 inches
this with:
½ slice tomato
son the tomato with:
A grating of pepper
A little salt
(A sprinkling of brown sugar)
nkle the top with:
Cooked diced bacon
e as in I, above.

Fill with:
Hot spicy puréed spinach
on it:
A smoked oyster
h with:
A little Cream Sauce, page 322
hich has been added:
Grated Swiss cheese
e as in I, above.

H COCKTAIL TART OR QUICHE
hysician in our family once took to
a scandalously obese patient. "But,
or," said the patient plaintively, "one
offer the stomach something from
to time." This is a favorite offering
ur family.
are any unsweetened:
Pie Dough, page 588
e as for tartlets and bake for only 5
tes in a 400° oven. Remove from the
♦ Lower the heat to 325°. Place in
bottom of each tart 1 tablespoon of
ollowing mixture:
beaten egg
cup cream
teaspoon grated Parmesan cheese
tablespoons sautéed mushrooms or
crab meat)
teaspoon salt
A small pinch coriander
the tarts for 15 minutes or until the
e has set. Keep them hot and toasty
electric skillet. For other Quiche
es, see page 227.

QUETTES FOR CANAPÉS
pare:
Biscuit Dough, page 583, or
Pie Dough, page 588
t until it is about ⅛ inch thick. Since
ettes are shaped like a scow or flat-
ned boat, but with pointed ends,
ither a barquette mold or something

similarly shaped to form the pastry. Place
in the barquettes a:
Filling for Pastry Canapés, page 56
Bake for about 10 minutes in a 425° oven.

II. Line the bottom of the barquettes with
a coating of:
Mayonnaise
Make a pattern of:
Chilled caviar
Pearl onions
Coat the top with:
Aspic Glaze, page 341
The aspic should be based on fish or
chicken stock. Flavor with:
Lemon
Refrigerate several hours before serving.

**STUFFED CHOUX, PUFF PASTE OR
PÂTÉ SHELLS**
I. Bake:
**1-inch Choux Paste Shells, page 597, or
Bouchées, page 596**
Split them on one side. Fill them with one
of the softer fillings, see:
Fillings for Pastry Canapés, page 56
Reheat the puffs in a 425° oven.

II. For a marvelous tea-teaser, put into the
base of a small cream puff shell a layer of:
Whipped cream
Lightly insert with the pointed end up:
A flawless ripe strawberry

III. Or, fill the puffs with:
Soft cream cheese
A dab of bright jelly

**TURNOVERS, RISSOLES OR
FRIED PIES**
These triangular or crescent-shaped pas-
tries make attractive canapés. If baked,
they are turnovers. If deep fat fried, you
may apply the homely title of fried pies or
the fancy one of rissoles.
Roll to the thickness of ⅛ inch any:
**Pie Crust, page 588 or Puff Paste,
page 593**
Cut it into 2½-inch rounds or squares.
Place in the center of each round any of
the:
Fillings for Pastry Canapés, page 56
Brush the edges of the rounds lightly with
water. Fold the dough over into crescents.
Be sure to seal the rissoles very firmly if
you are deep fat frying, so that none of the
filling escapes into and ruins the frying
fat. The tops of the turnovers may be
brushed with:
**1 egg yolk, diluted with 2 tablespoons
cream**
Bake them in a 400° oven until brown or
fry them in deep fat heated to 360° to
370°, page 124. Serve them around a

large garnish of:
    Fried parsley or chervil

CANAPÉ SNAILS
If the approval of guests is to be taken as
a criterion of excellence, this is the prize-
winning canapé, reminiscent of the guest
who hesitated to help himself, saying,
"Well, I shouldn't, I've had two already,"
Which remark was capped by his hostess'
brisk and crushing reply: "You've had six,
but who's counting?"
Roll into very thin oblongs any:
    **Pie Crust, page 588, or crustless soft
    bread**
The bread will be easier to cut if wrapped
in foil and chilled thoroughly. Spread the
oblongs with:
    Fillings for Pastry Canapés, below
Roll them like a jelly roll. Chill; cut in
½-inch slices and bake on a greased pan,
in a 425° oven, until light brown.

TACOS
This popular Mexican treat is called by
many names in different parts of the country. They are toasted tortillas cut into
thirds and filled with hot or mildly seasoned ingredients. This one is fairly mild.
Sauté until golden brown:
    1 finely chopped onion
in:
    2 tablespoons butter
Add and simmer for about 3 minutes:
    ½ cup tomato juice
    3 peeled minced green chilis
    **1 cup shredded cooked chicken or
    pork sausage meat**
    ⅛ teaspoon thyme
    1 teaspoon salt
    Dash of cayenne
Set this filling aside. Now fry in deep fat
at 380° until crisp:
    1 can tortillas: about 18
Remove them from the fat and drain. Cut
into thirds. Place 1 teaspoon of the above
filling on each piece. Fold in half, secure
with a toothpick and bake until crisp in
a 450° oven.

GLAZED CANAPÉS AND
SANDWICHES
Small glazed canapés are very showy for
cocktail service and in larger sizes make a
lovely luncheon plate when garnished with
a salad. ◗ But they must be kept refrigerated as they have a natural tendency to
sogginess.
Use:
    **Choux paste shells, tartlets or
    fancy-shaped thin toasts**
Coat these canapé bases first with:
    Mayonnaise
Then spread them with:
    **Well-seasoned fish paste, turkey,
    tomato slices, ham strips, asparagus
    tips**

or any combination suitable for ope
faced sandwiches. Cover with a ¼-inch
⅜-inch layer of:
    Well-seasoned aspic glaze
using 1⅓ cups stock or vegetable jui
1 tablespoon gelatin and 1 tablespo
lemon juice. Place the canapés on a ra
The aspic should be jelled to the thickn
of heavy cream partially beaten. Allow
to coat the surface of the tart or enve
the canapé. Refrigerate at once and all
the gelatin to set 1 to 2 hours. Then se
as soon as possible.

FILLINGS FOR PASTRY CANAPÉS
Place in the center of the preceding pa
cases 1 teaspoon or more of one of
following ingredients:
    Cheese Spreads, page 58
    Anchovy paste and soft cream che
    Well-seasoned or marinated oyster
    **Mushrooms, heavily creamed and
    seasoned**
    **Chicken or other croquette mixtu
    highly seasoned**
    Chicken, lobster, crab or fish sala
    Caviar and soft cream cheese
    **Liver sausage or braunschweiger,
    seasoned with catsup**
    Sausage meat, seasoned with must
    **Link sausages, seasoned with stuf
    olives**
    **Deviled ham, cream cheese and
    catsup**
    Minced clams or crab meat
    Calf brains with Hollandaise sauce
    Curried shrimp or poultry

ABOUT BUTTER SHAPES
Such a delicious staple deserves attrac
presentation. Try using a butter cu
our favorite because the light ⅛-inch-t
shell forms are such decorative assets
just the right texture for spreading.
the curler into warm water before pu
it lightly over firm butter. If the butt
too cold, the curls will crack. Put the c
at once into cold water and store in
refrigerator until ready to drain and se
Keep butter balls or molds described
in good form the same way until read
use.
    The easiest molds to handle are t
with a plunger. Both the molds and
paddles for butter balls must be co
tioned for use by pouring over them a
erous stream of boiling water. Then pl
them at once into ice water. Cut b
for molds into ⅓-inch thick slices.
mold will determine the size of the squ
For an easy way to make butter balls,
various-sized melon ballers. Dip them
in hot water. Scoop out the butter
and drop it into a dish of ice water. S
them piled in a small pyramid or con
a covered, sliding-domed, ice-racked
ter dish.

Another attractive way to serve butter is
a small clay crocks. Our favorite is one
that fits into a base which holds cold water. Squares of butter can be made attractive by even cutting. For a smooth cut,
sheath your knife trimly in the butter
wrapper before you make a cut. Decorate
with tiny herb leaves and/or flowers,
lightly pressed into the squares of butter.

BUTTER SPREADS

There are many ways of preparing good,
quick sandwich spreads with a butter
basis. Beat butter until soft. Add other
ingredients gradually. Chill the butter
mixture until it is of a good consistency to
spread or make it into a shape.
Use one of the simple suggestions in
this recipe or the more elaborate Seasoned
Butters that follow. Also see pages 338-
40.

Beat until soft:

   ¼ cup butter

Add to the butter slowly one or more of
the following:

   ½ teaspoon lemon juice
   ½ teaspoon Worcestershire sauce or
      ½ teaspoon dry mustard
   ½ teaspoon grated onion or
      minced garlic
   ⅛ teaspoon lemon rind)

Good additions to the butter mixture are a
choice of the following—either chopped or
made into a paste by using your mortar
and pestle:

   2 tablespoons chopped parsley
   2 tablespoons chopped chives
   1 tablespoon chopped dill
   1 tablespoon chopped mixed herbs:
      basil, tarragon, burnet and chervil
   2 tablespoons chopped watercress
   ¼ cup soft or grated cheese:
      Parmesan or Romano
   1 tablespoon anchovy or other
      fish paste
   1 tablespoon horseradish
   1 tablespoon olive paste
   2 tablespoons catsup or chili sauce

   1 tablespoon chutney
   ¼ teaspoon curry powder
      Correct the seasoning

⅄ SEAFOOD BUTTER

For a more economical form, see page 339.
Put through a sieve or blender or chop:

   1 cup cooked shrimp, lobster,
      lobster coral, etc.
   ¼ lb. butter
   1 teaspoon or more lemon juice
      A fresh grating of white pepper

Mold and chill to serve on an hors
d'oeuvre platter or use as a spread.

DRIED HERBS IN WINE
FOR BUTTER SPREADS

Combine:

   2 tablespoons crushed dried herbs:
      thyme, basil, tarragon, chervil
   ½ cup dry white wine or lemon juice

Permit the herbs to soak for 2 hours or
more. Follow the above recipe for Butter
Spreads, using a little of this mixture.
Keep the rest to use combined with melted
butter as a dressing for vegetables.

⅄ BLENDER MUSHROOM BUTTER

Sauté until golden brown:

   ½ lb. sliced mushrooms

in:

   ¼ cup butter

Put the mushrooms and butter into an
electric blender and add:

   ½ cup soft butter
   ¼ teaspoon black pepper
   ¼ teaspoon salt
   3 tablespoons dry sherry or brandy

Blend until smooth.

NUT BUTTERS

I. Cream until soft enough to stir:

   ½ cup butter

Stir in:

   1 cup ground pecans or walnuts
   2 tablespoons Worcestershire sauce

II. ⅄ In an electric blender combine:
   1 tablespoon salad oil
   1 cup salted nuts: peanuts,
      cashews or pecans

CREAM CHEESE SPREADS
What would we do without cream cheese?
The perfect emergency binder for the
many taste-provokers below.
Rub a bowl with:
   (Garlic)
Mash until soft and combine:
   1 package cream cheese: 3 oz.
   1 tablespoon cream
Add one or more of the following:
   ½ teaspoon onion juice
   1 teaspoon chopped onion or chives
   1 tablespoon lemon or lime juice
   1 tablespoon finely chopped Fines
      Herbes, page 540
   1 tablespoon finely chopped parsley
   1 tablespoon finely chopped celery
   ¼ cup chopped stuffed olives
   1 tablespoon horseradish
   3 tablespoons crisped chopped bacon
      or minced chipped beef
   ½ tablespoon anchovy or fish paste
   ½ cup shredded salted almonds
   1 tablespoon caviar
Season with:
   Salt, paprika or red pepper, if needed
For a tea canapé, use a:
   Bar-le-Duc mixture, page 708

CUCUMBER CREAM CHEESE
SPREAD
Mash with a fork:
   2 packages cream cheese: 6 oz.
Into a fine sieve or cheesecloth bag, grate:
   1 medium-sized cucumber
   1 onion
Press out the juice and combine with the
cream cheese. Add:
   Salt to taste
   ⅛ teaspoon hot pepper sauce
Now add until of spreading consistency:
   Mayonnaise

CHEESE PUFF CANAPÉS
Preheat Broiler
Beat until very stiff:
   2 egg whites
Fold in:
   1 cup grated American cheese
   1 teaspoon Worcestershire sauce
   ½ teaspoon paprika
   ½ teaspoon dry mustard
Toast on one side:
   Small rounds of bread or crackers
Spread the untoasted side with the cheese
mixture. Place the canapés under a broiler
for about 6 minutes, until the cheese is
well puffed and brown.

ROQUEFORT SPREAD
This delicious spread keeps well and improves with age—better when 1 week old

than when newly made.
Combine to a paste:
   ½ lb. Roquefort cheese
   2 packages soft cream cheese: 6 oz.
      or use an 8-oz. package
   2 tablespoons soft butter
   (1 small grated onion)
   1 tablespoon Worcestershire sauce
   2 tablespoons dry sherry
   Salt as needed
Keep the spread in a closely covered jar
the refrigerator. May be spread on cri
potato chips, crackers or on toast round
Decorate with:
   Radish slices and capers

PUFFED ROQUEFORT STICKS
Have ready:
   4 slices bread
The bread should be several days o
Coat with:
   Butter
Prepare:
   ¾ cup Béchamel Sauce, page 322
Combine with:
   2 oz. Roquefort cheese
   1 beaten egg
   Correct the seasoning
Spread the sauce on the bread and ▸
under the broiler for 5 to 8 minutes. Se
at once.

CHEESE SPREADS FOR
TOASTED SANDWICHES OR
CHEESE DREAMS
I. This practical sandwich spread ▸
keep for a week or more.
Scald in a double boiler:
   ½ cup milk
Add:
   1 beaten egg
   ¼ teaspoon dry mustard
   ½ teaspoon salt
   ¾ lb. diced American cheese
Cook these ingredients over hot water
15 minutes. Stir constantly. Cool the ▸
ture and keep it in a closed jar in the
frigerator. When ready to use, sprea
between:
   Rounds of bread
Place on each side of the canapés or s̄
wiches a generous dab of:
   Butter
Toast them in a 350° oven or unde
broiler until they are crisp.

II. ⅄ This filling is more quickly m
but not as bland as the preceding
Combine and stir to a smooth paste
blend in the electric blender:
   2 cups soft sharp cheese,
      grated if necessary
   ½ teaspoon salt
   A few grains cayenne
   1 teaspoon prepared mustard
   3 tablespoons cream or 1 to 2
      tablespoons soft butter

Cut the crusts from:
Thin slices of white bread
Spread and roll the slices. Toast as in I.
Serve the rolls very hot.

BACON AND CHEESE CANAPÉS
Preheat Broiler
Toast on one side:
Rounds of bread
Spread the untoasted side thickly with:
**2 cups grated cheese
2 slices minced sautéed bacon
¼ teaspoon dry mustard
A few grains cayenne
1 tablespoon Worcestershire sauce**
Broil the canapés until cheese is melted.

CHUTNEY AND CHEESE CANAPÉS
Preheat Broiler
Cover:
Round crackers or toast
with:
**Chutney
A thin slice of American cheese**
Broil the crackers to melt the cheese.

TOASTED CHEESE LOGS OR ROLLS
Preheat Oven to 350°
Trim the crusts from:
Thin slices of bread
Place on each slice, not quite covering it:
A thin slice of cheese
or place on each slice of bread:
An oblong block of cheese
Spread the cheese lightly with:
**Anchovy paste, prepared mustard or
horseradish**
Gather up 2 opposite corners and fasten
them with a toothpick or roll the bread.
Seal the ends, using:
Butter
Brush the outside of the logs with:
Melted butter
Toast them until light brown. Serve piping
hot on toothpicks.

SWEET TEA SPREADS
For those of us afflicted with a "sweet
tooth," it is always a welcome sight to be-
hold on the canapé tray something less
bland, spicy or tart than the usual fare. And
don't forget those good Nut Butters, page
586, and Cinnamon Toast, page 586.
I. Moisten:
Cream cheese
with:
Rich milk
Add:
**Chopped ginger
Chopped almonds**
This is very good spread on:
Brown bread

II. Spread on small toasts:
Bar-le-Duc, page 708

III. Combine:
1 package soft cream cheese: 3 oz.

**Rind of 1 orange or 2 tablespoons
orange or ginger marmalade
¼ teaspoon salt
⅛ teaspoon paprika**
Spread:
Thin slices of bread
with:
Mayonnaise or butter
Cover them with the cheese and:
Toasted chopped pecan meats

IV. Combine:
Equal parts soft butter and honey

V. Spread toast with:
**Butter
Apple butter**
Sprinkle with:
Grated cheese
Run under the broiler until the cheese is
toasted.

HARD-COOKED EGG SPREADS
I. Combine and mix to a paste with a
fork:
**2 hard-cooked eggs
1 tablespoon or more thick cultured
sour cream
¼ teaspoon salt
⅛ teaspoon paprika
1 tablespoon chopped chives
(1 teaspoon lemon juice)**
Garnish the canapé with a row of:
(Sliced stuffed olives)

II. Combine:
**4 chopped hard-cooked eggs
1 cup chopped pecan meats
2 dozen chopped stuffed olives
Well-seasoned mayonnaise**

III. Shell, then chop:
Hard-cooked eggs
Combine them with:
**Minced anchovies
Minced celery**
Moisten these ingredients with:
Mayonnaise

IV. Marinate for 30 minutes:
Shrimp or crab meat
in:
French dressing or lemon juice
Drain and combine, by making into a
paste with:
**Mayonnaise
A dash Worcestershire sauce
Hard-cooked eggs**

V. Combine:
**Finely chopped hard-cooked eggs
A liver pâté, page 432**

ROLLED ASPARAGUS CANAPÉS
OR SANDWICHES
Cut the crust from:
Thin slices of bread

Spread them thinly with:
  Butter and mayonnaise
Sprinkle lightly with:
  Chopped chives
Place on each slice a well-drained:
  Asparagus tip
Roll the canapés. Wrap the rolls in waxed paper until ready to serve. These sandwiches may be toasted.

AVOCADO SPREAD OR GUACAMOLE

★ A good holiday touch is a bit of pimiento or a slice of stuffed olive.
I. Pare:
  1 or 2 ripe avocados
Mash the pulp with a fork. Add:
  Onion juice and lemon juice
  Salt
  (**Tomato pulp—a very small amount**)
Heap this on small crackers or toast. Garnish with:
  Paprika and parsley

II. Have ready a combination of:
  1 peeled, seeded, chopped ripe tomato
  1 finely chopped scallion:
  2 inches green
  (**½ seeded, chopped green pepper**)
  ½ teaspoon chili powder
  1 teaspoon olive oil
  1 tablespoon lemon or lime juice
  ½ teaspoon coriander
  Salt and pepper
Add to the above, just before spreading:
  2 mashed ripe avocados

MUSHROOM CANAPÉS

Sauté, see page 126:
  Mushrooms
Mince the mushrooms. Prepare:
  Cream Sauce II, page 322
Make ½ as much sauce as mushrooms. Season it with:
  Salt and paprika
  Freshly grated nutmeg
Combine sauce and mushrooms. When cold, add a little:
  Whipped cream
Heap these ingredients on:
  Small rounds of bread or toast
Garnish the canapés with:
  Paprika and parsley
Serve immediately or run under the broiler.

ONION AND PARSLEY CANAPÉS

Parsley has the power to neutralize onion odors. Use it profusely in this decorative sandwich, so no one will know you have indulged.
Make a filling of:
  1 drained grated onion
  1 cup heavy mayonnaise
  ¼ teaspoon Worcestershire sauce
  A few drops hot pepper sauce

⅛ teaspoon turmeric
Put the filling between small rounds of:
  Brioche-type bread
or a bread that will not become sogg
Spread the outside edge of the sandwi
with:
  Mayonnaise
and roll these edges in:
  Finely chopped parsley

BLACK RADISH CANAPÉ

Peel and mince:
  2 black radishes
Combine with:
  1 small minced onion
  2 tablespoons cultured sour cream or yogurt
  1 tablespoon lemon juice
  ⅛ teaspoon salt
Just before serving, spread on thin sli
of:
  Pumpernickel bread

TOMATO OR CUCUMBER SANDWICHES

These sandwiches are very attractive fo
spring tea party.
Cut:
  Small rounds of bread
Spread them lightly with:
  Butter
Place on each round, covering it c
pletely:
  Small round of sliced tomato or a large round of pared sliced cucum. or both
Decorate each sandwich with a gener
  Dab of mayonnaise
For daintiness, but not for food va
slice tomatoes, then drain them fo
hours to keep the sandwiches from b
soggy.

CAVIAR AND ONION CANAPÉS

I. Sauté in butter:
  Rounds of thin toast
Combine and spread on the toast e
parts of:
  Caviar
  Finely chopped onion
Season with:
  Lemon juice
Garnish the edges of the canapés with
  Riced hard-cooked egg yolks
Top with:
  (**Tiny shrimp or prawns**)

II. Sauté:
  Chopped onions
in:
  Butter
Make a mound of the chopped onion
a round of:

Pumpernickel bread
n the scooped-out center, put some:
Cultured sour cream
nd a dab of:
Caviar

AVIAR AND CUCUMBER CANAPÉS
ip:
Slices of cucumber
:
French dressing
rain them. Prepare:
Small rounds of buttered toast
eel, then slice crosswise:
Mild onions
parate the slices into rings. Place a ring
each round of toast, so that it will form
wall. Place a slice of cucumber in each
g. Cover the cucumber with:
**Small mounds of caviar, seasoned
with lemon and onion juice or chives**
rnish the canapés with:
Capers
Riced hard-cooked eggs

NDERLOIN AND CAVIAR CANAPÉ
im half-frozen:
Tenderloin of beef
fit small squares of:
Melba toast
read the toast first with:
Onion Butter, page 57
n with a layer of the tenderloin and
ne:
Caviar

IICKEN OR HAM SALAD SPREAD
op until fine:
1 cup cooked chicken or ham
d:
2 tablespoons finely chopped celery
**¼ cup chopped blanched almonds or
other nut meats**
**¼ cup chopped pineapple or ½ cup
finely chopped green olives)**
mbine these ingredients with sufficient:
Highly-seasoned mayonnaise
make a paste that will spread easily.

ALL PIZZA CANAPÉ
d with cocktails, tea and for late eve-
g or barbecues.
ar in two, fairly evenly, but do not cut:
Small English muffins or biscuits
st on flat sides only, at least 5 inches
w broiler heat. On the broken sides,
ad:
1 teaspoon chili sauce
¼ teaspoon spaghetti sauce)
**Strips of sharp Cheddar or grated
mozzarella or Gruyère cheese**
¼ teaspoon oregano
with an:
Anchovy fillet
drizzle over all:
A little olive oil

Return to the broiler and toast until the
cheese is thoroughly melted. For a different flavored pizza, see page 226.

FOIE GRAS AND LIVER PASTES
You may serve pâté in the classic manner, page 434; cut it into rondelles on toast;
or incorporate it into Brioches, page 567,
Bouchées, page 596, pastry, barquettes or
turnovers. Use it for stuffing olives, artichoke hearts or mushrooms; or roll it up
like small cheroots, in the thinnest slices
of prosciutto. Use also in individual molds,
glazed with port wine or aspic jelly. See
pages 432-433 for a number of versions of
liver pastes, soufflés and pâtés—both simple and complex.

LIVER SAUSAGE CANAPÉS
I. Combine and mix to a paste:
¼ lb. liver sausage
1 or more tablespoons cream
Add:
¼ cup or more chopped watercress
Serve on rye bread or toast.

II. Make a paste of:
½ cup mashed liver sausage
2 tablespoons tomato paste
(A few drops Worcestershire sauce)
Spread on thinly-cut crustless bread, then
roll and toast.

CLAM PUFFS
Try some of the "Dips" on page 74, in
this same manner.
Combine:
1 package cream cheese: 3 oz.
2 tablespoons heavy cream
1 cup minced clams
¼ teaspoon dry mustard
1 tablespoon Worcestershire sauce
¼ teaspoon salt
½ teaspoon grated onion or onion juice
Heap the mixture on toast rounds and
broil.

CRAB OR LOBSTER PUFF BALLS
Serve these only if you have time to whip
the cream and fill the puff shells at the
last minute. The charm of this canapé
lies in the bland creaminess of the filling
and the dry crunchiness of the casing.
Shred or dice:
Cooked crab or lobster meat
Combine lightly 2 parts of the chilled sea-
food with:
1 part stiffly whipped seasoned cream
Put the mixture into:
Small cream puff shells, page 597
Sprinkle the tops with:
Chopped parsley and basil
Serve open or put puff lid on top after
filling. Good hot or cold, but serve at
once—and we mean at once.

MARINATED HERRING AND ONIONS ON TOAST

Drain:
   Marinated herring
Place fillets on:
   Squares or rounds of toast
Cover with:
   Thin slices of Bermuda onion
Sprinkle with:
   Chopped parsley or watercress

LOBSTER SPREAD

Combine:
   Chopped cooked lobster meat
   Chopped hard-cooked eggs
   Chopped cucumbers
   Well-seasoned mayonnaise

HOT LOBSTER, CRAB OR TUNA CANAPÉS

Combine:
   ½ lb. cooked lobster, crab or tuna meat
   ½ lb. Sautéed Mushrooms, page 281
   1 cup rich Cream Sauce II, page 322
   1 tablespoon finely chopped
      green pepper
   1 tablespoon chopped pimiento
   ¼ teaspoon curry powder or
   1 teaspoon Worcestershire sauce
   3 tablespoons dry white wine
   Salt and pepper
Heap the mixture on rounds of:
   Toast
which may be spread with:
   Anchovy paste
Sprinkle the tops with:
   Au Gratin II, page 342
Heat the canapés under a broiler until
slightly brown. Serve at once.

HOT CREAMED OYSTER CANAPÉS

Messy but good little things!
Prepare:
   Creamed Oysters, page 365
Place the pan containing the oysters over
hot water. Toast and butter lightly:
   Small rounds of bread
Place a coated oyster on each round.
Sprinkle with:
   Chopped parsley
Serve the canapés at once.

ANGELS ON HORSEBACK

May also be served as a savory, see page
708.
Toast lightly and butter:
   Small rounds of bread
Wrap:
   Large drained oysters
with:
   Thin pieces of bacon
Secure with toothpicks and place the ca-
napés in a pan. Bake at 400° for about 3
minutes or long enough to crisp the bacon.
Remove the toothpicks and serve on the
rounds of toast.

SMOKED SALMON CANAPÉS

If the salmon you are served is pale pin
and not salty, it has been truly smoked
but if it is a strong red in color and ver
salty, smoke salt extract, page 526, ha
been used in the processing. Salmon fo
canapés should be sliced across the grain
It is delicious served garnished with ci
cumber or egg and, when thinly sliced,
makes an ideal lining for tarts or ba
quettes.

I. Place on round waffle wafers
crackers:
   Squares of smoked salmon
Top them with a slice of:
   Stuffed olive
Brush the canapés with:
   Mustard or Aspic Glaze, page 341

II. Or, top the salmon with:
   Guacamole, page 60
and serve on toasted rounds.

SARDINE CANAPÉ ROLLS

Mash with a fork:
   12 skinless, boneless sardines
Add:
   ½ teaspoon Worcestershire sauce
   ½ teaspoon tomato catsup
   1 tablespoon finely cut celery or onion
   1 tablespoon chopped stuffed olives
Moisten these ingredients until they are
a good consistency to be spread with:
   Mayonnaise or French dressing
Season with:
   Salt and pepper
Cut the crusts from:
   Thin slices of white bread
Spread the sardine mixture on the bre
Roll the slices and secure them with too
picks. Toast the canapés in a 400° ov
and serve very hot.

SHRIMP PUFFS

                                                24 P

Preheat Broiler
Clean, then cut in half:
   12 shrimp
Whip until stiff:
   1 egg white
Fold in:
   ¼ cup grated cheese
   ⅛ teaspoon salt
   ⅛ teaspoon paprika
   A few grains red pepper
   ½ cup mayonnaise
Heap these ingredients lightly o
crackers or rounds of toast. Garnish e
one with ½ shrimp. Broil the puffs u
light brown. Serve hot.

HORS D'OEUVRE

[H]ors d'oeuvre and canapés are appetizers [se]rved with drinks. The canapé sits on its [o]wn little couch of crouton or pastry tid-[bi]t, while the hors d'oeuvre is independent [an]d ready to meet up with whatever bread [or] cracker is presented separately. Many [ho]rs d'oeuvre are themselves rich in fat or [ar]e combined with an oil or butter base to [bu]ffer the impact of alcohol on the sys-[te]m. If, during preprandial drinking, the [ap]petizer intake is too extensive, any true [en]joyment of the meal itself is destroyed. [T]he palate is too heavily coated, too over-[sti]mulated by spices and dulled by alcohol. [A] very hot, light soup is a help in clearing [th]e palate for the more delicate and subtle [fla]vors of the meal. The very name "hors [d']oeuvre," literally interpreted, means [o]utside the main works." These hold [th]emselves aloof as do the famed Russian [za]kuska or the Italian antipasto, the so-[cal]led "dry" soup of southern countries. [B]ut hors d'oeuvre and antipasto, in spite [of] their separatist quality, may even re-[pla]ce the soup course when the portions [off]ered are somewhat more generous in [siz]e or amount.

◆ Allow about 6 to 8 hors d'oeuvre per [pe]rson.

[S]erve imaginative combinations, but re-[me]mber that, unlike the opera overture the [ho]rs d'oeuvre course should not forecast [an]y of the joys that are to follow in its [tra]in. Never skip hors d'oeuvre or can-[apé]s when you are serving drinks, for they [pla]y a functional role, but there is no harm [in]keeping them simple—just olives, salted [nut]s and one or two interesting spreads or [can]apés, so the meal that is to follow can [be] truly relished. ◆Should you serve—either in the living [roo]m or at the table—caviar in pickled [bee]ts or anchovy eggs on tomatoes, forget [the] very existence of beet and tomato when [pla]nning the flavors of the dinner. This is [not] a superfluous caution, for one encoun-[ters] many unnecessarily repetitious meals. [◆C]hoose for living-room service bite-size [can]apés or hors d'oeuvre, unless you are [fur]nishing plates. ◆ If hors d'oeuvre are [mea]nt to be hot, serve them fresh from the [ove]n. If they are the type that will hold, [use] some form of heated dish. ◆ Have [col]d offerings right out of the refrigerator [on] platters set on cracked ice. Cheeses [shou]ld be presented at a temperature of [60 a]nd 70°.

[T]here are recipes given in other chap-[ters] of this book that are suitable for hors [d'oe]uvre. It is difficult to assign certain [recip]es to a single course, as they may be as [vers]atile as Alec Guinness. So, be sure to

look in Salads, Fruits and Luncheon dishes, as well as in the Index. The Index may not be literature but a careful perusal of it will sometimes produce a poem.

Set hors d'oeuvre off with plenty of attractively-cut vegetables, page 82, and garnishes of fresh herbs and greens, page 83.

Here are a few types of food which are particularly appropriate for the hors d'oeuvre course: caviar, pâté and terrines, vegetables à la grecque, stuffed artichoke hearts, mushrooms, beets, Brussels sprouts and cherry tomatoes. You may also use spreads and dips; deviled, pickled, truffled or chopped eggs; skewered or bacon wrapped tidbits; smoked, sauced or mayon-naised seafood; quenelles and timbales; choice sausages, both hot and cold; glazed or jelled foods; nuts, olives or cheeses. And, from the Salad chapter, choose indi-vidual aspics, a filled ring of aspic, page 95, one of the mousses, page 98, or an Italian Salad, page 84.

ABOUT WAYS TO SERVE
HORS D'OEUVRE AND CANAPÉS

Food often looks more dramatic if some of it can be presented on several levels. This old dodge has been manifested in some really frightening ways. Look at the com-plex, inedible architectural underpinnings by which the glories of ancient chefs used to be supported and still are today, on celebratory occasions, in some large hotels and restaurants. Artificial coloring, rigid aspics, fussy detailing abound. These tech-niques for presenting food in fancy form are unpleasantly obvious and eating qual-ity is sacrificed. Don't torture the food. Instead, play up its gustatory highlights and allow its natural subtle colors and textures to shine. Keep in mind what the platter will look like as it begins to be demolished. For this reason, it is often wiser to arrange several small plates which are easily replaced or replenished than one big one which may be difficult to resurrect to its pristine glory.

First described are some mechanical aids to give platters a lift. Here are a few of the simplest: cut a grapefruit in half or carve a solid base on an orange or apple, place cut-side down on a plate, stud with hors d'oeuvre—and surround with a gar-nish or canapés, as seen left, page 64. You may also cut a melon or use a small, deep bowl or a footed bowl as a receptacle for hors d'oeuvre and surround it with canapés, as shown on the right and center.

Stud a pineapple, cut as shown left below, or see other ways, page 119, to make this highly decorative fruit a focal point.

Try cabbages, especially savoys, among whose beautiful curly-veined, velvety leaves small shrimp can cascade down onto the plate surface. The center can be hollowed out to hold invisibly a glass container for a dip, or use red cabbages, whose color can be picked up with stuffed beets and modified with artichokes and pâté slices. Even plain, everyday cabbages can be made interesting if you persuade your green-grocer to let you have one from which the outer leaves have not been hacked or if you can get one direct from a garden. Then curl the leaves back carefully, so as not to bruise them and cut a cavity into which you can insert a sauce bowl, deep enough so the curled leaf edges will conceal its rim as shown right below.

Just by the placement of food on the platter you can bring about height variations and attractive color relationships. On an oblong plate, center some dainty triangular sandwiches, peaks up like a long mountain range. Alternate sandwiches of a fine ham spread or thinly sliced ham with others made of caviar or mushroom spread or with thin buttered bread. Place small, well-drained marinated shrimp along the base of the range, on either side, and accent the water cress garnished edge of the platter with French endive or celery filled with Guacamole, page 53, and smoked salmon, wrapped around asparagus tips.

Try to choose an edible garnish for hors d'oeuvre trays. You may want to use beautifully cut vegetables, see page 83.
♦ Should the vegetables for garnish or hors d'oeuvre be watery, like tomato or cucumber, be sure to rid them of excess moisture by draining well.

If platters are not passed and you want

a table accent, place hors d'oeuvre directly on crushed ice, on a layered trsimilar to the one shown on page 46 on a simple epergne.
♦ If you use a silver or metal tray, ymay want to protect it from food acidsan under-garnish of lettuce, grape leaor croutons.

We saw a chef friend rapidly arrangetray almost entirely from stored foods-gala quickie if you feel suddenly convivwhen an unexpected mob descends on ywith short warning. Garnish a large plter with lettuce. For the center, makelarge mound of Russian salad, pageusing canned drained vegetables, of shrisalad or of Spiced Cabbage Mound, pa69. Garnish it with slices of tomato whard-cooked egg slices on them—toppwith a tiny tip cluster of tarragon, thyor parsley; or, cut the eggs and tomatinto wedges and border the moundplacing the wedges against it, withyolk side against the salad, see page

If you want something less rich,might use a mound of cottage chedecorated with tender stalks of bupressed into the mound to resemble cofern fronds and accented with borblossoms. You may also make a dospiral of overlapping radish discs andthe interspace with chopped chives. Pat each end of the platter sardinesasparagus tips held by onion or lerings, page 82. Prepare onion cups, p82, to hold caviar and surround twith lemon slices. Use a crock of chea good cheddar or Liptauer, page 708Cucumber-Cheese Spread, page 58. Evcan of good white meat tuna, unmoand coated with mayonnaise and atttively garnished with ripe olives or calooks well with canned drained artichhearts or hearts of palm. Fill inshrimp or mussels. Sprinkle vinaig

uce, sour cream, mayonnaise or even cat-
p over one or another of these items; or
ace small bowls of sauces on the platter.
reen pepper, cucumber or onion cups,
ge 82, also make attractive containers
r the dips.
Don't forget an occasional garnish of
chovy or pimiento strip and even the
iquitous radish or gherkin, see page
. And remember that a plate of inter-
ing breads and crackers is a tremen-
usly attractive foil to all of this rich,
hly seasoned food.

OUT ANTIPASTO

is ever-present constituent of Italian
enus is a great snack bar of fine hard
sages; prosciutto with melon or figs; fish,
h as anchovies, sardines and Mediterra-
n tuna; pickled onions, beets, peppers,
chokes, cauliflower and mushrooms;
hly seasoned Garbanzos; and cold egg-
nt in tomato purée. It also includes
sh tomatoes, fennel, cheeses—the hard
es, as well as mozzarella and ricotta,
crusty breads, and deep-fat fried fish,
at, fowl or game, which go under the
ne of Fritto Misto when encased in a
t batter.
Like hors d'oeuvre, antipasto—or "what
es before the pasta course"—can be a
ck with drinks or the base of an entire
cheon.
ome recipes in this book, which are
able for antipasto, are listed below.
ve them on platters or make them up on
vidual plates.

Tomato slices cut lengthwise
Vegetables à la Grecque, page 255
Anchovies
Seviche, page 72
Smoked Salmon Rolls, page 73
Rollmops, page 73
Pickled Oysters, page 73
Marinated Mushrooms, page 70
Stuffed Celery, page 69
Pickled Beets and Caviar, page 69
Eggplant Casserole, page 278
Sardines
Slices of salami
Hard-cooked eggs
Masked Eggs, page 202
Garlic Olives, page 70
Cucumber and green pepper sticks
Stuffed Leeks, page 70
Black Radishes, page 70

UT SMORGASBORD

Scandinavian spread has been in this
try so thoroughly adapted to the cas-
ocktail hour that some of us have lost
of its original importance. Smorgas-
in its original country is a square
in itself, not the prelude to one. Its
stays of meat and fish—and the aqua-
which washes them down—are cli-
imperatives when subarctic weather
rs for months outside the door. Like

all native dishes, smorgasbord closely reflects a country's ecology and its people's
way of life.
The foods of which a smorgasbord is traditionally composed are sufficiently dissimilar to require at least three plates and
silver services per person, so that the flavors of one course do not disturb those of
the next. Typical of those first presented
are herring, hot and cold, smoked eel,
salmon or shellfish—all served with small
boiled potatoes, seasoned with dill—and at
least three kinds of bread with small moun-
tains of butter balls. In fact, it is bread
and butter that gives this kind of meal its
name.
With the first change of plate come
cheeses, deviled eggs, pancakes and omelets with lingonberries, sausages, marinated and pickled vegetables and aspics.
With the next, hot foods follow, such as
meatballs, ham with apples, goose with
prunes, tongue and baked beans. Although many of these foods are prepared
in advance, their true charm lies in the
freshness of their garnish and arrangement. Do not leave the platters with their
cut meats exposed too long to air on the
buffet table.
To assemble a smorgasbord from some
of the recipes in this book, see Herring,
page 73 and 356, Swedish Limpa Bread,
salmon hors d'oeuvre, page 73, Salmon in
Aspic, page 359, Swedish Meat Balls, page
429, Crêpes with Lingonberries, page 213,
shrimp dishes, Swedish Roll Cookies.

ABOUT CRACKERS AND BREADS
TO SERVE WITH HORS D'OEUVRE

Bought crackers and breads can be dressed
up into delightful additions to the hors
d'oeuvre table with the cut of a knife, a
few aromatic seeds, a bit of cheese and an
oven. See About Fancy Breads and Crackers for Soup, page 173, and Uses for Ready-
Baked and Leftover Breads, see page 586.
You may also bake small Biscuits, page
583, Beaten Biscuits, page 585, Corn Meal
Crackles, page 579, and Corn Zephyrs
Cockaigne, page 579. Bake Grissini, page
558, or some good rye, cheese or French
breads. Make Potato Chips, page 296, and
don't forget Cheese Straws, page 174, and
unsweetened pastries in variety, page 588-
591.

NUTS AS HORS D'OEUVRE

These can be roasted or deep-fat fried.
I. Preheat oven to 250° to 300°.
To roast, put in a greased shallow pan:
Blanched or unblanched nuts,
page 521
Bake until golden, about 20 minutes.
Sprinkle during baking with:
(**Melted butter**)
seasoned with:
(**Celery salt, onion salt, cayenne or**
paprika)

II. Preheat deep fryer to 360°
Have ready:
> **Blanched or unblanched nuts, page 521, almonds, pecans, peanuts, pistachios or cashews**

For every cup of nuts, allow:
> **½ cup cooking oil**

Cook the nuts in the hot oil until golden. Pecans and Spanish peanuts will need about 2 minutes. Skim off and drain nuts on absorbent paper. After salting store tightly covered.

NUTS TOASTED IN THE SHELL
These are delicious served hot with cheeses or as snacks.
Preheat oven to 425°.
Roast in the shell, in a shallow pan, in the oven for about 15 minutes before serving.
> **English walnuts**

CURRIED NUTS
Combine in a skillet:
> **¼ cup olive oil**
> **1 tablespoon curry powder**
> **1 tablespoon Worcestershire sauce**
> **⅛ teaspoon cayenne**

When this mixture is very hot, add:
> **2 cups nuts: walnuts, almonds, etc.**

Stir until well coated. Now line a baking pan with brown paper, pour in the nuts and bake at 300° for about 10 minutes or until crisp.

TOASTED SEEDS
Separate the fiber from:
> **Melon, pumpkin, squash, sunflower or watermelon seeds**

Cover with:
> **Salted water**

Bring to a boil and ♦ simmer for 2 hours. Drain and dry on brown paper. Then:

I. Deep-fat fry as for Nuts, above.

II. Spread the seeds in a shallow pan. Coat with:
> **Cooking oil**
> **(Salt)**

Bake in a 250° oven until golden brown. Stir from time to time.

PUFFED CEREALS FOR COCKTAILS
Melt in a skillet, over low heat:
> **1½ cups butter**

Stir in lightly:
> **2 packages crisp small cereals**
> **1 tablespoon curry**
> **Garlic**
> **Celery salt**
> **1 teaspoon Worcestershire sauce**
> **(1 cup pumpkin seeds or nuts)**

Mix gently until the cereal has absorbed the seasoned butter. Serve at once.

SEASONED POPCORN OR POPPED WILD RICE
Prepare:
> **Popcorn, page 738 or wild rice as for popcorn**

Season with:
> **Melted butter**
> **(Squeeze of garlic or onion juice)**
> **(Grated sharp cheese)**

STUFFED DRIED FRUIT APPETIZER
Prepare well in advance, as described Prunes in Wine, page 120:
> **Apricots, dates or prunes**

Drain the fruit and reserve the liquor f sauces, gravies, etc. Place in each cavi 1 or 2 of the following:
> **A walnut or other nutmeat**
> **A canned water chestnut**
> **A sautéed chicken liver**
> **Chutney**
> **Cheddar or Roquefort cheese**

The fruit may· be served cold or hot. Y may also wrap each piece with:
> **A narrow strip of bacon**

Secure it with a toothpick and bake in 375° oven until the bacon is crisp.

COLD SKEWERED TIDBITS
Alternate on small toothpicks:
> **Small onions with pieces of cockta sausages and burr gherkins**
> **Squares of cheese with pickle slice stuffed olives or small onions**
> **Slices of raw carrot and blocks of tongue or ham**
> **Shrimp, lightly flavored with must and pieces of celery**
> **Squares of cheese and slices of gr onion, topped with a ripe olive**
> **Chilled balls of cream cheese, sprinkled with paprika or mixed chopped olives and pieces of her or anchovy**
> **Pieces of ham or bacon and wate melon pickle**
> **Cubes of cooked turkey, honeyde melon and pistachio nut**
> **Pieces of kippered salmon or her and onions**

In short, use your imagination and y leftovers.

FILLED EDAM CHEESE
Fine for a buffet meal. Hollow:
> **An Edam or Gouda cheese**

Crumble the removed part.

I. Combine it with:
> **2 teaspoons or more Worcestershire sauce or red wine**
> **1 tablespoon prepared mustard**
> **A few grains cayenne**
> **1 or 2 tablespoons fresh or dried minced herbs**

II. Or, to preserve its lovely characte flavor, blend just enough:
> **Heavy cream**

with the cheese to make it easy to sp Refill the cheese shell. Serve it surrou by toasted crackers.

EDAM NUGGETS
About 16

Grate:
1 cup Edam cheese
Add:
2 tablespoons finely chopped celery
⅛ teaspoon dry mustard
2 tablespoons cream or ale
Make into small balls and roll in:
Finely chopped parsley

VICKSBURG CHEESE

Blend with a fork until smooth:
⅓ Roquefort cheese
⅓ Cheddar cheese
⅓ soft cream cheese
Sprinkle thickly a large piece of waxed paper with:
Paprika
Roll the cheese mixture into a sausage shape on the paper until it has a generous coating of paprika. You can cut it into slices later. You may also roll the mixture into a large ball, which can be coated with:
(Chopped nuts)
Place in refrigerator to chill.

NUT CHEESE BALLS

Work to a paste:
½ cup Roquefort cheese or part
Roquefort and part cream cheese
1 tablespoon butter
½ teaspoon Worcestershire sauce or
1 tablespoon brandy
½ teaspoon paprika
A few grains cayenne
Shape into 1-inch balls. Roll them in:
¼ cup ground nutmeats
Chopped herbs or watercress
Chill them. This is also effective made into one large cheese ball.

GELATIN CHEESE MOLD

Dissolve:
1¼ teaspoons gelatin
in:
¼ cup cold water
Add, when melted and mixed over hot water:
¾ cup American cheese
2 packages Neufchatel cheese
1 teaspoon paprika
Beat well and add:
1 cup whipped cream
Beat until light and put in buttered mold.
Ice for several hours before serving. Unmold and garnish with:
Fresh burnet sprigs

ANCHOVY CHEESE OR KLEINER LIPTAUER

Work until smooth:
2 packages cream cheese: 6 oz.
Work in:
3 tablespoons soft butter
2 minced anchovies

1½ tablespoons grated onion or
1 minced shallot
1½ teaspoons capers
½ teaspoon caraway seed
¾ teaspoon paprika
2 drops Worcestershire sauce
Salt, as needed
Shape the mixture into small patties. Chill thoroughly.

NUT CREAMS

Roll into ¾-inch balls:
Soft cream cheese
(Squeeze of garlic or lemon juice)
Flatten them slightly between:
2 salted English walnuts or pecans

CHEESE CARROTS

Grate:
Yellow cheese
Moisten it, until it is of a good consistency to handle, with:
Cream or salad dressing
Shape it into small carrots. In the blunt end, place:
A sprig of parsley

ABOUT DEEP-FAT FRIED HORS D'OEUVRE

If you can lick the service problem and get to your guests this type of hors d'oeuvre while hot and just out of the fryer, nothing is more delicious. Consider the many suggestions in this chapter and also both the Japanese Tempura, page 256, and the Italian Fritto Misto, page 256, which are deep-fat fried.

CHEESE BALLS FLORENTINE

◖ Please read about Deep Fat Frying, pages 124-126.
Preheat deep fryer to 375°.
Measure by packing closely:
1 cup cooked, well-drained spinach
Put it through a purée strainer or chop in the ⋏ blender until fine. Stir in:
2 beaten eggs
1½ cups fine dry bread crumbs
1 tablespoon grated onion
½ cup grated cheese
1 teaspoon salt
1 tablespoon lemon juice
Shape this mixture into 1½-inch balls. Fry them in deep fat until brown and crisp. Drain them on absorbent paper. Serve with:
Thickened Tomato Sauce, page 333
Spoonfuls of this mixture may be sautéed in hot butter. Good with Hollandaise Sauce, page 328. The balls may be rolled in 1 egg, beaten with 2 tablespoons water, then in sifted, seasoned bread crumbs and again in the egg mixture before being fried or sautéed. Permit the crumbs to dry for 20 minutes before frying.

FRIED CHEESE DREAMS

◖ Please read about Deep Fat Frying, pages 124-126.

Preheat deep fryer to 375°.
Mix:

>½ lb. grated Swiss cheese
>3 well-beaten eggs
>1 teaspoon double-acting
> baking powder
>1 tablespoon sherry
>⅛ teaspoon paprika

Put some flour in a narrow glass or cup. Drop a tablespoon of the mixture into the flour and swirl it until it is coated with flour. Fry until a golden brown.

PASTRY CHEESE BALLS

About 24

Preheat oven to 400°
Cream together:

>½ cup sharp spreading cheese
> or grated American cheese
>3 tablespoons butter

Sift, then add:

>¾ cup all-purpose flour
>½ teaspoon salt
>¼ teaspoon paprika
>¼ teaspoon curry

When well blended, pinch off pieces of dough and form them into ¾-inch balls. They should be chilled for 2 hours but they may be baked at once. Bake for about 10 minutes. Serve hot or cold.

ABOUT EGGS AS HORS D'OEUVRE

Perhaps no other single food plays such a varied role in hors d'oeuvre as do eggs. You find them plain hard-cooked as a bland foil for the many spicy items surrounding them; deviled in the most complex ways, with anchovies, curry, capers, caviar; truffled and En Gelée, page 99, or pickled, page 203. They are particularly useful cut into fancy shapes as garnishes for other hors d'oeuvre—or with the whites chopped fine and the yolks pulverized, to add fresh color in decorating all kinds of foods.

Overlap slices of hard-cooked egg as shown at the top on the right, or pink the whites with an hors d'oeuvre cutter as shown second from the top on the left. Garnish egg slices with herbs, caviar, small shrimp or rolled anchovy fillets as shown on the bottom left and on the far right in the second row. Deviled or plain hard-cooked eggs may be similarly garnished and the deviled ones may be further decorated by using a pastry tube filled with the softened yolk. On the bottom right are 3 cuts for deviled egg cups. Shown second on the left is a molded salad garnished with sliced sections arranged in a pinwheel around a center of parsley or chervil. Another mold to the right shows a center of sieved egg and shreds of white which form a casual chrysanthemum motif. To make the egg and tomato wedge border on the top left, see page 64.

EGG APPLES

Prepare:

>Hard-cooked eggs

While they are warm, shell them and press them gently between the palms of the hands until they are round. Color them by placing them in beet juice or red vegetable coloring. Place in 2 sides of each egg, to represent the blossom ends and the stems

>Cloves

Or shape the eggs, add the cloves and paint the cheeks of the eggs with a dash of red and a dash of green color.

CRAB-APPLE GARNISH

Roll into 1-inch balls:

>Coarsely grated yellow cheese

Place in one side of each ball:

>A whole clove

Place in the opposite side:

>The stem of a clove

Sprinkle one cheek of each ball with:

>Paprika

GARNISHED ASPARAGUS SPEARS

Drain:

>Canned white asparagus tips

Wrap around the base of each spear:

>Thinly sliced ham

Serve chilled.

AVOCADO AND CHUTNEY

Peel just before serving and slice lengthwise into 4 to 6 thick slices:

>Avocado

Fill the hollow at the base of each slice with:

>Chutney

MARINATED BEANS

Drain:

>2 cups canned Garbanzo beans or

freshly cooked haricots blancs
Prepare the following marinade and soak
the beans in it for four hours:
>   2 tablespoons lemon juice
>   2 tablespoons red wine vinegar
>   ½ cup olive oil
>   Garlic clove
>   Various herbs

Drain and serve chilled.

STUFFED BEETS COCKAIGNE

I. Prepare, leaving them whole, very small
shapely Beets, page 264 or canned beets.
If small beets are not available, shape large
ones with a melon scoop. Hollow the beets
slightly. Fill the hollows with:
>   Caviar

sprinkled with a very little:
>   Lemon juice

Garnish with:
>   A sprig of parsley or lemon thyme

II. Fill the beet cups with:
>   Frozen Horseradish Sauce, page 312

III. Or fill them with a combination of:
>   Chopped hard-cooked eggs
>   Mayonnaise
>   Herbs, preferably chives
>   and tarragon

IV. You may also fill them with:
>   Chopped vinaigretted cucumbers

and garnish with:
>   Anchovy

STUFFED BRUSSELS SPROUTS

Drain well:
>   Cooked or canned Brussels sprouts

Cut a small hollow in each one, preferably from the top. Drop into each hollow:
>   ½ teaspoon French dressing

Chill them. Fill them with any good:
>   Sandwich spread

Use liver sausage and tomato paste, cream
cheese and chives or anchovy, adding the
chopped center portion of the sprouts to
the spread. Garnish with:
>   A sprig of parsley, savory, basil, etc.

Serve several as a salad or use as hors
d'oeuvre.

SPICED CABBAGE MOUND

A decorative platter for a buffet or first
course.
Shred:
>   White cabbage

Dress it with equal parts of:
>   Mayonnaise
>   Chili sauce

Arrange it in a mound. Cover the top
with:
>   Marinated shrimp

Surround the mound with:
>   Deviled eggs, topped with caviar

MARINATED CARROTS

Slice as thin as soup noodles:
>   Carrots

Marinate the slices in:
>   Lemon or orange juice
>   A little sugar

Serve well chilled.

CELERY CURLS

Separate, then wash:
>   A stalk of celery

Trim leaves, cut several long gashes into
each rib. Soak in ice water until curled, as
sketched.

STUFFED CELERY OR FRENCH ENDIVE

I. Combine:
>   1 tablespoon butter
>   1 tablespoon Roquefort cheese
>   1 package cream cheese: 3 oz.
>   Salt
>   (1 teaspoon caraway, dill or
>   celery seed)

Place this mixture in:
>   Dwarf celery ribs or French endive

If you want them to look very elegant,
force the mixture through a large pastry
tube. Sprinkle with:
>   Paprika

Chill.

II. Or, fill celery with:
>   Guacamole, page 60

III. Another wonderful filling is:
>   Caviar and cultured sour cream,
>   with a little lemon juice

CUCUMBER LILY

Have ready:
>   Thinly sliced unpeeled
>   cucumber rings
>   3-inch carrot sticks

Gently fold the cucumber slice around the
base of the carrot stick. Fold a second
slice around the stick from the other side.
This forms the lily petals, with a carrot
stamen in the center. Fasten with a toothpick, being careful to catch all four lapped
edges of the cucumber as well as piercing
the carrot stick. Wrap flowers lightly in

a moistened paper towel and refrigerate until ready to use as garnish for the hors d'oeuvre or salad tray.

STUFFED LEEKS
18 to 24 Pieces
Cut into 1½-inch cross sections the white portions of:
3 large cooked leeks
When chilled, cut the cross sections in two, lengthwise.
Stuff the leeks with Shrimp or Shad Roe Salad, page 91. Coat the top with more:
(**Mayonnaise**)
or garnish with a tiny sprig of:
(**Fresh lemon thyme**)

MARINATED MUSHROOMS
Be sure to include in your repertoire Stuffed Mushrooms, page 281-282.

The ranchers of the West frequently resort to a repast of raw mushrooms. Here is a variation. Cut into thin vertical slices:
Large firm mushrooms or use very small button mushrooms
Marinate them for 1 hour or more in:
French dressing
(**Dash herb vinegar**)
Chopped chives or onion juice
Chopped parsley
Serve the mushrooms on:
Lettuce or water cress
or on toothpicks.

ABOUT OLIVES
So much fuss is made about commercial grading and typing of olives! The thing to remember is that size is not always a matter of quality. You don't have to be a connoisseur to know that the big dull-green woody Queen Olives can't compare in flavor or in texture with the Manzanillas fines—those small, succulent, yellowish green fruits.

Try various types in making up your hors d'oeuvre tray. The green ones, picked unripe, are treated with a potassium or ash solution and then pickled in brine. Since they have not been heat treated, a film sometimes forms after opening the bottle. If this happens, you may float olive oil on the surface of the liquid in the bottle before re-storing or rinse the olives in cold water, drain, place in a clean jar and re-cover with a solution of 1 teaspoon salt and 1 tablespoon white vinegar to a cup of water.

The black ones are picked ripe, put in a boiling brine and sold dried, pickled or in oil. To reduce the saltiness of dried or pickled olives, store them in olive oil that you can later use for dressing.

The ripe olives found on an hors d'oeuvre tray have usually been oil treated. There are many ways to stuff

them. For a real treat, put in a little foie gras and close with a pistachio nut.

GARLIC OLIVES
Drain the liquid from:
Green or ripe olives
Add:
12 peeled cloves garlic
Cover with:
Olive oil
Permit to stand for 24 hours or more under refrigeration. Drain. Use the oil for salad dressing. You may dust the olives with:
Chopped parsley

MARINATED ONIONS
Skin, then slice:
Bermuda onions
Soak them for 30 minutes in:
Brine: ⅔ cup water to 1 tablespoon salt
Drain. Soak them for 30 minutes in:
Vinegar
Drain, then chill them. They are then ready to be served side by side with celery, radishes, olives, etc.

PEPPER HORS D'OEUVRE
Remove skin from:
Peppers
by roasting under the grill until burned. Remove the core and seeds. Marinate in:
Olive oil
Lemon juice
for 15 minutes. Slice the peppers into thirds. On each strip, put:
1 tablespoon tuna salad or anchovies with capers
Roll the strips like small sausages. Garnish with the marinade and:
Chopped parsley

RADISH HORS D'OEUVRE
I. Dip whole or strips of:
White or red radishes
in:
Whipped cream
seasoned with:
Salt
Vinegar

II. Or serve red radishes cut in rose shapes, filled with:
Anchovy Butter or Other Seasoned Butters, page 338

III. Remove the rind from and slice thinly across the grain solid black radishes. Soak them covered in a little salted water for about 15 minutes. Drain, marinate in a mixture of:
Oil
Vinegar
White pepper
Serve chilled.

TIDBITS IN BACON OR HAM
Surround any of the following:
Pineapple chunks
Spiced cored crabapples
Prunes, stuffed with almonds
Watermelon pickles
Dates, stuffed with pineapple
Skinned grapefruit sections
Large stuffed olives
Pickled onions
Smoked oysters or mussels
Raw scallops or oysters
Cooked shrimp
Sautéed chicken livers
with:
Thin strips of ham or bacon
Secure them with picks. Broil until the
meat is crisp.

PROSCIUTTO AND FRUIT
On small toothpicks alternately interlace:
Prosciutto or Virginia ham slices
around:
Melon balls
Pineapple, pear or peach chunks
Fresh figs
The fruit may be marinated in:
(**Port wine**)
At the very tip of the toothpick, impale a
clustered tip of:
Mint leaves

MARROW HORS D'OEUVRE
Bake:
Beef marrow bones
Serve the marrow with long spoons. It is
delicious.

CANNIBAL MOUND OR
STEAK TARTARE
Combine:
2 lbs. raw, scraped or finely chopped,
fresh, lean steak
with:
2 raw egg yolks
½ cup finely chopped onions
4 mashed anchovies
and the following, to taste:
Capers
Chopped parsley and herbs
Worcestershire sauce
Olive oil
Serve in a mound, garnished with whole
anchovies and sprigs of parsley and surrounded by small squares of pumpernickel
bread, or shape small balls of the above
mixture and roll in:
Chopped parsley

MEAT BALL HORS D'OEUVRE
Prepare:
Tiny Meat Balls, Hamburgers, Nut-
burgers, Koenigsberger Klops,
page 428, or small size
Dolmas, page 431
Season them well. Serve them very hot on
toothpicks or between small biscuits.

TONGUE, CHIPPED BEEF OR
BOLOGNA CORNUCOPIAS
Prepare one of the following spreads:
Seasoned Cream Cheese, page 58
Hard-Cooked Egg Spread, page 59
Piccalilli, page 783
Cultured sour cream and horseradish
Spread the mixture on very thin slices of:
Smoked boiled tongue, chipped
beef or bologna
Roll into cornucopias. Or stack 6 slices.
Wrap them in waxed paper. Chill. Cut
into 6 or more pie-shaped wedges.

TINY BROILED SAUSAGES
Heat on a hibachi or broil:
Very small sausages
Serve them hot on toothpicks with:
Mustard Sauce, page 325

RUMAKI
Cut into bite-size pieces:
Chicken livers
sprinkle with:
(**Soy sauce**)
Prepare an equal number of:
¼-inch canned water chestnut slices
Marinate the chestnuts in:
(**Port wine**)
Wrap a slice of liver and one of water
chestnut together in:
½-inch-wide slice of bacon
Secure with a wooden toothpick and broil
slowly, until the bacon is crisp. Serve hot.

SHERRIED CHICKEN BITS
Stew and place while still warm into a
large jar:
Breasts of fat stewing hens
Leave the meat on the bone and cover
with:
Sherry
Cover the jar closely and refrigerate for 10
days before using. To serve, skin, bone
and cut the meat into bite-size pieces.
Serve cold on toothpicks.

CHOPPED GOOSE OR
CHICKEN LIVERS
For other liver hors d'oeuvre, see pages 432
and 434.
Drop into boiling seasoned water and simmer until barely done:
1 lb. chicken livers
Drain them and cool. Cook until hard,
shell, chop and add:
2 eggs
Chop coarsely, then sauté:
2 medium-size onions
in:
2 tablespoons butter
Chop or blend these ingredients until they
are a fine paste.
Correct the seasoning
Add:
(**2 tablespoons chopped parsley**)
(**1 oz. cognac or brandy**)

TURKEY AND OLIVE
HORS D'OEUVRE
Roll:

Thin slices of turkey

around:

Large pitted green olives

ABOUT CAVIAR AND OTHER ROES

A lady was once moved to ask plaintively why caviar is so expensive; to which a quick-witted maître d' replied: "After all, madam, it is a year's work for a sturgeon." The word caviar applies only to salted roe, but the best caviar is the roe of the sturgeon. The most sought-after form comes from Russia or Iran where highly-skilled workers prepare it. It is neither fishy nor briny in taste, as 2% of salt is enough to hold it. The eggs should be shiny, translucent, gray and large grained. ♦ As it spoils in a few hours in temperatures of 40° or above, always serve on ice. Its high oil content keeps it from freezing. To prepare caviar, see page 756.

To serve individual portions attractively, heat the back of a metal spoon, press it into an ice cube and fill the depression with the caviar—using a plastic spoon. ♦ Never allow the caviar itself to touch metal or to be served on it. If you spread it on canapés or in barquettes, see page 55, or stuff beets with it, page 69, be careful not to bruise the eggs. The classic accompaniments are lemon wedges, parsley, black bread or not-too-dry toast. Although egg whites, yolks and onions—all very finely minced and separately arranged—are more frequently served as the garnish, they are not considered by connoisseurs as suitable as the simpler lemon and parsley. Other favored ways of service are in Blinis with Sour Cream, page 214, or simply mixed half and half with sour cream and served with pumpernickel.

Other types of roe used as caviar are those of the salmon, cod, herring, tuna and gray mullet. Serve, as suggested for sturgeon roe, with slightly iced white wines, never red ones. To cook roes, see page

359. An ideal accompaniment to caviar dishes is champagne or vodka.

ABOUT SEA TIDBITS

When you go collecting at the shore, you can often find edible treats. Sketched are shellfish that can be eaten raw as hors d'oeuvre. Shown on the left are first 2 kinds of cockles, then an oyster. A sea urchin appears next to the right above the oyster. Known as a sea egg, it can be cooked just like soft boiled eggs and eaten with buttered toasted bread or puréed for tart filling. If cooked, cut the urchin on the concave side. The easiest way is to use scissors and remove the gut which surrounds the edible tangerine-like sections. In flavor it is not unlike brains. To eat out-of-doors, simply throw them on the rocks to crack them open. ♦ Just be certain to use gloves when handling sea urchins. Directly below the urchin is a clam, next 2 kinds of mussels and a razor clam. Following in the upper row, are first a limpet. You eat the foot and discard the visceral hump. Then you see a tiny winkle which can be extracted with a pin. Below the winkle is a bay scallop, and on the far right a sea scallop. In these the hinge muscle is edible. For other sea tidbits try small shellfish, page 363, in spicy sauces. Serve hot or cold. Due to red tides, mollusks may be poisonous during the summer months. Be sure to check local conditions.

SEVICHE

Marinated raw fish is very popular in South America as an hors d'oeuvre. If you are squeamish, you may prefer, as the Spaniards do—for a similar effect in their Escabèche—to poach the fish lightly and pour over it a hot marinade, based on olive oil and vinegar, rather than rely on the acid of lime juice. Refrigerate, covered, for 24 hours and serve cold; or,

I. Skin, remove bones from lemon sole, pompano or red snapper or use flaked crab meat. Dice:

2 lbs. very fresh, firm-fleshed fish

Marinate in a glass dish, covered, and refrigerate for 3 to 4 hours, entirely immersed in:

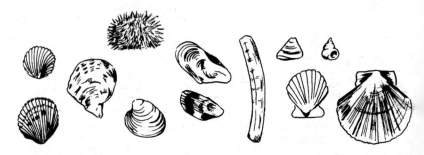

2 cups lime juice
½ cup finely chopped onions
¼ cup chopped green chilis
1 cup chopped, peeled and
seeded tomatoes
2 teaspoons salt
A few grains of cayenne
⅛ teaspoon oregano
Serve in small scallop shells. Garnish with:
Hot chili peppers
Serve with:
Cornmeal Crackles, page 579
tortillas or hot red peppers

II. Cut into quarters:
1 cup raw scallops
Cover with:
½ cup lime juice
and marinate refrigerated overnight. Drain.
Add:
2 tablespoons finely chopped onion
1 tablespoon finely chopped parsley
2 tablespoons finely chopped
green pepper
3 tablespoons olive oil
Correct the seasoning
Serve as a garnish in a bowl with individual toothpicks.

FISH BALLS
Prepare very small:
Codfish Balls, page 354
Serve them hot on toothpicks with:
Tartar Sauce

HERRING, ANCHOVY OR SMOKED SALMON ROLLS
I. Cut into ½-inch strips:
Pickled herring, smoked salmon
or anchovies
Roll the strips around tiny:
Sour-sweet or other gherkins
Secure and serve the rolls with picks.

II. Cut into very thin slices:
Smoked salmon
Spread them with:
Cream cheese, seasoned with cucumbers, horseradish, chopped chives or
parsley
Roll the strips. Secure and serve them
with toothpicks.

HERRING OR SARDINE HORS D'OEUVRE
Place on plates:
Lettuce leaves
Build up into a cone:
Finely shredded onion or pickled
pearl onions
Finely shredded cole slaw, topped
with pieces of pickled herring,
sardine or anchovy
Pour over the cone:
Cultured sour cream
The cream may be thinned with a few tablespoons of the liquor from the pickled
herring. Have all ingredients very cold.

ROLLMOPS
On a:
Herring fillet
place a layer of:
Capers
Chopped shallots
Chopped gherkins
A little prepared mustard
Roll the fillet and fasten with a wooden
toothpick. Place the rolled herrings in jars
and cover well with:
Wine vinegar
to which you add:
Slivers of lemon peel
Mustard seed
Sliced onion
Peppercorns
Allow the rollmops to steep for 10 days in
the refrigerator. Drain and serve cold,
lightly brushed with:
Olive oil

COLD OYSTER OR MUSSEL HORS D'OEUVRE
Mix together carefully:
Sour Cream Dip, page 74
Coat with this sauce:
18 oysters or mussels in the half shell
Decorate tops with:
Red caviar
Serve on a bowl of ice.

PICKLED OYSTERS
Combine in the top of a double boiler:
1 quart oysters
1 quart oyster liquor
Heat until the oysters are plump. Drain
and wipe the oysters. Reserve the liquor
and simmer it for 15 minutes with:
1 tablespoon peppercorns
1 tablespoon whole allspice
1 thinly sliced lemon
2 tablespoons vinegar
Dash of hot pepper sauce
Correct the seasoning
Pour the sauce over the oysters and refrigerate at least 24 hours before serving.

ASPIC-GLAZED SHRIMP
Clean and devein, page 376:
1½ lbs. boiled shrimp
Cut them lengthwise down the center, as
shown on page 376. Prepare:
Aspic Glaze, page 341
Chill the glaze until it begins to set. Spear
the shrimp on toothpicks. Dip them into
the glaze. When partly set, dip them again.
Chill well. Serve cold.

PICKLED SHRIMP
Warn your guests about these—they're
hot!
Cover:
5 lbs. shrimp
with:
Flat draft beer or ⅔ vinegar and
⅓ water

Add:

  1 tablespoon bruised peppercorns
  ¼ cup salt
  3 bay leaves
  1 teaspoon hot pepper sauce or
  ⅛ teaspoon cayenne pepper
  ¼ cup chopped celery tops

Bring to a boil and simmer for 15 minutes. Remove from the heat and let shrimp stand in the liquor for at least 1 hour in the refrigerator. Drain and serve on a platter of crushed ice.

▣ BROILED SHRIMP
Without cutting into the meat, shell, clean and devein, page 376:

  2 lbs. jumbo shrimp

Be sure to leave the tails on. Marinate the shrimp in the refrigerator for several hours in:

  1 clove pressed garlic
  1 cup olive oil
  ½ cup sauterne wine
  Juice of ½ lemon
  3 tablespoons parsley and basil,
    chopped together
  1 teaspoon salt
  ¼ teaspoon pepper

Grill or broil the shrimp for about 10 minutes, being careful not to scorch them. Serve at once with:

  Lemon Butter Sauce, page 338

flavored with:

  1 large pressed clove of garlic

FRIED SHRIMP BALLS
Mix and shape into balls:

  1¼ lbs. shelled, deveined,
    minced shrimp
  6 finely chopped canned
    water chestnuts
  1 piece finely chopped ginger
  1 small chopped onion
  1 egg white
  1 teaspoon cornstarch
  3 teaspoons wine
  1 teaspoon sesame or cooking oil
  Dash of pepper

Fry in deep fat, heated to about 360°, until golden brown.

ABOUT DIPS
Maybe overused, they are still the most popular type of hors d'oeuvre and the easiest to prepare. Good before dinner or for afternoon and late evening snacking. However, we feel that dips are not good for large groups, as it is too difficult to hand them around often enough. Don't forget to use some of the fine spreads listed earlier in Canapés. Make them juicier ♦ but still on the firm side, with a little cream, lemon juice or mayonnaise and choose additional seasonings to your own taste.

Try putting your favorite dip in this kind of bowl: a hollowed-out red cabbage, grapefruit or eggplant or a lovely scooped-out pineapple which, on fern or grape leaves, delights the eye and tantalizes the palate.

FOODS TO BE DIPPED
  Crackers
  Potato chips
  Small wheat biscuits
  Toast sticks
  Corn chips
  Fried Oysters, page 364
  Cooked shrimp
  Iced cucumber strips
  Iced green pepper strips
  Cauliflower florets
  Carrot sticks
  Radishes
  Celery sticks
  Peeled broccoli stems, etc.

SOUR CREAM DIPS
I. Combine:

  2 cups thick cultured sour cream
  2 tablespoons chopped parsley
  2 tablespoons chopped chives
  1 teaspoon dried herbs
  ⅛ teaspoon curry powder
  ½ teaspoon salt
  ¼ teaspoon paprika

II. Combine:

  1 cup cultured sour cream
  1 or more tablespoons horseradish
  ½ teaspoon salt
  ¼ teaspoon paprika

CHEESE DIPS
The mania for cheese dips, cold, has replaced that for cheese dips, hot—without which no party used to be complete. But don't forget those old favorites, Welsh Rarebit, made with beer, and Cheese Fondue, page 243.
I. Combine:

  ¾ lb. cheddar cheese
  ¼ lb. Roquefort cheese
  2 tablespoons butter
  ½ teaspoon Worcestershire sauce
  ½ teaspoon mustard
  ¼ teaspoon salt
  ½ pressed clove of garlic

and melt over heat with:

  1 cup beer

II. Beat until smooth:

  2 packages cream cheese: 6 oz.
  1½ tablespoons mayonnaise
  1 tablespoon cream
  ¼ teaspoon salt
  1 teaspoon grated onion
    or chives
  1 teaspoon Worcestershire sauce

LONG-KEEPING CHEESE SPREAD OR DIP
                              About 1½ Cups

This keeps well and makes excellent toasted cheese sandwiches or a sauce. Thin it as needed with a little milk in a double boiler.

Cut into small pieces and stir over very low heat, or in a double boiler, until melted:

½ lb. cheese

We find a soft cheese or a processed one preferable for this recipe. Add:

1 cup evaporated milk
¾ teaspoon salt
¾ teaspoon dry mustard
¼ teaspoon curry powder
¼ teaspoon dried herb

Remove from the heat and stir in:

1 beaten egg

Stir and cook the cheese mixture very slowly until the egg thickens slightly. Remove from the heat. Pour it into a dish. Cool it slowly. Beat it as it cools, to keep a crust from forming, cover and chill.

ORIENTAL DIP

Good with raw mushrooms and raw cauliflower.
Combine:

½ cup finely chopped green onions
½ teaspoon fresh coriander
¼ cup chopped parsley
2 tablespoons chopped fresh ginger
1 tablespoon soy sauce
2 tablespoons canned chopped
  water chestnuts
1 cup cultured sour cream
2 tablespoons mayonnaise

CAVIAR DIP

Whip:

½ cup whipping cream

Fold in:

2 to 3 tablespoons caviar
1 to 2 tablespoons finely
  chopped onion

Place in the center of a dish and garnish with:

Sliced hard-cooked eggs and
small toast rounds

CLAM DIP

Drain:

1 cup minced clams

Combine them with:

1 package soft cream cheese: 3 oz.
1 tablespoon Worcestershire sauce
  A pinch of dry mustard
  Salt, as needed
1 tablespoon, more or less, onion juice
¼ cup heavy cream

CRAB MEAT OR TUNA DIP

Flake:

1 cup crab meat or tuna

Stir in:

2 tablespoons mayonnaise
1 to 2 tablespoons tomato paste
  or catsup
  Juice of 1 lemon
  Seasoning, as needed
  (Chopped celery or olives)

SHRIMP DIP

I. Combine:

1 can cooked shrimp: 5 oz.
1 cup large curd creamy
  cottage cheese
3 tablespoons chili sauce
½ teaspoon onion juice
2 teaspoons lemon juice
1 to 2 tablespoons cream, if needed

II. Put through a coarse food chopper:

1½ lbs. cooked, cleaned shrimp
2 tablespoons capers
1 very small onion

Combine the above ingredients in a mixing bowl with:

¼ lb. soft butter
¼ cup heavy cream
¼ cup Pernod or dry white wine

Season with:

Salt
Hot pepper sauce
Tarragon
Chopped parsley

Mix well until of the consistency of whipped cream. Pack in a pretty mold which has been rinsed in cold water and refrigerate, covered, for 3 or 4 hours. Unmold and garnish with:

Cherry tomatoes

SALADS

We remember the final scene of a Maeterlinck play. The stage is strewn with personages dead and dying. The sweet young heroine whimpers, "I am not happy here." Then the head of the house—or what remains of it—an ancient noble, asks quaveringly, "Will there be a salad for supper?"

The primal craving for fresh greens can urge you out, seasonally, trowel in hand, to dig along the roadside and in the wild; or, like Willa Cather's Archbishop—no matter how torrid the climate, how dry the soil—to tend carefully a small patch of succulent leafage or herbs.

There is an ever-increasing demand for salads of all kinds, and a greater and greater appreciation of their contribution to our gastronomical enjoyment and our improved health. Salads figure prominently in reducing diets, too, for they are low in calories. But to achieve your goal, be sure to serve them with only a sprinkling of lemon juice, a touch of spiced vinegar or a low-calorie dressing, page 313.

When to serve the salad? It used to appear almost invariably after the main entrée but has taken, these days, to gadding about. In California, where people have a habit of doing things their own way, you may expect it on the table ready to eat when you sit down. In restaurants, if the service is leisurely, this priority is a lifesaver. At informal luncheons, salads often accompany the entrée or may even be the main dish. Don't neglect the possibility of using salads like Celeri-Rave Remoulade, page 85, as an hors d'oeuvre and, vice versa, appetizers like Vegetables à la Grecque, page 255, as a salad.

Originally, salads were the edible parts of various herbs or plants dressed only with salt—from which the word salad comes. But they now include a wide variety of ingredients, cooked and uncooked. Aside from fruits, vegetables and herbs, all kinds of meat, cheese and fish abound in salads—all served with some sort of moist dressing. The danger in this embarrassment of richness is that, in some carelessly planned meals, the salad tends to outshine the main entrée and plays the part of a "satisfier," rather than that of a stimulator.

◊ Keep the rest of the menu well in mind when preparing your salad and its dressing. A rich, heavy entrée demands a tart green salad. Slaws go well with casual meals, cookouts and impromptu suppers—at which hearty, uncomplicated foods are served. Elaborate salads, beautifully arranged and garnished, brilliant aspics and decorative chaud-froids. all look well on formal buffet tables or at special summer luncheons. In some cases, these are made as individual servings rather than as a grand "pièce de résistance."

◊ Always use your common sense and good taste in the matter of dressings. We have suggested suitable dressings for the individual salads in this chapter and want you to try some of the variations listed. Don't go overboard, however, in experimenting: a heavy dressing, undiluted, will make any lettuce, except iceberg, collapse just when you want to keep it crisp. Your dressing should enhance the salad by summoning forth its special flavor and texture and adding a delicate piquancy.

ABOUT CULTIVATED SALAD GREENS

◊ Do experiment with some of the greens sketched on the next page. On successive rows reading left to right are on the bottom row: Bibb lettuce, escarole, corn salad or màche and oak leaf lettuce; on the second row: Boston and water cress; on the top row, iceberg and Chinese or celery cabbage, Belgian, French or Witloof endive, romaine or Cos and curly endive.

ICEBERG OR CRISP HEAD LETTUCE:

Large, firm head, with crisp, brittle, tightly packed leaves. The outer leaves are medium green and fringed, the inner ones are pale green and tightly folded. Can be torn, shredded or sliced like cabbage for a salad. Adds "crunch" to it and does not wilt.

ROMAINE OR COS LETTUCE:

Elongated head, with long stiff leaves which are usually medium dark to dark green on the outside and become greenish-white near the center. Its more pungent flavor adds a tang to tossed salad.

BOSTON OR BUTTERHEAD LETTUCE:

Smaller, softer head than iceberg. Delicate leaves, of which the outer are green, the inner light yellow with a buttery feeling.

BIBB LETTUCE:

The aristocrat of all lettuce. Dark, succulent green leaves, loosely held together; tender and mild.

LEAF LETTUCE:

Crisp and, unless very young, a somewhat

tough, non-heading type. The loose leaves branch from a single stalk and are light or dark green. Frequently used as an undergarnish for molded salads, aspic or arrangements of salad vegetables and fruits.

OAKLEAF LETTUCE:

A type of leaf lettuce resembling its name. There are two types: one green, one bronze.

LAMB'S LETTUCE, MACHE, OR FIELD OR CORN SALAD:

Although found wild here, lamb's lettuce or mâche is cultivated extensively and in a number of varieties in France and Italy. It is an excellent winter salad and can be grown outside without protection. Small smooth green leaves, loosely formed into a head. Good for tossed salad and sometimes used as cooked greens.

CURLY ENDIVE OR CHICORY:

Curly fringed tendrils, coming from a yellow-white stem. It adds a bitter flavor and rather prickly texture to a tossed salad. Also used as a garnish.

ESCAROLE OR CHICORY ESCAROLE:

Also known as Batavian endive. The leaves are broader and less curly than endive, also a paler green. The taste is less bitter.

BELGIAN OR FRENCH ENDIVE OR WITLOOF:

These 6- to 8-inch, elongated, crisp yellow-white leaves look like a young unshucked corncob. The bitter flavor complements blander lettuces in a tossed salad or a bland filling for an hors d'oeuvre.

CHINESE OR CELERY CABBAGE:

About the size of a bunch of celery, its closely packed, whitish-green leaves are crisp and firm and, as the name implies, the flavor is between that of cabbage and celery.

WHITE MUSTARD:

A European annual, with small tender green leaves, usually cut about a week after the seeds have been sown and used with garden cress in salads or for garnish.

GARDEN CRESS:

Do not confuse with water cress. Has very tiny leaves, picked 14 days after sowing. It is frequently combined in sandwiches, hors d'oeuvre, etc., with mustard greens.

WATER CRESS:

Dime-size dark green glossy leaves, on sprigged stems. The leaves and tender part of stems are spicy and peppery additions to the tossed salad.

Water cress in France is the invariable accompaniment to a roast chicken. In America, it is one of our most interesting greens, frequently available in the wild. Its consumption, however, is often discouraged by the fact that it may be growing in ◆ polluted water. To settle any doubts you may have, soak the cress first in 2 quarts of water in which 1 tablet of water purifier has been dissolved. Then rinse the cress in clear water. Dry and chill before serving.

◆ To keep water cress, cut off ½ inch of the stems. Loosen the tie and set in a container which does not press it on the sides or top. Fill the container with 1 inch of cold water, cover and set in the refrigerator. Wash thoroughly when ready to use. Cut off the tough ends before tossing.

SEA KALE:

A native of most seacoasts of Western Europe, sea kale is cultivated for its leafstalks, but the curly leaves can be used uncooked in salad, either alone or with lettuce.

CELERY AND SPINACH:

Both these staples lend color variation to salads.

ABOUT WILD GREENS

These can add a different flavor and texture to your mixed green salads. Be absolutely sure, however, that you know the ones you are using and wash them very carefully. Here are some of the more common edible varieties, which can be identified fairly easily:

DANDELION, TARAXACUM OFFICINALE:

Abundant in lawns, fields, meadows and roadsides. It is easiest to handle and wash if it is cut off at the root crown, so that the cluster of leaves holds together. Its slightly acrid taste goes well with beetroot. After flowering, the plants become tough and rather bitter.

SORREL, RUMEX ACETOSELLA OR RUMEX ACETOSA:

There are many edible varieties of sorrel. Both grow in cultivated and recently filled soil, neglected fields and old grasslands. The leaves have a sour or acid taste and are best for salads when gathered young and small. Cooked and puréed sorrel is good with fish.

WINTER CRESS OR BARBAREA VULGARIS:

This cress has dark-green, smooth, shiny leaves and yellow flowers. It is common in waste and cultivated ground, fields, roadsides and streams. Use the rosette of root leaves for salad and gather the early spring growth and the new growth in late fall and early winter.

ABOUT TOSSED SALADS

We hesitate to admit how often we follow the injunction, "Serve with a tossed salad." A tossed salad arouses the appetite, complements a rich entrée and, incidentally, provides us with valuable vitamins and minerals.

The resigned acceptance of ready-made salad dressing has deprived many of us of a treasured prerogative—the making of French dressing at table. Presiding over cruets, seasonings and greens was, not so long ago, a ceremonial privilege of host or hostess. If the host officiated, it was apt to have a markedly meticulous and conver-

sational quality. Methods of mixing the dressing varied with individual taste, but there was no question of the importance of the moment or of its dignity.

◆ Salad ingredients prepared long in advance suffer a loss of nutritive value, and arrive at the table looking discouragingly limp. To serve one of the choicest treats of the table, take care ◆ to have salad ingredients fresh. ◆ In washing greens, be sure not to bruise them. ◆ Be sure, too, that they are well chilled, crisp and, especially, dry.

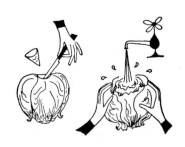

◆ To prepare lettuce, separate the leaves and wash them thoroughly. With iceberg lettuce this is difficult unless you core the solid part of the stem, either by using a sharp knife or pounding the bottom of the head quite hard on a wooden board, when the core will simply fall out. Hold the head upside down under running water. Water pressure pushes the leaves apart without bruising them. Boston and field lettuces must be inspected carefully for grit and sand. Try some of the wild as well as the cultivated salad greens previously listed, for their texture and flavors distinctively differ.

◆ Dry greens by letting them drip in a colander, wrapping them lightly in a soft absorbent towel until dry and chilling in the refrigerator until crisp and ready to use. Whirling greens in a wire salad basket is often recommended, but a Breton friend, observes that, at home, this kind of treatment is contemptuously referred to as "a ride in the jail wagon," because it manhandles the occupants. If you like to whirl, try doing it in a tea towel. To dry lettuces such as Bibb, that may be cleaned while still in head form, invert to drain, then place in the refrigerator on a turkish towel, cover with another plain towel and chill for several hours. Gravity and capillary action make them dry and crisp.

ABOUT MAKING A TOSSED SALAD

It is usual to tear rather than cut greens, except iceberg lettuce, which, if you desire smaller pieces, can be sliced or shredded. Place them in an ample bowl and give them a preliminary light coating of oil. About 1 tablespoon of salad oil will suffice for a medium-sized head of lettuce. Toss repeatedly by lifting the leaves gently with a large fork and spoon until each leaf is completely coated. This improves the salad from the standpoint of nutrition as well as that of gastronomy. Follow up with more oil, vinegar, and further tossing. If the salad is mixed on this principle, it will stay crisp, although it is usually eaten too rapidly to prove it.

Since vinegar and salt release juices and impair vitamin content, add them as close to serving time as possible. A good way to "toss" salad for a picnic is to have prepared, washed and drained greens in a large plastic bag. Take the dressing along in a separate container. Just before serving, pour the dressing into the bag and gently work it until the salad greens are coated. Serve from the bag or turn out into a large bowl.

The choice of salad oil is important. First in order of excellence is virgin-press olive oil, light in color and with a faint aroma. French and Italian groceries sell a very acceptable blend of olive, peanut and cotton seed oils which is more economical and has a greater degree of poly-unsaturated fats, page 508. You will also encounter an occasional gourmet who uses nothing but sesame oil or a cholesterol-conscious person who will eat only oil of safflower. An economical and effective substitute for straight safflower oil is a mixture of 20% safflower and 80% of another poly-unsaturated oil. If you find the taste of olive oil too strong, try combining it with one of the bland, more highly-poly-unsaturated salad oils. Your choice of a sour ingredient will depend on your own taste, but a good wine vinegar or lemon juice is the usual accompaniment to oil. Various kinds of herb vinegars are frequently chosen, but you may prefer to add these herbs separately later when you add the other seasonings. For a discussion of vinegars, see page 495. Remember the old admonition: "Be a spendthrift with oil, and a miser with vinegar." The classic proportions are 3 to 1.

Additional dressings, condiments and trimmings may be added after oil and vinegar to produce that infinite variety in flavor which is one of the chief charms of a tossed salad. Garlic is perhaps the most essential. There are two ways of giving to a salad a delicate touch of this pungent herb. Split a clove of garlic and rub the inside of the salad bowl with it, or rub a rather dry crust of bread on all sides with a split clove of garlic. This is called a "chapon." Place the bread in the bowl with the salad ingredients. Add the dressing and toss the salad lightly to distribute the flavor. Remove the chapon and serve the salad at once. If you wish to have a slightly stronger flavor of garlic, you may mash it at the bottom of your salad bowl with other seasonings before adding oil and vinegar. This seems to modify its heavy pungency. ♦ Never leave a whole clove of garlic in any food brought to the table. Withhold salt until all other ingredients have been incorporated. Salting your salad may be unnecessary. If, after a cautious taste-test, you decide that it will improve your mix, sprinkle it on very sparingly and give the salad a final thorough tossing.

♦ Additions to tossed salads may include sliced hard-cooked eggs, radishes, chopped olives, nut meats, pimiento or green pepper, sardines, anchovy, slivered cheese, julienned ham, chicken, tongue, grated carrots, cubed celery, onions—pickled, grated or as juice—and horseradish. Even a bit of cream or catsup may transfigure an otherwise lackluster mayonnaise, French or boiled dressing. ♦ In particular, the use of fresh herbs, page 530, may make a salad the high point of a meal.

♦ It is unwise to add cut-up tomatoes to a tossed salad, as their juices thin the dressing. Dress them separately and use them for garnishing the salad bowl. The French cut tomatoes in vertical slices, see page 90, since they bleed less this way. Another nice last-minute addition is small, hot Croutons, page 342, sprinkled over a tossed salad just before serving.

Well-seasoned wooden salad bowls have acquired a sort of sacred untouchability with some gourmets—which we think is misplaced. If the surface of a wooden salad bowl is protected by a varnish, as many are nowadays, the flavors of the oil, vinegar and herbs will not penetrate it, and you might just as well wash it in the usual way. An untreated wooden surface will certainly absorb some of the dressing used, but the residue left after wiping the bowl tends to become rancid, since we house our utensils in quarters warmer than they are abroad. This rancidity can noticeably affect the flavor of the salad. We prefer a bowl made of glass, of pottery with a glazed surface or of hard, dense, grease-proof plastic.

DRESSINGS FOR TOSSED SALADS

French Dressing, page 311
French Dressing with Cream Cheese
Roquefort or Bleu French Dressing,
page 312
Water Cress Dressing, page 312
Blender Cress Dressing, page 312
Chiffonade Dressing, page 312
Half and Half Dressing, page 316
Lorenzo Dressing, page 311
Thousand Island Dressing, page 316
Anchovy Dressing, page 311
Anchovy and Beet Dressing,
page 311
Low Calorie Dressings, page 313

CAESAR SALAD
4 Servings

For this famous recipe from California,
leave:
1 clove garlic, peeled and sliced
in:
½ cup olive oil: none other
for 24 hours. Sauté:
1 cup cubed French bread
in 2 tablespoons of the garlic oil, above.
Break up into 2-inch lengths:
2 heads romaine
Wash and dry well. Place the romaine in
a salad bowl. Sprinkle over it:
1½ teaspoons salt
¼ teaspoon dry mustard
A generous grating of black pepper
(5 fillets of anchovy, cut up small or
mashed to a paste, see page 539)
(A few drops of Worcestershire
sauce)
Add:
3 tablespoons wine vinegar
and the remaining 6 tablespoons garlic oil.
Cook gently in simmering water for 1 to
1½ minutes, or use raw:
1 egg
Drop the egg from the shell onto the ingredients in the bowl. Squeeze over the
egg:
The juice of 1 lemon
Add the croutons, and:
2 to 3 tablespoons Parmesan cheese
Toss the salad well. Serve it at once.

WESTERN SALAD
4 Servings

Prepare:
Caesar Salad, above
omitting the anchovies and adding:
2 tablespoons crumbled Blue cheese

WILTED GREENS
4 Servings

Sauté until crisp:
4 or 5 slices bacon

Remove from the pan, drain on absorbent
paper and cut or crumble in small pieces.
Heat:
2 tablespoons melted butter, bacon
drippings or oil
Add:
¼ cup mild vinegar
(1 teaspoon chopped fresh herbs,
page 530)
Add the bacon and also, at this time, if you
choose:
(1 teaspoon grated onion)
(1 teaspoon sugar)
Pour the dressing, while hot, over:
1 head lettuce, separated, shredded
cabbage, dandelion, young spinach
leaves or other greens
Serve it at once from a warm bowl onto
warm plates, garnished with:
Hard-cooked sliced eggs

CHICORY AND BEETROOT SALAD
4 Servings

This is a favorite winter salad in France.
Cut in ½-inch slices, into a salad bowl:
6 heads Belgian or French endive
Add:
2 cups sliced canned or cooked beets
Toss in:
French Dressing, page 311, or Water
Cress Dressing, page 312

ORIENTAL BEAN SPROUT SALAD
6 Servings

Place in a salad bowl:
4 cups crisp salad greens
1 cup drained bean sprouts
½ cup thinly sliced water chestnuts
¼ cup toasted, slivered almonds
Toss, just before serving, in:
¼ to ⅓ cup Oriental Dip, page 75
thinned with:
2 tablespoons cream

COLE SLAW
6 Servings

Red cabbage may be used. Very finely
shredded red and white cabbage may also
be combined with good effect. Pared and
diced pineapple or apple may be added.
Remove the outer leaves and the core
from:
A small head of cabbage
Shred or chop the remainder, cutting only
as much as is needed for immediate use.
Formerly, the chopped cabbage was
soaked in ice water for 1 hour. If soaked,
drain well, dry between towels and chill.
Immediately before serving, moisten with:
French Dressing, page 311, or
Boiled Dressing, page 316,
Sour Cream Dressing, page 317, or
equal parts mayonnaise and chili
sauce, or thick cream, sweet or
cultured sour
If you choose the cream, be sure to use a

little vinegar, salt and sugar. You may add
to any of these dressings:
   (Chopped anchovies)
   (Dill, caraway or celery seed)
   (Chopped parsley, chives or
   other herbs)

COLE SLAW DE LUXE
                                              8 Servings
Shortly before serving time, remove the
core of:
   A small head of cabbage
Cut into the thinnest shreds possible. Place
in a deep bowl. Add:
   1 to 2 tablespoons lemon juice
   (Fresh herbs: chopped parsley,
   chives, etc.)
Beat until stiff:
   ¾ cup whipping cream
Fold in:
   ½ teaspoon celery seed
   ½ teaspoon sugar
   ¾ teaspoon salt
   ¼ teaspoon freshly ground
   white pepper
   1 cup seedless green grapes
   ½ cup finely shredded blanched
   almonds
Pour it over the cabbage. Toss quickly until well coated. Serve at once with:
   Tomatoes or in an Aspic Ring,
   page 96

ROQUEFORT COLE SLAW
                                              4 Servings
This is based on a recipe from Herman
Smith. His splendid books, "Stina" and
"Kitchens Near and Far," should appeal to
all lovers of good eating and reading.
Shred finely:
   1½ cups red or green young cabbage
Peel and cut into long, narrow strips:
   1 cup apples
In order to keep them from discoloring,
sprinkle them with:
   Lemon juice
Toss salad lightly with:
   Roquefort Sour Cream Dressing
Serve at once, garnished with:
   Parsley

▤ COLE SLAW FOR BARBECUE
                                              6 Servings
The tangy dressing in this slaw goes well
with meat broiled or barbecued outdoors.
If you are cooking farther from home than
your own backyard or patio, try the plastic
bag method of "tossing" the slaw, described on page 79.
Combine:
   1 cup mayonnaise, page 313
   4 chopped scallions
   1 tablespoon tomato catsup
   2 teaspoons vinegar
   ⅛ teaspoon Worcestershire sauce
   ¼ teaspoon salt

   ⅛ teaspoon pepper
   ¼ teaspoon sugar
Add this mixture to:
   3 cups shredded cabbage
   3 cups salad greens
   1 thinly-sliced carrot
   ½ green pepper, cut in strips
Toss salad lightly and serve.

HOT SLAW WITH APPLE
                                              6 Servings
Place in a skillet:
   ½ lb. finely diced salt pork
Render it slowly, then remove the crisp,
browned pieces, drain them on absorbent
paper and reserve. Add to the rendered
fat in the skillet:
   3 tablespoons vinegar
   2 tablespoons water
   1 tablespoon sugar
   1 teaspoon caraway or celery seed
   1 teaspoon salt
Cook and stir these ingredients over quick
heat until they boil. ♦ Reduce the heat to
a simmer. Stir in:
   3 cups shredded cabbage
   1 large peeled, grated apple
Simmer the slaw for about one minute
longer and serve garnished with the tiny
browned cubes of salt pork. You may also
use the recipe for Wilted Greens, page 80,
using the crumbled bacon as a garnish
instead of hard-cooked eggs.

↿ BLENDER SLAW
                                              4 Servings
This can only be made satisfactorily in a
2-speed blender with a chopping action.
Quarter and core:
   1 small head of cabbage
Core, seed and remove membrane of:
   ½ green pepper
Peel:
   ½ medium onion
   1 carrot
Chop these vegetables coarsely into the
blender container, until it is half filled.
Add to within 1 inch of the top:
   Cold water
♦ Cover and blend for 2 seconds, no
longer, using the chopping speed. Empty
the vegetables into a sieve to drain and
repeat the process until all the vegetables
are shredded. Place them in a salad bowl
and sprinkle with:
   (1 teaspoon caraway seeds)
Toss lightly in:
   Mayonnaise, page 313, or Sour
   Cream Dressing, page 317
thinned with:
   2 tablespoons lemon juice

GINGHAM SALAD WITH
COTTAGE CHEESE
                                              4 Servings
Place in a mixing bowl and toss:

1½ cups coarsely chopped young
   spinach leaves
2 cups shredded red cabbage
⅓ teaspoon salt
¼ teaspoon celery seed
3 tablespoons chopped olives or chives
1 cup cottage cheese
Place these ingredients on:
   4 large lettuce leaves
Serve the salad with:
   Mayonnaise, page 313, Sour
   Cream Dressing, page 317, or Green
   Mayonnaise, page 315

ABOUT TOSSED COMBINATION SALADS

Serve combination salads as a luncheon
main dish, accompanied by Toasted Cheese
Rolls, page 59 or savory sandwiches,
page 244. Practically every restaurant
serves some kind of combination salad,
often named after its own inventive chef,
but each has the chief distinction of containing some form of protein such as meat,
chicken or cheese, in addition to the
greens and vegetables. Here are variations:

COMBINATION SALADS
I. Rub a salad bowl with:
   Garlic
Place in it:
   Lettuce or spinach leaves
   Cut-up anchovies
   Chopped, pitted, ripe olives
   Sliced radishes
   Sliced hard-cooked eggs
   Shredded Swiss cheese
Toss the salad with:
   French Dressing, page 311
Garnish it with:
   Peeled and quartered tomatoes

II. Combine:
   Lettuce
   Endive
   Romaine
   Water cress
Cut into narrow strips:
   Salami
   Sautéed bacon
   Anchovies
   Swiss cheese
Dice and add:
   Raw cauliflower
   Cooked string beans
Marinate these ingredients for ½ hour in:
   French Dressing, page 311
Serve the salad half wilted.

GARNISHES FOR SALADS
To garnish salads, use the following:
   Tomato slices, dipped in finely
   chopped parsley or chives
   Parsley or water cress in bunches or
   chopped
   Lettuce leaves, cress, endive,
   romaine, etc.
   Heads of lettuce, cut into slices
   or wedges
   Lemon slices with pinked edges,
   dipped in chopped parsley
   Shredded olives or sliced stuffed
   olives
   Cooked beets, cut into shapes
   or sticks
   Carrots, cut into shapes
   Pearl onions
   Pickles
   Capers
   Pomegranate seeds
   Fennel slices
   Cucumbers or Cucumber Slices,
   page 86
   Green and red peppers, shredded
   Pepper slices
   Mayonnaise or soft cream cheese,
   forced through a tube
   Aspic jellies in small molds or
   chopped aspic
   Eggs—hard-cooked, sliced, riced or
   stuffed
   Dwarf tomatoes, stuffed with cottage
   cheese
   Cherry tomatoes
   Fresh herbs, sprigs or chopped
   Mint leaves
   Nasturtium leaves
   Nut meats
   Chopped truffles
   Shaped truffles

ABOUT CUTTING VEGETABLE GARNISHES AND CASES

Use vegetables as cases for piquant
sauces, as sketched below. A pepper hollowed out, which can be lidded with its
handsomely fat stem portion; an onion
sliced to produce rings which will hold
vinaigretted asparagus upright on an hors
d'oeuvre tray; onion cups made from raw
or slightly blanched onions; a cucumber
slashed and hollowed to hold olives or
gherkins and a simpler scored cucumber
cup. Citrus rind rings or green or red pep-

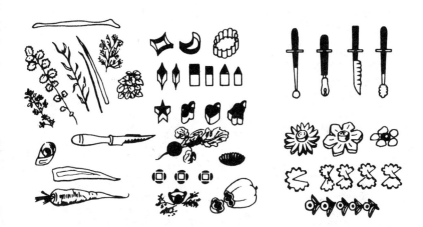

per rings can be used in the same manner to hold food upright.

Try your hand at carving vegetables and see what fun you can have and how attractive your trays can look with a little effort. Don't force effects. Use them sparingly. See illustration for some very simple suggestions. Begin on the left with carrots cut in scrolls, etc., radishes made into roses and pickles into fans. Make geometric accents with hors d'oeuvre cutters and scoops, shown at center and at the top on the right. Shape flowers and borders of olives, as shown on the lower right, also twists of cucumber. Make an ingenuous turnip or egg white and carrot daisy, gay for spinach dishes, or small daffodil blooms of carrots shown above. These can have chive stems and leaves if you like. Try for some asymmetric drawing-like effects, such as shrimps suggested by thin lines of red pepper. One of the loveliest decorations we ever saw were 2 small lobsters, cut in a modern feeling from red peppers and placed casually on the side and the top of a cream-covered mousse. Seaweed was indicated by fennel leaves and partially crowned the top. See also page 116, for varied lemon garnishes.

ABOUT VEGETABLES FOR SALAD

A welcome summertime alternative to the crisp green salads or slaws is a vegetable salad, attractively arranged and dressed. Try cooked and chilled vegetables, served with a vinaigrette or chiffonade dressing or use Vegetables à la Grecque, page 255, including podded peas, as occasion pieces, as well as in a whole salad. Your vegetables should have some "bite" to them and we prefer fresh, cooked or canned vegetables to frozen ones, which lose their crispness and tend to have tough skins when cooked.

COOKED VEGETABLE SALAD PLATTER

Cook separately a variety of:
> **Vegetables—cauliflower, carrots, snap beans, Lima beans, beets, soy beans, bean sprouts, etc.**

Marinate them in separate bowls for several hours with:
> **French Dressing, page 311**

Use about ¼ cup of dressing to 2 cups of vegetables. Drain well. Arrange in some attractive way on a large platter. For example, place the cauliflower or the beets in the center and alternate the other vegetables according to color in mounds, about them, on:
> **Lettuce leaves**

Garnish the platter with:
> **Curled celery, radishes, sliced or riced hard-cooked eggs or deviled eggs**

or, place in the center of a platter, chilled:
> **Snap Bean Salad, page 85**

Surround it with overlapping slices of skinned:
> **Tomatoes or cherry tomatoes filled with cottage cheese**

Garnish the platter with:
> **Shredded lettuce or watercress**
> **Deviled eggs or sardines**

RUSSIAN SALAD

6 Servings

This recipe is quickly made with canned vegetables, although it is not quite as good. If you wish, you may marinate your vegetables for 1 hour in French dressing, then drain and toss in the mayonnaise. Prepare and dice in ¼-inch cubes:
> **1 cup cooked carrots**
> **1 cup cooked waxy potatoes**
> **1 cup cooked beets**
> **½ cup cooked green beans**

Add:
> **½ cup cooked peas**

Toss the vegetables in:
Mayonnaise, page 313
with:
(**A few capers**)
(**Julienned strips of ham**)
Serve in mounds, on lettuce leaves.

ITALIAN SALAD
6 Servings

Prepare and dice:
1 cup cooked beets
1 cup cooked carrots
These proportions may be varied. Chill the
vegetables. Combine them with:
1 cup chopped celery
½ cup cooked or canned green peas
(**½ cup pared, seeded and diced**
cucumbers)
Moisten the vegetables with:
Boiled Salad Dressing, page 316,
mayonnaise thinned with cream, or
Sour Cream Dressing, page 317
Serve the salad in a bowl garnished with:
Lettuce
For more elegant occasions, mold the salad
into a fish shape and cover with thin, overlapping slices of cucumber for scales.

STUFFED ARTICHOKE SALADS
I. With Sea Food
Cook:
Artichokes, page 256
Chill, and remove the inedible choke. Mar-
inate:
Shrimp, crab meat, oysters or
bay scallops
with:
French Dressing, page 311
Fill the artichokes with the sea food and
serve with:
Mayonnaise
on a bed of:
Shredded lettuce

II. With Caviar
Fill the artichokes with:
Cultured sour cream
Caviar

III. With Meat
Fill with:
Ham, veal, tuna or chicken salad or
liver pâté, page 433

ARTICHOKE HEARTS SALAD
Cooked or canned, these are delicious in
salad. They may be cut up and added to
green salads or aspics or they may be used
as a basis on which to build up an attractive individual salad plate.

ASPARAGUS SALAD
Cook:
Asparagus, page 257
Drain and chill. Cover the tips with:
Mayonnaise or Boiled Salad
Dressing, page 316

Thin the dressing with a little:
Cultured sour cream
Add:
(**Chopped tarragon**)
If that is not available, add:
(**Chopped parsley or chives**)
or serve asparagus salad with:
Vinaigrette Dressing, page 311

ASPARAGUS TIP SALAD
Drain the contents of a can of:
Asparagus tips
Place around 4 or 5 tips a ring of:
Red or green pepper or pimiento
Place the asparagus in the ring on:
Shredded lettuce
Serve the salad with:
French Dressing, page 311, or
mayonnaise

ASPARAGUS AND EGG SALAD
6 Servings

Chill in a dish:
2 cups cooked, well-drained asparagus,
cut in pieces
3 sliced hard-cooked eggs
6 sliced stuffed olives
Wash, drain and place in refrigerator to
crisp:
1 bunch water cress
1 small head lettuce
When ready to serve, combine:
½ cup cultured sour cream
2 teaspoons grated onion or
chopped chives
2 tablespoons lemon juice,
caper liquor or vinegar
1 teaspoon salt
¼ teaspoon paprika
$\frac{1}{16}$ teaspoon curry powder
(**2 tablespoons capers**)
Line a serving dish with the larger lettuce
leaves. Break the rest into pieces. Add
these to the asparagus mixture. Chop and
add the water cress. Pour the dressing over
these ingredients. Toss them lightly. Place
them in the serving dish. Serve the salad
at once, garnished with:
Parsley

DRIED BEAN SALAD
4 to 6 Servings

Lentils, kidney, navy, Lima or miniature
green soy beans, cooked or canned, are the
basis of these "stick-to-the-ribs" salads.
Drain well and chill:
2½ cups canned or cooked kidney
or Lima beans
Combine with:
¼ cup French Dressing, page 311
(**A pinch of curry powder or ¼ cup**
chopped gherkins or pearl onions)
Serve on:
Lettuce leaves
Sprinkle with:
Chopped parsley
Chopped chives or grated onion

SNAP BEAN SALAD

4 to 6 Servings

This is a fine picnic salad.
Prepare:
  3 cups cooked Snap Beans, page 258
Drain well and toss, while warm, in:
  French Dressing, page 311, or
  Lorenzo Dressing, page 311
Chill thoroughly, then add:
  Chopped or grated onion, chives or
  pearl onions
Serve on:
  Lettuce leaves

HOT SNAP BEAN SALAD

6 Servings

Prepare:
  3 cups cooked Snap Beans, page 258
Drain them. Combine them with the dressing for:
  Wilted Greens, page 80
Season as desired or with:
  (Summer savory)
Serve from a warm bowl onto warm plates.

COLD BEET CUPS

Pressure cook:
  Large Beets, page 264
and chill. Fill the beets with:
  Marinated Cucumbers with
  cultured sour cream or
  Russian Salad, page 83
  Cole Slaw, page 80 or
  Deviled Eggs, page 203
Garnish with:
  Curly Endive

PICKLED BEET SALAD

Drain:
  2½ cups cooked or canned beets
Reserve the juice. Slice the beets. Place them in a fruit jar. Boil:
  ½ cup sharp vinegar
  ½ cup beet juice
Add and heat to boiling:
  2 tablespoons sugar
  2 cloves
  ½ teaspoon salt
  3 peppercorns
  ¼ bay leaf
  (1 sliced green pepper)
  (1 small sliced onion)
  (½ teaspoon horseradish)
Pour these ingredients over the beets. Cover the jar. Serve the beets very cold.

CARROT SALAD WITH RAISINS AND NUTS

4 Servings

Scrape well:
  4 large carrots
Place them on ice for 1 hour. Grate them coarsely into a bowl. Add and mix lightly:
  ½ cup seedless raisins
  ½ cup coarsely chopped pecans
  or peanuts
  ¾ teaspoon salt
  Freshly ground black pepper

  2 teaspoons grated lemon peel
  1 tablespoon lemon juice
Place the salad in a bowl. Pour over it:
  1 cup or more cultured sour cream
Toss the salad if you wish.

CELERY CABBAGE SALAD

Use celery cabbage in any recipe for hot or cold slaw, page 80, or in the colorful recipe below:
Wash well, then crisp:
  1 stalk celery cabbage
Cut it crosswise into shreds. Serve it very cold with:
  French Dressing, page 311
This cabbage combines superbly with:
  Water cress
Use any convenient proportion. Garnish the salad with:
  Pickled Beets, opposite

COOKED CELERY OR ENDIVE SALAD

I. Prepare:
  Braised Celery or Endive, page 271
and serve cold on:
  Lettuce leaves

II. Simmer until tender:
  Trimmed, halved dwarf celery or
  endive heads
in a quantity of:
  Veal or chicken stock
Drain. Reserve the juices for soup or sauces. Marinate the vegetable in:
  French Dressing, page 311
to which you may add:
  1 teaspoon anchovy paste
Chill and serve on:
  Lettuce

CELERIAC OR CELERY ROOT SALAD

Prepare:
  Celeriac, page 272
Chill it. Toss it in:
  Mayonnaise, well seasoned
  with mustard
or, best of all, in:
  French Dressing, page 311
to which you may add:
  Minced shallots or chives
Serve it on:
  Endive or water cress

CELERIAC OR CELERI-RAVE REMOULADE

5 to 6 Servings

One of the more classic ways is as follows:
Blanch for 1 to 2 minutes and chill:
  ½ lb. celeriac
Steep it in:
  Cold Mustard Sauce I, page 313
for 2 to 3 hours. Serve chilled.

CUCUMBER SALAD

Be sure to select firm, hard, green cucumbers. The slightly flabby or yellowing ones are old and often pithy and the skin seems to toughen. Some people who are allergic to cucumber find they can eat it if the skin is left on. It should have a slight sheen, but if highly polished it is probably waxed and in such case the skin should not be used. If you wish to make the cucumbers more decorative, leave unpared and score with a fork, as sketched, before slicing.

Chill, pare and slice:
> **Cucumbers**

Combine them with:
> **French Dressing, page 311, or Sour Cream Dressing, page 317**

to which you may add:
> **Finely minced parsley**

Serve at once.

WILTED CUCUMBERS

Although nutrients are undoubtedly lost in soaking, this process gives cucumbers a quality that is cherished by many. It rids the cucumber of a slightly acrid taste and produces an appetizing texture. So, on occasion, try soaking them.

I.
Peel and slice very thin:
> **Cucumbers**

A potato peeler does a fine job. Dispose them in layers in a bowl. Salt each layer and place a weight over the cucumbers. A plate with a heavy weight over all will do. Cover and refrigerate 3 to 6 hours. Drain and toss in:
> **Cultured sour cream**

Garnish with:
> **Chopped dill, basil or tarragon**

Serve chilled at once.

II.   3 Servings
Slice, leaving the skins on, if very young and unwaxed:
> **1½ to 2 cups cucumbers**

Salt and weight as above. Refrigerate 2

hours. Rinse in cold water, drain and dry. Place the cucumbers in a bowl and toss in:
> **¼ cup vinegar**

also:
> **1 tablespoon sugar**

dissolved in:
> **1 tablespoon water**
> **Correct the seasoning**

Chill 1 to 2 hours and serve garnished with:
> **Chopped dill or burnet or very thinly sliced Bermuda onion rings**

COLD STUFFED CUCUMBERS
Good for a luncheon plate or as hors d'oeuvre.
Chill:
> **Small, shapely cucumbers**

Pare them. Cut them in halves lengthwise or cut off a slice lengthwise and remove the seeds. The cucumber boats may be wrapped in waxed paper and chilled. Fill them with:
> **Chicken Salad, page 91, or a Fish Salad, page 90-91**

or anything suitable that you can think of, such as:
> **Celery, nut meats, green grapes, olives, etc.**

These ingredients may be moistened with or served with:
> **Mayonnaise, Beet and Anchovy Dressing, page 311, Chutney Dressing, page 313, etc.**

Serve the cucumbers on:
> **Shredded lettuce or water cress**

LOTUS ROOT SALAD
Peel and slice thin, crosswise:
> **1 lb. lotus root**

Soak for 10 minutes in:
> **Acidulated Water, page 494**

Drain and dip slices in:
> **Fresh, boiling, acidulated water**

Plunge quickly in:
> **Cold water**

and drain again. Heat and mix:
> **2 tablespoons sesame oil**
> **1 to 2 drops hot pepper sauce**
> **1½ tablespoons sugar**
> **2½ tablespoons soy sauce**

Pour this sauce over the drained lotus root and allow to stand about 1 hour. Serve chilled in the sauce.

OKRA SALAD
A fine hot-weather salad. The marinated pods are slightly reminiscent of oysters.
Prepare:
> **Stewed Okra, page 284**

Place the drained okra in a dish and cover with:
> **Well-seasoned French Dressing, page 311, Horseradish Dressing, page 312, Mayonnaise, page 313**

Chill. Serve very cold on:
> **Lettuce**

HEARTS OF PALM SALAD
I. Cut into lengthwise strips:
Chilled canned hearts of palm
Serve on:
Romaine
garnished with:
Stuffed olive slices
Green pepper rings
Sprinkle with:
Chopped parsley
Paprika
Serve with:
French Dressing, page 311, or
Mayonnaise, page 313

II. If you live in Florida, you can have
fresh:
Hearts of palm
But be sure to eat them as soon as peeled,
for they discolor quickly. Cut into dice,
sprinkle with:
Lemon juice
and serve with:
French Dressing, page 311, made
with lime juice
Another way to serve is to treat the hearts
as for Cole Slaw, page 80.

PEPPER SLICES WITH FILLINGS
8 to 10 Slices
These slices are highly decorative. They
make a pretty salad and are good as
canapés, on toast or crackers.
Wash:
2 medium-size red or green peppers
Cut a piece from the stem end and remove
the seeds and membranes. Stuff the peppers with a Cream Cheese Spread, page
58, or Ham Salad, page 92, and chill for
12 hours. Slice them with a sharp hot knife
and replace them on ice. Serve the slices
on:
Lettuce
with:
French Dressing, page 311, or
Mayonnaise, page 313

★ FILLED PIMIENTOS OR CHRISTMAS SALAD
6 Servings
A decorative and delicious salad, but do
not expect the peppers to look like fresh
ones. They are simply a casing for the soft
filling.
Drain:
6 large canned pimientos
Dice:
2½ cups drained canned pineapple
Add to it:
1½ cups diced celery
1 tablespoon tiny pickled pearl onions
Whip until stiff:
¼ cup whipping cream
Combine it with:
1 cup mayonnaise

Fold into these ingredients the pineapple,
celery and onions. Stuff the pimientos with
the mixture. Chill. Bed on a nest of:
Shredded lettuce
Roll into small balls:
6 oz. soft cream cheese
Roll the balls in:
Chopped parsley
Place them around the pimientos or, if they
are served individually, beside them.

POTATO SALAD
Potato salad is best made from potatoes
cooked in their jackets and peeled and
marinated while still warm. The small red
waxy potatoes hold their shape and don't
crumble when sliced or diced; furthermore,
they do not absorb an excessive amount of
dressing or become mushy. Do not try to
make potato salad with yesterday's cold
boiled potatoes—it is not good. For hot
weather picnics, use an eggless dressing to
avoid dangerous spoilage.

I.   **4 Servings**
Prepare as above:
2 cups sliced, boiled, waxy potatoes
Marinate them in:
½ cup heated French Dressing,
page 311
Mix in gently with a wooden spoon, just
before serving:
1 tablespoon chopped parsley
1 tablespoon chopped chives or
1 tablespoon finely grated onion
(1 cup sliced cooked scallops)
Serve tepid.

II.   **4 Servings**
Marinate the potatoes well with:
½ cup French Dressing, page 311,
soup stock or canned bouillon
Chop or slice and add discreetly a mixture
of any of the following:
Hard-cooked eggs, onions, olives,
pickles, celery with leaves, cucum-
bers, capers
1 tablespoon salt
Paprika
A few grains cayenne
(2 teaspoons horseradish)
After one hour or more of refrigeration,
add:
Mayonnaise, Boiled Salad Dressing,
page 316, or cultured sour cream
Refrigerate about 1 hour longer. Shortly
before serving, you may toss in:
(Coarsely chopped water cress)

POTATO AND HERRING SALAD
6 Servings
Place in a large bowl and toss gently:
2 cups diced boiled potatoes
1¼ cups diced marinated or pickled
herring fillets
¾ cup chopped celery with leaves

1 tablespoon minced parsley
1 tablespoon minced chives
6 tablespoons cultured sour cream
1½ tablespoons lemon juice
¾ teaspoon paprika
Serve the salad chilled in:
    Lettuce cups

GERMAN HOT POTATO SALAD
6 Servings

Cook in their jackets, in a covered sauce-pan, until tender:
    6 medium-size waxy potatoes
Peel and slice while they are hot. Heat in a skillet:
    4 strips minced bacon or 2 tablespoons
      bacon drippings
Add and sauté until brown:
    ¼ cup chopped onion
    ¼ cup chopped celery
    1 chopped dill pickle
Heat to the boiling point:
    ¼ cup water or stock
    ½ cup vinegar
    ½ teaspoon sugar
    ½ teaspoon salt
    ⅛ teaspoon paprika
    (¼ teaspoon dry mustard)
Pour these ingredients into the skillet. Combine them with the potatoes and serve at once with chopped parsley or chives.

POTATO SALAD NIÇOISE
12 Servings

Cook:
    3 cups new potatoes
in water to which a clove of garlic has been added. Peel and slice and, while still warm, sprinkle with:
    ½ cup heated white wine or ¼ cup
      wine vinegar and ¼ cup stock
Let stand at 70° for 1 hour. Have ready:
    3 cups chilled cooked green beans
    6 peeled quartered tomatoes
which have been marinating in:
    French Dressing, page 311
To serve, mound the potatoes in a volcano in the center of a platter garnished with:
    Salad greens
Garnish the potatoes with:
    Capers
    Small pitted black olives
    1 dozen anchovy fillets
Alternate the tomato quarters and small heaps of the green beans around the pota-toes. See the following Salad Niçoise for a version of this salad without potatoes, from the south of France.

SALAD NIÇOISE

Rub your salad bowl with garlic then place in it:
    2 peeled and quartered tomatoes
    1 peeled and finely cut cucumber
    6 coarsely cut fillets of anchovy
    12 coarsely chopped pitted black olives
    1 cup Bibb lettuce

    1 cup romaine
Toss in:
    French Dressing, page 311

RICE SALAD
4 Servings

Prepare:
    2 cups steamed rice
The grains must be dry and fluffy for the success of this salad. While the rice is warm, mix in:
    ¼ cup French Dressing, page 311
      preferably made with tarragon
      vinegar and olive oil
    A pinch of grated nutmeg
    ¼ cup coarsely chopped green pepper
    ¼ cup finely chopped celery
    10 black olives, pitted and halved
Garnish with:
    Peeled, quartered tomatoes
in a bowl lined with:
    Leaf lettuce
This goes well with cold chicken or cold smoked tongue. Serve the salad tepid.

ABOUT TOMATOES FOR SALAD

Good flavor and texture are particularly important in tomatoes for salad. If you can get vine-ripened tomatoes, they are in-finitely superior to those picked green and allowed to ripen on their way to the super-market. The latter often become mealy and almost tasteless in spite of their de-ceptively ruddy complexion. Use them for Stuffed Tomatoes, page 89, where they can be spiced up with a peppy filling.
Always cut out the stem-end core. It is tough and often tastes bitter. If you are going to stuff the tomato in one of the ways suggested later in this chapter, turn it upside down so that the cored end rests on the plate. If you wish, you can fake a stem and leaves by making a tiny hole in the lid and inserting a sprig of mint, pars-ley or some other fresh herb. Keep your eyes open at market for the topepo, a hybrid between a tomato and red pepper which makes a good substitute for tomato.

FRENCH TOMATO SALAD
Cut into very thin vertical slices, page 90:
    6 medium unpeeled tomatoes
Place them so that they overlap around a cold platter or across it. Pour over them a dressing made of:
    French dressing
    ¼ cup minced parsley
    2 minced shallots or green onions

CANNED TOMATO SALAD
Chill the contents of a can of:
    Whole tomatoes
or use the firm part of any canned toma-toes. Place them in individual dishes. Sprinkle them with:
    Celery salt
    Salt
    Lemon juice
    Brown sugar

or anything you like. The main thing is to serve them very cold.

ABOUT COLD STUFFED TOMATOES

A bit of tomato skin was once as much out of place at a dinner table as a bowie knife. The discovery that tomato skins contain highly valued vitamins makes them "salon-fähig"—so whether to serve tomatoes skinned or unskinned rests with the hostess' sense of delicacy or her desire for health.

♦ To skin tomatoes, first wash them and then use one of the following methods: stroke the skin with the dull edge of a knife blade until the skin wrinkles and can be lifted off; or, dip the tomato in boiling water for 1 minute and then immediately in cold water, drain and skin; or, pierce the tomato with a fork and rotate it over a burner until the skin is tight and shiny, plunge into cold water and peel.

♦ To prepare tomato cases, first skin the tomatoes as described above, then hollow them. Invert the tomatoes to drain for 20 minutes. Chill them and fill the hollows with one of the fillings suggested below.

Tomatoes can be cut and filled in a variety of attractive ways and they provide a gay splash of color for buffet salads. If you do not wish to serve large portions, cut the tomatoes in halves or in slices. Place on each slice a ring of green pepper ½ inch or more thick. Fill the ring.

You can also cut them crosswise in zig-zag fashion, fill them sandwich style and top with a mint leaf. Or slash into 6 sections, nearly to the base, and fill the center. Garnish with a stuffed olive.

Slice horizontally into quarters and fill as a club sandwich. Garnish with a slice of black olive or pimiento star or cover with a pepper lid as sketched.

FILLINGS
I. Pineapple and Nut Meats
Combine equal parts of:
> Chopped celery
> Fresh shredded pineapple
> A few walnut meats
> Mayonnaise

II. Eggs and Anchovies
Combine:
> Chopped hard-cooked eggs
> Chopped anchovies or anchovy paste
> Onion juice or grated onion
> Chopped parsley or other herb
> Mayonnaise or thick cultured sour cream
> Paprika and salt

III. Eggs and Ham
Combine:
> 2 chopped hard-cooked eggs
> 1 cup ground or minced ham
> ½ cup chopped celery
> 12 sliced olives
> Fresh or dried savory
> 2 chopped sweet pickles
> Sour Cream Dressing, page 317 or mayonnaise

IV. Deviled Eggs
Place in each tomato hollow:
> ½ Deviled Egg, page 203
Serve on:
> Lettuce
with:
> Anchovy Dressing, page 311

V. Aspic
For about 6 tomato cases prepare:
> 1½ cups aspic
This may be an Aspic Salad, page 96, to which chopped meat or fish and vegetables, etc., may be added. When the aspic is about to set, fill the tomato cases. Chill until firm. Garnish with:
> Olives, parsley, etc.
and serve with:
> Mayonnaise

VI. Some other good fillings are:
> Wilted Cucumbers I, page 86
> Crab Meat Salad, page 90, or
> A Fish Salad, pages 90-91
> Chicken Salad, page 91
> Guacamole I, page 60
> Cole Slaw, page 80
> Avocado chunks
> Shrimp with mayonnaise
> Cottage cheese or soft cream cheese mixed with mayonnaise and chopped chives

TOMATO AND ONION OR CUCUMBER SALAD
Skin and chill:
> Medium-size tomatoes
Cut 5 or 6 crosswise gashes in the tomatoes, equal distances apart. Place in each gash, as shown on next page, a thin slice of:
> Bermuda onion or cucumber
Serve the tomatoes on:
> Lettuce or water cress

with:
> French Dressing, page 311, or
> Sour Cream Dressing, page 317, etc.

MOLDED EGG AND CAVIAR SALAD
Also good as hors d'oeuvre. Crush with a fork:
> 8 hard-cooked eggs

Stir into them:
> 3 tablespoons soft butter
> ⅛ teaspoon dry mustard
> 2 oz. caviar
> 3 tablespoons lemon juice
> 1 tablespoon Worcestershire sauce

Pack these ingredients into a tall, oiled glass. Chill. Unmold and cut into ½- to 1-inch slices. Serve on:
> Thick tomato slices

or use to decorate a salad platter. Cover with a dab of:
> Mayonnaise
> (A rolled anchovy)

STUFFED LETTUCE ROLLS
Beat until smooth:
> Cottage cheese

Add all or some of the following:
> A sprinkling of chives or
> grated onion
> Chopped boiled ham
> Seedless raisins
> Chopped celery
> Chopped green peppers
> Chopped nut meats

Spread a thick layer of the cheese mixture on:
> Large lettuce leaves

Roll the leaves and secure with toothpicks. Chill. Allow 2 or 3 rolls to a person and serve with:
> Mayonnaise or French Dressing,
> page 313

You may also use a fancy cut vegetable garnish, as sketched on page 83.

MACARONI OR SPAGHETTI SALAD OR CALICO SALAD
5 Servings
Exact proportions are unimportant.
Prepare:
> 1 cup cooked elbow macaroni,
> page 186

Drain it. Beat well:
> 1½ tablespoons lemon juice or
> 2 tablespoons vinegar
> 1 tablespoon salad oil

Toss this into the cooked macaroni. There should be about 2 cups of it. Chill the salad for several hours. Toss into it:
> 1 teaspoon grated onion or
> 2 tablespoons chopped chives
> 1 cup diced celery with leaves
> 1 cup minced parsley
> ½ cup chopped stuffed olives
> ¾ teaspoon salt
> Freshly ground black pepper
> 3 tablespoons cultured sour cream
> 2 tablespoons chopped pimiento

Serve on:
> Lettuce

This makes an attractive filling for a tomato aspic ring.

CRAB MEAT OR LOBSTER SALAD
Combine:
> 1 cup crab meat or lobster
> 1 cup pared shredded apples
> ½ cup mayonnaise

CRAB LOUIS
4 Servings
This salad is a product of the West Coast, where the magnificent Pacific crab is frequently served in this way. Arrange around the inside of a bowl:
> Lettuce leaves

Place on the bottom:
> ¾ cup shredded lettuce leaves

Heap on these:
> 2 cups crab meat

Pour over the crab:
> 1 cup Pink Mayonnaise or Sauce
> Louis, page 316

Sometimes eggs are added to the salad. Slice:
> (2 hard-cooked eggs)

Place them on top of the crab. Sprinkle over them:
> Chopped chives

★ HERRING SALAD
About 20 Servings
Herring is a traditional dish for our family at Christmastime. Its rich color, thanks to the red beets, and elaborate garnishing make this dish an imposing sight.
Soak in water for 12 hours:
> 6 milter herring

Skin them, remove the milt and the bones. Rub the milt through a colander with:
> 1 cup dry red wine or vinegar

Cut into ¼-inch cubes the herring and:
> 1½ cups cold cooked veal
> 2 hard-cooked eggs
> 1½ cups Pickled Beet Salad, page 85
> ½ cup onions
> ½ cup pickles
> 2 stalks celery
> ½ cup cold boiled potatoes

Prepare and add:
> 3 cups diced apples

Blanch, shred and add:

> 1 cup almonds

Combine the milt mixture with:

> 1 cup sugar
> 2 tablespoons horseradish
> 2 tablespoons chopped parsley

Pour this over the other ingredients. Mix
well. Shape the salad into a mound or
place it in a bowl. Garnish it with:

> Riced hard-cooked eggs
> Pickles and olives
> Sardelles and parsley

LOBSTER SALAD

4 Servings

Dice:

> 1 cup canned or cooked lobster meat

Add:

> (Grated onion)

Marinate with:

> ¼ cup French dressing

Chill for 1 hour. Combine with:

> 1 cup chopped celery

Place on:

> Lettuce

Cover or combine with:

> ½ cup mayonnaise

to which you may add:

> (2 tablespoons dry sherry)

Garnish with:

> Lobster claws
> Olives and radishes
> Hard-cooked eggs
> Capers and pickles

or prepare:

> Tomato Aspic, page 100

Place it in a ring or in individual molds.
Invert the aspic on:

> Lettuce

Fill the ring or surround the molds with
lobster salad.

SHRIMP OR LOBSTER MOLD

4 Servings

This makes a lovely center for an hors
d'oeuvre tray. Grind together:

> 1 lb. cooked shrimp or lobster
> 1 tablespoon capers
> ⅛ of a small onion

Add and mix well:

> ⅓ cup softened butter
> 3 tablespoons heavy cream
> 2 tablespoons Pernod
> A dash of hot pepper sauce
> 1 teaspoon salt
> 1 teaspoon fresh tarragon

Pack into a mold. Refrigerate for 3 to 4
hours before serving. For a special occasion, mold the mixture flat in either individual molds or one large mold. Cover
with a thin icing of:

> Whipped cream

Cut large crescents from pieces of:

> Red peppers

to suggest the tails, claws and feelers of
lobster or shrimp. Apply them in these
patterns. For an added touch of realism,
garnish with seaweed made of:

> Wisps of finocchio leaf

and a few:

> Seedless green grapes

TUNA FISH, SHRIMP OR
SHAD ROE SALAD

4 Servings

Have ready:

> 1 cup canned fish

Flake it with a fork. Add:

> ½ to 1 cup diced celery or cucumber

Make a French dressing using:

> 2 tablespoons olive oil
> 2 tablespoons lemon juice

or use ¼ cup mayonnaise. Add:

> (1 tablespoon chopped chives)
> (1 tablespoon chopped parsley)

Serve very cold on:

> Lettuce

CHICKEN SALAD

8 Servings

A traditional "party" dish, chicken salad
should taste of chicken, the other ingredients being present only to add variety of
texture and to enhance the flavor. So always keep the proportions of at least twice
as much chicken as the total of your other
ingredients. Since it is usually combined
with mayonnaise, be careful to ♦ refrigerate it, particularly if you make it in advance.

Dice:

> 2 cups cooked chicken
> 1 cup celery
> (¼ cup salted almonds)

Chill these ingredients. They may be marinated lightly with:

> French Dressing, page 311

When ready to serve, combine with:

> 1 cup mayonnaise

Season the salad, as required, with:

> Salt and paprika

Serve it on:

> Lettuce

Garnish with:

> Pimiento and olives
> (Sliced hard-cooked eggs
> and capers)

Quantity note: Generous main dish servings for 50 will require:

> 1 gal. cooked cubed chicken

To obtain this amount, you need about 17
lbs. ready to cook chicken. If you substitute turkey, you need only a 12-pounder.

CHICKEN SALAD VARIATIONS

Follow the preceding recipe. You may
substitute cooked duck, turkey or veal for
the chicken, remembering to keep the proportions of 2 of meat or fowl to 1 of the
other ingredients.

> Chicken, celery and
> hard-cooked eggs

Chicken, bean sprouts
and water chestnuts
Chicken, cucumber and English
walnut meats
Chicken, Boiled Chestnuts, page 272,
and celery—pimiento may be added
Chicken and parboiled oysters
Chicken and fruit such as seedless
grapes, fresh chopped pineapple
and pomegranate seeds
You may add to the mayonnaise:
(Strained chili sauce)
See also Chicken Mousse, page 97.

HOT CHICKEN SALAD

4 Servings

Preheat oven to 350°.
Combine:
   2 cups cubed cooked chicken
   1 cup finely diced celery
   ½ teaspoon salt
   ½ teaspoon monosodium glutamate
   ¼ teaspoon tarragon
   ½ cup toasted almonds
   1 tablespoon chopped chives
   2 tablespoons lemon juice
   ½ cup mayonnaise
   ½ cup Béchamel Sauce, page 322
Bake in very shallow individual bakers for
10 to 15 minutes or until heated. Garnish
with:
   Parsley or small sprigs of
   lemon thyme

HAM, CORNED BEEF, VEAL
OR BEEF SALAD

Let this be a matter of inspiration.
Dice:
   Cooked ham, corned beef,
   veal or beef
   Hard-cooked eggs
   Celery with leaves
   (Green peppers or pickles)
Combine these ingredients with:
   Tart mayonnaise or
   French Dressing, page 311
Garnish with:
   Chopped chives, parsley or
   other herbs
Surround the meat with tomatoes, sliced
or whole.

ABOUT FRUIT SALADS

The purist frowns on fruit salads except for
dessert and we ourselves have shuddered
at the omnipresent peach half with cottage
cheese and a blob of mayonnaise. Nevertheless, such a wide variety of fruit is
available to us throughout the year, including many tropical ones, that we often
delight in their color and taste in salad
before or with the main entrée. Fruit
salads offer great scope for the artist. A
large arranged platter can substitute for
flowers as a centerpiece on a buffet. With

protein, such as chicken, meat, cheese, or
fish, fruits make wonderful summer luncheon dishes. As a general rule, keep the
dressings for pre-dessert fruit salads fairly
tart, so that the appetite is not dulled. As
a change from the usual base of salad
greens, serve fruit salads, where suitable,
in baskets, cups or cases made from fruit,
as described on page 118. In preparing
fruit salad in advance, ♦ store bananas,
peaches and other easily discolored fruit
covered with the acid dressing you plan on
using, to avoid discoloration.

APPLE, PEAR, OR PEACH SALAD

Try this with an omelet, French bread and
coffee.
Pare, core, slice and sprinkle with lemon
juice to keep them from discoloring:
   Well-flavored apples, pears,
   or peaches
Serve them on:
   Lettuce
with:
   Lemon and Sherry Dressing,
   page 318, or French Dressing
Garnish the salad with:
   Cream cheese and nut balls or
   Roquefort cheese balls
The apples may be cut into rings and the
cheese balls placed in the center.

WALDORF SALAD

6 Servings

Prepare:
   1 cup diced celery
   1 cup diced apples
   (1 cup Tokay grapes,
   halved and seeded)
Combine with:
   ½ cup walnut or pecan meats
   ¾ cup mayonnaise or Boiled Salad
   Dressing, page 316

ABOUT AVOCADO SALADS

Please read About Avocados, page 112. To
prepare avocado cups, cut the fruit in half
lengthwise, place between the palms of the
hands and gently twist the halves apart.
Tap the large seed with the edge of a
knife and lift or pry it out. ♦ To prevent
the fruit from darkening after cutting,
sprinkle with lemon juice. ♦ To store,
spread with mayonnaise, soft butter or
cream, allow the seed to remain in it and
cover well with wax paper or plastic. Avocado has a soft, buttery texture and taste
which combines best with citrus fruits or
tomatoes and a sharp or tangy dressing. It
also has an unexpected affinity with
shrimp, crab or lobster. All of these combinations offer a pleasing contrast of color,
as well as texture and taste—the hallmark
of a delectable salad.

AVOCADO SLICES

These may also be used as a garnish for

meats and fish.
Chill:
    Avocados
Pare and slice them. Marinate for about 5
minutes in chilled, highly seasoned:
    French Dressing, page 311
You may also add:
    (Hot pepper sauce, chili sauce,
    catsup, etc.)
Sprinkle with:
    Chopped parsley or chopped mint
Try these avocado slices in:
    (Tomato Aspic, page 100)

AVOCADO AND FRUIT SALAD

Pare:
    Avocados
Slice them lengthwise and arrange them
with skinned sections of:
    **Orange and grapefruit or
    pineapple slices**
in wheel shape, on:
    Lettuce
or, make a rounded salad by alternating
the fruit with the green avocado slices into
an approximate half globe on the lettuce.
Serve with:
    **French Dressing, page 311, or Lemon
    and Sherry Dressing, page 318**
Prepare the dressing with lime juice in
preference to lemon juice or vinegar.

AVOCADO SALAD CUPS

Cut into halves and remove the seeds
from:
    Chilled avocados
You may then fill the hollows with:
I. Chili sauce seasoned with horseradish

II. Marinated seedless grapes
Garnish with:
    **A sprig of parsley, mint or
    water cress**

III. Dress up:
    Crabmeat, chicken or fruit salad
with:
    Mayonnaise
thinned with a little:
    Lemon or lime juice
and fill the avocado cup.

IV. Fill with a **Tomato Ice** which can be
made like:
    Fruit Ice, page 722
only substitute tomato juice for the fruit
juice.

V. Scoop the pulp out of the skin, instead
of paring the avocado. Turn it into:
    Guacamole, page 60
Put the mixture back in the half shell and
garnish with:
    A slice of stuffed olive

BANANA AND NUT SALAD

For each serving, peel and split length-
wise:
    1 banana
Spread on the cut sides a thin coating of:
    Peanut butter
Sprinkle with:
    **Chopped peanuts or chopped
    English walnuts**
Serve on:
    Lettuce
Garnish with:
    Orange sections or red currant jelly
or sprinkle with:
    Honey Dressing, page 317

CHERRY AND HAZELNUT SALAD

Drain and pit:
    Canned white cherries
Insert in each cherry:
    A hazelnut meat
Serve very cold with:
    **Cottage cheese
    Mayonnaise**

ABOUT GRAPE SALADS

Grapes are not only delicious as part of
fruit and vegetable aspics but are superlative when served alone. Ever peel a grape?
Well, it takes time, but what is more luxurious than a lovely mound of peeled,
seeded grapes, lightly tossed in a mild
olive oil and vinegar dressing, served in
lettuce cups or as the center for a gelatin
ring mold! You may also toss a few peeled,
seeded grapes in a salad of tender lettuce.
To make a baroque grape finish on a gelatin top, see page 518. See also Seedless
Grape and Asparagus Aspic, page 99, or
mix seedless grapes with cultured sour
cream or yogurt as a fruit salad garnish.

GRAPE AND COTTAGE CHEESE
SALAD

Place in an oiled ring mold or in indi-
vidual ring molds:
    Cottage cheese
Chill and invert onto:
    Lettuce
Dust with:
    Paprika
Serve filled with:
    Seedless grapes
marinated in:
    French Dressing, page 311

GRAPEFRUIT SALAD

Prepare:
    Grapefruit segments, page 115
Serve them with:
    French Dressing, page 311
Use grapefruit juice in place of vinegar
and add a little:
    Confectioners' sugar

MELON SALAD
Prepare:
>Melon Baskets, page 118, or
>Melon Rounds

Fill the baskets with:
>Hulled berries
>Diced pineapple or seedless grapes

Moisten with chilled:
>French Dressing, page 311, or
>cultured sour cream

ORANGE AND ONION SALAD
Arrange:
>Skinned orange sections or peeled,
>sliced oranges
>Thin slices of Bermuda onion
>(Pink grapefruit sections)

on:
>Lettuce leaves, endive or escarole

Serve with:
>French Dressing, page 311

An Italian version of this salad adds:
>Pitted black olives

ORANGE AND GRAPEFRUIT SALAD
Prepare as directed, pages 116, 118:
>Orange and grapefruit segments

Place them on individual plates on:
>Lettuce or water cress

You may place between alternate segments of the fruit:
>Long slivers of green pepper
>and pimiento

Serve with:
>French Dressing, page 311

BLACK-EYED SUSAN SALAD
Skin unbroken whole or half sections of:
>Orange or grapefruit

Arrange them on:
>Lettuce

around a center of:
>Chopped dates and nuts

Serve with:
>French Dressing, page 311

ORANGE SALAD FOR GAME
4 Servings
Peel and separate the skin from the sections of:
>4 oranges

Arrange them on:
>Water cress

Combine and pour over them:
>2 tablespoons brandy
>2 tablespoons olive oil
>1 teaspoon sugar
>¼ teaspoon salt
>A few grains cayenne

Sprinkle the tops with:
>Chopped tarragon

FRESH PEACH AND CHEESE SALAD
6 Servings
Cut into 6 parts:
>3 oz. cream cheese

Roll the cheese into balls, then in:
>Chopped nut meats

Pare, cut into halves and pit:
>6 peaches

Place a ball of cheese between 2 peach halves. Press the peach into shape. Roll it in lemon juice. If the peaches are not to be served at once, chill them in closed containers. Serve the peaches on:
>Water cress

with:
>French Dressing, page 311

A bit of cress, a stem and several leaves may be placed in the stem end of each peach. Decorative—though it may affront a horticulturist.

PEAR SALAD
Chill and pare:
>Fresh pears or drained canned pears

Follow the preceding recipe for Peach Salad. Brush the side of each pear with:
>Red coloring or paprika

Place in the blossom ends:
>A clove

and in the stem ends:
>A bit of water cress

Serve with:
>French dressing

Garnish with:
>Nut Creams, page 67, or large
>black cherries, seeded and stuffed
>with cottage cheese

Or fill the hollows with cream cheese combined with chopped ginger.

PEAR AND GRAPE SALAD
Pare:
>Fresh pears

or drain:
>Canned pears

Place half a pear, cut side down, on a plate. Thin to spreading consistency:
>Cream cheese

with:
>Cream

Cover each pear half with a coating of cheese. Press into the cheese, close together to look like a bunch of grapes:
>Stemmed seedless grapes

Add a leaf of some kind, preferably grape, but an ivy leaf and a bit of stem is a good substitute. Serve with:
>Mayonnaise or French Dressing,
>pages 313, 311

JAPANESE PERSIMMON SALAD
This is an attractive-looking salad. If you wish to skin the fruit, rub it first with the blunt side of a knife and peel with the sharp edge.
Chill:
>Ripe Japanese persimmons

Serve them whole or cut lengthwise almost to the base and insert in the slashes:
>Slices of peeled orange,
>grapefruit and avocado

and serve with:
>Boiled Salad Dressing III, page 317

PINEAPPLE SALAD

Drain:
>Slices of canned pineapple

Serve them on:
>Lettuce with French Dressing,
>page 311

Add to the French dressing:
>A little confectioners' sugar

Or cover the slices with:
>Riced soft cream cheese

Topped with:
>A spoonful currant jelly

Serve the salad with:
>French Dressing, page 311
>or mayonnaise

ABOUT MOLDED SALADS

Any clever person can take a few desolate-looking refrigerator leftovers and glorify them into a tempting molded aspic salad or mousse. For utilizing leftovers, an aspic is second only to a soufflé. Well-combined scraps result in a dish that is sometimes as good as one composed of delicacies and with a further advantage to the busy housewife as it can be prepared a day in advance and chilled in the refrigerator until ready to serve. ♦ Do not freeze. Each of these salads depends on gelatin to hold its shape, so please read About Gelatin, page 516. Molds may be filled when dry; but a jellied mixture is more readily removed when a mold has been moistened with water. If the mixture is not a clarified one, you may lightly brush the mold with oil. Be sure to taste your salad before molding and correct the seasoning. ♦ Undersalt if it is to be held 24 hours.

Many of the recipes that follow can be made either in a large mold or in individual small ones. Ring molds can be used if you wish to fill the centers with some other kind of salad, such as chicken, Vegetables à la Grecque, page 255, fruit or cream cheese, dressed and garnished to your fancy. Fish-shaped molds can make a sea food aspic appear very professional. For large groups, you can even use small paper drinking cups for molding individual salads and tear off the cup when the salad is jellied and ready to serve. Or use large No. 2½ size cans and cut around the bottom of the can when ready to serve the salad. Push the salad out of the bottom of the can, slice and serve the rounds on lettuce.

♦ Aspics and other molded salads with a clear "body" lend themselves to highly decorative treatment, although their preparation can be time-consuming, page 517. However, certain ingredients naturally come to rest either at the top or bottom of a jelling salad and you can achieve interesting layered effects by using "floaters"

and "sinkers." See, on page 518, the list of ingredients which can be incorporated in your salad simultaneously.

ABOUT ASPICS

Nothing gives a cooler, lovelier effect on a hot summer night and nothing is easier to prepare than a brilliantly clear aspic. The problem, of course, is to keep the aspic properly chilled when serving. For small groups, chilled plates, individually served, will do, if you can control the timing. For large groups, if you want to use a quivery aspic, serve it molded in a crystal clear glass bowl set in another larger glass bowl with crushed ice between them or on a handsome, well-chilled platter, set on ice.

The most delicious aspics of all are reduced chicken and veal stocks, cooked down from the clarified gelatinous portions of these animals, page 96. Clarified strong meat, fish and fowl stocks with added gelatin are next in favor—but the average housewife seldom clarifies her own. She depends largely on canned bases for her jellies. ♦ Canned consommés, if over a year old, tend to lose some of their jelling power, so it is wise to refrigerate the can before using to test for texture. The consommé is still good to eat if it fails to jell just out of the can, but when used for aspic it will need about 1 teaspoon of gelatin per cup of consommé to firm it. To add gelatin, see page 517. If you save vegetable stocks, page 488, you can add them to meat or fish stocks to modify and enrich the otherwise easily identifiable canned flavors. It is wise to choose a stock that has the same general base as the food to be molded: fish stock for fish, meat stock for meat.

♦ To make aspics, allow 1 tablespoon gelatin to 1¾ to 2 cups liquid. Use the lesser amount of liquid if the solids to be incorporated are juicy or watery. ♦ Never reduce aspic made with added gelatin, with the idea of thickening it. It only wastes your good stock and never thickens. If you run into trouble, start the gelatin process over again, judging the amount of fresh gelatin you should add.

♦ The addition of wine or liqueur to your aspics can make them something rather special. Don't add too much ♦ one or two tablespoons per cup of liquid is sufficient to heighten the flavor significantly. Substitute the wine for part of the liquid called for in the recipe ♦ and add it when the gelatin has been dissolved and is beginning to cool. Dry white wine or a dry sherry go well with savory aspics such as chicken and veal. Sweeter wines, such as sauterne, cognac or fruit-flavored liqueurs, are good for molded fruit salads.

Aspic should be clarified unless you want to serve up something that resembles a molded London fog. If you decide to skip this process, be sure to plan to mask

your mold, see Mayonnaise Collée, page 341, or Sauce Chaud-froid, page 341.
♦ To clarify, see page 489. ♦ To make decorative molds, see page 517. Clear aspic jelly can make an attractive garnish for a meat or chicken aspic. Chill it in a refrigerator tray ♦ but do not freeze and, when ready to serve, cut in squares or fancy shapes or chop it rather fine and arrange it around the mold.

Many salads can become full-fledged luncheon dishes with the addition of various types of chopped meat, chicken or flaked fish. For other recipes including meat, fish and shellfish and Chicken Mousses see pages 97, 98.

A choice or a combination of the following ingredients may be included in a molded salad:

  Cooked diced meat or poultry
  Cooked flaked fish
  Hard-cooked eggs
  Cooked sweetbreads
  Shredded cabbage
  Diced celery
  Diced cucumbers
  Cooked celeriac
  Sliced green peppers
  Raw or cooked carrots
  Cooked beets
  Canned asparagus
  Halved cranberries
  Seedless grapes
  Skinned grapefruit sections
  Stuffed ripe or green olives
  Pickles
  Nut meats
  Chopped parsley, chives
  or other herbs

BASIC ASPIC OR GELATIN SALAD
5 Servings
Please read About Gelatin, page 516.
Soak:
  1 tablespoon gelatin
in:
  ¼ cup cold water
Dissolve it in:
  ¼ cup boiling stock
Add this to:
  1½ cups cold stock or 1¼ cups stock plus ¼ cup tomato juice
  2 tablespoons vinegar or 1½ tablespoons lemon juice
  Salt and paprika
  Celery salt
  (1 tablespoon grated onion)
If the aspic is to cover unseasoned food, make the gelatin mixture "peppy." Chill it and when about to set combine it with:
  1½ to 2 cups solid ingredients
Pour the aspic into a wet mold and chill until firm. Unmold. Surround with:
  Lettuce leaves
Serve with or without:
  Mayonnaise, Sour Cream Horseradish Dressing, page 317, etc.

ASPIC GARNISH
Prepare:
  Basic Aspic Salad, above
When firm and just before serving, chop the aspic so the light catches its many facets, and use it to garnish salads or meats.

LUNCHEON ASPIC SALAD
8 Servings
♦ Please read About Gelatin, page 516.
Drain, reserving the juices:
  2½ cups canned grapefruit sections
  ¼ cup green or white cooked asparagus
  1 cup canned or cooked crab meat or shrimp
Cut the asparagus into pieces. Pick over the crab meat or remove the intestinal vein from the shrimp. Add to the juices, to make 2¾ cups of liquid:
  Chicken broth, Stock, page 490, canned consommé or dissolved chicken bouillon cubes
Soak:
  1½ tablespoons gelatin
in ½ cup of this liquid.
Dissolve it in 1 cup hot liquid.
Combine the gelatin and the remaining liquid. Season well with:
  Juice of 1 or more lemons or with ¼ cup dry white wine
Add, if needed:
  Salt
Add:
  (3 or more tablespoons capers)
Chill the gelatin until it begins to thicken. Have ready a mold which has been rinsed in cold water. Pour part of the gelatin into it, sprinkle some grapefruit, crabmeat and asparagus over it, then alternate layers of gelatin and of the other ingredients. Wind up with gelatin on top. Chill the aspic until it is very cold. Serve on:
  Lettuce
with:
  Green Mayonnaise, page 315

JELLIED VEAL STOCK
4 to 6 Servings
Sometimes it is fun to make an aspic without added gelatin.
Place in a soup kettle:
  A knuckle of veal
  ¼ cup cut-up onion
  ½ carrot
  6 ribs celery with leaves
  1 teaspoon salt
  ¼ teaspoon pepper
Cover the veal with:
  Boiling water
Simmer the meat until it is tender. Strain the liquid. Reserve it. Remove the veal. When cold, cut the meat into small cubes. Remove the fat from the stock. Heat the stock. Add the veal or reserve it for other dishes and use the stock after clarifying it, page 489, to mold other ingredients.

Correct the seasoning
add:
  (1 teaspoon dried herb—basil,
     tarragon, etc.)
Rinse out a mold in cold water. Pour in
the veal mixture. Cover and keep in a
cold place to set. Unmold and slice.

CHICKEN ASPIC
                              6 to 8 Servings
Soak:
  1 tablespoon gelatin
in:
  ¼ cup cold water
Dissolve it in:
  2 cups boiling chicken broth or stock
Add:
  Seasoning, if needed
Chill and when the gelatin begins to set,
rinse a mold in cold water and fill it with:
  ½ inch of the jelly
Build up layers of:
  3 cups cooked, diced chicken
and the jelly. Ornament the layers with:
  1 cup canned mushroom caps
  2 hard-cooked eggs
  12 sliced stuffed olives
Chill the jelly until firm. Unmold it and
serve with or without:
  Mayonnaise

JELLIED CHICKEN OR VEAL MOUSSE
I.   10 Servings
Use the recipe for Jellied Ham Mousse,
below. Use chicken stock. Substitute
cooked ground chicken or veal for the ham
or use part chicken and part ham.

II.   8 Servings
Soak:
  1½ tablespoons gelatin
in:
  ¼ cup Chicken Stock, page 490
Dissolve it in:
  ½ cup hot stock
Beat:
  3 egg yolks
Add:
  1½ cups milk
Cook these ingredients in a double boiler
until they are smooth and fairly thick. Stir
in the dissolved gelatin. When the mixture
is cool, add:
  2 cups cooked minced or ground
     chicken or veal
  (½ cup diced seeded cucumber)
Season it with:
  Salt, white pepper and paprika
Chill the jelly and when it is about to set,
fold in:
  1 cup whipping cream
Place the mousse in a wet mold and chill
it until it is firm. Unmold it.

JELLIED HAM MOUSSE
                              10 Servings

Soak:
  1 tablespoon gelatin
in:
  ¼ cup cold water
Dissolve it in:
  1½ cups boiling Stock, page 490
Chill the jelly. When it is nearly set, combine it with:
  3 cups cooked ground or chopped ham
  ¼ cup chopped celery
  1 tablespoon grated onion
  ½ cup mayonnaise
  ¼ cup sour or sweet-sour chopped
     pickles
Add, if required:
  Worcestershire sauce
  Seasoning
Seasonal variation: Omit onion, olives and
pickles and add:
  (1 cup seedless green grapes)
Moisten a mold with cold water. If desired, decorate the sides and bottom with:
  Stuffed olives and sliced hard-cooked
     eggs
Add the other ingredients. Chill the
mousse until it is firm.

JELLIED CLAM JUICE RING
                              8 Servings
◗ Please read About Gelatin, page 516.
Dilute:
  Clam juice or minced clams
with:
  Water or vegetable juices
to make a palatable mixture. There should
be 4 cups of liquid. Season this with:
  Lemon juice and paprika
  A few drops Worcestershire sauce
Soak:
  2 tablespoons gelatin
in ½ cup of the liquid.
Heat ◗ just to the boiling point 1 cup of
the liquid. Dissolve the soaked gelatin in
it. Return it to the remaining liquid with
the minced clams if they were used. Pour
in a wet 9-inch ring mold. Chill until firm.
Invert the jelly onto a plate. Fill the cen-
ter with:
  Cottage cheese
Surround it with:
  Tomato and cucumber slices
Serve with:
  Mayonnaise

MADRILÈNE RING WITH SHAD ROE
A fine summer dish.
Fill a ring mold with:
  Canned Madrilène aspic or well-
     seasoned meat stock aspic
Chill. Invert on:
  Shredded lettuce
Place in the center:
  Chilled canned shad roe
Garnish with:
  Mayonnaise
  Lemon wedges or parsley
If the Madrilène is of a wobbly type, serve

it from a small dish, surrounded by pieces of roe on lettuce.

MOUSSELINE OF SHELLFISH
6 Servings

Line a 1½-quart fish mold with half-set:
Fish or Chicken Aspic, page 97
Refrigerate it. Prepare:
2 cups Fish Velouté, page 324
to which has been added:
1 tablespoon gelatin
soaked in:
¼ cup cold stock or water
Combine the cooled sauce with:
1 lb. cooked chopped shellfish meat
Add:
½ cup partially whipped cream
Correct the seasoning
and pour into the fish mold over the aspic. Chill before unmolding onto a cold serving platter.

JELLIED SEAFOOD RING OR MOLD
6 Servings

◆ Please read About Gelatin, page 516.
Prepare:
Basic Aspic Jelly, page 96
using a fish fumet or light meat stock. Dice.
Celery
Pare, seed and dice:
Cucumbers or green peppers
Drain and flake:
Salmon, crab or tuna fish: 1½ cups fish and vegetables in all
Add:
(2 chopped hard-cooked eggs)
(Sliced stuffed olives)
When the jelly is nearly set, combine it with the solid ingredients. Pour it into a wet mold and chill until firm. Unmold and serve on:
Lettuce
with:
Mayonnaise or boiled dressing

MOLDED CREAMED FISH
6 Servings

◆ Please read About Gelatin, page 516.
Soak:
¾ tablespoon gelatin
in:
2 tablespoons water
Combine in a double boiler, then stir constantly ◆ over—not in—boiling water until thickened:
2 egg yolks
1½ tablespoons soft butter
½ tablespoon flour
1½ teaspoons salt
2 teaspoons sugar
1 teaspoon Worcestershire sauce,
¾ teaspoon curry or 1 teaspoon dry mustard
1 teaspoon grated onion
A few grains red pepper
¼ cup lemon juice
¾ cup milk or tomato juice
Add gelatin and stir until it is dissolved.

Refrigerate. Prepare:
1½ cups seafood: cooked or canned shrimp, salmon, etc.
Or use part fish and part chopped celery. When the gelatin is nearly set, place part of it in the bottom of an oiled ring mold, add part of the fish, then more gelatin. Repeat this until all ingredients have been used, finishing with gelatin on top. Chill the salad until it is firm. Serve it on:
Water cress
Fill the ring with:
Marinated cucumbers
Surround it with:
Sliced tomatoes

SEAFOOD MOUSSE
6 Servings

◆ Please read About Gelatin, page 516.
Soak:
2 teaspoons gelatin
in:
¼ cup cold water
Dissolve it in:
¼ cup boiling water
Add it to:
¾ cup mayonnaise
Combine it with:
1 cup flaked crab meat or flaked tuna fish
½ cup chopped celery or carrots
2 tablespoons chopped parsley
½ cup chopped cucumber
2 tablespoons chopped stuffed olives
1 tablespoon or more lemon juice
Correct the seasoning
and place these ingredients in a wet mold. Chill them until they are firm. Unmold them on:
Cress or shredded lettuce
Serve with:
Cucumbers in Sour Cream
If you want a mousse based on whipped cream, see Lobster Mousse.

LOBSTER MOUSSE
6 Servings

◆ Please read About Gelatin, page 516.
This is an attractive salad, made in a 9-inch ring mold.
Soak:
1 tablespoon gelatin
in:
¼ cup water
Dissolve it over boiling water. Combine:
¾ cup minced celery
1½ cups canned or cooked lobster meat
(⅔ cup minced apple)
Season these ingredients with:
Salt and paprika
Stir the gelatin into:
¾ cup mayonnaise
3 tablespoons lemon juice
(1 teaspoon dry mustard)
(½ clove pressed garlic)
(A few drops hot pepper sauce)
Whip until stiff, then fold in:
⅛ cup whipping cream

Fold this mixture into the other ingredients. Place the mousse in a wet mold. Chill it thoroughly. Unmold it on a platter, garnished with:
>Water cress
>Marinated cucumbers

Serve it, if you like, filled with the following sauce. Simmer:
>1 cup tomatoes

When reduced to ½ cup, chill the tomatoes. Add to them:
>½ cup olive oil
>½ teaspoon sugar
>½ teaspoon salt
>1 tablespoon chopped parsley
>Freshly grated pepper
>½ teaspoon Worcestershire sauce

EGGS IN ASPIC OR OEUFS EN GELÉE

Make one of the above:
>Stock aspics, flavored with port and cognac

Have ready:
>Poached eggs, page 196

Swish cold water in individual molds until they are cold and wet. Drain but do not dry. Coat the interior with the jelling aspic so that it adheres to the sides. Chill until congealed. Place an egg in the center of each mold and fill with more aspic. Chill. Serve masked with:
>Mayonnaise Collée, page 341, or cold mayonnaise

EGGS IN ASPIC COCKAIGNE

Molded with one half egg this makes a pleasant hors d'oeuvre. With three halves, it makes enough for a luncheon salad. Prepare:
>Eggs in Aspic, above

using rich chicken stock for the aspic base and replacing the poached eggs with:
>Deviled Eggs, page 203

Place the molds on a bed of:
>Water cress

Mask the eggs with a coating of:
>Cultured sour cream

Garnish with:
>Finely chopped chives, basil and chervil
>Red caviar and tomato slices

MOLDED VEGETABLE GELATIN SALAD

6 Servings

Dissolve the contents of:
>1 package lime- or lemon-flavored gelatin

in:
>2 cups hot water

Prepare and add, when the jelly is about to set:
>1½ cups finely diced vegetables: cucumber, carrot, celery, unpeeled radishes, olive, pimiento
>½ diced green pepper

>2 teaspoons grated onion
>¾ teaspoon salt
>¼ teaspoon paprika

Place the salad in well-oiled individual ring molds. Chill thoroughly. Unmold on:
>Lettuce or water cress

Fill the centers with:
>Mayonnaise or Boiled Salad Dressing II, page 317

GOLDEN GLOW GELATIN SALAD

8 to 10 Servings

Good in flavor and lovely in color. Grate or grind:
>2 cups raw carrots

Drain, reserving the juice:
>1 cup canned crushed pineapple

Heat to the boiling point:
>⅞ cup pineapple juice
>⅞ cup water
>½ teaspoon salt

Dissolve in the hot liquid:
>1 package lemon-flavored gelatin

Chill and when the jelly is about to set, combine it with the carrots, the pineapple and:
>(½ cup chopped pecans)

Place in a wet mold. Chill until firm. Unmold on:
>Lettuce

Serve with:
>Mayonnaise

SEEDLESS GRAPE AND ASPARAGUS ASPIC

10 Servings

♦ Please read About Gelatin, page 516. A refreshing summer salad. Drain the contents of:
>2 cups canned asparagus tips

Reserve the liquor. The tips may be cut in two or they may be used whole as a garnish around the edge of the mold. Soak:
>1 tablespoon gelatin

in:
>3 tablespoons asparagus liquor

Heat the remaining asparagus liquor and dissolve the gelatin in it. Add to it to make 2 cups of liquor in all:
>Chicken bouillon or canned bouillon

Season these ingredients with:
>Salt and paprika

Chill them. When they are nearly set, combine them with:
>2 cups seedless grapes
>1 cup chopped celery

and the cut asparagus tips. Chill the salad until firm. Unmold and serve with:
>Mayonnaise

BEET GELATIN SALAD

8 Servings

Wash well, then boil:
>8 medium-size beets or use canned beets

Drain them. Reserve the beet juice. Peel the beets and dice them. There should be about 1 cup. Prepare:

 ¾ cup diced celery

Dissolve the contents of:

 1 package lemon-flavored gelatin

in:

 1 cup boiling water

Add to it:

 ¾ cup beet juice
 3 tablespoons vinegar
 ½ teaspoon salt
 2 teaspoons grated onion
 1 tablespoon prepared horseradish

Chill these ingredients until they are about to set. Fold in the beets and the celery. Place the salad in a wet mold. Chill until firm. Unmold on:

 Lettuce or endive

Serve with:

 Mayonnaise, Boiled Salad Dressing, page 316, or cultured sour cream

CUCUMBER GELATIN ON TOMATO SLICES

 8 Servings

◗ Please read About Gelatin, page 516.
Fine for a meat platter or a ring mold.
Pare and seed:

 Cucumbers

Grate them. There should be 4 cups of pulp and juice. Soak:

 2 tablespoons gelatin

in:

 ½ cup cold water or chicken stock

Dissolve it in:

 ¾ cup boiling water or chicken stock

Add:

 6 tablespoons lemon juice
 2 teaspoons grated onion

Add the gelatin mixture to the cucumber pulp with:

 1 teaspoon sugar
 Salt, as needed
 ¼ teaspoon paprika

Strain the jelly. Place it in small wet molds. When firm invert onto:

 Thick slices skinned tomatoes

Garnish the slices with:

 Water cress

Serve the salad with:

 Mayonnaise

or, place in a 9-inch wet ring mold. Chill the jelly. When firm, invert onto a platter. Fill the center with:

 Marinated shrimp

Garnish the edge with alternating:

 Tomato slices
 Cucumber slices

Serve the ring with:

 Green Mayonnaise, page 315, or
 Water Cress Dressing, page 312

CUCUMBER MOUSSE

 6 Servings

◗ Please read About Gelatin, page 516.
Soak:

 2 teaspoons gelatin

in:

 3 tablespoons cold water

Dissolve these ingredients over heat. Add:

 2 teaspoons vinegar or lemon juice
 1 teaspoon grated onion
 ¾ teaspoon salt
 ¼ teaspoon paprika

Chill until about to set. Drain well:

 1 cup pared, seeded, chopped cucumbers

Whip until stiff:

 1 cup whipping cream

Beat the gelatin mixture gradually into the cream. Fold in the cucumbers. Oil individual molds. Fill them with the mousse. When they are thoroughly chilled, invert the mousse onto a garnished platter.

CUCUMBER AND SOUR CREAM MOUSSE

 6 Servings

Dissolve:

 1 package lime-flavored gelatin

in:

 ¾ cup hot water

Add:

 ¼ cup lemon juice
 1 tablespoon grated onion

Chill until about to set, then stir in:

 1 cup cultured sour cream
 1 cup finely chopped unpared cucumber

Pour into 6 small oiled molds and chill until firm.

TOMATO ASPIC

 8 Servings, without the addition
 of solid ingredients

◗ Please read About Gelatin, page 516.
I. Simmer, for 30 minutes, then strain:

 3½ cups tomatoes
 1 teaspoon salt
 ½ teaspoon paprika
 1½ teaspoons sugar
 2 tablespoons lemon juice
 3 tablespoons chopped onion
 1 bay leaf
 4 ribs celery with leaves
 (1 teaspoon dried basil or tarragon)

Soak:

 2 tablespoons gelatin

in:

 ½ cup cold water

Dissolve it in the strained hot juice. Add water to make 4 cups of liquid. Chill the aspic. When it is about to set add 1 or 2 cups of solid ingredients—a choice or a combination of:

 Sliced olives
 Chopped celery
 Chopped green peppers
 Grated or chopped carrots

Chopped meat
Flaked fish
Well-drained oysters
Sliced avocados, etc.
Chill the aspic until firm. Unmold and
serve with:
     Mayonnaise or Boiled Salad
     Dressing, page 316

II. If you prefer a ring, keep the aspic simple and fill the center with:
     Cole slaw, marinated cucumbers or
     avocados, chicken or shrimp
     salad or cottage cheese and chives
Serve with a suitable dressing.

TOMATO ASPIC WITH
TASTY CENTERS
                                                   8 Servings
I. Prepare:
     Tomato Aspic, page 100
When it is about to set, pour into wet individual molds or ice cube molds and fill
them to ⅓ of their capacity. Combine and
roll into balls:
     1 package soft cream cheese: 3 oz.
     1 tablespoon anchovy paste
     2 drops Worcestershire sauce
Drop a ball into each mold and cover it
with aspic. Chill the aspic until firm. Unmold on lettuce leaves. Serve with:
     Mayonnaise

II. Use for the filling:
     Any small pieces of cooked meat,
     fowl or fish

CANNED TOMATO OR
VEGETABLE JUICE ASPIC
                                                   8 Servings
♦ Please read About Gelatin, page 516.
Soak:
     2 tablespoons gelatin
in:
     ½ cup cold canned tomato juice
Dissolve it in:
     3½ cups hot tomato juice or canned
     tomato and vegetable juice
Tomato juice varies. It is wise to taste the
aspic to see whether additional seasoning
is required. Lemon juice is good, so is a
teaspoon of chopped or dried herbs, page
530, preferably basil. Add, if desired, 1 or
2 cups of solid ingredients. See Tomato
Aspic, page 100. Mold, chill, unmold and
serve the aspic as directed.

BASIC GELATIN FOR
FRUIT SALADS
                                                   6 Servings
♦ Please read About Gelatin, page 516. It
is well to know that fresh pineapple cannot
be added to a gelatin salad without ruining
it. This also applies to frozen pineapple
juice, alone or combined with other frozen

juices such as orange or grapefruit. The
pineapple must be brought to ♦ a boil.
Canned pineapple complies with this rule
and may be used as is. The frozen juice is
usable if boiled.
Soak:
     1 tablespoon gelatin
in:
     ½ cup cold water
Dissolve it in:
     1 cup boiling water or fruit juice
Add:
     4 to 6 tablespoons sugar, less if
     sweetened fruit juice is used
     ⅛ teaspoon salt
     ¼ cup lemon juice
Chill the aspic and when it is about to set,
combine it with:
     1½ cups prepared drained fruit
Place it in a wet mold and chill until firm.
Serve with:
     Cream Mayonnaise, page 315

MINT GELATIN FOR FRUIT SALADS
Pour:
     1 cup boiling water
over:
     ¼ cup crushed mint leaves
Allow to steep for 5 minutes. Drain this
infusion. Add:
     A few drops of green
     vegetable coloring
Prepare, by the recipe above:
     Basic Fruit Salad Gelatin
substituting the mint infusion for the boiling water.

MOLDED AVOCADO SALAD
                                                   3 to 4 Servings
Soak:
     1 tablespoon gelatin
in:
     2 tablespoons water
Dissolve it in:
     1 cup boiling water
Add:
     ¼ cup lemon juice
     1 cup mashed avocado
     ¼ teaspoon celery salt
     1 teaspoon salt
     ½ teaspoon Worcestershire sauce
     A few grains cayenne
     ¼ cup chopped pimiento
Mold and serve.

BLACK CHERRY AND
ALMOND ASPIC
                                                   6 Servings
Prepare:
     Basic Fruit Salad Gelatin, above
Substitute for part of the boiling water:
     Fruit juice
Cool the gelatin mixture. When it is about
to set add:
     1¼ cups pitted black cherries
     ⅓ cup blanched shredded almonds
These proportions may be varied. Place

the aspic in a wet mold. Chill until firm.
Unmold and serve with:
  Mayonnaise

MOLDED CRANBERRY SALAD
                        6 to 8 Servings
♦ Please read About Gelatin, page 516.
Soak:
  1 tablespoon gelatin
in:
  3 tablespoons water
Cook until the skins pop:
  2 cups cranberries
in:
  1 cup boiling water or fruit juice
Use the cranberries strained or unstrained.
If the former, strain them at this time.
Add and cook for 5 minutes:
  ½ cup sugar
  ¼ teaspoon salt
Add the soaked gelatin. Chill the jelly.
When it is about to set, fold in:
  ⅔ cup diced celery
  (½ cup chopped nut meats)
  (1 cup canned, drained,
    crushed pineapple)
Place in a wet mold and chill until firm.
Serve with:
  Mayonnaise

MOLDED CRANBERRY AND
APPLE SALAD
                        8 to 10 Servings
♦ Please read About Gelatin, page 516.
Put through a food grinder:
  1 lb. cranberries
Add:
  The grated rind of 1 orange
  ½ cup orange juice
  3½ tablespoons lemon juice
  1½ cups sugar
Refrigerate overnight. Soak:
  1 tablespoon gelatin
in:
  3 tablespoons cold water
Dissolve:
  1 package lemon-flavored gelatin:
    3¼ oz.
in:
  1 cup boiling water
Add the soaked gelatin. Stir until dissolved. Combine these ingredients with the
cranberry mixture. Pare, then chop and
add:
  3 tart apples
Place the salad in a greased mold. When
firm, unmold and serve on:
  Water cress
with:

  Cream Mayonnaise, page 315

GINGER ALE SALAD
                        10 Servings
♦ Please read About Gelatin, page 516.
This is about the best molded fruit salad
given.
Soak:

  2 tablespoons gelatin
in:
  ¼ cup cold water
Dissolve it in:
  ½ cup boiling fruit juice
Add:
  ½ cup sugar
  ⅛ teaspoon salt
  2 cups ginger ale
  Juice of 1 lemon
Chill these ingredients until the jelly is
nearly set. Combine with:
  ½ lb. skinned, seeded Tokay grapes
  1 skinned, sliced orange
  1 grapefruit in skinned sections
  6 slices canned pineapple,
    cut in pieces
  3 teaspoons chopped preserved ginger
Place the salad in a wet mold. Chill and
unmold on:
  Lettuce
Serve with:
  Cream Mayonnaise, page 315

GRAPEFRUIT JELLY WITH SHERRY
                        10 Servings
♦ Please read About Gelatin, page 516.
Soak:
  2½ tablespoons gelatin
in:
  ½ cup cold water
Stir over heat until the sugar is dissolved:
  ½ cup water
  1 cup sugar
Dissolve the gelatin in the hot sirup. Cool.
Add:
  2 cups and 6 tablespoons fresh
    grapefruit juice
  3 tablespoons lemon juice
  ½ cup dry sherry
  ¼ teaspoon salt
Pour these ingredients into a well-oiled
9-inch ring mold. Chill the jelly until firm.
Turn it out on a platter. Fill the center
with:
  Soft cream cheese balls, rolled in
    chopped nuts
Garnish the outer edge of the platter with:
  Avocado slices
alternating with skinned:
  Grapefruit or orange sections
on:
  Water cress or shredded lettuce
Sprinkle with:
  Pomegranate seeds
Serve the salad with:
  Mayonnaise or French Dressing,
    pages 313, 311

MOLDED PEAR SALAD
                        6 Servings
♦ Please read About Gelatin, page 516.
Drain and reserve the juice from:
  3½ cups canned Bartlett pears
Soak:
  1 tablespoon gelatin

in:

    ¼ cup cold water

Add to the pear juice enough water to make 1¾ cups of liquid. Heat part of the liquid to the boiling point. Dissolve the soaked gelatin in it. Combine it with the rest of the liquid. Add:

    3 tablespoons lemon juice
    ¼ teaspoon salt

Cool these ingredients. Moisten:

    1 package soft cream cheese or
    pimiento cheese

with a very little:

    Cream

Use just enough to soften it. Add to the cheese:

    ¼ cup chopped nut meats
    (¼ teaspoon salt)

Form the cheese into balls. Place one in the center of a half pear and cover with another half pear. If the pears are large, do not cover them. Place the stuffed pears in a ring mold or in cups. Pour the gelatin mixture over them. Add, if desired:

    1 cup or more seedless grapes

Chill the gelatin until firm. Unmold on:

    Crisp lettuce

Serve with:

    Mayonnaise

This recipe may also be made with:

    1 package lime or lemon gelatin
    1 cup boiling water
    1 cup pear juice
    1½ tablespoons lemon juice
    ⅛ teaspoon ginger
    ¼ teaspoon salt

Substitute this for the gelatin mixture given in the recipe.

MOLDED STUFFED FRUITS

8 Servings

◗ Please read About Gelatin, page 516.
Soak:

    2½ tablespoons gelatin

in:

    ½ cup water

Drain and reserve the juice from:

    3½ cups canned peaches, apricots or pears

Combine and boil:

    2 cups of the juice
    1½ cups sugar

Dissolve the gelatin in it. Add these ingredients to the remaining juice with:

    ¾ cup lemon juice
    3 tablespoons lime juice
    ¼ teaspoon ginger

Add water or other fruit juice to make up 4 cups of liquid in all. Chill the gelatin until it is about to set. Soften:

    Cream cheese

with a little:

    Mayonnaise

Roll it into balls. Roll the balls in:

    Chopped nut meats

Stuff a cheese ball in each fruit, then place each fruit in an oiled individual mold. Chill well and invert onto:

    Water cress

Serve with:

    Mayonnaise

MOLDED PINEAPPLE RING

8 Servings

◗ Please read About Gelatin, page 516.
Soak:

    2 tablespoons gelatin

in:

    ½ cup cold water

Strain and reserve the juice of:

    2½ cups canned crushed pineapple

Add to the juice:

    ½ cup hot water

Bring these ingredients to the boiling point. Stir in the soaked gelatin until dissolved. Add:

    ⅝ cup sugar: ½ cup, plus
    2 tablespoons

Cool the mixture. Add the pineapple and:

    (2 cups grated cabbage)
    The grated rind of 1 orange
    or lemon
    ¾ cup orange juice
    5 tablespoons lemon juice

Pour these ingredients into a wet 9-inch ring mold. Chill the gelatin. Unmold on a bed of:

    Lettuce or water cress

Fill the center with:

    Cottage cheese, soft cream cheese
    balls rolled in chopped nut meats,
    chicken salad, etc.

Serve with or without:

    Mayonnaise

SEEDLESS GRAPE AND CELERY RING

8 to 10 Servings

Prepare:

    Lemon Jelly or Orange Jelly,
    or Basic Fruit Gelatin, page 101

When it is about to set, add to it:

    3 cups seedless grapes and diced
    celery, combined in any proportion

Place the jelly in a wet 9-inch mold and chill. Unmold on:

    Lettuce

Fill the center with:

    Cream Mayonnaise, page 315

FROSTED MELON OR PAPAYA SALAD

6 Servings

You may use this as salad or dessert.
Pare:

    1 large melon or papaya

leaving it whole. Cut off enough from one end so you can scrape out the seeds. Fill the cavity with water, pour it into a measuring cup; this is to guide you for the amount of gelatin you have to prepare. Stand the melon upside down to drain. Then fill, depending on the color of the

melon flesh, with:
>Fruit-flavored gelatin
>(Diced or small fruits)

Try a combination of:
>Orange-flavored gelatin, canned
>crushed pineapple, canned mandarin
>oranges or sliced bananas

or try:
>Raspberry gelatin with fresh
>raspberries

After the center is set, you may coat the
melon with:
>8 oz. cream cheese

softened with:
>A little milk

and whipped until fluffy. Chill until ready
to serve. Cut crosswise in 1-inch slices and
serve on:
>Lettuce

with:
>French Dressing, page 311

SOUFFLÉ FRUIT SALAD

4 Servings

Dissolve:
>1 package lime gelatin

in:
>1 cup hot water

Add:
>½ cup cold water
>½ cup mayonnaise
>2 tablespoons lemon juice
>¼ teaspoon salt

Whip with a rotary beater until well
blended. Pour into a refrigerator tray and
chill until firm at the edge but still soft in
the center. Turn into a bowl and whip in
the same manner until fluffy. Fold in:
>1 cup peeled and diced apples
>¼ cup chopped pecans
>¾ cup seeded Tokay grapes

Pour into a mold and refrigerate until firm.

STRAWBERRY AND RHUBARB
SALAD MOLDS

8 to 10 Servings

Dissolve:
>3 packages strawberry gelatin

in:
>3 cups hot water

Drop in:
>2 packages frozen rhubarb

Stir to separate the rhubarb. When the
jelly begins to set, add:
>1 quart sliced fresh strawberries

Pour into individual wet molds and chill
until set. Unmold on:
>Water cress

Garnish each with:
>A fresh whole strawberry

Serve with:
>Cream Mayonnaise, page 315, or
>Fruit Salad Mayonnaise, page 315

TWENTY-FOUR-HOUR FRUIT SALAD
WITH CREAM

12 to 14 Servings

Cook in a double boiler until thickened:
>2 egg yolks
>¼ cup sugar
>¼ cup cream
>Juice of 2 lemons
>⅛ teaspoon salt

Stir these ingredients constantly. Chill
them and add:
>6 diced slices canned pineapple
>2 cups pitted Queen Anne cherries
>1 cup blanched, shredded almonds
>½ lb. marshmallows, cut in pieces
>1 cup heavy cream, whipped
>(½ lb. peeled, seeded grapes)

Chill the salad for 24 hours. Serve on:
>Lettuce

with:
>Mayonnaise

or as a dessert, garnished with:
>Whipped cream

FRUITS

Too often the menu-builder takes herself too seriously and tops off a rich edifice with a disastrously rich dessert when fresh fruit with, perhaps, a cheese would be a far happier conclusion of the meal for all concerned. Well worth exploiting are the virtues of fruit—in either cup, compote, salad or sherbet form—as a "lightener" during, as well as after, a big meal.

If fruits lack flavor, serve them or prepare them with candied peels, ginger, zest or spices; or add a little lemon or lime juice to cooked fruits and fruit fillings. Vary the flavor of a particular fruit by processing it in the juices of other fruits, or in wine, or by blending it with other fruits in a purée. You may glaze poached fruit with contrasting fruit jellies, especially those of apple and quince, which are high in pectin. Also combine canned, frozen and fresh fruits—cold or slightly heated—in what the French call a compôte composée. Try presenting your "composed compôte" in a giant lidded snifter, laced with brandy or liqueur and serve it to your guests in smaller individual snifters.

Serve Fruit Soups, pages 109 and 149; Fruit with Custards, page 684, or Creams, page 645; Fruit Brûlé, page 108, or Flambé, page 108. For dried or preserved fruits used as garnishes, see About Candies and Glazed Fruits, page 741. For fresh fruit combinations, see below and also consult the chapter on Salads, pages 101-104.

ABOUT FRESH FRUITS

Andrew Marvell, the Puritan poet, wrote these lines:
  What wondrous life is this I lead!
  Ripe apples drop about my head;
  The luscious clusters of the vine
  Upon my mouth do crush their wine;
  The nectarine, the curious peach,
  Into my hands themselves do reach;
  Stumbling on melons, as I pass,
  Ensnared with flowers, I fall on grass.
Like Marvell, we have a passion for fruit. Like him also, we have encountered, in acquiring it, a few pitfalls.

Be wary of "fruit specials." Such produce may include pieces which are below standard in either quality or size. Therefore, they could prove to be no bargains at all. U. S. Government standards are of necessity variable, but you can judge for yourself as to size by the units packed to the box ♦ the smaller the number of fruits per box or basket, obviously, the larger the individual fruit.

If purchased underripe, fresh fruits

should be kept at room temperature in a dark place. Place them loosely so the fruits are separated in partially closed paper bags. Examine them twice daily, keep from bruising and, as soon as ripened, chill in the refrigerator before serving.

Most fresh fruits lose their flavor rapidly when soaked in water, so always ♦ wash them quickly in gently flowing water and dry at once. Below are some recipes for fresh fruit combinations.

FRUIT CUPS
Use attractive small bowls or glass cups. ♦ To frost them, see page 40. Use seedless grapes, citrus sections, watermelon, green and yellow melons, cut into balls with a French potato cutter, see page 83. Queen Anne cherries and cubed fresh pineapple combine well.
Chill and prepare for serving:
  Fresh fruit
Five minutes before serving, sprinkle lightly with:
  Powdered sugar
Immediately before serving, flavor with:
  Lime juice, lemon juice, sherry or
  lightly sweetened fruit juice
Garnish with:
  Candied Mint Leaves

AMBROSIA
                                4 Servings
This is a versatile old favorite, especially popular in the South.
Peel carefully, removing all membrane:
  2 large Valencia oranges
Peel and cut into thin slices:
  3 ripe bananas
Pineapple is sometimes added, as are other fruits. Combine and stir:
  ¼ cup confectioners' sugar
  1½ cups shredded coconut
Arrange alternate layers of oranges and bananas in individual serving dishes or in a bowl. Sprinkle each layer with part of the coconut mixture, reserving some for the top. Chill well before serving. Instead of coconut, try a garnish of:
  (Crushed mint and a cherry
  or a strawberry)

MACÉDOINE OF FRESH FRUITS
The following fruit and wine or liqueur combinations should be composed of ripe, perfect, pared, seeded and sliced seasonal fruits. Favorites for this dessert are strawberries, raspberries, peeled seedless green grapes, peaches, apricots, avocado slices, orange and grapefruit sections, melon balls, cherries and nectarines. Be sure to prick the fruits to allow the marinade to soak in. If you use raw apples or pears,

marinate the slices for several hours in wine or liqueur or they will be too hard. Some good marinating combinations are:

>   **Cognac with oranges**
>   **Brandy with cherries and clove-studded peaches**
>   **Port with melon balls**

A macedoine is usually served cold, but you may flambé it, see page 108, if the fruit is at room temperature—and if you add extra liqueur, slightly warmed.
Place in layers in a crystal bowl:

>   **Prepared fruit, see above**

Sprinkle each layer with:

>   **Powdered sugar**

Stir the fruit gently until the sugar is almost dissolved, then add for each quart of fruit:

>   **2 to 4 tablespoons cognac, brandy, rum or kirsch**

Serve very cold over:

>   **Vanilla ice cream, page 715**

or with:

>   **Cake**

FRUIT FOOLS

4 Servings

Long ago the word "fool" was used as a term of endearment. We have an old-fashioned fondness for the recipes in which fruit is combined with cream.
I. With Fresh Fruit
Prepare:

>   **Raspberries or strawberries**

Add to taste:

>   **Powdered sugar**

Let the mixture stand for 10 minutes. Now combine with an equal amount of:

>   **Thick cream**

Flavored with:

>   **(3 tablespoons kirsch, port or Madeira wine)**

Chill well before serving.

II. With Cooked Fruit
Whip until stiff:

>   **1 cup heavy cream**

Fold in:

>   **1 cup applesauce, rhubarb, berry, apricot, currant or other fruit purée**
>   **1½ teaspoons grated lemon rind or ¼ teaspoon almond extract**

Place the mixture in the bowl from which it is to be served. Sprinkle the top with:

>   **Crumbled macaroons**

Chill thoroughly. Serve with:

>   **(Ladyfingers, page 633)**

ABOUT COOKED FRUITS

A good reason for serving fruits uncooked is to retain fully their high vitamin content. But we can minimize the loss of vitamins and of natural sugars by using as little water as possible and by cooking briefly. Fruits may be poached, puréed, baked, broiled, sautéed or pickled, see Spiced Sirup, opposite.

Fruits should always be poached rather than stewed. ◆ Drop them into a boiling liquid ◆ reduce the heat at once and simmer until barely tender. Remove them from the heat and drain them immediately afterwards, so that they will not continue to cook in the pan and get mushy. Soft, very juicy fruits, like ripe peaches, are best poached if they are put, for a few moments, into heavy boiling sirup and if the pan is then plunged into a larger pan of cold water to arrest the cooking. Apples and other hard fruits should be poached in simmering water. Watch closely, so that they do not overcook. If necessary, add sugar, but only after poaching. A baked fruit compote or a mixture of cooked fruits makes a refreshing addition to a meat course, provided that fruit juices have not been used in basting the meat. Always pare fruit with a ◆ stainless knife to keep from discoloring.

SIRUPS FOR FRUIT
Thin Sirup
For apples, grapes and rhubarb.
Combine and heat:

>   **1 cup sugar**
>   **3 cups water**
>   **¹⁄₁₆ teaspoon salt**

Medium Sirup
For apricots, cherries, grapefruit, pears and prunes.
Combine and heat:

>   **1 cup sugar**
>   **2 cups water**
>   **⅛ teaspoon salt**

Heavy Sirup
For berries, figs, peaches and plums.
Combine and heat:

>   **1 cup sugar**
>   **1 cup water**
>   **⅛ teaspoon salt**

SPICED SIRUP FOR FRESH FRUITS
Enough for 1 to 1½ Pints Fruit
Tie in a cheesecloth bag:

>   **1½ teaspoons each cloves, allspice and cinnamon**

Add and boil for 5 minutes:

>   **1½ cups white or brown sugar or 2 cups honey**
>   **1 cup cider vinegar**
>   **1 cup water**

Remove the spice bag and discard. Drop the prepared fruit into the boiling sirup. Cool and serve.

SPICED SIRUP FOR CANNED FRUITS
Drain and reserve the sirup from:

>   **Canned peaches, apricots, pears or pineapple**

Measure the sirup and ◆ simmer until slightly reduced with:

>   **¼ to ½ as much wine vinegar**

Allow for every 2 cups of juice and vinegar:

>   **1 stick cinnamon**
>   **½ teaspoon cloves without heads**
>   **(2 or 3 pieces gingerroot)**

After simmering for about 10 minutes, add fruit. Remove the pan from the heat and allow the fruit to cool in the liquid. Serve hot or cold with meat.

POACHED OR "STEWED" PARED FRUIT
Boil for 3 minutes:
>Any sirup for Fruit, page 106

Drop, into the boiling sirup, about:
>1 quart prepared fruit

♦ Reduce the heat at once. Poach gently until tender. You may season the sirup with either of the following:
>Spices
>Crème de Menthe
>Wine
>Stick cinnamon
>Slice of lemon

Drain fruit and reduce sirup. Pour sirup over fruit and chill before serving.

POACHED OR "STEWED" THIN-SKINNED FRUIT
By adding the sugar late in the cooking as suggested here, you will need less of it to sweeten the same quantity of fruit than if you had used it from the start. This method will also keep the skin soft.
Boil:
>2 cups water

Prepare and add:
>1 quart unpared fruit: peaches, pears, apricots or nectarines

Reduce heat at once. Simmer fruit until nearly tender. Add:
>½ to ¾ cup sugar

During the last few minutes of cooking, add:
>(A Vanilla Bean, page 528)

POACHED OR "STEWED" THICK-SKINNED FRUIT
Use whole or cut into halves and remove the seeds from:
>4 cups thick-skinned fruit: plums, blueberries or cherries

Drop them into:
>1 to 1½ cups boiling water

Reduce heat at once. ♦ Simmer until nearly tender. Add:
>½ to 1 cup sugar

Cook a few minutes longer. ♦ After cooking blueberries, to which lemon juice is a good addition, shake the container to avoid clumping.

BAKED FRESH FRUIT COMPOTE
4 Servings
Use as is or as a garnish for custard or blancmange.
Preheat oven to 350°
Pare:
>8 small peaches, apples or pears

Place them whole or in thick slices in a baking dish. Combine, heat but do not boil, stir and pour over them:
>⅔ cup red wine or water
>⅔ cup sugar

>½ stick cinnamon
>4 whole cloves
>⅛ teaspoon salt
>½ thinly sliced seeded lemon or lime

Bake the fruit either covered or uncovered until tender when tested with a fork. If cooked uncovered ♦ it must be basted every 10 minutes. For more rapid and even cooking, some people prefer to turn the fruit over after the first two bastings.

ADDITIONS TO BAKED FRUITS
I. To be served with meats. Fill centers of fruits with:
>Mint, currant or cranberry jelly or Roquefort cheese

II. Add:
>Pearl onions and shredded candied ginger

PURÉED FRUITS
Puréed fruits are most delicate if cooked covered over gentle heat. ♦ We do not recommend pressure cooking of any fresh fruits. Apples, rhubarb and cranberries, especially, tend to sputter and obstruct the vent during cooking. However, should you be tempted to use a pressure cooker, do not remove the cover until all steam is exhausted. ♦ If you want to purée canned fruit, you should know that a No. 2½ can will yield 1¼ to 1½ cups.

GARNISHES FOR PURÉED FRUITS
Serve puréed fruit hot or cold, with one of the following toppings:
>Grated lemon rind, cinnamon or nutmeg and cream
>Chestnuts and marmalade
>6 crushed dry macaroons to 1 cup whipped cream
>Cultured sour cream, sugar, rum and nuts
>Bread or cake crumbs browned in butter with slivered chopped almonds
>Freshly chopped mint

BROILED FRUITS
Drain:
>Poached or canned peaches, pears or pineapple

Place them, hollow side up, in a shallow pan. Place in each hollow:
>A dab of butter

Sprinkle each piece of fruit lightly with:
>Salt and cinnamon

Broil the fruits under moderate heat until light brown. You may fill them with:
>(Cranberry or other jelly)

FRESH FRUIT KEBABS
Serve with meat course or as a dessert.
Marinate for about 30 minutes:
>6 canned peach halves—drained and cut in half
>3 thickly sliced bananas

2 apples, cut in sections
1 cubed fresh pineapple
3 sectioned grapefruits

in:

1 cup grapefruit juice
½ cup honey
2 tablespoons Cointreau
(1 teaspoon chopped mint)

Broil on skewers for about 5 minutes, basting often with the marinade.

ABOUT FLAMBÉING FRUITS

For a good effect, use at least 2 oz. of alcoholic liquor and remember that ♦ unless the temperature of the fruit is at least 75°, you may not get any effect at all. For best results, heat the fruit ♦ mildly in a ♦ covered chafing dish or electric skillet. ♦ Warm the liquor, too, but do not boil it. Sprinkle the fruit lightly with sugar and, after pouring the warm liquor over the warm fruit, re-cover the pan for a moment before lighting. Stand back—be careful.

FLAMBÉED FRUITS

This recipe makes 6 servings as a sauce, but only 3 if used as a main dessert dish. Caramelize, page 507, lightly over low heat:

3 tablespoons sugar

Add:

3 tablespoons butter

or, if you are lazy, melt the butter first and substitute brown sugar, stirring until dissolved. Cook over very low heat for 4 to 5 minutes. Add 2 of the following:

3 split bananas, peaches or
pears or 3 slices pineapple

Simmer until tender, basting occasionally. Since the banana will cook more rapidly than the rest of the fruit, it should be added later. Flambé the fruit, see above, with:

2 oz. cognac, dark rum or liqueur

FRUIT BRÛLÉ

4 to 5 Servings

This recipe is most often made with seedless green grapes, but it lends itself equally well to strawberries, raspberries and peaches.

Preheat broiler.

Fill the bottom of a 9-inch ovenproof baker or glass pie pan with an even layer of one of the above mentioned:

Fruits

Cover the fruit with:

1 cup cultured sour cream

mixed with:

1 teaspoon vanilla

The cream should then be dusted very evenly with:

About 1 cup light brown sugar

so that none of it shows through. Place the filled pan over a pan of equal size filled with:

Cracked ice

Put the stacked pans under the hot broiler until the sugar caramelizes, page 686. This is a moment of watchfulness, as the sugar must fuse but not scorch. Refrigerate, covered, for 5 hours before serving.

SAUTÉED FRUITS

Core and slice or cut in rings:

6 tart, well-flavored apples, peaches,
apricots or pineapple slices

Melt in a skillet over quick heat:

2 tablespoons butter or bacon
drippings

When the fat is hot, to the point of fragrance, fold in the fruit. Cover until steaming. Sprinkle with:

½ cup sugar or brown sugar
⅛ teaspoon salt

Cook, uncovered, over gentle heat until tender. Add, if needed:

(Butter)

Serve with a meat course or with:

Bacon

To serve with meat, you may begin making this dish by placing a layer of onions, about 1 cup, in the butter. Cook slowly for 5 minutes. Season with salt and paprika. Add the fruit, as directed.

CURRIED FRUIT

Fruit in season may be dipped into or served in a two-way hot sauce—hot with both spice and heating. Cut into cubes or finger-size sections:

4 doz. pieces of fruit—pineapple,
tropical mangoes, bananas, melons
and papaya

Combine and simmer, covered, for ½ hour:

1 cup chicken broth
1 cup dry white wine
1 tablespoon curry

Add:

1 tablespoon quick-cooking tapioca

dissolved in:

3 tablespoons water

Stir the sauce until thickened. Add:

1 cup freshly grated coconut
1 cup slivered, toasted almonds
½ cup white raisins

Keep the sauce hot in a chafing dish and add the fruit pieces or place them alongside as dippers.

ABOUT COOKED DRIED FRUITS

Do not wash or soak dried fruits unless it is called for on the package. The less water used, the more natural sugars will be retained within the fruit. If you must soak fruit such as dried apples, cover with water for about 12 hours and then use the soaking water in further preparation. Allow 1 pound dried for 3½ to 4 pounds fresh apples and proceed as for any apple recipe. In using dried dates, raisins and currants, see Ingredients, page 521-522.

Fine quality dried dessert fruits are an elegant note on the cheese platter, especially dried Malaga grapes. Only a few are needed, as they are nutritively rich, see page 521. Should any of the fruits have become unpleasantly dried out, steam them lightly—sprinkled with wine or water—in the top of a double boiler ♦ over—not in—hot water; or, prepare them for stuffing by steaming 10 to 15 minutes in a colander ♦ over boiling water, until tender enough to pit. Stuff with a hazelnut or with fillings suggested under confections, page 739. If you would like to use some of the smaller, drier types, do not wash or soak them unless it is called for on the package. The less water used in steaming—either for eating uncooked or processing for compote—the more natural sugar will be retained. Often no further sweetening is necessary.

ABOUT FRUITS FOR MEATS AND ENTRÉES

Fruit Compotes, page 105, Fruit Kebabs, page 107, Sautéed Fruits, page 108, or Pickled Fruits, pages 122, 786, served with meat are neglected delights. Consider using as occasional decorative fruit garnishes:

    Apple Rings
    Glazed Filled Apricots
    Kumquats
    Orange Slices with Cranberry
    or other jelly
    Ornamental Cranberries
    Filled Apples and the Filled Fruit
    Cases, page 223, stuffed with Farces,
    page 458

ABOUT FRUIT SOUPS

Soups of cooked fruit juice combinations, with cherries, orange slices or puréed fruits added, are delightful at the beginning or end of a summer meal. If served at the beginning, go easy on the sugar. Fruit soups are also refreshing when made from frozen fruits, in winter, as a dessert.

FRUIT SOUP COCKAIGNE

4 Servings

This good German fruit pudding, Rote Gruetze, long popular in our family, is usually made with raspberry juice. It is designed to end a meal, not, like the less sweet Fruit Soups, page 149, to begin it.

Strawberries, cherries or black currants may be used, but our favorite base is a combination of raspberry and strawberry juice, which may be strengthened with raspberry jelly or red wine. A wonderful fresh taste may be obtained in winter, if you cook frozen raspberries and strawberries and strain off the juice.

Bring to a boil:
    2 cups fruit juice
Sweeten it palatably with:
    Sugar
Season with:
    ⅛ teaspoon salt
Stir into the boiling juice:
    2 to 2⅔ tablespoons tapioca
Cook this mixture in the top of a double boiler ♦ over—not in—hot water for about 20 minutes. Stir until it thickens. Pour into individual serving dishes. Chill. Serve very cold with:
    Heavy cream

ORANGE FRUIT SOUP

6 Servings

Scrub and remove the orange-colored peel in shreds from:
    1 Valencia or navel orange
Add these peelings to a sirup of:
    1 cup sugar
    ½ cup currant jelly
    ¼ cup water
♦ Simmer for about 15 minutes. Meanwhile, section the peeled orange, page 116, and also:
    5 more peeled Valencia or
    navel oranges
♦ Cool the sirup to about 85°. Pour it over the orange sections. Add:
    2 tablespoons brandy
♦ Refrigerate, covered, for about 12 hours, before serving with:
    A crisp thin Ice Box Cookie, page
    659, or a Curled Cookie, page 666
Also good with:
    Cinnamon toast

INDIVIDUAL FRUITS

In the following pages we list various kinds of fruits, describing their particular charms and various ways to store and handle them. The exotic fruits shown on this page include, reading from left to right: the pomegranate, avocado, papaya, tropical mango and the oriental persimmon.

Above are sketched from left to right: figs, tamarind pods, akees, two forms of cherimoya, a guava, lichee nuts and a mangosteen.

PURÉED AKEE
3 Servings

Blighia sapida, named after the infamous Colonel Bligh, is one of the most strikingly beautiful, delicious and demanding of fruits for, unless it has ripened to the point of voluntary opening, it is a deadly poison. No fallen, discolored or unripe fruit dare be eaten and the greatest care must be used to ♦ remove all seeds before cooking, as these are always poisonous. When picked ripe, hulled and completely seeded, the akee is parboiled for use hot or cold. See illustration, above.

Remove the white pods from:

6 firm unbruised open akees

Discard every seed. Place the pods in:

Boiling water

to cover. ♦ Reduce the heat at once and simmer gently until soft. Strain and mash them until coarsely crushed. Season with:

Salt and pepper
(Grated Parmesan cheese)
(Toasted chopped cashews)

Although akee is technically a fruit it is served hot or cold with meats or fish like a vegetable.

ABOUT APPLES

Although apples are in the market the year around, they are not at their peak from January to June. The best month-to-month varieties are listed below. Check them and then turn to the next paragraphs which will tell you how to use the available apples at their prime. There is probably no flavor superior to that of the Greenups or Transparents, that fleetingly initiate the harvest. If you plan canning or freezing, do try to get the first picking for prompt preservation of this unusual tart flavor.

July to August: Early McIntosh, Gravenstein, Yellow Transparent
August to November: Wealthy
September to December: Grimes Golden
September to January: Jonathan, Late McIntosh
October to April: Red Delicious, Golden Delicious
October to January: Courtland, York Imperial, Rhode Island Greening
November to April: Newtown Pippin, Baldwin, Rome Beauty
December to March: Northern Spy, Stayman, Winesap
December to May: Winesaps

All-purpose apple varieties—good for eating, salads and for most cooking—are Yellow Transparent, Baldwin, Jonathan, Stayman, Winesap, Northern Spy, Wealthy, McIntosh, Gravenstein, Grimes Golden, York Imperial and Rhode Island Greening, which cooks best of all. So-called dessert apples—the firm types, most desirable for eating uncooked—are Delicious, Gold and Red Delicious and Newtown Pippin. Northern Spys, Wealthys and McIntoshes are not good bakers. ♦ Best for this purpose are Courtlands, Staymans, Winesaps, Baldwins and Rome Beautys, unless they are overripe. In that condition they become mealy.

Mealiness in apples may also denote too long or improper storage. Large apples tend to acquire greater mealiness during storage. If browning occurs near the core, the fruit has been stored at too low a temperature.

If you wonder why the apple in commercial pies has a firmer texture than yours, it is due to added calcium. If you notice also a more powerful apple flavor, this may be caused by the addition of a rather new product, made from the apple itself. If the flavor of your apples is poor, add lemon juice—but remember that nothing can really compensate for natural tartness. After paring, should apples seem dry, simmer their cores and skins, reduce the liquid and use it to moisten them during cooking.

If you receive a windfall from a friend's orchard and want to reserve some of it, let it stand in a cool, shady place for 24 hours. Inspect for blemishes. Wrap each fruit in paper and store in slotted boxes in a cool, dark, airy place.

The old saw about the doctor and the daily apple has been reinforced by recent discoveries. Raw apple, we now learn, has properties which help the digestive juices kill germs in the stomach; and dentists like apples as a tooth-cleaning aid. So keep them around for family munching.

For Fried Apples, see below. For other apple recipes, see below and the Index.

APPLE RINGS

Wash, core and cut crosswise into slices:

3 large, perfect cooking apples

Heat in a skillet:

3 tablespoons bacon fat or butter

Place in it a single layer of apple rings. Sprinkle lightly with:

Powdered sugar

Add to the skillet:

2 tablespoons water

Cover the skillet and ♦ simmer the apples until tender. Remove cover and brown rings on both sides. Serve hot, the centers filled with:

Bright red jelly

or dust the rings with:

Cinnamon

HONEY APPLES

An excellent way to use a dull-flavored apple. Heat in a small porcelain or stainless steel pan:

1 cup honey
½ cup vinegar

Peel, core and slice thinly:

2 cups apples

Drop the apples a few at a time into the simmering, bubbling honey mixture. Skim them out when transparent. Serve chilled or hot as a relish with pork, a tart filling, or a dessert with cream.

★ CINNAMON APPLES OR PEARS
4 Servings

Pare and core without cutting through the stem end:

4 baking apples or pears

Stir and boil in a saucepan until dissolved:

½ cup sugar
1 cup water
¼ cup cinnamon drops

Add the fruit slowly, one at a time. ♦ Simmer gently until tender. Test with a straw. Remove from sirup. Fill hollows with:

(Blanched almonds or other nut
meats and raisins)

Boil the sirup until it falls heavily from a spoon. Pour it over the apples. Chill.

SAUTÉED APPLES AND BACON
4 Servings

A fine breakfast or luncheon dish. Pare:

Tart winter apples

Cut them into cubes. There should be about 4 cups. Sauté in a heavy skillet, see page 128:

8 slices bacon

Remove the bacon when crisp. Keep it hot. Leave about 2 tablespoons of grease in the skillet. Add:

2 tablespoons cooking oil

Add the apples. Sauté uncovered over high heat until translucent. Sprinkle them with:

2 tablespoons white or brown sugar

Place them on a hot platter. Surround them

with the bacon. Serve garnished with:

Parsley

BAKED APPLES
I.
4 Servings

Preheat oven to 375°.

Wash, remove core to ½ inch of bottoms, then cut a strip of peel from the hollowed ends of:

4 large tart apples

Combine:

¼ cup sugar or brown sugar
(1 tablespoon cinnamon)

If the apples are bland, add:

(⅛ teaspoon grated lemon rind)

Fill the centers with this. Dot the tops with:

Butter

Put in an 8 x 8-inch pan with:

¾ cup boiling water
(2 tablespoons sugar)

Cover and bake forty to sixty minutes—or until tender but not mushy. Top the core holes with a:

(Marshmallow)

After removing from the heat, baste the apples several times with pan juices. Serve hot or chilled.

II.

Obviously a richer dish than that produced by recipe I.

Preheat oven to 425°.

Peel and core:

6 apples

Fill the cores with a mixture of:

½ cup chopped blanched almonds
or pecans
½ cup sugar
2 tablespoons raisins
(1 egg white)

Make another mixture of:

½ cup fine bread crumbs
2 tablespoons sugar
1 teaspoon cinnamon

Coat the apples with:

6 tablespoons melted butter

Roll them in the bread crumbs. Bake the apples in individual buttered bakers for about 25 minutes. Serve hot, covered with:

Caramelized Sugar, page 507

or cold with:

Cream

APPLES STUFFED WITH SAUERKRAUT
4 Servings

Preheat oven to 375°.

Pare the tops of:

4 large baking apples

Remove the pulp and discard the core, leaving a ½-inch shell. Chop the pulp, add to it:

2 cups drained canned or
cooked sauerkraut
⅛ teaspoon pepper
¼ teaspoon caraway seeds
Salt, as needed

Fill the shells. Place them in a dish with
¼ cup water or dry wine. Bake until
tender. Baste frequently.

BAKED APPLES FILLED WITH SAUSAGE MEAT

6 Servings

A 3-star winter dish.
Preheat oven to 375°.
Wash:

6 large tart apples

Cut a slice from the tops. Scoop out the
cores and pulp, leaving shells ¾ inch
thick. Cut the pulp from the cores and
chop it. Combine it with:

1 cup well-seasoned sausage meat or
sausage links

Sprinkle the shells with:

1 teaspoon salt
(2 tablespoons brown sugar)

Fill them heaping full with the sausage
mixture. Bake until tender. Serve with:

Potatoes or rice

or place them around a mound of:

Boiled Noodles, page 188

APPLESAUCE

♦ Please read About Puréed Fruits, page
107.
Wash, cut into quarters and core:

Apples

Place them in a saucepan and partly cover
them with water. Old apples require more
water than new ones. ♦ Simmer the apples
until tender. Put them through a purée
strainer or ricer or ⅃ blend, skin and all.
Return the strained apple pulp to the
saucepan. Add enough:

Sugar

to make it palatable. Cook gently for
about 3 minutes. Add to tasteless apples:

Sliced lemon or lemon juice

Canned applesauce may be seasoned in
the same way. Sprinkle it, if desired, with:

Cinnamon

Serve hot or cold. If served hot, add:

1 or 2 teaspoons butter

If served cold, add:

½ teaspoon vanilla or a few drops
almond extract

If it is to be served with pork, add:

1 or 2 tablespoons horseradish

You may also combine:

2 cups applesauce
1 cup puréed apricots or raspberries

or:

2 cups applesauce
1 cup crushed pineapple
1 teaspoon finely crushed
preserved ginger

CRANBERRY APPLESAUCE

Combine and stir:

2 cups cranberries
2 cups quartered apples
¾ cup water

Cook these ingredients slowly until the
fruit is soft. Put them all through a colander. Add:

1 cup sugar

Cook and stir the purée until the sugar is
dissolved. Sprinkle with:

Grated orange rind

ABOUT FRESH APRICOTS

Fresh apricots have a beautiful blush and
should be firm in texture. If they appear
wilted or shriveled, they lack flavor and
will decay quickly. Eat apricots raw or
cook them in a very light sirup and serve
them flambéed in Meringues, page 600.

DRIED APRICOTS

10 Servings

Place in a heavy pan:

1 lb. dried apricots
3 cups water

Simmer the fruit for about 35 minutes.
Add:

(½ to 1 cup sugar)

Heat until the sugar is dissolved, about 5
minutes longer.

ABOUT AVOCADOS

A native of America, this valuable fruit
harbors no less than 11 vitamins, including
large quantities of vitamin C. Buy it
slightly underripe and mature it at 70°,
hastening the process, if you like, by en-
closing it in a paper bag. The high and
perishable vitamin C content causes rapid
discoloration when the flesh of the avocado is exposed. To forestall browning,
sprinkle it with citrus or pineapple juice.
If using only half an avocado, keep the
unused part unpeeled, with the seed still
embedded in it, wrap it in foil and store at
a temperature between 40° and 70°. When
combining avocado with cooked foods
♦ add the last moment, away from heat.

BAKED AVOCADOS STUFFED WITH CREAMED FOOD

Preheat oven to 375°.
Cut into halves:

Avocados

Place in each half:

1 tablespoon Garlic Vinegar, page 496

Permit to stand for ½ hour. Empty the
shells. Fill them with hot creamed, well-
seasoned:

Crab, lobster, shrimp, chicken,
ham, etc.

Use ¼ as much sauce as filling. Place
them on waxed or buttered paper. Cover
the tops with:

Grated cheese, buttered crumbs
or cornflakes

Bake until just heated through.

ABOUT BANANAS

Cook all bananas called plantains, page
289. Others, picked green, are matured by

special moist processing, before reaching
the point of sale. They make beautiful arrangements while green, but should not be
eaten until further ripened by holding
them at 70° in a closed paper bag until
yellow in color. Once cut, they darken
rapidly and should be sprinkled with citrus
or pineapple juice.

As a rule use slightly underripe bananas
for cooking, except in Banana Bread.

▤ BAKED BANANAS
I. Preheat oven to 375°.
Bananas may be baked in their skins in
oven or on outdoor grill for about 20 min-
utes. On opening, sprinkle with:
Lemon juice
Confectioners' sugar
Salt

II.   2 Servings
This is a candied version.
Preheat oven to 375°.
In a small saucepan, melt together and
boil for about 5 minutes:
½ cup dark brown sugar
¼ cup water
Peel, slice in half the long way and then
laterally and place in a shallow buttered
dish:
1½ to 2 slightly underripe bananas
Sprinkle with:
Salt
Add to the cooled sirup:
Juice of ½ lemon or 1 lime
Pour the sirup over the bananas and bake
for about 30 minutes, turning the fruit
after the first 15 minutes. Serve on hot
dessert plates, sprinkled with:
Rum
Chopped candied ginger

BANANAS IN BLANKETS
Good as a breakfast dish or served with a
meat course.
Preheat broiler.
Cut into lengthwise halves:
Firm, ripe bananas
Place between the halves:
Canned pineapple sticks
Wrap the bananas with:
Slices of bacon
Broil in a pan, turning frequently until the
bacon is crisp

CARIBBEAN BANANA
For each serving, melt in a skillet:
1 tablespoon butter
Peel and split lengthwise:
A moderately ripe banana
Simmer the banana gently in the butter,
first on one side, then on the other. Baste
with:
2 tablespoons Sauce Cockaigne,
page 709
(A dash of lime juice)
Serve on a hot plate, flambé, page 127,
with:

Rum
and garnish with:
(A kumquat and sprig of
lemon thyme)
or, after flambéing the bananas, garnish
with:
Vanilla ice cream

ABOUT BERRIES
Strawberries, when ripe, keep their green
cap intact, but all other berries, when mature, come loose from the hull. Good color
is usually a test of prime condition, except
for cranberries, which differ in color, depending on variety. Currants, in their
dried form, taste delicious when used as a
garnish in or on sweet breads. Otherwise
these fruits, along with barberries and
gooseberries, are of interest chiefly for preserving. Gooseberries, when ripe, are a
light amber in color. Remember in preserving, see page 772, that the less ripe
berries contain more pectin. Store ripe
berries immediately in the refrigerator,
covered, unwashed and unstemmed. Do
not crowd or press.

For an attractive way to serve out of
doors, make some berry cones. We saw
them first in the shadows of the rain forest in Puerto Rico, where we were greeted
beside a waterfall by children with wild
berries in leaf cones, held in punctured
box tops. Glorify your box top with foil.

FRESH SELF-GARNISHED BERRIES
Clean:
1 quart berries
Reserve ⅔ and chill. Rub the remaining
⅓ through a sieve or blend, if using strawberries. Sweeten the pulp and juice with:
Powdered sugar
and stir until well dissolved. Serve the
whole berries chilled and garnished with
the sweetened pulp.

BERRIES WITH CREAM
Serve:
Unhulled berries
Arrange them on the plate around mounds
of:
White or brown sugar or shaved
maple sugar

Pass a dish of:
   Cultured sour cream, yogurt or whipped cream

FRESH STRAWBERRY VARIATIONS
Place in fruit cocktail glasses:
   Sliced strawberries
Simmer for 10 minutes equal parts of:
   Orange juice
   Strawberry juice
with:
   ¼ as much sugar or as much as is palatable
Chill the sirup. Season it well with:
   Sherry or kirsch
Add:
   Shaved ice
Or cover:
   Chilled strawberries
with:
   Chilled pineapple juice
Add, if needed:
   Confectioners' sugar
Or, sprinkle berries lightly with:
   Lemon juice
   Confectioners' sugar
Decorate fruit with:
   Mint leaves

STRAWBERRIES ROMANOFF
Prepare:
   2 quarts sugared strawberries
Whip slightly:
   1 pint ice cream
Fold into the ice cream:
   1 cup whipped cream
Add:
   6 tablespoons Cointreau
Blend the cream and the strawberries ♦ very lightly. Serve immediately.

BLUEBERRIES OR HUCKLEBERRIES
Pick before the dew is off:
   Huckleberries
which are richer in flavor than blueberries.
To cook, see:
   Poached Thick-Skinned Fruit, page 107

CRANBERRY SAUCE OR JELLY
New England sea captains were early aware of the cranberry's worth as a preventive against scurvy. Cranberries are so packed with vitamin C that they may retain a high degree of nutritive value even after being stored fresh for a year or more. If you are a vitamin buff, you may actually find more of it in the canned version, for this fruit will probably have been processed very soon after picking. Color differences in fresh cranberries have to do with variety, not with relative age. Wash and pick over:
   4 cups cranberries: 1 lb.
Place them in a saucepan. Cover with:
   2 cups boiling water
As soon as the water begins to boil again,
cover the saucepan with a lid. Boil the berries for 3 or 4 minutes or until the skins burst. Put them through a strainer or ricer. Stir into the juice:
   2 cups sugar
Place the juice over heat and bring it to a rolling boil. If you want cranberry sauce, remove at once. If you want to mold the cranberry jelly, boil for about 5 minutes, skim, then pour it into a wet mold. The cooking periods indicated are right for firm berries. Very ripe berries require a few minutes longer.

SPICED CRANBERRY JELLY
Prepare:
   Cranberry Jelly, above
adding to the water:
   2 inches stick cinnamon
   2 whole cloves
   ¼ teaspoon salt

WHOLE CRANBERRY SAUCE
Place in a saucepan and stir until the sugar is dissolved:
   2 cups water
   2 cups sugar
Boil the sirup for 5 minutes. Pick over, wash and add:
   4 cups cranberries: 1 lb.
Simmer the cranberries in the sirup ♦ uncovered, very gently without stirring, until the sauce is thick, about 5 minutes. Skim. Add:
   (2 teaspoons grated orange rind)
Pour the cranberries into 1 large or several individual molds which have been rinsed in cold water. Chill until firm. Unmold to serve.

UNCOOKED CRANBERRY RELISH
This relish is to be served like a compote. Grind:
   4 cups cranberries
Remove the seeds, then grind:
   1 whole orange
You may prefer to use only the yellow portion of the orange skin, as the white is often bitter. Stir into the cranberries the orange and:
   2 cups sugar
Place these ingredients in covered jars in the refrigerator. Let them ripen for 2 days before using. Serve the relish with meat or fowl or on bread.

ABOUT CHERIMOYA
The nineteenth century traveler, Humboldt, who left his scientific imprint over South America and Mexico, declared that this fruit is worth a trip across the Atlantic. It must be tree-ripened but still firm when picked and should be handled carefully so as to avoid bruising. Some-

times called custard apple, sherbet fruit or
sweetsop, this fruit shows on its light green
skin jacquarded engravings or longish
bumps. Discard the hard black seeds
which occur at random in the pulp, see
illustration on page 110.

ABOUT CHERRIES

Mark Twain claimed that we women
could, if given enough time and hairpins,
build a battleship. Hairpins, also mighty
useful as cherry-pitters, are growing
scarce. You may then prefer to substitute
a fresh, strong pen-point, inserted in a
clean holder. Whether pitted or not, cherries remain great favorites, especially the
dark Bing and Queen Anne, both sweet,
and the incomparable Tartarian pie cherries.
I. For Stewed Cherries, see page 107.

II. Cook until tender but still shapely,
page 107:
      Pitted sweet cherries
To each pound, allow:
      ½ cup currant jelly
melted in:
      ¼ cup kirsch or other liqueur
Drain the cherries. Reserve the juice for
pudding sauce or use it in basting meats
or in baking. Shake the drained cherries
in the jelly mixture until well coated. Chill
and serve.

ABOUT CITRUS FRUITS

ORANGES

The day, for many of us, begins with
oranges, which we often casually classify as
"juicers" or "eaters." Valencias, Temples,
Kings and blood oranges yield the sweetest
juice. For eating straight, try navel
oranges, one of the many tangerine types,
or tangelos, which are a cross between tangerine and grapefruit. For meat and fish
cooking, for garnishes, marmalades or
drinks, use Aurantium Seville, the bitter
orange, if available. For other garnishes,
watch the market for kumquats and calamondins. Although these smaller orange
types are more popular preserved, page
742, they are charmingly decorative when
fresh. Do not be misled by the color of
orange skin. Some of the best-flavored
fruit is green or russet, unless specially
dipped.

GRAPEFRUIT

The main types are whitish or pink-
fleshed. Late in the season, the skin may
change in tint from yellowish to greenish,
a sign of real maturity and high sugar content. But beware of late season grapefruit
if it seems unduly light in weight or if the
skins are puffy, for the flesh may then be
dry. ♦ Always chill grapefruit at once. It
will not ripen after picking and keeps better at lower temperatures.

To section grapefruit, remove the outer
skin, pull into halves, and split the membrane as shown. Pull the membrane parallel with the outer edge to the base of the
section. The segment may break but virtually none of the juice is lost. You may
prefer the method shown for oranges, page
116.

SWEETENED GRAPEFRUIT
                                 4 Servings
Peel, section and chill:
      2 large grapefruit
Place the fruit in cocktail glasses. Fifteen
minutes before serving, sprinkle it lightly
with:
      Confectioners' sugar
Immediately before serving, add to each
glass:
      (1 tablespoon Cointreau)
or fill each glass ¼ full of:
      Chilled orange juice

GRAPEFRUIT CUPS
I. Chill:
      Grapefruit
Cut in halves. Loosen the pulp from the
peel with a sharp-toothed, curved grapefruit knife or remove the seeds and cut out
the tough fibrous center with a grapefruit
corer. Five minutes before serving, sprinkle the grapefruit with:
      Confectioners' sugar
Add to each half immediately before serving:
      **1 tablespoon curaçao or a Crystallized
      Mint Leaf**

II. Preheat broiler to 350°.
Prepare:
      Grapefruit Cups, above
When grapefruit is very ripe it is inadvisable to loosen the pulp from the peel, as it
makes the fruit too juicy. Sprinkle each
half with:
      1 tablespoon or more sugar
Run the fruit under the broiler. When the
grapefruit is hot, pour over each half:
      1 tablespoon dry sherry
Serve the fruit at once.

KUMQUATS AND CALOMONDINS

These citrus fruits, oval in shape and a little less than two inches long, have largish
seeds and a distinctively bittersweet flavor.
Calomondins are a cross between a kum-

quat and a tangerine. They may be eaten raw, without paring. Use them as a garnish for meat. Parboil, unpeeled, for 5 minutes:

Kumquats

Drain and cool. Slice the top off of each. Remove seeds and fill each fruit with:

½ teaspoon sugar

Stand upright in a shallow buttered pan. Bake for about 15 minutes in a preheated 350° oven, basting frequently with:

Pineapple juice

For Preserved Kumquats, see page 742.

LEMONS

How could we ever get on without this versatile and delicious fruit? Many uses for juice and rind are indicated in individual recipes. For Beverages, see page 26, for flavoring suggestions and for use against the discoloration of fresh fruits and vegetables, see page 762. To cut it for use as a garnish, see below. · For **Limes,** see page 614.

POACHED ORANGES

6 Servings

Wash and cut into halves or thick crosswise slices:

3 navel oranges

Place them in a saucepan. Pour over them:

Boiling water to cover

◗ Simmer for 1 hour. Drain well. Discard the water. Cook for 5 minutes:

1 cup sugar
1¼ cups water
3 tablespoons lemon juice

Place the oranges in the sirup. Cook until tender, for about 1 hour. Place in a jar with the sirup. Keep in a cold place until ready to use. The centers may be slightly hollowed and filled with:

Crushed pineapple, chopped nut meats, maraschino cherries or a dab of tart jelly

Good served with baked ham, spoon bread and a green salad.

TO SECTION AN ORANGE

Wash and dry:

An orange

Hold the fruit over a bowl to catch all the juices and use a sharp knife to remove the

rind and the white skin. Pare it around and around like an apple so that the cells are exposed. Loosen the sections by cutting down along the membrane. Lift out the segment in one piece and remove any seeds. If the sections are large, use the method described for grapefruit, page 115.

ABOUT FIGS

When Cato advocated the conquest of Carthage, he used as his crowning argument the advantage of acquiring fruits as glorious as the North African figs, specimens of which he pulled from his toga as exhibits in the Roman Senate. These fruits have become so popular in America that many varieties—purplish, brownish and greenish—are grown in profusion. Even when shipped, they must be vine ripened. We grow a few ourselves; and every year we wonder how many will be spared us by the chipmunks and the frost, for making Antipasto with Prosciutto, page 71.

Fresh figs are very different from the dried ones we get from Smyrna and our South. They are ripe when soft to the touch and overripe when sour in odor, indicating a fermentation of the juice. See illustration, page 110. For dried fig confections, see page 738.

STUFFED FRESH FIGS

Fill stemmed fresh or canned:

Figs

with:

Cultured sour cream or Devonshire Cream

flavored with a touch of:

Grated orange peel

DRIED FIGS

Wash and remove the stems from:

1 lb. dried figs

Add:

> Cold water to cover well
> 1½ tablespoons lemon juice
> A piece of lemon rind
> (A large piece of gingerroot)

Stew the figs, covered, until they are soft and drain. Sweeten to taste with:

> Sugar: about 1 cup

Simmer the sirup until thick. Add:

> 1 tablespoon lemon juice

Replace the figs in the sirup. Cool. Add:

> (1 tablespoon dry sherry)

Chill and serve with:

> Cream

ABOUT GRAPES

For us, clusters of grapes, with their inimitable plastic charm, put the finishing touch to decorative fruit arrangements. Be sure to choose table varieties for eating raw. Best known of these are the pale green Thompson seedless, the white Malagas and Niagaras, the red Tokays, and Emperors. The latter feel quite hard, even when ripe. The blue Concords, the olive-shaped Cornichons and the late black Ribieros also look luscious. The fruits should be plump and have a bloom, the stems should not be brittle. When ripe for eating, grapes are highly perishable and should be stored refrigerated. Frost them, page 741, and serve in a fruit bowl or as a salad, page 83, or use seedless types as the foundation for a Brûlé Dessert, page 108.

GUAVAS

These fruits, when ripe, vary in color from white to dark red and in size from that of a walnut to that of an apple. They may be served puréed, baked or fresh, alone or in combination with other fruits such as bananas or pineapple. They have an exceptionally high vitamin content, much of which lies near the skin. Sprinkle:

> Peeled and sliced guavas

lightly with:

> Sugar

Chill and serve with:

> Cream

or bake in a 350° oven for about 30 minutes and then serve with the cream. See also Apple Cake Cockaigne page 606, and guava jelly with cream cheese, as for Bar le Duc, page 708.

TROPICAL MANGOES

These delicious flattish oval fruits are of a yellowish-green color, sometimes freckled with red or black and about 8 inches long. When chilled and eaten raw, they are as good as any peach-pineapple-apricot mousse you can concoct—rich and sweet but never cloying. If unchilled, they sometimes have an overtone of turpentine. The seed, which extends the length of the fruit, makes eating somewhat awkward, and special holders, not unlike those which bring corncobs under control, may be used. Pare, slice and serve mangoes on vanilla ice cream. Sauté ripe fruits. Use them when just mature in chutneys and when unripe for poaching or baking. If you want to freeze mangoes, see puréed fruits, page 762.

MANGOSTEEN

This 2- to 3-inch-diameter fruit has a most exquisite milky juice. Its sections—5 to 6 in number—may be easily scooped out and eaten with a spoon, see illustration on page 110.

MEDLARS

In Southern Europe these 2-inch fruits, which resemble crabapples, are eaten fresh-picked; but in England they are mellowed by frost and not attractive to look at, although the flavor is desirable, especially for jellies.

ABOUT MELONS

Melons are being developed into so many delicious strains that it is difficult to list them all by name. These fruits are usually eaten raw. The varieties can be served singly or in combination. Try a palette ranging from the pale greens of the honeydews, through the golden peach tones of the cantaloupes or cranshaws, to the blue-reds of the watermelon. They can be served from one end of a meal to the other in many attractive ways.

In order to be genuinely sweet—and this is one's perennial hope, as he bites into each fresh melon—the fruit must have matured on the vine. If it did, you will see that the scar at the stem end is slightly sunken and well calloused. The more fragrant the melon, the sweeter it will be. A watermelon, if truly ripe, will respond by giving up a thin green skin if scraped with a finger nail.

If you want to store melons for several days, keep them at 70°, away from sunlight and chill just before serving. To protect other food in your refrigerator from taking on a melon taste, cover the fruit with plastic or foil. Melons can be cut into highly decorative shapes. For an aspic-filled melon, see page 103, or cut Melon Baskets, as shown on the next page.

MELON BASKETS OR FRUIT CUPS
8 Servings

Cut into halves and remove the seeds from:

> 4 cantaloupes or other melons

Scallop the edges. Chill the fruit. Combine the following ingredients:

> 2 cups peeled, sliced oranges

2 cups peeled, sliced, fresh peaches
2 cups peeled, diced pineapple: fresh
    or canned
1 cup peeled, sliced bananas
(1 cup sugar, dissolved in the
    various fruit juices)
Chill thoroughly. Just before serving, fill
the cantaloupe cups with the fruit. Pour
over each cup:
    (1 tablespoon Cointreau or rum)
Top with:
    Orange and Lemon Ice, page 722, or
    Sherbet, page 723

MELON ROUNDS FILLED WITH RASPBERRIES OR STRAWBERRIES

Cut into 1- to 2-inch crosswise slices:
    Chilled honeydew melon or
    cantaloupe
Allow 1 slice for each person. Remove
seeds. Fill the centers with:
    Chilled, sugared raspberries or
    strawberries
Serve on individual plates with:
    Lime or lemon wedges
Melons are good sprinkled with ginger and
served with limes. Also see Melon Baskets,
above, for a decorative way to use melons.

SPIKED MELON

Cut a plug in the upper side of a:
    Melon
Dig out seeds and pulp with a long handled spoon. Pour in:
    ¾ to 1 cup port wine
Chill melon in ice in the refrigerator. Slice
and serve with rind removed and use the
marinating wine as a dressing.

ABOUT NECTARINES

This happy half-breed of plum and peach
can be used in any recipe calling for
peaches. It comes in both freestone and
cling types, but lacks the peach "fuzz."

PAWPAWS

These small native fruits should be picked
after the first heavy frost, individually
wrapped in tissue paper and stored in a
cool place until soft. A taste for them, we
feel, is an acquired one.

ABOUT PAPAYA

These fruits grow up to 20 inches in
length. When fully ripened, the flesh develops orangey tones and the greenish rind
turns soft and yellow. They are eaten like
melons. Their milky juice, when chilled
makes a pleasant drink. Their black seeds
which contain pepsin, are used for garnish
eaten raw or used as for capers. Many of
us know this plant only by its derivative
papain, the tenderizer made from the en
zymes of its leaves, page 383.
    Use underripe fruits for cooking. Process
as for summer squash types, page 383. I
serving papaya raw, chill and sprinkle with
lime or lemon juice. See sketch, page 109

ABOUT PEACHES

Choose firm but well-colored fruit—no
green ones. When plucked green peache
will not ripen. They merely soften and
wither, gaining nothing in flavor.
    In cooking, a few seeds are sometime
added to strengthen the flavor, but the
inner almond-like nut should never be
eaten, as it is high in prussic acid.

FILLED PEACHES

6 Servings

Peel and halve:
    4 chilled peaches
Place them in a bowl. Combine and stir:
    2 cups chilled berries
    6 tablespoons sugar
    1½ tablespoons lemon juice
If you live in a semi-tropical climate, try
adding a few fresh green almonds. Pour the
berries over the peaches. Serve with:
    Whipped cream

ABOUT PEARS

All pears seem to keep congenial compan
with cheese. Follow the season, beginning
with the tiny sugar-sweet Seckels, good
straight or pickled. By late summer the
Bartletts are prime, but they do not keep
well. With fall, come the buttery Comice
and, in midwinter, the russet-skinned Bosc
and the green-skinned Anjous. Kiefers
too, are acceptable winter pears, but need
a special approach in cooking, so that the
fruit is softened and the sugar absorbed.
    Pears are best if picked green and
ripened at 70° until soft for eating, but i
you plan to cook them, make sure to use
them while still firm. To store for eating
wrap the fruit in paper and put it away in
a slotted box, in a cool place. If you won
der why pears which look sound have be
come brown inside, it is because they have
been held too long at a too-low tempera
ture.

STUFFED PEARS

4 Servings

Preheat oven to 350°

Peel, core and halve:
4 firm pears
Mix together and stuff into the hollows:
¼ cup raisins
2 tablespoons chopped walnuts
2 tablespoons sugar
1 tablespoon lemon juice
Place the pears in a baking dish with:
2 tablespoons water
Pour over them:
½ cup light corn sirup
Cover and bake for 1½ hours. Baste during the cooking with:
(Pineapple juice and brown sugar)
or remove the cover and sprinkle the fruit lightly with:
(Granulated sugar)
(A light dusting of cinnamon)
then place under the broiler until golden brown and serve immediately.

PEARS IN LIQUEUR
4 Servings
Combine:
1 cup chilled orange juice
1 tablespoon powdered sugar
Before serving, add to the orange juice:
(2 tablespoons curaçao)
Pare, quarter, core and prick lightly:
4 pears
Cover them with the juice. Chill until ready to serve.

ABOUT PERSIMMONS

Be sure, in the recipes, to distinguish between our native **Diospyros virginiana** and **Kaki**, the oriental type. Ours are small, full of seeds and inedible until after frost. In fact, we wonder how we survived the many we consumed as children, because the skins resist digestion and can form obstructive waddy balls, as hard as the hair balls of animals.

Both native and oriental persimmons sometimes tend to be puckery, even when ripe—depending on variety. The orientals lose their astringency if stored for 2 to 4 days in a plastic bag with a ripe apple. The natives do not always prove so amenable. Eat both as fresh fruit; or puréed, fresh or frozen, combined in ice creams, custards or sherbets. See illustration on page 109.

ABOUT PINEAPPLE

So beloved was this fruit that on many Southern mansions it was carved above the door as a symbol of hospitality. In fact, the first fruits grown in England in a nobleman's "stove-house" were graciously rented to his friends for their table decorations. To be fully appreciated, the pineapple must be savored where the fruit is field-ripened, for it does not increase in sweetness if picked green. If field-ripened,

even the core is tender and can be eaten. ◗ A small compact crown usually denotes prime condition. When one of the inner leaves of the crown pulls out easily, the eyes are protruding and the whole fruit has developed a delightful aroma, it is apt to be ripe.

Store at 70° temperature away from sunlight. Pineapple lends itself magnificently to all kinds of combinations, but watch for one thing ◗ be sure to cook fresh pineapple before combining with any gelatin mixture, see page 516.

PINEAPPLE TIDBITS
I. 8 Servings
This dish is alluring in appearance, but needs very ripe pineapple. Trim ⅔ from the leafy top of:
1 chilled ripe pineapple
Cut the fruit into 8 lengthwise wedges. Cut off the core and place each part so that it will resemble a boat, as sketched. Pare the skin in 1 piece, leaving it in place, and cut the pulp downward into 5 or 6 slices, retaining the boat shape. Serve each boat on an individual plate, with a small mound of:
Confectioners' sugar
Add:
5 or 6 large unhulled strawberries
for each serving

II. A Texas girl taught us to prepare a pineapple this way. Loosen each section of a chilled pineapple by cutting it down to the core with a sharp knife. When all sections have been loosened, serve the pineapple, a toothpick stuck into each eye. Let the guests serve themselves.

III. Pineapple can make an attractive edible centerpiece. Cut off the top and bottom of a ripe pineapple and reserve them. Insert a long, sharp knife about ½ inch from the outer edge so the fruit is entirely loosened. Leaving the fruit in this cylindrical shell, cut it in about 12 long pie-shaped wedges. Set it back on its base and use the top for a lid.

FILLED PINEAPPLE
Cut in half, hollow out and chill:
A fresh pineapple
Cube the cut-out pineapple and also some:
Slices of melon

Fill the chilled pineapple shells with the cubed fruit and add:

> **A few raspberries**

Sprinkle the tops with:

> **Chopped mint leaves**
> **(2 tablespoons liqueur)**

FRESH PINEAPPLE CUP

6 Servings

Peel, core and dice:

> **1 fresh pineapple**

Chill it. Boil for 1 minute:

> **1 cup sugar**
> **⅓ cup water**

Chill this sirup. Add:

> **½ cup chilled orange juice**
> **3 tablespoons lime juice**

Place the pineapple in glasses and pour the sirup mixture over it.

GRILLED PINEAPPLE

4 Servings

Drain:

> **8 pineapple spears**

Wrap around them:

> **8 slices bacon**

Fasten the slices with toothpicks and broil the bacon under moderate heat.

QUICK-GLAZED PINEAPPLE

Drain:

> **Canned pineapple slices or spears**

Dip them in:

> **Brown sugar**

Brown them by simmering for about 3 to 5 minutes on each side in hot:

> **Bacon drippings, pan drippings**
> **or butter**

You may also dust them with:

> **Grated cheese**
> **A few grains red pepper**

and broil or bake them in a moderate oven to melt the cheese.

ABOUT PLUMS AND PRUNES

There are many varieties of plums, some for eating, some for cooking and some, like the very firm Damson, strictly for jellies and sauces; and then, of course, there are sugar plums.

Plums are best when soft but not mushy, shrivelled or brownish. Store them refrigerated. Two unusual varieties of plums are the Loquat and the Carissa Grandiflora. The Loquat, or Japanese Plum, has a downy fuzz over a smooth, thin, yellow-gold skin. Its pulp is juicy like a cherry and contains 4 or 5 large brown seeds. Use it as a garnish for salads or fresh, straight. The Carissa or Natal Plum is a thin-skinned crimson fruit with white mottling, which contains 12 small brown seeds. It has a mild flavor, slightly astringent, and a granular texture. The Natal is fine for jelly, a good vitamin C source, but does exude a harmless white latex which sticks to the cooking pan. Remove it by rubbing with a cloth soaked in salad oil.

DRIED PRUNES

◆ If the label calls for soaking, please read About Cooked Fruits, page 106. Otherwise, cover with cold water:

> **1 lb. dried prunes**

Bring to the boiling point. ◆ Reduce the heat and simmer gently for about 20 minutes. Add:

> **(¼ cup or more sugar)**

Cook about 10 minutes longer. You may add to the prunes, during this second cooking period:

> **(½ sliced lemon)**
> **(1 stick cinnamon)**

PRUNES IN WINE

4 Servings

Cook by the above method until almost tender:

> **½ lb. prunes**

Add:

> **3 tablespoons sugar**

Cook 5 minutes longer. Remove from heat and add:

> **½ cup or more dry sherry or ½ to ¾**
> **cup port wine**
> **(6 very thin slices lemon)**

Place in a screw-top jar. Chill thoroughly. Shortly before serving, the prunes may be pitted and filled with:

> **Halves of walnuts or blanched**
> **almonds**

PRUNES AND CHESTNUTS

4 to 6 Servings

Drain and place in a casserole:

> **1½ cups canned chestnuts**
> **¾ cup pitted canned prunes**

Combine, heat and pour over the above:

> **1 tablespoon butter**
> **¼ teaspoon salt**
> **(1 tablespoon sugar)**
> **½ cup dry white wine**

Heat thoroughly and serve as the compote in a meal in which the entrée is ham or fowl.

PICKLED PRUNES

Keep this delightful compote on hand, for it makes a decorative meat garnish and may be used drained in Stuffings, page 459. Place in a heavy pan:

> **3 cups water**
> **1 cup cider vinegar**
> **2 cups brown sugar**
> **2 cups dried prunes**
> **1 teaspoon whole cloves, with**
> **heads removed**
> **1 teaspoon whole allspice**
> **1½ sticks cinnamon**

◆ Simmer about 1 hour or until prunes are plump. Place the prunes in a jar and drain the liquid over them to cover, straining out the spices.

ABOUT POMEGRANATES

The shiny ruby seeds of this sophisticatedly-shaped fruit make a most beautiful garnish. Use them in French dressing or roll them in small cream cheese balls. When eating pomegranates fresh or when making jelly do not bruise the seed kernels, for then an unpleasant flavor develops. See illustration, page 109.

ABOUT PRICKLY PEARS

Also known as Indian fig, barbary fig or tuna, the prickly pear is now as much at home on the shores of the Mediterranean as in its native America. The red and yellow fruits, which are eaten raw, have sharp spines which can be removed by singeing before peeling.

BAKED QUINCE

Preheat oven to 350°
Wash:

Large whole quinces
Rub with:

Butter
and bake for about 45 minutes, until about ⅔ done. Hollow out about ⅔ and mix the pulp with:

Bread crumbs
Chopped nuts
Brown sugar
Grating of lemon rind
Salt
Return mixture to hollow rind and bake about 15 minutes longer or until tender. Serve hot or cold.

STEAMED RHUBARB

Rhubarb is tenderer and needs no peeling if hothouse grown. If the hardy, greenish type is used, young shoots are preferred. If you find it tough, peel it back like celery and remove the coarsest strings before cooking. In either case, use as little water as possible. Never cook the leaves, as they are heavy in oxalic acid.
Wash and cut, without peeling, into 1-inch blocks:

1 lb. rhubarb
Place in the upper part of a double boiler over boiling water or in a low oven. Cover closely. Steam for 20 or 30 minutes until nearly tender. Do not stir at any time.
Dissolve:

½ to ¾ cup sugar

in:
¼ cup hot water
Pour this over the rhubarb and steam it for about 2 minutes longer.
Dot with:

Butter
Cinnamon or ginger

BAKED RHUBARB AND JAM

Preheat oven to 350°

To give color to rhubarb and keep it whole, have ready:

¼ cup seedless red jam
Coat a small baker with ⅓ of the jam. Cut into 2-inch slices:

1 lb. rhubarb
Lay the slices in the jam base, in close patterns. Sprinkle with:

(½ teaspoon powdered ginger)
Add another layer of rhubarb and cover with the rest of the jam. Bake covered for about ½ hour.

ROSELLE SAUCE

A substitute for cranberries. To prepare a sauce, cut off the red part and discard the green pod of:

2 cups well-washed roselles
♦ Simmer them ♦ uncovered, for about 10 minutes in:

1 cup water
Add:

1½ cups sugar
2 tablespoons cornstarch
Cook about 5 minutes longer or until the cornstarch cannot be tasted. Serve cool with meat or dessert.

SAPODILLAS

The rough brown skin looks like that of a potato. Remove the seeds. It has a sweet, grainy but tender pulp—like brown sugar. Use it raw, for puddings and for desserts. A little lemon juice helps bring out the flavor.

WHITE SAPOTAS

This "peach of the tropics," a greenish yellow fruit, can be used as a peach.

SOURSOPS

Annona muricata is a heart-shaped fruit, weighing up to 5 lbs. It has a heavy, green, rough, spiny rind and a wet, soft, cottony interior. Press the pulp through a colander to remove the many shiny blackish-brown seeds. Used mostly for iced drinks and sherbets.

TAMARINDS

The 2- to 6-inch pods of this graceful tree, known as St. John's Bread, are fuzzy and cinnamon colored, see illustration, page 501. When fresh and tender, they can be either cooked with rice as "tamarind fish" or sucked raw for their spicy pulp, with its date-apricot kind of flavor. The leaves are used in curries and the dried, shiny, polished pods are ground into a meal called carob flour. To cook with this meal, see page 110. To keep the pulp, remove the seeds and pack it into jars with alternate layers of sugar and pod. Keep in a cool place.

THE FOODS WE HEAT

What do you think of when you think of cooking? Our own minds rush at once, with confidence, to a vision of food deliciously prepared, perfectly seasoned, beautifully presented—to, in short, the . final product. But somewhere along the line, in perhaps ninety-nine out of a hundred kitchen sequences, heat has been applied—and its application is of crucial importance. From Charles Lamb's legendary Bobo—you will remember him from your high school English classes as the boy who couldn't make roast pig without burning down the house—to the bride of the moment, described by her maid of honor as incapable of boiling an egg, heating food has often turned into a frustrating, sometimes even a disastrous, experience.

It needn't be. We have tried throughout our book, but especially in this chapter, to identify and explain the various types of cooking heat; to tell you simply and clearly how these heats are initiated, controlled and arrested to ensure best flavor, nutritive value, texture and color. We have tried to indicate what processes, when followed, will bring cooked food to the table in that ideal state of readiness the French call "à point."

Asking a cook why he heats food at all is, of course, like asking an architect why men do not live in caves. The obvious answer is that it usually tastes better that way. There are other reasons, too. Some are prosaic. Cooking destroys unwanted and sometimes unfavorable microorganisms. Contrary to some remarkably persistent notions, it makes many categories of food more digestible and of more nutritive value and less—to toss in a stylish term—allergenic.

Cooking, again, can seal up in food most of those natural juices which nourish and delight us, instead of squandering them away on pan or oven. For some kinds of preparation—Stocks, page 488, and soups are examples—the objective is just the reverse. It is true, also, that certain salted and variety meats, as well as a good many vegetables, profit by a precooking or blanching, page 132, which modifies texture or releases disagreeable odor and off-flavors.

Many cooks, like the rest of humankind, are born innovators, too. And they often introduce stimulating refinements in the heating of food, some of which—it must be said—emphasize taste at the expense of nutritional integrity.

▲ Cooking in mountainous country is an art all in itself. If high altitudes are new to you, watch for the high altitude cooking symbol ▲ which will give you formulas for adjusted ingredients or temperatures. Roasting procedure does not differ materially from that at sea level. But high altitudes do affect boiling considerably. In the following chart, we plot the difference in the boiling temperatures of water at sea level and at graduated elevations. Any process involving liquid will be proportionately lengthened as altitude increases.

	F.	C.
Sea level	212°	100°
2,000 ft	208°	98°
5,000 ft.	203°	95°
7,500 ft.	198°	92°
10,000 ft.	194°	90°
15,000 ft.	185°	85°
30,000 ft.	158°	70°

Adjustments required in using sea-level baking recipes at high altitudes are indicated where necessary for each baking category. Basic cake recipes for high altitudes and their baking temperatures marked ▲, may be found on pages 648-650.

If these hints are not sufficiently specialized for your area, write the Home Economics Department of your State College or call on your County Home Demonstration Agent for more information. And if you are doing any pressure cooking, the accuracy of the gauge is vital. These agencies can also tell you where to have gauges tested.

ABOUT HEATS

Let us consider first how heats are transferred to food, whether in air or in moisture, in fat or through a pan. Results each case will be quite astonishingly different. Cooking heats are generally known as ◗ dry or moist. In the text following we shall list types of each separate. Then, if a specific type of dry or moist heat involves more than one kind of food a detailed description of it will follow. On the other hand, should the heat-process apply only to a single food category, like meat, you will find it elsewhere, under the cooking instructions for that particular food.

ABOUT DRY HEATS

◗ Truly dry heats are achieved in a number of ways. Grilling over coals is one broiling or roasting in a ventilated oven another. When we say "barbecue," may be referring to Pit-Cooking, page in which case we refer to a moist heat process. Or we may mean skewer-cooking with its variants—spit, brochette or rotisserie—which is a dry one and itself a form of grilling. Parenthetically, the word " becue" has been traced back by some philologists to the Spanish "barbacoa," a raised platform for cooking; but we like to think of it, with other authorities, as originating among the French settlers in Florida, who roasted the native goats whole, "de barbe en queue"—from beard to tail. Some further remarks on barbecuing will be found farther along in this chapter, see Outdoor Cooking, page 133.

Baking is a dry heat process, too. In addition to the reflected and radiant heat of the oven, heat is transferred from the pan to the food and may be further diffused by the use of paper liners, temporary covers of foil or a dusting of flour between food and pan-bottom. Since, in baking, moisture is released from the food itself and, as warm vapor, continues to circulate in the closed oven chamber, this process is less dry than those previously mentioned.

Oddly enough, deep-fat frying is still another kind of dry heat cooking. Here the heat is not only transferred by the oil or grease used as a cooking medium, but by the moisture in the food itself—some of the steam from the food juices being forced into the fat and then out into the atmosphere. Among dry heat pan-processes, sautéing, page 253, uses the least fat. Pan-broiling and pan-frying are successive steps beyond sautéing and away from the driest heat. In pan-broiling and pan-frying, the food develops a greater amount of rendered fat than in sautéing and it absorbs a larger share of it. In doing so, it gives up proportionately more of its juices. To keep both pan-frying and pan-broiling at their best, excess fat should be poured off during cooking.

While reducing—or concentrating—food through heat usually involves liquids, it also counts technically as a dry heat process since no additional moisture is introduced in accomplishing it.

Among dry heat processes which may be described as "partial" are planking and flambéing—or flaming. Either way, the food is heated beforehand and through them is given only its final finishing touch.

BROILING

The principle of broiling, whether on a grill or in a range, is identical. The heat is a radiant glow; and the process differs from roasting or baking in that only one side of the food at a time is exposed to the heating source.

However, all three of these types of dry heat depend, for their effectiveness, on proper ventilation. In the great majority of modern ranges, either gas or electric, you are given no selectivity in broiling temperatures. And individual variations in wattage—coil or burner area—and venting capacity make it necessary that you become familiar with the special requirements of your own equipment. Some ranges, for example, must be preheated before broiling can begin; in others, broiler heat is almost instantaneous. Likewise, in some electric ranges, broiling takes place with the oven door ajar; in others, the door may, or even must, be kept closed.

When the heat indicator on a household range is turned to a ♦ broil position, the temperature is normally 550° or slightly above. If you wonder why you cannot always match the results you admire in some restaurant meat and fish cookery, remember that commercial installations deliver temperatures up to between 700° and 1000° and that these are quite beyond the reach of home equipment.

Under the limitations of the household range ♦ as much temperature control in broiling is exerted by the placement of the oven rack as by any other means. It is usually adjusted so that there is a 3-inch space between the source of heat and the top of the food. ♦ To lower the broiling heat for browning fragile sauces or delicate dishes like sweetbreads or for cooking very thick meats—where the heat must have time to penetrate deeply without charring—lower the broiling rack to make a 4- to 6-inch interval between food and broiler. Place food on a cold rack to prevent sticking. If the rack is hot, grease it—or grease the food. For details of broiling Steaks, etc., see page 385; Fowl, page 466; Fish, page 349; Vegetables, page 253.

SKEWER COOKING

From a marshmallow impaled on a stick to the most delicate bay scallops, this type of grilled food never seems to lose its charm for young or old. A most important first step is to ♦ choose items that will cook at the same rate of speed or to make the proper adjustment if they do not. When the meat or fish selected is a quick-cooking one, see that the onions, peppers or other more resistant vegetables which alternate with it are blanched in advance, so they will all be done at the same time. Should the meat need relatively longer cooking, skewer delicate alternates like tomatoes and mushrooms separately and mingle meat and vegetables in serving. Protect delicate meats—sweetbreads, liver, etc.—with breading or a wrapping of thinly sliced bacon. Choose skewers, whether of metal or wood, that are either square or oval in section, so that, as the food softens in cooking, it will not slip while revolving.

If using a grill, grease it and cook the skewered food over medium heat. Turn the skewers often. Food grilled in this way may take anywhere from 6 to 12 minutes.

If cooking in a range, broil on a greased grill about 3 inches from the source of heat or adjusted on a pan, as shown on the following illustration. You may, of

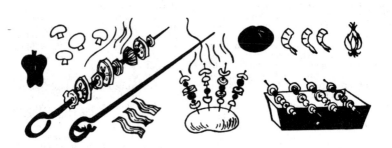

course, prefer to use the skewer element on your rotisserie. For more details about rotisserie or spit-cooking, see pages 136-137. Should you decide to precook any sort of skewered food, you may do so on the skewers themselves in a skillet, provided, of course, the skewers are no longer than the pan bottom. Sometimes partially precooked, skewered foods are coated with a sauce or with a bound breading and then cooked to completion in deep fat. When handled in this way, they are called atteraux. In flambéing skewered foods, page 127, provide some protection for your hand.

Attractive combinations for skewers or brochettes include the following: scallops, shrimps, or oysters with or wrapped in bacon, and firm miniature tomatoes; chicken livers or pieces of calf liver or kidney alternating with cocktail sausages and mushrooms; diced eggplant or squash, blanched small onions, firm small tomatoes and bacon; shrimp or diced lobster, diced cucumber and stuffed olives; pieces of fish, sections of blanched celery and bacon; pieces of sausage and pickled onions; bacon and pieces of unpeeled apple; scallops, bacon and blanched pieces of onion. In this sketch are some of the foods we have just mentioned as suitable for skewering and a decorative way to impale cocktail skewers in a potato or grapefruit, after they have had their turn at the grill.

DEEP-FAT FRYING

Deep-fat frying, like a number of other accomplishments in cooking, is an art in itself—an art in which experience is the best teacher. Even a novice, however, who follows our instructions to the letter, can succeed in turning out delicious dishes in this ever-popular category—and, what's more, food fried without excess fat absorption. A serving of French fried potatoes properly cooked may have a lower calorie count than a baked potato served with butter. Remember, too, that fat-absorption increases with the length of cooking time and with the amount of surface exposed to the fat.

We simply do not believe, as a cynic has remarked, at least in deep-fat frying, that "foresight is the last gift of the gods to man." While our directions may, at first glance, seem complicated, read them calmly and carefully and you will be rewarded with crisp, golden-brown fried foods every time.

♦ First, equipment need not be elaborate, for equally good French fried potatoes can come out of a black iron kettle as from the latest model electric fryer. This is not to underestimate the value of the fryer which offers the convenience of a built-in thermostat and furnishes also a storage space for the fat—after straining—between fryings. Proper fat storage is of considerable importance, as fat must be kept covered and in a cool place if it is to remain in good condition for repeated use.

Any deep kettle or saucepan, preferably a heavy one, serves nicely for deep frying. Use in a 3- or 4-quart kettle about pounds of fat. It isn't wise to try to skimp on the amount, for there must always be enough to cover the food and to permit it to move freely in the kettle. ♦ There must also be room in the kettle for the quick bubbling up of the fat which occurs naturally in frying potatoes, onions and other wet items. ♦ Never fill any container more than half full of fat. ♦ Remember, too, heat the fat gradually, so that any moisture in it will have evaporated by the time it reaches the required temperature.

The kettle should have a flat bottom, that it will set firmly on the burner. One without a long handle is desirable, to avoid the danger of accidentally overturning the hot fat and causing a small conflagration. In case fat should ever catch on fire, have a metal lid handy to drop over the kettle. You may also smother the flame with salt. ♦ Never, under any circumstances, use water, as this will only spread the fire.

For frying certain types of food such as doughnuts and fritters where bubbling is not a problem, a heavy skillet or electric fry-pan rather than a deep kettle is sometimes preferred, because of its wider surface, which permits frying more pieces at one time.

A wire basket is practically a necessity

for successful results in frying any quantity of material such as potatoes, oysters, onions, eggplant, etc. The food is then raised and lowered more easily, and even browning is assured.

Helpful, too, in deep frying, is a slotted metal spoon and long-handled metal tongs. A supply of absorbent paper for draining the fried food is important for the final disposal of excess fat.

For judging the temperature of the fat, use a frying thermometer, no other. Have the thermometer ready in a bowl of hot water to lessen the chance of breakage; but ◆ never plunge it into the fat without wiping it very dry. Nothing is more important in frying than proper temperatures. As that wise old gourmet, Alexander Dumas, so aptly put it, the food must be "surprised" by the hot fat, to give it the crusty, golden coating so characteristic and so desirable. And the easiest way to assure this is by using a thermometer.

When no thermometer is available, a simple test for temperature can be made with a small cube of bread about 1-inch square. When you think the fat is hot enough, drop in the bread cube and count slowly to sixty or use a timer for sixty seconds. If the cube browns in this time, the fat will be around 375°, satisfactory for frying most foods. A few—Soufflé Potatoes for instance, page 294—may require higher or lower temperatures, but these will always be noted in the specific recipes. Above all, do not wait for the fat to smoke before adding the food. This is not only hard on the fat, since smoke indicates that it is breaking down and may be spoiled for re-use, but the crust that forms on the food is likely to be overbrowned before the product is cooked through; and the result will be burned on the surface and raw inside. On the other hand, food introduced into fat that isn't hot enough to crust immediately will tend to be grease-soaked.

Once the proper temperature is established, you are ready to add the food.

◆ Do not try to fry too much at a time. This will lower the temperature unduly and may also cause the fat to bubble up too fast and go over the top of the kettle. Naturally, the colder the food when added to the fat, the more the fat temperature will be reduced.

◆ Whenever possible, foods should be at room temperature when introduced into the kettle. ◆ Always immerse gently with long-handled tongs or a slotted spoon or in a frying basket. ◆ Always dip these utensils into the hot fat first, so that the food will release quickly from them without sticking. And have a pan ready in which to rest the utensils when they come dripping from the fat.

After frying one batch ◆ let the temperature come up again to the required heat, so that you may continue to "surprise" each additional one. ◆ Skim out bits of food or crumbs frequently—as they collect in the fat during frying. If allowed to remain, they induce foaming, discolor the fat and affect the flavor of the food.

At the end of frying, and after the fat has cooled somewhat, strain it to remove all leftover particles. Return it to the container and store for re-use. Adding some fresh fat for each new frying materially increases its length of life. When the fat becomes dark and thickish-looking, it will no longer be satisfactory for frying. At this stage, the smoking point has dropped too low; the flavor that it contributes to the food will be unpleasant and absorption high. Discard it.

◆ The household cooking fat known as "all-purpose" or sometimes simply as "shortenings" are American favorites. These include the solid fats such as lard, the plastic and hydrogenated fats and the liquid oils, among which corn, cottonseed and peanut are most commonly available for household use. Except for lard, which has a characteristic odor and flavor, these fats are bland and very similar in appearance and composition. Most of them are 100% vegetable in origin. The oils, in

particular, are so much alike that unless one knows the source or examines the label, it is practically impossible to tell which is made from peanuts and which from corn or cottonseed. They all have smoking points well above those needed for deep frying.

Butter and margarines, valuable as they are for other purposes, are not considered suitable for deep frying, because of their low smoking points. As has been mentioned earlier, smoking of fat during frying should not be tolerated. It is hard on the food, hard on the fat itself and unpleasant when wafted through the house.

Various other fats are sometimes used for deep frying. Olive oil is popular where it is locally produced and soybean, safflower, rape and sesame oils are widely used where they are commonly grown and processed.

For special purposes and in certain circumstances chicken and goose fat are rendered in the home for frying, as are also veal, pork, suet and beef kidney fats. These are inclined to have low smoking points, but when handled with care they can be used to produce acceptable fried foods. If it seems desirable, the smoking point of these animal fats can be brought up to the required limit by blending them with any one of the cooking oils.

◊ The best way to render animal fats in the home is to cut them into small pieces—after removing bits of membrane, skin, etc. —and heat in a double boiler until melted. This process can be hastened by pressing down on the fatty pieces occasionally with a fork or spoon. Strain through cheese cloth to remove solid particles and store the rendered fat in a covered container in a cool place. ◊ Do not use drippings or fats skimmed from soups or gravies.

◊ For good results, the food to be fried must be properly prepared. Pieces should be uniform in size, preferably not thicker than 2 inches, so that they will all cook in the same length of time. Small pieces, obviously, will cook through faster than large ones. It is difficult here to give advice about length of cooking. When in doubt, it is wise to remove one piece and try for doneness.

Raw foods, ◊ especially wet ones, should be patted between towels or absorbent paper before cooking to remove excess surface moisture. This not only helps to keep the fat temperature from dropping too low, but it reduces the amount of bubbling when the food is introduced. In adding a batch of raw potatoes—French fries or chips—always lower the basket gradually so that you can observe the amount of bubbling and be ready to lift it up if it looks as though the fat might be going over the top. Until you have developed that "sixth sense," do not try to put too many pieces in the basket—rather fry several small batches than one large

one. The cooked food may be kept hot on a paper-lined pan in the oven, set at very low heat.

Certain types of food need special coating for proper browning and crust formation—croquettes, eggplant, fish, etc. For Breading, see page 502. The coating may be simply flour, cornmeal or finely crushed dry cereal. Or it may be a Fritter Batter, page 220, an egg and crumb mixture or even a pastry envelope. Whatever it is, it should cover the surface evenly.

Foods to be coated with batter—shrimp, for instance, or pineapple slices—should be surface-dried before applying the batter. Doughnuts, fritters and other batter-foods need no extra coating, as the egg-starch mixture browns nicely by itself when lowered into the hot fat. Many cooks do not realize that the richer a dough or batter mixture, the more fat it will absorb during frying. By adding even a little too much shortening or sugar to the mix, a doughnut may become so rich that it will end up by being grease-soaked. Or a fritter may simply disintegrate in the hot fat or the batter may slide off onion rings altogether.

✳ Frozen foods designed for deep frying are usually completely prepared. All that remains to be done is defrosting, which is better accomplished outside the package. Otherwise moisture may form on the surface and interfere with proper browning and crusting. Frozen foods that have to be coated should be defrosted, dried on the surface, if necessary, and the coating applied as usual.

In deep-fat frying ▲ at high altitudes you will find that the lower boiling point of the water inside moist foods will require lower fat temperatures. For instance French fries, which call for 375° in their final frying period, might need only 365° fat temperature at high altitudes.

SAUTÉING

"Sauter" literally means "to jump," and this is just what happens to the food you cook by this method. The cooking is done in an ◊ open pan, which is kept in motion. The process is rapid, the food usually thin or minced and the ◊ heat must be kept up, from the moment cooking starts until the food is tender. Any reduction in heat will draw juices. There are other requirements. The ◊ small quantity of fat used must be hot enough, when the food is added, to sear it at once—again to prevent the loss of juices. ◊ This can only be accomplished if the food is 70° or more, cut to a uniform thickness and size and dry on the surface. If it is too cold it will lower the heat, and if it is wet it will not brown properly. Worst of all, steam will form and break the seal holding the juices. To ensure a dry surface, food is frequently floured or breaded, see page 501. ◊ Steam will also form if the pan is crowded. There must be space between the pieces of food you are sautéing.

For the best sauté, use a Clarified Butter, page 338, or a combination of 3 parts butter and 4 parts oil. When these fats reach the point of fragrance, the 70° food is added, but not so much at a time as to reduce the heat in the pan. To keep the food, which should be heated to at least 340°, from too quick browning agitate the pan constantly. Too much turning of the food delays the quickness of heating. But food with a Bound Breading, page 502, especially if the coating has not been dried long enough before cooking, may steam. In this case, turning will help to release some of that steam more rapidly. Usually sautéed meat is browned or cooked on one side until the blood comes up to the surface of the exposed side, then turned and browned on the other side.

To serve sautéed food with a sauce, remove the food from the pan and keep it warm on a hot serving dish. Quickly deglaze the delicious brown residue in the sauté pan—unless you have been cooking strongly flavored fish—with stock or wine. Reduce the sauce and pour it over the sautéed food. If you heat sautéed food in sauce, you steam it too much.

PAN-FRYING

Dredge the food with seasoned breading, flour, cornmeal or a Bound Breading, see page 502. Melt a small amount of fat in a heavy pan over moderate heat. For meat, use fat from the meat you are cooking. Brown the meat on one side. When juice begins to appear on the upper surface, turn the meat with tongs and brown it on the other side. Drain and serve at once. Proceed in the same way for fish; but the cooking time is apt to be less. Cook on one side until golden brown before turning. Drain on paper towels and serve at once.

REDUCING LIQUIDS

This process is used mainly to intensify flavor: a wine, a broth or a sauce is evaporated and condensed over lively heat. A so-called "double consommé" is made in this way, the final product being half the original in volume. Naturally, reducing applies only to sauces without egg. And those which have a flour base must be watched carefully and stirred often to avoid scorching.

PLANKING

Why bother about planking? One reason is the attractive appearance of a planked meat, surrounded with a decorative band of Duchess Potatoes, page 296, beautifully browned on their fluted edges and garnished with colorful vegetables, after it emerges from the oven. Another reason is the delicious flavor an oak slab can give to meat. Planks are of 1-inch-thick kiln-dried oak. An 18-inch oval usually serves four to six. They often have a tree design cut down their length to drain juices into a shallow depression toward one end.

If all the cooking is done on the plank, it will char rapidly. Usually steaks are broiled on an oven grille fully on one side and partially on the other before being planked. To season a new plank ♦ brush it with cooking oil and heat in a 225° oven for at least one hour before using. To protect it when cooking, oil well any exposed part or cover, as suggested above, with a decoration of mashed potatoes or other puréed vegetables.

FLAMBÉING

Flaming always comes at a dramatic moment in the meal, sometimes a tragi-comical one if you manage to get only a mere flicker. To avoid anticlimax, remember that ♦ food to be flamed should be warm and that the brandy or liqueur used in flambéing should also be warm—but well under the boiling point. For meat, do not attempt this process with less than one ounce of liquor per serving. For nonsweet food served from a chafing dish or electric skillet, pour the warmed liquor over the surface of the food and ignite by touching the edge of the pan with the flame of a match or taper. For hot desserts in similar appliances, sprinkle the top surface with granulated sugar, add the warm liqueur and ignite as above.

ABOUT MOIST HEATS

What a number of processes can be assigned to the moist heat category! There are complete ones like boiling, pressure cooking, scalding, simmering, poaching, stewing, fricasseeing, braising, casseroling, cooking in wraps, double boiler cookery and steaming. Also, just as with dry heats, there are partial moist heat processes, like those in blanching and fireless cookery. We may as well mention here and now— although not on the side of simplification —that certain classic terms for kinds of moist heat cookery are broadly interpreted, even by the most knowledgeable cooks. Also a number are neither moist nor dry, but a combination of both. Some stews, for example, may be begun in a pan by browning, while others, like the Irish variety, never see the inside of a skillet. Similarly, a braise, a fricassee and a "smother" may all, like a browned stew, have their origin in dry heat sautéing and then are finished by cooking in a little stock.

BOILING

Discussing this process tempts us to mention stews again, in connection with the old adage "A stew boiled is a stew spoiled." And we may point out that the same sentiment can be applied to almost every other kind of food. While recipes often call for foods to be brought to the boiling point or to be plunged into boiling water, they hardly ever demand boiling for a protracted period. Even "boiled" eggs, so-called, should be simmered.

Quick evaporation—seldom advisable—is one of the few justifications for keeping a food at boiling point. When evaporating, never boil covered, as steam condenses on the lid and falls back into the pot, reducing the amount of liquid very little, if at all.

Adding foods to boiling water will lower the boiling point, unless the quantity of water is at least three times as much as will cover the food—to offset its lower temperature. Such compensation is recommended in Blanching, page 132, and in the cooking of cereals and pasta. When the pores of food are to be sealed, it may be plunged into rapidly boiling liquid, after which the temperature is usually reduced to a simmer.

✪ PRESSURE COOKING

A sound approach to pressure cooking involves an appreciation of its advantages and a knowledge of its limitations.

No matter how high the heat source, boiling in water in the presence of air can never produce a temperature over 212°. But, because in pressure cooking the air in the pan is withdrawn first, heat as high as 250° can be maintained at 15 lbs. gauge-reading. Some home cookers are geared to a range of from 3¾ to 20 pounds, although 15 pounds is commonly used. Cooking time at 15 pounds pressure takes only about ⅓ the total time—from the lidding of the pressure cooker through the capping of the vent and the release of pressure—that it takes to cook food in conventional ways at boiling temperatures. In pressure cooking vegetables over short periods at these higher temperatures, more than time is saved. Nutrients and flavor are also well conserved, see Steam Pressuring of Vegetables, page 252.

◗ In the pressure cooking of meats and soups, however, the higher heats involved tend both to toughen the protein and affect flavor adversely. Therefore, we recommend this method only when time is more important to you than choice results.

◗ In the canning of all nonacid foods, the higher heat of pressure cooking is essential to kill unwanted organisms, see page 751.

◗ Pressure cooking of beans and cereals and dried or puréed fruits, which may sputter and clog the vent, is not recommended because of this danger.

A pressure cooker may be used also for sterilizing baby bottles. Allow 10 minutes at 10 lbs. pressure.

It is essential in any pressure cooking to know your equipment well. ◗ Follow manufacturer's directions to the letter, observing these general principles. ◗ Never fill a pressure cooker with more food than ½ its capacity if there is much liquid or ⅔ if the contents are mainly solids. ◗ Be sure the required amount of liquid has been put in the cooker. ◗ Season lightly, as there is less liquid to dilute the flavor than in more traditional types of cooking. Solid foods may be placed at once over high heat. If soup or foods requiring more than the usual amount of water are to be cooked, the heat is brought up slowly. ◗ Always be sure to exhaust the air in the cooker before capping the vent, as trapped air will cause cold pockets and uneven cooking. Allow the steam to come out in a solid column before capping. When the ◗ indicator shows that the desired degree of pressure has been reached or when the gauge or weight jiggles reduce the heat to just maintain desired pressures. ◗ Time from the moment of capping the vent. The pressure pan should show a mild form of activity by hissing occasionally during the cooking period.

If you have a stop clock, use it; if not watch the time carefully as overcooking results very quickly. ◗ As soon as the time is up, to arrest further cooking and reduce the pressure in your cooker instantly, place it in cool water or let cool water run over the sides. Exceptions are steam pudding preserves and soups, which should be allowed to cool gradually. When the temperature is brought down, exhaust the steam fully by removing the gauge.

◗ The cover must not be removed until all the steam is out of the pressure cooker. Here again, handle your particular type of appliance exactly as you are instructed. ◗ When the cover is difficult to remove, do not force it; there is still steam in the container which will be exhausted if you wait a few minutes.

If the amount of food to be cooked increased, also increase the amount of liquid unless the units of the food are very small, when little or no additional liquid is necessary. But do not increase the amount of cooking time.

When cooking foods that require different periods of cooking, begin with the ingredient that requires the longest time. Always reduce the pressure, as directed in the manufacturer's booklet, before opening the lid to add the ingredient that requires the shorter period of cooking. Readjust the cover, place the cooker again over high heat and proceed as before. When the desired degree of pressure has been reached, reduce the heat and begin count the rest of the cooking time.

Or, when cooking together vegetables that require an unequal period of cooking equalize them by cutting into small dice those that require the longer period: potatoes, turnips, etc.

▲ A general rule for pressure cooking at high altitudes, whether you are cooking at 10, 15 or 20 pounds pressure, is to ◗ maintain the same timing as at sea level, but to increase the pressure by ½ lb. for every rise of 1,000 feet.

For additional details about High Altitude pressure cooking, see Vegetables, page 253, Meat, page 386, Canning, page 748. To use a pressure cooker as a steamer, see Steam Puddings, page 703.

SCALDING

As the term is used in this book, scalding means cooking at a temperature of about 185° or just below boiling. You will find this process discussed in relation to Milk, page 487, the food for which it is most frequently used.

SIMMERING

This ranks as one of the most important moist heats. The temperatures range from about 135° to 160°. Simmering protects fragile foods and tenderizes tough ones. The French verb for it is "mijoter" and they engagingly refer to low simmers— between 130° and 135°—as "making the pot smile." When food is simmering, bubbles come gently to the surface and barely seem to break. It is the heat best used in cooking, uncovered, for soups and, covered, for stews, braises, pot-roasts, poêles, étouffés, page 412, and fricassees, page 467.

POACHING

This kind of moist heat cooking is one that most people associate only with eggs, but its range is much wider. The principle of poaching never varies. The heat source is a liquid just under the boiling point and a distinguishing feature of the process is the basting or self-basting which is constant during the cooking period.

◗ When an egg is properly poached, it is floated on simmering water and then either basted with this simmering liquid or covered with a lid, so that steam accumulates to perform a self-basting action. Because the egg cooks in just a few minutes, the lid does not allow the formation of excess steam. In poaching meat or fish, where the cooking period is lengthened, entrapped steam may become too heavy. For these and delicate foods, therefore, a lid is not recommended. Instead, substitute a poaching paper, see sketch.

A poaching paper permits excess steam to escape through its small top vent and around the sides. The narrow vent also maintains better color in the food than when air is excluded altogether—as in other more tightly confined moist heat processes, such as casseroling. ◗ To make a poaching paper, take a piece of square parchment, the sides of which are a little larger than the diameter of the pan you wish to cover. Fold it in fourths and roll it diagonally: begin at the folded corner, as sketched. Hold it over the pan to determine the radius. Then snip off the part that projects beyond the edge of the pan. Cut a tiny tip off the pointed end to form a vent. When you unfold the paper you will have a circle just the area of your pan, with a perforation at its center. Place it over the food to form a self-baster. If the cooking process is a short one or if the food to be cooked is in small units, the liquid may be at simmering point when the food is added. If the food is chunky, like a whole chicken, the water is put on cold, the food added and the water brought to a simmer ◗ uncovered. The liquid may then be skimmed and the poaching paper applied. Should the liquid become too much reduced during the cooking process, it

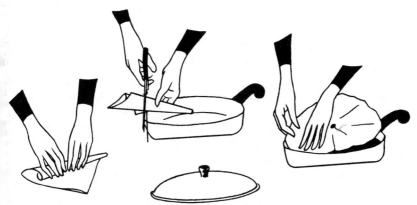

must be replenished. ◗ This type of poaching is often miscalled boiling or stewing.

CASSEROLING

The term casserole has been bandied about so carelessly that it is time we took stock of its meaning—or, rather, meanings. In correct parlance, a "casserole" is both a utensil—usually a lidded one—and the process used for cooking a raw food in that utensil. But it has also come to mean a favorite type of self-serve dish which graces so many American buffets, but is not in the least the real McCoy. This mock casserole is a mixture of several foods, one of which may be a pasta or rice in a sauce. The mixture is often precooked or consists of a combination of precooked and quick-cooking food; and it is served in the baker in which it was heated. ◗ Mock casseroles, if cooked covered, will develop too much steam and the sauce they are served in will break down. They often have a gratinéed top, page 342, to protect the food and absorb excess grease. ◗ It is wise to wipe "prefabricated" casserole dishes well before heating, so they will not show any browned spilled-over areas on the outside surface when served. Often, for large groups, a rather shallow dish is used, both to ensure its heating through quickly and the presence of plenty of gratinéed top for each serving. If topping with biscuit or corn pone, heat in a 375° to 400° oven.

Let's go back to the casserole as a utensil. The unglazed clay ware used in Europe today has not changed shape since very ancient times. It is squat, with bulging sides, easily grasped round handles and a slightly arched lid. ◗ To season unglazed casseroles and to prevent an "earthy" taste or the subsequent retention of unwanted flavors, rub them well, inside and out, with cut cloves of garlic. Then fill with water, add onion skins, celery and leek tops, put in a low oven, let the water come to a boil and simmer about 2 hours. Finally, discard the water, wash the dish and lid, after which the casserole is ready for use. ◗ To avoid cracking, never set clay casseroles on heating elements unless they have previously had butter, oil or other food put in them; and if your burner is not thermostatically controlled, it is wise to use an asbestos pad or wire trivet.

Today the word casserole is applied to any deepish pot in which cooking actually goes on, or even to pots more rightly called sauteuses or deep skillets. ◗ In true casseroling, as distinguished from "mock" casseroling, a tight lid is integral to the process. The very slow cooking goes on in about a 300° oven and develops a bare simmer. There is a continuous self-basting action, as steam condenses on the lid and falls back on the food. Inasmuch as only a small quantity of water has been used to begin with, the long, slow cooking condenses this and the food juices into a delicious residue. After the food is removed, the residue when degreased, if necessary, and then deglazed, forms the sauce for the dish. This form of closed cooking with only the barest escape of steam is also called cooking "à l'étouffée." Pot roasting of chicken or veal is sometimes carried on in a partially lidded casserole. This variant, because of greater evaporation, needs basting, and the meats should not be overcooked.

WRAP COOKERY

Food commonly needs heat; but we are forever inventing ways to protect it from drying out while cooking. Lids, as well as double boilers, are familiar to us all; but sometimes more interesting flavors and textures can be developed by other means. One of the most mouth-watering sights we ever saw was a movie of an Indonesian tribe on the march. When mealtime came, oldster to tot began devising cases for cooking their food in the coals: intricately folded leaves, large stoppered sections of bamboo, reed baskets. You knew at once that the cases all had enough moisture to withstand the heat of the coals they were buried in and that they would give special flavor and succulence to the food. Cooking in wraps may take other forms, too, and in less primitive company—from the clay enclosed meat pies of English kiln-workers to the "en croûte" cookery so esteemed in France, see page 387.

LEAF-WRAPPINGS

These make wonderful food cases. Choose only very fresh, unblemished green leaves. How to use them depends on the kind chosen.

◗ To prepare cabbage leaves: cut the stem from a head of cabbage deep enough to start a separation of the very outer leaves from the core. Dip the head in boiling water. This will loosen 3 or 4 leaves. Dip again and continue to remove the loosened leaves. Blanch, page 132, the leaves for 2 minutes, drain and plunge into cold water. To wrap meat in the leaves, see the illustration on the next page. Either tie the leaf-packet as shown or place it, if it is left untied, seam-side down. ◗ Cook the leaf-packets as follows.

I. Melt in casserole:
   2 tablespoons butter
Add:
   2 cups boiling water or stock

Put food in a single layer on bottom of casserole. Place a plate on top to give weight during cooking. If filling is uncooked, bake or simmer the packets, covered, 35 to 40 minutes—longer for pork

If filling is precooked, 10 minutes is enough to heat the food through.

II. If packets are tied, they may be dropped into simmering broth and cooked gently until done. See timing under I.

III. Or, as in Tamales, page 275, packets, see right above, may be steamed in a vegetable steamer. See timing under I.

◗ To prepare lettuce leaves: soak them very briefly in boiling water. Drain, dry and fill. Wrap as for cabbage leaves and cook as for I or III. They are not strong enough to cook as for II.

◗ To prepare fresh grape leaves for Dolmas, page 431, drop young pale-green leaves into boiling water and blanch till color darkens—about 4 to 5 minutes. Remove leaves. Drain them on a skimmer. Should you have to use large leaves, remove the tough part of the central rib. Place shiny side down on a board. Roll the filling in ¾-inch balls. If the filling is of rice, use not more than 2 teaspoons, as the rice will swell. Set one ball near the broad end of a leaf, fold over the left and right segments, as sketched. Then roll the leaf from beyond the filling ball toward its tip, just as though you were rolling a cigarette. Place it, loose end down, and cook as directed above.

◗ To prepare and separate canned grape leaves, place them briefly in hot water.

◗ To prepare papaya leaves, cover them with cold water. Bring ◗ just to the boiling point—uncovered. Drain. This will remove any bitterness. Plunge into boiling water to cover and ◗ simmer, uncovered, until tender.

◗ To prepare corn husks, place them in boiling water, remove from heat and allow ◗ stand 5 minutes before draining. To roll food in them, overlap two or three corn husks. Place the filling in an oblong shape centered on the leaves. Fold the leaves first from the sides and then from the ends, as shown, so they can be tied with one string.

OIL COOKERY

Aluminum foil solves many kitchen prob-

lems, but if you cook food wrapped in foil, please consider the following. The foil is impervious to air and moisture from the outside. Therefore, it traps within its case all the moisture released from the food during the cooking period. So, even if the heat source is dry, like that of an oven, the result will always be a steamed food, never a roasted one. Since the foil also has high insulating qualities, foil-wrapped food will require longer cooking at 75° higher heat. You may be willing to pay for both the foil and the extra heat needed to have the convenience of an effortless Pot Roast, see page 416. If you are cooking out of doors, see Campfire Vegetables and the comments in Outdoor Cooking, page 133.

COOKING EN PAPILLOTE

This is a delightful way to prepare delicate, quick-cooking, partially cooked or sauced foods. The dish, served in the parchment paper in which it was heated, retains the aromas until ready to be eaten. As the food cooks, some of the unwanted steam it generates evaporates through the paper. Just the same, the paper rises and puffs as heating progresses, putting considerable strain on the folded seam. So, note the following directions and sketches carefully.

To make a papillote: fold a parchment of appropriate size in half, crosswise. Cut from the folded edge to the open edge, a half heart shape, so that when the paper is opened, as shown, the full heart shape materializes.

Be generous in cutting—allowing almost twice again as much paper as the size of the object to be enclosed. Place the food near the fold—not too close to the seam. Turn the filled paper with the folded edge toward you. Holding the edges of the paper together, make a fold in a small section of the rim. Crease it with your fingers and fold it over again. Hold down this double fold with the fingers of one hand and with the other start a slightly overlapping and again another double overlapping fold. Each double fold overlaps the previous one. Repeat this folding, creasing and folding around the entire rim, finishing off at the pointed end of the heart with a tight twist of the parchment —locking the whole in place. Now butter the paper well. Place it in a buttered oven-proof dish in a 400° preheated oven for 5 to 6 minutes or until the paper puffs. In serving, snip about ¾ of the paper on the curved edge just next to the fold to reveal the lovely food and release the aroma.

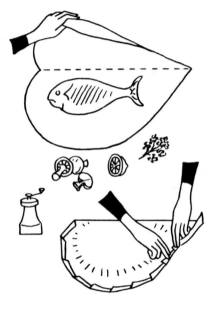

DOUBLE BOILER COOKING

For those foods which are quickly ruined beyond hope of resurrection if overheated, even for a short period—especially egg, cream or chocolate dishes—we recommend the use of a double boiler. It is a peaceful way to cook delicate sauces, particularly if you are obliged to make them at a time when preparing other dishes which need close surveillance.

Sometimes food is started over direct heat in the top of a double boiler and is finished ♦ over—not in—hot water. For sauces, we like a double boiler that is ra-ther wide. Deep and narrow vessels tend to overheat the sauce at the bottom even when it is stirred—if it is held for any time at all. ♦ The material of which the upper portion of the double boiler is made is very important. When the material is too thin, it transmits heat too fast. If it is too thick, it absorbs and retains too much heat. For years, we made magnificent Hollandaise in a stoneware bowl that fit the base of an aluminum double boiler. It was a com-pletely effortless procedure. Then the

bowl broke and the magic fled. We found stainless steel and aluminum too quick. A deluxe saucière of stoneware, deep set in a copper base, was too reluctant and, when it finally heated, too retentive of heat. A flame-resistant glass double boiler, for all the irritation of using a protective trivet at the heat source, has been a reliable sub-stitute for our favorite old makeshift and does allow us to keep track easily of the ♦ over—not in—hot water factor.

STEAMING

For cooking vegetables, steaming is an ex-cellent process to use. On page 252, we describe two methods for this purpose: di-rect steaming over boiling water and pres-sure steaming at greater temperatures. Di-rect steaming is also a good way to plump raisins, to release salt from smoked birds and, more importantly, to cook fish, page 348.

BLANCHING AND PARBOILING

These terms are among the most carelessly used in a cook's vocabulary. To introduce some order into traditional confusion we describe and differentiate between four dif-ferent types of blanching. Which type is re-quired will, we believe, be clear from the context of our individual descriptions.

♦ BLANCHING I

This means pouring boiling water over food to remove outer coverings, as in loos-ening the brown hulls of almonds and mak-ing the skins of peaches and tomatoes easier to peel off. This process is also used to soften herbs and vegetables for more flexible and longer-lived decoration.

♦ BLANCHING II OR PARBLANCHING

This involves placing food to be blanched into ♦ a large quantity of cold water ♦ bringing it slowly to a boil ♦ uncovered and continuing to ♦ simmer it for the length of time specified. Following this hot bath, the food is drained, plunged quickly into cold water to firm it and to arrest further hot water cooking and then finished, as directed in the recipe. This is the process used to leach excess salt from tongue, cured ham or salt pork and to re-move excess blood or strong flavors from variety meats. The cold water plunge after blanching effectively firms the more fragile variety meats, like brains and sweetbreads.

♦ BLANCHING III OR PARBOILING

This means that food is plunged into ♦ a large quantity of rapidly boiling water, little at a time so as not to disturb the boiling and then cooked for the period in-dicated in the recipe. The purpose of this particular kind of blanching or parboiling may be to set color or—by partial dehydra-tion—to help preserve nutrients and firm the tissues of vegetables. If further cooking follows immediately, the blanched food need not be chilled as above, but merely drained. Should an interval elapse before cooking and serving, use the cold water plunge, drain and store the food refrigerated. Blanching vegetables in this way preparatory to canning or freezing is described in greater detail on page 763. Small amounts of the vegetable are plunged into ◗ boiling water just long enough to retard enzymatic action and to shrink the product for more economical packaging. Then the vegetables are ◗ drained and quickly plunged into ◗ ice water, so that the cooking process is arrested at once.

◗ BLANCHING IV, STEAM BLANCHING OR PARSTEAMING

An alternate method for freezing and canning is also described on page 763.

FIRELESS COOKING

If fuel is scarce, and for food needing a long heating period, there is a possible advantage in using a fireless cooker. This appliance is enclosed on all sides by material that is a nonconductor of heat and is preheated to a desired temperature by an electric coil or by hot stones. Hot food set in it continues to cook without the addition of further heat.

OUTDOOR COOKING

Cooking out-of-doors may put to use all kinds of heat; but its enthusiasts do best when they stick to simple methods. As soon as cookouts get complicated, the whole party—in our perhaps jaundiced opinion—will do well to move back into the kitchen, where equipment is handy, controls positive and effects less problematical. We never attend a patio barbecue featuring paper chef's hats, aprons with printed wise-cracks, striped asbestos gloves, an infra-red broiler on white-walled wheels and yards and yards of extension cord and culinary red tape, without anticipating a deservedly heavy thunderstorm.

For campers, al fresco cooking is a necessity—rather than a pleasant indulgence. On long trips or in emergencies, very primitive heat sources will do a surprisingly good job. This is true especially if the camper's cooking utensils can be largely confined to kettle, coffee pot and skillet. The illustration to the left foreground shows perhaps the easiest of all outdoor cooking set-ups. It is called ◗ a hunter's fire. Two fairly chunky green logs are set directly on the ground, open-V fashion, and oriented so that the prevailing wind enters at the wide end of the V.

If big logs are not available, build the V of rocks. When the fire, which has been built inside, burns to embers, kettle, skillet and coffeepot can span the logs, as shown. ◆ Before bringing any sort of cooking container in close contact with a wood fire, remember to cover its under-surfaces with a film of soap or detergent. This precaution will greatly facilitate the removal of soot later, when the pan is cleaned.

Speaking of easy outdoor cooking devices, we once went on a picnic with some friends in a beech woods. Our host, toward supper-time, made criss-cross fires, just big enough for each individual steak. First, he set up log-cabin-like cribs about four layers high, with twigs approximately 1-inch thick. In these, he laid a handful of dry leaves and fine brush. On top of the cribs, he continued to build for about three inches an additional structure of pencil-like material. When, after firing, the wood had been reduced to a rectangular framework of glowing rods, he unlimbered some thin steaks from a hamper and, to our consternation, laid them calmly and directly on the embers. In a few moments he removed them with tongs, shook off whatever coals had adhered, turned the steaks over and repeated the process on the other side. They were delicious.

Another device for rough-and-ready outdoor cookery involves the principle of the crane. Two versions are illustrated, both for kettle cookery and both largely self-explanatory. A ring of rocks around a campfire will keep the flames from spreading and reflect the heat back into the cooking circle.

Pit-cooking is perhaps the most glamorous of all primitive types—glamorous because it is so largely associated with picturesque places, hearty group effort and holiday spirit. Pits may be small holes, of just sufficient depth and width to take a bean pot, a three-legged kettle or a true braizing pot with a depression on top for coals, as sketched; or they may be big enough to accommodate a king-size luau, replete with suckling pigs. Sometimes

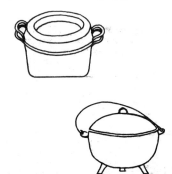

hardwood embers are left in the pit. Then steel rods are put across it—held a few inches above the fire on the rocks or logs set around its periphery. The rods, in turn, support a wire mesh grid on which the food is cooked. A switch from direct pit-firing to fireless pit-cooking and a completely different range of culinary effect can be achieved by a variant of this procedure.

Fairly large scale cookery of the latter type will require digging a pit, to begin with, not less than 2 feet deep, 3 feet across, and 4 feet long. If pit-cooking is more than occasional and the locale does not vary, you may find it more convenient to build a pit in reverse, by constructing a hollow rectangle of concrete blocks, about the same height as a true pit is deep.

The next step is to line the bottom and sides of the pit with medium-size flat rock ◆ never with shale, which may explode when heated. Toss in enough additional rock to approximate the area of the pit. Now spread over the rocks a substantial bonfire of hardwood deadfall or driftwood. Hickory, beech, maple or ironwood are prime for this purpose. And grape-vine cuttings lend grilled food special distinction. The French, incidentally, regard food broiled over grape-wood, or "sarments de vigne," as extraordinarily choice. When the fire has completely burned down—this should take not less than 2 hours—rake out the red embers and the top rock. Now, sprinkle a quart or so of water over the hot rock bed remaining and add a two-inch layer of green leaves—grape, beech, pawpaw, sassafras, cornhusks or seaweed. If you have remembered to bring along some handfuls of aromatic herbs, add these too. ◆ Work quickly at this point, so that the rocks do not lose their stored heat. On the bed of packed foliage arrange the elements of your meal: fish, cuts of meat, green peppers, onions, corn in its husk, unpeeled potatoes, acorn squash. Pile over them a second layer of green leafage, then a second grouping of food and, finally, a third layer of green leafage. Cap the stratification off with the remaining hot rocks, a tarpaulin or canvas cover and four inches of earth or sand to weight things down and to keep heat and steam at work inside—cooking your meal. How long this will take depends, of course, on what you're cooking—maximum time will probably be required for a small pig; it should test 190° when done and takes about 20 minutes per pound.

For shore dinners, with seaweed as filler, wire mesh is often placed over at least one layer to better support small crustacea, clams and oysters. For details of a Clam Bake, see page 368. Such tidbits may also be steamed in closed kettles—we have used a clean refuse can with a tight-fitting lid ◆ but be careful not to let such containers rest directly on the hot rocks or cook any food that is very acid directly in them. Allow one live lobster or three soft-shell crabs per person.

In Hawaii, and in the East Indies generally, food cooked in pits is frequently wrapped in papaya leaves which not only protect but tenderize, see page 131. In the West Indies, petate mats are used for this purpose. ♦ Wrapping food before introducing it into direct heat is almost as old as cooking itself. Primitive societies to this day surround pieces of food with a leaf and then with clay, to protect them from burning.

In France the technique has given rise to a branch of food preparation called "en croûte" cookery, page 387, in which the encasement is dough. Its principle is increasingly exploited in ♦ papillote, page 131. Both in the pastry and paper casings some steam escapes. But, in cookouts today, if ♦ wrapping the food in heavy duty aluminum foil, page 131, it must be remembered that the imperviousness of the foil makes for a truly steamed product and that texture and flavor are far removed from that of food typically cooked by direct heat. Indeed this is true of the closed-in type of pit-cookery, as described above, in general, but there the flavor of the charcoal and seaweed or leaves adds a delicious touch.

The whole pit-cookery operation, whether it is carried out on the beach or in the woods, has a distinctly adventurous character. And periodic tests for doneness performed on the foods closest to the edge of the pit are an essential part of the process.

In lifting the tarp and in removing it altogether when you are ready to serve, be extremely careful not to get food fouled up with sand or earth.

There are several ways to rig up simple stoves for camp cooking. One is made from a tin can of fairly large capacity—from a gallon on up, see the sketch at right, above. Its features are basic to stoves of any sort. The cylinder, or body, of the can shelters the fire from draft and supports the cooking pan; the fire below is kept supplied with oxygen by the bottom opening. The upper opening can be regulated to sustain the flow of heat and allows the release of smoke and hot gases. The holes punched in the top of the can steadily bring up a supply of heat to the pan. This can be fueled with canned heat or a small twig fire. ♦ You can cut a cooking utensil from a second can, but be sure to handle it with gloves!

Probably the most effective do-it-yourself device for smoking food is merely a modification of the tin-can stove—a can-on-can affair, with two hollow cylinders closely fitted together, as sketched. The fuel here is sawdust from nut or fruitwood, which is piled up to one-fourth the height of the lower can and which smolders

rather than burns, giving off, in so doing, the required abundance of smoke. The can should be preheated before the food is added. For smoking ham, meat, fowl or fish see pages 754-756. The food to be treated is hung from a crossbar or bars inserted across the upper cylinder. ♦ To retain as much smoke as possible in the curing area, the upper can has only a sin-

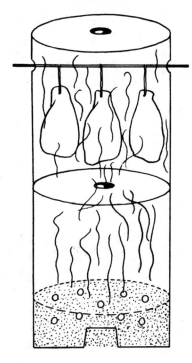

gle vent at the tops of the cans, some side-
perforations at the bottom, and a 4-inch
square base-vent.

By projecting the device just described
further, the Chinese, centuries ago, per-
fected a wholly distinctive type of food
preparation, which is gaining popularity in
this country today: smoke-cookery. A section through a typical smoke oven is L-
shaped. The horizontal leg of the L contains the firebox; the vertical portion is
fitted with horizontal bars or wire racks on
which the food is placed. After igniting
the fuel—generally fruitwood spiced with
dried herbs—the box is closed and firing
continued until the temperature of the
stack reaches 400° to 500°, at which time
the food to be smoke-cooked is introduced.

To return to the camper for a final
word: There is no law, of course, against
his availing himself of ready-made instead
of improvised cooking gear; and as much
of it as the traffic will bear. A gasoline or
propane-fired stove is a great convenience
and, if he expects to do any baking, a reflector oven a downright necessity. Shown
on page 133 is a folding oven. If that is
not available, use as a substitute a camp
skillet, as sketched, braced either by a
forked stick or rocks. There are even
available, for the Davy Crocketts of the
New Frontier, various solar heat cookers;
but it is suggested that they be given
home-side tryouts in advance.

We have described—at least briefly—
the elements of camp and pit cookery. The
disadvantages of the latter, as we have indicated, are several. The greatest, perhaps,
is its relative inconvenience. That is one
reason why the above-ground cookout—as
distinguished from the subterranean type
—is far and away the more popular.
There, again, we most enjoy the simpler
techniques and procedures: those which
involve direct heat from reduced charcoal.
Among them, we prefer, also, portable
rather than built-in cookers; and here we
seem to be following a definite trend. The
rather formidable backyard fireplace is less
and less favored. It had metal components
which were hard to clean and rusted in
the weather. These built-in features offered unintended hospitality to spiders,
wasps and field-mice. And its homely arch-
itecture can hardly be said to have graced
its surroundings. Now, the most popular
cookout stove is the portable brazier-type,
of which the hibachi is the Far-Eastern
representative. To accommodate a main
dish for groups of four or more, only the
larger Westernized brazier offers an adequate cooking surface. A hibachi-type
broiler or two will supplement this larger
grill in the preparation of side dishes, such
as hors d'oeuvre and vegetables. The circular grill shown boasts some improve-
ments over the original prototype. It has,
of course, fairly good-size wheels for easy
transport, as well as a hood or collar to

protect the grill surface against wind. The
grill itself may be twirled, to expose food
to the most active area of the heat and is
equipped with a screw device which raises
and lowers it for varied exposures. We
also show another model with a bellows,
which compensates for the small lower
draft-port found on the hibachi. This enables the cook to bring up quick high heat

for searing and rewarming. Some braziers
with horizontal grills have superimposed
over them a spit, in which case they are
commonly protected from wind by three
bent metal walls and a metal roof, rather
than a simple hood. Without an electrical
connection or making use of a cumbersome
counter-weight system, the only practical
way to turn a spit is by hand; and this—
make no mistake—is a real chore. On the
whole, should you go in extensively for
spit-cooking, we should advise either precooking the meat in the kitchen till nearly
done or investing in an electric rotisserie.

Remember that in all spit cooking, the weight losses due to shrinkage are great.

If you do cook out of doors electrically, you may want to make use of a vertical, rather than a horizontal, broiler which, in theory at least, exposes a maximum of food surface to the heat source. Newer still are infra-red broilers. But these, for what they are worth, we regard as strictly indoor appliances. Whatever equipment you use, pay close attention to the directions furnished with it by its manufacturer. Such brochures have become more and more informative and presently cover not only how to use the appliance itself, but how to cook a large number of typically outdoor dishes with it.

For cookout accessories, assuming a full scale operation, the following are recommended: a kettle for boiling water; a black iron pot for burgoos, stews or beans; a skillet or two; hinged wire basket grills with long handles—especially desirable for broiling fish and hamburgers; some sharp knives; a metal fork with an insulated handle; a spatula; tongs; a long pastry brush for glazing; a chopping block; skewers—these must be nonrusting ♦ square or oval, not round, in section and sharp-pointed; a roll of double-strength aluminum foil; a supply of potholders or a couple of pairs of asbestos mitts; individual serving trays; a pail of water and, with it, a flare-up quencher. For this last, an extra baster will do—or a water pistol. If you plan to roast a fowl or a joint, you will need, in addition, a baster, shown on page 386, and a meat thermometer.

♦ To prepare a brazier fire with charcoal, be sure that you build a big enough bed of coals to last out the cooking operation. We find prepared hardwood briquets most uniform and convenient. They should be put into the brazier approximately two deep—preferably over a layer of gravel—enough to level the bed out to the edge of the bowl.

A circle of aluminum foil, cut to size and put down over the gravel, will keep it from getting greasy and act as a heat reflector. Ignition may be helped along by pouring over the briquets a small amount of commercial lighter fluid ♦ before, not after, applying the match. Never use any strong-smelling substance as starter. To ready fuel for an extended firing period, arrange an extra circle of briquets around the edge of the brazier. As the center of your fire burns to embers, these may be pushed inward.¹

To ignite charcoal is often frustrating, especially if it is old and has been exposed to air—for it absorbs moisture so easily. A good way to avoid irritation is to keep a few briquettes soaking in lighter fluid ♦ in a tightly lidded metal container. You will find 1 or 2 of these saturated blocks is a great help.

Confect for yourself a 12- or 15-inch length of lightweight stove pipe, cut at the base every two inches with a tin snips to the depth of about 2½ inches to make a fluted edge—or punch holes in it about 1 inch up. Place it in the grill, put some paper near one of the fluted openings, place one or two of the saturated briquettes on the paper and then the other briquettes you are going to use on top. Light the paper. In about 5 to 10 minutes the briquettes will have become well ignited. Gently pull up the chimney with tongs and the briquettes will spread out so you can arrange them in whatever grilling pattern you plan to use—in one layer on one-half of the fire box of your circular twirl grill, as shown on page 136, or spaced at 1- to 2-inch intervals over the whole surface of the firebed or in a double ring around the edge for a spitted bird. If you use any kind of smoked or flavored chips, soak them in water for several hours beforehand and then wait until a few minutes before the charcoal is completely reduced, which should take anywhere from a half hour to 45 minutes, before placing them on the coals. ♦ When the charcoal is covered with a fine white ash, you are ready to begin cooking. Flick off the ash, which acts as insulation.

Judging the heat of a brazier fire is strictly a matter of manual training. Hold your hand above the grill at about the same distance from the coals that the food will be while cooking, while the name of a four-syllable state—"Massachusetts" or "Mississippi" will do nicely. If you can pronounce it once before snatching your hand away, your coals are delivering high heat; twice, medium heat; if three times, low heat.

Remember always that a number of factors influence the degree of heat transferred to food cooked on outdoor braziers; some of these being charcoals; their depth; distance between coals and grill; temperature of ingredients, which, if possible should be about 70°. You may also considerably influence heat transfer by your arrangement of coals: deepening them for concentration, spreading them apart for diffusion, etc. If you have the kind of brazier grill which twirls, heaping hot coals up on one side of the fire pot will make instantly available both very high and very moderate heat.

What food should be cooked out of doors? Just as we recommend simple cooking equipment in the open, so we now urge simple outdoor menus. The truth is that refined or fancy effects are—in the nature of things—all but impossible, not to say inappropriate. Again, certain kinds of food respond unfavorably or indifferently to outdoor cooking techniques: yeast breads are a conspicuous example; some vegetables are another; and among the meats, veal and pork, except, of course, pork sausages and—just because they are so delicious on a sparkling autumn afternoon—spareribs. But spareribs should be at least parboiled beforehand, page 132, and only finished off and rebasted on spit or grill out of doors.

Build your cookout meal around one basic delicious grilled or roasted meat course, complemented by crisp bread and a crisp salad. Let side dishes be strictly side-issues. The dessert should be correspondingly uncomplicated and, if baked, prepared beforehand in the kitchen. ◗ Remember with Picnic Food, page 25, to protect it always against insects.

Throughout this book you will find recipes which we regard as suitable for outdoor cookery marked with this grill-like symbol ☰. While, obviously, pan-broiled and pan-cooked food may be prepared over a brazier out of doors, you will not find such recipes singled out by the distinctive outdoor cookery symbol. We have, in large part, selected those in which the flavor is actually improved by the outdoor cooking medium.

Steaks and chops are extraordinarily well suited to flat-broiling on a brazier. ◗ Choose well-marbled meat—in other words, meat that is rather fatty in texture, page 381. But, by this, we definitely do not mean meat which has a rim or collar of fat. On the contrary, it is important ◗ to trim off all excess fat before broiling, to reduce the risk of flare-up. Also, cut through encircling sinew—being careful not to slice into the meat itself—so that the meat does not curl up under the high heat which initiates its cooking. ◗ Avoid excessively thick cuts: an inch and a half should be the limit for individual servings. Grease the grill first with some of the meat fat or with a vegetable oil. ◗ To sear the meat and seal in its juices, lower the grill close to the coals before laying the meat on it or use the bellows attachment if it is equipped with one.

Searing to seal is even more essential in flat-broil grilling than in pan or oven broiling, because the meat juices, once lost, are irrecoverable. After searing, raise the grill to about three inches from the fire and broil the meat until done. No specific time schedule for doneness can be set up because so much depends not only on the degree of heat itself, but on the age of the animal, how long the meat has been hung, the nature of the cut and, of course, individual preference.

Here are a few things to keep in mind: First, just as in indoor Timing, page 386, large cuts do not take weight for weight proportionately more cooking time. Second, to secure rareness in meat, turn it—but best practice is to turn as infrequently as possible. Third, if the cut is large, testing for doneness with a thermometer is safer than testing with a knife or fork. We would like to spare you the ordeal of an old friend of ours, whose enthusiasm for outdoor grilling is repeatedly dampened by his wife's low-voiced but grim injunction: "Remember, Orville, medium-burnt, not well-burnt."

◗ If you flat-broil chicken or other fowl, restrict the weight of the bird to two pounds or under. Split it in half, grease both sides with cooking oil, set the halves on the grill, cavity side down. The bony structure of the bird will transmit heat to the flesh above and at the same time provide insulation. Finish the cooking on the fleshy side; but ◗ to keep the skin from sticking, make sure to lower the heat before doing so.

Spit and rotisserie cooking are best for very small or large fowl; for joints, like leg of lamb, and for other chunky cuts of meat. Here again, consult the directions which come with your equipment to determine maximum weight, which will probably be in the neighborhood of ten pounds for roast meat and up to 15 for fowl. Smaller birds should be strung transversely on the spit, larger ones head to tail along the spit's axis, as illustrated.

For spare-ribs, get your butcher to cut them in half crosswise,· forming two long strips; prebake or parboil them in the kitchen and then string them, in turn—like an accordion—on your outdoor spit, as shown. Fowl and certain other types of meat must be trussed before spitting. Especially if they are heavy or of irregular shape, it is necessary, while adjusting them to the skewer, to determine their approxi-

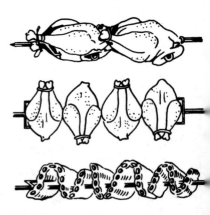

mate center of gravity. Fowl on a spit should be carefully coated in advance with melted butter or cooking oil. You may baste with butter or oil during the cooking period but ◗ do not apply any barbecue sauce until the last 15 to 20 minutes of cooking. For Barbecue Sauces, see page 332.

■ ♦ For cooking Vegetables, see page 253.
■ ♦ For Cooking on Skewers, see pages 124 and 138.

TIMING IN COOKING

How long to heat food? There are many answers. They lie in the interaction of the heat source, the equipment and the cooking medium, air, liquid or fat.

Consider the following rates of heat transferral. A dough that either bakes at 400° or steams at 212° for 20 minutes will cook in deep fat heated to 400° in 3 minutes. A hard-cooked egg will cool off in five minutes if plunged into ice water, but will need 20 minutes to cool in 32° air. A vegetable that will cook in 20 minutes in water at 212° will need only 2 minutes steaming under 15 lbs. pressure at 250°.

A great deal in timing depends on the freshness of food—this is especially true of vegetables—on the aging and fat content of meat and on the size of the food unit. Large, thick objects like roasts need lower heat and a longer cooking period than cutlets, to allow heat penetration to the deep center. The amount of surface exposed is also a factor, as you know from experience with whole as against diced vegetables.

Still another determinant is the reflective and absorptive quality of the pan. Recent tests have shown that a whole hour can be cut from the roasting time of a ten- or twelve-pound turkey if it is cooked in one of those dark enamel pans which absorbs heat rather than in a shiny metal one that reflects it. And we have discussed elsewhere, page 131, the insulative qualities of foil when used in wrap-cooking. Personal preference affects timing, of course, as well as the idiosyncrasies of equipment. Even placement in an oven, page 140, makes a difference and, last but not least, the temperature of food at the onset of heating. For all these reasons it is with some trepidation that we have indicated cooking periods in our individual recipes. And with some reluctance we have discarded the simple, safe admonition "cook until done." We know from our fan mail that cooking times are among the most worrisome of all problems for the beginning cook. Therefore, if our timing does not correspond to yours, we beg you to look for solutions in the facts we have set down above, before you take pen in hand.

HOLDING FOOD AT SERVING
TEMPERATURES AND REHEATING FOOD

Everyone knows that food which is held hot or reheated is not as tasty or nutritious as that served immediately after preparation. Unfortunately, laggards and leftovers are a cook's frequent fate. Here are a few hints on the best procedures.

♦ There are 2 ways to reheat dishes which are apt to curdle when subjected to high, direct temperatures. These include au gratin, egg or creamed dishes or any other dish rich in fat. One way is to put them in the oven in a container of hot water—allowing the water to come up about two thirds of the way on the cooking pan. The other way is to place under the pan a cookie tin, with the shiny side down —so that the heat is deflected. The latter suggestion is particularly handy in reheating pies or cakes to avoid overbrowning.

♦ Reheat other cream and egg-sauced foods in a double boiler ♦ over—not in— hot water.

♦ To retain color in vegetables which are reheated in a double boiler, use a vented lid.

♦ If reheating whole roasts, bring them to room temperature and then heat through in a moderate oven.

♦ If reheating roasted meat, slice it paper thin and put it on hot plates just before pouring over it ♦ boiling hot gravy. Any other method of reheating will toughen it and make it taste second-hand.

♦ To reheat deep-fat fried foods, which tend to go limp if steam develops, spread them on racks ♦ uncovered, in a 250° oven.

♦ To hold pancakes, place them on and between cloth towels in a 200° oven.

♦ To reheat casseroles, bring to 70° then place in a 325° preheated oven.

♦ To hold delicate sauces, use a wide-mouthed vacuum bottle.

♦ To reheat creamed or clear soups or sauces, heat to boiling point and serve immediately.

Devices which also hold foods for short periods are electrically controlled trays, individual retractable infra-red lamps, the age-old chafing dish and the bain-marie or steam table. None of these should be used for a protracted period, however, if you hope to preserve real flavor. Holding temperatures should be at about 140°.

ABOUT COOKING EQUIPMENT

Certain cooking effects we have admired away from home and would like to bring back with us seem to defy domestication. Part of the difficulty may have to do with the way food is grown elsewhere or to the fact that it is sometimes impossible to buy ingredients of comparable freshness. But, just as often, the loss in translation may be traced to special techniques which simply cannot be duplicated in the average kitchen. This is true of the following: the quick, intense, short-lived fires and the huge pans which are essential to Chinese stir-frying; the very low, long-retained heat of the "étuve" in old French kitchens—so ideal for drying out meringues or for simmering foods in covered pots; and, for that matter, the open-air charcoal grilling in our own country, which imparts its distinctive aroma to a steak, or the seaweed-smother which gives that authentic touch to lobsters pit-cooked at the shore.

Conditions like these may be approximated in cooking on modern ranges, but never completely reproduced.

If you grew up using gas for cooking heat, you appreciate its dynamic flexibility of control. If your experience has been with electric ranges, you value the evenness of their broiling heat and the stored warmth of their surface units. The relatively new infra-red cooking appliances—including infra-red attachments for the conventional electric range—have attracted favorable attention because of their ability to reduce heating time to a fraction of its former length. Should you decide to invest in this type of equipment, be sure to read the manufacturer's booklet with care, making some mental reservations about the feasibility of "plate dinner" cooking.

Indeed, whatever your source of cooking heat, learn the characteristics of your range, thoroughly. Find out if the broiling elements need a preheating period; if broiling in the oven requires an open or a closed door; whether, when you turn the switch to "Bake," you do better leaving the top oven element in or taking it out.

In purchasing, consider the safety value of controls which are located along the front of a range instead of at the rear, where they may be obstructed by tall pans or cause injuries by bringing the hand and clothing into too near proximity to the burners. Pay particular attention, also, to the quality of oven insulation in the range you plan buying and to its venting characteristics.

In loading ovens, we make the following suggestions. ◗ Place oven racks where you want them before heating, not after. For soufflés, arrange racks to bring the dish below center, as sketched. Often, in modern ovens, slight heat is provided by a top element, enough to harden the surface of a soufflé if set too close—keeping it from expanding. For cake-baking, the best position for the pan is just above center, as shown. Commercial ovens often feature

devices for introducing moisture into an oven, as needed. In the home range, a practical substitute—should the recipe require it—consists of a shallow pan partially filled with water, as sketched on the right, below.

◗ Make sure that the pans or sheets you are using will fit the oven shelf comfortably and at the same time leave at least a 2-inch margin between them and all four walls of the oven. Overcrowding of pans must also be avoided, with none touching. If space for air circulation is not provided for, your baking will burn at the bottom. Never use 2 shelves if you can avoid doing so; but if you must, stagger the pans, as shown below. For a discussion of heat and pan-size relationships, see page 618.

In baking, set the oven control for the temperature indicated and ◗ preheat for not less than 5 minutes—in some cases, where noted, longer—before inserting the pans as quickly as possible. Try not to peek until the time is up; but if you have any doubts, wait until almost the end of the baking period.

If you use a thermostatically controlled gas or electric oven, don't think you are speeding things up by setting the thermostat higher than the recipe indicates. You will get better results at the stated temperature. And don't, incidentally, press a thermostatically controlled oven into service as a kitchen heater. This will throw the thermostat out of gear. Ovens vary, however, and thermostats, even under normal use, need frequent adjustment—at least once every 12 or 14 months.

Keep in mind always that a clean oven will maintain temperature and reflect heat more accurately than an untidy one.

As to the range top, here again, as with its interior, familiarity breeds assurance. Questions about its use are, almost without exception, answered fully in the booklet which comes with the equipment. But, if you are confronted with a range for which printed instructions are lacking or if special problems arise, call your local utility company. They maintain a staff of the most obliging and well-trained consultants, prepared to give you advice, free of charge. A most important discovery to

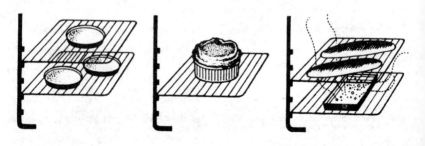

make in electric ranges is whether your surface heating units—one or several—are thermostatically controlled to level off disconcertingly when you most need sustained heat for a sauté. Also, learn if they are so differentiated as to provide all the potentials of an electric skillet.

In using gas burners, watch not only the dial, if you have a dial set, but the relation of flame to pan. ◗ The flame should never extend farther than ½ inch inside the outer edge of the pan-bottom.

ABOUT UTENSILS

The material of which pots and pans are made, as well as their size and shape, can often spell success or failure. So, often in this book we not only caution about too high heat, but especially warn against the combination of high heat and thin cooking pans. We do so because when our mail brings distress signals—which are few—they are run up, as often as not, by users of "The Joy" who have neglected this warning. In addition to their other disadvantages, too-thin pans develop hot-spots, to which food will invariably stick. ◗ Choose a pan, then, of fairly heavy gauge, the bottom of which will diffuse heat evenly.

HEAVY ALUMINUM

This has good diffusion but it will pit—no matter how expensive. And it will tend not only to discolor but will affect the color of some foods adversely. Don't clean aluminum with harsh soaps, alkalis or abrasives. To remove discoloration, boil in aluminum pans a solution of 2 teaspoons cream of tartar to 1 quart of water for 5 to 10 minutes.

COPPER

This is best in heavier gauges. It gives a quick, even heat distribution if kept clean. But, unless well tinned, or lined with stainless steel on surfaces contacting the food—it is affected by acids and can prove poisonous.

STAINLESS STEEL

Of course, this is the easiest material of all to keep clean. Its poor heat-conductivity is usually offset by thinning down the gauge, so that hot spots develop and food cooked in it is apt to burn easily.

IRON

This also has low conductivity, rusts easily and discolors acid foods. To treat new iron skillets or Dutch ovens, grease well and place in a 450° oven for 30 minutes. Scour with steel wool before using.

TEMPERED GLASS AND PORCELAIN ENAMEL

Both are poor heat conductors. The glass is apt to crack and the enamel chips. Unless of best quality and treated to resist acid foods, the glaze of enamel ware is quickly affected by them. It also is marked by metal spoons and beaters, so only wooden utensils should be used with it.

EARTHENWARE

While a poor conductor of heat, glazed or unglazed earthenware holds heat well and doesn't discolor foods. But it is heavy and breaks easily with sudden temperature changes. To treat an earthenware casserole, see page 130.

TINWARE

This has good conductivity, but it is apt to mar and then it rusts quickly. It turns dark after use and is affected by acid foods.

GREASELESS PANS

These are a delight to people suddenly put on fat-free diets, for cooking in such utensils resembles pan frying. The soapstone griddle is the ancestor of greaseless pans. And then there are skillets with nonsticking silicone and fluoro-carbon resin surfaces. These need care in handling. Use a wooden paddle for turning or a wooden spoon for stirring—to avoid marring the surface which will melt off at 450°. Eggs, breaded fish and meat will need added water.

If you are on a fat-free diet and get tired of broiling or using greaseless utensils, remember that poaching in skim milk, fruit juice, stock or wine can flavor food without the addition of fat.

PLASTICS

There are plastics which can stand high heat. But many storage containers, funnels and other kitchen utensils cannot be washed in water over 140°. Others are ruined by oil and grease. The surfaces of all plastic utensils retain grease, so don't try to get egg whites to whip in a plastic bowl, page 515.

You will wonder after reading these pros and cons what pan materials to choose. Fortunately there are on the market today a number of ◗ brands of cooking ware with good flat bottoms that combine metals to take advantage of the good diffusion of aluminum, the quick conductivity of copper and the noncorrosiveness of stainless steel. But while we are speaking of combinations of metal, let us say that ◗ copper, even when tin-lined, and iron pots must not be covered with aluminum foil if the food to be cooked is very acid, as the foil can be dissolved into it.

In fact, it is usually best to avoid dissimilar metal pots and lids when cooking any very acid foods. In the final analysis, you may still prefer a heavy iron Dutch oven for stews, an earthenware casserole for fondues, a flameproof glass vessel for sauce-making. ♦ Don't invest in large pan sets of a single material, until you know what your preference really is.

When you cook, choose a pan that fits the size of the burner. This correlation gives better cooking results and is more economical of fuel. Be sure that the lid is tight-fitting if the process calls for one. In vegetable cookery, see that the pan is filled ½ to ⅔ full if you are using a small amount of water, so enough steam can develop to cook quickly. ♦ Be sure the cooking pan is appropriate in size to its contents. Especially in braising and baking is this vital, see pages 412 and 618. Round pans will give you more even browning when baking. Square pans tend to brown too heavily at the corners. ♦ Note, too, that shiny metal baking pans deflect heat and that dark enamel or glass ones both catch and hold the heat more. Therefore, food cooked in glass or enameled pans needs at least a 25° reduction in the oven temperatures given in our recipes. While vitreous or dark metal materials may brown cookies too rapidly, they will insure better browning for pies and puff pastes. If cooking fuel is scarce, a great saving can be effected by the use of these heat-retaining pans.

In pan broiling or when using a griddle, utensils should be brought up slowly to cooking temperature. ♦ Do not make a habit of placing an unfilled pan on high heat unless it has grease or liquid in it.

♦ And should you scorch food by some unlucky chance, plunge the pan first into cold water before transferring the food to a clean container. This way the scorched taste is greatly lessened.

♦ To clean scorched pots, soak overnight with some detergent in the water. If that isn't enough, bring to boil with 1 teaspoon washing soda or cream of tartar for each quart of water.

♦ There is a certain pace in food preparation that an experienced cook learns to accept. This doesn't mean she scorns short cuts, but she comes to know when she has to take the long way 'round to get proper results. She senses, in short, not only the demands of her equipment but the reactions of her ingredients, page 482.

A man once summed up his wife's life with the epitaph, "She died of things." It might have happened to any of us. We are constantly encouraged to buy the latest gadget that will absolutely and positively make kitchen life sublime. No kitchen can ever have enough space at convenient levels to take care of even a normal array of equipment. So think hard before you buy so much as an extra skewer.

♦ Get pans that nest well. And if you can't resist a bulky mold, see that it hangs on an out-of-the-way pegboard panel or make it a decorative feature for an odd, unused nook. Buy square rather than round canisters for economical storage—see page 618 for area comparisons. Keep them and your spices in alphabetical arrangement for quick identification. ♦ And place these close to the areas where you will be using them most.

Most kitchens today are fairly scientifically laid out. Everyone is aware that the big kitchen is a time and energy waster; and that ♦ the U-shape or a triangular relationship of sink, stove and refrigerator—with their accompanying work spaces—are step-savers. But it pays occasionally to think about your work habits. See if you can make them more efficient.

♦ Nonrusting well-designed hand tools save your towels and your temper. The following is a basic, reasonably comprehensive equipment list.

HOUSEHOLD NEEDS

FOR COOKING

2 saucepans with lids
2 frying pans—large and small—with lids
1 large stewing or soup kettle
1 Dutch oven
1 double boiler
1 mold for steaming
1 dessert mold
1 deep-fat fryer
3 strainers
1 steamer
1 colander
1 bean pot
Coffee maker
Tea kettle
China teapot
Candy thermometer
Deep fat frying thermometer

FOR THE OVEN

1 open roasting pan with rack
3 round 9-inch cake pans
2 square 9-inch cake pans
2 loaf or bread pans
2 cake racks for cooling
1 muffin tin
2 pie pans—tin or glass
2 cookie sheets
1 large casserole
6 custard cups
1 9-inch tube pan
1 shallow 9 x 12-inch pan
1 8-inch soufflé baker
Meat thermometer

FOR PREPARATION

1 set of mixing bowls
1 8-oz. dry measuring cup
1 8-oz. liquid measuring cup

1 set of measuring spoons
Serving spoons
1 wooden slotted spoon for cake mixing
3 wooden spoons
1 large fork
1 small fork
2 paring knives
1 bread knife and 1 meat knife
1 French chopping knife
Grapefruit knife
Cutting board
Spatula
1 egg beater and mixer
Ladle
A 4-sided and a rotary grater
1 meat grinder
1 sugar or flour scoop
Funnel
Tongs
Flour sifter
Potato ricer or food mill
Potato masher
Wooden chopping bowl and chopper
Salad bowl
Doughnut cutter
Biscuit cutter
Pastry blender
Pastry board
Pastry brush
Vegetable brush
Rolling pin
Pastry cloth and cover for rolling pin
Pancake turner
Apple corer
Vegetable slicer or parer
Rubber scraper
Weighing spoon or scales
Ice-cream freezer
Griddle
Citrus fruit juicer
Food mill or ricer
Electric mixer
Blender
Pressure cooker
Toaster
Waffle iron

KITCHEN ACCESSORIES

4 canisters
1 bread box and 1 cake carrier
1 dish drainer
1 garbage can
1 waste basket
1 vegetable bin
1 or more trays
Bottle opener
Corkscrew
Can opener
Pot holders
1 bucket
Kitchen shears
Toothpicks for testing cake
Nutcracker
Salt and pepper shakers
Knife sharpener
Set of refrigerator containers
Waxed paper
Plastic storage bags

Aluminum foil
Paper towels
Dishpan
Whisk broom
1 broom
1 dust mop
1 scrubbing brush
Dust pan and brush
12 dish towels
4 dish cloths
2 dust cloths
Plastic detergent dispenser with brush
Plastic sponges
Asbestos pad

ABOUT BURNS AND BURNING

In the foregoing pages we have supplied, among other information, enough facts to keep our readers from ever burning the food they heat. Now for a few safeguards against burning the cook—and what to do should such an emergency occur.

♦ Never throw water on a grease fire. Use salt, soda or, if the area is a small one, a metal lid.

♦ Choose a range, if you can find one, on which the burners are level with the surrounding platform area, so pots cannot tip.

♦ Use flat-bottomed, well-balanced pans that are steady when empty. Be sure handles are not too heavy for the pot so they will tip; or so long that they can be knocked against or catch a sleeve.

♦ When deep-fat frying, please note the precautions given on pages 124-126.

♦ Put boiling liquid to the back of the stove, out of reach of small children.

♦ In pan-frying, keep a colander handy to place over the pan should the fat begin to sputter.

♦ In pouring hot liquids into glass, be sure to put a metal spoon in the glass to absorb excess heat.

♦ Watch that your hands or the cloths you are using are not damp in touching or wiping electrical equipment.

♦ Have polarized attachments put on your electrical appliances to avoid shock.

♦ Should you receive extensive or painful burns, call a doctor, lie down until skilled help comes and keep quiet and warm to avoid subsequent shock. If someone is with you, let her remove any loose clothing near the burned area, but do not let her touch any material that is sticking to the burned flesh. If you are burned over a limited area, cover the burn with a sterile petrolatum salve and sterile gauze. Never use cotton on a burned area. If the burn is more extensive but light, apply strips of sterile bandage that have been dipped in a solution of 3 tablespoons soda or Epsom salts to 1 quart clear water. A new therapy for the treatment of small burns about the hands is to plunge the burned area into cold water.

SOUPS

In the good old days, when a soup "bunch" cost a nickel and bones were lagniappe, pounds and pounds of meat trimmings and greenstuff were used in the household to concoct wonderful essences for everyday consumption. The best soups are still based on homemade stocks. ◗ Please read About Stocks, page 488, and all the suggestions offered for the long slow cooking of meat stocks or the rapid cooking of fish fumets and vegetable stocks, which apply to soup making. Fish and vegetable stocks are especially important in "au maigre" or meatless cooking.

To minimize cooking time, use your ⅄ blender as a preliminary step for the processing of raw vegetables, your ✿ pressure cooker for suitable meat scraps, fresh or leftover. See Quick Household Stock, page 490. Because not everyone wants to bother with the painstaking methods often required to extract soup stock, and because soups are such an interesting addition to or base for meals, we suggest toward the end of this chapter a large number of time-saving prepared soup combinations. Have on hand a supply of canned, dried or frozen bases to bring quick and revivifying soups into the range of even the most casual cook. No one can afford to be without a varied store of these consistently good, and often excellent products. However, just because they are so convenient and constantly served, even as our spoons stir up their aroma, our palates weary of these prepared soup flavors.

Learn to use herbs and seasonings, page 529-542. Keep your own economical stockpot, page 488, to dilute concentrated soups, and to enrich them with added minerals and vitamins. Astound your friends with effortlessly made and unusually flavored soup sensations!

No matter by what method made, soup should complement or contrast with what is to follow; and however enticing its name, it will fit into one of the categories below:

Some of the above are served hot, some cold, some either way, like bouillons, borsch and vichyssoise. ◗ To serve soups piping hot—use tureens, lidded bowls or well-heated cups. Especially if drinks and hors d'oeuvre have been offered before, a hot soup helps to recondition the palate.

◗ Cold soups should be very well chilled, and served in chilled dishes—especially jellied soups, which tend to break down more rapidly because they are relatively light in gelatin. Cold soups, when not jellied, may be prepared quickly by using a ⅄ blender and chilling in the freezer. On informal occasions, they may be chilled in a tall jug and served directly from it into chilled cups or bowls.

You should be able to count on about 6 servings from a quart of soup, unless it is being used as the mainstay for a lunch—as is so frequently the case with a potage, or a soup rich in solids. ◗ The quantities noted under the titles of individual recipes are consistently given in standard 8-ounce cups.

There are some classic dishes—Petite Marmite, New England Boiled Dinner or Goulash—that occupy middle ground between soups and stews.

▲ Above 2500 feet, soups need longer cooking periods than called for in the regular recipes, as the liquids boil at a lower temperature.

ABOUT SEASONING SOUP

Soup is as flavorful as the stock on which it is based. See page 488, and the comments on seasoning, page 489.

The addition of wine to soup frequently enhances its flavor, but ◗ do not oversalt soups to which wine is added, as the wine intensifies saltiness. Wines that blend well with bland soups, such as those made with chicken or veal, are a not too dry sherry or Madeira. Don't use more than ¼ cup wine to 1 quart soup. A strongly flavored soup, prepared with beef or oxtail, is improved by the addition of some dry red table wine—½ cup wine to 1 quart soup. A dry white table wine adds zest to a fish, crab or lobster bisque or chowder. Use ⅛ to ¼ cup wine to 1 quart soup. Wines should be added to the hot soup shortly before it is served. ♦ Do not boil the soup after adding the wine.

Beer adds a tang to bean, cabbage and vegetable soups. Use 1 cup for every 3 cups soup. Add the beer just before serving. Reheat the soup well, but ♦ do not boil.

ABOUT COLORING SOUP

If soups have been cooked with browned onions or onion skins, and if the amount of meat used has been substantial, they should have a good, rich color. Tomato skins also lend color interest. Caramelized Sugar II, page 508, may be added if necessary. We prefer it to commercial soup coloring, which is apt to overwhelm a delicately flavored soup with its own pervasive and telltale aroma. About Vegetables for Soup, see page 491.

ABOUT CEREALS FOR THICKENING SOUPS

Precooked cereal garnishes, such as rice, noodles and dumplings, give an effect of body to a clear soup, but a very different one from the more integral raw thickeners suggested below. These make for intriguing texture and elegance of flavor.

To add any of the following, bring the soup to a boil and reduce the heat again to a simmer as soon as the addition has been made. Stir ♦ raw cereals into soup for the last hour of cooking. For a light thickening, allow to the original amount of water approximately:

1 teaspoon barley to 1 cup water
1 teaspoon green kern to 1 cup water
1 teaspoon rice to 1 cup water
1 teaspoon oatmeal to 1 cup water
2 tablespoons wheat germ flour
   to 1 cup water
2 tablespoons peanut flour to
   1 cup water
2 tablespoons soya flour to 1 cup water
½ teaspoon quick-cooking tapioca
   to 1 cup water

If you wish to thicken cooked soup with flour, allow:

1½ teaspoons flour to 1 cup soup

Make a paste of the flour with about:

Twice as much cold stock, milk
   or water

Pour the paste slowly into the boiling soup, while stirring. Simmer and stir for 5 to 10 minutes. Or, as in cream sauce, make a roux, see page 319, of:

1½ teaspoons butter
1½ teaspoons flour

Pour the soup over this mixture, stirring constantly until smooth and boiling. Or add:

Flour and butter

to cooled soup in a ⅃ blender—then reheat the soup. Bring to a boil, lower heat and simmer for 5 minutes.

Additional thickenings for soup are dry, crustless French bread or Panades, page 155. Also, thick cream or a cream or Béchamel sauce, page 322, may be used.

ABOUT OTHER THICKENINGS FOR SOUPS

Egg yolks are one of the richest and best of soup thickeners—but they must be added just before serving. ♦ Care must be taken, when this is done, that the soup is not too hot.

Allow for each cup of soup:

1 egg yolk, beaten with
1 tablespoon cream or sherry

To avoid curdling, it is wise to add to this beaten mixture a small quantity of the hot soup before incorporating it into the soup pot. ♦ When using egg or cream-based thickeners, it is always essential that the soup, after their addition, be kept below the boiling point. You may prefer riced hard-cooked eggs. Allow:

2 yolks for each cup of soup

Add at the last minute and, of course, do not allow the soup to boil.

A good soup thickener, for those whose diet does not include flour, consists of:

3 tablespoons grated raw potato

for each cup of soup. Grate the potato directly into the soup about 15 minutes before it has finished cooking. Then simmer until the potato is tender, when it will form a thickener.

Soups cooked with starchy vegetables, such as dried beans, peas or lentils, will separate and must be bound. To do this, allow:

1 tablespoon melted butter
1 tablespoon flour

Well blended with a small amount of:

Cold water, stock or milk

Stir this mixture into about:

3 cups strained boiling soup

and simmer at least 5 minutes before serving.

ABOUT REMOVING GREASE FROM SOUP

I. Chill the soup. The grease rises at once and will solidify when cold. It is then a simple matter to remove it.

II. Float a paper towel on the surface of the soup and when it has absorbed as much grease as it will hold discard it; or roll a paper towel and use one end to skim over the soup surface to remove the fat. When the ends become coated with grease, cut off the used part with scissors and repeat the process.

III. Use your meat baster with bulb as a suction device.

ABOUT SOUP MEAT

Any meat that is ♦ immersed in cold water and simmered for a long period is bound to give its best flavor to the cooking liquor. But some food values remain in the meat and it may be heightened in flavor by serving it, when removed from the soup, with one of the sauces below:

Horseradish Sauce, page 325
Mustard Sauce, page 325
Tomato Sauce, page 333
Brown Onion Sauce, page 327

ABOUT CLEAR SOUPS

Because so much valuable material and expert time goes into the making of clear soups and because they taste so delicious, most of us assume that they have high nutritive value. It disappoints us to have to tell you that, while they are ♦ unsurpassed as appetite stimulators, the experts give them an indifferent rating as foods. If you have the time, do create these delicious broths by degreasing, clarifying and correcting the seasonings of stocks.
I. For chicken broth use:
Chicken Stock, page 490

II. For game broth use:
Fowl, Rabbit or Game Stock, page 491

III. For fish broth use:
Fumet or Fish Stock, page 491

IV. For vegetable broth use:
Vegetable Stock, page 492

♦ Be sure to see Garnishes for Soups, page 169.

CONSOMMÉ
Prepare:
Brown Stock I, page 490
and clarify it by the quick method, page 489. This will give you a clear, thin consommé. For double strength, clarify the stock by the second method.

CONSOMMÉ BRUNOISE
3 Cups
Make a mixture of the following finely diced vegetables:
1 rib of celery
1 small carrot
½ small turnip
½ small onion
Sauté them gently in:
1 tablespoon heated butter
Enough time should be allowed to let the vegetables absorb the grease but ♦ do not let them brown. Add:
1 cup consommé
and continue cooking, covered, until the vegetables are tender. Pour into:
2 cups hot consommé
Degrease and
Correct the seasoning
Just before serving, add:
1 tablespoon finely chopped chervil
1 tablespoon cooked peas
1 tablespoon finely diced cooked green beans

CONSOMMÉ MADRILÈNE
About 5 Cups
Heat to the boiling point and strain:
2 cups tomato juice
½ teaspoon grated onion
2 cups Chicken Stock, opposite
A piece of lemon rind
Salt and pepper
Flavor with:
Lemon juice, dry sherry or Worcestershire sauce
Or garnish with:
Cultured sour cream
dotted with:
Red caviar

CHICKEN OR TURKEY BROTH
♦ See the many cream soups, page 157 and egg garnished soups, page 169, based on this simple broth.
Prepare:
Fowl, Rabbit or Game Stock, page 491
or use canned stock.
When it is boiling, remove from heat. You may add for each 4 cups:
½ cup cream
Reheat but ♦ do not boil. Serve with chiffonade of herbs, page 173, with dumplings, page 170.

CHICKEN BROTH OR BOUILLON WITH EGG
Individual Serving
A good dish for an invalid, but not to be scorned by those in good health.
Degrease, clarify, and heat:
Chicken Broth, above
Correct the seasoning

SOUPS

For every cup added:
>(1 teaspoon lemon juice)
>(1 tablespoon chopped parsley)

When the soup is hot add:
>An egg drop, page 169

allowing 1 egg per serving. Serve at once.

POT-AU-FEU, POULE-AU-POT OR PETITE MARMITE
About 6 Cups Broth

A marmite is an earthenware lidded pot, higher than it is wide. Its material accounts in part for the flavor of the soup. In pot-au-feu, another name for petite marmite, the major meat is beef, with an addition of chicken wings and gizzards. In making poule-au-pot, the beef is cooked with a juicy hen—the hen which Henry IV wanted for every pot. Marrow bones are usually included, tied in cheesecloth. The vegetables may be seasonally varied. Blanched cabbage is often added.

Put in a marmite:
>2½ quarts cold water
>2 lbs. shank or chuck beef, cut in chunks

Tie in cheesecloth and add:
>(1 knucklebone)

Bring this mixture ◗ slowly to a boil and ◗ skim well. Cut Parisienne style, page 251, and add:
>2 carrots
>1 small turnip
>3 leeks: white parts only
>1 whole onion stuck with 1 clove
>1 teaspoon salt
>1 Bouquet Garni II, page 541

Bring these ingredients to a boil. ◗ Skim again. ◗ Cover and cook slowly for about 3 hours in a 350° oven. The bouillon should be clear and amber in color.

To serve, either start with the clear soup and offer the meat and vegetables on the side or reserve them for a second meal. Crusty thin slices of bread, which may be spread with Parmesan cheese, are delightful accompaniments to a pot-au-feu.

BOUILLON

Bouillon is an unsalted strong beef stock, not as sweet as consommé.

Clarify and reduce by ⅓:
>Brown Soup Stock I or II, page 490
>Correct the seasoning

Serve with:
>A Garnish for Clear Soups, page 169

TOMATO BOUILLON
About 3 Cups

Bring to the boiling point and simmer for about 5 minutes:
>3 cups strained tomato juice
>½ small bay leaf
>¼ cup cut up celery, with leaves
>2 tablespoons chopped fennel
>2 whole cloves
>1 tablespoon fresh basil
>(1 small skinned, chopped and sautéed onion)

Strain, and degrease if necessary.
>Correct the seasoning

Serve hot or cold in cups, topped with a teaspoon of:
>Whipped cream or cultured sour cream

BEEF TEA
About ¾ Cup

Grind twice:
>1 lb. lean round steak or neck bone meat

Place in a quart mason jar and add:
>1 cup cold water
>½ teaspoon salt

Cover the jar lightly. Place the jar on a cloth in a pan containing as much cold water as possible without upsetting the jar. Bring the water slowly to a gentle boil and continue for about 1 hour. Remove the jar. Place on a cake rack to cool as rapidly as possible. Strain the juice. Store it in a covered container in the refrigerator until ready to heat and serve.

KREPLACH SOUP
About 4 Cups

Prepare:
>Noodle Dough II, page 172

This will make about 20 pastries. Do not allow the dough to dry, however, before cutting it into 3-inch squares. Put about 1½ tablespoons of one of the following fillings in the center of each square.

I. Sauté in:
>1 tablespoon cooking oil
>½ cup minced onions
>½ lb. ground beef

Add:
>¾ teaspoon salt
>¼ teaspoon pepper

II. Or combine:
>1½ cups minced cooked chicken
>¼ cup minced sautéed onion
>1 egg yolk
>¾ teaspoon salt
>1 tablespoon chopped parsley

Fold the dough over into a triangular shape. Press the open edges carefully with a fork to seal them completely. Before cooking ◗ allow the kreplach to dry on a flour-dusted towel for 30 minutes on each side. Then drop them into:
>About 1 gallon rapidly boiling broth or salted water

and ◗ simmer gently for 7 to 10 minutes. Drain well and serve in:
>3 cups strong broth

WON TON SOUP
About 4 Cups

Prepare:
>Noodle Dough II, page 172

The fillings may be:
>Cooked pork, chicken, shrimp, crabmeat or Chicken Farce, page 458

Combine:
>½ lb. cooked pork or veal, etc.

2 finely chopped green onions, white
parts only
1 cup chopped spinach
1 beaten egg

There are many fancy wrappings for won
ton, which in most cases produce a high
proportion of paste to meat. If truly Chinese, won tons emerge with a rather loose
shape and a fluttery outline. Cook by putting all the won ton at once into:

About 1 gallon rapidly boiling water

Lower the heat at once to medium. When
the water again comes to a boil, add:

2 cups cold water

to temper the dough. About 10 minutes
should elapse from the time the won tons
are first added to the boiling water until
they are ready to serve. Put 5 won tons
for each serving into a soup bowl. Sprinkle them with:

(Soy sauce)

Have ready and pour over them:

3 cups hot, seasoned, clear chicken
broth or bouillon

A few prettily cut Chinese vegetables or
partially cooked spinach leaves with mid-
stems removed, usually garnish the broth.

VEGETABLE BROTH

About 3½ Cups

Quickly made and very good. Serve
strained or unstrained, hot or chilled.
Chop:

3 cups or more Vegetables for Soup,
page 492

Sauté them gently and slowly for 5 minutes in:

3 tablespoons butter

◗ Do not let them brown. Add:

4 cups boiling water or part water
and tomatoes or tomato juice

Simmer the soup, partially covered, for
about 1 hour. Season and add:

(1 bouillon cube)

MUSHROOM BROTH

I.   **About 6 Cups**

Prepare:

¾ lb. diced mature mushrooms
2 ribs celery, diced
½ skinned and diced carrot
¼ skinned and diced onion

Cover these vegetables with:

3 cups water

◗ Simmer partially covered for 45 minutes.
Strain the broth. Add, to make 6 cups of
liquid:

Chicken Stock, page 490, or Beef
Consommé, page 146

Add, if needed:

Salt and paprika

Serve very hot. Add to each cup:

1 tablespoon dry sherry

II. Blend or chop until fine:

¾ lb. mature mushrooms

Add them to:

6 cups Chicken Stock, page 490,
or consommé

Simmer, partially covered, for about 15
minutes or only 5 if you use the ⅃ blender.
Strain if you like or thicken, page 145.
Serve as for I, above.

ONION SOUP

6 Cups

Onion soup, with vegetable substituted for
meat stock, is used for meals "au maigre,"
also see Fish Stock, page 491.

Sauté until well browned, but not burned:

1½ cups thinly sliced onions

in:

3 tablespoons butter

Add:

6 cups beef or chicken broth
¼ teaspoon freshly ground
black pepper

Cover and cook over low heat or in a 275°
oven for 30 minutes. Either way, the soup
is now put into a casserole, covered with:

6 slices toasted French bread

Sprinkle over the toast:

1 cup grated Parmesan cheese

Heat in the oven for about 10 minutes or
until the cheese is melted. Add:

(A dash of cognac or dry sherry)

CLEAR WATER CRESS SOUP

About 5 Cups

Simmer together:

5 cups hot chicken broth
1½ cups chopped water cress

for 4 to 6 minutes or until water cress is
just dark green—not an olive green. Serve
at once.

COLD TOMATO SOUP
OR GAZPACHO

About 6 Cups

A summer delight—chilled vegetable soup
with fresh herbs.

Peel and seed:

2 large ripe tomatoes

Seed and remove membrane from:

1 large sweet pepper

Peel:

1 clove garlic

Wash:

½ cup or more fresh mixed herbs:
chives, parsley, basil, chervil, tarragon

Place all ingredients in a wooden chopping
bowl. Chop them. Stir in, gradually:

½ cup olive oil
3 tablespoons lemon or lime juice
3 cups chilled water or light stock

Add:

1 peeled, thinly sliced sweet
Spanish onion
1 cup peeled, seeded, diced
or grated cucumber
1½ teaspoons salt or more, if needed
½ teaspoon paprika

Some cooks prefer to use their ⅃ blender

for the above vegetables. Chill the soup
for 4 hours or more before serving.
To serve, place in each bowl:
  2 ice cubes
  1 tablespoon chopped parsley
Add the soup and sprinkle the tops with:
  ½ cup crumbled stale bread

JELLIED CLEAR SOUPS
These delicious warm weather soups may
be more highly seasoned than hot soups,
but ♦ watch their salt content. If you prepare them in advance, their saltiness is
intensified.
Serve with:
  A lemon and parsley garnish
You may add to the soup before jelling:
  A few drops of Worcestershire sauce
Or allow per cup:
  1 tablespoon sherry or 1 teaspoon
    lemon juice
If you add more lemon juice, be sure you
have allowed sufficient gelatin. Stock made
from veal knuckle and beef bone may jell
enough naturally to be served without
added gelatin. We have learned that if
canned consommé is from a new pack, it,
too, has enough gelatin in it to respond
favorably to mere chilling. If the pack is
as old as two years, it must be treated as
though it had no gelatin. ♦ Do not freeze
it, but try it out by refrigerating for at least
4 hours, to see how much additional thickening it will need. Keep in mind that, if
too stiff, soup jellies are not very attractive.
Allow, if necessary:
  1½ teaspoons gelatin
to each:
  2 cups consommé or broth
For rapid chilling, you may place clear
soups in a bowl over cracked ice or give
them a start by leaving them in the freezer
for a few minutes ♦ but not longer, as intense cold, if continued, destroys the texture.

JELLIED TOMATO BOUILLON
About 5 Cups
Soak for 5 minutes:
  2 tablespoons gelatin
in:
  ½ cup cold water
Heat to the boiling point and strain:
  2 cups tomato juice
  ½ teaspoon grated onion
  2 cups Light Soup Stock, page 490
  A piece of lemon rind
  Salt and pepper
Dissolve the gelatin in the hot stock. Cool.
Flavor with:
  Lemon juice, dry sherry or
    Worcestershire sauce
Pour stock into a wet mold. Chill. The
bouillon may be beaten slightly before
serving and garnished with:
  Lemon slices, chopped chives, mint,
    small nasturtium leaves, chopped
    olives, hard-cooked riced eggs, relish,
    horseradish, parsley or watercress

JELLIED BEET CONSOMMÉ
4 Servings
Combine and heat:
  1 cup beet juice
  1 cup consommé
Add:
  1 tablespoon gelatin dissolved over
    hot water, page 517
  Correct the seasoning
When about to jell add:
  (1 tablespoon lemon juice)
  1 cup minced cooked beets
Pour gelatin mixture into cups. In serving,
garnish each cup with:
  1 teaspoon caviar
  A slice of lemon decorated with
    minced fresh tarragon or basil, or
    a dab of cultured sour cream

BROTH ON THE ROCKS
For the guest who shuns an alcoholic
drink, offer a clear broth, such as:
  Chicken broth or bouillon
combined with:
  (Tomato and orange juice)
poured over ice cubes. ♦ Be sure the
broth is not too rich in gelatin, for it may
suddenly congeal.

FRUIT SOUPS
4 Cups
In Scandinavia, fruit soups are served as a
dessert, but in Germany, they constitute a
summertime chilled prelude to the entrée.
Either dried or fresh fruits, cooked until
they can be puréed easily, may be used.
Cherries are the most popular.
Prepare:
  1 lb. stoned cherries
Place in an enamel pan and cover with:
  2 cups water
  1 cup red wine
Add:
  ¼ cup sugar
  ½ teaspoon grated orange rind
Cook until the fruit is soft, about 10 minutes. Blend or sieve the fruit and thicken
the juice with:
  1 teaspoon arrowroot
mixed with a little of the cooled syrup. Return the mixture to the soup and cook
about 2 minutes. Serve hot or cold. Garnish with:
  Unsweetened whipped cream or
    croutons or dumplings, page 170

ABOUT THICK SOUPS
Purée, cream, bisque, velouté, potage—to
the connoisseur each of these is a quite
distinctive embodiment of the indispensable thick soup.
  If you like to attach a label to your crea-
tions, know that a purée is a soup which
gets its major thickening from the vegetable or other food put through a sieve and

has butter swirled into it at the very last moment. By omitting the butter or lessening the amount of it and adding cream and sometimes egg yolk, you get—guess what?—a cream soup! If that soup is on a shell fish base—and only if it is—you may call it a bisque. If you add both eggs and cream and a velouté sauce, see page 324, to a purée base, you achieve a velouté soup.

Potages, the most variable of soups, are likely to have the phrase "du jour" added, meaning that they are both the specialty of the day and, from the cook's point of view, seasonal and convenient to compose. Potages, which tend to be hefty, taste best when their vegetables are first braised in butter. For ways to thicken soups, see page 145.

Here are a few practical hints that will help you make the most of thickened soups. First, be sure to scrape the purée off the bottom of the strainer. ◗ If you use a ⊁ blender, first parblanch or cook any vegetables with strings, like celery, or hulls, like peas. After butter, cream or eggs are added ◗ never allow the soup to reach a boil. If you are not serving at once, heat it in a double boiler. To avoid a slight granular separation in legume soups, see page 145. Thick soups should not be served as the first course of a heavy meal. The wonderful thing about them is that they are nearly a meal by themselves. Balanced by a green salad or fruit, they make a complete luncheon.

BARLEY SOUP
I.   **About 9 to 10 Cups**
A favorite of French farmers. For the best flavor use stock from country cured hams, but not aged ones like Smithfield, Kentucky or Virginia.
Melt in a skillet:
   2 tablespoons salt pork
Cook, until translucent, in the above:
   3 tablespoons shallots or onions
Add:
   ½ cup barley
Agitate the pan to coat the barley well in the hot fat. After about 5 minutes, add:
   1 quart hot stock from
      country cured ham
Cook the mixture, covered, until the barley is tender, about 30 minutes. Bind or not as you like, depending on how rich and thick you want the soup, with:
   3 well-beaten egg yolks
   1 cup cream
◗ Heat, but do not boil after adding the eggs and cream. Before serving, add as a garnish:
   2 tablespoons finely chopped parsley
   1 cup sautéed, coarsely
      chopped mushrooms
To keep the mushrooms white, add:
   ½ tablespoon lemon juice

II. Scotch Broth
                                         About 10 to 12 Cups
Soak for 12 hours:
   ½ cup pearl barley
in:
   2 cups water
If you use other barley, soak it for 1 hour. Add this to:
   3 lbs. mutton or lamb with bones
   10 cups water
Simmer, covered, for 2 hours or until the meat is tender. Add for the last ½ hour of cooking:
   2 cups browned vegetables for soup,
      page 492
   (A dash of curry)
Remove the meat from the soup. Dice it, return it to the soup. You may use a flour or egg thickener, page 145, to bind the soup.
   Correct the seasoning
Serve garnished with:
   Chopped parsley

GREEN KERN SOUP
                                         About 9 Cups
If you are English, corn means wheat, if you are Scottish it means oats, but if you come from "down under" or are American, you know corn grows on a cob. Kern sounds as though it were somebody's word for corn, but it isn't. It's dried green wheat and makes a favorite European soup.
Soak for ½ hour:
   ½ to 1 cup green kern
in:
   4 cups water
Drain, then cook, as for Barley II, above, replacing the lamb with beef.

VEGETABLE SOUP OR
SOUP PAYSANNE
                                         5 Cups
Place in a large kettle or pressure cooker:
   2 tablespoons bacon fat or butter
Sauté briefly in the fat:
   ¼ cup diced carrots
   ½ cup diced onions
   ½ cup diced celery
Add:
   3 cups hot water or stock
   1 cup canned tomatoes
   (½ cup peeled, diced potatoes)
   (½ cup peeled, diced turnips)
   1 tablespoon chopped parsley
   ½ teaspoon salt
   ⅛ teaspoon pepper
Cover and cook for about 35 minutes; then add:
   (½ cup chopped cabbage,
      spinach or lettuce)
If using a ◷ pressure cooker, cook at 15 pounds pressure for 3 minutes. Remove from heat and let stand for 5 minutes, then reduce pressure instantly.
   Correct seasoning

and serve with:
> Melba Cheese Rounds, page 174

VEGETABLE CHOWDER
                                    About 6 Cups
Cut the stems from:
> 1 quart okra

Slice the okra. Prepare:
> 2 cups diced celery

Seed and dice:
> 1 green pepper

Skin and chop:
> 1 small onion

Sauté the vegetables for 5 minutes in:
> ¼ cup butter or bacon drippings

Skin, chop and add:
> 2 large ripe tomatoes or 1 cup
>   canned tomatoes
> 1 teaspoon brown sugar
> ¼ teaspoon paprika
> 4 cups boiling water

Stew the vegetables gently until they are
tender, for about 1 hour. Add, if required:
> Salt and paprika

Cooked chicken, meat, fish or crisp bacon
may be diced and added to the chowder.
Serve with:
> Boiled Rice, page 178

↫ BLENDER VEGETABLE SOUP
                                    About 4 Cups
Blend in:
> ¼ cup stock
> 2 cups mixed, coarsely cut vegetables

If cucumbers, celery, asparagus or onions
are used, blanch them first to soften seeds
or fibers and to make the onion flavor more
agreeable. Heat the blended vegetables
until tender in:
> 3 cups boiling stock

Serve at once.

BEET SOUP OR BORSCH
                                    About 5 Cups
There are probably as many versions of
borsch as there are Russians. For good,
quick versions, see page 166.
Peel and chop until very fine:
> ½ cup carrots
> 1 cup onions
> 2 cups beets

Barely cover these ingredients with boiling
water. Simmer gently, covered, for about
20 minutes. Add and simmer for 15 minutes more:
> 1 tablespoon butter
> 2 cups beef or other stock
> 1 cup very finely shredded cabbage
> 1 tablespoon vinegar

Place the soup in bowls. Add to each
serving:
> 1 tablespoon cultured sour cream

mixed with:
> Grated cucumber
> Correct the seasoning

and serve hot or cold with:
> Pumpernickel bread

Serve beer rather than wine with this dish.

CABBAGE SOUP
                                    About 6 Cups
This superb cabbage soup, quick and inexpensive, is from Herman Smith's book,
"Kitchens Near and Far." You will find it,
as well as his incomparable "Stina," most
rewarding.
Sauté gently in a saucepan until tender
and yellow:
> 1 large minced onion
> 1½ tablespoons butter

Grate or shred and add:
> 1 small head green cabbage:
>   about ¾ lb.

Bring to a boil:
> 4 cups Brown Stock I, page 490

Add the stock to the vegetables. Season
as needed with:
> Salt and pepper

Simmer the soup for about 10 minutes. If
you wish, use this delicious topping:
> ½ cup cultured sour cream
> 1 tablespoon minced parsley
> (½ teaspoon caraway seeds)

Place a spoonful of the sour cream mixture on each plate of soup.

CHICKEN CURRY OR
SENEGALESE SOUP
                                    About 2 Cups
Melt:
> 1 tablespoon butter

Add to it:
> ¾ to 1 teaspoon curry powder

Stir in, until blended:
> ¾ tablespoon flour

Stir in slowly:
> 1½ cups chicken broth

When the soup is boiling, season it with:
> Paprika

Reduce the heat. Beat:
> 1 egg yolk
> ¼ cup rich milk or cream

When the soup is no longer boiling, stir
these ingredients into it. Stir over low
heat until the egg has thickened slightly
▶ but do not boil. Add also, still not allowing the soup to boil:
> ¼ cup slivers of cooked
>   white chicken meat
> (2 tablespoons chutney)

Serve, hot or chilled, garnished with:
> Chopped chives

CHICKEN GUMBO
                                    About 12 Cups
Cut into pieces and dredge with flour:
> 1 stewing chicken

Brown it in:
> ¼ cup bacon grease

Pour over it:
> 4 cups boiling water

Simmer, uncovered, until the meat falls
from the bones. Drain the stock and chop
the meat. Place in the soup kettle and
simmer, uncovered, until the vegetables
are tender:
> 2 cups skinned tomatoes

½ cup green corn
1 cup sliced okra
(1 large green or
    2 small red peppers)
½ teaspoon salt
¼ cup diced onion
¼ cup rice
5 cups water

Combine these ingredients with the chicken meat and stock.

Correct the seasoning
Add:
(1 to 2 teaspoons filé powder,
    moistened with a little water)

After adding the filé ♦ do not boil the soup, as it will become stringy.

BEEF GUMBO

About 10 Cups

Melt in a skillet:
2 tablespoons butter
Add and sauté until dark brown:
    A soup bone with meat: 3 lbs.
Pour in:
12 cups water: 3 quarts
Simmer these ingredients, covered, for 2 hours. Add and simmer, covered, until the meat falls from the bone:
¼ cup chopped celery
¼ cup shredded parsley
¼ cup chopped onion
½ teaspoon salt
¼ teaspoon paprika
Strain, cool and skim the stock. Melt:
2 tablespoons butter
Add and sauté for 3 minutes:
½ cup chopped onion
½ cup fresh or canned sliced okra
1 cup chopped celery with leaves
Add:
2½ cups tomatoes
2 tablespoons quick-cooking tapioca
1 tablespoon sugar
The soup stock
Simmer the soup, covered, for 1 hour longer.

Correct the seasoning, and serve.

ABOUT LEGUME SOUPS
Lentils, Beans, Peas

Some packaged, dried legumes do not require soaking. Follow directions on the label. Soak if required, using ham stock, other stock, a broken-up turkey or chicken carcass, to which you may add ½ cup tomato juice or purée, making in all about 10 cups of liquid. Add flavor with bacon or scraps of ham or fresh pork fat. Try them out, page 510, then brown an onion in the fat. Reserve the cracklings to garnish the soup, or cook them in it. For vegetables and seasonings, see the following recipes.

For easy removal of fat, chill the soup, see page 145. Legume soups may be served unstrained, although they are usually more digestible if strained. They may be thinned with stock, tomato juice or milk. Navy bean soup always calls for milk.

Legume soups, whether made of fresh or dried materials, should be bound. To do this, melt 1 tablespoon butter, blend in 1 tablespoon flour and add a small amount of cold water, stock or milk. Stir this mixture into about 3 cups strained boiling soup and simmer at least 5 minutes before serving.

♀ We do not recommend the use of a pressure cooker for legume soups.

DRIED BEAN SOUP

4 Cups

If you use marrow beans and add the optional mashed potato, you will have come close to reproducing the famous United States Senate Bean Soup.
Soak, see above:
½ cup dried navy, kidney,
    Lima or marrow beans
Add:
A small piece of ham, a ham bone
    or ¼ lb. salt pork
4 cups boiling water
½ bay leaf
3 or 4 peppercorns
3 whole cloves
Cook the soup slowly until the beans are soft, for about 2½ to 3 hours. For the last 30 minutes, add:
1 diced carrot
3 ribs celery with leaves, chopped
½ sliced onion
(1 minced clove garlic)
(⅛ teaspoon saffron)
(½ cup freshly cooked mashed potatoes)
(½ cup chopped sorrel)
Remove and mince the meat. Put the soup through a food mill, ⅃ blender or sieve. Thin the soup, if required, with boiling water or milk.

Correct the seasoning
Serve with the meat and:
Croutons, page 174
Chopped chives or parsley

BLACK BEAN SOUP

About 9 or 10 Cups

Follow the recipe for Split Pea Soup, page 153.
Substitute for the peas:
2 cups black beans
As this soup is drier, add:
3, instead of 2, tablespoons butter
Serve garnished with:
2 teaspoons deviled or Smithfield
    ham for each cup
Thin slices of lemon
Thin slices of hard-cooked eggs
(1 tablespoon dry sherry for each cup)

BEAN SOUP WITH VEGETABLES
OR GARBURE

About 10 Cups

A highly variable soup. Perhaps the most famous version comes from Béarn. It includes preserved goose and is cooked in a glazed casserole. Exotic? It is made in season with freshly hulled haricot beans. Soak overnight:

1 cup dried haricot or navy or fava beans

You may blanch, page 132, or not, depending on its maturity:

2 lbs. green or white cabbage

Shred the cabbage finely the length of the leaf. Peel and slice:

1½ cups potatoes
1 cup carrots
1 cup white turnips
¼ cup leeks, using white portion only
½ cup onion
1 sprig thyme
(A ham bone)

Place all the above ingredients in a heavy pan and cover with:

Liquid

Use water if you plan to add salt pork; game stock, page 491, with game. Add:

1 lb. diced salt pork or boneless game or veal

♦ Simmer, partially covered, for 2½ hours or until the meat is tender.

Correct the seasoning

and serve the meat on the side. Pour the soup over:

Garlic buttered croutons, page 174

MINESTRONE
About 8 Cups

An Italian soup made with many kinds of vegetables, even zucchini blossoms. Sometimes elbow macaroni or other pasta and sometimes rice is added instead of dried beans. Sweet sausages and smoked spareribs may also be put in at the end. Simmer for about ¾ hour in a large soup kettle:

2 quarts stock
4 oz. diced fatty ham
1 cup chopped celery
½ cup fresh kidney beans
¾ cup fresh peas

Heat:

3 tablespoons olive oil

Sauté in it:

1 cup chopped spinach
1 small chopped vegetable marrow
¼ cup minced onion
1 diced carrot
1 cup chopped Savoy cabbage
1 cup diced tomatoes
1 diced leek

Pour the sautéed vegetables into the stock mixture and simmer about 25 minutes longer. Add:

1 tablespoon chopped parsley
1 tablespoon minced fresh sage
1 pressed garlic clove

Cook for 5 minutes more and

Correct the seasoning

Add:

½ cup Parmesan cheese

and serve with:

Italian Bread

LENTIL SOUP
About 8 Cups

Wash well and drain:

2 cups lentils

Add:

10 cups boiling water
¼ lb. salt pork or a piece of ham or a ham bone

♦ Simmer for about 4 hours. During the last hour, add:

1 large minced onion

which has been sautéed in:

3 tablespoons butter
Correct the seasoning

and serve puréed or not, as you prefer.

SPLIT PEA OR LENTIL SOUP
About 8 Cups

Try this on a cold winter day. Wash and soak, page 152:

2 cups split peas

Drain the peas, reserving the liquid. Add enough water to the reserved liquid to make 10 cups. Adding peas again, cook covered, for about 2½ to 3 hours with:

A turkey carcass, a ham bone or a 2-inch cube salt pork

Add and simmer, covered, for ½ hour longer until tender:

½ cup chopped onions
1 cup chopped celery with leaves
½ cup chopped carrots

Add:

(1 clove garlic)
(1 bay leaf)
(1 teaspoon sugar)
(A dash of cayenne or a pod of red pepper)
(¼ teaspoon thyme)

Remove bones, carcass or salt pork. Put the soup through a sieve. Chill. Remove grease. Melt:

2 tablespoons butter or soup fat

Stir in it until blended:

2 tablespoons flour

Add a little of the soup mixture, slowly. Cook and stir until it boils, then stir it into the rest of the reheated soup.

Correct the seasoning

Serve with:

Croutons, or sour black bread and Pickled Pigs' Feet

ㅅ BLENDER SPLIT PEA SOUP
About 1 Quart

Simmer about 45 minutes or until tender:

½ cup split peas

in:

2½ cups water

When slightly cooled, pour into a blender and add:

1 cup chopped pork luncheon sausage
1 small sliced onion
1 diced stalk celery with leaves
1 clove garlic
1 teaspoon salt
2 teaspoons Worcestershire sauce

A pinch of rosemary
⅛ teaspoon pepper
Blend until smooth. Return the soup to saucepan to heat. Rinse the blender with:
1 cup water
Add this to the soup and simmer for about 10 minutes. Garnish with:
Pieces of crisp bacon
Cultured sour cream

SPLIT PEA SOUP AU MAIGRE

Use the recipe for Split Pea Soup to make either a thick or thin soup. During the last 20 minutes of cooking, substitute for the fowl or ham bone any clean fish scraps —such as heads, tails and fins.

GREEN PEA SOUP OR POTAGE ST. GERMAIN

About 6 Cups

Do not attempt to make this soup with canned or frozen peas. ♦ If you do not have fresh peas, it is better to try the good Quick Pea Soup.
Hull:
3 lbs. green peas
There should be about 3 cups hulled peas.
Shred:
1 head Boston lettuce
1 peeled onion
½ cup or more celery with leaves
2 sprigs parsley
Sauté the vegetables gently, until tender, in:
2 tablespoons butter
Add:
2½ cups chicken stock
2 cups of the hulled peas
10 or 12 pea pods
(⅛ bay leaf)
Simmer these ingredients, covered, until the peas are very soft. Put the soup through a food mill or a potato ricer.
Simmer until tender:
1 cup of the hulled peas
in:
1½ cups chicken stock
Add them to the strained soup.
To bind the soup, see About Legume Soups, page 152.
Correct the seasoning
You may color the soup with a drop or two of:
Green vegetable coloring
and serve it with:
Butter Dumplings, or
Sponge Dumplings
(2 teaspoons chopped mint)

BOULA-BOULA

6 Servings

♦ Simmer in boiling water until tender:
2 cups green peas
Purée them through a fine sieve. Reheat and add:
2 tablespoons sweet butter
Correct the seasoning

Add:
2 cups canned green turtle soup
1 cup dry sherry
Heat ♦ but do not boil the soup. Spoon soup into heated cups. Top each with:
2 tablespoons whipped cream
Place briefly under broiler. Serve at once.

MULLIGATAWNY SOUP

About 4 Cups

Sauté lightly, but do not brown:
½ cup diced onion
1 diced carrot
2 stalks celery, diced
in:
¼ cup butter or olive oil
Stir in:
1½ tablespoons flour
2 teaspoons curry powder
Stir and cook these ingredients for about 3 minutes. Pour in and simmer for 30 minutes:
4 cups chicken broth
Add and simmer for 15 minutes longer:
¼ cup diced tart apples
½ cup boiled rice
½ cup diced cooked chicken
1 teaspoon salt
¼ teaspoon pepper
⅛ teaspoon thyme
Immediately before serving, stir in:
½ cup hot cream

OXTAIL SOUP

I. **About 7 Cups**

Brown:
1 disjointed oxtail or 2 veal tails:
about 2 lbs.
½ cup sliced onions
in:
2 tablespoons butter or fat
Add to the above and ♦ simmer, uncovered, for about 4½ hours:
8 cups water
1½ teaspoons salt
4 peppercorns
Add and simmer ½ hour longer or until the vegetables are tender:
¼ cup shredded parsley
½ cup diced carrots
1 cup diced celery
½ bay leaf
¼ cup barley
½ cup tomato pulp
1 teaspoon dried thyme, marjoram
or basil
Strain, chill, degrease and reheat the stock. The meat and vegetables may be diced or blended and added to the soup later.
Brown in a skillet:
1 tablespoon flour
Add and stir until blended:
2 tablespoons butter
Add the stock slowly and
Correct the seasoning
Shortly before serving you may pour in:
(¼ cup dry sherry or Madeira
or ½ cup red wine)

Serve the soup with:
  Fritter Garnish, or slices of lemon

II. ☉   About 3 Cups
Sear in a pressure cooker:
  1 oxtail, joints separated
  1 small diced onion
in:
  3 tablespoons fat
Add:
  4 cups hot water or ½ water,
  ½ tomato juice
  1 teaspoon salt
  2 peppercorns
Adjust cover. Cook at 15 pounds pressure
for 15 minutes. Reduce pressure quickly.
Remove the cover. Remove ox joints. Add
to liquid in cooker:
  1 diced carrot
  4 ribs celery, diced
Readjust cover. Pressure cook the soup for
5 minutes longer. Degrease the soup after
chilling it. Reheat and:
  Correct the seasoning
You may add:
  (2 tablespoons dry sherry
    or tomato catsup)
Separate meat from the joints. Add to
soup. Serve with:
  Chopped parsley

PANADES
                                   About 4 Cups
These bread-thickened vegetable soups are
practical and filling. They are a good way
of utilizing leftover bread. Panades combine well with leeks, celery and sorrel; but
watercress, spinach, lettuce, etc., may be
substituted.
Use:
  1 cup finely chopped celery,
    leeks or onions
Cook the vegetables slowly until soft, but
not brown, in:
  1 tablespoon butter
Cover with a lid. If a leafy vegetable is
used, add it to the butter, cover and cook
slowly until wilted and reduced to about
one fourth. Add:
  2 cups hot water or milk
  ½ teaspoon salt
  3 cups diced fresh or stale bread
Stir well and permit the mixture to boil.
Simmer for ½ hour. Beat well until smooth
with a wire whisk or in a ⅄ blender. Combine:
  1 cup rich milk
  1 large egg
Stir this slowly into the hot soup. Heat
but ♦ do not permit the soup to boil. Serve
it with:
  Chopped parsley
  Freshly grated nutmeg

PEPPER POT
                                   About 5 Cups
Cut into small pieces and sauté in a heavy
saucepan until clear:
  4 slices of bacon
Add and simmer for about 5 minutes:
  ⅓ cup minced onion
  ½ cup minced celery
  2 seeded, minced green peppers
  (1 teaspoon marjoram or
    summer savory)
Wash and cut into fine shreds:
  ¾ lb. cooked honeycomb Tripe,
    page 448
Put into the saucepan with:
  8 cups Brown Stock, page 490
  1 bay leaf
  ½ teaspoon freshly ground pepper
Bring these ingredients to the boiling
point. Add:
  1 cup raw, peeled and diced potatoes
Gently simmer the soup, uncovered, until
the potatoes are tender. Melt:
  2 tablespoons butter
Stir in, until blended:
  2 tablespoons flour
Add a little of the soup. Bring these ingredients to the boiling point, then pour
them into the rest of the soup.
  Correct the seasoning
Shortly before serving add:
  ½ cup warm cream

COCK-A-LEEKIE
                                   5 to 6 Cups
Old recipes for this leek, chicken and
cream soup start with a fowl or cock simmered in strong stock, and wind up with
the addition of prunes. The following version is delicious, if not traditional.
Remove the dark green part of the tops
and the roots from:
  6 leeks
Wash them carefully—they may be sandy.
Cut them in half lengthwise, then crosswise in ⅛-inch slices. There should be
about 4 cups. Place in a pan with:
  3 cups boiling water
  1½ teaspoons salt
Simmer from 5 to 7 minutes or until tender but not mushy. Add and heat to a boil:
  2 tablespoons chicken fat or butter
  1½ cups well-seasoned strong
    chicken broth
Scald and stir in:
  ½ cup cream
  Correct the seasoning
Serve the soup at once.

SAUERKRAUT SOUP
                                   About 7 Cups
Sauté until golden brown:
  ½ cup chopped onion
in:
  3 tablespoons bacon fat
Add:

½ clove minced garlic
½ lb. diced lean pork
Cover and cook over low heat for about 20 minutes. Add:
1 lb. chopped sauerkraut
6 cups stock
Cook until soft, about 45 minutes. Melt:
1½ tablespoons butter
Stir in:
1½ tablespoons flour
Stir in slowly a little of the hot soup, blend and return the mixture to kettle. Add:
(1 teaspoon sugar)
Correct the seasoning
and garnish with:
Diced salami or ham

SPINACH SOUP

About 6½ Cups
Pick over, wash, drain thoroughly, then chop fine or blend:
2 lbs. tender young spinach
You may use instead 4 cups cooked or two 14-ounce packages of frozen spinach, defrosted. Melt in a saucepan:
¼ cup butter
Sauté in it until golden brown:
¼ cup minced onion
Add the spinach. Stir to coat it well with the butter. Cover, and cook gently till the spinach is just tender. ⋌ Blend or put the spinach through a food mill or sieve. Return to pan and add:
4 cups chicken stock
A grating of nutmeg
Salt or paprika
Bring the soup slowly to a boil and serve; or you may serve it cold, garnished with:
Diced, seeded cucumbers or
chives and cultured sour cream

GREEN TURTLE SOUP

About 8 Cups
It is a timesaver to buy canned or frozen turtle meat. But if you can turn turtles, feel energetic and want to prepare your own, see page 380.
Place in a saucepan and bring to the boiling point:
1 lb. green turtle or terrapin meat cut into pieces
3 cups water
3 cups Brown Stock, page 490
1 bay leaf
1 sprig fresh thyme
2 cloves
¼ teaspoon ground allspice
Juice and thinly sliced peel of ½ lemon
A few grains cayenne
¼ teaspoon freshly ground black pepper
½ teaspoon salt
4 whole corianders
These pods will rise to the top by the end of the cooking period and can be skimmed out before serving.
Heat:
2 tablespoons cooking oil

Sauté in this for 2 minutes:
2 medium-sized chopped onions
Stir in:
1 tablespoon flour
Add:
1½ cups fresh skinned seeded tomatoes
Permit these ingredients to cook for 10 minutes. Combine them with the turtle mixture and:
1 tablespoon chopped parsley
2 cloves minced garlic
Simmer the soup until the meat is tender, at least 2 hours. You may add a few drops of caramel coloring. Add to each serving:
1 tablespoon dry sherry
Garnish the soup with:
2 chopped hard-cooked eggs
Lemon slices

MOCK TURTLE SOUP

About 12 Cups
This full-bodied, nourishing soup, served with crusty rolls, can be the main dish for any meal.
Cover:
5 lbs. veal bones
with:
14 cups water
Bring to the boiling point. Add and simmer for about 4 hours:
6 chopped celery ribs with leaves
5 coarsely cut carrots
1 cup chopped onion
2 cups canned tomatoes
1 small can Italian tomato paste
6 crushed peppercorns
1 tablespoon salt
2 teaspoons monosodium glutamate
6 whole cloves
2 bay leaves
½ teaspoon dried thyme
Degrease. Sauté for about 5 minutes in a greased skillet:
2 cloves minced garlic
2 lbs. ground beef
2 teaspoons salt
Add to the stock, with:
¼ teaspoon Worcestershire sauce
4 teaspoons sugar
Blend:
6 tablespoons browned flour, page 497
1 cup cooled stock
Stir this paste into the simmering soup. Permit it to simmer for 20 minutes more. Add:
2 thinly sliced lemons
1 set chopped, parboiled calf brains, page 443
Garnish the soup with:
3 sliced hard-cooked eggs

NEW YEAR'S SOUPS

Suggested below are traditional New Year's soups, served just before parties break up. They are also known as hangover soups, or Lumpensuppe, and are sometimes helpful for the morning after.
I. Onion Soup, page 148, with the addition of:
1 cup red wine

II. Lentil Soup with sour cream and sausage.

ABOUT CREAM SOUPS

These favored luncheon soups are also sometimes served at dinner. In this latter role, they satisfy what is, as often as not, a mechanical rather than a nutritional need. Like hors d'oeuvre, they act as a stabilizer for the cocktails which have just been drunk or as a buffer against the wines which are about to come.

For the richest of cream soups—the veloutés—first, sauté the vegetables in butter, purée them and combine the purée in equal parts with Velouté Sauce, page 324. Bind with egg yolk, allowing 2 to 4 yolks for each pint of soup. Simpler cream soups may be made on a Béchamel sauce base, page 322, or on this quick Béchamel: use 2 tablespoons butter to 1½ tablespoons flour, plus 2 cups cream and ¾ to 1 cup vegetable puree. Should you wish to thin these ingredients, use a little well-flavored stock.

For everyday cream soups, we find we can purée the tender vegetables raw or cook the more mature, fibrous ones and process them in a ⋏ blender. The soup is served without straining. ♦ If seafood or fowl is blended, it tends to be unpleasantly stringy and the entire soup will need straining before serving.

♦ All cream soups, whether bound with egg or not, are ruined by boiling, so be sure to heat just to the boiling point or cook them in the top of a double boiler ♦ over, not in, hot water. Reheat them this same way.

CREAM OF ASPARAGUS SOUP
About 6 Cups
Wash and remove the tips from:
1 lb. fresh green asparagus
Simmer the tips, covered, until they are tender in a small amount of:
Milk or water
Cut the stalks into pieces and place them in a saucepan. Add:
6 cups Veal or Chicken Stock, page 490
¼ cup chopped onion
½ cup chopped celery
Simmer these ingredients, covered, for about ½ hour. Rub them through a sieve. Melt:
3 tablespoons butter
Stir in, until blended:
3 tablespoons flour
Stir in slowly:
½ cup cream
Add the asparagus stock. Heat the soup well in a double boiler. Add the asparagus tips. Season the soup immediately before serving with:
Salt, paprika and white pepper
Garnish with:
A diced hard-cooked egg

CREAM OF CAULIFLOWER SOUP
About 6 Cups
Prepare:
1 large cauliflower, page 271
Drain it, reserving the water and about ⅓ of the florets. Put the remainder through a food mill, blender or sieve. Melt:
¼ cup butter
Sauté in it, until tender:
2 tablespoons chopped onion
3 celery ribs, minced
Stir in:
¼ cup flour
Stir in slowly and bring to the boiling point:
4 cups Veal or Chicken Stock, page 490
and the reserved cauliflower water
Add the strained cauliflower and:
2 cups scalded rich milk or cream
Add the florets and:
A grating of nutmeg
Salt and paprika
Garnish with:
(Grated cheese)

CREAM OF CELERY SOUP
About 4 Cups
Melt:
1 tablespoon butter
Add and sauté for 2 minutes:
1 cup or more chopped celery
with leaves
(⅛ cup sliced onion)
Pour in and simmer for about 10 minutes:
2 cups Veal or Chicken Stock
Strain the soup. Add and bring to the boiling point:
1½ cups milk
Dissolve:
1½ tablespoons cornstarch
in:
½ cup milk
Stir these ingredients gradually into the hot soup. Bring to the boiling point. Stir and cook for about 1 minute. You may add:
A grating of nutmeg
Serve with:
(2 tablespoons chopped parsley)

CHESTNUT SOUP
About 3 Cups
Prepare:
1 lb. chestnuts
Mash and beat them until smooth in:
2 cups milk
Melt:
¼ cup butter
Add and simmer until soft and golden:
1 minced onion
Sprinkle with:
1 tablespoon flour
1 teaspoon salt
⅛ teaspoon each nutmeg and pepper
½ cup chopped celery leaves
Stir and slowly add the chestnut and milk mixture. ♦ Simmer for about 10 minutes. Pour in:
1 cup cream

Heat ♦ but do not boil and serve immediately garnished with:
>   Parsley
>   Croutons, page 174

CREAM OF CHICKEN SOUP
About 4½ Cups
Simmer:
>   3 cups Chicken Stock, page 490
>   ½ cup finely chopped celery

When the celery is tender, add and cook for 5 minutes:
>   ½ cup cooked Rice, page 178

Add:
>   ½ cup hot cream
>   1 tablespoon chopped parsley
>   Salt and paprika

♦ Do not boil the soup after adding the cream.

CREAM OF CORN SOUP
About 5 Cups
Put through a food mill or coarse sieve:
>   2½ cups cream style canned corn or
>   2½ cups corn, cut from the ear,
>   simmered until tender in 1 cup milk

Melt:
>   3 tablespoons butter

Simmer in it until soft:
>   ½ medium-sized sliced onion

Stir in:
>   3 tablespoons flour
>   1½ teaspoons salt
>   A few grains freshly ground pepper
>   (A grating of nutmeg)

Stir in the corn and:
>   3 cups milk or 2½ cups milk and
>   ½ cup cream

Serve the soup sprinkled with:
>   3 tablespoons chopped parsley
>   or chives

CORN CHOWDER
About 6 Cups
Sauté slowly until lightly browned:
>   ½ cup chopped salt pork

Add and sauté until golden brown:
>   3 tablespoons chopped onion
>   ½ cup chopped celery
>   3 tablespoons chopped green pepper

Add and simmer:
>   1 cup raw, peeled, diced potatoes
>   2 cups water
>   ½ teaspoon salt
>   ¼ teaspoon paprika
>   ½ bay leaf

When the potatoes are tender, in about 45 minutes, combine until blended, bring to the boiling point, and add to the above:
>   3 tablespoons flour
>   ½ cup milk

Add:
>   1½ cups hot milk
>   2 cups whole kernel corn

Heat but do not boil the soup. Serve it sprinkled with:
>   Chopped parsley

COLD BULGARIAN CUCUMBER SOUP
About 3 Cups
"Nazdrave" as the Bulgarians say for "Bon appétit."

Two to 6 hours before serving, refrigerate, covered:
>   1½ cups peeled, diced cucumbers

marinated in a mixture of:
>   1 teaspoon salt
>   ¼ teaspoon pepper
>   ¼ to 1 cup chopped walnuts
>   2 tablespoons olive oil
>   1 clove minced garlic
>   2 tablespoons chopped fresh dill

♦ The fresh dill is the essential touch. When ready to serve, add:
>   1 to 1½ cups thick yogurt or 1 cup
>   cultured sour cream

Place 1 or 2 ice cubes in each soup bowl. Pour in the mixture. It should have the consistency of chilled borsch. If not thin enough, it can be thinned with a small amount of light stock. Serve at once.

CHILLED CREAM OF CUCUMBER HERB SOUP
6 Cups
Pare, seed and slice:
>   2 medium-sized cucumbers

Add to them:
>   1 cup water
>   2 slices onion
>   ¼ teaspoon salt
>   ⅛ teaspoon white pepper

Cook the cucumbers, covered, until very soft. Put them through a fine strainer or an ⋏ electric blender. Stir until smooth:
>   ¼ cup flour
>   ½ cup chicken stock

Stir into this flour paste:
>   1½ cups chicken stock

Add the cucumber purée and:
>   ¼ bay leaf or 2 cloves

Stir the soup over low heat. Simmer for 2 minutes. Strain and chill in a covered jar. Stir into these ingredients:
>   ¾ cup chilled cream or cultured sour
>   cream or yogurt
>   1 tablespoon finely chopped dill,
>   chives or other herb or grated
>   lemon rind
>   Correct the seasoning

Serve the soup very cold.

CREAM OF MUSHROOM SOUP
About 4½ Cups
The flavor of mushrooms is more pronounced if they have begun to color. Prepare for cooking:
>   ½ lb. mature mushrooms with stems

Sauté lightly in:
>   2 tablespoons butter

Add them to:
>   2 cups chicken stock or water
>   ½ cup chopped tender celery
>   ¼ cup sliced onion
>   ⅛ cup shredded parsley

Simmer, covered, for 20 minutes. Drain the vegetables, reserving the stock. ⅄ Blend them or put them through a food chopper. Prepare:

Cream Sauce I, page 322

Pour the liquid slowly into the cream sauce, cook and stir until the soup just reaches a boil. Add the ground vegetables. Heat ◗ but do not boil. Season the soup with:

1¼ teaspoons salt
⅛ teaspoon paprika
(⅛ teaspoon nutmeg)
(3 tablespoons dry white wine)

Serve, topped with:

(Whipped cream)

Garnish with:

Paprika
Sprigs of parsley or chopped chives

CREAM OF NETTLE SOUP

About 4 Cups

Using rubber gloves, remove the central stem from:

1 quart young nettle tops

Have boiling:

5 cups stock

Blend in:

2 tablespoons cooked rice or oatmeal

Add the nettles and simmer for about 15 minutes.

Correct the seasoning

and serve.

CREAM OF ONION SOUP OR ONION VELOUTÉ

About 4 Cups

Melt:

3 tablespoons butter

Add and sauté till a golden brown:

1½ cups thinly sliced onions

Stir in:

1 tablespoon flour
½ teaspoon salt

Add:

4 cups milk or cream and Stock, page 490

Simmer, covered, until the onions are very tender. Add:

4 beaten egg yolks

Heat but ◗ do not boil. Season with:

Salt and paprika
Freshly grated nutmeg or
(Worcestershire sauce)

Place in each cup:

1 teaspoon chopped parsley

Pour the hot soup over it.

POTATO SOUP

About 3 Cups

Peel and slice:

2 medium-sized potatoes

Skin and chop:

2 medium-sized onions
4 ribs celery

Sauté these ingredients in:

1½ tablespoons butter

Add:

Boiling water to cover
½ teaspoon salt
(½ bay leaf)

Boil the vegetables until the potatoes are tender or ◲ pressure cook them for 3 minutes at 15 pounds pressure. Put them through a ricer or ⅄ blender. Beat into them:

2 tablespoons butter

Thin the soup to the desired consistency with:

Rich milk and/or Chicken Stock, page 490

Add if required:

Salt and paprika
A dash Worcestershire sauce

Serve with:

Chopped parsley, chives or water-cress
1 cup sliced frankfurters, chopped, cooked shrimp or diced ham

POTATO SOUP WITH TOMATOES

About 10-12 Cups

A more sophisticated version of the previous recipe.

Prepare:

2 cups sliced onions

Sauté very gently until translucent in:

¼ cup butter

Add the onions to:

2 cups sliced potatoes
6 cups boiling water

Simmer for about ½ hour. Add and simmer, covered, for about 20 minutes:

5 cups sliced tomatoes or 3 cups canned tomatoes
2 teaspoons sugar
1 teaspoon salt
⅛ teaspoon paprika
A pinch of chervil

Put the soup through a fine strainer or ⅄ blender. Reheat and

Correct the seasoning

Scald and stir in:

1 cup cream

Heat ◗ but do not boil. Serve at once.

VICHYSSOISE OR LEEK POTATO SOUP

This leek soup may be served hot or very cold. Yes, the last "s" is pronounced. Most Americans shun it, in a "genteel" way, as though it were virtuous to ignore it. Be sure to serve the soup reduced to a velvety smoothness.

I.   **About 6 Cups**

Mince the white part of:

3 medium-sized leeks
1 medium-sized onion

Stir and sauté them for 3 minutes in:

2 tablespoons butter
Peel, slice very fine and add:
    4 medium-sized potatoes
Add:
    4 cups clarified Chicken Stock, page 490
Simmer the vegetables, covered, for 15
minutes or until tender. Put them through
a very fine sieve, food mill or ⅄ blender.
Add:
    1 to 2 cups cream
    (¼ teaspoon mace)
    Salt and white pepper
    Chopped watercress or chives

II.   **About 2½ Cups**
Superlative! Less rich and made in about
20 minutes by using a ⅄ blender and
♥ pressure cooker. Serve it hot or chill it
quickly by placing it in a refrigerator tray
or deep freeze.
Prepare as above:
    Vichyssoise
using ½ the amount of ingredients given.
After adding the potatoes and stock, pressure cook the soup for 3 minutes at 15
pounds pressure. Cool. Add:
    1 cup peeled, seeded and diced
    cucumbers
Blend covered until smooth, about 1 minute. Place the soup in a jar. Chill it thoroughly. You may add the cream, but you
will probably like the result just as well
without it. Hot or cold, sprinkle the top
with:
    Chopped chives

PUMPKIN SOUP
                                          About 4 Cups
Place:
    3 cups canned or 2 lbs. cooked fresh
    pumpkin
in:
    3 cups scalded milk
Add:
    1 tablespoon butter
    1 tablespoon sugar or 2 tablespoons
    brown sugar
    Salt and pepper
    (Nutmeg and cinnamon)
    A very small pinch saffron
    ½ cup finely julienned ham
Heat ♦ but do not boil. Serve at once.

CREAM OF SORREL SOUP
                                   About 5 to 6 Cups
Also known as **Potage Germiny** and a fa-
vorite combination with veal and fish
dishes. Because of the oxalic acid in sor-
rel ♦ use a stainless steel or enamel pan.
Clean, shred from the mid rib and chop:
    2 cups sorrel leaves
Sauté them, until wilted, in:
    1 to 2 tablespoons butter
When they are sufficiently wilted, there
will be only about 3 tablespoons of leaves.
Add:
    5 cups Chicken Stock, page 490
    (1 tablespoon fresh pea purée)

Simmer for about 2 minutes. Remove from
the heat and add:
    ½ cup cream
    3 beaten egg yolks
Heat until the soup thickens slightly ♦ but
do not boil. Serve garnished with:
    Chopped chervil

**CREAM OF SPINACH OR
LETTUCE SOUP**
                                          About 5 Cups
Pick over and wash:
    1 lb. spinach or 1 lb. leaf lettuce
Or you may use:
    1 cup frozen spinach
Place it, while moist or frozen, in a cov-
ered saucepan. Cook for about 6 minutes.
Drain. Put through a strainer or ⅄ blender.
Melt in a saucepan:
    2 tablespoons butter
Add and sauté for 3 minutes:
    1 tablespoon grated onion or 1 slice
    of onion which can be removed easily
Stir in and cook until blended:
    2 tablespoons flour
Stir in gradually:
    4 cups milk and/or stock
Season with:
    ¾ teaspoon or more salt
    ¼ teaspoon paprika
    (A grating of nutmeg)
Add the spinach or lettuce. Heat the soup
well. Serve sprinkled with:
    (Grated Parmesan cheese or
    sieved egg yolk)

CREAM OF TOMATO SOUP
                                          About 5½ Cups
Simmer, covered, for about 15 minutes:
    2 cups canned or fresh,
    cut-up tomatoes
    ½ cup chopped celery
    ¼ cup chopped onion
    2 teaspoons white or brown sugar
Prepare:
    4 cups Cream Sauce I, page 322
Strain into this the tomato and vegetable
stock.
    Correct the seasoning
and serve with:
    Croutons, page 174
    Chopped parsley, burnet or basil
If served chilled, garnish with:
    Chopped chives or whipped cream
    and paprika

**CREAM OF WATER CRESS OR
PURSLANE SOUP**
I.   **About 4 Cups**
Sauté:
    1 cup chopped cress or purslane
in:
    1 tablespoon butter
Add:
    Salt, white pepper and paprika
    ½ cup white wine
    4 cups cream
Heat but do not boil. Serve at once.

II. **About 5 Cups**
To:
5 cups hot Cream of Chicken Soup,
page 158
Add:
1½ cups chopped or ⅃ blended
watercress
Or, if you wish to try Gandhi's favorite
vegetable, use an equal amount of:
(Purslane)
Simmer the soup about 5 minutes. Add
and stir a small quantity of the soup into:
2 well-beaten eggs
Add this to the rest of the soup, stirring it
in slowly. Heat the soup ♦ but do not boil.
Serve at once.
An interesting taste variation results by
adding:
2 slices fresh ginger
which have been lightly sautéed in:
Butter
Salt
Remove ginger after reheating but before
serving the soup.

MILK TOAST OR SOUP
Individual Service
While not exactly a soup, this dish can
bring something like the same cozy com-
fort to the young or the ailing.
Toast lightly on both sides:
A slice of bread, ¾ inch thick
Spread it lightly with:
Butter
Sprinkle it with:
(Salt)
Place it in a bowl and pour over it:
1 cup hot milk

ABOUT FISH SOUPS
Making a good broth or fumet of fish is
like making a stock of any kind of meat in
that the process toughens the meat. It differs in that it takes a good deal less time.
Extraction is limited to a ♦ 20 to 30 minute period ♦ over relatively high heat, instead of the slow simmering recommended
for warm-blooded meat. ♦ As a consequence, most fish soups are quick soups.
When fisherman's stews are served, the
meat is often presented on the side; and in
the preparation of delicate bisques based
on shellfish, the shrimp or lobsters are
often poached separately, then pounded in
a mortar or minced before incorporation in
a separate stock, cream and egg base.
The original stock may be used as a
court bouillon for cooking other fish or reduced for use in "au maigre" or meatless
sauces. Bisques, as well as oyster, clam
and mussel soups and stews, need so little
heat that the stock bases are warmed first
and the shellfish then just heated through
in them, preferably in a double boiler
♦ over, not in, hot water. Serve fish soups
at once. If you must hold or reheat, be
sure to do so again ♦ over, not in, hot
water.

CLAM BROTH OR SOUP
About 4 Cups
Clams are of various types, see About
Clams, page 367. The broth is delicious
when fresh, but may be frozen until mushy
and served in small glasses or on the shells
with wedges of lemon. The meat of the
clams themselves may be used in various
sea-food dishes, see pages 237-240.
Wash and scrub well with a brush, then
place in a kettle:
2 quarts clams in shells
Add:
1¾ cups water
3 cut up ribs celery with leaves
A pinch of cayenne
♦ Cover the kettle closely. You may double the quantity of this soup, even though
the clam flavor will be lessened, by adding
about 4 cups of water and minced vegetables which are suitable for soup, see Court
Bouillon, page 493. ♦ Steam the clams until the shells open, page 369. Strain the
liquor through wet double cheesecloth to
remove any sand. It may be heated and
diluted with warm cream or rich milk.
Add:
1 teaspoon butter
Correct the seasoning
and serve.

COQUINA BROTH
If you are lucky enough to be on a beach
in Florida, collect in a sieve at ebb tide:
Coquinas
the little native periwinkle clams, in rain-
bow-hued shells.
Rinse them clean of sand, then barely
cover with:
Water
Bring slowly to a boil and ♦ simmer for
about 10 minutes. Pour the broth through
a fine sieve. When you imbibe it, remember the advice of an old German who said,
when serving a fine vintage, "Don't gullop
it, zipp it!"

CRAWFISH BISQUE
About 6 Cups
Wash and scrub with a brush under running water:
3 dozen crawfish
Soak for 30 minutes in salted water, 1 tablespoon salt to 4 cups of water. Rinse
thoroughly. Place the crawfish in a saucepan with:
6 cups boiling water
A few grains of cayenne
½ teaspoon salt
Bring to a boil, then ♦ simmer for 15 minutes. Drain, reserving the stock. Remove
the heads and reserve 18 of them to be
stuffed as a garnish for the bisque. Remove
the meat from the heads. Devein the
tails. Return all remaining shells to the
stock. Bring to a boil. Add:
4 ribs chopped celery
2 tablespoons chopped parsley

½ diced carrot
⅛ teaspoon thyme or a sprig of
fresh thyme
Simmer for 30 minutes. Strain. Meanwhile, prepare the stuffing for the heads. Mince the crawfish meat. Sauté until golden:

2 tablespoons minced onion

in:

2 tablespoons butter

Add and cook for 3 minutes:

2 tablespoons finely minced celery
1 tablespoon finely minced parsley

Remove from heat and add ½ the crawfish meat and:

½ cup bread crumbs

Beat and add:

1 egg
Salt and paprika as required

Stir lightly with a fork. Stuff the heads with this mixture. Place them on a greased shallow pan. Dot each head with butter. For 10 minutes, before serving the soup, bake the heads in a preheated 425° oven. Melt:

2 tablespoons butter

Sauté in it until delicately browned:

¼ cup minced onion

Add and stir until lightly browned:

2 tablespoons flour

Add the fish stock slowly, stirring until smooth. Add the remaining crawfish meat and

Correct the seasoning

♦ Simmer the bisque for about 5 minutes, stirring it often. To serve, place the heated heads in hot soup plates, then pour the bisque over them.

LOBSTER BISQUE

About 6 Cups

Remove the meat from:

2 medium-sized boiled lobsters

Dice the body meat and mince the tail and claw meat. Reserve it. Crush the shells. Add to them the tough end of the claws and:

2½ cups Chicken Stock, page 490, or
Fumet, page 493
1 sliced onion
4 ribs celery with leaves
2 whole cloves
1 bay leaf
6 peppercorns

Simmer these ingredients for ½ hour. Strain the stock. If there is coral roe, force it through a fine sieve, combine it with the butter in a mortar or bowl, add the flour and when well blended pour the heated milk slowly on it, stirring until the mixture is smooth.
Otherwise, melt:

¼ cup butter

Stir in:

¼ cup flour

Add gradually:

3 cups milk

¼ teaspoon nutmeg
Correct the seasoning

When the sauce is smooth and boiling, add the lobster and the stock. ♦ Simmer the bisque, covered, for 5 minutes. Turn off the heat. Stir in:

1 cup ♦ hot but not boiling cream

Serve at once with:

Minced parsley
Paprika
Dry sherry

MUSHROOM AND CLAM BISQUE

About 3 Cups

Sauté:

½ lb. chopped mushrooms

in:

2 tablespoons butter

Stir in:

2 tablespoons flour

Stir in slowly:

2½ cups clam broth

Simmer for 5 minutes. Remove from the heat. Heat ♦ but do not boil:

¾ cup cream

Add to the other ingredients.

Correct the seasoning

and serve with:

Chopped parsley or chives

SHRIMP BISQUE

About 5 Cups

Remove shells and intestines from:

1½ lbs. Poached Shrimp, page 377

Put the shrimp through a meat grinder or ⅃ blender. Cook, covered, in the top of a double boiler ♦ over, not in, hot water for 5 minutes:

6 tablespoons butter
2 tablespoons grated onion

Add the ground shrimp and:

3 cups warm milk

Cook for 2 minutes. Stir in slowly, heat ♦ but do not boil:

1 cup cream

Add:

Salt, if needed, and paprika or
freshly ground white pepper
A grating of nutmeg
3 tablespoons sherry
2 tablespoons parsley or chives

Serve at once.

OYSTER STEWS AND BISQUES

Here are 2 good recipes which differ in nutritive value and effort of preparation. The first calls for milk and is unthickened; the second, a bisque, calls for milk, cream and egg yolks.
To clean oysters, see page 364.

I.   **About 4 Cups**

Our instructions are foolproof, as the use of a double boiler prevents overcooking of the oysters. Combine in the top of a double boiler over, not in, hot water:

2 to 4 tablespoons butter

½ teaspoon or more grated onion or
leek, a sliver of garlic or ½ cup
stewed celery
Sauté lightly and add:
1 to 1½ pints oysters with liquor
1½ cups milk
½ cup cream
½ teaspoon salt
⅛ teaspoon white pepper or paprika .
Place the pan ♦ over, not in, boiling water.
When the milk is hot and the oysters float,
add:
2 tablespoons chopped parsley

II.   **About 4 Cups**
This is a true oyster bisque.
Prepare:
Oyster Stew I, above
Before adding the parsley, remove the soup
from the heat and pour a small quantity
over:
2 beaten egg yolks
After mixing, add them slowly to the hot
bisque. Heat slowly for 1 minute but
♦ do not allow to boil; or hold over hot
water in a double boiler until ready to
serve.

MUSSEL STEW
Clean the mussels and remove the beard,
page 366. Steam, strain and reserve the
liquor. Use either recipe for Oyster Stew,
above, substituting mussels for oysters.

LOBSTER STEW
About 5 Cups
Sauté for 3 or 4 minutes:
1 cup diced fresh lobster meat
in:
3 tablespoons butter
Add slowly:
4 cups scalded milk
2 teaspoons onion juice
A Maine correspondent writes that this
stew is much improved by the addition, at
this time, of ½ to 1 cup clam broth.
Correct the seasoning
and serve.

SHRIMP, CRAB AND OYSTER GUMBO
About 8 Cups
Melt:
1 tablespoon butter
Stir in and cook until golden:
¼ cup chopped onion
Stir in until blended:
2 tablespoons flour
Add and stir until smooth:
1½ cups strained tomatoes
4 cups Stock, page 490
or Fumet, page 491
1 quart thinly sliced okra
Break into small pieces and add:
½ lb. raw, shelled, cleaned shrimp
½ lb. raw crab meat
♦ Simmer these ingredients until the okra
is tender. Add:

16 shelled oysters
Correct the seasoning
and serve the gumbo as soon as the oysters
are plump. Sprinkle with:
Chopped parsley

ABOUT BOUILLABAISSE AND OTHER FISHERMAN'S STEWS

Necessity is the mother of invention; and
convenience gave birth to the can and the
frozen package. Use frozen or canned
fish, if you must, for fisherman's stews; but
remember that ♦ their fragrant, distinctive
and elusive charm can only be captured if
the fish which go into them are themselves
freshly caught. Curnonsky reminds us of
the legend that bouillabaisse, the most
celebrated of fisherman's stews, was first
brought by angels to the Three Marys,
when they were shipwrecked on the bleak
shores of the Camargue.

Divinely inspired or not, it is true that
bouillabaise can only be approximated in
this country, even if its ingredients are just
off the hook. For its unique flavor depends
on the use of fish which are native to the
Mediterranean alone: a regional rock fish,
high in gelatin content, for example, which
gives a slightly cloudy but still thin texture
to the soup, and numberless finny tidbits,
too small for market. We offer a free
translation of bouillabaisse into American
—realizing fully that we have succeeded
only in changing poetry to rich prose.

A similar accommodation has been made
for matelote or freshwater fish stew, in
which eel, carp, bream, tench and perch
are combined with wine. A certain amount
of freewheeling must be the rule, too, in
concocting chowders and stews of both sea
and fresh fish, which are milk-based and
often have potatoes added. Whatever fish
you use, see that it is as ♦ fresh as possible
and experiment with combinations of those
that are most quickly available.

BOUILLABAISSE
8 Cups
Have ready:
¼ cup finely chopped onion
4 finely julienned leeks: use the
white portions only
Skin and squeeze the pulp out of and then
dice:
4 medium-sized tomatoes
Combine:
5 cloves minced garlic
1 tablespoon finely chopped
fresh fennel
½ to 1 teaspoon saffron
2 pulverized bay leaves
1 teaspoon grated orange rind
2 tablespoons tomato paste
⅛ teaspoon celery seed
3 tablespoons chopped parsley
1 teaspoon freshly ground pepper
2 tablespoons salt

Heat in a large casserole:

¼ to ½ cup olive oil

When the oil is hot, add the prepared ingredients above and cook until the vegetables are transparent. Meanwhile, cut into 1-inch dice and then add:

4 lbs. very fresh fish in combination: red snapper, halibut, pompano, sea perch, scallops; also 1-inch pieces of well-scrubbed lobster, whole shrimp, clams and mussels—all in the shell

You may prefer to leave the fish in 2-inch-thick slices and use some of the smaller fish whole. If so, add the thinner pieces or small scrubbed shellfish to the pot slightly later than the thicker ones ♦ but do not disturb the boiling. Cover the fish with:

2½ cups hot Fumet, page 491, or water

♦ Keep the heat high and force the boiling, which should continue rapid for 15 to 20 minutes.

Correct the seasoning

To serve, have ready to arrange in the bottom of 8 hot bowls:

¾-inch slices of French bread

Dry the bread in the oven and brush with:

Garlic butter

When the bouillabaisse is ready, arrange attractively some of each kind of fish on and around the bread. You may remove the lobsters from the shell and remove the upper shells from the clams and mussels. Then pour the hot broth into the bowls and serve at once. Or, you may strain the broth onto the bread and serve the sea food on a separate platter. Plan the meal with a beverage other than wine.

MATELOTE

8 Cups

Depending upon the amount of wine used, this dish can be either a soup or a stew.
Cook separately and have ready to add as a garnish, just before serving the matelote:

12 small cooked onions, page 284
½ lb. sautéed mushrooms, page 281
½ lb. cooked shrimp, page 377

Now, clean and cut into 1-inch slices:

3 lbs. freshwater fish: eel, carp, tench, bream or perch

Cover first the fish that need the longest cooking with a combination of ½:

Good red wine

and ½:

Fish fumet or meat stock

Take note of the approximate amount needed, for this should be reduced by about one half later on. Add:

2 teaspoons chopped parsley
½ cup chopped celery
1 small bay leaf
2 cloves garlic
¼ teaspoon thyme
1 teaspoon salt

Bring the mixture to a boil, remove from heat and float on the surface:

2 tablespoons warm cognac

Ignite the cognac, and when the flame dies down, return the mixture to heat, add the remaining fish, cover the pan and simmer the soup for about 15 minutes. Now, remove the fish to a serving dish and strain the liquid into another pan. Thicken the soup with a beurre manié of:

3 tablespoons butter
2½ tablespoons flour

Add it a little at a time to the hot soup. Bring the soup just to a boil, stirring constantly. It should be creamy in texture, but will go thin if boiled.

Correct the seasoning

To serve, put the fish into soup bowls, cover first with the onions and mushrooms, then with the sauce; garnish the whole with the shrimp; and serve with:

Soup Croutons, page 174

MANHATTAN CLAM CHOWDER

About 8 Cups

Prepare:

1 quart quahog clams, page 367

Wash them in:

3 cups water

Drain through cheesecloth. Reserve liquid. Cut the hard part of the clams from the soft part. Chop finely:

The hard part of the clams
A 2-inch cube of salt pork or
3 slices of bacon
1 large onion

Sauté the salt pork very slowly. Remove and reserve the scraps. Add the minced onions and hard part of the clams to the grease. Stir and cook slowly for about 5 minutes. Sift over them and stir until blended:

3 tablespoons flour

Heat and stir in the reserved liquid. Peel, prepare and add:

2 cups raw diced potatoes
3 cups cooked or canned tomatoes
(½ cup diced green pepper)
(½ bay leaf)
(¼ cup catsup)

Cover the pan and simmer the chowder until the potatoes are done, but still firm. Add the pork scraps, the soft part of the clams and:

3 tablespoons butter

Simmer for 3 minutes more. Place the chowder in a hot tureen.

Correct the seasoning

Serve with:

Oyster crackers

You may substitute for the fresh clams:

2½ cups canned minced clams

Strain the juice. Add water to make 3 cups of liquid. Use this liquid in place of the water measurement given above.
Chowder should be allowed to ripen; it is always better the following day.

NEW ENGLAND CLAM CHOWDER

About 8 Cups

Most New Englanders consider the above recipe an illegitimate child. They omit the

matoes, green peppers and catsup, but
our in:

4 cups hot ♦ not boiling, milk

fter the pork scraps have been added.
Do not let the mixture boil. Serve with
rge crackers.

ONCH CHOWDER

repare:

Manhattan Clam Chowder, page 164

sing conch meat to replace the fish. ♦ To
repare conch in the shell, cover:

2 to 15 conchs or large whelks

ith cold water and ♦ simmer 20 to 30
inutes. Remove from shell and beat the
hite body meat in a canvas bag until it
egins to disintegate. Marinate 2 hours in:

¼ cup lime juice

fter adding the conch meat to the chow-
er, simmer about 3 to 5 minutes longer
an directed for Manhattan Clam Chow-
er.

BOUT QUICK SOUPS

Vhen we were very young, we were more
ppalled than edified by "Struwwelpeter,"
book of rhymed fables for children,
hich had been written in Germany by a
orpsbruder of our great grandfather.
Ve remember the story of Suppenkaspar,
little boy who resolutely refused to eat
is soup, wasted away for his stubbornness
nd was buried with a tureen as his head-
tone. Looking back and taking note of
ur wonderful present-day battery of
anned, frozen and dried soups, we can see
at Kaspar was born a century too soon
nd would, in this generation, have chosen,
eyond a doubt, to live.

Know the comfort and reassurance of a
rder well-stocked with processed soups.
Vith them, you may in a jiffy lay the
undation of a good, square meal. If
e unexpected guest prefers a clear soup,
se a canned consommé or chicken broth
ith any one of several quickly confected
gg-drops, page 169. If he fancies a more
lling dish, serve ⅄ Blender Borsch, page
66, or Quick Cucumber Soup Cockaigne,
age 166.

Very special effects may be achieved in
our canned and frozen soup repertory by
ixing with them the meat and vegetable
ocks which are the by-product of daily
ooking, page 488. Put these regularly by,
long with meat glazes, for just this pur-
ose. Occasionally, too, a bouillon cube
ill add interest. Please read About Soup
tock and Stock Substitutes, page 488. If
ou have a plot or some pots of fresh
erbs, now is the time to commandeer a
ipping all 'round.

♦ One word of caution. Normally, we
ilute ready-prepared soups considerably
ss than their manufacturers recommend,
hether we use home-cooked stocks, milk
r—less desirably—just plain water. But

we find that the more concentrated the
soup the more likely it is to taste over-
salted. Test your mix and correct this tendency.

For very sturdy potages, casseroles, etc.,
see suggestions in Brunch, Lunch and Supper Dishes, page 223. There is also the
possibility that you are harboring some
refrigerator scraps which will respond in a
constructive way to ⅄ blender treatment.
Before processing, add to them a few
mushrooms or a few leaves of spinach, lettuce or cress and a small amount of milk
and cream. Be sure, though, if you blend
uncooked vegetables, that they are tender
and will not spoil the texture of your soup
with stringy fibers or bits of hull.

If you have on hand some leftover
bones, lean fowl or meat trimmings and
have a little extra time, put your ✿ pressure cooker to work, too, at building a soup
base. Remember, in this connection, that
most fish soups are quick soups, even when
you start with raw materials. ♦ Please read
About Fish Soups, page 161.

QUICK CANNED CONSOMMÉ VARIATIONS

A clear soup is supposed to be as bracing
as a clear conscience.

Add to each serving of consommé, hot or
cold:

**A slice of lemon or 1 tablespoon
sherry or Madeira or diced avocado
A dollop of sour cream**

Or add to hot consommé:

**Egg Drops, page 169, Marrow Balls,
page 173, or Noodles, page 172**

QUICK TROPICAL CONSOMMÉ
About 3 Cups

Combine and heat the contents of:

**1 can condensed consommé
1 can condensed madrilene**

Stir in:

The juice of 1 large orange

Serve chilled "on the rocks."

⅄ BLENDER GAZPACHO
About 1 Cup

Blend together for 2 or 3 minutes:

**¼ cup skinned, seeded cucumbers
¾ cup skinned, seeded tomatoes
¼ cup consommé or water
½ teaspoon red pimiento**

Add and blend for a shorter time:

1 teaspoon to 1 tablespoon olive oil

Add, but do not blend, as the flavor would
be too strong:

**1 teaspoon chopped chives
Correct the seasoning**

and serve by pouring the broth over 2 ice
cubes. A good garnish is:

Garlic croutons

QUICK VEGETABLE SOUP
About 2½ Cups

Utilize the water in which vegetables have
been cooked. Melt:

2 tablespoons butter

Add and stir until blended:

1⅓ tablespoons flour

Add and stir until smooth:

1½ cups vegetable water

Bring to a boil and cook for 2 minutes.
Lower the heat and add:

½ cup cream or Stock, page 490

Add:

½ cup cooked, diced or strained
vegetables

2 tablespoons chopped parsley
(A dash of celery salt)
Correct the seasoning

Heat thoroughly ♦ but do not boil if you
have chosen to add the cream.

⅄ BLENDER CREAM OF
VEGETABLE SOUP

Blend:

1 can condensed cream of vegetable
soup

1 can condensed chicken rice soup

1 cup canned or strong asparagus stock

(¼ cup cream)

Heat ♦ but do not boil and serve at once.

QUICK CREAM OF
ASPARAGUS SOUP

4 to 5 Cups

Combine:

1 can condensed cream of asparagus
soup

1 can condensed chicken broth

(1 can condensed cream of
mushroom soup)

1 cup milk

Heat, stirring until smooth.

QUICK CHILLED CREAM OF
AVOCADO SOUP

3 Cups

Stir until smooth and at the boiling point:

2 cups condensed cream of
chicken soup

Remove from heat. Chill and add:

½ cup puréed avocado

When ready to serve, stir in:

½ cup chilled cream

⅛ teaspoon white pepper

Serve in cups, sprinkled with:

1 teaspoon chopped chives or chervil

⅄ BLENDER BORSCH
I.

About 4 Cups

Combine in a blender:

1 can condensed consommé

1 can condensed cream of
chicken soup

1 can beets: No. 2½

(1 clove minced garlic)

Half of the liquid from the beets may be
drained if a thick soup is desired. Blend
until smooth and chill. Serve with a garnish of:

Cultured sour cream and Fines
Herbes, page 540

II.

About 4 Cups

Combine in a blender:

2 cups tomato juice

2 cups canned beets

3 dill pickles

3 tablespoons finely grated onion

1 drop hot pepper sauce

(1 clove minced garlic)

Chill the soup and serve garnished with:

4 thinly sliced hard-boiled eggs

Cultured sour cream

Fresh chopped dill or fennel

QUICK PEA SOUP

About 6 Cups

Combine and bring to the boiling point:

1 can condensed consommé

1 can clear chicken soup

1 can condensed pea soup

Add:

1⅓ cups water or stock

¼ cup finely diced cooked ham

(4 oz. fine noodles)

(1 tablespoon Worcestershire sauce)

(1 tablespoon chili sauce)

Simmer, covered, until hot or the noodles
are done.

QUICK CREAM OF CHICKEN SOUP

Easy to make and very good.

Heat in a double boiler ♦ over, not in
hot water:

Chicken bouillon

Cream—about ¼ the amount of the
bouillon

Add, if you wish:

A dash of nutmeg

Chopped parsley

Add, if you want to be really luxurious:

Ground blanched almonds—use
about 2 tablespoons to 1 cup soup

QUICK CUCUMBER SOUP
COCKAIGNE

About 5 Cups

Bring to a boil:

2 cups strong chicken broth

Drop in about:

1½ cups peeled, seeded and
diced cucumbers

Simmer until translucent, about 15 minutes. Add:

1 can condensed cream of
chicken soup

blended with:

½ cup chicken broth

Again bring to a boil. Now add:

½ cup canned crab meat,
shrimp or minced clams

1 teaspoon fresh parsley or chervil

Heat ♦ but do not boil, and serve at once.

QUICK COLD CUCUMBER SOUP

About 5 Cups

Combine in a saucepan:

1 can frozen condensed cream of
potato soup

An equal amount of milk

1 chicken bouillon cube
1⅓ cups finely chopped cucumber

Heat slowly, stirring until very hot and until the cucumber is partially cooked, about 10 minutes. ↲ Blend or put through a food mill and refrigerate, covered, until chilled. Shortly before serving, stir in:

1 cup light cream
½ cup minced cucumber

QUICK CREAM OF CAULIFLOWER SOUP

About 3½ Cups

Heat:

2 tablespoons butter

Cook in the butter for 4 minutes:

¼ cup sliced onion
2 minced small ribs celery with leaves

Add:

1½ cups chicken broth
1 cup cooked cauliflower,
riced or mashed

Heat to the boiling point. Heat and add:

1 cup rich milk

♦ Do not let the soup boil after adding the milk.

Correct the seasoning

and serve with:

1 tablespoon chopped parsley
A light grating of nutmeg

QUICK CHEESE SOUP

About 4 Cups

Combine and stir over low heat:

1 can condensed celery soup
1 can condensed consommé
1¼ cups water or milk
½ cup grated cheddar or
pimiento cheese

Add:

(1 tablespoon chopped onion)
(¼ teaspoon Worcestershire sauce)

Stir over low heat until the cheese is melted. ♦ Do not let the soup boil. Serve with:

Chopped parsley

QUICK TOMATO CORN CHOWDER

3 Cups

Combine and heat, but ♦ do not boil:

1 can condensed tomato soup
An equal amount of milk
½ cup cream style corn
1 teaspoon sugar
(¼ teaspoon curry powder)
Correct the seasoning

and serve.

QUICK MUSHROOM SOUP

About 4 Cups

Combine, stir and heat:

1 can condensed mushroom soup
1 cup condensed beef or chicken
bouillon or consommé
1¼ cups water or milk

II.   4 Cups

Soak for 30 minutes:

Dried mushrooms

in:

2 cans condensed consommé

Add:

1 can condensed mushroom soup

Heat and serve.

QUICK ONION SOUP

About 2 Cups

Heat:

1 can condensed onion soup

Add:

2 teaspoons lemon juice
A grating of lemon rind
½ clove pressed garlic
⅛ teaspoon nutmeg
(¼ cup sherry)
Correct the seasoning

Top each serving with:

Melba Cheese Rounds

QUICK OXTAIL SOUP WITH WINE

About 2½ Cups

Pare thinly in several strips:

The rind of 1 lemon

Add to it:

1 cup water
1 can condensed oxtail soup
1 teaspoon grated onion

♦ Simmer these ingredients for 5 minutes. Remove the lemon rind and

Correct the seasoning

Reduce the heat. Stir in:

½ cup claret or ¼ cup very dry sherry
1 tablespoon minced parsley

Serve at once with:

Toasted crackers

QUICK SPINACH SOUP

About 2 Cups

Combine:

½ cup cooked spinach
1 can condensed cream of chicken soup

If the spinach has already been creamed, use instead:

(1 can chicken broth)

You may thin the soup with:

Spinach water, stock or milk
Correct the seasoning

heat and serve.

QUICK TOMATO SOUP

About 4 Cups

♦ Simmer, covered, for 15 minutes or steam for 2 minutes in a ❂ pressure cooker, then strain:

2½ cups canned tomatoes
¼ cup sliced onion
½ cup chopped celery with leaves

Melt:

2 tablespoons butter

Add and stir until blended:

2 tablespoons flour

Add, cook and stir until smooth and boiling:

2 cups Stock, page 490, or
    canned bouillon
½ teaspoon sugar
⅛ teaspoon paprika
    The strained tomato stock
    Correct the seasoning
and add, just before serving:
    (1 tablespoon chopped fresh basil or
    ¾ teaspoon anchovy paste or
    whipped cream)

QUICK CHILLED FRESH TOMATO CREAM SOUP
⋏ I.   About 3 Cups
One way to use surplus garden tomatoes.
Peel, seed and chop coarsely:
    2½ cups fresh, very ripe tomatoes
Blend briefly with:
    1 cup cream
    1 tablespoon parsley
    1 tablespoon basil
    Correct the seasoning
Chill and serve with:
    Lemon slices

II.   About 3 Cups
Combine in a cocktail shaker:
    2 cups chilled tomato juice
    1 cup chilled cream
    4 or more ribs raw celery, grated
    1 teaspoon grated onion
    A few drops hot pepper sauce
    A few grains cayenne
    Correct the seasoning
and add:
    ¼ cup chopped ice
Or, you may omit the onion and use:
    (¼ teaspoon dry ginger)
    (⅛ teaspoon allspice)
Shake well.

QUICK CLAM AND CHICKEN BROTH
Combine equal parts of:
    Clam broth
    Chicken stock
If the clam broth is very salty, you may
have to use more chicken stock or water.
You may use both clam and chicken stock
canned or one fresh and the other canned.
Season lightly with:
    White pepper
When the soup reaches a boil, remove
from heat and place in hot cups. Add to
each cup:
    1 tablespoon heavy cream or top it
    with 1 tablespoon whipped cream
Have the cream at room temperature.
Sprinkle the top, for color, with:
    Paprika or chopped chives or parsley
Serve at once.

QUICK CRAB OR LOBSTER MONGOLE
                             About 4 Cups
Sprinkle:
    3 tablespoons dry white wine or
    1 teaspoon Worcestershire sauce
over:
    1 cup flaked canned crab or lobster
Combine and heat to the boiling point:

1 can condensed cream of tomato soup
1 can condensed cream of
    green pea soup
Stir in slowly:
    1¼ cups rich hot milk or
    part cream and part bouillon
Add the crab. Heat the soup ♦ but do not
let it boil.

QUICK LOBSTER SUPREME
                            About 5 Cups
Combine:
    1 can condensed asparagus soup
    1 can condensed mushroom soup
Add:
    2 cups light cream
Pick over and add:
    6 to 8 oz. canned lobster meat
Heat this soup but do not let it boil. Add
    3 tablespoons dry sherry

QUICK LOBSTER CHOWDER
                            About 6 Cups
An easy-to-get soup meal.
Sauté in a saucepan for about 5 minutes:
    ¼ cup finely diced onion
    ½ cup finely diced celery
in:
    2 tablespoons butter
Add:
    1½ cups water
    1 small bay leaf
    1 package frozen mixed vegetables,
    defrosted
♦ Cover and bring to a boil. Cook the
vegetables until they are barely tender
about 5 to 10 minutes. Remove the bay
leaf. Drain, but reserve the liquor from:
    1 can chopped broiled
    mushrooms: 3 oz.
Stir into the liquor until smooth:
    1 tablespoon cornstarch
Add this to the mixture in the saucepan
stirring constantly until it thickens. Add
the drained mushrooms and:
    1 cup tomato sauce
    2 cups milk
    1 cup canned rock lobster
    Correct the seasoning
and heat slowly ♦ but do not boil. Serve
with an assortment of:
    Cheese
or, as they do in France, with:
    Crusty bread and sweet butter

QUICK SEAFOOD TUREEN
                            About 6 Cups
Melt in a saucepan:
    ¼ cup butter
Add:
    2 cups flounder fillets, cut in pieces
    1½ cups dry white wine
♦ Cover and simmer about 10 minutes
Add:
    1 cup cooked shrimp
    1 cup cooked lobster meat
    1 small can sliced mushrooms

1½ cups condensed cream of
   mushroom soup
2 tablespoons chopped pimientos
1 clove crushed garlic
⅛ teaspoon saffron
Simmer about 5 minutes longer. Add:
  (½ cup dry sherry)
   Correct the seasoning
and serve in a tureen with:
   Buttered toast or French bread

ABOUT GARNISHES FOR SOUP

Changing from marrow balls to a chiffonade of cress in the same clear soup can
change the temper of a meal. Scan the
parade of breads and garnishes below to
determine your pace-setter du jour. If
serving an informal buffet, arrange a group
of garnishes around a tureen to give your
guests a choice between rich, green or lean.
Whip up some satisfying dumplings for
hungry children or pass a rice ring, flavored with nutmeg. Tempt a finicky appetite with an egg drop. ♦ Be sure none
of the garnishes is chilled, unless the soup
is an iced one.

FOR CLEAR SOUPS

Drop into the soup:
   Thin slices of lemon or orange
   Minced parsley, chives, watercress,
   onion, mint, basil, chervil. For
   some classic flavor combinations, see
   Seasonings, 538
   Podded peas
   Cucumber balls
   Croutons, see many varieties, page
   174 and 342
   Vegetables Brunoise, page 146
   Noodles, page 172
   Gnocchi, page 177
   Won Ton, page 147
   Dumplings, page 170
   Marrow balls, page 173
   Quenelles, page 193
   Thin slices of lemon drenched
   avocado
   Thin slices of cooked root: parsley,
   chervil or celeriac
   Small choux paste puffs, page 597,
   farci or plain
   Spaetzle, page 192

FOR CREAM SOUPS

Garnish with:
   Salted whipped cream or sour cream
   and a dusting of mixed, finely
   chopped herbs
   Toasted cubed stuffing
   Chiffonade
   Blanched, shredded, toasted almonds
   or cashews
   Flavored popcorn or puffed cereals

FOR THICK SOUPS

Use:
   Thin slices of orange, lemon or lime
   Sliced small sausages or thin slices of
   hard sausages
   Sliced hard-cooked eggs
   Croutons, page 174
   Sour cream
   Julienne strips of ham, tongue,
   chicken or bits of sea food
   Grated cheeses or Pesto, page 539
And see Thickeners For Soups, page 145.

BREADS TO SERVE WITH SOUPS

   Fancy shapes in toasted white,
   rye or wholewheat
   Melba toast
   Toasted rye sticks
   Plain or toasted garlic bread or other
   herbed breads
   Crackers, hot and plain or spread
   with herb butters, cheese spreads or
   fish pastes
   Cheese crackers and straws
   Pastry Snails, page 56
   Hush Puppies, page 580
   Corn Dodgers, page 579, or Zephyrs,
   page 579
   Croutons, page 174

ABOUT EGG-GARNISHED SOUPS

If your travels have led you to the Mediterranean or China, you probably know the
trick of turning a cup of broth into a bracing midmorning pickup or a light nourishing lunch. Our friend Cecily Brownstone
gave us these infallible directions.

I.   2 Servings
Heat in a quart pan, until boiling vigorously:
   2 cups chicken broth or beef stock
Reduce the heat, so the broth ♦ simmers.
This means that the bubbles form slowly
and collapse below the surface of the
liquid. Break into a cup:
   1 egg, which has reached 75°
♦ Beat it with a fork, just long enough to
combine yolk and white. When the egg is
lifted high, it should run off the tines of
the fork in a watery stream. Now, with
the broth ♦ simmering, hold the cup with
one hand, 5 inches above the rim of the
saucepan. Pour a little of the beaten egg
slowly in a fine stream into the broth.
With a fork in the other hand, describe
wide circles on the surface of the broth to
catch the egg as it strikes and draw it out
into long filmy threads. Rather than pour
the egg in one fell swoop, break its fall 3
or 4 times, so as not to disturb the simmering broth. If you have a helper, he can
pour the egg through a strainer instead of
from a cup. Simmer for about 1 minute.

Add to taste:
Salt
(**A squeeze of lemon**)
Serve at once in hot cups.

II.   **6 Servings**
For a quick way to make a Mediterranean
egg drop that does not "flower" so profusely, heat to a rolling boil:
    3 cups chicken broth
    ¾ cup cooked rice or fine noodles
Beat in a large bowl, just long enough to
combine and be uniform in color:
    2 eggs
    2 tablespoons lemon juice or wine
From on high ♦ gradually, so as not to
curdle the eggs but to allow them to shred,
pour the hot soup over them, stirring constantly. Serve at once in hot cups.

III.   **8 Servings**
A still stauncher mix is made in Germany
and is called **Baumwollsuppe.**
♦ Simmer:
    4 cups strong brown stock
Mix together:
    2 eggs
    1 tablespoon flour
    ¼ cup cream
    (**1 tablespoon butter**)
    (**Pinch of nutmeg**)
Mix and cook as described in I. Serve in
hot cups.

IV.   **4 Servings**
In Italy a ragged fluffy drop is made by
beating until well combined:
    1 egg
    1½ teaspoons grated Parmesan cheese
    1 tablespoon grated dry bread crumbs
    (**½ clove pressed garlic**)
Stir this mixture rapidly into:
    3 cups ♦ simmering consommé
Continue to simmer and stir until egg is
set. Serve at once.

SOUP CUSTARD OR ROYALE
Preheat Oven to 325°.

These tender drops are used in clear soups.
Bake them as for Cup Custard, page 684.
They may be poured initially to ½-inch
thickness into a well-buttered 9-inch pie
pan. Because of their fragile consistency,
they must always be ♦ well cooled in a
mold before handling. Any slight crusting
may be trimmed.
Beat well:
    ½ cup milk or stock
    ⅛ teaspoon each salt, paprika, and
      nutmeg
    1 egg
    (**1 egg yolk**)
Bake about 25 minutes, then ♦ cool, before
cutting into dice or fancy shapes. Simmer
the soup and drop the royales into it, just
long enough to heat them through. Serve
at once, allowing 3 or 4 small drops to
each cup of broth.

HARD-COOKED EGG DROPS
Crush with a fork:
    2 hard-cooked egg yolks
Add to them and blend well:
    1 tablespoon soft butter
    1 raw egg yolk
    A few grains of cayenne
    A light grating of nutmeg
    ⅛ teaspoon salt
Form these ingredients into ½-inch balls.
Roll them in:
    Flour
Cook the drops in ♦ simmering consommé
for about 1 minute.

ABOUT DUMPLINGS

The secret of making light dumplings is to
keep them steaming on top of ♦ simmering
liquid. And be sure the temperature of the
stock, gravy or water in which you are
cooking them never goes higher than a
simmer. Most dumplings are bound together by egg, and the protein in the egg
must not be allowed to toughen. ♦ Use
ample liquid in a wide-topped cooking
vessel, giving each ball or drop a chance
to expand. ♦ Never crowd the pan. The
minute the batter is floating in the liquid
♦ cover the pot, so the steam can begin
functioning. ♦ Do not lift the lid until the
dumpling is done. This is not as hard to
do as it sounds if you cover the pan with
a tight-fitting heat-resistant glass pie pan
or lid, so you can watch the swelling of the
batter. When the dumplings look fluffy
♦ test them for doneness, as you would a
cake, by inserting a toothpick. If it comes
out clean, the dumplings are done. Once
you are expert at timing, try simmering
dumplings in a ◐ pressure pan. Proceed
to cook as above, but instead of the glass
cover use the pressure pan lid. ♦ Keep the
vent off the entire time. Some good additions to dumpling dough are parsley or
other herbs, cheese or grated onion. We
have given ♦ dumpling amounts in cups,

for some people like large dumplings, others small. A cup of dough will usually yield about eighteen to twenty 1-inch balls, but marrow, liver and meat balls do not expand as do those high in cereal and egg. ♦ For other dumplings more suitable for luncheon dishes or as an accompaniment to meat dishes, see pages 191-193.

SOUP OR STEW NOCKERLN
About 1 Cup
Beat until creamy:
   ¼ cup soft butter
   1 egg
Stir in:
   1 cup all-purpose flour
   ⅛ teaspoon salt
Add gradually, until a firm batter is formed, about:
   6 tablespoons milk
Cut out the batter with a teaspoon to form small balls. Drop them into boiling water or directly into the clear soup in which they will be served. Reduce the liquid to a ♦ simmer and continue to simmer, covered, for about 10 minutes. For a stew, cook nockerln in water, drain, and drop them into the meat mixture just before serving.

MATZO OR CRACKER MEAL DUMPLINGS
About 2 Cups
These light Passover soup drops are made with the finely crushed crumbs of special unleavened crackers.
Beat until thick and well blended:
   2 egg yolks
   3 tablespoons soft chicken fat
Pour over them and beat well:
   ½ cup hot stock
Stir in gently a mixture of:
   ¾ cup matzo meal or cracker meal
   ½ teaspoon salt
   (⅛ teaspoon ginger)
   (⅛ teaspoon nutmeg)
   (1 tablespoon finely chopped parsley)
   (1 tablespoon finely grated onion)
Beat until ♦ stiff, but not dry:

   2 egg whites
Fold the egg whites into the cracker mixture and chill, covered, for ½ to 1 hour. About ½ hour before you are ready to serve, form this dough lightly into small balls. If you wet your hands with cold water, the job will be easier. Drop them into:
   6 cups boiling stock
Reduce heat at once to a ♦ simmer and cook, covered, for about 15 minutes.

FARINA BALLS COCKAIGNE
About 3 Cups
Serve these stout but light dumplings with a soup-and-salad meal.
Have ready at about 75°:
   2 eggs
Heat to the boiling point:
   2 cups milk
Add, stir and cook until thick:
   ½ cup farina
   1 tablespoon butter
   ½ teaspoon salt
   ⅛ teaspoon paprika
   (⅛ teaspoon nutmeg)
Remove the batter from the heat and beat in the eggs vigorously ♦ one at a time. The heat of the mixture will thicken the eggs. Drop the batter, a generous teaspoon at a time, into ♦ simmering soup stock. Cook, covered, for about 2 minutes and serve.

LIVER DUMPLINGS OR LEBERKLOESSE
About 3 Cups
Being the descendants of South Germans, we cannot well compile a cookbook without including a recipe that is typical of that neck of the woods—not exactly a handsome dish, but it has qualities.
Skin and remove the fiber from:
   1 lb. calf liver or chicken livers
Grind or chop until very fine. Slightly frozen liver is easy to grind. Soak in water for 3 minutes, then wring the water from:
   2 slices white bread: 1 cup
Beat, then stir into liver and bread:
   2 egg yolks
   ¼ cup soft butter
   2 teaspoons chopped onion
   2 tablespoons chopped parsley
   1½ teaspoons salt
   ½ teaspoon pepper
   2 tablespoons flour
Beat until stiff:
   2 egg whites
Fold them into the other ingredients. Shape this mixture into 1½-inch balls. Drop them into gently boiling:
   Soup Stock, page 490
Cook them for 5 or 6 minutes. Serve them with the soup; or drop them into boiling water, drain them and serve with:
   Sautéed Onions, page 285

CHOUX PASTE GARNISH
About 1½ Cups

You may add:
 (4 to 6 tablespoons grated
   Parmesan cheese)
to the dough, for either of these garnishes.

I. Use a pastry bag with a ¼-inch-diameter tube. Fill with:
   **Unsweetened or cheese-flavored
   Choux Paste, page 597**
Squeeze onto a greased baking tin pea-sized bits of dough. Bake in a preheated 400° oven for about 10 minutes. Add these to the soup the instant before serving.

II. Fill a pastry bag with:
   Unsweetened Choux Paste, page 597
Make 1-inch rounds. Flatten carefully with a moistened finger any points remaining after the bag is lifted off. Glaze with:
   French Egg Wash, page 682
Bake in a preheated 400° oven for about 10 minutes. Be sure the puffs are well dried out before removing them from the oven. ♦ Fill them, the last minute before serving, with a farce that combines well with the soup. ♦ Place in soup the instant before serving to avoid sogginess.

FRITTER GARNISH
                                    About ¾ Cup
Preheat Deep Fryer to 360°.
Beat until light:
   1 egg
Add:
   **¼ teaspoon salt
   ⅛ teaspoon paprika
   ½ cup flour
   2 tablespoons milk**
When the fat is ready, page 125, allow the batter to drop into it through a colander. Fry until the garnish is brown. Drain on paper. Place in the soup just before serving.

MEAT PASTRIES FOR SOUPS
Some pastry wrapped meats are used in soup itself, others as accompaniments, but with all of them the aim is the same—to make a covering of dough which is tender, yet strong enough to hold the filling. Chinese Won Ton, page 147, are frequently served in soup. They are very much like ravioli and can also be served with a sauce as an entrée or sautéed in butter and coated with cheese. If made in small sizes, they also make interesting cocktail snacks. Other soup accompaniments of this type are rissoles, turnovers or Piroshki, page 224.

BUTTER DUMPLINGS OR BUTTERKLOESSE
                                    About ¾ Cup
Beat until soft:
   2 tablespoons butter
Beat and add:
   2 eggs

Stir in:
   **6 tablespoons flour
   ¼ teaspoon salt**
Drop the batter from a spoon into ♦ simmering soup and simmer the dumplings, covered, for about 8 minutes. You may also simmer them in the soup for about 4 minutes in a ♥ pressure cooker on which you keep the vent open the entire time.

WHITE OR GREEN NOODLE DOUGH OR FETTUCINI
                        **About ½ Lb. Dry or
                        4 Cups Cooked Noodles**
♦ If you are a beginner, do not try to make noodles in damp weather.
I. On a large pastry board or marble table top make a well, page 594, of:
   ⅔ cup all-purpose flour
Drop into it:
   1 egg
barely combined with:
   **1 tablespoon water
   ½ teaspoon salt
   1 teaspoon oil**
Work the mixture with your hands, folding the flour over the egg until the dough can be rolled in a ball and comes clean from the hands. If you want to make green noodles, at this point, add:
   **(2 to 4 tablespoons very well pressed
   and dried, finely chopped cooked
   spinach)**
Knead the dough as for bread, page 554, about 10 minutes. Then let it stand, covered, for about 1 hour. Now roll the dough, pulling it as you wrap it around the rolling pin, stretching it a little more each time. Continue to sprinkle it with flour between each rolling and stretching to keep the dough from sticking to the pin or board or developing holes. Repeat this procedure about 10 times or until the dough is paper-thin and translucent. Let it dry for about 30 minutes. You can hang it as the Neapolitans do—like laundry on a

line—over a piece of foil or plastic. Before it is brittle, roll it up like a scroll and cut it on the bias into strips of any width you prefer: ⅛ inch for soup or 1 inch for lasagna. Allow about 3 tablespoons uncooked noodles for each quart of soup. Cook the noodles in ♦ rapidly boiling salted water for about 10 minutes. Drain and quickly add them to the soup. If stored for future use, keep them, dry and uncooked, in a closed jar.

II. In making casing for Won Ton, Ravioli, etc., proceed as for above, but ♦ do not allow the dough to dry before cutting. Cut into 3-inch squares, fill and use at once.

SPATZEN FOR SOUP
About 1½ Cups

Prepare:

Spatzen or Spaetzle, page 192

making these delicious dumplings in a smaller size. Drop the batter as directed into ♦ simmering soup, instead of water.

MEAT BALLS FOR SOUP

A superb main dish may be had by adding these to vegetable soup. Make up ½ the recipe for:

German Meat Balls, page 428

You may use more bread, if desired. Mix the ingredients lightly with a fork. Shape them without pressure into 1-inch balls and drop into boiling soup or stock. ♦ Simmer them until done for about 10 minutes.

QUENELLES FOR SOUP

Prepare:

Quenelles, page 193

As with all protein-based foods, these delicately poached drops should be added to simmering soup and cooked only until they are heated through thoroughly.

MARROW BALLS
About ¾ Cup

These delicate drops may be prepared several hours in advance and refrigerated. Combine and beat until creamy:

¼ cup fresh marrow
2 tablespoons butter

Add:

3 egg yolks
¼ teaspoon salt
⅛ teaspoon paprika
2 tablespoons chopped parsley
Cracker crumbs

Use just enough cracker crumbs, at least ½ cup, to make the mixture of the right consistency to shape into balls. Now, fold in:

3 stiffly beaten egg whites

Cook the balls in ♦ simmering soup for about 15 minutes or until they rise to the surface.

LIVER SAUSAGE DUMPLINGS
About 1 Cup

Combine and work with a fork:

¼ lb. liver sausage
½ egg or 1 egg white or yolk
½ cup cracker crumbs
1 tablespoon chopped parsley
or chives
(1 tablespoon catsup)

Shape the mixture into 1-inch balls. ♦ Simmer gently for about 2 minutes in soup stock.

SAUSAGE BALLS FOR SOUP
About 1½ Cups

Good in pea, bean or lentil soup. Combine:

½ lb. raw sausage meat
1 egg white
2 teaspoons chopped parsley
⅛ teaspoon fresh basil
¼ teaspoon fresh rosemary
3 tablespoons toasted bread crumbs

Roll this mixture into 1-inch balls. Drop them into boiling stock. Reduce the heat at once and ♦ simmer the soup until the balls are done, for about 30 minutes.

CHEESE BALLS FOR SOUP
About 1½ Cups

Combine:

2 beaten egg yolks
2 tablespoons grated cheese:
preferably Parmesan
2 tablespoons dry bread crumbs
⅛ teaspoon paprika
½ teaspoon dried herbs, fresh chives
or parsley

Beat until stiff ♦ but not dry, then fold in:

2 egg whites
⅛ teaspoon salt

Drop the batter from a spoon into ♦ simmering soup. Simmer for only 1 or 2 minutes.

CHIFFONADE OF HERBS FOR SOUPS

To prepare a chiffonade, always use the freshest and most tender of greens ♦ being sure to remove stems and coarse mid ribs—lettuce, sorrel or parsley, alone or in combination with whatever fresh herbs you have on hand that are compatible with the flavor of your soup. Allow:

1 or 2 tablespoons fresh herbs
or greens

to:

1 pint broth

Add the herbs to a small quantity of broth and chop in a ⅄ blender until fine. Combine the blended herbs with the remaining broth. If you have no blender, mince a combination of herbs very, very fine.

ABOUT FANCY BREADS AND CRACKERS FOR SOUP

We suggest in the following recipes a number of quick fancy breads, wafers and crackers, but ask that you consider also Bread Sticks and toasted Cheese Bread, page 556, and look at things to do with Ready Baked Bread, page 586.

✳ **PUFFED BREAD BLOCKS**
                    About Thirty 1½-Inch Blocks
These may be prepared in advance. Keep
at room temperature until soft, then blend
well:
    ½ lb. cheddar cheese
    ¼ lb. butter: 1 stick
Season palatably with:
    Mustard
    Curry powder
    Caraway or celery seed
    Salt and pepper or paprika
Cut bread into 1½ x ¾ x ¾-inch blocks.
Cover them with the cheese spread. Keep
them chilled until ready for use. Pop them
into a 375° oven. They should brown
lightly and puff.

SOUP CROUTONS
For other Croutons, see page 342.
To retain the crispness of these ever-popular diced toasts, serve them in individual
dishes and let the guests add them to the
soup as they are ready for them. Or, use
them diced small, so they are much like
buttered toasted crumbs to garnish spinach,
noodles or game. They may be flavored by
sautéing in:
    Butter and olive oil
or dusting them with:
    Grated cheese
while still hot.

**CHEESE OR BUTTER
BREAD CUBES**
Preheat Oven to 375°.
I. Beat together:
    1 egg
    1½ tablespoons melted butter
Cut into cubes or blocks of any size:
    Fresh bread
Roll the cubes in the egg mixture, then in:
    Finely grated American cheese
    Salt and cayenne or paprika
Toast the cubes on a buttered sheet until
the cheese is melted. Serve them hot as
appetizers. Good with soup or salads.

II. Spread bread cubes with a paste made
of:
    Butter
    Grated Parmesan cheese
    Caraway or celery seed
    Salt and a few grains cayenne
    (Mustard)
Toast and serve, as above.

SEEDED CRACKERS
Brush:
    Small crisp salt crackers
with:
    **Melted butter or partially
    beaten egg white**
Sprinkle lightly with:
    Caraway, celery or sesame seeds
Toast and serve.

**REFRIGERATOR CHEESE WAFERS
OR STRAWS**
These keep for weeks in a refrigerator or
freezer and are quickly sliced and baked
for the unexpected guest. Or just after
mixing put the dough in a pastry tube to
make straws. Or use the 1½-inch ribbon
disk on a cookie press to make ribbons
Cut into 2 inch lengths.
I.   **4 Dozen**
Preheat oven to 475°.
Grate or grind:
    ½ lb. aged cheddar cheese
Combine with:
    3 tablespoons soft butter
    ¾ cup all-purpose flour
    (1 teaspoon Worcestershire sauce)
    ½ teaspoon salt
    Dash of hot pepper sauce
Form the dough into 1-inch rolls. Wrap in
foil and refrigerate or freeze till cold
enough to slice as thin as possible, under
a quarter of an inch. Bake for about 1
minutes.

II.
Preheat oven to 475°.
Cream:
    ¼ cup butter
and mix it well with:
    ¾ cup all-purpose flour
    ¼ lb. grated aged cheddar cheese
    ⅛ teaspoon salt
    A dash of white pepper
Shape and bake as above.

MELBA CHEESE ROUNDS
Spread:
    Melba rounds
lightly with:
    Butter
Sprinkle generously with:
    Parmesan cheese
Just before using, run them under a broil
until toasted. Serve at once, floating one
two on:
    Onion or other soup

CEREALS AND PASTAS

ABOUT CEREALS

On a train trip from Palermo to Syracuse, a stranger leaned toward us to say in the most casual tone that this was the field where Pluto abducted Persephone — and rushed her to his dark abode. This brought to mind the lamentations of her mother Ceres and a speculation as to how much greater those lamentations would have been had she known what today's processing was to do to the grains that bear her name. Until a century ago the entire kernel, including the germ, could be ground between cool millstones without risking rancidity. Today, the heat of steel grinding necessitates removal of the germ.

In spite of the incomplete protein make-up of cereals, they form almost a fourth of the average diet. So let's look at their values more closely. Especially, note that grain mixtures—when served with milk, cheese, egg or even small quantities of meat and fish—have a greatly increased nutritive protein content. If you buy ready-to-eat cereals, the grains have been highly processed. They are either exploded into puffs, under high steam, or malted, sugared and shattered into flakes under rollers; or mixed into pastes and formed. You pay as much for the processing, and the expensive packaging to keep these cereals crisp, as you pay for the cereal itself. You may have to give more time to the proper cooking of whole-grains but there is no question of nutritive and monetary savings. For further details about Whole-Grains, see About Flours, page 496.

Partially precooked cereals in which the heat has been great enough to destroy the enzymes—which cause rancidity—keep better than raw cereals. They should be finish-cooked according to the directions on the label. ▶ All cereals should be stored covered against insect infestation and moisture absorption. Raw cereals will further profit by storage in a cool place, as even mild heat induces more rapid development of rancidity.

ABOUT COOKING CEREALS

Scientists tell us that cereals are edible as soon as the starch granules swell to their fullest capacity in hot liquid. This state they speak of glibly as gelatinization, although it remains something of a chemical mystery. To cooks, this phenomenon is evident in the thickening of cereals and sauces. While the technical-minded insist that the starch and protein in cereals are adequately cooked in a short period of time, many cooks claim that the results are not so nutty and sweet as when the older, slow-heat methods are used. Whether you back the cook or the scientist, on these points they agree: cereals must be added ▶ slowly to ▶ very rapidly boiling water and ▶ stirred in, so that each individual grain is surrounded and quickly penetrated by the hot liquid. The boiling point of the water ▶ 212°, must be maintained throughout as the cereal is added.

With cereals that tend to gumminess, this slow addition to the boiling water allows the outer starch layers to stabilize and keeps the grains separated after swelling. Coarsely ground cereals may be added dry. Granular fine cereals may be moistened with part of the measured cold water to form a loose mush and may be poured so slowly into the boiling water that they do not disturb the boiling point. They are then cooked 2 to 3 minutes over direct heat and 5 to 20 minutes more in a double boiler. If you want to cook any of these cereals longer, start out as directed above and, if necessary, add more milk or water during the cooking period. If you cook cereals or starches in an acid liquid like fruit juices with sugar, the thickening power is lowered.

The cereal is done when it looks translucent. The grains should still be separated, retaining their individual shape even though they are soft. Serve at once. Cereals increase in bulk depending on the amount of water they absorb. You may count 4 to 6 servings for each cup of uncooked cereal. If you cook cereal in advance of serving ▶ cover it at once while it is still hot from the first cooking—so no crust forms on the top. If you plan to use it more than an hour after the first cooking, refrigerate it. ▶ To avoid lumps on reheating, place the cereal over hot water and allow the cereal to become hot all the way through before stirring.

To make a gruel for the baby, cook the cereal with 3 times the called for amount of water or milk and cook twice as long. Strain and serve.

FINELY MILLED CEREALS

About 4 to 6 Servings

▶ Please read About Cooking Cereals, above. To prepare the fine granular cereals listed below, have water heated in the bottom of a double boiler. In the top of the boiler, over direct heat, bring to a rolling boil, 212°:

4 to 6 cups water or milk
1 teaspoon salt

Very slowly ♦ without disturbing the boiling point, dribble into the water:

   **1 cup dry corn meal, farina or
   hominy grits**

Continue to cook over direct heat for 2 to 3 minutes, then cook covered over, not in, hot water 5 to 20 minutes. To avoid gumminess ♦ do not stir. If you do not serve at once see About Cooking Cereals, page 175, for reheating or storing. During the last few minutes of cooking, you may fold in lightly:

   **3 tablespoons dry skim-milk solids
   2 teaspoons debittered yeast powder**

for each cup dry cereal. These ingredients make no noticeable change in taste and are a great addition in food value. You may at that time also add:

   **Dates, figs, raisins and cooked
   dried fruits**

Or serve with:

   **Cold or hot sliced canned or fresh
   fruits
   A cinnamon-sugar mixture
   Sugar and cream
   Maple sirup
   Jams and preserves**

COARSELY MILLED CEREALS
                              About 4 to 6 Servings

These coarsely ground or cracked grains have many different names, but all are cooked the same way. The wheats, wholegrain and cracked, also include bulghur—a parched cracked wheat—and couscous. Groats may be cracked wheat, buckwheat or oats. Coarsely ground buckwheat barley or millet is also called kasha. Cracked corn is called samp. Coarse oats come in a number of forms, steel cut or rolled. Prepare any of these as for the finely milled cereals above. Because they are coarser in grind, you need to use in all:

   **2 to 4 cups water, milk or fruit juice
   1 teaspoon salt**

for every:

   1 cup dry cereal

Cook about one hour as directed above.

ABOUT WHOLE CEREALS

Whole cereals like rice or barley may be cooked on two principles—the one described above for coarsely ground cereals or by the so-called fried method, in which the cereal is sautéed in oil or clarified butter before the liquid is added. For a detailed description of this method, see Risotto, page 183. For other ways to cook rice, see page 178, and the Index.

ABOUT HOMINY

Hominy is corn with the hull and germ removed. In an attempt to give it calcium values, it is sometimes also soaked in wood ash lye. It has recently gained favor as an antistrontium absorbent. Hominy grits are the broken grains.

HOMINY
I.   **Yield 1 Quart**

Shell and wash:

   1 quart of dried corn

Put it in an enamel or stainless steel pan. Cover with:

   2 quarts water

Add:

   2 tablespoons baking soda

Cover the pan and let this mixture set 12 hours. Then bring it to a boil in the liquid in which it has soaked. Simmer about 3 hours or until the hulls loosen. If necessary, add water. Drain. Rub corn until hulls are removed. Bring to a boil in:

   2 quarts cold water

Drain. Repeat this boiling process again in fresh water, adding:

   1 teaspoon salt

Drain once more and serve. Season with:

   Melted butter

II.   **6 Servings**

Preheat oven to 400°.
Combine and place in a greased baking dish:

   **2 cups drained, cooked hominy, above
   1 cup Cheese Sauce, page 326
   ½ cup minced green pepper**

Cover the top with:

   Strips of bacon

Bake the dish for about 20 minutes.

HOMINY CAKES
                                                       5 Servings

These cakes are a variation on potatoes. Drain:

   2½ cups cooked or canned hominy

Combine it with:

   **2 tablespoons flour
   1 egg
   Salt and pepper**

Form these ingredients into flat cakes. Sauté them until they are brown in:

   Butter or drippings

Serve them hot—plain or with:

   Honey or sirup

SCALLOPED HOMINY AND HAM
                                                       4 Servings

Preheat oven to 375°.
Combine:

   **½ cup water
   1 can condensed tomato soup or
   2 cups Cream Sauce I, page 322**

Add:

   **1 cup diced cooked ham
   ½ teaspoon salt
   ½ teaspoon sugar
   ⅛ teaspoon paprika or pepper**

Drain and add:

   2½ cups cooked or canned hominy

Heat these ingredients. Combine:

   **1 cup soft bread crumbs
   1 cup grated cheese
   ⅛ teaspoon paprika
   ¼ teaspoon salt**

Place ½ the hominy mixture in a greased

king dish, cover it with ½ the bread
xture. Dot the top with:
    1 tablespoon butter
peat the process. Bake the dish until
: top is brown, about 12 minutes.

CORN MEAL MUSH
                                    4 Servings
ombine and stir:
    1 cup water-ground corn meal
    1 cup cold water
    1 teaspoon salt
ace in the top of a double boiler:
    4 cups boiling water
r corn meal mixture in gradually. Cook
d stir the mush over quick heat from 2
3 minutes. Steam it, covered, over, not
hot water about 15 minutes. Stir it fre-
ently. Serve with:
    Maple sirup, honey or molasses

POLENTA
st as our greatest architectural surprise
Italy was to find St. Francis' first church
og cabin, so were we amazed to discover
at the Italians do even more delicious
d interesting things with corn meal than
u can find in the deep South.
eese is sometimes cooked with it, and
metimes it is served sprinkled over it.
mato sauce, meat or a combination of
th is another favorite accompaniment.
Prepare:
    Corn Meal Mush, above
ld to it for the last 15 minutes of cooking:
    ⅛ teaspoon paprika
    A few grains red pepper
(½ cup grated cheese)

. Prepare as above and sauté it in:
    Olive oil or butter

BUCKWHEAT GROATS OR KASHA
                                    4 Servings
eheat oven to 350°.
ave ready:
    1 cup kasha
own it in hot skillet with:
    2 tablespoons hot chicken fat or butter
ir with fork until each grain is coated.
ld:
    3½ cups boiling water
over and cook for about 15 minutes, then
nsfer to greased casserole and bake for
out one hour.

. As a luncheon dish, add:
    Sautéed onions
    Salt and pepper
    Some almonds
d proceed as above.

GNOCCHI WITH FLOUR
                                    4 Servings
rve as a separate course in place of pota-
es or as a soup garnish.

Scald:
    1 cup milk
Melt in a skillet:
    2 tablespoons butter
Stir and blend in until smooth:
    2 tablespoons flour
    2 tablespoons cornstarch
    ½ teaspoon salt
Stir in the scalded milk. Reduce the heat
and add:
    1 egg yolk
    (½ cup grated cheese)
Beat the batter until the egg has thickened
and the cheese has melted. Pour it onto a
shallow greased platter or pan.
Preheat oven to 375°.
When the batter is cool, cut it into strips
2 inches long. Place the strips in a pan
and pour over them:
    Melted butter
Sprinkle them with:
    (Grated cheese)
Heat them in the oven. We prefer poaching
the batter after it has been cut into strips.
Poach in gently boiling water or stock for
1 or 2 minutes. Drain the strips and serve
them with melted butter.

GNOCCHI WITH FARINA
                                    4 Servings
Scald:
    2 cups milk
Stir in, all at once:
    ¾ cup farina
Stir the mush over low heat until thick.
Remove from heat and beat in until smooth:
    1 tablespoon butter
    1 egg yolk
    ¼ teaspoon salt
You may spread the mixture evenly in an
8 x 8-inch pan lined with foil to make
handling easier. Chill for about 3 hours.
Preheat oven to 425°.
Cut the farina mixture into 1½-inch squares.
Place the squares in a well-greased oven-
proof dish, letting them overlap slightly.
Dot with:
    2 tablespoons butter
Pour over them slowly:
    1 cup Hunters' Sauce, page 327
      or Aurore Sauce, page 324
Sprinkle the top with:
    6 tablespoons grated Parmesan cheese
Bake for about 10 minutes.

GNOCCHI WITH POTATOES
                                    6 Servings
◆ The potatoes must be freshly cooked and
used at once. Boil, then put through a ricer:
    2 medium-sized potatoes
Heat to the boiling point:
    ½ cup milk
    5 tablespoons butter
Stir in, until the dough forms a ball:
    1 cup flour
Remove from heat. Beat in:
    2 eggs
    1 teaspoon salt

178   CEREALS AND PAST

¼ teaspoon paprika
(3 tablespoons grated cheese)
and the potatoes. Sprinkle the dough with
flour. Roll it into sticks ½ inch thick. Cut
it into 1-inch lengths. Drop the gnocchi
into simmering salted water. Or force the
gnocchi dough through a pastry bag. Cut
into desired lengths as shown above before
letting the gnocchi fall into the water.
Simmer uncovered for 3 to 5 minutes.
Drain. Place them on a greased pan in a
hot oven for about 3 minutes. The baking
is optional. Serve the gnocchi dressed with
melted butter and grated cheese.

ABOUT RICE

"May your rice never burn," is the New
Year's greeting of the Chinese. "May it
never be gummy," is ours. So many people
complain to us about the variability of their
results in rice cookery. Like flour, it may
have more or less moisture in its makeup
when you start to use it. In Japan they have
a standard ratio, allowing 8 cups of water
to 8 cups of rice for the first six weeks after
harvest. The amount of water then rises
steadily. And when the rice is 11 months
old, 8 cups of rice need 10 cups of water.
Not only is there moisture variability in
rice, but the type must also be reckoned
with. Brown rice, which retains its bran
coat and germ, is much slower to tenderize
—although more valuable nutritionally—
than highly polished white rice.
There are also differences in the grain
hybrids. Use short grain types—which cook
up tender and moist—in recipes calling for
sauces. Long grain types are best for
soups, molding or stuffing. Also on the
market are preprocessed rices, for which
you must follow the directions on the
label. Some of these which are parboiled
before milling have greater nutritive value
than polished white rice. Wild rice is not
a true rice. The seed comes from a strictly
American plant and needs its own recipes,
see page 179.
♦ To keep rice white when cooking in
hard water, add 1 teaspoon lemon juice or
1 tablespoon vinegar to the cooking water.
♦ One cup raw rice equals 3½ cups when

cooked. If using preprocessed rice,
volume will be less. This is also true
recipes in which rice is browned in
skillet—with or without fat—prior to co
ing it with moisture. But this browni
helps to keep the granules separate a
does contribute to good flavor.

BOILED RICE
6 to 7 Servin
I. Bring to a ♦ rolling boil:
1¾ to 2½ cups water or stock
Add:
¾ teaspoon salt
You may add:
(1 tablespoon melted butter)
to the rice before cooking, to keep it fr
sticking to the pot. Stir slowly into t
water, so as not to disturb the boiling:
1 cup white or brown rice
Cover and cook over slow heat. Wh
rice will take from 20 to 30 minutes, bro
from 40 to 50. If the rice becomes t
dry, add ¼ cup or more ♦ boiling wat
When the grains have swelled to capaci
uncover the pot for about the last 5 minu
of cooking. Continue to cook the rice o
♦ very low heat, shaking the pot from ti
to time until the grains have separate
Or fluff the cooked rice with a fork.

3 Servin
II. A moist Oriental-type rice.
Wash and drain:
½ cup rice
Place in a deep, heavy kettle with:
1½ cups cold water
Boil for 5 minutes until most of the surfa
water is gone and air bubbles can be se
on the surface of the rice. ♦ Reduce t
heat and continue to cook ♦ covered,
about 20 minutes longer. Remove fro
heat and let the rice stand covered f
about 20 minutes more. It is then rea
to serve.

BAKED RICE
6 to 7 Servin
Preheat oven to 375°.
Sauté:
½ chopped onion
in:
¼ cup butter
until translucent. Add, and stir until w
coated:
1 cup long-grain rice
Add:
2 cups boiling chicken broth or
boiling salted water
Cover and bake for about 18 minute
Gently mix with the rice:
2 tablespoons melted butter
Serve the rice at once.

BAKED GREEN RICE
3 Servin
Outstanding alone or as a stuffing for
veal breast. This amount will fill a 7-in
ring mold.

Preheat oven to 325°.
Beat:
  1 egg
Add and mix well:
  1 cup milk
  ½ cup finely chopped parsley
  1 finely chopped clove garlic
  1 small minced onion
  2 cups cooked rice
  ½ cup sharp grated cheese or
  2 tablespoons butter
  ⅛ teaspoon curry
  Salt to taste
Place these ingredients in a baking dish, in which has been poured:
  2 tablespoons olive oil
Bake for 30 to 40 minutes.

RICE COOKED IN CHICKEN STOCK
3 Servings

Melt in a saucepan:
  2 tablespoons butter
Add and stir until golden brown:
  ½ chopped onion
Add and shake until the grains are coated:
  1 cup rice
Add:
  2 cups hot chicken stock
Cover the pot and simmer the rice, or bake it in a 375° oven until the liquid is absorbed. Add:
  2 tablespoons melted butter
Toss the rice with a fork to distribute it.

CURRIED RICE
3 Servings

An unusual and delicious rice dish. Its popularity is undoubtedly due to the restraint with which the spice is used.
Pour:
  2 cups hot water
over:
  ½ cup rice
Place the rice where it will remain hot, but will not cook, for about 45 minutes.
Preheat oven to 350°.
Add to the rice:
  ½ cup tomatoes
  ¾ teaspoon salt
  ¼ cup finely sliced onion
  ¼ cup sliced green peppers
  2 tablespoons melted butter
  ¾ teaspoon curry powder
Bake these ingredients in a baking dish for 1½ hours or until done. Stir them from time to time. At first, there will be a great preponderance of liquid, but gradually the rice will absorb it. Remove the dish from the oven while the rice is still moist. Good served with beer.

ABOUT WILD RICE
Wild rice is a seed from a grass growing wild in the northern United States and remains a luxury because of the difficulty of harvesting it. For economy, combine cooked wild rice with cooked white or brown rice.
One cup of wild rice equals 3 to 3½ cups of cooked wild rice. Add 1 teaspoon salt to each cup uncooked rice.

WILD RICE
4 Servings

Wash well in several waters, pouring off the foreign particles from the top:
  1 cup wild rice
Drain it. Stir it slowly into:
  4 cups boiling water
  1 teaspoon salt
Cook it without stirring until tender, for about 40 minutes.

WILD RICE RING
4 Servings

Preheat oven to 350°.
Prepare as above:
  1 cup wild rice
You may add:
  1 sliced clove garlic
Cook the rice as above. Add:
  ¼ cup butter
  ½ teaspoon poultry seasoning or freshly grated nutmeg
  (1 cup sautéed onions and mushrooms)
  (¼ cup dry sherry)
Place it in a well-greased 7-inch ring mold. Set the mold in a pan of hot water and bake for about 20 minutes. Loosen the edges with a knife, invert the contents onto a platter and fill the center with:
  Creamed Mushrooms, page 281
  Chicken Livers Lyonnaise, page 439
  or Sautéed Onions, page 285

CHINESE FRIED RICE
6 Servings

The rice for this recipe must be ♦ cooked, fluffy and at least one day old. Heat in a heavy skillet:
  ¼ cup cooking oil
Toss in it:
  3 cups Boiled Rice, page 178
until hot and golden. Add:
  4 minced scallions
  ¾ teaspoon salt
  (½ cup cooked julienned roast pork or ham or 1 cup cooked diced shrimp)
When these ingredients are well mixed, hollow a center in the rice. Break:
  3 eggs
into the hollow and scramble until semi-cooked—then stir them into the rice mixture. Sprinkle with:
  1½ tablespoons soy sauce
  (¼ cup minced Chinese parsley leaves)
and serve with:
  Podded Peas, page 288

CHEESE RICE
6 to 7 Servings

This is a good dish to serve with a cold supper.

Boil, page 178:
 1 cup rice
When the water is nearly absorbed, add:
 ½ to ¾ cup or more grated cheese
 ¼ teaspoon paprika
  A few grains cayenne
Add:
 1 can condensed tomato or mushroom
  soup: 10½ oz.
Stir the rice over low heat until the cheese is melted.

SPANISH RICE
                                   3 to 4 Servings
Sauté until brown:
 3 slices minced bacon
Remove the bacon. Stir and cook in the drippings until brown:
 ½ cup rice
Add and cook until brown:
 ½ cup thinly sliced onions
Add the bacon and:
 1¼ cups canned tomatoes
 ½ teaspoon salt
 1 teaspoon paprika
 1 seeded and minced green pepper
 (1 clove garlic)
Steam the rice in a double boiler for about 1 hour. Stir it frequently. Add water or stock if the rice becomes too dry. It may be served with:
 Cheese Sauce, page 326

RICE LOAF OR CASSEROLE
I.   **5 Servings**
Boil, page 178:
 ⅔ cup rice
Line a buttered mold with it. Reserve ½ cup for the top. Preheat oven to 375°.
Cook:
 1 cup Cream Sauce II, page 322
Stir in and thicken over low heat:
 1 egg yolk
Add:
 1 cup diced canned salmon, cooked
  fish or meat
 ½ cup bread crumbs
 1 tablespoon chopped parsley
 1 tablespoon chopped onion
 ½ cup chopped celery
 1 teaspoon lemon juice or 1 teaspoon
  Worcestershire sauce
  Salt, paprika, nutmeg
Fill the mold and place the reserved rice over the top. Cover this with a piece of buttered paper. Set the mold in a pan of hot water and bake or steam it until it is set, for about 30 minutes. Invert the loaf onto a platter. Garnish it with:
 Sprigs of parsley
Serve it with:
 Tomato Sauce, page 333, or
 Mushroom Sauce, page 327, etc.

II.   **6 Servings**
Preheat oven to 400°.
The proportions of rice and fish in this dish may be varied. Use about ½ as much cream sauce as you do of the other main ingredients combined. Boil, page 178:

 ⅔ cup rice
There should be about 2 cups cooked rice.
Drain:
 1 cup tuna fish
Break the tuna into pieces with a fork.
Cook:
 2 cups Cream Sauce II, page 322
Add:
 ½ teaspoon salt—more if rice is
  unsalted
 ½ teaspoon paprika
  A few grains red pepper
Reduce the heat to low. Stir in until melted:
 2 cups grated cheese
Place in a baking dish alternate layers of rice, fish and sauce. Dot the top with:
 Au Gratin II, page 342
Bake the dish until the crumbs are brown. If preferred, bake the ingredients in a ring, invert and serve it with the center filled with Sautéed Mushrooms, page 281.

NUT LOAF
                                        4 Servings
Serve with broccoli or any green leafy vegetable.
Preheat oven to 375°.
Melt:
 3 tablespoons butter
Sauté in it until soft:
 1 minced onion
 1 seeded chopped green pepper
Add:
 1 cup cooked rice
 ⅓ cup bread crumbs
 1 cup chopped tomatoes
 1 cup chopped or ground walnut
  or other nut meats
 1 beaten egg
 2 tablespoons chopped parsley
 ¾ teaspoon salt
 ¼ teaspoon paprika
 (1 teaspoon grated lemon peel)
Place these ingredients in a greased baking dish. Bake them for about 30 minutes. Cover the top with:
 Mashed potatoes
Dot them generously with:
 Butter
Brown them under a broiler. Serve the loaf with:
 Tomato Sauce, page 333

RICE RING OR MOLD
A molded rice ring is a handsome way to enclose your main course. For color, include chopped parsley with the cooked rice, or try some of the following recipes.
I.   **6 Servings**
Preheat oven to 350°.
Boil, page 178:
 1 cup rice
Season it with:
 ½ teaspoon grated nutmeg
Place it in a well-greased 7-inch ring mold.
Melt and pour over it:
 ¼ cup butter
You may add:

(¾ cup blanched, coarsely chopped
  almonds)
Set the mold in a pan of hot water. Bake
the rice for about 20 minutes. Loosen the
edges, invert the contents of the mold onto
a platter.
Fill the center with:
    Creamed Chicken, page 235,
    Creamed Mushrooms, page 281, or
    a creamed or buttered vegetable

II. This works fine for any recipe not using
egg to bind it. Otherwise use I, above.
We have had success packing the hot
cooked rice firmly into a well-buttered
ring mold. Rest it 3 or 4 minutes and
then turn it out onto the serving platter
to be filled with the hot entrée.

CHEESE RICE RING
                                    3 Servings
Preheat oven to 350°.
Boil:
    ½ cup Rice, page 178
Add:
    1 beaten egg
    2 tablespoons olive oil or melted
      butter
    ¼ cup milk
    ⅓ cup grated cheese
    ¼ tablespoon grated onion
    1 teaspoon Worcestershire sauce
    ¼ teaspoon salt
    3 tablespoons chopped parsley
Grease a 7-inch ring mold. Fill it with the
rice mixture. Bake it, set in a pan of hot
water, for about 45 minutes.

MUSHROOM RICE RING
                                    6 Servings
No need to bake this mold.
Boil, page 178:
    1 cup rice
Grind, chop fine or ⅃ blend:
    ½ to 1 lb. mushrooms
Sauté them for 2 or 3 minutes in:
    2 tablespoons butter
Add:
    ¼ cup hot stock or water
Combine the mushrooms and rice. Add:
    (¾ cup blanched coarsely chopped
      almonds)
    Correct the seasoning
Press the rice firmly in a greased 7-inch
ring mold and let stand for 3 or 4 minutes.
Invert the rice onto a platter. Fill the
center with a buttered vegetable, creamed
fish, etc.

RICE AND HAM RING
                                    6 Servings
Preheat oven to 375°.
Combine:
    2 cups cooked rice
    1 cup diced cooked ham
Combine and beat:
    1 egg
    ⅔ cup condensed mushroom soup

    ½ cup milk
    ¼ teaspoon salt
    (½ teaspoon dried basil)
Grease a 9-inch ring mold. Place in it
layers of rice and ham. Pour the liquid
ingredients over them. Sprinkle the top
with:
    1 cup crushed potato chips or
      bread crumbs
Bake the ring in 1 inch of hot water, for
about ½ hour. Invert it onto a platter.
Fill the center with:
    A cooked vegetable, carrots and
    peas, snap beans, etc.

RICE AND ONION CASSEROLE
                                    3 to 4 Servings
Heat in a skillet:
    2 tablespoons butter
Sauté in it, until lightly browned:
    ½ cup uncooked rice
    ⅛ cup sliced fresh or canned
      mushrooms
Stir in:
    1 package dried onion soup
    1 cup water
Cover and cook over low heat, about 25
minutes, until the rice is tender.

RICE WITH SPINACH AND CHESTNUTS
                                    6 to 8 Servings
Preheat oven to 350°.
Combine:
    1 cup cooked rice
    1 cup cooked chopped spinach
    1 cup cooked chestnuts
    ½ to 1 cup grated cheese
Cover with:
    Au Gratin II, page 342
Bake about 35 minutes or until thoroughly
heated. Garnish with:
    Sprigs of water cress and ribbons
    of pimiento
before serving.

BACON AND RICE CUSTARD
                                    4 Servings
Preheat oven to 325°.
Cook until partly done:
    8 slices bacon
Use 4 muffin tins. Line each one with 2
slices of bacon. Fill them with the follow-
ing mixture. Combine:
    2 cups cooked rice
    1 beaten egg
    2 tablespoons cream
    1 tablespoon melted butter
    1 tablespoon grated onion
    1 tablespoon chopped parsley
    ⅛ teaspoon salt
    ⅛ teaspoon paprika
Bake the custard until firm, for about ½
hour. Serve with:
    Tomato or other sauce

BAKED PINEAPPLE RICE
                                    6 Servings
This good dish may be served with baked

ham or fried chicken or as a dessert with
cream.
Preheat oven to 350°.
Boil, page 178:
   1 cup rice
Drain, then cut into pieces:
   3½ cups cubed pineapple
Place in a buttered baking dish ⅓ the rice.
Cover with ½ the pineapple. Repeat the
layer of rice and pineapple. Place the
last ⅓ of the rice on top. Dot each layer
with:
   1½ tablespoons butter
   ¼ cup brown sugar
Use in all 5½ tablespoons butter and ¾
cup sugar. Pour over all:
   ¾ cup pineapple juice
Bake the rice, covered, for about 1 hour.

ROMBAUER RICE DISH
4 Servings

Freely varied each time it is made, but
in such demand that we shall try to write
a general rule for it.
Prepare:
   ½ cup Boiled Rice, page 178
Prepare:
   Veal stew: 1½ lbs. meat
Pare, slice and add for the last 20 minutes
of cooking:
   ½ parsnip
   2 carrots
   2 onions
   6 sliced ribs celery
   3 sprigs parsley
Drain the stew. To make the gravy, see
page 322. There should be about 3 cups
of stock. If there is not enough, add
chicken bouillon, a bouillon or vegetable
cube and water, rice water or sweet or
sour cream to make up the difference. If
there is not enough fat, add butter. The
better the gravy, the better the dish. Combine the rice, meat, vegetables and gravy
and reheat them. Garnish with:
   Parsley
You may add a dash of curry powder and
some herbs—thyme, basil, etc., page 530.
You may use leftover meat, gravy and vegetables. You may serve the stew in a baking
dish, au gratin or in individual bakers.
A de luxe dish is this recipe made with rice,
chicken, sauce—with cream and chicken
gravy—and blanched slivered almonds. An
everyday dish is this recipe made with
corned beef and some canned soup to
substitute for gravy.

VEGETABLE RICE OR JAMBALAYA
4 Servings

Ideal for a picnic supper.
Steam:
   ⅔ cup rice
Sauté lightly in butter:
   ¾ to 1 lb. mushrooms
Chop and add:
   2 medium-sized green peppers,
     seeds and membrane removed
   1 medium-sized onion

   1 stalk of celery
   2 canned pimientos
   1¼ cups cooked or canned tomatoes
Season these ingredients with:
   ¾ teaspoon salt
   A few grains cayenne
   ½ teaspoon paprika
Add:
   ¼ lb. melted butter
These proportions may be varied.
Preheat oven to 300°.
Combine the rice and other ingredients
Place in a greased baking dish. Bake
covered for about 1 hour. The sautéed
mushroom caps and the pimientos may be
used to garnish the top of the dish. They
are highly decorative with a bunch of
parsley in the center.

JAMBALAYA WITH MEAT OR FISH
6 to 8 Servings

Sauté lightly in a saucepan:
   2 slices diced bacon
Add and sauté until golden:
   ¼ cup chopped onion
Stir in:
   1 tablespoon flour
Add:
   1 cup tomato pulp
   ⅓ cup water
Bring these ingredients to the boiling point
Stir in:
   3 cups cooked rice
   2 cups coarsely diced cooked ham,
     chicken, sausage, tongue or shrimp,
     crab, etc., alone or in combination
Season these ingredients with:
   ¼ teaspoon thyme
   (Worcestershire sauce)
   Correct the seasoning
Stir over very low heat for about 10 minutes or heat over boiling water for about
½ hour. Serve sprinkled with:
   Chopped parsley

CHICKEN JAMBALAYA
4 to 6 Servings

Cut into pieces:
   A young chicken
Sauté for about 5 minutes in:
   ¼ cup cooking oil or butter
Remove meat from pan. Sauté in the
grease, also for about 3 minutes:
   ⅓ cup minced onion
   ½ cup skinned, seeded and chopped
     tomato
Stir in:
   1 diced green pepper, seeds and
     membrane removed
   ½ cup diced celery
   1 cup rice
When the rice is well coated with grease
stir in the sautéed chicken. Cover these
ingredients well with:
   Boiling water
Add:
   1 bay leaf
   ¼ teaspoon thyme
   ¼ cup chopped parsley

1 teaspoon salt
¼ teaspoon pepper
Simmer these ingredients until the chicken
is tender and the rice almost done. Add:
½ lb. finely diced cooked ham
Correct the seasoning
Dry out the jambalaya by placing it for
about 5 or 10 minutes in a 350° oven.

ITALIAN RICE OR RISOTTO
A LA MILANÈSE
8 to 10 Servings

This dish needs fairly constant watching
for about 20 minutes and ♦ must be served
at once to prevent gumminess. Melt in a
heavy pan:
¼ cup Clarified Butter, page 338
Sauté in it, until golden:
1 small minced onion
Add and stir well with a wooden spoon
until all the butter is absorbed:
2 cups rice
Have ready:
8 to 10 cups hot beef or chicken stock
After the rice is well coated with the fat,
add 1 cup of the stock. Continue to stir,
adding about ⅔ of the hot stock over a
10 minute period. Dissolve in a little of
the stock:
(A tiny pinch of saffron)
Or add:
(½ teaspoon fennel seed)
Continue to stir and add stock for about
to 8 minutes longer, by which time the
rice should have absorbed all of the
liquid. ♦ Do not let it dry out.
Correct the seasoning
Place the rice in a hot serving dish. Pour
over it and mix:
¼ cup melted butter
(Sautéed chicken livers and giblets)
Sprinkle over it:
1 cup grated Parmesan cheese

PAELLA
8 Servings

Preheat oven to 350°.
If you do not own a paellero, the vessel
which gives this dish its name, you will
need a generous lidded casserole in which
to cook and serve it.
Have ready:
2 cups cooked chicken, cut in about 1-
to 1½-inch pieces
4 cups hot chicken stock
Heat briefly in the casserole:
¼ cup olive oil
2 cloves garlic
Remove the garlic. Over moderate heat
add, stirring until lightly browned:
2 cups rice
Add the hot stock, in which has been dissolved a small quantity of:
Saffron—or up to 2 teaspoons if you
are Spanish
Add:
1 cup peas
2 sliced sweet red peppers
(6 artichoke hearts)

8 thin slices chorizo or hard
Spanish sausage
Correct the seasoning
Also put in the chicken, arranging it toward
the top of the mixture. Cover and bake
in a 350° oven for about 15 minutes. Add,
arranging them attractively on the top:
8 raw shrimp
16 well-scrubbed clams in their shells
Cover and steam about 10 minutes longer.
Serve at once.

PILAF
4 Servings

A rice dish combined with shrimp or chick-
en livers, etc. It has many variations.
Boil, page 178:
⅔ cup long grained rice
Sauté until golden:
3 tablespoons chopped onion
in:
1 to 2 tablespoons butter
Add to the rice. Simmer until thick:
2½ cups tomatoes
½ bay leaf
3 ribs of celery with leaves
⅓ teaspoon salt
¼ teaspoon paprika
½ teaspoon brown sugar
Strain these ingredients.
Add:
1 cup cooked shrimp, lobster meat,
crab meat or sautéed or boiled
chicken livers
Combine these ingredients with the rice.
Correct the seasoning
Place the rice in a greased baking dish.
Sprinkle with:
¼ cup grated cheese and bread crumbs
Run under a heated broiler to brown.

FRUIT, NUT AND RICE CASSEROLE
10 Servings

Cover with water and soak for ½ hour:
2 cups dried apricots
1 cup white raisins
Boil, page 178:
2 cups rice
Preheat oven to 375°.
In a skillet, melt:
½ cup butter
Sauté:
1 cup minced onion
½ cup chopped green pepper
(½ teaspoon curry powder)
Add:
(1 cup toasted almonds)
and the drained, chopped apricots and raisins and the cooked rice.
Correct the seasoning
and put into a greased baking dish to bake
for about 30 minutes.

RICE TABLE OR RIJSTTAFEL
8 Servings

As this Javanese dish is very filling, it is
ideal for suppers. Serve it with ice cold
beer, followed by salad. It may be made

as elaborate or as simple as you wish. If
you object to coconut or if you do not like
the flavor of curry, do not discard this dish.
Instead, carry out the idea of the rijsttafel
by substituting creamed chicken, ragoût
fin or a lamb curry you do like, followed
by vegetable and condiments served in
some attractive way.

Grate:

    **A fresh coconut or use about 2 cups
    canned coconut**

Heat but do not scald:

    4 cups milk or coconut milk

Add the coconut. Permit these ingredients
to stand for 2 hours in a cool place. Melt:

    1 tablespoon butter

Sauté in it, until light brown:

    ½ cup finely chopped onion

Add:

    Chopped gingerroot, a 2-inch length
    1 chopped clove garlic
    1½ tablespoons curry powder

Strain and add the coconut. Add to the
cooled, strained milk:

    1 cup milk or Chicken Stock, page 490

Mix with 3 tablespoons of the above liquid:

    1 tablespoon flour
    1 tablespoon cornstarch

Heat the remaining liquid and stir the starch
paste into it. Cook and stir the sauce until
it is hot and thickened.

    Correct the seasoning

Place ½ of the sauce in the top of a double
boiler. Add the coconut mixture and:

    3 cups cooked diced chicken, shrimp,
    fish, veal, sweetbreads, mushrooms,
    etc., either alone or in combination

Heat rest of sauce in another double boiler.
Have ready:

    2 cups steamed rice, page 178

Have it rather dry and flaky.
The ceremony of serving this dish is part
of its charm. In Java one refers to it by
the separate dishes, as a "One boy curry"
or a "Twenty-two boy curry," each boy
representing one dish. Pass the rice first.
Spread it generously over your plate, forming a base or "table." Pass the food in the
sauce next. Follow this with:

    Onion Rings
    Sieved hard-cooked eggs
    Grated peanuts or toasted almonds
    Grated coconut, if there is none
    in the sauce
    Relish
    Chutney, raisins, preserved ginger
    or kumquats
    Halved fried bananas
    Mixed pickles

Now pass the extra heated sauce.

To simplify matters, the last 4 or 5 dishes
may be served from one large condiment
dish. Servings from these various dishes
are placed upon the rice table. Cut through
the layers and proceed to feast.

"LONG RICE" OR HARUSAME

This is not a rice at all, but an orienta
pasta made of soy bean powder. It is bes
described, we feel, as threadlike cellophane
noodles, but we infinitely prefer its native
name of "Spring Rain."

To prepare, pour:

    Boiling water

over:

    Harusame

Let stand 15 minutes or until it is limp
Cut into desired lengths. Add as a garnish
for soup, meat or vegetables. It shoul
then ◆ simmer during the last 15 minute
of the cooking of these foods.

ABOUT SPAGHETTI, MACARONI
AND NOODLES

So popular are these hearty fillers that there
are over 500 kinds and shapes to choose
from. Do we ever graduate from loving the
alphabets or sea shells and those large maca-
ronis that can be stuffed? When freshly
cooked and tossed in or served with a meat
fish or cheese sauce, pastas need only a salad
to make a nutritious, inexpensive and quic
meal.

◆ If pastas must be cooked in advance
moisten them with butter, milk, bouillon, to
mato juice or a sauce to keep them from
drying out. Rarely are any of the past
types—except Noodles, page 172—made i
the home. This is partly because they re
quire unavailable hard-wheat flours.

◆ Always use a pot large enough to hol
without boiling over, water 3 times the vo
ume of the pasta to be cooked. For ½ lb
pasta, use not less than 2 qts. water, sea
soned with 2 teaspoons salt. Bring water t
a ◆ rolling boil. You may put ◆ a tablespoo
of fat in the water to help keep the past
from clumping. It is said this will also dete
the water from boiling over, but our exper
ence does not validate this theory. Watc
the pot to keep the boil active during th
cooking period. The pasta should b
◆ added to the water so gradually that th
brisk boiling is not disturbed. To cook lon
macaroni or spaghetti, hold it as shown an
as it softens, push it farther into the boilin
water.

♦ Do not overcook. Italians usually prefer pasta "al dente," a state in which it still offers some resistance to the teeth. If pastas are freshly made, like homemade noodles, they may require as little as 5 minutes' cooking. If they have been on a shelf a long time, 8 to 10 minutes is long enough for thin types. If thick, they may need all of 15 minutes. Try pastas "al burro," simply tossed in butter with a freshly grated Parmesan cheese topping.

BOILED SPAGHETTI
4 Cups

About 2 cups or ½ lb. uncooked spaghetti yields 4 cups cooked.
In a large pan, have boiling:
      2 quarts water
seasoned with:
      2 teaspoons salt
Slowly add, so as not to disturb boiling:
      ½ lb. or about 2 cups spaghetti
Cook until tender—about 10 minutes more or less—to your own taste satisfaction.
Drain it. Keep it hot. Heat a salad or large bowl. Rub it with a cut:
      Clove of garlic
Place in it:
      ¼ teaspoon salt
      ¼ teaspoon paprika
      ¼ cup hot oil or melted butter
      1 cup grated cheese
Toss the spaghetti in the above dressing like a salad and serve at once.

BAKED SPAGHETTI
Preheat oven to 375°.
Prepare:
      Boiled Spaghetti, above
Alternate in a greased baking dish layers of spaghetti and:
      1 cup grated cheese
Pour over all:
      Tomato Sauce, page 333
Dot with:
      Butter
and bake about 15 minutes.

ITALIAN SPAGHETTI WITH SAUCE
About 6 Servings

In Italy spaghetti is served in one dish, the sauce in another and grated cheese in a third. The sauce may be poured over the spaghetti, which is tossed until the two are well blended. Prepare:
      A Pasta Sauce, page 335
Cook:
      1 lb. unbroken spaghetti
When well drained, pour over it:
      ¼ cup melted butter
Put the spaghetti in a bowl. Pour the sauce over it and toss until well coated.

SPAGHETTI WITH EGG AND CHEESE
4 to 6 Servings

Not the usual cheese sauce, but an Italian version.

Cook in boiling salted water for 8 to 10 minutes:
      1 lb. spaghetti
In the meantime, cook in a small skillet:
      2 tablespoons olive oil
      6 slices finely cut bacon
until the bacon is crisp. Add:
      ⅓ cup dry white wine
and reduce until the wine has evaporated.
Beat together:
      3 eggs
      ⅔ cup mixed Parmesan and Romano
            grated cheese
Drain the spaghetti and return it to the hot saucepan. Add the egg and cheese mixture and the hot bacon fat and bits, stirring it in quickly. The heat of the spaghetti will cook the egg mixture.
      Correct the seasoning
Serve immediately.

QUICK SPAGHETTI WITH TUNA FISH, SALMON OR BEEF
4 Servings

Drain and reserve the oil from:
      1 can tuna fish or salmon
Sauté in the oil:
      ⅛ cup chopped onion
Or use the onion and:
      ½ lb. ground beef
Sauté in:
      ¼ cup drippings
Add to the onion the contents of:
      1 can condensed tomato soup: 10½ oz.
      2½ cups canned spaghetti
Fold in the flaked fish. Season with:
      ½ teaspoon sugar
      A few grains cayenne
      Salt and paprika
Cook it until it is thoroughly heated. You may rub a bowl with:
      (A cut clove garlic)
Add the spaghetti. Garnish it with:
      2 tablespoons chopped parsley
This dish may be served in an ovenproof baking dish, au gratin. Use a hot oven—400°—or a broiler to melt the cheese.

QUICK SPAGHETTI MEAT PIE
4 Servings

Preheat oven to 375°.
Sauté lightly:
      2 cups cooked cubed meat
      2 teaspoons grated onion
in:
      2 tablespoons butter
Add:
      ¼ cup cream
Season it with:
      Salt and pepper
      (½ teaspoon basil)
Place in a greased dish the contents of:
      1 can spaghetti: 24 oz.
Make a depression in the center. Place the meat in it. Sprinkle the top with:
      Au Gratin II, page 342
Bake for about 25 minutes.

QUICK SPAGHETTI WITH SOUP AND BACON

4 Servings

Preheat oven to 375°.
Sauté until nearly crisp:
> 8 slices bacon or 1 cup chopped tongue, ham or potted meat

Cut them into large pieces. Combine the contents of:
> 1 can condensed mock turtle or pepper pot soup: 10½ oz.
> 2½ cups canned spaghetti

If preferred, cook and substitute 1¼ cups spaghetti or use 2½ cups cooked spaghetti. Add:
> ¼ cup hot water

Place alternate layers of this mixture and the bacon in a greased ovenproof dish. Cover the top with:
> Buttered crumbs

Bake the dish for about 20 minutes, until it is thoroughly heated. If you wish, omit the soup and season the spaghetti with:
> 1 teaspoon prepared mustard
> 1 teaspoon grated onion

CHICKEN OR TURKEY TETRAZZINI

8 to 10 Servings

A fan writes that she prefers using ¼ lb. macaroni and 1 lb. mushrooms. A bit more extravagant but very good.
Cut the meat from the bones of:
> A boiled chicken

There should be 2 to 3 cups of shredded meat. Cook:
> ½ lb. macaroni or spaghetti

Add to this:
> ½ to ¾ lb. Sautéed Mushrooms, page 281
> (½ cup blanched, slivered almonds)

Make a sauce of:
> 3 tablespoons butter or chicken fat
> 2 tablespoons flour
> 2 cups chicken broth
> Seasoning

Remove from heat. Stir in:
> 1 cup heated whipping cream
> 3 tablespoons dry white wine

Preheat oven to 375°.
Add ½ the sauce to the chicken and ½ to the macaroni and mushrooms. Place the macaroni in a greased baking dish. Make a hole in the center. Place the chicken in it. Sprinkle the top with:
> Grated Parmesan cheese

Bake the dish until it is lightly browned.

SEAFOOD TETRAZZINI

8 Servings

Preheat broiler.
Boil:
> ½ lb. spaghetti

Sauté until golden:
> 6 tablespoons chopped onion

in:
> 2 tablespoons olive oil

Add:
> 2 cans cream of mushroom soup: 10½ oz.

> 1⅓ cups water
> ¼ cup grated Romano cheese

Stir in and heat thoroughly:
> 2 cups flaked, drained tuna, shrimp, or clams, etc.
> ⅔ cup sliced pitted ripe olives

Add:
> 2 tablespoons chopped parsley
> 2 teaspoons lemon juice
> ⅛ teaspoon dried thyme and marjoram

In a buttered casserole, mix the sauces and the drained spaghetti. Top with:
> ¼ cup grated Romano cheese

Heat under the broiler until golden brown.

BOILED MACARONI WITH CHEESE

6 Servings

In a large pan have boiling:
> 2 quarts water

seasoned with:
> 2 teaspoons salt

Slowly add so as not to disturb boiling:
> ½ lb. or about 2 cups macaroni

Cook until tender, about 10 to 12 minutes. Drain. Return to the saucepan. Stir and reheat over slow heat with:
> ½ cup cream or rich milk

Place it in a dish and sprinkle it with:
> ½ cup or more grated cheese

Serve it with any of the Pasta Sauces on page 335, or with the Tomato Sauces on page 333.

BAKED MACARONI

I.   **4 Servings**

Preheat oven to 350°.
Cook:
> 4 oz. macaroni: 1 cup

Drain it. Place layers of macaroni in a buttered baking dish. Sprinkle the layers with:
> 1 cup grated cheese

Beat until blended:
> 1 or 2 eggs
> ⅔ cup milk
> ¼ teaspoon salt
> ⅛ teaspoon paprika
> A few grains cayenne

Pour this mixture over the macaroni. Sprinkle the top with:
> Au Gratin III, page 342

Bake the macaroni about 40 to 50 minutes.

II. Alternate layers of:
> Macaroni, as in I, above

and:
> ¼ lb. sliced dried beef

III. Follow the above recipe. Substitute for the milk:
> ½ cup tomato juice
> ¼ cup cream

Add:
> ½ teaspoon sugar
> (1 tablespoon chopped parsley or 1 teaspoon dried basil or thyme)

IV. One cup well-seasoned Cream Sauce, page 322, may be substituted for the egg and milk mixture. Bake at 400° about 30 minutes.

MACARONI BAKED WITH SOUR CREAM

4 Servings

Preheat oven to 400°.
Cook:
      1½ cups macaroni
Drain it well. Toss it in:
      3 tablespoons melted butter
Place it in a greased oven-proof dish. Make a hollow in the center into which pour:
      1 cup cultured sour cream
You may sprinkle this with:
      ½ cup grated cheese
Bake the macaroni until the top is brown.

MACARONI LOAF

5 Servings

Preheat oven to 350°.
This delectable dish is very attractive in appearance. It makes a fine ring dish.
Boil:
      5 cups water
      1½ teaspoons salt
Add:
      ¾ cup macaroni or spaghetti
Boil for about 10 minutes. Drain in a colander. Place in a bowl. Scald:
      ½ cup milk or cream
Beat into it:
      2 or 3 eggs
Melt and add:
      3 tablespoons butter
Pour this over the macaroni. Add:
      ½ cup soft bread crumbs, without crusts
      ½ cup grated cheese
      1½ sliced pimientos
      ¼ cup chopped green peppers or 2 tablespoons chopped parsley
      1 tablespoon grated onion
      ¼ teaspoon salt
      ⅛ teaspoon paprika
      A few grains cayenne
Place these ingredients in a buttered baking dish. Bake them for about 1 hour. Serve with:
      Mushroom Sauce, page 327, or
      Quick Tomato Sauce, page 334
It makes a somewhat lighter dish if you add only the egg yolks to the scalded milk. The whites, beaten until stiff, are then folded into the other ingredients at the last moment.

MACARONI WITH TOMATOES, LIVERS, MUSHROOMS AND CHEESE

About 2 Quarts

Preheat oven to 400°.
Cook, page 178:
      ½ lb. macaroni
Drain. Place in a deep casserole. Sauté:
      ½ lb. Mushrooms, page 281
Sauté or boil until tender:
      ½ cup chicken livers or calf liver

Chop the mushrooms and the liver. Simmer until fairly thick:
      4 cups canned tomatoes
Strain them. Season with:
      ¾ tablespoon salt
      1 teaspoon brown sugar
      A few grains cayenne
      (1 teaspoon dried basil)
Sauté:
      1 minced onion
      (½ minced clove garlic)
in:
      2 tablespoons butter
Combine these with the other ingredients and pour them over the macaroni. Mix them well with 2 forks. Sprinkle the top with:
      Grated cheese
Bake the macaroni until the cheese is golden.

MACARONI WITH SHELLFISH

4 Servings

Preheat oven to 350°.
Cook, page 178:
      1½ cups macaroni
Drain it. Sauté:
      1 tablespoon minced onion
in:
      3 tablespoons butter
Stir in until blended:
      1½ tablespoons flour
Stir in until smooth:
      1½ cups milk
      ¾ cup grated cheese
      1 teaspoon Worcestershire sauce
      ½ teaspoon lemon juice
      1 teaspoon salt
      ¼ teaspoon paprika
      A few grains cayenne
Have ready:
      1½ to 2 cups cleaned shrimp, oysters or clams, etc.
Place layers of macaroni and fish in a baking dish. Pour the sauce over them. Cover the top with:
      Au Gratin III, page 342
Bake the dish for about 45 minutes.

MOSTACCIOLI

5 Servings

Melt:
      1 tablespoon butter
Stir and brown in it:
      ¾ to 1 lb. ground round steak
      1 large chopped onion
      1 clove garlic cut into halves
Cover these ingredients with boiling water.
Add:
      ¾ teaspoon salt
      ⅛ teaspoon pepper
Simmer covered until almost dry. Fish out the garlic. Add:
      2 cups canned tomatoes
Continue to simmer, stirring frequently. Cook until the sauce is thick, from 1 to 1½ hours. Add mushrooms when the sauce is partly done. Wash well in warm water, then drain:

¼ lb. dried reconstituted mushrooms,
    page 541
When the sauce is almost done add:
    ¼ cup olive oil
Cook until tender, page 184:
    ½ lb. mostaccioli: about 2 cups
Serve the mostaccioli on a hot platter.
First a layer of the pasta, then a layer of
sauce, then a layer of the pasta and again
a layer of sauce. Sprinkle each meat sauce
layer generously with:
        Grated Parmesan cheese
        Freshly grated black pepper

BOILED NOODLES

                                            5 Servings
Drop:
        2 cups Noodles, page 172
into:
    3 quarts boiling, salted water—
        ½ teaspoon salt to the quart—or
        chicken stock, consommé, etc.
Boil for about 8 to 10 minutes, depending
on size and your taste preference. Drain in
a colander and immediately put back in
cooking pot, set over very low heat and
moisten them generously with:
        Melted butter or cream
        (Chicken Stock, page 490)
Serve with:
        Au Gratin II, or III, page 342
Additions may be:
        Chopped hard-cooked eggs
        Chopped chives
        2 tablespoons poppy seeds
    (¾ cup cultured sour cream)
or:
        ½ cup blanched chopped almonds
sautéed in:
        1 tablespoon butter
Boiled noodles may be arranged in a ring
on a platter and the center filled with a
creamed meat, vegetable or a hash.

BUTTERED NOODLES OR
FETTUCCINI AL BURRO

                                        4 to 6 Servings
Alfredo II came to Cincinnati to demonstrate the making of those noodles which
brought both him and his father fame. He
carried along from Italy the hard special
flour needed for the dough and the hard
Parmesan cheese and sweet butter for the
tossing. Yet when the noodles were presented, he wished he had brought with him
the Roman water in which to cook them.
Cook:
        2 cups noodles
In:
        3 quarts boiling salted water
for 6 to 8 minutes or until "al dente".
Drain. Put on a hot platter:
        ½ cup butter
Cover with drained noodles. Toss until the
noodles are coated with the butter. Have
ready:
        ¾ cup grated Parmesan cheese
to pass at table.

FRIED NOODLES
To be served in the place of a starchy
vegetable or as a garnish on vegetables or
other dishes, notably Chinese mixtures.
Boil in water for about 5 minutes:
        Thin noodles
Place them in a colander and rinse them
with cold water to rid of surface starch
Drain, separate and dry well.
Preheat deep fryer to 390°.
Fry them, a small amount at a time, until
they are a delicate brown. Drain them on
absorbent paper. Sprinkle them lightly
with:
        Salt
Keep them hot or reheat in a 400° oven.

NOODLE BASKETS
Preheat deep fryer to 390°.
For these you need a tea strainer about
3 inches in diameter and a second strainer
about ⅜ inch smaller that fits into it but
leaves space for the swelling of the noodles
Prepare:
        Noodle Dough, page 172
Before the dough is dry fold it over and cut
it into ¼ inch strips. Dip the strainers in
hot fat to keep the noodles from sticking
Line the larger strainer with 2 layers of
noodles, giving them a crisscross effect
Snip off the ragged edges. Place the
smaller strainer over the noodle basket
Fry the noodle basket in deep fat, page
124, until lightly browned. Remove it
carefully from the strainers and fry the
next one. You may fill the fried basket
at once with creamed food, etc., or you
may cool them and reheat them later by
dipping them briefly in hot fat without the
strainers.
Drain them on absorbent paper.

BAKED NOODLE RING

                                            4 Servings
Preheat oven to 350°.
I. Cook:
        1½ cups Noodles, page 172
Drain them. Beat:
        2 egg yolks
        ½ cup milk
        ¾ tablespoon melted butter
        ¼ teaspoon salt
        ⅛ teaspoon paprika
        (½ cup grated cheese)
        (⅛ teaspoon nutmeg)
Combine this mixture with the noodles
Beat until stiff but not dry:
        2 egg whites
Fold them lightly into the noodles. Butter
a 7-inch ring mold or individual ring molds
Fill them with the noodle mixture and bake
them set in a pan of hot water in the oven
until done, about 45 minutes for a large
mold or 30 minutes for the small ones
Invert the contents of the molds on hot
plates and fill the centers with:

Creamed spinach, peas, mushrooms, hash, stewed tomatoes, Chicken à la King, etc.

II. Made with cheese this is our favorite. Follow the above recipe. Use in all:
　¾ cup milk
Add to the noodle mixture before folding in the egg whites:
　1½ teaspoons Worcestershire sauce
　½ tablespoon catsup
　¾ cup grated cheese
Also good made with:
　Cottage cheese

NOODLE RING WITH WHIPPED CREAM

10 Servings

Preheat oven to 350°.
Use a 9-inch ring. For 5 servings take half the recipe and use a 7-inch ring. Cook:
　2 cups fine Noodles, page 188
Drain. Beat and pour over the noodles:
　4 egg yolks
　¼ teaspoon paprika
　½ cup melted butter
Whip until stiff:
　4 egg whites
　¼ teaspoon salt
Beat until stiff:
　1 cup whipping cream or use 1 cup cultured sour cream
Fold the egg whites and the cream lightly into the noodle mixture. Fill a well-greased ring. Place it in a pan of hot water. Bake it until firm, for about 1 hour or more. Invert the ring and fill it with:
　Green peas or creamed food, sweetbreads, fish, etc.

NOODLES, STEWED PRUNES AND CROUTONS

This is a traditional Good Friday dish in a number of European countries. It is a reminder of how good simple food may be in a tempting combination. Prepare:
　Boiled Noodles, page 188
　Dried Prunes, page 120
　Croutons, page 342
Serve the noodles hot with the croutons poured over them. Serve the prunes from a separate bowl.

HAM NOODLES

8 Servings

Preheat oven to 350°.
This recipe is capable of a wide interpretation and its proportions may be varied. Cook:
　1½ cups Noodles, page 188
Grease a baking dish. Place in it layers of noodles sprinkled with:
　¾ cup cooked diced or ground ham
　(½ cup grated cheese)
　(½ cup shredded green pepper and celery)
Combine:
　1½ cups milk
　1 or 2 eggs
　¼ teaspoon paprika
　¼ to ½ teaspoon salt—omit if the ham is very salty
Pour this over the noodles. The top may be covered with:
　Bread or cracker crumbs
Bake the dish for about 45 minutes.

LEFTOVER NOODLE DISH

Follow the previous recipe. Substitute for the ham:
　Diced cooked roast, chicken, crab, shrimp, chipped beef, mushrooms and other vegetables
Part gravy may be substituted for milk or you may like to try a ham and chicken combination in a Cream Sauce, page 322.

NOODLE RAREBIT

Prepare:
　Cheese Rarebit I, page 242
When blended and hot stir in:
　1 to 2 cups diced ham or smoked tongue
　8 oz. cooked noodles

ROMANIAN NOODLE AND PORK CASSEROLE

8 Servings

Preheat oven to 350°.
Cook until slightly underdone:
　1 lb. fine noodles
Combine:
　1 lb. ground cooked pork
　1 slice bread which has been soaked in milk and wrung out
　1 minced leek
　½ to 1 teaspoon fennel seeds
　¼ cup chopped parsley
　1 teaspoon salt
　½ teaspoon pepper
In a shallow large baking pan, arrange alternate layers of noodles and pork mixture, ending with noodles. Beat together:
　4 eggs
　⅔ cup cream
　¼ cup grated cheese
Pour this mixture over the noodles and dot with:
　¼ cup butter
Bake for about 45 minutes.

QUANTITY NOODLE AND CHEESE LOAF

18 Servings

Preheat oven to 325°.
Cook:
　5 cups Noodles, page 188
and drain them. Have ready:
　1 lb. grated sharp cheese
　1½ cups dry bread crumbs
Mix together half the cheese and one cup of the crumbs with:
　¼ cup melted butter

Mix the rest of the crumbs and the cheese and the noodles with:

> 7 beaten eggs
> 1¾ cups milk
> 3 tablespoons grated onion
> ⅓ cup chopped pimiento
> ⅓ cup chopped green peppers, seeds and membranes removed
> 1 teaspoon salt
> ½ teaspoon white pepper
> (1 cup finely chopped celery)
> (½ cup sliced stuffed olives)

Divide the mixture in two parts and place in two 9 x 9 inch baking pans. Cover with the cheese, butter and crumb mixture. Bake for about 25 minutes or until the custard sets and the top is golden brown.
To test the custard for doneness, see page 684.
Serve with:

> Mushroom Sauce, page 327
> Tomato Sauce, page 333
> Creole Sauce, page 333

TUNA, NOODLE AND MUSHROOM SOUP CASSEROLE

                                          4 Large Servings

Preheat oven to 450°.
An excellent emergency dish. Cook until tender:

> 2 cups Noodles, page 188

Drain them in a colander. Drain:

> 1 cup canned tuna fish

Separate it with a fork into large flakes. Do not mince it. Grease an ovenproof dish. Arrange a layer of noodles, then sprinkle it with fish and so on. Have noodles on top.
Pour over this mixture:

> 1 can condensed mushroom soup:
>   10½ oz.

Season the soup with:

> Worcestershire sauce, curry powder, dry sherry, etc.

Cover the top with:

> Buttered cornflakes or cracker crumbs

Bake the dish until the top is brown.

LASAGNE

                                          16 Servings

The sauce may be made the day before.
Combine in a large saucepan:

> 2 cans Italian-style peeled tomatoes: No. 2½
> 4 cans tomato sauce: 8 oz. each
> 2 teaspoons salt
> 3 teaspoons dried orégano
> (2 teaspoons onion salt)

Start simmering these ingredients uncovered. Sauté until golden:

> 2 cups minced onions
> 2 minced cloves garlic

in:

> ⅓ cup olive oil

Add:

> 2 lbs. ground chuck roast or round

> 2 teaspoons salt

and cook until meat loses its red color. Add to the tomato sauce above. Simmer about 2½ hours longer. Prepare:

> ¾ lb. lasagne noodles

according to package directions—usually in generous quantities of water—and cook for about 25 minutes. Add to the water:

> 2 tablespoons cooking or olive oil

Stir occasionally. Drain and separate noodles.
Preheat oven to 350°.
Now let's build the lasagne! Put into the bottoms of two 13 x 9 x 2½-inch baking dishes a thin layer of sauce, then a crisscross layer of the lasagne noodles and a layer of cheese.
In all, use:

> ¾ lb. Ricotta cheese
> ⅓ lb. thinly sliced or crumbled Mozzarella cheese
> ½ lb. grated Parmesan cheese

Repeat twice with sauce, noodles and cheese. The final cheese layer is covered once more with sauce and a dusting of Parmesan.
Bake for about 40 minutes. Remove and let stand for 10 minutes. The lasagne can then be cut for serving.

CANNELONI OR MANICOTTI

                         Ten 4 x 6 Inch Rolled Square

Wrapped around fillings and served with a sauce, the charm of these "channels" or "little muffs" lies in the freshness of the dough; although the wrappings may be made in advance and held between wax papers in the refrigerator for several hours.
Have ready a filling made by mixing together until well blended:

> 1 cup grated Parmesan cheese
> ½ cup Mozzarella cheese
> 1¾ cups Ricotta cheese
> ⅛ teaspoon nutmeg
> 1 beaten egg
> ¼ cup Béchamel Sauce, page 322, or Cream Sauce IV, page 322

You may use instead of the above filling a good chicken or sausage farce, page 458.

> Correct the seasoning

Make a well and mix as described, page 594:

> 2 cups flour
> ¾ teaspoon salt
> 2 eggs
> 2 to 4 tablespoons water

Knead for about 10 minutes or until the dough is smooth. Rest the dough ♦ covered under a cloth about 10 minutes. Divide the dough in half and roll each part paper thin. Cut into 4 x 6 inch squares. Have ready in a large pan:

> 8 quarts boiling water

Cook 5 squares at a time by dropping them into the boiling water ♦ reducing the heat at once and simmering about 5 minutes. Remove with a skimmer, and when drained

place between moist towels until all the
dough is cooked and ready to fill.
Preheat oven to 400°.
Divide the filling into 10 oval parts. Place
on the center of the squares, fold over
the two edges and put seam-side down in
a greased ovenproof dish, or in individual
bakers allowing 2 per person.
Cover generously with:
    A tomato sauce or butter and a
    sprinkling of fresh basil
Bake about 10 minutes.
Serve with:
    Grated Parmesan cheese

RAVIOLI
If you are fond of this Italian savory pastry
buy a mold for mass-producing it.
Prepare:
    Noodle Dough II, page 172
Cover it with a cloth and permit it to stand
for 10 minutes. Roll the dough until it is
very thin. Cut it into 2 sheets. On one
sheet put a teaspoon of one of the ravioli
fillings, in little mounds 2 inches apart.
Cover them with the second sheet which
may be brushed lightly with water. Press
the top sheet gently around the ravioli
mounds. Press the edges. Cut the dough
into squares with a mound in each center.
Use a pie jagger. Dry the ravioli for about
2 hours. Drop them into boiling, salted
water or into chicken broth. Simmer them
for about 10 minutes. Remove them from
the liquid with a skimmer onto a hot platter. Sprinkle them with:
    Grated Parmesan cheese
Serve with:
    A tomato sauce, page 333

RAVIOLI FILLING
This is usually a spinach and meat mixture
very finely chopped or put through a purée
strainer. Grated cheese and light seasoning
may be added. Sometimes the filling is
thickened slightly with bread crumbs or
egg. There can be much leeway in the
composition of the filling and you may
use any combination of meat and vegetables you like. For other fillings, see
Farces, page 458.

I.
Combine:
    ¼ cup cooked puréed spinach
    ¼ cup chopped cooked meat
    1 egg
    2 tablespoons toasted bread crumbs
    2 tablespoons grated cheese
        Stock, cream or gravy to form a
        stiff paste
    ½ teaspoon dried basil
    (½ clove minced garlic)

II.
Combine:
    ½ cup cooked drained spinach

    ½ cup cooked minced chicken
    2 tablespoons grated cheese
        Salt and pepper
    ½ teaspoon dried basil or ⅛ teaspoon
        nutmeg
    (½ clove minced garlic)

DUMPLINGS
                                4 Servings
♦ Please read About Dumplings, page 170,
where you will find other recipes suitable
for use with meats.
Measure, then sift 3 times:
    1 cup cake flour
    2 teaspoons double-acting baking
        powder
    ½ teaspoon salt
Break into a measuring cup:
    1 egg
Add until the cup is half full:
    Milk
Beat well and stir the liquid slowly into the
sifted ingredients. Add more milk if necessary but keep the batter as stiff as possible.
Add:
    (¼ cup finely chopped parsley or
    1 tablespoon fresh chopped herbs) or
    (½ teaspoon grated onion and 3
        tablespoons minced green peppers)
Thicken:
    2 or 3 cups stock
with:
    Flour—allow 1½ tablespoons flour
        to 1 cup stock
Heat the stock in a 9-inch saucepan. To
drop dumpling batter from a spoon easily,
dip the spoon in water first. Then dip the
spoon in the batter, fill it and drop the
batter into the stock. Continue doing this
until the dumplings are barely touching.
Then cover them and simmer for 5 minutes,
turn them, cook them 5 minutes longer.
They should be served at once.
If using a ❂ pressure cooker, drop the
batter from a spoon into at least 3 cups
hot stock or water. Adjust cover, steam
over low heat, vent open, for 5 minutes.

CHEESE DUMPLINGS
To the above recipe for:
    Dumplings
Add:
    2 tablespoons grated cheese
Cook the dumplings in:
    Tomato juice

QUICK CHEESE DUMPLINGS
                        Ten 2-Inch Dumplings
Have ready:
    ⅔ cup grated cheese
Add 2 tablespoons of this cheese to:
    2 cups commercial biscuit mix
and prepare the recipe on the label. Pat
out the dough to a ⅛ inch thickness and
cut into 3 inch rounds. Place in the center
of each round a tablespoon of the cheese.
Wet the edges of the rounds with cold
water. Gather them up to form a ball.

Pinch them well. Have ready in a lidded pot:

6 to 8 cups boiling water

Drop the dumplings in, cover at once and ♦ reduce heat. ♦ Simmer covered about 15 minutes. Meanwhile heat:

Quick Tomato Sauce, page 334

Drain the dumplings and serve at once on hot plates covered with the sauce and:

Finely chopped parsley

CORN MEAL DUMPLINGS

Cooking in the United States is on the up and coming side but it seemed to us that a peak was reached in a small Kentucky town where we were served chicken with dumplings. The latter were like thistledown. "Oh yes!" said the hotel proprietress wearily when we exclaimed over them. "They are always like that when our cook is drunk."

Far be it from us to limit your sources of inspiration, but we are convinced that the following recipe will give you superlative dumplings without dissipation.

Have simmering:

5 or 6 cups corned beef stock,
  consommé or any clear soup or stock

Sift:

1 cup corn meal
¼ cup all-purpose flour
1 teaspoon any baking powder.
½ teaspoon salt

Beat:

2 eggs
½ cup milk

Combine the egg mixture and the dry ingredients. Stir in:

1 tablespoon melted butter

Drop the batter from a spoon into the hot stock. Cover the pan closely. Simmer the dumplings for about 15 minutes. Remove them at once from the liquor.

FARINA DUMPLINGS COCKAIGNE

6 Servings

Please read About Dumplings, page 170. Prepare:

Farina Balls Cockaigne, page 171

These remain after many tests the queen of dumplings. Though usually served in soup they may be simmered in stock or boiling water, then served with meat gravy. They may be drained, placed in a greased baking dish and covered with a cup of cream sauce, to which you may add onion juice and parsley, or chopped chives. Sprinkle the top with ¼ cup grated Parmesan cheese, dot it with butter and bake the dish in an oven for about 15 minutes.

SPATZEN, SPAETZLE OR GERMAN EGG DUMPLINGS

4 Servings

Spatzen are good at any time but they are particularly good served with roast veal. Beat:

2 eggs

Combine them with:

1½ cups flour
½ cup water
½ teaspoon salt
¼ teaspoon any baking powder
  (A small grating of nutmeg)

Beat these ingredients well. Drop small bits of the batter from a spoon into simmering salted water or stock, or put the batter through a colander, or a sliding cutter as shown below or use a pastry bag as shown on page 178. Spatzen should be very light and delicate. Try out a sample and if it is too heavy, add water to the batter. Simmer them until they are done. Drain them, place them in a dish and cover them with:

Croutons, or ¼ cup bread crumbs
  sautéed in ½ cup butter

Spatzen may be cooked and served in soup. Pie Dough, page 588, cut into strips or shapes, simmered in stock, is frequently substituted for a dumpling mixture. Remember the good Vegetable Noodles on page 172.

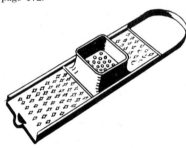

POTATO DUMPLINGS OR KARTOFFELKLOESSE

These are light and tender, especially good with beef à la mode or other roast gravy. It is traditional to serve them with Sauerbraten.

Boil uncovered in their jackets until tender:

6 medium-sized mature baking
  potatoes

Peel and coarsely grate or rice them. Add:

2 eggs
1½ teaspoons salt
½ cup flour

Beat the batter with a fork until it is fluffy. Roll it lightly into balls 1 inch in diameter. Many cooks prefer to put croutons in the balls. Put 1 crouton into the center of each 1 inch ball. If you wish to make large balls, roll several croutons into each ball. Drop them into gently boiling salted water for about 10 minutes. Drain them well. Melt:

½ cup butter or drippings

Stir in:

¼ cup dry bread crumbs

Or prepare:

½ cup Croutons, page 342

Pour them over the dumplings.

KARTOFFELKLOESSE WITH RAW POTATOES

6 to 8 Servings

This recipe, contributed by Claire Gregory, is a favorite of her far West German village. Coarsely grate into a bowl of cold water:

5 lbs. peeled mature baking potatoes

Reserve the small ends and pieces that cannot be grated and put them in a small pan covered with water. Squeeze the grated potatoes in a muslin towel until dry and in a firm ball, saving the pressed-out water in a bowl and letting it stand to settle the potato starch. In the meantime, cook the small pieces of potato in a small amount of water until tender. Drain, mash and add:

3 cups boiling milk

to make a smooth paste.

Correct the seasoning

then add the grated raw potato. Drain off the water from the settled potato starch and add the starch to the potato and paste mixture. Mix together by hand and form patties 3 inches in diameter and about ¼ inch thick. Place in the center of each patty:

Small diced buttered croutons, diced liverwurst or sausage

Then press the potato patty around this to enclose it in the center of the ball. Drop these balls into a large pot of:

Boiling salted water

When the pot begins to boil again ♦ reduce the heat and simmer for 25 to 30 minutes. Serve with:

Fat meats
Game
Cabbage with hot melted butter

ABOUT QUENELLES

Once eaten, never forgotten is the texture of a well-made quenelle. Success lies not only in the mixing but in the very shaping. The ground mixture, which may be fish, chicken, veal or game, is placed in a large bowl ♦ set in a bowl of ice, see below. It is then worked into a smooth paste with a wooden spoon.

♦ To shape, you may roll quenelles in flour but this is not the method for best results. We suggest the following classic spoon molding—letting the size of the spoon determine the size of the quenelle. They will expand to about double their original size. Have ready a well-buttered cooking pan and 2 spoons of equal size. Put one spoon in a bowl of hot water. With the other spoon, lightly scoop out enough of the quenelle mixture to just fill it. Invert the other hot, moist spoon over the filled spoon, shaping as shown. ♦ Do not press hard—only smooth the surface. After shaping the point, invert the little egg shapes into the buttered pan. Continue to shape and place the quenelles in neat rows, allowing for expansion space. ♦ To poach the quenelles, pour almost boiling salted water or stock very gently into the pan from the sides so as not to dislodge them. The stock should come halfway up the quenelles. ♦ Simmer gently for 8 to 10 minutes. The water should be barely quivering. As quenelles cook on the bottom, they become light and rise and turn over, but the weight of the uncooked portion will keep them submerged until they are thoroughly done and float.

Although they are not quite as delicate as when served at once, you may hold the quenelles for several hours if you poach them as described above. Place them gently in a bowl of cold water to cool, then drain off onto a cloth and place on a plate. ♦ Butter the surfaces to keep from crusting.

If you want quenelles very small, as a garnish, cut a parchment paper the size of the pan in which you plan to poach them. Use a decorating bag with a small round tip, fill with the quenelle mixture and force out small units on the parchment paper in uniformly spaced rows. Lift the whole paper into the pan and as with larger quenelles, pour the water gently from the side of the pan until the quenelles are only half-covered. As they simmer for 5 to 8 minutes, they will float free and roll over. When floating, skim off and place in a bowl of warm mildly salted water until ready to use.

If fancy shapes are desired, pack the quenelle mixture into buttered decorative individual molds. To poach, place the molds into a pan of hot water so that they are completely covered. When the quenelle mixture is cooked, it will release itself, rise to the surface and can be removed for serving.

Reheat quenelles by simmering them in the sauce or soup in which they are to be served. Or place the quenelles in a buttered mold in a pan of hot water. Cover with a buttered poaching paper, page 129, and bake for 50 to 60 minutes at 350° until firm.

POACHED OR BAKED QUENELLES
6 Servings
◗ Please read About Quenelles, above.
Run through the finest blade of a food chopper 3 times:
1½ lbs. fresh pike, sole, shrimp
or lobster
Place the ground mixture in a large bowl ◗ set in a bowl of ice. With a wooden spoon, work it to a smooth paste. Gradually ◗ by small additions work in:
2 egg whites
Season with:
Grated fresh nutmeg
Salt
White pepper
Dash of cognac
Dash of cayenne or hot pepper sauce
Mix well. At this point the quenelle mixture should be very firm. Still over ice, add ◗ very, very gradually and mix well with a wooden spoon:
3 cups well-chilled whipping cream
The consistency now should be like a firm whipped cream. To form and poach or bake, follow above directions. Serve with:
Newburg Sauce, page 323
Poulette Sauce, page 324

FISH QUENELLE IN LOBSTER SAUCE
6 Servings
Preheat oven to 350°.
This is a deluxe fish course for a special dinner party.
Prepare the mixture for:
Quenelles, page 193

using:
Dover sole
Put the quenelle mixture into a buttered mold. Place the mold in a pan of hot water. Cover with a buttered poaching paper and bake 50 to 60 minutes until firm.
◗ Test for doneness as for cake, page 617.
Remove the hot mold from the oven, allowing it to rest 5 minutes before unmolding. Then drain off the accumulated liquid and unmold onto a hot deep serving tray and cover with:
Newburg Sauce, page 323
Garnish with:
Parsley
and serve immediately.

YORKSHIRE PUDDING
6 Servings
Preheat oven to 400°.
It was customary to cook this old and delicious dish in the pan with the roast or under the roast, letting the drippings fall upon it. As many of us now cook roast beef in a slow oven and no longer have extravagant drippings, we must revise the preparation of Yorkshire pudding. It is best to cook it separately in the hot oven required to puff it up and brown it quickly. Serve it from the dish in which it was cooked, cut into squares. In Yorkshire it is served before the meat course as a hefty pudding. We always substitute the pudding for the usual starch served with a main course.
◗ The ingredients must be at room temperature when mixed or they will not puff
Sift into a bowl:
⅞ cup flour
½ teaspoon salt
Make a well in the center, into which pour
½ cup milk
Stir in the milk. Beat until fluffy:
2 eggs
Beat them into the batter. Add:
½ cup water
Beat the batter well until large bubbles rise to the surface. You may permit this to stand covered and refrigerated for 1 hour and then beat it again. Have ready a hot ovenproof dish about 9 x 12, or hot muffin tin containing about ¼ inch hot beef drippings or melted butter. Pour in the batter. It should be about ⅝ inch high. Bake the pudding for about 20 minutes. ◗ Reduce the heat to 350° and bake it 10 to 15 minutes longer. Some cooks recommend a 350° oven for ½ hour or longer. Serve it at once

EGGS, SOUFFLÉS AND TIMBALES

ABOUT EGG DISHES

Egg dishes are maids of all work in most households. They are nutritious, economical, usually quickly assembled and can be served in any number of appealing combinations—pleasing to the eye and to the palate. Every country in the world seems to have its own special knack of cooking eggs or combining them with something which brings up their flavor. The light, fluffy, golden omelet was born in France. East Indians like their eggs curried. And the Chinese, while partial to Eggs Foo Yoong, are reputed to be connoisseurs of vintage eggs.

To us, no egg dish can be good unless the eggs are "strictly fresh" and cooked with due regard for their delicacy and great sensitivity to heat. Let us not say of an egg, like the curate breakfasting with the bishop, "Oh, no, my Lord, parts of it are excellent!" For more details ♦ please read About Eggs, page 514. Eggs and egg dishes can be served at any meal in the day: fried, scrambled, boiled, poached, baked or cooked in omelets or soufflés. And almost unlimited variations of meat, vegetables or fish may accompany or be folded into them. They are an excellent means of adding extra protein to a light meal, whether it be hot or cold.

♦ Always keep in mind that eggs must cook on very gentle heat. In combining eggs with soufflés and sauces let them partially cook on the stored heat in the pan. Do not put them back on direct heat—because they never will have as good a texture in sauces and will not function properly in soufflés.

SOFT, HARD-COOKED AND CODDLED EGGS

The difference in soft-cooked, hard-cooked and coddled eggs is more a matter of timing than method.

Place in a sauce pan, preferably glass or enamel:

Unshelled eggs

Cover them with:

Cold water

Put the pan over medium heat and bring the water to boiling point. ♦ Reduce the heat to below boiling point and let the water ♦ simmer. Now watch your time, which will depend on how large and how cold your eggs are. Allow the following times for 70° eggs. If they come right out of the refrigerator, you will have to add at least 2 minutes to the timing given below:

I. Soft-Cooked Eggs
Remove them from the water 2 to 3 minutes after you reduce the heat.

II. Medium-Soft-Cooked Eggs
Allow about 4 minutes after you reduce the heat.

III. Hard-Cooked Eggs
Allow about 15 minutes after you reduce the heat. Plunge the finished hard-cooked eggs in cold water at once to arrest further cooking and to prevent the yolks from discoloring.

IV. Coddled Eggs
Place the eggs in boiling water by lowering them in gently with a tablespoon. Turn off the heat and cover the pan. Allow 6 minutes for delicately coddled eggs; 8 minutes for firmly coddled eggs; and 30 to 35 minutes for hard-cooked eggs. We repeat, plunge hard-cooked eggs, when done, into cold water. If you want the eggs to remain shapely, turn them several times within the first few minutes of coddling so that the white of the egg solidifies evenly in the air space and the yolk is centered.

♦ To shell hard-cooked eggs, crack the shell and roll the egg between the palms of the hands to free the thin tough skin from the egg and make shelling easier. If eggs are very fresh, they are more difficult to shell. If you want to slice the eggs smoothly, dip a knife in water before using.

Soft-cooked eggs may be served shelled, in the various ways suggested for Poached Eggs, page 196.

Recipes and suggestions for serving hard-cooked eggs follow. Others will be found in Hors d'Oeuvre and Salads.

SAUTÉED OR FRIED EGGS
4 Servings

Melt in a skillet over low heat:

1 or 2 tablespoons butter

Break into a saucer one at a time and slip from the saucer into the skillet:

4 eggs

Baste the eggs with the hot butter. Cook them over a very low heat until they are done. To get a firm white ♦ cover the pan with a lid at once. If you like a softer white, you may at once pour over the eggs:

1 tablespoon boiling water

then cover the skillet and cook for about 1 minute. When the eggs are firm, serve them seasoned with:

Salt and pepper

ADDITIONS TO SAUTÉED EGGS
It is the extras that often give punch to eggs, especially in brunch and luncheon dishes. Try eggs on a small mound of:

> Boiled rice, noodles, potatoes or
> rounds of toast

Pour over them:

> Well-seasoned leftover gravy
> Mushroom, tomato or onion sauce
> Canned Soup Sauce, page 333
> Cream sauce seasoned with mustard
> or curry powder, herbs, onion, celery,
> green peppers, capers, anchovies or
> cheese, Black Butter, page 338, with a
> few capers, or Brown Butter, page 338

POACHED EGGS
Individual Serving
I. Poached eggs, unless made in individual molds, are apt to produce "streamers" that you may trim off with scissors before serving.

Grease the bottom of a 6 to 8-inch pot. Put in enough slightly salted boiling water to fill to twice the depth of an egg. While the water comes to a boil, put in a small bowl:

> 1 egg

Swirl the water into a mad vortex with a wooden spoon. Drop the egg into the well formed in the center of the pot. ◗ The swirling water should round the egg. ◗ Reduce the heat. ◗ Simmer 4 to 5 minutes or let stand off the heat for 8 minutes. The white should be firm and the yolk soft by this time. Remove with a skimmer and drain well. If not using the egg immediately, plunge at once into cold water to stop the cooking. Repeat the process for each egg. To reheat the eggs, use hot—not boiling—water.

II. This method will produce a flattened poached egg rather than the rounded "egg-shaped" one described previously.
Put enough water to cover the eggs in a shallow skillet. Add:

> ½ teaspoon salt
> 1 teaspoon vinegar

Bring to a boil. Break into a saucer:

> 1 egg

Take the skillet from the heat and slip the egg into the hot water. Repeat the process for as many eggs as you require. Let the eggs stand in hot water for about 3 to 5 minutes, or until the white is firm. Remove with a skimmer and drain well. Eggs may be poached in a small amount of milk, cream or stock. If these liquids are used, omit the vinegar. For other additions, see below. To store for later use—but not later than 24 hours after the original cooking—put the poached eggs in a bowl of ice-cold water in the refrigerator. This is a good way to prepare eggs in advance for use the following day in Eggs Benedict, page 197, or any other recipe calling

for poached eggs. The heat from platter, toast and sauce warms up the egg.

ADDITIONS TO POACHED EGGS
I. Arrange them in a shallow buttered baking dish.
Cover with:

> Sauce Mornay, page 323

Sprinkle with:

> Grated cheese
> Bread crumbs

and brown quickly under a hot broiler.

II. Cover the bottom of a shallow buttered baking dish with:

> Creamed Spinach, page 300

Arrange the poached eggs on the spinach and proceed as for Poached Eggs Mornay, above, to produce **Eggs Florentine.**

III. Hollow out a hard roll, insert egg, cover with Seafood Spaghetti Sauce, page 335, and garnish with cooked shrimp, mussels and oysters.

IV. Serve on toast, covered with Hunters' Sauce or Aurore Sauce, pages 327, 324.

V. Poach eggs in:

> Creole Sauce, page 336

EGGS POACHED IN SOUP
4 Servings
The following recipe makes a good, attractive, light meal—prepared in a few minutes. Combine in an 8-inch skillet and heat to the boiling point over low heat:

> 1 can tomato soup: 10½ oz.

diluted with:

> ½ cup water

Add:

> (½ teaspoon dried basil)
> (¼ teaspoon sugar)

◗ Reduce the heat and keep the liquid below the boiling point. Add to the soup:

> 4 eggs

◗ Simmer 4 to 5 minutes or until the eggs firm up. Serve the eggs on:

> Rounds of toast

covered with the soup. Sprinkle them with:

> Chopped parsley

EGGS POACHED IN WINE
6 Servings
Combine in a skillet:

> 1 cup dry red wine
> 1 crushed clove garlic
> 2 tablespoons minced onion or shallot
> ¼ teaspoon salt
> ⅛ teaspoon pepper
> A Bouquet Garni, page 541

Heat to boiling point ◗ reduce heat and simmer for about 3 minutes, then remove the bouquet garni. Slide into the wine from a saucer, one at a time:

> 6 eggs

Poach them until the whites are firm. Remove and put them on:

Slices of fried bread (rubbed with
garlic)
Strain the wine, put it back into the skillet
and thicken with:
Kneaded Butter, page 321
Pour the sauce over the eggs.

EGGS BENEDICT
6 Servings
Toast:
6 rounds of bread or halves of
English muffins
Cover each with:
A thin slice of cold or hot ham,
minced cooked bacon or deviled ham
Top with:
A Poached Egg, page 196
Serve them hot, covered with:
Hollandaise Sauce, page 328

POACHED EGGS BLACKSTONE
6 Servings
Sauté, then mince:
3 slices bacon
Reserve the drippings. Cut:
6 slices tomato, ½ inch thick
Season them with:
Salt and white pepper
Dip the slices in flour. Sauté them in the
bacon fat. Sprinkle them with the minced
bacon. Cover each slice with:
A Poached Egg, page 196
Pour over the eggs:
Hollandaise Sauce, page 328

SMOKED SALMON WITH EGGS
A good winter breakfast or luncheon dish.
Prepare:
Buttered toast or a slice of
pumpernickel bread
Dip into boiling water:
Very thin slices smoked salmon
Dry them. Place them on the toast. Cover
them with:
Poached or sautéed eggs
Sprinkle with:
(Dill seed)

HUEVOS RANCHEROS OR
COWBOY EGGS
4 Servings
A traditional Spanish and Latin American
dish. These eggs can be baked in the following sauce or poached or sautéed with
the sauce poured over afterward. Heat in
a skillet:
¼ cup olive oil
and sauté in it for 5 minutes:
1 crushed clove garlic
Remove the garlic and add, sautéing until
soft:
2 medium-sized finely chopped onions
1 large finely chopped green pepper
Add:
1 cup peeled, seeded and chopped
fresh tomatoes
½ teaspoon salt
¼ teaspoon freshly ground black pepper

2 teaspoons chili powder
¼ teaspoon oregano
⅛ teaspoon powdered cumin
Simmer covered until thick and well
blended.
Correct the seasoning
The sauce should be very hot and well
flavored. At this point, pour it over:
8 poached or sautéed eggs
allowing 2 eggs per serving.
Or, to bake, preheat oven to 450°.
Pour the sauce into a heatproof shallow
dish or 4 individual casseroles and nest the
uncooked eggs in the same. Garnish with:
Strips of red pimiento
Sprinkle with:
A little grated cheese
Bake until eggs are set. Serve with:
Hot Pepper Sauce, or
Mexican Sauce, page 334

ABOUT OMELETS

The name "omelet" is loosely applied to
many kinds of egg dishes. In America, you
often get a great puffy, soufflélike, rather
dry dish in which the egg whites have
been beaten separately and folded into the
yolks. In France an entire mystique surrounds a simple process in which the egg
is combined as unobtrusively as possible
to avoid incorporating air and this mar-
bleized mixture quickly turned into a
three-fold delicacy, filled or unfilled. In
an Italian frittata, the food is often mixed
at once with the stirred egg and this thin
pancakelike mixture is cooked in a little
oil, first on one side and then on the other,
with a result not unlike a large edition of
Eggs Foo Yoong, page 199.
Since omelet making is so rapid, see that
you have ready everything you are going
to serve the omelet with or on and be sure
you have your diners captive. For more
details about equipment, see French Omelet, following.
The quality that all of these so-called
omelets have in common is that ♦ the pan
and the fat in which they are cooked must
be hot enough to form an envelope almost
at once to hold together the softer egg
layers above it, but not too hot to let it
toughen before the rest of the egg cooks.
♦ Eggs, therefore, and any food incorporated with them, must be at least 70° before being put in the pan. More omelet
failures are due to eggs used direct from
the refrigerator than to any other cause.
There is always, too, discussion about salting. As salt tends to toughen the egg structure, this flavoring can be allowed to come
in the delicate tidbits added to the omelet.
Glazing omelets makes them look pret-
tier but also tends to toughen them. ♦ To
glaze an omelet, brush it with butter. Or,
if it is a sweet omelet, sprinkle it with
sugar and run it under the broiler briefly or
use a hot salamander or brander. If you

want a real finished job, put the omelet on an ovenproof server. Coat it lightly with a thin Mornay Sauce, page 323, and run it under a broiler for 2 minutes.

♦ To fill and garnish an omelet with mushrooms, seafood, ham, truffles or tongue, put them into the hot butter before the eggs are added. Creamed food, cheese, herbs, garlic or any foods demanding low heat go on top of the eggs the minute the eggs are added to the pan and before stirring begins. Have ready about ½ to ¾ of a cup of the mixture. Place ¼ cup on the upper half of the omelet. Reserve the remaining mixture for the final garnish on top. Or, a simple method is to fold the omelet as sketched below, then cut an incision along the top and insert the hot food. For other fillings, see Additions for Scrambled Eggs, page 200.

ABOUT OMELET PANS

Much fuss is always made about an omelet pan. It is said that it should be kept for that purpose and that alone and should never be washed but simply rubbed with a handful of salt and soft toweling. The argument for a separate pan goes further. For not only should this surface smoothness be maintained, but any pan used for braising is apt to have developed hot spots. But those of us who resent giving kitchen space to a pan for one use only find an all-purpose skillet—cleaned with modern detergents—usable ♦ provided the pan surface is smooth so the eggs can slide freely over it. The pan should be heavy enough and slowly but thoroughly heated. Otherwise the egg cannot stand what one French authority calls the too great brutality of the quick heat. The next thing to consider is the omelet in relation to the pan size. Since French omelets are made so quickly, we never try more than 2 to 3 eggs at a

time—cooked in 1 tablespoon of sweet butter. If more than one omelet is needed have some extra butter already melted to save preparation time. We use a skillet with a long handle and a 5-inch base flaring gently to a 7-inch top, as shown in the sketches. For larger omelets—and they can be made successfully with up to 8 to 10 eggs—see that the similarly-shaped pan is big enough to keep the egg no deeper than ¼ inch, and add a proportionate amount of butter.

FRENCH OMELET

♦ Please read About Omelets, above. Remember that an omelet of this type takes only 30 to 50 seconds to make, depending on your preference for soft or firm results. Mix briefly in a bowl with a dinner fork:

   3 eggs

Put in a 7-inch omelet pan:

   1 tablespoon clarified sweet butter

To avoid sticking, clarified butter is best. Roll it over the bottom and sides of the pan. When it is hot and ♦ has reached the point of fragrance, but is not brown, pour in the eggs. Meanwhile, agitate the pan forward and backward with the left hand. Keep the egg mass sliding as a whole over the pan bottom. Quickly pick up a dinner fork and swirl the eggs with a circular motion, as shown on the left below. Hold the fork so the tines are parallel to, but not scraping, the base of the pan. At this point the heat in the pan may be sufficient to cook the eggs and you may want to lift the pan from the heat as you gently swirl the eggs, as illustrated, in circular scrolls from the edges to the center. Pay no attention to the ridges formed by the fork. The rhythm of the pan and the stirring is like a child's trick of patting the head while rubbing the stomach. ♦ Have ready a hot serving plate—a heat-resistant one if you

plan to glaze the omelet. A heated plate helps to inflate the omelet. To fold it—whether you fill, see page 198, or serve a plain omelet—grasp the handle of the pan so the right palm is up, as shown. Tip the pan down away from the handle and, with the fork, flip about one third of the omelet over, away from the handle, as shown in the center. If the omelet shows any tendency to stick, discard the fork and, by giving the pan handle a sharp rap or two with the fist, as sketched, the omelet will even flip over without the use of a fork and will start to slide. Slant the pan to 90° or more until the omelet makes a second fold in sliding out of the pan and lies with its ends folded under on the plate—ready to serve. Glaze and garnish if you wish and serve at once. For fillings, see About Omelets.

FLUFFY OR SOUFFLÉD OMELET
4 Servings
If you have 1 or 2 extra egg whites, add these and omit the baking powder. You may add some grated Parmesan cheese or chopped parsley, chives and chervil to the egg mixture before cooking it, or sprinkle these on top before putting the omelet in the oven.
Combine and beat with a fork:
> ¼ cup milk
> 4 egg yolks
> 1 teaspoon any baking powder

Beat until stiff, but not dry:
> 4 egg whites

Melt in a heavy skillet over slow heat:
> 1 tablespoon butter

Fold the yolk mixture lightly into the egg whites. Pour the batter into the skillet. Cover the skillet with a lid. As the omelet cooks, slash through it several times with a knife to permit the heat to penetrate the lower crust. When the omelet is half done—after about 5 minutes—it may be placed uncovered on the center rack of a 350° oven until the top is set. Jet-propel this to the table as it comes out of the oven, as it will collapse quite quickly. Do not try to fold it as it will crack and become flat and tough. It may be garnished with any of the fillings or sauces suggested for a French omelet, or use poached, drained, chopped oysters. Serve it cut in pie-shaped wedges.

BAKED OMELET
4 Servings
Preheat oven to 325°.
Beat until very light:
> 4 egg yolks
> ¼ cup sugar

Add:
> ½ teaspoon vanilla

Whip until stiff:
> 4 egg whites

Fold them lightly into the yolk mixture. Place these ingredients in a flat, 8-inch, round baking dish. Slash the top lightly.

The soufflé should be about 1-inch high. Bake it until firm, about 25 minutes. Dust it with:
> Powdered sugar

Warm and pour over it:
> ¼ cup rum, Cointreau or kirsch

Ignite the rum at table and let it burn down. This may be served with:
> Crushed sweetened berries

FIRM OMELET
4 Servings
For the beginner, the texture of this omelet is a little more manageable.
Beat with a fork until blended:
> 4 eggs

Beat in:
> ¼ cup milk or cream
> ½ teaspoon salt
> ⅛ teaspoon paprika

Melt in a skillet:
> 1½ tablespoons butter

When this is fairly hot, add the egg mixture. Cook it over low heat. Lift the edges with a pancake turner and tilt the skillet to permit the uncooked custard to run to the bottom or stick it with a fork in the soft spots to permit the heat to penetrate the bottom crust. When it is all an even consistency, fold the omelet over and serve it. The Japanese make a good omelet by this rule, substituting stock for milk or cream.

SWEET OMELET
See page 692 for other sweet omelets.
I. Follow the preceding recipe for:
> Fluffy Omelet

Add to the yolk mixture:
> 1 tablespoon sugar

Just before serving spread the omelet with:
with:
> Jam or jelly

Sprinkle the top with:
> Confectioners' sugar

Fruit juice may be substituted for the milk and the omelet may be spread with cooked or raw sweetened fruit instead of jelly.

II. Prepare:
> Fluffy Omelet, above

Add to the egg yolks:
> 1 tablespoon brandy
> 1 tablespoon curaçao

When finished, sprinkle with:
> Castor sugar

and Flambé, page 127.

SHRIMP EGGS FOO YOONG
Foo Yoong is really a rich omelet made with additions of cooked vegetables, fish and meat.
Clean or drain:
> 2 cups bean sprouts

Heat:
> A little cooking oil

in a skillet and stir-fry, page 253, until translucent and crisp:
> 1 slice minced gingerroot
> 6 chopped green onions

1 stalk thinly sliced celery
1 cup shredded cooked fish or finely
  diced cooked meat
Have ready and combine with the above
ingredients:
  6 well-beaten eggs
  1 teaspoon salt
  ½ teaspoon pepper
Heat an additional:
  1 tablespoon cooking oil
in another small skillet. Drop the above
mixture into it to form small omelets,
golden brown on both sides. Serve with:
  Soy sauce

FRITTATA

3 Servings

This Italian omelet usually has the filling
mixed into the eggs before they are cooked.
You may use any of the suggested fillings
for the basic French omelet, except the
creamed or sauced ones, allowing about 1
cup of filling to 3 eggs. The frittata is
usually turned when the bottom has set
firm.

Prepare and keep warm:
  2 cups diced cooked vegetables,
    chicken, seafood, ham, etc., in any
    combination
Beat with a fork until blended:
  6 eggs
Stir in the filling and
  Correct the seasoning
How much salt and pepper you add will
depend on how highly seasoned your filling is. Have ready a 10-inch greased omelet
pan. Into another 10-inch pan which has
been heated, put:
  1½ tablespoons olive oil
Pour in the egg mixture and proceed as in
the basic French Omelet, above, until the
bottom of the frittata is set and the top is
still like creamy scrambled eggs. Place the
greased skillet with the greased side over
the frittata like a lid. Reverse the position
of the skillets so the ungreased side of the
frittata falls into the lid, and this lid then
becomes the skillet which is heated to
complete the cooking of the dish, a matter
of 1 to 2 minutes more. Serve at once on
a hot platter.

SCRAMBLED EGGS

2 Servings

Beaten egg whites may be added to whole
eggs in the proportion of one additional
white to 3 whole eggs.
Melt in a skillet over slow heat or in a
well-greased double boiler ♦ over—not in
—hot water:
  1 tablespoon butter
Beat and pour in:
  3 eggs
  ⅛ teaspoon salt
  ⅛ teaspoon paprika
  (3 tablespoons cream)
When the eggs begin to thicken, break

them into shreds with a fork or stir with a
wooden spoon. When they have thickened,
serve them on:
  Hot toast lightly buttered or spread
    with fish paste, deviled ham or liver
    sausage; or in a hollowed-out
    hard roll
An attractive way to serve scrambled eggs
is to put them in individual well-buttered
ring molds while the eggs are still rather
creamy in consistency. Let them finish
cooking in their own heat, which will set
them. Turn out and fill the center with
any of the additions listed below.

ADDITIONS TO SCRAMBLED EGGS

Small amounts of the following may be
stirred into the egg mixture before scram-
bling. They should be at least 70°.
  Grated or crumbled cheese
  Chopped, peeled, seeded, sautéed
    tomatoes flavored with basil
  Cultured sour cream and chives
  Canned chopped sardines
  Crab meat, seasoned with
    curry powder
  Capers
  Chopped canned anchovies
  Chopped sautéed onions
  Crisp bacon bits
  Small pieces of broiled sausage
  Sautéed mushrooms
  Poached calf brains

EGGS SCRAMBLED WITH CREAM
CHEESE

4 Servings

Melt in a double boiler over simmering
water:
  1 package cream cheese: 3 oz.
  1 tablespoon butter
Scald and stir in:
  1 cup cream
Add:
  ½ teaspoon salt
  ¼ teaspoon paprika
Break into the sauce:
  6 eggs
Before the egg whites are firm, stir the
eggs gently with a fork until thick. Add:
  1½ tablespoons sherry

SCOTCH WOODCOCK

2 Servings

Toast:
  2 slices bread
Cut it into fingers. Butter well and spread
with a thin layer of:
  Anchovy paste
Beat together:
  3 or 4 egg yolks
  ½ cup cream
  ⅛ teaspoon pepper
  ⅛ teaspoon salt
Melt in a double boiler:
  2 tablespoons butter
Add the egg mixture and scramble until
creamy. Arrange the anchovy toast on a

hot dish and cover with the egg mixture.
Garnish with:
Chopped parsley

SHIRRED OR BAKED EGGS
OR EGGS EN COCOTTE
Individual Serving
Baked eggs always have great "eye appeal"
served in little ramekins, casseroles or co-
cotte dishes. Care must be taken that they
are not overcooked, as the white can become quite hard and rubbery and the
ramekin will retain the heat and continue
to cook the egg after it is removed from
the oven. If you put a poaching paper,
page 129, over the ramekin, this will return enough heat to the topside of the egg
to set it. The centers should be soft, the
whites just set. Don't try to hurry baked
eggs; they must be cooked in a gentle oven
heat.
Preheat oven to 350°.
Grease small bakers or ramekins. Break
carefully into each one:
1 egg
Add lightly:
Salt
Sprinkle over the top:
1 teaspoon cream or melted butter
Bake for about 8 to 10 minutes. You may
garnish with:
Chopped or sliced truffles
Sautéed pieces of chicken liver

BAKED EGGS ON TOAST
Individual Serving
Carefully prepared, this makes a delicious
dish.
Preheat oven to 325°.
Grease warmed individual molds with:
Butter
Place in each one:
1 teaspoon chopped celery, chives
or parsley
Break into each one:
1 or 2 eggs
Season them with:
Salt and paprika
Cover each mold with a small poaching
paper. Place the molds in a pan of hot wa-
ter, deep enough to reach to within ½ inch
of the top of the mold. Bake until the eggs
are firm. Turn them out on:
Rounds of hot buttered toast
Serve them with well-seasoned:
Cream Sauce I, page 322, or
Tomato Sauce, page 333
Or serve with one of the Additions to
Baked Eggs, listed below.

ADDITIONS TO BAKED EGGS
For interesting variations to baked eggs
try adding: cooked mushrooms, asparagus
tips, tomatoes or other vegetables, such as
creamed spinach. Or add chicken hash,
small bits of bacon, sausage or anchovy.
Or place a round of toast covered with

Gruyère cheese in the bottom of the baker
before the eggs are added. Instead of butter, you may also cover the eggs with a
cheese or tomato sauce before baking.
Other tasteful sauce additions are: one cup
cream sauce flavored with 1 teaspoon prepared mustard; creamed mushrooms or
canned soup—celery, mushroom, asparagus, etc. Dilute the latter with milk or water to the consistency of cream sauce. Eggs
are also good baked in 1 cup or more of
Creamed Onions, page 284.

EGGS IN A NEST
1 to 2 Servings
A gala-looking dish:
Preheat oven to 350°.
Beat until very stiff:
2 egg whites
Heap them in a greased ovenproof dish.
Make 2 cavities an equal distance apart,
not too near the edge. Slip into them:
2 unbroken egg yolks
Bake for 10 minutes or until the eggs are
set. Season with:
Salt and white pepper
Sprinkle with:
(Chopped chives)

EGGS BAKED IN BACON RINGS
Individual Servings
Preheat oven to 325°.
Sauté or broil lightly:
Strips of bacon
Grease the bottom of muffin pans. Line the
sides with the bacon. Place in each pan:
(1 tablespoon chili sauce)
Drop into it:
1 egg
Pour over the egg:
1 teaspoon melted butter
Sprinkle with:
Salt and paprika
Bake for about 10 minutes or until the
eggs are set. Turn them out onto:
Rounds of toast or slices of
drained pineapple
Garnish with:
Parsley

HAM CAKES AND EGGS
4 Servings
Preheat oven to 325°.
Combine:
1 cup cooked ground ham
1 egg
1 tablespoon water
⅛ teaspoon paprika or pepper
Press these ingredients into 4 greased muf-
fin tins. Leave a large hollow in each one.
Drop into the hollows:
4 eggs
Bake the cakes until the eggs are firm.
Turn out the cakes on:
Rounds of toast
Garnish them with:
Parsley or chopped chervil

HARD-COOKED EGG AND VEGETABLE CASSEROLE

5 Servings

Preheat oven to 350°.
Combine:

  1 cup cooked vegetables
  1 cup Cream Sauce I, page 322
  1 cup Creole Sauce, page 336

You may add:

  2 teaspoons chopped fresh parsley,
    thyme, basil, etc.

Dill or celery seeds are wonderful. Prepare:

  5 Hard-Cooked Eggs, page 195

Slice them. Grease a baking dish. Place alternate layers of eggs, etc., and sauce in the dish. Top with:

  Au Gratin III, page 342

Bake for about 15 minutes.

CURRIED EGGS

4 Servings

An occasional curry dish is a treat.
Cook:

  6 Hard-Cooked Eggs, page 195

Shell and slice them or cut them in half, lengthwise. Prepare:

  2 cups Curry Sauce I or II, page 325

You may pound and add:

  (¼ cup blanched almonds)

Add the eggs. Heat them well. Serve on:

  Hot buttered toast

garnished with:

  Parsley

CREAMED EGGS AND ASPARAGUS COCKAIGNE

6 Servings

We use both versions of this, depending on the time at hand. The texture is lovely if the asparagus is well drained and the sauce is not overheated.
I. Drain well and cut in 1-inch pieces:

  2 cups cooked or canned asparagus tips

Reserve the liquid. Have ready:

  6 hard-cooked, shelled, sliced eggs

Prepare:

  2 cups Quick White Sauce, page 323

using milk and the reserved asparagus liquor. When the sauce is hot, gently fold in the asparagus and sliced eggs. Either heat this further in the top of a double boiler ♦ over—not in—hot water or preheat oven to 350° and place in a baker. Cover with:

  Au Gratin I, page 342

and bake until the eggs and asparagus are heated through. Serve with:

  Slices of ham
  Hot French Bread, page 557

II.

4 Servings

Preheat oven to 350°.
Have ready:

  4 to 6 sliced hard-cooked eggs
  1½ cups well-drained canned asparagus,
    cut in 1-inch lengths
  1 can cream of chicken soup

diluted with:

  ¼ cup asparagus liquor

Place in 4 individual baking dishes. Alternate layers of eggs and asparagus. Cover each dish equally with soup mixture. Cover and bake about 15 minutes or until thoroughly heated.

CREAMED EGGS AU GRATIN

4 Servings

Preheat broiler.
Slice into a baking dish:

  4 hard-cooked eggs

Combine:

  1½ cups Cream Sauce II, page 322
  ¼ cup chili sauce

Pour this mixture over the eggs. Top with:

  Au Gratin III, page 342

Place the dish under the broiler until the crumbs are golden.

SCOTCH EGGS

Individual Servings

Preheat deep fryer to 375°.
♦ Please read About Deep-Fat Frying, pages 124-126.
Some people use pork sausage meat, bound with egg and bread crumbs for the coating.
Make a forcemeat with:

  Finely chopped or minced cooked
    ham
  2 or 3 mashed anchovies in oil
  Fresh bread crumbs
  Salt
  Pepper

Coat thickly with the forcemeat:

  Hard-cooked eggs

Bind with:

  Raw egg

Dip in:

  Egg and bread crumbs

Deep fry until the coating is brown. Slice in half and serve on:

  Croutons

MASKED EGGS

Allow 1 Egg to a Person

Chill and shell:

  Hard-Cooked Eggs, page 195

Cut them into halves, lengthwise. Place them cut side down on:

  Water cress or shredded lettuce

Pour over them:

  Mayonnaise thinned with a little
    lemon juice or cream, Mayonnaise
    Collée, page 341, or Chaud-Froid
    Sauce, page 341

Sprinkle them with:

Capers, chopped anchovies, bits
of ham or cooked bacon

STUFFED EGGS ON ROSETTES WITH SAVORY SAUCE

8 Servings

This dish is elaborate, but capable of pre-fabrication. The rosettes, the sauce and eggs may be made the day before they are served.
Prepare:

8 hard-cooked eggs

Cut them crosswise into halves. Remove the yolks. Combine them with an equal part of:

Cooked, finely chopped seasoned spinach or Creamed Spinach, page 300

Fill the egg whites with the mixture. Prepare:

2 cups Cream Sauce I, page 322

Season it with:

2 tablespoons Worcestershire sauce
2 tablespoons dry sherry
¾ cup chili sauce
Salt and pepper

When the sauce is smooth and hot, add:

2 cups cooked or canned shrimp or diced cooked sweetbreads

Prepare:

16 Rosettes, page 223

Place a stuffed egg half on each rosette and cover with sauce. Serve them at once or, if you have made the sauce and the rosettes ahead of time, reheat the sauce in a double boiler. Reheat the rosettes in a 400° oven.

PICKLED EGGS

Prepare:

6 hard-cooked eggs

Shell and stick into each egg:

4 cloves—24 in all

Boil:

2 cups vinegar

Make a smooth paste of:

½ teaspoon ground mustard
½ teaspoon salt
½ teaspoon pepper

with a little cold vinegar and add to the boiling vinegar. Stir for about 1 minute. Put the eggs in a glass fruit jar and pour the boiling vinegar over them. Cover and refrigerate for about 2 weeks. Use with cold cuts and in salads.

DEVILED OR STUFFED EGGS

The blandness of hard-cooked eggs is a challenge to adventurous cooks and a few suggestions to vary this basic ingredient with supplies from your pantry shelves follow.
Prepare:

Hard-Cooked Eggs, page 195

Shell the eggs. Cut them in half lengthwise or slice off both ends, which leaves a barrel-shaped container. Remove yolks carefully so as not to damage the whites. Crush the yolks without packing them and moisten them pleasantly with:

French dressing or mayonnaise, sweet or cultured sour cream, soft butter with vinegar and sugar, lemon juice or sweet pickle juice

Season to taste with:

Salt and paprika

Or one or more of the following:

A little dry mustard
Catsup
A dash of cayenne, curry, or hot pepper sauce
Worcestershire sauce

Exotic additions to the yolks are:

Anchovy or sardine paste
Liver sausage paste or foie gras
Chopped sautéed chicken livers
Chopped ginger and cream cheese
Chutney
Caviar
Smoked salmon
Deviled ham or tongue
Grated Roquefort
Chopped chives, tarragon, chervil, parsley, burnet or basil

Garnish with:

Olives, capers or truffles

Put the filling back in the whites. You may use a pastry tube for elaborate effects. Remove from the refrigerator ½ hour before serving for improved flavor and texture.

DEVILED EGGS IN SAUCE

4 Servings

Preheat oven to 425°.
Prepare:

4 Deviled Eggs, above

Place the halves in a greased dish. Pour over them:

1 cup Tomato Sauce, page 333, Mornay Sauce, page 323, Béchamel Sauce, page 322, or Mushroom Sauce, page 327, or a Shrimp Sauce for Fish, page 334

Coat the sauce with:

Au Gratin II or III, page 342

Bake the dish until the top is brown.

ABOUT SOUFFLÉS AND TIMBALES

The soufflé is considered the prima donna of the culinary world. The timbale is her more even-tempered relative. On closer acquaintance, both become quite tractable and are great glamorizers for leftover foods. ♦ Cooked foods are best to use, as they release less moisture into the mixture than do raw ones.

The soufflé is usually based on a Béchamel or cream sauce, the timbale often on cream and eggs only. The timbale may seem the more fragile of the two, but ♦ steaming—the distinctive process in the timbale—gives this custardlike dish much more stamina. The soufflé, which is baked ♦ must always be kept away from drafts and be served at once in the ovenproof straight-sided dish in which it is cooked.

A timbale is made in a mold and can be reversed onto a hot dish or into a pastry shell that was previously baked and cooled. It looks particularly attractive in a ring mold. It is often coated or served with a sauce. If a delay is even a possibility, turn your ingredients into a timbale, which will even submit to the indignity of reheating.

If your guests are assembled, prepare a soufflé. If not it may be like the beauty Horace Walpole commented on: "She is pretty with the bloom of youth but has no features and her beauty cannot last."

ABOUT SOUFFLÉS

Soufflés have the same kind of life as the "breath" for which they are named, some slightly longer than others, but with a predictable endurance for puffiness. If well made, you can count on about 10 short minutes in a holding oven ♦ but beware of drafts. Since they ♦ depend on egg white and steam for their ascent ♦ no second should be wasted from the beating of the whites until the soufflé is popped quickly into the ♦ preheated oven. With very few exceptions, every action, including ♦ immediate serving after baking, should contribute to hold their "breath" as long as possible. These tours de force, based on cream sauce with egg yolks and whipped whites, are easy to make if the pointers are carefully heeded. The cream sauce should be a rather firm one ♦ heated just to a boil. Remove it from the heat for ½ minute before the 70° eggs and any other ingredients—also at 70°—are added. The egg whites should be ♦ stiff, but not dry, page 515. ♦ Soufflés can always be made lighter if an extra egg white is added for every 2 whole eggs.

♦ To prepare soufflé dishes for baking, use a straight-sided ovenproof baker. Grease the bottoms and sides well with butter and then coat the buttered surfaces with a thorough dusting of flour, sugar or dry grated cheese—depending on the flavor of your soufflé. It will also climb up the sides of an ungreased baker, but it will not rise as high and the lovely brown crust will stick and have to be scraped off the sides rather than form a glossy coating which adds so much to the look of the individual serving.

Next, be sure the oven is heated to the indicated temperature. ♦ A soufflé needs quick bottom heat. ♦ If your electric oven has a top element, be sure to remove it, as the heat in it is often enough to stiffen the top surface of the soufflé too quickly and not allow for its fullest expansion during the baking period. ♦ For oven placement of soufflé bakers, see sketch, page 140. Some recipes suggest making soufflés in

the top of a double boiler ♦ over—not in—hot water. This is advisable only if an oven is not available, as the resulting texture is closer to a timbale than a soufflé. ♦ To make a soufflé with a crown—a "high-hat soufflé"—just before putting the soufflé into the oven take a large spoon or a rubber scraper and run a groove about 1½ inches deep all around the top, about 1¼ inches from the edge of the dish. A crown may also be made by extending the height of the baker with a piece of parchment paper tied firmly around the dish. We find this satisfactory only with so-called cold soufflés based on cream gelatins, page 693.

MADE-IN-ADVANCE CHEESE SOUFFLÉ

6 Servings

Preheat oven to 475°.
You can mix this soufflé as much as 3 hours before baking time, if you like, and set in the refrigerator. Remove it about 20 minutes before putting it in the preheated oven.
Prepare a 10-inch soufflé baker, opposite.
Melt:

½ cup butter

in a double boiler ♦ over—not in—boiling water. Add:

½ cup sifted flour
1½ teaspoons salt
½ teaspoon paprika
Dash cayenne or hot pepper sauce

Mix well. Gradually stir in:

2 cups milk

Cook ♦ stirring constantly until sauce is thick. Dice:

½ lb. sharp cheddar cheese

Stir into cream sauce until cheese melts. Remove from heat. Beat until light:

8 egg yolks

♦ Gradually pour yolks into cheese sauce, stirring constantly. Wash beater. Beat ♦ until stiff, but not dry:

8 egg whites

Fold cheese sauce into egg whites. Pour mixture into baker and refrigerate if you wish. Bake 10 minutes. ♦ Reduce heat to 400° and bake 25 minutes longer. Serve with:

Tossed Green Salad, page 79, or Grapefruit and Orange Salad, page 94

⅄ BLENDER CHEESE SOUFFLÉ

4 to 5 Servings

A somewhat firm but acceptable soufflé. ♦ To prepare baker, please read About Soufflés, above.
Preheat oven to 325°.
Dice into cubes:

6 oz. sharp cheddar cheese

Heat to just below boiling:

1½ cups milk

Pour the milk into blender container and quickly add:

　　2 tablespoons butter
　　6 to 8 pieces crustless bread, torn
　　　　into large pieces
　　½ teaspoon salt
　　⅛ teaspoon pepper or a few grains
　　　　of cayenne
　　(⅛ teaspoon mustard)

Blend until thickened. Add the cubed cheese. Beat in a large bowl until lemon colored:

　　4 egg yolks

Add the blended cheese mixture ♦ very slowly, beating constantly. Beat until stiff, but not dry and fold in gently:

　　4 egg whites

Place the mixture in a prepared 8-inch soufflé baker and bake about 50 minutes or until set.

ADDITIONS TO CHEESE SOUFFLÉS

For a more complete dish, consider adding one of the following to cheese soufflé:

　　½ cup ground or finely chopped ham
　　½ to 1 cup cooked, well-drained
　　　　and chopped or ground vegetables,
　　　　such as celery or carrots
　　3 tablespoons Italian tomato paste

CHEESE SOUFFLÉ COCKAIGNE
4 Servings

Preheat oven to 350°.
♦ Please read About Soufflés, page 204.
Prepare:

　　1 cup Cream Sauce II, page 322

Bring to a boil. Remove from heat ½ minute. Add, stirring well:

　　5 tablespoons grated Parmesan cheese
　　2 tablespoons grated Gruyère cheese
　　3 beaten egg yolks

Beat until stiff, but not dry:

　　4 egg whites

Fold into the cheese mixture. Pour into one 7-inch or 4 individual ♦ prepared soufflé bakers. You may decorate the soufflés before baking with:

　　Paper thin slices of Swiss cheese
　　　　cut into fancy shapes

Bake for about 25 to 30 minutes or until set.

VEGETABLE SOUFFLÉ
4 Servings

Preheat oven to 350°.
Cooked oyster plant, eggplant, cauliflower, peas, onions, carrots, celery, canned or fresh asparagus, etc., may be used alone or in any good combination. Small quantities of leftover vegetables may be combined with minced raw carrots, celery and onions.
Prepare:

　　1 cup Cream Sauce II, page 322:
　　⅓ cup cream and ⅔ cup vegetable
　　　　stock

When the sauce is boiling, stir in:

　　1 cup minced drained vegetables

When the vegetables are hot, reduce the heat and add:

　　3 beaten egg yolks

Cook and stir for 1 minute longer to permit the yolks to thicken. Season as required with:

　　Salt and pepper
　　(Nutmeg)

Cool this mixture slightly. Whip until stiff, but not dry:

　　3 egg whites

Fold them lightly into the vegetable mixture. Bake the soufflé in a greased 7-inch baking dish for about 40 minutes or until firm. If you wish a dish that is a course in itself, serve the soufflé with:

　　Mushroom Sauce, page 327

CORN SOUFFLÉ

Follow the preceding recipe. Use in place of the minced vegetables:

　　¾ cup well-drained corn, canned
　　　　or cooked, cut from the cob

Add:

　　(1 chopped pimiento)
　　(1 chopped green pepper)

ONION SOUFFLÉ
4 Servings

One of our pet accompaniments to an otherwise slim meal.
Preheat oven to 325°.
Prepare:

　　1 cup Steamed Onions, page 284

Drain and mince them. Melt:

　　2 tablespoons butter

Stir in until blended:

　　2 tablespoons flour

Combine and stir in slowly:

　　½ cup milk
　　½ cup evaporated milk or cream

When the sauce is smooth and hot, stir in the minced onion. When the onions are hot ♦ remove them from the heat and stir in:

　　3 beaten egg yolks

Cook ♦ but do not boil, and stir for about 1 minute longer to permit the yolks to thicken. Season with:

　　Salt, paprika and nutmeg
　　2 tablespoons chopped parsley
　　　　or ½ teaspoon dried basil

Cool these ingredients slightly. Whip until stiff, but not dry:

　　3 egg whites

Fold them lightly into the onion mixture. Bake the soufflé in a greased or prepared 7-inch baker until it is firm, about 40 minutes.

SWEET POTATO AND PINEAPPLE
OR APPLESAUCE SOUFFLÉ
6 Servings

This is fine with cold or hot ham.
Preheat oven to 350°.
Prepare:

　　3 cups Boiled Sweet Potatoes,
　　　　page 298

Add and beat with a fork until the potatoes are fluffy:

3 tablespoons butter
½ teaspoon salt
½ teaspoon grated lemon rind
2 beaten egg yolks

Drain well and fold in:

½ to ¾ cup drained crushed pineapple or tart applesauce

Cool these ingredients slightly. Whip until stiff and fold in:

2 egg whites

Bake the soufflé in a greased 7-inch baker for about 40 minutes.

EGGPLANT SOUFFLÉ

Preheat oven to 325°.
Prepare:

A Stuffed Eggplant, page 278

Combine the cooked mashed pulp with:

¾ cup soft bread crumbs
2 beaten egg yolks
1 tablespoon melted butter
½ cup chopped nut meats or grated cheese
Salt and pepper
Grated nutmeg

If the filling seems stiff, add:

1 tablespoon or more milk

Beat until stiff but not dry:

2 egg whites

Fold them lightly into the other ingredients. Fill the shells. Cover the tops with:

Buttered crumbs or cornflakes

Place them in a pan with a little water and bake for about 30 minutes.

CHICKEN SOUFFLÉ
16 Individual Soufflés

This soufflé makes a good luncheon dish, as it has more "body" than most of the other soufflé recipes. Serve in individual bakers.
♦ Please read About Soufflés, page 204.
Preheat oven to 325°.
Mince:

2¼ cups cooked chicken

Prepare:

3 cups Cream Sauce II, page 322

using chicken fat to replace the butter and stock or cream as the liquid. When the sauce is hot, stir in the minced chicken and:

1 cup chopped nut meats
1 cup chopped cooked vegetables or raw celery, carrots and onions

When these ingredients are hot, remove from the heat and add:

9 beaten egg yolks

Season with:

Salt and pepper
Nutmeg

Let cool slightly. Whip ♦ until stiff, but not dry:

9 egg whites

Fold them lightly into the chicken mixture. Pour until ⅔ full into prepared soufflé bakers, page 204. Bake until firm about 20

to 25 minutes. Serve the soufflé with:

Mushroom Sauce, page 327, or Poulette Sauce, page 324, etc.

LEFTOVER CHICKEN SOUFFLÉ
5 Servings

A glamorous way to use chicken leftovers.
Preheat oven to 325°.
Prepare:

1 cup Cream Sauce II, page 322

using Chicken Stock and cream for the liquid. When the sauce is hot, add:

1 cup solids: minced chicken, nut meats, minced and drained cooked vegetables

Remove from the heat and add:

3 beaten egg yolks

Season with:

Salt and pepper
Freshly grated nutmeg

Let cool slightly. Whip ♦ until stiff, but not dry:

3 or 4 egg whites

Fold them lightly into the chicken mixture.
Bake the soufflé in a prepared 8-inch baker until firm, about 40 minutes.

COOKED FISH OR MEAT SOUFFLÉ
4 Servings

♦ Please read About Soufflés, page 204.
Preheat oven to 325°.
Prepare:

1 cup Cream Sauce II, page 322

When it is smooth and hot, stir in:

¾ to 1 cup flaked cooked fish: tuna, crab, clams, lobster, shrimp, etc., or finely chopped, cooked meat
¼ cup finely chopped raw carrots, celery and parsley

When these ingredients are hot, remove from the heat and stir in:

3 beaten egg yolks

Season with:

Salt and paprika
Nutmeg
Lemon juice, Worcestershire sauce or tomato catsup
(⅛ cup sliced olives)

Let cool slightly. Whip ♦ until stiff, but not dry:

3 to 4 egg whites

Fold them lightly into the mixture. Bake in a greased 7-inch soufflé baker until firm, about 40 minutes. Serve the soufflé with:

(Tomato Sauce, page 333)

OYSTER SOUFFLÉ
4 Servings

This soufflé is very delicate.
Preheat oven to 325°.
Drain, but save the liquor from:

½ to 1 pint oysters

Dry on a towel. Prepare:

1 cup Cream Sauce II, page 322
using part cream and part oyster liquor

When it is hot, remove from heat and add:

he oysters. Add:
3 beaten egg yolks
Season with:
Salt and pepper
Nutmeg
(Lemon juice)
Let cool slightly. Whip ◗ until stiff, but not dry:
3 to 4 egg whites
Fold them lightly into the oyster mixture. Bake in a ◗ prepared 7-inch soufflé baker until firm, about 40 minutes.

SHAD ROE SOUFFLÉ
4 Servings
◗ Please read About Soufflés and Timbales, page 204.
Preheat oven to 375°.
Poach for 3 to 5 minutes:
1 fresh shad roe
Remove outer integument and veins. Crumble the roe and combine it with:
2 beaten eggs
1 cup whipped cream
A grating of nutmeg
Correct the seasoning
Fill individual molds ¾ full of this mixture. Set molds in a pan of hot water. Bake about 25 minutes. Serve with:
Allemande Sauce, page 324, or
Béarnaise Sauce, page 329

ABOUT TIMBALES
◗ Please read About Soufflés and Timbales, page 203.
Butter individual or larger molds lightly. Fill them about two-thirds full with timbale mixture. ◗ Place them on a rack in a pan of hot, but not boiling, water. The water should be as high as the filling in the molds. If a rack is not available, fold several thicknesses of paper and place the molds on it. ◗ Check the heat occasionally to make sure that the water around the mold never boils—just simmers.
It is wise to protect the top of the timbale with a poaching paper, page 129.
Bake the timbales in a ◗ moderate oven, about 325°, for about 20 to 50 minutes, depending on the size of the mold. The timbales are done when a knife blade inserted in the center of the mold comes out uncoated.

CUSTARD FOR VEGETABLE TIMBALES
4 Servings
In France the salad is served with the meat course and the vegetable is served in solitary state. It is usually worthy of this exalted position. Sometimes it is accompanied by a mound or ring of delicious custard.
Preheat oven to 325°.
Combine and beat with a wire whisk:
1½ cups warm cream or ½ cup cream and 1 cup chicken stock
4 eggs

¾ teaspoon salt
½ teaspoon paprika
(⅛ teaspoon grated nutmeg or celery salt)
(1 tablespoon chopped parsley)
(A few drops onion or lemon juice)
To bake, unmold and serve, see About Soufflés and Timbales, page 203. Serve the timbales with:
Creamed vegetables or Mushroom Sauce, page 327
For a brunch, garnish with:
Crisp bacon
Parsley

LEFTOVER TIMBALES
5 to 6 Servings
Use any good combination of cooked vegetables and meat.
Preheat oven to 325°.
Follow the rule for:
Custard for Vegetable Timbales, above
using milk instead of cream. Omit the seasoning. Cut into small pieces and add:
1 to 1½ cups leftover food
(Chopped parsley)
(Grated onion)
After the food has been added to the timbale mixture, season it to taste. If the food is dry, no additional thickening is needed. If it is slightly moist, add to the leftovers, before combining them with the custard, until they form a moderately thick paste:
Cracker crumbs or bread crumbs
To bake, unmold and serve, see About Soufflés and Timbales, page 203. Serve with:
Tomato Sauce, page 333

BROCCOLI OR CAULIFLOWER TIMBALES
5 to 6 Servings
Preheat oven to 325°.
Prepare:
Custard for Vegetable Timbales, opposite
Add to the custard:
1 to 1½ cups cooked well-drained broccoli or cauliflower, chopped or put through a food mill
Add seasoning if required. To bake, unmold and serve, see About Soufflés and Timbales, page 203. Garnish with:
Hollandaise Sauce, page 329

MUSHROOM TIMBALES
5 to 6 Servings
Preheat oven to 325°.
Prepare:
Custard for Vegetable Timbales, opposite
Add:
2 cups drained, chopped, sautéed mushrooms
To bake, unmold and serve, see About Soufflés and Timbales, page 203.

SPINACH TIMBALES

5 to 6 Servings

Preheat oven to 325°.

Prepare:

Cream Sauce I, page 322

Add to it:

2 cups cooked, drained, finely
chopped spinach
3 beaten eggs
½ cup grated cheese
¼ cup Veal Stock or other stock,
page 490
Salt and pepper
A few grains cayenne

To bake, unmold and serve, see About
Soufflés and Timbales, page 203.

CORN, EGG AND CHEESE
TIMBALES

4 Servings

Preheat oven to 325°.

Combine:

1½ cups canned cream style corn
½ cup grated Swiss cheese
2 to 3 beaten eggs
¼ teaspoon salt
⅛ teaspoon paprika
¼ teaspoon mustard
A few grains cayenne

To bake, unmold and serve, see About
Soufflés and Timbales, page 203.

ASPARAGUS TIMBALES

4 Servings

Wonderful balanced by a fruit or vegetable
salad.

Preheat oven to 325°.

Grease 4 deep custard cups or a 7-inch
ring mold. Place around the sides of each
container:

3 to 5 well-drained canned or cooked
asparagus tips, heads down

Fill the cups with:

Custard for Vegetable Timbales,
page 207

To bake, unmold and serve, see About
Soufflés and Timbales, page 203. Place
between the inverted timbales:

Hollandaise Sauce, page 329

Garnish them with:

Parsley

and surround them with:

Broiled or boiled link sausages

CHEESE TIMBALES OR CRUSTLESS
QUICHE

Preheat oven to 325°.

Prepare the filling for:

Cheese Custard Pie, page 227

To bake, unmold and serve, see About
Soufflés and Timbales, page 203. Good
served with:

Green peas, spinach or broccoli

RICE TIMBALES

A good garnish for a fish platter.

Preheat oven to 350°.

Pack greased molds with leftover:

Vegetable Rice, page 182
Pilaf, page 183
Curried Rice, page 179, or
Spanish Rice, page 180

Bake them in a pan of hot water for 10
minutes. Invert them and garnish with:

Parsley

Serve with:

Onion Sauce, page 325

CHICKEN OR HAM TIMBALES

6 Servings

Preheat oven to 325°.

Grind twice or blend:

2 cups cooked white chicken meat or
1 cup each chicken and cooked ham

Stir into it very slowly to form a paste:

¾ cup cold thick cream
¼ teaspoon salt
⅛ teaspoon paprika

Whip until stiff:

4 egg whites

Fold them lightly into the chicken mixture.
Line greased timbale molds with:

(Pieces of truffles, ripe olives
or pimiento)

To bake, unmold and serve, see About
Soufflés and Timbales, page 203. Serve
them with:

Mushroom Sauce, or
chicken gravy with chopped parsley

CHICKEN LIVER TIMBALES

4 Servings

Very light and delicate.

Preheat oven to 325°.

Put through a ricer, grinder or ⅄ blender:

¾ cup cooked chicken livers
½ cup Boiled Rice, page 178

Add:

A scant ¼ teaspoon salt
A few grains cayenne and nutmeg
½ teaspoon prepared mustard

Whip until stiff:

2 egg whites

In a separate bowl, whip until stiff:

¼ cup whipping cream

Fold these ingredients lightly into the
chicken-liver mixture. To bake, unmold
and serve, see About Soufflés and Timbales, page 203. Serve with:

Mushroom Sauce, page 327, or
Poulette Sauce, page 324

VEAL TIMBALES

4 Servings

Preheat oven to 325°.

Grind twice or blend:

1¼ cups cold cooked veal

Beat slightly and add:

3 egg yolks

Stir the ingredients well. Our French
recipe says pound them in a mortar. Continue to stir while adding:

⅓ cup whipping cream
¼ cup dry white wine or 2 tablespoons
lemon juice

⅛ teaspoon paprika
    Salt, as needed
Beat until stiff:
    3 egg whites
    (¼ teaspoon mace)
Fold these into the other ingredients. To
bake, unmold and serve, see About Soufflés and Timbales, page 203. Serve with:
    Mushroom Sauce, page 327, or
    Tomato Sauce, page 333

FISH TIMBALES

                                5 to 6 Servings
Preheat oven to 325°.
Flake and chop until very fine:
    2 cups cooked fish
Season it with:
    ¼ teaspoon salt
    ⅛ teaspoon paprika
    ½ teaspoon grated lemon rind
    1½ teaspoons lemon juice
Whip until stiff:
    ½ cup whipping cream
In a separate bowl, whip until stiff:
    3 egg whites
Fold the cream into the fish mixture, then
fold in the egg whites. To bake, unmold
and serve, see About Soufflés and Tim-
bales, page 203. Serve them with:
    Shrimp Sauce, page 334, Béchamel
    Sauce, page 322, or Tartare Sauce,
    page 316

FISH TIMBALE OR MOUSSE

                                   6 Servings
Cooked fish may be substituted, but un-
cooked fish gives a better result.
♦ Please read About Soufflés and Timbales,
page 203.
Preheat oven to 350°.
Grind, put through a ricer or ⅃ blend:
    1 lb. uncooked fish: 2 cups
Heat over a low burner:
    1½ tablespoons butter
Stir in, until blended:
    1 tablespoon flour
Stir in:
    ¼ cup milk
♦ Remove from heat. Beat and stir in:
    2 egg yolks
Season these ingredients with:
    ½ teaspoon salt
    ⅛ teaspoon paprika
Stir the yolks for 1 or 2 minutes. Permit
them to thicken slightly. Add the ground
fish. Cool the mixture. Whip ♦ until stiff,
but not dry:
    2 egg whites
Whip until stiff:
    1 cup whipping cream
Fold these ingredients lightly into the fish
mixture. Garnish a greased 9-inch ring
mold with:
    Strips of pimiento
    (Strips of green pepper)
Pour the fish mixture into the mold. Set
the mold in a pan of hot water. Bake it

for about ½ hour. Serve it with:
    Hollandaise Sauce, page 328
    Hot Shrimp Sauce, page 334
    Horseradish Sauce, page 324
    Oyster Sauce, page 324

SPINACH OR BROCCOLI RING MOLD
                                    4 Servings
♦ Please read About Soufflés and Timbales,
page 203.
Preheat oven to 325°.
Have ready:
    1 cup cooked spinach or broccoli
Drain, chop until fine, put through a purée
strainer or ⅃ blend. Melt in a skillet:
    3 tablespoons butter
Add and sauté for about 1 minute:
    1 tablespoon chopped onion
Stir in until blended:
    3 tablespoons flour
Combine and stir in slowly:
    ½ cup milk or Stock, page 490
    ½ cup cream or evaporated milk
When the sauce is boiling, stir in the spin-
ach. Remove from heat and stir in:
    3 beaten egg yolks
Cook and stir for about 1 minute longer to
permit the yolks to thicken. Season with:
    Salt and pepper
    Nutmeg
    (½ cup grated cheese)
Cool slightly. You may add just for looks:
    A few drops green coloring
Whip until ♦ stiff, but not dry:
    3 egg whites
Fold them lightly into the spinach mixture.
Place these ingredients in a greased 7-inch
ring mold set in a pan of hot water. Bake
the mixture until it is firm, about 30 minutes. Invert it on a platter and serve it
filled with:
    Creamed Mushrooms, page 281
    Some other creamed dish

CELERY ROOT RING MOLD
                                    6 Servings
♦ Please read About Soufflés and Timbales,
page 203.
Preheat oven to 325°.
Cook, page 272:
    4 medium-sized celery roots
Drain them well. Put them through a
grinder, using a coarse knife, or through a
ricer. Soak:
    2 slices white bread
in:
    3 tablespoons milk
Stir this into the celery and add:
    2 tablespoons melted butter
    1 teaspoon grated onion
    2 tablespoons cream
    4 beaten egg yolks
    ¾ teaspoon salt
    ½ teaspoon paprika
    A fresh grating nutmeg
Whip until ♦ stiff, but not dry:
    4 egg whites
Fold them into the celery mixture. Bake

the mixture in a greased ring mold set in a pan of hot water for about 45 minutes. Invert it onto a hot plate. Fill the center with:

Buttered peas, sautéed mushrooms, etc.

CHESTNUT RING MOLD

4 Servings

A delightful way to use chestnuts—the egg white lightens the consistency of the mixture.

♦ Please read About Soufflés and Timbales, page 203.

Preheat oven to 325°.

Combine:

2 tablespoons flour
1 teaspoon salt
¼ teaspoon paprika
1 cup riced Boiled Chestnuts, page 272
½ teaspoon grated onion

Add gradually:

½ cup milk

Stir and cook these ingredients over low heat for about 5 minutes. Cool slightly. Whip until ♦ stiff, but not dry, then fold in:

3 egg whites

Bake the mixture in a 7-inch ring mold set in a pan of hot water for about ½ hour. Invert it onto a hot plate. Fill it with:

Buttered green peas
Chopped parsley

It may be served with:

Mushroom Sauce, page 327

to which add:

2 tablespoons dry sherry

MUSHROOM RING MOLD WITH SWEETBREADS OR CHICKEN

8 Servings

♦ Please read About Soufflés and Timbales, page 203.

Preheat oven to 325°.

Parboil, page 441:

1 pair sweetbreads or use 1 cup cooked minced chicken

Remove the skin and membrane and mince the sweetbreads. Prepare:

1 cup Cream Sauce II, page 322

Melt in a pan:

2 tablespoons butter

Add and sauté for about 3 minutes:

2 slices onion

Remove the onion. Add to the pan:

1½ cups finely minced mushrooms

and the sweetbreads or chicken. Heat the cream sauce to the boiling point and combine it with the mushroom mixture. Remove from heat and stir in:

¼ cup dry bread crumbs
1 chopped pimiento
¼ teaspoon salt
2 beaten egg yolks

Cook and stir about 1 minute longer to permit the yolks to thicken. Cool these ingredients slightly. Whip until ♦ stiff, but

not dry:

2 egg whites

Fold them lightly into the mushroom mixture. Place the mixture in a greased ring mold set in a pan of hot water and bake covered with a piece of buttered paper for 35 minutes or until firm. Invert the mold onto a platter and serve filled with:

Asparagus spears
Peas, etc.

and pass with:

Suprême Sauce, page 325

STEAMED VEAL MOLD

8 Servings

The following is an excellent pudding.

Combine:

1½ lbs. ground veal
½ lb. ground pork
1½ cups finely rolled cracker crumbs
3 egg yolks
¾ cup milk
¼ teaspoon nutmeg
1 tablespoon melted butter
1 tablespoon onion juice
1¼ teaspoons salt
¼ teaspoon pepper
¼ cup chopped celery
⅛ cup chopped parsley

Beat until ♦ stiff, but not dry:

3 egg whites

Fold them into the other ingredients. Grease a pudding mold, fill it with the mixture, close it tightly and steam for 2¼ hours. ♦ Please read about Steamed Puddings, page 702. Serve with:

Mushroom Sauce, page 327, or
Poulette Sauce, page 324

or with the always admirable:

Quick Tomato Sauce, page 334

HALIBUT RING MOLD

4 Servings

♦ Please read About Soufflés and Timbales, page 203.

Preheat oven to 350°.

Combine and cook to a paste:

1 cup bread crumbs
½ cup cream

When it is hot, add:

½ lb. finely chopped raw halibut

Season with:

¼ teaspoon salt
⅛ teaspoon paprika

Cool these ingredients slightly. Whip until ♦ stiff, but not dry:

2 egg whites

Fold them lightly into the fish mixture. Place the mixture in a 7-inch buttered baking dish; set it in a pan of hot water. Bake it for about 40 minutes. Serve with:

Oyster Sauce, page 324, or
Poulette Sauce, page 324

Garnish with:

Tomatoes
Water cress

PANCAKES, WAFFLES, CROQUETTES AND FRITTERS

ABOUT PANCAKES, GRIDDLE OR BATTER CAKES

No matter what your source of heat, a hot rock or an electric skillet, no matter how fancy the name, blintzes, crêpes or Nockerl, all these confections are easily mixed and made from simple batters.

There are three equally important things to control in producing such cakes: the consistency of your batter, the surface of your griddle or pan and its even heat. Mix the liquid ingredients quickly into the dry ingredients. ◗ Don't overbeat. Give just enough quick strokes to barely moisten the dry ingredients. ◗ Ignore the lumps. Superior results are gained if most pancake doughs are mixed and ◗ rested, covered, for 3 to 6 hours or longer before cooking. This resting period does not apply to recipes which include separately beaten egg whites or to yeast-raised cakes that have the word "raised" in the title. Variation in moisture content of flours, see page 497, makes it wise to test the batter by cooking one trial cake first. Adjust the batter ◗ if too thick, by diluting it with a little water ◗ if too thin, by adding a little flour.

If your griddle is a modern one or is of soapstone, you may not need to use any type of grease. Nor should you need to grease any seasoned pan surface if you have at least two tablespoons of butter for every cup of liquid in the recipe. If you are using a skillet or crêpe pan, you may grease it lightly and continue to do so between bakings. ◗ Before baking, test the griddle by letting a few drops of cold water fall on it. If the water bounces and sputters, the griddle is ready to use. If the water just sits and boils, the griddle is not hot enough. If the water vanishes, the griddle is too hot.

◗ To assure a well rounded cake, don't

drop the batter from on high but let it pour from the tip of a spoon. After you pour the dough from the spoon, it will be two to three minutes before the cakes are ready to turn. When bubbles appear on the upper surfaces, but before they break, lift the cakes with a spatula to see how well they have browned. ◗ Turn the cakes only once and continue baking them until the second side is done. Cooking this second side takes only about half as long as cooking the first side. The second side never browns as evenly as the first. Serve the cakes at once. If this is not possible, keep them on a toweled baking sheet—well separated by a tea towel—in a 200° oven. Or fold for yourself a sort of cloth file in which to store them. ◗ Never stack one on the other without the protection of cloth—for the steam they produce will make the cakes flabby.

▲ In high altitudes, use about ¼ less baking powder or soda than indicated in the following recipes.

Several egg dishes approximate pancakes, see Eggs Foo Yoong, page 199, and Italian Frittata, page 200.

Pancakes are delicious stuffed, rolled or glazed with a sauce and run under the broiler. Try filling with prunes and cinnamon or with creamed seafood, page 237. You may incorporate in the doughs chopped nuts, candied fruits or currants; or wheat germ, flaked bran or corn. To do this, let the cereal or fruit rest in the liquid called for in the recipe for about half an hour before making it up. For additional garnishes and sauces, see Dessert Sauces.

PANCAKES, GRIDDLE OR BATTER CAKES
About Fourteen 4-Inch Cakes
Sift before measuring:
1½ cups all-purpose flour

Resift with:
    1 teaspoon salt
    3 tablespoons sugar
    1¾ teaspoons double-acting baking
        powder
Beat lightly:
    1 or 2 eggs
When using 2 eggs, you may separate
them. Add the yolks to the milk mixture.
Beat the whites until ◗ stiff, but not dry
and fold them lightly into the blended batter, after adding the milk and butter. Add:
    3 tablespoons melted butter
    1 to 1¼ cups milk
◗ To test griddle and bake, see About Pancakes.

WHOLE-GRAIN GRIDDLE CAKES
Prepare:
    Griddle Cakes, above
Use in all:
    ¾ cup cake flour
    ¾ cup whole-grain flour
Add to the liquid ingredients:
    2 tablespoons molasses
Serve the cakes with:
    (Sausages and sirup)

GRAHAM GRIDDLE CAKES
               About Fourteen 4-Inch Cakes
Sift before measuring:
    ½ cup all-purpose flour
Resift with:
    2 tablespoons sugar
    ½ teaspoon salt
    ½ teaspoon double-acting baking
        powder
    ¾ teaspoon soda
Stir in:
    1 cup graham or finely milled whole-
        wheat flour
Combine and beat:
    1 egg
    2 cups sour milk
    2 tablespoons melted butter or bacon
        drippings
◗ To test griddle and bake, see About Pan-
cakes, page 211.

FRENCH PANCAKES
              About Fourteen to Sixteen
                      5-Inch Cakes
Sift:
    ¾ cup all-purpose flour
Resift with:
    ½ teaspoon salt
    1 teaspoon double-acting baking
        powder
    2 tablespoons powdered sugar
Beat:
    2 eggs
Add and beat:
    ⅔ cup milk
    ⅓ cup water
    ½ teaspoon vanilla or ½ teaspoon
        grated lemon rind
Make a well in the sifted ingredients. Pour

in the liquid ingredients. Combine them
with a few swift strokes. Ignore the lumps;
they will take care of themselves. Heat a
5-inch skillet. Grease it with a few drops
of oil. Add a small quantity of batter. Tip
the skillet and let the batter spread over
the bottom. Cook the pancake over moderate heat. When it is brown underneath,
reverse it and brown the other side. Use a
few drops of oil for each pancake. Spread
the cake with:
    Jelly
Roll it and sprinkle with:
    Confectioners' sugar

STUFFED FRENCH PANCAKES
OR CRÊPES
I. With Seafood
Prepare but omit the sugar:
    French Pancakes
Prepare:
    Creamed Oysters, page 365
or use any available canned or frozen seafood. Spread the pancakes with the
creamed mixture. Roll them. Cover with
the remaining sauce. Sprinkle with:
    (Grated cheese)
Brown them lightly under a broiler.

II. With Meat or Vegetables
Follow the above recipe, filling the pancakes with:
    Hash with gravy or creamed
        vegetables, chicken, ham, chipped
        beef or other precooked meat
The cream sauce may be made from a condensed cream soup.

III. Roll in the pancakes:
    Precooked pork sausages
Serve very hot with:
    Applesauce

GÂTEAU CRÊPE
                      10-Inch Skillet
An unusual way to make a Torte.
Prepare batter for:
    French Pancakes
Make four or five large pancakes. Cool
them.
Spread between the layers:
    Lemon, Orange or Lime Sauce,
        page 709, or Lemon or Orange
        Filling, pages 646, 647
You may spread over the top layer:
    Caramelized sugar, see Dobos
        Torte, page 638
or simply sprinkle the top with:
    Powdered sugar

FRUIT PANCAKES
Prepare batter for:
    French Pancakes
Melt in a skillet:
    1 tablespoon butter
    1 tablespoon shortening
When the fat is hot, pour in ½ the batter.
Sprinkle it with:

1 cup or more pared, cored, thinly
sliced apples, peaches, bananas or
blueberries, or ½ cup elderberry
blossoms, stripped from the stem
Pour the remaining batter over the fruit.
Turn the cakes when they are brown underneath. Brown the other side. After browning the cakes on both sides, you may keep
them on a rack in a preheated 250°
oven for about 5 minutes to assure that the
center is sufficiently cooked. Serve the
pancakes hot with:
Powdered sugar

BLINTZES OR COTTAGE CHEESE PANCAKES

4 Servings

Prepare:
French Pancakes
Use a 5-inch skillet. Cook very thin cakes
on one side only, until the top is bubbly.
Place them on a damp tea towel, cooked
side up. Prepare the following filling.
Mix well:
1½ cups smooth, rather dry, cottage
cheese: 12 oz.
1 egg yolk
1 teaspoon soft butter
1 teaspoon vanilla or grated lemon rind
Place about 2 tablespoons of filling on the
center of each cake. Roll the edges up and
over from either side. At this point the
blintzes may be placed seam side down in
a closely covered dish and chilled for
several hours or they may be cooked at
once. Melt in a large skillet:
½ tablespoon oil
½ tablespoon butter
Place several blintzes in it, seam side down.
Fry them to a golden brown, turning them
once. Repeat, adding more oil or butter to
the skillet, until all are done. Serve them
hot, sprinkled with:
Sugar and cinnamon
You may pass:
Cultured sour cream

CRÊPES SUZETTE

4 Servings

At the age of 14 the famous Franco-
American cook, Henri Charpentier, invented crêpes Suzette—a glorified French
pancake. His patron was Albert, Prince of
Wales, whose penchant for all that was
bright and gay seemed a defense against
his incredibly dull upbringing. In "Life à
la Henri," he tells amusingly of his delight
in tempting the jaded palate of the royal
gourmet.
One day he was composing a crêpe sauce
—a most complicated affair—a blend of
orange and lemon peel, sugar, butter, maraschino, curaçao and kirsch. By accident
the cordials caught fire and the poor boy
thought that both he and his sauce were
ruined. The Prince was waiting. How
could Henri begin all over? He tasted the

sauce—it was delicious. Quickly he
plunged the crêpes into the boiling liquid,
added more of the cordials and let the
sauce burn again. The dish was a triumph.
Asked by the Prince what he called these
fabulous cakes, Henri stammered, "Crêpes
Princesse." The Prince, acknowledging the
compliment to himself, answered gallantly
that there was a lady present. There was,
a very small girl—would Henri consent to
changing the name to Crêpes Suzette?
Henri would and did. Later he received
from the Prince a jeweled ring, a hat and
a cane, but best of all he had put his foot
on the first rung of the ladder to his future
success.
This is Henri's recipe, condensed and put
into what approximates American form. It
makes 8 cakes—"enough for 4 people," says
Henri.
Combine and stir until the ingredients are
the consistency of thin cream:
3 eggs
2 tablespoons all-purpose flour
1 tablespoon water
1 tablespoon milk
A pinch of salt
We recommend keeping this batter 3 hours
to overnight, covered and refrigerated.
Place in a skillet:
Butter "as one joint of your thumb"
When this bubbles, pour in enough paste to
cover the bottom of the pan with a thin
coating—"almost like the white of an egg."
Keep the pan moving, for this is a delicate
substance. A minute of cooking and the
job is ¾ done. Turn the cake. Now again
and again and again until the cake is well
browned. Fold the cake twice. It will be
triangular in shape "like a lady's handker-
chief." The crêpes may be stacked, with
foil or waxed paper in between, and reheated much later in sauce. Reheating and
freezing are often suggested and, while
possible, the crêpes are not improved.

Henri's Butter Sauce for Crêpes Suzette

This may be made in advance and kept for
months refrigerated. Cut into very thin
strips pieces of:
Lemon rind, ¾-inch square
Orange rind, ¾-inch square
"Enough to put a patch on the ball of your
thumb." Use only the thin yellow rind.
Add:
1 teaspoon Vanilla Sugar, page 508
We say—not Henri—you may substitute a
few drops of vanilla and 1 teaspoonful of
sugar. Permit these ingredients to stand
closely covered for 12 hours or more. Melt
in a large thin skillet:
½ cup sweet butter
When it starts to bubble, add:
1 pony maraschino
1 pony curaçao
1 pony kirsch
Put a lighted match to the sauce. As the
flame dies down, add the lemon and orange

214		PANCAKES, WAFFLES, CROQUETTES AND FRITTERS

mixture. Place the sauce in a cool place until ready to use, if you wish. Make the crêpes. Plunge the cakes in boiling sauce. Turn them. Add:

 1 pony maraschino
 1 pony curaçao
 1 pony kirsch

Put a lighted match to the sauce. Permit it to flame. Serve the cakes at once. The final performance—plunging the folded crêpes into the hot sauce, adding and burning the liquor—is done in the presence of the one to be feted.

PFANNKUCHEN OR GERMAN PANCAKES

2 Servings

Henriette Davides, the German counterpart of the fabulous English Mrs. Beeton, says that the heat under this pancake must be neither "too weak nor too strong," that it is advisable to put "enough butter in the skillet, but not too much" and that the best results are obtained in making this simple great pancake with not more than 4 eggs. Henriette's recipes make mouth-watering reading. But only a strongly intuitive person on speaking terms with his imagination has a chance of success. Firming up Henriette's rule, will you try our version of this large pancake?

Combine and stir until smooth:

 4 beaten egg yolks
 2 tablespoons cornstarch
 ¼ cup lukewarm milk
 ¼ cup lukewarm water
 ¾ teaspoon salt
 1 tablespoon sugar
  Grated rind of 1 lemon

Beat until stiff:

 4 to 5 egg whites

Fold them into the yolk mixture. Melt in a heavy 10-inch skillet:

 2 tablespoons butter

When the skillet is hot, pour in the pancake batter. Cook it over low to medium heat, partly covered with a lid, for about 5 minutes. Or the batter may be cooked until it begins to set and then be placed in a preheated 400° oven until it is puffed and firm. Cooking time in all is about 7 minutes. It should puff up well, but it may fall. So serve it at once with:

 Confectioners' sugar and cinnamon
 or lemon juice, covered with jam or
 jelly and rolled, or with wine, fruit or
 rum sauce

AUSTRIAN PANCAKES OR NOCKERLN

Four Small Servings—
If You Are Not Very Hungry

In Salzburg few visitors failed to indulge in one or more of these fluffy globular puffs between the delights of the Annual Musical Festival. This rich soufléd pancake is good as a breakfast, a supper dish or a dessert with rum or fruit sauce. Make it immedi-ately before serving, as it has very little body and shrinks quickly.

Melt in a 9- or 10-inch skillet:

 1 tablespoon butter

The butter should be hot when the soufflé mixture is put into it. Beat until very light:

 4 egg yolks
 2 to 4 tablespoons sugar

Add:

 ⅛ to ¼ teaspoon vanilla

Whip until stiff:

 4 to 6 egg whites

Fold the yolk mixture lightly into the egg whites. Heap the soufflé into the hot skillet by the spoonful. Allow about 5 minutes in all for cooking. Brown the underside lightly, turn the puffs and brown the other side—also lightly. The center should remain soft. If you are serving the Nockerln without fruit or sauce, sprinkle them with:

 Confectioners' sugar

RUSSIAN RAISED PANCAKES OR BLINI

About Twenty-Four 2-Inch Cakes

Dissolve:

 ½ cake compressed yeast

in:

 2 cups scalded milk which has
  cooled to 85°

Stir in, until well blended:

 1½ cups sifted all-purpose flour
 2 tablespoons sugar

Set this sponge to rise in a warm place for about 1½ hours. Cover the bowl with a cloth. Beat until well blended:

 3 egg yolks
 6 tablespoons soft butter

Stir in:

 1½ cups sifted all-purpose flour
 ¾ teaspoon salt

Beat these ingredients into the sponge. Permit the sponge to rise again for about 1½ hours or until almost double in bulk. Whip until stiff, but not dry:

 3 egg whites

Fold them into the batter. After 10 minutes bake the batter, a very small quantity at a time, in a greased skillet or on a griddle. See About Griddle Cakes, page 211. Turn to brown lightly on the other side. Serve each blini filled with:

 1 tablespoon caviar

Garnished with:

 Cultured sour cream

SOUR MILK PANCAKES

About Ten 4-Inch Cakes

Sift before measuring:

 1 cup cake flour

Resift with:

 1 teaspoon sugar
 ½ teaspoon salt
 ¾ teaspoon double-acting baking
  powder
 ½ teaspoon soda

Beat until light:

1 egg
Add:
 1 cup buttermilk
Combine the sifted and the liquid ingredients with a few swift strokes. Beat in:
 1 to 2 tablespoons melted butter
To bake, see About Pancakes, page 211.

CORN MEAL PANCAKES
About Twelve 4-Inch Cakes
Delicate and good.
Measure:
 1 cup white or yellow corn meal
Place it in a bowl. Add:
 1 teaspoon salt
 1 to 2 tablespoons sirup or sugar
Stir in slowly:
 1 cup boiling water
Cover these ingredients and permit them to stand for 10 minutes. Beat:
 1 egg
 ½ cup milk
 2 tablespoons melted butter
Add these ingredients to the corn meal. Sift before measuring:
 ½ cup all-purpose flour
Resift with:
 2 teaspoons double-acting baking
  powder
Stir the sifted ingredients into the batter with a few swift strokes. To bake, see About Pancakes, page 211.

▣ CRISP CORN FLAPJACKS
About Twenty Thin 2-Inch Cakes
A distinguished botanist friend had as visitors on a field trip a Parisian confrére who traveled accompanied by his gifted Indonesian chef. To amuse the chef, our friend cooked his favorite corn cakes for him over a campfire. As he tossed the flapjacks, the chef cried out in delight, "Crêpes Sauvages!"
If you make this version up without the eggs, the pancakes become lacy.
Place in a bowl:
 1⅛ cups white corn meal
 1¼ teaspoons salt
 ½ teaspoon soda
 ¼ cup sifted all-purpose flour
Cut into this with a pastry blender:
 ¼ cup butter
Combine and beat:
 2 cups buttermilk
 (1 to 2 eggs)
Stir the liquid into the sifted ingredients with a few swift strokes. Make the cakes small for easier turning. The batter settles readily, so beat it between spoonings. To test griddle, bake and serve, see About Pancakes, page 211.

RICE CORN MEAL GRIDDLE CAKES
Twelve 4-Inch Cakes
Sift before measuring:
 ½ cup all-purpose flour

Resift with:
 1 teaspoon salt
 ½ teaspoon soda
 1 tablespoon sugar
Add:
 ½ cup water-ground corn meal
 1 cup cold boiled rice
Combine, beat, then stir into the sifted ingredients with a few swift strokes:
 2 cups buttermilk
 2 egg yolks
 2 tablespoons melted, cooled
  shortening
♦ Beat until stiff, but not dry:
 2 egg whites
Fold them into the batter. To test griddle and bake, see About Pancakes, page 211.

OATMEAL GRIDDLE CAKES
About Twelve 4-Inch Cakes
Sift before measuring:
 ½ cup all-purpose flour
Resift with:
 1 teaspoon double-acting baking
  powder
 ½ teaspoon salt
Beat:
 1 egg
Stir in:
 1½ cups cooked oatmeal
 ½ cup evaporated milk
 ¼ cup water
 2 tablespoons melted butter or bacon
  drippings
Stir this mixture into the sifted ingredients. To bake and serve, see About Pancakes, page 211.

BUCKWHEAT CAKES
About Forty 3-Inch Cakes
This batter is so light that it makes a lot of cakes. It keeps well covered in the refrigerator for several days. Sift before measuring:
 ½ cup all-purpose flour
Resift with:
 ½ teaspoon double-acting baking
  powder
 ½ teaspoon salt
 1 teaspoon soda
 2 teaspoons sugar
Two teaspoonfuls molasses may be substituted. Add it to the milk.
Add:
 1½ cups buckwheat flour
Pour into a bowl:
 3¼ cups buttermilk
Add:
 2 tablespoons melted shortening
Add the dry ingredients. Beat the batter until it is blended only. To bake and serve, see About Pancakes, page 211.

RAISED BUCKWHEAT CAKES
About Eighteen 2½-Inch Cakes
Scald, then cool to about 85°:
 2 cups milk
Add and stir until dissolved:

¼ crumbled cake compressed yeast
Add and stir to a smooth batter:
    1¾ cups buckwheat flour
    ½ teaspoon salt
Cover the batter with a cloth and permit it
to rise at room temperature for 12 hours.
Stir in:
    1 tablespoon molasses
    ½ teaspoon soda, dissolved in ¼ cup
        lukewarm water
    1 egg or ¼ cup melted shortening
To bake, see About Pancakes, page 211.
Serve with:
    Maple sirup

ONION GRIDDLE CAKES
About Fourteen 4-Inch Cakes
Serve these filled with seafood, Creamed
Sweetbreads, or chicken. Use a tomato or
other suitable sauce and a green salad.
Prepare:
    Griddle Cakes, page 211
using only:
    1 tablespoon of butter
Sauté until tender and golden:
    1½ cups finely chopped onion
in:
    2 tablespoons butter
Add them to the batter. To test griddle
and bake, see About Pancakes, page 211.

RICE FLOUR GRIDDLE CAKES
About Eighteen 4-Inch Cakes
Mix, then sift:
    2 cups rice flour
    4½ teaspoons double-acting baking
        powder
    2 teaspoons maple sugar
    2 teaspoons salt
Beat the mixture while adding:
    2 cups milk
Add and barely blend:
    1 beaten egg
    1 tablespoon melted butter
To bake and serve, see About Pancakes,
page 211.

ABOUT WAFFLES
You don't have to be told how good these
are with sirup, honey, marmalade and
stewed fruit. But you may not realize what
attractive cases they make for serving

creamed foods, leftovers and ice creams.
You can even cook raw bacon directly into
the dough, as illustrated, and have it come
out crisp and nut brown. But be sure to
treat your iron with care. Manufacturer's
directions should be followed exactly in
seasoning a new electric waffle iron. Once
conditioned ♦ the grids are neither greased
nor washed. You may brush the iron out
to remove any crumbs. ♦ The iron itself is
never immersed in water. After use, merely
wipe down the outside with a cloth well
wrung out in hot water.

Heat a waffle iron until the indicator
shows it is ready to use. If it has been
properly conditioned, it will need no greasing, as most waffle batters are heavy in
butter. Have the batter ready in a pitcher.
Cover the grid surface about ⅔ full, as
sketched on the left. Close the lid and
wait about 4 minutes. When the waffle is
ready, all steam will have stopped emerging from the crack of the iron. If you try
to lift the top of the iron and the top shows
resistance, it probably means the waffle is
not quite done. Cook about 1 minute more
and try again.

You may think our waffle recipes heavy
in fat. But the richer the waffle dough, the
crisper it becomes. With the butter flavor
baked in, there is then no reason for ladling
butter on top of it. We also suggest ♦ beating egg whites separately for a superbly
light waffle. Since waffles are made from
a batter ♦ keep them tender by not overbeating or overmixing the dough. See
About Muffin Batters, page 580.

▲ In high altitudes, use about ¼ less
baking powder or soda than indicated in
our recipes.

WAFFLES
6 Waffles
If used with savory foods, omit the sugar.
Sift before measuring:
    1¾ cups cake flour
Resift with:
    2 teaspoons double-acting baking
        powder
    ½ teaspoon salt
    1 tablespoon sugar
Beat well:

3 egg yolks
Add:
  2 to 7 tablespoons melted butter
    or salad oil
  1½ cups milk
Make a hole in the center of the sifted ingredients. Pour in the liquid ingredients.
Combine them with a few swift strokes.
The batter should have a pebbled look,
similar to a muffin batter. ♦ Beat until stiff,
but not dry:
  3 egg whites
Fold them into the batter until they are
barely blended. To bake, see About Waffles, above. Good served with:
  Maple sirup or Honey Butter
  Sweetened strawberries
Be sure to check under Dessert Sauces,
page 709, for other toppings.

FRUIT WAFFLES
6 Waffles

Prepare:
  Waffles
Add to the sifted ingredients:
  1 tablespoon sugar
  1 teaspoon grated lemon rind
Beat in with the last few strokes before
adding the egg whites:
  1 cup thinly sliced ripe bananas, or
  ½ cup drained crushed pineapple, or
  ¾ cup puréed apricots or prunes or
  1 cup blueberries

RAISIN, NUT OR COCONUT WAFFLES
6 Waffles

Prepare:
  Waffles
Add to the sifted ingredients:
  ½ cup chopped seeded raisins and
  ½ cup chopped nut meats or ¾ cup
  shredded coconut or ¾ cup broken
  pecans

CHEESE WAFFLES
6 Waffles

Prepare but omit the sugar:
  Waffles
Use in all:
  2 tablespoons butter and ½ cup
  grated sharp cheese
  (1 cup finely diced cooked ham)

GOLDEN YAM WAFFLES
6 Servings

Prepare:
  ½ cup boiled mashed yams, page 298
Add:
  3 well-beaten eggs
  1½ cups milk
  2 tablespoons melted shortening
Sift together and add to the yam mixture:
  1 cup sifted flour
  ½ teaspoon salt
  2 teaspoons double-acting baking
  powder

2 tablespoons sugar
♦ Stir only enough to moisten. To bake, see
About Waffles, page 216. Serve with:
  Honey and butter or Sauce
  Cockaigne, page 709
The sauce makes this a dessert waffle.

BUTTERMILK WAFFLES
6 Waffles

Sift before measuring:
  2 cups all-purpose flour
Resift with:
  ¼ teaspoon soda
  1⅓ teaspoons double-acting baking
  powder
  1 tablespoon sugar
  ½ teaspoon salt
Beat in a separate bowl until light:
  2 egg yolks
Add and beat:
  1¾ cups buttermilk
  6 tablespoons melted butter
Combine the liquid and the dry ingredients
with a few swift strokes. ♦ Beat until stiff,
but not dry:
  2 egg whites
Fold them into the batter. To bake, see
About Waffles, page 216.

SOUR CREAM WAFFLES
About 4 Waffles

These waffles are superlative.
Sift before measuring:
  1 cup cake flour
Resift with:
  1⅛ teaspoons double-acting baking
  powder
  ⅛ teaspoon salt
  1 teaspoon sugar
  1 teaspoon soda
Beat in a separate bowl, until light:
  3 egg yolks
Add:
  2 cups thick cultured sour cream
Combine the liquid and the dry ingredients
with a few swift strokes. ♦ Beat until stiff,
but not dry:
  3 egg whites
Fold them into the batter. To bake, see
About Waffles, page 216.

BACON CORN MEAL WAFFLES
6 Waffles

Don't worry about too much grease from
the bacon, as this is all absorbed in the
cooking of the waffles.
Beat slightly:
  2 eggs
Add:
  1¾ cups milk
Sift:
  1 cup cake flour or ⅞ cup all-purpose
  flour
  2½ teaspoons double-acting baking
  powder
  1 tablespoon sugar
  ½ teaspoon salt

Add:

1 cup yellow water-ground corn meal

Combine these ingredients with the eggs and milk in a few quick strokes. Add:

**5 tablespoons melted bacon fat or
other shortening**

Cut into halves or quarters:

6 to 12 very thin slices bacon

Place a piece of bacon on each waffle iron section after pouring the batter, see illustration, page 216. To bake, see About Waffles, page 216.

CHOCOLATE WAFFLES
                                      6 Waffles

Delectable with ice cream.

Sift before measuring:

1½ cups cake flour

Resift with:

**2 teaspoons double-acting baking
powder**

¼ teaspoon salt

(¼ teaspoon cinnamon)

(¼ teaspoon nutmeg)

Cream:

½ cup butter

with:

1 cup sugar

Beat in, one at a time:

2 eggs

Add:

1 teaspoon vanilla

Melt, cool and add:

2 oz. chocolate

Add the sifted ingredients in about 3 parts, alternately with:

½ cup milk

To bake, see About Waffles, page 216.

FRENCH TOAST WAFFLES

Combine:

1 beaten egg

¼ cup milk

2 tablespoons melted butter

⅛ teaspoon salt

Cut into pieces to fit a waffle iron:

Sliced bread

Coat the bread well in the batter. ~~Toast it~~ on a hot waffle iron.

ABOUT CROQUETTES

While croquettes are frequently made with freshly cooked ingredients—minced chicken, mushrooms, sweetbreads, lobster, oysters—these breaded deep-fat fried delicacies are also a good means for utilizing leftover food. ♦ Use about ¾ cup of heavy cream or brown sauce to 2 cups of ground or minced solids, meat or fish and vegetables. ♦ The solids should not be watery —always well drained. You may add to the hot sauce 1 to 2 egg yolks and let them thicken slightly off the heat. Add enough sauce to the solids so they are well bound, but still of a rather stiff consistency. There is a good deal of leeway in this relationship, provided—after chilling—the mixture can be easily handled. Spread it in a

greased pan and chill thoroughly. You may also brush the top of the mixture lightly with butter to avoid crusting. When cool, form into shapes not larger than 1 x 1 x 2½ inches or in small balls or cones. Roll in flour, then coat carefully in a bound breading, page 502. Allow them to dry on a rack for an hour, if possible. To avoid bursting, if the mixture is a soft one, you may coat as described. Then dry for about 10 minutes, recoat and dry for 1 hour before frying. ♦ Please read About Deep-Fat Frying, pages 124-126. Preheat deep-fat fryer to 375° to 385° and immerse the croquettes, not too many at a time, in a basket, so they will have exactly the same amount of cooking time. They will be golden in 2 to 4 minutes, unless otherwise indicated. Drain on absorbent paper. You may hold them briefly before serving on a rack in a 350° oven. ♦ To reheat croquettes, use a 400° oven.

CROQUETTES OF COOKED FOOD
                              About 12 Croquettes

♦ Please read About Croquettes, above, and About Deep-Fat Frying, pages 124-126.

Prepare:

Cream Sauce III, page 322

When the sauce is smooth and hot, remove from heat and add:

1 to 2 egg yolks

allowing them to thicken slightly. Add to the sauce until it binds:

**2 cups minced solid food: cooked
meat, fish or vegetables**

1 tablespoon chopped onion

2 tablespoons chopped parsley

Return the pan to very low heat and season the food well with a choice of:

Salt, pepper or paprika

Freshly grated nutmeg or celery salt

2 teaspoons lemon juice

1 teaspoon Worcestershire sauce

½ teaspoon hot pepper sauce

2 teaspoons cooking sherry

½ teaspoon dried herbs

½ teaspoon curry powder

Cool and, in shaping, place in the center of each croquette either:

A sautéed mushroom

A piece cooked chicken liver

A pimiento olive

**A well-drained, seasoned or
marinated oyster**

Bread, dry and deep-fat fry the croquettes as directed. Drain on absorbent paper.

You may serve the croquettes with one of the following if suitable to your croquette mixture:

Onion Sauce, page 325

Mushroom Sauce, page 327

**Tomato Sauce, page 333, or leftover
gravy, etc.**

HAM AND CORN CROQUETTES
                                      8 Croquettes

♦ Please read About Croquettes, above, and

About Deep-Fat Frying, pages 124-126.
Combine and mix well:
 1¼ cups cream-style corn
 2 tablespoons chopped green pepper
 1 cup ground or minced ham
 1 beaten egg
 ½ cup dry bread crumbs
Chill these ingredients. Shape them into
8 croquettes. Bread, dry and deep-fat fry
as directed. Drain on absorbent paper.
Serve the croquettes with:
 Tomato Sauce, page 333

RICE CROQUETTES
About 8 Croquettes
♦ Please read About Croquettes, page 218,
and About Deep-fat Frying, pages 124-
126.
Place in a double boiler:
 2 cups cooked rice
Soften with:
 2 or 3 tablespoons hot milk
Add:
 2 tablespoons butter
 ¼ teaspoon nutmeg
 1 or 2 beaten eggs
 (1½ tablespoons chopped parsley)
 Correct the seasoning
Cook and stir the rice until the egg thickens.
Cool the mixture. In shaping, imbed in
center:
 Small pieces of ham or cheese
Bread, dry and deep-fat fry as directed.
Drain on absorbent paper and serve.

CHEESE AND RICE CROQUETTES
About 10 Croquettes
♦ Please read About Croquettes, page 218,
and About Deep-Fat Frying, pages 124-
126.
Combine:
 2 cups Boiled Rice, page 178
 ½ cup grated sharp cheese
 ½ cup Cream Sauce III, page 322
 1 tablespoon chopped parsley
 ½ teaspoon paprika
 A few grains cayenne
 Salt
Cool and shape these ingredients into cones
or croquette balls. Bread, dry and deep-
fat fry as directed. Drain on absorbent
paper and serve at once.

SWEET RICE CROQUETTES
About 12 Croquettes
♦ Please read About Croquettes, page 218,
and About Deep-Fat Frying, pages 124-
126.
Combine:
 1 cup chopped walnuts
 ½ cup toasted white bread crumbs
 2 cups Boiled Rice, page 178
 1 teaspoon sugar
 ½ teaspoon salt
 1 beaten egg
 1 teaspoon grated lemon rind or vanilla

Cool, if necessary, shape, bread, dry and
deep-fat fry as directed. Drain on absorbent
paper. Serve them with:
 Tart jelly

MUSHROOM CROQUETTES
About 6 Croquettes
♦ Please read About Croquettes, page 218,
and About Deep-Fat Frying, pages 124-
126.
Prepare:
 ½ cup Cream Sauce III, page 322
Remove it from the heat. Add:
 ½ teaspoon Worcestershire sauce
 ⅛ teaspoon curry powder
 1 slightly beaten egg
 2 tablespoons cracker crumbs
 1 cup chopped mushrooms
 ½ teaspoon salt
 ¼ teaspoon paprika
Cool, shape into croquettes or cones. Bread,
dry and deep-fat fry the croquettes as directed. Drain on absorbent paper. Serve at
once.

CHEESE CROQUETTES
12 Croquettes
♦ Please read About Croquettes, page 218,
and About Deep-Fat Frying, pages 124-
126.
Melt:
 ¼ cup butter
Stir in:
 5 tablespoons flour
Stir in gradually until thickened:
 1 cup milk
 ⅛ cup cream
Stir in, over low heat:
 ½ lb. grated Swiss cheese
Cool slightly. Stir in:
 3 beaten egg yolks
 ¾ teaspoon salt
 ⅛ teaspoon paprika
Pour the custard into a well-greased pan,
about 6 x 9 inches. Chill well. When
ready to use, immerse pan for a moment
in hot water, reverse it and turn the custard onto a flat surface. Cut into shapes.
Bread and dry twice and deep-fat fry as
directed. Drain on absorbent paper. Serve
with:
 Hot Tomato Sauce, page 333

CHICKEN OR VEAL CROQUETTES
♦ Please read About Croquettes, page 218,
and About Deep-Fat Frying, pages 124-
126. Try adding poached sweetbreads or
brains.
Combine:
 1½ cups minced chicken or veal
with:
 ½ cup sautéed mushrooms, minced
 celery or minced nuts
Add, until these ingredients are well bound:
 About ¾ cup hot Velouté Sauce,
 page 324
Cool, shape, bread, dry and deep-fat fry
the croquettes as directed. Drain on ab-

sorbent paper. Serve them with:

Mushroom Sauce, page 327, or
Poulette Sauce, page 324

OYSTER AND CHICKEN CROQUETTES

About 12 Croquettes

◆ Please read About Croquettes, page 218, and About Deep-Fat Frying, pages 124-126.

These whole oysters in a chicken croquette mixture are very good. Heat in their liquor until they are plump:

1 pint oysters

Drain them. Reserve the liquor. Dry them. Melt:

2 tablespoons butter

Sauté slowly in the butter until golden:

(3 tablespoons minced onion)

Stir in, until blended:

¼ cup flour

Slowly add:

1 cup oyster liquor and Chicken Stock, page 490
Correct the seasoning

and add:

A few grains cayenne
A few grains nutmeg

Stir in:

½ cup cooked minced chicken

Reduce the heat and add:

3 beaten egg yolks
1 tablespoon minced parsley

Allow mixture to thicken. Whip until stiff and fold into the chicken mixture:

½ cup heavy cream

Spread the mixture on a platter. Cool. Dip the oysters one at a time in the chicken mixture until they are well coated. Shape, bread, dry and fry the croquettes, as directed. Drain them on absorbent paper. Serve them garnished with:

Lemon slices
Parsley or water cress

SALMON CROQUETTES

About 12 Croquettes

◆ Please read About Croquettes, page 218. Mix:

2 cups flaked cooked or canned salmon
2 cups mashed potatoes
1½ teaspoons salt or anchovy paste
⅛ teaspoon pepper
1 beaten egg
1 tablespoon minced parsley
1 teaspoon lemon juice or Worcestershire sauce

Shape, bread, dry and fry the croquettes as directed. Drain on absorbent paper before serving.

ABOUT FRITTERS

The term fritter is rather confusingly used to cover three quite different types of food. We think of a truly light, good fritter as a delicately flavored batter, heavy in egg and deep-fat fried. While they are not called fritters, crullers and doughnuts, see pages 705-707, are very closely related to them —the crullers usually richer in fat, the doughnuts heavier in flour. The success of these simple batters depends on the care and skill with which they are mixed and fried, so please read About Deep-Fat Frying, pages 124-126.

◆ Don't confuse the texture of any of these fritters with certain pan-fried mixtures like corn fritters, page 274. The term fritter also applies to bits of meat, fish, vegetable or fruit dipped in a batter and dried before deep-fat frying. In this last type, the fritter batter acts as a protective coating and we prefer to think of these delicacies as frittered foods. Examples are Deep Fat Fried Vegetables, page 256.

Variations of this completely encased food are rosettes and timbale cases or cassoulettes in which the deep-fat fried casing is a free-standing affair, so shaped that it may be filled. ◆ Be sure to choose fillings that are rather on the stable side with these types and put them in just before serving so the fritterlike casing will stay crisp.

To prepare frittered vegetables, use almost any leftover or raw vegetables. Tomatoes or seafood are also delectable served this way. ◆ But veal, pork and pork products should always be cooked and brains must be parboiled before frying. ◆ To cook, please read About Deep-Fat Frying, pages 124-126.

▲ Doughs for deep-fat fried fritters and doughnuts have to be adjusted and the temperature of the fat usually has to be lowered when cooking at high altitudes.

ABOUT FRITTER BATTERS

These are really much like simple pancake mixtures, but they ◆ must have the consistency that makes them stick to the food to be fried. As in all recipes involving flour, measurements can only be approximate, see page 497. But don't despair. There is an easy test. And if the surface of the food you are frying is as dry as possible, the dough will adhere. ◆ Take a generous spoonful of batter and hold it above the mixing bowl. Instead of running from the spoon in a broad shining band that the French call "en ruban," the batter should start to run for about a 1½-inch length, then drop in successive long triangular "splats." When the batter is this consistency, ◆ beat it until very smooth. ◆ Cover it refrigerated for at least two hours. It may even be stored this way overnight. This resting period allows a fermentation which is even greater if beer or wine forms part of the liquid used and any rubberiness in the batter is broken down.

◆ If you do not have time to let the dough rest, mix it to smoothness with as few strokes as possible so as not to build up the gluten in the flour. Batters heavy in egg yolk resist fat penetration during frying. Use whole eggs if you wish, but if you separate them and plan to rest the dough, fold in the whites beaten ♦ stiff, but not dry, at the last minute before coating the food. ♦ To fry, see about Deep-Fat Frying, pages 124-126. Either cooked or uncooked foods may be fried in batter, although uncooked meats are more satisfactory if minced. Time depends on the size of the fritter. If slightly smaller than doughnut size, precooked food requires only about 2 to 3 minutes at about 375°. Uncooked food in larger units is better at around 350° to 360° and will need from 5 to 7 minutes. This allows more time for thorough cooking of the interior.

FRITTER BATTER FOR VEGETABLES, MEAT AND FISH

♦ Please read About Fritter Batters, above.

**Enough to Coat About
2 Cups Food**

Put in a bowl and mix well:

1⅛ cups all-purpose flour
1 teaspoon salt
¼ teaspoon pepper
1 tablespoon melted butter
    or cooking oil
2 beaten egg yolks

Add gradually, stirring constantly:

¾ cup flat beer

Allow the batter to rest covered and refrigerated 3 to 12 hours. Just before using, you may add:

(2 stiffly beaten egg whites)

To coat food and fry it, see About Fritter Batters, page 220.

ABOUT FRUIT FRITTERS

Fritter batter for fruit, like any other batter, profits by resting at least 2 hours after mixing. ♦ Please read about Fritter Batters, on page 220.

It is very important that fruit used in these desserts be ripe but not mushy. Keep fruit slices about ½-inch thick. Use apples —cored and cut crosswise—pineapple and orange wedges, halves of canned or stewed apricots or bananas cut in 3 or 4 diagonal pieces. In season, even try fuzzy white elderberry blossoms. Dusted with powdered sugar and sprinkled with kirsch, they are dreamy.

The fruit is often marinated in advance in a little wine, kirsch, rum or brandy. This marinade may also be used in the batter, but in this case you must marinate and drain prior to mixing the batter and adjust the amount of liquid to that called for in the recipe. Even beer can be used as a liquid. Both beer and wine help to break down the gluten and make a tender batter. After marination of about 2 hours, be sure to ♦ drain the fruit well and dust it with confectioners' sugar just before immersing it in the batter. To cook, please read

About Doughnuts, on page 705. Fritters are good either dusted with sugar or served with a sauce like Sabayon, see page 710

If a variety of fruits are served in this way, they are called a Fritto Misto.

FRITTER BATTER FOR FRUIT

About 8 to 10 Servings

This batter can be used either to encase about 2 cups diced fruit or to hold the same amount of small fruits and berries that are mixed directly and gently into it. See About Fruit Fritters, above.

Heat deep fat to 375°

I. Beat together:

2 egg yolks
⅔ cup milk or the liquid from
    the fruit marinade
1 tablespoon melted butter

Sift before measuring:

1 cup all-purpose flour

Resift with:

¼ teaspoon salt
1 tablespoon sugar

Combine liquid and dry ingredients. **If you have the time, rest the dough at least 2 hours,** covered and refrigerated. Then beat this mixture well, until smooth. Otherwise, stir until just blended. Just before using the batter, whip ♦ until stiff, but not dry:

2 egg whites

Fold them into the dough. Dip into the batter or mix with it the well-drained sugared fruit. To cook, please read About Deep-Fat Frying, on pages 124-126. The fritters will take from 3 to 5 minutes to brown. Drain them on absorbent paper. Dust with:

Confectioners' sugar

II. Prepare:

Fritter Batter for Vegetables, above

omitting the pepper and adding:

1 to 2 tablespoons sugar

To coat food and fry it, see About Fritter Batters, page 220.

III. Mix together and beat until smooth:

1¼ cups sifted all-purpose flour
1 cup white wine
1 tablespoon sugar
½ teaspoon grated lemon rind
¼ teaspoon salt

Rest the batter refrigerated and covered 3 to 12 hours. Just before using ♦ whip until stiff but not dry:

1 egg white

To coat food and fry it, see About Fritter Batters, page 220.

UNSWEETENED CHOUX PASTE FRITTERS

Prepare:

Choux Paste, page 597

Omit the sugar. Shape dough with greased spoons or a small greased self-releasing ice cream scoop. Fry in 370° deep fat for about 6 minutes. For sweetened choux paste fritters, see Beignets, page 706.

PURÉED VEGETABLE FRITTERS
3 Servings

Preheat deep fryer to 375°.
Beat until light:
    1 egg
Add and beat well:
    1 cup cooked mashed or puréed carrots, parsnips, butter beans, etc.
Stir in:
    ¼ teaspoon salt
    1½ tablespoons melted butter
    1½ tablespoons flour
    6 tablespoons milk
    1 tablespoon Worcestershire sauce or
    2½ teaspoons onion juice
    ½ teaspoon dried herb, or
    2 tablespoons chopped parsley
Spread these ingredients on a greased platter. When they are cold, shape them into 1-inch balls. Flour and roll the balls in:
    Bound Beading, page 502
Fry the balls in deep fat, pages 124-126.

EGGPLANT FRITTERS
6 Servings

Preheat deep fryer to 365°.
Pare and slice:
    A small-sized eggplant
Cook it until it is tender in:
    Boiling water to cover
Add:
    1 teaspoon vinegar
Drain the eggplant. Mash it. Beat in:
    1 egg
    ½ teaspoon salt
    3 tablespoons flour
    ½ teaspoon any baking powder
♦ To fry, see About Fritter Batters, page 220.
Serve the fritters with a meat course.

CALF BRAIN FRITTERS
3 Servings

Preheat deep fryer to 375°.
♦ Please read About Deep-Fat Frying, pages 124-126.
Prepare and blanch:
    1 set Calf Brains, page 443
Dry them between towels. Pull them into small pieces. Sift:
    1 cup all-purpose flour
    1 teaspoon double-acting baking powder
    ¼ teaspoon salt
Beat until light:
    2 egg yolks
Beat in the sifted ingredients until blended.
Beat in:
    1 tablespoon melted butter
    1 teaspoon grated lemon rind

A grating nutmeg
    ½ cup milk
    (1 tablespoon wine or brandy)
Beat until stiff ♦ but not dry:
    2 egg whites
Fold them into the batter. Add the brains. Drop the batter into hot deep fat. Serve when golden.

COOKED MEAT FRITTERS

Prepare as for:
    Calf Brain Fritters
substituting for the brains about:
    1½ cups chopped cooked meat
Add to the meat, if desired:
    2 tablespoons chopped parsley
    1 tablespoon lemon juice or 1 teaspoon Worcestershire sauce
Serve the fritters with:
    Gravy, Tomato Sauce, page 333, or Horseradish Sauce, page 324

CORN AND HAM FRITTERS
6 Servings

Preheat deep fryer to 375°.
Beat until light:
    2 egg yolks
Add and combine with a few swift strokes:
    ½ cup milk
    1⅛ cups sifted flour
    2 teaspoons double-acting baking powder
    ¾ teaspoon salt
    ¼ teaspoon paprika
Fold in:
    2 tablespoons minced parsley or onion
    ¼ cup drained cream-style corn
    ¾ cup cooked minced ham
    2 stiffly beaten egg whites
To fry the fritters, see Deep-Fat Frying, pages 124-126.

BLOOMS IN BATTER

There is a chichi revival of the age-old custom of eating flowers. If you are an organic gardener and if you know your flowers, all is well. A lily of the valley which always looks good enough to eat is very poisonous and the sprays used on roses are not only lethal to pests, but to you. From sprayed gardens, save petals for fragrance only—not eating. Wash well any kind of blooms and leaves you use for garnish.
♦ To make fritters of blossoms, please read About Fritter Batter, page 220, and About Deep-Fat Frying, pages 124-126.
Pick with the dew on them and dry well:
    Unsprayed elderberry, squash or hemerocallis blooms
Dip them in:
    Fritter Batter for Fruit II, page 221
Fry them in deep fat preheated to 350°.

BRUNCH, LUNCH, AND SUPPER DISHES

This is a chapter, we admit, for which we have a special fondness. In it, we call attention to the many delicious ways you can combine those foods you have already cooked, as well as the staples in your larder—whether they are dried, preserved, canned or frozen. Do not neglect other combinations in the egg, pasta and cereal chapters. From many of these recipes attractive meals may be prepared in less than half an hour's time.

Care in cooking, distinction in seasoning and presentation, can make even a tin of tuna memorable. The large gratinéed casserole, the individual lidded baking dish or one of the following cases for food—as well as garnishes made from simple materials—all lend distinction in making a quick dish a gracious one.

Keep in mind that many fresh fish and shellfish recipes are almost as rapidly cooked as those involving a preprocessed food. For other quick dishes, refer also to the section on Ground Meats, page 426, Variety Meats, page 438, and Vegetables, page 250. For the quickest of sauces, see Soup-Based Sauces, page 333.

ABOUT CASES FOR FOOD

We have left behind the era of trenchers—those coarse loaves that served as dishes and were eaten when empty by trenchermen. But none of us has lost a taste for the sauce-flavored pastry, pancake, tortilla or toast. All manner of creamed foods—meat, vegetables or fish mixtures, cheese concoctions, as well as farces and stews can be placed in one of the following cases and then served with a sauce.

Patty Shells, page 596
Popovers, page 582
Brioches, page 567
Rounds of buttered and toasted bread or French Toast, page 587
Rusks lightly buttered and heated
A loaf of bread that has been hollowed, buttered lightly and toasted in a 300° oven
A Rice Loaf, page 180
Pies or Tart Shells, page 588
Large or individual Noodle Rings, page 188
Large or individual Rice Rings, page 180
A Pastry Roll, page 225
Biscuits or Shortcakes, page 583
A Mashed Potato Ring, page 290
A Bread Dressing Ring, page 234
Stuffed Pancakes, page 212
Waffles, page 216
Noodle Baskets or Potato Baskets, page 297

Stuffed vegetables
Sandwich Loaf, page 54
Barquettes, page 55
Turnovers, page 55
Leaf Wrappings, page 130
Coconut shells
Sea shells
And the 9 recipes that follow.

ROLL CASES
Preheat oven to 300°.
Hollow out:
  Small rolls
Spread the hollows with:
  Melted butter
Toast in the oven until crisp.

BREAD CASES
Preheat oven to 300°.
With a biscuit cutter make rounds from:
  1¼-inch-thick slices of bread
With a smaller cutter, press out an inner round, but do not let the cutter go beyond 1 inch deep. Hollow out these smaller rounds and brush the hollows with:
  Melted butter
Toast in the oven until crisp and golden.

MELBA TOAST BASKETS
Preheat oven to 275°.
Lightly butter on both sides:
  Thin crustless bread slices
Press them into muffin tins, letting the corners of the bread protrude slightly. Toast in the oven until crisp and golden.

ROSETTES
            About Thirty-Six 2½-Inch Rosettes
Rosettes are shaped with a small iron made for the purpose. They are very good served as a base for creamed chicken or sweetbreads. For dessert, serve with sweet sauce, stewed fruit or alone with coffee.
  ◆ This batter makes a thinner, crisper confection if it is allowed to rest refrigerated for 2 hours or more.
Beat until blended:
  2 eggs
Add and beat:
  ¼ teaspoon salt
  1 tablespoon sugar
If the rosettes are to be used as patties, omit the sugar. Sift before measuring:
  1 cup all-purpose flour
Stir it into the egg mixture, alternately with:
  1 cup milk
  2 tablespoons melted butter
To deep fry rosettes, prepare the iron by immersing the head of it in deep fat. You can use a rather small deep pan, slightly larger than the head of the iron, with

about 2½ inches of fat in it. Heat the fat
to 375°. Dip the hot iron in the batter,
but do not let it run over the top of the
iron, for then it is difficult to get the
rosette off when cooked. Return the bat-
ter-coated iron to the fat, immersing it

completely from 20 to 35 seconds. Remove the rosette with a fork. Reheat the
iron in the deep fat and repeat the process.
Drain the rosettes on absorbent paper and,
if served as a dessert, dust with:
    Confectioners' sugar

TIMBALE CASES FOR FOOD
Select a timbale iron that is fluted, see
above. It is easier to handle than a plain
one.
Sift:
    ¾ cup all-purpose flour
    ½ teaspoon salt
Combine and beat:
    1 egg
    ½ cup milk
Combine the liquid and the sifted ingredients with a few swift strokes. Add:
    1 teaspoon olive oil or melted butter
Let the batter stand for 1 hour to avoid
bubbles which disfigure the timbales. For
a crisper, thinner case, rest the batter 2
hours or longer covered and refrigerated.
To fry timbale cases, prepare the iron by
immersing its head in deep fat. Heat the
fat to 370°—hot enough to brown a cube
of bread in 1 minute. Wipe the iron with
a cloth wrapped around a fork. Plunge
the iron into the batter, within ¾ inch of
the top. Remove it. Allow the batter to
dry slightly on the iron. Fry the timbale
in the hot fat until it is golden brown,
about 1 to 1½ minutes. Remove it from
the iron and drain it on a paper towel. Repeat the process.

ABOUT MEAT PASTRIES
How we'd love to judge a competition of
housewives, each turning out her native
meat pastry! The doughs would range
from the resilient to the flaky, with fillings
running a full gamut of flavor. They would
include: Won Ton, Ravioli, Kreplach,
Piroshki, Rissoles, Enchiladas, Pot Pies. It
is in such homely functional dishes, varied
according to the season and by the individual cook, that the true cuisine of a
country dwells. Many of these specialties
call for precooked fillings which, already

encased, need only a brief cooking of the
dough and reheating of the filler, either by
simmering in a broth, deep-fat frying,
sautéing or baking.
Take your pick of the recipes following
and those in hors d'oeuvre and soup garnishes. Size often dictates their placement
in the menu.
    ♦ Cooking method will determine
whether or not to vent the pastry. A baked
meat pie will need a vent. Some cooks
leave a hole in the center by which to add
more gravy, if necessary. Others just prick
the surface to allow the steam to escape
and to prevent a soggy crust. If simmered
like Won Ton, page 147, or fried like Rissoles, page 55, do not vent. If covering a
stew with biscuits, allow steam to escape
by leaving spaces between the biscuits.
This wide spacing also applies to dumpling toppings.

**TURNOVERS, PIROSHKI OR ROLLS
FILLED WITH MEAT, ETC.**
                                    6 Servings
Preheat oven to 450°.
This recipe and the following one make
excellent hot canapés. For canapés, cut
the dough into small, attractive shapes.
For hot luncheon sandwiches, make them
a more generous size. If prepared in advance, keep them chilled until ready to
bake.
Prepare, using about 2 cups of flour:
    Biscuit or Pie Dough, pages 583, 588
Pat or roll it until thin. This is a matter of
taste—about ¼ inch for biscuit dough, ⅛
inch for pie dough. Cut it into 3 x 3-inch
squares or rounds. Place a filling on each
piece of dough—as much as they will hold
properly. Moisten the edges, fold over and
pinch down with a fork. Place the triangles or crescents in a pan. Brush them
lightly with:
    (Soft butter)
Bake them until the dough is done, about
20 minutes. This may be served with:
    Brown Sauce, page 326
Fillings
I. Lightly moisten:
    Ground or minced cooked meat
with:
    Gravy or cream, Brown Sauce, page
    326, or canned Soup Sauce, page 333
Season it well with:
    Salt and pepper
    Worcestershire sauce or chili sauce

II. Moisten braunschweiger sausage with
chili sauce or tomato soup.

III. Use:
    1½ cups cooked ground ham
    ½ cup Cream Sauce II, page 322
        thick cream or evaporated milk
    2 tablespoons chopped pickles
    1 tablespoon chopped onion

1½ tablespoons catsup
    Salt and pepper, if needed

IV. Sauté gently until yellow:
    2 cups chopped onions
in:
    3 tablespoons olive or anchovy oil
Add:
    ¼ cup or more chopped ripe olives
    6 or 8 chopped anchovies

V. Use any good cooked seafood filling and taste before seasoning.

MEAT PIE ROLL OR PIN WHEELS
4 Servings

Preheat oven to 450°.
This is a palatable, quickly made, everyday dish—an attractive way to serve a small quantity of leftover meat.
Use one of the fillings given in the previous recipe.
Use the recipes on pages 583, 588, or a biscuit mix to make:
    Biscuit Dough or Pie Dough: use 2
    cups of flour
If you use biscuit dough, make it a little drier than for ordinary biscuits, otherwise it will be difficult to handle. Roll it until very thin. Cut it into an oblong. Use a pastry brush and brush it lightly with:
    1 egg white or soft butter
This will keep the crust from being soggy. Spread the dough with the meat filling, being careful to leave about 1 inch at the sides uncovered. Begin to roll it loosely. Moisten the end with water and plaster it down. Moisten the sides and pinch them together. Bake the roll until it is done, about 20 minutes. Or cut the roll into ¼-inch slices. Place the slices in a lightly greased pan. Dot the tops with:
    Butter
This roll may be prepared in advance and placed in the refrigerator until ready for use. Bake the slices until the dough is done. Serve tnem very hot with:
    Brown Sauce, page 326, or Tomato
    Sauce, page 333

MEAT SHORTCAKES
10 Cakes

Preheat oven to 350°.
Prepare, omitting the sugar:
    Fluffy Buscuit Dough, page 584
If a richer dough is desired, use an additional tablespoon of butter. Combine:
    ¼ cup cream
    ¾ cup deviled ham
Ground cooked ham or other meat may be substituted. In that case ¼ teaspoon prepared mustard, 2 teaspoons minced onion or other seasoning may be added. Roll out the dough on a lightly floured board to the thickness of ¼ to ⅓ inch. Spread ½ of it with the ham mixture. Fold over the other ½, so that the ham is between the layers

of dough. Cut the dough with a biscuit cutter. Bake the cakes for about 15 minutes until done.

QUICK CHICKEN OR BEEF POT PIE
Preheat oven to 400°.
An easy dish if you have precooked chicken or beef and precooked pie crust shells. We find the precooked shell more convenient and tastier than the crust which has to be exposed to long, slow cooking.
Have ready:
    A baked Pie Shell, page 590
formed to fit your casserole or individual bakers. Heat.
    Creamed chicken, Chicken or Turkey
    Hash, page 235, or Beef Hash,
    page 233
Fill the shell with the meat filling and top with:
    A prebaked pie topping, Biscuit
    Dough, page 583, or slices of bread
    buttered on both sides
Bake until thoroughly heated and the top is light brown.

CORN BREAD TAMALE PIE
6 Servings

Preheat oven to 425°.
This can be prepared up to the point of adding the corn bread topping; then cooled and refrigerated until 45 minutes before serving time. Place the casserole in the oven and let it warm while you are mixing the corn bread topping.
Sauté in a lightly greased skillet:
    1 pound ground beef
    1 chopped onion
When the meat is lightly browned and the onion translucent, add:
    1 can tomato soup
    1 cup water or stock
    ¼ teaspoon pepper
    1 teaspoon salt
    1 tablespoon chili powder
    1 cup drained whole kernel corn
    ½ cup chopped green pepper, seeds
    and fiber removed
Simmer for 15 minutes. Meanwhile, sift and mix together:
    ¾ cup corn meal
    1 tablespoon flour
    1 tablespoon sugar
    ½ teaspoon salt
    1½ teaspoons baking powder
Moisten with:
    1 beaten egg
    ⅓ cup milk
Mix lightly and fold in:
    1 tablespoon cooking oil
Place meat mixture in a greased 2-quart casserole and cover with the corn bread topping. The topping will disappear into the meat mixture, but will rise during baking and form a good layer of corn bread. Place in oven and bake for about 20 to 25 minutes or until corn bread is brown.

CHINESE EGG ROLLS
6 Servings or 12 Egg Rolls
Egg rolls are frequently used for hors
d'oeuvre or you may serve them as the
main dish at luncheon. The pancake-like
skins are available at Chinese grocery
stores, although in an emergency you may
make a thin Won Ton dough, page 147, or
use the following:
Sift into a bowl:
> 1 cup flour

Beat in:
> 2 eggs
> ½ teaspoon salt

Add gradually to make a thin, smooth
batter:
> 2 cups water

Grease a 6-inch-diameter skillet and put
over ♦ low heat. Beat the batter again and
pour 1 tablespoon into the pan. Let it
spread over the surface of the pan to form
a very thin, flexible pancake. When it
shrinks away from the sides, turn it and
let it set on the other side. Do not let it
become brown or crisp. Remove each pancake to a dish when done and cover all
with a damp cloth until ready to use.
You may prepare the filling the day before,
as it should be chilled before being enclosed in the pancake envelope. Bring
to a boil in ½ cup water, then drain:
> ½ cup finely chopped celery
> ¾ cup shredded cabbage

Heat in a skillet:
> 3 tablespoons salad oil

Stir-fry, see page 253, for 3 minutes:
> ½ cup diced cooked shrimp
> ½ cup diced cooked pork

Add and stir-fry for 5 more minutes:
> 4 finely chopped scallions
> ½ cup drained and finely chopped
>   water chestnuts
> 1 minced clove garlic
> ¼ cup soy sauce

Place 4 tablespoons of filling in rectangular shape on the center of each pancake
and fold up envelope-style, sealing the last
flap with a paste made of:
> 1 tablespoon flour
> 2 tablespoons cold water

Preheat deep fryer to 375°.
Fry rolls until golden brown. Or fill a
deep skillet with oil about 1 inch deep up
the sides and fry the egg rolls until golden
brown. Serve with:
> Chinese Mustard
> Soy sauce
> Chinese Sweet-Sour Sauce I,
> page 330

PIZZAS
These Italian pies—pizza is the Italian
word for pie—have become very popular
luncheon and supper dishes. The pizza
began as a use for leftover bread dough.
The Italians sometimes use pastry as the
base and, in an emergency, we have successfully used sliced English muffins. A
slice of cheese over the whole first—before
the sauce—keeps it from getting soggy.
To make pizza dough, mix as for Bread,
page 556, using the following ingredients,
but do not let it rise a second time:
> 4 cups sifted flour
> 1 cake yeast in 1⅛ cups 85° water
> 2 tablespoons salad or olive oil
> 1 teaspoon salt

Knead for 10 minutes. Cover with damp
cloth and let rise about 2 hours. Have ready
two oiled 12-inch pizza pans. Pat and stretch
the dough in the pans, pinching up a collar
around the edge to hold the filling. Prick
dough in about 6 places.
Preheat oven to 400°.
Spread each pizza with your preferred filling and rest it for about 10 minutes. (At
this stage the pizzas may be frozen for at
least a week before baking.) Bake for about
25 minutes until light brown and serve at
once very hot.

I. Spread the pizza with:
> (A thin slice of cheese)
> Thickened Tomato Sauce, page 333,
> or Italian Tomato Paste, page 334

Arrange on top:
> 12 to 14 anchovies or sliced Italian
>   sausage, pepperoni, Prosciutto ham
>   or Salami

Sprinkle with:
> Orégano
> Olive oil
> Chopped parsley
> (Parmesan or Romano cheese)

II. Use a highly seasoned:
> Meat Sauce for Spaghetti, page 335,
> or other meat pasta sauce

Cover with a layer of:
> Fontina or Mozzarella cheese

III. Use as a base:
> Thickened Tomato Sauce, page 333

Add:
> 1 cup chopped or sliced mushrooms

IV. Cover the base with:
> Lightly sautéed onions
> Black olives
> Anchovies

Brush with:
> Olive oil

ENCHILADAS
About 2 Dozen
Preheat oven to 350°.
Have ready:
> Baked tortillas

In a heavy saucepan, heat:
> 2 tablespoons olive oil

Sauté until golden:
> ½ cup chopped onion
> 1 minced clove garlic

Add:
> 2 teaspoons to 1 tablespoon chili
>   powder

1 cup tomato purée
½ cup chicken or beef stock
Season with:
Salt and pepper
1 teaspoon cumin
Spread some sauce over the tortillas and fill
the centers with equal quantities of:
Chopped raw onion
Chopped Mozzarella cheese
Roll the tortillas and place in an oven-
proof dish. Pour more sauce over the tops
and sprinkle with:
Chopped Mozzarella cheese
Heat thoroughly about 15 minutes in the
oven.

ABOUT QUICHES

Early recipes for Quiche called for bacon
and cream, but gradually cheese was
added. When sautéed onions were included, the dish was called **Alsacienne.**
Cool the onions before adding them.

Quiche makes a hefty brunch or an hors
d'oeuvre baked in tiny tarts no larger than
the lining of muffin tins. As it is always
served lukewarm, time it accordingly. Following are several variations on a Quiche
theme.

QUICHE LORRAINE

6 Servings

Preheat oven to 375°.
Prepare a 9-inch pie shell of:
A Pie Crust, page 588
Brush it with:
The white of an egg
and prick it well. Slice in 1-inch lengths:
¼ lb. sliced bacon
Cook the bacon in a heavy skillet, stirring
constantly, until the fat is almost rendered
out but the bacon is not yet crisp. Drain
on absorbent toweling. Scald to hasten
the cooking time:
2 cups milk or cream
Cool slightly, then beat together with:
3 whole eggs
¼ teaspoon salt
⅛ teaspoon white pepper
A fresh grating of nutmeg
1 teaspoon chopped chives
Sprinkle in the bottom of the pie shell the
bacon and:
½ cup diced Swiss cheese
Pour the custard mixture over it. Bake 35
to 40 minutes or until the top is a golden
brown. For safety, you may test as for
Custard, page 684.

CHEESE CUSTARD PIE

4 Servings

Preheat oven to 325°.
In Switzerland we had a vile-tempered
cook named Marguerite. Her one idea,
after being generally disagreeable, was to
earn enough to own a small chalet on some
high peak where she could cater to mountain climbers. While she was certainly not
born with a silver spoon in her mouth—

although it was large enough to accommodate several—she did arrive with a cooking spoon in her hand. If she has attained
her ideal, many a climber will feel it worth
while to scale a perilous peak to reach her
kitchen. The following Cheese Custard
Pie was always served in solitary state. Its
flavor varied with Marguerite's moods and
her supply of cheese. It was never twice
the same, as she had no written recipe, but
we have endeavored to make one like hers,
for it would be a pity to relegate so good
a dish to inaccessible roosts.
Prepare and bake:
An 8-inch baked Pie Crust, page 588
It should be at least 2 inches deep. When
cool, brush with:
Egg white
Scald:
1¾ cups milk or cream
Reduce the heat and add:
1 cup grated cheese
Stir until the cheese is melted. Add:
½ teaspoon salt
¼ teaspoon paprika
½ teaspoon grated onion
A few grains cayenne
Remove the mixture from the heat and
beat in, one at a time:
3 eggs
Fill the pie crust and bake it until the custard is firm, about 45 minutes.

ONION SHORTCAKE

6 Servings

Preheat oven to 425°.
Peel and slice:
10 medium-sized white onions
Sprinkle them with:
½ teaspoon salt
Melt in a saucepan:
3 tablespoons butter
Add the onions. Cover and simmer until
they are tender. Cool them. Prepare ½
the amount on page 584:
Fluffy Biscuit Dough
omitting the sugar.
Spread the dough in a deep greased ovenproof dish. Cover it with the cooked
onions. Add:
¼ teaspoon paprika
2 teaspoons chopped parsley
(½ cup diced cooked ham)
A grating nutmeg or white pepper
Prepare:
1 cup Cream Sauce I, page 322
Beat into the sauce:
1 egg
Pour the sauce over the onions. The top
may be sprinkled with:
¼ cup grated cheese
Bake the cake for about 20 minutes or until the dough is done.

ONION OR LEEK PIE

Preheat oven to 450°.
Richer and more sophisticated than **the**
preceding Onion Shortcake. Serve Onion

Shortcake with a meat course. Have Onion Pie as a main dish with a green salad.

Line a 9-inch pie pan with:

Pie Dough, page 588

Prick and chill it. Skin and slice thinly:

2½ lbs. Bermuda onions or leeks

Melt in a heavy saucepan:

3 tablespoons butter

Add the onions. Stir and cook them over low heat until they are clear. Cool them well. Combine and heat slowly until blended:

3 eggs
1 cup cultured sour cream
¼ cup dry sherry
1 teaspoon salt
¼ teaspoon freshly ground pepper
(1 tablespoon minced fresh herb or
1 teaspoon dill or celery seed)

Stir this mixture into the onions. Brush the bottom of the cooled pie shell with:

1 slightly beaten egg white

Fill it with the slightly cooled onion mixture. Place over the top:

(4 strips bacon cut into squares)
(Small cooked link sausages)

Bake the pie in a 450° oven for 10 minutes. ◆ Reduce the heat to 300° and bake the pie until the crust is light brown, about ½ hour. Serve it piping hot.

QUICK TOMATO TART

6 Servings

Preheat oven to 350°.

Have ready:

2 baked, unsweetened, 2½-inch tart
shells, page 590

Slice ½ inch thick:

6 peeled seeded fresh tomatoes

Mix and heat well:

¼ cup sautéed sliced mushrooms
¼ cup canned cream of chicken soup
¼ cup Italian tomato purée
¼ teaspoon sugar
¼ cup softened liver sausage
4 large chopped stuffed olives
2 teaspoons fresh chopped basil
¼ teaspoon salt

First place a layer of this hot sauce in each tart shell, then a tomato slice. Cover with the remaining hot mixture. Dust each tart with:

Grated Parmesan cheese

Heat the filled tarts on a baking sheet in the oven for about 15 minutes or until well heated.

MIXED VEGETABLE GRILL

A good Lenten dish if you omit the bacon and sausages.

Preheat broiler.

Cut into slices:

Tomatoes

Brush them with:

Melted butter

Season them with:

Salt and pepper
Brown sugar

Prepare for cooking:

Mushrooms

Brush them with:

Melted butter or heavy cream

Season them lightly with:

Salt
(Lemon juice)

Grease the broiler. Place on it the tomato slices, mushrooms and:

(Sliced bacon)
(Sausages)

Broil these ingredients until they are done. Meanwhile sauté or poach:

Eggs

Serve the eggs on a hot platter, surrounded by the grilled food. Garnish the platter with:

Parsley, olives, radishes, etc.

ROAST BEEF IN SAUCE

I.   4 Servings

Cut into ½-inch cubes:

2 cups cooked roast beef

Prepare:

Hot Cumberland Sauce, page 331

Add the beef and heat the sauce, but do not boil. Serve at once on:

Hot toast

II. Prepare:

Creole Sauce, page 336, or Curry
Sauce II, page 325

Arrange very thin slices of:

Cooked roast beef

on a hot platter. Pour the hot sauce over them. Sprinkle the top with:

Chopped parsley or chopped chives

BOEUF MIROTON

Make a sauce by melting:

2 tablespoons butter

Sauté in it until golden:

1 coarsely sliced onion

Sprinkle over all and mix rapidly with a wooden spoon:

1 tablespoon flour

Add and stir until boiling:

1 cup bouillon
Salt and pepper

Reduce the heat and add:

1 to 2 teaspoons vinegar

Simmer about 15 minutes. Arrange on a heatproof platter:

Thin slices of boiled or roasted beef

Cover the slices with the above hot sauce. Keep on low heat for about 20 minutes and serve.

DEVILED LEFTOVER MEAT

Preheat broiler.

Spread:

Cooked sliced meat

with:

Prepared mustard or catsup

Roll the slices in:

Buttered bread crumbs

Broil them until browned. Serve the meat with:

Leftover gravy, Piquant Sauce, page
327, or Brown Onion Sauce, page 327

CREAMED LEFTOVER VEAL
6 Servings

Melt in a chafing dish or electric skillet:
- ¼ cup butter

Add and sauté for about 5 minutes:
- ½ lb. sliced mushrooms
- ¼ cup diced green pepper, seeds
  and membranes removed

Add and stir well:
- ¼ cup flour

Pour over the mixture and stir until thickened:
- ½ cup cream
- 1 cup veal or chicken stock

Correct the seasoning and add:
- 2 cups diced cooked veal
- 2 tablespoons minced pimiento
- ¼ teaspoon marjoram
- ½ cup dry white wine

Simmer about 5 minutes longer and serve over:
- Rice, noodles or macaroni

Garnish with:
- Chopped parsley

VEAL AND SPINACH DISH

Preheat oven to 425°.

Place in a casserole a 1-inch layer or more of:
- Creamed spinach

which has been delicately flavored with a little:
- Grated onion

Place over it:
- Slices of roast veal or lamb, etc.

If you have gravy, pour a little of it over the meat or use a little thick cream. Cover the top with:
- Au Gratin III, page 342

Bake the dish until the top is brown. Garnish it with:
- Parsley

COOKED CURRIED VEAL OR LAMB AND RICE
4 Servings

This combination of meat, apple and curry is luscious. Peel and slice:
- 1 cup onions
- (½ cup celery)

Core, peel and slice:
- 2 medium-sized apples

Melt in a saucepan:
- 3 tablespoons butter

Add:
- ½ to 1 teaspoon curry powder

Caution: use only ½ teaspoon curry to begin with if you are unfamiliar with it. Add the onions and apples and sauté until the onions are tender. Remove them from the pan. Brown lightly in the pan about:
- 2 cups sliced or diced cooked veal
  or lamb

Remove it from the pan. Stir into the pan juices:
- 2 teaspoons flour

Stir in slowly:
- 1 cup Stock, page 490

When the sauce is smooth and boiling, add the onions, apples and meat. Stir in:
- 1 tablespoon lemon juice
- Correct the seasoning

and serve the meat with:
- Steamed or boiled rice

LAMB TERRAPIN
4 Servings

Cut into dice:
- 2 cups cold cooked lamb

Chop or rice:
- 2 hard-cooked eggs

Combine the lamb, the eggs and:
- 2 tablespoons olive oil
- 1 tablespoon lemon juice

Melt:
- 2 tablespoons butter

Stir in until blended:
- 3 tablespoons flour
- 1 teaspoon dry mustard

Stir in slowly:
- 2 cups lamb stock or milk

Add:
- 1 teaspoon Worcestershire sauce
- Salt, as needed

Cook and stir the sauce until it is boiling. Add the lamb and egg mixture. Heat the terrapin thoroughly. Serve it on:
- Hot toast

CHOP SUEY OR CHOW MEIN
4 Servings

These vaguely Chinese dishes which can be made with cooked pork, chicken or seafood, differ in that Chop Suey is served over steamed rice, and Chow Mein over fried noodles. They resemble some Chinese porcelain patterns originally made strictly for export. To get the feeling of true Chinese food, read Mrs. Buwei Yang Chao's delightful "How to Cook and Eat in Chinese."

Cut into 2 inch julienne strips about ¼ inch in section:
- 2 cups cooked pork roast

Sliced diagonally, see page 407:
- ½ cup celery with tender leaves
- ½ cup green onions
- 1 cup mushrooms

Chop coarsely:
- 1 green pepper, seeds and membrane
  removed

Drain:
- 1 cup bean sprouts

Heat well in a deep heavy skillet:
- 2 tablespoons cooking oil

Stir-fry, page 253, the onion and celery for about 3 minutes. Then add the mushrooms, pork, peppers and the bean sprouts. Continue to stir-fry for 2 to 3 minutes longer. Then add:
- (½ cup fresh, peeled, seeded, and
  slivered tomatoes)
- Jellied juices from the roast or a bit
  of Meat Glaze, page 492
- 1 cup strong consommé

Season with:
> Salt and pepper
> 1 tablespoon soy sauce
> 3 tablespoons dry sherry

You may thicken the juices with:
> Cornstarch

Serve at once.

LEFTOVERS IN BACON

Preheat oven to 450°.
Measure:
> Cooked ground meat, meat loaf, etc.

Add ⅓ this measure of:
> Boiled Rice

Moisten it lightly with:
> Gravy or cream

Season it well with:
> Salt and pepper
> Minced onion or onion juice

Roll the mixture into small balls, flatten them slightly and wrap around them:
> Slices of bacon

Secure the bacon with toothpicks. Place the patties in a greased pan or dish and bake them until the bacon is crisp, about 15 minutes. Serve them with:
> Tomato Sauce, page 333

HAM LOAF WITH COOKED HAM
6 Servings

Preheat oven to 350°.
Combine:
> 2 cups cooked ground ham
> 1 cup bread or cracker crumbs or crushed cornflakes
> 2 eggs
> 2 tablespoons grated onion
> ⅛ teaspoon pepper
> 1 cup milk
> 2 tablespoons chili sauce
> 2 to 4 tablespoons chopped parsley or celery

Bake these ingredients in a greased loaf pan for about 45 minutes. Serve the loaf with:
> Tomato, Horseradish, Mustard, Mushroom or some other sauce, page 327

STUFFED HAM ROLLS

I.   4 Servings
Make these when you have leftover rice.
Preheat oven to 400°.
Trim:
> 8 thin slices baked or boiled ham

Spread them lightly with:
> Mustard

Place on each slice part of the following filling. Combine:
> 1½ cups cooked rice
> ⅛ cup chopped raisins
> 1 beaten egg
> ¼ teaspoon paprika
> ½ teaspoon Worcestershire sauce

> (¼ cup chopped celery)
> (½ teaspoon basil)

Roll the slices and secure them with toothpicks. Brush them with:
> Milk

Bake the rolls until they are thoroughly heated. Serve them with:
> Hot Cumberland Sauce, page 331

II. Prepare, as for above:
> Slices of ham

Place on each slice:
> 4 asparagus tips

Roll, brush and heat the ham, as directed. Serve the rolls with:
> 1½ cups Cheese Sauce, page 326

III.   4 Servings
Preheat oven to 350°.
Prepare, as for above:
> 8 large slices ham

Combine and mix well:
> ¾ cup cultured sour cream
> 1 cup sieved creamy cottage cheese
> 1 slightly beaten egg
> ¼ cup minced onions
> ½ cup drained chopped cooked spinach
> ½ teaspoon dry mustard
> ¼ teaspoon salt

Place about 2 tablespoons filling on each slice of ham. Roll and tuck in the edges. Put in a shallow baking dish and cover with the following mixture:
> 1 can cream of mushroom soup: 10½ oz.
> ¼ cup cultured sour cream

Bake for 20 to 25 minutes.

GROUND HAM ON PINEAPPLE SLICES
4 Servings

Preheat oven to 400°.
Combine:
> 1 cup cooked ground ham
> 1 teaspoon prepared mustard
> 2 tablespoons mayonnaise

Spread this mixture on:
> 4 slices drained pineapple

Bake the slices in a greased pan for about 10 minutes.

HAM AND POTATO CAKES
4 Servings

Combine:
> 1 cup mashed potatoes
> 1 cup ground cooked ham
> 1 tablespoon chopped parsley
> ½ teaspoon grated onion
> ⅛ teaspoon pepper
> Salt, if needed

Shape this mixture into flat cakes. Dip them lightly in:
> Flour

Sauté them in:
> Bacon drippings or other fat

HAM CAKES WITH PINEAPPLE AND SWEET POTATOES
6 Servings

Boil by the recipe on page 298:

3 large sweet potatoes

Preheat oven to 375°.

Combine:

2 cups cooked chopped or ground ham
½ cup dry bread crumbs
2 eggs
⅛ teaspoon salt
1 teaspoon prepared mustard

Shape these ingredients into 6 flat cakes. Melt in a skillet:

5 tablespoons bacon drippings

Brown lightly in the skillet:

6 slices drained pineapple

Remove them and brown the ham cakes in the skillet. Place the pineapple slices in a baking dish and cover each slice with a ham cake. Peel the sweet potatoes. Cut them lengthwise into halves. Combine and sprinkle over them:

¼ teaspoon cloves
¼ cup brown sugar

Cook them slowly in the skillet until they are well caramelized. Place them in the baking dish. Baste them with:

Pineapple juice

Bake the dish for about 10 minutes.

HAM À LA KING
6 Servings

Prepare:

2 cups Cream Sauce I, page 322

When the sauce is boiling, add:

2 cups cooked diced ham
2 diced hard-cooked eggs
1 cup Sautéed Mushrooms, page 281
or canned mushrooms with sliced stuffed olives
1 tablespoon chopped green pepper
1 tablespoon chopped pimiento

Serve the ham very hot on:

Rounds of toast, on rusks, in bread cases or on corn bread squares

Garnish with:

Chopped parsley

▤ BARBECUED FRANKFURTERS, WIENERS OR HOT DOGS

Preheat broiler or grill.

Grill or put:

Frankfurters, wieners or hot dogs

on a rack in a roasting pan. During the cooking baste them ♦ constantly with:

Barbecue Sauce, page 332

▤ FRANKFURTER KEBABS
8 Servings

Preheat grill or broiler.

Cut into about 4 pieces each:

8 frankfurters

Marinate about 30 minutes in:

French Dressing, page 311

Skewer the pieces alternately with bits of:

Bacon
Small canned pickled onions
Green pepper

Grill or broil, turning often.

FRANKFURTERS OR SAUSAGE IN SAUCES
I.   **3 Servings**

Preheat oven to 400°.

Place in a shallow pan:

6 frankfurter sausages

Prepare:

1 cup Tomato Sauce, page 333
or Barbecue Sauce, page 332

Add:

(Chopped green peppers, seeded and veined)
(Grated onions or chives)

Pour these ingredients over the sausages. Bake them until they swell and the sauce thickens.

II. Prepare, using no salt:

Creole Sauce, page 336, or Quick Tomato Sauce, page 333

Season it well with:

Paprika

Cook:

Vienna Sausages, page 437

Drain them. Heat them in the sauce. Serve with:

Boiled Rice, Noodles, page 188
or Mashed Potatoes, page 290

SAUSAGE BAKED WITH APPLES
4 Servings

Preheat oven to 400°.

Arrange in a baking dish:

8 partially cooked pork sausages

Core:

6 tart apples

Cut them into ¼-inch slices and place them around the sausages. Sprinkle them with:

¾ cup brown sugar

Bake the dish in a hot oven 400° for 10 minutes. ♦ Reduce the heat to 350° and continue baking for about 15 minutes longer. Baste with the drippings.

SAUSAGES AND MUSHROOMS

Fine for brunch.

Prepare:

Mashed Potatoes, page 290, or
Boiled Mashed Chestnuts, page 272

Heap them in a mound on a hot platter. Keep them hot. Cook:

Sausages, page 437

Place them around the potatoes. Sauté in the drippings:

Mushrooms, page 281

Garnish the platter with them and:

Sprigs of parsley

Pour the drippings over the potatoes.

SAUSAGE AND ONIONS
4 Servings

Heat in a skillet:

2 tablespoons oil or fat

Add:

1½ cups slivered onions

Cook and stir these over low heat for about 15 minutes until light brown. Cut a lengthwise slit in:

8 wiener sausages or frankfurters
Fill them with the onions. Fasten them with toothpicks. Broil them slowly on both sides. You may place them in:
Lightly toasted buns

LENTIL AND SAUSAGE CASSEROLE
4 Servings
Preheat oven to 400°.
Place in a greased ovenproof dish:
1 cup cooked lentils
Place in boiling water and simmer for 10 minutes:
1 lb. small link or other sausages
Drain them. Place them on top of the lentils. Bake the dish uncovered until the sausages are brown.

PIGS IN POTATOES
3 Servings
Preheat deep-fat fryer to 375°.
Combine and beat well:
1 teaspoon minced onion
1 teaspoon minced parsley
2 cups Mashed Potatoes, page 290
1 egg yolk
Cook:
6 small Vienna sausages
or use:
Precooked pork sausages
Coat them with the potato mixture. Roll in:
Finely crushed bread crumbs
then in:
1 egg diluted with 1 tablespoon water or milk
then again in the crumbs. Fry the piggies until they are a golden brown.

BAKED CORNED BEEF
Preheat oven to 350°.
Remove whole from the can:
Corned beef
Stud it with:
Whole cloves
Make a paste by stirring a little water into:
¼ cup brown sugar
1 teaspoon chili powder
Add to it:
2 tablespoons chopped pickles
Spread the beef with the paste. Bake it for about 10 minutes.

CREAMED CHIPPED BEEF
4 Large Servings
◗ Do not oversalt.
Pull apart:
8 oz. chipped beef
Melt:
3 tablespoons butter
Sauté in it until light brown:
3 tablespoons minced onion
3 tablespoons minced green pepper
Sprinkle these with:
3 tablespoons flour
Add slowly, stirring constantly:
2 cups milk
Add the beef. Simmer these ingredients until they thicken. Remove from the heat and season with:

1 tablespoon chopped parsley or chives
¼ teaspoon paprika
2 tablespoons dry sherry
(2 tablespoons capers or chopped pickles)
Serve the beef on:
Hot buttered toast

CHIPPED BEEF IN CREOLE SAUCE
3 Servings
◗ Do not oversalt.
Prepare:
Quick Creole Sauce, page 333
Melt:
1 tablespoon butter
Sauté in it for 1 minute:
4 oz. shredded chipped beef
Add the sauce. Heat the dish. Serve it on:
Buttered toast

CHIPPED BEEF IN CHEESE SAUCE
2 Servings
◗ Do not oversalt.
Prepare:
1 cup Cheese Sauce, page 326
Add to it:
4 oz. or more shredded chipped beef
Heat it. Serve it over:
Hot corn bread squares
This may be served in pancakes.

CHIPPED BEEF AND
SWEET POTATO CASSEROLE
5 Servings
Preheat oven to 375°.
◗ Do not oversalt.
Cut into cubes:
5 cooked or canned sweet potatoes
Shred:
¼ lb. dried beef
Prepare:
¼ cup grated onion
1½ cups Cream Sauce I, page 322, or canned cream soup
Place these ingredients in layers in a greased casserole. Cover the top with:
Crushed cornflakes
Dot it with:
Butter or cheese
Bake for ½ hour.

CHIPPED BEEF OR CORNED BEEF
IN CANNED SOUP
4 to 5 Servings
◗ Do not oversalt.
Combine and heat:
1 can cream soup—mushroom, celery, asparagus, etc.: 10½ oz.
6 tablespoons milk or Stock, page 490
⅛ teaspoon freshly ground nutmeg
A grating of black pepper
Add:
8 oz. shredded chipped beef or 1 cup canned diced corned beef
1 cup leftover vegetables
Heat these ingredients. Serve them on:
Toast or hot biscuits

sprinkled with:
> Chopped parsley, chives or grated
> cheese

Or you may boil until nearly tender:
> 10 small onions

Drain them and place them in a baking dish, pour the soup and beef mixture over them. Cover the top with:
> Crushed potato chips

Bake the dish in a 400° oven for about 15 minutes.

ABOUT HASH

Hash has its ups and downs.

The Irish cook was praised for her hash and she said: "Beef ain't nothing. Onions ain't nothing. Seasoning's nothing. But when I throw myself into my hash, that's hash!" The usual way to make hash is to cut the meat from a chicken or turkey carcass or from a roast beef, combine it with leftover gravy, reheat it briefly and season it acceptably. Never overcook it. There should be about ½ as much gravy as other ingredients. Have sauce or gravy boiling vigorously. Put in the solids ♦ reduce the heat at once and let them warm through thoroughly. If heating hash in the oven, be sure to use a lid or a topping, see Gratins, page 342.

You may add, in addition to the meat, cooked mushrooms, celery or potatoes, chopped olives, green peppers, parsley or some other herb or anything else that seems suitable. The proportions may be varied. This is a matter of taste and expediency. In the absence of gravy, sweet or sour cream or a sauce—cream, tomato, creole, etc.—may be substituted. Or you may add a sauce or cream to the gravy to obtain the desired amount. When using cream, reheat the hash in a double boiler as boiling thins it. Sherry, Madeira or dry wine may be added. Hash may be served in a pastry shell, in a rice or noodle ring, etc.

BEEF AND HAM HASH WITH POTATOES AND MUSHROOMS

Cut into cubes equal parts of:
> Cooked roast beef and cooked or
> smoked ham
> Raw pared potatoes

Reserve the beef. Place in a saucepan the ham and potatoes. Cover them with:
> Brown Sauce, page 326

Cover these ingredients and simmer for 15 minutes. Add:
> ½ lb. or more sliced mushrooms

Simmer them covered for 15 minutes longer. Add the beef. Reheat the hash, but do not permit it to boil. Season it with:
> Garlic salt
> A pinch basil, thyme or savory
> Dry sherry
> Salt, if needed

Serve it on:
> Hot toast

garnished with:
> Chopped parsley

This dish may be made without the ham.

SAUTÉED OR BROWNED HASH
4 Servings

Combine and grind:
> 1½ cups cooked meat
> ½ cup raw cubed potatoes with or
> without skins
> 1 medium-sized onion

Season with:
> Salt, pepper, celery seed

Turn these ingredients into a hot well-greased skillet. Cook the hash over medium heat until a crust forms on the bottom, turn it and brown the other side. Stir it from time to time to let the hash brown throughout. Shortly before it is done, pat it down firmly to form an unbroken cake. This requires about ½ hour cooking in all. Serve the hash with:
> Catsup or Tomato Sauce, page 333

QUICK HASH
4 Servings

Heat over very low heat:
> 1 can cream of mushroom soup: 10½ oz.

Stir in gradually:
> ¼ cup milk

Add:
> 1 cup cubed cooked ham or meat:
> frankfurters, hamburgers, etc.
> 2 sliced hard-cooked eggs

Season the hash with:
> A pinch dried basil or thyme
> Salt and pepper
> (Chopped parsley)

Serve it over:
> Hot corn bread or toast

HASH WITH VEGETABLES
6 Servings

This is an excellent combination. If it is not feasible to use all the ingredients given, it will still be good.
Preheat oven to 350°.
Prepare:
> ½ cup cooked diced potatoes
> ⅓ cup cooked diced onions
> ⅓ cup seeded sliced green peppers
> ⅓ cup cooked chopped celery
> 3 tablespoons diced pimientos
> 2 cups cold cooked meat, cut into
> ⅛-inch cubes

Combine and heat to boiling:
> 1 cup leftover gravy
> ⅓ cup tomato purée
> 1 tablespoon butter
> Salt and pepper, as required
> 1 teaspoon Worcestershire sauce

Add the meat and vegetables. If there is no available gravy, make it with 2 tablespoons butter, 2 tablespoons flour and 1 cup of vegetable stock or water in which 1 beef cube has been dissolved. **Pour the** hash into 1 large baking dish or into 6 individual baking dishes. Sprinkle the top with:

Au Gratin III, page 342

Or cover it with green pepper rings and seasoned slices of tomatoes dotted with butter. Brown the dish in the oven.

HASH IN CREAMED CABBAGE

Preheat oven to 400°.
Prepare:

Creamed Cabbage III, page 267

Place ½ the cabbage in a greased oven-proof dish. Place on top of it a layer of:

Hash moistened lightly with gravy or cream

Cover it with the remaining cabbage. Sprinkle the top with:

Au Gratin II or III, page 342

Bake the cabbage until the top is light brown.

SHEPHERD'S PIE

I. Preheat oven to 400°.
Prepare:

Hash

Spread it in a baking dish. Cover it with fresh hot:

Mashed Potatoes, page 290

Spread the top with:

Melted butter

Bake the dish until the potatoes are brown.

II. Preheat oven to 400°.
A very good way of using a small quantity of cold mashed potatoes and bits of meat or vegetable scraps.
Line individual molds with a wall ¼ inch thick of:

Leftover mashed potatoes

If the potatoes are very hard, soften them with:

1 or 2 tablespoons hot milk

Brush the inner walls with:

1 egg white

Moisten:

Chopped cooked meat and vegetables

with a small amount of:

Gravy, Tomato Sauce, page 333, Cream Sauce, page 322, or cream

Fill the molds and cover them with a layer of mashed potatoes. Brush the tops with:

Soft butter

Place the molds in a pan of hot water in the oven for 15 minutes or until the potatoes are brown.

BREAD DRESSING IN A RING FILLED WITH HASH, ETC.

Preheat oven to 400°.
Grease a ring mold. Fill it with:

Bread Dressing, page 456, Apple and Onion Dressing, page 458, etc.

Bake it until it is brown. Invert it onto a hot plate. Fill the center with:

Hash, or stewed creamed fresh or leftover vegetables

Good served with:

Leftover gravy or other sauce

CORNED BEEF HASH AND POTATOES

6 Servings

Grind, using coarse blade, or dice:

1½ lbs. cooked or canned corned beef: about 3 cups

Dice:

2 cups boiled potatoes

Melt in a large saucepan:

2 tablespoons butter

Stir in and simmer until tender:

**½ cup chopped onion
1 diced green pepper, seeds and fibers removed
2 ribs chopped celery
(1 clove garlic)
(1 cup mushrooms)**

Remove the garlic. Add the beef and potatoes and:

**1 tablespoon Worcestershire sauce
2 tablespoons minced parsley or chives
Salt and pepper, as needed**

Cook and stir lightly over medium heat while adding gradually:

⅛ to ⅔ cup Stock, page 490, or Cream Sauce III, page 322

Stir and cook till well blended and thoroughly heated. Place on a hot platter and serve topped with:

6 Poached Eggs, page 196

Or sauté the hash in a greased skillet until well browned on the bottom. Remove carefully, folding like an omelet, to serve.

CANNED CORNED BEEF HASH PATTIES

4 Servings

Sauté:

3 tablespoons chopped onion

in:

2 tablespoons butter

Add:

**2 tablespoons horseradish
½ teaspoon thyme
2 cups canned corned beef hash**

Form patties of this mixture. Sauté them on both sides in:

Hot butter or drippings

Sauté in the same pan:

Slices firm tomato

Season them with:

**Brown sugar
Salt and pepper**

Arrange the tomatoes and patties on a platter, garnished with:

Parsley

Or serve the patties with:

1½ cups Cream Sauce I, page 322

to which you may add:

2 chopped hard-cooked eggs
2 tablespoons chopped pickles

CHICKEN OR TURKEY HASH
4 Servings
♦ Please read About Hash, page 233.
Combine and heat:
   1½ cups diced cooked chicken or turkey
   ½ cup cooked drained celery or
      boiled potato cubes
   1 cup leftover chicken or turkey gravy
      or sauce
   1 tablespoon chopped parsley or chives
      Seasoning, as required
Serve the hash as suggested in About Hash,
page 233.

CREAMED CHICKEN OR VEAL
4 Servings
There is no reason why this dish should
not be delicious, whether it is made in a
luxurious way or with leftover food. Proportions, seasonings, etc., are unimportant,
provided that good combinations are
chosen.
Prepare:
   1 cup Cream Sauce I, page 322
Use cream and chicken stock or vegetable
water, with part gravy and part milk, etc.
Add:
   2 tablespoons chopped parsley
   2 cups minced cooked chicken or veal
   (¼ cup Sautéed Mushrooms, page 281)
Part of this may be cooked or canned vegetables. Season these ingredients with:
   1 teaspoon lemon juice or ½ teaspoon
      Worcestershire sauce or 2 teaspoons
      dry sherry
   (3 tablespoons chopped pickles or
      olives)
Add:
   Salt and pepper
   (Celery salt)
Grease a baking dish and put the creamed
mixture in it. Sprinkle the top with:
   Au Gratin II or III, page 342
   (½ cup blanched shredded almonds)
Place the dish under the broiler until the
crumbs are brown. The creamed ingredi-
ents may be served unbreaded on:
   Hot Waffles or in a Noodle or Rice
   Ring, pages 188, 180

CHICKEN À LA KING
4 Servings
Cut into dice:
   1 cup cooked chicken
   ½ cup Sautéed Mushrooms, page 281
   ¼ cup canned pimiento
Melt:
   3 tablespoons chicken fat or butter
Stir in and blend:
   3 tablespoons flour
Add slowly:
   1½ cups Chicken Stock, page 490,
      or cream
When the sauce is smooth and boiling, add

the chicken, mushrooms and pimiento. Reduce the heat. Pour some sauce over:
   1 egg yolk
Return mixture to pan. Stir and permit it
to thicken slightly. Add:
   Seasoning, if required
   (¼ cup blanched slivered almonds)
   (1 tablespoon dry sherry)
Serve the chicken at once. To reheat, place
in a saucepan over boiling water.

TURKEY OR CHICKEN CASSEROLE
WITH VEGETABLES
4 Servings
Prepare by cutting into cubes:
   2 cups cooked turkey or chicken
Melt:
   3 tablespoons butter
Stir in and sauté gently until lightly
browned:
   ½ cup diced celery
   ⅓ cup thinly sliced onions
   ⅓ cup thinly sliced green pepper,
      seeds and fibrous portions removed
Sprinkle over the top, stir in and cook
slowly for 5 minutes:
   3 tablespoons flour
Stir in gradually:
   1½ cups turkey or chicken stock
Remove the pot from the heat. Stir in:
   2 lightly beaten egg yolks
   Seasoning, as required
and the turkey meat. Stir over low heat
just long enough to let the sauce thicken
slightly. You may add:
   3 tablespoons dry white wine
   Correct the seasoning
Place the mixture in one large or in individual casseroles. Sprinkle the top with:
   Minced chives or parsley, nut meats
   or grated cheese
Serve at once. Good with rice or spoon
bread or on toast.

QUICK CHICKEN CREOLE
4 Servings
Melt:
   3 tablespoons chicken fat
Sauté in it:
   2 tablespoons chopped onion
   2 tablespoons chopped green pepper
   (1 minced clove garlic)
Stir in:
   3 tablespoons flour
   ¼ teaspoon salt
   ¼ teaspoon paprika
Add:
   ½ cup tomato purée or strained tomatoes
   1 cup chicken broth
Stir and cook these ingredients until they
boil. Add:
   1 teaspoon lemon juice
   ½ teaspoon horseradish
   2 cups cooked diced chicken meat
   ½ cup sliced Sautéed Mushrooms,
      page 281
   ½ cup chopped pimiento
   Salt, as needed

Serve the chicken in a:
>Rice Ring, page 180, or Noodle
>Ring, page 188

Just before serving, top with:
>(1 cup cultured sour cream)

COOKED TURKEY, CHICKEN OR VEAL LOAF
>4 to 6 Servings

Preheat oven to 350°.
Cook and stir for 1 minute:
>1½ tablespoons grated onion

in:
>1 tablespoon butter

Add it to:
>2 cups diced cooked turkey, chicken
>or veal
>¾ teaspoon salt
>1 cup cracker crumbs
>¾ cup gravy or thickened Chicken
>Stock, page 490
>¾ cup milk
>2 beaten eggs
>(½ cup finely chopped celery)
>(¾ teaspoon chili powder)

Place these ingredients in a well-greased loaf pan set in a pan of hot water. Bake the loaf for about 50 minutes. Serve it with:
>Leftover gravy with chopped olives
>Mushroom Sauce, page 281, or
>cream sauce with lots of chopped
>parsley or chives

QUANTITY CHICKEN LOAF
>16 to 24 Servings

This is a wonderfully stretchable recipe to serve at group meetings. It is rather firm and serves well sliced, covered with a sauce.
Preheat oven to 350°.
Remove meat carefully from:
>A 4 to 5 lb. stewed chicken

Shred it. Combine lightly with a fork:
>2 to 4 cups dry bread crumbs
>1 to 3 cups cooked rice
>1½ to 2 cups chicken broth, depending
>on how much rice and crumbs are
>added
>3 to 4 lightly-beaten eggs
>Correct the seasoning
>(½ cup chopped ripe olives)
>(½ cup slivered pistachio nuts)

Bake ♦ uncovered for about 25 to 30 minutes. Serve with:
>Chicken pan gravy, page 322, seasoned with a little lemon rind,
>parsley and 1/16 teaspoon saffron

or with:
>Quick à la King Sauce, page 333, or
>Mushroom Sauce, page 327, or
>Poulette Sauce, page 324

SWEETBREAD AND CHICKEN IN PATTY SHELLS OR BOUCHÉES À LA REINE
>4 Servings

A good party dish.
Prepare and keep warm:
>Timbale Cases, Bread Cases, page
>223, or Patty Shells, page 596

Prepare:
>1 cup Cream Sauce I, page 322

seasoned with a small amount of:
>Chablis or dry sherry

Add:
>½ cup blanched button mushroom caps
>¾ cup coarsely chopped cooked white
>chicken meat
>1 pair coarsely diced cooked
>sweetbreads

Heat thoroughly, but do not boil and, just before serving, fill the above cases to overflowing with the creamed mixture. Garnish with:
>Chopped parsley

CHICKEN OR TURKEY DIVAN
>4 Servings

Preheat oven to 400°.
Butter a 12 x 9-inch shallow heatproof dish or use individual oval steak platters. Place on the dish:
>(4 slices hot buttered toast or make a
>layer of butter crackers)

Next place a layer of:
>Slices of cooked chicken or turkey

The white meat is best. Allow 2 or 3 slices per serving. Partially cook and lay on top of the meat:
>1 package frozen broccoli or
>asparagus spears, cooked and well
>drained

Or use leftover cooked broccoli or asparagus. Cover the whole with:
>2 cups Mornay Sauce, page 323

Sprinkle with:
>Grated Parmesan cheese

and heat in the oven until the sauce is browned and bubbling. Serve at once.

DUCK PILAF
>4 Servings

A leftover duck and rice dish.
Remove the meat from:
>Roast duck

There should be about 2 cups. Break the carcasses apart. Add to them:
>4 cups water
>1 chopped onion
>Some celery leaves

Simmer this stock covered for 1 hour. Strain. Bring to boiling point. Stir in slowly, not disturbing the boiling:
>⅔ cup rice

Cook the rice until it is tender, for about ½ hour. Strain it. Reserve the liquor. Melt:
>2 tablespoons butter

Add and sauté covered for 5 minutes:
>¾ cup finely chopped celery
>1 teaspoon grated onion

Add the duck scraps, the rice and:
>1 cup leftover gravy, duck liquor
>or cream combined

Mix these ingredients well with a fork. Season them, if needed, with:
>Salt and paprika

Serve the pilaf hot with:
>Stewed plums or apricots

SEAFOOD À LA KING
4 Servings

Combine:
  1 cup canned lobster, crab meat, etc.
  3 peeled, diced, hard-cooked eggs
  1 chopped pimiento
Sauté, page 281, and add:
  ½ cup chopped mushrooms
Cook until tender in boiling water, drain and add:
  ¼ cup chopped sweet red peppers
Prepare:
  Cream Sauce I, page 322
When the sauce is smooth and boiling, add the other ingredients.
  Correct the seasoning
and add:
  1 teaspoon Worcestershire sauce,
  1 tablespoon lemon juice or 2 tablespoons dry white wine
Serve the seafood over:
  French Toast, page 587, rusks, or in a patty shell or au gratin in ramekins
Or toast bread triangles and spread with:
  Mashed avocado and lemon juice

CREAMED SEAFOOD AU GRATIN
6 Servings

Preheat oven to 350°.
Combine 3 or 4 kinds of raw fish or shellfish.
For example:
  ½ lb. chopped lobster meat
  1 cup drained oysters
  1 cup minced fillet of haddock
Prepare:
  1½ cups Sautéed Mushrooms, page 281
  4 cups Cream Sauce I, page 322
using cream as the liquid. When the sauce is smooth and hot, fold in the fish. Add the mushrooms.
  Correct the seasoning
Fill ramekins or shells with the mixture. Cover the tops with:
  Au Gratin II, page 342
Bake the fish for about 25 minutes.

QUICK TUNA OR SEAFOOD CASSEROLE
4 Servings

Prepare:
  1½ cups Cream Sauce I, page 322, or Poulette Sauce, page 324
Add:
  1 cup canned tuna, shrimp, clams, etc.
Just before serving, heat through and add:
  ½ to 1 cup coarsely chopped watercress
  1 diced avocado
Serve over:
  Toast or rusks

CREAMED SEAFOOD AND VEGETABLES
4 Servings

Preheat broiler.
Cook:
  1 cup chopped celery, eggplant or cucumber
Drain it well. Prepare:
  ¾ cup Cream Sauce I, page 322
When the sauce is boiling, add the celery and:
  ¾ lb. cooked shrimp, crab meat, etc.
Season with:
  Salt, if needed
  ⅛ teaspoon paprika
  (½ teaspoon Worcestershire sauce)
Place these ingredients in greased ramekins. Cover with:
  Au Gratin I, page 342
Brown them under the broiler.

SHRIMP WITH CHEESE AND ONION SAUCE
4 Servings

Preheat broiler.
Shell and clean:
  1 lb. poached Shrimp, page 377
Melt:
  ¼ cup butter
Add:
  ½ cup minced onion
Sauté the onion for about 3 minutes. Stir in:
  ½ cup grated cheese
  ½ teaspoon dry mustard
  ½ teaspoon salt
  (½ minced clove garlic)
Cook and stir these ingredients over very low heat until the cheese has melted. Add the shrimp and:
  6 tablespoons dry sherry
Butter individual baking dishes. Place the shrimp in them. Brown lightly under a broiler. Shortly before they are done sprinkle the tops with:
  Grated coconut
Serve very hot when the coconut is light brown.

KEDGEREE OF LOBSTER OR OTHER FISH
6 Servings

Combine:
  2 cups cooked rice
  1 lb. cooked flaked lobster or cod fillets
  4 minced hard-cooked eggs
  ¼ cup butter
  ¼ cup cream
  2 tablespoons minced parsley
  Salt and cayenne
Heat these ingredients in a double boiler.

SEAFOOD CASSEROLE IN CREOLE SAUCE
4 Servings

Prepare:
  ¾ lb. cooked shrimp or other seafood
Melt in a skillet:
  2 tablespoons butter
Add the shrimp. Stir and cook over high

heat for about 2 minutes. Add:
  2 cups Creole Sauce, page 336
  ¼ cup dry white wine
Simmer the shrimp covered for about 5
minutes. You may add:
  (Salt and pepper)
  (A few grains cayenne)
  (3 diced hard-cooked eggs)
Serve the shrimp with:
  Boiled Rice

LOBSTER OR SEAFOOD CURRY
                                          4 Servings
Heat in a double boiler:
  2 cups Curry Sauce I, page 325
Add, stir and cook for about 3 minutes:
  2 cups boiled diced lobster meat or
  2 cups cooked seafood
You may add:
  (3 chopped sautéed ribs celery)
  (½ chopped sautéed green pepper, seeds
    and fibrous portions removed)
  (1 teaspoon grated sautéed onion)
  Correct the seasoning
❯ Simmer until well heated. May be served
at once with:
  Boiled Rice, Chutney, page 786,
  or slivered almonds
Or place in individual baking dishes or a
casserole and cover with:
  Au Gratin II, page 342
Heat in a 425° oven until the crumbs are
lightly browned.

LOBSTER OR SEAFOOD NEWBURG
                                          4 Servings
I.
Melt in a double boiler:
  4 tablespoons butter
Add, stir and cook for 3 minutes:
  2 cups boiled diced lobster meat
Add:
  ¼ cup dry sherry or Madeira
Cook gently about 2 minutes more. Add:
  ½ teaspoon paprika
  (⅛ teaspoon nutmeg)
Beat and add:
  3 egg yolks
  1 cup cream
Cook and stir these ingredients until they
thicken. Do not permit them to boil.
  Correct the seasoning
Serve the lobster at once on:
  Hot buttered toast

II. Heat in a double boiler:
  2 cups Newburg Sauce, page 323
Add, stir and cook for about 3 minutes:
  2 cups boiled diced lobster meat or
  2 cups cooked seafood
You may add:
  (1 lb. sliced sautéed mushrooms)
  Correct the seasoning
Serve at once on:
  Hot buttered toast or Boiled Rice

QUICK SEAFOOD DIVAN
                                          4 Servings
Preheat oven to 325°.
Prepare and heat:
  1½ cups Cream Sauce I, page 322,
    condensed cream of celery or
    mushroom soup sauce, or Quick
    Creole Sauce, page 333
Have ready:
  1 cup cooked shrimp, crab meat, etc.
  Correct the seasoning
Put in a hot baking dish:
  2 cups cooked asparagus, broccoli,
    cauliflower, etc.
  ½ cup Sautéed Mushrooms
  2 teaspoons diced pimientos
Cover the vegetables with a close layer of
the seafood. Pour the hot sauce over the
seafood. Sprinkle lightly all over:
  Grated cheese
Bake for about 25 minutes.

QUICK CRAB MEAT OR
LOBSTER MONGOLE
                                          4 Servings
For a perfect luncheon or supper, serve
with rice and a salad.
Combine and heat in a double boiler:
  ¾ cup canned tomato soup
  ¾ cup canned pea soup
  ¾ cup cream
Heat in a double boiler:
  1 cup canned crab or lobster meat
Pour a little of the sauce over it. Serve it
garnished with:
  Parsley
  Boiled Rice, page 178
and the remaining sauce. All the sauce
may be added to the crab. In that case,
the dish becomes a thick soup.

CRAB MEAT CUSTARD
                                          8 Servings
Preheat oven to 325°.
In the bottom of a large buttered casserole
place:
  4 slices crustless bread
Place on top of the bread:
  1 large can flaked crab meat: 2 cups
  ½ cup grated American cheese
  Salt and pepper
Beat together:
  4 eggs
  3 cups milk
  ½ teaspoon salt
  Dash of cayenne
Pour this mixture over the fish and top
with:
  ½ cup grated American cheese
Bake as for a Custard, page 684, until
done. Serve with:
  A mixed green salad

DEVILED CRAB

4 Servings

Flake and pick over:

    1½ cups canned or cooked crab meat

Melt in a saucepan:

    1 tablespoon butter

Add:

    1½ tablespoons cracker crumbs

    ¾ cup milk or cream

Cook these ingredients until they are thick.
Remove from the heat. Beat and add:

    2 small eggs

    ¼ teaspoon salt

    1½ teaspoons prepared mustard

    A few grains cayenne

Add the crab meat. Pack these ingredients
into crab shells or ramekins. Brush the
tops with:

    Melted butter

Brown them in a 400° oven or under a
broiler.

INDIVIDUAL TUNA FISH PIES

6 Servings

Any other fish or seafood may be substituted. Bake 6 individual Pie Shells, page
590.

Combine:

    1 cup flaked tuna fish

    1 or 1½ cups thick Cream Sauce II,
        page 322, or condensed cream soup
        slightly diluted with milk

Heat this mixture. Season it with a choice
of:

    2 tablespoons fresh chopped parsley
        or chervil

    ¼ teaspoon curry powder

    ½ teaspoon Worcestershire sauce

Place the hot tuna mixture in the hot pie
shells. Serve them garnished with:

    Parsley sprigs

Sprinkle with:

    Parmesan cheese or chives

TUNA AND POTATO CHIP LOAF

4 Servings

Preheat oven to 350°.

Pat lightly until broken:

    3 oz. potato chips

Flake and add:

    1 cup canned tuna fish

Combine these ingredients lightly with:

    1 can mushroom soup: 10½ oz.

Add, if desired:

    Chopped pimiento, stuffed olives
        or chopped parsley

Bake the loaf in a greased pan for about
½ hour.

LOBSTER PARFAIT

6 Servings

This is an exceedingly elegant way of serving cold lobster—fit for a pavilion! Serve
with iced champagne.

Purée in the ✴ blender:

    The meat of 1 freshly killed and
        cooked 2½ lb. lobster or 2 cups
        cooked meat from frozen lobster tails

with:

    3 tablespoons tomato purée

    2 tablespoons lemon juice

    1 tablespoon dry sherry

    2 teaspoons cognac

    ½ cup water

Mix in:

    1 minced clove garlic

    1 finely chopped shallot

Cook the mixture over a low heat until
reduced by ⅓. Cool, then add:

    2 cups mayonnaise

    1½ tablespoons heavy cream

    ½ teaspoon paprika

    1 teaspoon salt

    ½ teaspoon monosodium glutamate

Chill for 1½ hours. Arrange additional:

    4 oz. lobster meat per serving

in 6 parfait glasses. Cover the meat with
the above sauce, letting it trickle down in
parfait style. Garnish with:

    Chilled whipped cream

    Water cress

Serve at once.

HOT LOBSTER RING

5 Servings

Preheat oven to 325°.

Melt:

    2 tablespoons butter

Stir in, until blended:

    3 tablespoons flour

Stir in gradually:

    2 cups chicken bouillon or 1 cup
        bouillon and 1 cup cream

Add:

    1 tablespoon minced parsley

    ½ cup grated bread crumbs—not toasted

    4 beaten egg yolks

    2 cups boiled diced lobster meat

    Salt and white pepper

Whip until stiff, but not dry:

    4 egg whites

Fold lightly into the other ingredients.
Bake in a well-oiled 9-inch ring mold until firm, about 20 minutes. Unmold and serve with:

    Mushroom Sauce, page 327

QUICK FISH LOAF

4 Servings

Preheat oven to 400°.

Drain, then flake:

    1 lb. cooked or canned fish: 2 cups

Combine and beat:

    1 egg

    ¼ cup undiluted evaporated milk
        or rich cream

    ¾ cup soft bread crumbs

    ½ teaspoon salt

    ¼ teaspoon paprika

    2 teaspoons lemon juice or 1 teaspoon
        Worcestershire sauce

    1 tablespoon melted butter

    3 tablespoons minced parsley

    2 tablespoons chopped celery, onion,
        green pepper or olives

Add the fish. Place these ingredients in a greased baking dish. Bake them for about 30 minutes. This loaf may be served hot with:

> Cream, Tomato or Cheese Sauce,
> or Caper Sauce

or cold with:

> Mayonnaise

TUNA FISH BALLS
About 4 Servings

Also use as a hot hors d'oeuvre.
Combine and mix well:

> 1 cup grated or flaked tuna fish
> 1 cup mashed potatoes
> 4 or 6 chopped olives
> 6 or 8 capers
> ½ minced clove garlic or 1 teaspoon grated onion
> 1 tablespoon minced parsley
> Salt and paprika
> 1 teaspoon brandy or dry sherry
> (1 teaspoon dried basil)

Shape the mixture into 1-inch balls. Sauté them for 2 or 3 minutes in:

> ½ cup hot olive oil or butter

Drain the balls, roll them in:

> ¾ cup ground nut meats

EMERGENCY FISH CAKES

Excellent cakes may be made quickly by combining cooked seafood with condensed cream soup. Keep your mixture rather stiff. Treat it as you would any other fish ball or cake.

CRAB, CLAM OR OYSTER CAKES
Six 3-Inch Cakes

You may combine the fish or use them separately.
Melt:

> 2 tablespoons butter

Add, stir and simmer for 3 minutes:

> 2 tablespoons minced onion
> ½ cup soft bread crumbs

Combine and add:

> 2 beaten eggs
> ½ cup cream
> 2 cups minced oysters, canned clams or flaked crab meat
> ½ cup minced celery
> ½ teaspoon dry mustard or 1 tablespoon lemon juice
> 2 tablespoons chopped parsley
> ½ teaspoon salt
> ½ teaspoon paprika

Chill this mixture for 2 hours. Shape into cakes. Dust them lightly with:

> Flour or bread crumbs

Melt in a skillet:

> 1 tablespoon butter

Quickly brown the cakes on both sides. ◗ Lower the heat and cook the cakes slowly for about 6 minutes longer. You may dip the cakes in crumbs, then in 1 egg diluted with 1 tablespoon water and again in crumbs. If you do, permit them to dry

for 15 minutes, then fry until golden in deep fat heated to 375°.

SALMON CAKES
6 Servings

Flake the contents of:

> 2 cups canned salmon

Stir in:

> ½ cup cracker crumbs
> 2 beaten eggs
> ½ teaspoon salt
> ⅛ teaspoon paprika

Form these ingredients into cakes. Sauté them until brown in:

> Butter

Serve the cakes with:

> Mushroom Sauce, page 327
> Celery Soup Sauce III, page 333, etc.

SALMON POTATO CAKES
6 Servings

Prepare:

> Leftover Potato Cakes, page 297

Use the egg and 2 cups mashed potatoes. Add in small flakes:

> 1 cup or more cooked salmon

Season with:

> Chopped parsley, onion juice or celery seed

Shape the mixture into cakes. Dip them in:

> Crushed cornflakes or bread crumbs

Sauté them slowly in:

> Butter, oil or drippings

SALMON PUFFS
6 Servings

Preheat oven to 350°.
Remove skin and bones, drain, then flake:

> 2 cups canned salmon

Add and stir lightly to blend:

> ½ cup fresh bread crumbs
> 2 tablespoons grated onion
> 1 tablespoon lemon juice
> 1 tablespoon melted butter
> ¼ teaspoon salt
> ¼ teaspoon pepper

Beat:

> 1 egg

Add and beat in:

> ½ cup milk

Combine with the salmon mixture. Place in 6 well-greased baking cups set in hot water. Bake for about 45 minutes. Unmold onto a hot platter. Serve with:

> Velouté Sauce, page 324

SALMON CASSEROLE
4 Servings

Preheat oven to 425°.
Skin, bone and flake:

> 2 cups cooked or canned salmon or other fish

Add:

> Salt—lightly
> Freshly ground pepper
> Freshly ground nutmeg

Place the fish in a greased baking dish

Pour over it:
> Béchamel Sauce, page 322, Cream
> Sauce, page 322, or Canned Soup
> Sauce, page 333, etc.

Cover the top with:
> Au Gratin II, page 342

You may add a border of:
> Mashed potatoes

Bake the dish until the top is lightly browned.

SALMON LOAF WITH CHEESE SAUCE
                                        6 Servings

Preheat oven to 350°.
Prepare:
> 1 cup Cream Sauce I, page 322

Stir in over low heat until melted:
> ¼ lb. grated cheese

Season the sauce with:
> ¼ teaspoon salt
> ⅛ teaspoon paprika
> A few grains cayenne

Prepare:
> 1½ cups Mashed Potatoes, page 290

Grease a baking dish and spread the mashed potatoes in it. Cover them with ½ the sauce. Drain, skin, then flake the contents of:
> 2 cups canned salmon

Place it over the sauce. Cover it with the remaining sauce. Bake the dish for about 30 minutes. Serve it with:
> Tomato Sauce, page 333

The cheese may be omitted in the cream sauce and a well-seasoned Cream Sauce I page 322, may be used. Add herbs.

SALMON POT PIE
                                        8 Servings

Preheat oven to 425°.
A meal in one dish. The salmon mixture may be prepared in advance, so may the dough, and combined shortly before baking. A fine thing for the hurry-up house-keeper. Canned vegetables—peas, aspara-gus, etc.—and, of course, other fish—crab, shrimp, tuna, etc.—may be substituted.
Drain, reserving the oil:
> 2 cups canned salmon

Prepare:
> Biscuit Dough, page 583

Prepare:
> 1 cup cooked celery
> 1 cup cooked peas

Drain the vegetables, reserving the liquid.
Melt:
> ¼ cup butter

Sauté in it for about 2 minutes:
> 1½ tablespoons minced onion

Stir in until smooth:
> 6 tablespoons flour

Stir in until boiling:
> ¾ cup vegetable water
> 1½ cups milk

Add:
> 1 teaspoon salt
> ⅛ teaspoon paprika
> 1 tablespoon lemon juice or 1 teaspoon
> Worcestershire sauce
> 1 teaspoon or more chopped parsley
> or chives

Break the salmon into large pieces. Fold the vegetables and the salmon into the cream sauce. Add, if needed, more salt and flavoring. Place the mixture in a large casserole. Roll the biscuit dough to the thickness of about ¼ inch. Cut it into rounds. Top the salmon mixture with bis-cuits. Bake until it is done, for about 12 minutes.

SALMON AND TOMATO SCALLOP
                                   4 Large Servings

Preheat oven to 375°.
Drain:
> 2 cups canned salmon

Combine them with:
> 3 cups soft bread crumbs
> 2 tablespoons butter
> ¼ cup chopped onion
> ½ teaspoon salt
> 1 teaspoon sugar
> ¼ teaspoon paprika or pepper
> 2½ cups tomatoes
> (1 chopped seeded green pepper)
> (1 beaten egg)
> (1 teaspoon Worcestershire sauce
> or lemon juice)
> (¼ cup white wine)

Place these ingredients in a greased baking dish. The top may be sprinkled with:
> Grated cheese

Bake the dish until the top is brown and the interior heated.

SALMON IN PARSLEY SAUCE WITH RICE OR NOODLE RING
                                        6 Servings

Drain:
> 2 cups canned salmon

Remove skin and bones. Break the fish into large flakes. Combine:
> 1½ teaspoons dry mustard
> 1½ teaspoons salt
> ⅛ teaspoon pepper
> ½ teaspoon paprika
> 3 tablespoons flour

Combine and beat into the dry ingredients:
> 1 cup milk
> ¾ cup salmon liquid and water

Place in double boiler ◗ over—not in—boiling water and beat with a wire whisk:
> 1 egg
> 2 tablespoons lemon juice

Add the milk mixture and stir and cook until the sauce has thickened. Add the salmon and:
> 2 tablespoons butter
> ½ cup finely minced parsley
> 1 teaspoon Worcestershire sauce

Heat well and serve in:
> Rice Ring, page 180, or Noodle
> Ring, page 188

CREAMED CANNED SHAD ROE
2 Servings

Sauté:
    1 cup canned shad roe
in:
    Butter
with:
    ½ teaspoon curry powder
Add:
    Salt and paprika
    ¾ cup cream
Reheat but do not boil the roe. Serve it on:
    Toast
See other roe recipes on page 360.

BROILED CANNED SHAD ROE
2 Servings

Preheat broiler.
Separate into pieces:
    1 cup canned shad roe or other
    canned fish roe
Dry them with a paper towel. Brush them
with:
    Melted butter
Sprinkle them with:
    Lemon juice
    Paprika
Place them in a shallow greased pan or on
a greased broiler. Broil the roe gently for
about 10 minutes. Turn it once. Baste it
frequently with:
    Melted butter
Serve it on toast, garnished with:
    Slices of lemon
    Chopped parsley

CANNED FISH ROE IN RAMEKINS
3 Servings

Preheat oven to 325°.
Combine:
    1 cup drained canned fish roe
    1½ teaspoons bread crumbs
    1½ teaspoons butter
    1 beaten egg
    Salt, if needed
    ¼ teaspoon paprika
    2 teaspoons chopped parsley
    ½ cup milk
Fill four greased ramekins. Bake them in
a pan of hot water until firm—about 20
minutes. Serve the roe with:
    Slices of lemon

ABOUT CHEESE DISHES

If you want to know the secrets of cheese
cookery, please read About Cheeses, page
512.

WELSH RAREBITS

Our correspondence is closed on the sub-
ject of rarebit vs. rabbit. We stick to rare-
bit because rabbit already means something else. But we can only answer the
controversy with a story. A stranger molli-
fying a small crying boy: "I wouldn't cry
like that if I were you!" Small boy, "You
cry your way and I'll cry mine." Good

Welsh rarebit can now be bought canned,
ready to be heated and served.

I. With Beer
6 to 8 Servings

Grate or grind:
    1 lb. aged yellow cheese
Melt in a double boiler:
    1 tablespoon butter
Stir in:
    1 cup beer
When the beer is warm, stir in the cheese.
Stir constantly with a fork until the cheese
is melted. Beat slightly and add:
    1 whole egg
Season the rarebit with:
    1 teaspoon Worcestershire sauce
    1 teaspoon salt
    (½ teaspoon paprika)
    A few grains red pepper
    (¼ teaspoon curry powder)
    ¼ teaspoon mustard
Serve the rarebit at once on:
    Crackers, hot toast or Grilled
    Tomatoes

II. With Milk
4 Servings

Melt in a pan over hot water:
    1 tablespoon butter
Stir in and melt:
    1½ cups diced aged cheese
Add:
    ⅛ teaspoon salt
    ¼ teaspoon dry mustard
    A few grains cayenne
    1 teaspoon Worcestershire sauce
Stir in slowly:
    ½ to ¾ cup cream or top milk
When the mixture is hot, remove the pan
from the heat. Beat in:
    1 egg yolk
Serve the rarebit at once over:
    Hot toasted crackers or bread

TOMATO RAREBIT OR WOODCHUCK
I.
4 Servings

Combine and bring to the boiling point:
    1 can tomato soup: 10½ oz.
    ½ cup water
Add and cook slowly until tender:
    (¾ cup thinly sliced onions)
Add and stir until melted:
    ¾ lb. or more thinly sliced aged cheese
Remove the pan from the heat. Combine,
beat and add:
    2 egg yolks
    1 teaspoon Worcestershire sauce
    1 teaspoon dry mustard
    1 teaspoon salt
    ¼ teaspoon paprika
    ⅛ teaspoon white pepper
Stir these ingredients over low heat for 1
or 2 minutes to permit the yolks to thicken
slightly. Whip until ♦ stiff, but not dry:
    2 egg whites
Fold them into the hot cheese mixture.
Serve the rarebit on:
    Hot toast or crackers

II.   4 Servings
Stir and melt over low heat:
    ½ lb. grated aged cheese: 2 cups
Add, stir and heat:
    1 can condensed tomato soup: 10½ oz.
    3 tablespoons water
    ½ teaspoon salt
    A few grains cayenne
Serve the rarebit on:
    Toast or toasted crackers

CHEESE CASSEROLE
This inexpensive luncheon or supper dish
is good balanced by a green vegetable,
a salad or orange and grapefruit cups. A
fine addition to this dish is ½ pound
cooked or canned shrimp.

I.   4 Servings
Preheat oven to 350°.
Cut ½ inch thick:
    7 slices bread
Spread the slices lightly with:
    Butter
Cut 2 of the slices twice across on the bias,
making 8 triangular pieces. Cut the re-
maining bread into cubes. There should be
about 4 cups of diced buttered bread.
Place layers of diced bread in a buttered
baking dish. Sprinkle the layers with:
    1 cup grated cheese
Combine and beat:
    2 eggs
    1 cup milk
    1 teaspoon salt
    ¼ teaspoon paprika
    A few grains cayenne
    ½ teaspoon dry mustard
Pour these ingredients over the cheese.
Place the triangles of bread upright around
the edge to form a crown. Bake the dish
for about 25 minutes. Serve at once.

II.   4 Servings
Preheat oven to 350°.
Trim the crust from:
    8 slices bread
Cut them in half on the bias. Place ½ of
them in the bottom of a greased 8-inch
ovenproof dish, spiral fashion, not letting
them overlap. They should resemble a
pinwheel. Cut into slices ¼-inch thick:
    6 oz. cheese: cheddar,
        American, Swiss, etc.
Cover the bread layer with the cheese
slices, not letting them overlap. Cover the
cheese with the rest of the bread, again in
spiral fashion. Beat lightly:
    3 eggs
Add and beat well:
    ¼ teaspoon salt
    ⅛ teaspoon paprika
    A few grains cayenne
    2 cups rich milk
    (1 teaspoon grated onion, 1 tablespoon
        parsley or chives or ¼ teaspoon
        mustard)
Pour this mixture over the bread. Permit
the dish to stand for 1 hour. Bake it for

about 1 hour or until well browned. Serve
it hot.

CHEESE NUT AND BREAD LOAF
                                            6 Servings
Preheat oven to 350°.
Combine well:
    2 cups fresh bread crumbs
    1 cup minced walnut or pecan meats
    1 cup grated American cheese
    1 cup milk
    ¾ teaspoon salt
    ½ teaspoon paprika
    1 tablespoon finely chopped onion
    1 tablespoon minced parsley
    1 beaten egg
Shape these ingredients in a loaf by plac-
ing them in a bread pan. Bake the loaf
for about 25 minutes. Serve it with:
    Quick Tomato Sauce, page 334,
    Mushroom Sauce, page 327, or
    Onion Sauce, page 325

ABOUT FONDUE

For so simple an affair, the controversy involved in the making of this dish is vast
indeed. Its confecting is a ritual that varies with each Swiss household. Experiment
has led to the following conclusions, no
matter how simple or how complex a version you choose to make. The cheese or
combination of cheeses used must be
♦ natural cheeses, not pasteurized types.
Whatever kind of wine, it must be ♦ a dry
white wine. Although kirsch is de rigeur,
you may substitute a nonsweet liqueur like

slivovitz, a cognac or an applejack.
♦ Measure all ingredients and have them
ready to add with one hand. For your
other hand will be busy stirring the mixture with a wooden spoon—from the time
the wine is hot enough for the cheese until
the fondue is ready to be eaten. Altogether, this is a matter of about 10 minutes of cooking.
    Have ready a bread basket or bowl filled
with crusty French or Italian bread cut
into 1 x 1 x ¾-inch pieces, making sure

that each piece has one side of crust. At this point the guests, each equipped with a heatproof-handled fork—preferably two or three-tined—spear the bread from the soft side and dip the impaled bit into the well-warmed cheese. The fondue will at first be on the thin side, but will thicken as the process progresses. There is seldom much left by the time another 10 minutes has elapsed. Serve with fresh fruit and tea.

FONDUE

4 Servings

Grate:
  1 lb. Emmenthaler or ½ lb. Emmenthaler and ½ lb. Gruyère cheese
Rub a heavy sauce pan with:
  A clove of garlic
Put into the pan:
  2 cups dry white wine
While this is heating ♦ uncovered, over moderately high heat, pour into a cup:
  3 tablespoons kirsch
This is the classic flavoring, although one of the other dry liqueurs mentioned above may be used. Stir into the kirsch until well dissolved:
  1 teaspoon cornstarch
By this time the wine will begin to show small foamy bubbles over its surface. When it is almost covered with this fine foam ♦ but is not yet boiling, add the coarsely shredded cheese gradually ♦ stirring constantly. Keep the heat high, but do not let the fondue boil. Continue to add the cheese until you can feel a very slight resistance to the spoon as you stir. Then, still stirring vigorously, add the kirsch and cornstarch mixture. Continue to cook until the fondue begins to thicken. Add to taste:
  Nutmeg, white pepper or paprika
Quickly transfer it to a heatproof heavy pan which can be placed over an alcohol lamp or chafing dish or transfer it to an electric skillet adjusted to ♦ low heat. After this transferral the cooking continues on low heat and the guests take over as described previously.

ABOUT SANDWICHES

Innumerable hostesses—not to mention quick-lunch stands—keep green the memory of Lord Sandwich, whose mania for gambling gave the world the well-known concoction that bears his name.

Sandwiches range in size and complexity until they rival a Dagwood. But don't neglect the Canapé chapter, where many delectable smaller versions are found. To keep sandwiches fresh, wrap in wax paper, foil or a dampened cloth.

TOASTED SANDWICHES

These are offered as luncheon suggestions. Many of the sandwich fillings given in the chapter on Canapés, page 58, may be

spread between slices of toast. The sandwiches may be served with a hot sauce or a cold dressing.
Put between:
  2 slices toast
any of the following combinations:
  Sliced chicken
  2 strips sautéed bacon
  Grated cheese
  Mushroom Sauce, page 327

  Creamed chicken
  Parmesan cheese
  Grilled tomatoes and bacon

  Baked ham
  Creamed chicken and mushrooms

  Ham, chicken and lettuce, with mayonnaise

  Braunschweiger
  Sliced tomatoes
  Lettuce
  Tart mayonnaise

  Sliced tongue
  Sliced tomatoes
  Mayonnaise
  Sautéed bacon

  Creamed mushrooms
  Sliced tomatoes
  Grated cheese on top, broiled until it is melted

  Sliced ham
  Creamed mushrooms

  Lettuce, French dressing
  Sliced tomato and avocado
  2 slices crisp sautéed bacon

  Asparagus tips
  2 slices crisp bacon
  Welsh Rarebit, page 242

  Lettuce, sliced tomato
  Sliced chicken
  Crumbled Roquefort cheese
  2 slices crisp bacon

SAUTÉED OR GRILLED SANDWICHES

Melt in a small skillet large enough to accommodate one sandwich:
  1½ teaspoons butter
Sauté a sandwich slowly on one side until browned. Add to the skillet:
  1½ teaspoons butter
Brown the second side. Especially good with a thin slice of cheese, mustard, salt and paprika between the bread slices or with deviled ham, meat mixtures, jam or jelly.

WAFFLE OR TOASTED SANDWICHES

Cut into thin slices:

White or dark bread

Spread it lightly with:

Soft butter

Cut off the crusts and spread between the slices:

Cheese Spread or other sandwich fillings, pages 58 and 244

Cut the sandwiches to fit the sections of a waffle iron. Wrap them in a moist cloth until ready to toast. Heat a waffle iron, arrange the sandwiches upon the iron, lower the top and toast them until they are crisp.

FINGER ROLL FILLINGS

Very good picnic sandwiches.

Cut into lengthwise halves:

Soft finger rolls

Hollow them slightly. Fill the hollows with any palatable sandwich spread. These are easy to handle. They are delicious filled with:

Chicken Salad, page 91
Tuna Fish Salad, page 91
Braunschweiger sausage
Canapé Filling, page 58
Chopped celery and mayonnaise
Chopped olives and cream cheese, etc.

Also see the many spreads in Canapés, pages 58 to 61.

HOT BISCUITS BAKED WITH FILLINGS

About Eighteen 2½-Inch Biscuits

Combine:

1 cup cooked, shredded meat: chicken, fish, ham, veal, roast, etc.
½ cup thick gravy, cream sauce or condensed soup
1 tablespoon grated onion
1 chopped hard-cooked egg
2 tablespoons chopped pickles or olives
Seasoning

Prepare:

Baking Powder Biscuit Dough, page 583

Roll it to the thickness of ¼ inch. Cut it into rounds. Place on one round 1 tablespoon of the above meat mixture.

Moisten the edges and cover it with another round. Seal the edges with a fork. Prick the tops. Place the biscuits on a baking sheet and bake them until brown in a very hot oven—450°. You may serve these with:

Mushroom Sauce, page 327

MEAL-IN-ONE SANDWICH

4 Servings—But Better Call It 2

Be on your toes when you make this. It's easy if you have all your ingredients ready before you poach the eggs.

Prepare:

4 large slices of toast
8 sautéed bacon slices
4 skinned and sliced large tomatoes
½ cup French dressing
1 cup Cream Sauce I, page 322
1 cup grated cheese

Place the toast on a baking sheet, cover it with the bacon, tomatoes and dressing.

Poach:

4 eggs

Place an egg on each piece of garnished toast, cover it with ¼ of the cream sauce and ¼ of the grated cheese. Place the toast under the broiler until the cheese melts. Serve the sandwiches piping hot.

HOT ROAST BEEF SANDWICH

4 Servings

Slice:

Cold roast beef

Prepare:

1 cup Brown Sauce, page 326

Add to it:

1 tablespoon finely minced sour pickle or ½ cup chopped olives

Cut:

6 thin slices of light or dark bread

Beat until soft:

2 tablespoons butter
¼ teaspoon prepared mustard or 1 teaspoon horseradish

Spread the bread with this mixture. Dip the beef slices in the hot sauce. Place them between the slices of bread. Serve the sandwiches on a hot platter, covered with remaining sauce.

CORNED BEEF OR DRIED BEEF AND CHEESE SANDWICHES

6 Servings

Cut into tiny slivers:

¼ cup sharp American cheese

Cream the cheese well with:

2 tablespoons mayonnaise

Shred finely and add:

4 oz. canned corned beef or dried beef

Chop until fine and add:

¼ cup sweet-sour pickles
1 tablespoon grated onion
(2 tablespoons minced celery or parsley)

Season the spread, as needed, with:

Salt and pepper
Curry powder, mustard or Worcestershire sauce

Spread it between:

Slices of bread

The sandwiches may be toasted or served with sliced tomatoes and lettuce between the layers.

CORNED BEEF AND TOMATO SANDWICHES

Preheat broiler.

Prepare:
  Slices of buttered toast
Cover them with:
  Sliced corned beef
seasoned with:
  Mustard or horseradish
  Tomatoes seasoned with French
    dressing
Sprinkle the tops with:
  Grated cheese
Broil the sandwiches until the cheese is
melted.

SANDWICH SAVOYARDE
                                           1 Serving
Preheat broiler.
Place on a shallow baker:
  ½ English muffin
Then add:
  A large thin slice of ham
Make a:
  2 egg French Omelet, page 198
large enough to cover the ham. Do not
fold the omelet, but slip it flat onto the
above. Sprinkle with:
  Grated Swiss cheese
Run under broiler until cheese melts. Serve
at once.

HAM OR TONGUE SALAD
SANDWICHES
I. Combine:
  Ground cooked ham or tongue
  Chopped onion or chives
  Chopped celery
Moisten them with:
  Cream or salad dressing
If cream is used, season with:
  Paprika and salt, if needed
Spread the filling between:
  Thin slices of bread

II. Combine and mix:
  2 tablespoons chopped onion
  2 tablespoons catsup
  2 tablespoons chopped green pepper
  2 tablespoons chopped pickles
  ½ lb. chopped sharp cheese
  3 oz. deviled ham or ½ cup finely
    cut cooked ham
  ¼ cup cream, melted butter or oil
Serve in hollowed hard rolls.

HAWAIIAN TOAST WITH BACON
SANDWICH
                                           4 Servings
Cut:
  4 to 6 slices stale bread, ½ inch thick
Beat until light:
  2 eggs
Beat in:
  1 cup pineapple juice
  ½ teaspoon salt
Dip the bread in the egg mixture. Soak it
well. Sauté in a skillet:
  8 slices bacon
Remove them to a hot platter. Keep them

hot. Fry the bread in the bacon drippings
brown one side and then the other. Re
move the bread to the hot platter. Saut
in the bacon drippings:
  4 slices drained pineapple, cut into
    halves
Garnish the platter with the bacon and th
pineapple. Serve the toast at once.

HAM, TOMATO AND EGG
SANDWICH
Slice and butter:
  Rye bread
Place on it:
  Slices boiled ham
  Lettuce leaves
  Sliced tomatoes
Garnish the sandwiches with:
  Slices hard-cooked egg
  Sprigs parsley
Serve them with:
  Horseradish Dressing, page 312, or
  Russian Dressing, page 316

TOAST ROLLS WITH HAM
AND ASPARAGUS
                                           4 Serving
A fine luncheon or supper dish with
molded grapefruit salad and coffee.
Preheat oven to 400°.
Drain:
  2 cups asparagus tips
Remove the crusts from:
  8 thin slices bread
Brush them lightly on both sides with:
  Melted butter
Place on each slice:
  A slice boiled ham
  Several asparagus tips
Roll the bread around the tips or bring
corners together. Fasten the bread wit
toothpicks. Bake these rolls on a bakin
sheet until they are lightly browned. Us
the asparagus water and cream to make:
  Cream Sauce, page 322
Serve the rolls piping hot with the sauce

HAM AND PINEAPPLE FRENCH
TOAST SANDWICH
Combine equal parts:
  Ground ham
  Crushed pineapple
Season these ingredients with:
  French mustard
Spread this filling between slices of:
  Buttered bread
See French Toast, page 587. Spread th
outside of the sandwiches with the eg
mixture and sauté them as directed.

TOASTED DEVILED HAM AND
CHEESE SANDWICHES
Cover:
  Thin slices of toast
with a paste made of:
  Deviled ham, French mustard or
  horseradish

Or use:
    (Thin slices boiled ham)
Cover the ham with thin slices of:
    American cheese
Dot with:
    Capers
Press the sandwiches and refrigerate 6
hours. Then sauté until toasted in:
    Butter
Serve hot.

POOR BOY, SUBMARINE OR HERO SANDWICH
                                            4 Servings
Cut in half lengthwise a long loaf of:
    French Bread, page 557
Spread both cuts with:
    Butter
On the bottom half, arrange layers of:
    Sliced salami sausage
    Sliced sharp cheese
    Thinly sliced boiled ham
    (Thin slices tomato)
Put the top half of bread on to make a
sandwich and cut into 4 pieces. Mix to-
gether:
    ¼ cup dry mustard
    1 tablespoon dry white wine
Serve this with the sandwich.

TOASTED BRAUNSCHWEIGER SANDWICH
Braunschweiger is a refined version of the
other heavy smoked liver sausage.
Combine and stir to a smooth paste:
    Braunschweiger sausage
    Canned tomato soup or tomato paste
    (A few drops of cream or
    Worcestershire sauce)
Cut the crusts from:
    Thin slices of bread
Spread them with the sausage mixture.
Roll the bread or make double-deck sand-
wiches. Toast and serve them very hot.

BACON AND CHEESE SANDWICH
                                            4 Servings
Preheat broiler.
Toast on either one or both sides, or use
untoasted:
    4 slices bread
Place on each slice:
    (A thick slice tomato)
    (Chopped onion and green peppers)
    (Sliced olives or pickles)
    A slice of American cheese
Spread the cheese with:
    Mustard or chili sauce
Cover each sandwich with:
    2 slices bacon
Crisp the slices of bacon under the broiler
and serve immediately. Also good with:
    (Hot Cheese Sauce)

EGG AND CHEESE SANDWICH WITH TOMATO SAUCE
                                            4 Servings
Rub:

    4 slices French bread
with:
    (Garlic)
Dip them quickly in:
    Milk seasoned with a pinch of salt
Brown them in:
    Olive oil
Place them on a hot ovenproof plate.
Cover them with:
    4 chopped hard-cooked eggs
    1 cup or more grated cheese
    6 or more chopped olives
    Dots of butter
Place the slices under a broiler until the
cheese is melted. Serve them with:
    Tomato Sauce, page 333

FRENCH TOAST AND CHEESE
                                            4 Servings
Preheat oven to 350°.
Prepare, omitting the sugar:
    French Toast, page 587
Toast the bread in the oven on a buttered
ovenproof plate for about 5 minutes. Stir
over very low heat until smooth:
    ½ lb. grated or minced cheese
    ½ teaspoon salt
    A few grains cayenne
    ¼ cup milk
    3 tablespoons butter
Spread the toast with the cheese mixture.
Return it to the oven to brown lightly.

FRENCH TOMATO TOAST
Beat until light:
    2 eggs
    ½ teaspoon salt
    ¼ teaspoon paprika
    ½ cup condensed tomato soup
Dip in this:
    6 slices of bread
Sauté the slices in hot:
    Butter or drippings
When a good brown, serve them with:
    Cheese Sauce, page 326
    Minced parsley or chives

CHEESE SANDWICH WITH MUSHROOM SAUCE
Trim the crusts from:
    Slices light or dark bread
Spread them with:
    Butter
Place on each piece:
    Slices of cheese
    Lettuce leaves
    Slices tomato or cucumber
    Slices hard-cooked egg
    Sliced olives or pickles
Serve the sandwiches with:
    Mushroom Sauce, page 327

PUFFED CHEESE WITH MUSHROOMS ON TOAST
                                            4 Servings
Preheat oven to 375°.
Melt in a saucepan:
    1 tablespoon butter

Add and sauté until tender:
    ½ cup finely sliced mushrooms
    1 teaspoon grated onion
Combine:
    2 unbeaten egg yolks
    ½ lb. grated Swiss cheese: 2 cups
    ¾ teaspoon salt
    ¼ teaspoon pepper
    A few grains cayenne
Stir in the mushroom and onion mixture.
Beat until stiff, but not dry:
    2 egg whites
Fold them into the mixture. Toast on one
side:
    6 slices bread
Place them toasted side down on a cookie
sheet. Spread the untoasted sides lightly
with:
    Butter
Heap the cheese mixture on the bread.
Bake the slices until they are firm to the
touch and well puffed.

PEANUT BUTTER AND TOMATO
SANDWICH
Preheat broiler.
Toast on one side:
    A slice of bread
Spread the untoasted side with:
    Peanut butter
mixed with:
    Chopped cooked bacon
    Bacon drippings
You may top this with:
    A thick slice of tomato
Season the tomato with:
    ¼ teaspoon brown sugar
    Salt and paprika
Put the sandwich under a broiler for a
minute or two.

PEANUT BUTTER AND BACON
SANDWICH
                                        4 Servings
Preheat broiler.
Virtue, however admirable, is frequently
dull. Peanut butter needs enlivening. Try
this mixture on the unconverted.
Combine:
    ¾ cup peanut butter
    ¼ cup mayonnaise
    ¼ teaspoon salt
    2 tablespoons pickle relish or chili
      sauce
    ¼ cup cooked minced bacon
Toast on one side:
    4 slices bread
Spread the untoasted side with the mix-
ture. Broil the sandwiches until the tops
are brown. Slice them diagonally.

CLUB SANDWICH
                                Individual Serving
Prepare:
    3 large square slices of toast
Cover slice 1 with:
    A lettuce leaf

    3 crisp slices hot bacon
    Slices of tomato
    1 tablespoon mayonnaise
    (Drained slices pineapple)
Place slice 2 over slice 1 mixture and cover
it with:
    Slices of cold cooked chicken
    1 tablespoon mayonnaise
Place slice 3 over slice 2 mixture and cut
the sandwich on the bias.

FRUIT STICKS
I. Cut into strips 3 by 1½ inches wide and
½ inch thick:
    White bread
Toast them on 3 sides. Place them on a
baking sheet with the untoasted side up.
Drain:
    Pineapple or apricot slices
Place them on the untoasted sides. Sprin-
kle them well with a mixture of:
    Brown sugar and cinnamon
Dot them with:
    Butter
Brown them under a broiler.

II. Preheat oven to 450°.
Prepare:
    Pie Dough, page 588
Roll it until very thin. Cut it into oblongs. Sprinkle:
    Pineapple or apricot slices
with:
    Cinnamon and brown sugar
Wrap the slices in the oblongs. Moisten
the edges with water. Bake the slices for
about 20 minutes.

LAMB OR CHICKEN SANDWICH
Trim the crusts from:
    Large slices rye bread
Spread them with:
    Butter
Place on each piece:
    Slices cold lamb or chicken
    Lettuce leaves
    Slices tomato
    Slices hard-cooked egg
Serve the sandwich with:
    Russian Dressing, page 316

CHICKEN AND CREAM CHEESE
SANDWICHES
Spread:
    Slices of whole-wheat bread
with:
    Cream cheese softened with cream
Add:
    Slices of cooked chicken
    Chopped green olives
    Salt

HOT CHICKEN SANDWICHES
I. Cut into slices:
    Cold cooked chicken
Dip the slices in:
    Mayonnaise
Prepare:
    Biscuits, page 583

While hot, open and spread them with:
Butter
Place the chicken slices in the biscuits.
Serve them hot with:
**Chicken gravy, Cheese Sauce,
page 326, or Mushroom Sauce,
page 327**

II. Using biscuits, as in the previous recipe, fill with:
Chicken Salad, page 91
or combine:
**½ cup cooked minced chicken
1 chopped hard-cooked egg
6 chopped stuffed olives
¼ cup mayonnaise
(2 tablespoons chopped parsley)**
Serve hot with one of the sauces mentioned previously.

III.
Preheat oven to 375°.
Prepare:
Buttered toast
Cover the toast with:
Sliced chicken
Sprinkle it with:
Crumbled Roquefort cheese
Cover it with:
Strips of notched bacon
Bake for about 10 minutes, until the bacon is crisp. Sliced tomatoes may be placed on the toast.

**OPEN-FACED SEAFOOD SALAD
AND TOMATO SANDWICHES**
I. Prepare:
Slices of buttered bread
Cover them with:
Slices of tomato
Top the tomatoes with mounds of:
**Tuna Salad, page 91, or
other seafood**
Garnish with:
**Chopped parsley, olives or chives
Chopped sautéed bacon**

II. Cut crosswise into 2 sections:
A large round loaf of bread
Spread cut sides with:
Butter
Place around the outer edges of each piece:
Thinly sliced tomatoes
Sprinkle with:
**Salt and pepper
Chopped fresh basil or chives**
Arrange like spokes of a wagon wheel, in the center of each piece:
Canned sardines
Decorate with:

Sliced black olives
Sprinkle some of the sardine oil over all, cut the pieces into 6 wedges each and serve.

**TOASTED ROLLS WITH CRAB
MEAT AND CHEESE**

4 Servings

Fine with beer or cider.
Preheat broiler.
Cut into halves:
4 rolls
Cover the 4 lower halves with:
Lettuce leaves
Combine:
**¾ cup canned crab meat
¼ cup mayonnaise**
Spread this on the lettuce. Spread the remaining halves with:
**Butter
Slices of cheese
(Mustard)**
Toast the cheese under a broiler until it is soft. Combine the halves.

LOBSTER SANDWICHES
Flake:
6 oz. canned lobster or other seafood
Sprinkle over it:
1 teaspoon lemon juice
Add:
**½ cup minced celery
1 tablespoon minced onion or chives
½ cup mayonnaise**
Mayonnaise, if too thick, is fine thinned with sour cream. Season with:
**(Worcestershire sauce, curry powder
or freshly grated nutmeg)**
Add:
**(Capers, chopped olives, pickles or
parsley, etc.)**
Spread these ingredients on:
Buttered rye bread
You may add:
Crisp lettuce leaves

**SHRIMP SANDWICHES WITH
CHEESE SAUCE**

3 Servings

Clean:
1½ cups cooked shrimp
Melt:
2 tablespoons butter
Add:
**1 tablespoon grated onion
(1 sliced pimiento)**
and the shrimp. Stir over low heat for 1 minute. Prepare:
6 slices toast
Heap the shrimp on the toast. Serve with:
Cheese Sauce, page 326

VEGETABLES

It is probably true that more outrages are perpetrated against vegetables than against any other basic foods. These outrages often begin when the seeds are sown—in impoverished ground; they may continue during the plant's development, because of inadequate moisture; and then reach some sort of climax in the almost uniformly careless handling that produce is subjected to on its way to the point of sale.

To preserve their true, delicate flavor, as well as their natural sugars and nutrients and to enjoy green vegetables at their wholesome best, they should be ♦ washed just before cooking ♦ cooked just after picking ♦ just to the point of doneness, not a moment more, and ♦ eaten just off the heat.

♦ The longer vegetables take to reach maturity, the coarser their cellulose. The greater the period between picking and cooking, the longer the time needed to make them palatable. Naturally, longer cooking periods impair nutritive values, color and especially flavor—that quality a family considers first.

Here are ways to get the best out of the less than perfect vegetables we are often forced to buy. Market on days when supplies reach your store—buying so that you hold them the least possible time before use. ♦ Apply to each kind of vegetable the tests for ripeness we describe later.

If stocks are limited, always prefer a fresh, fluffy, country or garden lettuce over a bruised Bibb and a crisp bunch of carrots over darkened, leathery artichokes. Care in cooking, piquancy of seasoning and ingenuity in combining familiar varieties can compensate for the more commonplace choice.

If the vegetable is old, dress it up with seasoned butters, herbs, spices and sauces. If young, drain it, toss it in butter, allowing 1 tablespoon to every cup of vegetable, and season it very lightly, so that its own tender flavor prevails. You will find that young vegetables have an abundance of natural sugars but that ♦ older ones often profit by an added pinch of sugar in cooking. You will notice varied seasonings suggested in our individual recipes. Add them with a light hand; the exception being dried legumes and canned vegetables, which are greatly improved by a bold and imaginative approach. ♦ Salting just after the onset of cooking will slightly firm vegetable structure and help retain color and flavor. ♦ Allow about ¼ tea-spoon of salt to each cup of water. But see the steaming method we prefer, page 252.

ABOUT STORING VEGETABLES

Certain vegetables and fruits should not be stored together. Apples give off an ethylene gas that makes carrots bitter, for example, and onions hasten the spoilage of potatoes. Watch for other such relationships. Do not wash vegetables until you are ready to use them and then do not soak them, except as indicated, because moisture tends to leach away the water-soluble vitamins.

A good general rule ♦ for leaf vegetables, peas and green beans is to store them unwashed at about 45° in plastic bags. There is enough moisture within the vegetables to keep them fresh this way. The exception is water cress, page 77. Cut the leaves from root vegetables before storing, for the flow of sap continues to the leaf at the expense of the root. Store thick-skinned vegetables like potatoes, rutabagas and turnips unwashed in a dry, dark, cool place. The ideal temperature is 55° to 65°.

ABOUT PREPARING VEGETABLES FOR COOKING

Some vegetables may simply be scrubbed and steamed or baked unpeeled. These methods keep vitamin losses to a minimum, provided cooking is not overly prolonged. Sometimes vegetables are scrubbed, scraped or thinly pared before cooking. Remember that most of the vitamins lie near the skin and that deep paring will mean losing them. Prepare peeled vegetables and cook them immediately to minimize their exposure to air. ♦ Never soak after slicing, if the greatest amount of nutrient values is to be retained. Whether you cook vegetables whole or sliced ♦ see that pieces are uniform in size, so they will all be done and tender simultaneously.

Many chopping and slicing devices are advertised, but nothing can replace a skilled relaxed wrist and a sharp French knife. Acquire this indispensable trick and you will be forever grateful. Practice with a mushroom, which is yielding and no slippery when placed cap down, and work up to an onion, which is resistant and evasive. In either case ♦ to slice, first cut the onion or apple or whatever you are slicing so that it rests on a flat, not a rolling base; then hold this object as shown in the sketch on the next page. For a good view showing how the knife handle is held re-laxed between the thumb and forefinger, see Soufflé Potatoes, page 295. ♦ The point of the knife is never lifted from the cutting board but forms a pivot. The cutting edge is never lifted above the first

joint of the left forefinger. The handle end of the knife is raised high enough to be eased gently up and down, its wide blade guided by the perpendicular left forefinger and mid-finger. As the slicing progresses, inch a slow retreat with the left hand without releasing a firm grasp on the object.

If celery or Chinese cabbage, for instance, are to be sliced on the diagonal, the two guide fingers are set at an angle, as shown next. But the knife in the right hand continues its relaxed accurate slicing, while the left makes way without losing control of the stalks. To peel very hard, round vegetables, see a trick sketched on page 309.

If you are really determined to lure your family into eating vegetables, you will find they will respond more readily if the vegetables are attractive in shape and perhaps rather sparse in number. Think of the irresistible charm of vegetables floating like flowers in a Japanese lacquered bowl. The French are also very adept at presentation, if more lavish, and they disguise the same old carrots, beans and potatoes under a mass of impressive aliases. As **printanière,** they are spring-grown, young, tender and thinly sliced. As **brunoise, salpicon, mirepoix** and **macédoine,** they are ageless, and sliced respectively from ⅛ to ¼ to ⅜ inch, which latter size we call just plain "diced." As **jardinière, julienne** or **allumette,** they are taller and thinner, about 2 to 3 inches long and ⅛ inch through. When they are round in shape and small, you may call them **pearls;** if they are elliptical, call them **olivette** at ⅜ inch, **noisette** at ½ inch and **Parisienne,** if about 1 inch at their narrowest diameter. Utilize whatever scraps are left over in ⅃ blender soups or, unless they are starchy ones, in the stockpot.

ABOUT MAINTAINING FLAVOR AND COLOR DURING VEGETABLE COOKING

There are bound to be some nutritional losses, especially of vitamin C, in any cooking process. It does not follow that eating vegetables raw is the whole answer. Cooked carrots and spinach, in spite of losses during cooking, will have more nutrients available for absorption by the body than raw. ♦ The greatest losses probably come in mashing and puréeing. If done when the vegetables are hot, exposure to air during these processes will involve losses of ¼ to ½ of the vitamin C content. If you prepare mashed or puréed vegetables, compensate by serving a salad or citrus fruit at the same meal. All in all, you will do best nutritionally with fresh vegetables; next, with frozen ones that have been held below 0° for less than 2 months; last, with canned vegetables, provided the liquid in the can is utilized. Dehydrated vegetables, frozen and nonfrozen, suffer great loss of nutrients, the latter, especially, if improperly packaged. For cooking frozen vegetables, see pages 253, 765.

No one method of vegetable cooking can claim superiority over all other methods, but ♦ those processes which retain the best color and flavor are most apt to retain the most nutrients.

♦ Color should never be maintained by the addition of baking soda, for this method not only destroys nutrient values but makes the vegetable mushy in texture. Color may, however, be lost without accompanying nutrient loss if you cook in hard water, see page 493. ♦ The addition of vinegar or lemon juice to the cooking water will stabilize color. Greens, cauliflower, cabbage, onions, turnips and beets will need about 1 teaspoon for each 2 cups of water. Another method of preserving color without losing nutrients is to cook vegetables in milk. This tenderizes them more rapidly too, although sometimes, due to acid in the vegetable, the milk may curdle harmlessly.

It is advisable to cook most vegetables ♦ covered and with a small amount of water. ♦ Exceptions are the cabbage and onion tribes, turnips, parsnips, beets and wild greens which, when boiled, require water to cover. All are cooked uncovered. They react adversely under too great heat and too long a period of cooking. The greens become slimy and the strong, volatile oils of all these vegetables give off unpleasant odors—and they discolor. It is often wise to parblanch, page 132, this whole group of vegetables, briefly. ♦ Both when putting them into hot water which has reached a rolling boil for the blanching and again for the cooking, add them gradually so as not to disturb the boiling. These vegetables also tend to discolor badly, especially if covered. Blanching, page 132, helps to retain their color, as does cooking Cauliflower à blanc, page 493. Do not cover any vegetable completely after the cooking is over, but allow the steam to escape and the dish will have much better color.

No matter which method of cooking you use, be sure ♦ to keep the vegetable waters unless they taste too strong. Use them for their invaluable nutritional qualities and flavoring powers, page 488.

ABOUT STEAMING VEGETABLES

Steaming vegetables, we find, gives the most consistently good results. See the sketches of steamers below. Our favorite method ♦ when time is short, is a French steamer used with a pressure cooker. If you ✪ pressure-steam, add a minute or two to the time we indicate for pressure cooked vegetables. Expel air from the pan before closing the vent. Time carefully, for vegetables may be quickly overcooked by this method. Or use regular heat under a double boiler with a specially built steamer inset—sketched on the right. Steaming is

such a superior method, we feel, that, if you have no adequate equipment, it is worthwhile to improvise a steamer by placing a colander in any pot with a tight-fitting lid.

In any steaming, no matter what accessory you use, be sure that ♦ the water is boiling before you set the perforated container over it. ♦ Cover at once and cook 3 to 5 minutes longer than when vegetables are processed in boiling water.

ABOUT PANNING VEGETABLES

Panning, also known as braising or covered-skillet cooking, as well as stir-frying—discussed later—are very good and quick methods for tender vegetables and those very finely and evenly sliced. ♦ They are prepared the same way for both methods: sliced fine and usually cut on the diagonal for any that tend to be stringy. If leaves are coarse, remove mid-ribs and stem ends. For 4 servings, allow about 1 lb. kale, cabbage, okra, celery or celery cabbage, about 1½ lbs. of spinach or chard, ¾ lb. beans.

Skillet and panning cookery requires about 1 tablespoon of oil or butter per pound of vegetables. If the vegetables are dry, sprinkle them lightly with water before adding them to the hot fat. To pan, braise or skillet-cook any tender vegetable, have ready a pan with a tight-fitting lid. Heat the pan, put in the fat and heat to the point of fragrance. Quickly add the ♦ uniformly sliced vegetables and clap the lid on at once to retain as much steam as possible. When the steam comes up vigorously ♦ reduce the heat at once and cook over low heat until the vegetable is just tender. Shake the pan repeatedly to be sure the contents do not stick.

The braising or panning method is also an effective, if somewhat slower, way to do small quantities of podded vegetables. Let them remain in the pod and shell them just before serving. Allow about 1½ to 2 lbs. of these vegetables—depending on

how full the pods are—for 4 servings. Depending also on the thickness of the pod, add from ⅓ to ¾ cup boiling water for each pound of vegetable and cook 15 to 20 minutes or until tender. No fat is necessary if the vegetables are podded. Butter them after shelling.

ABOUT STIR-FRYING

This is the method so typical of Chinese cooking, which allows the vegetables to remain tender, crisp and of very good color. They are traditionally stirred in a big open conical pan held erect by a ring stand ♦ over really fierce heat. Stir-frying is an ideal way to cook mixed tender vegetables quickly—the whole process lasting only 3 or 4 minutes. Preparation is the slow part, as the vegetables must all be cut uniformly as for panning, page 252. Those which need longer cooking are put in first and the tenderer ones later, so they are all done at the same time.

Use any cooking oil, other than olive. Allow 2 teaspoons of oil to 1 pound of vegetables. ♦ Have the pan very hot and heat the oil to the point of fragrance. A slice or two of fresh ginger root or garlic may be put in at this time and discarded before the vegetables are added. Stir the vegetables rapidly to make sure they are well coated with the oil. Continue to cook ♦ uncovered, over high heat, stirring constantly until the vegetables are just tender.

Watery vegetables like cucumber, tomato and zucchini, and thin-leafed types like spinach, Chinese cabbage, bean sprouts and salad greens may need no water. Beans and root vegetables will require about ¾ cup of stock or water for each pound. Cook these a little longer—about 5 to 8 minutes in all.

When the vegetables are just tender, you may add Chinese Sauce for Vegetables, page 331. Stir it into the vegetables—and cooked meat, if you are using any. ♦ Cover the pan briefly until the sauce reaches the boiling point and serve at once.

♦ To ensure crispness, bring your guests to the table the moment you have finished cooking. Be sure also ♦ to preheat lidded dishes from which to serve the food.

The preceding description applies primarily to meat-and-vegetable dishes, but may be ♦ adapted to meat combinations, too—although ♦ we do not recommend it for raw pork. First, cook thin slices or slivers of lean meat briefly in the pan. Remove the meat and set it aside—keeping warm. Cook the vegetables in the same fat with the meat juices. When they are ready, add the meat to them just before serving. It is advisable to cook no more than one pound of meat at a time by this method.

✪ ABOUT PRESSURE COOKED VEGETABLES

Please see About Pressure Cooking, page 128. Rather than cook directly in a small amount of water, we prefer to pressure steam, as described previously in About Steamed Vegetables. For pressure timing, see individual recipes. Be sure to save the cooking juices for the stock pot.

⅄ ABOUT BLENDED PURÉED VEGETABLES

The blender is a real find for mothers of young children who want to cook fresh vegetables all at once for the whole family and then purée the very young children's portion. As an alternative, well-washed and scrubbed, tender, raw vegetables may be blended and then cooked to the boiling point. Tough ones should be briefly parboiled, cooled and then blended. You may reheat briefly in butter or cream before serving.

🗎 ABOUT CAMPFIRE VEGETABLES

Here are 2 simple, potless ways to cook vegetables for an outdoor barbecue. For the first, use frozen or sliced and washed vegetables. Place them on heavy-weight aluminum foil and season them. Use the drugstore wrap, page 759. Place the foil-wrapped vegetables on a grill or under or on hot coals for 10 to 15 minutes.

For the second method, place—directly on a greased grill above the coals—thick slices of tomato, mushroom, pepper, parboiled onion. Cover with an inverted colander. Cook until tender.

✳ ABOUT COOKING FROZEN VEGETABLES

♦ Please read about Thawing and Cooking of Frozen Foods, page 760. To cook these convenience foods so they are all heated through at the same time, use a frozen-food steamer.

♦ To pressure cook frozen foods, allow about ½ as long as for the regular pressure cooking times given in individual recipes, but use the same amounts of water.

If using an electric skillet, place the hard-frozen vegetables, except for spinach and corn on the cob, which must be partially thawed, in the skillet and cover. Set at 350° until steam escapes. Then turn to 300° until the vegetable is tender.

▲ ABOUT COOKING VEGETABLES AT HIGH ALTITUDES

In baking vegetables at high altitudes, use approximately the same temperatures and timing given for sea-level cooking. In cooking vegetables at high altitude by any process involving moisture, both more liquid and a longer cooking time are needed, as the vegetables boil at lower temperatures. Frequently, the longer time can be reduced if the vegetables are thinly sliced or cut into small units. To avoid tough stems and overcooked leaves in leafy vegetables, remove the mid rib and use it in the stock pot.

Make these adjustments as an approximate time guide: for each 1000 feet of elevation, add to the cooking time given in the recipes about 10% for whole beets, carrots and onions and about 7% for green beans, squash, green cabbage, turnips and parsnips. ▲ ✳ In cooking frozen vegetables at high altitudes, whole carrots and beans may require as much as 5 to 12 minutes of additional cooking, while other frozen vegetables may need only 1 to 2 more minutes.

The extension division of most land grant colleges will test the gauge of your pressure cooker and probably provide a pressure chart for your area free of charge.

In pressuring vegetables at high altitude, you will have to increase the liquid in your cooker ¼ to ½ cup for every 2 cups of vegetables, depending on their respective length of cooking time. As with other vegetable-cooking at high altitudes, sliced or shredded vegetables, as well as peas, corn and spinach may cook almost as rapidly as at sea level, at 15 lbs. pressure. But you may find that, with some of the leafy greens, 10 lbs. of pressure and a slightly longer cooking period gives a better result. This has been found true for asparagus, celery, turnips and cauliflower. Don't be surprised if whole potatoes, beets, yams and beans need considerably more time than at sea level.

ABOUT REHEATED VEGETABLES

Reheating vegetables is frowned on—both from a culinary and health standpoint. If you do reheat them, put them with a few teaspoons of water or stock in the top of a covered double boiler or reheat or bake them in a hot sauce. Allow about ¼ to ½ as much sauce as vegetables. Reheating in a sauce is one of the best ways to serve vegetables which must be held. The sautéing and browning of cooked vegetables diminish vitamins. Try serving leftover vegetables vinaigretted in a salad, remembering—contrary to at least one precept we learned at mother's knee—that cold food is as nutritious as hot.

Canned or frozen vegetables have, of course, already suffered some loss of flavor and vitamins. Reheating before serving increases this loss. ◗ Be sure to retain the canning or cooking water for use in soup or sauce or as the medium in which to reheat.

◗ Always clean off tops before opening cans, as they may be dusty or have been sprayed with poisonous insecticides while in the store. Also ◗ avoid metal slivers in opening a can, by starting to open it beyond the side seam and stopping before you cut through it. Food may be stored safely in opened cans, covered and refrigerated, but a metallic taste results, especially if the food is acid.

ABOUT CREAMED, BUTTERED AND SAUCED VEGETABLES

Practically any vegetables may be served in or with a sauce. They may be steamed or even deep fried before saucing. ◗ Drain them well before combining with sauces or butter. The amount to allow for garnishing will depend so largely on the richness of the sauce, from ½ to 1 tablespoon of butter per cup of cooked vegetables— on up to 4 tablespoons of a cream sauce garnish. If the vegetable is heated in the sauce, allow about 2 to 3 tablespoons for each cup of vegetables, using less if it is a rich sour cream dressing—more, perhaps, if based on cream soup. Consider, too, if the vegetable is to be presented in individual deep dishes or from a big serving bowl onto a flat plate.

If you are casseroling the vegetable in a sauce, allow enough sauce to just cover the vegetables. Such casseroles are often finished off Au Gratin, page 342.

Add to vegetable butters and sauces, if not already indicated in the recipe, citrus juices and pinches of zests, page 540, fresh or dried herbs, curry powder, mustard, chili powder, horseradish or grated cheese; and don't forget the onions, page 534.

ABOUT VEGETABLE FONDUES

Although the term fondue is usually associated with cheese, page 252, or Boeuf Bourguignonne, page 401, it applies also to vegetables reduced to a pulp by very, very slow cooking in butter, as for Tomato Pudding II. Some other vegetables that lend themselves well to such dishes are carrots, celery, eggplant, sweet pepper, onion, leek and lettuce.

To prepare them for this method of cooking, first rid them of excess moisture in one of the following ways. Except for tomatoes, they ,may be parblanched, page 132, from 3 to 5 minutes. Eggplant and cucumber may be sliced, salted generously and allowed to drain on a rack. Salting clears them of a rather unpleasant astringent quality they sometimes acquire. They may also be thinly sliced, salted, placed in a bowl and weighted to force out excess moisture.

Mushrooms and green onions may be wrapped in a dish towel and wrung out. If you are strong enough, you may be able to extract enough juices for the stock pot. Tomatoes for fondues may be cut at the stem end and squeezed toward the cut end to get rid of both moisture and seeds.

Cook fondue vegetables covered, until they reach a naturally puréed state.

ABOUT STUFFED VEGETABLES

Tomatoes, peppers, squashes, cucumbers, onions, mushrooms, all make decorative and delicious vegetable cases. For a "new dimension," fill them with other vegetables, contrasting in color or flavor; or point up the bland ones with a farce of cooked food, with buttered, crumbed, cooked vegetables or with creamed mixtures. Raw foods needing long cooking should not be used in vegetable stuffings.

As vegetable cases need different timing for blanching, see recipes under individual vegetables for this information. Other factors remain the same. After draining, place the filled cases on a rack, in a pan containing about ¼ inch of water.

Heat the cases through in a 400° oven, unless otherwise indicated, before serving. Or, if you want to serve them Au Gratin I or II, page 342, you may find they have better color if you run them first under a broiler and then bake as above to heat them. With Au Gratin III, the cheese will probably brown the tops sufficiently in the baking alone without using a broiler at all.

ABOUT VEGETABLES À LA GRECQUE

These mixed vegetables, left whole if small or cut into attractive shapes, see page 251, become aromatic as the result of being boiled in a court bouillon of highly seasoned oil and water. They are served at between 70° and 90° or, at most, slightly chilled, so that the oil will not be evident. They make convenient hors d'oeuvre, meat tray or salad garnishes, as they keep well covered and refrigerated. They are excellent for an antipasto tray. Prepare one of the following court bouillons in which to cook:

1 lb. mixed vegetables

Suitable vegetables include artichoke hearts, julienned carrots, cauliflower florets, celery, fennel, green beans, leeks, mushrooms, pearl onions, peppers and pickled whole olives. Cucumber and eggplant slices or strips are delicious but these should have excess moisture removed, see page 176.

Squeeze over the cut vegetables, to keep them white:

Juice of 2 lemons

Place in a 3-quart stainless or enamel pan:

    4 cups water
    ⅓ to ½ cup olive oil
    1 teaspoon salt
    2 peeled cloves garlic
    (3 peeled shallots)

Add the following herbs and spices, tied in a cheesecloth bag:

    6 sprigs parsley

    2 teaspoons fresh thyme
    12 peppercorns
    (3 coriander seeds or ¼ teaspoon
      orégano)
    (⅛ teaspoon fennel or celery seeds)

Add for flavor 2 of the squeezed lemon halves. Bring the mixture to a boil, then remove from the heat to season for about 15 minutes. Remove the spice bag and garlic. Bring the court bouillon again slowly to a ▶ simmer. Add in turn the most delicately flavored of the prepared vegetables. Once more bring the oil just to a boil, reduce the heat and let the vegetables heat through and then cool in the marinade. Drain them and place them in a jar, using a slotted wooden spoon. Now, use the marinade to cook the next most delicately flavored vegetable. Continue till each one has been cooked and cooled in the marinade. When they are all in the jar, mixed or separate, cover them with the marinade to store. After the vegetables have been eaten, use the marinade for sauces.

II. Combine in a stainless or enamel pan:
    1 cup wine
    2 cups olive oil
    ½ cup vinegar
    ½ to ¾ cup water
    2 cloves garlic
    3 sprigs parsley
    6 peppercorns
    2 sliced lemons
    ¼ teaspoon salt
Cook the vegetables in the heated mixture, as in I.

III. This rather off-beat version is a pleasant change.
Combine in a stainless or enamel pan:
    ¾ cup olive oil
    ½ cup wine vinegar
    ¾ cup catsup
    ½ cup chili sauce
    1 clove garlic
    1 teaspoon Worcestershire sauce
Cook the vegetables in the heated mixture, as in I.

ABOUT VEGETABLES BAKED UNPEELED

We have always liked the snug phrase "baked in their jackets" to describe this process. But we are told that at least one young cook, after encountering it, called a home economist of the local utility company and complained that her grocer was unable to supply her with potato-jackets!

Only to a degree true is the concept that unpeeled baking is the very best way of cooking to preserve vitamins in vegetables. Since most vitamins lie just under the skin ▶ those most sensitive to heat will be destroyed if baking is too protracted and the skin becomes too crusty. Proper baking, however, destroys few and we can cheerfully put up with the loss in gaining the distinctive baked flavor.

ABOUT VEGETABLES FOR A ROAST

To cook vegetables for a roast, it is better on several scores to process them separately. For one thing, if they are placed in the roasting pan, the steam they exude tends to give a moister oven heat than is desirable for meat roasting. For another, typical root vegetables such as potatoes, carrots, onions and turnips themselves profit by separate cooking. Steam them, page 252, first, then drain and dry. Cook them in butter in a ♦ heavy, covered pan until almost tender and finish browning them uncovered.

GLAZED ROOT VEGETABLES
Choose:
> 2 cups young vegetables—onions,
>   carrots, turnips or potatoes

Simmer, covered, in a very heavy pan with:
> 1 cup veal or chicken stock
> ½ teaspoon salt
> 2 teaspoons sugar
> 2 tablespoons butter

When the vegetables are tender and the liquid has been almost absorbed ♦ uncover and continue to cook, shaking the pan constantly over brisk heat until they are coated with a golden glaze.

ABOUT DEEP FAT FRIED VEGETABLES

The French have made the fried potato famous in floured strips, page 295, the English in chips, page 350. The Italians, by using either a beaten egg coating or a batter, produce their famous vegetable and other mixtures as fritto misto—and the Japanese, who learned this trick from Portuguese sailors way back in the 16th century, prepare them today under the term tempura.

Since success depends so largely on the ♦ quality of the fat and avoiding its excess absorption, please read About Deep Fat Frying, page 124. ♦ Be sure to have the vegetables dry before applying the coating. It is also best to let the coating dry for about 10 minutes before immersing the food in fat brought to between 350° and 375°. Cook until the vegetables are golden.

Vegetables suitable for this type of cooking are long green beans; ⅓ inch thick eggplant slices—barely nicked with tiny knife marks at ½ inch intervals, all around the bands of skin; mushrooms and tiny green peppers—whole or cut in half vertically; cucumber, squash, zucchini or sweet potato rounds, cut lotus roots or bamboo shoots, small bundles of julienned onions, asparagus tips, finely shredded cabbage, cauli-flower or broccoli florets, artichoke hearts or stems.

After preparing the vegetables, be sure to sprinkle any which may discolor with lemon juice.

ARTICHOKES
Artichokes of the globe type, sketched, differ in shape, taste and method of cooking from Jerusalem artichokes, page 257. If the leaves are spreading or discolored, the artichokes are not tender. They are served whole or cored and eaten with the fingers after cooking. Serve one to each diner. The leaves are dipped, one at a time, in a sauce and the lower end is simply pulled through the teeth to extract the tender edible portion. The leaf is then discarded. Continue to eat them until a light-colored cone of young leaves appears. Pull this up with one movement. Then lift the fuzzy center out and discard it. Eat the remaining heart with a fork, dipping each piece in sauce first.

To prepare, hold by the stem end and dash up and down, quickly, in a deep bowl of water:
> Artichokes

Cut off the stems. Pull off the tough bottom row of leaves and cut off ¼ of the tops. For this, you may use scissors. To avoid discoloration, dip the cut parts in:
> Lemon juice

♦ Steam, page 252, or place the artichokes upright on a trivet, with 1 to 2 inches of boiling water beneath. Add:
> 1 sliced onion or 1 mashed clove garlic
> 2 celery ribs with leaves
> 1½ tablespoons lemon juice, wine
>   or vinegar
> (2 tablespoons salad oil)
> (A bay leaf)

Cook them covered for 45 minutes or until tender. Drain and serve them hot with:
> Melted butter, Mayonnaise, page 313,
> Hollandaise Sauce, page 328,
> Béchamel Sauce, page 322, or
> Vinaigrette Sauce, page 311

Cooked artichokes may be served chilled. ◒ Pressure cook large artichokes at 15 lb. about 15 minutes, small ones 8 minutes at 15 lbs.

CORED ARTICHOKES
Clean and trim, as described previously:
> Artichokes

urn them upside down. Press hard to orce the leaves apart. Reverse and insert grapefruit corer. Press the handles down o cut out the choke. Remove it. Tie rtichokes into shape with string. ◗ Steam hem, page 252, or cook as in previous ecipe. Drain them well, untie and serve ither warm or cold, the centers filled vith:

Hollandaise Sauce, page 328

f they are too hot when filled, the Hollandaise may separate. Or serve cold with:

Marinated shrimp and mayonnaise

RTICHOKE HEARTS
emove all leaves and chokes from:

Artichokes

team them, page 252, or drop the hearts ito 1 inch of:

Boiling water

◗ which you may add:

Lemon juice

mmer them, covered, for 20 minutes or ntil tender. Serve them with:

Brown Butter, page 338, or
Hollandaise Sauce, page 328

ooked or canned artichoke hearts, well ained, may be sautéed until hot in:

Butter or drippings

which you may add:

Garlic, shallots or onions

ason them with:

Salt and paprika
Lemon juice

rve hot or cold. For a good way to stuff ld artichoke hearts, see Salads, page 84.

UFFED BAKED ARTICHOKES
eheat oven to 350°.

Roman Style

ean, trim and blanch, page 132:

Artichokes

ain them well. Make a dressing of:

Bread crumbs
Minced garlic or onion
Chopped celery
Chopped anchovies or anchovy paste
Grated Parmesan cheese
Chopped parsley
Salt and paprika

sh the dressing down between the ves. The choke may be removed, as scribed previously, if desired, and the ter filled with the dressing. Pour over artichokes a little:

Olive oil

ce them in a baking dish and cover the ttom of the dish with ½ inch of:

Boiling water or stock

ke them, covered, until they are done, out 1 hour.

Or fill the artichokes with either:

Ham or sausage stuffing, or
Stuffed Mushrooms, page 281, or

Creamed Spinach, page 300, and grated cheese

JERUSALEM ARTICHOKES
This tall, yellow blooming composite of our roadsides has been miraculously hybridized and should be better known. Its nubbly roots proliferate to furnish us that extra vegetable we always wish we could find. They do need watching while being cooked.

Wash:

1½ lbs. Jerusalem artichokes

◗ Steam them, page 252, or drop them into:

Boiling water

To prevent discoloration, add:

1 teaspoon mild vinegar or white wine

Cook them ◗ covered, until they are tender only. If permitted to cook beyond this point, they will again become tough. Test them with a toothpick after 15 minutes. Drain them. Remove the peel. Melt:

2 to 3 tablespoons butter

Add:

2 drops hot pepper sauce
2 tablespoons chopped parsley

Pour these ingredients over the artichokes or cream them, page 254. Or, cut into halves and ✪ pressure cook at 15 lbs. for 10 minutes.

ASPARAGUS
The Romans used to say if they wanted to do something in a hurry, "Do it in less time than it takes to cook asparagus."

I.   4 to 6 Servings

Wash:

2 lbs. asparagus

Cut off or snap off the lower part of the stalks. Keep the trimmings for soup. It is seldom necessary to skin green asparagus. If it is white, skin from below the head, increasing the depth of cut into the stalk as you approach the base to remove any bitter flavor in the skin. Tie the asparagus in serving bunches with white string. Place them upright in a deep stewpan or in the bottom part of a double boiler, the lower ends in:

½ cup boiling water

Cook the asparagus ◗ closely covered 12

minutes or until tender. An inverted double boiler top may be used. The steam will

cook the tips. Drain the asparagus well.
Reserve the liquor. Add:
    ½ teaspoon salt
Melt:
    ⅓ cup butter
Sauté in it, for 1 minute:
    1 cup bread crumbs
Pour this mixture over the tips of the as-
paragus or serve them with:
    1 cup Cream Sauce I, page 322, made
      with half cream and half asparagus
      liquor, Egg Sauce, page 323, or
      Hollandaise Sauce, page 328

II. Sometimes, if asparagus must be held,
both the color and texture are improved if
this recipe is used—although we do not
guarantee nutritive value.
Arrange in a flat pan:
    2 lbs. cleaned asparagus
Place them not more than 3 or 4 deep.
Add:
    ½ teaspoon salt
Cover with cold water. Prepare and cover
with a poaching paper, page 129. Bring
them to a boil, reduce the heat at once and
♦ simmer about 15 minutes. Keep lukewarm until ready to serve.
Drain when ready to serve.

BAMBOO SHOOTS
These slightly acid shoots, which complement mushrooms and meat, must be young
and tender and from an edible bamboo
plant.
If fresh, boil:
    Bamboo shoots
in:
    Water
about 10 to 15 minutes. Discard the water and then the shoots are ready to use.
If using canned shoots, scrape off the calcium deposits. If you want to use only
part of a can, store the remainder by first
draining. Re-cover with cold water and
refrigerate ♦ covered, for about 1 week.

ABOUT FRESH BEANS
Green or snap beans, formerly called
string because their strings had to be removed, have in many instances been hybridized so that now they snap clean and
need only have the ends snipped off. Kentucky wonders and wax beans, however,
still need both snipping and stringing. To
prepare broad beans, see Lima Beans, page
262. To prepare immature fava beans or
marrow-fat beans, see Podded Peas, page
288. For mature green favas, see Lima
Beans. For dried favas, see Dried Legumes,
page 259. Haricots verts, with their okra-
like flavored overtones, are otherwise much
like green beans. ♦ To avoid toughening
any beans, salt when cooking is half finished.

GREEN OR SNAP BEANS
                     4 Serving
This vegetable is available fresh the yea
around and lends itself to endless varia
tions.
Wash:
    1 lb. green beans
Snip off the ends. You may then slive
them, French them on the diagonal o
leave them whole. If the latter, tie the
in individual bunches before cooking
When cooked and drained, arrange the
on a platter and cover with one of th
garnishes or sauces suggested below. T
cook green beans ♦ steam, page 252,
drop them into:
    Boiling water or part water and
    part stock
Reduce the heat at once. Place on top
the beans:
    (1 whole peeled onion)
Cook partially covered, page 251, if yo
wish to preserve the color; or covered,
you wish to preserve more nutrients. Sin
mer until barely tender, no longer—abo
20 minutes. Before draining, you may r
move the onion.
    Correct the seasoning
Cover with:
    1 tablespoon melted butter

ADDITIONS TO GREEN BEANS
To further flavor beans during the coo
ing, add:
    (1 small cut-up onion)
    (1- to 2-inch cube of salt pork)
To garnish or sauce, use for 1 lb. of bea
    1 tablespoon butter or browned
      butter, or ¼ cup buttered crumbs,
      or 2 tablespoons brown onion butter,
      or 2 tablespoons crumbled bacon
      and drippings
Add to the above fats:
    (1 teaspoon celery or dill seed) or
      (1 teaspoon fresh summer savory
      or basil)
Or garnish with:
    Anchovy Butter or Oil, page 339,
    Almond Garnish, page 343
Or add:
    ½ cup sautéed mushrooms
    ⅛ to ½ cup cultured sour cream
    2 tablespoons chopped parsley
Or add:
    2 tablespoons wine vinegar
    ¼ teaspoon mustard
    1 tablespoon Worcestershire sauce
    A drop of hot pepper sauce
Or add:
    2 tablespoons butter
    ¼ cup toasted slivered almonds
    ¼ cup sliced water chestnuts
    ¼ cup sliced cooked mushrooms
If the beans are left long, cover with:
    A Cream Sauce Variation, page 32
    or 1 can Cream of Chicken or Mus
    room Soup and herbs, or Quick

Tomato Sauce, page 334, or Egg
Sauce I, page 323

CASSEROLE GREEN BEANS
I.   6 Servings
Preheat oven to 350°.
What becomes of the onions and peppers?
They frequently disappear, leaving mar-
velously seasoned beans. An easy dish for
the hostess who cooks her own dinner.
Trim:
  1 lb. green beans
Skin and chop:
  4 medium-size white onions
Remove the seeds and membrane from:
  2 medium-size green peppers
Chop the peppers. Butter a baking dish.
Place in it alternate layers of the vegeta-
bles, beginning and ending with a layer of
beans. Sprinkle each layer with:
  Salt and paprika
Dot each layer with:
  Butter
Bake the vegetables ♦ covered, for about
1¼ hours or until the beans are tender.
Before serving, garnish with:
  Au Gratin II, page 342

II. Preheat oven to 350°.
Prepare for cooking:
  1 lb. green beans
Place them in a greased casserole. Cover
with:
  1 can cream of tomato soup
  3 tablespoons prepared horseradish
  2 teaspoons Worcestershire sauce
  ¼ teaspoon salt
  ¼ teaspoon paprika
Bake ♦ covered, for about 1 hour or until
tender. Remove the lid and garnish with:
  Au Gratin III, page 342
Serve when the cheese is melted.

GREEN BEANS, POTATOES
AND SMOKED MEAT
                                 4 Servings
Cook until nearly tender in water to cover:
  A piece of smoked meat: ham,
  picnic, Canadian bacon, etc.
If using already cooked or leftover ham or
bone, just bring to a boil before adding:
  1 lb. green beans
  4 halved, pared, medium potatoes
  (1 onion)
Simmer, covered, about 20 to 25 minutes.
  Correct the seasoning.
Serve from a large platter, garnished with:
  Lemon wedges

SWEET-SOUR BEANS
                                 4 Servings
Trim and shred lengthwise:
  1 lb. green beans
♦ Steam them, page 252, or drop them
into:
  Boiling water

to barely cover. Cook them, covered,
about 20 minutes. Now, render the fat
slowly from:
  3 pieces lean bacon
Cook with it:
  2 tablespoons chopped onions
When the bacon is crisp, remove it and
swirl in the pan:
  1 tablespoon white wine vinegar
  1 tablespoon sugar
  ½ teaspoon salt
Drain the liquid from the beans and add it
to the skillet mixture. Then combine with
the beans and cut-up bacon and serve. A
good variation to this dish is the addition
of:
  Bean sprouts

PURÉED GREEN BEANS, PEAS
OR LIMAS
In winter, these are a fresh note if used as
a base for soup, as a lining in serving
sautéed mushrooms or as a puréed vegetable, garnished with parsley.
Purée:
  2 cups cooked beans or peas
Use a ⅃ blender or a food mill. Add:
  2 tablespoons butter
  Correct the seasoning
and serve as soon as possible after puréeing. If the purée must be held over, cover
it while hot with whipping cream and, in
reheating in a double boiler ♦ over hot water, beat in the cream before serving.

COOKED BEAN SPROUTS
                                 4 Servings
As with other vegetables, cooked sprouted
beans have less vitamin C than if eaten
raw just after sprouting.
Bring to a boil:
  ¾ cup water
Add:
  4 cups sprouted beans, Mung or edible
  soybeans or lentils
♦ Simmer, covered, until almost soft, just
long enough to remove the raw bean
flavor. Season with:
  Salt
  (Soy sauce)

ABOUT DRIED LEGUMES
Dried peas and beans, being rather on the
dull side, much like dull people respond
readily to the right contacts. Do not scorn
them, for they have valuable, if incomplete, proteins, see page 2. Combine
them with tomatoes, onions, chili and
cheese. They are also much more tempera-
mental than one would think. Their cooking time depends on the locality in which
they were grown and on their age—usually
two unknowns for the cook; plus the type
of water used in cooking them, see About
Water, page 493. Wash, unless the package states otherwise. Do not use soda, see
About Soda, page 504. Soak in 3 to 4

times as much water as beans. Remove any beans that float. If the beans are not preprocessed, usually they are soaked overnight. Bring the beans to a slow boil in the water in which they were soaked, unless it is bitter, as happens sometimes with soybeans. Reduce the heat and ‣ simmer them. All beans should be cooked until tender. One test, provided you discard the beans you have tested, is to blow on a few of them in a spoon. If the skins burst, they are sufficiently cooked.

If you have forgotten to soak, a quick method to tenderize them for cooking is to cover with cold water. Bring up to a boil and simmer for 2 minutes. Remove from heat and let stand, tightly covered, for 1 hour. Or, blanching the beans for 2 minutes is almost equivalent to 8 hours of soaking.

You may use pre-processed beans which require no soaking. But remember that some nutrients have been lost in the preparation. Lentils and split peas are better for soaking, but do not require it.

Remember that 1 cup of beans, peas or lentils will expand to 2 to 2½ cups after cooking.

There are over 25 types of beans and peas available in our stores. They include red, kidney, black-eyed peas or beans, edible soys, pinto, strawberry, cow peas or Mexican frijoles, chick peas or Garbanzos or flageolets—which is the French haricot, dried and shelled.

White beans, which the white man learned of from the Indians and then took sailing, became our navy beans. They are usually the toughest beans and take up to 3 hours simmering. Dried Limas, after soaking for 8 hours, may cook almost as rapidly as the fresh ones—in about ½ hour. Lentils take about 1½ hours to cook.

Other people know a trick or two with navy beans. In Europe, where chestnuts are highly prized, bean purée often replaces chestnut purée in strongly seasoned chestnut dishes. ✪ Dried legumes can be pressure cooked, but can be dangerous, see page 128; therefore, long, slow cooking is preferable. Never fill the pressure cooker more than ¾ full of liquid. Pressure cook at 15 lbs.: black-eyed peas for 10 minutes; Great Northern beans for 20 minutes; kidney beans for 30 minutes; lentils for 20 minutes; Lima beans, small, for 25 minutes—large for 30 minutes; navy beans for 30 minutes; pea beans for 20 minutes and soy beans for 35 minutes. Cool pan normally for all dried vegetables for about 5 minutes, then place under cold water faucet.

PURÉE OF DRIED LEGUMES
Cook until tender:
   Dried Lentils, Beans or Peas, page 259
You may add:
   A clove of garlic

After draining the lentils, put them through a fine sieve, a purée strainer or ⅃ blender. Allow to every cup of purée:
   1 tablespoon butter
   A scant ½ teaspoon salt
   ¼ teaspoon pepper or paprika or a dash of clove
You may brown in the butter:
   1 tablespoon flour
Whip the purée over a high heat. Serve in a mound, garnished with:
   Sautéed onions
   Chopped parsley
✪ For pressure cooking time, see About Dried Legumes, above.

DRIED BEAN PATTIES
4 Servings
Grind and mash:
   2 cups cooked dried beans: soy, Lima, navy
Add to them:
   1 chopped onion
   ¼ cup chopped parsley
Beat and add:
   2 egg yolks
   2 tablespoons cream or evaporated milk
   ¼ teaspoon pepper
   1 teaspoon salt
Shape these ingredients into balls. Flatten them. Dip them in:
   Flour
Chill the patties for 1 hour or more. Sauté them slowly, until brown, in:
   Butter, drippings or other fat
Serve them with any:
   Barbecue Sauce, page 332

GREEN SOYBEANS
Use the young vegetable type, not field varieties of beans. The fuzzy pods should still be green. Immerse them in boiling water. ‣ Cover the pot. After 5 minutes, drain and cool them. Squeeze the pods to press out the beans. Cook the beans in boiling water until tender, approximately 10 to 15 minutes. Use them as directed in About Lima Beans, etc., page 262.

The cooked beans may also be spread in a greased pan, dotted with butter and roasted in a 350° oven until brown or they may be browned in deep fat, page 124. Soy milk, see page 487, and cheese can also be made from them.

BEAN DINNER IN ONE DISH
4 Servings
Preheat oven to 350°
Combine:
   1 cup cooked corn
   1 cup cooked navy beans
   1 cup lightly drained canned tomatoes
   ¾ teaspoon salt
   ¼ teaspoon paprika
   ½ teaspoon brown sugar
   1 teaspoon grated onion
Place in a greased baking dish. Sprinkle

the top with:
  **Browned bread crumbs or grated
  peanuts**
Bake ♦ covered, for about 45 minutes.

BAKED BEANS
Did you know that baked beans are as traditional in Sweden as they are in Boston?
♦ Please read About Dried Legumes, pages
259-260.

                                    4 Servings
If quick-cooking or precooked beans are
used, follow the directions on the package.
Otherwise, soak:
  1½ cups dried beans
Cover them with water. Bring them to a
boil, then simmer them slowly for ½ hour
or more, until tender.
Preheat oven to 250°.
Drain the beans, reserving the cooking
water and add:
  ¼ cup chopped onion
  2 tablespoons or more dark molasses
  2 or 3 tablespoons catsup
  1 tablespoon dry mustard
  1 teaspoon salt
  ½ cup boiling bean water or beer
  (½ teaspoon vinegar)
  (1 teaspoon curry powder)
  (1 tablespoon Worcestershire sauce)
Place them in a greased baker, decorate
them with:
  ¼ lb. sliced salt pork
and bake them, covered, for 6 to 9 hours.
If they become dry, add a little:
  **Well-seasoned stock or reserved
  bean water**
Uncover the beans for the last hour of
cooking.

CANNED BAKED BEANS
WITH FRUIT
                                    6 Servings
This is a good brunch dish.
Preheat oven to 250°.
Arrange:
  2 cans beans without sauce
in layers in a casserole with:
  2 sliced apples
  **2 sliced oranges or 4 canned apricot
  halves or pineapple slices**
  (2 large onions, sliced)
Top with:
  ½ lb. salt pork
Cover with:
  1 cup molasses
Bake about 1 to 3 hours.

BOILED BEANS
                                    5 Servings
Soak, page 259, then drain:
  **1 lb. dried beans: kidney, navy,
  marrow-fat or Limas**
Place them in a heavy saucepan. Cover
them with water. Add:
  6 tablespoons butter
  ⅓ cup chopped onion
  3 whole cloves
  2 teaspoons salt

  ¼ teaspoon freshly ground pepper
  ¼ teaspoon dried thyme
Simmer the beans, covered, from 1 to 1½
hours. Stir them from time to time. Add
and cook for about 20 minutes longer:
  1 cup dry red wine or stock
When the beans are tender, serve them
hot, garnished with:
  Chopped chives or parsley
❂ We do not recommend the pressure
cooking of dried beans, because of the
danger of frothing.

▤ CAMPFIRE BEANS
Have ready at least 2 to 3 quarts of hot
coals. Dig a hole deep enough and wide
enough to hold a covered iron kettle, allowing about 4 extra inches to the depth
of the hole. Get ready for cooking:
  Baked Beans
Put half the coals in the bottom of the
hole. Sink the covered kettle. Cover the
lid with a large piece of foil to keep out
dirt. Put the rest of the coals on the kettle
lid. Now, fill in the rest of the hole with
dirt and put at least 3 inches of dirt on top
of the kettle. Don't dig in to peek for at
least 4 hours.

CANNED BAKED BEANS AND
BACON OR FRANKFURTERS
                                    6 Servings
Preheat oven to 350°.
To jazz up pepless canned beans, add to:
  2½ cups canned beans
approximately:
  ¼ cup catsup
  2 tablespoons molasses
  2 tablespoons brown sugar
  2 tablespoons bacon drippings
  **Minced onion, celery and green
  pepper**
  Salt, if needed
  **(3 drops hot pepper sauce, a few grains
  of red pepper or 1 tablespoon
  mustard)**
to make them moist and palatable. Place
the beans in a greased, shallow, ovenproof
dish. Cover the top with:
  **Bacon, very thin strips of salt pork
  or skinned sliced frankfurters**
Bake beans ♦ covered, about 30 minutes.
♦ Uncover. Bake 30 minutes more.

CANNED KIDNEY BEANS
AND TOMATOES
                                 4 Large Servings
Preheat oven to 350°.
Grease a baking dish. Have ready:
  2½ cups canned red kidney beans
  **1 cup canned tomatoes or diluted
  tomato soup**
  ¼ cup chopped onion
  ¼ lb. chopped bacon
Cover the bottom of the dish with a layer
of beans. Sprinkle it with some of the
bacon and onions. Repeat the process.
Pour the tomatoes over the whole. Cover
the top with:

Bread crumbs or cornflakes
Dot it with:
Butter
or sprinkle it with:
Grated cheese
Bake the dish until the top is browned, for about 30 minutes.

PINTO BEANS AND RICE
4 Servings
A combination often found in South American countries.
Soak:
½ **cup pinto beans**
in:
3 cups ham broth
Gently boil the beans in the broth until they are almost done. Add:
½ **cup chopped cooked ham**
½ **cup rice**
Cover and cook for about 20 to 30 minutes, until the rice is tender.

LENTILS
6 Servings
◆ Please read About Dried Legumes, pages 259-260.
I. Add to:
2 cups lentils
3 sprigs parsley or a celery rib with leaves
¼ **cup sliced onions**
½ **bay leaf**
(A piece of fat corned beef, ham skin or bacon rind, tried-out pork fat or smoked sausage)
(2 cloves without heads)
(A slice of garlic)
Cover with:
4 cups water
Cook, covered, about 1½ hours. Add boiling water, if necessary, during the cooking. Drain the lentils and serve with:
Tomato Sauce, page 333
Or serve as a Purée, page 253. If you omit the bacon or pork flavorings above, serve the lentils with:
Roast Pork, page 407

II. Wash but do not soak:
1 cup lentils
Sauté, until golden brown:
1 minced onion
in:
¼ **cup olive oil**
Add the lentils and let them absorb the oil. Pour over them:
3½ cups boiling water
Cover the pan and simmer about 1½ hours.
Correct the seasoning
and serve hot or cold. If used for a salad, serve with French dressing and hard-cooked egg slices.

LENTILS AND PRUNES
4 Servings
Please read About Dried Legumes, pages 259-260. Wash and cook:
1 cup lentils
Cook:
1 cup Stewed Dried Prunes, page 120
Pit the prunes and mash them. Add them to the lentils with:
¼ **cup dry sherry**
1 teaspoon salt
(Lemon juice and spices)
Cook over low heat until thoroughly heated.

ABOUT LIMA, BUTTER OR BROAD BEANS

The following cooked beans, whether canned, frozen, fresh or dry, may be substituted for one another in most recipes: Fordhooks or baby Limas, Sieva types or fava beans and the European broad beans —which really taste more like peas.
If you are hulling fresh Limas, cut a thin strip along inner edge of the pod to which the beans are attached. The beans will pop out easily. One pound in the pods will yield 2 servings.
For that famous combination called Succotash, see page 274.

LIMA BEANS
6 Servings
◆ Steam, page 252, or cover:
1 quart fresh shelled Lima beans
with:
1 inch boiling water
Add:
1 tablespoon butter
Simmer the beans for 15 minutes. Add:
1 teaspoon salt
Simmer the beans, covered, until tender, for about 20 minutes more. Add:
1 tablespoon butter or olive oil
1½ tablespoons lemon juice
1 tablespoon chopped parsley, chives or dill
Or dress them with:
Warm cultured sour cream and freshly ground white pepper
Or serve them with:
Sautéed onions, creamed mushrooms or a sprinkling of crisp bacon
❂ Pressure cook Lima beans at 15 lbs. for about 2 minutes.

LIMA BEANS WITH PIQUANT SAUCE

4 Servings

In order to provide a canned Lima bean with glamor, you must do a fan dance with it!

Drain:

  1½ cups canned or cooked Lima beans

Reserve the liquor. If necessary, add to it, to make 1½ cups of liquid:

  Cream

Melt:

  3 tablespoons butter or drippings

Sauté in it until golden brown:

  ¼ cup chopped onion
  (¼ cup chopped celery)

Stir in, until it bubbles:

  2½ tablespoons flour

Stir in the liquid slowly. Reduce the heat and stir in until melted:

  ¼ cup or more minced cheese

Season the sauce with:

  ½ teaspoon salt
  ⅛ teaspoon paprika
  A few grains red pepper
  ¼ teaspoon mustard
  2 teaspoons Worcestershire sauce
  A pinch of 3 herbs—marjoram, thyme, savory, etc.

Add the beans and heat them. Serve them garnished with:

  Chopped parsley

FRENCH LIMA BEANS

4 Servings

Place in a heavy saucepan:

  1 quart fresh Lima beans
  1 small clove garlic
  2 tablespoons peeled, seeded, finely diced tomatoes

Barely cover with:

  1 inch water or half water and half olive oil

Cover and simmer about 15 minutes. Remove garlic. Add:

  2 tablespoons butter
  ¼ teaspoon salt
  1 tablespoon chopped parsley

Continue cooking, covered, until beans are tender.

LIMA BEAN CASSEROLE

4 Servings

This is a fine main dish.
Preheat oven to 375°.
To:

  1 cup cooked or canned Lima beans

add:

  6 sliced frankfurters or sausages
  1 chopped and seeded green pepper
  2 chopped tomatoes

You may wish to purée the beans, page 253. Place these ingredients in a baking dish and cover the top with:

  Au Gratin II, page 342

Bake the beans for about 15 minutes. This dish, puréed, makes a fine stuffing for peppers or onions.

LIMA BEANS WITH CHEESE

4 Servings

Preheat oven to 350°.
Prepare:

  2½ cups cooked Lima beans

Stir into them:

  ½ cup chicken stock

Or melt:

  2 tablespoons butter

Add and sauté for 3 minutes:

  ¼ cup minced onion

Stir into the stock or butter, over low heat, until melted:

  ½ lb. grated cheese

Add the beans and:

  ½ teaspoon salt
  ¼ teaspoon pepper
  1 teaspoon dried basil or thyme
  A few grains cayenne
  (1 cup chopped nut meats)

Bake the beans for about ½ hour. Serve them with:

  Tomato Sauce, page 333

CHILI LIMA BEANS

6 Servings

Preheat oven to 350°.
Drain:

  2 cups cooked Lima beans

Add:

  ¼ lb. salt pork, cut in strips
  1 large minced onion
  1 tablespoon molasses
  2 cups cooked tomatoes
  1 tablespoon brown sugar
  ¼ teaspoon chili powder or pepper
  1 teaspoon salt

Bake these ingredients in a greased casserole for about 1 hour.

LIMA BEANS AND MUSHROOMS

6 Servings

Serve this with crisp bacon and grapefruit salad.
Have ready:

  2 cups fresh, cooked or canned Lima beans

Drain them. Sauté:

  ½ lb. mushrooms

Drain them, saving the liquor if there is any. Add to the liquor and melt:

  1 tablespoon butter

Stir in:

  2 tablespoons flour

Cook and stir these ingredients until they are well blended. Stir in slowly:

  ½ cup Chicken Stock, page 490, or stock and bean liquor
  ½ cup top milk
  Correct the seasoning.

Add the beans and mushrooms. Heat them.
Add before serving:

  (1 tablespoon sherry)

The dish may be served with:

  Au Gratin II, page 342

Place it under a broiler until the crumbs are brown.

BEETS

8 Servings

Cut the tops from:

2 lbs. beets

leaving 1 inch of stem. Wash the beets.
♦ Steam them, page 252, or half cover
them with:

Boiling water

Cover pot and cook until tender. Allow ½
to 1 hour for young beets, 1 to 2 hours for
old beets. Add boiling water as needed.
When the beets are done, cool them
slightly and slip off the skins. Cut them
into quarters, chop or put them through a
ricer.

Correct the seasoning

Then either pour over them:

Melted butter
Chopped parsley

or serve the beets in:

Cream Sauce II, page 322

seasoned with:

Mustard, curry powder, horseradish
or ¼ cup sautéed onions

or prepare:

Cream Sauce II, page 322

using in place of the milk, half orange
juice and half water. Add:

3 tablespoons brown sugar
2 teaspoons grated orange rind

❷ Pressure cook small beets 12 minutes,
large beets 18 minutes at 15 lbs.

CASSEROLED BEETS

8 Servings

Preheat oven to 400°.
Pare, then slice or chop fine:

16 medium-sized beets

Grease a 7-inch baking dish. Place the
beets in it in layers. Season them with:

¼ cup sugar
¾ teaspoon salt
¼ teaspoon paprika

Dot them with:

3 tablespoons butter

Add:

1 tablespoon lemon juice or a
sliver of fresh ginger
⅛ cup water
(Grated or sliced onions)

Cover the dish closely and bake the beets
for 30 minutes or until they are tender.
Stir them twice.

SWEET-SOUR OR HARVARD BEETS

6 Servings

For a cold version of sweet-sour, see Pickled Beet Salad, page 85.
Slice or dice:

3 cups freshly cooked or canned beets

Stir in a double boiler until smooth:

½ cup sugar
1 tablespoon cornstarch
½ teaspoon salt
2 whole cloves
½ cup mild cider vinegar or dry
white wine

Cook and stir these ingredients until they
are clear. Add the beets and place them
over hot water for about 30 minutes. Just
before serving, heat, but do not boil, the
beets and add:

2 tablespoons butter
(1 tablespoon orange marmalade)

BOILED BEETS IN SOUR CREAM

4 Servings

Combine in a double boiler:

3 cups cooked or canned sliced beets
½ cup cultured sour cream
1 tablespoon prepared horseradish
1 tablespoon chopped chives
Salt, as needed
(1 teaspoon grated onion)

Heat these ingredients ♦ over hot water.

SWEET-SOUR APPLE BEETS

4 Servings

Preheat oven to 325°.
Grease a casserole. Mix together and put
into it:

2 cups chopped cooked beets
2 cups chopped tart apples
¼ to ½ cup thinly sliced onions
1½ teaspoons salt
A generous grating of nutmeg

If the apples are very tart, add:

(1 tablespoon sugar)

If they are bland:

(2 tablespoons lemon juice)

Dot with:

2 to 3 tablespoons butter

Cover and bake for about 1 hour.

BAKED BEETS

I. Beets may be baked like potatoes—in
their jackets.
Preheat oven to 325°.
Wash:

Beets

Trim the tops, leaving 1 inch of stem.
Place them on a pan and bake them until
they are tender. Allow at least ½ hour for
young beets and 1 hour for old beets. Pull
off the skins. Season the beets with:

Salt and paprika

Serve them with:

Melted butter

II. Have ready a preheated 325° oven or
▤ hot coals in the grill. Pare and slice:

Beets
Correct the seasoning

and add:

Butter

to each serving, before wrapping in aluminum foil. Bake until tender.

YOUNG BEETS AND LEAVES

4 Servings

Scrub well and dice, unpared, into ¼-inch
cubes:

6 or 8 beet roots

Drop them into:

¾ cup hot milk

Stir until you are sure that all surfaces have been coated with the milk. Cook, covered, over slow heat, 8 to 12 minutes, depending on age of beets. Cut into ½-inch shreds:

Beet leaves

Add them to the diced beets. Re-cover the pan and continue to simmer 6 to 8 minutes longer. Season with:

Salt and paprika
Freshly ground nutmeg or cloves

BEET GREENS

4 Servings

Beet greens may be prepared like Spinach, page 300. Put the beets in a ring, serve the greens in the center, dressed with melted butter, and garnish with horseradish sauce. Or, heat in a frying pan:

2 tablespoons butter or cooking oil

Add and simmer:

2 cups cooked, chopped beet greens
1 teaspoon grated onion
¼ teaspoon salt
½ tablespoon prepared mustard
1 tablespoon horseradish

Remove from the heat and add:

½ cup cultured sour cream

✪ Pressure cook at 15 lbs. for about 3 minutes.

BREADFRUIT

If ever your fate is that of Robinson Crusoe, remember that you can eat raw any breadfruit that has seeds. The seeds are treated like Chestnuts, page 272. All seedless varieties must be cooked.

The breadfruit is one of the most beautiful of tropical trees, with a highly romantic history. The fruit is 6 to 8 inches in diameter and greenish brown or yellow when ripe. The slightly fibrous meat is light yellow and sweet. You may remove the center core with its seed, if it has one, before or after cooking. Season and serve it as you would sweet potato.

I. To boil, choose mature, firm fruit, with rind still green in color. Core and dice:

4 cups peeled breadfruit

Drop into:

3 cups boiling water

and simmer, covered, about 1 hour, until tender. Drain, season and serve.

II. Preheat oven to 375°.
To bake, place in a baking pan:

1 unpeeled breadfruit

Have enough water in the pan to keep it from burning. Bake until tender, about 1 hour, then the stem and core will pull out easily. Cut in half. Season with:

Salt and pepper or sugar and butter

III. To steam, remove skin, stem and core:

1 breadfruit

Cut into halves or quarters and place the pieces in a pan to steam, covered, page 252, for 2 hours. Season with:

Butter

Salt and pepper

You may steam ¾-inch-thick breadfruit slices, roll in flour and fry in deep fat until a golden brown color.

BREADFRUIT SEEDS

These are so close to chestnuts in flavor and texture that they may be substituted in any chestnut recipe. Wash well:

1 lb. breadfruit seeds

Drop them into:

1 quart boiling water
3 tablespoons salt

Cook covered for about 45 minutes. Drain and serve hot.

BROCCOLI

4 Servings

Choose heads that are all green. If yellow appears, the bloom is coming up and the broccoli is apt to be tough. Soak for 10 minutes in cold water:

2 lbs. broccoli

Drain it well. Remove the large leaves and the tough part of the stalks. Cut deep gashes in the bottom of the stalks. If the broccoli is mature, cook it like cabbage, page 266. If it is young ▶ steam it, page 252, or place it upright so only the stems are in water and the heads steam, see Asparagus. page 257. Or, to retain excellent color, use a poaching paper, page 129. Add:

1 inch boiling water

Cook it ▶ closely covered, until it is barely tender, 10 to 12 minutes. Drain and sprinkle with:

½ teaspoon salt

Serve it with:

Buttered crumbs, melted butter or lemon juice

to which add:

(¼ cup chopped salted almonds)

or try serving it:

Au Gratin II, page 342

or with one of the following sauces:

Hot Vinaigrette Sauce, page 311
Hollandaise Sauce, page 342
Cheese Sauce, page 326
Onion Sauce, page 325
Sour Cream Dressing, page 317
Allemande Sauce, page 324

✪ Pressure cook broccoli at 15 lbs. for about 2 minutes.

QUICK CREAMED BROCCOLI

4 Servings

Preheat broiler to 550°.
Prepare:

2 cups hot, cooked broccoli

Drain. Either cover it with:

Hot canned cream soup sauce

or dice the broccoli and fold it gently into the sauce. Place it in a buttered casserole and sprinkle with:

Crushed cornflakes
(Grated Romano cheese)

Run it under the broiler until golden.

DEEP FRIED BROCCOLI
Preheat deep fryer to 375°.
Prepare:

> **Cooked broccoli**

Drain it before it is tender. Cut it into quarters. Dip in:

> **Batter for Vegetables, page 221**

Fry the broccoli in deep fat, page 124, until golden brown.

BRAISED BROCCOLI
6 Servings

Preheat oven to 350°.
Cut off the tough stems and slice:

> **2 lbs. broccoli**

Wash and drain it. Prepare and place in a baking dish:

> **¼ cup chopped celery or carrots**
> **¼ cup chopped onions**

Add the broccoli, cover it with:

> **Well-seasoned Chicken Stock,**
> **page 490**

Bake the vegetables, covered, until they are tender—about 1 hour. Serve:

> **Au Gratin I or III, page 342**

❂ Pressure cook broccoli at 15 lbs. for about 2 minutes.

BRUSSELS SPROUTS
6 Servings

If wilted, pull the outer leaves from:

> **1 lb. Brussels sprouts**

Cut off the stems. Soak the sprouts for 10 minutes in cold water to which a little salt has been added. Drain them. Cut crosswise gashes into the stem ends. ◗ Steam, page 252, or drop them into a quantity of rapidly boiling:

> **Water**

◗ Reduce heat and simmer, uncovered, until they are barely tender, about 10 minutes. Do not overcook. Drain and serve with:

> **1 tablespoon melted butter**
> **(Grated Parmesan cheese and**
> **chopped parsley or 1 tablespoon**
> **lemon juice or a grating of nutmeg)**

or sauté in the butter:

> **1 tablespoon grated onion, or**
> **2 tablespoons bread crumbs and**
> **¼ teaspoon mustard**

or serve with:

> **Canned Cream Soup Sauce, page 333**

into which you may put at the last moment:

> **(½ cup finely chopped fresh celery)**

or, best of all, with lots of:

> **Hollandaise Sauce, page 328**

❂ Pressure cook Brussels sprouts at 15 lbs. for about 3 minutes.

BAKED BRUSSELS SPROUTS AND CHESTNUTS
6 Servings

Preheat oven to 350°.
Have ready:

> **2 cups cooked Brussels sprouts**

> **½ lb. cooked chestnuts**

Butter a baking dish. Fill it with alternate layers of sprouts and chestnuts. Dot the layers with:

> **Butter**
> **Correct the seasoning**

Moisten them lightly with:

> **Stock**

Cover with:

> **Au Gratin II, page 342**

Bake them, uncovered, for about 20 to 30 minutes.

ABOUT CABBAGE

Cabbage types are as different as the uses of the word. In France, "mon petit chou" is a term of endearment—but call anyone a cabbage in English and see what happens!

Savoys, which are a loose-leaved cabbage, endear themselves to us for their elegance of texture. They are usually available only in the fall. As a rule, whether cabbage is green or red, choose a head that is firm. Cabbage lends itself to stuffing as do the leaves, see Dolmas, page 431.

All cabbage types, if fresh, are a high and inexpensive source for vitamin C. To preserve the vitamins, keep cabbage wrapped before cooking. And use the cooked cabbage water in sauces and soups. The old way of cooking cabbage is to cut it in sections and boil it for hours. The new way is to shred it finely or quarter it and barely cook it—allowing only 7 minutes if shredded, 15 if quartered. ◗ To shred cabbage, cut the head in half and place flat side down on a board. Hold the cabbage with the left hand and slice into long shreds with a sharp knife. The longer growing periods required for winter and Savoy cabbages demand in turn more time to break down their coarser cellulose. Use a longer cooking period, about 20 minutes. ❂ Pressure cook 2- to 3-inch wedges of cabbage at 15 lbs. pressure for 3 to 5 minutes.

I. Remove the outer leaves from:

> **½ head cabbage**

Drop it into a quantity of rapidly boiling:

> **Water**

◗ Reduce the heat to a simmer. Cook it ◗ uncovered, until it is tender but still crisp. Drain it. Add:

> **½ teaspoon salt**

Place it in a serving dish and pour over it:

> **Melted butter—1 tablespoon to**
> **1 cup cabbage**

Add to the butter:

> **(Bread crumbs or caraway, chilis, or**
> **poppy seeds or a few drops lemon**
> **juice and a tablespoon chopped**
> **parsley)**

or place the cooked cabbage in a baking dish and cover with:

> **A Creole Sauce, page 336, or**
> **Au Gratin III, page 342**

Heat through in a 350° oven.

II. All rules have exceptions, so try out this cabbage dish which calls for little water. Cut into wedges:
> A head of cabbage

Trim off part of the core. Drop the wedges into:
> ½ inch boiling water

Cover and cook the cabbage for about 10 minutes. Drain it well. Dress it with:
> 1 cup Cream Sauce I, page 322

to which has been added:
> ½ teaspoon freshly grated nutmeg or
> 2 teaspoons prepared mustard or
> ½ cup grated cheese

or use:
> 1 cup Horseradish Cream Sauce, page 324, or 1 cup creamed canned condensed soup, or Allemande Sauce, page 324

No matter which sauce you use, combine it with the cabbage and serve at once.

III. 6 Servings
This method makes young cabbage very delicate and is a great help in disguising the age of a mature cabbage, but you may be losing some nutrients. Cut into very fine shreds:
> 3 cups cabbage

Drop it gradually into:
> ¾ cup boiling milk

Boil it for 2 minutes. Drain and discard the milk. Drop the cabbage into hot:
> Cream Sauce I, page 322

Simmer for 3 minutes longer and serve at once with:
> Broiled sausages

CABBAGE, POTATOES AND HAM
4 Servings
Cook until nearly tender, in water to cover:
> A piece of smoked ham: Cali, picnic, butt, shank or cottage ham or roll

If using already cooked or leftover ham or bone, just bring to a boil before adding:
> 1 large quartered cabbage
> 4 halved and pared medium size potatoes

Simmer, covered, about 20 to 25 minutes.
> Correct the seasoning

Serve from a large platter, garnished with:
> Lemon wedges

BAKED CABBAGE
4 Servings
Preheat oven to 325°.
Put in a buttered baking dish:
> 3 cups shredded cabbage

Pour over it a mixture of:
> ¾ cup cream
> 1 tablespoon sugar
> ½ teaspoon salt
> ½ teaspoon paprika
> (½ cup chopped nuts)

Sprinkle the top with:
> ½ cup bread crumbs

Bake for about 45 minutes. Just before serving, sprinkle the top with:
> ⅛ cup grated cheese

and run under the broiler until melted.

SAUTÉED CABBAGE
4 Servings
Preheat oven to 375°.
Shred:
> A small head cabbage

Sauté it lightly in:
> Butter or bacon drippings

Add to the hot fat:
> ½ teaspoon salt
> ¼ teaspoon paprika
> Minced garlic or onion

Place the cabbage in a greased baking dish. Pour over it:
> 1 cup cultured sour or sweet cream

Bake it for about 20 minutes.

FRENCH FRIED CABBAGE
Preheat deep fryer to 375°.
Crisp in cold water:
> Finely shredded cabbage

Drain and dry it. Dip it in:
> Milk

then in:
> Flour

Fry a small amount at a time in deep fat, see page 256. Drain it on absorbent paper.
> Correct the seasoning

CABBAGE OR LETTUCE AND RICE DISH
6 Servings
This is a good dish to make in the trail of a salad luncheon. You may use the outer leaves of lettuce. Melt:
> 2 tablespoons bacon drippings
> 2 tablespoons butter or 3 tablespoons other fat

Stir in, cover and cook gently for about 10 minutes:
> 3 cups finely shredded cabbage or lettuce
> ½ cup finely chopped onion
> 1 seeded, chopped green pepper

Stir these ingredients frequently. Stir in and cook until well heated:
> 1 cup cooked rice
> 2 cups tomato pulp or thick stewed tomatoes
> Salt and pepper

This is good served with:
> Crisp bacon or cold ham

CABBAGE OR SAVORY STRUDEL
12 to 14 Servings
Prepare:
> Strudel Dough, page 598

Steam blanch, page 133, for 5 minutes:
> 4 lbs. shredded cabbage

Press out any excess moisture and place on the dough with:
> 1½ cups heavy cultured sour cream
> (1 teaspoon caraway seed)
> (4 chopped hard-cooked eggs)

To roll and bake the strudel, see page 599.

SCALLOPED CABBAGE

8 Servings

Rather luxurious treatment for this good bourgeois vegetable.
Preheat oven to 375°.
Chop, then cook:

> 1 medium-sized head cabbage

Drain it well. Prepare:

> 1½ cups Cream Sauce I, page 322

Prepare:

> 2 tablespoons chopped seeded green peppers
> 2 tablespoons chopped pimientos

Sauté and mince:

> (6 slices bacon)

Melt:

> 2 tablespoons bacon fat or butter

Toss lightly in this:

> ½ cup bread crumbs

Place layers of drained cabbage in a greased baking dish. Sprinkle them with the minced bacon and peppers and:

> 1 cup or less grated cheese

Cover them with the cream sauce. Top the dish with the sautéed bread crumbs. Bake the cabbage for about 10 minutes.

CABBAGE WITH TOMATO SAUCE

6 Servings

A practical, all-purpose vegetable dish. Good made with Brussels sprouts as well.
Prepare by any recipe for Cooked Cabbage, page 266:

> A small, firm head cabbage

While the cabbage boils, prepare this sauce. Dice and sauté until crisp:

> 4 slices bacon

Remove and reserve the bacon. Sauté in the bacon fat, until tender:

> 1 small minced onion

Add:

> 1 cup tomato purée
> Salt and pepper
> (2 teaspoons brown sugar)

When the sauce is boiling, add the well-drained cabbage and the bits of bacon. Serve very hot, garnished with:

> 2 tablespoons minced parsley

CABBAGE, TOMATO AND CHEESE DISH

6 Servings

Preheat oven to 325°
Cook for 5 minutes, page 266:

> 3 cups finely shredded cabbage

Drain it well. Cook:

> 1½ cups Stewed Tomatoes, page 305
> ¾ teaspoon salt
> ¼ teaspoon paprika
> (2 teaspoons brown sugar)

Butter a baking dish. Place in it alternate layers of tomatoes and cabbage, beginning with tomatoes. Sprinkle the layers with:

> Au Gratin III, page 342

Bake the dish for about ½ hour or until the crumbs are brown.

CABBAGE ROLLS STUFFED WITH RICE AND CHEESE

6 Servings

To prepare, see:

> Dolmas, page 431

Omit the vegetables if desired. Substitute for the meat:

> ¾ cup grated American cheese

Season well with:

> Cayenne, paprika and salt

CABBAGE STUFFED WITH CORNED BEEF HASH

4 Servings

Trim the outer leaves and the stem from:

> A medium-sized head of cabbage

Cook it, uncovered, until it is barely tender in:

> 2 quarts boiling water

Do not overcook cabbage. It is best when still slightly crisp. Drain it well. Scoop out the inside, leaving a 1½-inch shell. Place the shell in a greased ovenproof dish. Keep it hot. Chop the removed part. Add it to the contents of:

> 1 can minced corned beef hash: 16 oz.
> ¼ cup or more sautéed onions
> A pinch of thyme

Moisten it with:

> (Cream, evaporated milk or bacon drippings)

Heat these ingredients. Fill the shell. Cover the top with:

> Buttered cornflakes

The cabbage may be heated in a 425° oven for about 10 minutes. It may be served with:

> Dried Onion Soup Sauce, page 333

CABBAGE STUFFED WITH HAM AND CHEESE

6 Servings

Trim the loose outer leaves from:

> A firm head cabbage

Cut out enough from the stem end to make a deep well. Prepare a filling by combining:

> 2 cups cooked ground or chopped ham
> 1 cup bread crumbs
> ¾ cup grated American cheese
> ½ teaspoon dry mustard
> Salt
> ½ teaspoon paprika
> A few grains cayenne

Fill the center of the cabbage with this filling. Steam in an improvised steamer made of a colander or frying basket, if necessary, until it is tender—from 1 to 2 hours. Place it over boiling water. Cover it with a bowl or lid or wrap the cabbage in heavy foil and bake it from 1 to 2 hours. Serve it with:

> Cheese Sauce, page 326, or Tomato Cheese Sauce, page 333

RED CABBAGE

An old favorite to serve with game—cooked either for a long time as in this recipe or for a shorter time as in the next.

4 Servings
Pull the outer leaves from:

A head of red cabbage: about 2 lbs.

Cut it into sections. Remove the hard core, shred the cabbage and soak in cold water. Cook over low heat until some fat is rendered out:

4 slices chopped bacon or use 3 tablespoons melted butter

Sauté with the bacon or butter, until golden:

3 or 4 tablespoons finely chopped onions

Lift the cabbage from the water with the hands, leaving it moist. Place it in a heat-proof glass or enameled iron casserole, cover it and let it simmer for 10 minutes. Core and cut into very thin slices:

2 apples

(⅛ teaspoon caraway seeds)

Add them to the cabbage with:

¼ teaspoon salt, if bacon is used, or 1 teaspoon salt, if unsalted butter is used

¼ cup vinegar or ½ cup red wine or a mixture of 2 tablespoons honey and 2 tablespoons vinegar

Add the sautéed onion and stir these ingredients. Cover the pan and simmer the cabbage very slowly for 1 hour and 20 minutes. Add boiling water during cooking, if necessary. If the water has not been absorbed when the cabbage is done, uncover the pot and cook it gently until it is absorbed.

RED CABBAGE AND CHESTNUTS

6 Servings
In "The House of Exile," the Chinese serve red cabbage in green peppers, see Stuffed Peppers, page 288. This dish is attractive. Have ready:

1 cup blanched chopped chestnuts

Shred until very fine:

1 small head red cabbage

Place it in a bowl. Cover it with:

Boiling water

Add:

¼ cup dry white wine or vinegar

Permit it to soak for 15 minutes. Drain it well. Heat in a saucepan:

2½ tablespoons bacon drippings or butter

Add the cabbage. Sprinkle it lightly with:

Salt and pepper

Sauté the cabbage until it is limp. Cover and simmer for ten minutes. Sprinkle over the cabbage:

1 tablespoon flour

Meanwhile, in a separate saucepan, combine the chestnuts with:

1 cup water

1½ tablespoons sugar

¼ cup dry white wine or vinegar

⅓ cup seedless raisins

1 peeled, thinly sliced apple

Simmer these ingredients, covered, until the chestnuts are tender. Add to the cab-

bage mixture. Cook these ingredients until they are well blended.

Correct the seasoning

and serve them hot.

SAUERKRAUT

6 Servings
The healthful quality of sauerkraut was recognized in 200 B.C. when, history records, it was served to the laborers working on the Great Wall of China. To retain its full flavor, serve it raw or barely heated through. Cooking makes kraut milder. Melt in a skillet:

2 tablespoons butter or bacon drippings

Add and sauté until clear:

½ cup sliced onion or shallots

Add and sauté for about 5 minutes:

1 quart fresh or canned sauerkraut

Peel, grate and add:

1 medium-sized potato or tart apple

Cover the kraut with:

Boiling Stock, page 490, or water (¼ cup dry wine)

Cook the kraut, uncovered, for 30 minutes, cover it and cook or bake it in a 325° oven for about 30 minutes longer. It may be seasoned with:

1 or 2 tablespoons brown sugar

1 teaspoon caraway or celery seed

Serve with:

Frankfurters, roast pork or spareribs

SAUERKRAUT AND TOMATO CASSEROLE

8 Servings
Lovers of sauerkraut will welcome this old friend in a new guise.
Preheat oven to 350°
Drain well:

4 cups canned sauerkraut

Put through a strainer:

3½ cups canned tomatoes

Melt:

2 tablespoons bacon or other fat

Add, cook and stir about until golden:

1 small chopped onion

Add the strained tomatoes and:

¼ cup brown sugar

Freshly ground pepper

Add the drained sauerkraut. Place the mixture in a covered casserole and bake for about 1 hour. ♦ Uncover the last 20 minutes of cooking. Garnish the top with:

Crumbled crisp bacon

CARDOONS

A vegetable of the thistle family, like artichoke—but the tender stalks and root are eaten, rather than the flower. Generally used for soups. Wash well. Discard outside stalks, trim the strings as for celery. Leave the heart whole. Cut into 3-inch pieces:

Tender stalks of cardoon

Parblanch, page 132, in:

Court Bouillon Blanc, page 493

for 5 to 7 minutes, to keep it from discoloring. Drain and rinse at once in cold water to remove bitterness. Simmer, covered, for about 1½ to 2 hours or until tender in:

Boiling Acidulated Water, page 494, to cover
Correct the seasoning

and serve with:

Cream, butter or Cream Sauce I, page 322

Slice the heart and arrange it as a garnish.

CARROTS

Carrots are frequently boring—but that may be the cook's fault. For good results, combine them with onions, celery, green peppers, olives, mushrooms, etc. Peel or scrape them; or use unpeeled, cut into slices, or diced. If small, they may be served whole. If large, they may be more attractive if cut Parisienne, page 251. Wash and scrape:

Carrots

◗ Steam, page 252, or place them in a small quantity of:

Boiling water or stock

Cook them, covered, until they are tender, from 20 to 30 minutes. Allow a shorter cooking period for cut-up carrots. Permit them to absorb the water in which they are cooked. If necessary, add a small quantity of boiling water. Celery, onions, etc., may be cooked with peeled carrots or they may be cooked separately and added later. Serve the carrots with:

(Seasoned chopped parsley)
Bercy Butter, page 339, or
Cream Sauce I, page 322

or add to 2 cups cooked carrots:

1 or 2 tablespoons butter
1 to 2 tablespoons sugar, honey or orange marmalade
(½ teaspoon ginger, ginger root or cinnamon)

Simmer the carrots in this mixture until well glazed. Or try the glaze in:

Candied Sweet Potatoes, page 298

✪ Pressure cook carrots whole for 4 minutes—sliced, 2½ minutes—at 15 lbs.

CARROTS IN BUNCHES

Steam or cook as in preceding recipe:

Small, shapely carrots in their jackets

Cool them. Skin them. Reheat them by placing them over steam or by sautéing them for about 12 minutes in a little butter. Serve them in 2 bunches—one at each end of a meat platter. Place at the blunt ends, to represent carrot greens:

Sprigs of parsley

Pour over them:

Melted seasoned butter

Season with:

A dash of cloves

MASHED CARROTS OR CARROT RING

4 Servings

Cook as above:

2 bunches young carrots in their jackets

Skin the carrots and use a ⅃ blender or put them through a ricer or mash them with a potato masher. Beat in:

1 tablespoon butter
Salt and pepper
1 tablespoon chopped parsley or chives
(A dash of cloves)

Heap the carrots in a mound or in individual mounds. Garnish them with:

Sprigs of parsley

To make a ring, beat in:

1 to 2 egg yolks

Place in a greased mold and heat over hot water in a 350° oven until set, for about 20 to 30 minutes. Invert the mold. Fill the center of the ring with:

Green Peas, page 287

CARROTS VICHY

4 Servings

Place in a saucepan:

2 cups scraped, sliced carrots
½ cup boiling water
2 tablespoons butter
1 tablespoon sugar
¼ teaspoon salt
(1 teaspoon lemon juice)

Cover the pan closely. Cook the carrots over quick heat until the water evaporates. Permit them to brown in the butter. Serve them sprinkled with:

Chopped chives or parsley

BAKED CARROTS

4 Servings

Preheat oven to 350°.
Melt:

3 tablespoons butter

Sauté in it for about 3 minutes:

¼ cup chopped onion

Add:

2 cups peeled, shredded carrots

Place these ingredients in a baking dish. Sprinkle them with:

¾ teaspoon salt
1 teaspoon sugar

Pour over them:

½ cup water or stock

Cover the dish. Bake the carrots until they are tender.

WATERLESS CARROTS

5 Servings

Peel or scrape:

2 bunches carrots

Slice them in long, thin strips. Place them in a heavy saucepan with:

2 tablespoons butter
½ teaspoon sugar
½ teaspoon salt
1 tablespoon chopped parsley

You may sauté in the butter:

3 tablespoons chopped onion

Cover the pan closely. Simmer the carrots on top of the stove for about 20 minutes or place them in a 350° oven until they are done. Add:

1 tablespoon cream
Cook them about 2 minutes longer.

CARAMELIZED CARROTS
A good way to treat mature carrots.
Steam in their jackets, page 252:
Carrots
Skin them. Cut them into halves or quarters. Dip them in:
Melted butter
Sprinkle them with:
Salt, paprika and brown sugar
Place them in a heavy skillet over low heat until they are well glazed. Baste them from time to time with a little melted butter.

CAULIFLOWER
4 Servings
Cut off the tough end of the stem, remove the leaves and soak in cold salted water, head down for 10 minutes:
1 medium-sized head cauliflower
Drain it. You may break it into florets. Cut deep gashes into the stalks. ♦ Steam, page 252, or place it uncovered, head up, in about 1 inch of:
Boiling water or milk
The milk will help keep it white, as will:
(Juice of ½ lemon)
Reduce the heat to a simmer and cook ♦ partially covered, until the stalk is barely tender. Test for tenderness after 12 minutes. Drain the cauliflower well and place it in a serving dish. Serve it with:
Brown Buttered Bread Crumbs, page 501
and you have prepared Cauliflower Polonaise.
Or cream it, page 254. Or use:
Hollandaise Sauce, page 328
Egg Sauce I, page 323 (with crumbled bacon)
Creole Sauce, page 336
Lemon Butter, page 338
✪ Pressure cook whole cauliflower at 15 lbs. for about 7 minutes.

SAUTÉED CAULIFLOWER
5 Servings
Cook as above:
Boiled or steamed cauliflower
Break it into florets. Heat:
2 tablespoons butter
2 tablespoons salad oil
Add and cook for 2 minutes:
½ clove garlic or 2 teaspoons grated onion
Remove the garlic. Sauté the florets in the fat until they are well coated. Cover and cook for several minutes. Season with:
Salt and paprika
A fresh grating of nutmeg
or serve the cauliflower with:
Chopped parsley or chives

DEEP FRIED CAULIFLOWER
Drain:

Cooked cauliflower
Separate the florets.
Preheat deep fryer to 380°.
Dip each section of cauliflower in:
Fritter Batter for Vegetables, page 221
Drain, and deep fry, page 124, until golden. Serve with:
Hollandaise Sauce, page 328, or
Sour Cream Dressing, page 317
or cream them, page 254.

CAULIFLOWER AND MUSHROOMS IN CHEESE SAUCE
6 Servings
Cook:
1 large cauliflower
Drain it well and put it in a greased baking dish. Place it where it will keep hot. Melt in a skillet:
2 tablespoons butter
Sauté in it for 2 minutes:
½ lb. mushrooms
Cook:
1½ cups Cream Sauce I, page 322
Stir into the hot sauce ♦ off the heat:
¾ cup grated cheese
When the cheese is melted, add the sautéed mushrooms and pour the sauce over the cauliflower. Serve it at once.

CELERY
4 Servings
Wash:
2 cups chopped celery
♦ Steam, page 252, or drop it gradually into:
½ inch boiling water
Cook it, covered, until it is tender, for about 8 minutes, allowing it to absorb the water. Should there be any liquid, drain the celery and reserve the liquid for the sauce. Brown the celery in:
Seasoned butter
Or, drop the celery into:
1 cup Cream Sauce I, page 322, made with cream and celery liquor
Season the sauce with:
Curry powder
Celery, dill or sunflower seeds
Freshly grated nutmeg
Herbs, page 529
Serve:
Au Gratin III, page 342
✪ Pressure cook celery at 15 lbs. pressure for 1½ minutes.

BRAISED OR GLAZED CELERY
4 Servings
Not only celery, but Belgian endive and Boston lettuce are choice prepared in this way. Do blanch the endive and lettuce briefly first.
Wash and trim:
1½ lbs. celery
Cut into 3- to 4-inch lengths. Arrange them attractively in the bottom of a buttered heatproof ♦ glass, enamel or stainless

steel casserole. Squeeze over them:
    3 tablespoons lemon juice
Add:
    ½ cup chicken or veal stock
    ½ teaspoon salt
    1 tablespoon sugar
    2 tablespoons butter
Bring the liquid to a boil, then cover with
a poaching paper, page 129. Now, cover
the casserole with a lid and simmer for
about 25 minutes or until tender. Place
the celery on a heated serving dish and
keep warm. Reduce the pan liquid to
about ½ a cup. Add:
    1 tablespoon butter or Beurre Manié,
    page 321
Pour this glaze over the celery.

CELERY CABBAGE OR CHINESE CABBAGE

Use raw as a salad or prepare this vegetable by any of the recipes for cabbage; or
stir-fry it as the Chinese do, page 253.
If young, it may require only a few minutes' cooking.
♦ Steam page 252, or place a stalk of:
    Whole or shredded celery cabbage
in:
    ½ cup boiling water
Cook until it is barely tender. Drain thoroughly. Add:
    ½ teaspoon salt
Serve it with:
    Melted butter or Mock Hollandaise
    Sauce, page 329
or season with:
    ½ teaspoon turmeric
and garnish with:
    ¼ cup freshly grated coconut

CELERY ROOT OR CELERIAC

4 Servings
This knobby tough root, also called **celeri-**
rave, is often woody if too old, but can be
one of the most subtly flavored vegetables.
It is difficult to peel, so cut into slices first.
See page 309. To make the flavor more
delicate for use in salads and hors d'oeuvre,
blanch 1 to 2 minutes after peeling to keep
it white—by using lemon juice or ascorbic
acid in the water. Scrub well:
    1½ lbs. celery root
♦ Steam, page 252, or cover it with:
    Boiling water
Cook uncovered, until it is tender—about
25 minutes. Drain the celery root. Cover
with:
    1½ cups Cream Sauce II, page 322
or serve with:
    Au Gratin III, page 342
♥ Pressure cook at 15 lbs. about 5 minutes.

SWISS CHARD

Prepare:
    Chard leaves
as you would spinach, but remove the
coarse middle rib before cooking. If cooking the ribs, cook as for asparagus.

CHAYOTES

4 Servings
This pear-shaped vegetable belongs to the
gourd family and is also called **Christo-**
phenes. Treat it much as you would zucchini or other squash. It may be served
chilled with mayonnaise, combines well
with meats, seafoods and is even good in
some desserts.
Pare and cut crosswise in ¾-inch slices:
    1 lb. chayotes
Drop into:
    Boiling water to cover
Reduce the heat at once and ♦ simmer 45
minutes, if young, or as long as 1 hour, if
mature—or until tender. Drain it. You
may also ♥ pressure cook whole chayotes
at 15 lbs. for 6 to 8 minutes and, if diced,
for 2 minutes. Dress with:
    Salt
    Butter
    Black Butter, page 338, etc., or
    cream sauce and grated cheese
They are delicious if steamed whole and
stuffed with:
    Mushrooms and cheese

BOILED CHESTNUTS

4 Servings
To use as a vegetable, shell and skin, page
520:
    1 lb. chestnuts
or use ½ lb. dried chestnuts that have been
soaked overnight. Use this water. Drop
the chestnuts into:
    Boiling water or milk
To which add:
    3 chopped ribs celery
    1 small, peeled, chopped onion
    (1 tablespoon vinegar)
    (⅛ teaspoon anise)
Cook them until they are tender. Drain
them well. Mash them with:
    1 tablespoon butter
    Correct the seasoning
Add:
    2 or more tablespoons warm cream
Beat the chestnuts until they are fluffy.
Keep them hot over hot water. Immedi-
ately before serving them, stir in:
    (1 cup or more finely diced raw celery)

II. To use as a compote, shell, skin, boil,
as above:
    1 lb. chestnuts
in:
    Boiling water or milk
Drain. Save the liquid and add sufficient
to make about 2 cups. Make a sirup by
adding:
    2 cups sugar
    Juice and grated rind of 2 lemons
    Juice and grated rind of 1 orange
    4 whole cloves
    1 stick cinnamon
    ¼ teaspoon ground ginger
    (½ cup raisins)
    (½ cup chopped nuts)

Simmer the sirup gently until slightly reduced, then fold into the mashed chestnuts and serve.

BAKED CHESTNUTS
4 Servings
Preheat oven to 325°.
Prepare and cook:
  3 cups chestnuts, above
Season them with:
  (2 tablespoons or more brown sugar)
Grease a baking dish. Place the chestnuts in it. Pour over them:
  1¾ cups chicken stock
Cover them and bake for about 3 hours. Pour off the stock and reserve. Melt:
  2 tablespoons butter
Stir in until blended:
  1 tablespoon flour
Stir the stock in slowly. When the sauce is smooth and boiling, pour it over the chestnuts and serve them.

CHICORY
Witloof chicory and **French** or **Belgian endive** may be treated just as for any recipe calling for cooked lettuce or celery. Differentiate the above from the sunburst-centered, highly ruffled or frisée endive, common in our stores and usually used raw only.

ABOUT CORN

Some years ago a Frenchman wrote to the Paris Herald to ask: "Why do Americans put their elbows on the table?" The answer, published the following day, was conclusive: "It comes from eating green corn."

When cooked corn is called for in the following recipes, it can be canned, fresh cooked or frozen cooked. Cooked just after picking, young corn is naturally sweet. A few hours off the stalk brings about changes which lessen this flavor. Try cutting fresh corn for puddings and fritters by scraping with either of the tools sketched here—and notice the superior results this

preparation gives. If you must use a knife to cut off the kernels, do not cut deeply. Then press along the rows with the dull side of a knife to retrieve the richly flavored juice and heart of the kernel. ♦ To avoid toughness in cooking corn, add salt when the cooking period is half over.

If ♦ pressure cooking ✱ frozen corn on the cob ♦ be sure to thaw partially before cooking at 15 lbs. for about 4 minutes.

CORN ON THE COB
I. Remove the husks and silk from:
  Ears of fresh corn
♦ Steam, page 252, or drop them, ear by ear, so as not to disturb the boiling, into:
  **1 inch boiling water or half milk and
  half water**
Add:
  (1 tablespoon or more sugar)
Cover the kettle and boil the corn rapidly until it is tender, from 4 to 10 minutes, depending on maturity. Drain and serve it with:
  Butter
  Salt
  Freshly ground pepper

II. Remove the husks and silk from:
  Very young, freshly picked corn
In a large kettle which you can cover tightly, bring to a rolling boil:
  **Enough water to cover corn
  generously**
Slip the ears into the water one by one. Cover the kettle and remove it from the heat at once. Allow the corn to remain in the hot water for about 5 minutes or until tender. Drain and serve at once.

FRESH CORN CUT FROM THE COB
Cut or grate from the cob:
  Fresh corn
Simmer it, covered, for several minutes, until it is tender, in its own juice and a little:
  Butter
Season it with:
  Salt and white pepper
Moisten it with:
  Milk or cream
You may devil it by adding:
  1 tablespoon Worcestershire sauce
  Minced garlic

▤ GRILLED OR ROASTED CORN
Preheat oven to 400° or have ready a good bed of coals.
I. Pull down husk to remove silk and any damaged portions of the ear on:
  Young roasting corn
Replace the husk. Run into the husk as much:
  Water
as it will hold. Drain and close the husk by twisting it. Put the ears on a rack over the hot coals or in the preheated oven and bake 20 to 25 minutes. Husk before serving.

II. Strip the husk and silk from:
  Roasting ears
Remove any damaged portions. Rub with:

Butter
Salt and pepper
Wrap in foil and roast 20 to 30 minutes, depending on the size of the ears.

FRESH CORN PUDDING COCKAIGNE
8 Servings

This is a luscious dish, but it is a little difficult to give an exact recipe for it because the corn differs with the season. If the corn is watery when scraped, it is sometimes necessary to add a tablespoon of flour. This is apt to be the case early in the season. Later on, it may be necessary to use more cream—up to 1 cup. When the corn mixture is right, it looks like thick, curdled cream when scraped.
Preheat oven to 325°.
Scrape, but ♦ do not cut:

2 cups fresh corn

Add:

1 teaspoon sugar
½ to ¾ cup cream
Salt and white pepper

Place these ingredients in a generously buttered flat baking dish. Dot the top with:

Butter

Bake the pudding for about 1 hour. ✻ This dish may be frozen.

CORN PUDDING
5 Servings

A good hefty corn dish.
Preheat oven to 350°.
Drain:

1 No. 2 can kernel corn: 2½ cups

Reserve the liquid. Melt:

2 tablespoons butter

Stir in until blended:

2 tablespoons flour

Combine and stir in slowly:

The corn liquid and enough cream
to make 1 cup

When the sauce is smooth and hot, stir in the drained corn and:

¼ cup chopped seeded green pepper
1 chopped pimiento

When this mixture reaches a boil ♦ reduce heat. Beat well:

2 egg yolks

Pour part of the corn mixture over them off the heat. Beat it and return to corn mixture. Stir and cook for several minutes to permit the yolks to thicken slightly.
Add:

¾ teaspoon salt
¼ teaspoon paprika
(¼ cup crisply cooked, crumbled bacon)

or you may cover the bottom of the dish with:

(Minced ham)

Place on a platter and whip ♦ until stiff, but not dry:

2 egg whites

Fold them lightly into the corn mixture.

Bake the pudding in a baking dish ♦ prepared as for a soufflé baker, page 204, for about 30 minutes.

SCALLOPED CORN
4 Servings

Preheat oven to 325°.
Combine:

2 cups uncooked corn, scraped or
cut from the ear
2 beaten eggs
½ teaspoon salt
(¼ cup minced seeded green peppers
with membrane removed, or chopped
olives)
¾ cup cream

Place in a baking dish, prepared as for a soufflé baker, page 204. Sprinkle with:

Au Gratin II, page 342

Bake the corn for about ½ hour.

CORN SUCCOTASH

This is also good made with canned or frozen vegetables.
4 Servings

Combine, then heat in a double boiler ♦ over—not in—hot water:

1 cup cooked fresh corn
1 cup cooked fresh Lima or finely
shredded green beans
2 tablespoons butter
½ teaspoon salt
⅛ teaspoon paprika
Chopped parsley

CORN CREOLE
6 Servings

Seed, remove membranes and chop:

¼ cup green pepper

Skin and chop:

1 small onion

Melt:

2 tablespoons butter

Sauté the vegetables in the butter until they are translucent. Heat in the top of a double boiler:

1 cup drained canned or fresh
cooked tomatoes

Add the sautéed vegetables and:

½ teaspoon salt
⅛ teaspoon pepper
A few grains cayenne

Cook and stir these ingredients ♦ over—not in—hot water about 5 minutes. Add:

⅔ cup cooked corn

Heat 2 minutes longer. Stir in, until melted:

1⅓ cups grated cheese

CORN FRITTERS WITH FRESH CORN

For a short period one of our local newspapers devoted a column to masculine taste in culinary matters. The author of the following graciously permitted us to use it when we told him how much it pleased us.
"When I was a child, one of eight, my

father frequently promised us a marvelous treat. He, being an amateur horticulturist and arboriculturist, would tell us of a fritter tree he was going to plant on the banks of a small lake filled with molasses, maple sirup or honey, to be located in our back yard. When one of us children felt the urge for the most delectable repast, all we had to do was to shake the tree, the fritters would drop into the lake and we could fish them out and eat fritters to our hearts' content.

"Mother was a good cook and a good helpmate, so she developed the fritter that was to grow on and fall from the tree into the lake of molasses or maple sirup or honey, as the case might be. Her recipe, as preserved in our family, is:

"Grate 12 ears of corn, preferably sugar corn, then beat the yolks of 3 eggs with a very small amount of flour—about a teaspoonful—and a scant teaspoon of salt; beat the whites thoroughly. Mix the grated corn and yolks, then fold in the beaten whites.

"Fry in butter like pancakes and serve hot. You will want more; so will your guests."

Who could resist the delightful idea of a fritter tree in full fruit?

For 4 Servings

Grate:
  2½ cups fresh corn
Add:
  1 well-beaten egg yolk
  (2 teaspoons flour)
  ¼ teaspoon salt
Whip until ◗ stiff, but not dry:
  1 egg white
Fold the egg white into the corn mixture. Into a hot buttered skillet, drop the mixture as for pancakes and sauté until light brown and fluffy. Do not overcook.

CORN FRITTERS OR CORN OYSTERS WITH FRESH OR CANNED CORN
About 16 Fritters
For best results, make the batter immediately before using it. Drain, then mash with a potato masher:
  1 cup freshly scraped corn or canned, cream-style corn
Beat until light and add:
  2 eggs
Add:
  6 tablespoons flour
  ½ teaspoon double-acting baking powder
  ¼ teaspoon salt
  ⅛ teaspoon nutmeg
Melt in a small skillet:
  3 tablespoons butter
When it has reached the point of fragrance, add the batter with a tablespoon. Permit the bottom of the cakes to brown, reverse them and brown the other side. Serve at once with:
  Mushroom Sauce, page 327, or maple sirup

TAMALES
20 Tamales
A curious call used to rend the air on hot summer nights, one that brought a sense of adventure to our limited childhood world. It was the Mexican tamale man, whose forbidden, hence desirable, wares long remained a mystery. These varied, leaf-wrapped confections, like individual puddings, may be spicy as mole, filled with cheese and peppers, or sweet with almond, citron and coconut.

Tamales steam slowly to allow the wrapping, either corn husks or banana leaves, to both protect and flavor the contents. Soften the leaves by soaking for 5 minutes in hot water and then draining before using. Most tamales have two ingredients not easily available. First a pastate or tortilla base—that moistened mixture of unslaked lime and dried corn which is ground into flour in a matate; and second, a combination of tequesquite and transparent green tomato parings which make the puddings puff up. The following tamale filling, for which we can get authentic ingredients, is made from fresh corn.

Remove the husks from 20 ears of:
  Tender corn
and reserve the largest leaves. Soak for 5 minutes in hot water and drain. You will need 3 to 4 large leaves for each tamale. Scrape the kernels from the cobs, using the scraper illustrated on page 273. Mix these tender bits with:
  ¾ cup cultured sour cream
  1 to 1¼ cups milk
Use the larger quantity if the corn is absolutely not fresh picked. Add:
  ¼ cup sugar
  ½ teaspoon salt
  ½ cup raisins
Overlap 3 or 4 leaves, see page 131. Place about 3 tablespoons of the corn mixture lengthwise down the center of the overlapped leaves. Roll the filling so the husks completely encase it, tucking up the short ends and tying with a white string. Put several layers of the remaining husks in the bottom element of the steamer and cover with about 1 to 1½ inches of boiling water. Place the carefully wrapped rolls ◗ upright in some form of vegetable steamer, see types illustrated on page 252. Close the steamer tightly and steam the tamales over low heat for about 1 hour. Remove the strings, allow the puddings to cool slightly and serve still wrapped in the inedible husks. The fillings should be firm enough to leave the husks easily. You may pass as a garnish:
  Cultured sour cream
  Cinnamon

ABOUT CUCUMBERS

How often the Japanese draw these decorative plants! That their formal values were missed when the cold weather came was poignantly noted by Isaiah when he said, "as desolate as a cottage in a cucumber garden abandoned in winter."

A cucumber ready to use is rigid and all green. It should have a lustrous skin—but do not be misled by the heavy, waxy, man-applied finish on some of those now in the markets. Never use a skin so waxed. If not waxed, it is perfectly edible. Some people who are allergic to this delicious vegetable find they can enjoy it if it is cooked. ♦ Use any recipe for summer squash or one of the following.

MULLED CUCUMBERS
I.   **4 Servings**
Pare, seed and cut into strips:
>   **2 cups cucumbers**
Drop them into:
>   **1½ cups boiling water**
♦ Simmer them until they are nearly tender—but no longer, as they will not retain their color. Drain them well. Place in a double boiler:
>   **¾ cup Cream Sauce I, page 322**
Season the sauce with:
>   **Salt and white pepper**
>   **Freshly grated nutmeg or 1 teaspoon**
>   **chopped fresh herbs or dill or**
>   **celery seeds**
>   **1 teaspoon or more lemon juice**
When the sauce reaches a boil, add the drained cucumbers. Place the pan over hot water and steam them, uncovered, for a few minutes before serving.

II. Prepare:
>   **Mulled Cucumbers I, above**
substituting for the Cream Sauce:
>   **Lemon Butter, page 338, with**
>   **capers or Tomato Sauce, page 333,**
>   **with basil or Soubise or Onion**
>   **Sauce, page 325**

CUCUMBER OR MOCK-OYSTER CASSEROLE
                                                                          4 Servings
Preheat oven to 400°.
Prepare:
>   **2 cups Mulled Cucumbers, as above**
Drain the vegetable well. Prepare:
>   **1 cup Cream Sauce, page 322**
seasoned with:
>   **1 tablespoon anchovy paste**
Place the vegetable in a baking dish. Pour the hot sauce over it. Cover the top with:
>   **Au Gratin III, page 342**
Bake the dish until the top is brown.

CUCUMBER CREOLE CASSEROLE
                                                                          4 Servings
Preheat oven to 375°.
Pare and seed:
>   **3 large cucumbers**

Cut them into ¼-inch slices. Combine with half the recipe for:
>   **Creole Sauce, page 336**
Place in the bottom of a greased ovenproof dish:
>   **½ cup dry bread crumbs**
Add the cucumbers. Pour the sauce over them. Cover it with:
>   **Au Gratin I, page 342**
Bake the dish for about 35 minutes.

ABOUT DASHEEN OR TARO

This versatile vegetable, a form of the elephant ears we all know as a decorative plant, has a potato-like root that becomes grayish or violet when cooked. It is used as a vegetable or as a base for puddings and confections. Fermented, it is the famous **poi** of tropical countries, see following recipe. The spinach-flavored leaves are boiled as for greens but must be cooked from 45 minutes to 1 hour.

To bake, parboil the unpared root for 15 minutes and then time as for potato baking, but make certain the oven is not over 375°.

POI
                                                                   About 5 Cups
Poi may be held at room temperature if unmixed with water. If refrigerated, mix with water.
Dice into 1-inch cubes:
>   **2½ lbs. cooked taro roots, above**
Mash in a wooden bowl with a wooden potato masher until starchy paste forms. Work in gradually with the hands:
>   **2½ cups water**
To remove lumps and fiber, force through several thicknesses of cheesecloth. Store in a cool place and serve at once or let it stand 2 to 3 days until it ferments and has a sour taste.

ABOUT EGGPLANT OR AUBERGINE

These vegetables, lovely when stuffed, also make beautiful individual servings with their green caps against the polished purple of the cases. We have tried alternating them with green and red stuffed peppers for an effective buffet platter.

There are several important things to keep in mind in cooking eggplant. ♦ It may become very watery. Get rid of excess moisture by salting and draining on a rack before using in unthickened recipes; or stack the slices, cover with a plate, place a heavy weight on top and let stand until moisture is squeezed out. ♦ Eggplant discolors quickly when cut and should be sprinkled or rubbed with lemon juice. Also, because of discoloration ♦ cook in pottery, enamel, glass or stainless steel. One lb. of eggplant equals 3 cups diced.

Eggplant has a blotter-like capacity for oil or butter, well pointed up by this Near

East tale. The imam or priest was so fetched by the eggplant dish his fiancée prepared that he asked that her dowry be the oil in which to cook it. Great Ali Baba jars of oil were stored in their new home. The first night the eggplant was delicious, also the second; but on the third night, his favorite dish was not waiting for him. "Alas," said the wife, "the first two nights have exhausted the supply of oil." And then the priest fainted! Imam Baaldi, the current and classic dish which carries the priest's name, calls for halved egg-plant, stuffed and completely covered in oil and casseroled covered, page 130, for 1½ hours.

EGGPLANT SLICES
These slices, after frying, sautéeing or broiling, are used in many ways.
I. Top with:
  Creamed Spinach, page 300
Sprinkle with:
  Gruyère cheese
and run under broiler.

II. Put in a casserole and cover with:
  Creole Sauce, page 336
Sprinkle with:
  Au Gratin I, page 342
Run under a broiler.

III. Place on each slice:
  A slice of Tomato Provençale, page 305

IV. Place on eggplant slice:
  A grilled tomato slice
Cover with:
  A poached egg
Serve with:
  Cheese Sauce, page 326

V. Place on an eggplant slice:
  Creamed ham or hash

BAKED EGGPLANT SLICES
                                    4 Servings
Preheat oven to 400°.
Pare:
  An eggplant
Cut it crosswise into slices ½ inch thick. Spread the slices on both sides with a mixture of:
  Soft butter or salad oil
Seasoned with:
  Salt and pepper
  Grated onion, lemon juice or basil
Place them on a baking sheet and bake until tender, about 12 minutes, turning them once. Garnish with:
  Chopped parsley or chervil

BAKED EGGPLANT HALVES
                                    4 Servings
Preheat oven to 400°.

Wash, dry, then cut into halves lengthwise:
  An eggplant
Crisscross the top with gashes about 1 inch deep. Sauté the halves cut side down for about 10 minutes in:
  3 tablespoons hot olive oil
Set them upright in a shallow ovenproof dish. Make a paste by mashing together until well blended:
  8 flat, minced anchovy fillets
  2 skinned, chopped cloves garlic
  ¼ cup bread crumbs
  2 tablespoons strong beef stock
  ⅛ teaspoon freshly ground pepper
Spread this over the tops of the eggplant. Sprinkle them with:
  Dry bread crumbs
  Finely minced parsley
  A little oil or dabs of butter
Bake the dish for about ½ hour.

SCALLOPED EGGPLANT
                                    4 Servings
Preheat oven to 375°.
Pare and cut into dice:
  A medium-sized eggplant
Simmer it until tender in:
  ½ cup boiling water
Drain it well. Sprinkle it with:
  (2 tablespoons chopped parsley)
Chop until very fine:
  1 small onion
Melt:
  1 tablespoon butter
Sauté the onion in this until it is golden. Add it to the eggplant with:
  ½ cup milk
  (2 well-beaten eggs)
Melt:
  3 tablespoons butter
Stir into it, until the butter is absorbed:
  ¾ cup cracker crumbs or ½ cup bread crumbs
Place layers of eggplant and layers of crumbs in a baking dish. Season them, if the crackers are unsalted, with:
  ¼ teaspoon salt
  ⅛ teaspoon paprika
Have the top layer of crumbs. Place on the top:
  (Thin slices of cheese or grated cheese)
Bake the eggplant for about ½ hour. Garnish it with:
  Crisp crumbled bacon, page 411, or thin strips of pepperoni

DEEP FRIED EGGPLANT SLICES
                                    4 Servings
The classic method is to dip eggplant in batter and fry it in deep fat.
♦ Please read About Deep Fat Fried Vegetables, page 256.
Preheat deep fryer to 370°.
Pare, cut into ½-inch slices or sticks:
  An eggplant
Dip it in:

Fritter Batter for Vegetables,
page 221
Fry it in deep fat until golden. Drain on
absorbent paper and serve after adding:
Salt

SAUTÉED EGGPLANT SLICES
4 Servings
Peel and cut into ½-inch slices, cubes or
sticks:
An eggplant
Dip the pieces in:
Milk
Dredge them in:
Seasoned flour, crumbs or cornmeal
For easier handling, place slices on a rack
to dry for 15 minutes before cooking.
Melt in a skillet:
Butter or oil
Sauté the pieces until tender. Serve while
very hot with:
Chopped parsley or tarragon
A sliced lemon or Tomato Sauce,
page 333

EGGPLANT CASSEROLE OR RATATOUILLE PROVENÇALE
8 Servings
This ends up looking in color like a Braque
still life.
Put in a deep skillet or heavy casserole:
⅓ cup olive oil
Sauté until golden:
¾ cup thinly sliced onions
2 cloves garlic
Remove the onions and garlic from the
casserole and combine in layers with:
4 julienned green peppers
2½ cups peeled, diced eggplant
3 cups zucchini in ½-inch slices
2 cups peeled, seeded, quartered
tomatoes
Add to each layer:
Salt and pepper
Sprinkle the top with:
Olive oil
Simmer, covered, over very low heat 35 to
45 minutes. ♦ Uncover and continue to
heat 10 minutes longer to reduce the
amount of liquid. Serve hot or cold.

STUFFED EGGPLANT OR EGGPLANT FARCIE
4 Servings
Eggplant makes a wonderful "background"
food, due to its color and shape. Cut eggplant, just under and following the lines
of the leafy green cap. This then forms an
attractive lid. Or slice it into two oval
halves. The cases may be filled with any
desired combination of food, to which the
cooked eggplant pulp is added.
Preheat oven to 400°.
Cut as described:
A medium-sized eggplant

Scoop out the pulp, leaving a thick shell.
Then, drop the pulp into a small quantity
of boiling water or stock and cook it until
it is tender. Drain it well and mash it.
Combine with:
Farce, page 458, or chopped or
ground cooked meat: lamb or ham
or rice and shrimp

Fill the shell. Cover the top with the cap
or
Au Gratin II or III, page 342
Bake the eggplant until filling is heated.

STUFFED EGGPLANT CREOLE
4 Servings
Cut into halves:
A small eggplant
Scoop out the pulp and chop it. Leave a
shell ¼ inch thick. Mince and heat in a
skillet:
2 strips bacon
Add to it and sauté until the bacon is
cooked:
¼ cup minced onion
¼ cup minced seeded green pepper
with membrane removed
Add the eggplant pulp and:
2 cups drained canned tomatoes
¼ cup diced celery
Simmer these ingredients until the eggplant is tender. Beat them with a fork until they are well blended. Thicken them
with:
⅓ cup bread crumbs
Season them with:
Salt and freshly ground pepper
Add to them:
½ cup Sautéed Mushrooms, page 281
Preheat oven to 350°.
Fill the eggplant shells with the mixture.
Cover the tops with:
Au Gratin III, page 342
Place the eggplant in a pan with a very
little water and bake until it is thoroughly
heated, about 15 minutes.

BRAISED OR GLAZED ENDIVE
Prepare as for:
Braised Celery, page 271

ABOUT FENNEL OR ANISE
Florence fennel, which is found in season
at Italian markets, can be eaten raw and is

a choice hors d'oeuvre or a substitute for celery with rice in stuffings. If you enjoy the anise flavor, use the bulbous root and stalk as for celery and try seasoning with olive oil. The leaves can also be used discreetly for seasoning, but the usual plant for this purpose is Foeniculium vulgare, page 532.

ABOUT FERN SHOOTS OR FRESH BRACKEN

In the Spring, cut ferns while the shoots are still curled in crosiers. Wash and tie in bundles of 6 to 8 fronds. Stand upright and steam about 20 minutes or until just tender.
Serve with:
    Hollandaise Sauce, page 328

ABOUT GREENS

Greens, such as turnips, mustard, kale, collards, corn salad, comfrey, borage, etc.—are seldom creamed. However, there is no reason why they should not be. The old-fashioned custom is to cook them to death, for an hour or more, with bacon, salt pork or ham hocks and to serve them with vinegar. To retain color and nutrients, try cooking by the following methods.
I. Prepare greens by washing carefully to remove grit and cut out any blemished areas or tough stems. Simmer for 2 hours in water to cover:
    A 2 lb. piece side meat: bacon or
        cottage ham
Add:
    2 to 3 lbs. greens
And simmer about 35 to 40 minutes, until just tender.

II. If the greens are very young, cook them as for:
    Panned Spinach, page 301
allowing about 15 minutes cooking time.

ABOUT WILD GREENS

If you are in earnest about pursuing the hobby of greens collecting, try to consult a local enthusiast. If he is not available, make a slow approach, trying the greens you are absolutely sure of, like dandelion. Then experiment with poke, dock, lambs quarters, marsh marigold leaves, emerging ferns, yellow rocket cress, young milkweed shoots, pigweed, mustard, purslane.
    Many plants are poisonous in part or in whole and most wild greens are bitter unless blanched, page 132, sometimes more than once before cooking. Young milkweeds, marsh marigold, plantains, purslane and nettles are relatively mild, while dock and dandelion, even when young, are better blanched.
    Poke, for instance, has a poisonous root and leaf, although the shoot is both edible

and delicious. In any case, use these wild greens in small quantities until you know your own reaction to them.

KOHLRABI
4 Servings
Wash:
    8 large kohlrabi
Cut off the tops and pare the roots. Slice the roots and drop them into a quantity of rapidly:
    Boiling water
Cook them, uncovered, until they are barely tender. Drain them well. Boil the tops separately in the same manner. Drain them well, chop them until they are very fine or purée them and combine them with the roots. Prepare:
    Cream Sauce I, page 322
Add:
    (A grating of nutmeg)
When the sauce is smooth and hot, add the kohlrabi.

ABOUT LEEKS OR POIREAUX

How we wish that leeks were as common here as in France, where they are known as the "asparagus of the poor." Leeks, like other onion types, page 534, make a wonderful seasoning. When cooked as a vegetable, they must be carefully washed to free the interlacing leaves from grit; and only the white portion is used. Cook as for Asparagus, page 257, or braise as for Celery, page 271.

PURÉE OF LEEKS

Good as a meat garnish or stuffing in tomatoes.
Prepare and cook:
    Leeks, as above
Drain them well. Chop them coarsely. For each cup add:
    2 tablespoons butter
    ½ cup fresh bread crumbs
    Salt and pepper
Stir and simmer them gently until blended. If they become too thick, add:
    A little cream
Serve the purée very hot with:
    Finely chopped parsley

COOKED LETTUCE

Home gardeners in their enthusiasm find themselves with sudden surpluses of lettuce and wish they had rabbits instead of children—failing to realize that nibbling is not the only approach to this vegetable. Try these delectable alternatives: cook lettuce as a Cream Soup, page 160; cream it like Spinach, page 300; cook with peas; stuff it like Cabbage, page 268; cook and smother it with stewed tomatoes or braise as for Celery, page 271, allowing the lettuce to simmer only a few minutes before reducing the sauce.

ABOUT MUSHROOMS

Who would expect a lot of sunshine vitamin D in plants that flourish in cellars and caves? Yet this is only one of the many valuable nutrients in mushrooms. They delight us too with their almost total lack of calories and then promptly fool us by a blotter-like capacity for butter, oil and cream.

They can fool the experts in other ways. Some of the poisonous types resemble edible forms during various stages of development. ♦ There is no simple way to identify mushrooms and other edible fungi. Experts prefer to have about 10 specimens for identification before committing themselves.

The amanitas, for instance, include types so deadly they may well have been the rumored secret poison of the Borgias. These rather common growths are white gilled and they have a ruptured basal cup and a torn veil or ring left by that veil on the stem. So, collectors should stick to a safer family, like the puffballs, which have neither stems nor gills. They are edible if they grow above ground and the flesh inside is white. Lycoperdon giganteum, shown first on the left, varies from marble to canteloupe size and Lycoperdon craniforme resembles a skull slightly shrivelled, even when in prime eating condition.

Rural families return, season after season, to the same mushroom clumps and fairy rings which appear like magic when moisture conditions are just right. The hidden roots of mushrooms are often as stable as an oak. To preserve these seasonal mushrooms, see page 541. ♦ Never use any mushroom that shows signs of decay. It harbors ptomaines and toxins just like any other decaying vegetation. ♦ Never cook light-colored mushrooms in aluminum as it darkens them. And don't worry about mushrooms packaged by reputable firms. These firms guard their beds intensively against harmful invading spores. Don't bother to buy spawn blocks to grow your own mushrooms if your cellar is warmer than about 55°.

Agaricus campestris, shown in the center, is the type most often found fresh at the market. The young, pale buttons are succulent, the older, drier ones are best for sauces, as the flavor lies in the dark gills. The completely dried Gyromitra esculenta usually imported from Europe is also very strong in flavor when reconstituted, see

below. Strangely enough, it can never be eaten raw as it has a poisonous alkaloid which, with this mushroom, disappears entirely in drying or parboiling. But cooking will not destroy the poison ♦ with the most poisonous types.

Shown second from the left, above are a morel, a spring growth, and second from the right, chanterelle, a summer one. On the far right is Boletus edulis, a great European favorite known to gourmets as cèpe or Steinpilz. For truffles, those diamonds of the kitchen, see page 283.

♦ To prepare fresh mushrooms, brush or wipe with a cloth. If they must be washed, dry thoroughly. As the most intense flavor lies in the skin, do not remove it. Some people use only the caps, as the stems tend to be tougher. Should you be so extravagant, turn the mushroom on its side and cut the stem so enough is left within the cap to prevent subsequent shrinkage at the center during cooking. Be sure to use the stems in Stock Making, page 490, in Farces, page 468, or in Duxelles, page 540. Another way to keep the mushroom plump and to use most of the stem is to turn them, as sketched, and slice lengthwise.

One of the choicest garnishes for looks is the channelled mushroom. To channel these curving lines on the rather firm but spongy textured mushroom evenly with a sharp knife requires considerable skill, but we find the point of a curved grapefruit knife is quick and easy for the amateur. We have even been tempted to use a V-shaped linoleum carving tool.

♦ To keep mushrooms light in color, sprinkle with lemon juice or white wine or cook À Blanc, page 493. ♦ To reconstitute dried mushrooms, soak from ½ to 4 hours in tepid water to cover. Drain and use as for fresh mushrooms. Use the water for sauces or soups. Store dried mushrooms, uncovered, in a glass container in a light place. ♦ 3 oz. dried mushrooms reconstituted equal 1 lb.

To keep mushrooms or truffles impaled on food as a garnish, use tiny lemon thyme branches as picks.

STEAMED MUSHROOMS

This is a fine way to prepare very large mushrooms for stuffing.
♦ Please read About Mushrooms, above.
Prepare:

    1 lb. mushrooms

Place them in the top of a double boiler ♦ over—not in—hot water. Dot them with:

    2 tablespoons butter

Add:

    ¼ teaspoon salt
    ⅛ teaspoon paprika
    (½ cup milk)

Cover closely. Steam for about 20 minutes or until tender. The broth that results is superlative. Serve with salt or use this broth in sauces.

SAUTÉED MUSHROOMS

                                 4 Servings

Prepare for cooking, using caps or pieces sliced to uniform thickness:

    1 lb. mushrooms

Melt in a skillet over moderately high heat until they reach the point of fragrance:

    2 tablespoons butter
    1 tablespoon cooking oil

or use:

    (3 tablespoons clarified butter)

Add the mushrooms and ♦ shake the pan, so the mushrooms are coated without scorching. Drop in:

    (1 clove garlic)

Continue to cook over moderately high heat ♦ uncovered, shaking the pan frequently. At first the mushrooms will seem dry and will almost invisibly absorb the fat. Continue to shake the pan for 3 to 5 minutes, depending on the size of the pieces. Remove the garlic. If you are holding the mushrooms to add to other food, do not cover, as this will draw out their juices. If using as a garnish or vegetable, serve at once on:

    Toast rounds
    Grilled tomatoes or eggplant

or on a bed of:

    Puréed Peas, page 288

CREAMED MUSHROOMS

                                 4 Servings

Sauté, as for Sautéed Mushrooms, above:

    1 lb. sliced mushrooms
    1 tablespoon finely chopped onion

Combine the above with:

    1 cup hot Cream Sauce II, page 322,
      or Velouté Sauce, page 324

Season with:

    Salt and paprika
    2 tablespoons dry white wine
    A pinch of herbs

Marjoram is the traditional touch. Chives and parsley are recommended too. Serve over a baked potato or serve in a casserole, covered with:

    Au Gratin II, page 342

MUSHROOMS À LA SCHOENER

                                 4 Servings

A Viennese specialty.
Wipe off with a clean cloth:

    1 lb. button mushrooms

Choose mushrooms with about a 1- to 1½-inch cap and cut off the stems ¼ to ½ inch below the caps. Sprinkle with:

    Lemon juice
    Salt

Dip them in:

    Fritter Batter with Beer, page 221

and deep-fat fry them at 375°, until a golden brown. You may hold them for a very short time in a 200° oven, covered with a paper towel. Just before serving, dust them with:

    Chopped parsley or chervil

Serve with:

    Cold Tartare Sauce, page 316

BROILED MUSHROOMS

Preheat broiler.
Wipe with a dry cloth and remove the stems from:

    Mushrooms

Brush them lightly with:

    Butter or oil

Place them cap side down on a hot greased broiler and broil them for about 2½ minutes to a side, turning them once. Put in each cap a small lump of:

    Butter or a square of bacon

Season the mushrooms with:

    Salt, as needed and paprika
    Chopped parsley and lemon juice

They are usually done when the butter has been absorbed. Serve them at once on:

    Hot toast

After adding the butter, keep the cap side up to preserve the juices.

BROILED STUFFED MUSHROOMS COCKAIGNE

                          4 Small Servings

Preheat broiler.
There are wonderful farces of sweetbreads, sausages or just seasoned puréed peas with a sprig of lemon thyme. The mushroom stems may be incorporated with them to form the stuffings. Our particular favorite is given below.
Remove stems. Wipe with a damp cloth:

    12 large mushroom caps

Chop the stems. Simmer them for 2 minutes in:

    1 tablespoon butter

or, if the stems are very large, cook them, first in the top of a double boiler in:

    Milk

Add:

1½ cups dry bread crumbs
¼ cup chopped blanched almonds,
   pecans or other nut meats
(1 pressed clove garlic)
1½ tablespoons chopped chives, basil
   or tarragon
Bind these ingredients with:
2 tablespoons cream, stock or part
   stock and part sherry
Season with:
Salt and paprika
Brush the caps with:
Butter or olive oil
Fill them with the above dressing and
sprinkle with:
Grated Parmesan cheese
Place them cap side up on a well-greased
pan. Broil for about 5 minutes and serve
them sizzling hot on:
Toast

MUSHROOMS STUFFED WITH CLAMS OR OYSTERS

Preheat broiler.
Remove the stems and wipe with a dry
cloth:
Large mushrooms
Dip the caps in:
Melted butter
Place on each one:
A clam or oyster
Cover each clam with:
1 teaspoon horseradish
1 teaspoon or more mayonnaise
A drop or 2 hot pepper sauce or
   Worcestershire sauce
Place the mushrooms in a pan. Broil them
about 6 inches from the source of heat, un-
til the tops begin to color. Serve them hot.

MUSHROOMS FLORENTINE

4 Servings

Preheat broiler.
Prepare as for Broiled Stuffed Mushrooms
Cockaigne, page 281:
12 large mushrooms
Add to the stems and the juice in the pan:
2 teaspoons grated onion
2 tablespoons chopped parsley
(1 teaspoon anchovy paste)
Cook these ingredients gently for about 3
minutes. Add:
⅓ cup or more creamed spinach
Brush the caps with:
Butter or olive oil
Fill them with the above mixture and broil
them cap side up on a greased pan for
about 5 minutes. Serve as a garnish for
individual steaks or scrambled eggs.

MUSHROOMS STUFFED WITH SEAFOOD OR SNAILS

4 Servings

Preheat broiler.
Remove the stems from:
8 large mushrooms
Wipe caps and stems with a dry cloth.
Chop the stems. Shell, then chop:

½ lb. cooked shrimp, snails or crab
   meat
Prepare the sauce. Melt:
3 tablespoons olive oil or butter
Stir in:
¼ cup flour
Add:
2 cups shrimp, chicken or clam stock
Add the mushroom stems. ◆ Lower the
heat. Stir and simmer the sauce for 2 minutes. Add the seafood and:
2 teaspoons chopped chives, parsley
   or other herb
Stir gently until well blended.
Correct the seasoning
and add:
⅛ teaspoon curry powder or 1
   tablespoon sherry
Brush the caps with:
Butter or olive oil
Fill them with the above dressing, place
cap side up on a well-greased pan and
broil for about 5 minutes. While the caps
are cooking, prepare:
8 rounds of buttered toast, about same
   size as mushrooms
Place the cooked caps on the toast. Put
the remaining filling in the center of a
platter and surround it with the caps on
toast. Garnish with:
Parsley
If you want to make this a main dish, add
curls of:
Broiled bacon

MUSHROOMS AND ONIONS IN WINE

4 Servings

Fine for a chafing dish.
Prepare for cooking:
1 lb. mushrooms
Melt:
½ cup butter
Skin, add, stir and sauté for 5 minutes:
16 tiny white onions
Add the mushrooms. When they are
coated with butter, add:
2 tablespoons flour
¼ cup chopped parsley
½ bay leaf
¼ teaspoon freshly grated nutmeg
½ cup bouillon or stock
Cook and stir these ingredients until the
onions are tender. Add:
¼ cup Madeira or dry sherry
Serve garnished with:
Croutons, page 342
Sprigs of parsley

MUSHROOM RING OR MOUSSE

6 Servings

Preheat oven to 325°.
Put through a food chopper:
1 lb. mushrooms
Melt:
2 tablespoons butter
Stir in:
2 tablespoons flour
Brown the flour slightly. Sauté the mush-

rooms in this mixture for 2 minutes. Cool them. Beat in:

4 beaten egg yolks
½ teaspoon salt
¼ teaspoon paprika

Whip until stiff:

1 cup heavy cream

In another bowl ♦ whip until stiff, but not dry:

2 egg whites

Fold the cream lightly into the mushroom mixture. Fold in the egg whites. Butter a 9-inch ring mold. Pour in the mousse. Cover it with a piece of buttered paper. Place the ring mold in a pan of hot water. Bake it for about 1 hour. Invert the mousse onto a platter. Fill center with:

Buttered peas and parsley

MUSHROOMS UNDER GLASS
                                        4 Servings

In former years the following dish was always a mark of extreme luxury. Today it is within the reach of anyone with an oven-proof glass bowl that fits closely over a baking dish.

Preheat oven to 375°.

Trim the stems from and channel, page 280:

1 lb. mushrooms

Beat until creamy:

¼ cup butter

Stir in very slowly:

2 teaspoons lemon juice

Add:

1 tablespoon chopped parsley
⅛ teaspoon salt
¼ teaspoon paprika

Cut with a biscuit cutter and toast:

4 rounds bread, ½ inch thick

When cold, spread them on both sides with ½ the butter mixture. Spread the rest on the tops of the mushroom caps. Place the toast in the bottom of a small baking dish and heap the mushrooms upon them. Pour over them:

½ cup cream

Cover them closely with a glass bowl. Bake them for about 25 minutes. Add more cream if they become dry. Just before serving, add:

2 tablespoons dry sherry

Serve the mushrooms garnished with:

Parsley

ABOUT TRUFFLES

When we found them at a gas stop in the Indiana hills one winter day, in their imported cans, both as rubbings and whole, we knew they had become common currency. So common that when a friend asked the proprietor of a small fruit market if he had any truffles, he, being a little hard of hearing, shrugged his shoulders eloquently and replied, "And who hasn't?"

Like other "storied" foods, truffles are best appreciated where they are grown: in Périgord, they lock them up in hotel safes.

For even where they are most plentiful they are expensive and treasured, as they defy cultivation. French are the black truffles, rooted from their underground depths by trick pigs. Dogs are used in Italy for digging the whites. They are called white only in contrast to the best French ones, for they are really pale brown and beige and are in season from October to March.

Too bad there isn't a truffle Geiger counter, but since these fungi have a symbiotic relationship to oak trees, that's the place to start digging.

The terms **Périgordine**, **Piémontaise** or **Lucullus** are often applied to truffled dishes. Famous dishes seasoned with truffles are:

Pâté de foie in pastry
Scrambled eggs
Garnishes for hors d'oeuvres
Farce for artichokes

♦ To prepare truffles, wash fresh ones in several waters. As the skin is rough, scrub them. They should be sliced very thin, for their aroma is overpowering. To take advantage of it, place thin slices on food and store overnight in a closed container in the refrigerator. Save all parings and mince finely for sauce or soup. Add truffles to dishes at the end of the cooking period, as they should be cooked with the food to flavor it—but not overcooked. If using canned truffles, merely heat with the food or use as a garnish. If you open a can and use only a portion, cover the remainder with oil or sherry. It will keep refrigerated a month.

✱ Truffles may be frozen in their own juice; or add some Madeira wine if juice is lacking.

⅄ TRUFFLE GARNISHES

I. To get truffles in economical quantity for decorating, put in a blender:

7 tablespoons truffle bits, peelings
and juice
1 tablespoon gelatin

Dissolved in:

¾ cup water

If this blended mixture is not dark enough to suit you, heat it over hot water until it colors to your satisfaction. Spread the mixture thin on a cookie tin and cool it in the refrigerator. Cut into any desired form and use on cold food, see Chaud-froid, page 341. This same process may be used for pimientos.

II. White truffles can be used raw over risotto or fondue, puréed for canapés, processed in foie gras or cooked 2 to 3 minutes in butter with Parmesan cheese.

ABOUT OKRA

This vegetable is often combined in stews, where its gluey sap helps thicken the sauce and gives to such dishes the name of **Gumbo.** See also page 152.

STEWED OKRA

3 Servings

Wash:

2 cups young okra

If the pods are small, leave them whole, in which case less sap is released. If they are large, cut off the stems and slice into 1-inch pieces. Drop the okra into a small amount of:

Boiling water

enough to cover the bottom of the pan by ⅛ inch. Simmer it, covered, until tender. If whole, it will take about 8 minutes—if cut, about 5. Or the okra may be cooked until half tender, drained and then cooked, covered, in the butter over low heat until it is tender. Drain it.

Correct the seasoning.

Serve it hot with:

Melted butter—1 tablespoon to 1 cup okra

or serve with:

Hollandaise Sauce, page 328

or serve it:

Vinaigrette, page 311

◐ Pressure cook okra cut into 1-inch slices at 15 lbs. for 4 minutes.

SAUTÉED OKRA

6 Servings

Wash:

1 quart okra: 1 lb.

Dry it well, cut off the stem ends and slice the okra crosswise in thin slices. Melt:

2 tablespoons butter

Add the okra, cover it and simmer gently for about 10 minutes. Stir it frequently. Remove the cover and continue cooking the okra until it is tender and a golden brown.

ABOUT ONIONS

Onions are supposed to be the secret of health. But how can they keep that secret? For various suggestions to disguise their

lesser virtues and exploit their potential ◖ please read About Onions as Seasoning, page 534, where you will also find a full discussion of this marvelous family with the qualities each member contributes.

A pleasant way to skin onions is to drop them into rapidly boiling water and leave for about 8 seconds. Drain, chill; and the skin should slip off.

To avoid weeping, you may also pare them under running water, as sketched. Onions all rebel under high heat or too long a cooking period by both discoloring and releasing an unpleasant clinging odor from their sulphur compounds. In sautéing them, be sure they are evenly sliced so they all cook golden at the same time and none remains raw and unpleasant in taste. Give them care in cooking and you will be amply rewarded by the flavor that results.

STEAMED ONIONS

4 Servings

This method is recommended in place of stewing because onion, like cabbage, releases sulphur compounds under too great heat, causing odors and discoloration.

Place on a rack ◖ over—not in—hot water:

10 medium, dry, unpeeled onions

Cover the pan and cook them until tender, for 30 minutes or more. Peel and serve with:

(1 cup browned buttered bread crumbs, page 501)

or dress them with:

¼ cup melted butter
½ teaspoon salt
½ teaspoon cinnamon or cloves
(1 teaspoon sugar)

CREAMED ONIONS

4 Servings

Prepare:

Steamed Onions, above

Cover with:

1 cup Cream Sauce I, page 322, and Au Gratin III, page 342, 1 cup Allemande Sauce, page 324, or 1 cup Tomato Sauce, page 333

You may use ¼ onion water and ¾ cream. Cook the onions and the sauce together for 1 minute. Add:

¼ cup chopped parsley
A dash of cloves
¼ teaspoon paprika
(2 tablespoons sherry)

A wonderful addition is:

(½ cup Sautéed Mushrooms, page 281)

or:

(Minced celery, cooked or raw)

If using one of the above sauces, you may serve the onions on:

(Toast)

YOUNG GREEN ONIONS OR SCALLIONS

Place:

Young green onions

in a very small quantity of:

Boiling water

Cook them, uncovered, until they are nearly tender, about 25 minutes. Drain them well. Place them in rows, on very thin:

Slices of toast

Season them with:

Salt and freshly grated white pepper or nutmeg

Pour over them:

Melted butter or Hollandaise Sauce, page 328

Or cut the onions into small pieces, cook them and combine them with other cooked vegetables—peas, beans, or new potatoes.

WHOLE BAKED ONIONS

I. Preheat oven to 375°.

Wash:

Medium-sized onions

Bake them in a buttered baking dish until they are tender, for about 1½ hours. Cut a slice from the root end. Squeeze the onions to force out the centers. Discard the outer shells. Pour over the onions:

Melted butter

Season them with:

Salt and paprika

Cover them with:

(Grated cheese or chopped parsley)

II. ▣ Cook, as you would potatoes, in a bed of coals for about 45 minutes:

Whole onions

The outer skin forms a protection. When they are tender, puncture the skin to let the steam escape. Scoop out the centers and serve with:

Salt and pepper

SAUTÉED ONIONS

2 Servings

These can be useful also as a garnish for a greater number than two.

Skin:

4 medium-sized onions

Cut them into very thin slices or chop them. Melt in a skillet:

2 tablespoons butter or bacon drippings

Add the onions and sauté them until they are golden brown. Stir them frequently to keep them from burning. Before serving, season with:

Salt

(Worcestershire sauce)

SMALL BRAISED ONIONS

Skin:

Small onions

Pour over them, to the depth of ½ inch:

Boiling Stock, page 490

Simmer them, covered, over slow heat. Let them absorb the liquid until they are tender, about 35 minutes. Add additional stock, if necessary. When they are tender

Correct the seasoning

and add:

(Seeded raisins)

GLAZED ONIONS

4 Servings

These onions are good with pork roast.

Skin:

12 small onions

Prick them through the center and place them on a rack above:

1 inch boiling water

Cook them, covered, until they are nearly tender, for about 25 minutes. Dry them on a cloth. Melt:

¼ cup butter

Add:

½ teaspoon salt

2 tablespoons brown sugar

Cook this sirup for 1 minute. Add the onions and move them about until they are well coated. Cook them over low heat for about 15 minutes, using an asbestos mat under the pot, if needed, toward the end.

SCALLOPED ONIONS WITH CHEESE

4 Servings

Preheat oven to 350°.

I. Peel, slice crosswise and poach in:

Milk

until tender:

6 large white onions

Drain them well. Place in a buttered baking dish:

4 slices buttered toast

Arrange the onions on the toast. Sprinkle them with:

½ cup grated American cheese

Beat well:

1 egg

1 cup milk

½ teaspoon salt

⅛ teaspoon paprika

Pour this mixture over the onions. Dot the top with:

1 tablespoon butter

Bake the dish for 40 minutes. Serve with:

Crisp bacon

Parsley

II. Or, as a substitute for scalloping which gives much the same result, cook the onions, as described above, until tender. Then make a generous spread of grated cheese, Worcestershire sauce and seasonings. Place the parboiled onions on the toast, spread them with the paste, broil them until the cheese is melted.

FRENCH FRIED ONION RINGS OR SHOESTRING ONIONS

4 Servings

▶ Please read About Deep-Fat Frying, pages 124-126.

Skin and cut crosswise into ¼-inch slices or shred paper-thin:

2 large onions

Combine:

1 cup milk

1 cup water

Soak the onions in this for ½ hour. Drain them, spread them on absorbent paper and dredge them with:

Fritter Batter for Vegetables, page 221

Fry in a deep fryer, preheated to 350°-370°, until light brown. Drain on absorbent paper.

STUFFED ONIONS

Onions make attractive garnishes or individual servings when filled.
◗ Please read About Stuffed Vegetables, page 255.
Skin and parboil, page 132, for about 10 minutes:

Medium-sized onions

Drain well. Cut a slice from the top and remove all but ¾ inch of shell. Chop the removed pulp with:

Bread crumbs or cooked rice, chopped cooked fish, meat or sausage, baked beans, mushrooms and bacon, deviled ham or nutmeats

Moisten these ingredients with:

Cream Sauce I, page 322, melted butter, stock, cream or gravy
Correct the seasoning

and add:

Chopped fresh herbs

Fill the onion cases. Cover the tops with:

Au Gratin III, page 342

Place the filled onions in a pan with enough water to keep them from scorching and bake them in a preheated 375° oven until they are tender, about 30 to 40 minutes, depending on size and type. If they are too soft to hold their shape well, bake them in well-greased muffin tins.

ONIONS STUFFED WITH SAUERKRAUT

4 Servings

Preheat oven to 400°.
Prepare:

6 onion cases, above

Combine the chopped pulp and:

1 cup drained sauerkraut
½ cup soft bread crumbs
¼ teaspoon salt
(¼ teaspoon caraway or celery seed)

Heap the mixture into the onion cases. Sprinkle the tops generously with:

Buttered crumbs

Bake the onions in a pan with a very little water until they are well heated and tender, about 35 minutes.

ONION AND APPLE CASSEROLE

4 Servings

This is a complete meal served with green salad, a beverage and bread.
Preheat oven to 375°.
Peel and cut crosswise into ⅛-inch slices:

6 medium-sized onions

Peel, core and cut in the same way:

4 medium-sized apples

Sauté, remove from the pan and mince:

8 slices bacon

Take out 2 tablespoons of the bacon fat. In the remainder, toss:

½ cup soft bread crumbs

Grease a baking dish. Arrange the onions, apples and bacon in alternate layers. Combine and pour over them:

¾ cup hot Stock, page 490, or water
½ teaspoon salt

Cover the top with the bread crumbs. Cover the dish and bake it for 30 minutes. Uncover and cook it about 15 minutes longer.

ABOUT OYSTER PLANT OR SALSIFY

Salsify, as usually found in the market, is white-skinned. If you plan growing a salsify, pick **scorzonera**—the black-skinned type which is better flavored. The best flavor results if the vegetable is stored for several weeks at temperatures just above 32°.

This root discolors on exposure to air. To avoid this, cook it unpeeled or, if peeled, cook it à blanc, as below.

OYSTER PLANT À BLANC

Have ready:

3 cups boiling water

in which you have dissolved:

1 tablespoon flour
2 teaspoons lemon juice
½ teaspoon salt

Drop in:

2 cups peeled oyster plant

and cook for 7 to 10 minutes. Serve in:

Cream Sauce I, page 322

or with:

2 tablespoons melted butter
(Chopped chives or parsley)

or season it with:

1 tablespoon brown sugar
A grating of nutmeg
½ cup whipping cream

SAUTÉED OYSTER PLANT

Wash and peel:

Oyster plant

Dip at once in:

Milk

Drain and season it with:

Salt and pepper

Roll it in:

Flour, bread crumbs or crushed cornflakes

Sauté it slowly until golden in:

Butter

ABOUT HEARTS OF PALM

This ivory-layered vegetable, also known as swamp cabbage, usually weighs between 2 to 3 lbs. when trimmed. Unless avail-

ble where grown, it is found canned—for
loses flavor and discolors quickly after
emoval from its sheath.
♦ To boil, remove the outer covering of
ae heart, leaving a cylindrical portion, the
ase of which should be tested for bitter-
ess. Remove fibrous upper portion. Slice
nin and soak for 1 hour. Use the same
ater to blanch à blanc, page 493, the
alm for 5 minutes—if there is any trace
f bitterness. Now drain and plunge into
oiling water again. Cook, covered, about
5 minutes. Drain and serve with:

> Hollandaise Sauce, page 328

r in:

> Cream Sauce I, page 322

To roast, leave the heart in its sheath.
oast in a 400° oven until tender. Lay
ack the sheath. Slice the heart crosswise
nd serve with:

> Lemon juice and salt

EEP FRIED PARSLEY
Please read About Deep-Fat Frying,
ages 124-126.
ried parsley was used merely as a decora-
on by Ranhofer, the great chef at Del-
onicos, who wrote "The Epicurean." To-
ay, try to keep guests from eating it!
his is so delicious if properly fried, but
ecomes limp if the fat is not hot enough
nd olive green if the fat is too hot. It
ould be both crisp and a bright dark
een. To obtain this crispness and color
ave at least 2 to 3 inches of fat per cup of
arsley and bring the fat you are using just
the smoking point. The parsley must be
arefully stemmed, washed and placed be-
veen towels until absolutely dry. Put in
frying basket:

> 1 cup clean, fresh, well-dried,
> stemmed parsley

nmerse the basket in:

> Hot cooking oil

hich has just reached the smoking point
nd leave it 1 to 2 minutes or until no
ssing noise is heard. Remove and drain
n paper. Serve immediately!

ARSNIPS
                                                    4 Servings
o bring out the best flavor of this vegeta-
e, store for several weeks at tempera-
res just above 32°. Parsnips discolor
asily. To avoid this see Oyster Plant, page
36.
reheat oven to 375°.
are, then cut into halves:

> 4 medium-sized parsnips: 1 lb.

lace them in a buttered ovenproof dish.
rush them with:

> 2½ tablespoons butter

prinkle them with:

> ½ teaspoon salt

dd to the dish:

> ¾ cup stock or water

over the dish and bake until the parsnips

are tender, for about 45 minutes. **Serve**
with:

> Parsley butter

✿ Pressure cook parsnips at 15 lbs. for 7
minutes.

FRENCH PARSNIPS
Prepare as for:

> Carrots Vichy, page 270

GREEN PEAS
                                                    2 to 3 Servings
Young peas have always elicited paeans of
praise, but what to do with old ones? The
skins toughen easily. Try salting when
cooking is about half over or try Puréed
Peas I, below. ♦ One pound of fairly well-
filled pods will yield about 1 cup hulled
peas. Wash, then hull:

> 1 lb. green peas

Steam them, page 252, or cook them, covered, in:

> ⅛ inch boiling water or light stock

to keep them from scorching. Add:

> ½ teaspoon lemon juice

to help preserve color. There is a tradition
that one must add to peas:

> (A pinch of sugar)

Two or three pea pods may be cooked
with the peas for flavor. Simmer 10 to 15
minutes. When the peas are tender, drain
them if there is any water left. Season
them with:

> Melted butter or hot cream

to which you may add:

> Chopped parsley or mint

✿ Pressure cook peas at 15 lbs. for 2 minutes.

GREEN PEAS AND LETTUCE
I.   2 to 3 Servings
Wash, and remove the heart from:

> A head of lettuce

Wash, then hull:

> 1 cup green peas

Season them with:

> Salt and pepper
> Pinch of sugar

Fill the head of lettuce with the peas, tie
up the leaves and place the head in a small
quantity of:

> Boiling water

Steam the peas, covered, until tender,
about 30 minutes. Serve them with:

> Melted butter or cream

The lettuce leaves may be chopped and
served with the peas.

II.   2 to 3 Servings
Wash, then hull:

> 1 cup green peas

Place them in the top of a double boiler.
Cover them with large moist:

> Lettuce leaves or purslane

Cook them, covered, until tender, over
boiling water. This is sometimes a slow
process, dependent upon the size of the
peas, about ¾ of an hour. Remove the
lettuce or purslane.

Correct the seasoning
and add:
  Butter or cream
Serve the peas sprinkled with:
  Chopped parsley

PURÉE OF PEAS
These make a lovely base on which to
place stuffed mushrooms.
I. Prepare:
  2 cups cooked frozen peas
♪ Blend them, when tender, with:
  3 tablespoons cream
  Correct the seasoning
and serve at once.

II. Prepare:
  ¼ cup minced onion, scallions
  or chives
Sauté them until tender in:
  3 tablespoons butter
Heat in a double boiler the contents of:
  2 cans condensed cream of pea soup:
  21 oz.
Stir in the onions. Serve:
  Au Gratin, page 342

PEAS AND CARROTS
Prepare:
  Hot, drained Carrots, page 270
Combine them in any proportion with:
  Hot canned or cooked green peas
Drain the vegetables well.
  Correct the seasoning
Pour over them:
  Melted butter: 1 tablespoon to 1 cup
  vegetables
  Chopped parsley
Serve at once.

PEAS AND MUSHROOMS
Prepare as for:
  Peas and Carrots, above
substituting for the carrots:
  Sautéed Mushrooms, page 281

PODDED PEAS
These sought-after varieties, known also as
sugar peas, snow peas and mange-tout,
are often available in Chinese shops. If
they are not young, slice them diagonally,
page 251.
Wash, cut off the ends, string and cook as
for:
  Green or Snap Beans, page 258
or you may stir-fry, page 253, about 5
minutes. Serve while still crisp.

ABOUT SWEET PEPPERS
OR PIMIENTOES
Many people in the Midwest call sweet
bell peppers mangoes. Do not confuse
them with the tropical fruit of the same
name, page 117. Peppers and their hot
cousins, page 536, are chock-full of vitamin
C and are also reported as having antibacterial values as well. The seeds cause

excruciating pain when in contact with
eyes or lips, so ♪ always remove, before
use, the stem and fibrous portions that hold
the seeds. ♪ To peel peppers, put under
the broiler and turn often until they
blister.
  These are one of the few vegetables that
can be ✳ frozen without blanching. So
buy when they are plentiful. Peppers are
delicious stuffed, but ♪ never overcook
them as they become bitter.

GREEN PEPPERS IN SAUCE
Stewed green peppers combine well with
other vegetables—for example, green pep-
pers with celery or onions. Remove stem,
seeds and fibrous portions from:
  Green peppers
Cut the peppers into oblongs or strips.
Drop them into:
  ½ inch boiling water
Boil them until they are tender, for about
10 minutes. Drain them well. Serve them
in:
  Cheese sauce or a canned soup sauce
Season either one with:
  Salt
  Worcestershire sauce
Allow about ½ as much sauce as peppers.

ONIONS AND GREEN PEPPERS
                                   4 Servings
This is a good accompaniment to cold
meat.
Skin, then cut into thin slices:
  6 medium-sized onions
Cut coarsely, after removing seeds and
membranes:
  3 green peppers
Melt in a large skillet:
  3 tablespoons butter, ham fat
  or olive oil
Sauté the onions and peppers in this for
about 10 minutes. Add:
  2 tablespoons stock or water
  Correct the seasoning
Cover the skillet. Simmer the vegetables
until the onions are tender, for about 5
minutes. Serve with:
  Tomato Sauce, page 333

STUFFED PEPPERS
Should you want to fill peppers with
heated, precooked food, blanch them, page
132, for about 5 minutes. Fill and serve.
Or, cover the filling with Au Gratin I, II
or III, page 342, and run briefly under a
broiler until the crumbs are golden. You
may fill pepper cases with any of the fillings suggested for Stuffed Tomato, page
307, or one of the following: parsli
buttered Lima beans; creamed spinach
peas or celery; creamed asparagus with
shredded almonds; Stuffings of precooked
food; Macaroni and Cheese au Gratin,
page 186, or Corn Creole, page 274.

PPERS STUFFED WITH CHOVY DRESSING
4 Servings
lease read About Stuffed Vegetables,
e 255.
heat oven to 350°.
pare:
4 pepper cases
the pepper cases with a mixture of:
¼ cups dried bread crumbs
2 tablespoons melted butter
6 crushed anchovy fillets
2 tablespoons capers
½ cup sliced green olives
½ teaspoon salt
¼ cups undrained canned tomatoes
e, as directed, about 10 to 15 minutes.

PPERS STUFFED WITH RICE
4 Servings
lease read About Stuffed Vegetables,
e 255.
heat broiler.
pare:
4 pepper cases
/e ready:
1 cup hot cooked rice
i:
½ cup stock, cream or tomato pulp
Salt and pepper
A few grains cayenne
½ teaspoon curry powder or a bare
pinch of oregano
½ cup or more grated cheese
the pepper cases. Cover the tops with:
Au Gratin I or II, page 342
wn briefly under a broiler.

PPERS STUFFED WITH FISH MEAT
e for creamed turkey or shrimp.
lease read About Stuffed Vegetables,
e 255.
e individual molds with:
Pimientos, whole or in strips
pare in Cream Sauce II, page 322.
Chopped cooked fish or meat
½ as much cream sauce as fish or
t. Season these ingredients with:
Worcestershire sauce, lemon juice
or sherry
the molds and place them in a pan of
water on top of the stove. Steam them
tly until they are well heated, about
minutes. Serve them hot with:
Thickened Tomato Sauce, page 333
/hich add:
2 tablespoons chopped parsley
chill them, unmold and serve cold with:
Mayonnaise

PPERS STUFFED WITH MEAT D RICE
4 Servings
ease read About Stuffed Vegetables,
e 255.
heat oven to 350°.
k until nearly tender:
4 pepper cases

Melt:
2 tablespoons drippings or butter
Add, stir and sauté until light colored:
½ lb. ground beef
3 tablespoons minced onions
Add:
1 cup hot cooked rice
2 well-beaten eggs
½ teaspoon salt
⅛ teaspoon paprika
¼ teaspoon celery seed, curry powder,
dried herb or Worcestershire sauce
Fill the pepper cases. Bake, as directed,
about 10 or 15 minutes.

PEPPERS STUFFED WITH CORN À LA KING
6 Servings
♦ Please read About Stuffed Vegetables,
page 255.
Prepare:
6 pepper cases
Place in a double boiler and cook for 20
minutes:
2½ cups corn niblets: 1 No. 2 can
1 shredded green pepper
1 chopped pimiento
You may add:
(4 slices sautéed minced bacon)
2 tablespoons minced onion that has
been sautéed in the bacon fat
and drained
Combine and beat:
1 egg
½ cup milk
1 tablespoon soft butter
¾ teaspoon salt
⅛ teaspoon paprika
Add these ingredients to the vegetables.
Cook and stir over low heat until they are
slightly thickened. Fill the peppers with
this hot mixture and serve.

PEPPERS STUFFED WITH CREAMED OYSTERS
4 Servings
♦ Please read About Stuffed Vegetables,
page 255.
Preheat broiler.
Prepare:
4 pepper cases
½ pint Creamed Oysters, page 365
using ½ the amount
Add:
2 tablespoons chopped parsley
Fill the pepper cases with the hot oysters.
Cover the tops with:
Au Gratin II or III, page 342
Brown the tops briefly under a broiler.

ABOUT PLANTAIN

These 9- to 12-inch bananas must be
cooked to avoid a starchy, raw flavor. They
are not sweet, even when ripe. They get
bitter when overcooked, due to a tannin
component, but can be put into omelets,
soups or stews if finely diced and added the
last minutes before serving.

Remove the fibrous strings before cooking, as they darken. Peel green plantains under running water to keep from staining the hands. ◖ Simmer 30 minutes in rapidly boiling water. Season and serve with butter. If plantains are ripe, slice fine and deep-fat fry as for Potato Chips, page 296, or cook as for Candied Sweet Potatoes, page 298. The purple bud end of the banana can be roasted in its husk. Only the heart is eaten. Serve with crumbled bacon or cracklings.

ABOUT POTATOES
Anyone who has visited Hirschhorn, in the sweetly romantic Neckar Valley, and who has climbed the hill to the partly ruined castle that dominates the little village, will remember being confronted by a "Potato Monument" dedicated piously "To God and Francis Drake, who brought to Europe for the everlasting benefit of the poor —the Potato."

But, in recent years, potatoes have been maligned as too caloric—although they are only equal to the same-sized apple or a baking powder biscuit. They are full of B, C, and G vitamins, plus many minerals and even some high-class protein. Do include them regularly in the diet, but don't use potatoes whose skins are greenish, as they are apt to be bitter, or sprouted potatoes or frost-bitten ones, which are watery and have a black ring under the skin when cut in cross sections.

If you wonder why there are no recommendations for ✳ freezing potatoes in this chapter, let us say that this operation is not possible with success in home freezers. Potatoes purchased frozen have all been treated to a quick-vacuum partial dehydration and instant freezing, to which home freezing equipment does not lend itself.

In the following recipes we have tried to give these delicious vegetables a renewed status. ◖ Be sure, if a potato type is specified, to use that type only—and remember that ◖ once a potato is cold, mealiness can never be returned to it.

Potatoes are often combined and mashed with other cooked vegetables, as: ⅔ celeriac, ⅓ potato, or in equal parts with turnips or ¼ fresh avocado, ¾ potato.

BOILED MATURE POTATOES
4 Servings
Wash well, remove sprouts and blemishes, then pare:
6 medium-sized potatoes
When in haste, cut them into quarters. Cook them, covered, from 20 to 40 minutes in:
4 cups boiling water
½ teaspoon salt
When they are tender, drain them well. Reserve the stock for a thick soup base. To make the potatoes mealy, place a folded towel over the pot for 5 minutes. Shake

the pot well. Remove the towel, wh will have absorbed excess steam. Roll potatoes in:
2 to 3 tablespoons melted butter
3 to 4 tablespoons chopped parsley or chives
✪ Pressure cook large potatoes at 15 for about 15 minutes.

BOILED NEW POTATOES
There are many lovely things to do v small new potatoes, one of which is serv them in their skins, so all of their delic goodness is held until the very mom they are eaten.
4 Servi
Wash well:
12 new potatoes
Drop them in:
Boiling water to cover
Cook them, covered, until they are ten from 20 to 30 minutes. Remove the s and serve the potatoes with:
Chopped parsley, mint or chives
Or melt in a skillet:
3 to 6 tablespoons butter
Add the potatoes and shake them ge over low heat until they are well coa Serve them sprinkled with:
Salt
Chopped parsley or chopped fresh dill or fennel
Or add to the butter in the pan:
3 to 4 tablespoons freshly grated horseradish
and shake the potatoes until coated. last is particularly good with cold cuts.
✪ Pressure cook small new potatoes at lbs. for about 2½ minutes.

RICED POTATOES
6 Serv
A fine foil for meat with a rich gravy.
Prepare:
Boiled Mature Potatoes, this page
When the potatoes are tender and dr put them through a food mill, ricer strainer. Heap them on a dish and over them:
(2 tablespoons melted butter)

MASHED POTATOES
6 Serv
Mashed potatoes should be served at but, in a pinch, can be kept warm by p ing the pan in a larger pan of hot wε Or put them in a greased casserole, ru slight film of cream over the top and in a warm oven. The cream should br to an attractive color.
Prepare:
Boiled Mature Potatoes, this page
You may add to the water a small onio a cut clove of garlic, a piece of bay and a rib of celery with leaves. Rer these extraneous ingredients. Mash potatoes with a fork or a potato mashe put them through a food mill, ⅃ ble or electric mixer. Add to them:

3 tablespoons butter
1 teaspoon salt
⅛ cup hot milk or cream

Beat them with a fork or heavy whisk until they are creamy. Grated or sautéed onions with the drippings, minced crisp bacon, chopped parsley, chives or water cress are good additions to mashed potatoes. To help fluff the potatoes, cover the pan after they are mashed and place over very slow heat for about 5 minutes.

MASHED POTATO CHEESE PUFFS
6 Puffs

This is a tempting potato dish and a good-looking one.
Preheat oven to 350°.
Beat:
2 egg yolks
Add and beat until fluffy:
1⅓ cups hot or cold Mashed Potatoes, page 290
3 tablespoons hot milk
⅛ cup grated cheese
Season these ingredients with:
¼ teaspoon salt
¼ teaspoon paprika
¼ teaspoon celery salt
½ teaspoon finely grated onion
1 teaspoon chopped green pepper or parsley
Beat until stiff, then fold in:
2 egg whites
Place the batter in mounds in a greased pan. Brush the tops with:
1½ tablespoons soft butter
Bake the potatoes for about 20 minutes.

CHANTILLY POTATOES
6 Servings

The use of whipping cream is what makes dish Chantilly.
Preheat oven to 375°.
Prepare:
3 cups Mashed Potatoes, page 290
Whip until stiff:
½ cup whipping cream
Season it with:
Salt and white pepper
A few grains cayenne
Combine it with:
½ cup grated cheese
Shape the potatoes into a mound on an ovenproof plate. Cover the mound with the whipped cream mixture. Bake the plate until the cheese is melted and the potatoes are lightly browned.

BAKED MASHED POTATO BALLS
4 Servings

Preheat oven to 350°.
Have ready:
2 cups well-seasoned, hot Mashed Potatoes, page 290; 4 medium-sized potatoes
Beat in:
2 egg yolks
1 tablespoon chopped parsley

Cool these ingredients slightly. Beat until stiff:
2 egg whites
Fold them lightly into the potato mixture. Shape the mixture into balls. Bake the potatoes in lightly greased muffin tins or drop them on a greased sheet. Bake them until crisp. Turn them to brown evenly.

CREAMED POTATOES
Prepare:
Boiled New Potatoes, page 290
Drain and dry off potatoes over very low heat. Peel and cut into ½-inch dice. Serve at once in:
Cream Sauce II, page 322
flavored with:
Dill seed

CREAMED POTATO CASSEROLE
Prepare as for:
Boiled New Potatoes, page 290
using mature baking potatoes. When nearly done, in about 35 to 40 minutes, drain and dry off the potatoes by shaking the pan over low heat. Peel and cut into ½-inch dice.
Preheat oven to 400°.
Prepare, for every 2 cups diced potatoes:
1 cup Cream Sauce II, page 322
Line a buttered casserole with the potatoes. Add the cream sauce and sprinkle the top with:
Au Gratin III, page 342
Bake the potatoes for 20 minutes, longer if the casserole has been refrigerated.

SCALLOPED POTATOES
4 Servings

Preheat oven to 350°.
I. Grease a 10-inch baking dish. Place in it, in 3 layers:
3 cups pared, very thinly sliced potatoes
Dredge the layers with flour and dot them with butter. Use in all:
2 tablespoons flour
3 to 6 tablespoons butter
There are many tidbits you can put between the layers. Try:
(¼ cup finely chopped chives or onions)
(12 anchovies or 3 slices minced crisp bacon—but then reduce the salt in the recipe)
(¼ cup finely sliced sweet peppers)
Heat:
1¼ cups milk or cream
Season with:
1¼ teaspoons salt
¼ teaspoon paprika
(¼ teaspoon mustard)
Pour the milk over the potatoes. Bake them for about 1½ hours. They may be covered for the first ½ hour.

II. Prepare:
Scalloped Potatoes I, above
Omit the flour, using, instead of the hot milk mixture:

1¼ cups hot condensed mushroom or
celery soup or hot Cheese Sauce,
page 326
Bake, as directed above.

POTATOES SCALLOPED IN BUTTER
6 Servings
Preheat oven to 425°.
Wash and pare:
4 cups mature baking potatoes
Cut them in slices ⅛ inch thick. Place
them in cold water to cover for 15 minutes.
Drain them. Dry them between towels.
Butter a shallow 9-inch baking dish gener-
ously. Sprinkle it with:
Fine dry bread crumbs
Cover the bottom carefully with the po-
tato slices. Dot them generously with:
Butter
Use in all about ⅓ cup. Sprinkle them
lightly with:
Salt and white pepper
(Grated Swiss cheese)
Repeat this process until the dish is filled.
Cover the dish. Bake the potatoes for
about ¾ hour or until tender. Turn them
out onto a platter. Garnish them with:
Parsley

BAKED POTATOES
The best baked potatoes are flaky when
served—so start with mature baking types
like Idahos. Although new potatoes can be
used, they will never have the desired
quality and will need only half as much
baking time. The present rage for wrapping potatoes in foil will not allow them to
become flaky as too much moisture is retained. In fact, to draw moisture out of
bakers, they are often placed on a bed of
rock salt. One of the treats of baked potatoes is eating the skin, under which the
greatest proportion of its minerals, vitamins and protein lie.
Preheat oven to 425°.
Wash and scrub even-sized, shapely:
Baking potatoes
Dry them and grease them lightly with:
Butter
Bake the potatoes for 40 minutes to 1
hour, depending on their size. When potatoes are ½ done, pull out rack, quickly
puncture skin once with fork, permitting
steam to escape. Return to oven and finish baking. When done, serve them at
once with:
Butter or thick sweet or cultured
sour cream
Chopped chives or parsley
1 tablespoon deviled ham
or serve with:
Cheese Sauce, page 326

STUFFED POTATOES
6 Servings
Prepare:
6 Baked Potatoes, above
Cut them in halves crosswise, lengthwise
like boats, or leave them whole, cutting a

small ellipse on the flat top. Scoop out the
pulp. Add to the pulp:
3 to 4 tablespoons butter
3 tablespoons hot milk or cream
1 teaspoon salt
Sauté:
(2 tablespoons grated onion)
in the butter or, if you plan to serve them
with fish, add, for piquancy:
(1 tablespoon horseradish)
along with the butter and cream. Beat
these ingredients until they are smooth.
Whip until stiff:
(2 egg whites)
Fold them into the potato mixture. Fill
the potato shells. Sprinkle the exposed potato with:
½ cup grated cheese
Paprika
Broil them under low heat until the cheese
is melted.

BAKED POTATOES STUFFED WITH
VEGETABLES
8 Servings
Preheat oven to 400°.
Prepare:
4 Baked Potatoes, this page
Have ready:
1 cup Cream Sauce I, page 322
Mix into the sauce:
¼ teaspoon salt
½ cup grated cheese
½ cup cooked peas
½ cup cooked chopped carrots
¼ cup diced green peppers
2 tablespoons diced pimientos
Cut the potatoes lengthwise into halves.
Remove the pulp without breaking the
skin. Mash the pulp and fold in the sauce
and vegetables. Fill the potato shells with
the mixture. Cover them with:
Au Gratin II, page 342
Place the potato shells in the oven until
the tops are brown. Serve with:
Hot or cold meat

BAKED POTATOES STUFFED WITH
HASH
6 Servings
Creamed leftover vegetables and/or meat
or fish may be substituted.
Preheat oven to 400°.
Bake:
6 medium-sized baking potatoes
Cut a thin slice off the flat side. With a
spoon, remove as much as you can of the
potato without breaking the skin. Do not
mash the potato. Add to it and work it
lightly with a fork until blended:
1 tablespoon butter
1 tablespoon cream
½ teaspoon salt
¼ teaspoon paprika
1 teaspoon onion juice
1 tablespoon minced parsley
1 cup chopped cooked meat
(¼ cup minced celery)
Moisten these ingredients with:

Gravy or stock
eason them with:
  2 teaspoons Worcestershire sauce
ombine them with the potato mixture.
ill the skins, heap the tops. Place on each
otato:
  ½ teaspoon butter
r sprinkle it with:
  Grated cheese
rown the potatoes in the oven.

TUFFED POTATO CUPS

Please read About Deep-Fat Frying,
ages 124-126.
reheat deep fryer to 385°.
are oval:
  Potatoes
[ollow out the centers to make cups or
oat shapes. Parboil for 10 minutes in:
  Boiling water
rain and dry them. Fry the potato cups
the hot deep fat until they are well
rowned. Drain well and sprinkle them
ith:
  Salt
ill them with hot:
  Creamed meat, fish or vegetables

INY NEW POTATOES, SAUTÉED

4 Servings

crub and scrape well:
  24 very small whole new potatoes
eat in a heavy saucepan:
  2 to 3 tablespoons olive oil or
    clarified butter
urn the potatoes in the oil, cover them
osely and cook them slowly until tender.
hake the pan from time to time. Sprinkle
e potatoes with:
  Salt and paprika
  (Chopped chives or parsley)

YONNAISE POTATOES

repare:
  6 medium, waxy, Boiled New
    Potatoes, page 290
/hile hot, peel and slice thinly. Sauté
em to an even brown in a heavy skillet
:
  2 tablespoons butter
  2 tablespoons cooking oil
/hile they are cooking, sauté until golden
another pan:
  ½ cup finely sliced onions
:
  2 tablespoons butter
ix onions and potatoes together gently.
  Correct the seasoning
prinkle with:
  Parsley
d serve at once.

RANCONIA OR BROWNED OTATOES

'e love browned potatoes, but have an
version to the hard-crusted, grease-soaked
ariety so often served. To insure a tender
ust, we suggest preparing:

6 boiled mature potatoes, about 2-inch
  diameter
Cook them until they are ♦ not quite done,
so that there is still resistance to the testing fork.
Preheat oven to 350°.
Melt in a small, heavy iron skillet or casserole a mixture of:
  Butter and cooking oil
to the depth of about ¼ inch. When the
fat is hot, but not quite to the point of
fragrance, put in the potatoes. Let them
cook ♦ covered, in the oven for about 20
minutes, turning them for even coloring.
On the last turn, put in:
  2 tablespoons finely chopped parsley
Bake them ♦ uncovered, about 10 minutes
longer.

POTATOES ANNA

6 Servings

One of the most beautiful of all culinary
wares is the lidded copper Potatoes Anna
dish, about 8 inches in diameter and 3½
inches high. The lid, which has side handles, fits down over it to a 1½ inch depth
during the oven period, but is reversed to
hold the potatoes for serving. You may
substitute a heavy skillet.
To get even rounds, cut cylinders from
big potatoes with a corer the size of a
small biscuit cutter. Cut the cylinders into
³⁄₁₆-inch even slices to make:
  4 cups potatoes
Soak them in ice water for 10 minutes.
Drain. Dry carefully in a towel. Heat in
an 8-inch skillet with sloping sides:
  2 to 3 tablespoons butter
  2 tablespoons cooking oil
Do not brown the fats, but let them just
reach the point of fragrance. Put the potatoes in the butter in slightly overlapping
spirals until the base of the pan is filled.
Shake vigorously while filling, so the potatoes will not stick. Add a sprinkling of:
  Salt
  Grated onion
  Parmesan cheese
The butter will bubble up. But make sure,
before adding another layer of slightly
overlapping potato slices, that the first
layer is coated with additional:
  Butter
Continue this process for the first 2 layers,
letting the potatoes color slightly. Be sure
the layers are welded together. Add a
sprinkling of salt, onion and butter each
time. It is not necessary to continue adding butter if you have used about ½ cup.
The moisture from the cooking potatoes
will make it bubble up. In building the
next layer or two, omit the butter. Shake
the pan constantly to make sure the contents are not sticking. Cover the pan and
bake in a 375° oven for 45 minutes to 1
hour. Just before the potatoes are done,
turn the entire mass over—to brown the
upper side.

HASHED BROWN POTATOES
4 Servings

Combine with a fork:
3 cups finely diced raw potatoes
1 teaspoon grated onion
1 tablespoon chopped parsley
½ teaspoon salt
¼ teaspoon black pepper
(1 teaspoon lemon juice)
Heat in a 9-inch skillet:
3 tablespoons bacon drippings, oil
or other fat
Spread the potato mixture over this. Press it with a broad knife into a cake. Sauté the potatoes slowly, shaking them from time to time to keep them from sticking. When the bottom is brown, cut the potato layer in half and turn each half with 2 spatulas. Pour over them slowly:
¼ cup cream
Brown the second side and serve the potatoes piping hot.

POTATO PANCAKES
About Twelve 3-Inch Cakes
◆ This recipe demands mature potatoes.
Pare and grate coarsely until you have:
2 cups grated mature potatoes
Place the gratings on a muslin towel and wring the towel to extract as much moisture from the potatoes as possible. Place them in a bowl. Beat well, then stir in:
3 eggs
Combine and sift:
1½ tablespoons all-purpose flour
1¼ teaspoons salt
Add the flour to the potato mixture with:
(1 to 3 teaspoons grated onion)
Shape it into ¼-inch thick 3-inch diameter patties. Sauté in ¼ inch or more hot fat. Turn and brown the second side until crisp. These are usually served hot with:
Applesauce, page 112
They are best, like all pancakes, served hot out of the pan. If you must hold them until all the batter is cooked, place them on a rack above a baking sheet in a 200° oven. Then serve all of them at once after draining on absorbent paper to remove any excess grease.

GRATED POTATOES, PAN-BROILED
4 Servings
Very good, quick—something like a potato pancake. Wash, grate on a medium grater, skin and all:
3 medium-sized mature baking
potatoes
(2 tablespoons grated onion)
Melt in a skillet to the point of fragrance:
2 tablespoons butter
2 tablespoons cooking oil
Spread the potatoes in the skillet to a depth of about ¼ inch. Cook, covered, over medium slow heat until the bottom is brown. Reverse and brown the other side.

Season with:
Salt
Serve piping hot.

SOUFFLÉ OR PUFFED POTATOES
6 Servings
◆ Please read About Deep-Fat Frying pages 124-126.
Legendary or not, we like this version the origin of these delicacies. Louis XI diverted for the moment by his favorite pastime of fighting the Dutch, was inspecting his army at the front. He was to dine at a given point, at a given time, and a fitting repast had been prepared for him.

His sumptuous traveling coach, that little palace on wheels which was the scene of so many intrigues—or so many tender affairs—was swinging along on its great springs when it was delayed by torrential rains that made the rough roads almost impassable.

Whenever the King made his entrance he would undoubtedly demand food at once to appease his phenomenal appetite. The cook was frantic. His delicious dinner was kept hot over steam, but the potatoes, unfortunately fried ones, appeared limp and cold. A tremendous bustle heralded the arrival of the King and, in despair, the unfortunate cook immersed the potatoes in the hot fat for the second time, agitated them madly, and, behold—the dish that was to make him rich and famous!

There were several more coincidences that the cook may not have been aware of. His potatoes must have been old, so that the starch content was just right to make them puff. He must have had a very systematic apprentice who cut the potato all with the grain and to a very uniform thickness, as sketched. In his relief at having something to serve, he evidently didn't mind a 10% failure, for even experts who make these daily count on that great a percentage of duds. All this is just to encourage you if, like us, you expect a 100% return on your efforts. The duds, by the way, are edible as good French fries, not as glamorous as the puffs.
Choose:
8 large mature potatoes
Restaurants famous for this dish age their own to the point where you can no longer pierce or scrape the skin off with your fingernail, but must use a knife to pierce it. There should be about 80% starch in the potato. Idahos and Burbanks are especially recommended, although Pierre Adrian, who is very expert at this, says there is nothing like a Holland potato grown on Spanish soil. Cut from the unpared potato the largest possible oblong ◆ with the grain—that is, the long way, sketched—into ◆ ⅛-inch slices that are uniform thickness from one end to the other. In restaurants, this accuracy is produced by a slicing machine. Once you

have these long, even slices, you can cut them into the classic shape with polygonal ends, as sketched, or into triangles, circles or fancy ovals with crimped edges. ♦ But whatever the final shape, always start with the long piece—cut with the grain—and have it ⅛ inch thick for its entire length. Soak the slices for at least 25 minutes in:

Ice water

Dry them thoroughly. Have ready a deep-fat frying kettle ⅓ filled with:

Rendered kidney suet or cooking oil

heated to 250°. Drop the slices in separately. ♦ Do not crowd the pan. The slices will sink. This next admonition is not without danger for the unskilled. ♦ When, after a few seconds, they rise, use a continuous shaking motion with the pan, which will set up a wave-like action to keep the floating strips bathed in the fat. Continue to cook them at 250° until they begin to clarify toward the centers and show a marked difference in texture at the cut edges, to a depth of about 1/16 of an inch. Drain them on absorbent paper. If you do not want to use them at once, they may be refrigerated before the second cooking, but ♦ bring them to room temperature before immersing them in the hot fat the second time. If you want to proceed at once, let them cool off and drain for about 5 minutes before the second cooking.

Just before you are ready to serve them, drop them again one by one into a kettle filled ⅓ full with frying oil which has reached 375°. Again agitate the pan, as described. The once-fried slices should puff at once, although they always retain a seam wherever you have made an original perimeter cut. Cook to a golden brown. Drain. Dry them on absorbent paper. Salt and serve the puffed ones at once. If they

are not crisp enough, return them to the fat for a few seconds. Drain again. Sometimes it is worth trying the duds once more, after they have cooled.

NEVER-FAIL FRENCH FRIES

The following recipe, like Soufflé Potatoes, calls for a two-stage frying operation. After the first stage, you may drain and cool the potatoes on absorbent paper. Cook the second stage just before serving.
♦ Please read About Deep-Fat Frying, pages 124-126.
Preheat deep fryer to 300° to 330°.
As with all successful potato frying, much depends on the maturity of the potato, so choose:

Mature baking potatoes

Pare and slice them into strips about 2¼ inches long and about ⅜ inches through. If you are using cold storage potatoes and want a good, light-colored result, soak the potatoes for 15 minutes in 90° water. Wipe well with a towel to remove surface moisture and excess starch. Slowly heat to 300° to 330°:

Cooking oil or rendered beef kidney fat

When the fat is ready, drop in the potatoes—about 1 cup at a time—and cook about 2 minutes, until all sputtering ceases. Skim out the rather limp potatoes, drain on absorbent paper and cool at least 5 minutes before starting the second stage.
♦ Heat the oil to 375°. Place the potatoes in a frying basket. This will assure quick and easy removal from the fat, in just the right condition. Finish frying them for about 3 minutes. They should be golden brown and will be crisp when drained on absorbent paper. ♦ Never cover them, as they will get flabby. Serve at once, in a napkin-lined basket.

SHOESTRING POTATOES

Cut into very thin strips, not more than 3/16 inch thick:

Mature baking potatoes

Cook as for:

Never-Fail French Fries, above

BAKED "FRENCH FRIED" POTATOES
4 Servings

Preheat oven to 450°.
Pare:

4 medium-sized potatoes: 2 cups

Cut them lengthwise into strips about ½ inch thick. You may soak them in cold water for 10 minutes. Dry them well between towels. Spread them in a single layer in a flat ovenproof dish. Pour over them:

¼ cup melted butter, bacon drippings or cooking oil

Stir them about until coated. Bake them for about 30 to 40 minutes. Turn them several times during this period. Drain them on absorbent paper. Sprinkle them

with:
  ½ teaspoon salt
  ¼ teaspoon paprika

POTATO PUFFS
                                    4 Servings
Preheat deep fryer to 385°.
Combine:
  ½ cup sifted flour
  1 teaspoon double-acting
    baking powder
  ¼ teaspoon salt
Add and mix:
  1 cup mashed potatoes
The potatoes should be soft at room temperature. If they are not, add a little hot milk or water and beat. Add:
  1 slightly beaten egg
  1 teaspoon minced parsley
Drop by spoonfuls into hot fat. Fry to a golden brown. Drain on absorbent paper.

BAKED POTATO WAFERS
Potatoes prepared in this way have a distinctive flavor.
Preheat oven to 375°.
Select large, well-shaped:
  Potatoes
Scrub them well. Rub them with:
  Butter
Cut them, without peeling, in rounds ¼ inch thick. Place them in a generously buttered skillet or baking pan, flat side down. Sprinkle them with:
  Salt and white pepper
Cover and bake for 20 minutes or until they are tender. Turn the slices as they brown. Serve them, garnished with:
  Minced parsley

POTATO OR SARATOGA CHIPS
♦ Please read About Deep-Fat Frying, pages 124-126.
As with Soufflé Potatoes, page 294, and French Fries, page 295, it is very important to have properly aged potatoes. Or try unpeeled sweet potatoes. Use either of these chips as a vegetable, a garnish or a cocktail snack.
Using a vegetable slicer, slice as thin as possible:
  Peeled Idaho potatoes
Soak the slices for 2 hours in cold water, changing the water twice. Drain and dry well. ♦ Very slowly, heat to 380°:
  Peanut or corn oil
If you want a good luster on your cooled chips, bring the cooking oil to 75° before heating it. Drop the separated slices into the hot fat in a frying basket. Shake the basket or stir the potatoes several times to prevent the chips from sticking together. Cook until they are golden. Drain and place on absorbent paper to get rid of excess fat.

POTATO BASKETS
♦ Please read About Noodle Baskets, page 188.

Preheat deep fryer to 390°.
Use a shredder to cut into long ¼-inch strips:
  Peeled potatoes
Soak them for 30 minutes in ice water. Drain them well and dry them between towels. Line the larger strainer, as directed for noodle baskets. Fit the smaller strainer over it. Fry the potato baskets 3 to 4 minutes. Remove from the fat and drain. Bring the fryer up to 390° again and immerse basket for 1 minute more. Drain on absorbent paper and serve at once.

DUCHESS POTATOES
                                    4 Servings
I. Prepare:
  Riced Potatoes, page 290
Add:
  ¼ cup butter
  2 beaten egg yolks
  (A dash of mustard)
  Correct the seasoning
and allow this mixture to cool briefly.
Preheat oven to 400°.
Now shape the potato mixture into flat cakes on a floured board. Place the cakes on a buttered baking sheet. Brush with:
  A slightly beaten egg
Bake until golden and serve at once.

II. This version is for decorating the edges of planks or baking dishes.
Prepare:
  Duchess Potatoes I, above
using
  1 egg yolk
  3 to 4 tablespoons milk
Be sure there are no lumps to block the nozzle of the pastry tube or to destroy the smooth surface. Use a fluted tube to shape ruffles or wavy scallops. Brown in oven.

DAUPHINE POTATOES
If you add about 2 tablespoons of grated Gruyère cheese to each cup of potatoes called for in this recipe, you will have Potatoes Lorette.
♦ Please read About Deep-Fat Frying pages 124-126.
Preheat deep fryer to 350°.
For every cup:
  Freshly Mashed Potatoes, page 290
add:
  ⅓ to ½ cup Pâte à Choux, page 597
made without sugar and seasoned with:
  A grating of nutmeg
Shape the potato mixture into 1 to 1½ inch balls or fill into a pastry bag with a large plain tube. If you use the tube, shape as for Spaetzle, page 192.
Roll in:
  (White dry bread crumbs)
Deep-fat fry for 3 or 4 minutes and allow the heat of the fat to increase to 370° until the potato balls are golden. Drain on absorbent paper. Add:
  Salt
and serve at once.

FRIED POTATO BALLS
                                        6 Servings
A simpler version, not unlike Dauphine
Potatoes.
♦ Please read About Deep-Fat Frying,
pages 124-126.
Preheat deep fryer to 385°.
Prepare:
    2 cups hot Riced Potatoes, page 290:
        4 medium-sized potatoes
Add to them:
    2 tablespoons butter
    ½ cup grated cheese
    ½ teaspoon salt
    A few grains cayenne
    2 tablespoons cream
    2 beaten egg yolks
    ½ teaspoon any baking powder
Whip these ingredients until they are light.
Shape them into balls. Roll the balls in:
    Flour
then in:
    1 egg, diluted and beaten with
        2 tablespoons water
and in:
    Sifted bread crumbs
Fry the balls in deep fat. Drain them on
absorbent paper. Serve at once.

ABOUT LEFTOVER POTATOES

Not for nothing do we use the phrase
"cold potato" as a disagreeable appella-
tion. Once cold after cooking, potatoes
lose their mealiness and the good, earthy
flavor of a freshly cooked potato is forever
gone. They are probably most frugally
used ↄ blended into or used with a soup
base. If you do use them, see that the
base liquid is hot before combining with
the cold potato. We give the following
recipes as rather sorry bargains.

LEFTOVER MASHED POTATOES
To reheat, try placing in the top of a double boiler:
    Leftover mashed potatoes
Add, if necessary:
    A little hot milk
Beat the mixture well with a fork. Cover
and cook ♦ over—not in—hot water until
thoroughly heated.

LEFTOVER BAKED POTATOES
Have ready:
    2 baked potatoes, 24 hours old
Grate them on the coarsest side of a hand
grater. Melt in a 10-inch skillet:
    2 tablespoons cooking oil
When the oil is hot, sprinkle the potato
evenly and thinly over the bottom of the
pan. Cook until the entire mass can be
turned as one. Before turning, dribble
over the uncooked surface of the potatoes:
    2 tablespoons melted butter
Now cook the second side until glazed and
brown. Serve at once, garnished with:
    2 tablespoons yogurt and chives

LEFTOVER GERMAN FRIED POTATOES
                                        4 Servings
Melt in a skillet:
    2 or more tablespoons fat
Add:
    2 cups cold, sliced, boiled potatoes
    Salt and paprika
    (1 or more teaspoons minced onion)
Sauté the potatoes slowly until they are
light brown. Turn them frequently.

LEFTOVER POTATOES O'BRIEN
                                        6 Servings
Preheat oven to 350°.
Dice:
    6 medium-sized leftover boiled
        potatoes
Add:
    1 chopped seeded green pepper
    1 chopped onion
    1 tablespoon flour
    Salt and pepper
    A few grains cayenne
    (¾ cup grated cheese)
Place these ingredients in a greased bak-
ing dish. Pour over them:
    1 cup hot milk
Cover them with:
    Au Gratin II, page 342
Bake them for about 30 minutes.

LEFTOVER POTATO CAKES
I. Shape into little cakes:
    Leftover mashed potatoes
Add:
    (A beaten egg)
    (Chopped parsley)
    (Chopped celery)
    (Celery seed)
    (Grated onion or ¼ cup chopped
    sautéed onions)
    (A grating of nutmeg)
Dip the cakes in:
    Flour, bread crumbs or crushed
    cornflakes
Melt in a skillet:
    Butter or other fat
Brown the cakes in this on one side, re-
verse them and brown the other side.

II. Preheat oven to 375°.
Have ready:
    2 cups leftover mashed potatoes
Roll the potatoes into balls and flatten
them. Dip in:
    Melted butter
Roll in:
    Crushed cornflakes
Place them in a greased pan. Bake the
balls until they are well heated.

LEFTOVER AU GRATIN POTATOES
Cut into dice:
    Leftover boiled potatoes
Prepare:
    Cream Sauce—½ as much sauce as
    there are potatoes, page 322
Combine the potatoes and the sauce. Add:

**(Chopped parsley, minced onion
or chives)**
Heat these ingredients in a double boiler
for 30 minutes or put them in a greased
baking dish. Cover them with:
Au Gratin II, page 342
Bake them in a 400° oven until the crumbs
are brown. To prepare the potatoes with
cheese, omit the parsley, etc., and substi-
tute grated cheese or place alternate layers
of potatoes and cream sauce in a baking
dish and sprinkle the layers with:
Grated cheese
Season with:
Paprika or a dash of cayenne
Cover top with:
Au Gratin III, page 342
Bake the potatoes, as directed.

ABOUT SWEET POTATOES OR YAMS

It was George Washington Carver who
really brought attention to the many ways
in which this highly nutritious tuber could
increase the health of our South. Sweet
potatoes, whether the light yellow, dryish
Jersey types or the orangey, moist varieties
affectionately called yams, are both extremely high in vitamin A. Buy only
enough for immediate use as they spoil
rather easily.

They lend themselves to most of the
cooking methods used for potatoes, and are
especially good when combined with fruits
and fruit flavoring.

Six medium-sized sweet potatoes will
yield about 2 cups of riced sweet potatoes.
Cooked sweet potatoes lend themselves to
reheating better than leftover "Irish" potatoes, page 254.

BOILED SWEET POTATOES

To cook sweet potatoes in their jackets,
drop them into boiling water to cover and
cook ♦ covered, until tender, about 25
minutes. They may also be pared, dropped
in ¼ cup boiling water and cook ♦ uncovered, until tender, about 15 minutes. Salt
before serving.

MASHED SWEET POTATOES
4 Servings
Prepare:
6 Boiled Sweet Potatoes, above
Put them through a ricer or mash them
with a potato masher. Add:
2 tablespoons butter
½ teaspoon salt
**A little hot milk, cream, lemon juice
or dry sherry**
(2 teaspoons brown sugar)
Beat them with a fork or whisk until they
are very light. Sprinkle them with:
**Grated orange or lemon rind, cloves
or cinnamon**
Chopped dates and nut meats may be
added. Good served with ham.

BAKED SWEET POTATOES
Follow the recipe for:
Baked Potatoes, page 292
♦ Be sure to cut a small slice off one end
or to puncture a sweet potato when half
cooked, as a safety valve to prevent its
bursting.

STUFFED SWEET POTATOES
4 to 6 Servings
Preheat oven to 375°.
I. Prepare and bake as for Baked Potatoes,
page 292:
6 shapely sweet potatoes
Cut them lengthwise into halves and
scrape out the pulp. Add:
2 tablespoons butter
**¼ cup hot cream or ¾ cup crushed
pineapple**
½ teaspoon salt
(1 tablespoon dry sherry)
Southern people say "use lots of butter,
some brown sugar, nutmeg and black walnut meats; and replace the sherry with 2
tablespoons bourbon whisky."
Beat these ingredients with a fork until
they are fluffy. Fill the shells and cover
the tops with:
Au Gratin II, page 342
Marshmallows may be substituted for the
bread crumbs and butter. These are a matter of taste, or lack of taste. Bake the potatoes until they are brown.

II. These make a good cold weather lunch.
Bake:
Sweet potatoes
Just before serving, insert in each potato:
1 tablespoon deviled ham

CANDIED SWEET POTATOES
4 Servings
Cook, covered, in boiling water to cover
until nearly tender:
6 sweet potatoes
Preheat oven to 375°.
Pare and cut them lengthwise in ½-inch
slices. Place them in a shallow greased
baking dish. Season with:
Salt and paprika
Sprinkle with:
**¾ cup brown sugar or ⅓ cup maple
sirup**
½ teaspoon grated lemon rind
**1½ tablespoons lemon juice or ⅛
teaspoon ginger**
Dot them with:
2 tablespoons butter
Bake them, uncovered, for about 20 minutes.

CARAMELIZED SWEET POTATOES
Slice:
4 medium-sized boiled sweet potatoes
Melt:
**3 tablespoons orange marmalade or
Sauce Cockaigne, page 709**
Cook the sweet potatoes gently in the sauce
until they are glazed and brown.

SAUTÉED SWEET POTATOES
Slice into a skillet:
    4 medium-sized boiled or baked hot
        sweet potatoes
Add to them:
    3 tablespoons melted butter
    Grated rind and juice of 1 small
        orange
    ½ cup brown sugar
    2 tablespoons chopped parsley
        or chives
Shake the sweet potatoes over quick heat
until they are hot.

DEEP-FRIED SWEET POTATOES
Please read About Deep-Fat Frying,
pages 124-126.
Preheat deep fryer to 380°.
    Wash, then parboil for 10 minutes:
        Large sweet potatoes
Pare and cut them into strips. Fry the
sweet potato strips in the deep fat until
they are a golden brown. Drain them on
absorbent paper. Sprinkle with:
        Salt
To flambé, just before serving, put the
drained potatoes in a pan. Sprinkle over
them:
    2 tablespoons warm brandy, applejack
        or rum
Light and tilt the pan back and forth until
the flame burns low.

II. Pare, then cut into ¼-inch slices:
        Sweet potatoes
Deep fry them in hot fat until done. Drain
them on absorbent paper. Sprinkle with:
        Brown sugar
        Salt
        Freshly grated nutmeg

SWEET POTATO PUFFS
Preheat oven to 500°.
Have ready:
    2 cups riced, cooked sweet potatoes
Peel, mash and add:
    1 large ripe banana
Combine these ingredients and beat them
into:
    1½ tablespoons melted butter
    1 egg yolk
    1½ teaspoons salt
    ⅛ to ¼ cup hot milk or cream
    (⅛ teaspoon nutmeg or ginger)
Beat until stiff:
    1 egg white
Fold it lightly into the potato mixture.
Drop the batter with a tablespoon in
mounds—well apart—on a greased tin, or
place the mixture in buttered ramekins.
Bake the puffs for about 12 minutes.

SWEET POTATOES AND APPLES
                                    4 Servings
This tart dish is exceptionally good with
roast pork, baked ham or game. Cook,
covered, until nearly done in boiling wa-
ter to cover:
    6 medium-sized sweet potatoes
Peel and cut them into ½-inch slices.
Cook, covered, until nearly done in a very
little boiling water:
    1½ to 2 cups thinly sliced apples
If the apples are not tart, sprinkle them
with:
    Lemon juice
Preheat oven to 350°.
Grease a baking dish and place in it alter-
nate layers of sweet potatoes and apples.
Sprinkle the layers with:
    ½ cup or more brown sugar
    A dash cinnamon or grated lemon
        rind
Dot them with:
    ¼ cup butter
Pour over them:
    ½ cup apple water or water
Bake them for about 1 hour.

SWEET POTATOES WITH OTHER FRUITS
Follow the recipe for:
    Sweet Potatoes and Apples, above
Omit the sugar and substitute for the ap-
ples:
    ½ cup puréed, sweetened, dried
        apricots, page 112, ½ cup Sauce
        Cockaigne, page 709, or ½ cup
        crushed pineapple

SWEET POTATOES AND ORANGE JUICE
Preheat oven to 375°.
Cook and mash:
    Sweet potatoes
Allow to every cup of potatoes:
    1¼ tablespoons butter
    1 tablespoon brown sugar
    ½ teaspoon grated orange or
        lemon rind
    3 tablespoons orange juice
    ½ teaspoon salt
Combine these ingredients and place them
in a baking dish or in hollow orange rinds
made into cups, placed in a baking pan.
Sprinkle the top with:
    Brown sugar
    Paprika
Cover the dish or the cups closely. Bake
the potatoes for 30 minutes in the dish, 15
minutes in the cups. Remove the cover
and bake them until they are brown.

PURSLANE
                                    3 Servings
Wash well:
    2 lbs. purslane
Use only the tender tips and leaves. Blanch,
page 132, briefly in:
    Salted boiling water
Drain well. Reheat in:
    2 tablespoons butter
    Correct the seasoning
and serve at once.

ABOUT RADISHES

We all enjoy red and white radish garnishes and, if we've read Pepys, we know he ate them buttered at William Penn's—worth trying, too, especially with black radishes. Radishes are also good prepared as for Celeriac Remoulade, page 85. The large Japanese radish, Daikon, and the red and white ones, if you have a plethora in your garden, are good cooked by any recipe for Turnips, pages 308-309.

To store radishes before using, cut off the leaves.

COOKED RADISHES

Peel and slice:
  Radishes
Drop them into:
  Boiling salted water to cover
Simmer, uncovered, about 6 to 8 minutes or until tender. Drain.
  Correct the seasoning
Serve in:
  Cream or Cream Sauce I, page 322

RUTABAGAS OR SWEDES
                                                    4 Servings
These may be French fried as for Shoestring Potatoes, page 295, or baked like Potatoes, page 292.
To boil, pare and dice:
  4 medium rutabagas
♦ Do not use the leaves. Drop the pieces into:
  Boiling water
Cook them, uncovered, until tender, about ½ hour. Drain them well. Add:
  ½ teaspoon salt
Serve them with:
  Melted butter
to which you have added generously:
  Lemon juice
  Chopped parsley
or mash the turnips and add them in any proportion to mashed potatoes with lots of:
  Chopped parsley or cultured sour cream and nutmeg

ABOUT SKIRRET

Cook as for any recipe using carrots, but never peel before boiling as the flavor is lost. Be sure to remove the inner hard core before serving.

ABOUT SORREL

Rather heavy in oxalic acid, this vegetable is seldom served by itself, but is combined with spinach, chard or other greens. It lends itself to flavoring with meat glaze, eggs and cream.

Prepare as for Panned Spinach, page 301, and season with butter; or purée it and season with mustard and tarragon as a bed for fish.

ABOUT SPINACH

Forced down the throats of a generation as a source of iron, spinach is today in bad repute for its calcium-robbing activity. Perhaps we had better forget both these factors and just eat it in moderation for its true goodness. It is a special treat as a garnish with other foods, where its presence is usually heralded by the title **Florentine.**

We suggest 3 servings to the pound as the cooked amount is so variable—depending on age.

Spinach requires little salt. Its astringent taste comes from alum and iron. Never serve it in silver.

✳ If using frozen spinach, thaw partially before cooking.

❂ Pressure cook spinach at 15 lbs. for 1 minute.

BOILED SPINACH
                                                    3 to 4 Servings
Pick over and cut the roots and tough stems from:
  ¼ peck spinach: 1 lb.
Wash it quickly in several waters until it is free from sand and soil. If it is young and tender, cook it as for Panned Spinach, page 301. If old, place the spinach in:
  2 cups rapidly boiling water
♦ Reduce heat and simmer, covered, until tender, for about 20 minutes. Discard the water if it is strong in flavor. If not, keep it for use in soups and sauces. Drain the spinach well. ⅄ Blend briefly or cut up the spinach with 2 sharp knives or a triple chopper until it is as fine as you like it. Sauté:
  2 tablespoons diced sweet red pepper,
  2 tablespoons minced onion or a clove of garlic
in:
  Butter or drippings
Add:
  Lemon juice
  Correct the seasoning
♦ being careful not to oversalt. Serve the seasonings over the spinach. Other garnishes for spinach include:
  Hard-boiled egg
  Crumbled bacon
  Fine buttered croutons
  Hollandaise Sauce, page 328
  Au Gratin III, page 342

CREAMED SPINACH
                                                    3 Servings
Prepare:
  2 cups Boiled Spinach, above
⅄ Blend, rice or chop it until it is a fine purée. Melt in a skillet which may be rubbed lightly with a clove of garlic:
  1½ to 2 tablespoons butter
Add and cook for 1 minute or, if preferred, until golden:
  (1 tablespoon or more very finely chopped onion)

in, until blended:
1 tablespoon flour or 2 tablespoons
    browned flour
    in slowly:
½ cup hot cream, top milk or stock
1 teaspoon sugar
en the sauce is smooth and hot, add the
nach. Stir and cook it for 3 minutes.
son it well with:
    Salt and pepper
    (Freshly grated nutmeg or grated
        rind of ½ lemon)
ve it garnished with slices of:
1 hard-cooked egg

NNED OR SICILIAN SPINACH
                                         3 Servings
e seasonings in this dish are also good
d with canned spinach.
sh well and remove the coarse stems
m:
1 lb. spinach
ake off as much water as possible. Heat
a large, heavy skillet:
1 tablespoon butter
2 tablespoons olive oil
d:
(1 clove minced garlic)
d the spinach. Cover at once and cook
er high heat until steam appears. ◗ Re-
ce the heat and simmer until tender, 5
6 minutes in all.
    Correct the seasoning
turn this into Sicilian Spinach, add:
(2 or more chopped anchovies)

INACH WITH TOMATOES
                                         4 Servings
ok:
1 lb. spinach
ain and ⅃ blend or chop fine. Add:
6 or 8 oz. Italian tomato paste or
    tomato purée
uté:
1 pressed clove garlic or 3 tablespoons
    minced onion

3 or 4 tablespoons olive oil
d the spinach mixture and
    Correct the seasoning

INACH, TOMATO AND
EESE LOAF
                                         8 Servings
eheat oven to 350°.
ace in a bowl:
2 cups cooked, drained spinach
2¼ cups canned tomatoes
¼ cup chili sauce
½ lb. grated cheese
1 cup cracker crumbs
    Juice of ½ onion
¼ teaspoon salt
¼ teaspoon freshly ground pepper
oss these ingredients until they are
ended. Place them in a greased loaf pan.
ake the dish for about 1 hour. Serve it

garnished with:
    Crisp Bacon, page 411

SPINACH IN PANCAKES
Prepare:
    Creamed Spinach, page 300
Prepare:
    French Pancakes, page 212
    Chopped Sautéed Mushrooms,
        page 281
Place the spinach and mushrooms on the
pancakes. Roll them like a jelly roll. The
tops may be sprinkled with:
    Grated cheese
Place the rolls under a broiler until the
cheese is melted. Serve at once.

⅃ BLENDER SPINACH
                                         3 Servings
Cook and drain:
    Boiled Spinach, page 300
Put it very briefly through a blender. Stir
into it:
    ¼ cup cultured sour cream or
        condensed cream of chicken soup
    A grinding of nutmeg or ⅛ teaspoon
        prepared mustard
    (1 teaspoon horseradish)
    Correct the seasoning
Heat briefly and serve.

GROUND SPINACH
                                         3 Servings
Cooked in this way, spinach seems to re-
tain all its flavor.
Wash:
    1 lb. spinach
Drain it well. Shortly before you are ready
to serve the spinach, run it through a food
chopper with:
    1 small onion
Reserve the juices. Place it in a saucepan
with the juices and:
    ½ teaspoon sugar
Cover and cook it slowly for 3 minutes.
Add before serving:
    1½ to 2 tablespoons butter
    (2 teaspoons lemon juice)
    Correct the seasoning

ABOUT SQUASHES
Perhaps no other vegetable has so wide a
tolerance of growing conditions. You will
quickly know after cooking if the variety
you have is cultivated, for the wild ones
are very bitter. Cross-pollination from
wild species grown in subtropical climates
may explain the occasional bitterness you
find in squash from the market.
    These plants divide into summer and
winter types. We often call for special
varieties of each type in the recipes which
follow; but others may be substituted, as
long as they belong to the respective type.

SUMMER SQUASHES OR CYMLINGS

Whether green, yellow, white, long, round

or scalloped, these are all thin-skinned and easily punctured with a fingernail—the classic marketer's gesture and the grocer's despair. They should be firm and heavy. Avoid them if the rind is tough or the stem dry or black. If they are young, there is no need to pare nor to discard the seeds. If only hard-rinded ones are available, do both. Summer squash do not store well.

You may have your favorites. Ours are undoubtedly zucchini or the closely related cocozelle. Remember these squash may also be prepared by recipes for cucumber and eggplant. As shown above, from left to right, they are **straight neck, crooked neck, cymling, cocozelle** and **zucchini.**

WINTER SQUASHES

These are of many colors and shapes and remain on the market from fall to early spring. Except for butternut, they have hard-shelled skins. Choose the others for their hard rinds. Avoid winter squash with watery spots which indicate decay. The winter types sketched, from left to right below, are **Golden Delicious, acorn, buttercup** or **turban, butternut** and **Hubbard.** For ways to cook pumpkin, the most famous winter squash, see page 605. Unless you bake them whole, remove the seeds and stringy portions. Peel and cut into small pieces. They need from 10 to 45 minutes of cooking.

Because squash is so bland in flavor, it can stand a good deal of "doctoring" and is ideal for stuffing. Cut small squash into boats and fill. ♦ To stuff a whole squash

cut off the ends, core the center and, a stuffing, secure the ends with tooth closures. For fillings, see Farces, page

If it is a tender summer type, you combine the removed portion with farce, which may include vegetables, bi crumbs, nuts, mushrooms or cooked m

STEAMED SUMMER SQUASH

4 Serv
♦ Please read About Squashes, above.
I. Wash and cut into small pieces:
   2 cups any summer squash: zucchini, yellow crooked neck, etc.
If very tender, the squash may even left whole. Steam it, covered, in a stra over boiling water until it is tender. D it very well. Sprinkle it generously wit
   Grated Parmesan cheese and melted butter

II. Prepare the squash as above, then m it with a fork. Beat it until it is flu Beat in:
   1 tablespoon cream
   1 tablespoon butter or olive oil
   ⅛ teaspoon pepper
   (1 teaspoon grated onion or chopped fresh herb or a touch of saffron)
Reheat the squash briefly and serve.

STUFFED SQUASH BLOSSOMS

Do you wonder why so many of y squash blossoms fall off without maturi These are male blooms and after they cl and drop make decorative, as well as ble, cases for Forcemeat, see page 4 Open each flower and put in only enov

the forcemeat to allow the petals to
se again. Place stuffed blossoms side by
: in a greased baking dish, in a moder-
oven, until thoroughly heated. Serve
m alone or as a platter garnish.

KED SUMMER SQUASH
4 Servings

lease read About Squashes, page 301.
heat oven to 350°.
ummer squash is young, it need not be
ed. Cut into strips:
  3 cups any summer squash
:e in a greased baking dish. Dot with:
  2 tablespoons butter
inkle with:
  1 teaspoon salt
  ¼ teaspoon paprika
    **(A grating of nutmeg or 1 teaspoon
    fresh lemon thyme)**
r over it:
  ¼ cup milk
  (1 teaspoon grated onion)
ver the dish. Bake the squash for about
our or until it is tender. Garnish with:
  Crisp crumbled bacon

UTÉED SUMMER SQUASH
4 Servings

'lease read About Squashes, page 301.
ish and cut into dice:
  2 cups any summer squash
lt in a saucepan:
  3 tablespoons butter or olive oil
d and sauté until golden:
  1 cup minced onion
d the squash and:
  ½ teaspoon salt
  **¼ teaspoon freshly ground white
  pepper**
ver the pan and cook the squash until
der, for about 10 minutes, shaking the
occasionally to keep from sticking.
ve it sprinkled with:
  Chopped parsley or basil
  **Grated Parmesan cheese or Tomato
  Sauce, page 333**

UFFED COOKED SUMMER SQUASH
4 Servings

'lease read About Squashes, page 301.
ish thoroughly, then cut the stem ends
m:
  4 small summer squashes
am them as for Steamed Summer
uash, but leave them whole. When al-
st tender, drain the squashes, cool them.
oop out the centers, leaving a shell
ut ½ inch thick. Chop the removed
p.. Add to it:
  ¼ teaspoon paprika
  ½ teaspoon Worcestershire sauce
  Minced garlic or onion
  ¼ teaspoon salt
  1 tablespoon butter
  3 tablespoons dry bread crumbs
  ¼ cup grated cheese
  A few grains cayenne

  **⅛ teaspoon curry powder or dry
  mustard**
Preheat oven to 400°.
Refill the shells. Place them in a pan, in a
very little water or on a rack above the
water. Bake until hot, about 10 minutes.

II. Or fill these cooked squash cases while
hot with:
  **Heated creamed chicken, ham, fish
  or spinach**
Garnish with:
  Parsley or tiny sprigs of lemon thyme

STUFFED RAW SUMMER SQUASH
4 Servings

♦ Please read About Squashes, page 301.
Preheat oven to 350°.
Wash:
  4 small squashes
Cut them down the middle, either crosswise or horizontally. Scoop out the pulp,
leaving a ½-inch shell. Combine the squash
pulp and:
  2 tablespoons chopped sautéed onions
  ½ cup grated cheese
  ½ teaspoon salt
  ¼ teaspoon paprika
  A dash of nutmeg or cloves
Stir and cook these ingredients until hot.
Remove from the heat. Add:
  1 beaten egg
  ½ cup dry bread crumbs
You may rub the squash shells with:
  Butter or drippings
Fill them with the stuffing. Place them in
an ovenproof dish. Cover the bottom with
⅛ inch water or stock. Sprinkle the tops
with:
  Au Gratin II, page 342
Bake the squashes until tender, about 20
to 25 minutes, depending on their size.

SUMMER SQUASH CREOLE
♦ Please read About Squashes, page 301.
Have ready:
  **2½ cups well-drained, cooked zucchini,
  yellow crooked neck, etc. summer
  squash**
Place it in a greased baking dish and proceed as for:
  Stuffed Eggplant Creole, page 278
substituting the squash for the eggplant.

DEEP FRIED ZUCCHINI
♦ Please read About Deep-Fat Frying,
page 124, and About Squashes, page 301.
Preheat deep fryer to 365°.
Wash, dry and slice into ¼- to ½-inch
slices:
  Zucchini
Dry it well. Dip it in:
  **Fritter Batter for Vegetables,
  page 221**
Fry it in deep fat until golden. Serve at
once.

SUMMER SQUASH CASSEROLE COCKAIGNE

4 Servings

We are particularly fond of zucchini in this dish.

♦ Please read About Squashes, page 301.

Cut into small pieces:

3 cups summer squash

Simmer the squash, covered, until tender, for about 6 to 8 minutes, in a small amount of boiling water. Shake the pan to keep from sticking. Drain well. Combine:

¼ cup cultured sour cream
1 tablespoon butter
1 tablespoon grated cheese
½ teaspoon salt
⅛ teaspoon paprika

Stir this mixture over low heat until the cheese is melted. Remove it from the heat. Stir in:

1 beaten egg yolk
1 tablespoon chopped chives

Add the squash. Place the mixture in a baking dish. Cover the top with:

Au Gratin III, page 342

Brown it in a heated 375° oven.

BAKED WINTER SQUASH

♦ Please read About Squashes, page 301.

Preheat oven to 375°.

If the squash is small, like:

Acorn or butternut squash

it may be washed, dried, greased and treated just like Baked Potatoes, page 292. Bake at least 1 to 1½ hours. The smaller baked winter squashes make attractive cases for:

Creamed spinach, ham, etc., or buttered vegetables

Serve garnished with:

(Pimiento strips or Au Gratin, page 342)

MASHED WINTER SQUASH

♦ Please read About Squashes, page 301.

I.

Preheat oven to 375°.

Scrub:

A 3 to 4 lb. Hubbard or other winter squash

Place it on a rack and bake it until it can be pierced easily with a toothpick. Cut it in halves, remove the seeds. Peel the squash and mash the pulp. To:

1 cup squash

add:

1 tablespoon butter
1 teaspoon brown sugar
¼ teaspoon salt
⅛ teaspoon ginger

Beat this well, with enough:

Warm cream or orange juice

to make it a good consistency. Place it in a serving dish. Sprinkle it with:

Raisins or nut meats
¼ cup crushed pineapple

II. ✳ If using frozen or canned squash, season with:

Sautéed onions
Cultured sour cream
A pinch allspice
Chopped parsley

Heat it in a double boiler.

STUFFED WINTER SQUASH

Small acorn or butternut squash are id for individual service. You may fill raw shell as in I or bake it first, as Baked Winter Squash, and then fill it w the hot, creamed foods suggested below

♦ Please read About Stuffed Vegetab page 255, and About Squashes, page 3

I. Preheat oven to 375°.

Prepare uncooked:

Acorn squash cases

by washing, cutting the squash in l lengthwise and scooping out the see

Fill them with:

Sausage meat or Ham à la King page 231

Bake them for about 1 hour.

II. Prepare cooked:

Acorn squash cases, see above

Fill them with:

Creamed oysters, chicken, chipped beef, crab, fish, mushrooms, hash, hash and vegetables, hot applesau or crushed pineapple

Garnish the tops with:

Parsley

Reheat for 10 to 15 minutes in a 3! oven.

ABOUT PUMPKIN

We think of this squash first as pie, p 605, and next as soup, but it is also go as a vegetable. Cook by any recipe call for a winter squash. About ½ lb. will se 1 person.

ABOUT TOMATOES

Really a fruit, beautifully colored and surpassed for flavoring, tomatoes, lemons, are one of the most satisfact things to have on hand fresh or canned also in the form of juice, purée, paste, c sup or chili sauce. Since they are an a fruit and often home grown, they can easily home processed, page 751. growing the more meaty pear-shaped I ian varieties, which are both sweeter a sharper than American types.

To use fresh tomatoes in cooking, wh their juiciness is sometimes not an as slit the stem end and remove it. Hold your hand palm down above a bowl, pr the tomato tightly in the palm to eject cess juice and seeds. To skin tomatoes, pages 89 and 751.

When recipes call for strained, canr tomatoes, watch for 2 things: Be sure force the pulp through the sieve well, you make the most of its thickening a seasoning powers; also watch your brands: the cheaper ones are often watery.

We cannot leave this eulogy without comment on the high vitamin C and A values of tomatoes. To retain them and the best color ♦ store in good light, not sunlight, unwrapped, between 65° and 75°. If you have any choice in the matter, do not pick until they have reached their full size. Ripened 5 to 6 days off the vine, unless overripe, they retain good vitamin values. Once ripe, store refrigerated. ♦ Immature green tomatoes will not ripen off the vine, so use at once for pickles. To retain food value, prepare tomatoes just before using.

Prepare them stuffed, not only for Salads, page 89, but as cases for other Vegetables, page 255.

STEWED TOMATOES
                                            4 Servings
Wash and skin, page 751:
  6 large quartered tomatoes or
  2½ cups canned tomatoes
Place them in a heavy pan over slow heat, about 20 minutes for the fresh tomatoes—10 for the canned. You may add:
  (1 teaspoon minced onion)
  (½ cup chopped celery)
  (2 or 3 cloves)
Stir them occasionally to keep them from scorching. Season them with:
  ¾ teaspoon salt
  ¼ teaspoon paprika
  2 teaspoons white or brown sugar
  ⅛ teaspoon curry powder or 1 teaspoon
    chopped parsley or basil
  1 tablespoon butter
Tomatoes may be thickened with:
  (½ cup bread crumbs)

STEWED GREEN TOMATOES
                                            4 Servings
Sauté until light brown:
  2 tablespoons minced onion
in:
  2 tablespoons butter
Add:
  2 cups sliced green tomatoes
Stir and cook the tomatoes slowly until they are tender. Season with:
  ¾ teaspoon salt
  ¼ teaspoon paprika
  ½ teaspoon curry powder
Garnish the tomatoes with:
  1 tablespoon chopped parsley

SEASONED SAUTÉED TOMATOES
                                            4 Servings
This recipe is much like the preceding one, but it may be useful when broiling or baking is out of the question. Wash:
  6 firm, medium-sized, red or green
    tomatoes
Slice them in ¼-inch slices. Bread them with:
  Seasoned Flour, page 502

Rub a skillet with garlic. Melt in it:
  3 tablespoons butter or bacon
    drippings
Add the tomato slices. Sauté them gently on both sides. Place the tomatoes on:
  Rounds of toast or squares of corn
  bread
Blend the butter and crumbs left in the skillet with:
  ¾ cup cream
  1 teaspoon chopped fresh basil
  or chopped parsley
When the sauce is smooth and hot ♦ but not boiling, pour it over the tomatoes.

CREAMED CANNED TOMATOES
                                            4 Servings
Simmer gently for about 10 minutes:
  2 cups canned tomatoes
  2 tablespoons minced onion
  ¾ teaspoon salt
  ¼ teaspoon paprika
  2 teaspoons brown sugar
  (½ cup chopped celery)
Combine until smooth and bring just to a boil:
  1 tablespoon flour
  ½ cup cream or milk
If you use the milk, add 2 tablespoons of butter to the tomato mixture. Add the tomato mixture slowly to the cream or milk. ♦ To avoid curdling, be careful not to reverse the process, and stir constantly over very low heat until the raw-flour taste is gone, about 3 to 5 minutes.

BAKED TOMATOES
                                            4 Servings
Preheat oven to 400°.
Cut deep, narrow holes in:
  6 firm tomatoes
Season them—pushing the seasoning into the hollows—with:
  3 tablespoons brown sugar
  1½ teaspoons salt
  2 tablespoons butter
Fill the remaining space with:
  (¼ cup Au Gratin II, page 342)
Place the tomatoes in a well-buttered shallow baking dish on a rack or in greased muffin tins. Bake them for about 15 minutes. You may top each tomato with:
  Crisp crumbled bacon

TOMATO PROVENCALE
This garnish looks very professional if you have a broiler and an oven you can use in quick succession. Choose:
  Firm ripe tomatoes
Slice off a deep enough section horizontally on the stem end to get an even surface. Do the same on the base. Divide the remaining tomato horizontally. Place these thick slices on a rack to drain. Sprinkle on top of each:
  Salt and black pepper
  Sweet basil

A slight pinch of orégano
Melt enough:
  Butter
to coat the tomato slices. Place in the butter
  A split clove of garlic
Or, as an alternative to the butter, squeeze a little garlic on a thin square of:
  (Parmesan cheese)
that will almost cover the tomato slice. Allow the seasoned tomatoes to remain at 70° for 1 hour.
Preheat broiler and preheat oven to 350°.
Put the slices on a greased baking sheet. Run them under a broiler first to brown slightly and then bake them for 15 minutes. Serve at once.

GRILLED TOMATOES

4 Servings

Preheat broiler.
Wash:
  4 large, firm tomatoes
Cut them crosswise into even ½-inch slices. Season them well with:
  1 teaspoon salt
  ¼ teaspoon pepper
  White or brown sugar
  (Celery salt)
Place in a greased pan and cover them closely with:
  About 1 cup Au Gratin III, page 342
  (2 tablespoons or more grated onion)
Broil them for about 10 minutes ♦ about 5 inches from the heat source.

BROILED BREADED TOMATOES

Preheat oven to 375°.
Wash and cut a piece off the stem end horizontally, so the surface is even, and cut another off the base of:
  Tomatoes
Cut them in half, crosswise and sprinkle the halves with:
  Salt and pepper
  (Brown sugar)
Dip them in:
  Bound Breading III, page 502
Bake them on a greased sheet until they are nearly soft, then broil them under moderate heat, turning them once, until they are brown.

CANDIED TOMATOES

4 Servings

Melt:
  2 tablespoons butter
Sauté in the butter until brown:
  ¼ cup chopped onion
Add:
  1 quart canned tomatoes
  6 tablespoons brown sugar
Cook these ingredients very slowly, using an asbestos mat, until the juice has been absorbed. Place the tomatoes in a baking dish. Sprinkle them with:
  ¾ teaspoon salt

  2 tablespoons brown sugar
  1½ cups buttered bread crumbs
Bake them in a 375° oven until the crumbs are brown.

TOMATOES CREOLE

4 Servings

In contrast to the above, a very good quickie!
Melt in a saucepan:
  2 tablespoons butter
Add:
  4 large, skinned, sliced, seeded tomatoes or 1½ cups canned tomatoes
  1 large minced onion
  2 tablespoons minced celery
  (1 shredded green pepper)
Cook the vegetables until they are tender, about 12 minutes. Add:
  ¾ teaspoon salt
  ¼ teaspoon paprika
  2½ teaspoons brown sugar
  (¾ teaspoon curry powder)
Strain the juice from the vegetables and add to it enough:
  Cream
to make 1½ cups of liquid. Stir in:
  1½ tablespoons flour
Simmer and stir the sauce until it is thick and smooth. Combine it with the vegetables and serve them hot on:
  Toast
with:
  Sautéed bacon
Or use to fill pepper or squash cases.

TOMATO OLIVE CASSEROLE

3 Servings

If you have any prejudice against tapioca, please dismiss it long enough to try out this fine dish. Serve it with ham, scrambled eggs, omelet, etc.
Preheat oven to 350°.
Heat and ♦ strain well, discarding the seeds:
  1½ cups canned tomatoes
Melt in the top of a double boiler:
  1 tablespoon butter
Add and sauté until golden:
  ¼ cup minced onion or 1 pressed clove garlic
Add the strained tomato and:
  3 tablespoons quick-cooking tapioca
  ½ teaspoon salt
  ½ teaspoon sugar
  ⅛ teaspoon paprika
Cook and stir these ingredients in a double boiler ♦ over—not in—hot water for about 7 minutes. Chop coarsely:
  18 stuffed or ripe olives
Grease a baking dish. Fill it with alternate layers of tomato mixture and olives. Sprinkle the layers with:
  (½ cup grated cheese)
Cover the top with:
  Au Gratin I, page 342
Bake the dish for about 30 minutes.

TOMATO CUSTARD

6 Servings

Preheat oven to 325°.
Skin and squeeze well, page 304, to rid
them of excess liquid and seeds and put
through a coarse sieve:

Enough tomatoes to make 2 cups

Beat together with:

3 eggs
1 cup milk
¼ to ½ cup sugar
½ teaspoon salt
⅛ teaspoon nutmeg

Bake in custard cups for about 30 minutes
or until set. Serve hot or cold.

TOMATO PUDDING COCKAIGNE

Either of these recipes should serve 6, but
we find the demand for this favorite makes
4 servings a safer count.
I. Preheat oven to 375°.
In winter, place in a saucepan:

1¼ cups tomato purée
¼ cup boiling water

Heat to the boiling point and add:

¼ teaspoon salt
6 tablespoons brown sugar
½ teaspoon dried basil

Place in a 9-inch baking dish:

**1 cup fresh white bread crumbs,
page 501**

Pour over them:

¼ cup melted butter

Add the tomato mixture and:

(2 tablespoons chopped stuffed olives)

◗ Cover the dish closely. Bake the pudding about 30 minutes. Do not lift the lid
until ready to serve.

II. Preheat oven to 325°.
In summer, substitute for the dried basil:

1½ to 2 teaspoons fresh chopped basil
1 teaspoon chopped chives
1 teaspoon chopped parsley

and for the tomato purée and water, substitute:

14 skinned, seeded, sliced tomatoes

Bake the dish for 2½ to 3 hours until it
has cooked down to a pastelike consistency.

TOMATO TART

6 Servings

Have ready:

6 baked 3-inch Tart Shells, page 590

Prepare a filling of:

¾ cup tomato purée
¾ cup Cream Sauce III, page 322
3 tablespoons sautéed chopped onions
½ cup sautéed chopped chicken livers
2 tablespoons chopped stuffed olives

Just before serving, preheat the oven to
400°. Fill the tarts and bake until thoroughly heated. Serve at once.

ABOUT HOT STUFFED TOMATOES

◗ Please read About Stuffed Vegetables,
page 255.

To prepare cases for hot food, cut large
hollows in very firm unpeeled tomatoes.
Salt them and invert them on a rack to
drain for about 15 minutes. Fill the tomato
cases with any of the following cooked
foods and cover the tops with:

Au Gratin I, II, or III, page 342

Place the tomato cases in a pan with
enough water to keep them from scorching and bake them in a preheated 350°
oven for 10 or 15 minutes. If they are too
soft to hold their shape, bake them in well-
greased muffin tins. For fillings, try:

**Creamed ham or sausage and
mushrooms**
Bread crumbs and deviled ham
**Chestnuts and rice or wild rice,
seasoned with salt and brown sugar**
**Creamed green peas, parsley or
mushrooms**
Mashed potatoes and nuts
Creamed Spinach, or Florentine

Or see Farces, page 458, Fillings for Vegetable Cases, page 89; or use one of the
following recipes.

TOMATOES STUFFED WITH PINEAPPLE

4 Servings

◗ Please read About Stuffed Tomatoes,
above.
Preheat oven to 350°.
Prepare:

4 medium-sized tomato cases

Sprinkle each hollow with:

1 teaspoon brown sugar

Place in each hollow some of the following mixture:

1 tablespoon chili sauce
1 cup drained crushed pineapple
2 tablespoons dry bread crumbs

Sprinkle the tops with:

Au Gratin II, page 342

Bake, as directed above and serve on:

Toast rounds

TOMATOES STUFFED WITH CORN

4 Servings

◗ Please read About Stuffed Tomatoes,
above.
Preheat oven to 350°.
Prepare:

4 tomato cases

Sauté, then mince:

4 slices bacon

Combine:

1 cup cooked, drained corn
1 chopped pimiento
½ chopped green pepper
2 tablespoons chopped celery
½ cup bread crumbs
2 tablespoons corn liquor or cream
½ teaspoon salt
¼ teaspoon paprika
½ teaspoon sugar, if the corn is green

Add the minced bacon. Fill the tomato
cases. Sprinkle the tops with:

Au Gratin I or III, page 342

Bake as directed above.

TOMATOES FILLED WITH ONIONS
6 Servings
◗ Please read About Stuffed Tomatoes, page 307.
Preheat oven to 350°.
Prepare:
  6 tomato cases
Melt:
  **2 tablespoons bacon drippings
  or butter**
Add and sauté until golden:
  ½ cup finely chopped onion
Chop the pulp taken from the tomatoes and combine it with the onions. Add:
  **1½ teaspoons brown sugar
  ½ teaspoon salt
  1 tablespoon celery seed**
Simmer these ingredients for about 10 minutes. If the filling is too moist, it may be thickened with:
  (Bread crumbs)
If it is too dry, it may be moistened with:
  Cream or milk
Fill the tomato cases. Cover the tops with:
  Au Gratin II or III, page 342
Bake them, as directed above.

TOMATOES STUFFED WITH BREAD CRUMBS AND ANCHOVIES
6 Servings
◗ Please read About Stuffed Tomatoes, page 307.
Preheat oven to 350°.
Prepare:
  6 medium-sized tomato cases
Season the cases with:
  3 tablespoons brown sugar
Chop the pulp taken from the tomatoes. Combine it with an equal amount of:
  Soft bread crumbs
add:
  **2 tablespoons sautéed chopped onion
  2 tablespoons sautéed chopped pepper
  4 chopped anchovies**
Taste before
  Correcting the seasoning
as anchovies are salty. Fill the tomato cases. Bake, as directed above.

TOMATOES STUFFED WITH CREAMED SWEETBREADS
6 Servings
◗ Please read About Stuffed Tomatoes, page 307.
Prepare:
  6 tomato cases
Sauté:
  ¼ lb. Mushrooms, page 281
Cook:
  ¼ lb. Sweetbreads, page 441
The mushrooms and sweetbread proportions may be varied. Cook by the recipe on page 322:
  **Cream Sauce I—as much as there
  are mushrooms and sweetbreads
  combined**
Add the other ingredients to the boiling cream sauce. Thicken them with:

  (¼ cup bread crumbs)
Preheat oven to 350°.
Fill the tomato cases. Cover the tops with:
  Au Gratin II or III, page 342
Bake them, as directed above.

TOMATOES STUFFED WITH CRAB MEAT
6 Servings
◗ Please read About Stuffed Tomatoes, page 307.
Preheat oven to 350°
Prepare:
  6 tomato cases
Melt over low heat:
  1½ tablespoons butter
Add and cook for 3 minutes:
  **3 tablespoons minced green pepper
  3 tablespoons minced onion**
Stir in, until blended:
  1½ tablespoons flour
Stir in slowly:
  1½ cups milk
When sauce is thick and hot, add:
  **1½ cups crab meat
  ⅓ teaspoon salt
  A few grains red pepper
  2 teaspoons Worcestershire sauce
  1 cup grated American cheese**
Simmer and stir these ingredients until the cheese is melted. Fill the tomato cases with this mixture. Bake, as directed above.

TOMATOES STUFFED WITH SHRIMP
6 Servings
◗ Please read About Stuffed Tomatoes, page 307.
Preheat oven to 350°.
Prepare:
  6 tomato cases
Chop the tomato pulp removed from the centers. Melt:
  1 tablespoon butter
Sauté in it for 2 minutes:
  2 tablespoons finely chopped onion
Add the tomato pulp and:
  **1 cup chopped, cooked or canned
  shrimp**
Stir in:
  **1 tablespoon chopped parsley
  3 tablespoons crushed cracker crumbs
  Paprika and salt, if needed**
Fill the tomatoes with this mixture. Dust the tops with:
  Au Gratin I or II, page 342
Bake them, as directed in the 2 previous recipes.

ABOUT TURNIPS

A turnip is not necessarily a depressant, as so many people seem to feel. Children often enjoy them well-washed and raw, like apples; and the knowing choose them as an accompaniment to game. They make good change, if browned, to serve instead of potatoes around a roast, page 256. A favorite peasanty dish, **Himmel und Erde**, is made of mashed turnips, potatoes and seasoned apples, combined in any proportion.

Discard woody turnips and parblanch old ones for 3 to 5 minutes before cooking. ♦ One pound turnips will yield about 3½ cups sliced and 2½ cups cooked.

Cut off the tops at once and store in a dark cool place. The tops, if tender, may be used as greens, page 279.

♦ Pressure cook turnips at 15 lbs. for 5 minutes.

COOKED TURNIPS

4 Servings

. If young, wash, pare and place in a steamer:

1 lb. sliced young turnips

Steam, page 252, for 20 to 30 minutes. Drain.

Correct the seasoning

and dress with:
Butter
Lemon juice and vinegar
Or mash or cream as for Potatoes, page 290.

II. If old, you may parblanch, page 132, 3 to 5 minutes:

Sliced or whole turnips
Drop them into rapidly boiling water to cover. Add:

½ teaspoon salt
½ teaspoon sugar
Cook, uncovered, 15 to 20 minutes if sliced, 20 to 25 minutes if whole or until tender. Proceed as for I.

SCALLOPED TURNIPS

Prepare:

Scalloped Potatoes, page 291
substituting just turnips or turnips and sliced onions for the potatoes.

GLAZED TURNIPS

Cook as directed previously:

Young turnips
Drain and dry them well. Brown them in:

Hot melted butter
Season them with:

Paprika and sugar
The sugar helps with the browning. Use Meat Glaze, page 492, or dissolve in a little boiling water:

A beef cube
Pour it over the turnips.

Correct the seasoning
Serve them at once, rolled in:

Chopped parsley

STUFFED TURNIP CUPS

8 Servings

♦ Please read About Stuffed Vegetables, page 255.

Preheat oven to 350°.

I. Pare, then blanch, page 132, for 3 to 5 minutes:

8 medium-sized turnips
Hollow into cups, reserving and chopping the pulp. Melt:

1 tablespoon butter
Sauté in it for about 3 minutes:

1 tablespoon grated onion
2 tablespoons cooked, seasoned peas
You may use the peas alone, omitting the onion. Combine the pulp with the onion and peas. Season with:

Salt and pepper
Thicken it slightly with:

Cracker crumbs or bread crumbs
Fill the turnip cups with this mixture. Place them in a greased baking dish. Combine and pour around them:

½ cup milk
⅛ teaspoon salt
Bake until tender, about 15 minutes.

II. Proceed as above, using a filling of leftover sauced foods, a cooked Farce, page 458, or creamed peas.

ABOUT WATER CRESS

Usually thought of only as salad and sandwich material, water cress not only adds greatly in flavoring soups and vegetables but is good cooked with other greens or by itself. Prepare as for Creamed Spinach, page 300. Serve with grills or chops.

WATER CHESTNUTS

Please read About Water Chestnuts, page 520.

These crisp vegetables are added usually as a garnish to other vegetables.

♦ Add for the last 2 or 3 minutes of cooking only.

SALAD DRESSINGS, SAUCES, GRAVIES, MARINADES, GLAZES AND SEASONED BUTTERS

ABOUT COLD SAUCES AND DRESSINGS

Some dressings seem designed to turn a salad into a costume piece. To demonstrate how welcome a switch to simplicity can be—after more elaborate recipes—follow our instructions for Tossed Salad, page 79. This dressing consists of nothing whatever but oil and vinegar, both of first quality, plus a sprinkling of salt. Good salad dressings should complement—never repeat—the salad ingredients they grace.

A word to dieters: while a salad is an unimpeachable slenderizer, a salad dressing most definitely is not. The fat content in commercial French dressings may be 35% and generally goes up to 40%; commercial mayonnaise must, by law, consist of 65% fat; and these amounts are almost always exceeded in their homemade counterparts. If you diet, then, be a spendthrift with the greenstuff, a miser with dressing. To help along, we have included in this section some low calorie formulas. The recipes given later may inspire you to make spiced or herb vinegars in quantity; also to add to individual bottles of salad dressing that certain something which gives them a personalized appeal. ♦ Store refrigerated, in closed containers, all egg-based dressings like mayonnaise. Please read About Salads, page 76, About Oil, page 510, and Vinegar, page 495. For heavier dressings, see Dips, page 74.

ABOUT SAUCE TOOLS

Handy-size simple tools hanging above the cooking area encourage the addition of interesting ingredients to sauces. ♦ The 3 hand-beaters, sketched on the left, make lumps vanish. The third from the left is particularly useful for beating an egg in a cup. For that little grating of cheese onion or bread crumbs, try the rotary grater shown next. Kitchen shears with a self-releasing hinge are easy to keep clean and unrusted. Use them to snip herbs quickly, right into the sauce.

A garlic press, center, will squeeze enough juice to give an ineffable flavor to your sauces, and the hand grater is good for a shaving of lemon rind or nutmeg Also have ready a bar-type strainer for the quick clearing of very small quantities of sauce. For larger ones, use a Chinese hat or conical strainer, shown on page 170, and for very careful straining, line this with muslin.

By all means have some very hard wooden spoons for delicate sauces which may be broken down by the more vigorous metal tools. A sauce spoon with one pointed end will scrape the pan edge clean easily and help avoid lumping. I you should use a metal spoon, make sure it is stainless steel, so as not to discolor a delicate sauce.

♦ If the recipe calls for beating over ice, please see illustration, page 193.

Electric beaters and ⅄ blenders are great labor-savers in the kitchen and wil beat out lumps very quickly. They do however, change the texture and flavor o the sauce as they whip in a great deal o air and will make a thickened sauce foamy and less tasty and a brown sauce much lighter in color.

OIL DRESSING
Pour the following over salad greens:
  ½ **cup olive oil**
  1 **clove garlic**
  ½ **teaspoon salt**
Before serving, grate over greens:
  Fresh lemon peel

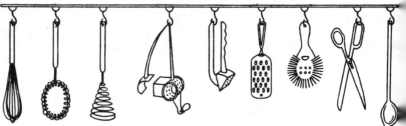

FRENCH DRESSING OR SAUCE VINAIGRETTE
About ½ Cup

This dressing is best made just before use and can become part of the salad-making if you like. See Tossed Salad, page 79. The classic proportions are 3 to 4 parts of oil to one part lemon juice, lime juice or vinegar, and salt and pepper to taste. Many other condiments may be added, including Worcestershire sauce, chili sauce, chutney, Roquefort cheese, spices, sweet and sour cream and, of course, herbs and garlic. The garlic clove should be removed after 24 hours if the dressing is to be stored refrigerated. ◗ Fresh herbs should be added only when the sauce is to be used at once, because they become strong and unpleasant if left in the oil for any length of time.

Combine in a small bowl:
   ¼ teaspoon salt
   ¼ teaspoon pepper
   1 tablespoon olive oil
   1 tablespoon vinegar or lemon juice
   (¼ teaspoon dry mustard)
Beat these ingredients well with a wire whisk or a fork until they are smooth. Add:
   2 tablespoons olive oil
Beat well again. Add:
   1 tablespoon vinegar or lemon juice
   3 tablespoons olive oil
Peel and add:
   (1 clove garlic)
Place the dressing in a jar, cover it well. Put it in a cold place ready for use. Shake well before using.

FRENCH FRUIT-SALAD DRESSING
About ⅔ Cup
Prepare:
   ½ cup French dressing
Substitute for the vinegar:
   3 tablespoons grapefruit or lemon juice

FRENCH DRESSING WITH CREAM CHEESE
About ⅞ Cup
Serve this dressing over a green salad or a vegetable salad.
Mash with a fork and beat until smooth:
   1 package cream cheese: 3 oz.
Beat in:
   1 teaspoon finely minced onion
   ½ teaspoon dry mustard
   1 teaspoon salt
   Freshly ground black pepper
   2 tablespoons chopped parsley
Beat in gradually:
   ¼ cup salad oil
   1½ tablespoons vinegar

AVOCADO DRESSING
I.   **About ¾ Cup**
Good on sliced tomatoes.
Peel and mash:
   ½ avocado

Add gradually:
   ½ cup French dressing
and beat until smooth. Use immediately.

II. Use this as a heavy dressing or as a filling for tomatoes, cucumbers, celery or endive. See Salads, page 79, and Hors d'Oeuvre, page 63.
Mash:
   A ripe avocado
with:
   Lemon juice or vinegar to taste
and
   Correct the seasoning.

RAVIGOTE SAUCE
About 1⅓ Cups
Good with cold meat or fish.
Prepare:
   1 cup French dressing
Add:
   ½ cup finely chopped onion
   1 tablespoon finely chopped capers
   1 teaspoon chopped parsley
   ½ teaspoon chopped fresh tarragon
   ½ teaspoon chopped fresh chervil

LORENZO DRESSING
About ½ Cup
Combine:
   ½ cup French dressing
   2 tablespoons chili sauce
   2 tablespoons chopped water cress

ANCHOVY DRESSING
About ½ Cup
Prepare:
   ½ cup French dressing
Beat into it:
   1 tablespoon or more anchovy or other fish paste

ANCHOVY AND BEET DRESSING
About 1 Cup
Place in a jar with a screw top:
   ½ cup French dressing
   3 or 4 chopped anchovies
   2 small chopped cooked beets
   1 chopped hard-cooked egg
Season the dressing highly. Shake the jar well. Pour the dressing over a large bowlful of:
   Endive or lettuce

SALSA VERDE
About ¾ Cup
To be used with salads and fish.
Combine:
   ½ cup chopped parsley
   1½ tablespoons capers
   2 garlic cloves
   3 anchovy fillets or ½ teaspoon anchovy paste
Add:
   1 crustless slice white bread
soaked in:
   ¼ cup vinegar
   3 tablespoons olive oil

~~2 tablespoons sugar~~
   Correct the seasoning
Any of the following may be added:
   (Horseradish, pickles, green olives,
   green peppers)

ROQUEFORT OR BLEU CHEESE FRENCH DRESSING
About ⅔ Cup

Prepare:
   ½ cup French dressing
Beat into it:
   **2 tablespoons or more crumbled
   Roquefort or bleu cheese**

⅃ BLENDER ANCHOVY AND ROQUEFORT DRESSING
About 1½ Cups

Place in container of electric blender and blend until smooth:
   **⅔ cup olive oil
   1 can anchovies with oil
   3 tablespoons vinegar
   3 tablespoons lemon juice
   ¼ teaspoon paprika
   (1 clove garlic)
   ½ teaspoon mustard
   ½ teaspoon sugar
   ½ teaspoon celery salt
      A dash of Worcestershire sauce and
      hot pepper sauce
      A 3-inch wedge Roquefort cheese**

HORSERADISH DRESSING
About ½ Cup

Prepare:
   ½ cup French dressing
Beat into it:
   **1 tablespoon or more fresh or
   prepared horseradish**

FROZEN HORSERADISH SAUCE
About 1½ Cups

This comes out rather like a sherbet and is delicious with boiled beef.
Combine:
   **¼ cup grated horseradish
   ¼ cup fresh orange juice
   1 teaspoon sugar**
and fold into:
   1 cup stiffly whipped cream
Freeze about 3 to 4 hours in a tray and spoon out into a bowl to serve. Do not hold frozen for long periods.

CUMBERLAND SAUCE
About ¾ Cup

Good with cold ham and game.
Combine and blend well:
   **Grated rind of 1 lemon
   Juice of 1 lemon
   Grated rind of 1 orange
   1 tablespoon confectioners' sugar
   1 teaspoon prepared mustard
   ½ cup melted red currant jelly
   1 tablespoon port wine**

If the jelly is very stiff, it may have to be diluted over heat with:
   (1 or 2 tablespoons hot water)

WATER CRESS DRESSING
About 2 Cups

Excellent over salad greens or Cucumber Gelatin Salad, page 100, and Shrimp, page 376.
Combine:
   **2 tablespoons lemon juice
   1 tablespoon tarragon vinegar
   ½ cup olive oil
   1 teaspoon salt
   ⅛ teaspoon pepper**
Stir in:
   2 finely chopped bunches water cress

⅃ BLENDER CRESS DRESSING

Blend to a paste in an electric blender:
   **2 hard-cooked eggs
   2 tablespoons olive oil
   ¾ cup cut water cress, packed lightly**
Dilute this paste with:
   French dressing
to the consistency you like.

⅃ BLENDER VEGETABLE SAUCE
About 1 Cup

Serve this sauce over bland foods, sweetbreads, cold veal, hot or cold fish.
Combine:
   **¾ cup tomato purée or 2 large, raw,
      skinned tomatoes—the juice pressed
      from them
   1 medium-sized onion
   1 green pepper, seeds and
      membrane removed
   ¼ cup celery or 1 teaspoon
      celery and/or dill seeds
   2 tablespoons parsley or chives
   ½ teaspoon salt
   ¼ teaspoon freshly ground pepper
   (2 tablespoons French dressing)**
Chill the sauce for about ½ hour.

CHIFFONADE DRESSING
About 1½ Cups

Prepare:
   ½ cup French dressing
Add to it:
   **2 chopped hard-cooked eggs
   2 tablespoons julienned cooked
      beet root
   2 tablespoons chopped parsley
   2 teaspoons chopped chives
   1 teaspoon chopped onion**

COCKTAIL SAUCE
About 1 Cup

Good for dunking or garnishing shellfish, small sausages or other hors d'oeuvre.
Combine:
   **¾ cup catsup
   ⅛ to ¼ cup prepared horseradish
   Juice of 1 lemon
   1 dash hot pepper sauce**

CHUTNEY DRESSING
About 1 Cup

Combine in a bottle and chill:
1 tablespoon chopped hard-cooked egg
1 tablespoon chopped chutney
¼ teaspoon curry powder
1 tablespoon lemon juice
½ cup olive oil
3 tablespoons vinegar
¼ teaspoon salt
1 teaspoon sugar
A few grains black pepper

Shortly before serving the dressing, beat it well with a fork.

COLD MUSTARD SAUCE

For boiled or cold meats or fish. This is in the nature of a relish.
Combine:
2 teaspoons grated onion
1 tablespoon prepared mustard
1½ teaspoons sugar
1 to 2 tablespoons oil
2 tablespoons vinegar
(2 hard-cooked egg yolks)
(1 tablespoon cream)

I.
About 1 Cup

Try this over raw or cooked vegetables or seafood.
Combine:
¾ cup Italian tomato paste
1 teaspoon dry mustard
1 tablespoon sugar
½ teaspoon salt
1 tablespoon vinegar
1 tablespoon drained horseradish
(1 tablespoon chopped onion, chives
or fresh herbs)

II.

A highly seasoned sauce for cold meats or broiled sausages. Blend gradually:
2 tablespoons or more dry mustard
with a little:
Water
until it is the consistency of thick cream.
Fold this paste into:
½ cup heavy cream or evaporated
milk, whipped, page 484
Season the sauce, if desired, with:
Salt and paprika

DRESSING WITHOUT OIL
About ¾ Cup

No, it isn't particularly good, but it may be eaten by the bulging with a clear conscience.
Soak:
1 teaspoon gelatin
in:
1 tablespoon cold water
Dissolve it in:
¼ cup boiling water
Add:
1 tablespoon sugar
½ teaspoon salt

Cool this mixture. Add:
1 teaspoon grated lemon rind
½ cup lemon juice
⅛ teaspoon dry mustard
¼ teaspoon paprika
A few grains cayenne
⅛ teaspoon pepper
¼ teaspoon onion juice
(⅛ teaspoon curry powder)

Shake the dressing. Chill it. Before serving it, beat it well with a wire beater. Add, if you wish:
2 tablespoons minced parsley
1 tablespoon minced chives

SWEET-SOUR LOW CALORIE DRESSING
1 Cup

Serve on a green salad.
Combine:
⅓ cup lemon juice
⅔ cup water
1 teaspoon sugar
¼ teaspoon salt

CHINESE LOW CALORIE DRESSING
About ½ Cup

Good on sliced cucumber and tomato.
Combine:
3 tablespoons lemon juice
3 tablespoons soy sauce
1 tablespoon sugar
(1 teaspoon finely chopped candied
ginger)

LOW CALORIE THOUSAND ISLAND DRESSING
About 2 Cups

Combine in a large screw-top jar:
¾ cup tarragon vinegar
1 can condensed tomato soup: 10½ oz.
1 minced garlic clove
A few grains cayenne
2 tablespoons chopped dill pickle
2 tablespoons finely chopped celery
2 tablespoons finely chopped parsley
1 tablespoon Worcestershire sauce
1 teaspoon paprika
1 teaspoon prepared mustard

MAYONNAISE

The making of a perfect mayonnaise is the Sunday job for Papa in France and rivalry for quality between households is intense. Mayonnaise or Mahonnaise—as it was first called, after a French victory over the British at Port Mahon on the Island of Minorca—is a great favorite, not only as a dressing, but for combining with other foods. It has been made by hand for some 300 years. But, with care, we can now make it with an electric mixer or in the ↄ blender. Blender mayonnaise is made more quickly, has greater volume and fluffier texture, but cannot duplicate the smooth, rich-looking glisten of hand-beaten mayonnaise. We believe it is slightly less adaptable to some mayonnaise variations, such as mayonnaise collée. Care must be used in ♦ storing all mayonnaise combinations under refrigeration, as they are subject to bacterial activity which may be very toxic without showing any evidence of spoilage. Cooked foods to be mixed with mayonnaise keep much better and help deter bacteria if they have been marinated in vinegar or lemon juice or are mixed with pickle. But, even if they have this added acid content, they must be kept thoroughly refrigerated. Freezing mayonnaise combinations is also chancy, as the spoilage is only arrested and not destroyed and then accelerates when the food is defrosted. ♦ Don't try to make mayonnaise if a thunderstorm threatens or is in progress, as it simply will not bind.

If you have to resort to bottled mayonnaise, beating in 1 to 2 tablespoons good olive oil until all trace of it has disappeared will give it a good flavor and make it stiffer and heavier. Sour cream, according to taste, can also do wonders for commercial mayonnaise—if well beaten in. Please note that commercial "Salad Dressing" is not mayonnaise and the above suggestions will not work if it is used.

♦ Eggs, oil, bowl and mixer must all be at room temperature, 70°. Warm the oil slightly if it has been refrigerated, rinse your bowl in hot water and dry it.

I.   About 1¼ Cups
Place in a medium-sized bowl and beat with a wire whisk or wooden spoon until lemon color:

2 egg yolks

Beat in:

¼ to ½ teaspoon dry mustard
½ teaspoon salt
A few grains cayenne
½ teaspoon vinegar or lemon juice
½ teaspoon confectioners' sugar

Beat in, very slowly, ½ teaspoon at a time:

½ cup olive oil

The mixture will begin to thicken and emulsify. Now you can relax! Combine in a cup or small pitcher:

1½ tablespoons vinegar
2 tablespoons lemon juice

Have ready:

½ cup olive oil

Alternate the oil ♦ drop by drop, with a few drops of the lemon and vinegar mixture. If the oil is added slowly during constant beating, this will make a good thick sauce. Sometimes the sauce will break, because you have either added your oil too fast toward the end or added too much of it—figure no more than ½ to ¾ cup oil to each large yolk. It may also break if your oil has been cold and your egg yolks warm. Do not despair: a curdled mayonnaise can be reconstituted by placing 1 egg yolk in a bowl. Stir it constantly and add the curdled dressing to it very, very slowly at first and continue slowly as the mixture thickens. If the dressing is too heavy, thin it with cream.

II.   About 1½ Cups
You may make the above recipe following exactly the same procedure, in the same order, using an electric mixer on medium speed or the speed indicated for whipping cream.

III. ⚘   About 1¾ Cup
Blender mayonnaise differs from the first recipe in that it uses a whole egg. If your beating arm is rather weak, we suggest you try this method as the emulsifying is taken care of by the action of the blender.

Put in blender container:

1 egg
1 teaspoon ground mustard
1 teaspoon salt
A dash of cayenne
1 teaspoon sugar
¼ cup salad oil

Cover and blend until thoroughly combined. With blender still running, take off the cover and slowly add:

½ cup salad oil

and then:

3 tablespoons lemon juice

until thoroughly blended. Then add slowly:

½ cup salad oil

and blend until thick. You may have to stop and start the blender to stir down the mayonnaise.

AIOLI OR GARLIC SAUCE
                                              1 Cup
This is a garlic sauce very popular in France where it is sometimes known as "Beurre de Provence." Some recipes omit the eggs. Serve over fish, cold boiled potatoes, beet rounds and boiled beef.

Skin, then chop very finely the:

4 garlic clove sections

that give the sauce its name. Beat in:

2 egg yolks
⅛ teaspoon salt
(1 slice dry French bread without crust, soaked in milk and wrung out)

Add, as for mayonnaise, very slowly and beating constantly:

1 cup olive oil

As the sauce thickens, beat in:

½ teaspoon cold water
1 teaspoon lemon juice

In the case the sauce fails to thicken, treat as a defeated Mayonnaise, above.

SKORDALIA
                                              1 Cup
Prepare:

Aioli Sauce, as above

adding, after the sauce has thickened:

¼ cup ground almonds
¼ cup fresh bread crumbs
3 teaspoons lemon juice
2 tablespoons chopped parsley

ROUILLE SAUCE

A strongly flavored sauce, served with Mediterranean fish soups or bouillabaisse. Pound together in a bowl or mortar to make a smooth paste:

1 blanched, seeded, skinned red
  pimiento or 1 canned pimiento
1 small red chili, boiled until tender
  or a dash of hot pepper sauce
¼ cup white bread crumbs soaked in
  water and squeezed dry
2 mashed cloves garlic

Beat in, very slowly, as in Mayonnaise:

¼ cup olive oil

Thin the sauce just before serving with:

2 to 3 tablespoons of the soup you
  are serving

Pass with the soup.

SAUCE FOR SMOKED FOOD

Combine:

2 tablespoons mayonnaise
1 teaspoon horseradish
1 tablespoon cultured sour cream

ANDALOUSE SAUCE

2 Cups

For vegetable salads, cold fish or egg dishes.
Combine:

2 cups mayonnaise
1 chopped tomato, with seeds and
  juice removed or ½ cup tomato
  purée
¼ julienned red pimiento

FRUIT-SALAD MAYONNAISE

1½ Cups

Combine:

1 cup mayonnaise
½ cup pineapple juice
1 teaspoon grated orange rind
1 tablespoon orange curaçao

CREAM OR CHANTILLY MAYONNAISE

2 Cups

Serve with fruit salad.
Prepare:

1 cup mayonnaise

Add to it, shortly before serving:

1 cup whipped cream

CURRY MAYONNAISE

About 1 Cup

For fruit or fish.
Combine:

1 cup mayonnaise
¼ teaspoon ginger
½ to 1 teaspoon curry powder
1 mashed clove garlic
1 teaspoon honey
1 tablespoon lime juice

It is very good for molded chicken salad or shrimp with these additions:

(1 tablespoon chopped chutney)
(1 tablespoon chopped kumquats)
(1 tablespoon blanched slivered
  almonds)

MAYONNAISE GRENACHE

About 2½ Cups

Serve with smoked turkey or smoked tongue.
Combine:

1 cup mayonnaise
½ cup red currant jelly
3 tablespoons grated horseradish
¼ teaspoon salt
⅛ teaspoon freshly ground pepper
2 tablespoons dessert sherry
  or Madeira

Fold in:

½ cup whipped cream

GREEN GODDESS DRESSING

About 2 Cups

Use on fish or shellfish.
Combine:

1 cup mayonnaise
1 minced clove garlic
3 minced anchovy fillets
¼ cup finely minced chives or
  green onions
¼ cup minced parsley
1 tablespoon lemon juice
1 tablespoon tarragon vinegar
½ teaspoon salt
  Ground black pepper
½ cup cultured sour cream

GREEN MAYONNAISE OR SAUCE VERTE

1 Cup

For cold shellfish or vegetables.
Chop, blanch, page 132, for 2 minutes and drain:

2 tablespoons parsley
2 tablespoons tarragon, fennel or dill
2 tablespoons chives
2 tablespoons spinach or finely
  chopped cucumber
2 tablespoons water cress

Rub through a sieve and combine to make a paste with:

2 hard-cooked egg yolks

Add to:

1 cup stiff mayonnaise

HARD-COOKED EGG MAYONNAISE OR SAUCE GRIBICHE

About 3 Cups

For fish and cold meat.
Mash in a bowl until smooth:

3 hard-cooked egg yolks

Add:

½ teaspoon salt
  A dash of pepper
1 teaspoon prepared Dijon-type
  mustard

Add very gradually and beat constantly:

1½ cups olive oil
½ cup vinegar

The mixture will thicken. Then stir in:

3 finely julienned egg whites
½ cup mixed, finely chopped sour
    pickles and capers, with the moisture
    squeezed out
2 tablespoons finely chopped mixed
    parsley, chervil, tarragon and chives

REMOULADE SAUCE
About 1⅛ Cups

For cold meat and poultry—also shellfish,
with which it is especially good.
Combine:

1 cup mayonnaise
1 tablespoon drained, finely chopped
    cucumber pickle
1 tablespoon drained, chopped capers
2 teaspoons French mustard
1 teaspoon finely chopped parsley
½ teaspoon chopped fresh tarragon
½ teaspoon chervil
(½ teaspoon anchovy paste)

RUSSIAN DRESSING
About 1¾ Cups

Use on arranged salads, eggs, shellfish or
in chicken sandwiches, instead of butter or
mayonnaise.
Combine:

1 cup mayonnaise
1 tablespoon grated horseradish
(3 tablespoons imported caviar)
(1 teaspoon Worcestershire sauce)
¼ cup chili sauce or catsup
1 teaspoon grated onion

TARTARE SAUCE
About 1⅛ Cups

A good old stand-by for fried fish.
Combine:

1 cup firm mayonnaise
1 teaspoon French mustard
1 tablespoon finely chopped parsley
1 teaspoon minced shallots
1 tablespoon chopped, drained
    sweet pickle
(1 tablespoon chopped, drained
    green olives)
1 finely chopped hard-boiled egg
1 tablespoon chopped, drained capers
    Correct the seasoning

You may thin the sauce with:

A little wine vinegar or lemon juice

THOUSAND ISLAND DRESSING
About 1½ Cups

Serve over iceberg lettuce wedges, eggs,
etc.
Combine:

1 cup mayonnaise
¼ cup chili sauce or catsup
2 tablespoons minced stuffed olives
1 tablespoon chopped green pepper
1 tablespoon minced onion or chives
1 chopped hard-cooked egg
2 teaspoons chopped parsley

WATER CRESS SAUCE OR SAUCE AU CRESSON
About 1 Cup

This is excellent with cold fish dishes.
Combine:

¼ cup finely chopped water cress
¾ cup mayonnaise
1 tablespoon lemon juice
    Correct the seasoning

SAUCE LOUIS
About 2 Cups

This is good with stuffed artichokes,
shrimp or crab. It is the sauce used for
Crab Louis, page 90.
Combine:

1 cup mayonnaise
¼ cup heavy cream
¼ cup chili sauce
1 teaspoon Worcestershire sauce
¼ cup chopped green pepper
¼ cup chopped green onion
2 tablespoons lemon juice
    Correct the seasoning

HALF AND HALF DRESSING
About 2½ Cups

Serve on tossed salad, combination salad
or hearts of lettuce.
Combine:

1 cup mayonnaise
1 cup French dressing
1 minced garlic clove
1 teaspoon mashed anchovies
½ cup Parmesan cheese

BOILED SALAD DRESSINGS

Three recipes for boiled salad dressings
are given. No. I, made with 1 egg or 2
yolks, is a very economical, acceptable
boiled dressing. It may be thinned with
cream, but is good as it is over vegetable
and potato salad. No. II is made with
milk and whole eggs. Use this dressing
over slaw, tomatoes, aspics, etc. No. III is
a fruit salad dressing. Keep these dressings
well refrigerated.

I.   About 1¼ Cups

Dissolve:

½ to 1 teaspoon dry mustard
1 to 2 tablespoons sugar
½ teaspoon salt
2 tablespoons flour
¼ teaspoon paprika

in:

½ cup cold water

Beat in the top of double boiler:

1 whole egg or 2 yolks
¼ cup vinegar

Add the dissolved ingredients. Cook and
stir the dressing ♦ over—not in—boiling
water, until it is thick and smooth. Add

2 tablespoons butter

Chill the dressing. It may be thinned with

Sweet or cultured sour cream

About 1½ Cups

?at in the top of a double boiler:
  2 egg yolks
  2 teaspoons sugar
  1 tablespoon melted butter
  ⅔ cup milk
  ¼ cup vinegar
  2 teaspoons salt
    A few grains cayenne
  1 teaspoon dry mustard
'ssolve:
  2 teaspoons cornstarch

  ⅛ cup milk
ld it to the ingredients in the double
iler. Cook and stir the dressing ♦ over—
t in—boiling water, until it is thick.
ol it. You may add chopped parsley,
ives or other herbs, celery or dill seeds,
. Fold it into:
  2 stiffly beaten egg whites

About 1¼ Cups

at in the top of a double boiler:
  1 teaspoon salt
  ⅛ teaspoon paprika
  ¼ to ½ cup sugar
  2 tablespoons melted butter
  6 tablespoons cream
  3 eggs
  (½ teaspoon mustard)
r and cook the dressing ♦ over—not in
boiling water, until it is thick. Add
wly:
  6 tablespoons lemon juice
e dressing may be thinned with:
    Fruit juice or cream

UR CREAM HORSERADISH
RESSING OR DRESDEN SAUCE
                                    1 Cup
ine change from the well-liked but often
notonous butter or cream sauce. Usually
ved with smoked or boiled fish. Com-
e and stir:
  1 cup cultured sour cream
  ½ teaspoon prepared mustard
  ½ teaspoon horseradish
  ¼ teaspoon salt

EAM HORSERADISH DRESSING
About 1¼ Cups
is dressing is good with cold meat.
at until stiff:
  ½ cup heavy cream
d slowly, beating constantly:
  3 tablespoons lemon juice or vinegar
  ¼ teaspoon salt
  ⅛ teaspoon paprika
    A few grains cayenne
  2 tablespoons grated horseradish
  (3 tablespoons mayonnaise)

UR CREAM DRESSING FOR
GETABLE SALAD
                              About 1 Cup
t until smooth:
  1 cup thick cultured sour cream

Add to it:
  1 teaspoon grated onion or fresh
    onion juice
  1 teaspoon celery or dill seed
  ½ teaspoon salt
    A fresh grating of white pepper
  (2 tablespoons chopped green or sweet
    red pepper)

CUCUMBER SAUCE
                              About 1½ Cups
For fish or meat, preferably cold food,
such as salmon.
Beat until stiff:
  ¾ cup heavy sweet or cultured
    sour cream
If the cream is sweet, add slowly:
  2 tablespoons vinegar or lemon juice
Season the sauce with:
  ¼ teaspoon salt
  ⅛ teaspoon paprika
Pare, seed, cut finely and drain well:
  1 large cucumber
Add it to the sauce with:
  (2 teaspoons finely chopped chives
    or dill)

YOGURT DRESSING
Yogurt, page 485, simple and unadorned,
is excellent on honeydew and cantaloupe
melon balls in a lettuce cup. Try it on
other fresh fruits or on crisp salad greens
on hot summer days. Good for dieters,
too.

SOUR CREAM SAUCE FOR
BAKED POTATOES
                                    1 Cup
Combine:
  1 cup cultured sour cream
  1 teaspoon Worcestershire sauce
    A dash of hot pepper sauce
  ½ teaspoon monosodium glutamate
  ½ teaspoon salt
    Freshly ground black pepper
Garnish with:
    Chopped chives

CAVIAR SAUCE
                              About 1⅛ Cups
Try on baked potatoes or as a dip for cold
vegetables in hors d'oeuvre or salad.
Combine:
  1 cup cultured sour cream
  1 teaspoon onion or shallot juice
  2 teaspoons capers
  ¼ cup red caviar

HONEY DRESSING
                                    1 Cup
For fruit salads:
Combine:
  ½ cup honey
  ½ cup lime juice
    (A pinch of ground ginger)

CELERY SEED DRESSING
                              About 2 Cups
Add to fruit salad just before serving. This

may be made with an electric ⅃ blender or mixer. Constant beating to blend the ingredients is the secret of success here.
Combine:

½ cup sugar
1 teaspoon dry mustard
1 teaspoon salt
1 to 2 teaspoons celery seed

Add:

3 tablespoons grated onion

Gradually add, beating constantly:

1 cup salad oil
⅓ cup vinegar

Garnish with:

(A few finely cut sprigs lemon thyme)

CREAM CHEESE DRESSING FOR FRUIT SALAD
About 1¼ Cups
Mash with a fork and beat until smooth:

1 package cream cheese: 3 oz.

Beat in slowly:

1 tablespoon lemon juice
2 tablespoons currant jelly
¾ cup cream

Chill the dressing for 1 hour or more before serving it.

LEMON AND SHERRY DRESSING FOR FRUIT SALAD
About ½ Cup
Delightful over tart fruit, apples, grapefruit, etc.
Combine:

¼ cup lemon juice
⅛ teaspoon salt

Stir in slowly:

¼ cup sugar

Add:

2 tablespoons dry sherry

CURRY DRESSING FOR FRUIT SALAD
About 1 Cup
Combine:

2 tablespoons mild vinegar
1 tablespoon lemon juice
¼ to ½ teaspoon curry
1 teaspoon sugar

Stir in:

1 cup cultured sour cream

See also Curry Mayonnaise, page 315.

ABOUT HOT SAUCE TYPES

There are certain old dowagers who try to dominate "sauciety." Call them the mother sauces, as the French do, if you like. Each has her strong peculiarities of individual makeup; each traditionally queens it over a whole coterie of dishes. The ubiquitous member of the clan—the one who is always close by—is pan gravy: she knows what's cooking, because she carries its true essence.

Her roux-based cousins have more solid and dependable backgrounds and take more abuse in heating, reheating and stor-

ing—for their flour and butter base combines into as stable an ingredient as any in the kitchen. There are the delicate pale members of the roux family, descended from Béchamel, who accept the company of eggs, cream and even shallots. There are the robust characters originating in browned flours, who have picked up acquaintanceships with strange foreign spices, who love tomatoes and who, on occasion, set their caps for garlic. Both rely for authenticity on two principles. The roux base must be cooked to rid it and them of any trace of plebeian floury origin; and must always be hot when added to cold liquids or cold when added to hot.

There are the plush sauce aristocrats who scorn flour altogether and derive their stamina from eggs. Like a lot of other sauces for cold food, the mayonnaise branch performs this elegant trick without requiring heat. While its cousins, the Hollandaise-Béarnaise group, must have heat, they need it only in small doses and for short periods.

Most showy and demonstrative of all are the wine sauces, the vinaigrettes, the playful tenderizing sweet-sours or agrodulce, the marinades, the barbecues and, of course, the truly sweet dessert sauces, page 709, which are the simpering sentimentalists of the whole colony.

Although these rather simple divisions mark the major sauce families, don't feel overconfident about your acquaintanceship until you can spot a rare nonidentical twin—with arrowroot as thickener—or an occasional reveler in fancy dress, tricked out with beurre manié or butter swirls. The wayward collaterals are among the most treasured, if fleeting, personalities of all.

When you once feel at home in sauce circles, you will learn rapidly how to make them welcome members of your culinary life. You will learn how to skillfully blend the hot ingredients, so that they may receive food without thinning. You will discover that adding the wine before—not after—the eggs and cream will avoid curdling and that a mixture can be stabilized with that extra bit of cream when separation threatens.

Of course, there is always the ⅃ blender to fall back on in a crisis of this kind, but the texture of the sauce can never be as smooth or thick as if it had been properly made in the first place. In sauces based on cornstarch, overbeating itself can disturb consistency—and this factor alone may cause thinning. The use of a light whisk or a wooden spoon is a help in avoiding this condition. Another reason for thinning in sauces may be the addition of acid in the form of fruit juice or wine. Sauces will also lose body if covered and hot heated, for the excess steam created them and tends to cause separation. ♦ To lessen separation in frozen sauces, see Waxy Rice Flour, page 499.

ABOUT COLOR IN SAUCES

A well-prepared sauce really has its color built in and should need no artificial coloring. ♦ To maintain and develop color for sauces, see page 318.

Rich beef stock combined with some tomato, browned meat—in the case of a stew—browned onions and carrots and a brown roux will result in a rich brown sauce needing no addition of caramel to bring up the color. If you feel obliged to add caramel to gravies, add it sparingly. Some cooks use yellow coloring for thicken gravies and sauces to try to hide the omission of chicken fat and egg yolks. Should you use saffron, do beware of its overpowering flavor. A tomato sauce will keep a good color if you do not cook it too quickly or too long.

ABOUT SAUCES IN QUANTITY

If you are making gravies or sauces in quantity, it will take considerably longer to get rid of the raw flour taste after the liquid has been added to the roux than when you are making only 1 or 2 cups for immediate family use. We advise heating these larger amounts ♦ uncovered, in a low oven for ½ to ¾ of an hour and straining the sauce before serving, to remove any crusting or lumps. But if you stir the sauce from time to time, it may not be necessary to strain it.

When doubling the ingredients in sauce recipes, taste before adding the full amount of seasoning. It is easy to overdo.

ABOUT KEEPING SAUCES

You may keep Velouté, Tomato and Brown sauces in the refrigerator for at least a week. To store, strain the sauce, pour it into a container and cover with a thin layer of fat or sherry. If you have not used all the sauce at the end of a week, you may reheat it, put it in a clean jar, over again with a little melted fat and return it to the refrigerator, where it will keep at least another week.

You can also ✻ freeze the sauces mentioned above, as well as Béchamel, in ice-cube trays and keep the cubes in your freezer in a plastic bag, taking out as many as you need for immediate use. They may be melted in a double boiler—4 large cubes melt down to about ½ cup of sauce. You may also freeze Hollandaise Sauce, page 328, but be very careful when reheating. Do not try to freeze mayonnaise; it will break. And, in general, do not try to keep sauces made with eggs, cream or milk for more than 2 or 3 days in the refrigerator.

ABOUT SAUCE INGREDIENTS

Sauces in general are spoken of as savory or sweet. Many of those in the first category are made with some sort of pan gravy. Pan residues, unless from fish or from strong variety meats, like kidneys, are a most desirable flavoring ingredient. ♦ To make pan gravies, see page 322.

Pan residues for sauces also include those which are left over from browning and sautéing meats. Browning lends attractive color and the addition of some rendered fat serves to intensify the characteristic meat flavor. It is always best, if you sauté with butter—and the butter should be sweet, not salted—to clarify it, page 338, or to combine it with a little cooking oil to raise its smoking point, so as to prevent scorching and bitter overtones. If economy is a factor and margarine has been substituted for butter, you may wish to improve the flavor of the final product by finishing the sauce off with a Butter Swirl, page 321.

Good strong, fat-free Stocks, page 488, are invaluable sauce ingredients, too, especially when reduced to a Glaze, page 492. Where possible, the stock should reflect the food it is to flavor: chicken stock for chicken, lamb stock for lamb, etc. Although meat stocks, including those of poultry and game, are often combined in sauce-making—favorites being those of chicken and veal—fish and shellfish Fumets, page 491, should be reserved only for fish and shellfish dishes.

Such broths always make better sauce ingredients if left to stand refrigerated for 24 hours and then de-fatted.

When pan residues or stocks are scanty, turn to wine. ♦ Please read About Cooking With Wine, page 494. Use, as a rule of thumb, dry white wines in sauces for fish or white meats; dry red wines for red meats. Strong game sauces sometimes support stronger liquors like rum, brandy or Madeira, but whisky is never added to them.

♦ In any wine sauce, add egg, milk, cream or butter swirls after the wine has been incorporated.

ABOUT THICKENERS FOR SAUCES

Sauces not made by deglazing with liquids, as described above, are generally ♦ thickened just enough to coat food lightly and yet not run off it.

ROUX

The most common thickeners for savory sauces are the ♦ roux—white, blonde or brown. All of these are made of the same ingredients to begin with, but change in character as heat is applied. These mixtures of flour and fats are blended gently ♦ over very low heat from 5 minutes to a much longer period, depending on your available time and your patience. White roux should not color; blonde, barely; and brown should reach the color of hazelnut and smell deliciously baked. ◗ Unless a roux is cooked long enough to dispel the raw taste of flour, this unpleasant flavor will dominate the strongest stocks and seasonings. And unless the flour and butter are stirred to distribute the heat and to allow the starch granules to swell evenly, they will later fail to absorb the liquid. Therefore the sauce will be thin. ◗ This heated blending period is important. Using too high heat to try hurrying it will burn the flour, giving it a bitter taste and it will shrink the starch, making it incapable of continuing to swell.

For white roux-based sauces, see Béchamel, page 322; for blonde, see Blanquette de Veau, page 419; for brown, see Sauce Espagnole, page 326. Since most cooks use some form of roux every day, you may find it a time-saver to make one in advance and store it in tablespoon-sized units under refrigeration. It will keep in the ✳ freezer, too, for several months if you do the following: when the roux has been cooked to the desired color and is still soft, measure it by tablespoons on a baking sheet and freeze. Transfer the frozen wafers to a plastic bag or wide-topped container and store in the freezer. To thicken sauce, drop several wafers of the original roux in the sauce to reach the thickness desired. Or you may soften the wafers in a double boiler over hot water and proceed as usual with the making of the sauce.

BROWNED FLOUR

This variant is used in gravies to enhance color and flavor. The slow but inexpensive procedure by which it is made is worth trying. Place:

1 cup all-purpose flour

in a heavy dry skillet. ◗ Stir constantly over very low direct heat until golden brown; or place the skillet in a 350° oven until the flour is golden brown, about 30 minutes. Stir frequently, scraping the flour from the sides and bottom of the pan. In a very slow oven, the flour, when ready, should let it nutty and baked. Do not let it get too dark or, as with brown roux, it will become bitter and lose its thickening power altogether. ◗ Even properly browned flour has only about ½ the thickening power of all-purpose flour. It may be stored in a tightly covered jar in a cool place.

FLOUR PASTE

This is sometimes pressed into service to thicken emergency gravies and sauces, but

the results are never as palatable as when even a quick roux is used. Make a paste of flour and cold water or stock. Use about 2 parts water and one part flour. Stir as much of the paste as needed into the boiling stock or drippings. Permit the sauce to heat until it thickens and ◗ simmer for at least 3 minutes more to reduce the raw taste of the flour. Stir frequently with a wire whisk.

CORNSTARCH

Cornstarch is often used where translucency is desirable, as in some Chinese or dessert sauces. It should be mixed with a little cold water before being added to the hot liquid. One tablespoon cornstarch will thicken 1½ to 2 cups of liquid. Most Chinese sauces are finished over direct heat. But dessert sauces are better cooked in the top of a double boiler ◗ over—not in—hot water until the raw taste of the cornstarch disappears. ◗ Do not overbeat cornstarch based sauces for this thins them.

ARROWROOT

Of all the thickeners, this makes the most delicately textured sauces. ◗ But use it only when the sauce is to be served within 10 minutes of thickening. It will not hold nor will it reheat. Since the flavor of arrowroot is neutral and it does not have to be cooked to remove rawness, as do flour and cornstarch, and since it thickens at a lower temperature than either of them, it is ideal for use in egg and other sauces which should not boil. Allow 2½ teaspoons to 1 cup liquid. See also page 500.

POTATO STARCH OR FECULA

This is preferred by some cooks, rather than flour, as a thickener in certain delicate sauces. When it is used, less simmering is required and the sauce gains some transparency. ◗ Heated beyond 176° the sauce will thin out. Serve soon after it has thickened, as it has no holding power. One tablespoon of potato starch will moderately thicken 1 cup of liquid.

EGG YOLKS

Egg yolks not only thicken but also enrich a sauce. ◗ Never add egg yolks directly to hot liquid. Stir them into a little cream, then incorporate with them some of the hot sauce you want to thicken. Stir this mixture into the remainder of the hot liquid and continue to stir over low heat until the sauce thickens. ◗ Do not allow the sauce to boil, or it will curdle. If this happens, plunge pot into cold water and stir; or beat in a small amount of chilled cream. It is generally safer to add egg yolks to a mixture in a double boiler ◗ over —not in—hot water, unless you can control the heat source very exactly. Two or three egg yolks with a little cream will thicken 1 cup of liquid. Egg yolks added very slowly to melted butter or oil with constant stirring will produce an emulsion which is quite thick. Suitably seasoned, this becomes the base for Hollandaise or mayonnaise. Hard-cooked egg yolks and oil will also emulsify, see Sauce Gribiche, page 315.

BLOOD

Blood from the animal or bird the sauce is to accompany is a desirable thickener. To have the blood from a freshly killed hare, rabbit or chicken, see page 752. You may store it refrigerated for a day or two, mixed with 1 or 2 tablespoons vinegar to prevent clotting. Strain it and add it to the sauce at the last minute just before serving, swirling it in as you would butter, below. Simmer gently, but ♦ never allow the sauce to boil after the blood is added. For other thickening suggestions, see Thickeners for Soups, page 145, and ingredients.

REDUCTION

This is another classic way to thicken sauces. Béchamel and Espagnole may be thickened during very slow simmering by the evaporation of liquid to achieve a more perfect consistency. If you intend to thicken a sauce by reducing it, season after you have brought it down to the right viscosity, otherwise you may find it highly overseasoned or unpleasantly salty. There are a good many recipes for tomato sauces which demand long cooking and reducing. Unless you can keep these sauces—or, in fact, any thickened sauces—in very low heat, they will cook too fast and flavor will be impaired. In the case of roux-thickened sauces which call for reducing, do use an oven. It is a great labor-saver and the heat can be controlled much more exactly. ♦ Almost all reduced sauces, to be perfect in texture, should be strained before serving.

BUTTER SWIRLS

These finish off many fine, rich sauces, both white and brown, after straining and final heating. This can only be done if the sauce is to be served at once. ♦ It must not be reheated after the butter has been added. In addition to improving the flavor, the butter swirl also, very slightly, thickens the sauce. To make a sauce "finie au beurre" after straining and heating, add unsalted, unmelted butter bit by bit to the sauce, moving the pan in a circular motion, so that the butter makes an actual swirl in the hot sauce as it melts. Remove the pan from the heat before the butter is fully melted and continue to swirl. ♦ Do

not use a spoon to stir it and do not try to reheat it About 1 tablespoon butter is generally used to "finish" 1 cup of sauce.

KNEADED BUTTER OR BEURRE MANIE

This is a magic panacea for rectifying sauces or thickening thin ones at the end of the cooking process. Do not use it for those which require long simmering. After adding kneaded butter ♦ do not boil the sauce. Simmer only long enough to dispel the floury taste. Manipulate with your fingers, as though you were rubbing for fine pastry, 2 tablespoons butter and 2 tablespoons flour. Form into small balls and drop into the hot liquid, stirring constantly until the ingredients are well blended and the sauce thickens. This amount will be sufficient for 1 cup of thin liquid.

ABOUT ATTRACTIVE WAYS TO SERVE SAUCES

Apart from the usual gravy boat or deep bowl and ladle, there are a number of attractive ways to serve sauces. Cold sauces and dips with a mayonnaise or sour cream base may be served in a crisp hollowed-out cabbage, page 64, or individually in tomato or pepper cases, page 82. Suggest the marine flavor of cold shrimp or poached salmon with a delicate pink mayonnaise or Remoulade Sauce in a large sea shell.

Hot sauces can be served in ramekins, tin-lined copper pans or other small heatproof containers. The doll house instinct rises in all of us at the sight of these miniature individual pitchers and pots that are so appropriate when serving hot lobster, artichokes or asparagus. Sauces on the buffet table may be kept hot in small French three-legged saucepans, placed over a candle or—in the case of egg-based sauces—in wide-mouthed vacuum bottles or in chafing dishes. Like the food it accompanies, sauce, if it is meant to be hot, must be kept hot. However, ♦ any sauce that is worth its salt won't keep indefinitely on a steam table or in a casserole. There is a point of maximum goodness at which it should be served.

Cold sauces and seasoned butters can be kept chilled on a mound of crushed ice. Molds and pats of seasoned butter may be placed directly on the ice. Don't use ice cubes—the butter slips down between them.

ABOUT SAUCES MADE BY DEGLAZING

These are such a welcome change after the monotonous flour-thickened type. Pan juices and scrapings are precious and are frequently used as the base for many delicious sauces accompanying sautéed as

well as roasted fowl and meat dishes. In
initially roasting meat, be sure to grease
the pans lightly to keep from burning any
juices which may drip, before the fats from
the meat have covered the bottom of the
roasting pan. The addition of a cup of
Mirepoix, page 541, to the pan after the
browning period will make both roast and
pan gravy more flavorful. When the meat
is done, remove it from the pan and pour
off the fat. Add ¼ cup or more hot water
or stock to the pan and cook on top of the
stove—stirring and scraping the solidified
juices from the bottom and sides. The addition of wine or dry sherry will hasten the
deglazing process and heighten the flavorful aroma. Use the stock appropriate to
your meat or fowl and the kind of wine
you would normally drink with it. This,
with a Butter Swirl, page 321, or Beurre
Manié, page 321, or a little cream or more
wine, can make the finest of all sauces.

ABOUT PAN GRAVY

If you use drippings for sauces, you may
want to strain them first and remove excess fat. Reheat some of the fat because it
will absorb the flour better. Add flour until it has the consistency of heavy cream.

PAN GRAVY

1 Cup

Remove the meat from the pan. Place it
where it will remain hot. Pour off all but:

2 tablespoons drippings

Blend into them:

1 or 2 tablespoons flour

Stir with a wire whisk until the flour has
thickened and until well combined and
smooth. Continue to cook slowly and stir
constantly, while adding:

**The degreased pan juices and enough
milk, water, stock, cream or beer to
make 1 cup**

The beer may be "still." Season the gravy
with:

Salt
Pepper
Fresh or dried minced herbs
Grated lemon rind, etc.

Color, if necessary, with:

A few drops Caramel, page 508

You may strain the gravy, reheat and serve
it. If you are using a thickener other than
flour, please read About Thickeners, page
319, for the correct amount of cornstarch
or arrowroot to be added for the above
amount of liquid.

CHICKEN PAN GRAVY

About 2 Cups

Strain the juices from the roast chicken.
Pour off the fat. Heat:

¼ cup fat

Add and stir until blended:

¼ cup flour

Stir in slowly:

**2 cups pan juices and Chicken Stock,
page 490**

Cook and stir the gravy until smooth and
♦ simmer for 5 minutes. Add:

**The cooked chopped chicken giblets
(¼ cup or more cream)**

♦ If the gravy is very rich, it may separate
Add the cream slowly. Stir it constantly
This will usually forestall any difficulty.

Correct the seasoning

and serve.

CREAM SAUCE I OR BÉCHAMEL

1 Cup

This sauce, actually made with milk, i
used for creaming foods like vegetable
and fish and as a base for other sauces
Melt over low heat:

2 tablespoons butter

For a delicate flavor, even commercial es
tablishments have found no substitute fo
butter. Add and blend over low heat for
to 5 minutes:

1½ to 2 tablespoons flour

Stir in slowly:

1 cup milk

For better consistency, you may scald th
milk beforehand; but be sure—to avoi
lumping—that the roux is cool when yo
add it. Add:

**1 small onion studded with 2 or 3
whole cloves**
½ small bay leaf

Cook and stir the sauce with a wire whis
or wooden spoon until thickened an
smooth. Place in a 350° oven for 20 min
utes to cook slowly. The oven interva
also saves your time and hands for othe
kitchen jobs. Strain the sauce,

Correct the seasoning

and serve. For creamed dishes, use abou
½ as much sauce as solids.

CREAM SAUCE II OR HEAVY
BÉCHAMEL

1 Cu

This sauce is used in soufflés.
Prepare:

Cream Sauce I

Use in all:

3 tablespoons butter
3 tablespoons flour
1 cup liquid

CREAM SAUCE III OR BINDING
BÉCHAMEL

1 Cu

This sauce is used in croquettes.
Prepare:

Cream Sauce I, above

Use in all:

3 tablespoons butter
⅛ cup flour
1 cup liquid

CREAM SAUCE IV OR ENRICHED
BÉCHAMEL

Reduce:

1 cup Cream Sauce I

to ¾ of its volume. Stir in:
    ¼ cup heavy cream
and bring to boiling point. If the sauce is
for fish, add:
    (½ to 1 teaspoon lemon juice)

QUICK WHITE SAUCE
If you are in a hurry, this base can be flavored and modified in many ways. Melt
over low heat:
    2 tablespoons butter
Add ♦ still over low heat and stirring about
3 to 4 minutes or until well blended and
the taste of raw flour has vanished:
    1½ to 2 tablespoons flour
Stir in slowly:
    1 cup milk, milk and light stock, light
        stock or light stock and cream
    Correct the seasoning
and vary the flavor with one or more of
the following:
    Celery salt
    A grating of nutmeg
    1 teaspoon lemon juice
    ½ teaspoon Worcestershire sauce
    1 teaspoon sherry
    1 teaspoon onion juice
    2 tablespoons chopped parsley
    2 tablespoons chopped chives
♦ Simmer and stir the sauce with a wire
whisk until it has thickened and is smooth
and hot. Combine it with other ingredients
just as it boils, so that it will not become
watery. For creamed dishes, use about ½
as much sauce as there are solids.

CREAM SAUCE MIX
                            4 Cups Dry Mix
This can be stored in a covered container,
refrigerated several months. It will
thicken, in all, about 2½ to 3 quarts of
sauce. Rub:
    1 cup butter
into:
    1 cup flour
Stir in and blend thoroughly:
    2 cups nonfat milk solids
To make sauce, stir to a paste in a saucepan ⅓ cup of the above mixture with:
    ⅓ cup water or stock
then add:
    ⅔ cup water or stock
gradually over low heat and stir constantly
until the sauce thickens.
    Correct the seasoning

EGG CREAM SAUCE
                                1¼ Cups
This is good made with chicken stock and
cream.
Prepare:
    Cream Sauce I, page 322
Add to it:
    2 chopped hard-cooked eggs
    1 tablespoon capers or chopped pickles

FLORENTINE SAUCE
                            About 2 Cups

Combine:
    1 cup Cream Sauce I, page 322
    A dash of hot pepper sauce
    2 drops Worcestershire sauce
    (A dash of monosodium glutamate)
    1 cup finely chopped spinach
    A fresh grating of nutmeg
    1 tablespoon finely chopped parsley
If using cold for fish, do not thin. If you
use it hot, you may thin it with:
    Cream or dry white wine

MORNAY SAUCE
                            About 1¼ Cups
Excellent for masking fish, egg and vegetable dishes. If you are using it in a dish
to be browned in the oven or under the
broiler, sprinkle a little grated cheese over
the top first. Prepare:
    1 cup Cream Sauce I, flavored with
        onion or shallot, page 322
Beat together until blended:
    1 egg yolk
    2 tablespoons cream
♦ Add a little of the sauce to the egg yolk
and cream, stirring constantly, then return
the mixture to the rest of the sauce and
cook until well heated. Then add:
    2 tablespoons grated Parmesan cheese
    2 tablespoons grated Gruyère cheese
Keep stirring with a small whisk to help
melt the cheese and keep the sauce smooth
while it thickens.
    Correct the seasoning
with:
    Salt and a few grains of cayenne

NANTUA SAUCE
                            About 1½ Cups
For fish.
Prepare:
    1 cup Cream Sauce I, page 322
Add:
    ½ cup whipping cream
Rub through a fine sieve:
    2 tablespoons Shrimp Butter, page 339
Instead of the shrimp butter, you may add
1 tablespoon finely ground shrimp made
into a smooth paste with 1 tablespoon but-
ter. Heat to boiling point.
    Correct the seasoning
Garnish with:
    Finely chopped shrimp

NEWBURG SAUCE
I.   About 1 Cup
Melt in a double boiler:
    ½ cup Lobster Butter, page 339
Add and cook gently until translucent:
    1 teaspoon finely chopped shallots
Add and continue to cook about 3 minutes:
    ¼ cup sherry or Madeira
Into:
    1 cup cream
beat:
    3 egg yolks
Add the two mixtures, stirring constantly
until the sauce thickens. Use at once.

II. If you want a pink sauce for shrimp or lobster, add to the above:

    1 tablespoon tomato paste
    (1 tablespoon cognac or brandy)

OYSTER SAUCE FOR FISH
About 2 Cups

Prepare:

    1 cup Cream Sauce II, page 322

Season it well with:

    Salt
    (1 teaspoon Worcestershire sauce)

Shortly before serving, bring the sauce to the boiling point and add:

    3 tablespoons chopped parsley
    1 cup finely chopped poached oysters and juice

ANCHOVY SAUCE FOR FISH
1 Cup

Prepare:

    Cream Sauce I, page 322

Add to it:

    3 fillets of anchovy, washed and pounded to a paste

Blend it well with the sauce.

HORSERADISH SAUCE OR SAUCE ALBERT
1 Cup

Usually used with boiled beef or corned beef.

Prepare:

    Cream Sauce I, page 322

Remove it from the heat. Add:

    3 tablespoons prepared horseradish
    2 tablespoons whipping cream
    1 teaspoon sugar
    1 teaspoon dry mustard
    1 tablespoon vinegar

Reheat but do not boil. Serve immediately.

VELOUTÉ SAUCE OR SAUCE BLANCHE
1½ Cups

This is a white cream sauce made from a roux and stock base. The stock may be chicken, veal or fish, depending on the dish the sauce is to accompany. A quick Velouté may be made like Cream Sauce I, using stock in place of milk, but for a classic sauce of fine texture, proceed as directed below. ♦ The sauce should never be cooked in aluminum pans because they discolor it badly. Melt in the top of a double boiler:

    2 tablespoons butter

Stir in:

    2 tablespoons flour

When blended, add gradually:

    2 cups chicken, veal or fish stock

and stir over low heat until well combined and thickened. Add:

    ¼ cup mushroom peelings

Place in the double boiler and simmer ♦ over—not in—hot water for about 1 hour, stirring occasionally. Strain through a fine sieve, then add:

    A pinch of nutmeg
    Correct the seasoning

and stir occasionally during the cooling process to prevent a crust from forming.

AURORE SAUCE
About 2 Cups

Fine with fish.

Prepare:

    Velouté Sauce

Add:

    2 tablespoons tomato purée

to the sauce and mix. Let boil a little before pouring through a sieve and adding:

    A Butter Swirl

ALLEMANDE SAUCE OR THICKENED VELOUTÉ
1½ Cups

This is an enriched Velouté Sauce, to be used with poached chicken or vegetables. ♦ Do not let this sauce boil or it will curdle.

Prepare:

    1½ cups Velouté Sauce, above

Stir in:

    ¾ cup strong chicken stock

Blend well and reduce on medium heat to ⅔ of its original volume. Remove from the heat and add:

    1 egg yolk mixed with 2 tablespoons cream

Stir the sauce until it is slightly thickened. Just before serving, stir in:

    1 tablespoon lemon juice
    1 tablespoon butter

POULETTE SAUCE
1½ Cups

Prepare:

    1½ cups Allemande Sauce, above

Just before serving, add:

    1 tablespoon finely chopped parsley

PAPRIKA OR HUNGARIAN SAUCE
About 1½ Cups

Use for fish, poultry or veal.

Sauté until golden:

    1 finely chopped onion

in:

    1 tablespoon butter

Add:

    2 tablespoons mild Hungarian paprika

and stir for 1 minute. Add gradually, stirring constantly:

    1 cup cream
    ⅛ cup Velouté Sauce, above
    Correct the seasoning

CAPER SAUCE
1½ Cups

For poached or broiled fish, or mutton.

Prepare:

    1½ cups Velouté or Allemande Sauce, above

Just before serving, add:

    2 tablespoons drained chopped capers

CURRY SAUCE

I.   **1½ Cups**

Pour over whole poached fish or fish fillets.
Prepare:

1½ cups Allemande Sauce, page 324

A few minutes before serving, stir in:

1 teaspoon good curry powder

II.   **About 2 Cups**

Sauté slowly until tender:

¼ cup chopped onion
¼ cup chopped tart apple

in:

¼ cup butter

Stir in and cook, without browning, for 4
or 5 minutes:

2½ tablespoons flour
½ to 2 teaspoons curry powder

Add slowly, stirring constantly and simmer
until well blended:

1 cup chicken broth
1 cup cream
½ teaspoon grated lemon peel

If you wish to have a perfectly smooth
sauce, add the chicken broth and grated
lemon peel only, cook for 10 minutes, strain
through a sieve, add the cream and bring
back to a boil. You may liven up this sauce,
if you like a hot curry, with dashes of:

Hot pepper sauce
Cayenne
Ginger
Chopped chutney
Dry sherry

MUSTARD SAUCE

1½ Cups

Serve with poached or broiled fish.
Prepare:

1½ cups Allemande Sauce, page 324

Add, just before serving:

½ teaspoon dry mustard or 1 teaspoon
prepared mustard
¼ teaspoon salt
½ teaspoon freshly ground black
pepper

SOUBISE OR WHITE ONION SAUCE

About 1½ Cups

This is a delicate onion-flavored sauce for
fish, poultry or vegetables.
Prepare:

1½ cups Velouté Sauce, page 324

Sauté until transparent:

2 medium chopped onions

in:

2 tablespoons butter

Add the onions to the Velouté Sauce and
simmer over low heat for 30 minutes, stir-
ing occasionally. Rub the whole sauce
through a fine sieve. Finish off the sauce
with:

2 tablespoons whipping cream
Correct the seasoning

SUPREME SAUCE

About 2 Cups

For fish, poultry and eggs. The special
characteristics of Supreme Sauce are its
perfect whiteness and delicacy.
Prepare:

1½ cups Velouté Sauce, page 324, made
with chicken stock

Add:

1 cup strong white chicken stock
¼ cup mushroom peelings

Bring to a boil, reduce the heat and simmer, stirring occasionally, until the sauce
is reduced to 1½ cups. Strain through a
fine sieve and add, stirring constantly:

½ cup whipping cream

Stir in:

1 tablespoon butter
Correct the seasoning

HOT RAVIGOTE SAUCE

This sauce is served lukewarm over variety
meats, boiled fish, light meats and poultry.
Chop until very fine:

2 shallots

Add:

1 tablespoon wine vinegar

Cook these ingredients rapidly, stirring
constantly for about 3 minutes. Add:

1 cup Velouté Sauce, page 324

to the shallots and simmer the sauce for
about 10 minutes. Stir it from time to time.
Add:

Salt and freshly ground pepper

Cool the sauce to lukewarm. Add:

1 tablespoon chopped parsley
(1 teaspoon prepared mustard)
1 tablespoon chopped chervil
1 tablespoon chopped capers
½ teaspoon chopped chives
½ teaspoon chopped tarragon
(A grating of fresh nutmeg)

SMITANE SAUCE

About 2 Cups

Use for roast poultry or game—especially
pheasant.
Melt in a saucepan:

1 tablespoon butter

Add:

¼ cup finely chopped onions

and cook until transparent, then add:

½ cup dry white wine

and cook until the mixture is reduced to
½. Add:

1 cup Velouté, page 324, or Brown
Sauce, page 326

Blend and simmer 5 minutes then add:

1 cup cultured sour cream
Correct the seasoning

If a sourer effect is wanted, add:

(A little lemon juice)

Do not allow the sauce to boil after adding
the sour cream or it will curdle.

BREAD SAUCE

About 3 Cups

Usually served with small roasted wild
birds or roast meat.
Skin:

A small onion
Stud it with:
   3 whole cloves
Place the onion in a saucepan with:
   2 cups milk
   2 tablespoons butter
Bring the milk to a boil. Add:
   1 cup fresh white bread crumbs
Simmer for 15 minutes. Remove the onion. Beat the sauce smooth and stir in, until blended:
   3 tablespoons cream

CHEESE SAUCE

About 2 Cups

Melt in a saucepan:
   3 tablespoons butter
Stir in, until blended:
   3 tablespoons flour
Stir in slowly:
   1½ cups milk
When the sauce is smooth and hot, reduce the heat and stir in:
   1 cup or less mild grated cheese or diced processed cheese
Season the sauce with:
   ½ teaspoon salt
   ⅛ teaspoon paprika
   A few grains cayenne
   (½ teaspoon dry mustard)
Stir the sauce until the cheese is melted.

BROWN SAUCE OR SAUCE ESPAGNOLE

About 6 Cups

This is one of the "sauces mères" of the French cuisine, the basis for many other sauces and dishes. Diat has said that the making of a good Espagnole is the mark of an accomplished saucier.
   ▶ Always stir, never whip, a Brown Sauce and use good, strong, clear beef stock. The flavor comes from the gradual "reduction" of the sauce by very slow simmering, which, if you are a perfectionist, can be 8 to 12 hours. Here is a rather more time-saving method.
Melt in a heavy saucepan:
   ½ cup beef or veal drippings
Add:
   1 cup Mirepoix, page 541
When this begins to brown, add:
   ½ cup flour
and stir until the flour is a good brown. Then add:
   10 black peppercorns
   2 cups drained, peeled tomatoes or 2 cups tomato purée
   ½ cup coarsely chopped parsley
Stir and mix well, then add:
   8 cups good beef stock
Simmer on the stove for about 2 to 2½ hours or until reduced by ½. Stir occasionally and skim off the fat as it rises to the top. Strain the sauce and stir occasionally as it cools to prevent a skin forming. The sauce should be the consistency

of whipping cream, no thicker. If you are using this sauce "as is,"
   Correct the seasoning

DEMI-GLAZE SAUCE

About 4½ Cups

This is the Espagnole, above, reduced to the nth degree. Serve with filet mignon or any meat with which Madeira Sauce is generally used.
Combine in a heavy saucepan:
   4 cups Brown Sauce, above
   4 cups good beef stock, flavored with mushroom trimmings
Simmer slowly, until reduced by half. Strain into a double boiler and keep warm over hot water, while adding:
   ½ cup dry sherry

ORANGE SAUCE FOR DUCK OR GOOSE

About 2 Cups

For a true Bigarade, see page 474.
Pour off the fat from the pan in which you have roasted the bird. Deglaze the pan with:
   1 cup Game Stock, page 491
Thicken with:
   1 teaspoon arrowroot or cornstarch
mixed first with a little of the stock. In another pan, cook together until light brown:
   2 tablespoons vinegar
   2 tablespoons sugar
Add the sauce from the roasting pan and cook 4 or 5 minutes, then add:
   1 tablespoon julienned and blanched orange rind
   ½ cup hot orange juice
   1 teaspoon lemon juice
   2 tablespoons curaçao
   Correct the seasoning
Serve immediately over goose or wild or domestic duck and garnish with:
   Orange sections

BORDELAISE SAUCE

For sweetbreads, chops, steaks, grilled meats.
Cook together in a saucepan:
   ½ cup dry red wine
   4 or 5 crushed black peppercorns
until reduced to ¾, then add:
   1 cup Brown Sauce, above
Simmer for 15 minutes. Add, just before serving:
   ¼ cup diced beef marrow, poached for a few minutes and drained
   (½ teaspoon lemon juice)
   ½ teaspoon chopped parsley

QUICK BROWN SAUCE OR GRAVY

About 1 Cup

You may rub your pan with:
   ½ clove garlic
Melt:

2 tablespoons butter
Stir in, until blended:
2 tablespoons flour
Stir in:
1 cup canned bouillon or 1 or 2
bouillon cubes dissolved in 1 cup
boiling water
Permit the gravy to reach the boiling
point. Stir it constantly. Season it as re-
quired with:
Salt and pepper or paprika
Dry sherry or Worcestershire sauce
Lemon juice, catsup or chili sauce
Dried herbs

HUNTER'S SAUCE OR SAUCE CHASSEUR
About 2 Cups
Sauté gently until very tender:
2 tablespoons minced onion or shallots
in:
2 tablespoons butter
Stir in and sauté gently for about 2 minutes:
1 cup sliced mushrooms
Add:
½ cup dry white wine
(2 tablespoons brandy)
Simmer until reduced by ½. Add:
½ cup tomato sauce or purée
1 cup Brown Sauce, page 326
Cook for 5 minutes, then:
Correct the seasoning
and add:
1 teaspoon chopped parsley

MADEIRA SAUCE
About 1 Cup
This sauce may also be made with dry
sherry. It is good with game or fillet of
beef.
Reduce:
1 cup Brown Sauce, page 326
to ¾ its volume, then add:
¼ cup Madeira
(1 teaspoon Meat Glaze, page 492)
Finish with a:
Butter Swirl, page 321
and another:
2 tablespoons Madeira
Keep hot, but do not allow to boil after
adding the butter. You may also make
this in the pan in which you have sautéed
the meat. Remove the meat and pour off
the fat. Deglaze the pan with the above
quantity of Madeira until the wine is reduced by half, then add the Brown Sauce
and cook for 10 minutes before finishing,
as described above.

LYONNAISE SAUCE OR BROWN ONION SAUCE
1¼ Cups
A good sauce to use for leftover meat.
Melt in a saucepan:
2 tablespoons butter
Add:
2 finely chopped onions

and cook until golden brown. Add:
⅓ cup dry white wine or 2
tablespoons vinegar
If you use the wine, simmer until reduced
by ½. Then add:
1 cup Brown Sauce, page 326
and simmer for 15 minutes. Just before
serving, add:
1 tablespoon finely chopped parsley

MARCHAND DE VIN SAUCE
About 2 Cups
Serve with broiled steak.
Sauté:
1 cup finely sliced mushrooms
in:
2 tablespoons butter
Add:
½ cup hot beef stock
♦ Simmer for 10 minutes. Add:
1 cup Brown Sauce, page 326
½ cup dry red wine
♦ Simmer for 20 minutes, then:
Correct the seasoning
You may add:
(Juice of ½ lemon)

MUSHROOM SAUCE
About 2 Cups
For roast meat, chicken and casseroles.
Sauté:
¼ lb. sliced mushrooms
in:
2 tablespoons butter
Remove the mushrooms from the skillet.
Add to the drippings:
1 cup Brown Sauce, page 326, or
Quick Brown Sauce, page 326
When the sauce is heated, add the sautéed
mushrooms.

SAUCE PÉRIGUEUX
1 Cup
Use for croquettes, shirred eggs and
chicken.
Prepare:
Madeira Sauce, page 327
Just before adding the butter swirl, stir in:
1 tablespoon chopped truffles
Very similar is Sauce Périgourdine, but the
truffles are finely diced instead of chopped
and a dice of foie gras is added.

PIQUANT SAUCE
About 1¼ Cups
This sauce is excellent for giving extra zip
to bland meats and for reheating leftover
meat. A good sauce for pork and pigs'
feet.
Lightly brown:
2 tablespoons minced onion
in:
1 tablespoon butter
Add:
2 tablespoons dry white wine or
2 tablespoons vinegar or lemon juice
and cook until the liquid is almost evapo-

rated. Add:
>1 cup Brown Sauce, page 326

and simmer for 10 minutes. Just before
serving, add:
>1 tablespoon chopped parsley or
>chopped mixed parsley, tarragon
>and chervil
>1 tablespoon chopped sour pickles
>1 tablespoon chopped capers
>Correct the seasoning

SAUCE ROBERT

1¼ Cups

Prepare:
>Piquant Sauce, above

doubling the amount of onion and omitting
the parsley, chervil and tarragon. Just before serving, stir in:
>1 teaspoon prepared Dijon-type
>mustard
>A pinch of powdered sugar

POIVRADE OR PEPPER SAUCE

3 Cups

This is the traditional sauce to serve with
venison and constitutes the basis of several other game sauces. As the name suggests, it is quite peppery.
Heat:
>¼ cup cooking oil

Sauté in it, until brown:
>1 chopped carrot
>1 chopped onion
>(Game bones, trimmings and giblets,
>if available)

Add:
>3 sprigs parsley
>1 bay leaf
>A pinch of thyme
>¼ cup vinegar or ¼ cup marinade
>liquid, if the game has been
>marinated before cooking

Simmer until reduced to ⅓ original quantity. Add:
>3 cups Brown Sauce, page 326

Bring to a boil ♦ reduce heat and simmer
for 1 hour. Add:
>10 peppercorns

and simmer 5 more minutes. Strain the
sauce into another saucepan and add
again:
>¼ cup marinade liquid

Cook slowly for 30 minutes more, then
add:
>½ cup dry red wine
>Correct the seasoning

Add enough:
>Freshly ground black pepper

to make a hot sauce.

ROSEMARY WINE SAUCE

1 Cup

Serve with Calf's Head, or turtle meat.
Heat to boiling point:
>½ cup good Madeira or dry sherry

Add:
>1 teaspoon mixed dried marjoram,

>rosemary, sage, bay leaf, thyme and
>basil

This strongly flavored combination of
herbs is known as herbs "à tortue" in
France. Remove from heat and let stand
5 to 10 minutes. Strain off the herb-flavored wine and add it to:
>1 cup hot Brown Sauce, page 326

ABOUT HOLLANDAISE AND OTHER EGG-THICKENED SAUCES

These delicious sauces, loaded with calories, make a superb dish out of the plainest and simplest cooked vegetables or
broiled or roasted meat. But nothing can
make a cook more frenzied than a Hollandaise which suddenly breaks or fails to
thicken just as dinner is to be served. To
avoid such disasters, here are a few tricks.
Don't try to make Hollandaise or Béarnaise, on a very humid day, unless you use
Clarified Butter, page 338. You will remove the cords from the egg yolks as they
make the sauce lumpy. Cook these sauces
♦ over—not in—hot, but not boiling, water. If you use a heatproof glass double
boiler you can see when the water begins
to boil and add 1 or 2 tablespoons of cold
water. ♦ Keep stirring the sauce all the
time and ♦ add the melted butter very,
very slowly at first. Scrape the mixture
away from the sides and bottom of the pan
as you stir, to keep the sauce smooth. As
with Mayonnaise, page 313, a wooden
spoon or a whisk is the best tool for making Hollandaise. A professional chef will
make Hollandaise over low direct heat,
but don't try this unless you have a drum-
mer's quick wrist—as it needs both fast
and practiced stirring. ♦ To hold egg
sauces for several hours, prepare and store
in wide-mouthed vacuum bottles, as
sketched. Some of our friends freeze Hollandaise just as one can roux-based sauces.

Reheat it in a double boiler ♦ over—not in—hot water, stirring constantly so that it does not break. Should any of these egg sauces break, beat into them at once 1 to 2 tablespoons cream. Or a slightly curdled sauce can be rescued in a blender, although the texture will not be as good as an originally well-made sauce. Or it can be reconstituted, using a fresh egg yolk as for Mayonnaise, page 313.

NEVER-FAIL HOLLANDAISE SAUCE
♦ Please read About Hollandaise Sauce above.

1 Cup

Our cook calls this "holiday sauce"—isn't that a grand name for it?
Melt slowly and keep warm:
    ½ cup butter
Barely heat:
    1½ tablespoons lemon juice, dry sherry
        or tarragon vinegar
Have ready a small saucepan of boiling water and a tablespoon with which to measure it when ready. Place in the top of a double boiler ♦ over—not in—hot water:
    3 egg yolks
Beat the yolks with a wire whisk until they begin to thicken. Add:
    1 tablespoon boiling water
Beat again until the eggs begin to thicken. Repeat this process until you have added:
    3 more tablespoons water
Then beat in the warm lemon juice. Remove the double boiler from the heat. Beat the sauce well with a wire whisk. Beat constantly while adding the melted butter slowly and:
    ¼ teaspoon salt
        A few grains cayenne
Beat until the sauce is thick. Serve at once.

⅄ BLENDER HOLLANDAISE
About 1 Cup

This is easy, but not as flavorful as handmade Hollandaise. It is also paler in color. ♦ Do not make in a smaller quantity than given here, as there is, then, not enough heat to cook the eggs properly.
Have ready in your blender:
    3 egg yolks
    2 tablespoons lemon juice
        A pinch of cayenne
    ¼ teaspoon salt
Heat to bubbling stage, but do not brown:
    ½ cup butter
Cover container and turn motor on "High." After 3 seconds, remove the lid and pour the butter over the eggs in a steady stream. By the time the butter is poured in—about 30 seconds—the sauce should be finished. If not, blend on "High" about 5 seconds longer. Serve at once or keep warm by immersing blender container in warm water. This sauce may be frozen and reconstituted over hot water.

MOCK HOLLANDAISE
For less rich versions, try one of the following or if you are in a hurry, prepare Hot Mayonnaise.

I.   **About 1¼ Cups**
Mix in the top of a double boiler:
    1 cup cultured sour cream
        Juice of 1 lemon
    2 egg yolks
    ½ teaspoon salt
    ¼ teaspoon paprika
Stir ♦ over—not in—hot water until thick.

II.   **4 Servings**
Good over vegetables such as Cauliflower, see page 271.
Place in a double boiler ♦ over—not in—boiling water:
    2 beaten eggs
    ¼ cup cream
    ⅛ teaspoon salt
    ⅛ teaspoon freshly ground nutmeg
    1 tablespoon lemon juice
Cook and stir these ingredients until they are thick, then add a little at a time:
    2 tablespoons butter
Serve at once.

HOT MAYONNAISE SAUCE
About 1 Cup
Good over steak and fish.
Heat in a double boiler and stir:
    1 cup mayonnaise
Add:
    Lemon juice and capers

MOUSSELINE SAUCE
1¼ Cups
Use for any vegetable or fish on which Hollandaise is served.
Just before serving, add:
    ½ cup whipped cream
to:
    1 cup Hollandaise Sauce, above
Serve hot or cold.

FIGARO SAUCE
Prepare:
    1 cup Hollandaise Sauce, above
Beat in very slowly:
    ¼ cup warm tomato purée
Add:
    1 to 2 tablespoons chopped parsley
        Correct the seasoning
and serve.

MALTAISE SAUCE
About 1 Cup
Interesting on asparagus.
Add:
    2 to 3 tablespoons orange juice
    1 teaspoon grated orange rind
to:
    1 cup Hollandaise Sauce, above

SAUCE BÉARNAISE
About 1½ Cups
Heavenly on most broiled red meat, espe-

cially beef tenderloin. It is also quite at
home on fish and eggs.
Combine in the top of a double boiler:

> ½ cup white wine or red wine
> 2 tablespoons tarragon vinegar
> 1 tablespoon finely chopped shallots
>   or onion
> 2 crushed peppercorns
> 2 sprigs chopped tarragon
> 1 sprig finely chopped chervil
> (1 sprig parsley)

Cook over direct heat until reduced by
half. ◗ If you have used dried tarragon or
coarsely chopped onion, now strain the
mixture. Allow it to cool. Then, beating
briskly ◗ over—not in—hot water, add alternately a little at a time and beat steadily so that they are well combined before
you add in all:

> 3 egg yolks
> ¾ cup melted butter
> Correct the seasoning

When you have added all the butter, the
sauce should have the consistency of Hollandaise.

SOUFFLÉD MAYONNAISE SAUCE
FOR FISH

6 Servings

This is also good as a masking for broiled
tomatoes.
Broil until nearly done, see page 349:

> 3 lbs. fish

Transfer them to a hot ovenproof dish.
Combine and beat well:

> ½ cup mayonnaise
> ¼ cup pickle relish
> 2 tablespoons chopped parsley
> 1 tablespoon lemon juice
> ¼ teaspoon salt
> A few grains cayenne

Beat until stiff, but not dry:

> 2 egg whites

Fold them into the mayonnaise mixture.
Spread the sauce evenly on the fish. Broil
it until the sauce is puffed and golden.

MINT SAUCE

About 1 Cup

The usual accompaniment to roast lamb.
Heat:

> 3 tablespoons water

Dissolve in it:

> 1½ tablespoons confectioners' sugar

Cool the sirup and add:

> ⅓ cup finely chopped mint leaves
> ½ cup strong vinegar

This is best made ½ hour before serving.

SWEET-SOUR MUSTARD SAUCE

About 2½ Cups

Use for ham or tongue.
Combine in a double boiler ◗ over—not in
—hot water:

> ½ cup sugar

> 1 tablespoon flour
> 4 teaspoons dry mustard

Add gradually:

> 2 cups cream

mixed with:

> 2 egg yolks

Cook until thick. Stir in, gradually:

> ½ cup vinegar

SWEET-SOUR CREAM DRESSING

About 1 Cup

For snap beans, cabbage, etc. Combine
and stir over very low heat until the sauce
thickens slightly:

> 1 beaten egg
> ½ cup cultured sour cream
> 2 tablespoons sugar
> ¼ cup vinegar
> ½ teaspoon salt
> ¼ teaspoon paprika

Serve it hot over hot vegetables or cold
over chilled vegetables.

SWEET-SOUR BACON SAUCE

About 1 Cup

Fine for green beans.
Slowly render, until crisp:

> 4 thin slices of cut-up bacon

At the same time, you may cook until
transparent:

> (1 teaspoon minced onion)

Remove the bacon and onion and pour off
all but:

> 2 tablespoons bacon grease

Add to the grease:

> ¾ cup of the bean or vegetable stock
> 2 tablespoons vinegar
> 1 to 2 tablespoons sugar

Heat and pour over the vegetables. Garnish with the bacon and onion bits.

CHINESE SWEET-SOUR SAUCE
I.   **1 Cup**

Heat:

> ½ cup pineapple juice
> 3 tablespoons oil
> 2 tablespoons brown sugar
> 1 teaspoon soy sauce or salt
> ½ teaspoon pepper
> ¼ cup mild vinegar

II.   **2½ to 3 Cups**

Serve with Chinese Meat Balls, page 429,
or Sweet-Sour Pork, page 409.
Have ready a paste of:

> 2 tablespoons cornstarch
> ½ cup chicken broth
> 2 tablespoons soy sauce

Melt in a heavy pan:

> 2 tablespoons butter

Add:

> 1 cup chicken broth
> ¾ to 1 cup diced green peppers
> 6 slices diced canned pineapple

Cover and simmer for 5 minutes. Add the
cornstarch paste and the following ingredients to the peppers and pineapple:

½ cup vinegar
¾ cups pineapple juice
½ cup sugar
½ teaspoon salt
¼ teaspoon ginger

Simmer, stirring constantly, until the mixture thickens.

CHINESE SAUCE FOR VEGETABLES
For About 1 lb. Vegetables

Blend until smooth:
    1 tablespoon cornstarch
    3 tablespoons cold water
Add:
    ½ teaspoon salt
    1 tablespoon soy sauce
    ½ teaspoon finely grated gingerroot

Pour over vegetables that are cooking. Stir well until the whole mixture comes to a boil.

CURRANT JELLY SAUCES
I.   **About 1¼ Cups**

For game or cold meat.
Heat in a double boiler just before serving:
    ¾ cup currant jelly
Stir in:
    ½ cup Indian chutney
    1 teaspoon lemon juice
    1 tablespoon brandy
    Salt

II.   **About ½ Cup**

Make a simplified version by mixing:
    ½ cup jelly
    2 tablespoons horseradish
    ½ teaspoon dry mustard

HOT CUMBERLAND SAUCE
About 2 Cups

This calls for many ingredients, but you may omit some or substitute others.
Combine:
    1 teaspoon dry mustard
    1 tablespoon brown sugar
    ¼ teaspoon powdered ginger
    A few grains cayenne
    ¼ teaspoon salt
    ¼ teaspoon ground cloves
    1½ cups red wine, preferably port
    (½ cup seedless raisins)
    (½ cup blanched slivered almonds)

Simmer the sauce, covered, for 8 minutes. Dissolve:
    2 teaspoons cornstarch
in:
    2 tablespoons cold water
Stir this into the sauce. Let it simmer for about 2 minutes. Stir in:
    ¼ cup red currant jelly
    1 tablespoon grated orange and
        lemon rind
    ¼ cup orange juice
    2 tablespoons lemon juice

BURGUNDY SAUCE OR SAUCE BOURGUIGNONNE
1 Cup

For snails and egg dishes.

Reduce by ½ a mixture of:
    2 cups dry red wine, preferably
        red Burgundy
    2 minced shallots
    A few sprigs parsley
    A pinch of thyme
    ¼ bay leaf
    (Mushroom peelings)

Strain the mixture. When ready to serve, heat and add:
    1 to 1½ tablespoons Kneaded Butter,
        page 321
    (A dash of cayenne)

RAISIN CIDER OR BEER SAUCE
About 1½ Cups

Good with hot or cold ham or smoked tongue.
Combine in a saucepan:
    ¼ cup firmly packed brown sugar
    1½ tablespoons cornstarch
    ⅛ teaspoon salt
Stir in:
    1 cup fresh cider or beer
    ¼ cup raisins, cut in halves

Put in a cheesecloth bag and hang it in the cooking sauce from the edge of the pan:
    8 whole cloves
    1 two-inch stick cinnamon

Cook and stir for about 10 minutes. Add:
    1 tablespoon butter

Remove the spices. Serve the sauce very hot.

SAUCE FOR LIGHT MEAT GAME

After roasting the game bird, which is barded with salt pork or bacon and basted with equal quantities of butter and white wine, flame it in:
    ⅛ cup cognac: 1 oz.

Remove the game and keep warm. Degrease the pan juices and reduce them over low heat for 1 minute. Then add, for each small bird:
    1 egg yolk
Beat in:
    ½ cup whipping cream

Stir until thickened ♦ but do not allow the sauce to boil. Season well.

BERCY SAUCE
¼ Cup

White wine is best for this sauce, which is served on fish.
Cook until transparent:
    1 teaspoon finely chopped shallots
in:
    1 tablespoon butter
Add:
    ¼ cup dry white or red wine
    ¼ cup Fish Fumet, page 491
and simmer until reduced by ½. Thicken the mixture with:
    Kneaded butter, made by creaming
        together 1 teaspoon flour and
    2 tablespoons butter
stirring it in briskly until well blended.

Add:
  1 teaspoon chopped parsley
  Correct the seasoning

WHITE WINE SAUCE FOR FISH
About 1¼ Cups

Reduce by ½ over medium heat a mixture of:
  ¼ cup white wine
  1 bay leaf
  2 cloves
  2 black peppercorns
  (1½-inch piece gingerroot)
  ¼ cup fish stock
  1 teaspoon chopped shallot
Strain and add to:
  1 cup strained Cream Sauce I,
    page 322
To make a sauce that coats well and browns beautifully, add:
  2 tablespoons whipped cream

WHITE WINE SAUCE FOR LIGHT MEATS
About 1 Cup

Serve over Sautéed Brains, page 443, or other light meats.
Add to the pan drippings and sauté until light yellow:
  1 tablespoon chopped onion
Stir in until smooth:
  1½ tablespoons flour
Stir in gradually, until the sauce is smooth and very hot:
  ½ cup chicken or veal stock
  ½ cup dry white wine
Add:
  1 tablespoon chopped parsley or chives
  Salt, as needed

SOYER'S UNIVERSAL DEVIL SAUCE
We have chosen this sauce from Alexis Soyer's "Culinary Campaign," a fabulous account of the Crimean War, through which he cooked his way with abandon. No one brought more conviction to his work, whether changing the diet of the British armed forces, cooking at the Reform Club or remolding the cooking habits of the English lower classes—which he attempted through his Shilling Cook Book. The original recipe called for a tablespoon of cayenne pepper. We have changed it to a small pinch, for in Soyer's day cayenne was baked into a sort of bread and then ground, making it about the same strength as a mild paprika.
Rub any deviled food with the following mixture:
  1 good tablespoon Durham mustard
  ¼ cup chili vinegar
  1 tablespoon grated horseradish
  2 bruised shallots
  1 teaspoon salt
  A few grains cayenne
  ½ teaspoon black pepper
  1 teaspoon sugar
  (2 teaspoons chopped chilies)
  (2 raw egg yolks)
Soyer's instructions are to "broil slowly at first and end as near as possible the Pandemonium Fire."

BARBECUE SAUCES
Please read About Skewer Cooking, page 123. It is important to ♦ baste with barbecue sauces only during the last 15 minutes of cooking. Too long cooking of the sauce will make the spices bitter.

I. **About 2 Cups**
Sauté until brown:
  ¼ cup chopped onions
in:
  1 tablespoon drippings or other fat
Add and simmer for 20 minutes:
  ½ cup water
  2 tablespoons vinegar
  1 tablespoon Worcestershire sauce
  ¼ cup lemon juice
  2 tablespoons brown sugar
  1 cup chili sauce
  ½ teaspoon salt
  ¼ teaspoon paprika
  1 teaspoon pepper
  1 teaspoon mustard

II. **About 1½ Cups**
Simmer for 15 minutes, stirring frequently:
  12 to 14 oz. tomato catsup
  ½ cup white distilled vinegar
  1 teaspoon sugar
  A liberal seasoning of red and black
    pepper
  ⅛ teaspoon salt

FEROCIOUS BARBECUE SAUCE
Combine and heat:
  1½ cups Barbecue Sauce II, above
  ¼ of a seeded lemon, diced fine
  ½ teaspoon ground cumin
  1 teaspoon ground coriander
  ⅛ teaspoon Spanish paprika
  ⅛ teaspoon saffron
  ¼ teaspoon ground ginger

BARBECUE SAUCE FOR FOWL
For 1 Fowl

I. Combine and heat:
  4 teaspoons lemon juice
  1 teaspoon Worcestershire sauce
  1 teaspoon tomato catsup
  1 tablespoon butter

II. Cook slowly until golden:
  1 medium chopped onion
  1 minced clove garlic
in:
  3 tablespoons fat
Add and simmer for 30 minutes:
  3 tablespoons soy or Worcestershire
    sauce
  1 cup water
  1 red pepper
  2 tablespoons vinegar

2 to 4 tablespoons brown sugar
1 cup catsup
1 teaspoon prepared mustard
½ cup celery
½ teaspoon salt
Then add:
    ¼ cup lemon juice

QUICK CANNED SOUP SAUCES

Not only can the thin canned consommés and broths be used for flavoring sauces, but some of the condensed cream soups can be quickly made into acceptable sauces. ◗ Taste before salting them.

I.   1¼ Cups
For chicken, veal and fish.
Heat:
    1 cup condensed cream of chicken
      soup
    2 tablespoons butter
    2 to 4 tablespoons rich chicken or
      vegetable stock
    A grating of lemon rind

II.   1¼ Cups
For beef hash.
Heat:
    1 cup cream of mushroom soup
    2 to 4 tablespoons strong beef stock
    ½ teaspoon meat glaze
    Few drops garlic juice
    1 tablespoon butter

III.   1¼ Cups
For creaming vegetables.
Heat:
    1 cup cream of celery soup
    2 tablespoons butter
    2 to 4 tablespoons chicken stock
    1 tablespoon chopped chives

DRIED SOUP SAUCES
4 Servings

These are not as quick as the canned ones but can provide a well-flavored base when reconstituted with half the amount of liquid called for normally. Use in making sauces for casseroles. The dried vegetables swell as the casserole cooks.
Try heating:
    1 package dried cream of leek, cream
      of mushroom or smoky pea soup
    1½ cups light cream or top milk
Use with leftover chicken or veal, with rice or noodles in a casserole. Or combine and heat:
    1 package dried onion soup
    1½ to 2 cups water
and add to meat and vegetables in a casserole. Again, do not salt—and go easy on other seasonings in these sauces—until they have cooked for about 20 minutes and you have tasted them.

QUICK À LA KING SAUCE
About 1½ Cups
To the rescue, whenever this type of sauce is required.

Sauté until tender:
    1 minced green pepper
in:
    1 tablespoon butter
Add the contents of:
    1 can condensed mushroom soup:
      10½ oz.
    ¼ cup milk
Heat the sauce and add:
    1 pimiento, cut into strips
    (2 tablespoons dry sherry)

QUICK CREOLE SAUCE
2½ Cups
To:
    2 cups Quick Tomato Sauce, page 334
Add:
    ½ cup finely chopped green peppers,
      onion, celery, olives and pimiento

QUICK TOMATO CHEESE SAUCE
About 1½ Cups
Good over eggs.
Heat in a double boiler:
    1 can condensed tomato soup: 10½ oz.
Add:
    ¼ teaspoon salt
    ¼ teaspoon pepper or paprika
Stir and cook these ingredients until they are hot. Beat in:
    1 cup or more grated cheese
Use a wire whisk. Beat the sauce until the cheese is melted.

UNTHICKENED TOMATO SAUCE
About 4 Cups
Place over low heat:
    3 tablespoons olive oil
Add and stir for about 3 minutes:
    1 large chopped Bermuda onion
    2 chopped celery ribs with leaves
    1 carrot, cut in small pieces
    (½ chopped green pepper, seeds and
      fibrous portions removed)
    (1 chopped clove garlic)
Add:
    4 cups canned tomatoes or 6 large
      fresh tomatoes
If these are very juicy, peel and squeeze slightly to get rid of excess liquid and seeds. Add:
    1 sprig thyme, basil or tarragon
    1 teaspoon salt
    ⅛ teaspoon pepper
    1 teaspoon sugar
Cook the sauce gently, uncovered, until thick, for about 45 minutes. ◗ Watch it, so that it does not burn. Put it through a fine strainer. Add seasoning, if needed. This sauce will keep for several days.

THICKENED TOMATO SAUCE
About 1½ Cups
Bring to a boil and then ◗ simmer for 30

SALAD DRESSINGS, SAUCES, GRAVIES AND GLAZES

334

minutes before sieving:
2 cups canned tomatoes
1 onion, stuck with 3 cloves
2 chopped celery ribs with leaves
1 diced carrot
1 Bouquet Garni, page 541
1 bay leaf
(½ chopped green pepper)
♦ Be sure to get all the pulpy residue when
sieving, so that only cloves, leaves and
seeds remain in the sieve. This well-flavored pulp helps thicken the sauce. Melt
in a saucepan:
3 tablespoons butter
Stir in, until blended:
2 tablespoons flour
Add the strained thickish stock slowly
with:
¼ teaspoon sugar
♦ Simmer and stir the stock for about 5 to
10 minutes.
Correct the seasoning
Flavor with:
(1 tablespoon fresh basil)

QUICK TOMATO SAUCE
About 3 Cups
Strain:
1 large can Italian tomatoes
Add:
½ can tomato paste: 6 oz.
½ teaspoon salt
1 tablespoon onion juice or 2
tablespoons finely grated onion
½ teaspoon sugar
Bring to a boil and simmer gently for 15 to
20 minutes.

SHRIMP SAUCE FOR FISH
3½ Cups
This is an elaborate sauce. Do not hesitate to deduct from, add to or alter it.
Prepare:
2 cups Thickened Tomato Sauce, page
333, or 2 cups Cream Sauce I,
page 322
Season the sauce well. Add and heat to
the boiling point:
1 teaspoon Worcestershire or 2
teaspoons chili sauce
2 tablespoons chopped parsley
¼ cup chopped olives
½ cup boiled or canned shrimp
½ cup sautéed or canned mushrooms
¼ cup finely chopped celery
Serve the sauce with baked or boiled fish
or place the fish on a platter and pour the
sauce over it. Heat it under a broiler.

ITALIAN TOMATO PASTE
This flavorful paste is diluted in a little
boiling water or stock and added to sauces
and soups. Fine in spaghetti and noodle
dishes and as a dressing for cooked vegetables or salads.
Wash and cut into slices:

1½ pecks ripe Italian tomatoes: 6 quarts
Add:
3 teaspoons salt
You may add:
1 large celery stalk, cut up with some
leaves
¾ cup chopped onion
3 tablespoons fresh herbs or 1
tablespoon dried herbs
¾ teaspoon peppercorns
12 cloves
1 two-inch stick cinnamon
(1 minced clove garlic)
Simmer these ingredients until the tomatoes are soft. Stir frequently. Put the vegetables through a fine sieve. Simmer the
pulp over hot water or simmer it over direct heat with some means of protecting it
from the bottom by using an asbestos
pad. Stir it frequently, as it burns easily.
After several hours, when the pulp is thick
and reduced by about ½, spread the paste
to the depth of ½ inch on moist plates.
Cut into the paste to permit the air to
penetrate. Place the paste in the sun to
dry or dry it in a 250° oven. When the
paste is dry enough, roll it into balls. They
may be dipped in salad oil. Store them in
airtight jars or store the paste in a tin box
with waxed paper between the layers.

TOMATO PASTE OR VELVET
About ¾ Cup
Wash, then mash:
6 large ripe tomatoes
Melt:
2 tablespoons butter
Add the tomatoes and:
1 teaspoon brown sugar
¼ teaspoon paprika
¾ teaspoon salt
Cook the tomatoes over low heat, stirring
constantly or in a double boiler, until they
are the consistency of thick paste. Put the
paste through a strainer. This makes a
relish or fine addition to sauces.

MEXICAN SAUCE
About 1 Cup
Just what you might expect. You will feel
hot inside, down to your toes. Use with
Cowboy Eggs, page 197.
Place in a small saucepan and simmer until fairly thick:
¾ cup canned tomatoes or about 3
large, skinned and quartered, peeled
and seeded fresh tomatoes
6 tablespoons chili sauce
2 teaspoons dry mustard
3 tablespoons grated or prepared
horseradish
½ teaspoon sugar
¾ teaspoon salt
¼ teaspoon pepper
A few grains cayenne
¾ teaspoon curry powder
6 tablespoons vinegar
1 teaspoon onion juice
1 sliced clove garlic

Strain the sauce. Add:
  1 teaspoon dried or 1 tablespoon
    fresh herbs
This may be served—in discreet quantities—by itself but it combines excellently with hot cream sauce or hot or cold mayonnaise. Use as much of the Mexican sauce as you find palatable.

SPAGHETTI MEAT SAUCE
                              About 2½ Quarts
Mince and cook over very slow heat:
  3 slices bacon
Stir in and sauté:
  ¼ cup chopped onion
  ½ lb. ground round steak
When the meat is nearly done, add:
  2½ cups pressed drained tomatoes
  ½ cup chopped green peppers
  1 cup chopped mushrooms or ½ lb.
    to 1 lb. fresh sliced Sautéed
    Mushrooms, page 281
    Salt, cayenne or paprika
  ½ lb. grated cheese: 2 cups
Simmer ◗ uncovered 20 or 30 minutes. If more liquid is needed after adding the spaghetti, add:
  ½ cup hot stock or canned bouillon

ITALIAN MEAT SAUCE FOR SPAGHETTI
                              About 1 Quart
Heat:
  ½ cup olive oil
Add:
  1 pressed clove garlic
  1 lb. ground round steak
  ¼ lb. ground lean pork
  2 cups Italian tomatoes
  ½ cup Italian tomato paste
  ½ cup beef or veal stock
  1½ teaspoons salt
  ¼ teaspoon pepper
  1 bay leaf
Simmer the sauce uncovered for about 1 hour. Add for the last 15 minutes:
  (½ cup sliced mushrooms)
Season it with:
  1 to 2 tablespoons fresh basil
Serve over:
  Cooked spaghetti or noodles
with:
  Grated Parmesan cheese

SPAGHETTI SAUCE WITH LIVER
                              4 Servings
Melt:
  2 tablespoons butter or drippings
Sauté in it until light brown:
  ½ cup chopped onions
Add and sauté very lightly:
  1 cup cubed liver or chicken livers
Add and simmer for about 15 minutes:
  ½ cup tomato sauce
Season with:
  1 teaspoon salt
  ⅛ teaspoon pepper
  (¼ teaspoon basil)

Serve the sauce over noodles, spaghetti, etc., garnished with:
  Parsley

BOLOGNESE SAUCE
                              About 2 Cups
This is an interesting variation on the usual meat sauce for pasta.
Melt in a large saucepan:
  ⅓ cup butter
Add:
  ¼ cup minced lean ham or
    Canadian bacon
  ¼ cup finely chopped carrot
  ¼ cup finely chopped onion
Stir and cook for 1 or 2 minutes. Add:
  1 cup chopped lean beef
and brown it over medium heat, stirring occasionally, then add:
  2 tablespoons tomato paste
  1 strip lemon peel
  A pinch of nutmeg
  1 cup beef stock
  (½ cup dry white wine)
Partially cover and simmer slowly for 1 hour. Remove from heat, take out the lemon peel and stir in:
  ¼ cup whipping cream
just before serving with:
  Green Noodles, page 172, or
  Lasagne, page 190

MARINARA SAUCE
                              About 1½ Cups
Keep this sauce on hand. Use a little on green beans or serve over meatless spaghetti.
Sauté lightly:
  1 minced clove garlic
in:
  2 tablespoons olive oil and the oil
    from the anchovies
Add slowly:
  2½ cups canned pressed and drained
    whole or Italian tomatoes
then stir in:
  6 finely chopped anchovies
  ½ teaspoon orégano
  1 tablespoon chopped parsley
Bring to a boil then ◗ reduce heat and simmer uncovered 15 to 20 minutes, stirring occasionally. If served with spaghetti, pass with:
  Grated Parmesan cheese
Try omitting the orégano and adding:
  (5 chopped canned artichoke hearts)
Simmer 3 or 4 minutes more.

SEA FOOD SPAGHETTI SAUCE
                              About 1 Quart
Heat:
  1½ cups condensed tomato soup
Melt in a saucepan over slow heat:
  ¼ cup olive oil or butter
Stir in and cook until transparent:
  ¼ cup or more chopped onion
  ¾ cup chopped green pepper
Stir in slowly:

½ cup Stock, page 491
When the sauce is hot, add very slowly,
stirring constantly:
  ½ lb. cooked or canned diced lobster,
    crab, shrimp or tuna
Remove from heat and add:
  ½ lb. diced cheese: Mozzarella or
    Scámorza
  Correct the seasoning
and stir in cheese until melted. Pour over
cooked spaghetti.

QUICK SHRIMP AND CLAM SAUCE FOR PASTA
Enough for 1 lb. Pasta

Heat in a skillet:
  6 tablespoons olive oil
Add:
  3 minced cloves garlic
and cook gently for 5 minutes. Add:
  ¾ cup finely chopped parsley
  1 cup minced clams or mussels with
    liquid
  ½ lb. shelled raw shrimp, cut in bite
    size pieces
  (⅛ teaspoon orégano)
Heat until bubbling and the shrimp is
pink. Serve at once over hot cooked sea
shell pasta—conchiglie—to complete the
marine flavor. This goes down well with
seafood addicts who don't care for the
usual tomato sauces. Pass with:
  Grated Parmesan or Romano cheese

OCTOPUS PASTA SAUCE
For 1 lb. Linguini Pasta

Heat in a large saucepan:
  1 to 1¼ cups olive oil
Add:
  1¼ cups seeded, peeled fresh tomatoes
  ⅔ to 1 cup finely chopped parsley
  1 teaspoon salt
  2 cloves garlic
To remove the garlic before serving, see
page 534. Simmer the mixture for 15 to
20 minutes. Add:
  1½ cups cooked octopus, cut into bite
    size pieces
Simmer for another 15 to 20 minutes. Toss
with the cooked, drained pasta and serve
at once.

CREOLE SAUCE
About 2 Cups

Melt over low heat:
  2 tablespoons butter
Add and cook, covered, for about 2 minutes:
  ¼ cup chopped onion
  1 minced clove garlic
  6 shredded green olives
Add and cook until the sauce is thick,
about 50 minutes:
  1½ cups canned tomatoes or ½ cup
    tomatoes and 1 cup Brown Sauce,
    page 326
  ½ chopped green pepper, with seeds
    and membranes removed

  ½ bay leaf
    A pinch of thyme
  1 teaspoon chopped parsley
  1 teaspoon white or brown sugar
  ⅓ teaspoon salt
    A few grains cayenne
  (1 tablespoon dry sherry)
  (¼ cup chili sauce)
  (2 tablespoons diced ham)
  (½ cup sliced mushrooms)

ABOUT MARINADES

Never underestimate the power of a marinade. ◆ Choose your type carefully if an
originally delicate food flavor is to be preserved. These aromatic tenderizing liquids
are easily abused. There is usually an acid
in their make-up, so any dish in which
they are soaked should be glass, glazed or
impervious metal—like stainless steel or
stainless enamel. Use wooden spoons in
stirring or turning.

The simplest marinades are, first, a
means of spreading flavor or preserving a
better color; and immersion may last only
a few minutes. Spicier, stronger marinades
may be devised to make bland food more
interesting or to mask off-flavor. But perhaps the most important function of a
marinade is to tenderize tougher foods.
Sometimes these replace and sometimes
are combined with, papaya extract, which
tenderizes.

Marinades may be either raw or cooked.
◆ The cooked ones make their flavor more
available to the food and should be prepared in advance and ◆ thoroughly chilled
before use. They are best to use if the
marinade exceeds 12 hours. Marinating is
hastened by higher temperatures, but so is
the danger of bacterial activity.

◆ Refrigerate any foods in their marinade if the marination period indicated is 1
hour or more or if the weather is hot or
stormy.

A marinade is also used in finishing a
sauce. So do not discard it before decid-
ing whether you need it for your meat
when it has been cooked. Sauce Poivrade
for venison is an example. And some
dishes, such as Hasenpfeffer and Sauerbraten, are cooked in the marinade, which
is then converted into a sauce proper—
just before serving.

When using the same marinade for
cubed meat or one whole piece, soak the
cubes for only 2 to 3 hours and the whole
4- or 5-lb. piece overnight. Longer marination may be too pungent and kill the flavor
of the meat. In an emergency, try mixing
oil and vinegar with packaged dried salad
seasonings for a quickly prepared marinade.

MARINADES FOR VEGETABLES

Marinated vegetables are usually served

cold as hors d'oeuvre or salads. French dressing seasoned with herbs, Vinaigrette and Ravigote Sauces are all suitable for the short-term marinating of vegetables. See also Vegetables à la Grecque, page 255.

FISH OR LAMB MARINADE
Enough for 1 lb. Lamb Kebabs
I. Combine:
    2 tablespoons lemon juice
    ¼ cup olive oil
    1 teaspoon salt
    ⅛ teaspoon pepper
Marinate refrigerated and covered for at least 3 hours. Turn frequently.

II. Combine:
    ½ teaspoon turmeric
    ½ teaspoon powdered ginger
    1 small pressed clove garlic
    1 tablespoon lemon juice
    ½ teaspoon grated lemon rind
Toss the meat in this mixture and leave to marinate covered and refrigerated for 24 hours.

III. Combine:
    ¼ cup pineapple juice
    2 teaspoons soy sauce
    2 teaspoons lemon juice
    1 minced clove garlic
Marinate covered and refrigerated for 2 hours, turning the meat frequently.

LAMB OR GAME MARINADE
About 1 Cup
For marinated leg of lamb.
Combine:
    ½ cup dry red wine
    ¼ cup vinegar
    ¼ cup olive oil
    3 or 4 juniper berries
    A sprig of parsley
    A sprig of thyme
    2 bay leaves
    1 crushed clove garlic
    2 slices onion
    A pinch of nutmeg
    1 tablespoon sugar
    1 teaspoon salt
    A dash of hot pepper sauce
Marinate the meat, covered and refrigerated, for 24 hours.

MARINADE FOR VENISON
For 5 lbs. Meat
Cover venison with:
    1 cup each of water and dry red wine
Add:
    6 or 8 black peppercorns
    1 bay leaf
    8 to 10 whole cloves
    1 sliced onion
    (1 small sprig rosemary)
Permit the meat to remain in the marinade,

covered and refrigerated, from 1 to 3 days. Turn it from time to time.

SASSATIES SAUCE OR MARINADE
For a 3-lb. Lamb
Soak overnight:
    ½ cup dried apricots
Cook them until soft and press through a sieve or purée in the ⅄ blender. Sauté until golden:
    3 large sliced onions
    1 minced clove garlic
in:
    2 tablespoons butter
Add and cook for a minute longer:
    1 tablespoon curry powder
Then add the apricot purée with:
    1 tablespoon sugar
    ½ teaspoon salt
    3 tablespoons vinegar
    A few grains cayenne
    6 lemon or orange leaves
Bring to a boil, then remove from heat, cool and pour over raw meat, which marinates overnight in the sauce. Fry or grill the meat, which should be cut into small, thin, round pieces. Heat the sauce to boiling and pour over the grilled pieces of meat. Serve with rice.

COOKED MARINADE FOR GAME
About 8 Cups
This is a cooked marinade, which can be stored in the refrigerator and used as needed for venison, mutton or hare.
Sauté a combination of:
    1 cup chopped celery
    1 cup chopped carrot
    1 cup chopped onion
in:
    ¼ cup cooking oil
until they begin to color. Then add:
    8 cups vinegar
    4 cups water
    ½ cup coarsely chopped parsley
    3 bay leaves
    1 tablespoon thyme
    1 tablespoon basil
    1 tablespoon cloves
    1 tablespoon allspice berries
    A pinch of mace
    1 tablespoon crushed peppercorns
    6 crushed cloves garlic
Simmer for 1 hour. Strain and cool.

BEER MARINADE
I.   2 Cups
Use for beef.
Combine:
    1½ cups beer
    ½ cup salad oil
stirring the oil in slowly. Then add:
    1 clove garlic
    2 tablespoons lemon juice
    1 tablespoon sugar
    1 teaspoon salt
    3 cloves

II. **2 Cups**
A more pungent mix for beef or pork.
Combine:
  1½ cups beer
  ½ teaspoon salt
  1 tablespoon dry mustard
  1 teaspoon ground ginger
  3 tablespoons soy sauce
  ⅛ teaspoon hot pepper sauce
  2 tablespoons sugar
  4 tablespoons marmalade
  2 cloves minced garlic

PORK MARINADE
Enough for 1 lb. of Pork Chops
Combine:
  3 tablespoons chili sauce
  1½ tablespoons lemon juice
  1 tablespoon grated onion
  ¼ teaspoon dry mustard
  2 teaspoons Worcestershire sauce
  ½ teaspoon salt
  ¼ teaspoon paprika

MARINADE FOR CHICKEN
¾ Cup
Use for chicken to be broiled or grilled.
Combine:
  ¼ cup cooking oil
  ½ cup dry white wine
  1 minced clove garlic
  1 finely chopped medium-sized onion
  ½ teaspoon celery salt
  ½ teaspoon salt
  ½ teaspoon coarsely ground black
    pepper
  ¼ teaspoon dried thyme, tarragon or
    rosemary
Mix well. Chill several hours in covered
jar or dish. Shake well, then pour over
chicken pieces. Chill about 3 hours, turning pieces at least once.

ABOUT SEASONED BUTTERS AND BUTTER SAUCES

Butter sauces are quick, tasty and simple.
The main thing is to use fresh, good butter, preferably unsalted. For other seasoned butters used as Spreads, see page
57. For Snail Butters, see page 339.
  Allow about 1 tablespoon butter per
serving for butter sauces. A few butter
sauces are melted, but most seasoned butters are creamed and served in solid form,
being allowed to melt on the hot fish,
meat or vegetables. You may form the
butter into fancy shapes and molds, see
page 56. Most of the solid seasoned butters may be prepared more quickly and
taste almost as good, when made, as
melted butter sauces. But if you use
melted butter, dress the food in the
kitchen. Make sure you spoon out the seasonings with the butter. They will sink to
the bottom if you serve the melted butter
at table in a sauce boat. There are some

butters, such as shrimp and lobster, which
are used to flavor and finish sauces, but
rarely are served by themselves as sauces.
  Seasoned butters may be ✳ frozen for
several weeks. But they ◗ should not be
refrigerated longer than 24 hours, as the
herbs deteriorate quickly.

DRAWN OR CLARIFIED BUTTER
There is no mystery about drawn or clarified butter. It is merely melted butter
with the sediment removed. But, as it is
used in so many different ways—as a
sauce for cooked lobster, to make brown
and black butter and as a baking ingredient—here is the recipe.
Melt over low heat:
    Butter
When completely melted, remove from
heat, let stand for a few minutes, allowing
the milk solids to settle to the bottom.
Skim the butter fat from the top and place
in a container. This is the clarified drawn
butter ready for use.

BROWN BUTTER OR BEURRE NOISETTE
4 Servings
Brown and black butters can only be made
successfully with clarified butter. The
sediment in unclarified butter will tend to
brown and make sauce speckled and bitter. Use for asparagus, broccoli and
brains.
Melt in a saucepan and cook slowly until
light brown:
    ¼ cup clarified butter

BLACK BUTTER OR BEURRE NOIR
4 Servings
Use for fish, eggs, vegetables and brains.
Melt very slowly, until very dark brown:
    ¼ cup clarified butter
Stir in at once:
    1 teaspoon vinegar or lemon juice
If served with brains or fish, you may add:
    1 tablespoon chopped capers
Serve immediately.

MEUNIÈRE OR LEMON BUTTER
4 Servings
Prepare:
    Brown Butter, above
Add:
    1 tablespoon chopped parsley
    1 teaspoon lemon juice
    Correct the seasoning

ALMOND BUTTER
⅓ Cup
This is often used in cream sauces, for
sautéed chicken and other "amandine"
dishes. Another version for such dishes is
Amandine Garnish, page 343.
Cream:
    ¼ cup butter
Blanch:
    ¼ cup Almonds, page 521

Remove the skins and pound the almonds to a paste with:

1 teaspoon water

Add gradually to the butter, blending well. Rub through a fine sieve.

ANCHOVY BUTTER

4 Servings

Fine spread on hot broiled fish, steak or canapés.

Cream until soft:

¼ cup butter

Beat in:

1 teaspoon anchovy paste
⅛ teaspoon onion juice
¼ teaspoon lemon juice
A few grains cayenne

BERCY BUTTER

4 Servings

Simmer in a saucepan:

2 teaspoons finely chopped shallots
¾ cup dry white wine

until reduced to ¼ original quantity. Cool. Cream together and blend into the wine and shallot mixture:

¼ cup butter
2 teaspoons finely chopped parsley
Correct the seasoning

and serve on broiled meats.

CAVIAR BUTTER

6 to 8 Servings

A lovely fish garnish.

Cream:

½ cup butter

Add:

1 tablespoon lemon juice
¼ cup black caviar
Salt, if necessary

Chill slightly, mold or cut into shapes and serve.

MAÎTRE D'HÔTEL BUTTER

4 Servings

Good over broiled steak.

Cream until it is soft:

¼ cup butter

Add:

½ teaspoon salt
⅛ teaspoon white pepper
1 teaspoon chopped parsley

Add very slowly, stirring the sauce constantly:

¾ to 1½ tablespoons lemon juice

COLBERT BUTTER

4 Servings

Use on fish and roasted meats.

Cream together:

¼ cup Maître d'Hôtel Butter, above
½ teaspoon melted beef extract or meat glaze
¼ teaspoon finely chopped fresh tarragon

SNAIL BUTTER

About 1 Cup

Should any of this be left from stuffing the snails ✻ freeze for a short period for use on steaks, fish or vegetables.

Cream until soft:

¾ cup butter

Work into it:

1 to 2 tablespoons minced shallots
1 to 2 well-crushed cloves garlic
(1 tablespoon minced celery)
1 tablespoon minced parsley
½ teaspoon salt
Freshly ground pepper

DEVILED BUTTER FOR SEAFOOD

4 Servings

Work until soft:

¼ cup butter

Combine it with:

½ teaspoon dry mustard
2 teaspoons wine vinegar
2 teaspoons Worcestershire sauce
¼ teaspoon salt
1/16 teaspoon cayenne
2 egg yolks

Beat well.

GARLIC BUTTER

4 Servings

This is good on steak, if you are a garlic fancier, or it can be used for garlic bread.

Boil in a little water for 5 or 6 minutes:

1 to 3 cloves garlic

Drain, crush and pound well in a mortar with:

¼ cup butter

GREEN OR RAVIGOTE BUTTER

Use for broiled fish, to give sauces a green color or in the making of Ravigote Sauce, page 325.

Chop until fine:

2 shallots
1 teaspoon fresh tarragon
1 teaspoon fresh chervil
1 teaspoon fresh parsley
6 to 8 spinach leaves

Blanch these ingredients for 5 minutes, then plunge in cold water, drain and dry in a towel. Pound them in a mortar or bowl. Work in gradually:

¼ cup butter
Salt, if needed

SHRIMP OR LOBSTER BUTTER

½ Cup

This should appeal to frugal cooks. It uses every last bit of your shellfish, and a deliciously flavored pinkish butter is the result. Use for finishing cream sauces served with fish or with the shellfish you have used for the butter.

Dry the shells from:

1 lb. shrimp or 1 large lobster

in a low oven for a short time. Pound them in a mortar or put them through the food grinder, so that they are broken up as finely as possible. Melt:

½ cup butter

in a double boiler ♦ over—not in—hot water. Add the shells and:

    2 tablespoons water

Simmer for 10 minutes. ♦ Do not let the butter boil. Line a sieve with cheesecloth or fine muslin and strain the hot butter into a bowl of ice water. Refrigerate and skim off the butter when it hardens.

WHITE BUTTER

                              4 Servings

Use for poached fish, making the fumet required from the same type of fish. Simmer together, until reduced to ¼ original volume:

    1 teaspoon finely chopped shallots
    ¼ cup wine vinegar
    ¼ cup Fish Fumet, page 491

Cool and add, a little at a time:

    ¼ cup softened butter

beating constantly with a sauce whisk until the sauce is creamy and whitened, rather like whipped cream.

    Correct the seasoning

Add:

    (1 teaspoon chopped parsley)
    2 tablespoons mixture of chopped fresh
        fennel, parsley, chives, basil, chervil
        or tarragon or 1 tablespoon of the
        dried herbs

POLONAISE OR BROWNED CRUMB SAUCE

                              4 Servings

A garnish for vegetables.

Brown:

    ⅓ cup fine dry bread crumbs

in:

    Meunière Butter, page 338

Garnish the vegetable with:

    Hard-cooked, finely chopped egg

and pour the sauce over it. If you wish, you may sauté:

    (1 tablespoon minced onion)

in the butter, until transparent, before adding the bread crumbs.

BUTTER SAUCE FOR CANNED OR BOILED VEGETABLES

Drain the vegetables. Permit the stock or juice to boil until it is reduced by ½. Add to it:

    Melted butter
    Seasonings

ABOUT GLAZES AND GLAÇAGE

These terms are among the very trickiest in the cooking vocabulary and we might try to straighten them out right here. They apply to both glazes for candies, nuts and desserts and to the desserts themselves. They also apply to a number of important processes and coatings for savory items.

Let's get rid of the sweet ones first, by referring to the following: Glace or Ice, page 721; Crème Glacé or Ice Cream, page 715; Glacé, as in Meringue, page 741; Fruit Glaze for Tarts, page 683; and Caramel Glaze as in Crème Brulée, page 685; transparent glaze as in Nuts Glacé, page 736, and Fruits Glacé, page 741.

And then turn to the nonsweet processes and coatings, which do so much to add color and flavor to food. ♦ To glaze meats is an expression that can be interpreted in a number of ways. If food has been Braised, page 442, or prepared à l'étouffée, page 130, it acquires, in the cooking, reduced juices which may be further reduced. Place it ♦ uncovered in an oven if the food was braised. Or hold it ♦ covered in the skillet or poêle if the food is covered with a poaching paper, before lidding. Meats may also be glazed by the use of Glace de Viande, or Meat Glaze, page 492—a specially prepared, potent and wonderful substance to use with discretion.

♦ To glaze a sauce can mean to run it under a hot broiler until it becomes golden brown.

♦ To glaze an hors d'oeuvre or sandwich may mean to apply to it an aspic jelly coating.

♦ You can, in cooking vegetables, let the butter in which they are cooked combine with their reduced juices to form a glaze. This is usually done over carefully controlled heat. Often a little sugar or honey is added, see page 341.

♦ You can coat eggs or fish with a rich white sauce—which process can be referred to as glazing them.

And last but not least, let's read about ♦ deglazing, a most vital process—usually neglected—but one that can mean so much, see page 321.

TO GLAZE A SAUCE ON A CASSEROLE

Preheat broiler.

Try this only if you have preheated your broiler well. Then run your dish quickly under the heat, until it browns delicately. Should the broiler not be hot enough and your sauce boil before it colors, it will separate into an oily, watery mass. ♦ Be sure the sauce does not touch the edge of the pot. Allow an empty area all around for expansion. It is also a wise precaution to protect the casserole by putting it in a pan of hot water. Do not leave it longer than 3 minutes. A perfect all-over brown glaze on the sauce coating fish dishes or Chicken Divan can be achieved by the following method: Reserve some of the Béchamel or Mornay Sauce and fold in whipped cream, at least 4 tablespoons to 1 cup of sauce. The more whipped cream, the smoother the browning. Put under the hot broiler and watch closely.

SPIRIT GLAZE FOR HAM

Combine:

    ½ to 1 cup dry red wine

½ to 1 cup bourbon whisky
1 cup brown sugar
6 cloves
2 tablespoons grated orange peel

Spread on the ham after it is skinned and continue to baste during the last ½ hour of cooking.

CRANBERRY GLAZE FOR FOWL
Combine:
1 cup canned cranberries
½ cup brown sugar
2 tablespoons lemon juice

HONEY GLAZE FOR MEAT OR ONIONS
Combine:
¼ cup honey
¼ cup soy sauce
1 teaspoon mustard

ASPIC GLAZE
Use this for cold meats, fish, salads and canapés.
Soak:
1 tablespoon gelatin
in:
½ cup meat or vegetable stock
Dissolve it over hot water. Add it to:
1½ cups clarified stock
Season it mildly. Chill it until it thickens somewhat. Spoon it over cold roast, cold fish, canapés, etc.

MAYONNAISE COLLÉE OR GELATIN MAYONNAISE
This coating, also known as Mayonnaise Chaud-Froid, is ordinarily used to coat or mask aspics, cold fish, meat or fowl dishes. But if you make it fairly stiff, it can be piped through a pastry tube and you can achieve the same rococo flights of fancy as when icing a wedding cake. You may also use delicately tinted mayonnaise collée, made from Green Mayonnaise, see page 315, but please avoid highly colored mayonnaise which looks unappetizingly artificial. Note that this stiffened mayonnaise serves much the same purpose as the Béchamel-based Chaud Froid Sauce opposite, but it does not hold as well or as long for the heavy oil content may cause oozing. ◖ Have the dish you wish to coat well chilled and dry.

I. Soak:
1½ to 2 teaspoons gelatin
in:
1½ to 2 tablespoons water
Beat into:
1 cup heavy mayonnaise

II. Or beat:
1 cup mayonnaise
into:
¼ cup Aspic Glaze, above
The Aspic Glaze should be at about 70° —tepid and still liquid. Once it has begun to jell, it will not beat into the mayonnaise properly. Spread it as you would frosting, with firm strokes of a spatula. Work quickly, for this mayonnaise will set at room temperature. Chill the dish until the mayonnaise is set, then decorate as described later. After the decorations have set, place the whole dish on a rack with a platter under it and glaze it with aspic glaze, which should be about the consistency of thick sirup. Your food should be very cold, so that the aspic almost sets at the moment of contact. Use a ladle which holds about 1 cup glaze and pour it on with the motion illustrated for Petits Fours, page 634. You should give the whole dish two or three coats, which should be perfectly smooth. There should be no streaks or lumps if you have used aspic of the consistency described. You may re-use the aspic which has fallen through the rack onto the platter, after straining, for the second and third coats.

SAUCE CHAUD-FROID
Chaud-Froid is so-called because it begins as a heated sauce and is served as a cold one. It has an advantage over Mayonnaise Collée, because it emphasizes the flavor of the dish it coats—for you make the sauce with the stock resulting from the dish itself. It is often used to coat whole cooked chickens, ham or veal roasts, fish or other cold buffet items.
Prepare:
2 cups Béchamel Sauce, page 322, slightly overseasoned
using chicken or veal stock or Fish Fumet, page 491—according to the dish you intend to mask. Chaud-Froid may also be made with a Brown Sauce for meats or chicken. The brown color is more appetizing to many people. Add:
2 tablespoons gelatin
softened in:
3 or 4 tablespoons stock
again using the appropriate flavor for the dish. Stir constantly over medium heat until thoroughly combined. Remove from heat and cool, stirring from time to time to prevent a skin forming. ◖ When cool enough to coat a spoon, but not set, ladle it over the cold chicken or fish in the way described above. Chill to set. The dish may need more than one coat of the sauce. Decorate and glaze.

ABOUT DECORATIONS FOR CHAUD-FROID
Decorations on dishes masked with Sauce Chaud-Froid or Mayonnaise Collée, can be as fanciful as you wish. And professional chefs achieve masterful effects. With a little practice, you can produce the same elegantly curving sprays of flowers, leaves and stems from leeks, chives, eggplant skin or green peppers. To make them pliable,

they must be blanched for about 3 minutes in salted water, then cooled immediately on crushed ice to retain their color. Chives form the stems, and leeks, etc. can be cut into leaf shapes—free-hand or with fancy cutters sketched in the illustration on page 83.

Lemon rind, carrot and red pepper, blanched as above, can be used for flower petals. Or use paper-thin slices of ham. Other materials suitable for decoration are: truffles; black olives—you can use the skins of ripe olives as a truffle substitute; pickles, hard-cooked eggs and grapes; parsley and other herbs—blanched for 1 minute; peas, capers and wilted cucumber slices.

The decorations are first dipped in clear Aspic Glaze, page 341, then applied to the dish to be ornamented, as described on page 341. If they slip after the first application of clear glaze, replace carefully with tweezers. If the decorating proves slow, be sure to chill periodically so that the chaud-froid does not darken.

Chaud-froids are often garnished with aspic jelly, chopped or cut in fancy shapes; and you may use on a suitable meat dish, foie gras balls rolled in chopped Truffles, see page 283. Lemon wedges, sprinkled with finely chopped parsley and other fancy lemon shapes are shown, page 116. To garnish with hard-cooked eggs, see page 68.

ABOUT AU GRATIN

"Au gratin" is a term that, in America, is usually associated with cheese. But the term may merely refer to a light but thorough coating of fine fresh or dry bread crumbs or even crushed corn flakes, cracker crumbs or finely ground nuts placed on top of scalloped or sauced dishes. These are then browned in the oven or under the broiler to form a crisp golden crust. Such dishes are usually combinations of cooked shellfish, fish, meats, vegetables or eggs, bound by a white or brown sauce and served in the dish in which they are cooked. If the sauce is heavy in fat, it is wise to place the scalloped dish in a pan of hot water before running it under a broiler. Or you may set the casserole or baking dish on a piece of foil, with the shiny side down to deflect the heat. Or just put the casserole in a baking tin.

Raw food may also be covered with one of the above toppings before cooking. See Scalloped Potatoes, page 291. ♦ To make au gratin mixtures quickly, put them in a blender ⅃ in the proportion and amount you need.

AU GRATIN
I. Place:
    Dry bread crumbs
in a thorough, but light, covering over the

sauced food. Bake in a 350° to 375° oven—or run it under a preheated broiler, 3 inches below the source of heat until a golden brown crisp crust forms.

II. Place:
    Dry bread crumbs and dots of butter
to make a thorough but light covering over the food, before baking it in a 350° oven—or running it under a preheated broiler, 5 inches from the source of heat, to produce a crisp golden crust.

III. Completely cover the food to be au gratined with:
    Dry bread crumbs, dots of butter
    and grated cheese
Run it under a preheated broiler, 5 inches below the source of heat, to form a glazed golden crust. The finished result should be neither powdery nor rubbery but "fondant." It will be more "fondant" if you use natural-aged American or cheddar cheese, and drier if you use Parmesan or Romano.

BUTTERED CRUMBS
Sauté:
    1 cup bread crumbs
in:
    ⅛ cup hot butter or bacon drippings
You may add a choice of:
    Chopped minced bacon
    Minced onions
    Chopped parsley
    Chopped nut meats
    Curry powder
    Paprika
    Grated cheese

CROUTONS
These dry or fried seasoned fresh breads come in all sizes. As coarse crumbs, they are an attractive garnish for noodles, dumplings or Spaetzle. In small dice, they add glamour to pea and other soups. Use in tiny dice and mound them around game, or, as larger toasts, under game or a chop. They can be spread with a pâté or be used as a spongy surface for the natural juices. In large size, they can also be placed under a dripping rack during the roasting of meats to catch and hold the juices.

I. Dice bread, fresh or dry, and sauté it in butter until it is an even brown. Or butter slices of bread, cut them into dice and brown them in a 375° oven.

II. When croutons have been sautéed or browned in the oven, drop them while still hot into a bag containing:
    1 teaspoon salt
    1 teaspoon paprika
    Ground Parmesan cheese or very
    finely minced fresh herbs
Close the bag. Shake it until the croutons are evenly coated. Add them to hot soup.

III. Use for soup, noodles or Caesar Salad.
Cut into ½-inch cubes:

> **Bread**

Sauté the cubes in:

> **Hot butter or olive oil**

You may rub the skillet with garlic or add
grated onion to the butter. Stir them gently
or shake the skillet until they are coated.
Sprinkle with:

> **Grated cheese or herbs**

ELABORATE TOPPING OR GRATIN
About 1½ Cups

Combine:

> ¼ cup melted butter
> 2 tablespoons crumbled potato chips
> ½ cup cracker or bread crumbs
> ½ teaspoon paprika
> 2 tablespoons grated Parmesan
> ½ cup dry sherry

ALMOND OR AMANDINE GARNISH
A Scant ½ Cup

This garnish is a classic. It glorifies the
most commonplace dish.
Melt:

> ¼ cup butter

Stir and sauté in it over low heat, to avoid
scorching, until lightly browned:

> ¼ cup blanched shredded almonds
> Salt, as needed

As a variation on almonds as a vegetable
garnish, try:

> (Roasted pumpkin, squash or sesame
> seeds)

EGG AND CHEESE GRATIN
About 1 Cup

This is a good topping for spaghetti or
noodle casserole dishes which have to wait
for tardy guests, as it prevents the spaghetti from drying out.
Beat until light yellow and foamy:

> **3 eggs**

Stir in, to form a thick paste:

> **⅔ cup grated Parmesan chese**

Spread over the top of the dish and bake
in a 400° oven until the eggs and cheese
are set and browned.

CHICKEN LIVER TOPPING FOR PASTA DISHES

Sauté until just done:

> **1 cup chicken livers**

in:

> **¼ cup cooking or olive oil**

Remove the livers from the pan and cut up
coarsely. In the same pan, sauté for 5 minutes:

> **1 cup sliced mushrooms**

then add:

> **½ cup halved, ripe, pitted olives**

and the chicken liver pieces. Stir and deglaze the pan with:

> **½ cup dry sherry**

Spread the topping over the spaghetti in
an even layer and sprinkle as evenly as
possible with:

> **½ cup chopped hard New York cheese**

Run under the broiler until the cheese is
toasted, about 2 minutes.

FISH

ABOUT FISH

As demographers concern themselves about our exploding population they begin more and more to consider—as a source of abundant high-grade protein—the creatures of the lakes, the rivers, and the seven seas. There are schemes for reaping the fantastically numerous, infinitely tiny plankton. There are projects for fertilizing the spawning ground of the world's more conventionally edible water-life and so harvesting familiar species more intensively than ever before.

The amateur angler, too, has been doing his bit. With America gone fishing-crazy, no housewife knows when she will answer a knock at the kitchen door and be suddenly faced with a neighbor's surplus catch in all its chill, scaly impersonality. This need not be a moment of consternation. If it happens to you, judge the gift—after, of course, enthusiastically thanking the donor—as critically as you would judge a fish offered at market. To test its freshness ♦ make sure that its eyes are bulging and its gills are reddish, that the scales are adhering firmly to the skin, and that the flesh, when you press it, is firm to the touch. The scales should have a high sheen. Also be certain that the fish has no offensive odor—especially around the gills or the belly. If it is very fresh, and you cannot use it at once ♦ see directions for freezing fish and for cooking frozen fish, page 347, and page 767. Should you be buying fish, remember that in some stores ♦ thawed frozen fish is sold with no sign or comment to indicate the important fact that it should be used at once and never refrozen. If you are in doubt about the freshness of a fish, place it in cold water. A fresh fish will float.

♦ To choose a method of cooking appropriate to a particular type of fish and to the kind of meat at hand—whether whole, filleted or cut for steaks—see the generalized recipes which come first in this chapter.

Many fish are seasonal delicacies. Available all year round are rock bass, carp, cod, eel, flounder, grouper, haddock, hake, halibut, herring, mullet, red snapper, sole and tuna.

If you are adventuring with eel, herring, some types of sole—or an officious stranger like octopus—consult the Index to see if we have some extra special suggestions for preparing, cooking or seasoning them.

SEAFISH

These include: bass, bluefish, butterfish, cod, croaker, cusk, flounder, grouper, haddock, hake, halibut, Atlantic herring, Pacific herring, lingcod, mackerel, mullet, pilchard, pollock, pompano, porgy, red snapper, rosefish, sea bass, sea trout, shad, the soles, swordfish, tuna, turbot and whiting.

FRESH-WATER FISH

These include: buffalo fish, carp, catfish, crappie, lake herring, mullet, muskellunge, yellow perch, yellow pike, pickerel, sheepshead, sucker, sunfish, brook trout, lake trout, and whitefish.

Either sea or fresh fish—depending on age and season—are eel, elver and salmon.

For those of you concerned with lean and fat fish, the following are considered in the fattest category: bloaters, bluefish, herring, kipper, pilchard, salmon, sardine, shad, smelt, and sprat, beginning at 15% fat and achieving about 30% with eel.

Now, a few more general comments. Many fish respond to Deep Fat Frying, pages 124-126, Sautéing, page 126, Pan-Frying, page 127, Broiling, page 349, and Baking, page 350. And there are fish that steam or poach well. In the latter category—a more descriptive term with which we like to replace the word "boiled"—are: cod, buffalo fish, hake, haddock, sheepshead, red snapper, grouper, pollock, halibut and salmon. Some very oily fish respond to smoking, page 756. Some others are available fresh or salted, page 354. Some fish, strong in flavor or dry in texture, respond to Marinating, pages 355, 356.

Whatever kind of fish you choose ♦ don't overcook it.

ABOUT CLEANING AND PREPARING FISH

♦ To prepare a fish for baking and stuffing, begin by spreading on a firm work surface several layers of newsprint covered with 3 thicknesses of brown paper. If the fish needs scaling, cut off the fins with scissors so they will not nick you while you are working. Wash the fish briefly in cold water—scales are more easily removed from a wet fish. Grasp the fish firmly near the base of the tail. If it is very slippery you may want to hold it in a cloth. Begin at the tail, pressing a rigid knife blade at slight angle from the vertical position to raise the scales as you strip them off. Work against the "nap"—up toward the head. A serrated scaler or a grater will be of great help in scaling. Be sure to remove the scales around the base of the head and the fins. After scaling, discard the first layer of brown paper with the scales on it. Next draw the fish. Cut the entire length of the belly from the vent to the head and remove the entrails. As they are all contained in a pouch-like integument which is easily freed from the flesh, evisceration need not be a messy job. Now, cut around the pelvic and ventral fins on the lower side and remove them. If you are removing the head, cut above the collarbone and break

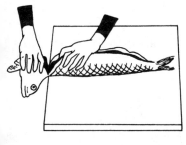

the backbone by snapping it off on the edge of the work surface as shown above. The head and pectoral fins, if they were not previously cut off, should come with it. Then remove the tail by slicing right through the body just above it. Wrap and discard the entrails, keeping the choicer trimmings for making Fumet, page 491.

If the fish does not need scaling and you are preparing it for stuffing, you can remove the dorsal fin in such a way as to release unwanted bones. Cut first down to either side of it for its full length. Then give a quick pull forward toward the head and to release it, and with it the bones that are attached to it, as sketched below.

Wash the fish in cold running water, removing any blood, bits of viscera or membrane. ♦ Be sure the blood line under the backbone has been removed. Dry the fish well. It is then ready to use steamed, baked, stuffed or unstuffed, or as steaks.

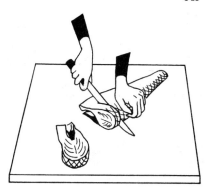

♦ To cut a fish into steaks or darnes, begin at the head end and cut evenly, as shown, into cross sections of desired thickness.
♦ To clean small fish like smelts, spread open the outer gills, take hold of the inner gills with the forefinger and pull gently. The parts unfit for food are all attached to these inner gills and come out together, leaving the fish ready to cook after rinsing.

If you cannot use a fish at once, store it at 39° temperature, preferably lidded, so that its penetrating odor does not permeate other foods in the refrigerator. Fish may be kept directly on ice if drainage is provided to prevent it from soaking up water. Length of fish storage depends largely on the condition in which it reaches you. The sooner it can be used the better, for its fragile gelatinous substances break down and dry out quickly as the fish ages, destroying flavor as they dry.

ABOUT FILLETING FISH

To prepare skinned fillets, you need not scale the fish, remove its fins, or draw it.

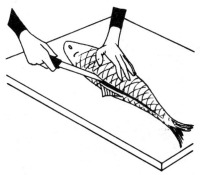

♦ To fillet—place on the work surface several thicknesses of newsprint covered by brown paper. Cut the fish, as shown, along the back ridge from the tail to a point just behind the head. Then slice down at a slight angle behind the collar bone beyond the gill—until you feel the backbone against the knife. Turn the knife flat with the cutting edge toward the tail and the point toward the cut edge of the backbone. Keep the blade flat and in the same plane with the backbone. Now, cut with a sliding motion along the backbone until you have freed the fillet all the way to the tail, see below. It should come off in one piece.

◗ To skin, place the fillet skin side down. Hold the tail firmly with your free hand as shown. Cut through the flesh of the fillet about ½ inch above the tail. Flatten the knife against the skin with the blade pointing toward the top of the fillet. Work the knife forward, keeping in the same plane and close against the skin while your left hand continues to hold the skin taut.

An exception to the above procedure must be made with a certain group of very flat fish, some of which, rather disconcertingly, have both eyes on their upper surface. All of them are skinned and filleted in a special way; and they may all be cooked by recipes for sole or flounder, including turbot, which is less flat than most.

The true English or Dover sole, whose eyes are normally situated, has the most delicate flavor and texture of them all. But fillets of flounder, plaice, dab, lemon or gray sole are often palmed off on the unsuspecting purchaser as the genuine article.

◗ To fillet these flat varieties, first skin the fish by cutting a gash through the skin above the tail. Peel back the skin for about ¾ of an inch. Grasp the released skin firmly in the right hand as shown. Hold the tail flat in the left hand while pulling steadily toward the head with the right. When skinned, flat fish reveal an indentation down the center which separates a double set of fillets—2 on the dark side and 2 on the light side. Cut through the flesh on either side of the spine. Slip the knife under the fillet—close to the bone—and cut the fillet loose from the backbone toward the outside edge of the fish. Having freed the fillets, refrigerate them, and wrap for discard in the papers on which you were working all the unusable entrails. You may keep the bone structure, skin, heads and tails for Fumet, page 491, unless the fish is a strong-flavored or oily one.

ABOUT COOKING FISH

◗ While in cooking and timing, the size and shape of the fish, and whether it is whole or divided, must be taken into consideration, the methods themselves are much the same. A good cook knows through experience how long to cook her fish, but even she will watch the proceedings with a vigilant eye to guard against overdoneness. For details of each method of cooking see the following pages. ◗ Cooking times in individual recipes apply to fish which has been removed from the refrigerator long enough to reach 70°, but no warmer.

You will sometimes see ◗ suggestions for gashing fish before cooking. This procedure is adopted chiefly for firm-fleshed fish when cooked unskinned, to prevent them from curling. Slashes may be made, too, before baking, if the fish is a very tough skinned one, to allow the heat to penetrate, or when the area of skin is large, as in turbot, to keep the skin from bursting.

◗ To test a fish for doneness you may insert a thermometer at an angle in the thickest portion of the flesh behind the gills. Fish is edible when the internal heat reaches 140°. At 150° its tissues begin to break down, allowing both juices and flavors to escape. Remove the fish from the heat, surely by 145°. Remember that because fish needs so little heat to cook, it will continue to do so on a hot platter.

If you have no thermometer, stick

toothpick into the thickest part of the fish near the backbone and separate the meat from the bone. The fish is done when the flesh is no longer translucent and flakes readily. One of the best ways ♦ to test a soft-fleshed fish is to touch it as you would a cake to see if the flesh responds by returning to its original shape after imprinting a finger.

Many fish are bland in flavor and profit by a sauce. If, on the contrary, the fish is strong in flavor, many expert cooks ♦ discard the butter or cooking oil in which it has been cooked. Otherwise, deglaze the pan, page 321.

♦ Most of our fish recipes call for cooking in ovenproof dishes. Service is simplified if such dishes are attractive enough to appear at table. This way, fish—being fragile—undergoes less handling, and you have fewer "fishy" dishes to clean up later. Single-dish service also, of course, keeps the fish warmer; but do watch for overcooking from the added heat of the dish.

♦ To keep a whole fish warm, put it on a heated serving platter in a very low oven. Leave the door ajar. For fillets, treat as above, but cover them with a damp warm paper towel or cloth. ♦ Be sure that any sauce served on the fish is very hot.

♦ To keep a sauced fish warm, use a double boiler ♦ uncovered, or place the baker in which you plan to serve the fish in a pan of boiling water and hold ♦ uncovered.

♦ If cooked fish is to be served cold keep refrigerated until the very last minute. If served buffet, place it over cracked ice.

♦ Allow per serving 1 lb. whole small fish, ¾ lb. if entrails, head, tail and fins are removed; ½ lb. fish steaks; or ⅓ lb. fish fillets.

♦ To minimize fish tastes and odors, use lemon, wine, vinegar, ginger, spring onions, or garlic in the marinating or cooking.

To remove the odor of fish from utensils and dishcloths use a solution of 1 teaspoon baking soda to 1 quart water. Pans may be washed in hot suds, rinsed and dried, and then scalded with a little vinegar. To remove the odor of fish from the hands, rub them with lemon juice, vinegar or salt before washing them.

FROZEN FISH

Frozen fish should preferably be thawed before cooking but may be cooked while still frozen. ♦ Use thawed fish immediately, and do not re-freeze. You may also thaw at room temperature if you are in a hurry, and speed up the process even more by covering the fish and placing it in front of an electric fan, see page 767. ♦ Frozen fish, when thawed, may be cooked in the

same way as its fresh counterpart. ♦ If cooked frozen, it is best baked, broiled, or cooked "en papillote" or in aluminum foil. Double the cooking time given for fresh fish, and in foil cooking add another 15 minutes to allow the heat to penetrate the foil. Freezing processes for fish have improved greatly in the last few years, and have brought us varieties hitherto not available, such as rainbow trout. But we still think that frozen fish cannot compare with fresh fish for flavor and texture. It is apt to be dry, as the gelatins lose their delicate quality, and thus needs a well-flavored sauce or a good deal of moisture or fat in the cooking process. ♦ If you are buying frozen fish from frozen food cabinets, buy only solidly frozen packages. They should not be torn or misshapen or show evidence of refreezing. ♦ Skin frozen fish before cooking it.

CURED FISH

Smoked, dried, salted or pickled—some of these cured fish can be eaten as they come, others must be cooked first. Haddock and several kinds of herring are usually ♦ Cold-Smoked, page 756. They have been salted and smoked over a smoldering fire to the dry stage, but have not been cooked. Whitefish, chub and salmon are usually ♦ Hot-Smoked, page 756, so that they cook in the heat of the smoking fire, and so can be used without further cooking. Haddock, when smoked, becomes finnan haddie. A smoked herring is known as a kipper—actually, the general term for any smoked fish. An unsalted, smoked herring is known as a bloater. It will not keep as long as a kipper. ♦ Store all smoked fish refrigerated in airtight containers to lengthen their keeping period.

Cod, mackerel and herring are often ♦ salted and air-dried, and before cooking should be soaked in water for several hours —skin side down. If soaking in fresh running water is not practical, change the water frequently during the soaking period. For ways to cook, see Salt Cod, page 354. Fish was often ♦ pickled in the days before refrigeration, and in eighteenth century English and American cookbooks you will find recipes for "caveaching" fish in spices, oil and vinegar. We imagine there is a close relationship between the French "Escabèche," and its Spanish variant, page 353, in both word derivation and method. Nowadays, herring and mackerel are usually reserved for pickling, although Escabèche can be used for small fish, like fresh anchovies, sardines, young mullet and whiting.

♦ To prepare fish dishes based on cooked fish and shellfish, see Luncheon Dishes, pages 237-242, and Hors d'Oeuvre, page 72, and Canapés, page 61. ♦ To prepare Fish Stews and Soups, see pages 161-165.

There are any number of attractive ways to serve and garnish fish. Handsome bases for cold dishes are salmon, lake trout, chicken halibut, turbot, filleted Dover sole, wall-eyed pike and carp. For directions for Cold Salmon, see page 359.

A gala way to serve a hot fish in summer is to place it on a grill above a bed of dry fennel stalks and flame it for several seconds before serving. This may also be done directly on a heat-proof platter. Another decorative and delicious addition to fish is Fried Parsley, page 287.

ABOUT STEAMING, POACHING OR BRAISING FISH

Steaming is one of the better ways to treat a delicate lean fish as far as retaining flavor is concerned; although—unlike meat—fish will lose more weight processed in this way than in poaching. Poaching—sometimes also called braising in fish cookery—runs steaming a close second.

A steamer has a perforated tray support designed to hold the fish above the water level. In a poacher, which is otherwise very similar, the tray is not elevated and allows the fish to be immersed in the liquid. ◗ A poaching tray is always greased before the fish is placed on it. Fish may be poached in Fumets, page 491, Court Bouillons, page 493, in Light Stocks, page 490, or à Blanc, page 493—depending on the flavor you wish to impart or the degree of whiteness you desire. If you are chiefly concerned with preserving the· true flavor of the fish, salted water may be all you care to use. Allow 1 tablespoon of salt for every quart of water. For details, see individual recipes.

◗ If fumet or light stock is used for the steaming or poaching liquid, you may want to use some of it either as it is, or reduced, in the fish sauce. ◗ Court bouillons are not used in this way, nor are à blanc liquids, because they are both apt to contain too much vinegar and salt.

◗ Please read the general principles of Poaching, page 129, which apply here. Small fish or cut pieces are started in a boiling liquid which is at once reduced to a simmer. ◗ Large pieces are started in cold liquid. This is especially important because immersing a fish of any considerable size in boiling water causes the skin to shrink and burst. Fragile fillets profit by the use of a poaching paper. Large fish will tolerate more liquid. In either case, allow about 5 to 8 minutes to the pound, depending on the size of the fish, from the moment the cooking liquid reaches the boiling point, and then ◗ reduce to a simmer for the remainder of the cooking period. If you do not have a poacher there is the problem, with large fish, of keeping them constantly bathed in liquid; and after cooking, of lifting them out of the pan

without breaking them. Both can be solved either by cooking them tied in a muslin

cloth or by using a cloth as described below.

A roasting or baking pan is best. If a large pan is not available, cut the fish in two and place it in a smaller pan with the halves dovetailed. The fish can be reassembled on a platter later. If served hot or cold, it can be masked with a sauce without anyone being the wiser for your subterfuge. Put in the pan with the fish several onion and lemon slices, a chopped carrot and a few celery stalks. Fill the pan with Court Bouillon, page 493, to within an inch of the top. Cover the fish completely with a piece of turkish toweling or a heavy muslin which is large enough to hang down into the liquid. Baste the cloth with the court bouillon in which the fish is cooking as it ◗ simmers on the stove or in the oven. ◗ See that the cloth is always completely soaked. The top of the fish will then cook as quickly as the bottom. If you have already wrapped the fish in muslin as described previously, it will serve exactly the same purpose as a piece of cloth over the top; so will a close-fitting domed lid or a poaching paper if the pot is sufficiently deep.

After the cooking period the fish is sometimes allowed to cool in the water. We do not recommend this practice, as it leads to overcooking and waterlogging. ◗ If the fish is to be served cold it is easier to remove the skin and trim the fish while it is still warm.

ABOUT COOKING FISH "AU BLEU"

It is the skin of the fish only, of course, which turns blue during this cooking process. The important point about cooking

ı bleu" is to have available a very fresh
ı—alive, if possible. The fish should not
washed or scaled, and should be han-
d as little as possible, merely being
iscerated. Small fish are sometimes
aned through the gills, see page 344.
rger ones, such as carp and pike, are slit
ng the belly to clean them. And, if this
olves less handling, slit the small fish,
. Both may then be poached in a vine-
· Court Bouillon, page 493. The natural
ıne of the fish, coupled if you wish with
preliminary sprinkling of boiling hot
egar all over, "blues" the skin. See
ıe Trout, page 362. They may be served
: or cold.

OUT BROILING FISH

ıling a large kingdom," observed Lao-
ı, "is like cooking a small fish." What
meant was that both should be gently
dled, and the treatment never over-
ıe. We have usually respected the
philosopher's advice. But in broiling
we have discovered that they taste
ı better when they can be subjected to
te high and intense, rather than gentle,
t. The following cooking procedure,
instance, is most effective.

'or a 2½-lb. fish, unskinned, broil in the
tom of a preheated broiler at 400° for
inutes, then move to a top broiler for 5
utes more at a preheated 800°. The
° is not a misprint. But it requires coil
burner capacity that most household
ıes are simply not equipped to supply,
page 123. The closest practical home

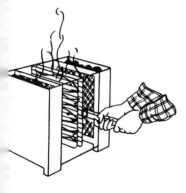

oach is to use a vertical pair of char-
grills—set as sketched—which pro-
what is known in France as a "roti"
ır than a grill. But most of us must
ontent with our range broilers pre-
ed to 550°. ♦ It helps to warm up the
ing rack in advance—thus transferring
heat at once to the fish; but be sure
grease the rack after heating so the
will not stick. If the fish is to be

turned, the hinged rack which fits into the
vertical grill, as sketched, may also be conveniently used in the oven broiler pan.
Grease it with cooking oil, and the fish
with clarified butter. A lean fish may be
floured before dotting with butter.

Fillets, flat and split fish are usually
placed about two inches from the source
of heat. If unskinned, place them skin side
down. It is not necessary to turn them, but
advisable to baste several times during the
cooking period.

If thick fish steaks or large fish are being
broiled, place the rack about 6 inches from
the source of heat. They may take as long
to cook as 5 or 6 minutes to a side.

Types of fish good for broiling include:
halibut or salmon steaks, sole and its cousins, split herring, mackerel and sea trout.
For swordfish steaks, be sure to baste with
plenty of butter, as they tend to become
dry. Melted butter, lemon wedges and
parsley adequately garnish broiled fish. If
the fish is fat, try a spicy sauce, like Tomato, page 333, Mustard, page 325, Tartare, page 316, or Devil Sauce, page 332;
if lean, Hollandaise, page 328, Béarnaise,
page 329, or one of the seasoned butters.

🗗 FISH KEBABS
Serves 6

Prepare:
    2 lbs. firm-fleshed fish: swordfish,
        halibut, cod or haddock
Cut into 1-inch cubes. Place in a glass,
enameled or stainless steel pan and mari-
nate for 30 minutes in:
    ¾ cup cooking oil
    ½ cup lemon juice
    ¼ teaspoon powdered bay leaf
    4 drops soy sauce
Stir once or twice to thoroughly coat fish.
Preheat broiler.
Thread on skewers alternating with thick
slices of:
    2 cucumbers, and
    Stuffed olives
Broil or grill for 10 minutes, turning fre-
quently and basting with the marinade.

FRIED FISH
Scale, if necessary, and clean, page 344:
    A large fish or several small pan fish:
    crappie, brook trout, sun fish, or
    perch
Cut the large fish into Steaks or Darnes,
page 345, before rolling them in:
    Seasoned flour or corn meal
    or Bound Breading, page 501
Melt in a skillet to the depth of ⅛ inch:
    Clarified butter and cooking oil
♦ It is inadvisable to use butter, when
sautéing large fish, without the addition of
cooking oil, as it burns more readily than
other shortening or drippings. When the
fat is hot place the fish in it. To keep
the fat from spattering your hands you may

cover the pan with an inverted colander.
Reduce the heat slightly and cook the fish
until done, from 3 to 5 minutes. Our
former cook, Virginia Turner, taught us
to complete cooking one side of the fish
entirely before turning and cooking the
other side until done. Larger fish may be
sautéed on both sides until seared, then
placed in a 375° oven about 10 minutes.

DEEP FAT FRIED FISH
Allow About ⅓ Pound Per Serving
Preheat deep fryer to 370°
◖ Please read About Deep Fat Frying,
pages 124-126. Have fish at 70° Clean
and prepare for cooking:
Small fish or pieces of fish not
thicker than 1 inch
Dip them in:
Fritter Batter for Fish, page 221, or
Bound Breading, page 501
Fry in deep fat for 5 to 8 minutes, or until
a golden brown. The fish will rise to the
surface when done. Drain on absorbent
paper. Serve very hot with:
Lemon wedges or Tartare Sauce,
page 316

MARINATED DEEP FAT FRIED FISH
3 Servings
Preheat deep fryer to 370°.
◖ Please read about Deep Fat Frying,
pages 124-126. Skin and cut into pieces:
1½ lbs. fish steaks
Marinate for 30 minutes in:
6 tablespoons dry white wine or
2 tablespoons lemon juice
Drain dry and dip each piece separately in:
6 tablespoons cream
then in:
Flour
Fry the fish in deep fat for about 7 minutes. Serve with:
Tartare Sauce, page 316

FISH AND CHIPS
4 Servings
Preheat deep fryer to 375°.
◖ Please read about Deep Fat Frying,
pages 124-126.
Cut into uniform serving pieces:
1½ lbs. fillet of flounder
Coat with:
Fritter Batter for Fish, page 221
Cut into thick uniform strips, slightly
larger than for French fries:
1½ lbs. mature baking potatoes
Soak in cold water for ½ hour. Drain and
dry thoroughly. Fry in the hot fat until
golden brown. Remove, drain and keep
warm. Deep fry the breaded fish until
golden brown. Arrange the potatoes and
fish on a platter and serve as a dip:
Hot cider vinegar

OVEN-FRIED SMALL FISH FILLETS OR STICKS
Allow About ⅓ Pound Per Serving
Prepare for cooking:

Small fish, pieces of fish or fish fillets
Dip the fish in:
¼ cup rich milk or cream
then in:
Seasoned bread crumbs or crushed
cornflakes
Let the fish dry on a rack for ½ hou
Preheat oven to 350°. Bake in an ove
proof dish until firm and golden. Bas
twice during the cooking period with:
Melted butter

FILLETS OF FISH SAUTÉED AMANDINE
Allow ⅓ Pound Per Servi
Dip:
Fillets of Sole
in:
Milk
Dust with:
Flour
Melt in a skillet enough to cover the b
tom well:
Butter
Sauté the fillets in the pan. Turn on
Place on a hot platter. Melt additional:
Butter
Brown in it lightly:
Blanched shredded almonds
Pour them over the fillets. Garnish
dish with:
Lemon and parsley

FRESH FILLETS SAUTÉED PALM BEACH
2 Servi
Bread if you like:
2 small skinned fish fillets
Sauté until golden brown in:
2 tablespoons clarified butter
Serve with 3 or 4 alternate sections of:
Grapefruit and orange
on each fillet. Pour the pan gravy over
garnished fillets and serve at once.

BAKED UNSTUFFED FISH
Allow ½ Pound Per Per
Preheat oven to 325°.
Scale, remove the entrails and clean:
A 3-lb. fish
A larger fish may be used, but will req
longer, but not proportionately lon
baking, see page 346. If the fish ha
tough skin slash it in several places. Pl
it on a well-greased ovenproof plat
Rub generously with:
Clarified Butter, page 338
If the fish is ◖ lean, you may bard it, p
383. If it is not barded, baste it
quently with:
Clarified Butter
Bake about 30 minutes or until do
Serve on a hot platter garnished with:
Slices of lemon
Sprigs of parsley
Stuffed Tomatoes, page 307

‹itable sauces are:

Almond Sauce, page 343, Shrimp Sauce, page 334, or Mustard Sauce, page 325

To carve an unstuffed fish, remove the ›in and cut a line down the middle of the ›posed side from head to tail. To either ›e of this line, cut pieces 2½ to 3 inches ›de. Lift off above the bone structure ›d serve. Pry up the backbone, beginning ›the tail. Slide it up and out the dorsal ‹ge. Break the spine at the neck. Lift it ‹t and lay it aside. The exposed lower ›et will then be ready to carve just as the ›per one was.

›ACHED FISH STEAKS
3 Servings

‹t into pieces suitable for individual serv-
›s:

½ lbs. halibut or other fish steak

‹ce it in a skillet. Cover with:

Boiling water

‹ason with:

4 whole peppercorns
½ bay leaf
2 teaspoons lemon juice

›mer about 10 minutes, or until tender. ›move to a hot platter. Strain the stock ‹l use it to make the sauce. Try:

Curry Sauce I, page 325, or
Poulette Sauce, page 324, or
Mustard Sauce, page 325, or
Anchovy Sauce for Fish, page 324

›H FILLETS À LA BONNE ›MME
4 Servings

‹t, wipe with a damp cloth and dry:

4 Flatfish Fillets, page 346

‹ce in a buttered shallow casserole. ›ver with:

¾ cup finely sliced mushrooms
1 minced shallot
1 teaspoon chopped parsley

‹ır gently into the dish:

⅔ cup dry white wine

›ver with a Poaching Paper, page 131, ‹ ♦ simmer 10 to 15 minutes. Remove ‹ fish onto a hot shallow ovenproof serv-
‹dish. Reduce the wine by half. Stir ♦ it gradually until well blended:

‹ cup Velouté Sauce, page 324

‹g fish stock. You may swirl in:

2 tablespoons butter

‹r the sauce over the fillets and run ›n under a broiler until the sauce is ‹tly browned. Serve with:

Boiled New Potatoes, page 293

›H STEAKS OR FILLETS ›RGUÉRY BAKED IN SEA FOOD ›CE
6 Servings

›neat oven to 350°.
‹e in boiling water or milk and simmer ‹l nearly tender:

6 fillets or 3 steaks

This will be a quick process if the fillets are thin. Drain the fillets. Place in a greased baking dish or platter. Keep them where they will remain hot. Melt:

¼ cup butter

Stir and sauté in it until done:

½ lb. mushrooms

Stir in:

¼ cup flour

Stir in gradually:

1¾ cups milk

Simmer in their liquor until plump:

½ pint oysters: 1 cup

Strain and reserve the liquor. Dry in a towel and add the oysters to the hot cream sauce. Stir in:

¼ lb. cooked shelled shrimp, split lengthwise

Remove the sauce from the heat. Add the oyster liquor and:

½ cup dry white wine
Correct the seasoning

Pour the sauce over the fillets. Bake about 10 minutes or until firm when pressed.

FILLETS OF FISH ON SPINACH WITH SHRIMP AND MUSHROOMS
3 Servings

Cook, page 300, drain and chop:

1 lb. spinach or broccoli

Poach, page 348:

1 lb. fish fillets

Cook, then shell, page 376:

½ lb. shrimp cut lengthwise

Sauté:

½ lb. mushrooms

Prepare:

1 cup Cream Sauce, page 322

using part of the stock in which the fish was poached, and part cream. Combine:

1 egg yolk
¼ cup dry white wine

Add these ingredients to the cream sauce. Thicken the sauce by stirring over low heat, but do not let it boil. Place the spinach on a buttered ovenproof dish, place the fillets on it. Pour the sauce over them. Surround them with the mushrooms and shrimp. Place the dish in a preheated 400° oven until well heated.

QUICK BAKED FILLETS OF FISH
3 Servings

Preheat oven to 350°.
Place in an ovenproof dish:

1 lb. small skinned fish fillets

Stir and heat until smooth:

⅔ cup condensed soup: tomato, celery, mushroom or asparagus
2 tablespoons milk, stock, or dry white wine

Add:

A few grains cayenne

Pour the sauce over the fish. Bake ♦ uncovered 10 minutes. Serve with:

Steamed Rice

BAKED STUFFED FISH
6 Servings

♦ If you bone a fish before stuffing, be sure to leave the skin intact. Stuffed fish, like stuffed meats, need a longer baking period to the pound. See About Cooking Fish, page 346.

Dressing for fish should not be so bold in seasoning as to destroy the naturally delicate fish flavor. Scandinavians would object to this counsel, and make lavish use of fennel in preparing many of their traditional seafood dishes.
Scale, eviscerate and clean:
A 3-lb. fish
Preheat oven to 325°.
Stuff fish with:
1½ cups Oyster Bread Dressing, page 457, or Bread Dressing for Fish, page 457, or Green Dressing, page 457
or with a combination of:
Pressed cucumbers, bread crumbs and almonds
Bake about 40 minutes or until done.
Serve with a sauce of equal parts of:
Butter and sauterne
and:
Lime wedges

BAKED FILLETS OF FISH IN WINE
4 Servings

Preheat oven to 350°.
Place in a greased ovenproof dish:
1½ lbs. fillets of sole or other fish
If the fillets are large they may be cut in half. Pour over them:
1 cup dry white wine
(2 tablespoons dry sherry)
Bake until just done, see page 346. Serve covered with the liquid from the dish, which you may reduce slightly. Garnish with:
Lemon wedges
Sautéed mushroom caps

BAKED FISH WITH SOUR CREAM
8 Servings

Preheat oven to 350°.
Split and remove the bones from:
A 4-lb. whitefish
Flatten it out. Rub inside and out with:
Paprika and butter
Place on an ovenproof dish. Cover with:
2 cups cultured sour cream
Lid the dish. Bake the fish for about ¾ hour, or until done, see page 346. Before serving sprinkle with:
Chopped parsley

FISH BAKED IN A COVERED DISH
4 Servings

Preheat oven to 350°.
This is a simple way to bring out the flavor of a delicate fish.
Combine:
2 tablespoons Clarified Butter, page 338

¼ teaspoon pepper or paprika
A fresh grating of nutmeg
Rub well over:
2 lbs. fish, preferably in 1 chunky piece
Place the fish in an ovenproof dish. Cov with a closely fitting lid. Bake 20 to ? minutes, or until done. The time depend largely on the shape of the fish. Add wh cooking:
(2 tablespoons dry white wine)
Place the fish on a hot platter. Melt:
3 tablespoons butter
Add:
2 tablespoons capers
1 teaspoon chopped parsley
1 teaspoon chopped chives
2 teaspoons lemon juice
Correct the seasoning
Pour this or some other suitable sauce ov the fish.

▤ FISH BAKED IN FOIL
Individual Servi

Preheat oven to 350°.
Clean a small fish. Rub with:
Seasoned Butter, page 338
Place on a piece of buttered aluminum large enough to make a generous fold the edges. Do not include more than 1 in each packet. Bake 35 to 40 minutes the pound.

MOLDED FILLED FILLETS OF FISH OR PAUPIETTES
4 Servi

Preheat oven to 375°.
Have ready:
8 fillets of Dover sole or blue fish, or any other very thin fillet
Butter 4 individual molds. Line each m by placing 2 fillets crisscrossed at right gles, filling the center with the farce low, or with a Fish Quenelle Mixture, p 193, and overlapping the ends of the fill to make a casing. Combine and stir w a fork a farce made of:
¼ cup melted butter
1½ cups soft bread crumbs
¼ cup chopped celery
1 teaspoon grated onion
1 tablespoon chopped parsley
(⅛ teaspoon dried burnet or basil)
¼ teaspoon salt
Fill the molds with this filling. Place molds in a pan of hot water. Bake about ½ hour. Unmold on a hot plat Garnish with:
Lemon wedges
Parsley or watercress
Serve with:
Lemon Butter, page 338, or a seaf sauce, page 334, or Oyster Sauce for Fish, page 324

PLANKED FISH
6 Serv

♦ Please read about Planking, page 127
Preheat oven to 350°.

ale, clean, wash in running water and
y:
> A 3 to 4 lb. fish

ush with:
> Clarified butter or cooking oil

ace the fish on a well-greased ovenproof
metal platter, about 18 x 13 inches. A
asoned Plank, page 127, may be used
but if used, should in the future be re-
rved solely for fish. Bake the fish 40 to
minutes; ◗ if stuffed, about 10 minutes
iger.
eheat broiler.
rnish the platter with a decorative
ging of:
> Duchess Potatoes, page 296

oil 6 to 8 minutes, 8 inches from the
rce of heat or until the potato garnish
delicately browned. Further garnish the
nk with:
> A stuffed vegetable
> Parsley, fennel or watercress

d serve.

SH IN ASPIC COCKAIGNE
> 5 Servings

pare for cooking, page 344, then cut
o 4 or 5 pieces:
> A fish weighing about 2½ lbs.

ng to the boiling point:
> 5 cups water
> 3 or 4 ribs celery with leaves
> 1 small sliced onion
> 4 or 5 sprigs parsley
> 3 tablespoons lemon juice
> 1 inch lemon rind
> 3 peppercorns
> ½ teaspoon dried herbs: tarragon,
>   basil, etc.
> ½ teaspoon paprika
> 1 teaspoon salt

p the fish into the boiling stock. ◗ Sim-
: until tender. Do not let it boil at any
e. This is a quick process, requiring
y 12 to 15 minutes or so. To test for
ieness, see page 346. Remove it at once
m the stock. Strain the stock. There
uld be about 3½ cups. If there is not,
water or chicken stock to make up the
erence. Soak:
> 2 tablespoons gelatin

4 cup cold fish stock
solve it in the hot stock. Add:
> 2 tablespoons or more capers
> 2 to 3 tablespoons lemon juice
>   or dry white wine
> Correct the seasoning

ll until it begins to thicken. Remove
skin and bone from the fish. Leave it
arge flakes or pieces. Place a layer of
in a wet mold, cover it with flaked
and repeat this process, winding up
aspic on top. Chill. Serve the aspic
cold with:
> Mayonnaise, page 313, or cultured
>   sour cream

ither of which you may add:
> to 2 tablespoons chopped herbs:

chives, tarragon, parsley, etc.
> Diced cucumbers

Decorate the platter with watercress or
shredded lettuce, and surround it with
deviled eggs, radishes and olives. Serve
with:
> Brioche Loaf Cockaigne, page 557,
> or Garlic Bread, page 586

PICKLED FISH OR ESCABECHE
> Allow ½ Pound Per Serving

Preheat deep fryer to 375°.
◗ Please read About Deep Fat Frying,
pages 124-126.
Use smelts, fresh anchovies, sardines, whit-
ings or mullets not over ½ inch thick. For
an alternate method, see page 72.
Clean, wash, dry and flour:
> 1 lb. small whole fish

Plunge them into:
> Hot cooking oil

for 5 to 10 seconds, according to size. Remove them, drain, and arrange in a shallow
ovenproof glass or earthenware dish. Using
3 tablespoons of the oil, sauté until the
onion is translucent:
> 2 tablespoons finely minced carrot
> 1 small finely minced onion
> 4 whole cloves garlic

Add:
> ⅔ cup wine vinegar
> ¼ cup water
> A small bay leaf
> A sprig of thyme
> Salt
> 2 small red hot peppers

Simmer for 10 minutes, then pour sauce
over the fish. When cooled, refrigerate for
24 hours. Serve the fish in the same dish
in which it was marinated.

GEFÜLLTE FISH OR POACHED
FISH BALLS
> Allow ½ Pound Per Person

Using two varieties of fish, lean and fat,
remove the skin and bone from:
> 3 lbs. of fish: jack salmon and white

Put the fish through a fine food chopper
with:
> 3 large onions

Place this ground mixture in a large bowl.
Slowly add, mixing well until fluffy:
> 1 well-beaten egg
> ¾ cup cold water
> 1 teaspoon salt
> ¼ cup soft white bread crumbs
>   or matzo meal
> ½ teaspoon pepper

Place heads, skins and bones of fish in a
large pan and add:
> Water to cover
> 1 large sliced onion
> 2 thinly sliced carrots
> Salt and pepper

Bring to a boil. Wet hands to facilitate
handling. Form the ground fish mixture
into small balls. Drop the balls into the
boiling stock. Reduce the heat, cover the
kettle and ◗ simmer for 2 hours. Remove

the fish balls. The fish liquid may be strained and thickened with egg yolks, page 320, to make the sauce.

SOUTHERN FRIED CATFISH
Preheat deep fryer to 370°
Clean and skin:
>**A catfish**
Dredge with:
>**Seasoned white corn meal**
Fry in hot fat until golden brown. Serve with:
>**Hush Puppies, page 580**
>**Sliced Tomatoes, page 88**

ABOUT CARP

These great, languid, soft-finned fish, whose portraits we admire on Chinese scrolls, can be admirable eating too. But be sure to hold them alive for several days in clear, running water—to rid them of the muddiness they acquire in their native haunts. To enjoy carp at their best, they should be killed just before cooking. If you cannot appoint a Lord High Executioner and must perform the act yourself, we recommend a preliminary perusal of the chapter called "Murder in the Kitchen," in Alice B. Toklas' weird and wonderful "Cookbook."

Carp lend themselves to cooking Au Bleu, page 348; are delicious baked, stuffed or braised; in red wine, page 494; and eaten hot or cold. Serve with new potatoes and Celeriac, page 272.

ABOUT COD

Through the ages cod has been one of the mainstays of the Lenten diet. It has endless variations. Salt cod, often very tough, is pounded before desalting. To freshen salt cod, leave it under running water for 6 hours; or soak it up to 48 hours in several changes of water in a glass, enamel or stainless steel pan.

Salt cod is most often used flaked. To prepare for flaking, put the desalted fish in cold unsalted Court Bouillon, page 493, to cover, then bring it to a boil and ◗ simmer for 20 to 30 minutes. Skin, bone and flake it. One lb. dried salt cod will yield about 2 cups cooked flaked fish.

SCALLOPED COD

>4 Servings

Preheat oven to 375°.
◗ Please read About Cod, above.
Cook and flake:
>**1 lb. dried salt cod**
Combine:
>**1 tablespoon flour**
>**2 cups milk**
>**1 well-beaten egg**
Cook and stir these ingredients until they are thick in the top of a double boiler ◗ over, not in, hot water.
>**Correct the seasoning**
Prepare:
>**1½ cups bread crumbs**

>**1½ cups finely chopped celery**
Grease a baking dish. Place in it ½ the fish and a layer of ⅓ the crumbs and celery. Cover with ½ the sauce and repeat the process. Sprinkle the remaining crumbs on the top. Dot with:
>**Butter or grated cheese**
Bake for about 20 minutes, or until the crumbs are golden brown.

CODFISH BALLS OR CAKES

>4 Servings

◗ Please read About Cod, this page.
Soak in water for 12 hours, drain, place in boiling water, and simmer for 15 minutes:
>**1 cup salt cod**
Drain and flake it. Rice or mash:
>**6 medium-sized boiled potatoes**
Combine the fish and potatoes. Beat one at a time:
>**2 eggs**
Beat in until fluffy:
>**2 tablespoons cream**
>**(1 teaspoon grated onion)**
>**Correct the seasoning**
Shape the mixture into balls or patties, and use one of the following cooking methods:

I. Form the mixture into 2-inch cakes, dip in flour and sauté in butter until brown. Serve at once.

II. Preheat deep fryer to 375°.
Form into 1-inch balls, dip in milk, roll in flour. Fry until golden brown.

III. Preheat oven to 375°.
Form into patties and bake in a greased pan about ½ hour. Dot with butter and serve.

FRESH COD À LA PORTUGAISE

>4 Servings

Season:
>**4 thick cod fillets**
with:
>**Pepper**
Place the fish in a heavy saucepan. Add:
>**1 finely chopped onion**
>**1 crushed clove garlic**
>**¼ cup coarsely chopped parsley**
>**A sprig of thyme**
>**3 peeled, seeded and coarsely chopped tomatoes**
>**½ cup dry white wine**
Bring to boiling point, ◗ reduce the heat and simmer gently ◗ covered for about 10 minutes. Remove the fish carefully. Arrange it on a hot serving dish and keep warm. Reduce the cooking liquid by ½.
>**Correct the seasoning**
and finish with a Butter Swirl, page 338. Pour the sauce over the fish and serve at once.

SALT COD OR MORUE À LA PROVENÇALE

>4 Servings

◗ Please read About Cod, this page.

Cook, drain, cut into 2-inch cubes and reserve:

    1 lb. salt cod

In a large saucepan fry gently until golden:

    3 tablespoons olive oil
    1 minced clove garlic
    3 large chopped onions
    1 large sliced leek, white part only

Add and simmer gently for about 15 minutes:

    1 quart hot water
    ¼ cup tomato paste
    ¼ teaspoon each dried sage, thyme, and rosemary
    1 bay leaf
    1 small hot Spanish pepper
    1 chopped green pepper, seeds and membrane removed

Add to the sauce and simmer until tender:

    2 cups peeled potatoes cut Parisienne, page 251

Add the cod to the hot sauce and set the pan over very low heat until the cod is heated through. Garnish with:

    Triangles of fried French bread
    Chopped parsley

COD SOUNDS AND TONGUES
        Allow About ¼ Pound Per Serving

Sounds — or cheeks — and tongues may come fresh or salted. If salted, they must be soaked overnight, drained, simmered for 5 minutes in water started cold, then drained again.

To poach, cover with boiling water, ◖ reduce the heat and simmer about 5 minutes. Drain. Serve this way with Mornay Sauce, page 323, or Poulette Sauce, page 324. Or you may sauté them until golden brown. Serve with Maître d'Hôtel Butter, page 339.

FRESH COD BOULANGÈRE
                    4 Servings

Preheat oven to 350°.
Parboil in separate pans:

    16 small peeled potatoes
    12 small white onions

Place in a shallow buttered heatproof dish:

    A center cut of cod or a whole small cleaned cod

Arrange the onions and potatoes around it and sprinkle with:

    A pinch of thyme
    Correct the seasoning

Brush with:

    Melted butter

Baste frequently with melted butter during the baking process. Bake about ½ hour. Serve in the same dish garnished with:

    Chopped parsley
    Slices of lemon

BROILED FRESH SCROD
        Allow ½ Pound Per Serving

Split, then remove the bones from:

    A young codfish: scrod

Leave it whole, flatten it out, or cut it in pieces. Broil as described on page 349.

ABOUT EEL

The eel is a fish which believes in long journeys. It is spawned in the Sargasso Sea in the western Atlantic, and from there will travel back to its fresh water haunts in this country or in Europe to feed and grow up in the rivers and streams frequented by its parents. The young eel or elver is still only 2 or 3 inches longer after its immense journey, and is transparent and yellowish. Little eels can be cooked and larger ones smoked or pickled to make a delicious addition to Hors d'Oeuvre or Antipasto, page 65. As with cats, there is more than one way to skin a fresh eel. We prefer the following. Slip a noose around the eel's head and hang the other end of the cord on a hook, high on the wall. Cut the eel skin about 3 inches below the head all around, so as not to penetrate the gall bladder which lies close to the head. Peel the skin back, pulling down hard—if necessary with a pair of pliers—until the whole skin comes off like a glove. Clean the fish by slitting the white belly and removing the gut which lies close to the thin belly skin.

Eel may be sautéed as for:

    Trout à la Meunière, page 361

poached for 9 to 10 minutes and then served with a:

    Velouté Sauce, page 324

or one of its variations, made from the eel stock. Skinned, cleaned, boned and cut into 3-inch pieces and dried, eel may be dipped in:

    Batter, page 221, or
    Bound Breading, page 502

and deep fried until golden brown. Serve this way with:

    Fried Parsley, page 287, and
    lemon wedges, Tartare Sauce or
    Tomato Sauce, page 333

Eel may also be broiled as for any fat fish, page 349.

MARINATED FLOUNDER FILLETS
                    6 Servings

Marinate for 10 minutes:

    2 lbs. flounder fillets

in:

    1 cup tarragon vinegar

Drain, and coat with a mixture of:

    ½ cup yellow corn meal
    ½ cup flour
    ¼ teaspoon salt
    ⅛ teaspoon freshly ground pepper

Sauté the fillets in:

    ¼ cup butter

until golden brown, about 4 minutes on each side. Serve with:

    Hot Ravigote Sauce, page 325, or
    Cucumber Sauce, page 317

ABOUT HADDOCK

Fresh haddock may be prepared as in any recipe for cod, flounder or other lean white fish. It may be baked plain or stuffed, its fillets fried, sautéed, or poached. Smoked haddock—or **finnan haddie**—may be broiled, well basted in butter, or baked, as in the following recipe.

CREAMED FINNAN HADDIE

Barely cover:
> **Finnan haddie: smoked haddock**

with:
> **Milk**

Soak for 1 hour. Bring slowly to the boiling point. Simmer for 20 minutes. Drain. Flake and remove the skin and bones. Place the fiish in very hot:
> **Cream Sauce I, page 322**

Use about ⅔ as much sauce as you have fish. Add for each cup of flaked fish:
> 1 chopped hard-cooked egg
> 1 teaspoon chopped green pepper, seeds and membrane removed
> 1 teaspoon chopped pimiento

Serve fish on:
> **Rounds of toast**

sprinkled with:
> **Lemon juice**
> **Chopped chives or parsley**

BAKED STUFFED FRESH HADDOCK
6 Servings

Preheat oven to 375°.
Sauté in a large saucepan for about 5 minutes:
> ½ cup chopped onion
> ¼ cup chopped celery
> ½ cup chopped fresh mushrooms

in:
> 3 tablespoons butter

Stir into the sautéed vegetables:
> 2 cups soft bread crumbs
> 1 teaspoon salt
> ⅛ teaspoon pepper
> **A pinch of dried tarragon**
> (A pinch of dried rosemary)

Arrange in a layer on a greased large shallow baking dish:
> **2 lbs. haddock fillets**

Sprinkle the fish with:
> **Lemon juice**

and spread the stuffing over it. Cover with:
> 3 or 4 peeled sliced tomatoes

Bake uncovered for 35 to 40 minutes. Serve with:
> **Boiled Potatoes, page 290**

BAKED FINNAN HADDIE
6 Servings

Preheat oven to 350°.
Prepare for cooking:
> **2 lbs. finnan haddie: smoked haddock**

Soak it in warm water for ½ hour, skin side down. Pour off the water. Put the fish on a greased ovenproof pan and cover it with:

> 1 cup cream

Dot generously with:
> **Butter**

Sprinkle with:
> ¼ cup chopped onions
> **Paprika**

Bake for about 40 minutes. If cream evaporates, use additional cream. The dish may be served with:
> **Cream Sauce I, page 322**

BAKED FRESH FILLETS OF HADDOCK IN CREAM SAUCE
4 Servings

Preheat oven to 350°.
Place on an ovenproof dish:
> **4 haddock or other lean fish fillets**

Prepare:
> **2 cups Cream Sauce I, page 322, or**
> **Cheese Sauce, page 326**

Season the sauce well, adding:
> 1 teaspoon Worcestershire sauce or
> ½ teaspoon dry mustard or 1 teaspoon fennel, dill or celery seed
> (2 tablespoons dry sherry)

Pour it over the fillets. Bake the fish until done, see page 346. You may sprinkle over it:
> 1 cup or more freshly cooked or canned shrimp or crab meat

Place the dish under a broiler until the top is heated. Sprinkle with:
> **Chopped parsley**

ABOUT HERRING

Herring is one of the cheapest, most nutritious and plentiful fish one can buy. It is very fat, with a calcium content twice that of milk. Split, salted and smoked, it is known as a **kipper;** smoke-cured without salt, as a **bloater.** Bloaters are very perishable and should be eaten right after curing. Perhaps the reason herring is not more popular is because it has innumerable tiny, fine bones. If you split a herring down the center of the back with a sharp knife, lever up the backbone and carefully pull it out, most of these small bones will come with it. After cleaning, page 344, you may then cook the herring in one piece or split it in two.

Marinated herring comes in various disguises. **Rollmops** are fresh herring fillets seasoned and rolled—like Paupiettes, page 352—around a pickle or cucumber. **Bismarck herring** is the flat fillet in a sour marinade; **matjes** or virgin herring can be sour or salted. Herring also comes with the roe or milt sieved and thinned with sour cream as a dressing over the fish, pages 317 and 359.

BAKED HERRING AND POTATOES
4 Servings

Preheat oven to 375°.
I. To prepare salt herring, soak overnight in water or milk to cover:

2 large salt herring

Drain and split them. Remove and discard skin and bones. They can now be used as garnish for hors d'oeuvre, on lasagne; or as follows. Cut fillets into 1-inch-wide pieces. Pare and slice very thinly:

6 raw potatoes
2 medium-sized onions

Butter a baking dish. Place in it alternate layers of potatoes, onions and herring, beginning and ending with potatoes. Cover the top with:

Au Gratin II, page 342

Bake for 45 minutes or more.

I. A Yorkshire version substitutes:

Sour apples

for the onions, and uses:

Fresh herring

In this case, prepare as above, but season with:

Salt and pepper

after each layer of herring.

MARINATED HERRING

12 Servings

Soak for 3 hours in water to cover:

24 milter herring

Change the water twice. Cut off the heads and tails. Split the herring. Remove the milt, page 359. Reserve it. Remove the bones as described, page 356. Discard them. Cut the fillets into pieces about 3 inches long. Place in a crock in alternate layers with the herring:

½ the milt
2 very thinly sliced lemons
2 skinned and thinly sliced onions
⅓ cup mixed pickle spices
1 tablespoon sugar

Cover these ingredients with:

Malt vinegar or other vinegar

Crush with a fork and add:

The remaining milt

Dilute the vinegar with a little water if it very strong. ◗ Cover the crock and put in a cool place. The herring will be ready to serve after 2 weeks.

MARINATED HERRING WITH SOUR CREAM

Prepare, as above:

6 milter herring

using only 1 lemon, 1 onion, 2½ tablespoons mixed spices and ¼ cup vinegar. Add:

1 cup cultured sour cream

Keep in a cool place. Serve after 48 hours.

SCOTCH FRIED HERRING

Allow 1 Herring Per Serving

This must be made with:

Fresh caught herring

You may fry them whole but they are better split down the backbone and boned, as described, page 356. Cut off head, tail and fins. Roll in:

Medium-ground seasoned Scotch oatmeal

pressing a little to make it stick. Fry the herring on both sides in:

Bacon fat or olive oil

Serve with:

Lemon wedges
A pat of butter

or with:

Mustard Sauce, page 325

Garnish with:

Parsley

GRILLED OR BAKED KIPPERS OR BLOATERS

Allow ½ Pound Per Serving

Preheat broiler.
An excellent breakfast dish with scrambled eggs. Do not try to grill canned kippers; they are too wet. Place:

Kippers or bloaters

skin side down on a hot oiled grill. Dot with:

Butter

Grill 5 to 7 minutes. Serve very hot. You may also bake them in a 350° oven for 10 minutes, or En Papillote, page 131, for 15 minutes at the same temperature. Season with:

A little lemon juice
Pepper

ABOUT OCTOPUS AND SQUID

These fish are similar in shape, treatment and taste. They both have long edible arms, a body that can be formed into a natural sack for stuffing if desired, and an ink-expelling mechanism. The transparent cartilage must be removed from squid and octopus before they are ready for the kitchen; and some of it, after heating and drying, becomes the cuttlebone one sees in birdcages.

Of much greater importance to us is the ink. Not only does it furnish the pigment known as sepia, but it may be used in recipes just as blood is used, page 321, to color, flavor and give body to a sauce. When the ink is not available, it is sometimes "faked" by the use of chocolate, as in Mole Sauce, page 473.

To prepare octopus and squid, remove the beaklike mouth, anal portion and the eyes—being careful not to pierce the ink sack which lies close by. If inkfish are small, this may be done with scissors; if large and tough, you will need a knife to penetrate far enough to slip them inside out and remove and discard the yellowish pouch and the attached membranes. On octopus the very ends of the tentacles are also discarded. Wash well in running water to remove gelatinous portions. Octopus, which has 8 arms, comes in enormous sizes, but is apt to be very tough if over 2 to 2½ lbs. in weight. Both these and the 8 to 12 inch squid, which have 6 arms and 2 tentacles, need tenderizing. This can be done in 2 ways: by merciless beating—native fishermen pound them on the rocks—or by adding tenderizer to a marinade.

The arms and tentacles are cut crosswise in 1 to 1¼ inch rounds and the white portions of the body meat are often cut in diamond shapes of about the same size to equalize the cooking time. ♦ To skin these sections, Parblanch, page 132, briefly 1 to 2 minutes, and arrest further cooking by plunging them into cold water. If you do not deep fat fry as for other fish, page 350—a matter of 3 to 4 minutes at 375°—long slow cooking is necessary. Even after marinating, the simmering time may run close to 3 hours, unless the specimens are very young and well pounded, when 45 minutes should suffice.

Squid is available ready to use in cans and is sometimes found frozen or dried. ♦ To use dried squid, marinate in a combination of water, gin and ginger for 45 minutes and then use in recipes as for the fresh meat. ♦ Allow about ½ lb. of fresh squid or octopus per serving.

CASSEROLED OCTOPUS
Allow ½ lb. Per Person
Clean, pound, and cut up as described previously and place in a casserole:
  6 small octopus
  ½ cup olive oil
  ⅓ cup vinegar or ½ cup dry wine
  2 cups julienned mushrooms
  1 cup chopped onions
  1 pressed clove garlic
  1 tablespoon each fresh chopped parsley, chervil and basil
  ⅓ bay leaf
Cover and bring just to a boil. ♦ Reduce the heat at once and ♦ simmer, very tightly covered, 2½ to 3 hours. You may add the ink to the pan drippings just before serving. ♦ Do not boil. Serve with:
  Creamed Spinach, page 300

BOILED SALT MACKEREL
Allow ⅓ to ½ Pound Per Serving
Soak overnight, skin side up, well covered with cold water:
  Salt mackerel
Drain, place in a shallow pan, cover with water and simmer until tender, for about 12 minutes. Drain well. Place on a hot platter. Pour over the fish:
  Melted butter
to which add:
  Chopped chives or parsley, lemon juice or Worcestershire sauce

BROILED FRESH MACKEREL
Preheat broiler.
Split and bone:
  A Mackerel, page 344

Place it skin down in a greased pan. Sprir kle with:
  Paprika
Brush with:
  Melted butter or olive oil
Broil slowly on one side only until firm about 20 minutes. Baste with the drip pings while cooking. Remove to a he platter. Spread with:
  Anchovy Butter, page 339
Garnish with:
  Parsley and lemon slices

BROILED SALT MACKEREL
Allow ⅓ to ½ Pound Per Servin
Soak by the preceding recipe:
  Salt mackerel
Drain, then wipe dry.
Preheat broiler.
Brush with:
  Melted butter
Broil, skin side down. Baste twice wit melted butter while cooking. Remove to hot platter. Pour over the fish:
  ½ cup Cream Sauce I, page 322
Garnish with:
  Chopped parsley

ABOUT PIKE, PICKEREL AND MUSKELLUNGE

These fish, which are naturally dry, ma be marinated or not, as desired, befor cooking. Many cooks prefer to bake o braised them, page 348.

POMPANO EN PAPILLOTE
                                              Individual Servin
Preheat oven to 450°.
Place on heart-shaped parchment paper page 131:
  2 medium-sized skinned pompano fillets
Cover with:
  2 tablespoons Veloutè Sauce, page 324
  2 chopped cooked shrimp
  2 tablespoons chopped cooked crab meat
Close the parchment paper, fold the edg and bake for about 15 minutes until th paper is browned and puffed. Serve imme diately. For a party, make individua packets ahead of time, refrigerate and before serving, allow them to reach abou 60°. Preheat oven and bake as above.

ABOUT SALMON

Atlantic salmon, pink and prized, comes t our markets mainly in fresh form. Pacifi salmon reaches us in many forms. Thes include the choice King or Chinook from Alaska and the Columbia River areas. The may be pink or white-fleshed, and are about 17% fat. Included also are the red fleshed sockeye, the pinkish silver Coh and the yellowish-fleshed, almost fat-free dog salmon. ◗ All smoked salmon is highly perishable and should be kept refrigerated even when canned. Regular canned salmon, if in tall cans, is tail meat; if in squat cans it comes from the center cuts.

BROILED SALMON STEAKS OR DARNES
Allow ½ Pound Per Serving

Preheat broiler.
To cut steaks or darnes, see page 345.
Brush preheated broiler rack and:
   ¾-inch-thick salmon steaks
well with:
   Clarified Butter, page 338
Place rack 6 inches from the source of heat. Broil 5 minutes. Baste, turn, baste again and continue to broil 5 to 8 minutes. To test for doneness, see if you can lift out the central bone without bringing any of the flesh with it. Serve with:
   Freshly grated horseradish
The steak shape lends itself to attractive service as the hollow may be filled with:
   A stuffed tomato, or
   A mound of vegetables, or
   Potatoes garnished with parsley

COLD GLAZED SALMON
Allow ½ Pound Per Serving

This method of preparation applies to any fish you wish to glaze and serve cold.
Poach, page 348, leaving head and tail on:
   1 large cleaned salmon
Remove from the poaching water as soon as it is done. Leaving the head and tail as it is, and working with the grain, skin and trim the rest of the fish, removing the fins and the gray, fatty portions until just the pink flesh is left. Place on a large serving platter and refrigerate. If you have an emergency, the fish may be eaten just this way with mayonnaise. But to glaze—read on. ◗ Work quickly to prevent the glaze from darkening, and keep chilling between processes. Coat the visible pink portion of the fish evenly and smoothly with:
   Mayonnaise Collée, page 341, or
   Sauce Chaud-Froid, page 341
Rechill until this sauce has set. Decorate as described in the Sauce Chaud-Froid recipe. Chill again. Coat the whole surface, head and tail too, with:
   Aspic Glaze, page 341
Chill and continue coating and chilling until you have built up an even clear ¼ inch of aspic. Clean the platter by removing aspic dribbles. Save any leftover aspic and chill it in sheet form. Chop it fine and surround the fish with an edging of little sparkling tidbits. Serve the fish with:
   Cold Mousseline Sauce, page 329, or
   Green Mayonnaise, page 315
The classic garnish is:
   Tiny tomatoes stuffed with Russian Salad, page 83
We suggest also:
   Cold Leeks Vinaigrette

ABOUT SARDINES

Sardines were to us something that came out of a can on laundry day until one summer we had a Breton guest. Her family had for centuries lived an amicably divided life in seaside castles on opposite sides of a river inlet. Her uncle's fleets dredged seaweed from which chemicals were produced. Her father's fleet sailed from Maine to Spain—following those Atlantic sardines which were fit even for the Czar of Russia, himself, to whom they were purveyed. But fish, like people, may change habits suddenly. For three years the fleet failed to find the sardine runs. Sonar might have changed Odette's fate, but Brittany's loss was our vivacious and warmhearted gain.

Pacific sardines are almost twice as large as the Atlantic kind, and both are bigger than the type of pilchards originally caught off Sardinia. Anchovies are even smaller sardines. When smoked, sardines are referred to as sprats. Treat fresh sardines as for Smelts, page 360.

If you want to present canned sardines in an interesting way, skin and bone:
   12 canned sardines
Mash 6 of them with:
   1 teaspoon minced onion
   2 teaspoons butter
   ½ teaspoon prepared mustard
   1 teaspoon lemon juice
Spread:
   6 narrow toasts
with this mixture. Place a whole sardine on each toast and run under the broiler. Before serving garnish with:
   Finely chopped fennel
   A grating of black pepper

ABOUT SEA SQUAB OR BLOWFISH
These puffers are related to the sought after Japanese fugu. As the ovaries and liver are very poisonous be sure to discard all but the back flesh before cooking. Prepare as for any delicate fish.

ABOUT ROE AND MILT

The eggs of the female fish are known as roe or hard roe; the male fish's sperm is known as milt or soft roe, as its texture is creamy rather than grainy. Both types are used in cooking and the roe of certain fish is more valued than the fish itself, see Caviar, page 72.

Shad roe is considered choice. You may serve the roe or milt of other fish such as herring, mackerel, flounder, salmon, or cod as in the following recipes for shad roe. The milt of salmon must have the vein removed.

Hard roe, to be cooked and served alone, should be pricked with a needle to prevent the membrane from bursting and splattering the little eggs. Cook roe gently

---

with very slow heat. Overcooked, it is hard, dry and tasteless. It may be served as a luncheon dish; as a savory; as stuffing or garnish for the fish from which it comes. Or it may be used raw, as in Marinated Herring, page 357, or as an hors d'oeuvre. Also see Canned Roe Dishes, page 242.

♦ Allow 6 oz. Per Serving.

PARBOILED SHAD ROE

♦ Please read About Roe, above.

Prick with a needle in several places and cover with boiling water:

    Shad roe

Add to it:

    2 tablespoons lemon juice or
    3 tablespoons dry white wine

Simmer from 3 to 12 minutes, according to size. Drain and cool. Remove the membrane. Add salt if needed. The roe is now ready to be sautéed, sauced, or used in a garnish or hors d'oeuvre.

BAKED SHAD ROE

Preheat oven to 375°.

Parboil:

    Shad roe

Place in a buttered pan. Cover with:

    Creole Sauce, page 333, or
    Mushroom Sauce, page 327

Bake for 15 or 20 minutes, basting every 5 minutes.

SAUTÉED SHAD ROE

Heat until light brown:

    2 tablespoons Clarified Butter,
    page 338

Sauté in this until delicately browned on both sides:

    Parboiled Shad Roe, see above
    Correct the seasoning

Remove to a hot platter. Add to the drippings and heat:

    2 teaspoons lemon juice
    ½ teaspoon chopped chives
    ½ teaspoon chopped parsley
    1 minced shallot
    ½ teaspoon dried tarragon, chervil
    or basil

Pour the sauce over the roe. Sautéed roe is frequently served with Tartare Sauce, page 316. Or sprinkle with:

    Chopped parsley, lemon juice
    and Brown Butter, page 338

Surround with:

    Orange sections

BROILED SHAD ROE

Preheat broiler.

Parboil, page 132, wipe dry and place on a greased rack:

    Shad roe

Sprinkle with:

    Lemon juice

Bard with:

    Bacon

Broil from 5 to 7 minutes. If the roe is large, you may have to turn it, baste with

drippings and cook until firm. Serve on toast garnished with:

    Maître d'Hôtel Butter, page 339
    Parsley

BAKED SHAD WITH CREAMED ROE

6 to 8 Servings

Preheat oven to 350°.

Parboil, page 132:

    Shad roe

♦ Simmer for 15 minutes. Drain. Remove the outside membrane. Mash the roe. Melt in a saucepan:

    2 tablespoons butter

You may add and sauté for about 3 minutes:

    1 tablespoon grated onion

Add the roe and stir in:

    2 tablespoons flour
    ½ cup cream

When these ingredients begin to boil, remove from heat. Stir in:

    2 egg yolks

Season the roe mixture well with:

    Dry white wine or lemon juice

Keep hot. Bone, page 346:

    A 3 or 4 lb. shad

Place it skin side down on a well-greased broiler rack or a flat pan. Brush it with:

    Melted butter

Bake, allowing about 8 minutes per pound. Remove from the oven and spread the thin part of the fish with the creamed roe. Cover the fish with:

    Au Gratin Sauce II, page 342

Return to the broiler and brown evenly. Serve at once garnished with:

    Lemon slices
    Parsley or water cress
    Pickled beets or cucumbers

ABOUT CARVING SHAD

Carving shad is a very direct process. Before cooking, every effort must be made to remove as many bones as possible. Even tweezers may be resorted to. When carving time comes, the fish is sliced completely through its entire thickness in about 4-inch parallel widths. Any exposed bones may again be removed with tweezers before the cut pieces are put on the individual plates.

ABOUT SHARK

If you care to adventure, you will find that shark meat—close to and along the backbone—responds to recipes for Fish Fillets, pages 350-352, or to Poaching, page 348. The belly sections need long simmering.

SMELTS

2 Servings

Clean, see page 344, rinse thoroughly and wipe dry:

    12 smelts

Leave whole. Season with:

    Lemon juice

Let them stand covered for 15 minutes.
Roll the smelts in:
Cream
Dip in:
Flour or corn meal

I. Melt:
¼ cup butter
Sauté the smelts gently until they are done.

II. Bake smelts in a buttered pan in a
450° oven for about 5 minutes. Place
them on a hot platter. Add to the butter
in the pan:
Juice of 1 lemon
**2 tablespoons chopped parsley or
chives**
Pour the sauce over the smelts.

III. ♦ Please read About Deep Fat Frying,
pages 124-126. Smelts may be dipped in
crumbs or egg and crumbs and fried in
deep fat at 370° about 3 minutes. Serve
with:
Tartare Sauce, page 316

BAKED RED SNAPPER WITH
SAVORY TOMATO SAUCE
                                    4 to 6 Servings
Preheat oven to 350°.
Prepare for cooking:
**A 3-lb. red snapper or other
large fish**
Dredge it inside and out with:
Seasoned flour
Place in a baking pan. Melt:
6 tablespoons butter
Add and simmer for 15 minutes:
½ cup chopped onion
2 cups chopped celery
**¼ cup chopped green pepper, seeds
and membrane removed**
Add and simmer until the celery is tender:
3 cups canned tomatoes
1 tablespoon Worcestershire sauce
1 tablespoon catsup
1 teaspoon chili powder
½ finely sliced lemon
2 bay leaves
1 minced clove garlic
1 teaspoon salt
A few grains red pepper
Press these ingredients through a potato
ricer or food mill. Pour the sauce around
the fish. Bake the fish for about ¾ hour,
basting frequently with the sauce.

SOLE AMBASSADOR
                            Allow ½ lb. Per Person
Prepare for poaching:
**10 fillets of sole, lemon or English, trout
or halibut**
Place them in a buttered heatproof dish or
skillet and sprinkle with:
**1 tablespoon finely chopped shallot
or onion**
Salt and pepper
Add:
½ cup dry white wine
Juice of 1 lemon

Cover with a buttered poaching paper,
page 129, and simmer until the fillets are
done, see page 346. While they are cooking, melt in a heavy casserole:
1 tablespoon butter
Sauté:
1 cup finely chopped mushrooms
Juice of ½ lemon
Salt and pepper
Cook over high heat for about 3 minutes,
until the juices disappear. Reduce heat.
Add:
½ cup whipping cream
♦ Simmer until reduced by ⅓. Remove
from the heat and beat in:
1 egg yolk
Drain and save the stock from the fish. On
a heatproof serving platter, spread the
mushroom mixture, and arrange the fillets
over it. Heat the fish stock and add:
Kneaded Butter, page 321
Beat in well until thickened. Add:
½ cup whipping cream
Heat to the boiling point. ♦ Remove from
the heat and add:
3 egg yolks
Strain the sauce and pour it over the fish
fillets. Glaze under the broiler until brown.
Serve at once.

FILLET OF SOLE FLORENTINE
                                    6 Servings
Poach, page 348:
6 fillets of sole or other fish
In the bottom of an ovenproof platter, put
a layer of:
1½ cups Creamed Spinach, page 300
Arrange the poached, drained fillets on
top. Cover with:
**1 cup seasoned Cream Sauce II,
page 322**
Sprinkle over it:
Au Gratin III, page 342
Run under the broiler to heat through until the sauce is glazed.

SWORDFISH STEAKS
Prepare as for:
Salmon Steaks, page 359
As this fish dries out even when in prime
condition, be sure to use plenty of butter
in the cooking.

BROOK TROUT MEUNIÈRE
                                    4 Servings
Clean and wash:
4 brook trout: 8 inches each
Cut off the fins. Leave the head and tail
on. Dip in:
Seasoned flour
Melt:
¼ cup Clarified Butter, page 338
Sauté the trout until they are firm and
nicely browned. Remove to a hot platter.
Add to the drippings in the pan:
3 tablespoons clarified butter
Let it brown. Cover the fish with:
Chopped parsley

Pour the browned butter over the fish.
Garnish with:
    Lemon wedges

BROILED LAKE TROUT
OR WHITEFISH
                Allow About ½ Pound Per Serving
Preheat broiler.
Bone, page 344:
    A large fish, lake trout, whitefish, etc.
Flatten it out or cut it into pieces. Rub a
saucer with
    Garlic
Place in it and mix:
    1 or 2 tablespoons olive oil
    ¼ teaspoon white pepper
Rub the fish on both sides with these in-
gredients. Place it in a greased shallow
pan. Broil until brown, turning it once.
Spread with:
    Maître d'Hôtel Butter, page 339,
    or Lemon Butter, page 338
Garnish with:
    Parsley
    Cucumbers in Sour Cream, page 86

BLUE TROUT OR TRUITE AU BLEU
                Allow One 4 to 6½ Ounce Trout
                                        Per Person
Please read About Cooking Fish "Au Bleu,"
page 348. The amazingly brilliant blue
color of this dish can be achieved only if
your fish is alive when ready for the pot.
We ate these first in the Black Forest at an
inn bordering a stream, but we think of
them always in connection with Joseph
Wechsberg's zestful book, "Blue Trout and
Black Truffles."
Have ready and boiling:
    Seasoned Acidulated Water with
    lemon juice or vinegar, page 494
allowing 2 tablespoons acid per fish. Kill
the fish with one sharp blow on the head.
Split and clean it with one stroke if possible. Be careful not to disturb the slime
on the body of the fish. Plunge it at once
into the boiling water. Let this come to a
boil again, then remove the pan from the
heat and cover it. Let stand for about 5
minutes. Slightly larger fish may need another 2 or 3 minutes. The white eyeballs
pop out when the fish is done. Remove the
fish and drain well. The classic service is
on a napkin on your best silver salver, accompanied by a garnish of:
    Parsley
with:
    Boiled or steamed potatoes and

    sweet butter balls, or melted butter
You may also serve other fancy butters or:
    Hoilandaise Sauce, page 328
But why add earrings to an elephant? If
you serve the fish cold, pass:
    Gribiche Sauce, page 315 or
    Ravigote Sauce, page 311

FRESH TUNA OR BONITO
                Allow ½ Pound Per Serving
Clean:
    A fresh tuna or bonito
Braise or roast as for veal, or brush the
delicate stomach sections with:
    Cooking oil
and broil. For recipes for canned tuna
see Index.

POACHED TURBOT
                Allow ½ Pound Per Serving
This firm-fleshed, very white flat fish may
be skinned and filleted, page 346, and
poached in Court Bouillon, page 493, part
wine or part milk to reinforce its white
ness, and cooked as for any recipe for
Sole, page 361. As both the skin and the
gelatinous areas near the fins are consid
ered delicacies, turbot is often prepared
and served unskinned. To keep it from
curling or bursting cut a long gash down
the center of the under or brown side be
fore poaching.
To cook in the skin, place the fish in a
greased pan; float it in a cool:
    Court Bouillon
Cover with a poaching paper, page 129.
Bring the liquid to a boil. ♦ Reduce the
heat at once. Barely simmer for about 30
minutes, basting several times during the
cooking. Be sure to replace the paper
after each basting.

WHALE
                Allow ½ Pound Per Serving
Last—but vast.
If whale meat is frozen, thaw before cook
ing. Whether fresh or frozen, soak for
hour in a solution of:
    1 tablespoon baking soda to
    1 quart water
Rinse well and marinate 1 to 2 hour
♦ covered with a liquid made up of:
    3 cups water
    1 cup vinegar
Cut across the grain into thin steaks no
over ½-inch thick. Sprinkle with:
    Lemon juice
and pound, page 383, to tenderize further
Stew, braise or sauté as for beef, which i
resembles more than it does fish.

SHELLFISH

ABOUT MOLLUSKS AND CRUSTACEANS

Connoisseurs dispute as to which stretches of the world's seacoast provide the best breeding grounds for shellfish and are ready to do battle over the relative merits of oysters and mussels versus lobsters and crabs. We hope to sidestep most of these controversies in the pages which follow. We hope also to clarify the distinction, along the way, between lobster, page 372, langouste, page 373, and langoustine, page 376, and between crevettes, scampi, page 378, and écrevisses, page 378; sneaking in a few succulent freshwater anomalies like crawfish and frogs, as well as the land-based snail. And we will put our chief emphasis on how to cook so as to retain just-caught flavor. Details for handling and keeping are given in each shellfish category.

In cooking, we beg you to ♦ use low heat, unless otherwise indicated, to ♦ use the shortest possible cooking period and to serve at once. If these delicacies are eaten raw, be sure they are served properly chilled. Shrimps, prawns, lobsters and crabs are regarded as rather indigestible. Consider an accompanying citrus or vinegar sauce, which will both stimulate the gastric juices and help break down food fibers. Keep in mind that ♦ commercial shellfish collection is permitted only in areas where the waters are unpolluted and that if you collect on your own, be sure the water in the area is safe. ♦ Recipes for mussels, oysters and clams are fairly interchangeable; and some exciting dishes may be created by combining mollusks and crustaceans.

Seafood is often seasoned with wines. For every 6 servings, allow 2 tablespoons dry sherry, 4 tablespoons white wine or 1 tablespoon cognac.

SHELLFISH COCKTAILS

Serve these well chilled, preferably in glasses imbedded in ice. If serving individually, allow about ⅓ cup of seafood per person with about ¼ cup sauce. You may pour the sauce over the seafood, serve it separately for dipping or toss the seafood in the sauce and serve it on lettuce, endive or cress. For appropriate sauces, see:
Russian, page 316, or Seafood Dips and Sauces, pages 74 and 312
Serve with these cocktails:
Oyster crackers
Cheese crackers
Pretzel sticks
Potato chips
Olives

ADDED COLOR AND FLAVOR IN SEAFOOD DISHES

To 3 well crushed lobster shells and 2 lbs. shrimp shells, add ½ bottle of white wine. Reduce to ½ to ⅓. A bright red sauce results which, when tepid, can be added with puréed shrimp or lobster to Hollandaise Sauce. Purée of pimiento can also be used.

ABOUT OYSTERS

These shellfish, edible at any time, are best in flavor when they are not spawning. As Southern oysters spawn all during the year, they do not have the fine flavor of Northern types and are, therefore, often served highly condimented. These bivalves have one shallow and one deep shell and it is in the deeper shell that they are served raw or baked. Some canny diners have been known to ask for them in restaurants on the shallow shell, in the hope of getting them absolutely freshly opened. Oysters in the shell should be alive. If they gape and do not close quickly in handling, discard them. Also discard any with broken shells.

♦ To open oyster shells, provide yourself first with a strainer and a bowl in which to catch the juices. Hold a well-scrubbed oyster, deep shell down, in a folded napkin in the palm of one hand—work over the strainer and bowl. Insert the edge of an oyster knife into the hinge of the shell. Turn the knife to pry and lift the upper shell enough to insert the knife to cut the hinge muscle. Then run the knife along between the shells to open. The oysters are then ready to be served on the half shell. This procedure is not easy until you have the knack. Should you grow desperate in this shucking process, you may be willing to sacrifice some flavor for convenience. If so, place the oysters in a 400° oven from 5 to 7 minutes, depending on size, drop them briefly into ice water and drain. They should open easily. ♦ To shuck, no matter how you open them, release the oysters from the shell with a knife. Examine each oyster with your fingers to be sure no bit of shell is adhering to it. Drop the oyster into a strainer. If the oysters are sandy, you may rinse them in a separate bowl, allowing ½ cup cold water to each quart of shucked oysters. Pour it over the oysters and reserve the water. In using the oyster liquor and the water mixture, be sure to strain it through a fine muslin to free it from grit. ♦ Before using oysters in any fried or creamed dish, dry them carefully in an absorbent towel.

If oysters have been bought already opened, in bulk, be sure to free them of bits of shell. They should be plump and creamy in color. The liquor should be clear, not cloudy, and should have no sour or unpleasant odor. If plump oysters burst during the cooking, they have been previously soaked in fresh water to plump them and their flavor as well as their texture has been ruined. Oystermen claim they can easily tell the sex of oysters and insist that females should be fried and males should be stewed. ♦ Allow 1 quart undrained, shucked oysters for 6 servings. It is hard to estimate amounts for oysters on the shell, as they vary in size—6 moderate-sized Eastern oysters would equal about 20 Olympia West Coast oysters.

♦ To store oysters in the shell, refrigerate at 39°, not directly on ice. Keep dry. Store shucked oysters at the same temperature, covered by their liquor, in a closed container. The container may be put in crushed ice, up to about ¾ its height. If you received them fresh, oysters may be stored in this way up to 5 days.

For other oyster suggestions, see Hors d'Oeuvre and Canapés, pages 62 and 73. For cooked oyster suggestions and oyster cakes, see Luncheon Dishes, page 237. Champagne is a fine accompaniment.

OYSTERS ON THE HALF SHELL
Allow 5 to 6 Oysters per Serving
♦ Please read About Oysters, page 363.
Scrub well and ♦ open just before serving:
> Oysters

Chill them well. Arrange them in cracked ice on the serving plates. You may place, in the center, a small glass of:
> Cocktail Sauce, page 312, or
> Lorenzo Dressing, page 311

or you may serve them with:
> Lemon wedges and horseradish sauce

BROILED OYSTERS
Allow 6 Oysters per Serving
♦ Please read About Oysters, page 363.

Preheat broiler.
Shuck, drain and dry in a towel:
> Oysters

Place them on a well-buttered baking sheet. Broil them for about 3 minutes, turning once during this time. They should be lightly browned. Serve them with:
> Lemon wedges, Parsley or Lemon Butter

☰ GRILLED OYSTERS
Allow 6 Oysters per Serving
You may grill Western oysters—except Olympias—right on the coals without toughening them, but if you have Eastern oysters put them on a piece of foil in which you have punched holes, before placing them on your grill over a bed of coals.
I. Put on the foil:
> Scrubbed, unopened oysters in their shells

Grill until the shells pop. Season and serve with:
> Lemon wedges
> Melted butter

II. Open:
> Scrubbed oysters

Sprinkle them with a:
> Gremolata, page 541

Heat for a few minutes on the grill over moderate coals.

DEEP-FAT FRIED OYSTERS
2 Servings
♦ Please read About Deep-Fat Frying, pages 124-126.
Preheat deep fryer to 375°.
Drain:
> 12 large shucked oysters

Dry them well between towels. Beat together:
> 1 egg
> 2 tablespoons water

Inserting a fork in the tough muscle of the oysters, dip them in the egg, then in:
> Seasoned bread crumbs

in the egg again and again in the crumbs. Permit the oysters to dry on a rack for ½ hour. Fry them in deep fat for about ½ minutes.

SAUTÉED OYSTERS
2 Servings
Bread, as above, for Deep-Fat Fried Oysters:
> 12 large shucked oysters

When they are dry, sauté them until they are golden in a combination of:
> 3 tablespoons cooking oil
> 2 tablespoons butter

Serve at once.

BAKED OYSTERS
6 Oysters per Serving
Preheat oven to 475°.

Have ready:
    Oysters on the half shell
Cover them with:
    1 tablespoon Creamed Seafood,
      this page
Sprinkle them with:
    Bread crumbs
Bake for about 10 minutes or until golden.

CREAMED OYSTERS
                    4 Servings
Please read About Oysters, page 363.
Drain and dry:
    1 pint oysters
Reserve the liquor. Melt in a saucepan:
    2 tablespoons butter
Add and stir until blended:
    2 tablespoons flour
Stir in slowly:
    1 cup oyster liquor or oyster liquor
      and cream, milk or chicken stock
Add:
    ½ teaspoon salt
    ⅛ teaspoon paprika or cayenne
    (½ to 1 teaspoon curry powder)
When the sauce is smooth and hot, add the
drained oysters. Heat them to the boiling
point, but do not allow the sauce to boil.
When the oysters are thoroughly heated,
season them with:
    1 teaspoon lemon juice, ½ teaspoon
      Worcestershire sauce or
    2 tablespoons dry sherry
Serve them at once in:
    Bread Cases, page 223, patty shells
      or on hot buttered toast
Sprinkle them generously with:
    Chopped parsley

SCALLOPED OYSTERS
                    6 Servings
Preheat oven to 350°.
Have ready:
    1 quart shucked oysters in their liquor
Find a deep buttered casserole. Place in
the bottom a:
    ½-inch layer of coarsely crushed soda
      crackers
Put in a layer of the oysters. Season with:
    Salt and pepper
    Bits of butter
    2 cups cream
Sprinkle with another layer of:
    Crushed crackers
Bake 45 to 50 minutes.

OYSTERS SCALLOPED IN CANNED SOUP
                    6 Servings
Please read About Oysters, page 363.
Preheat broiler.
Drain and dry, reserving the liquor:
    1 pint small oysters: 2 cups
Combine:
    1 cup dry bread or cracker crumbs
    3 tablespoons melted butter
    ¼ teaspoon salt
    1 teaspoon minced parsley

Heat to the boiling point:
    1 can cream of celery, mushroom or
      chicken soup: 10½ oz.
    The oyster liquor or 4 tablespoons
      water
or replace 1 tablespoon of the liquor with:
    (Catsup)
Add the oysters. Cook them until the edges
begin to curl. Place ½ the buttered crumbs
in a hot casserole, add the oysters and soup.
Top with the remaining crumbs. Place
the dish under a broiler until the top is
brown.

OYSTER CELERY
                    4 Servings
Preheat oven to 350°.
Prepare:
    Creamed Oysters, this page
Before adding the oysters thicken with:
    2 egg yolks
Season with:
    Dry sherry
Place in a baking dish:
    ¾ cup white, peeled, diced celery
Cover with the creamed oysters and dust
with:
    Parmesan cheese
Bake until golden, about 15 minutes.

BAKED CREAMED OYSTERS AND SEAFOOD
                    6 Servings
Do not take this dish too literally. Change
the proportions and substitute crab, tuna,
etc., to suit yourself. It's a grand basic dish
with which to work.
Preheat oven to 375°.
Prepare:
    Creamed Oysters, this page
Add:
    1 cup cooked chopped shrimp, lobster,
      crab meat, tuna, scallops or leftover
      cooked fish
Cover with:
    Au Gratin II or III, page 342
Bake about 10 minutes.

OYSTERS IN MUSHROOMS AU GRATIN
                    4 Servings
Preheat oven to 375°.
Sauté, page 281:
    20 large mushroom caps
in:
    3 tablespoons butter
Place the mushrooms, cavity side up, in a
greased baking dish. Fill them with:
    20 large drained oysters
and cover them with:
    1 cup hot Cream Sauce I, page 322
seasoned with:
    Dry sherry
Sprinkle the top with:
    —Grated Parmesan cheese
Place the dish in the oven until the top is

brown or omit the cream sauce and dot each oyster with:

    ¼ teaspoon butter
    A few drops lemon juice

Bake about 10 minutes, until the oysters are plump. Serve on:

    Creamed Spinach, page 300

OYSTER RAREBIT

4 Servings

Cook in their liquor until plump:

    2 cups oysters: 1 pint

Drain. Keep them hot and reserve the liquor. Cook in a double boiler and stir until smooth:

    2 tablespoons butter
    ¼ lb. diced Swiss or Gruyère cheese
    ½ teaspoon salt
    A few grains cayenne

Add and stir until thick:

    The oyster liquor

If there is not enough oyster liquor to make a good sauce, add rich milk until it is the right consistency. Add:

    2 beaten eggs

Add the oysters and:

    Salt
    1 teaspoon Worcestershire sauce or
    2 tablespoons dry sherry

Serve it on:

    Toast or rusks

Garnish it with a sprinkling of:

    Paprika

OYSTERS ROCKEFELLER

Allow 6 Oysters per Serving

Preheat oven to 475°.

I. This dish is best with oysters in the shell but, if they are not available, this recipe is a good way to dress up bulk oysters in separately bought shells.

Season and cover the oysters in turn with:

    Butter, creamed with onion juice
    and chopped parsley—reserve some
    of this
    Salt
    A few grains cayenne
    Cooked, minced bacon
    Puréed spinach
    Bread crumbs and some of the
    remaining butter
    A dash of Spice Parisienne

It is a New Orleans idea to sprinkle the oysters with absinthe. The shells are then imbedded in pans of rock salt. Bake for about 10 minutes or until plump. Run them under a broiler to brown and serve at once.

II. A simpler version.
Half fill a shell with:

    Creamed Spinach, page 300

Place on spinach:

    1 large oyster

Cover with:

    1 teaspoon chopped parsley

    A few drops lemon juice and
    Worcestershire sauce
    A square inch of bacon

Cook as in I.

III. Fill half the shell, as above, with:

    Creamed Spinach, page 300

Place the oyster on the spinach and cover with:

    1 teaspoon well-seasoned Cream
    Sauce I, page 322
    1 teaspoon grated Parmesan cheese

Bake as above.

OYSTERS CASINO

4 Servings

♦ Please read About Oysters, page 363.
Preheat oven to 450°
Prepare:

    24 oysters on the half shell

Imbed them in pans of rock salt. Cream together:

    ½ cup sweet butter
    ⅛ cup finely chopped shallots
    ¼ cup finely chopped parsley
    ¼ cup finely chopped green pepper
    ¼ cup finely chopped white celery
    Juice of 1 lemon

Put a piece of the butter mixture on each oyster, plus:

    ½ teaspoon of chopped pimiento
    Small square of partially cooked
    bacon

Bake until the bacon is browned, from 5 to 8 minutes.

ABOUT MUSSELS

Mussels are sometimes called "the oyster of the poor," which only goes to show that there are various definitions of poverty. These delicious mollusks do, however, deteriorate rapidly and, if uncooked, may be the cause of infections.

    ♦ To test mussels for freshness, try to slide the two halves of the shell across each other. If they budge, the shell is probably filled with mud, not mussel. Mussels are distinguished by a beard. They may be served either with or without it.

Wash mussels in a colander in running water. Keep agitating the colander, so as to keep them from opening their shells and dying. Scrub them with a stiff brush. You may clip the beards with scissors. Mussels may be steamed, removed from the shell, bearded and served much like oysters or clams or served with a sauce, shell and all. It is permissible—probably because it is necessary—to use the hands in separating the shells. Gourmets suggest that a half shell be used to spoon up the liquor to the last drop. ♦ For 4 servings allow about 1 quart undrained shucked or 3 quarts unshucked mussels. Cockles may also be cooked as for mussels.

STEAMED MUSSELS OR MOULES MARINIÈRE

3 to 4 Servings

Please read About Mussels, page 366.
in:

¼ cup butter

Sauté until golden:

6 chopped shallots
1 clove garlic

Cook in a deep, heavy skillet for about 2
minutes:

¼ cup dry white wine
⅓ bay leaf

Add the sautéed shallots and:

3 quarts scrubbed, bearded mussels

Cook ♦ closely covered, over lively heat
about 6 to 8 minutes. Agitate the pan
sufficiently during this time to cook the
mussels evenly but ♦ remove from heat the
moment the shells are open. Pour the
mussels, shells and all, and the sauce into
heated bowls and serve garnished with:

¼ cup chopped parsley

If you prefer, you may drain the sauce off
and quickly thicken it with:

2 tablespoons fresh bread crumbs

before pouring it over the mussels.

BAKED BUTTERED MUSSELS

Preheat oven to 450°.

Place well-cleaned mussels in a large pan,
:

2 tablespoons olive oil

in the oven until the shells open. Do not
overcook them. Remove the upper shell
and beard or fringe. Reserve the liquor.
If any has escaped to the pan, strain and
add it to the reserved liquor from the shell.
Serve the mussels on the lower shell with:

Melted butter or melted garlic butter

and the liquor in small cups or glasses. See
Steamed Clams, page 369.

ABOUT CLAMS

All clams are sandy, especially surf clams.
Unshucked, they should be scrubbed and
washed in several waters, then soaked in
cold brine of ⅓ cup salt to 1 gallon of
water; and it may even be necessary later
to put the cooked clams under cold running
water to rid them completely of sand. Clams
are sold in the shell or shucked. If in the
shell ♦ test to see that the clams are tightly
closed or, if slightly open, that they close
tightly at once upon being touched. ♦ Discard any that float, or have broken shells.
♦ Eight quarts of clams in the shell will
yield about 1 quart of clams shucked.
Allow about 1 quart of unshucked clams
per person for steamed clams, 6 to 8 clams
if served in some other way.

SOFT OR LONGNECK CLAMS

Found mostly north of Cape Cod, these are
the preferred East Coast type for eating
raw or steamed whole. They are easily
opened by running a sharp knife along the
edge of the top shell. Work over a bowl,
so as to trap the juices. Cut the meat
from the bottom shell. Slit the skin of the
neck or siphon, as sketched, and pull off
the neck skin.

This skin is too tough to eat as it is, but
may be chopped or ground and used in
chowders or creamed dishes with other
clam meat.

HARD-SHELL CLAMS

These include **butter clams** and **quahogs**
which in turn are called **cherrystones** in
junior sizes; in medium sizes, they are
called **littlenecks**. The large, strongly flavored hard-shells are preferred for chowders. The smaller sizes are suitable for
eating on the half shell. If in the shell,
you may wash them in several waters.
Then cover them with a cold brine of ⅓
cup salt for each gallon of water and sprinkle on the top ¼ cup corn meal to every
quart of clams. Leave them in this bath
3 to, preferably, 12 hours. This whitens
them, rids them of sand and causes them
to eject the black material in their stomachs.
After soaking, wash them again in clear
water.

Quahogs are difficult to open but, if
covered for 5 minutes with water and then
gently picked up, you may be able to insert a knife quickly in the opening. Or, if
you are using them in a cooked dish and

do not mind a small loss in flavor, you may
place them in a pan in a moderate oven
until they open. After opening, cut through

the muscle holding the shells together. If they have not had a corn meal bath, open the stomachs with sharp shears and scrape out and discard the contents. Large hard-shelled clams have a tough portion, which may be separated from the tender portion, chopped or ground and used in various dishes, creamed, scalloped, in fritters, chowders, etc., using any of the recipes for oysters, or any of the following clam recipes.

RAZOR CLAMS

Especially the Pacific Coast variety, these are unsurpassed for flavor.

SURF CLAMS

These may be used in chowders, broth or cocktails, but their sweetness should be counteracted with salt. They are the sandiest of all clams.
♦ For other recipes, see Soups and Chowders, page 163, or Luncheon Dishes, page 238.

ABOUT CLAMBAKES

Whatever the size of your bake, dig your clams the day before. Scrub them well to remove sand. Put them in a bucket, well covered with sea water. Add corn meal, allowing ½ cup to 2 quarts water. The cereal helps rid the clams of sand and internal waste. Leave the clams in a ♦ cool place. Rinse and drain them just before using. A big bake is described in I; a smaller one, often more practical, in II, with amounts proportionately cut.

▤ CLAMBAKE
I.   20 Servings
Allow:
  200 soft-shell clams
  (50 hard-shell clams)
Start preparations at least 4 hours before you plan to serve. Dig a sand pit about 1 foot deep and 3½ feet across. Line it with smooth round rocks. ♦ Be sure the rocks have not been baked before. Have a wet tarpaulin—generous enough to overlap the pit area by 1 foot all around—and a few rocks handy to weight the edges. Build a fire over the rock surface, using hardwood, and keep feeding it for the next 2½ to 3 hours while the rocks are heating. Gather and wash about 4 bushels of wet rock seaweed. In fact, it is wise to soak the seaweed for at least 45 minutes before use. Have a pail of sea water at hand. Partially husk about:
  4 dozen ears of corn
Do not pull them quite clean but leave on the last layer or two. Rip these back far enough to remove the silk. Then replace them, so the kernels are fully protected. Reserve the pulled husks. Quarter:
  5 broiling chickens
Have ready:

  10 sweet potatoes
  (20 frankfurters)
You may wrap the chicken pieces in cheese cloth or divide the food into 20 individual cheesecloth-wrapped servings, so that each person's food can later be removed as one unit. Scrub:
  20 1½-lb. lobsters or 5 pecks soft shell crabs
Now you are ready to arrange for the "bake." Rake the embers free of the hot stones, remove them from the pit and line it with the wet seaweed covering the stones. The lining should be about six inches deep. Put over it, if you wish, a piece of chicken wire. If you haven't wrapped the individual servings in cheese cloth, now pack the pit in layers. For added flavor, put down first a layer of hard shell clams, then the frankfurters if you use them, then the lobsters or crabs, the chicken, the corn and the soft-shell clams. You may also put seaweed between the layers. Cover the layered food with the reserved corn husks and sprinkle the whole with the bucket of sea water. Quickly cover with the wet tarp. ♦ Weight the tarp down well with rocks. The whole should steam ♦ covered about 1 hour. During the steaming, it will puff up, which is a sign of a satisfactory "bake." To test, lift the tarp carefully at one corner ♦ so as not to get sand into the pit and see if the clams have opened. If so, the whole feast should be cooked just to the right point. Have handy plenty of towels and:
  Melted butter
Serve with the "bake":
  Beer
and afterwards:
  Watermelon
  Coffee

II.   8 Servings
A well-timed bake in a wash boiler on a stove or outdoor grill.
Soak for 45 minutes and remove sand from seaweed in several rinsings. Line the bottom of the boiler with a 4-inch layer of it. Add about:
  1 quart water
When water boils, add:
  8 foil-wrapped potatoes
♦ Cover boiler and cook gently 15 minutes. Wrap in cheesecloth:
  2 cut-up broiler chickens
and place on top of the potatoes. Cook 15 minutes more, before adding:
  8 well-scrubbed 1½ lb. lobsters
Cover and cook 8 minutes more, then place on top of the lobsters:
  8 shucked foil-wrapped ears of corn
Cook 10 minutes, still covered and add:
  48 well-scrubbed soft-shell clams
Cover and steam until the clams open, from 5 to 10 minutes longer. In serving, use:
  Melted butter

The drained kettle liquid is to be drunk, but it is wise to drain this through a cloth-lined sieve before serving.

II.   4 Servings
For amounts, cut those in II in half. Use a clean 8-inch stove pipe, about 20 inches deep. Dig and line a circular 18-inch-diameter pit with stones, as described in I—about 12 inches deep—and build the same type fire. When ready to cook, center the stove pipe over the embers. Put in an 8-inch layer of well-soaked seaweed, followed by 4 units of food wrapped in cheese-cloth, as described in I, placing seaweed between them. Top with 8 inches of sea-weed and heap sand against the stove pipe in volcano shape. Put a wet tarp over the top and weight with rocks. Cook about 1 hour.

STEAMED SOFT-SHELL CLAMS WITH BROTH
Allow 2 Dozen Unshucked Clams per Serving
Scrub thoroughly with a brush and wash in several waters:
Soft-shell clams
Place them close together in the top of a steamer, as sketched on the right, page 348, or on a rack in a stock pot with a spigot, as shown on page 488. Place in the bottom of the steamer or stock pot:
½ inch water
Cover the kettle closely. Steam the clams over moderate heat until they open, but no longer—from 5 to 10 minutes. Overcooking makes clams tough. Lift them out. Place in individual soup bowls. Serve with individual dishes of:
Melted butter
Lemon wedges
The broth is served in cups along with the clams or it is used for clam juice cocktail later. ♦ To eat clams, pick them up from the shell by the neck with the fingers, dip in broth to remove any possible sand, then in butter. All of the clam is edible, except the neck sheath. The broth is delicious to drink, but don't entirely drain the cup, so as to avoid the sand at the bottom.

BAKED SOFT-SHELL CLAMS
4 Servings
Preheat oven to 425°.
Scrub with a brush and wash in several waters:
36 soft-shell clams
Place them flat in a pan in depressions in crumpled foil or rock salt to keep shells steady. Bake them about 15 minutes until the shells open. Remove the top shell carefully to avoid spilling the juices. Serve the clams in individual plates with:
Butter and celery salt
Pepper and lemon wedges

CLAMS BROILED ON THE HALF SHELL
Allow 6 to 8 Clams per Person
Preheat broiler.
Place on an ovenproof dish, in which foil has been crumpled to keep shells steady:
Cherrystone clams on the half shell
Cover each clam with:
A dash of Worcestershire sauce
A square of bacon
Broil the clams until the bacon is done.

FRIED CLAMS
Allow 6 to 8 Clams per Person
♦ Please read About Clams, page 367.
Shuck, wash well in a colander under running water:
Soft-shell clams
Dry them between towels. Cut away the black skin of the neck or siphon. Prepare as for Fried Oysters, page 364. Serve with
Tartare Sauce, page 316, or catsup

CLAM BROTH FROM STEAMED HARD-SHELL CLAMS
The meat of these clams is used for chowder, fritters or sauced dishes, the broth for soup or as sauce stock. Prepare as for:
Steamed Soft-shell Clams, opposite
Strain the broth through 2 thicknesses of cheesecloth. You will have about 1 quart of strong broth. It may be diluted with scalded cream or milk but do not boil it after these additions. Or it may be combined with:
Water, chicken broth, consommé
or tomato juice
Each cup of broth may be topped with a spoonful of:
(Unsweetened whipped cream)
Sprinkled with:
(Chopped chives)
To prepare the clam meat for use ♦ please read About Hard-Shell Clams, page 367, and add to broth, if desired.

ABOUT SCALLOPS

These beautiful mollusks known on menus as Coquilles St. Jacques are emblematic of the pilgrims who visited the shrine of St. James of Compostella. They ate the mollusks as penance—surely not a rigorous one—and afterwards fastened the cockle shells to their hats. Scallops are also responsible for the cooking term "scalloped," which originally meant seafood creamed, heated and served in a shell. If you get scallops in the shell, wash and scrub them thoroughly. Place in a 300° oven, deep shell down, until they open. Remove the hinge muscle. In Europe, the handsome beanlike coral and beard are both used. The former is treated as for any roe and the latter cut up, sautéed briefly and then simmered ♦ covered, in white wine for ½ hour. When you buy scallops, try for the small, tender, creamy pink or tan **bay scallops** rather than the large, firmer, whiter **sea scallops.** Both types are illustrated on page 72. If only the large ones are available, slice them—after cooking—in 3 parts, against the grain, for use in salads and creamed dishes or sauces.

◗ To test scallops for freshness, see that they have a sweetish odor. If in bulk, they should be free of liquid. Allow about ⅓ lb. of sea scallops or ¼ lb. of bay scallops per serving for sautéing or broiling. Cooked scallops may be used in any recipe for fish salads or creamed fish or may be skewered and grilled, see below. See also seafood suggestions in Luncheon Dishes, page 237.

SCALLOPS MEUNIÈRE

4 Servings

In:

A Bound Breading, page 502

dip:

1 lb. bay or sea scallops

You may let them dry on a rack about 15 minutes. Heat in a heavy skillet large enough so the scallops will be only 1 layer deep:

2 tablespoons butter
2 tablespoons cooking oil

Sauté ◗ agitating frequently, about 5 minutes for bay scallops, 8 minutes for sea scallops. Just before the cooking time is over, sprinkle with:

Lemon juice
Finely chopped parsley

Serve with:

Tomatoes Florentine, page 307

BAY SCALLOPS FONDU BOURGUIGNONNE

4 Servings

◗ Please read about Boeuf Fondu Bourguignonne, page 401, using instead of beef:

1 lb. bay scallops

Serve as sauces:

Seasoned Butters for Fish, page 338, or Hollandaise Sauce, page 328

▤ SCALLOP KEBABS

Allow ¼ lb. Bay or ⅓ lb. Sea Scallops per Person

Preheat broiler or grill.

If scallops are large or old, drop into boiling water and allow them to stay immersed, but removed from heat, for 1 minute. Drain and dry. If tender, simply brush:

Scallops

with:

Cooking oil

Dip in:

Fine bread crumbs

Skewer alternately with:

1-inch squares of bacon

Grill over moderate heat for 10 minutes or until golden brown or broil 4 inches from the source of heat, turning several times during the cooking period. Serve with:

Lemon wedges
Fried Parsley, page 287

DEEP-FAT FRIED SCALLOPS

6 to 8 Servings

Preheat deep fryer to 385°.

Wash and pick over:

1 quart scallops: about 2 lbs.

Drain. Dry between towels. Season with:

White pepper
Celery salt

Dip them in a:

Bound Breading, page 502

Fry for 2 minutes in deep fat. Drain on absorbent paper. Serve with:

Tartare Sauce, page 316, Béarnaise Sauce, page 329, or Tomato Sauce, page 333

SCALLOPS IN WINE

6 to 8 Servings

Wash well:

2 lbs. scallops

◗ Simmer in:

2 cups dry white wine

Drain and reserve the liquid. Melt:

¼ cup butter

Sauté:

4 finely chopped shallots
24 finely sliced mushroom caps
2 tablespoons minced parsley

Stir in, until blended:

2 tablespoons flour

Add the reserved liquid and:

2 to 4 tablespoons whipping cream

Add the scallops to the hot sauce. Place in a shallow casserole. Cover with·

Au Gratin II, page 342

and run under a broiler until golden brown.

CREAMED SCALLOPS OR OYSTERS AND MUSHROOMS

4 Servings

Simmer until tender, for about 5 minutes:

2 cups scallops

in:

Water or light stock to cover

Drain well. Sauté for 5 minutes:

½ lb. mushrooms

in:

2 tablespoons butter

Prepare:

1 cup Cream Sauce I, page 322

using half cream and half chicken broth milk. When the sauce is smooth and hot stir in the scallops and the mushrooms. Simmer gently for about 3 minutes if bay scallops, 5 minutes if sea scallops.

Correct the seasoning

An unusual variation is to add:

2 cups of minced cooked ham

to the above mixture. When oysters are substituted, cook them in their own juice until the edges begin to curl. Drain. Substitute the juice for part of the milk.

SCALLOPED SCALLOPS OR SCALLOPS MORNAY

6 Servings

Preheat broiler.

Poach:

3 cups scallops

n:
1½ cups dry white wine and Light
Stock, page 490, or Fumet, page 491
Drain and slice the scallops. Coat each of
the deep halves of 12 scallop shells with:
1 tablespoon hot Mornay Sauce,
page 323
You may edge the shell, using a forcing
bag, with a decorative rim of:
(Duchess Potato, page 296)
Almost fill the shell with the sliced scallops.
Coat each shell, staying within the rim of
the potatoes, with:
Hot Mornay Sauce, page 323
Dust the sauce coating with:
Grated Parmesan or Gruyère cheese
Run under a broiler until the sauce is lightly
browned. Serve at once.

ABOUT ABALONE

The foot of this delicious shellfish—contra-
and if shipped from California—comes to
our markets canned or frozen from Mexico
and Japan, shelled, pounded and ready to
cook. If you get it in the shell, remove the
edible portion by running a knife between
the shell and the meat. Trim off the
dark portion. Abalone, like inkfish, needs
prodigious pounding to tenderize it, if it
has died in a state of tension. Leave it
whole or cut it in ¼-inch strips for pounding with an even, not too hard, motion.
The meat is ready to cook when it looks like
Dali's limp watches. ♦ For steaks, slice
against the grain. Bread it if you like and
sauté or boil as for any fish, page 349.
Beat and chop it for Chowder, or for Fritters, page 220. ♦ Allow 1 lb. for 2 to 3
servings.

SAUTÉED ABALONE

2 to 3 Servings
Cut into ⅜-inch-thick steaks across the
grain and pound:
1 lb. abalone
Dip in a:
Bound Breading, page 502
Melt in a heavy skillet:
2 tablespoons cooking oil or
clarified butter
When the fat reaches the point of fragrance,
sauté the abalone steaks, allowing 1½ to
minutes to each side.

ABOUT CRABS

Recipes for cooking crab meat apply to
most all species of edible crab, but both
the type of crab and the part of the crab
from which the meat is taken may make a
difference in color, taste and texture.

BLUE CRABS

These comprise three-fourths of the fresh
crabs in the market. Lump or back-fin
meat, taken from the body, is choice for
looks and white in color. Flake meat, while
less shapely, is also white. Claw meat is
brownish, but very choice as to taste.

DUNGENESS AND ROCK CRABS

These are both packaged in one grade,
combining body and claw meat. The rock
crab flesh is brownish. Dungeness is best
in 2½ to 3 lb. size.

KING CRABS

These are pinkish in tone, and consist
mainly of leg meat.

OYSTER CRABS AND HERMIT CRABS

There are two edible types of miniature
crabs. Oyster crabs are crispy ½-inch
pinkish "boarders," found living right in
the shell with live oysters and may be eaten
raw. They may also be sautéed or deep-
fat fried, as is. When deep fried, several
dozen may be served with several dozen
fried whitebait as one portion. Tiny hermit
crabs are found in vacated univalve shells
and respond to deep-fat frying and sautéing, but not to being eaten raw.
Preheat deep fryer to 390°.
To deep fry either of these crabs or whitebait, keep them on ice until the last minute.
Wash and dry carefully and put in a bag
to dust with flour, page 502, then in a
sieve to bounce off as much flour as possible. Place a few at a time in a frying
basket and cook only 2 to 3 seconds until
crisp.

HARD-SHELL CRABS

These do not ship well. ♦ From a 5 oz.
hard crab, you can expect about 1½ oz. of
crab meat. ♦ Crabs must be alive and
lively when cooked.

SOFT-SHELL OR EASTERN BLUE CRABS

These are crabs that have just molted and
not yet hardened. Their hardening up is
a matter of only a few days. They ship very
satisfactorily.
♦ Freshly cooked crab meat in partially
aerated cans must be under constant refrigeration until used. It should have no
ammonialike odor. The completely sealed
canned crab meats, Japanese and Korean,
are all nonperishable until the cans are
opened.
♦ To prepare crab shells for restuffing,
select large, perfect shells and scrub them

well with a brush until clean. Place them in a large kettle, covered with hot water. Add one teaspoon baking soda. Cover the kettle closely. Bring to a boil and simmer for 20 minutes. Drain, wash and dry. They are then ready for refilling.

♦ For crab dishes made with cooked or canned crab, see page 237. In using canned meat, be sure to pick it over for small bits of shell and bone.

♦ To prepare soft-shell crabs, wash them in several waters. Place live crab face down on a board. Make an incision just back of the eyes and cut out the face. Lift the tapering points on each side of the back shell to remove sandbag and spongy gills, as shown in sketch. Turn crab on its back and with a pointed knife remove the small pointed apron at the lower part of the shell. These crabs, since the shell is edible, are usually broiled or breaded and sautéed, or are deep-fat fried as follows.

DEEP-FAT FRIED SOFT-SHELL CRABS

Preheat Deep Fryer to 375°.
♦ Please read About Deep-Fat Frying, pages 124-126. Dip:
    Cleaned soft-shell crabs
in:
    A Bound Breading, page 502
Fry from 3 to 5 minutes or until golden brown, in deep fat. Turn them once while they are frying. Drain on absorbent paper. Sprinkle well with:
    Salt and pepper
Serve at once with:
    Tartare Sauce, page 316
    Remoulade Sauce, page 316, with parsley

BROILED SOFT-SHELL CRABS

Preheat broiler.
Prepare for cooking:
    Soft-shell crabs
Combine:
    ¼ cup butter
    2 tablespoons lemon juice
    A few grains cayenne
    A few grains pepper
Roll the crabs in the butter mixture, then lightly in:
    Flour
Place them on the broiling rack, 2 inches from the heat. Broil for about 10 minutes. Turn once.

SAUTEED SOFT-SHELL CRABS

Follow the above recipe for:
    Broiled Soft-Shell Crabs
Sauté them in butter or other fat over moderate heat. Place on a platter. Serve with:
    Fried Parsley, page 287

STEAMED HARD-SHELL CRABS

We are very grateful to a Maryland fan who put us wise to handling this type of crab. She says, "When I moved into this crab country, I began to boil hard crab and threw the natives into fainting fits. They were right."

This is the way she describes the Maryland method: "Dump the crabs into a large vessel or deep sink and cover them with water a little hotter than the hand can bear. The crabs sometimes drop their claws at the contact with hot water—but it is no matter—just pile the claws on top when steaming.

"This hot water bath anesthetizes them quickly with 2 good results: first, you can handle them safely, like soft-shells, and second, they do not appear to suffer when they are placed over the steam. Otherwise they struggle woefully in the pot while the steam is rising. I scrub the muck from each crab with a vegetable brush. This is my own discovery—the natives do not bother. But somehow I like to suck a clean crab better. If you have suitable rack, place it in a large pot with close lid and put a little water in the bottom, but not nearly enough to touch the rack. If a rack is lacking, moisten the bottom of the vessel with 2 or 3 tablespoons of water. In any case, lay in the crabs and set upon the rack. Sprinkle well with:

    About 1 teaspoon red pepper
    2 tablespoons salt
    ½ cup vinegar or lemon juice
    (2 tablespoons Crab Boil)
    1 tablespoon monosodium glutamate
    ½ cup beer or what-have-you

Have no fear that the pot will get dry while steaming. It never does, for the crab put out a lot of moisture. The problem, on the contrary, is to keep them from getting sodden. Cover and steam until the aprons begin to rise, about 30 minutes or a little more. Eat hot or cold, preferably over newspapers, and dip each bit in melted butter. Some people use simple French dressing, but not me. If you pull off the apron and open the crab from that point with the fingers, it is easy.

"For the uninitiated we might interpolate: eat only the meat and discard the intestines and spongy gills. Otherwise, a knife is useful to pry off the shell. A mallet or hammer is then better than crackers for opening the claws. And don't forget to pry in the points of the top shell for a bite of fat. Some crabs are lean, but some are not. Many crabs—followed by a general hand washing—and then green salad, French bread and dessert make a fine dinner for the fanciest guests."

ABOUT LOBSTERS

The **Northern lobster** or French "homard" with its great delicious claw meat, sketched on page 374. It is caught from

New England to the Carolinas and in North European waters.

The **spiny rock lobster,** or **langouste,** as it is also called, is shipped from Florida, California, Australia, South Africa and the Mediterranean. It has extra-long antennae and most of the meat is in the heavy tail. These are also sometimes called crawfish, in contradistinction to the freshwater écrevisses or crayfish of both continents. The Northerns are reputed most delicious when served hot. The spinys, when frozen, especially if over 10 oz., may be tough. If fresh, they are often preferred in cold dishes. The Northerns, when caught, are a dark mottled blue green. The spinys vary from tan to reddish orange and maroon with more or less light spotting and more or fewer spines. Both kinds require about the same cooking time and may be cut and cleaned as shown on page 374. But as lobster ritual is more complicated in the Northern type, we will discuss it in further detail below.

The female is considered finer in flavor. Look for the soft, leathery, finlike appendages on the underside, just where the body and tail meet. In the male, these appendages are bony. In opening the female lobster, you may find a delicious roe or coral that reddens in cooking. Use it as a garnish or to color a sauce. The flesh of the male stays firmer when boiled. The greenish substance in both of them is the liver or tomalley.

◆ Allow ½ large lobster or 1 small lobster per serving. Buy active live lobsters weighing from 1¼ to 2½ pounds. Lobsters weighing 3 pounds and over are apt to be coarse and tough. A 2½-pound lobster will yield about 2 cups of cooked meat.

◆ To store live lobsters until ready to use, place them in the refrigerator, but not directly on ice. The claws should be plugged with a small piece of wood and held together with rubber bands. Before cooking, test to make sure lobsters are lively and that, when picked up, if the tail is stretched out flat, it snaps back.

POACHED OR "BOILED" LOBSTER

I. To boil or poach lobster for hot family-type table service, put a folded towel on the bottom of a large, heavy pan. Place on it:

A 1½ to 2½ lb. live lobster

Cover with:

Cold sea or salted water

Bring the water to a boil and cook for minutes. ◆ Reduce the heat and simmer for 15 minutes, slightly less if the lobsters have recently shed and are soft. Drain. Serve at once, leaving the head, body and tail intact, and surrounding this portion with the claws. Garnish with a small bowl of:

Drawn Butter, page 338
Lemon wedges

And provide each person with a finger bowl, a bib and abundant napkins. The uninitiated are sometimes balked by the ferocious appearance of a lobster at table. They may take comfort from the little cannibal who, threading his way through the jungle one day at his mother's side, saw a strange object roar overhead. "Ma, what's that?" he quavered. "Don't worry, sonny," said Ma. "It's an airplane. Airplanes are pretty much like lobsters. There's an awful lot you have to throw away, but the insides are delicious."

All the lobster components lie on your plate—the body, head and tail intact, arched shell up, surrounded by the large claws which, on removal before serving, have been cracked to allow excess moisture to drain off. Pick the lobster up in your fingers, turn it soft side up and arch it until the tail cracks off the body. Then break off and discard the tail flippers by bending them back. Pick up the tail piece, again upside down, and push the meat at the small flipper end of the tail with the oyster fork. The tail meat should emerge in one piece out of the large end. Unhinge the back from the back shell and crack open the back by pulling it open. Be sure to eat the greenish tomalley or liver and all the meat. At this point, we call your attention to the finger bowl.

II. To boil lobster for salad, hors d'oeuvre or sauced dishes, prepare as for I, using:

A 2½ to 3 lb. lobster

Larger ones are apt to be tough. After the cooking period, drain and plunge into cold water to arrest further cooking. When cool ◆ to remove the meat from the shell, place the lobster on its back. With sharp scissors cut a lengthwise gash in the soft underside as sketched on page 375. Draw out the tail meat in one piece. Remove and discard the lady, or sandbag, and the intestinal vein, as well as the spongy lungs which, while harmless, are tough. Add the red coral, if any, and the green liver, or tomalley, to the lobster meat or reserve it for use in sauces.

If you buy pre-boiled lobster in the shell, see that the color is bright red and that it has a fresh seashore aroma. ◆ Most important of all, the tail should be curled and, when pulled, should roll back into place under the body. This means the lobster was alive, as it should have been, when cooked.

To remove lobster meat from the large claws, crack them with a nutcracker or a mallet. If you want them in a single piece for garnish, break the claw off at the first joint. Place it on a flat surface, the lighter underside up. Using a mallet, hit the shell at the inner hump. This will crack it, so that the meat in the entire larger pincer claw is released. Crack off the small pincer shell and its meat will slide out. For attractive service, you may want to keep the lobster shell to refill with the seasoned sauced meat or you may want to use it to make Lobster Butter, page 339.

⊟ BROILED LOBSTER

1 Serving

Preheat broiler.
Prepare for broiling:

A 1¼ lb. live lobster

Sever the vein at the base of the neck. Place the lobster on his back. Hold him with your left hand firmly over the head. Be sure to protect your hand with a towel. Draw the knife from the head down through the base of the abdomen, as shown below, so the lobster will lie flat with the meat evenly exposed to the heat. All the lobster meat is edible, except for the stom-

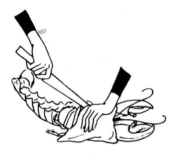

ach, or lady—a hard sac near the head—and the intestinal vein that runs through the middle of the underside of the tail meat. Remove and discard these inedible parts. The spongy substance to either side of the body—the lungs—is harmless. It may or may not be removed when the lobster is cooked in the half shell. Beyond a doubt edible are the delicious red coral and the greenish liver or tomalley. You may prepare a stuffing by removing and mixing together:

The coral
The tomalley
1 tablespoon toasted bread crumbs
1 teaspoon of lemon juice or

dry sherry
Replace in the cavity and brush with:
Melted butter
Also brush with:
Melted butter
the exposed lobster meat. ♦ If broiling stuffed, place shell side down on the oven grill and broil about 16 minutes. If broiling unstuffed or grilling over charcoal, place shell side toward heat for 7 to 8 minutes, turn and broil, flesh side to heat, for about 8 minutes more. In either case serve with:

Lemon wedges and Drawn Butter,
page 338

♦ To eat broiled lobster served to you on the half-shell, begin with the tail meat first, using the small, sharp-pronged lobster or oyster fork, see sketches below. You may twist off bite-size pieces with the fork. This needs some skill, and we often wish, when dining out, for a good European fish knife. Dip the pieces in the sauce. You may also squeeze lemon juice from the garnish wedges over the lobster meat. Twist off a large claw with the fingers and, if necessary, also use the cracker which should always be provided. Crack the claw, as shown, to release the delicate rich meat. You may then pull off the small side claws, one by one, with the fingers, and suck out the meat. As you empty the shells, place them on the bone tray or extra plate and make use of the finger bowl when needed. Continue to eat the contents of the shell: it is good to the last shred. Some people even suck the knuckle after releasing it from the grey gristle.

LOBSTER AMÉRICAINE OR ARMORICAINE

2 Servings
Who really cares how it's spelled? This method of cooking lobster is good enough to credit regional inventiveness on both sides of the Atlantic.
Have ready:

½ cup Fish Fumet, page 491

Place on a flat pan, so as to be able to reserve any juice that results from cutting

2 live 1½ lb. hen lobsters

With a sharp knife, sever the vein at the the base of the neck. Cut off the claws

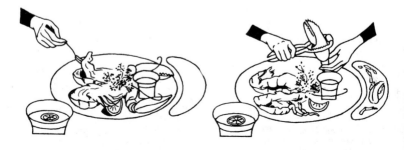

Divide the body at the tail and cut the tail in 3 or 4 pieces at the segmentations. Divide the shell in half, lengthwise. Remove and discard the sac. Reserve the coral, if any, and the tomalley, for the sauce. Have ready 2 heavy skillets. In one, sauté:

    3 tablespoons butter
    1 cup Mirepoix, page 541
    ½ cup chopped shallots

Heat in the other, to the point of fragrance:

    ½ cup olive oil
    1 clove garlic

Sauté in the oil for about 4 minutes ▶ still in the shell, the cut-up lobster. Keep the pan moving. When the lobster shell is red and the flesh firm, add it to the mirepoix in the first skillet. Flambé, page 127, the lobster mixture in:

    1 oz. brandy

Place in the second skillet and simmer about 5 minutes:

    ½ cup tomato purée
    1 cup white wine
    3 peeled, seeded, chopped tomatoes

In winter use the small Italian-type canned tomatoes.
Add the sautéed lobster pieces still in the shell, the fumet and:

    1 teaspoon chopped fresh tarragon
    The juice or "blood" of the lobster
    The coral and tomalley

to the tomato mixture. Heat the sauce.
Correct the seasoning
Thicken the sauce slightly with:

    (Beurre Manié, page 321)

Serve the lobster with the hot sauce poured over it and garnish with:

    Chopped parsley

▤ GRILLED LOBSTER TAILS
                                    4 Servings
Preheat broiler or grill.
Marinate for several hours:

    4 spiny lobster tails

in a mixture of:

    ¼ cup lemon or lime juice
    ¼ cup salad oil
    1 teaspoon each salt and paprika
    ¼ cup minced shallots

Remove with scissors the soft under-cover of the lobster tails, as sketched above.

Slightly crack the hard upper shell with a cleaver so the tails will lie flat, and grease the meat lightly. Broil for about 5 minutes to a side, basting the exposed side well with the marinade. Hold about 4 inches above coals or under broiler. These make an attractive plate when served with:

    Asparagus spears

placed to either side and garnished with:

    Polonaise Sauce, page 340

▤ CHARCOAL-GRILLED BAHAMIAN LOBSTER TAILS WITH LIME BUTTER SAUCE

You can use fresh or frozen lobster tails for this recipe and grill them outdoors or in a broiler. Split:

    Lobster tails

Do not remove meat from the shells. Several hours before cooking, marinate lobster tails in:

    Melted butter or olive oil

or a mixture of the two, allowing 2 to 3 tablespoons of fat for each lobster, plus:

    Freshly ground black pepper
    1 teaspoon lime or lemon juice

Broil until top is crisp and golden brown, 10 to 15 minutes. Keep basting with the marinade. Serve hot, with the drippings or extra butter and cut limes or lemons, if desired.

BAKED STUFFED LOBSTER
                                    2 Servings
Split in half, as for Broiled Lobster, page 374:

    A freshly Boiled Lobster, page 373:
    about 2½ lbs.

Remove the meat. Chop it. Melt:

    ¾ tablespoon butter

Stir in until blended:

    ¾ tablespoon flour

Stir in slowly:

    ½ cup Chicken Stock, page 490,
    or Fumet, page 491

Season the sauce with:

    1¼ teaspoons dry mustard
    1 teaspoon chopped onion
    Salt
    Paprika

Melt in a separate saucepan:

    2 tablespoons butter

Sauté the lobster meat in the butter until it is heated. Add the boiling sauce. Simmer these ingredients for about 2 minutes. Remove them from the heat.
Preheat broiler.
Beat, then stir in:

    1 tablespoon cream
    2 egg yolks

Add:

    (½ cup chopped Sautéed Mushrooms,
    page 281)

Fill the lobster shells with the mixture. Cover them with:

    Buttered Crumbs, page 501, or
    Au Gratin I or II, page 342

Broil the lobster until the crumbs are brown. Season it, as it is removed from the oven, by pouring over it:

(2 tablespoons sherry)

LOBSTER THERMIDOR

2 Servings

This calls for cream, as well as stock. Split in halves:

2 freshly Boiled Lobsters, page 373:
1 to 1½ lbs. each

Remove the meat, as directed. Dice the meat. Melt:

2 teaspoons butter

Stir in, until blended:

2 teaspoons flour

Add the lobster meat. Stir in slowly:

¼ cup rich cream
1 cup Stock, page 490

Simmer these ingredients for about 10 minutes. Stir them frequently. Season them lightly, if required, with:

Salt, paprika and celery salt
A few grains cayenne

Preheat broiler.
Remove the lobster from the pan. Add:

1 tablespoon dry sherry

Melt:

3 tablespoons butter

Add:

1½ cups shredded white bread

Cook and stir these ingredients until all the butter is absorbed. Wash the lobster shells thoroughly. Fill them with the mixture. Spread the tops with the bread crumbs. Brown them under a broiler. Serve the lobster with:

Wilted Cucumbers, page 86

ABOUT SHRIMP

Formerly our Southern shrimp or **crevette** was the only one available in most of our markets. Today we can buy many members of this family. So let us remind you of the tiny forms from our West coast and from Scandinavia—now widely used as hors d'oeuvre; **scampi, Dublin prawns** or **langoustines**—all large—from Europe; and the

giants from India—shrimp so large that 2 or 3 suffice for a serving. In spite of slight differences in flavor and texture, all can be substituted for one another if size is taken into consideration for serving amounts and cooking time. If poaching cooking varies from 3 to 8 minutes.

♦ To test shrimp for freshness, see that they are dry and firm. Allow about ⅓ pound of shrimp in the shell—these are called "green" shrimp—½ pound of cooked shrimp without shells for 3 servings. In buying, remember, 2 to 2½ lbs. of shrimp in the shell gives only about 1 lb. cooked shelled shrimp, or 2 cups. While shrimp may be cooked in the shell or unshelled, the shells add considerable flavor. Shelling is easy—either before or after cooking. A slight tug releases the body shell from the tail.

Devein before or after cooking, using a small pointed knife or the end of a toothpick, as sketched. This is essential.

♦ If using canned shrimp, you may rinse briefly in cold water to remove excess salt. Large shrimp may be made more decorative by slicing lengthwise, as shown below. ♦ To

butterfly shrimp, peel the shrimp down to the tail, leaving it on. Devein. Hold so the underside is up. Slice down its length almost to the vein, to form the hinge. Spread and flatten to form the butterfly shape.

♦ Never overcook shrimp. If they are fresh, drop them into boiling stock or water ♦ reduce the heat at once and simmer 3 to 4 minutes. But be sure to remove them from the heat before they begin to curl up ♦ Drain at once, to prevent curling and also overcooking. To cook frozen shrimp, peeled and deveined, and also the "green" types, start from the frozen state, drop into boiling stock or water and count the time when the stock comes to a boil again.

For other shrimp recipes, see Hors d'Oeuvre chapter, pages 73 and 74.

BUTTERFLY SHRIMP

♦ Please read About Deep-Fat Frying

ages 124-126. To cut for butterfly shape, see About Shrimp, page 376.

Preheat deep fryer to 370°.

Don't flour or crumb the tails, but do coat the body of the shrimp with:

Bread crumbs or grated coconut or flour or egg or both; or in a batter

Fry 8 to 10 minutes or until golden. Drain on absorbent paper. Serve at once with:

Soy Sauce, Tartare Sauce, page 316, or Chinese Sweet-Sour Sauce, page 330

POTTED SHRIMP OR LOBSTER

This terrine can be used as a luncheon or hors d'oeuvre spread. Cook:

Raw shrimp or lobster

Drain and remove meat from shells. Chop coarsely. Reserve shells. Allow for every cup of seafood:

2 to 3 tablespoons butter

To ½ the butter, add the reserved shells to make:

Shrimp or Lobster Butter, page 339

Season with:

⅛ teaspoon mustard or mace
⅛ teaspoon salt
A few grains cayenne

Stir the seafood into the heated shrimp or lobster butter until well coated. Place it in a small terrine. Clarify the remaining butter. ♦ Do not let it color. Pour it while hot over the seafood, making sure the food is well covered. Refrigerate covered.

SHRIMP TERIYAKI

3 Servings

Marinate:

1 lb. shelled, deveined "green" shrimp

for about 15 minutes, in:

½ cup pineapple juice
2 to 4 tablespoons soy sauce
½ cup bland cooking oil

Drain and broil or grill 3 or 4 minutes on each side, 4 inches from heat. Serve with:

Rice, page 178

POACHED SHRIMP

6 Servings

Simmer for about 5 minutes:

8 cups water
¼ cup sliced onion
1 clove garlic
1 bay leaf
2 celery ribs with leaves
1½ tablespoons salt

Wash, drain and add:

2 lbs. "green" shrimp

Dice and add:

½ lemon

Simmer the shrimp for about 5 minutes or until pink. Drain immediately and chill. Serve very cold in their shells—to be shelled at table—with a bowl of:

Russian Dressing, page 316, or
Remoulade Sauce, page 316

or shell them, remove the intestinal vein and use them as desired.

SHRIMP CASSEROLE WITH SNAIL BUTTER

4 Servings

Preheat oven to 400°.

Prepare:

1½ lbs. Poached Shrimp, see above

Have ready in refrigerator:

Colbert or Snail Butter, page 339

Put a ¼-inch layer of the butter in the bottom of a shallow casserole. Lay shrimp in rows and press into the butter. Cover the shrimp with the remaining butter and bake about 10 minutes. Broil for a few minutes to let top brown. Serve at once.

DEEP FAT FRIED SHRIMP

3 Servings

Shell:

1 lb. raw shrimp

Remove the intestinal vein. Combine:

⅔ cup milk
⅛ teaspoon paprika
¼ teaspoon salt

Soak the shrimp in the milk for 30 minutes.

Preheat deep fryer to 375°.

Drain the shrimp well. Sprinkle with:

Lemon juice
Salt

Roll in:

Corn meal

Fry in deep fat until golden brown. Drain on absorbent paper. Serve hot with:

Lemon juice or mayonnaise seasoned with puréed chutney

DEEP FAT FRIED STUFFED SHRIMP

2 Dozen Shrimp

Shell and devein:

10 jumbo-size shrimp

Chop them into a pulp and add:

6 water chestnuts

which have been smashed with a cleaver and finely chopped. Shell, leaving the tails intact, and devein:

14 jumbo-size shrimp

Split lengthwise along the deveined edge ♦ but not far enough to separate. Spread them flat and lay along each crevice:

A thin julienne of Prosciutto or Westphalian ham

Spread the shrimp and chestnut mixture in the crevices above the ham and mold it into the form of a wide beveled edge when you partially reclose the shrimp for breading. Dip into:

Beaten egg

then into:

Flour

Allow to dry on a rack 15 to 20 minutes.

♦ Please read About Deep-Fat Frying, pages 124-126.

Preheat deep fryer to 370°.

Lift the shrimp by the tails and slide them gently into the heated fat. Fry for about 5 minutes or until golden. Drain on absorbent paper. Serve at once with:

Chinese Sweet-Sour Sauce, page 330

adding some:

Plum jam

SHRIMP FRIED IN BATTER

3 Servings

Preheat deep fryer to 370°.
Shell and clean, page 376:

1 lb. "green" shrimp

You may leave the tails on. Prepare:

Fritter Batter for Fish, page 221

Dip a few shrimp at a time in the batter,
holding them by the tail. ♦ Do not cover
the tail with batter. Fry in deep fat until
golden brown. Drain on absorbent paper.
Serve with:

**Lemon wedges or mayonnaise
seasoned with catsup and mustard**

SHRIMP TEMPURA

♦ Please read About Deep-Fat Frying,
pages 124-126.
Preheat deep fat fryer to 350°.
Prepare:

Butterfly Shrimp, page 376

Dip them in:

Fritter Batter for Fish, page 221

Fry until golden.
Serve with:

**Hot Mustard Sauce, page 325, soy
sauce, Chinese Sweet-Sour Sauce,
page 330**

NEW ORLEANS SHRIMP

4 to 6 Servings

Poach:

2 lbs. fresh shrimp, page 377

Shell and clean them. Serve well chilled on:

Lettuce

Prepare the following sauce. Rub a bowl
with:

Garlic

Add:

**½ cup finely chopped celery
1 stalk finely chopped green onion
1 tablespoon chopped chives
6 tablespoons olive oil
3 tablespoons lemon juice
¼ teaspoon hot pepper sauce
5 tablespoons horseradish
2 tablespoons prepared mustard
¼ teaspoon paprika
¾ teaspoon salt
½ teaspoon white pepper**

You may marinate the shrimp in this sauce
for 12 hours, or the time may be much
shorter. A clove of garlic may be added
to the mixture for 2 hours.

SHRIMP NEWBURG

3 to 4 Servings

Prepare, page 377:

1 lb. Poached Shrimp

Serve with:

Newburg Sauce, page 323

using 1 to 1½ cups of sauce. Serve in a:

Rice Ring, page 180

or over:

Baked Green Rice, page 178

ABOUT CRAYFISH, CRAWFISH, OR ECREVISSES

♦ Allow about one dozen per servi
One of the thrills of our grandparents w
to find in Missouri streams the crayfish th
had so relished in Europe. These crust
ceans, looking like miniature lobsters, we
brought to the table in great steami
crimson mounds, garnished with dill
swimming in their own juices, that is, "à
nage."

To cook, wash well in several waters:

Crayfish

If they have been kept in fresh runni
water for several days, they need not
eviscerated. If they have not, they
cleaned while still alive. Grasp the mido
tail fin, as sketched, give a long firm tw
and pull to remove the stomach and
testinal vein. Have ready a large pot of:

Boiling water

seasoned with:

**A leek—white part only
Parsley
1 chopped carrot**

Drop the crayfish one by one into the bo
ing water at a rate which will not distu
the boiling. Cook not longer than 5 to
minutes. Serve in the shell. Have on t
side plenty of:

Melted butter

seasoned with:

Fresh dill

They are eaten with the fingers. Separ
tail from body. Crack open tail by holo
between thumb and finger of both ha
and force it back against the curve of
shell. Be sure to serve with finger bov
If you are preparing them for hors d'oeuv
cook only until the water is boiling v
after they are all immersed. Then rem

from heat. Let them cool in the liqu
Shelled, they lend themselves to all ki
of combinations and sauces, but the c
noisseur usually wants them for themse
alone.

ABOUT SNAILS

The Romans, who were addicted to sn
grew them on ranches where they were
special foods like bay, wine and spicy sc
to preseason them. Only snail types that

ealed in their opercula before hibernating are edible. If your snails are less privileged than the Roman ones, be sure to let them fast for about 10 days to get rid of any possible poisons they may have imbibed from foliage inimical to humans. After the fast, they may be fattened for the feast before cooking. ♦ Allow about 1 dozen snails per serving.

Before cooking, scrub and remove the membrane which closes them. Place in water to cover and add ½ cup salt or ¼ cup vinegar for every 50 snails. Change the water several times during this 3 to 4 hour soaking. Then rinse in several waters until the slime is removed. Blanch à blanc, page 493, 8 minutes. After draining from the cold water, place the snails in a court bouillon to cover, made with:

    ½ water or stock and ½ white wine

seasoned with:

    A Bouquet Garni, page 541
    An onion stuck with cloves
    2 cloves garlic

Simmer gently for 3 to 4 hours, depending on the size of the snails. After cooling in the court bouillon, drain.

Remove snails from shells. Cut off and discard the black end. Dry the snails and shells in a cloth. Place a dab of Snail

utter, page 339, in each shell. Replace the snails. Pack them firmly in the shell, generously covered that only the lovely green herbed butter is visible at the opening. You may chill the snails for later use or bake them at once on a pan lightly sprinkled with water in a 425° oven just long enough to get them piping hot—a matter of a few minutes only. Have ready heated, grooved, snail dishes. The shell holder has a spring in the handle which allows you to regulate its viselike end to the size of the snail. The long, closely tined fork is used with a slight twist to remove the snail. See sketch above.

For those of us who have to rely on canned snails, the following is a snail rejuvenation.

Prepare enough to fill 48 snails:
    Snail Butter, page 339
Reduce to 1 cup over high heat:
    1 cup consommé
    1 cup dry white wine
cooked with:
    ½ bay leaf
    1 clove garlic
Put in a colander:
    48 canned snails
Pour over them:
    1 quart warm water
Drain well. Simmer the snails briefly in the hot reduced consommé and wine. Wash the snail shells well and drain. Pack, as above, with:
    Snail Butter, page 339
Heat and serve as for I.

III. Or, replace the shells with:
    Sautéed Mushroom Caps, page 281
Fill the mushrooms with one or more snails, depending on size. Coat the snails with:
    Snail Butter, page 339
and run under a broiler briefly until heated.

ABOUT FROG LEGS

Frog legs resemble chicken in texture and flavor. They are usually bought skinned and ready to use. Allow 2 large or 6 small frog legs per person. If the frogs are not prepared, cut off the hind legs—the only part of the frog used—close to the body. Separate and wash them in cold water. Begin at the top and strip off the skin like a glove. Through an experiment with a twitching frog leg, Galvani discovered the electric current that bears his name. Should you prefer keeping your kitchen and your scientific activities separate and distinct, chill the frog legs before skinning.

BRAISED FROG LEGS

                    4 Servings

Clean:
    8 large frog legs
Roll them in:
    Seasoned flour
Melt in a skillet:
    6 tablespoons clarified butter
Add to it:
    ½ cup chopped onions
Brown the frog legs in the butter. Reduce the heat and add:
    ¾ cup boiling Stock, page 490
Cover the skillet closely and cook the frog legs until they are tender, for about 10 minutes. Melt:
    6 tablespoons butter
Sauté in the butter:
    1¼ cups seasoned bread crumbs
    ¾ cup finely chopped hazelnuts
Add:
    1 teaspoon lemon juice
Roll the frog legs in the bread crumbs and serve them garnished with:
    Fennel
or, if you have used the hazelnuts, with:
    Parsley

DEEP-FAT FRIED FROG LEGS

◆ Please read About Deep-Fat Frying, pages 124-126.
Preheat deep fryer to 375°.
Clean:

Frog legs

Dip them in:

A Bound Breading, page 502

Let dry for 1 hour. Fry the frog legs until golden. Drain. Serve with:

Tartare Sauce, page 316

FROG LEGS IN MUSHROOM SAUCE

3 Servings

Clean:

6 large frog legs

Cut the meat into 3 or 4 pieces. Place in a saucepan. Cover with:

Boiling water or Light Stock, page 490

Add:

2 thin slices lemon
⅛ teaspoon white pepper
(Celery, parsley, onion or vegetables suitable for soup)

Simmer the frog meat, covered, until it is tender. Drain well. Melt in a saucepan:

3 tablespoons butter

Add to it and sauté until light brown:

1 cup sliced mushrooms

Stir in:

1½ tablespoons flour

Stir in slowly:

1½ cups chicken stock or stock in which the frog legs were cooked
Correct the seasoning

When the sauce is hot, add the frog meat. Reduce the heat to low. Beat well:

3 egg yolks
3 tablespoons rich cream

Stir these ingredients into the sauce. Let them thicken off the heat. Add:

1½ teaspoons lemon juice or 2 teaspoons dry sherry

Serve the meat at once, covered with the sauce.

FROG LEGS FORESTIÈRE

Allow 5 Per Serving

Sprinkle small frog legs with:

Brandy

Let stand about 2 hours and wipe dry. Sauté them in:

Clarified Butter, page 338

During the last few minutes of cooking when the frog legs become firm to the touch, sauté with the meat for each portion:

2 thinly sliced mushrooms
(1 tablespoon very finely sliced fresh sweet red pepper)
1 tablespoon chopped parsley
1 teaspoon lemon juice
Correct the seasoning

ABOUT TURTLES AND TERRAPIN

Sea turtles attain huge size and their habits are nowhere more fascinatingly described than in "The Windward Road" by Archie Carr.

Handling and cooking these monsters, some of which weigh over 100 pounds, is not a usual household procedure. Therefore most of us are content to enjoy the highly prized, highly priced, gelatinous meat ready-diced and in cans. The greenish meat from the top shell is considered the best—that taken from the bottom is whitish.

The **terrapin** is a freshwater snapping turtle: our children bring them home from the creeks in our neighborhood, as yours may, too. If you cannot use them at once or wish to keep them at least long enough to make certain that they are rid of waste or pollution, you may put them in a deep open box—and don't forget a wire screening on top—give them a dish of water and feed them for a week or so on 3 or 4 small handouts of ground meat.

◆ To cook, place in a pan of cold water:

A 7-inch terrapin

Bring water slowly to a boil and parblanch for at least 10 minutes. Drain. Plunge into cold water and leave until cool enough to handle. Scrub the terrapin well. Place in rapidly boiling water, and add:

(A Bouquet Garni, page 541)
(An onion stuck with cloves)
(3 stalks celery)

◆ Reduce the heat at once and simmer 30 to 45 minutes or until the claws can be removed by pulling. Drain, reserving the stock. Allow the terrapin to cool on its back in order to trap the juices as it cools. When cool, pry the flat plastron free from the curved carapace—easier said than done. Near the head you will find the liver. ◆ Free it carefully from the gall. Discard the gall. Slice the liver thin and reserve it, as well as the eggs, if any. You may or may not want to reserve the small intestines, which may be chopped and added to the meat or sauce. Remove the meat both from the carapace and the skinned legs. When ready to serve, you may toss the meat, including the ground liver and intestines, in:

6 tablespoons melted butter

until heated. Garnish with parsley and serve with:

Sherry, as a drink

or you may heat the meat briefly over very low heat or in the top of a double boiler ◆ over—not in—hot water in a sauce made by combining:

1 cup Brown Sauce, page 326
The chopped, cooked eggs, if any
1 teaspoon mixed herbs: including basil, sweet marjoram, thyme, with a touch of rosemary, bay and sage
3 tablespoons Madeira or dry sherry

MEAT

BOUT MEATS

When a novice approaches the meat counter, she may also approach a state of panic. The friendly informative butcher of a generation ago has often been succeeded by an automaton, mysteriously cutting, grinding, and packaging behind a glass partition. The meats he so impersonally presents in transparent film look bafflingly similar and equally attractive. As a result, they often react in the pan or on the palate in a totally unexpected way. We hope, if you are a rank amateur, that the charts in this chapter will give you the skill of an expert in choosing the right cut for the right dish. For each animal, the charts show you first the general layout of the bone structure; next, the relation of bone to common commercial cuts.

Tender cuts, you will note, lie in those sections where the least body movement and stress occurs and respond to dry heat cooking: roasting, broiling, pan-broiling and sautéing.

Meats with more connective tissue will need very slow cooking with moisture: braising, stewing, fricasseeing, pot roasting ' poaching. ◗ In these processes, the liquid should never go above the simmering point, 185°. For this reason, we do not recommend the pressure cooking of meats, although expediency sometimes overcomes our better judgment. If you pressure cook meat, follow the directions given by the manufacturer of your appliance.

The third chart shows how these commercial cuts are further subdivided into the meat shapes we are familiar with at table. Listed nearby are the recipes appropriate for each cut. Meat cuts and their names vary not only from country to country but even from region to region in the United States. This makes us wish that there were, in plants, a sound Linnaean classification. We hope that the charts will not only identify the names most commonly used, but correlate for you the meat and bone relationships involved and—along with the government grading—give you some relative ideas of fat and lean content.

But there is much about meat that must learned the hard way. How the animal was fed—on grass or corn—and how it was killed, are important factors. Also important are the temperatures at which meat has been held; whether it is watered, or whether treated with preservatives, page 6; how long it has been packaged; and whether it is fairly priced. These are all factors in which you must rely partly on experience and mostly on ◗ the integrity of the butcher.

ABOUT THE GRADING OF MEAT

Before you plunge into purchasing, a word about ◗ grades and prices. The U.S. Government gives you grade protection by stamping all meat sold in interstate commerce. And some states and cities have their own inspection laws. Federal standards of sanitation are rigid, but do be critical of any uninspected locally butchered meats. U.S. grading falls into six classes.

PRIME

This is not commonly available in neighborhood markets. Lean portions, unless the meat is aged, are bright red and well-marbled with fat. Because it comes from young, specially fed cattle, "prime" is well-flavored, fine-textured, tender and encased in white fat. It is very expensive because you pay for the excess fat, much of which is rendered out in cooking.

CHOICE

This grade has less fat than "prime" in its marbling of the lean portions. And, in its coloring, it has a slightly darker tone in both of these portions, but retains high, tender, juicy eating quality.

GOOD

This is still a relatively tender grade, but has a higher ratio of lean to fat meat than either of the above. The lean meat is darker, with little fat marbling, the encasing fat is yellowish and thin.

STANDARD

This grade is cut from young low-quality animals with a very thin fat covering and virtually no marbling in the lean portions. The youth of the animals gives this meat a bland flavor. Tenderness cannot be counted on.

COMMERCIAL AND UTILITY

These are very lean grades and come from old animals. While they are by reason of maturity better in flavor than those in "standard," such meats are coarse in flesh texture and tough, even when carefully cooked, because of their great proportion of connective tissue and their lack of fat.

Although we are always being assured that ◗ the food value of the meat from older animals is comparable to that from younger, more tender ones, we know that they rarely match them in eating quality. One definite exception applies to stocks and soups, page 488. Both are enhanced by extractives from more mature animals. Whatever grade or cut of meat you buy, there is a great deal that you as a cook can do to make less tender cuts pleasanter to eat.

But before we discuss the cook's role, let's consider ♦ how much to purchase per serving. ♦ While price may go down for bonier cuts, the amount you need per serving goes up. So that ♦ for highly processed and canned meats you need less poundage per person. Another thing to watch is the weight of meat, trimmed and untrimmed. In buying trimmed meats, allow: ♦ for boneless cuts, ¼ to ⅓ lb. per serving. This category includes ground beef, lamb and veal, boneless stew, boned roasts and steaks, flank tenderloin and most variety meats. ♦ For meat with some bone, allow ⅓ to ½ lb. per serving. These cuts include rib roasts, unboned steaks, chops and ham. ♦ For bony cuts, allow ¾ to 1 lb. per serving. In this bracket are short ribs, spareribs, lamb shanks, shoulder, breast and plate cuts, brisket and hock.

ABOUT STORING MEAT BEFORE COOKING

We assume that the meat you buy is properly aged, page 766. ♦ Raw meat should be stored at once at 42°, loosely wrapped; or, if encased in fat, uncovered. You will see a typical butcher wrap illustrated on page 759. If you simply pull out the ends of the paper and loosen them, adequate protection and proper ventilation are usually ensured. As a general rule, the larger the piece of meat the longer it will store.

Ground meat, fresh sausage and variety meats are among the most perishable kinds —both as to flavor-retention and safety. Use them within 24 hours of purchase; and, if the ground meat is in amounts over a pound, make sure it is stored, loosely covered, in a container not more than 2½ inches thick in depth, so that the chill of the refrigerator penetrates it quickly. Uncooked diced and cubed meats should be used within 48 hours or so. Roasts will hold 3 to 5 days, steaks 2 to 4.

Pork, lamb and veal are slightly less stable than beef. Prepackaged cured or smoked meat and sausages may be stored refrigerated in the original wrapper. Tenderized hams can be kept much longer in the refrigerator—about 2 weeks—provided the seal of the original wrapper is not broken; only one week otherwise. Once opened, the cut surfaces should be protected. The only exception to an invariable rule is so-called "dry sausage," which need not be refrigerated.

ABOUT SEASONING MEAT

Early salting brings the juices of meat to the surface and into the pan. These juices, which are themselves quite salty, are retained if the meat is seared before season-

ing. If meat is breaded or dredged, pag 501, or if it is browned before stewing an the pan drippings or liquors used in gravy salt may be added when cooking begin In cooking ground meat, allow ¾ teaspoo salt to 1 pound, but do not apply it t patties until the first side is seared an turned. Allow 1 teaspoon to 2 pounds c solid meat with bone.

There are other ways to accent flavo About half an hour before cooking, eithe rub meat with garlic, onion, herbs or spice or insert slivers of garlic or onion near th bone of a roast or else distribute them ove a cut surface of steak or roast. Remove an exposed garlic before cooking, as i scorched flavor is not attractive.

Delicacy of flavor may be preserved i meat heavy with fat by pouring off an excess grease after the first half hour c cooking.

ABOUT COOKING TOUGH MEATS

Tenderness in raw meats depends not onl on the comparative youth of the anima but on the strain of cattle to which it be longs and the way it was fed. ♦ Toughne is due to the presence of connective tissue and lack of fat in the muscle. Larding an Barding, page 383, can help to make u somewhat for the lack of fat. The best wa to convert stringy to tenderer tissue is b very long and ♦ very slow covered cookin in the presence of moisture. See Braisin Pot-Roasting and Stewing, page 41 Grinding and mincing make chewing easie But the texture of the meat, if basical tough, remains so and it should never l used in luxury dishes like galantines or, f that matter, even in those as humdrum hamburger.

Any meat can be made more palatab by seasonings and by added fats or dres ings. Pounding and scoring are a help cuts that are normally treated by dry he methods, like sautéing and pan-frying. A other favorite technique is marinating, a though it involves nutritive losses, some which can be recaptured if the marina itself is subsequently used in making t the dish.

Chemical tenderizing is a modern d velopment. One controversial innovation this type is beyond the control of the co sumer. The live animal is given an inje tion of vegetable enzyme, the tenderizi effects of which are carried throughout th body before butchering. Special aging a storing techniques must accompany th method. The enzyme is reactivated at 13 and reduces cooking time. A 22-lb. pie of beef will cook at 400° in about 1 hot

Unfortunately all meat tissues—tho which need it and those which do not—a affected by enzyme injection. As a resu the prime portions are usually flabby a somewhat tasteless and the meat general has a jellied consistency which we find u pleasant. Nor can we say much for the older methods of injecting or dusting the meat with papain, a derivative of papaya, which also tenderizes. We feel that both the flavor and the texture of the meat itself are adversely affected. Meat may be tenderized with a papain derivative of the household type. Usually it is sprinkled on both sides, allowing 1 teaspoon of tenderizer per lb. Prick the meat all over with a fork after applying the tenderizer. Recent studies indicate that papain enzymes seem to tenderize meat as it warms up to between 140° and 176°, so apply the tenderizer as the meat is put in the oven.

ABOUT MINCING, GRINDING AND POUNDING MEAT

The effect of the first two processes is quite different. Particles of minced meat remain separate in further preparation; but ground meat, especially if ground 2 or 3 times, tends to pack. ◗ Always handle ground meat lightly to avoid a dense finished texture.

Pounding, which breaks down the tough fibers of the meat, may be done with a wooden mallet or the flat side of a cleaver. Shown below is a Chinese cleaver which can also be used for chopping, just like a French knife, page 251. ◗ If you are inexperienced, hold the cleaver in both hands and be sure the handle projects beyond the board or table surface—so that you don't pound your fingers.

If you strike with a glancing motion or if you slightly moisten the cleaver, the meat is not so apt to stick. If you are pounding something delicate, like capon breasts, and don't want the fillets to separate, put them in a fold of oiled parchment paper. This allows a sliding and slipping comparable to the glancing action the professional achieves and keeps the meat intact, even when it is pounded paper thin. A chef friend has suggested that if you find the appearance of a very thin piece of meat

disappointing, it can be pounded and then folded over for the cooking—to make it more presentable when served.

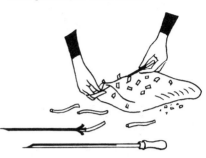

ABOUT LARDING AND BARDING MEAT

Lean meat is frequently "larded" to give it additional juiciness and flavor. ◗ Lardoons are thin strips of salted pork or bacon. They may be first blanched briefly, page 132, and dried before use. French cooks rub them with garlic and other herbs or dust them with cloves and cinnamon. They are cut into 2- or 3-inch strips ¼ inch thick for heavy meat cuts, ⅛ inch thick for small fowl. A larding needle may be used to draw lardoons through the surface of the meat or, as a stopgap measure, a thin knife or ice pick can be pressed into service. Insert lardoons about 1 inch apart. When larding a fowl, place the lardoons at right angles to the breast bone. Larger strips of salt pork may be forced through such meat cuts as chuck and round from surface to surface. After pulling the lardoons through, the ends may be cut off. Allow about 3 oz. of fat per pound of meat.

Lardoons are sometimes placed so their ends form rosettes or decorations. Larding needles are of 2 types. The one in use above is also shown, center left, before the lardoon is firmly tightened in it by pinching the pliable fringed ends together. The lower needle has a more than semicircular profile and can be used to form the lardoon itself by plunging it into the salt pork. Then turn the needle to cut the lardoon free. It is shown loaded and ready to run through the meat. To keep the lardoon in the meat, after forcing the needle in, place your thumb or forefinger at the base of the needle groove and slip the needle out with an even, steady pressure. If salt pork is used to lard a meat, as in Galantine, page 436, the lardoons are placed with the grain of the meat, as sketched above. Then, in carving, the pork shows attractively in cross section.

LARDOONS

Enough for 2½ Lbs. of Meat

I. Rub:
    ¼ lb. salt pork or bacon

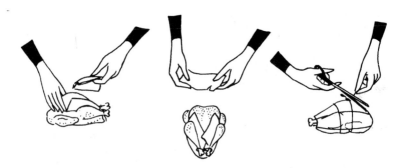

with a cut:
> **Clove of garlic**

Cut into small strips. Dip into:
> **Freshly ground pepper**
> **Ground cloves**
> **Minced parsley or chives**

II. Marinate:
> **¼ lb. salt pork lardoons**

in:
> **A few tablespoons of brandy**

Just before using, sprinkle with:
> **Nutmeg**
> **Chopped parsley**

III. Lardoons or Cracklings
These are also called grattons.
Dice:
> **Salt pork**

Try it out, page 511, in a skillet until
brown and crisp or place the dice in a very
slow oven until golden brown. Use for
garnishing.

Any lean meat or that of fowl, like guinea
or partridge, which is low in fat content, or
any fowl from which the skin has been removed can profit by barding before roasting. Meat cuts are simply covered with
slices of salt pork, about ¼ inch thick, or fat
bacon, as shown on the left in the sketch.
For fowl, truss the bird. For each small
bird, use 4 pieces of ¼-inch-thick salt pork
or fat bacon about 3 x 3½ inches square.
Slip one on either side between the leg
and breast, see sketch above, left and center. Cover the bird—legs and all—with 2
other pieces and tie, as shown on the right,
♦ making sure that the high exposed surfaces of the bird are blanketed. After cooking, the salt pork or bacon which has served
its protective purpose is discarded.

ABOUT MARINATING MEAT

Although you may gain tenderness through
marination, you also stand to lose substantial nutritive value, since, by this
method, a good many proteins and vitamins are leached away. Marinades are

made of both raw and cooked materials
and ♦ just to remind you of the importance
of using them in making up the finished
dish, you will find them in Sauces, page
336. ♦ Marinating for 12 hours or more
cuts the cooking time by approximately ⅓.
Allow about ½ cup of marinade for every
pound of food to be processed.

ABOUT RETAINING MEAT JUICES
IN COOKING

When raw meat is put into a cold liquid,
as in the making of stocks, page 488, the
meat juices are released into the liquid.
But when we cook meat for the table, we
want these juices to stay in the meat itself.
♦ Do not cook chilled meats or ✳ frozen
meat unthawed. Temperature and cooking
times in all of our recipes are given for
meat at 70°. Of course, this method does
not apply if the meat is salt, like ham and
tongue, when it may first be blanched,
page 132, or unless the broth is being used
for stock. In a stew, one approved method
of preparation is to drop the meat into
boiling water—disturbing the boiling as
little as possible— ♦ and as soon as the
meat turns in color, to reduce the heat to
a simmer. This method is effective with
veal or poultry and is called cooking "à
blanc."

But the proper browning, see below, of
most meats not only does a sealing job but
adds immeasurably to flavor.

ABOUT SEARING OR
BROWNING MEAT

Before browning meat, be sure that it is
wiped ♦ dry. It is best to use as little fat
as possible in browning, but be sure it
covers the entire bottom of the pan. If
there is not enough fat to keep the meat
from burning, the charring will give a bitter taste to the sauces or gravies which may
be prepared from it later. Use fat that
comes from the meat you are browning or
one that complements it in flavor. The
♦ heavy pan should be thoroughly and
slowly heated before the fat is added and

ie meat ♦ slowly browned. Turn it frequently. ♦ Be sure not to crowd the pan,
ecause this lowers the heat and the meat
ecomes greyish rather than the desired
rown. If necessary, until you learn to
rown without burning, use a little more
at and pour it off after the searing. In
act, it is always wise to pour off most of
ie excess grease which may accumulate in
ie pan before adding a liquid for stewing.
Vhen browning a meat, it is often desir-
ble to cook a few chopped onions or other
egetables with it. Since vegetables are
pt to cook more rapidly, the meat may be
artially browned before they are added.
eep the vegetables moving so they, too,
ook without scorching. You may, if you
refer, brown them separately in order to
ontrol the heat more easily and then add
iem to the meat pan. If you are cooking
ie onions separately, sprinkle them with a
ery small amount of sugar. It caramelizes
iem attractively and gives good color to
stew. For vegetables used as meat flavor-
ig, see Mirepoix, page 541.

To braise, stew or pot-roast, see page
12.

BOUT BROILING MEAT

Please read About Broiling, page 123,
ien choose tender cuts, see Chart, pages
90-397, like beef steak and lamb chops.
lank is also handled this way, but should
e cooked rare. See London Broil, page
01. The broiling of veal and fresh pork
not recommended. Sauté or pan-fry such
 its instead.

For broiling ♦ have the meat at room
mperature. Score it about every 2 inches
round the edge to keep it from curling.
ut off excess fat, if any.

Place the meat ♦ on a cold rack to keep
from sticking or, should your rack be
ot, grease the meat or rack. Set the meat
n the middle of the broiler rack, 3 inches
om the heating unit.

Broil the meat until the top side is well
rowned. Turn, season and broil until the
cond side is browned. ♦ Only one turn-
ig is necessary for a 1-inch steak or chop.
urn frequently for thicker ones and lower
ie rack about 1 inch for each successive
ich of meat thickness—although 2 inches
considered the limit for broiling. Season
nd serve the meat on a hot platter. Broil-
ig time depends largely upon the thick-
ess of the meat, the length of time it has
een hung, its fat content and the degree
: doneness desired. If you use a ther-
iometer, rare steaks are broiled to an
iternal temperature of 130°; medium to
50°. Lamb chops are broiled to 155° for
ire and to 170° if well done. Ham is
oked well done. The time for broiling
icon is influenced by personal preference
s to crispness, but ♦ to keep it from curl-
ig, the heat should be low. Should your
roiler be an infrared one, follow manu-
icturer's directions.

ABOUT PANBROILING MEAT

♦ Preheat a heavy skillet. Rub the pan with
a small quantity of fat if the meat is not
prime. Sear the meat on one side until the
blood rises to the surface. Then turn at
once and sear it on the other side. ♦ Reduce the heat and continue to process the
meat uncovered. If cooked too long, it
toughens badly and dries out. In the case
of a steak about 1½ inches thick, cooking
time may be 10 minutes or more if you
want it medium to well done. During the
cooking, pour excess fat from the pan for,
if allowed to accumulate, the meat is
"fried" rather than "broiled" in quality.

If meat is solid and well-marbled or if fat
has been incorporated with it—as is often
the case with ground meats, like hamburger—it can go directly into a preheated
ungreased pan. Sometimes a salt base is
suggested, allowing 1 teaspoon salt for
each pound of meat. This rather surprising
technique works but is, in our judgment,
best avoided, since the salt extracts meat
juices which, of course, are promptly discarded when broiling is over. If you are
obliged to follow fat-free procedures, try
oven broiling, a soapstone griddle or a pan
whose surface has been specially treated
for fat-free frying. With such treated pans,
follow the manufacturer's directions.

ABOUT ROASTING MEAT

After trying out different methods of roasting meat over a long period of years, we
are convinced that the quality of the meat
is the decisive factor. We suggest you
choose a method best suited to the meat at
hand. ♦ To cook vegetables with a roast,
see page 256.

I. If the meat is Prime or Choice, we get
the best flavor by placing not less than 2
ribs at about 70° temperature ♦ on a rack
in a pan greased with suet or oil, in a preheated 500° oven, fat side up. The rack
allows proper circulation of air. As soon
as the oven door is closed ♦ reduce the
heat to 350° and time the cooking from
that point, depending on the size of the
roast and the degree of doneness wanted.
Timings are given in the individual recipes.

No basting is necessary in this procedure, there being sufficient fat in the meat.
You will get minimal, but very precious,
juice in the pan. To make gravy from pan
drippings, see page 322.

II. ♦ If meat is Good or Standard grade
and its weight not under 4 lbs., place it
when it has reached 70° ♦ uncovered in a
preheated 325° oven—except for pork, for
which we prefer an oven heated to 350°.
Sometimes we first brown the roast, page
384. But usually we put a thermometer in
it and simply place the meat, unbrowned,
on a rack, in a pan directly in the preheated oven and forget about it until it is
almost time to check for internal tempera-

ture. The method just described produces practically no fat or juice in the pan, and needs a gravy confected from precooked stocks, see page 488. In adopting either of the above methods, remember that if the roast is carved in the kitchen rather than at the table, the juices which run into the carving dish can and should be quickly de-fatted and incorporated into any gravy previously prepared—to give it a final authentic flavor. Meanwhile, keep the already sliced meat warm on a hot platter.

♦ Sometimes very low, slow roasting is suggested. ♦ It is important not to have the oven under 275°, for unwanted microorganisms may not be destroyed below this temperature, no matter how long the cooking. ♦ The insertion of metal pins in a roast cuts down cooking time somewhat and the meat will be juicier but not quite as tender.

ABOUT BASTING MEAT

In roasting and broiling, everything is done to preserve the dry quality of the heat. If roasts are Prime grade, they are so heavy in fat that basting is not necessary. In fact, with prime meats, fat losses run as high as 40% of weight. Just brush a small amount of fat in the base of the pan to tide over until some from the meat is rendered. An exception is tenderloin, which may be simply rubbed with fat or oil or be larded or barded, page 383.

The leaner cuts profit by basting ♦ with melted fat. But the moment you baste with stocks or water, excess steam is created which lessens the dry heat quality that makes a roast so delicious. ♦ Baste preferably with fatty pan drippings by using a bulb-type baster, as sketched on the left, or with a spoon as shown on the right.

There are also 2 types of self-basting. One is with fat, in barding, page 384. The other is with steam, which takes place in a covered pan—when the steam rising from the food falls back from the lid onto the braising meat or stew. This kind of basting never goes on in roasting—where, to achieve the essential dry heat ♦ no cover is used.

ABOUT TIMING IN COOKING MEAT

Timing is given in each recipe, but it [is] most difficult to advise about this accurate[ly] without knowing the thickness of the mea[t,] its quality, its shape and how much bon[e] it contains. Ovens and broilers should a[l]ways be preheated. All meat, we repea[t,] should be at about 70° throughout befo[re] roasting or broiling begins. If meat [is] chemically tenderized, the papain deriv[a]tives used in the household, see page 38[,] begin to take effect during cooking an[d] greatly shorten its cooking period.

If meats have been ✱ frozen, bring the[m] to 70° and time as for fresh meat. Thaw[]ing before cooking keeps to a minimu[m] the amount of juices released. But the[re] are times—occasional emergencies—whe[n] one must cook meat before thawing it.

In roasting unthawed frozen meat, pr[e]heat the oven to about 25° less than ind[i]cated in the recipes and allow about [twice] again as much time for the cooking perio[d.]

In broiling unthawed meat, regardless [of] its thickness, place it at least 5 to 6 inch[es] below the heat source. Again allow [at] least ½ again as much time as normally in[]dicated. For further comments on timin[g,] see page 139. ♦ To test for doneness, se[e] below.

▲ In high altitudes, roasted and bake[d] meats require no adjustment up to 7000 f[t.] After that a longer cooking period ma[y] be needed. We recommend the pressur[e] cooking of meats only in cases of emer[]gency. Tests show that these have le[ss] shrinkage and more flavor if cooked at 1[0] rather than at 15 pounds pressure.

ABOUT DONENESS IN MEAT

Rare, medium, or well done—these are suc[h] personal preferences that set rules becom[e] difficult to prescribe. What you shoul[d] realize is that ♦ in cooking any meats, hea[t] should at some point be high enough [to] destroy unwanted and harmful organism[s.] We give these necessary internal tempera[]tures for various meats in our individua[l] recipes and elsewhere in this chapter. B[ut] we ask you to realize that meat roasted f[or] as long as 12 hours and to as high a tem[]

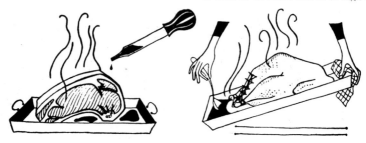

perature as 200° may still be insufficiently cooked to ensure safety—since roasting is merely a reflected heat; whereas stewing at a simmering temperature of 180° over a comparably long period will be sufficient—this heat being moist, and a more penetrating one. ◗ Reaching the proper temperature is especially vital for safety in cooking pork, page 406. We suggest in recipes for roasts, steaks and stews a certain timing—usually minutes to the pound at a given temperature. But with this rough and ready formula you may not get the result you expected. The reasons are many: if you have not allowed the meat to reach 70°, if its shape is very thick or if it is not well aged, it will require longer cooking. Or the meat may have much fat, which will allow the heat to be transmitted more rapidly.

Since it requires a trained eye to judge the doneness of meat from its external appearance ◗ use a meat thermometer for accurate results. Before broiling meat over 3 inches thick or before roasting it, insert the thermometer in the center and fleshy portion of the meat, away from bony or fatty sections. Unless the glass of the thermometer is metal-shielded, make a gash with a pointed sharp knife to ease the insertion of the thermometer. Place the top so that it is as far away from the source of heat as possible.

If you have no thermometer, there are two ways to judge doneness. In the touch method, firm meat is well done. If it responds as a cake does, page 617—is soft yet resilient—the meat is medium rare. You can also detect the degree of doneness by pricking roasted or broiled meats, but when you do you lose valuable juices. If the juice runs red, the meat is rare; pink, medium rare; colorless, well done.

◗ Pork and fowl with light meat must be cooked until the juice is colorless. Most other meats are overdone at this point.

To test for braised meats, use a sharply pointed knife near the bone. The juice should run clear.

ABOUT COOKING MEAT EN CROÛTE

Meat in a crust, or en croûte, lends itself particularly to buffet service. If served hot, the meat remains "à point," page 122, for at least half an hour. Hot or cold, the finished dish is beautiful to behold. The crust is not eaten. It serves only as a medium for retaining aromas. You may encase ham, fowl, lamb or beef roast when cooked to within ½ to ¾ of an hour of doneness. Starting with uncooked fowl or roast is described later.

Cool the meat while you prepare the following crust, heavy in egg, which lends the tensile strength necessary to keep large or heavy meats covered. Have all ingredients at 70°. Mix together, to the consistency of coarse corn meal:

    4 cups all-purpose flour
    1 cup shortening
    1½ teaspoons salt
Make a well, page 594, of these ingredients and work in one at a time:
    3 to 4 eggs
    ½ cup water
Knead the dough until well bound. Roll into a ball and rest covered for several hours at 70°. Preheat the oven to 450°. Roll the dough into a large sheet, about ³⁄₁₆ inch thick. Place the meat you want to cover so that the top surface is down on the dough. Then fold the dough over it, as neatly as possible, pressing it to take the form of the meat. Be careful to keep the covering intact. Then turn the covered meat right side up. Brush any excess flour off the dough with a dry brush.

Now the fun begins. From the pastry scraps that remain, cut rounds, flowers and leaves or any decorations that suit your mood. If you like, score them with a fork to give their surfaces a variation that will show up markedly after baking. You may even use Puff Paste, page 593, for such trimmings. Space them out on the dough up to three thicknesses by applying French Egg Wash, page 682, to each, as a glue. When you are satisfied with your design—and don't make it too cluttered—brush the surfaces with egg wash again. Cut a series of decorative gashes in the dough casing, as for a covered pie, to let the steam escape and to keep the crust from buckling. Put the covered meat in the hot oven, and ◗ reduce the heat at once to 350°. Allow the crust to bake until it is delicately browned. Repeat the egg glazing at the end of baking, for an even effect. You may also brush the crust with butter on removal from the oven.

Another way to bake en croûte is to use, instead of the dough indicated above, a stiff bread dough. Punch it down once before rolling it out and cover as previously described.

◗ To cook uncooked meat en croûte, prepare the dough described previously. Coat the meat to be covered with Egg Wash, page 682. Fold the pastry around the meat and decorate as described above.

Bake the meat in a preheated 280° to 300° oven, 2 to 3 hours, depending on size. Hams and legs of lamb may be boned and stuffed before wrapping. If a stuffing is used, be sure the food it is made of is precooked, as the heat may not penetrate it sufficiently otherwise to cook it through.

ABOUT STORING COOKED MEAT

It is much safer to ◗ put meat into the refrigerator while still fairly hot and this is only a slightly more expensive way to refrigerate. ◗ Cover it.

If you prefer, you may also leave meat that has been cooked to cool ◗ covered for 2 hours before refrigerating.

Do not store ◖ meat in hot gravy in quantities larger than 1 quart. Drain off the gravy and allow it to cool separately if the amounts are larger. If meats are ◖ stuffed, unstuff them and store the stuffing separately.

ABOUT REHEATING MEAT

It is a great temptation to try to prepare large joints of meat in advance and reheat them just before serving. This is not good practice. For the heat to penetrate on reheating, a very long period is necessary and the meat tends to dry out.

With hash or sauced meats, be sure the sauce is ◖ just to the point of boiling before the meat is added. ◖ Reduce the heat at once and allow the meat to heat thoroughly. Serve at once. An even better way to reheat thin sliced meats is described on page 139.

ABOUT CARVING MEAT

The convenient ready-to-serve platter, or so-called Russian service, has almost displaced carving. Fortunately, a few hosts still delight in practicing this gracious skill. And, given a very sharp knife, a large platter and the most rudimentary knowledge of animal anatomy, almost anyone can learn to carve.

Illustrations throughout this chapter show the general direction taken in approaching major cuts. Most meats are cut against the grain, although a leg of lamb or mutton may also be cut with it. If you are trying out in the kitchen, use a board until you become worthy of the art and can carve on a platter without scratching it. Ply the knife with a long, light, pulling and pushing, sawlike action. Always try to keep your fork-hand behind, not in front of,

the blade. Protect yourself further by using a fork with a thumb piece.

Slicing knives for ham, roast beef, big turkeys and pot roasts have a very flexible 10-inch blade, about 1¼ inches wide. Carving knives for game, loin of pork, rack of lamb or lobster are about a foot in length. Their 8½-inch pointed, rigidly firm blades, about 1¾ inches wide, are so shaped that at the blade edge they come to a fine V. ◖ Keeping the knife blade sharp and under easy control is important. But of equal importance to the successful carver is keeping the V-edge true by the use of a steel. And the following procedure should precede the use of the knife before each carving period. The steel, which must be kept magnetized, realigns the molecular structure of the blade.

◖ To true a blade, hold the steel firmly in the left hand, thumb on top of handle. Hold the knife in the right hand, point upward, and the hand slightly away from the body. Place the heel of the blade against the far side of the tip of the steel, as illustrated. The steel and blade should meet at about a 15° to 25° angle.

◖ Draw the blade across the steel, bringing it down toward the left hand, with a quick swinging motion of the right wrist. ◖ The entire blade should pass lightly over the steel. To start the second stroke, bring the knife into the same position as in the first, but this time the steel should lie behind the blade, away from you, as shown on the right. About twelve strokes are enough to true the edge.

Some carvers feel the results are better if they allow a roast to set—that is rest outside the oven on a hot platter. With very large joints which retain their heat well, this setting period may be from 30 to 45 minutes.

GUIDE TO APPROXIMATE YIELD OR CUTS FROM 250 LB. SIDE OF BEEF, CUT FROM AN 800 LB. STEER

Please read About Steaks, page 399, and Fillet of Beef, page 399.

FROM 26 LBS. OF SHORTLOIN

You have a choice of club, sirloin and porterhouse steaks—which are a combination of T-bone, sirloin and fillet. But, if you want 5 lbs. of fillet from the shortloin, you must forego the porterhouse steaks, which will leave you 21 lbs. of shortloin for sirloin steaks, T-bone and club steaks. If you choose to have the fillet, see page 399 to utilize it to the best advantage.

FROM	CHOICE OF
21 lbs. of loin end	Butt steaks and roasts
2 lbs. of flank steak	Ground beef—flank steak
45 lbs. of boneless round	Top and bottom, Swiss steak, pot roasts, hamburger, cubed steak
23 lbs. of rib	7-rib roast, rolled roast, rib steaks
42 lbs. of boneless chuck	Ground beef, stew, pot roast
10 lbs. of boneless brisket	For braising, stewing, ground, corned beef
17 lbs. of plate	Ground beef, stew
10 lbs. of shank	Soup meat, marrow bones
49 lbs. of fat, bone and waste	Also, tripe, tongue, liver, heart, sweet-
5 lbs. loss in trimming	breads, brains, kidneys, oxtail and head.

ABOUT ECONOMICAL USE OF LARGE CUTS OF MEAT

If shopping for a household of two, there are times when you may look longingly at the "weekly special" on meat. How tempting the standing rib roast of beef, the rump of beef, the leg of spring lamb, the loin of pork, the round of veal or the half or whole ham! But unless you are planning to have guests, it looks as if it is far more meat than you care to buy for two. But by taking advantage of special sales prices and planning ahead to freeze a part of the cut for future use, it is an economy to buy the larger piece. You can have your delicious roast for just two—or steaks from the ham or veal, chops from lamb or pork, short ribs from beef. Then the remainder may be used in many interesting leftover dishes.

2 RIBS OF BEEF—5 lbs.

Have butcher cut off:
Short Ribs, page 417; Roast Beef, page 398. The leftover beef can be reheated in: Cumberland Sauce, page 331. Or used in Hot Roast Beef Sandwich with Olive Sauce, page 245; Shepherd's Pie, page 234; Leftover in Bacon, page 230; Peppers filled with Meat and Rice, page 289; Cold Roast Beef and Tomato Sauce, page 333; Acorn Squash Filled with Creamed Food, page 304.

RUMP OF BEEF—4 to 5 lbs.

Have butcher cut off a piece about 2 inches thick, dice into 1-inch cubes for:
Beef Stew with Wine, page 415. Or use in one piece for Pot Roast, page 414. Use the leftovers as Cold Roast Beef and Curry Sauce, page 325; or hot as beef reheated in Cucumberland Sauce, page 331.

Or use in Hot Roast Beef Sandwich, page 245; Turnovers filled with meat, page 224; or Leftover Timbales, page 207.

ROUND OF VEAL

Have butcher cut off 1 or 2 thin slices of veal for:

Veal Birds	Page 420
Veal Scallopini	403
Mexican Veal Steak	420
Wiener Schnitzel	404

Have another slice cut off to dice into 1-inch cubes for:

Blanquette de Veau	419
Cubed Veal Baked in Sour Cream	421

Use the remainder for:

Veal Roast	402

Use leftovers in:

Curried Veal and Rice	229
Creamed Veal	229
Veal and Spinach	229
Veal Timbales	208
Meat Shortcakes	225

LEG OF LAMB—5 to 6 lbs.

Have butcher cut off:

4 chops for:

Broiled II	Page 406
Stuffed Lamb Chops	406

Also a slice about 2 inches thick, diced into 1-inch cubes for:

Curried Lamb	423
Lamb Stew	422
Roast the remaining shank end	405

Leftovers may be used in:

Veal or Lamb and Spinach Dish	229
Eggplant Filled with Leftover Food	278
Lamb Terrapin	229
Lamb Sandwich	248
Scotch Broth	150

DIVISIONS OF COMMERCIAL CUTS AND RETAIL CUTS OF BEEF

BEEF

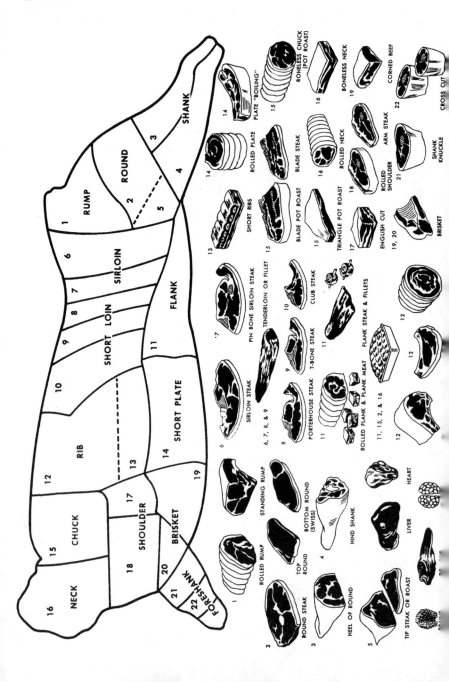

RECIPES KEYED TO CHART

Roast of Beef, Page 398: Rib 12; Sirloin 6-7; Short Loin 8-9-10.

Pot Roasts, Page 414: Shoulder 18; Chuck 15; Rump 1; or Brisket 19.

Sauerbraten, and Boeuf à la Mode, Page 415; Shoulder 18.

Steaks: For details of beef cuts bearing this name, see Page 399. For Chart of Fillet Steaks, see Page 411; also see Broiled Steaks, Page 400 and Pan-Broiled Steaks, Page 400, for which you can use Shoulder 18; Rib Steak 12; Tip Steak 5; Ground Round 2.

Boeuf Fondu Bourguignonne, Page 401: Fillet 6-9; Sirloin 6-7.

Beef Stroganoff, Page 401: Fillets 6-9.

Beef Kebabs, Page 402: Round 2; Sirloin 6-7; Fillets 6-9.

Beef Rolls, Roulades or Paupiettes, Page 418: Round 2; Flank 11.

Burgoo, Page 418: Chuck 15; Neck 16; Shoulder 18; Foreshank 21-22.

Sukiyaki, Page 402: Tenderloin 6-9; Sirloin Tip 6; Eye of Round 2.

Beef Goulash, Page 417: Round 2; Shinbone 21-22.

Flank Steak With Dressing, Page 416: Flank 11.

Oxtail Stew, Page 418: Tailbones.

Corned Beef, Page 412: Brisket 19.

Ground Beef and Meat Loaves, Page 431, and Hamburgers, Page 427: Chuck 15; Flank 11; Neck 16; Round 2.

Heart, Page 447, Tongue, Page 445, and Tripe, Page 448, are the favored beef variety meats.

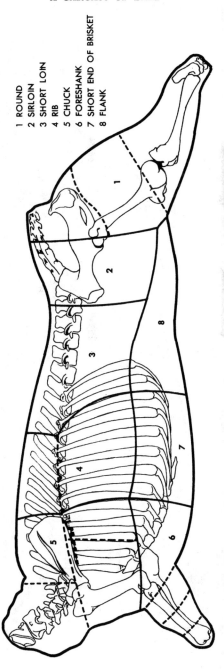

1 ROUND
2 SIRLOIN
3 SHORT LOIN
4 RIB
5 CHUCK
6 FORESHANK
7 SHORT END OF BRISKET
8 FLANK

DIVISIONS OF COMMERCIAL CUTS AND RETAIL CUTS OF VEAL

VEAL

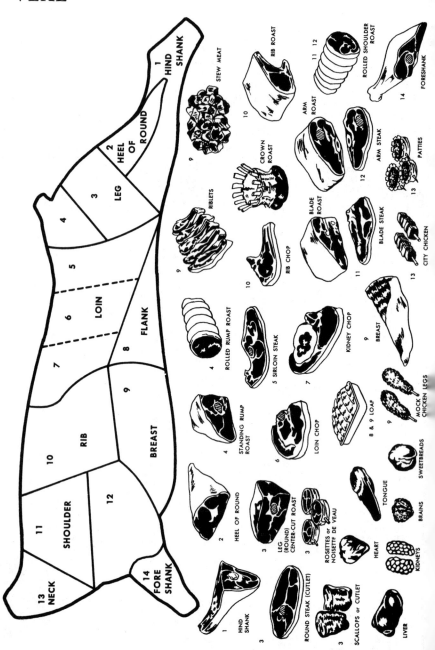

BONE STRUCTURE AND
COMMERCIAL CUTS FROM
A CARCASS OF VEAL

RECIPES KEYED TO CHART

Roast of Veal, Page 403: Rib 10.

Stuffed or Rolled Veal Roast, Page 402:
Shoulder 11-12; Breast 9.

Veal Kidney Roast, Page 403: Loin 7.

Veal Pot Roast, Page 420 or Veal Pot
Roast In Red Wine, Page 419: Rump 4.

Veal Cutlet, Scaloppini or Schnitzel or Veal
Parmigiana, Page 403-404: Leg 3;
Loin 5-6-7.

Veal Stew, or Veal Stew in Red Wine,
Page 419: Breast 9; Neck 13.

Blanquette de Veau, Page 419:
Shoulder 11-12.

Veal Porkolt, Page 417: Leg 3; Shoulder
11-12; Neck 13.

Mock Chicken Drumsticks or City Chicken,
Page 420: Breast 9; Neck 13.

Osso Buco, Page 421: Shank 14.

Veal Patties, Page 428: Flank 8; Breast 9.

Terrine, Page 435: Leg 3.

Veal Birds or Paupiettes, Page 420: Leg 3.

All Veal Variety Meats are considered
choice.

See Index for Liver, Sweetbreads, Brains,
and Kidneys; Also Steak and Kidney
Pie, Page 420, and Head Cheese and
Brawn, Page 449.

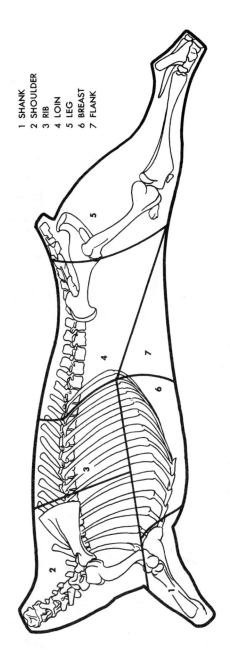

1 SHANK
2 SHOULDER
3 RIB
4 LOIN
5 LEG
6 BREAST
7 FLANK

DIVISIONS OF COMMERCIAL CUTS AND RETAIL CUTS OF LAMB

LAMB

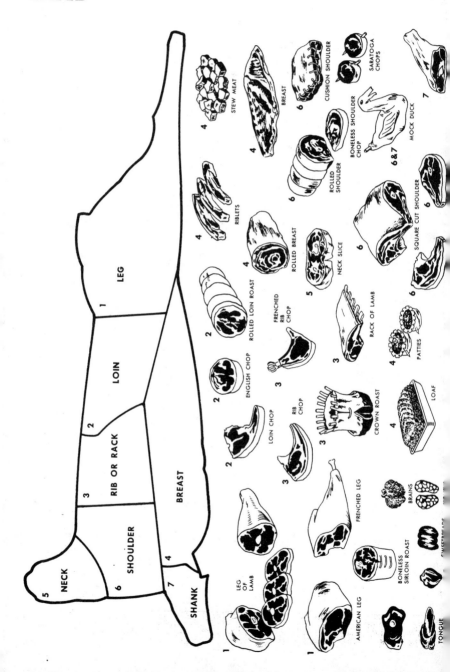

BONE STRUCTURE AND
COMMERCIAL CUTS FROM
A CARCASS OF LAMB

RECIPES KEYED TO CHART

Lamb or Mutton Roast, Page 405: Rib 3.

Broiled Lamb Chops, Page 406: Rib 3;
Loin 2; Leg 1.

Broiled Lamb Kebabs, Page 406:
Shoulder 6.

Hamburgers, Page 428: Shoulder 6.

Since lamb is a relatively tender meat,
almost any cut, especially of young lamb,
can be cooked by the dry heat methods
above. Also see pages 405-406. Cuts from
active areas where the muscle is firmer
may be cooked according to the following moist heat methods on pages
421-423.

Braised Stuffed Shoulder or Farce of Lamb,
Page 421: Shoulder 6.

Braised Lamb Shanks or Trotters, Page
422: Shank 7.

Irish Stew, Page 423: Shoulder 6; Breast 4.

Navarin Printanier, Page 422: Shoulder 6;
Breast 4.

Try cooked lamb in Curry of Lamb, Page
423; Lamb and Eggplant Casserole,
Page 430; Stuffed Eggplant, Page 278.

For Variety Meat Recipes, see Tongue in
Creole Sauce, Page 446; Steak and
Kidney Pie, Page 418.

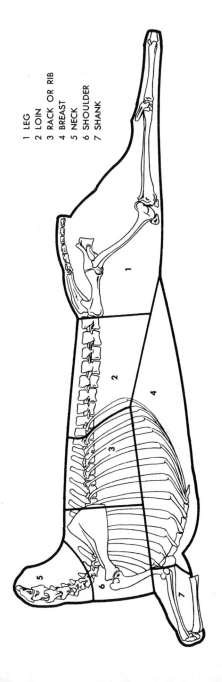

1 LEG
2 LOIN
3 RACK OR RIB
4 BREAST
5 NECK
6 SHOULDER
7 SHANK

DIVISIONS OF COMMERCIAL CUTS AND RETAIL CUTS OF PORK

PORK

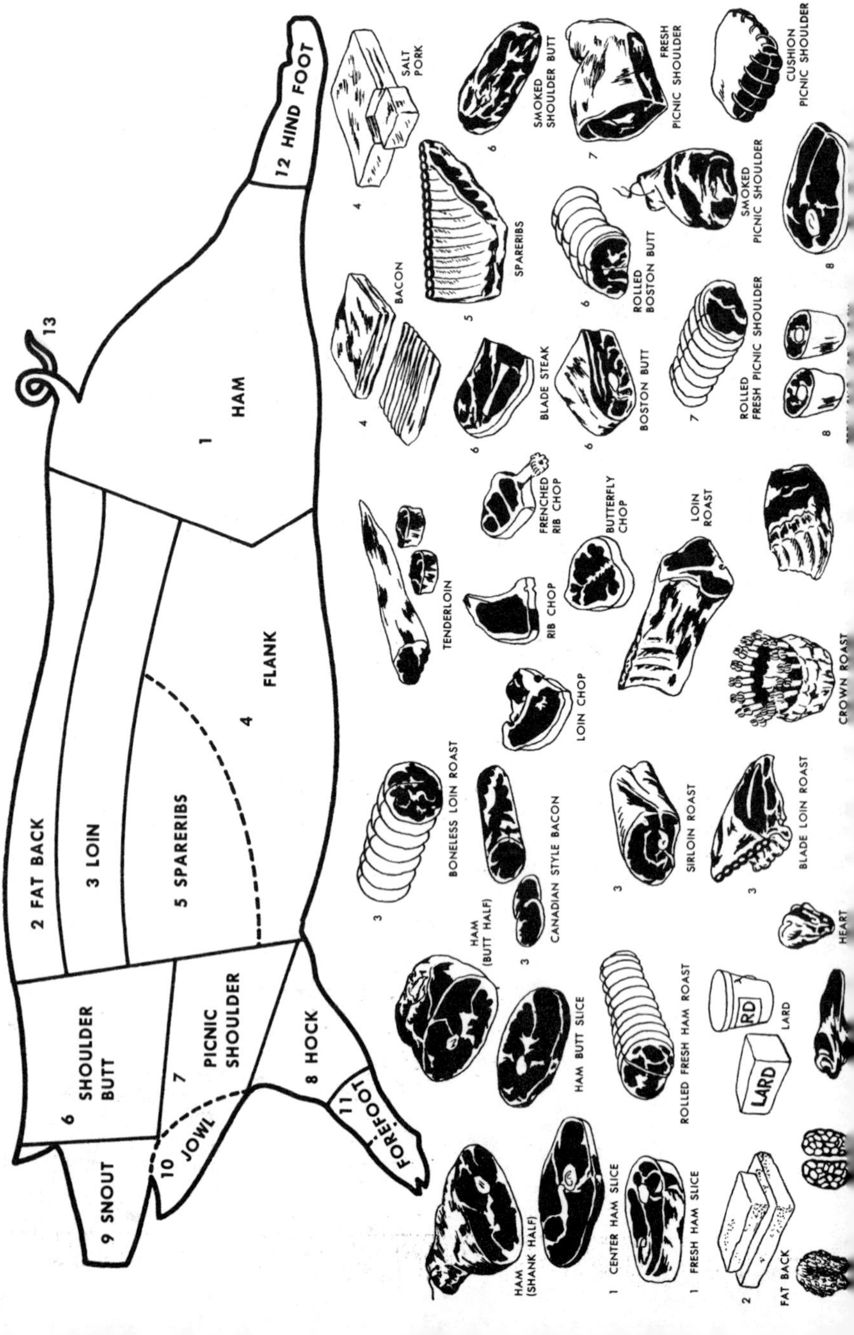

SALT PORK

SMOKED SHOULDER BUTT

FRESH PICNIC SHOULDER

CUSHION PICNIC SHOULDER

12 HIND FOOT

13

BACON

SPARERIBS

ROLLED BOSTON BUTT

SMOKED PICNIC SHOULDER

1 HAM

BLADE STEAK

BOSTON BUTT

ROLLED FRESH PICNIC SHOULDER

FRENCHED RIB CHOP

BUTTERFLY CHOP

LOIN ROAST

TENDERLOIN

RIB CHOP

FLANK

4

CROWN ROAST

LOIN CHOP

2 FAT BACK

3 LOIN

5 SPARERIBS

BONELESS LOIN ROAST

CANADIAN STYLE BACON

SIRLOIN ROAST

BLADE LOIN ROAST

HEART

HAM (BUTT HALF)

6 SHOULDER BUTT

7 PICNIC SHOULDER

8 HOCK

HAM BUTT SLICE

ROLLED FRESH HAM ROAST

LARD

LARD

9 SNOUT

10 JOWL

11 FOREFOOT

HAM (SHANK HALF)

1 CENTER HAM SLICE

1 FRESH HAM SLICE

2 FAT BACK

RECIPES KEYED TO CHART

Roast of Pork, Page 407: Loin 3.

Roast of Pork Stuffed with Sauerkraut, Page 408: Shoulder Butt 6.

Pork Tenderloin, Page 408: Loin 3.

Frenched Fruit Casserole, Page 409; Loin 3; with Mushrooms, Page 424: Loin 3.

Rib Pork Chops Broiled, Page 408: Loin 3.

Rib or Loin Chops, Page 424 or with Fruit, or Stuffed, Page 425: Loin 3.

Sweet and Sour Pork, Page 426: Boned Ribs 5.

Baked Spareribs, or Ribs With Sauerkraut, Page 425 or Barbecued Ribs, Page 138: Ribs 5.

Stewed Pork Hocks, Page 426: Hock 8.

Hams, Pages 409-411, or Ham En Croûte, Page 387, or Ham Slices Casseroled or with Fruit, Page 411: Ham 1.

Rolled Smoked Picnic Shoulder, Page 411: Picnic Shoulder 7.

Broiled or Sautéed Bacon, Page 411: Flank 4.

Broiled Sautéed or Baked Canadian Bacon, Page 412: Loin 3.

Parblanched Salt Pork, Page 510: Flank 4.

Pigs' Feet, Page 450: Forefoot 11.

Pork Scrapple or Goetta, Page 438: Shoulder Butt 6.

Pork Variety Meats are not choice with the exception of Suckling Pig's Livers, see Pâté En Croûte, Page 433; for Suckling Pig, see page 407.

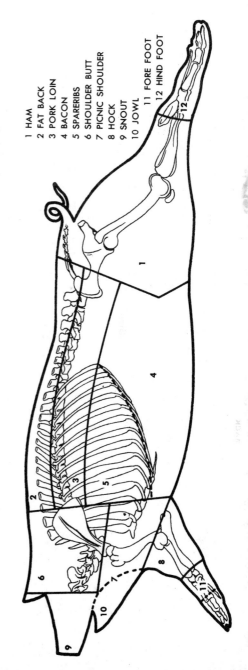

BONE STRUCTURE AND
COMMERCIAL CUTS FROM
A CARCASS OF PORK

1 HAM
2 FAT BACK
3 PORK LOIN
4 BACON
5 SPARERIBS
6 SHOULDER BUTT
7 PICNIC SHOULDER
8 HOCK
9 SNOUT
10 JOWL
11 FORE FOOT
12 HIND FOOT

LOIN OF PORK—9 to 10 lbs.

Have butcher cut off:

4 chops from center of loin for:

Pork Chops	Page 408
Deviled Pork Chops	424
Pork Chops Baked in Sour Cream	424

Use one end for:

Pork Roast	407

Freeze the other end for:

Pork Roast with Sauerkraut	408

Use leftovers in:

Meat Pie Roll	225
Chop Suey	229
Shepherd's Pie	234
Pizza	226
Scrapple or Goetta	438

HALF HAM—4 to 7 lbs.

Have butcher cut off 1 or 2 slices to use for:

Broiled Ham	Page 411
Stuffed Ham Rolls, III	230
Ham with Fruit	411

Use remainder as:

Baked Ham	409-410

Use leftovers for:

Ham and Corn Croquettes	218
Ham à la King	231
Ham Rolls with Asparagus	230
Jellied Ham Mousse	97
Split Pea or Lentil Soup	153
Ham Cakes with Pineapple and Sweet Potatoes	230
Ham Loaf with Cooked Ham	230
Lima Bean Casserole with Ham	263
Ham Waffles with À la King Sauce	333

TO MAKE A FRILL FOR A SHANK BONE

To make a frill for a shank ham, a lamb bone or drumsticks, fold in half stiff paper dinner napkins, about 12 x 8 inches. Cut through fold at ½-inch intervals to within 1 inch of open edge. Reverse the fold, bringing the open edges together. Begin to roll the uncut portion of the newly folded paper, leaving an opening at the folded open edge big enough to slip over the bone. Fasten this roll with scotch tape and slide the frill over the bone.

ABOUT BEEF

Beef, its aging, grading and general characteristics are described in About Meats, page 381. With the exception of game, no meat profits more by proper aging. Few households are able to buy, not for lack of money, but for lack of supply, the kind of beef purchased by hotels and clubs. The scarce superior grades are almost always reserved for these commercial establishments.

The American woman, through visual advertising, has been made to feel tha' bright red lean beef is the desirable grade, but actually beef for best flavor should be well aged to a purplish tone and show definite evidence of mottling, as well as heavy fat coverings.

ROAST BEEF
3 to 4 Servings to the Pound

Preheat oven to 550°.

When buying a standing rib of beef, be sure to have your butcher remove the spinal cord, the shoulder bone and the chine. Have him tie the chine back on—to keep the contour of the meat and to protect the eye of the roast during the cooking period. If the roast is made oven-ready in this way, the carving, illustrated, is very simple. Remove the roast from the refrigerator at least 3 hours before preparing for cooking. Trim off the excess fat and hard edges of:

A rib roast of beef

Place the roast, fat side up, on a rack in a pan in the oven. ◗ Reduce the heat immediately to 350° and cook 18 to 20 minutes to the pound for medium rare. To cook vegetables with roast, see page 256.

A rolled roast will require 5 to 10 minutes longer to the pound. To make gravy from pan drippings, see page 322. Serve the roast with:

Macaroni Loaf, page 187
Yorkshire Pudding, page 194, or
Tomato Pudding, page 307

To carve see below.

For ways to utilize leftover roasted meat, see Boeuf Miroton, page 228, and Luncheon Dishes, page 223.

ROAST STRIP SIRLOIN
24 to 30 Servings

Preheat oven to 550°.
Have the meat at 70° and trim excess top fat from:

**An 18 to 22 lb. eye of the
strip sirloin**

Place on a rack in a pan, fat side up, in the oven. ♦ Reduce heat at once to 350°. Roast uncovered 1½ hours for rare meat.

ABOUT FILLET OF BEEF

This choicest, most tender cut can be utilized in many ways; but trim off, first of all, the fat and sinew. Loosen fat at the small or tail end and tear this off as well as the clods of fat, near the wing-shaped portion of the fillet. Then, with a sharp pointed knife, remove the thin, tough, bluish sinew that lies underneath. To cook whole, either cut off about 6 inches of the tail end and save it for Stroganoff or Sukiyaki—or fold thin end under to equalize the thickness of the whole before roasting. To make the classic cuts, start at the upper end on the left and cut Filet Mignon, below, in slices 1½ to 2 inches thick. As you approach the center or Châteaubriand area, below, the small wing pieces will cut free. The Châteaubriand section is always cooked whole, either roasted or broiled, and is sliced at the table before serving. The narrower portion can be cut into 1-inch-thick slices called Tournedos, to within about 4 inches of the end. Use the tail again for Stroganoff, page 401, or Steak Tartare, page 71.

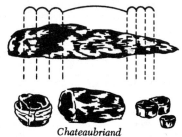

Filet Mignon

Chateaubriand

Tournedos

♦FILLET OR TENDERLOIN OF BEEF
Allow ⅓ Pound per Serving

♦Preheat oven to 500°.
♦Have the meat at room temperature. Remove the surplus fat and skin from:

At least a 5 lb. fillet of beef

You may lard, page 383, with narrow strips of:

(Salt pork or country bacon)

Fold over the thin ends of the fillet and secure them with string. If not larded, spread the meat generously with butter or tie strips of bacon over it. Do not cover or baste it. Place on a rack in a roasting pan in the oven. You may oil the pan. ♦ Reduce the heat immediately to 350° and bake from 18 to 30 minutes in all. A fillet is usually cooked rare when the internal temperature reaches 120°. Season when done. You may surround the fillet with:

Broiled Mushrooms, page 281

Garnish the platter with:

**Sprigs of parsley
Soufflé Potatoes, page 294**

Serve with:

**Marchand de Vin Sauce, page 327
Bordelaise Sauce, page 326
Béarnaise Sauce, page 329**

ABOUT STEAKS

When in doubt, the stock answer to the menu problem is, "Let's have steak!" Steak—from ▤ charcoal grill to planked Châteaubriand, page 127—does duty for so many different occasions that we would like to discuss steak varieties below. Unless special recipes are given, they may all be broiled, page 385, or pan-broiled, page 385. The meat should of course ♦ be at least 70° and the ♦ grill should be hot and oiled ♦ the broiler preheated. ♦ Season at the end of cooking and not before.

Steak, hot or cold, is greatly enhanced by a sauce and the most usual accompaniments are one of the following:

**Colbert Butter, page 339
Béarnaise Sauce, page 329
Bordelaise Sauce, page 326
Marchand de Vin Sauce, page 327
Sour Cream Horseradish Sauce,
page 317
Mushroom Sauce, page 327**

FLANK STEAK

This is considered the least choice cut, probably because so often poorly prepared. It is a treat if properly cooked, see London Broil, page 401.

HAMBURGER

This, too, can be a real treat, not just a stopgap, see page 426.

RUMP, SWISS AND ROUND STEAK

Made from the round, these are prized for their flavor but are never truly tender. Since they must be braised and do not respond to dry heat methods, they are steaks only in name, see Moist Heats, page 127. Scrape and serve raw for Steak Tartare, page 71.

CUBE STEAKS

These are top butt or round and macerated to tenderize for grilling. They are usually tough.

RIB OR SPENCER STEAKS

These are comparable in price but varying in flavor and texture and cut from a choice area of the eye of the rib.

CLUB OR MINUTE STEAK

This is cut from the end of the shortloin and makes a good individual serving.

T-BONE STEAK

This also is cut from the shortloin but near the middle. It combines the tail of fillet and the tail of the sirloin.

PORTERHOUSE STEAK

Another shortloin cut. It is very like T-bone—but a larger version—and includes the choice fillet and choice sirloin.

SIRLOIN

Cut from the shortloin, it is comparable to a French entrecôte. Its flavor is the one associated most often with the word steak.

SIRLOIN STRIP STEAK

This is the eye of the sirloin—the choice cut most often met with in hotels. In serving large groups, the eye of the sirloin, 18 to 22 lbs., from which these strip steaks come, is often roasted whole, page 399, and sliced.

TENDERLOIN OR FILLET STEAKS

These include Filet Mignon, Châteaubriand, Tournedos, Steak Tartare. They vary in name and size, depending on the portion of the fillet from which they are cut. For details, see the illustration on page 399. Prized for their tenderness, they are somewhat lacking in flavor and require an interesting sauce.

BROILED STEAK
Preheat broiler.
Prepare for cooking a 2-inch-thick:
  Sirloin, T-bone, strip or
  porterhouse steak
Have the meat at room temperature. You may rub the steak with:
  (A cut clove of garlic)
You may spread it an hour before it is cooked with:
  (Olive oil)
Add:
  (Grated onion and prepared mustard)
Or spread when ¾ cooked with:
  French Dressing
A very thick steak may be browned on both sides, then cooked until done, 4 inches from the heat. When done, spread with:
  Butter and the pan drippings,
  after removing most of the fat
Add:
  Chopped parsley or chives
If the drippings are meager, you may add:

(1 to 2 tablespoons butter or wine)
Serve the steak garnished with:
  Sautéed Mushrooms, page 281
  French Fried Onions, page 285
Or serve with:
  Bordelaise Sauce, page 326
  Béarnaise Sauce, page 329
  Maître d'Hôtel Butter, page 339
  Marchand de Vin Sauce, page 327
  Garlic Butter, page 339
  Colbert Butter, page 339

PAN-BROILED STEAK
Prepare for cooking:
  A beefsteak
Heat a heavy frying pan over lively heat until very hot. If the meat is not prime, rub the pan very lightly with:
  A bit of beef fat
Put the steak in the pan and sear for 1 minute or until the blood rises on the uncooked surface. Turn and sear the other side.
  ♦ Reduce the heat and continue cooking the steak until done, about 10 minutes for a 1½-inch steak. Pour off any fat in the pan for, if it is allowed to remain, the steak will be "fried" and not "broiled."
Season the steak with:
  Salt and freshly ground pepper
Make with the drippings:
  Pan Gravy, page 322
or use:
  Maître d'Hôtel Butter, page 339
For suggestions for steak sauces, see Broiled Steak, above.
Serve with:
  Franconia Potatoes, page 293

PAN-BROILED FILLET STEAK
Pan-broil, as above:
  Four 1-inch fillet steaks
using, to prevent sticking, a small amount of:
  Butter
When the meat is done—not more than 3 minutes to a side—deglaze the pan, page 321, with:
  ¼ cup dry red wine
  2 tablespoons beef stock
  1 teaspoon Meat Glaze, page 492
Serve with:
  Artichoke hearts, stuffed with
  Creamed Spinach, page 300

**BROILED TOURNEDOS OR
FILET MIGNON STEAK**
Preheat broiler.
Upon request a butcher usually will cut fillet steaks, shape them and surround them with a strip of bacon secured by a wooden pick. Otherwise follow instructions and sketch on page 399, to find from which portion of the fillet these cuts come. The thickness of the steaks may vary from ¾ to 1 inch or more.
Prepare for cooking:
  Fillet steaks: 1 to 2 inches thick

Spread with:
    Butter
Broil as for:
    Broiled Steak, page 400
When done, remove the bacon. Serve on:
    A fried or toasted crouton, page 342
with:
    Béarnaise Sauce, page 329
    Lemon and parsley
    Broiled Mushrooms, page 281
    Potatoes Anna, page 293, or
    Duchess Potatoes, page 296

STEAK AU POIVRE OR PEPPERED STEAK

Use:
    Trimmed 1-inch-thick strip sirloin, club or filet mignon steaks
Crush:
    1 to 2 tablespoons peppercorns
The pepper should not be ground but crushed coarsely on a board with a pressing, rolling movement, using the bottom of a pan. Press the steaks into the crushed pepper and work it into both sides of the meat with the heel of your palm or with the flat side of a cleaver. Sprinkle the bottom of a skillet with:
    2 teaspoons salt
When it begins to brown, put the steaks into the pan and brown ♦ uncovered over high heat.
♦ Reduce to medium heat, turn the steaks and cook to desired degree of rareness. In a separate pan, prepare:
    ¼ cup butter
    1 teaspoon Worcestershire sauce
    2 tablespoons lemon juice
Remove the steaks from the pan in which they have been cooked and discard the pan drippings. Pour the butter mixture over steaks. Flambé steaks, page 127, with:
    (2 oz. cognac)

LONDON BROIL OR FLANK STEAK

Preheat broiler.
Place on a greased broiler rack:
    A 2 to 3 lb. flank steak
Broil within 2 inches of source of heat—the hotter the better—about 5 minutes on each side ♦ making sure the meat is kept rare. If a flank steak is cooked medium or well done, it becomes extremely tough.
♦ Carve by slicing against or across the grain to make it more tender.
Serve with:
    Bearnaise Sauce, page 329
    Bordelaise Sauce, page 326

BOEUF FONDU BOURGUIGNONNE
6 Servings
This dish is cooked at table in a special deep metal pot which narrows at the top to keep the butter from sputtering. It can be cooked in an electric skillet ♦ if the butter is sweet and clarified, which keeps it from popping. We love this dish inordinately. It gives the hostess an easy time, both from the cooking angle and from the entertaining one—as the guests quickly reveal their individual characteristics. They are all there—the hoarder, the cooperator, the kibitzer, the boss. ♦ Don't try to get more than 5 or 6 guests around one heat source. Allow for each person ⅓ to ½ lb. fillet of beef. Cut into ¾-inch dice:
    About 3 lbs. fillet of beef
Have ready 2 to 4 sauces:
    Mustard with capers
    Thickened Tomato Sauce, page 333
    Mayonnaise with garlic and herbs
    Marchand de Vin with Mushrooms, page 327
    A curry sauce
    A chutney-based sauce
    A sweet-sour sauce
Melt in an electric skillet:
    1 cup clarified butter
When the butter is brownish, announce the rules of the game. Allow to each guest only one to two pieces of meat at a time, so as to keep the cooking heat constant. Impale the beef on long forks, worry it around in the butter until it is done to your liking. If rare is your choice, the time is very short. Arrange the sauces on your plate like oils on a palette. The plate can be a compartmented one, but this is not necessary. Dip the hot browned meat in the sauce of your choice. Serve with the beef crusty French bread or rolls and a tossed salad—with green grapes or avocado slices.

BEEF STROGANOFF
4 Servings
This dish ✱ freezes well and is economical when made with fillet ends. See chart, page 399.
I. Cut into ½-inch slices:
    1½ lbs. fillet of beef
Pound them with a mallet until thin. Cut into strips about 1 inch wide. Melt in a pan:
    1 tablespoon butter
Sauté in the butter for about 2 minutes:
    ¾ tablespoon grated onion
Sauté the beef quickly in the butter for about 5 minutes. Turn so that it will be browned evenly. Remove and keep it hot. Add to the pan:
    2 tablespoons butter
Stir and sauté in the butter:
    ¾ lb. sliced mushrooms
Add the beef. Season with:
    Salt and pepper
    A grating of nutmeg
    (½ teaspoon basil)
Add and heat, but do not boil:
    ¼ cup white wine
    1 cup warm sweet or cultured sour cream
Serve with:
    Green Noodles, page 172

II. Or have ready:
    1¼ lbs. hot cooked fillet
Slice as described above, but omit the first sauté and add the grated onion to the mushrooms.

◩ BEEF KEBABS OR BEEF ON SKEWERS

4 Servings

◗ Please read About Skewer Cooking, page 123, and About Marinades, page 336.
Preheat broiler or grill.
Use:

1½ lbs. better or good grade round

Cut the marinated beef, page 336, into about 1½-inch cubes. You may alternate the cubes on skewers with:

> **Parboiled onion slices**
> **Firm tomato chunks**
> **Mushrooms**
> **Bacon, etc.**

Or put the vegetables on separate skewers to cook more slowly at the side of the grill. Roll the filled skewers in:

> **Melted butter**

Broil or grill about 3 inches from the source of heat. Brush while cooking with the melted butter. Turn to cook evenly, about 18 minutes for rare, 25 for well done.

> **Correct the seasoning**

and serve hot. The meat may be presented flambé by igniting a brandy-soaked bit of cotton impaled on the sharp end of the skewer.

SUKIYAKI

4 Servings

Known in Japan as a "friendship dish," this one-plate meal, which may be cooked in the kitchen in a heavy skillet, lends itself to pleasant preparation at table in an electric skillet. The cooking proceeds as an orderly ritual which lasts about 25 minutes, while the uniformly sliced ingredients are taken from a beautifully arranged platter. Have ready on the platter:

> **2 lbs. thinly sliced beef: sirloin tip,**
> **eye of the round or fillet of beef**

The meat can be sliced most easily if put in the freezer about 20 minutes and then cut on a #5 slicer. When ready to cook, however, it should be ◗ at room temperature—as should all the other ingredients. Have ready:

> **2 strips beef suet, about 1 oz. each,**
> **or 3 tablespoons cooking oil**

A small dish to hold:

> **½ cup thinly sliced onions**
> **½ cup ¾-inch squares bean curd: Tofu**

Arrange also on the platter in uniform diagonally cut sizes, see page 251:

> **6 scallions with 3 inches of green**
> **left on**
> **6 ribs celery or Chinese cabbage**
> **2 cups thinly sliced mushrooms**
> **1 lb. spinach, cut in 1-inch strips**
> **after stem is removed, or water cress**
> **2 cups bean sprouts or cooked,**
> **drained Shirataki**

These last are spaghetti-shaped yam shreds. We find that if a single skillet is used for cooking, it is best to cook only half the amount on the platter at one time, sharing the first batch and then cooking the "sec-

onds" later. Put the suet in the hot skillet over medium heat and, when it reaches the point of fragrance, remove the unmelted bits and add the thin beef slices. Cook ◗ without browning, turning frequently for about 3 minutes, then push the meat to one side of the skillet and sauté the vegetables. Add them in sequence, beginning with those that need longer cooking. First sauté the onions until almost golden, then as you incorporate the other vegetables, pour in a little at a time a mixture of:

> **½ cup soy sauce**
> **½ cup stock**

This procedure gives a quickly rising steam but not enough moisture to waterlog the vegetables. Sprinkle over the vegetables while stirring them:

> **1 teaspoon sugar**
> **½ teaspoon monosodium glutamate**

From the sautéing of the onions through the rest of the vegetable cooking, count about 7 minutes. Then push the meat into the center of the skillet and combine with the sprouts or Shirataki, continuing to heat and stir for about 4 minutes more. The vegetables should retain their crispness and good color.

> **Correct the seasoning**

Serve this mixture at once over:

> **Boiled Rice, page 178**

As an authentic detail, you may have a room temperature a raw egg in a small dish into which bits of the Sukiyaki can be dipped before eating.

ABOUT VEAL

In America veal is a very misunderstood meat—and the milk-fed variety is hard to come by. Veal should be tender, succulent and white. If it is not, there are two ways to improve it. One is to blanch briefly starting in cold water. The other is to soak refrigerated in milk overnight before using. Veal needs a careful cooking approach, as it is lacking in fat and may toughen quickly. Although abroad certain dishes—like Veal à la Meunière or à la Crème—are served both rosy and juicy, veal here is generally served after reaching an internal temperature of 175°. It is roasted 25 to 30 minutes per lb. until well done. Although a leg of veal may be roasted, most large pieces of veal are pot-roasted. The long round muscle of the leg, when cut across the grain, produces **scallops**.

VEAL ROAST STUFFED OR FARCI

The meat may be rubbed first with garlic or gashes may be cut in a shoulder roast in which fine slivers of garlic, marjoram, peppercorns, anchovies or anchovy paste may be inserted.
Preheat oven to 450°.
Have a pocket cut in:

> **A breast or shoulder of veal**

Remove the meat from the refrigerator least ½ hour before preparing. Rub with

Garlic

Dust the pocket lightly with:

Ginger

before filling with:

3 cups Dry Dressing, page 456,
Bread Dressing, page 456, with 2
slices chopped salt pork added,
Oyster Dressing, page 457, or Green
Rice, page 179, the cheese omitted

Sew the pocket up with a coarse needle
and thread. If the meat is not fat, rub with:

Butter

Dredge with:

Seasoned flour

Place in the oven in a greased roasting pan
and ♦ reduce the heat to 300°. Bake ♦ uncovered about 25 to 30 minutes to the
pound until done. You may place on the
roast several strips of:

(Bacon)

Make:

Pan gravy, page 322

When the gravy is done, you may remove
from the heat and add:

(¼ cup cultured sour cream)
(1 or 2 tablespoons dry white wine)

Heat the gravy but ♦ do not let it boil. To
carve a stuffed veal shoulder, see illustration. For ways to utilize roasted meat, see
Luncheon Dishes, page 223.

VEAL ROAST, KIDNEY, LOIN, ETC.,
OR ROLLED ROAST

Follow the preceding recipe for preparing
and cooking breast or shoulder—but allow
30 to 40 minutes to the pound for rolled
roast. Turn every ½ hour. You may add
parboiled vegetables—potatoes, carrots, etc.
—for the last ½ hour or so of cooking. If
there are insufficient drippings, add a little
water to the pan. This roast is good served
with:

Dumplings, page 192
Spatzen, page 192, and
Pickled Prunes, page 120

ABOUT VEAL CUTLETS

From these thin flattened pieces of meat
come collops, scallops, scallopini and
schnitzels—all of which may be cooked
with or without breading.

So-called "natural" cutlets, unflavored or
very lightly so, are one of the easiest,
quickest and most delightful of all.

For any of these dishes a white veal is
best, sometimes hard to obtain. You may
soak the veal in milk overnight, as suggested previously, or in lemon juice for 1
hour. Dry well before flouring or breading.

All these cutlets should be cut as thin as
possible and may be pounded. The pounding gives a very different texture. Watch
your thumb during this process. ♦ To
pound, see illustration, page 383.

In the following recipes use about 1½
lbs. of veal that has been carefully trimmed
and from which the bone has been removed. There is often a thin membrane
that holds the meat taut as it cooks. Be
sure it is slashed in a number of places
before cooking. This should serve 3 to
4 persons. If you are serving more and
have to repeat your sautéing, keep the already finished cutlets ♦ uncovered in a
250° oven until all the rest are ready.

VEAL CUTLET OR SCALLOPINI

Please read About Veal Cutlets, above.
Dredge lightly with flour on one side only:

Thin pounded veal scallops

Sauté them, floured-side first in:

¼ cup butter

heated until fragrant. In about 3 minutes,
when the juices begin to emerge on the
upper side, turn the meat and continue to
sauté for about 3 minutes more. Shake the
skillet vigorously from time to time, until
the meat is done. Veal is never served
rare. Remove from the skillet and keep
warm.

Deglaze the pan juices with:

½ cup veal or chicken stock or ¼ cup
stock and ¼ cup Marsala or Madeira
Correct the seasoning.

You may swirl in, at the end:

(1 tablespoon butter)

If you do not use the wine, you may add:

(1 tablespoon lemon juice)

Pour the sauce over the cutlets and serve
at once.

VEAL SCALLOPINI WITH
TOMATOES

3 to 4 Servings

Preheat oven to 325°.

Cut into 1-inch squares:

1½ lbs. veal cut thin, trimmed, boned
and pounded

Dredge with:

Flour

Brown in a mixture of:

1 tablespoon butter
1 tablespoon olive oil

Add:

½ lb. thinly sliced mushrooms
½ to 1 clove pressed garlic
2 tablespoons chopped parsley
2 tablespoons chopped fresh basil
½ cup peeled, seeded, diced, fresh
tomatoes
½ cup Marsala
2 tablespoons Parmesan cheese

Cover and cook in a 325° oven for about 45 minutes.

VEAL PAPILLOTE
Veal lends itself very well to this method of cooking, see Papillote, page 132. Trim veal for cutlet. To season and cook, see Chicken Suprême Papillote, page 471.

VEAL PARMIGIANA
Slice a ¼-inch-thick:
Veal cutlet
into 2 x 2-inch slices. Pound thin until they reach about 3 x 3 inches. Dip into a:
Bound Breading, page 502
using equal parts bread crumbs and Parmesan cheese. Sauté the pieces until crisp in:
Clarified Butter, page 338
about 2 minutes on each side. Serve with:
Tomato Sauce, page 333

VEAL SCALLOP OR ESCALOPE DE VEAU ORLOFF
A good party dish, as it can be partially prepared in advance.
Preheat oven to 350°.
Slice:
A ¼-inch-thick veal cutlet
into 2 x 2-inch slices. Pound them until they reach about 3 x 3 inches. Sauté until barely frizzled on both sides in:
Clarified Butter, page 338
Remove from pan and drain on absorbent paper. To make a **Soubise,** mix and grind in a food chopper:
½ cup cooked rice
½ cup white onions
½ cup mushrooms
Season with:
Salt and pepper
Cover each scallop of veal with:
1 tablespoon liver paste
Then press on firmly over each scallop the soubise mixture. Sprinkle over each:
1 teaspoon brandy or sherry
Dust generously with:
Grated Parmesan cheese
Place the scallop in an ovenproof serving platter and bake for about 15 minutes until the cheese is golden.

PAPRIKA SCHNITZEL OR CUTLET
♦ Please read About Veal Cutlets, page 403.
Trim the edges and remove the bone from:
A ¼- to ½-inch-thick slice of veal from the round
Dredge one side only in:
Seasoned flour
Heat in a skillet:
¼ cup butter or bacon drippings
Sauté lightly in the fat:
(½ cup or more sliced onions)
Sauté the meat, first on the seasoned side, in the hot fat, until lightly browned. Turn, then add until the fat becomes red:
Paprika
Remove the pan from the heat and add:
1 cup boiling vegetable or chicken stock

Cover the skillet and cook the veal ♦ ove very low heat until it is almost tender about 15 minutes. Add:
½ cup cultured sour cream
Correct the seasoning
Serve garnished with:
Parsley, capers, sardelles
Applesauce, page 112
Creamed Spinach, page 300

WIENER SCHNITZEL OR BREADED VEAL CUTLET
3 to 4 Serving
Viennese friends insist that the true Wiene Schnitzel is deep-fat fried—other authori ties insist it is sautéed. But most typica Viennese recipes put up to ¾ cup of butte in the sauté pan which virtually gives deep fat, rather than a sautéed result any way, see page 126. Although there ar many variations, we suggest the following ♦ Please read About Veal Cutlets, page 403 Just before cooking, bread, page 502:
1½ lbs. veal cutlet
Sauté over low heat for 2 minutes on on side in:
½ to ¾ cup butter
Turn and cook 2 minutes on the other side Turn again and cook until done—about 1 to 15 minutes in all. Garnish with:
Lemon slices and rolled anchovies
If you also cap the garnished cutlet abov with a fried egg, you may call it **Holstei**

VEAL SCALLOPS WITH HAM
4 Serving
This recipe is also good using pounde chicken breasts.
Pound:
2 veal cutlets
and slice into about 12 three-inch square Sauté the pieces until barely frizzled o both sides in:
Clarified Butter, page 338
Remove from pan and drain on absorbe paper. Cut into 6 thin slices:
Prosciutto or smoked ham
Place the ham on 6 slices of veal. To with a similar sized slice of:
Swiss cheese
Cover each piece with the remaining ve slices. Gently pat in:
Bound Breading, page 502
Sauté in:
Clarified Butter, page 338
until golden on each side, about 3 minute Or you may bake the meat on an ovenpro platter in a 350° oven about 15 minutes.

ABOUT LAMB AND MUTTON
Since lamb is shipped from different c mates it is no longer referred to as spri lamb. When it is from 3 to 5 months ol lamb is now called baby or milk-finishe lamb. From 5 months to a year and a ha it is simply called lamb, and from there out—mutton. Mutton may be substitut

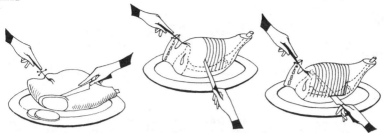

or lamb, but the cooking time is usually increased from 5 to 10 minutes to the pound. Both lamb and mutton are covered with a whitish brittle fat, called the fell, which is usually removed before cooking, as it tends to make the flavor of the meat strong. Almost any cut of lamb may be cooked by the dry heat methods which follow. For ground lamb recipes, see page 426. For moist heat methods, see Braises and Pot Roasts, page 412, and for cooked meat recipes, see Luncheon Dishes, page 223.

LAMB OR MUTTON ROAST
About 8 Servings
Please see Economical Use of Large Cuts, page 389.
Preheat oven to 450°.
Remove from the refrigerator at least ½ hour before cooking:

>   A 5-lb. leg of lamb or mutton

Remove the fell or papery outer covering. Rub the meat with:

>   (Cut garlic or lemon and rosemary)

Insert under the skin, using a pointed knife:

>   (Slivers of garlic or herbs)

Place the meat fat side up on a rack in an uncovered pan. Immediately after putting it in the oven ♦ reduce the heat to 350°. Roast it 30 minutes to the pound if you want it well done or until the internal temperature is 175° to 180°. Most Europeans like lamb slightly rare or at an internal temperature of 160° to 165°. ♦ Do not cover or baste. Make:

>   Pan Gravy, page 322, using cultured sour cream or milk

Or serve the roast with:

>   Deglazed drippings, page 321

and:

>   Mint Sauce, page 330

If the mint sauce is not desired, see:

>   Cumberland Sauce, page 312

To carve a lamb roast, see the illustration above, or carve it parallel to the bone. For ways of reusing roasted meat, see Leftover and Luncheon Dishes, page 223.

BARBECUED LEG OF LAMB
Preheat grill.
Have butcher bone and flatten:

>   A leg of lamb

At least 2 hours before cooking, cover the leg with:

>   Fresh mint

Rub with:

>   Dry mustard
>   Pepper
>   Onion juice

While the charcoal is burning down to embers, cook gently for about 5 minutes a sauce of:

>   ¼ cup butter
>   ½ clove garlic
>   1 tablespoon grated onion

Take out the garlic and add:

>   ½ cup chopped fresh mint leaves
>   ¼ cup butter

Put the lamb on the grill and brush often with the warm sauce. After about 20 minutes, salt and pepper and turn the meat. If you like lamb pink, it should be "à point" in 35 to 45 minutes, depending on the heat of the coals. Well-done lamb will take 15 minutes longer.

CROWN ROAST OF LAMB
Allow 2 Ribs per Person
Preheat oven to 450°.
Wipe with a cloth:

>   A crown roast of lamb

Protect the ends of the bones by covering with aluminum foil. Immediately after putting the meat in the oven ♦ reduce the heat to 350°. Process as directed for Lamb Roast, above, but remove the roast before the last hour of cooking. Fill the center with:

>   3 cups Bread Dressing, page 456, or
>   Dressing for Cornish Hen, page 458

Return to the oven and complete the cooking. Remove the covering from the bones. Garnish them with a paper frill, a slice of pickle or a stuffed olive and carve as shown, page 407. Make:

>   Pan Gravy, page 322

An unfilled crown roast may be cooked upside down. Omit covering the bones. When done, fill the hollow of the roast with:

>   Green Peas, page 287

or with:

>   Baked Chestnuts, page 272

Garnish with:

>   Parsley

Serve with the gravy and:

>   Mint Sauce, page 330, or currant jelly

LAMB SHOULDER ROAST
About 8 Servings
Preheat oven to 450°.
Prepare or have prepared with one side
left open for inserting dressing:
A 4- to 5-lb. cushion shoulder of lamb
Rub the meat with:
A cut clove of garlic
Fill the cavity with:
Bread or other dressing, page 456
Sew or skewer up the open side. Place
the roast uncovered on a rack in a pan in
the oven. ◗ Reduce the heat immediately
to 350° until done, about 30 minutes to
the pound. Serve with:
Pan Gravy, page 322

▤ BROILED LAMB KEBABS
4 Servings
Take:
1 lb. lamb shoulder
Cut the meat into 2-inch squares. Marinate
if you like for 3 hours in Marinade I, page
336, turning several times.
Preheat broiler.
Place the meat on skewers, alternately
with:
Pineapple slices
Blanched Bermuda onion slices
Tomatoes
Stuffed olives
Place 4 inches from the heat source and
broil. Turn frequently. Baste while cook-
ing with:
Butter or olive oil
and cook about 15 minutes or until done.
Serve on a shallow bed of:
Cooked Green Rice, page 178

LAMB CHOPS
2 Chops per Person
◗ Trim the outer skin, which is strong in
flavor, from:
Lamb chops

I. Pan-broiled
Sear the chops in a hot dry skillet. ◗ Re-
duce the heat and cook slowly until done.
Allow for well-done 2-inch chops about 20
minutes, for 1½-inch chops about 16 min-
utes. Pour off the fat as it accumulates in
the pan. Season the chops with:
Salt and freshly ground pepper
Serve very hot. Garnish with:
Parsley

II. Broiled
Follow directions for:
Broiled Steak, page 400
allowing a shorter time for cooking, according to the thickness of the chops.

STUFFED LAMB CHOPS
6 Servings
I.
Preheat broiler.
To prepare for stuffing, see:
Braised Stuffed Pork Chops
Cockaigne, page 425

Substitute:
6 double lamb chops
The chops may be wrapped before cooking
with:
Strips of bacon
Use toothpicks-to hold it in place.

II. Or cut out the bone from:
Lamb chops
Wrap the tail around:
1-inch balls of sausage meat
Secure them with a toothpick. Broil or
pan-broil the chops.

GARNISHED ENGLISH MIXED GRILL
1 to 2 Servings
While this is the classic serving for one, it
does very well for 2 in our family.
Preheat broiler.
Grease the broiling rack. Arrange on it:
2 single lamb chops
2 small link sausages
2 chicken livers
½ blanched veal kidney
1 slice of bacon
½ small tomato seasoned with salt,
pepper and butter
½ cup mushroom caps dipped in butter
3 to 4 small whole blanched onions
Place the broiler rack about 3 inches from
the source of heat. During the cooking
process, turn the meats and mushrooms.
Baste if necessary with clarified butter.
The cooking time is dependent on the
thickness of the chops and the degree of
doneness desired. Arrange ingredients on
hot plates or a platter and serve with:
Sauce Béarnaise, page 329

ABOUT PORK

Someone has observed that a pig resembles
a saint in that he is more honored after
death than during his lifetime. Speaking
further of his social standing, we have noticed that, when smoked, he is allowed to
appear at quite fashionable functions; but
that only one's best friends will confess to
anything more than a bowing acquaintance
with pork and sauerkraut or pickled pigs'
feet.
High-grade pork is fine-grained and firm
—the shoulder cuts finely marbled, the fat
white. Because of the heavy fat content,
all parts of pork can be roasted. Because
of the pervasive fat, too, the meat is virtually self-basting. ◗ Pork demands thorough cooking. Otherwise the very harmful trichinae or parasites which often exist
in it may be transmitted to the eater. Rule
of thumb for judging doneness are to cook
the meat until the juices run clear when
the flesh is pricked and to make sure, when
cut into, that the meat is white or greyish
◗ never pink. Slow cooking is desirable,
allowing 30 to 45 minutes to the pound,
to 10 minutes longer per pound for rolled

or stuffed roasts. Internal temperature should register 185°. The choice roasts are rib, loin and shoulder. The lower half of the foreleg—also called picnic—may be boned, rolled or flattened or rolled and stuffed. Fresh hams or legs of pork are good either roasted or braised. For details about cuts, consult the charts and compare them with the recipes listed. Also read Economical Use of Large Cuts, page 398.

For uses of cooked pork, see Luncheon Dishes, page 223.

ROAST OF PORK
Preheat oven to 450°.
Use for a fine, juicy roast:
> **A rib end of loin**

Or roll or stuff a shoulder or loin, which will need about 10 minutes more cooking to the lb. than recommended here, even when the meat is at 70° before cooking. Rub the roast well with:
> **A cut clove of garlic, fresh sage,
> dried rosemary, tarragon or thyme**

Dredge with:
> **Seasoned Flour, page 501**

Place fat side up on a rack in a pan in the oven. ◗ Reduce the heat at once to 350°. Cook ◗ uncovered 30 to 35 minutes to the pound. The internal temperature should be 185°. Make:
> **Pan Gravy, page 322**

You may roast alongside the meat for the last 35 minutes of cooking:
> **Peeled and parboiled sweet potatoes
> or parsnips**

or on top of the roast:
> **Prunes and apricots**

or serve the roast with:
> **Applesauce, page 112, seasoned
> with 2 tablespoons horseradish and
> a grating of nutmeg
> Sweet Potatoes and Apples, page 299
> Apples with Sauerkraut, page 111, or
> other sauerkraut variations
> Apple and Onion Dish, page 286
> Turnips and Apples, page 309
> Puree of Lentils or Peas, page 288**

◗ Please read about the Economical Use of Large Cuts, page 398; and for other ways of using leftover roasted meats, see Luncheon Dishes, page 223.

CROWN ROAST OF PORK
> **Allow 2 Ribs per Person**

Preheat oven to 450°.
Wipe with a cloth:
> **A crown roast of pork**

Protect the ends of the bones by covering with aluminum foil. Immediately after putting the roast in the oven ◗ reduce the heat to 350°, allowing 30 to 45 minutes to the pound. If the crown is not to be filled with dressing, omit covering the bones and cook the roast upside down. Serve filled with a cooked vegetable; or, if the roast is to be stuffed, remove it 1 hour before it is done and fill the center with:
> **Sausage Dressing, page 457
> Apple and Onion Dressing, page 458
> or fruit dressing**

Return the roast to the oven and complete the cooking. Make
> **Pan Gravy, page 322**

To garnish and to carve, see illustration. Serve with:
> **Glazed Onions, page 285
> Cinnamon Apples, page 111
> Water cress, or broiled canned
> apricots and crystallized ginger
> slices**

ROAST SUCKLING PIG
We never think of suckling pig without thinking of our friend Amy, an American, long a resident of Mexico but determined to reconstruct in alien surroundings the traditional Christmas dinners of her youth. Describing the preparation of roast pig to her skilled Indian cook, she wound up with the announcement, "The pig is brought to table on plenty of greenery, with an apple in the mouth." The cook looked first baffled, then resentful and finally burst out with a succession of "no's." Her employer persisted patiently, but with increasing firmness. When the pig was served, she discovered that her cook could effect an entrée which surpassed her wildest expectations. There was plenty of greenery and a distinct air of martyrdom; but the apple was clenched, not in the pig's mouth, but in that of the desperate cook!

10 Servings

Preheat oven to 450°.

Dress, by drawing, scraping and cleaning:
>   **A suckling pig**

Remove eyeballs and lower the lids. The dressed pig should weigh about 12 pounds. Fill it with:
>   **Onion Dressing, page 457, or**
>   **Forcemeat, page 458**

It takes 2½ quarts of dressing to stuff a pig of this size. Multiply all your ingredients, but not the seasonings. Use these sparingly until the dressing is combined, then taste it and add what is lacking. Sew up the pig. Put a block of wood in its mouth to hold it open. Skewer the legs into position, pulling the forelegs forward and bending the hindlegs into a crouching stance. Rub the pig with:
>   **Oil or soft butter**
>   **(A cut clove of garlic)**

Dredge it with:
>   **Flour**

Cover the ears and the tail with aluminum foil. Place the pig in a pan ▶ uncovered, in the oven for 15 minutes. ▶ Reduce the heat to 325° and roast until tender, allowing 30 minutes to the pound. Baste every 15 minutes with:
>   **About 2 cups boiling stock and the**
>   **pan drippings**

Remove the foil from ears and tail before serving. Place the pig on a platter. Remove the wood from the mouth. Replace it with a small:
>   **Apple, lemon or carrot**

Place in the eyes:
>   **Raisins or cranberries**

Drape around the neck a wreath of:
>   **Small green leaves**

or garnish the platter or board with:
>   **Water cress**

The pig may be surrounded with:
>   **Cinnamon Apples, page 111, Apples**
>   **Stuffed with Sweet Potatoes, page**
>   **111, Apples Stuffed with Mincemeat,**
>   **page 603, Tomatoes Florentine,**
>   **page 307, etc.**

Make:
>   **Pan Gravy, page 322**

To carve, place head to left of carver. Remove forelegs and hams. Divide meat down center of back. Separate the ribs. Serve a section of crackling skin to each person.

FRESH HAM

I. You may place a fresh leg of pork called:
>   **A fresh ham**

in a marinade, page 336, and refrigerate covered for 24 to 48 hours.

Preheat oven to 450°.

Remove the ham from the marinade. Wipe dry. Cook as for:
>   **Pork Roast, page 407**

basting every ½ hour with part of the mar-

inade or with the traditional:
>   **(Beer)**

Make:
>   **Pan Gravy, page 322**

Serve with any of the accompaniments suggested in Pork Roast.

II. Or cook a:
>   **Boned fresh ham**

as for:
>   **Veal Pot Roast, page 420**

PORK ROAST STUFFED WITH SAUERKRAUT

Preheat oven to 350°.

Have the butcher remove the bones from:
>   **A pork shoulder**

Fill it with:
>   **Drained sauerkraut**

Dredge with:
>   **Flour**

Prepare and cook as for:
>   **Roast Shoulder of Lamb, page 406**

PORK TENDERLOIN

Preheat oven to 350°.

Split lengthwise:
>   **A pork tenderloin**

Flatten it out. Rub lightly with:
>   **Butter**
>   **(Garlic)**

Spread with:
>   **Bread Dressing, page 456, using**
>   **¼ the amount given or with Apple**
>   **and Sweet Potato Dressing, page**
>   **459, using about ⅛ the amount**
>   **given, or with stewed, drained,**
>   **pitted prunes**

Sew or tie it up. Dredge with:
>   **Seasoned flour**

or brush with an unsalted fat. Place the tenderloin on a rack. Bake 30 to 45 minutes to the pound. Make:
>   **Pan Gravy, page 322**

You may add to the gravy:
>   **(Cultured sour cream and cooked**
>   **mushrooms or sweet cream and**
>   **currant jelly)**

FRENCHED PORK TENDERLOIN

Cut crosswise into ¾-inch slices:
>   **Pork tenderloin**

Flatten the slices slightly with a cleaver, as shown on page 383. Dredge with:
>   **(Flour)**

Sauté as for:
>   **Pork Chops, below**

Add to the pan juices or the gravy you serve with the meat:
>   **½ teaspoon grated lemon rind**

PORK CHOPS

I. Sear in a hot pan:
>   **Pork chops**

in just enough cooking oil or rendered pork fat to keep them from sticking. Before searing, they may be rubbed with:

(Garlic or powdered rosemary)
fter searing ♦ reduce the heat. Cook the
1ops slowly, covered or uncovered, until
one. Pour off the excess grease as they
ook. Season with:
Salt and pepper
(ake:
Pan Gravy, page 322

, Preheat oven to 350°.
good way to do thick chops.
fter searing them as above, bake covered
r about 1 hour:
4 pork chops
uring the last half hour, you may add for
asoning:
3 tablespoons minced green pepper
and celery
1 clove garlic
1 piece ginger root mashed in
1 tablespoon vinegar
3 slices orange
½ cup orange juice

)RK TENDERLOIN FRUIT
ASSEROLE
6 Servings
Please read About Deep-Fat Frying,
iges 124-126.
eheat deep fryer to 375°.
it into ½-inch cubes:
1 lb. pork tenderloin
ip the pieces into:
2 beaten eggs
en roll in:
2 tablespoons cornstarch
eep fry for about 10 minutes. Drain. In
large, deep skillet, melt:
2 tablespoons cooking oil
dd the pork and:
2 tablespoons wine vinegar
2 tablespoons sugar
1 cup chicken stock
1 tablespoon catsup
1 cup canned pineapple pieces
1 chopped green pepper
½ cup thinly sliced carrots
1 teaspoon salt
A grating of fresh black pepper
ix and cook over high heat for about 5
nutes, stirring constantly. Serve at once.

READED PORK CHOPS
4 Servings
b with garlic:
4 half-inch-thick pork chops
ead them, page 502. Brown lightly,
ing a heavy hot pan, in:
2 to 3 tablespoons rendered pork fat
or cooking oil
duce the heat. Cook uncovered for
out 20 minutes longer or until done.
ake:
Pan Gravy, page 322

VEET AND SOUR PORK
6 Servings
'lease read About Deep-Fat Frying,
ges 124-126.

Preheat deep fryer to 375°.
Cut into ½-inch squares:
2 lbs. boned pork loin
Toss with:
3 teaspoons soy sauce
3 tablespoons flour
Fry in deep fat until the squares come to
the surface and float. When crisp and
golden brown, drain on absorbent paper.
Have ready and ♦ simmering the following
sauce. Mix:
2 tablespoons water
1½ teaspoons cornstarch
Heat:
2 tablespoons lard
Sauté until golden:
1 very small chopped onion
Add:
6 tablespoons sugar
½ cup water
¼ finely chopped garlic clove
1 tablespoon soy sauce
¼ cup vinegar
½ cup chopped sweet and sour pickle
(6 pieces of red haw)
and the cornstarch mixture. Cook and stir
for 1 minute. Add the meat and heat.
Serve with:
Rice, page 178

ABOUT SALTED MEATS

Because of the prevalence of refrigeration,
Ham, page 754, Tongue, page 445, Corned
Beef, page 412, and Salt Pork, page 755,
today are subjected to much weaker brining than formerly. Therefore a preliminary soaking or blanching in the kitchen,
see Blanching II, page 132, can often be
skipped. ♦ But all of these salted meats,
of course, like brined vegetables, still are
less valuable nutritionally than fresh meats.
They are particularly enjoyed because of
their "cured" flavors. If the meats were
♦ given heavy brines or aged like "old"
hams, page 410, be sure to soak 12 hours—
allowing 1 quart of water to 1 lb. of ham.
Or ♦ parblanch them before cooking. After
blanching, put the meat into rapidly boiling water, bring to a boil again and ♦ at
once reduce the heat to a simmer. Salted
meats are always cooked à blanc, see
page 493. Cook ♦ uncovered until tender.
Time indications are given in the recipes.

UNPROCESSED BAKED HAM
♦ Please read About Ham, page 754.
If it has not been processed, scrub well:
A smoked ham
Place it in a kettle of ♦ simmering:
Water, cider, beer or ginger ale
Add:
Vegetables suitable for soup
1 bay leaf
8 peppercorns
(6 allspice)
Simmer 20 to 30 minutes per lb. Allow a
longer time per lb. for a small ham than

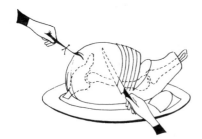 

for a large one. The thermometer will register 165° when the meat is done. This takes care of the actual cooking, but to make it look attractive at table proceed as follows.

Let it partially cool in the liquid in which it was cooked. Drain. Strip off skin.
Preheat oven to 425°.
Cover the top of the ham with:

Brown sugar
(A little dry mustard)

Stud with:

Whole cloves

Place in the oven and ♦ lower heat at once to 325° for about 20 minutes. Baste with a choice of:

1 cup cider, pineapple or orange juice, the juice of pickled peaches, cooked prunes or apricots, wine, ginger ale, molasses or beer

Cook for 30 minutes longer, without basting, after dredging with:

Brown sugar

sprinkling with:

Grated orange rind

and garnishing the top with:

Pineapple slices
Maraschino cherries

Serve with:

Raisin Cider Sauce, page 331, Sour Cream and Horseradish Sauce, page 324, Barbecue Sauce, page 332, Hot Cumberland Sauce, page 331, or horseradish

And:

Scalloped Potatoes, page 291, or a barquette of Puréed Chestnuts, page 272

To carve see sketch above.

PROCESSED BAKED HAM

♦ Please read About Ham, page 754.
Preheat oven to 325°.
Unwrap and wipe with a damp cloth:

A processed ham

Bake on a rack, uncovered. Allow 30 minutes to the pound for ½ a ham, 25 minutes for a whole ham. The meat is done when the thermometer registers 160°. Take the ham from the oven about 1 hour before it is done. Remove the rind, all but a collar around the shank bone. Cut diagonal gashes across the fat side of the ham, in

diamond shapes. Combine and glaze t top fat side of the ham with:

1⅛ cups brown sugar
2 teaspoons dry mustard
¼ cup fine bread crumbs

Moisten these ingredients with:

3 tablespoons cider vinegar, prune juice, wine or ham drippings

Stud the fat at the intersections or cent of each diamond with:

Whole cloves

Return the ham to the oven for about minutes. ♦ Increase the heat to 42! Bake 15 minutes longer. Place on a pl ter. Garnish with:

Cranberries and Orange Slices, page 102 or
Pineapple slices

heated in the pan for the last 15 minut Or with already cooked:

Apple Cups filled with sweet potatoes, page 111

The ham may be served with:

Marchand de Vin Sauce, page 327

or some other sauce for ham.

COUNTRY HAMS: VIRGINIA, SMITHFIELD, KENTUCKY, ETC.

It is the custom in some parts of the U to hang hams, after special processing, several years, after which time, of cour they develop a heavy exterior mold. ♦ prepare one of these old hams, soak it cold water to cover for 24 to 36 hou Then scrub it well, using a brush and y low soap, if necessary, to remove the mo Rinse thoroughly and place in a kettle simmering water, skin side down. All 20 minutes to the pound until the me reaches an internal heat of 150°. Add the water before last ¼ of cooking time:

1 quart cider
¼ cup brown sugar

Drain when the cooking time has elaps Remove the skin while the ham is s warm, being careful not to tear the Trim the fat partially. Dust the ham w a mixture of:

Black pepper
Corn meal
Brown sugar

Put it in a 425° oven long enough to gl it. If you want more of a baked quali allow the ham to reach an internal heat

160° to 165°. Serve hot or cold. Be sure to slice very, very thin.

CASSEROLED HAM SLICES

Good dishes variously flavored are easily made from raw ham slices.

2 to 3 Servings

Preheat oven to 350°.
Place in a casserole:

>A slice of smoked ham, about
>1 inch thick

Pour over the ham:

>Barbecue Sauce I or II, page 332
>or Hot Cumberland Sauce, page 331

Bake ◗ covered, until tender, about 1 hour.

HAM SLICE WITH FRUIT

2 to 3 Servings

Preheat oven to 325°.
Ham lends itself to combination with fruit —almost better than any other meat. You may arrange the fruit either between layers and on top of several ham slices or just on top of a single slice. If the ham is not fat, grease the bottom of a casserole lightly. Place in it:

>A slice of ham, about 1 inch thick

Cover the ham with fruit seasoned to taste.

>Sliced apples, oranges or cranberries

Sprinkled with:

>Brown sugar or honey

Or cover with drained:

>Slices of canned pineapple, apricots,
>peaches, red plums, prunes, cherries
>or raisins

These may be sprinkled with:

>Cinnamon, cloves or curry powder

◗ Cover the casserole with a lid. Baste several times with the pot juices or additional:

>Fruit juice, sherry or cider

Bake about 45 minutes or until done. Uncover for the last 10 minutes of cooking.

HAM BAKED WITH TOMATOES AND CHEESE

2 to 3 Servings

Preheat oven to 350°.
Place in a baking dish:

>A slice of smoked ham, about
>1 inch thick

Pour over it:

>1 cup seeded, chopped, canned
>tomatoes

◗ Cover the dish. Bake the ham until tender, about ¾ hour. Uncover for the last 15 minutes of cooking. When you uncover, sprinkle over the ham:

>¼ cup grated Parmesan cheese

BROILED HAM

Allow ⅓ lb. per person

Preheat broiler.
Slash in several places the fat edge of:

>A piece of smoked ham, about
>1 inch thick

Place it on a broiler rack, 3 inches below the heating unit. Broil 10 to 12 minutes to a side. A processed ham slice will require from 8 to 10 minutes to a side. You may brush the ham after cooking it on one side and turning it for final broiling with a mixture of:

>1 teaspoon mustard
>1 tablespoon lemon juice
>¼ cup grape jelly

If you do not use the glaze, a traditional accompaniment is:

>Corn Fritters, page 274
>Tomato Slices, page 306

SAUTEED HAM AND EGGS

Trim the edges of:

>A thin slice of smoked ham

Rub a skillet with ham fat. Heat it. Brown the ham on one side, reverse it and brown on the other. Remove to a hot platter. Keep hot. Reduce the heat. Sauté gently in the tried-out ham fat:

>Eggs, page 195

HAM BUTT, SHANK OR PICNIC HAM

Use these comparatively small cuts of ham as for:

>New England Boiled Dinner,
>page 412

Cook the ham until nearly tender or until the internal temperature is 170°. Add the vegetables the last ½ hour of cooking.

SMOKED SHOULDER BUTT OR COTTAGE ROLL

This cut may be boned. You may cut slices from this piece for broiling or sautéing or you may roast or "boil" it.

ABOUT BACON

Crisp, thin, properly cured breakfast bacon is attainable, but sometimes the search is long. Bacon should have a good proportion of lean meat and not taste too salty. It cannot take much heat. Broil it or start it in a cold pan to keep it from curling. We have found this a better method than the use of pressure or of specialized gadgets. In pan-broiling, keep pouring off accumulated grease and watch carefully. Bacon burns in seconds and old bacon burns twice as fast as fresh.

Canadian bacon is from the eye of a pork loin, which accounts for its leanness and high cost. It should be treated more like ham. In England a side of salted smoked or dried bacon is called a **gammon** and a slice or portion is a **rasher.**

◗ Allow about 2 slices per person.

BROILED BACON

Preheat broiler.
Place on a fine wire broiler or rack in a dripping pan:

>Strips of bacon

Keep the bacon about 5 inches from source of heat and broil until crisp. Drain on absorbent paper.

SAUTÉED BACON
♦ Please read About Bacon, page 411.
Place in a cold skillet:
    Strips of bacon
Sauté slowly until done. You may pour off the drippings while cooking. Turn frequently. Place it between paper towels to drain.

CANADIAN BACON
If you are a twosome with a craving for ham but don't want leftovers, try this smoked substitute.
I. Place in boiling water to cover:
    1 lb. or more Canadian bacon
♦ Simmer until tender, about 1 hour.

II.   **8 Servings**
Preheat oven to 325°
Combine and have ready:
    ½ cup brown sugar
    ½ teaspoon dry mustard
    2 tablespoons fine bread crumbs
    1 tablespoon cider vinegar
Bake uncovered for 1 hour. Baste every 15 minutes for 45 minutes with:
    ½ cup pineapple or other acid fruit
    juice, dry sherry, cider, ginger ale
    or a cola drink
Then spread the brown sugar mixture over it. Bake for about 15 minutes more or until the sugar has glazed.

III. Place in a heavy skillet:
    ⅛-to ¼-inch slices Canadian bacon
Cook them over low heat for 3 to 5 minutes. Turn frequently. When done, the lean part is a red brown and the fat a light golden brown. Serve with:
    Hot Cumberland Sauce, page 331
    Raisin Cider Sauce, page 331

ABOUT CORNED BEEF
At this printing, for want of a better substance the government still allows the use of sodium nitrate or saltpeter in commercial meat packing to prevent botulism. Packers also like the color it gives their meats.
To corn, combine:
    4 quarts hot water
    2 cups coarse salt
    ¼ cup sugar
    2 tablespoons mixed whole spice
    (1½ teaspoons saltpeter, for color)
When cool, pour over:
    A 5 lb. piece of beef: brisket or tongue
which has been placed in a large enameled pot or stone jar. Add:
    3 cloves garlic
Weight the meat to keep it submerged and cover the jar. Cure in the refrigerator for 3 weeks, turning the meat every 5 days.

♦ To cook corned beef, wash under running water to remove surface brine. Cover with boiling water and simmer 4 hours until a fork can penetrate to the center.
Serve hot with:
    Horseradish Sauce, page 324
    Boiled Potatoes, page 290
    Gnocchi with Farina, page 177
Serve cold with:
    Horseradish
♦ To press for slicing cold, when cool force into a deep pan. Cover and refrigerate weighted. The moisture pressed from the meat should form a jellied coating.

CORNED BEEF AND CABBAGE OR NEW ENGLAND BOILED DINNER
I.   **10 to 12 Servings**
This is a delicious dinner using only corned beef, onions and cabbage, but it is customary to cook and serve separately:
    10 to 12 beets
Skin and serve them with the rest of the dinner, garnished with:
    Parsley
Prepare and cook:
    Corned Beef, above
You may add about:
    ½ lb. salt pork
for the last 2 hours. Remove the meat from the pot. Peel, quarter and simmer in the stock for 30 minutes:
    3 small parsnips
    6 large carrots
    3 large yellow turnips
Skin and add:
    8 small onions
Peel, quarter and simmer in the stock for 15 minutes longer:
    6 medium-sized potatoes
Cut into wedges, add and simmer until tender, for about 10 to 15 minutes:
    A head of cabbage
Reheat the meat in the stock. Serve it on a platter, surrounded by the vegetables.

II. If using a ✪ pressure cooker, use the ingredients above but cook for 10 minutes before adding the salt pork. Reduce heat. Add the salt pork. Bring up to pressure and cook 10 minutes more. Reduce pressure. Add the vegetables, except for beets. Bring up to pressure. Cook for 2 minutes more. Reduce pressure and serve at once, using the separately cooked beets as a garnish.

ABOUT BRAISING, POT-ROASTING AND STEWING
Escoffier believed that braising was a process which warranted the use of choice meats and the exercise of all his immense skill and patience. We concur. However, we wish to point out that quite inexpensive meat cuts can also be made to re-

spond well not only to braising, but to other kinds of moist heat, like stewing and pot-roasting. Time, with most of them, is of the essence: relax and resign yourself to cooking ♦ very, very slowly and ♦ very, very long.

More exact directions will be given in each recipe. You can of course shortcut by using a ♦ pressure cooker, but the necessarily high heat of this process will give you a less desirable result and a "canned" taste. Instead—and preferably—find yourself a ♦ heavy, covered pot or casserole, slightly bigger than the piece or quantity of meat you customarily cook. ♦ Do not use this process for a piece of meat over 4 to 5 pounds. If it is larger, cut it into pieces and make a stew of it, following the same method described for braising.

♦ If the meat is lean, you may want to lard it with seasoned Lardoons, page 383. If salt pork is called for and if it is very fat or salty, you may parblanch it, page 132, before rendering or before cooking it in a stew. ♦ Do not worry if the meat comes from an older animal. Maturity will add to its flavor. So will a good browning, page 384, in rendered fat of the same type, unless you are cooking veal or fowl. These are usually cooked "à blanc"—the term in this instance meaning that the meat is not seared before stewing. You may want to ♦ tenderize the meat by marinating, page 384; and you may dredge the meat with flour or not, as you like. ♦ If you do not dredge, be sure that the meat is wiped dry. When you have browned it on one side and are browning it on the other, you may add finely chopped onions. After it is seared, pour off all but 1 or 2 tablespoons of the fat which may have been rendered out of it. Then set the meat on a bed of about 1 cup Mirepoix, page 541, on a rack, or on a rind of pork. Have ready enough ♦ boiling stock to cover the bottom of the pan, at least 1 to 2 inches. In any case, if you use more, barely cover the meat. ♦ Cover the pan tightly. As soon as the liquid reaches a boil, reduce the heat at once to ♦ maintain a simmer. Do not allow the liquid to get too low during the cooking. Replenish it with boiling stock or water, if necessary. Turn the meat over occasionally to keep it moist.

Vegetables may be cooked entirely in the pot-roasting pan. ♦ Allow about ¼ lb. vegetables to ¾ lb. meat. If cooking on top of the stove and if the vegetables are of medium size, add them during the last ¾ hour of cooking. But if they are very mature—especially carrots, onions, turnips, parsnips and the outer ribs of celery—they may profit by a brief blanching, see Blanching II, page 132. Or you may cook vegetables partially and separately before adding them toward the end of the pot-roasting. Should the stew or braise be cooked in the oven, the vegetables may need as long as 1½ hours. When the stew

is served, the sauce will not be thick, but should have good body—what the French call "du corps."

♦ Always allow a stew to stand for at least 5 minutes off the heat so that grease rises and can be skimmed, page 145. To reheat leftover stews, see page 388. Also note recipes for cooked meats in Luncheon Dishes, page 223.

ABOUT MEAT PIES AND PIE TOPPING

To make meat pies taste and look well, be sure to have ♦ sufficient tastily seasoned gravy to almost cover the meat. There are several ways to top meat pies, but the trick in each instance is to assure the escape of steam, so that the under part of the crust will not be soggy. We find that unless the crusts are prebaked, it is difficult not to end up with some soggy surface. If you do not prebake, do brush the under surfaces exposed to moisture or steam with white of egg. ♦ Vent the crust well.

Prepare:

Any unsweetened Pie Dough, page 588

I. For a surefire method, cut and bake separately on a baking tin a piece, or pieces, of dough to cover the large or individual dishes in which you will serve the meat pie. To bake the dough, see page 590. Remember that pie dough shrinks in baking, so cut it slightly larger than the dish. Don't forget that this separate baking means you will have to cover your stew in some other way during the heating—such as with a tight-fitting lid. Just before serving, when the casserole has been heated through, place the prebaked crust on top and serve at once.

II. If you want to put the topping on before heating, preheat the oven to 350°. Fill the baking dish to be covered to within 1 inch of the top.

Place the dough on rather generously—to allow for shrinkage. Brush with Egg Wash, page 682. Be sure to vent it well. Heat the dish for 45 minutes to 1 hour, when the stew should be thoroughly heated and the crust golden. You may brush the crust with butter before serving. When the stew is done, the sauce should not be thick, but should have good body.

BOILED BEEF OR BOEUF BOUILLI
4 to 6 Servings

In his witty book about Viennese gourmandising, "Blue Trout and Black Truffles," Joseph Wechsberg describes no less than 24 different kinds of boiled beef specialties and announces categorically that in Imperial days only the best beef was "boiled." Viennese beef owes its special flavor to a special feed of sugar beet mash. Special feeding is the reason that the French, as well as the Viennese, consider this dish a treat, rather than the boarding-

house stopgap it has come to be considered here. If you add Spaetzle, page 192, Noodles, page 188, or Dampfnudeln, page 608, the result can become quite extraordinary.
Bring to a boil, in a heavy pot:
> 6 cups water

Put in:
> 3 lbs. lean, first cut brisket, bottom round or plate beef

Bring to a boil and skim the pot. Add:
> 1 onion stuck with 3 cloves
> ½ cup sliced carrots
> ½ cup sliced celery with leaves
> 1 teaspoon salt
> (1 sliced turnip)

♦ Cover the pot closely and simmer the meat until tender, about 3 to 4 hours. Drain and reserve the stock. Melt:
> ¼ cup butter

Brown lightly in the butter:
> ¼ cup chopped onions

Stir until blended:
> 2 tablespoons flour

Stir in slowly 2 cups of the degreased stock. Season the sauce with:
> 2 tablespoons freshly grated horseradish
> Salt
> Vinegar or lemon juice
> (Sugar)

Prepared horseradish contains vinegar and it is difficult to give exact proportions. So:
> Correct the seasoning

Cut the meat into thin slices against the grain and reheat ♦ very briefly in the boiling gravy. Garnish with:
> Chopped parsley

Serve with:
> Boiled New Potatoes in their jackets, page 290
> Sauerkraut, page 269
> Dumplings, page 191

BEEF POT ROAST
6 Servings
Please read About Pot Roasts, Braises and Stews, page 412.
Preheat oven to 300°.
Prepare for cooking:
> 3 to 4 lbs. beef shoulder, chuck, blade, boneless neck, rump or brisket

If the meat is lean, you may lard it, page 383. Rub the meat with:
> (Garlic)

Dredge it in:
> (Flour)

Heat in a heavy pan over lively heat:
> 2 tablespoons rendered suet or cooking oil

Brown the meat on all sides in the fat.
♦ Do not let it scorch. Add to the pot when the meat is half browned:
> 1 chopped carrot
> 1 rib diced celery
> (1 small diced white turnip)
> (2 tablespoons chopped green pepper)

When the meat is browned, pour off excess fat. Add to the pot:
> 1 small onion stuck with 3 cloves
> 2 cups boiling meat or vegetable stock or part stock and part dry wine

Cover and bake 2 to 3 hours. During this time turn the meat several times and, if necessary, add additional:
> Hot stock

When the meat is firm,
> Correct the seasoning

Pour off excess fat and serve with the pot liquor as it is or slightly thickened with:
> Kneaded Butter, page 321

You may, if you wish, add to the pot roast drained boiled vegetables. Serve with:
> Potato Pancakes, page 294, Kasha, page 177, or Green Noodles, page 188
> Blue Plum Compote, page 107

BEEF POT ROAST IN SOUR CREAM AND WINE
Prepare:
> Beef Pot Roast, above

Add to the liquid for gravy:
> 1 cup dry wine, preferably red
> ½ cup water

Pour it around the roast and cook until done. Heat over hot water and stir in just before serving:
> ¾ cup warm cultured sour cream

GASTON BEEF STEW
6 Servings
This one-dish meal seems to taste better when cooked a day ahead.
Cut into small pieces and, if very salty, parblanch, page 132, briefly:
> ½ lb. salt pork

Dry the pork and sauté it slowly in a large skillet. Cut into pieces suitable for stewing:
> 2 lbs. beef

Brown the beef in the hot drippings over high heat. Pour off most of the accumulated fat. Sprinkle the meat with:
> Seasoned flour

Combine and heat until boiling:
> 1½ chopped cloves garlic
> 1 large chopped onion
> 1 cup bouillon
> 1 cup canned tomato sauce
> 12 peppercorns
> 3 whole cloves
> ¼ cup chopped parsley
> ⅓ bay leaf

Place the meat in a heavy saucepan. Pour the above ingredients over it. Simmer closely covered for about 2 to 3 hours or until the meat can be easily pierced with a fork. During the last hour of cooking, add:
> ½ cup dry sherry or dry white wine

Cook separately until nearly tender:
> 6 medium-sized pared quartered potatoes
> 6 pared quartered carrots
> 1 stalk chopped celery

Add these vegetables for the last 15 minutes of cooking.

BEEF STEW WITH WINE OR BOEUF BOURGUIGNONNE
4 to 6 Servings

For an added bouquet, you may marinate the diced meat overnight in wine. Drain the wine for later use in cooking. Preheat oven to 300°.
Try out:
>½ lb. thinly sliced salt pork or use
>3 tablespoons butter

Peel, add and sauté lightly:
>12 small onions or 4 shallots

Remove pork and onions from the pan. Cut into 1-inch dice and sauté in the hot fat until light brown:
>2 lbs. lean beef

Sprinkle the meat with:
>(1½ tablespoons flour)

Place it in an ovenproof dish with:
>1 teaspoon salt
>4 peppercorns
>½ bay leaf
>(½ teaspoon thyme or marjoram)

Cover the meat with:
>Dry red wine and water—
>¾ part wine to ¼ part water

Cook ♦ covered in oven for 1 hour. Place the pork and onions on top and continue to cook for another hour or until the beef is tender. Or simmer the beef covered on top of the stove for about 1½ hours in all. You may add:
>(1 cup sautéed mushrooms)
>Correct the seasoning

and serve the stew sprinkled with:
>Chopped parsley

Flambé at the last minute with:
>(¼ cup brandy)

BEEF BRISKET WITH SAUERKRAUT
6 Servings

Tie into a compact shape:
>3 lbs. beef brisket

Melt in a deep kettle:
>3 tablespoons bacon or other fat

Add, stir about and brown lightly:
>(¼ cup chopped onions)

Add the meat and place over it:
>2 lbs. sauerkraut

which then acts as a marinade. We prefer to add the sauerkraut after the meat has cooked about an hour. Add:
>2 cups boiling water

Simmer the meat covered for about 2½ hours or until tender. Season with:
>Salt and pepper
>Dry white wine
>(Caraway seed)

Serve with:
>Boiled Potatoes, page 290

Pour over them:
>Cultured sour cream
>Chopped parsley or chives

SOUP MEAT
Sometimes, for reasons of economy, soup meat is served at table, but by and large it has, by this time, been deprived of most nutrients and flavor. Therefore, it must be presented with a self-assertive sauce. Brisket or other soup meat may be taken from the kettle before the vegetables are added. Serve it with:
>Horseradish Sauce, page 324
>Mustard Sauce, page 325, Thickened
>Tomato Sauce, page 333, or Brown
>Onion Sauce, page 327

SAUERBRATEN
6 Servings

Prepare for cooking:
>3 lbs. beef shoulder

Lard it, page 383, with:
>18 seasoned lardoons, ¼ inch thick

or choose a fat cut of meat. Rub with:
>Pepper
>(Garlic)

Place in a deep crock or glass bowl. Heat but do not boil:
>Equal parts mild vinegar or dry
>wine and water

Use in all about:
>1 quart of liquid
>½ cup sliced onion
>2 bay leaves
>1 teaspoon peppercorns
>¼ cup sugar

Pour this mixture while hot over the beef, so that it is more than ½ covered. Place a lid over the crock and refrigerate 24 hours to a week. The longer you leave it, the sourer the meat will get. Drain it, saving the marinade, and cook like:
>Pot Roast, page 414

Use the vinegar mixture in place of stock. When the meat is tender, remove from the pot. Thicken the stock with:
>Flour, see Pan Gravy, page 322

Add:
>1 cup sweet or cultured sour cream

We like the gravy "straight." Some cooks add:
>(Raisins, catsup and gingersnaps)

Serve the roast with:
>Potato Dumplings, page 192, or
>Potato Pancakes, page 294

and you will have a treat. ♦ This dish does not freeze successfully.

BOEUF À LA MODE
A pot roast de luxe, because so elegantly presented. The meat is sliced very thin and even, covered with a sauce, and the platter garnished with beautifully arranged vegetables.
Prepare the beef as for:
>Sauerbraten, above

larding it but marinating only for 4 to 5 hours in a mixture of:
>1½ to 2 cups dry red wine
>¼ cup brandy

When ready to cook, add:
>2 boned blanched calf feet

Use Blanch II, page 132, simmering for 10 minutes. ♦ Simmer covered for 3½ to 4 hours. You may, toward the last hour of cooking, add to the degreased sauce and cook with the meat:

1 cup parboiled, lightly sautéed carrots
1 cup parboiled, lightly sautéed onions

Just before serving, heat with the dish:

1 cup sautéed mushrooms

Serve the meat cut as described above, garnished with the vegetables and with the calf feet cut in one-inch squares.

SPICED BEEF

8 Servings

Good served hot. Fine for a cold meat platter. Cover:

4 to 5 lbs. chuck roast

with:

Cider vinegar, dry wine or cider
2 sliced onions
½ bay leaf
1 teaspoon each cinnamon, allspice and cloves
1½ teaspoons salt
1 teaspoon pepper

Let the roast stand refrigerated in this marinade for 12 hours or more. Drain it and reserve the liquor.
Preheat oven to 275°.
Place the meat in a roasting pan. Heat to the boiling point and pour over it ½ the vinegar and:

2 cups water

Cover closely and roast for about 3 hours. Put through a grinder or mince, then saute in butter until a golden brown:

2 onions
4 large carrots
1 medium yellow turnip
1 stalk celery

Add these ingredients to the roast for the last ½ hour of cooking. Add, if needed:

Salt

The stock may be thickened with:

Flour, see Gravy, page 322

CHUCK ROAST IN FOIL

12 Servings

Foil-cooked meats often have a pasty look about them, but the use in this recipe of dehydrated onion soup gives great vigor of color and flavor, in spite of the fact that the meat is not browned first. Try this for informal company.
Preheat oven to 300°.
Have ready 2 or 3 large pieces of heavy-duty foil. You may wipe the top of a:

7 lb. chuck roast

with:

Cooking oil

Sprinkle with:

½ to 1 package dehydrated onion soup

Place the center of the foil over it and turn the meat and foil over. Sprinkle the other side with:

½ to 1 package dehydrated onion soup

Now wrap the roast very carefully with the pieces of foil, so that no juices can escape. Place the package in a pan and

bake for 3½ to 4 hours. If your company is informal, do not cut the foil until you are at table and ready to carve. The sudden burst of fragrance adds to the anticipation. Serve with:

Spaetzle, page 192
A rice ring with mushrooms filled with Parslied Peas, page 288

SWISS STEAK

6 Servings

Preheat oven to 300°.
Trim the edges of a ¾-inch thick:

2 lb. round steak

Rub with:

½ clove garlic

Pound into both sides of the steak, with the edge of a heavy plate or a mallet:

As much seasoned flour as the steak will hold

Cut it into pieces or leave it whole. If left whole, gash the edges to prevent curling. Heat in a large heavy casserole:

¼ cup bacon or ham drippings

Sear the steak on one side until brown. After you turn it over, add:

½ cup finely chopped onions
1 cup mixed finely chopped carrots, peppers and celery

Do not allow them to brown.

Correct the seasoning

Add:

(½ cup strained boiling tomatoes)
1 cup stock

Cover the casserole closely and place in the oven for 2 hours or more. Remove the steak to a hot platter. Strain the drippings. Degrease the drippings and make:

Pan Gravy, page 322

Pour the gravy over the steak. Serve with:

Mashed Potatoes, page 290

FLANK STEAK WITH DRESSING

4 Servings

If you use sharp seasonings this gives a deviled effect.
Have ready:

A 2 lb. flank steak, page 399

Trim the edges. Season with and pound in:

1 teaspoon salt
⅛ teaspoon paprika
¼ teaspoon mustard
(⅛ teaspoon ginger)
(1 teaspoon Worcestershire sauce)

Melt:

¼ cup butter or bacon drippings

Add and sauté until brown:

2 tablespoons chopped onion

Add:

1 cup bread crumbs
¼ teaspoon salt
A few grains paprika
2 tablespoons chopped parsley
3 tablespoons chopped celery
1 slightly beaten egg

Spread this dressing over the flank steak, roll it loosely and tie it. For variety, try Sausage Dressing and apples, page 457.
Heat in a skillet:

3 tablespoons cooking oil

Sear the steak in the hot oil on all sides. Preheat oven to 325°. Place the steak in a casserole or closely covered dish. Stir into the oil in the skillet:

2 tablespoons flour

Add:

1 cup water or stock
1 cup tomato juice or dry wine
¼ teaspoon salt

Pour this mixture over the steak. Bake closely covered for about 1½ hours. Add seasoning, if required. Serve the steak with a:

Green vegetable

SHORT RIBS OF BEEF

2 Servings

Cut into about 3-inch pieces:

2 lbs. lean short ribs of beef

Place in a heavy pot with a lid:

5 cups water
1 small sliced onion
1 small sliced carrot
4 or more ribs celery with leaves

Bring these ingredients to the boiling point. Add the short ribs. Simmer ♦ covered until nearly tender, about 2 hours. Take out the meat. Strain and degrease the stock. Make about 3 cups of thin gravy, page 322, using:

¼ cup fat
¼ cup flour
3 cups stock

Season the gravy mildly with:

Salt and pepper
A few drops brown coloring

Preheat oven to 325°.
Heat in a heavy skillet:

¼ cup fat

Slice, add and stir about until light brown:

1 small onion

Brown the meat in the hot fat. Pour over it ½ the gravy. Bake ♦ uncovered for about 45 minutes and let it get brown and crisp. It may be basted occasionally with the drippings. Reheat the remaining gravy. Add:

1 teaspoon fresh marjoram
Correct the seasoning

Place the meat on a hot platter. Garnish with:

Mashed potatoes

Serve piping hot with gravy.

ABOUT GOULASH, GULYAS OR PÖRKOLT

This Hungarian specialty is cooked in many ways, but its most distinguishing seasoning is usually sweet paprika, page 536. In Beef Goulash, the meat is browned. In the variations that follow it is cooked à blanc—that is, without even browning at all. Beef, veal, and other meats are used separately and in combination. If lamb and pork are included in some of the following recipes, the dish may be called **Pörkolt**. Vegetables are sometimes added for the last hour of cooking. Goulash is always highly spiced. Some epicures insist that freshly ground peppercorns are a requisite, others prefer the imported Rosen paprika. Some cooks use water as the liquid, others prefer stock or dry red wine.

BEEF GOULASH

6 Servings

Cut into 1-inch cubes:

2 lbs. beef: round steak, shinbone or
1 lb. beef and 1 lb. lean veal

Melt in a heavy pot:

¼ cup butter or cooking oil

Brown the meat on both sides in the hot oil. Add and sauté:

1½ cups chopped onion

Add:

1 cup boiling Stock, page 490, or
tomato juice
1 teaspoon salt
½ teaspoon paprika

Use just enough stock to keep the meat from scorching and add more gradually during the cooking, as necessary. Cover the pot closely and simmer the meat for 1½ hours. Six small peeled potatoes may be added for the last ½ hour of cooking, but they do soak up the gravy which is apt to be the best part of the goulash. Remove the meat from the pot and thicken the stock for:

Gravy, page 322

It may be necessary to add stock or tomato juice.

Correct the seasoning

If potatoes have not been made an ingredient, serve the goulash with:

Polenta, page 177, Spaetzle, page
192, or Noodles, page 188

LAMB OR PORK GOULASH AU BLANC

Sauté in:

¾ cup butter
1½ to 2 cups chopped onions

Mash in a mortar and add:

1 teaspoon caraway
2 teaspoons marjoram
A grating of lemon rind
1 clove garlic
1 tablespoon sweet paprika

Add and bring to a boil:

1 cup water or stock

Add:

2 lbs. pork or lamb in 1½-inch cubes

Simmer covered for 1½ hours.
Garnish with:

Slivered red or green peppers

VEAL AND PORK GOULASH

4 Servings

Sauté until light brown:

6 tablespoons chopped onions

in:

2 tablespoons butter

Add:

½ lb. one-inch veal cubes

½ lb. one-inch lean pork cubes
Heat and add:
1 lb. sauerkraut
1 teaspoon caraway seed
Simmer these ingredients covered for about
1 hour. Heat and add:
1 cup cultured sour cream
A generous grating of freshly
ground pepper
Serve at once.

BELGIAN BEEF STEW OR CARBONNADE FLAMANDE

4 Servings

Cut into 1½-inch cubes and coat in seasoned flour:
2 lbs. boneless beef: chuck, etc.
Sauté lightly in:
1 tablespoon butter
¼ cup thinly sliced onions
Put them to one side. Add:
1 tablespoon butter
and brown the floured meat. Drain off any
excess fat. Combine and bring to a boil:
1 cup dark beer
1 pressed clove garlic
½ teaspoon sugar
Pour over the meat and onion mixture.
Cover and simmer 2 to 2½ hours. After
straining the sauce, you may add:
(½ teaspoon vinegar)
To serve, garnish meat with:
Parsley or dill new potatoes
Use sauce as gravy.

OXTAIL STEW

6 Servings

Preheat oven to 350°.
Brown, page 384, in a heavy-lidded pan:
3 oxtails with separated joints
in:
3 tablespoons beef fat
with:
¼ cup diced onion
Add:
¼ cup Mirepoix, page 541
4 cups hot stock or ½ stock and
½ tomato juice or water
1 teaspoon salt
2 peppercorns
Simmer 3½ to 4 hours. During the last 35
minutes of cooking you may add:
½ cup diced celery
½ cup diced carrots
(¼ cup tomato paste)
When the meat is tender and the stew degreased, page 145
Correct the seasoning
Thicken the liquid with:
2 tablespoons of Beurre Manié,
page 321
Add:
2 tablespoons chopped parsley

ABOUT BEEF ROLLS, ROULADES OR PAUPIETTES

Thin strips of meat or fish rolled around
vegetables or other stuffing are known also
as Roulades or Paupiettes. They may be

further wrapped in salt pork or bacon.
To make them with beef, use:
Thin strips of round or flank steak,
3 x 4 inches
Season with:
Salt and pepper
You may pound the meat. Place on each
strip about 2 tablespoons of one of the
following fillings:
I. A well-seasoned smoked or cooked sau-
sage, 1 teaspoon chopped parsley or a
sliver of dill pickle.

II. A thick julienned carrot, a rib of celery, 2 teaspoons minced ham.

III. 2 tablespoons seasoned cooked rice, 2
chopped stuffed olives.
Roll the meat and tie with string near
both ends or wrap as for cabbage leaves,
sketched on page 130. Dredge in:
Flour
Brown in bacon grease or rendered salt
pork. Place in a casserole and use for
every 6 rolls:
1½ cups stock or dry red wine
1½ to 2 tablespoons tomato paste
♦ Cover and cook slowly in a preheated
325° oven or on direct low heat for about
1 hour and 15 minutes.

STEAK AND KIDNEY PIE

4 Servings

Preheat oven to 350°.
Classic recipes for this dish often call for
beef kidneys. If they are used, they must
be blanched, page 132, and the cooking
time must be increased to assure tenderness. If a crust lines and covers the baker
—a process we do not recommend, see below—the top should be protected until the
final browning with a foil lightly placed
over it. Cut into small, ½-inch-thick slices:
1½ lbs. round or other beef steak
Wash, skin and slice thin:
¾ lb. veal or lamb kidneys
Melt in a skillet:
3 tablespoons butter or beef fat
Sauté the kidneys in this over high heat
for 1 to 2 minutes. Shake constantly.
Shake the beef in a bag of:
Seasoned flour
Lightly grease an ovenproof baker. Place
in it a layer of meat, then a layer of kidneys. Or you may reserve the kidneys and
add them the last 15 minutes before placing the pastry cover. Add:
2 cups Brown Stock, page 490
1 cup dry red wine or beer
Cover the dish and bake for 1½ to 2 hours.
Cool slightly. Raise oven heat to 400°.
Cover the meat with:
Pâte Brisée, page 591
Bake about 12 to 15 minutes.

▤ BURGOO

10-12 Servings

One of those mixtures not unlike Mulligan
and Brunswick Stews—a combination of

[m]eats, fowl and gleanings from the garden
[p]atch. Addicts—and there are many in
[K]entucky—claim this stew is best if served
[th]e day after it is made. Put in a heavy-
[li]dded kettle with:

    3 qts. water or stock
    ¾ lb. lean inch-diced stewing beef
    ¾ lb. inch-diced pork shoulder

[B]ring slowly to a boil. ◗ Reduce heat at
[on]ce and simmer about 2½ hours. In an-
[ot]her heavy kettle put:

    1 disjointed 3½ lb. chicken
with:
    Enough water to just cover

[B]ring these ingredients to a boil. ◗ Reduce
[th]e heat at once and simmer about 1 hour
[or] until the meat can easily be removed
[fr]om the bones. Put the chicken meat and
[th]e water in which it was cooked into the
[fir]st kettle with the other meat after it has
[si]mmered the 2½ hours as directed. At
[th]is time, also add:

    2½ cups quartered ripe, peeled and
      seeded tomatoes
    1 cup fresh Lima beans
    ½ diced red pepper
    4 diced green peppers
    ¾ cup diced onions
    1 cup diced carrots
    2 cups diced potatoes
    1 bay leaf
    1 tablespoon Worcestershire sauce

[Si]mmer this whole mixture ½ hour or more
[be]fore adding:

    2 cups corn, cut freshly from the cob

[Co]ok about 15 minutes more or until all
[th]e vegetables are soft.

    Correct the seasoning

[Se]rve hot in deep bowls with:

    Chunks of French bread

[on] the side, to be used—you know how!
[I]s that kind of a dish.

[V]EAL STEW
                              4 Servings

[Se]lect:
    1½ lbs. veal with little bone or
    2 lbs. neck or shanks

[T]he meat may be cooked in one piece, cut
[in]to 3-inch pieces or into 1½-inch cubes.
[M]elt in a heavy pot or saucepan over mod-
[er]ate heat:

    3 tablespoons butter or drippings

[Br]own the meat in the hot drippings. Re-
[du]ce the heat. Cover the bottom of the
[po]t ½ inch with boiling:

    Vegetable Stock, page 492

[C]over the pot closely and ◗ simmer the
[m]eat until tender, 45 minutes or more.
[R]emove it from the pot. Strain the stock.
[T]hicken it with:

    Flour, see Pan Gravy, page 322

[T]he browning of the meat in the fat is
[op]tional. For a pleasant change drop it
[di]rectly into boiling vegetable stock and
[co]ok as directed. Serve the stew with:

    Chopped parsley
    Noodles, page 188
    Farina Balls, page 171, or Rice

      Ring, page 180, and Fried Apples,
      page 111
or serve it in:
      A Hominy Grits Ring, page 176
Veal stew is also good with a baked top
crust. Follow the recipe for Quick Chicken
Pot Pie, page 225.

VEAL STEW WITH RED WINE
                              4 Servings

Cut into 12 chunks:
    1½ lbs. boneless veal or beef
Roll each piece in:
    ½ slice bacon: 6 slices in all
Dredge the meat lightly with:
    Flour
Melt in a heavy skillet:
    2 tablespoons bacon or other fat
Add the meat and:
    12 small peeled onions
Stir these ingredients about and permit
them to brown on all sides. Remove them
from the pan. Pour off all but 1 tablespoon
of fat. Stir in:
    1 tablespoon flour
Add and stir until smooth:
    1½ cups consommé or stock
    ½ cup dry red wine
Add the meat and onions. Simmer closely
covered 1½ to 2 hours until the meat is
very tender. Season and serve with some
baked dish like:
    Crusty or Soft-Centered Spoon
    Bread, page 579

BLANQUETTE DE VEAU OR
ELABORATE VEAL STEW
                              6 Servings

Cut into 1-inch pieces:
    1½ lbs. veal shoulder
    1½ lbs. veal breast
Parblanch, page 132, the pieces of veal
about 2 minutes in salted water. Drain
and wash well under cold running water,
removing all the scum. Put the meat in a
heavy pan and add:
    5 cups chicken or veal stock
    1 large onion studded with 1 clove
    1 peeled carrot
    1 stalk chopped white celery
    A Bouquet Garni, page 541
Simmer uncovered for about 1¼ to 1½
hours until the veal is tender and may be
pierced with a fork. Now skim out the
vegetables and the bouquet. Add:
    24 small blanched white onions
    2 cups fresh button mushroom caps
Simmer for about 10 minutes. Combine:
    ¼ cup flour
    ¼ cup butter
Add this thickener to the veal and simmer
for another 10 minutes. Remove pan from
heat. Mix together:
    3 beaten egg yolks
    ½ cup whipping cream
Stir about 2 tablespoons of the hot veal
stock into the egg mixture and return it to
the pan. Add:

2 to 3 tablespoons lemon juice
    Correct the seasoning
Serve with:
    Noodles or rice
Garnished with:
    Chopped parsley

VEAL AND PORK PIE

4 Servings

Cut into 1-inch pieces:
    ½ lb. veal
    ½ lb. lean pork
Stir and brown the meat lightly in:
    2 tablespoons butter or cooking oil
Add and simmer covered for about 15
minutes:
    3 cups boiling water
    1 teaspoon salt
    ½ teaspoon paprika
    ½ bay leaf
    2 whole cloves
Remove spices. Add:
    ¼ cup diced carrots
    ¾ cup diced celery
    1 cup diced potatoes
    12 small onions
Bring the stew to the boiling point ▶ re-
duce the heat and simmer covered until
the meat is tender, about 30 minutes
longer.
    Correct the seasoning
Make:
    Pan Gravy, page 322
Preheat oven to 450°.
Place the stew in a baking dish. Top it
while hot with:
    Pie Crust, page 588
Bake for about 20 minutes.

MOCK CHICKEN DRUMSTICKS
OR CITY CHICKEN

6 Servings

Preheat oven to 325°.
Cut into 1 x 1½-inch pieces:
    1 lb. veal steak
    1 lb. pork steak
Arrange the veal and pork cubes alter-
nately on 6 skewers. Press the pieces close
together into the shape of a drumstick.
Roll the meat in:
    Seasoned flour
Beat:
    1 egg
    2 tablespoons water
Dip the sticks in the diluted egg, then
roll in:
    Bread crumbs
Melt in a skillet:
    ¼ cup butter
Brown the meat partially in the fat. Add:
    1 tablespoon grated onion
Continue to brown the meat. Cover the
bottom of the skillet with:
    Boiling Stock, page 490
Cover the skillet and place in oven, about
50 minutes or until the meat is tender.
Make:
    Pan Gravy, page 322

VEAL BIRDS OR PAUPIETTES

For other stuffings, see About Beef Rolls,
page 418.
Trim the edges from ⅓-inch-thick:
    Slices of veal from the round
Pound the meat with a cleaver and cut
into pieces about 2 x 4 inches. Make the
following dressing. Chop the meat trimmings and combine them with an equal
amount of chopped:
    Salt pork
Measure the salt pork and trimmings and
add to them ½ the amount of:
    Bread crumbs
Add:
    Chopped onion, chopped raisins or
        seedless grapes
    Chopped celery
    (A grating of lemon rind)
Moisten these ingredients with sufficient:
    Cream or stock
to hold them together. Spread the meat
lightly with the dressing and roll it. Secure with skewers or thread. Roll the birds
in:
    Flour
Sauté them in hot:
    Butter or cooking oil
until golden in color. Reduce the heat
and add:
    Hot cream, milk, stock or dry wine
until the meat is half covered. ▶ Cover
the pot closely and simmer until tender,
about 20 minutes.
    Correct the seasoning
Add:
    (½ lb. Sautéed Mushrooms, page 281)
Make:
    Pan Gravy, page 322

VEAL POT ROAST

Please read About Pot Roasts, page 412.
Prepare by boning and rolling:
    A rump roast of veal
Cook as for any unbrowned Stew, see
à blanc, page 413. Classically, veal is not
browned—but we've eaten some mighty
good browned veal pot roasts! Use:
    ½ cup water for every lb. of meat
Or prepare:
    Pot Roast in Sour Cream and Wine,
        page 414
omitting the browning. Add to the finished
gravy:
    (Capers, basil or thyme)

MEXICAN VEAL STEAK
WITH NOODLES

6 Servings

Cut into small slices:
    1 lb. thin veal steak
Dredge with:
    ¼ cup flour
Heat:
    3 teaspoons butter or olive oil
Sauté the meat quickly on both sides until
brown. ▶ Reduce the heat. Cover the
meat with:
    1½ cups sliced onions

6 tablespoons chili sauce
1¼ cups boiling stock
♦ Simmer closely covered about ½ hour. Meanwhile, cook and drain:
2 cups Noodles, page 188
Toss them in:
¾ cup cream of chicken soup
Serve the noodles mounded, covered with:
¼ cup buttered crumbs
2 tablespoons grated Parmesan cheese
Surround the noodles with the steak. Garnish with:
(Parsley)

CUBED VEAL BAKED IN SOUR CREAM

4 Servings

Preheat oven to 300°.
Cut into cubes:
1½ lbs. boneless veal
Brown lightly in:
1½ tablespoons butter
Remove the meat to an ovenproof baking dish. Add to the butter, stir and sauté lightly:
1 tablespoon chopped onion
½ lb. sliced mushrooms
Remove from the heat. Stir in slowly:
1 tablespoon flour
⅓ cup stock
¾ cup cultured sour cream
½ teaspoon salt
⅛ teaspoon pepper
Pour sauce over the meat. Cover the dish. Bake for about 1 hour.

BAKED MARROW BONES OR OSSO BUCO

3 Servings

Preheat oven to 300°.
♦ To make this dish really delectable, the animal should not be more than 2 months old. Saw into 2½ to 3 inch pieces:
2 lbs. shin bone of veal
Dip the bones first in:
Olive oil
Then in:
Seasoned flour
Heat in the pan:
¼ cup olive oil
To keep the marrow intact, set the bones upright. To conserve stock, place them as close as possible on the base of a heavy pan just large enough to hold them. Brown the bones very slowly for about 15 minutes. Pour over them:
½ cup white wine
(½ cup skinned, diced, seeded, fresh tomatoes)
Seasoned stock—enough to come at least ⅓ up the bones
Cover and bake for 1 to 1½ hours until the meat falls from them. Before serving, sprinkle the tops with:
Gremolata, page 541
Serve garnished with:
Fried Chipolata sausage and Boiled Chestnuts, page 272, or Risotto, page 183

BRAISED SHOULDER OF LAMB

6 Servings

Melt in a heavy pot:
¼ cup cooking oil or butter
Sear on all sides in the hot fat:
A rolled shoulder of lamb
Remove it from the pot. Cook slowly in the fat for 10 minutes:
½ cup chopped onion
¼ cup chopped carrots
¼ cup chopped turnips
½ cup chopped celery with leaves
(1 sliced clove garlic)
Return the meat to the pot. Add:
½ bay leaf
4 whole peppercorns
1 teaspoon salt
4 cups boiling vegetable stock or
3 cups stock and 1 cup tomato pulp
♦ Cover the pot closely. ♦ Simmer the meat until tender, about 2 hours. When the meat is done, degrease the stew and thicken the stock slightly with:
Kneaded Butter, page 321
Serve the roast surrounded by the vegetables.

BRAISED STUFFED SHOULDER OR FARCE OF LAMB

6 Servings

This cut is hard to carve unless boned. Its flavor is highly prized.
Preheat oven to 325°.
Bone:
A shoulder of lamb
You may rub it with:
(Garlic)
or insert slivers of garlic under the skin. Prepare about:
3 cups Bread Dressing, page 456
Spread it on the meat. Roll like a jelly roll. Secure with string, or fasten with spiral skewers, page 463. Brown in:
3 tablespoons cooking oil or butter
Place in a roasting pan:
1 cup Vegetable Stock, page 492
Put the browned roast in it and cook ♦ covered, allowing about 40 minutes to the pound. You may put some of the bones in the pan. Meanwhile, prepare for cooking:
3 cups diced vegetables: celery, carrots, onions, potatoes
After the meat has cooked about 45 minutes, place the vegetables in the pan with:
1 cup vegetable stock
Cover and continue to cook the meat about 1 hour after adding the vegetables or until the internal temperature of the meat is 175° to 180°. Pour off, but reserve most of the liquid and allow the meat and vegetables to glaze by cooking them ♦ uncovered for about 10 minutes longer. Meanwhile, to make the sauce, degrease the reserved liquid and reduce it somewhat.
Correct the seasoning
before serving.

LAMB FORESTIÈRE OR MOCK VENISON

Wipe with a damp cloth:
A leg of lamb or mutton
Cover it with:
Buttermilk
Soak it refrigerated for 24 hours or more.
Preheat oven to 450°.
Drain, wipe dry and lard the meat, page 383, with:
Salt pork or bacon
Dot it with:
Butter
Dredge with:
Flour
Put the roast on a rack in a pan in the oven and bake for 15 minutes. Add:
⅓ cup hot Vegetable Stock, page 492
Cover closely. ♦ Reduce heat at once to 325°. When the roast is nearly done, allowing 35 minutes to the pound, remove the cover and add:
1 cup Sautéed Mushrooms, page 281
Pour over the roast:
1 cup cultured sour cream
Cook ♦ uncovered for 10 minutes.
Correct the seasoning
Make:
Pan Gravy, page 322
Serve the roast surrounded by:
Browned Potatoes, page 293
Garnish with:
Parsley

BRAISED LEG OF MUTTON OR LAMB

About 8 Servings
If cooked this way, the flavor is almost like venison.
Remove the fell from:
A 5 lb. leg of mutton or lamb
You may place the meat for several hours in a marinade, page 336, or you may rub it all over with:
(A cut clove of garlic)
Rub the meat with:
Butter
Melt in a heavy pan:
¼ cup fat or drippings
Brown the meat in it on all sides. Add:
4 cups boiling stock
Cover the pot. ♦ Simmer the meat until tender, allowing 30 minutes to the pound. Add boiling water, if necessary. After the meat has cooked for 1 hour, add:
2 small whole onions
3 peppercorns
3 cloves
A sprig of thyme or ½ teaspoon dried thyme
½ bay leaf
When the meat is tender, remove from the pot. Season with:
Salt
Place the meat where it will remain hot. Serve with:
Caper Sauce, page 324
and:
Puréed Turnips, page 309

BRAISED LAMB SHANKS OR TROTTERS

4 Servings
Rub:
4 lamb shanks: 3½ to 4 lbs.
with:
Garlic
Roll in:
Seasoned flour
Melt until fragrant:
2 tablespoons cooking oil
Partially sear the shanks and add:
2 tablespoons diced onion
Continue to cook the meat until browned on all sides. Pour off the fat. Place the meat on a rack in a lidded pan. Add:
1½ cups boiling stock
¼ teaspoon pepper
1½ teaspoons salt
½ bay leaf
Cover the pan closely. ♦ Simmer the meat or bake covered in a 325° oven for about 1½ hours or until tender. You may add for the last ½ hour of cooking:
3 cups diced vegetables
½ cup boiling stock or water
The vegetables may be onions, carrots, celery, peppers, turnips, tomatoes and/or potatoes—a matter of choice and expediency. Strain, degrease and reduce the stock. Serve as it is or make:
Pan Gravy, page 322
If you have not added the vegetables, you may serve the shanks with:
Creole Sauce, page 336

LAMB STEW OR NAVARIN PRINTANIER

8 Servings
Cut into about 1½-inch pieces:
1 lb. shoulder of lamb
1 lb. breast of lamb
Brown the meat in a heavy skillet in:
2 tablespoons fat
Remove the meat to a casserole. Pour off the fat and deglaze the pan with:
2 cups light stock
to which you may add:
2 tablespoons tomato paste
Bring to a boil and pour over the meat. ♦ Simmer covered. Meanwhile, peel and shape into ovals about 1½ inches long:
2 cups new potatoes
6 carrots
3 white turnips
Add:
18 small onions: about 1 inch
After the lamb has cooked about 1 hour, skim off the fat, add the vegetables to the casserole and ♦ simmer covered for about 1 hour longer or until the vegetables are tender. Have ready to add:
1 cup cooked fresh peas
1 cup cooked fresh green beans,
cut in 1-inch lengths
When the lamb and vegetables in the casserole are tender, skim any fat from the casserole and gently fold in the cooked

peas and beans. Serve at once, sprinkled
with ½ cup finely chopped parsley.

IRISH STEW
4 to 6 Servings
This famous stew is not browned.
Cut into 1½-inch cubes:
    1½ lbs. lamb or mutton
Peel and slice to ⅛-inch thickness:
    ¾ cup onions
    2½ lbs. potatoes
Put in the bottom of a heavy pan a layer
of potatoes, a layer of meat, a few slices
of onion. Repeat this twice, ending with
potatoes on top. Season each layer with:
    Salt and pepper
Add to the pot:
    1 bay leaf
Pour over the layers:
    2 cups boiling water or stock
    2 tablespoons finely chopped parsley
Bring to a boil. ◗ Cover closely. Simmer
gently over very low heat for about 2½
hours or until done. Shake the pot periodically so that the potatoes do not stick.
When done, all the moisture should have
been absorbed by the potatoes.

CURRY OF LAMB WITH RICE
4 Servings
Remove the gristle and fat from:
    A 2 lb. lamb shoulder
Cut the meat into 1-inch cubes. Heat:
    3 tablespoons fat or cooking oil
Brown the meat in the hot fat with:
    1 tablespoon chopped onion
    ¾ teaspoon curry powder
Add:
    1 cup light Stock, page 490
    ¼ cup or more chopped celery
    2 tablespoons chopped parsley
    (1 tablespoon chopped pimiento)
    (¼ cup peeled, seeded, diced
    cucumbers)
Cover the meat and simmer until done,
about ½ hour. Stir frequently.
    Correct the seasoning
Make:
    Pan Gravy, page 322
Place on a platter a mound of:
    Rice, page 178
Arrange the meat and gravy around it.
Garnish the platter with:
    Parsley

CASSOULET
About 12 Servings
With a thicker texture than a pot au feu,
this controversial dish from the South of
France has one solid pivot—white beans.
They are cooked usually with fresh pork
and sausage; but often with mutton and
"confit d'oie"—potted goose, page 474—or
with duck, partridge or bacon. Goose fat
is a frequent component, also an onion
stuck with cloves. Vegetables vary seasonally. Garlic is essential. For this recipe you almost need a routing sheet. The
beans soak overnight and are cooked the
next day with meat and other trimmings.

The pork roasts for a while before the lamb
joins it. Then the meats that have been
cooking with the beans are taken from the
bone and sliced before they are returned
to the beans. This way the flavors unite in
a single casserole and make a final trium-
phant appearance under a golden crust of
crumbs.
Soak overnight in cold water:
    1 lb. white beans: haricots, marrow-
    fat or broad beans
Roast in a 350° oven for about 2½ hours
or until tender:
    3 lbs. Loin of Pork, page 407
Blanch, page 132, by placing in cold water and just bringing to a boil:
    1 ham shank
    1 lb. salt pork
Drain the beans. Heat the water in which
they soaked, adding:
    Enough water to make 4 quarts
Bring to a boil and skim the pot. Add the
drained, blanched ham shank and salt pork
and:
    A Bouquet Garni, page 541
    3 cloves garlic
Simmer covered for about 1½ hours. Add:
    6 small white onions
    ½ lb. hard Italian sausage, like
    Salcisetta
◗ Simmer about 1 hour longer, until the
beans are tender but still intact. Brown,
page 384, in a heavy skillet:
    3 lbs. rolled lamb shoulder
in:
    1 tablespoon butter
Drain off any excess fat. Roast the meat
and the bones from the lamb with the pork
◗ uncovered. ◗ After about 1½ hours, pour
over it:
    Thickened Tomato Sauce, page 333
and roast for about ½ hour more. ◗ Lower
oven heat to 300°, then drain off and reserve the sauce and drippings. Remove and
slice the meat of both the lamb and the
pork roast. Drain the beans, adding the
juice to the drained tomato sauce. Trim
and slice the ham, the sausage and the salt
pork in bite-sized pieces. Layer these
meats with the beans in a casserole and
skim excess fat from the combined tomato
and bean juices before adding them to the
other ingredients. Top with:
    1 cup buttered dry bread crumbs
Bake about 1 hour longer in the oven,
when the crumbs should have turned a
golden color.

COUSCOUS
6 Servings
As with most basic native dishes, variations
of this North African specialty abound.
The following version comes from friends
in Libya.
Soak overnight and cook the following day
until about half tender:
    1 cup Chick Peas, page 260
Drain them. Cut into about 10 pieces:

2 lbs. lamb, mutton or beef
Brown lightly in:
   1 tablespoon olive oil
   2 tablespoons butter
While browning slowly for about 10 minutes, add:
   ¾ cup minced onion
When the onion is translucent, add:
   2 teaspoons salt
   ½ teaspoon freshly ground pepper
   ⅛ teaspoon red pepper
   ½ teaspoon turmeric
   2 tablespoons tomato paste
◗ Reduce heat and barely simmer this thick mixture for about 10 minutes more. Place in a heavy pot with:
   2 knuckle bones
and enough:
   Water to cover
◗ Simmer covered until the meat can be pierced with a fork, but still offers slight resistance. Add:
   3 cups potatoes, cut Parisienne, page 251
   2 cups coarsely diced yellow or white squash
   2 cups coarsely diced zucchini
and the drained cooked chick peas. Add, if necessary:
   Stock, page 490
◗ Simmer covered until the meat and vegetables are tender, about ¾ of an hour longer. Remove from heat and reserve this meat and vegetable mixture. When the fat rises to the top, skim and reserve 2 tablespoons of it. Rinse briefly and place in the top of a perforated steamer or a couscous pot:
   1 lb. semolina, cracked millet, cracked wheat or kasha
Steam the cereal ◗ uncovered for 15 minutes, timing after you see steam rising from the top. Meanwhile reheat the meat and vegetable mixture. Drain the liquid and reserve it. Now ◗ working quickly so everything stays warm, remove the cereal from the steamer and add:
   2 tablespoons orange flower water
   ¼ teaspoon cinnamon
   ¼ teaspoon cloves
Toss the seasoned couscous lightly in the 2 tablespoons of fat, reserved from the meat mixture, and put it in a serving dish. Pour over it 1 cup of the drained liquid. Put the meat, vegetables and chick peas on top of the couscous. Use the remaining liquid as a separate sauce. Serve at once.

PORK TENDERLOIN WITH MUSHROOMS AND OLIVES
                                    4 Servings
Cut into 1-inch crosswise slices:
   1 lb. or more pork tenderloin
Roll in:
   Seasoned flour
Sauté until golden in:
   2 tablespoons butter

with:
   A sliced onion
Bring just to the boiling point:
   ½ cup dry white wine
Pour over the meat. Add at this time:
   ⅓ lb. sliced mushrooms
   (⅛ teaspoon fresh rosemary)
Cover the skillet closely. ◗ Simmer the rounds until they are done, about 30 minutes. Add:
   6 sliced green olives, stuffed with almonds
   (2 tablespoons lemon juice)
Serve the pork garnished with:
   2 tablespoons chopped parsley

PORK CHOPS BAKED IN SOUR CREAM
                                    4 Servings
Preheat oven to 350°.
Dredge:
   4 loin pork chops: ½ inch thick
with:
   Seasoned flour or bread crumbs
Insert in each chop:
   1 clove
Brown lightly in a little hot pork fat or lard. Place in a baking dish. Combine, heat and pour over the meat:
   ½ cup water or stock
   ½ bay leaf
   2 tablespoons vinegar
   1 tablespoon sugar
   ½ cup cultured sour cream
   (¼ teaspoon summer savory)
Bake the chops ◗ covered for about 1 hour.

BRAISED PORK CHOPS CREOLE
                                    6 Servings
Preheat oven to 350°.
Dredge:
   6 pork chops, ½ inch or more thick
with:
   Flour
Brown them in:
   Hot fat or cooking oil
Place in a baking dish. Combine, heat and pour around them:
   1 can condensed tomato soup: 10½ oz.
   1 can water or stock
   ½ cup chopped celery
   1 chopped green pepper—seeds and membrane removed
   ¾ cup minced onions
   ¾ teaspoon salt
   ¼ teaspoon paprika
Bake ◗ covered for about 1¼ hours. ◗ Remove the cover for the last 15 minutes. Cover the top for this last period with:
   Crushed cornflakes

BRAISED DEVILED PORK CHOPS
                                    4 Servings
Preheat oven to 325°.
Place in a dish:
   4 pork chops, 1 inch thick
Marinate them for 3 to 6 hours covered and refrigerated in:

Pork Marinade, page 338
Drain the chops, reserving the marinade. Wipe them dry. Brown in a hot greased skillet. Heat the marinade and:

½ cup water or stock

Pour it around the chops. Bake ◗ covered until tender, about 1 hour.

BRAISED PORK CHOPS WITH FRUIT
Allow 1 Chop per Person
Preheat oven to 350°.
Sear in a hot, lightly greased skillet:

Trimmed pork chops, ¾ inch thick
or more

Season lightly. Place on the chops, skin side down:

Halved, cored apples, pitted
apricots, prunes or pineapple slices

Fill the centers of the fruit with:

Brown sugar

Cover the bottom of the skillet to ½ inch with:

Chicken stock and/or some of the
fruit juice

◗ Cover the pan closely. Bake for about 50 minutes. Remove the chops from the pan carefully, so as not to disturb the fruit. Keep warm. Partially degrease and add to the pan juices:

¾ to 1 cup sweet or cultured sour cream

Serve this sauce with the chops and fruit.

BRAISED STUFFED PORK CHOPS COCKAIGNE
6 Servings
Preheat oven to 350°.
Cut from the bone:

6 rib pork chops, ¾ to 1 inch thick

Cut the bone from the meat. Trim off the excess fat and cut a large gash or pocket into the side of each chop. Prepare a dressing of:

1 cup bread crumbs
¼ cup chopped celery
¼ cup chopped onions
2 tablespoons chopped parsley
Milk to moisten the dressing
¼ teaspoon salt
⅛ teaspoon paprika

These proportions and ingredients may be varied. Fill the pockets with the dressing. Skewer them. Sear the chops in a hot skillet and place in a pan with a little:

Milk or stock

◗ Cover the pan and bake about 1 hour and 15 minutes or until tender. Make:

Pan Gravy, page 322

PORK BIRDS
6 Servings
Pound to the thickness of ¼ inch:

2 lbs. pork steaks which have been
cut from the shoulder

Cut them into 6 oblong pieces. Spread them with half the recipe for:

Apricot or Prune Dressing, page 459

Roll them. Secure the rolls with string or toothpicks. Dredge in:

2 tablespoons flour

Brown in:

2 tablespoons fat

Add:

1 cup boiling water or Stock, page 490

Simmer covered for about 50 minutes or until tender. Serve with the liquor in the pan, degreased and thickened as:

Pan Gravy, page 322

or just reduced.

▤ ABOUT SPARERIBS
◗ Allow at Least 1 lb. per Person
These gloriously messy old favorites can simply be baked in a 325° oven about 1½ hours; but there are a good many more lively things to do with them. We find parboiling, page 132, the ribs for about 3 or 4 minutes not only removes unwanted fat, but makes the end result very palatable. After parboiling, try one of the following recipes or barbecue them, page 138.

BAKED SPARERIBS WITH DRESSING
4 Servings
Preheat oven to 500°.
As there is much bone and little meat to spareribs—we love the self-explanatory name—it is well to allow 1 pound of them to a person. Parboil for 2 minutes:

4 lbs. spareribs

Cut into 2 pieces. Spread 1 piece with:

Apple Onion Dressing, page 458

Cover the dressing with the other piece of meat. Tie the 2 pieces together. Rub the outside of the meat with:

2 tablespoons flour
⅛ teaspoon salt
A few grains pepper

Place on a rack in an uncovered roasting pan and ◗ reduce the heat at once to 325°. Bake for about 1 hour. Baste the meat every 10 minutes with the fat in the pan.

BAKED SPARERIBS WITH SAUERKRAUT
4 Servings
Preheat oven to 400°.
Place in a mound, in the center of a small roasting pan:

1½ quarts Sauerkraut, page 269

Season:

4 lbs. parboiled spareribs, see above

lightly with:

Salt and pepper

Fold the ribs in half. Place between them:

Slices of onion

Cover the kraut with the folded spareribs. Bake ◗ uncovered in a hot oven until nicely browned. Baste frequently with kraut juice. Turn the ribs and brown the other side. Add water, if necessary. ◗ Cover the pan. ◗ Reduce the temperature to 350°. Parboil until nearly tender:

6 peeled medium-sized potatoes

When the meat is nearly done, after about 1¼ hours cooking in all, uncover it and place the whole potatoes around it, turning them frequently to permit them to brown.

Serve the ribs and vegetables when the meat is tender.

BOILED SPARERIBS
Place:

    Spareribs

in:

    Boiling water to cover

Add:

    Salt and pepper
    Chopped onion, celery, parsley
    and carrots
    (1 teaspoon caraway seed)

◗ Simmer the meat covered until tender, from 1½ to 2 hours. Drain and serve on a mound of hot:

    Sauerkraut or Red Cabbage, page 269

surrounded by:

    Mashed Potatoes, page 290

SWEET-SOUR SPARERIBS
Preheat oven to 350°.

Cut into 2-inch pieces:

    2 lbs. spareribs

Parboil, page 132, 3 to 4 minutes. Drain and dry. Brush with:

    Soy sauce

Bake ◗ uncovered on a rack in a pan in the oven for 1 hour. Have ready the following sauce. Boil briefly:

    ½ cup vinegar
    ½ cup sugar
    ¼ cup sherry
    1 tablespoon soy sauce
    1 teaspoon fresh ginger

Mix together and add:

    2 teaspoons cornstarch
    1 tablespoon water

Cook until cornstarch is transparent. Pour the sauce over the cooked spareribs and serve at once with:

    Baked Green Rice, page 178

STEWED PORK NECK BONES
Partly cover with seasoned boiling water:

    Pork neck bones

◗ Simmer covered until tender, about 1½ hours. Vegetables may be added to the stew for the last ½ hour or so of cooking.

STEWED PORK HOCKS
Cover with seasoned boiling water:

    Pork hocks

Simmer covered from 1½ to 3 hours. You may add potatoes for the last ½ hour of cooking or greens or cabbage for the last 20 minutes.

SALT PORK AND MILK GRAVY
                       4 Servings

Dip thin slices of:

    1 lb. salt pork

in:

    Boiling water

Drain and dip in:

    Corn meal

Brown slowly in a skillet, turning frequently. Thicken:

    2 tablespoons drippings

With:

    2 tablespoons flour, see Gravy,
    page 322

Pour in slowly:

    1 cup milk

Serve with:

    Boiled or baked potatoes

ABOUT GROUND MEAT VARIATIONS

When emergencies demand all our ingenuity to make meat stretch graciously or otherwise, we have discovered the incontrovertible fact that by grinding meat it can be made to seem in much more ample supply than it really is. This does not mean that all the variations listed in this section are economical—although some are definitely so. But many provide interesting blends, seasoning and combinations that give a much-sought variety in menu building. No one needs an introduction to hamburger, although many people should be alerted to the best actual handling of the meat and the best ways to retain its tenderness and flavor during cooking. Meat loaves, pâtés and galantines, meat balls, croquettes, timbales, farces and mousses—all have their own individuality, which we hope you will discover and exploit.

Many other dishes using already cooked, diced, slivered and minced meats—which are rather different in texture—will be found in Luncheon and Supper Dishes, page 223. While grinding does, of course, help with tough and old meats, remember that ◗ the distinctive succulence of pâtés and galantines depends on a base of moist young meat. ◗ Do not store any uncooked ground meat longer than 24 hours. ◗ Be sure the mass is not more than 2 inches thick, so the cold can penetrate it quickly and thoroughly.

ABOUT HAMBURGER

A mother we know has made the disheartening discovery that her children will eat nothing but hamburger. She calls it "The Daily Grind." At home and abroad, indoors and out, the dispensing and downing of these meat patties is so nearly universal that it is worth considering for a moment from just what beef the commercial variety is built. So all-embracing did some butchers find the term "hamburger" that the law saw fit to define any beef sold under this term as at least 70% meat, 30% fat. Federal statute further forbids the use of sodium sulphite, an additive which keeps the meat rosy. Recent surveys, however, indicate that the practice is far from dead. Should you find the color of ground meat too persistently red—expose a sample to bright sunlight. Untreated meat will darken.

If, as many people do, **you have lean**

beef ground specially for hamburgers, use chuck, flank, shank, neck, heel, round or hanging tenderloin. ◗ Twice-ground meat will compact more than once-ground. You may be surprised at the apparently large amount of fat you didn't see go into the grinder. Grinders are so constructed that often as much as a fourth of every pound of meat that goes in stays in; and the unexpected fat may come from the grinding of the previous order.

✳ To freeze beef for hamburger, see pages 760 and 766.

Good quality beef, freshly ground and used at once, needs only ◗ light shaping. You may want to incorporate into it some onion juice or finely chopped chives. ◗ If the beef has to be kept ground for 12 to 18 hours, it profits by having worked into it with a fork about 2 tablespoons beef stock for each pound of meat. This is done before shaping.

◗ If beef is to be "stretched," you may add to each pound about ½ cup soft bread crumbs, page 501, soaking them briefly in about ½ cup seasoned milk or stock. Or you may use ½ cup finely grated raw carrots, potatoes or ground and cooked soy beans, page 260, or 1 cup dry processed cereal. ◗ Incorporate these ingredients into the meat lightly with a fork and, with a light touch, shape the mixture into patties. Always decide before you put the meat into the pan how thick you want the finished hamburger. ◗ Never compact it in the pan by pressing down on it with a spatula.

◗ To cook hamburger, consider your grind. The degree of fattiness is important in helping determine how you will treat the pan for sautéing or whether you will brush the patties with butter during broiling.

If you use ◗ ready ground hamburger, preheat an ungreased heavy skillet slowly, to the point where a small sample of meat when added will sizzle, not hiss sharply. Drop the patties in the pan and leave them, cooking over medium heat ◗ uncovered, for 3 or 4 minutes. During this time sufficient fat should be available from the patty itself to permit the hamburger to be turned without sticking. Turn and cook on the other side another 3 minutes or even longer, depending on the thickness of the patty and the whims of your diners.

Another prevalent, if flavor-destroying, way of preparing a fat-free pan is to preheat it slowly and scatter over the surface of it about 1 teaspoon salt for each pound of meat. The salt will keep quite lean meat from sticking—and for a very good reason. It draws the juices from the meat, see page 525. Because of this, too, we prefer ◗ withholding seasoning from hamburgers until after at least one side of the meat is seared. If you use ◗ very lean beef, you will need at least 1 tablespoon butter or suet added to the preheated

skillet. Heat the fat to the point of fragrance before you add the meat, and proceed to cook as for ready-ground hamburger.

SAUTEED HAMBURGERS
4 Servings
◗ Please read About Hamburger, page 426. Shape lightly into patties, allowing 2 for each serving:

> 1 lb. ground beef

You may mix in lightly with a fork any one of the following. To stretch, add:

> ½ cup soft bread crumbs, page 501

soaked briefly in:

> ⅛ to ½ cup milk or stock

or add:

> ½ cup finely grated raw carrots
> or potatoes

moistened with:

> 2 tablespoons beef stock, cream,
> tomato paste or lemon juice

To flavor, use:

> 2 teaspoons chili sauce, 1 teaspoon
> ground anchovy or anchovy paste,
> 3 tablespoons sautéed mushrooms,
> 1 tablespoon finely diced stuffed
> olives or 1 teaspoon capers

or:

> ¼ teaspoon thyme
> 1 squeeze garlic clove
> 1 teaspoon Worcestershire sauce

or:

> 2 tablespoons fresh chopped parsley
> and chives or 1 tablespoon sautéed
> chopped shallots or onions

After turning to complete the cooking, season with about:

> 1 teaspoon salt
> ⅛ teaspoon pepper
> (1 teaspoon monosodium glutamate)

Defat the pan drippings. Deglaze them with:

> Stock

Reduce the juices slightly and pour over the patties before serving. Or mix with the pan juices a little:

> Barbecue, chili sauce, tomato
> catsup, horseradish, a few chopped
> olives or sauteed onions or mushrooms

Or spread over them:

> Herb butters or mustard, page 338
> A slice of Swiss cheese, crumbled
> blue cheese or grated cheddar
> or Parmesan

Run the patties briefly under a broiler. You may garnish the tops with one of the following:

> Very thin, sweet, raw or sautéed
> onion slice
> A slice of tomato or cucumber

BROILED HAMBURGERS
4 Servings
Preheat broiler.
◗ Please read About Hamburger, page 426. Shape lightly into ¾-inch-thick patties:

> 1 lb. ground beef

Place them on a broiler pan, 4 inches from

the heat or place them so they cover the untoasted side of:

A piece of bread toasted on one side only

If on the bread broil about 10 minutes. If not broil 6 minutes on one side, turn and broil about 4 minutes on the other. If the meat is very lean, you may brush it during broiling with:

Butter

▤ GRILLED HAMBURGERS

We have watched with agony as good juices fed the flames of barbecues and the guests were dealt dry chips. If you must grill ground meat, please see page 137.
Prepare previous recipe for:

Hamburgers

To make the meat adhere well during handling, you may add to it:

1 beaten egg for each pound

Proceed as for:

Broiled Hamburgers, above

▤ SLOPPY JOES

                                                        8 Sandwiches

Sauté in:

2 tablespoons butter
½ cup minced onions
½ cup chopped green pepper, seeds and membrane removed

When these are translucent, add:

1½ lbs. ground beef

Cook and stir until meat is lightly browned. Add:

½ cup chopped mushrooms
2 to 4 tablespoons chili sauce
Correct the seasoning

Cook, uncovered, over low heat until the mushrooms are done. Fill with this hot mixture:

8 slightly toasted sandwich buns

▤ FILLED BEEF OR LAMBURGERS

                                                        6 Servings

Preheat broiler.
Vary the fillings by using chopped celery, pickles, chili sauce, bread dressing, chopped leftover vegetables.
◗ Please read About Hamburger, page 426.
Sauté lightly:

(6 slices bacon)

Divide into 12 portions:

1½ lbs. ground beef or lamb

Shape into flat cakes and fill with:

I.
6 tablespoons chopped nut meats
3 tablespoons chopped parsley
2 tablespoons grated onion

II.
Anchovy and a few capers for each patty

III.
Slice of Roquefort or cheddar cheese or liverwurst

Spread it on 6 of the cakes. Top them with those remaining. Bind the edges with the partially sautéed bacon strips and

fasten with a toothpick. Broil for 10 to 15 minutes, turning them once.

LIVER PATTIES

                                                        6 Servings

Preheat oven to 350°.
Combine:

1 lb. ground liver
1 slice chopped bacon
½ cup dry bread crumbs
¼ cup evaporated milk or cream
½ teaspoon salt
⅛ teaspoon pepper
2 teaspoons grated onion
2 tablespoons chopped parsley

Shape these ingredients into 6 flat cakes. Wrap around them:

6 slices bacon

Secure the bacon with toothpicks. Place the cakes in a lightly greased pan. Bake until well browned, about 6 minutes. Turn to insure even baking.

CHICKEN, VEAL OR LAMB PATTIES

                                                12 to 14 Servings

Preheat broiler.
The French make many attractive dishes by grinding uncooked meat or fish, shaping it with other ingredients and poaching, broiling or sautéing the patties.
Cut the meat from:

A 4½ lb. chicken or use 3½ lbs. veal or lamb

Pick over the carcass for all edible bits of meat. Put the meat through a grinder, using a coarse knife. Save the juices, if any. Combine the ground meat, the juices and:

¾ cup whipping cream
1½ cups soft bread crumbs
1 teaspoon salt
1 teaspoon dried basil or 1 tablespoon chopped parsley
A grating of lemon rind
¼ teaspoon paprika
A grating of nutmeg

Shape the mixture into 10 patties. Roll them in a:

Bound Breading, page 501

Place them in a ◗ shallow greased pan. Broil under moderate heat about 10 minutes to a side or until lightly browned. The patties may be left unbreaded and poached in a pan in the oven in a small amount of milk or stock to cover, enough to cover the bottom of the skillet, until done. This means very low heat. Serve with:

Béarnaise Sauce, page 329, or
Soubise Sauce, page 325

GERMAN MEATBALLS OR KOENIGSBERGER KLOPS

                        6 Servings—About Ten 2-Inch Balls

A good buffet dish.
Soak in water, milk or stock to cover:

1 slice of bread, 1 inch thick

Put through a meat grinder twice:

1½ lbs. meat: ½ lb. beef, ½ lb. veal
½ lb. pork or liver

Beat well and add:
  2 eggs
Melt:
  1 tablespoon butter
Sauté in it until golden:
  ¼ cup finely minced onion
Add them to the meat. Wring the liquid from the bread. Add the bread to the meat and:
  3 tablespoons chopped parsley
  1¼ teaspoons salt
  ¼ teaspoon paprika
  ½ teaspoon grated lemon rind
  1 teaspoon lemon juice
  1 teaspoon Worcestershire sauce
  or a grating of nutmeg
A few minced sardelles or ¼ herring may be added to the meatballs at this time or they may be added later to the gravy. Combine these ingredients well. Do this lightly with the hands—a better method than using a fork or spoon. Shape lightly in 2-inch balls. Drop into:
  5 cups boiling Vegetable Stock,
  page 492
♦ Simmer covered for about 15 minutes. Remove from the stock. Measure the stock. Make Gravy of it, page 322, by using, for every cup stock:
  2 tablespoons butter
  2 tablespoons flour
  Correct the seasoning
Cook and stir until smooth and hot. Add:
  2 tablespoons capers, or 2 tablespoons
  chopped pickles, lemon juice or
  cultured sour cream
  2 tablespoons chopped parsley
Reheat the meatballs in the gravy. Serve with a platter of:
  Boiled Noodles, page 188, or
  Spaetzle, page 192
Cover generously with:
  Buttered Crumbs, page 342

ITALIAN MEATBALLS
Preheat oven to 350°.
Follow the preceding rule for:
  German Meatballs
Omit the Worcestershire sauce. Add to the meat mixture:
  ½ chopped clove garlic
  3 tablespoons grated Parmesan cheese
  ¼ teaspoon orégano
Mix and form into balls. Brown lightly in:
  2 tablespoons butter
Place in a casserole. Half cover with:
  Unthickened Tomato Sauce, page
  333, or Marinara Sauce, page 335
Bake covered for about 30 minutes.

SWEDISH MEATBALLS
                    6 Servings of About Eighteen
                    1½-Inch Balls
There are many recipes for this dish, all similar to and, in our opinion, none superior to:
  German Meatballs, page 428
Shape the meat into 1½-inch balls. Brown in:

  1 tablespoon butter or drippings
Simmer closely covered until done, about 15 minutes, in:
  2 cups consommé or other stock
Make:
  Pan Gravy, page 322
Season it with:
  Sherry
Reheat the balls in the gravy. This is attractive served in a chafing dish, garnished with:
  Potato Dumplings, page 192

CHINESE MEATBALLS
                                        6 Servings
Shape into 18 balls:
  1½ lbs. ground beef
Season with:
  1½ teaspoon salt
  1 teaspoon monosodium glutamate
  1 tablespoon finely chopped parsley
Coat the balls with:
  Fritter Batter for Meat, page 221
Let them dry on a rack for 30 minutes. Deep-fat fry, pages 124-126, at 375°, until golden brown. Serve at once, covered with a:
  Chinese Sweet-Sour Sauce, page 330

PORK BALLS IN TOMATO SAUCE
                                        4 Servings
Soak in water to cover:
  A slice of bread, 1½ inches thick
Wring the water from it. Add to the bread:
  1 lb. ground pork
  ⅓ cup chopped onion
  1 beaten egg
  ¾ teaspoon salt
  ¼ teaspoon paprika
Combine these ingredients lightly with the hands until well blended. Shape into 2-inch balls. Combine the contents of:
  1 can tomato soup: 10½ oz.
  An equal amount of water
Bring the liquid to the boiling point. Drop the balls into it. ♦ Reduce the heat at once. Cover the pan and simmer until done, about ½ hour.

SAUERKRAUT BALLS
                    4 Dozen 1¼-Inch Balls
The sauerkraut helps tenderize as well as flavor these meat balls.
♦ Please read About Deep-Fat Frying, pages 124-126.
Preheat deep fryer to 375°.
Grind with a medium blade:
  ½ lb. each ham, corned beef and
  lean pork
Sauté the meat in:
  3 tablespoons butter or fat
with:
  ⅓ cup finely chopped onion
Mix, stir in and ♦ simmer until thick, stirring constantly:
  2 cups flour
  ½ to 1 teaspoon dry mustard
  1 teaspoon salt

2 cups milk
When this mixture has cooked, combine it with:
　　2 lbs. cooked, drained sauerkraut
Then regrind the entire mixture. Form into 1¼-inch balls. Roll them in:
　　Bound Breading, page 501
Deep fry until golden brown. Drain on absorbent paper and serve at once.

CHILI CON CARNE
　　　　　　　　　　　　　　　　8 Servings
Melt:
　　2 to 3 tablespoons bacon drippings
　　　or butter
Sauté in the fat:
　　½ cup chopped onion or ½ chopped
　　　clove garlic
Add:
　　1 to 2 lbs. ground beef or lamb
Stir and sauté the beef until well done.
Add:
　　1¼ cups canned tomatoes
　　4 cups canned kidney beans
　　¾ teaspoon or more salt
　　½ bay leaf
　　(1 teaspoon sugar)
　　2 teaspoons to 2 tablespoons chili
　　　powder
depending on your taste and the strength of the chili powder. Cover and cook slowly for about 1 hour. Serve with:
　　Tortillas or crackers

PORCUPINES
　　　　　　　　　　　　　　　　6 Servings
Combine:
　　1 lb. ground beef
　　½ cup bread crumbs
　　1 egg
　　¾ teaspoon salt
　　¼ teaspoon paprika
　　(2 tablespoons chopped green peppers)
Roll these ingredients ♦ lightly into balls. Press into flat cakes. Roll in:
　　¼ cup raw rice
Heat in a heavy pot:
　　Thickened Tomato Sauce, page 333
Add:
　　(1 teaspoon chili powder)
Add the meat cakes. Cover the pot. Simmer the meat for about 45 minutes.
　　Correct the seasoning
and serve.

SPANISH CASSEROLE WITH RICE
　　　　　　　　　　　　　　　　6 Servings
This is a one-dish meal.
Preheat oven to 350°
Steam:
　　⅔ cup rice
Prepare:
　　1 cup chopped celery
　　¼ cup chopped green pepper
Melt in a saucepan:
　　2 tablespoons butter or other fat
Peel, chop and sauté in the butter until golden:
　　1 medium-sized onion

Add and sear:
　　1 lb. ground round steak
Season with:
　　¾ teaspoon salt
　　¼ teaspoon paprika
Place in a greased baking dish ⅓ of the rice and ½ of the meat. Sprinkle over it ½ of the celery and pepper. Repeat this process. Place the last of the rice on top. Pour over these ingredients:
　　1 can condensed tomato soup: 10½ oz.
　　Seasonings
Cover the dish and bake about ½ hour.

LAMB AND EGGPLANT CASSEROLE
　　　　　　　　　　　　　　　　4 Servings
Preheat oven to 350°.
Pare and chop until fine:
　　1 medium-sized eggplant
Combine with:
　　2 cups ground lamb: 1 lb.
　　½ cup chopped onion
　　3 tablespoons chopped parsley
　　1 teaspoon salt
　　¼ teaspoon paprika
　　(½ teaspoon curry powder)
　　1 cup canned chopped tomatoes
Butter a casserole. Fill it with the lamb mixture. Bake covered for about ¾ hour. Remove the cover and let the top brown.

HAMBURGER CASSEROLE
　　　　　　　　　　　　　　　　4 Servings
Preheat oven to 400°.
Melt in a skillet:
　　¼ cup butter
Sauté in it until the meat loses its ruddiness:
　　1 lb. ground steak or veal
　　1 cup minced celery
　　1 medium-sized cubed onion
　　½ lb. mushrooms
Add:
　　1 teaspoon salt
Place the ingredients in a casserole. Cover with:
　　1 cup condensed tomato soup
Bake for about 45 minutes. Serve with:
　　Fried Noodles, page 188

STUFFED CABBAGE OR
GEFUELLTER KRAUTKOPF
　　　　　　　　　　　　　　　　6 Servings
Separate and prepare by blanching for about 5 minutes, page 132:
　　The leaves from a head of cabbage
Reserve the liquor. Place the leaves at once on towels to drain. Prepare one of the following meat dressings.
I.
Soak in water for 2 minutes:
　　1 slice of bread, 1 inch thick
Press the water from it. Combine the bread with:
　　½ lb. ground pork
　　½ lb. ground beef
　　½ lb. ground veal

3 beaten eggs
¾ teaspoon salt
¼ teaspoon paprika

I.

Or use a filling of:
1 lb. fresh pork sausage meat
3 half-inch slices of bread
1 beaten egg

Line a bowl with a large napkin or cloth
and fill it with alternate layers of the
leaves and the meat dressing. Cover the
top with 1 or 2 large leaves, gather up the
cloth and tie it with a string. Place the
bag in boiling water—the water in which
the cabbage was boiled and as much fresh
boiling water as needed to cover well.
◆ Simmer the cabbage gently for 2 hours if
you are old-fashioned, but 45 minutes
should be ample time. Drain it in a colander, untie the bag and place the cabbage
on a hot serving dish. Serve with the following onion sauce. Brown in the top of a
double boiler:
¼ cup butter
Add and stir until brown:
2 tablespoons flour
Have ready:
2 cups Stock, page 490, or cabbage
water
Stir ½ cup of this into the butter mixture.
Add:
½ cup or more chopped onion
If required,
Correct the seasoning
Cook the onions covered ◆ over—not in—
hot water, until they are very tender. Add
the remainder of the stock gradually. The
gravy is best when it is thick with onions.

GROUND BEEF IN CABBAGE
LEAVES

4 Servings

Preheat oven to 375°.
Wash and parblanch, page 132:
8 large cabbage leaves
Drain and dry them on a towel. Combine:
1 lb. ground beef or a mixture of beef
veal, pork and liver
3 tablespoons finely chopped onion
2 tablespoons finely chopped parsley
¾ teaspoon salt
½ teaspoon thyme
½ mashed clove garlic
A few grains cayenne
If you want a sweet-sour effect, add:
2 tablespoons vinegar
3 tablespoons brown sugar
1 teaspoon capers
Divide the meat mixture into 8 parts. Put
one part on each cabbage leaf. Roll the
leaves, as shown on page 131. Tie or secure them with toothpicks. Place them
close together in a buttered baking dish.
Dot each roll with:
½ teaspoon butter
Pour into the dish:
½ cup boiling Stock, page 490
or you may use:

½ cup water, tomato juice or
cultured sour cream and paprika
Bake the rolls, covered, until the cabbage
leaves are very tender, about 50 minutes.

STUFFED GRAPE LEAVES
OR DOLMAS

30 Dolmas or 9 to 10 Portions
Prepare for stuffing:
30 tender Grape Leaves, page 131
Fill each one with a tablespoon of the following mixture:
2 cups finely chopped onions
½ cup rice
⅓ cup olive oil
2 tablespoons finely chopped parsley
2 tablespoons finely chopped dill
¼ cup pine nuts
¼ cup currants
(1 cup finely minced lamb)
Do not roll the leaves too tightly, as the
rice will swell. Cook as directed, page
131, weighted, over low heat about 1½
hours. Serve chilled.

ABOUT MEAT LOAF

Although proportions of beef, veal and
pork are specified in the following recipes,
they may be varied, provided the total
amount of meat remains the same. Be sure
to ◆ cook thoroughly if pork is used. Handle ingredients for meat loaf ◆ lightly,
mixing with a two-tined fork. To stretch,
see About Hamburger, page 426.
Meat loaf may be mounded on a flat
greased pan or put into a greased ring
mold or loaf pan. Also, it may be baked
in 2 layers with a good stuffing between.
You may pour about ½ cup of catsup in
the bottom of the mold or pan before you
fill it with the meat; or you may pour
about 2 tablespoons of chili sauce over the
meat loaf when it is half baked. This
gives it a good flavor and a light crust.
For more rapid cooking, individual meat
loaves take only about 15 minutes and—
for attractive service—may be baked in
greased muffin tins and glazed. Bake the
loaf and baste it, as directed in the following recipes. You may cover it with a piece
of foil. Remove the foil for the last ¼
hour of the baking period. If using chili
sauce on top or covering the loaf with foil,
do not baste it. Invert the mold.
Serve a ring hot, filled with green peas
or some other vegetable and surrounded
by browned potatoes. Or serve cold, filled
with potato or some other vegetable salad.

MEAT LOAF

4 Servings

Preheat oven to 350°.
Combine and shape into a loaf:
1 lb. ground beef: ¼ this amount
may be pork
(1 egg yolk)
2 tablespoons chopped parsley
1 tablespoon soft butter
1 tablespoon bread crumbs

1 teaspoon lemon juice
1 teaspoon salt
¼ teaspoon pepper
½ teaspoon onion juice

Place the loaf in a lightly greased pan.
Bake it for 1 hour. Pour some over the
top and baste at intervals with the remainder of:

¼ cup butter
1 cup Vegetable Stock, page 492, or
    1 cup boiling water plus ½ package
    dried soup mix

Serve the loaf with:
    Sweet Potato Puffs, page 299

II.   4 Servings

Preheat oven to 350°.
Place in a bowl:
    1 lb. ground round steak
    1 to 2 tablespoons horseradish
    2 tablespoons catsup
    1 teaspoon salt
    ¼ teaspoon pepper
    ½ cup cream

Grind in a food chopper then add:
    6 slices bacon
    2 medium-sized onions
    1 cup broken-up crackers

Mix with a fork. Mold into a loaf. Roll
it in:
    ¼ cup cracker crumbs

Place the loaf in a shallow baking pan.
Pour into the pan:
    ½ cup stock

Bake the loaf for about 1½ hours. Baste
occasionally, adding more liquid, if necessary. Make:
    Pan Gravy, page 322

MEAT LOAF COCKAIGNE
                                                             6 Servings

Preheat oven to 350°.
Mix lightly with:
    1½ lbs. lean ground beef—be sure beef
        has only been ground once
    1 can condensed cream of chicken
        or mushroom soup
    ¾ cup dry bread crumbs
    ¼ cup mixed fresh tarragon, parsley,
        basil or chives
    1 teaspoon salt
    1 pressed clove garlic
    10 or more chopped stuffed olives or
        ¼ cup chopped water chestnuts

Place the mixture in a 4 x 8 x 4-inch pan.
Bake about 45 minutes. Serve hot with:
    (Thickened Tomato Sauce, page 333)

VEAL LOAF
                                                         8 to 10 Servings

Preheat oven to 350°.
Grind:
    2 lbs. veal
    1 lb. smoked ham or sausage

Add and ♦ mix together very lightly:
    1 tablespoon minced onion
    ¼ cup seeded chopped green pepper
    2 beaten eggs
    ½ teaspoon salt

⅛ teaspoon paprika
¾ cup dry bread crumbs
1 cup condensed mushroom soup

Place ½ to ⅓ of this mixture in a 4 x 8
4-inch loaf pan. You may then press whole
mushrooms or hard-cooked eggs, stuffed
olives or pistachio nuts into the meat in a
pattern. Cover with another third of mea
and repeat the pattern or cover with ha
the meat. Bake for about 1 hour. Serve
hot or cold.

LIVER LOAF
                                                          6 to 8 Serving

This makes a most appetizing everyday
liver spread.
Preheat oven to 350°.
Boil for 5 minutes:
    1 cup water
    1 medium-sized chopped onion
    3 ribs celery with leaves

Prepare for cooking, page 439, slice, add
and simmer for 2 minutes:
    1 lb. liver: beef, lamb or pork

Drain, reserving liquid. Put liver and
vegetables through a meat chopper with:
    2 slices bacon or a 1½-inch cube
        salt pork

Add and blend well:
    1 or 2 beaten eggs
    ¾ teaspoon salt
    ⅛ teaspoon pepper
    1 cup cracker or dry bread crumbs
    ½ teaspoon dried marjoram or thyme
    1 cup liquid: liver stock, milk,
        tomato juice, etc.

Pour into a greased loaf pan:
    (½ cup catsup)

Place the meat in the pan. Bake for abou
40 minutes.

RAW SMOKED HAM LOAF
                                                          4 to 6 Serving

You may dress this up or down.
Preheat oven to 350°.
Try using:
    ½ cup crushed pineapple
    ½ teaspoon dry mustard

in the bottom of the pan or end up with
the glazes suggested below. Grind:
    1 lb. raw smoked ham
    ½ lb. lean pork
    (½ onion)

Add and mix together with the hands:
    2 well-beaten eggs
    ½ to 1 cup cracker or dry bread crumbs
        An equal amount of milk
    ⅛ teaspoon pepper
    3 tablespoons mixed fresh herbs

Shape into a loaf, place in a greased bread
pan and bake for about 2 hours, basting
frequently with:
    Honey Glaze, page 341, or
    Spirit Glaze for Ham, page 340

ABOUT PÂTÉ DE FOIE

The famed foie gras of Europe is produced by the forced feeding of geese,

which causes their livers to become marbled in appearance and so increases their
bulk that they often account for ¼ the
bird's weight. In this country the law forbids this practice, although unfatted goose
liver is available. As a matter of fact, the
liver of which American pâtés are usually
composed—that of chickens—makes a
more than merely acceptable substitute.

◀* PÂTÉ DE FOIE DE VOLAILLE OR CHICKEN LIVER PÂTÉ

About Twenty ½-Inch Slices

Divide into 3 parts:

1½ lbs. chicken livers

Blend one part with:

2 eggs

Blend the second part briefly with:

¼ cup whipping cream

Blend the third part with:

4 slices chopped bacon
1 egg
3 tablespoons cognac
2 tablespoons port wine
¼ cup flour

Mix these three blends together ◀ very
lightly with:

1 teaspoon ginger
2 teaspoons salt
½ teaspoon black pepper
1 teaspoon allspice or nutmeg

Line a loaf pan with dough for a pâté,
see this page.
Preheat oven to 325°.
Put ½ the above mixture in the loaf pan.
You may add:

1 to 2 sliced truffles

Cover with the remaining mixture. Top
with:

Thin-sliced salt pork

Cover tightly with foil. Bake the pâté in a
pan of hot water for 1½ to 2 hours. Test
for doneness, as for poultry.

II. *

About 40 Slices, ½ Inch Thick

Should the veal be red, as it is so often in
our markets, marinate it overnight covered
with milk and refrigerated.
◀ Please read About Pâté En Croûte below.
Preheat oven to 325°.
Pound:

1 lb. white veal

Add to it and ◀ grind 3 times:

1½ lbs. chicken livers
¼ lb. salt pork
2 anchovy fillets

Mix in lightly until very smooth:

4 beaten eggs
½ cup whipping cream
3 tablespoons grated onion
2 tablespoons chopped parsley
    or chervil
⅛ teaspoon freshly ground
    black pepper
¼ cup cognac
1 tablespoon Madeira
2 tablespoons chopped truffles

You may put this mixture in a loaf pan
lined with dough for pâté, page 434, or
directly into a greased loaf pan. If you do

not use the pastry liner on page 434, set the
pan in a larger one of hot water. Bake for
about 1½ hours or to an internal temperature of 180°. To test for doneness, see
page 617. The pâté should still be pink in
color when done. After cooling, you may
glaze the pastry case with:

Aspic, page 341

if you do not plan freezing it.

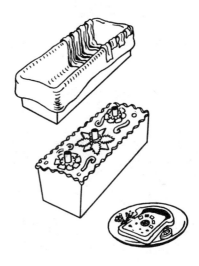

ABOUT PÂTÉ EN CROÛTE

The term alone evokes an instant image of
glamorous dining. But for those of us who
know pâtés only in canned form—where
the heat necessary to preserve them destroys their bloom—a good pâté maison is
a revelation. And it makes us want at once
to develop our own pâté ménagère. Basically this isn't any harder than making a
meat pie. Pâté en croûte is beautiful to
see in its glazed case. And it is even
lovelier when sliced, revealing first the
crusty edge and, within, the nugget-filled
farce, with its clear gelatin top—see illustration. The novice does not realize that
the crust is not really meant to be eaten,
but is the protection the pâté needs to develop flavor to the fullest and to retain the
juices.

Our friend, Chef Pierre Adrian, worried
so about his American diners' insistence on
consuming this tough protective coating
that he now customarily uses a more appetizing, if harder to handle, pâte brisée,
page 591, to line his molds. He also suggests that the conventional hinged pâté
molds nearly always leak and, should the
pâté crust break in any way, the delicious
juices run into the oven. If, instead, you
use a loaf pan, 9 x 4½ x 4½ inches, you
will still retain the characteristic shape, and

the juices, if released, are trapped for later use. Also your oven does not become a mess.

First choose one of the Fillings or Farces on page 433, for your pâté. Endless combinations and textures are possible. Some people—if the materials are beef, veal and pork—prefer a coarse grind, some a fine one. Chicken is nearly always ground fine. Calf liver and chicken liver, diced or ground, are sometimes used for reasons of economy. Suckling pigs' livers are a real treat.

◗ Cut into dice only the tenderest, choicest parts of young meat—free from all connective tissue or sinew. Marinate these and any liver in white wine refrigerated for 24 hours. Foie gras is often marinated in cognac. Mix with at least ½, up to twice, as much fat as meat. Then grind both meat and fat together 3 times, with the finest meat grinder blade. You may be tempted to use a blender, but we find the texture that results is both stringy and pasty. The ground meat is then folded into the yolks, spices, cream and the other ingredients to form the pâté.

Now it's time to prepare the pâte or crust, which for easier handling should rest covered for several hours. Have ready the tenderloins, livers, truffles, tongue or other choice bits which will form the eventual mosaiclike pattern in cross section when the pâté is cut. Now, line the pâté mold with the crust. You may roll and fit it in by making a ⅓-inch-thick circular shape of ¾ of the dough. Reserve the other fourth for the lid. We find it easier to form ¾ of the dough into a thick oval approximately the size of the base of the mold and line the bottom. With the sides of the hands, used in chopping motions, gradually work the dough from the base so that it thins out and creeps up the sides. Then, with the fingers patting it thin, form the rest of the crust to lap over the top, page 433. Do not stretch the dough or tear it. Next, line the mold with thin strips of fat bacon in parallel U shapes, as sketched. Allow them to rest, temporarily, over the side. When the pâté is built up to the top, fold the bacon ends over to encase it completely. Now back to the lining. First spread on it a ¾-inch layer of farce. Begin then to imbed the choice solids called for in the recipe, separating and surrounding them with more of the farce, so that the pâté when cut shows a pattern in cross section. When the mold is filled and the bacon placed over the top of the filling, crimp the edge of the dough and cut off the excess.

From the remaining ¼ amount of dough, roll a ⁹⁄₁₆-inch-thick section of crust for the lid. Brush the edges of the mold with Egg Wash, page 682. In applying the top, pinch it onto the already crimped top edges. Do not stretch the dough, but leave it lax enough so that it will not crack or become distorted during baking. Cut from the scraps small geometric or floral shapes to ornament the top. Work your pattern around 2 or 3 circles which can hold pastry vents, as shown in the drawing. These will later form a guide for the funnel when the aspic is carefully poured between the pâté and the upper crust. Apply the ornaments with egg wash and brush the top with it before baking. Vent the top crust with a few fancy cuts, as you would for a pie. Preheat the oven to 400°. To avoid too rapid browning of the crust, you may have ready a piece of foil to put loosely over the top. This will protect it in the early stages of baking. As soon as you put the pâté in the oven ◗ lower the heat to 325°. Pâtés are usually cooked about 1½ hours. Test for doneness as for cake, page 617.

Allow the pâté, still in the pan, to cool on a rack. When cold, fill the space which will have formed at the top between the filling and the crust by pouring through the vents enough flavorful aspic which—when it solidifies—will support the crust. Use a firm gelatin, allowing 1 tablespoon of gelatin for each cup of meat stock. Hold a funnel in one of the vents and pour the mixture—being careful not to moisten the crust on the outside. Allow the pâté to remain in the pan refrigerated until the aspic is set. To unmold the pâté, proceed as for unmolding a gelatin, page 518. Use a rack, however, on which to reverse it—to facilitate turning the pâté right side up onto a serving platter.

Pâtés should, of course, be stored refrigerated and most pâtés profit by ◗ resting refrigerated for at least 48 hours before serving—so that the flavors blend and the contents are firm enough for even slicing.

When served, the whole pâté may be garnished with a border of chopped aspic jelly, parsley and lemon wedges. When serving, cut it with a warm knife. An individual serving should be at least ⅜ to ½ of an inch thick and garnished with parsley and a lemon wedge.

For the size described here, you can produce 40 servings this way: slice about ½ inch thick, then cut each slice in half on the diagonal.

CRUST OR PÂTE FOR PÂTÉ

Work together with your fingers until you have achieved the consistency of coarse corn meal:

> **6 cups sifted all-purpose flour**
> **2 teaspoons salt**
> **1½ cups lard or shortening**

Make a well, page 594, of these ingredients and break into the center, one at a time:

> **2 eggs**

working them into the flour mixture from the inside and adding gradually:

> **About 3 cups water**

ou may need a little more water to make
dough that can be worked into a smooth
ass and rolled into a ball. The mold is
sier to form if you rest it covered at
out 70° for several hours. To mold, see
bout Pâté en Croûte, page 433.

IVER PÂTÉ

less luxurious version of this dish may
e made more quickly by omitting the
elatin and consommé.
lend with a fork:
1½ cups liver sausage
½ can condensed cream of tomato soup
issolve:
1 tablespoon gelatin
:
¼ cup cold water
ring to a boil:
1 can condensed consommé
d combine with the dissolved gelatin.
eserve ¾ cup of this mixture to line a
nt mold. Add to the remainder:
1 teaspoon Worcestershire sauce
¼ teaspoon salt
(1 pressed clove garlic)
(1 tablespoon finely chopped parsley)
d the blended liver mixture. Fold into
e mold. Let set. Reverse to serve.

UFFLÉED LIVER PÂTÉ

eheat oven to 350°.
Have ready two 9-inch bread pans, one
used in cold water, the other prepared as
r a soufflé baker, page 204. Into the
used pan, pour ½ inch of the following
latin mixture and place it in the refrig-
ator.
ak for 3 minutes:
2 teaspoons gelatin
¼ cup cold water
mbine it with:
2 cups well-seasoned Double
Consommé, page 146
serve the rest of the gelatin mixture and
ep it at room temperature. Grind:
1 lb. raw chicken livers
Or if you use ↄ a blender put the liver
d the following ingredients into it and
nd briefly. Beat in:
2 eggs
2 egg yolks
2 teaspoons onion juice
2 tablespoons chopped parsley
ld in:
2 cups whipping cream
2 stiffly beaten egg whites
ke this mixture in the greased pan at
)° until set, about 1 hour. Before plac-
it in the oven, you may set the pan in a
arger one of warm water. When the loaf
thoroughly cold, remove from the pan
d place on top of the chilled and set
atin. Pour the reserved gelatin over the
ersed bottom of the loaf, letting it run
wn the sides so that it is entirely en-
sed in the gelatin. Let the added gela-
set and the loaf become thoroughly

chilled before serving. Unmold and deco-
rate the top with:
Thinly sliced limes
Garnish the platter with:
Parsley

II. An alternate suggestion for glazing this
loaf is to replace the consommé with a
combination of 1 cup water or stock and 1
cup port wine. Jell and mold it in 2 steps,
as described previously.

ABOUT TERRINES

Terrines are the poor relations of the pâté.
They are often made from leftovers, game
or rabbit. Like pâté, the meat must be
succulent and is often in the form of me-
dallions or scallops. ♦ There should be
about ⅓ fresh veal to jelly the whole when
it cools. Terrines are baked without a
crust in lidded earthenware dishes. Set
them in a pan of water. For an 11½ x 9
x 4½-inch size, allow about 2 hours of
baking in a 300° oven. Use the following
method or make up your own meat mixture which you may reinforce with liver.
The meat may, if you like, be placed in a
wine marinade before cooking.

✱ VEAL OR CHICKEN TERRINE

Line the bottom and sides of a mold with
strips of bacon, overlapping them ever so
slightly. Strew with:
1 tablespoon chopped parsley
1 tablespoon chopped onion
Pound very thin:
2 lbs. veal scallops, cut in ¼-inch-
thick slices
In pounding veal, use your mallet with a
glancing action, as sketched, page 383, and
the meat will not stick to it. Have ready:
2 lbs. finely sliced ham, chicken or pork
Overlay the bacon with a layer of the thin
pounded veal. Season it with:
A grind of pepper
A pinch of thyme
A pinch of powdered bay leaf
Put down a layer of the thin-sliced ham.
Continue to build layers of parsley and
onion and veal, seasoning and ham. Cover
the top with overlapping bacon strips.
Pour about:
A cup of white wine
A dash of brandy
over the meat layers until all the crevices
are filled with liquid. Set the pan in a
larger pan of hot water. Bake at 300° about
2 hours or until done As soon as you remove the meat from the oven, cover with
heavy aluminum foil and weight the layers
with a brick. When the meat has cooled,
a grease-covered jelly will have formed,
which keeps the meat in prime condition.
To serve, slice very thin. Use for hors
d'oeuvre or as a main informal luncheon
dish. Store refrigerated any that remains,
covered with:
Clarified butter

ABOUT GALANTINES

When galantines appear in all their truf-fled chaud-froid splendor, it is hard to be-lieve that they started out with the boning of a bird, page 462. Begin with a slit down the spine but it is vital that during the rest of the boning the skin be kept intact. If cut, as around the leg and wing joints, it must be patched by sewing.

GALANTINE OF TURKEY

If Served Hot, 12 to 15 Servings—
if Served Cold, 30 Servings

Bone, page 462:

A 12 to 15 lb. turkey

Reserve the meat, including that cut from the drumsticks and the breast. Make a Stock, page 491, of the bones. Reserve ½ the breast meat for decorations and cut it into ½-inch strips. Grind 3 times and put into a large bowl:

1 lb. lean white veal
1 lb. lean pork

as well as all the turkey meat, except the reserved portion. Season the mixture with:

¼ cup cognac, dry sherry
or Madeira
1 teaspoon freshly grated nutmeg
Ground black pepper
2 teaspoons Worcestershire sauce
1 tablespoon salt
A dash hot pepper sauce
2 teaspoons monosodium glutamate

Add:

8 eggs
½ cup finely chopped parsley

Mix these ingredients into a smooth paste.

Correct the seasoning

Spread a large piece of clean linen or cheesecloth on the table. Place in the center of the cloth the turkey skin, outer side down, as shown in the center below. Carefully follow the instructions under Boned Chicken, page 472, about arranging the skin. Pat the meat mixture onto it in an even rectangular shape, extending it all the way to the edges. Arrange in neat al-ternating rows down the center, as shown:

Strips of cooked ham or tongue

and the reserved strips of turkey brea
Arrange a center row of:

Small whole truffles, page 283

Over the whole, sprinkle:

¾ cup pistachio nuts
¼ cup finely chopped parsley

Starting at the long side farthest away fro you, pull the cloth toward you gently-rolling the filled turkey skin into a sausag like shape. You do not want the cloth be inside the turkey roll, but keep manip lating it until it forms an outside casin You may need help. Tie the cloth s curely at both ends. The roll should smooth and even. Also tie it lengthwis as sketched. Place it on a rack, seam si down, in a large poaching kettle. Add:

Mirepoix, page 541
Enough turkey or chicken Stock
to cover, page 490

Cover the kettle and bring to a boil th reduce the heat and simmer very gent for 1½ to 2 hours until the roll is firm the touch. Carefully remove it from t broth. You may serve it hot, sliced, w buttered toast. Or let it cool—wrapped on a large platter. You may weight it you wish. When it has reached at le room temperature, remove the outsi wrapping and refrigerate thoroughly. decorate, either use:

Chaud-Froid, page 341

or cover with a savory:

Aspic Glaze, page 341

made from the poaching broth. Ser thinly sliced with:

Buttered toast

as an hors d'oeuvre or an entrée.

ABOUT SAUSAGE

One of our early European memories the rapt stance of the citizenry as th gazed at window displays of sausage. made us aware for the first time of th wealth of choice and, on a considera more limited scale, of our own. There freshly ground sausage meat or Coun Sausage, page 437, which must be used once. There are smoked sausages: fra furters, wieners or Vienna sausage,

na and Mettwurst—all of which may be
en as bought, but may also be sim-
red, baked or broiled for serving with
sta, hot vegetables and fruit garnish. See
ewed Fruits, page 107. ♦ To make
noked Sausages, see page 755.

If you broil or pan-fry these cased saus-
es ♦ prick them to keep the skins from
rsting. This is not necessary if you
ve added a small quantity of water to
: pan at the beginning of cooking or
ve first blanched, dried and floured them
htly before frying. Even then, if they
ell quickly, prick them lightly before
ey burst, to give greater protection to
: meat.

♦ For 4 servings, allow about 1 lb. of
shly ground sausage meat or the smoked
nes, slightly less for the more aged and
er types.

Dry sausages are also available: hard
l soft cervelat, salami, saucisson de
on, mortadella, pepperoni and chorizo.
ey are delicious as hors d'oeuvre, in
dwiches and for seasoning bland dishes.
Be sure that any kind of sausage you
y or make involves good quality meats.
real "stretchers" are almost certainly
sent in commercial sausages unless they
marked "pure" or "all meat." When
perly made and if the casing is intact,
: sausages may be kept indefinitely in a
l place. For this reason, they have be-
ne known as "summer sausages"—al-
ugh they are available the year round.
y types are particularly prized when re-
geration is lacking. Available, too—
nough they need constant refrigeration—
spiced meats like liver loaf or Braun-
weiger, blood sausage, deviled minced
n and veal loaves. ♦ Once the sausage
ing is cut open, smoked or cooked
sage can be stored refrigerated about 1
ek; semidry and dry types, 2 weeks or
re.

UNTRY SAUSAGE

butchering time in our valley, the popu-
man is the one who knows how to fla-
the sausage—not too much pepper or
e and just enough coriander. This proc-
has to be played by ear, for ♦ uncooked
at cannot be tasted to correct the sea-
ing and the strength of spices is so
iable. The best way to learn is to mix
mall batch and cook up a sample for
always hungry helpers to test.
To each part:
      Firm diced lard
:
    2 parts lean ground pork
son the lard with a mixture of:
      Thyme
      Summer savory
      Coriander
      Sweet marjoram
      Pulverized bay leaf
      Freshly ground pepper
o cook fresh sausage patties, start them

in a ♦ cold ungreased pan over moderate
heat and cook until medium brown on
both sides and done throughout.

II.   6 Medium Patties
If you have a sudden hankering for one of
these small-scale recipes, grind ♦ twice
with the finest grinder knives:
      ½ lb. lean pork
      ½ lb. pork fat
      ½ lb. lean veal
Mix in a large bowl:
      1 cup bread crumbs
      Grated rind of 1 lemon
      **¼ teaspoon each sage, sweet marjoram
        and thyme**
      ⅛ teaspoon summer savory
      **½ teaspoon freshly ground black
        pepper**
      2 teaspoons salt
      A grating of fresh nutmeg
Add the ground meat and form this mixture into a 1½-inch layer. Store overnight
refrigerated and covered to blend the seasoning. ♦ To cook, see I, above.

SAUTEED SAUSAGE MEAT PATTIES
                                   4 Servings
Combine:
      1 lb. sausage meat
      2 tablespoons flour
      **(¼ cup drained crushed pineapple
        or grated fresh apple)**
Shape the meat into cakes ½ inch thick.
Sprinkle with:
      Flour
Heat a skillet. No fat is required. Brown
the cakes quickly on both sides. Cover
with a lid. ♦ Reduce the heat and cook
about 10 minutes on one side. Pour off
excess fat. Turn and cook 10 minutes on
the other side or until done. Serve with:
      Sautéed Onions, page 285
      Applesauce, page 112

▤ PAN-BROILED SAUSAGE
                                   4 Servings
♦ Please read About Sausage, page 436.
Cut apart and place in a skillet:
      8 sausages
Add:
      ½ cup boiling water
Cover the pan. Simmer gently, not over
190°, for 8 to 10 minutes or until almost
done. Pour off the liquid. Return the
sausages to the pan. Cook them over low
heat, shaking the pan constantly until they
are an even brown. Drain. Serve with:
      Prepared mustard
For picnics, serve between:
      Rolls

BROILED SAUSAGE PATTIES
                                   2 Servings
Preheat broiler.
Shape into 4 flat cakes:
      ½ lb. sausage meat
Roll the cakes in:
      1 tablespoon flour
Broil under moderate heat for 8 to 10 min-

utes or until done. Arrange on a hot platter:

Apple Rings, page 111
Place the sausage cakes on them. Serve garnished with:

Parsley

BOILED SAUSAGE
Place in a kettle:

Smoked sausage
Cover with:

Boiling water
Simmer for about 10 minutes. Drain, skin, slice and serve with:

Sauerkraut, page 269

BAKED SAUSAGE MEAT RING
                                                    6 Servings
Preheat oven to 350°.
Grease lightly a 7-inch ring mold. Press onto the bottom:

3 tablespoons cornflakes
Combine well:

1 lb. sausage meat
1 tablespoon minced onion
¾ cup fine bread crumbs
2 tablespoons chopped parsley
1 beaten egg

Place these ingredients in the mold. Bake the ring 15 minutes. Drain the fat from it. Bake 15 minutes longer or until done. Invert the ring onto a hot platter and fill the center with:

8 Scrambled Eggs, page 200
Garnish the top with:

Chopped parsley or paprika

BAKED SAUSAGE MEAT, SWEET POTATOES AND FRUIT
                                                    4 Servings
Preheat oven to 350°.
This is a good dish for large groups.
Cook:

4 large sweet potatoes
Peel and cut them into thin slices. Grease a baking dish. Cover the bottom with ½ the sweet potatoes. Shape into 4 flat cakes:

1 lb. sausage meat
Brown the cakes lightly in a greased pan, to which you may add:

1 tablespoon minced bacon
Peel and cut into thick slices:

4 large apples or pineapple slices
Place the drained meat cakes on the sweet potatoes and cover with apple slices. Sprinkle lightly with:

Salt and brown sugar
Place the remaining sweet potatoes over the fruit. Brush the potatoes with:

Milk
and sprinkle with:

Brown sugar
Bake for about ¾ hour.

PORK SCRAPPLE OR GOETTA
                                                    About 6 Servings
If you use corn meal, call it scrapple. If you use oats, call it goetta. This may also

be made with ¾ cup cooked pork. U stock from the pork bones in cooking cereal. Place in a pan:

2 lbs. pork neck bones or other bony pieces
Add:

1½ quarts boiling water
1 sliced onion
6 peppercorns
(1 small bay leaf)
Simmer the pork until the meat falls fr the bones. Strain, reserving the liqu There should be about 4 cups. Add wa or light stock if necessary to make t amount. Prepare, using this liquid in pl of boiling water:

Corn Meal Mush, page 177
You may substitute 1 cup oatmeal for corn meal. In cooking oatmeal, you m want to reduce the liquid by one cup. move all meat from the pork bones a chop or grind it fine. Add it to the cook mush. Season with:

Salt, if required
1 teaspoon or more grated onion
(½ teaspoon dried thyme or sage)
A grating of fresh nutmeg
A little cayenne
Pour the scrapple into a bread pan t has been rinsed with cold water. Let stand until cold and firm. Slice it. serve, sauté slowly in:

Melted butter or drippings

BLOOD SAUSAGE, BOUDIN NOIR OR BLACK PUDDING
Have sausage casings ready.
Cook gently without browning:

¾ cup finely chopped onions
in:

2 tablespoons lard
Dice into ½-inch cubes and half melt:

1 lb. fresh pork fat
Cool slightly and mix in a bowl with:

⅛ cup whipping cream
2 beaten eggs
A grind of fresh pepper
⅛ teaspoon fresh thyme
½ pulverized bay leaf
When these ingredients have been gen combined, mix in:

2 cups fresh pork blood
Fill casings about ⅘ full, as this mixtu will swell during the poaching peri Without overcrowding, put the sealed c ings into a wire basket. Plunge them i boiling water. ♦ Reduce heat at once 200° to 203° and continue to cook at t temperature for about 20 minutes. Shou any of the sausages rise to the surface the simmering liquid, pierce them to lease the air that might burst the skins. serve, split and grill them very gently.

ABOUT VARIETY MEATS

Variety, we know, is the spice of life. A variety meats provide welcome relief fr the **weekly** round of beef, pork, ve

icken and fish. Variety meats include
gan meats like sweetbreads, brains, liver
d kidney; muscle meats like heart,
ngue and tripe; and very bony-struc-
red meats like tails, knucklebones and
eir delicious marrow centers. Time was
nen most of these tidbits were ours al-
ost for the asking. Today, hospital au-
orities—aware of the special virtues of
gan meats—purchase them in large
antity. And the remainder are increas-
gly used in meat processing. As a result,
e American housewife is apt to find
riety meats of all types scarcer and con-
derably more expensive than they were a
cade ago. ♦ It is essential that these
eats be very, very fresh. Even when they
e, the pan drippings from kidney and
er may sometimes be strong, and some
oks prefer to discard them. If in doubt,
te the drippings before serving.

OUT LIVER

icken and calf livers are the tenderest
d most desirable unless, of course, you
n secure extra-fat goose livers—the kind
ich in Europe almost invariably find
eir way into Pâtés, page 432. Baby beef
er comes next for quality. It should be
ndled like that of lamb, sheep, pork and
der beef livers—that is, soaked for about
♦ minutes in a marinade, page 336, or in
lk. Before cooking, all these stronger
es of liver should be dried and the
uids in which they have been soaked
scarded.
♦ To prepare any liver for cooking, wipe
first with a damp cloth, then remove the
n outer skin and veining. Except for
e timing noted in individual recipes, the
oking method for liver generally is the
ne. ♦ Never toughen it by cooking it
o long or over excessive heat. ♦ Never
ok it beyond the point of tenderness.
metimes the drippings in which liver
s been cooked are bitter. Test them by
sting before you use them as sauce. Al-
w 1 pound liver for 4 servings.

ALF OR CHICKEN LIVER ONNAISE

2 Servings

Please read About Liver, above.
ave sliced to a ⅓-inch even thickness:
   ½ lb. calf liver or 12 chicken livers
   cut in half
ason with:
   Salt and pepper
at on both sides with:
   Flour
atting well between your hands to make
e flour adhere and to remove the excess.
uté until golden brown in:
   2 tablespoons butter
   ¼ cup sliced onions
   (¼ cup sliced mushrooms)
d set aside nearby. Now melt over high
at in a heavy skillet:
   1 tablespoon butter

Heat it until it starts making slight crackling noises. Put the floured liver into the
skillet, allowing 1 minute to each side. Remove the liver and discard the butter it
was cooked in, which may be bitter. Put
the liver on a hot plate, cover with the
onion butter and:
   Chopped parsley
Serve at once. We hate to add this, because we feel liver should be rare—but if
you don't like it this way, cook it over
medium heat 2 minutes to the side for
medium doneness.

GOOSE LIVER

Goose liver is considered a great delicacy.
Remove the gall bladder. Soak in cold
salted water for 2 hours:
   A goose liver
Dry it with a cloth.
I. Sprinkle it with:
   ⅛ teaspoon paprika
   ½ teaspoon sugar
   ⅛ teaspoon ginger
Sauté it in hot goose fat until it is tender.
Excellent served with sautéed onions and
apples and with a little dry sherry.

II. Prepare and soak as directed previously:
   A goose liver
Place it in an ovenproof dish. Cover it
with:
   1 cup brown sugar
   ¼ teaspoon salt
   1 cup dry sherry
Broil it slowly for ½ hour. Watch it so
that it does not burn. Baste it frequently
to prevent a crust from forming. Cook
sliced apples in a thick sirup until well
glazed. Place them around the liver. Continue to baste with apple sirup until the
liver is tender.

▤ BROILED LIVER

♦ Please read About Liver, above.
I. Preheat broiler.
Some epicures have a preference for liver
prepared in the following way—doctors
have, too. We lean toward sauteed liver,
but must acknowledge the good qualities
of this recipe which accents liver—pure
and simple.
Place on a broiling rack, about 3 inches
from the source of heat:
   Slices of calf liver, ⅛ inch thick
You may brush them with:
   (Butter or cooking oil)
Leave the door of the broiling oven open.
Broil the liver exactly 1 minute on each
side.
   Correct the seasoning
It is remarkably good as it is.

II. Preheat broiler.
Allowing 2 to 3 slices of bacon and onion
for each slice of liver, broil:
   Slices of lean thin bacon
   Thin slices of Bermuda onion

Prepare:
Broiled Liver I, page 439
Serve the liver, bacon and onions on a hot
platter garnished with:
Parsley
A lemon cut into quarters

BRAISED LIVER WITH
VEGETABLES

6 Servings

♦ Please read About Liver, page 439.
Cut into 1-inch slices:
1½ lbs. beef or calf liver
If you substitute beef liver, you may lard
it, page 383. Dredge with:
Seasoned flour
Brown the liver in:
¼ cup hot bacon drippings
Combine and heap on the slices:
2 diced carrots
2 seeded chopped green peppers
6 small onions
1 cup sliced celery
Add to the pan:
1 cup boiling water or stock
Cover and simmer until the liver is tender.
Add, if necessary, more boiling stock. Calf
liver will be tender in about 15 minutes,
beef liver in about 30.

BRAISED LIVER COCKAIGNE
WITH WINE

8 Servings

♦ Please read About Liver, page 439.
Place:
2½ lbs. calf liver in 1 piece
in the following marinade for 1 hour or
more:
⅛ cup salad oil
1½ tablespoons lemon juice
¼ teaspoon salt
⅛ teaspoon paprika
¼ bay leaf
Turn it from time to time.
Preheat oven to 325°.
Melt in an ovenproof baking dish:
3 tablespoons butter
Add and stir about until lightly cooked:
1 small chopped onion or leek
1 diced carrot
2 or 3 diced ribs celery
2 or 3 sprigs minced parsley
1 tablespoon fresh basil or tarragon
Place the liver, marinade and all, in the
ovenproof dish. Cover closely and bake
until nearly tender, for about 50 minutes.
Baste from time to time. If you wish to
serve the liver without further additions,
continue cooking it until very tender. The
following ingredients are optional, but they
complement the dish. While the liver is
cooking, place in a heavy skillet:
4 slices diced bacon
Cook over very slow heat until the bacon
is clear. Add and stir until well glazed:
18 small peeled shallots or onions
6 large or 8 small sliced carrots
3 ribs sliced celery

Add:
1 cup Stock, page 490, or canned
consommé
Cover the skillet and cook the vegetabl
over direct low heat for 15 minutes. Ad
them to the liver in the baking dish, cov
and cook for 15 minutes longer. Drain th
contents of the baking dish, reserving th
liquor. Place the liver on a hot platte
Add to the liquor:
½ cup dry white wine, or ¼ cup
dry sherry
(2 beaten egg yolks)
Cook and stir the sauce over low heat u
til hot. If you have added the eggs, do n
permit it to boil. Pour the sauce over th
liver. Serve with:
Small new browned potatoes
garnished with:
Parsley

BEEF LIVER CREOLE

4 Servin

♦ Please read About Liver, page 439.
Cut into thin slices:
1 lb. beef liver
Dust the slices lightly with:
Flour
Melt, then brown the liver in:
3 tablespoons hot butter or drippings
Add:
1¼ cups sliced onions
1½ cups heated canned tomatoes
½ cup diced celery
1 thinly sliced green pepper
½ teaspoon salt
A few grains cayenne
Cover the pan and simmer these ingr
dients for about 20 minutes. Drain the
Thicken the liquid with:
Flour, see Pan Gravy, page 322
Add the liver and vegetables. Simmer
minutes longer. Serve with:
Boiled Rice, page 178, or
Noodles, page 188

▤ LIVER, PEPPER, ONIONS AND
OLIVES ON SKEWERS

4 Servir

Preheat broiler.
Simmer covered in a little boiling wa
until nearly tender:
¾ lb. calf liver
Drain the liver. Cut it into 1-inch cub
Cut into quarters:
4 medium-sized onions
Place them in water to separate the s
tions. Cut into 1-inch pieces:
6 strips bacon
Cut into 1-inch pieces:
2 green peppers, seeds and
membrane removed
Alternate on skewers pieces of liver, oni
green pepper, bacon and:
Stuffed olives
Heat in a skillet over low heat a few
con scraps or butter. Add the filled sk
ers. Move them about and cook them
about 3 minutes. Place them under

broiler until the bacon is crisp and the liver
is tender.

CHICKEN LIVERS À LA KING
Prepare:
    1 cup or more Chicken Liver
        Lyonnaise, page 439
Serve in:
    1 cup à la King Sauce, page 333

CHICKEN LIVERS IN BATTER
Preheat deep fryer to 375°.
Wipe with a cloth:
    Chicken livers
Season them lightly with:
    Salt and pepper
Dip them into:
    Fritter Batter for Meat, page 221
Fry them in deep fat, pages 124-126, until
well browned. Serve with:
    Herb Omelet, page 198
or as a garnish for a hot vegetable plate.

ABOUT SWEETBREADS

To paraphrase Puck: "What foods these
morsels be!" Veal sweetbreads are those
most favored. But beef sweetbreads are
sometimes incorporated into mixtures like
meat pies, pâté and terrines. Sweetbreads,
properly so-called, are the rounded more
desirable "heart" or "kernel" types, the
pancreas. Also sold as sweetbread is the
less desirable "throat," which is the thy-
mus gland of the animal.

♦ Like all organ meats, sweetbreads are
highly perishable and should be prepared
or use as soon as purchased. First soak
them at least 1 hour in a large quantity of
cold water to release any blood. You may
change the water several times during this
period. Next they must be blanched. This
is done by putting them into cold acidulated water to cover, page 494. Bring them
slowly to a boil and simmer uncovered
from 2 to 5 minutes depending on their
size. Drain. Firm them by plunging them
at once into cold water. When they have
cooled, drain again and trim them by removing cartilage, tubes, connective tissue
and tougher membrane. Weight them refrigerated for several hours if you plan using them whole. If you are not using them
in one piece, break them into smaller sections with your hands, being careful not
to disturb the very fine membrane that surrounds the smaller units. Allow 1 pair for
servings.
After these preliminary processes, to
which all sweetbreads must be subjected,
you may poach, braise, broil or sauce them.

SAUCED POACHED SWEETBREADS
                              2 Servings
♦ Please read About Sweetbreads, above.
Soak, blanch, firm, drain and trim:

    1 pair calf sweetbreads
Bring to the boiling point:
    Enough water to cover
to which you may add:
    ¼ cup chopped onions
    3 ribs celery with yellow leaves
    2 peppercorns
Drop the sweetbreads into the liquid and
♦ lower the heat at once. Simmer covered
with a parchment paper, page 129, for
about 15 to 20 minutes depending on size.
♦ Do not overcook. Serve in a delicate
sauce flavored with:
    1 tablespoon sherry, Madeira
        or brandy
Add a few:
    Toasted English walnuts and/or
        almonds
Allow about:
    1 cup Béchamel, Poulette, Mushroom
        or Wine Sauce for Light Meats
Sauced sweetbreads are often served on:
    A thin slice of Virginia ham
or with a:
    Spinach Ring, page 209, a Vegetable
        Soufflé, page 205, or Wild Rice,
        page 179

SAUTÉED SWEETBREADS
                              2 Servings
♦ Please read About Sweetbreads, this
page.
Blanch, firm, dry, trim and poach for about
25 minutes:
    1 pair calf sweetbreads
Bread with a:
    Seasoned Bound Breading, page 502
Sauté them in:
    Hot butter
until they are a rich brown. Serve them
with:
    Cream sauce of sweetbread stock
        and cream
Season the stock with:
    Sherry or lemon juice
    Chopped parsley
Serve the sweetbreads with:
    New potatoes and green peas
garnished with:
    Watercress

BROILED SWEETBREADS
                              2 Servings
♦ Please read About Sweetbreads, this
page.
Soak, blanch, firm, drain, trim and poach
for about 25 minutes:
    1 pair calf sweetbreads
Preheat broiler.
Place the broiling rack about 6 inches
from the heat source. Break the sweet-
breads into large pieces. Roll them in:
    Seasoned flour
Surround them with:
    Strips of bacon
Secure it with toothpicks. While broiling

them, baste frequently with the juices that drip and, if they are rather dry, use additional:

Butter

Add to the drippings a small amount of:

(Sherry or lemon juice)

Serve with:

Madeira Sauce, Poulette Sauce or broiled tomatoes

or on a bed of:

Spinach

BRAISED SWEETBREADS

2 Servings

Make this as simple or as fancy as you like.

◗ Please read About Sweetbreads, page 441.

Soak, blanch for 5 minutes, firm, drain and trim:

1 pair calf sweetbreads

You may press them between 2 plates under a weight if you want them to have uniform thickness and to mellow.

Preheat oven to 375°.

Break sweetbread into several large pieces. You may lard, page 383, the pieces or surround each one with:

(**Strips of lean bacon, very thin pieces of Virginia ham or smoked tongue**)

Sauté in a casserole in:

2 tablespoons melted butter

for about 10 minutes or until the onions are transparent:

**⅓ cup finely chopped onions
2 tablespoons finely minced carrot
⅓ cup chopped celery**

Add:

**½ cup dry white wine and ¾ cup light stock, or 1¼ cups stock
½ teaspoon salt
¼ teaspoon freshly ground white pepper**

Arrange the sweetbreads on this bed of sautéed vegetables. ◗ Cover and bake for about 30 minutes.

This is an added touch, particularly good if you have used the ham or bacon. In a skillet, sauté for about 5 minutes:

(**½ cup sliced mushrooms**)
(**¾ cup chopped cooked chestnuts, page 272**)

in:

2 tablespoons butter

GLAZED SWEETBREADS

2 Servings

◗ Please read About Sweetbreads, page 441.

Soak, blanch, firm, drain and trim:

1 pair calf sweetbreads

Melt in a casserole and sauté for about 10 minutes or until the onions are transparent:

**3 tablespoons butter
2 tablespoons finely julienned carrots
2 tablespoons finely chopped shallots or onions**

Add:

1½ cups veal stock

Simmer closely covered for about 20 minutes. ◗ Make sure that the vegetables do not brown. Add more stock, if necessary. When the sweetbreads are cooked, help to deglaze the pan by the addition of:

**½ cup dry white wine
Correct the seasoning**

Preheat oven to 400° for glazing.

Now, remove the sweetbreads from the pan, but keep warm in an ovenproof dish on which they can be served. Reduce the pan liquors to a demi-glaze. Cover the sweetbreads, allowing about 2 tablespoons of glaze for each one, and place the dish in the oven, basting often for about 1 minutes. Serve at once, garnished with:

Chervil or parsley

Serve with:

**Fresh young peas
Soufflé Potatoes, page 294**

RAGOÛT FIN

4 Servings

A delicate and far-reaching dish.

◗ Please read About Sweetbreads, page 441.

Prepare and drain:

1 pair poached sweetbreads

Drain and cut in two:

2 cups cooked asparagus tips

Reserve the liquid. Melt in a heavy skillet:

¼ cup butter

Sauté in the butter for about 3 minutes:

½ lb. mushrooms
(**¼ cup chopped shallots**)

Remove them from the skillet. Add to the fat in it:

6 tablespoons butter

Add and stir until blended:

6 tablespoons flour

Stir in slowly:

3 cups liquid: milk or cream, asparagus water or Stock, page 490

When the sauce is smooth and boiling, add gradually the asparagus tips, the mushrooms and the sweetbreads. ◗ Reduce the heat. Put a small amount of sauce in a separate pan and beat in:

2 egg yolks

Combine the sauces and ◗ without letting them boil, stir for about 1 minute very gently, so as not to mash the asparagus. Season with:

**Salt and paprika
Freshly grated nutmeg**

Just before serving, add:

(**2 tablespoons dry sherry or
1 teaspoon Worcestershire sauce**)

Serve the ragoût at once in:

Hot patty shells, on hot buttered toast, in Bread Cases, page 223, in a baked Noodle Ring, page 188, or on hot Waffles, page 216

⊟ SWEETBREADS ON SKEWERS

2 Servings

Preheat oven to 400°.

◗ Please read About Sweetbreads, page 441.

Soak, blanch for about 10 minutes, firm
and trim:

 1 pair calf sweetbreads

Break them into 1-inch chunks. Partially
cook:

 Thin slices of lean bacon

enough to surround the pieces of sweetbread. Spread:

 Mushroom caps

lightly with:

 Butter

Place the sweetbreads and the mushrooms
alternately on skewers. Put them over the
edge of a pan and bake for about 10 minutes or grill over charcoal until the bacon
is crisp.

ABOUT BRAINS

Calf, sheep, lamb, pork and beef brains are
listed in order of preference. Brains may
be used in all recipes calling for sweetbreads but in both cases they must be very
fresh.

‣ To prepare them, give them a preliminary soaking of about 3 hours in cold
acidulated water, page 494. After skinning, soak them in lukewarm water to free
them from all traces of blood. Then, as
they are rather mushy in texture, firm them
by again blanching in acidulated water
to cover for about 20 minutes for calf
brains, 25 for the others. ‣ Be sure the
water does not boil. Allow 1 pound of
brains for 4 servings or 1 set for 2 servings.

Brains are often combined with eggs or
in ragoût and soufflés with sweetbreads.
Because they are bland, be sure to give the
dish in which they are used a piquant flavoring, as suggested below.

SAUTEED BRAINS

                                        4 Servings

‣ Please read About Brains, above.
Prepare:

 2 sets cooked brains

Cut in two, lengthwise. Dry them between
towels. Season them with:

 Salt and paprika

Roll them in:

 Corn meal or flour

Melt in a skillet rubbed with:

 Garlic

 ⅓ cup butter or bacon grease

When the fat reaches the point of fragrance, cook the brains on each side for
about 2 minutes. Cover them, reduce the
heat and complete the cooking, about 10
minutes in all. Serve them with:

 Lemon wedges
 Thickened Tomato Sauce, page 333,
 or Worcestershire sauce
 Buerre Noir, page 338

with a few:

 Capers or black olives

BAKED BRAINS

                                        3 Servings

‣ Please read About Brains, above.
Preheat oven to 400°.

Chop coarsely:

 1 set cooked brains

Combine them with:

 ½ cup bread crumbs
 2 chopped hard-cooked eggs
 6 tablespoons cream
 1 tablespoon catsup
 2 peeled chopped green chilis
 ½ tablespoon lemon juice
 Correct the seasoning

Place in a greased baking dish or in individual dishes. Sprinkle the top with:

 Au Gratin II, page 342

Bake for about 15 minutes.

BAKED BRAINS AND EGGS

                                        4 Servings

‣ Please read About Brains, this page.
Preheat oven to 350°.
Cut into 1-inch dice:

 2 sets cooked brains

Place them in 4 small greased casseroles.
Peel, seed and dice:

 4 tomatoes

Combine them with:

 1½ tablespoons hot olive oil
 1 teaspoon chopped parsley
 1 teaspoon chopped onion or chives
 Salt and paprika
 1 teaspoon brown sugar

Pour these ingredients into the casseroles.
Break into each one:

 1 egg

Bake for about 5 minutes until the eggs are
firm. Melt and brown lightly:

 ¼ cup butter

Add:

 2 teaspoons lemon juice

Pour this over the eggs. Garnish with:

 Parsley

Serve at once.

BROILED BRAINS

‣ Please read About Brains, this page.
Preheat broiler.
Brush:

 Cooked brains

with:

 Oil or melted butter

Dust with:

 Paprika

Place the broiler about 6 inches from the
source of heat and broil the brains for
about 8 minutes on each side or until done.
Baste with oil or butter. Serve piping hot
with:

 Broiled Bacon, page 411
 Chopped parsley and lemon wedges

or

 Grilled Tomato Slices, page 306
 Water Cress

ABOUT KIDNEYS

Veal kidneys are the most delicious. Those
of lamb are somewhat soft and flat in flavor, but especially suitable for grilling.
Large beef kidneys tend to be hard and
strong in flavor. Soak them first for 2

hours in cold salted water. Off-flavors may be withdrawn either by blanching, page 132, in acidulated water or by drying after soaking and sautéing briefly over brisk heat, after which the kidneys are allowed to cool partially before further cooking.

Beef, mutton and pork kidneys, which are prepared as for beef, are most often used in terrines, braises and stews where very slow cooking helps make them tender.

The white membrane should be snipped from all kidneys before they are washed. Curved scissors makes the job easier. Another way to remove the membrane conveniently is to sauté the kidneys first for about 1 minute in fat. Discard the fat.

◗ To prepare for broiling, almost halve them and keep from curling during cooking by skewering them open. Expose the cut side first to the heat.

Veal and lamb kidneys should be cooked for as short a time as possible over medium heat. ◗ Do not overcook. The center should be slightly pink. If kidneys are of the best quality, pan juices may be used. If not, discard the juices and use freshly melted butter or wine sauce. In any case, ◗ never allow kidneys to boil in a sauce, as this only hardens them. Pour the hot sauce over them or toss them in it for a moment or two.

Beef, mutton and pork kidneys need slow, moist cooking which is described in some of the following recipes. Allow 1 medium veal, 2 or 3 lamb, 1½ to 2 mutton, ½ beef or 1 small pork kidney per person. The veal kidney is surrounded by delicious delicate fat which you can use for seasoning or render for deep-fat frying, pages 124-126. If kidneys are to be ◗ flambéed, never do it for more than 1 minute. Longer exposure to this high heat will toughen them.

BAKED VEAL KIDNEYS
◗ Please read About Kidneys, above.
Preheat oven to 300°.
Note for the lone housekeeper: 1 kidney makes a fine little roast for 1 person. Prepare and bake kidneys, leaving the fat on. Place in a pan, fat side up:
    Veal kidneys
Bake them uncovered until tender, about 1 hour.

KIDNEY NUGGETS
2 Servings
◗ Please read About Kidneys, this page.
Preheat oven to 375°.
Prepare for cooking and slice in half:
    4 lamb kidneys
Prepare:
    Dressing for Stuffed Pork Chops,
        page 425
adding:
    1 beaten egg
Spread the dressing on:
    8 slices of thin lean bacon

Wrap the spread bacon around the kidney halves and fasten it with a toothpick. Bake about 20 minutes.

SAUTÉED KIDNEYS
3 Servings
This could be called Kidneys Bercy because it has both shallots and dry white wine.
◗ Please read About Kidneys, this page.
Remove some of the fat from:
    3 veal kidneys
Cut them crosswise into slices, removing all the white tissue. Rub a pan with:
    (Garlic)
Melt in it:
    ¼ cup butter
Sauté in the butter until golden:
    ½ cup sliced onions or shallots
Remove the onions and keep hot. Then sauté the kidneys in the hot fat, a quick process, about 5 minutes. Add the onions and season with:
    Salt and paprika
    1 tablespoon lemon juice or ¼ cup
        dry white wine
You may serve this flambé, page 127, with:
    Mushrooms on toast

SAUTEED KIDNEYS WITH CELERY AND MUSHROOMS
4 Servings
If you can get very young fresh kidneys and follow this recipe closely, you may imagine yourself—for a mealtime—in France.
◗ Please read About Kidneys, this page.
Prepare:
    8 lamb kidneys
Skin and quarter them. Sprinkle them with:
    Lemon juice
Heat:
    3 tablespoons butter or drippings
Sauté lightly in this:
    1 cup chopped celery
    ¼ cup chopped onion
Add the kidneys. ◗ Simmer them covered for about 5 minutes. Stir in:
    1 tablespoon flour
    1 cup hot Stock, page 490
When these ingredients are blended, add:
    ½ lb. chopped mushrooms
Season the kidneys lightly with:
    Paprika
    Worcestershire sauce
Simmer them covered for about 15 minutes. Add:
    2 tablespoons dry sherry
    1 tablespoon chopped parsley
    Correct the seasoning
and serve.

▤ BROILED KIDNEYS
Allow 1 Kidney per Person

◗ Please read About Kidneys, page 443.
Preheat broiler.
Remove most of the fat from:
   Veal kidneys
Cut them crosswise into slices. Broil them
for about 5 minutes or until done. Turn
them, baste with:
   Melted butter
and broil for about 5 minutes longer. Sea-
son with:
   Lemon juice
   Salt and paprika

BROILED BEEF KIDNEYS, TOMATOES AND ONIONS

2 Servings

◗ Please read About Kidneys, page 443.
Soak and blanch, page 132, in acidulated
water for about 20 minutes or until tender:
   A beef kidney
Cut it into ⅓-inch slices.
Preheat broiler.
Meanwhile, simmer until nearly tender:
   Sliced onions
in:
   Milk or water
Drain these ingredients. Dry them between
towels. Grease an ovenproof dish. Ar-
range the kidneys and onions upon it with:
   Thick slices tomato
Season the vegetables with:
   Salt and pepper
Dot them and the meat with:
   Butter
Place the broiler pan about 6 inches from
the heat source and broil until the toma-
toes are done. Dust with:
   Finely chopped parsley

▤ KIDNEYS EN BROCHETTE

Individual Serving

◗ Please read About Kidneys, page 443.
Prepare for cooking, allowing per serving:
   1 veal or 3 lamb kidneys
Blanch in:
   Milk or cold water and lemon juice
about 2 to 3 minutes or until tender. Dry.
Cut in quarters. Wrap in:
   Bacon
Arrange on skewers and broil 3 inches
from the heat source, about 3 minutes.
Turn and broil 3 minutes more. Serve at
once.

VEAL KIDNEY CASSEROLE

4 Servings

◗ Please read About Kidneys, page 443.
Preheat oven to 350°.
Wash and core:
   4 veal kidneys
Skin and dice after heating them for about
1 minute in:
   2 tablespoons fat
Discard the fat. Put the kidneys in a
heated ovenproof dish. Then heat in a
skillet:
   1 tablespoon butter
Sauté in the butter:

   ¼ to ½ lb. sliced mushrooms
   2 tablespoons minced onion or
   ¼ clove garlic
   1 tablespoon minced parsley
Stir and cook these ingredients for about 2
minutes. Stir in:
   3 tablespoons flour
Stir in:
   1 cup boiling veal or light stock
Bring these ingredients to the boiling point.
Add:
   ¼ cup dry white wine or ½ cup
   orange juice
   Correct the seasoning
Pour these ingredients into the casserole.
Cover it closely. Bake for about 20 minutes or until tender. If you want to reduce
the juices slightly, remove the kidneys and
keep warm, then pour the thickened hot
gravy over them. Have ready, by cutting
into triangles:
   4 thick slices bread
Sprinkle them with:
   Grated cheese
Place them on top of the kidneys. Broil
them until the cheese is melted.

KIDNEY STEW

4 Servings

A favorite for Sunday breakfast.
◗ Please read About Kidneys, page 443.
Cut away all the white tissue from:
   2 small beef kidneys
Drop them into acidulated water to cover
and blanch, page 132, for 30 minutes or
until tender. Remove the kidneys from the
liquid and cool them. For easier slicing,
you may place them in a covered dish in
the refrigerator. When cold, cut the meat
into wafer-thin slices. Melt:
   1 or 2 tablespoons butter
Sauté the kidneys lightly in the hot butter.
Remove the kidneys and keep them warm.
Stir into the drippings:
   1½ to 2 tablespoons flour
Pour in:
   1 cup stock or ½ cup stock
   and ½ cup beer
Stir until the gravy is smooth and boiling.
Flavor by adding:
   1 slice lemon or 2 tablespoons
   tomato paste
   Salt and paprika, as needed
Toss the kidneys in the hot sauce and
serve on:
   Noodles, page 188, toast or
   Corn Meal Waffles, page 217
Garnished with:
   Chopped parsley

ABOUT TONGUE

No matter from which source—beef, calf,
lamb or pork—the smaller-size tongues are
usually preferable. The most commonly
used and best flavored, whether fresh,
smoked or pickled, is beef tongue. For
prime texture, it should be under 3 pounds.
◗ Scrub the tongue well. If it is smoked

or pickled, you may wish to blanch it first, page 132, simmering for about 10 minutes. Immerse the tongue in cold water. After draining, put it into seasoned boiling water to cover. ♦ Reduce the heat immediately and simmer uncovered 2 to 3 hours or until tender.

If the tongue is to be served hot, drain it from the hot water, plunge it into cold water for a moment so you can handle it, skin it and trim it by removing the roots, small bones and gristle and return it very briefly to the hot cooking water to reheat before serving.

If the tongue is to be served cold, take the pot from the heat when the tongue is tender, remove the tongue and allow it to cool just enough to handle comfortably. It skins easily at this point ♦ but not if you let it get cold. Trim it and return it to the pot to cool completely in the cooking liquor. It is attractive served with Chaud-Froid Sauce, page 341, or in the Aspic, page 447.

♦ To carve tongue, cut nearly through at the hump parallel to the base. But toward the tip, better-looking slices can be made if the cut is diagonal.

BOILED FRESH BEEF TONGUE
6 to 8 Servings

♦ Please read About Tongue, above.
Place in a kettle:
A fresh beef or calf tongue:
about 2 lbs.
Peel and add:
2 medium-sized onions
1 large carrot
3 or more ribs celery with leaves
6 sprigs parsley
8 peppercorns
Barely cover these ingredients with boiling water. Simmer the tongue uncovered until it is tender, about 3 hours for beef, about 2 hours for calf. Drain it. Skin and trim the tongue. Serve it with:
Mustard Sauce, page 325
Piquant Sauce, page 327
Hot Vinaigrette Sauce, page 311
Harvard Beets, page 264
Horseradish, capers or chopped
pickle

BEEF TONGUE WITH RAISIN SAUCE

An undemanding dish to prepare while working on other things in the kitchen.
♦ Please read About Tongue, this page.
Cook, as in previous recipe:
A fresh beef tongue, boiled
After it has been skinned and trimmed, place it where it will keep hot.
Sauce:
Blanch, page 132, and split:
½ cup almonds
Place them in:
2 cups water
and simmer for 20 minutes. Add and sim-

mer for ½ hour longer:
⅔ cup seedless raisins
Drain the sauce. Reserve the liquid. Melt:
6 tablespoons fat from the tongue
stock or butter
Stir in until blended:
3 tablespoons flour
Stir in gradually:
The raisins, almond liquid and
tongue stock to make 3 cups
liquid in all
¼ cup crushed ginger snaps
(2 teaspoons Caramel II, page 508)
Add the almonds, raisins and:
1 teaspoon grated lemon rind
Correct the seasoning
Serve the tongue with:
A Rice or Noodle Ring, pages 188,
and 189, filled with green peas

BOILED CORNED OR PICKLED TONGUE

Keeps better in a refrigerator than ham and is a less usual emergency dish.
♦ Please read About Tongue, page 445.
If the tongue is very salty, soak it or blanch it, page 132, in cold water to cover for several hours. Prepare as for Fresh Beef Tongue, Boiled, above, using:
A corned or pickled beef tongue

BOILED SMOKED TONGUE
6 to 8 Servings

♦ Please read About Tongue, page 445.
Cover with cold water and soak in a cool place for 12 hours or blanch, page 132:
A 2 lb. smoked beef tongue
Drain, then cover the tongue with:
Fresh water
Add:
1 sliced or whole onion stuck with
3 cloves
½ cup chopped celery with leaves
3 bay leaves
1 teaspoon peppercorns
Simmer it uncovered until it is tender, from 2 to 4 hours. Skin and trim, as directed. Slice and serve hot with:
Creamed Spinach, page 300
Horseradish Sauce, page 324
or cold in:
Aspic, page 447

TONGUE BAKED IN CREOLE SAUCE
6 Servings

♦ Please read About Tongue, page 445.
Cook:
A fresh or smoked beef tongue, about
1½ lbs., or 2 veal or 8 lamb tongues
Skin and trim as directed.
Preheat oven to 375°.
Prepare:
Creole Sauce, page 336
Place the drained tongue, sliced or unsliced, in a casserole. Pour the sauce over it. Bake it covered for ½ hour. Serve it with:
Chopped parsley

TONGUE IN ASPIC

8 Servings

A fine-looking dish.
Cook:

A Smoked Beef Tongue, page 446

Leave it in the stock until it is cool, then prepare it as directed. Make the following aspic. Soak:

1½ tablespoons gelatin

in:

½ cup cold beef stock

Dissolve it in:

2½ cups boiling beef stock
½ cup dry white wine or the juice of
2 lemons
1 tablespoon sugar
Salt, if required
A few drops Caramel II, page 508, or
commercial coloring
1 teaspoon Worcestershire sauce

Chill the aspic and, when it is about to set, add:

½ cup chopped sweet-sour pickles
1 cup chopped celery
½ cup chopped green peppers

Have ready a mold or bread pan moistened with cold water. Place a small amount of aspic in the bottom of the mold. If desired, mold into this carrots, cooked beets, canned mushrooms, etc. Put the tongue into the mold and pour the remaining aspic around and over it. When well chilled, unmold the aspic on a platter. Garnish it with:

Lettuce leaves
Deviled eggs
Parsley
Slices of lemon

Serve it with:

Mayonnaise or see Mayonnaise
Collée, page 341

ABOUT HEART

Heart, which is firm and rather dry, is best prepared by slow cooking. In texture, it more nearly resembles muscle than organ meat and so may be used in many recipes calling for ground meat. An especially good way to prepare heart is to stuff it with a savory dressing. Before cooking, wash it well, removing fat, arteries, veins and blood and dry carefully. A 4- to 5-lb. beef heart will serve 6, a veal heart will serve 1.

BAKED STUFFED HEART

3 Servings

♦ Please read About Heart, above.
Preheat oven to 325°.
Prepare:

A small beef heart or 3 veal hearts

Tie with a string to hold its shape if necessary. Place on a rack in an ovenproof dish and pour over it:

2 cups stock or diluted tomato soup

Place over the heart:

4 slices bacon

Cover the dish closely and bake until tender—if beef, a matter of 3 to 4 hours, if veal, about 2 hours. Remove the heart to a plate and cool it slightly. Heat in a double boiler, then fill the heart cavity with:

Apple and Onion Dressing,
page 458, or Olive and Celery
Dressing, page 457

You will need about 1 cup for a veal heart, about 3 cups for a beef heart. ♦ To allow for expansion, do not pack the dressing tightly. Sprinkle the heart with:

Paprika

Return it to a 400° oven long enough to heat quickly before serving. The drippings may be thickened with:

Flour, see Pan Gravy, page 322

HEART EN PAPILLOTE

3 Servings

Preheat oven to 400°.
Prepare:

Baked Stuffed Heart, this page

using a small beef heart. Before cooking wrap it in greased parchment paper, as shown on page 129. Put the wrapped heart on a rack in the oven. ♦ Reduce the heat at once to 300° and continue to bake for 2½ to 3 hours. About 15 minutes before serving, remove the paper and discard it. Baste the heart for about 10 minutes, allowing it to glaze in the drippings. Thicken the drippings with:

Flour, see Pan Gravy, page 322

and serve.

BRAISED HEART SLICES
IN SOUR SAUCE

6 Servings

A homey treat.
♦ Please read About Heart, this page.
Prepare:

A 4 to 5 lb. beef heart or
6 veal hearts

If veal, you may halve the heart, if beef, cut it across the fiber into ¼-inch slices. Pour into a saucepan or ovenproof dish to the depth of ¾ inch:

Boiling water

Add:

¼ cup diced carrots
¼ cup chopped celery with leaves
¼ cup sliced onion
½ teaspoon salt
(¼ cup diced green pepper)

Place the heart slices on a rack in the pan, well above the water. Cover closely. Steam the meat until tender for about 1½ hours. Strain the stock. Chill and degrease it. Save the fat. Reserve the stock. Melt:

3 tablespoons butter or fat from
the stock

Stir in:

3 tablespoons flour

Then add:

1½ cups stock

When it reaches a boil, add the meat and

vegetables and ♦ reduce the heat. You may add:

>**2 tablespoons lemon juice or dry wine**
>**½ teaspoon sweet marjoram or**
>**2 tablespoons chopped parsley**
>**or olives**
>**Correct the seasoning**

Good with Spoon Bread, page 580, rice or Potato Dumplings, page 192.

ABOUT TRIPE

If you start from scratch, cooking tripe is a long-drawn-out affair—as you will see by the following description. But today you will find almost everywhere that you can buy it partially precooked, so that your job is just the final seasoning and heating. Using the following recipes, you need only cook it about ½ hour, as in Spanish Tripe.

Tripe is the muscular lining of beef stomach. There are 4 kinds, all of which, as you will note, are used in at least one classic recipe. The fat part of the belly, called in France "gras double," usually comes already cooked. Then there are 3 different sections of honeycomb tripe which comes from the second stomach of beef—the extremity of the belly, which is only partially honeycombed, the dark and the light.

Fresh whole tripe calls for a minimum of 12 hours of cooking, some time-honored recipes demanding as much as 24. Sometimes tripe is pickled after cooking and served hot or cold in a marinade.

♦ To prepare fresh tripe, trim if necessary. ♦ Wash it thoroughly, soaking overnight, and blanch it, page 132, for ½ hour in salted water. Wash well again, drain and cut for cooking. When cooked, the texture of tripe should be like that of soft gristle. More often, alas, because the heat has not been kept low enough, it has the consistency of wet shoe leather.

COOKED TRIPE

                                   4 to 5 Servings
♦ Please read About Tripe, above.
Trim, wash, soak, blanch, wash again and drain:

>**2 lbs. fresh honeycomb tripe**

Cut it into 1½- to 2-inch squares. Have ready a heavy pot that you can lid tightly later. Add to:

>**Enough water to cover**
>**¼ teaspoon salt**
>**¼ teaspoon sugar**
>**1 clove garlic**
>**⅔ cup chopped onion**
>**1 cup chopped mixed celery**
>**and parsley**
>**4 peppercorns**

Bring to a boil and add the tripe. ♦ Reduce the heat at once. Seal the lid with a strip of pastry or tape, page 588, and simmer for 12 hours. When the tripe is tender, you may serve it with:

>**Pan Gravy, page 322**

seasoned with:

>**Salt**
>**½ teaspoon mustard**
>**1 teaspoon Worcestershire sauce**

TRIPE A LA MODE DE CAEN

                                        8 Servings
This famous Normandy dish demands a deep earthenware casserole and the inclusion of all 4 types of beef tripe.
♦ Please read About Tripe, this page.
Preheat oven to 250°.
Trim, wash, soak, blanch, wash again, drain and cut into 1½-inch squares:

>**3 lbs. fresh tripe**

Wash and blanch:

>**A split calf's foot**

Peel and slice:

>**2 lbs. onions**

Dice:

>**¼ lb. beef suet**

Line the bottom of the casserole with a layer of onions, then a layer of tripe and a sprinkling of the beef suet. Continue to build successive layers, topping with the split calf's foot and:

>**An onion stuck with 3 cloves**
>**A bay leaf**
>**A Bouquet Garni, page 541**

Pour over this:

>**¼ cup brandy**

or, if you can get it:

>**¼ cup Calvados**

and enough:

>**Cider or water**

to cover all the ingredients. Bring just to a boil. Seal the casserole with a strip of Pastry Dough, page 588. Bake in the oven at least 12 hours. When ready to serve, break the seal on the casserole, remove the bouquet garni, the bay leaf and the whole onion. Degrease the sauce and pick the meat from the calf's foot. Return the meat to the casserole to heat through and serve the tripe in individual hot covered casseroles, garnished with:

>**Boiled parsley potatoes**

FRIED TRIPE

♦ Please read About Tripe, this page.
Cut into squares or strips:

>**Cooked Tripe, this page, or**
>**precooked tripe**

Sprinkle with:

>**Salt and paprika**

Dip it into:

>**Fritter Batter for Meat, page 221**

Fry in deep fat, pages 124-126. Serve with:

>**Tartare Sauce, page 316**

SPANISH TRIPE

♦ Please read About Tripe, this page.
Wash partially precooked:

>**Tripe**

Follow the directions for Cooked Tripe, this page, and add to the vegetables:

>**1 cup more or less tomato puree**

A few grains cayenne
1 teaspoon Worcestershire sauce
Simmer at least ½ hour and add for the
last 15 minutes:
    ½ cup cooked minced ham
    ½ cup sliced mushrooms
Good served with:
    Boiled Rice, page 178

LAMB FRIES
                                         2 Servings
Skin, cut into quarters:
    4 medium lamb fries
You may marinate them for about 1 hour
in:
    (¼ cup olive oil)
    (2 tablespoons lemon juice)
If you marinated them, dry them before
rolling them in:
    Bound Breading, page 502
Sauté until golden brown in:
    ¼ cup butter
Garnish with:
    Fried Parsley, page 287
and serve with:
    Tomato sauce

CALF OR LAMB HEAD
            4 Servings for a Calf Head—
            2 Servings for Lamb
It is always so easy to say, "Let the butcher
prepare, etc." In this case, it is assumed
that the head is skinned and the eyes removed. The head is split the long way, so
the brains can be removed. We prefer to
cook the Brains, page 443, and the Tongue,
page 446, separately. Scrape away any
clots. Soak overnight in salted cold water
to cover:
    1 calf or lamb head
Wash again in cold water. You may dry
the head and brown it in butter or put
in a large kettle and bring to a boil:
    Enough water to cover the head
with:
    1 carrot
    1 onion
    ½ sliced lemon
    1 bay leaf
    4 cloves
    1 tablespoon salt
    ¼ teaspoon pepper
In actuality you may also add, to keep the
bones white:
    (½ cup veal kidney fat or suet)
When this reaches a boil, add the head.
♦ Reduce the heat at once and simmer uncovered until the meat is tender, about 1
hour for lamb, about 2 hours for calf. If
you have included the tongue, it may take
a little longer. When the meat is tender,
drain and remove it from the bones and
dice it. Keep the meat warm. Skin, trim
and slice the tongue. Meanwhile prepare
a double portion of:
    Rosemary Wine Sauce, page 328
using as stock the liquid in which the calf
head was cooked.
    Correct the seasoning

You may want to spice the sauce with:
    Mild white wine vinegar, lemon
    juice or wine
Reheat the meat, the tongue and the
cooked brains in the sauce. ♦ Do not boil.
Serve this dish garnished with:
    Chopped parsley
It is sometimes served with the addition at
the last moment of:
    ½ cup scalded cream
Or part of the sauce is drained off into:
    2 beaten egg yolks
Return this mixture to the pot. Heat, but
do not boil, the sauce after adding the
yolks. But ♦ if you add cream or egg yolks,
to avoid curdling do not add lemon, vinegar or wine until the last moment.

HEAD CHEESE OR BRAWN
                                         4 Servings
A well-liked old-fashioned dish.
Quarter:
    A calf head
Clean teeth with a stiff brush, remove
ears, brains, eyes, snout and most of the
fat. Soak the quarters about 6 hours in
cold water to extract the blood. Wash
them. Cover with cold water, to which
you may add:
    2 onions
    5 celery stalks
Simmer until the meat is ready to fall from
the bones, about 2 to 3 hours. Drain but
reserve stock. Chip the meat off the bones.
Dice it. Cover it well with the stock. Reserve the brains. Now add:
    Salt
    Pepper
    Herbs
Cook for ½ hour. Pour into a mold and
cover with a cloth. Put a weight on top.
Chill. Serve, cut into slices, with:
    Vinaigrette Sauce, page 311
to which you have added the diced cooked
brains.

CALF LUNGS OR LIGHTS
                                         6 Servings
Cut into julienne strips, wash well and
simmer in stock until just tender, about 1½
hours:
    3 lbs. calf lungs
Remove lungs and keep warm. Reduce the
stock by ½, adding:
    A Bouquet Garni, page 541, of
    bayleaf, thyme and lemon rind
Brown in a heavy skillet:
    ½ cup flour
    1 teaspoon sugar
Add:
    ½ cup butter
Stir until smooth and add:
    ½ cup finely minced onion
Strain the reduced stock and add it gradu-
ally to the flour mixture. Cook and stir
until thickened. Add:
    1 tablespoon anchovy paste
Preheat oven to 325°.

Put the cooked lungs in a casserole. Cover with the sauce. Cover the whole tightly with a lid. Bake for about ½ hour. Before serving

Correct the seasoning

and stir in gently:

1 cup cream or cultured sour cream
1 tablespoon capers

Continue to bake until cream is heated through.

CHITTERLINGS

6 to 7 Servings

We were well along in years before we discovered that the name of this dish had an "e," an "r," a "g"—and 3 syllables. Just after slaughtering, empty the large intestines of a young pig while still warm by turning them inside out and scraping as clean as possible. Soak 24 hours in cold salted water to cover. Then wash in 5 or 6 waters. Remove excess fat, but leave some for flavor. To:

10 lbs. chitterlings

allow:

1 garlic clove
½ sliced lemon
½ teaspoon salt
½ teaspoon pepper
½ teaspoon each thyme, clove, mace
and allspice
1 bay leaf
¼ cup sliced onions
(3 red pepper pods)
2 tablespoons fresh parsley
2 tablespoons white wine vinegar
Enough cold water to cover

Add:

Chitterlings, cut up in 2-inch lengths

Bring slowly to a boil. ♦ Reduce the heat at once and simmer for about 3 hours. During the last 30 minutes of cooking, you may add:

(¼ cup tomato catsup)
Correct the seasoning

and serve with:

Corn Bread, page 578
Cole Slaw, page 80

SAUTÉED CHITTERLINGS

Prepare previous recipe for:

Chitterlings

omitting the vinegar and catsup. Drain and dry well. Dip in:

Seasoned flour

Sauté them gently in:

Butter

until a delicate brown.

STEWED PIGS' FEET

4 Servings

Wash, leave whole or split in halves and blanch, page 132:

4 pigs' or calves' feet

You may wrap them in cheesecloth to retain their shape. Cover them with water. Bring just to a boil. ♦ Reduce the heat at

once and simmer for about 4 hours uncovered. During the last 30 minutes of simmering, add:

1½ to 2 lbs. green beans, cabbage or
sauerkraut

Cook the vegetables until they are tender.

Correct the seasoning

and serve hot.

JELLIED PIGS' OR CALVES' FEET

6 Servings

Wash, leave whole or split in halves and blanch, page 132:

6 pigs' or calves' feet

You may wrap them in cheesecloth to retain their shape. Cover them with water. Add:

1 large sliced onion
1 cut clove garlic
1 sliced lemon
2 bay leaves
3 or 4 whole black peppercorns
6 or 8 whole cloves

Bring this mixture to the boiling point. ♦ Reduce the heat and simmer uncovered for about 4 hours. Add boiling water, if needed. Strain the stock through a sieve and reserve it. Remove the skin and the bones from the pigs' feet. Place the meat in the stock. Season to taste with:

White vinegar or dry wine

and

Correct the seasoning

Chop and add:

(1 pimiento, decorative but optional)

Pour the pigs' or calves' feet into a mold and chill until the stock is firm.

BAKED PIGS' FEET

Prepare:

Stewed Pigs' Feet, above

Preheat oven to 375°.

Cut the pig's feet in two, lengthwise. Roll them in:

Melted butter

then in:

Corn meal or cracker crumbs

Bake them about 20 to 30 minutes or until tender. Serve with:

Sweet-sour Beets, page 264, or
lemon wedges

BRAISED OXTAILS

5 to 6 Servings

Preheat oven to 350°.

Cut into joints:

2 oxtails

Melt in a skillet:

¼ cup butter or beef drippings

Sauté the oxtail sections until they are browned. Season them with:

Salt and paprika

Add:

2 cups boiling Brown Stock I, page
490, or tomato juice

Bring these ingredients to the boiling point. Place them in a casserole. Cover it closely. Bake until the oxtails are tender, 3 to 5 hours. Add additional stock, as needed. For the last 45 minutes of cooking, add:

8 small peeled onions
½ cup diced celery
¼ cup peeled diced carrots

When the oxtails are tender, strain the stock from them. Skim off most of the fat. Thicken the stock with:

Flour, see Pan Gravy, page 322
Correct the seasoning

Return the meat, the vegetables and the gravy to the casserole. Serve with a platter of:

Noodles, page 188

Cover the noodles with:

Au Gratin II, page 342

VARIETY MEAT PATTIES

4 Servings

◗ Please read About Kidneys, page 443, About Liver, page 439, or About Brains, page 443. Prepare one of the following for cooking and then chop until fine:

2 pairs steamed brains, ½ lb. raw liver
or 1 beef, 2 pork or veal or
5 lamb kidneys

Sprinkle them with:

1 tablespoon lemon juice

Rub a skillet with:

Garlic

Heat in it:

2 tablespoons butter

Sauté in this lightly:

1 chopped onion or leek
½ cup minced celery
2 tablespoons minced green pepper

Remove from heat. Add the chopped variety meat and:

¼ cup dry bread crumbs
¼ cup milk
1 egg
¼ teaspoon salt
¼ teaspoon freshly ground pepper
4 drops Worcestershire sauce
(¼ teaspoon caraway or dill seed)

Drop this mixture by the tablespoon into a hot pan, in which you have:

2 tablespoons hot bacon drippings

Brown the patties lightly on both sides. Serve them with:

Tomato sauce, slaw or
Vegetables à la Grecque, page 255

CHICKEN GIBLETS

Dice, put in boiling water or stock, then ◗ reduce the heat at once and simmer until tender, about 1 hour:

Chicken giblets: gizzards and hearts

You may add, for the last 15 minutes of cooking:

Chopped green pepper

Chopped celery

Drain these ingredients, reserving the stock. Make:

Gravy, page 322

using:

2 tablespoons butter
2 tablespoons flour to 1 cup stock or
stock and dry wine
Correct the seasoning

Add the giblets and vegetables and simmer ◗ but do not boil. Serve on:

Toast

COCKSCOMBS

These have been used since the time of Apicius as a garnish.
Blanch:

Cockscombs

Peel off the outer skin. ◗ Steam, covered, on a:

Mirepoix, page 541

moistened with:

1 cup Mushroom Stock, page 492

until tender, about 45 to 50 minutes.
Preheat deep fryer to 375°.
Drain well, cut an incision and stuff with:

Duxelles, page page 540, or Chicken Farce, page 458

Cover with:

Allemande Sauce, page 324

Dip in crumbs and deep-fat fry till crumbs color.

ABOUT MARROW

Spinal marrow, which is really a continuation of the brain, may be substituted in any of the recipes for brains. Bone marrow may be removed from split large bones. ◗ It must not be overcooked, as it is very fat and simply disintegrates under too high heat. Bone marrow may be cut into ½-inch slices and softened in the top of a double boiler or gently and briefly poached in a little stock, for about 1½ to 2 minutes. You may serve it this way for hors d'oeuvre. It may also be gently poached in the bone in water barely to cover or roasted in a 300° oven for about 1 hour. See also Marrow Balls, page 176, for soup and Osso Buco, page 421.

MARROW

I. Cut into ¼-inch rounds:

Marrow

Poach it gently in:

Stock, page 490

for a few minutes. Drain and serve at once on:

Toast rounds

II. Or use raw in a:

Sauce Bordelaise, page 326

GAME

ABOUT SMALL GAME

Small game such as rabbit, squirrel and muskrat may be substituted in most recipes calling for chicken. But following are some classic, and not so classic, recipes which take the special characteristics of these small animals into account. If you are a novice, the most important things to remember is ♦ never handle rabbit or any wild meat without using gloves, because of the danger of tularemia infection. ♦ Always make sure the meat of wild animals is sufficiently cooked. Be guided in your choice of recipe by the age of the animal. ♦ Use a moist heat process, page 127, for older animals.

ABOUT RABBITS AND HARES

When rabbit or hare is young and fresh, the cleft in the lip is narrow, the claws smooth and sharp. Test for the youth of the animal, also, by turning the claws sideways to see if they crack. The ears should be soft and bend easily. A young hare has a stumpy neck and long legs. To ensure tender meat, hang the animals by the feet from 1 to 4 days. They will, however, be tender without hanging if used before they have time to stiffen. Once stiffened, they are edible as long as the hind legs are rigid. Some of the most delicious game sauces use blood as a thickener. To trap and preserve the blood, see page 752. To incorporate it in a sauce, see page 321. Hares may weigh up to 10 to 14 pounds. European hare is all dark meat, while American domestic hare is all white.

♦ To dress rabbit or hare, sever the front legs at the joint, as shown opposite on the dotted line. Cut through the skin around the hind legs, as shown again by a dotted line. Tie the feet together securely. Hang the rabbit on a hook where tied. Pull the skin down off the legs, stripping it inside out like a glove, and over the body and forelegs. Sever the head and discard it with the skin. Slit the rabbit down the front. Remove the entrails and discard them, except for the heart and liver. Wash the carcass inside and out with acidulated water—water to which 1 or 2 tablespoons of vinegar are added. Rinse and dry carefully.

RABBIT OR HARE À LA MODE, HASENPFEFFER OR CIVET
Skin:
A rabbit

Cut into pieces by severing the legs at the joints and cutting the back in 3 sections. Place the pieces in a crock or jar. Marinate refrigerated for 24 to 48 hours in:
Cooked Marinade for Game, Page 337
Drain and reserve the marinade. Dry the pieces of rabbit. Dip them in:
Flour
Brown until golden in:
3 tablespoons bacon drippings
Remove the browned rabbit to an ovenproof casserole.
Preheat oven to 350°.
Sauté in the pan the rabbit was browned in:
1 cup finely sliced onions
2 tablespoons butter
Add the sauté to the casserole with the warmed marinade and bring to a boil on top of the stove. ♦ Cover and remove to oven for about 1½ hours or until tender. Correct the seasoning. Place rabbit on a serving dish. Pour sauce over it. Serve with:
Noodles, page 188

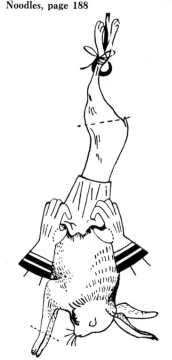

SAUTÉED RABBIT

If rabbit is very young, prepare as for:
Sautéed Chicken, page 466
Serve with:
Elderberry preserves

SMOTHERED RABBIT OR HARE WITH ONIONS

Skin, clean and cut into pieces:
A rabbit
Dredge with:
Seasoned flour
Melt in a pot or skillet:
3 tablespoons drippings or butter
Sauté the rabbit in the drippings until browned. Cover thickly with:
Sliced onions
Pour over them:
1 cup cultured sour cream
Cover the pot closely and simmer for 1 hour or place the pot in a slow oven—300°—and bake the rabbit until tender, 1 hour or more.

ROAST RABBIT OR HARE

Preheat oven to 450°.
Skin and clean:
A rabbit or hare
Stuff it with any recipe suitable for fowl, using the sautéed chopped liver. Close the opening and truss it. Brush the rabbit all over with:
Melted butter or cooking oil
Dredge with:
Seasoned flour
Place on a rack on its side in a roasting pan in the oven. ♦ Reduce the heat to 350°. Baste every 15 minutes with the drippings in the pan or, if necessary, with:
(Additional butter)
Turn the rabbit when cooking time is about ½ over. Cook until tender, about 1½ hours. Make:
Pan Gravy, page 322

FRICASSEE OF RABBIT OR HARE

Skin, clean and cut into pieces:
A rabbit
Dredge with:
Seasoned flour

Melt in a skillet:
¼ cup butter
or you may use:
(¼ lb. diced, lightly rendered salt pork—a wonderful substitution)
Add:
¼ cup chopped shallots or onions
(1 cup cut-up mushrooms)
Remove the shallots and mushrooms before sautéing the meat in the drippings until lightly browned. To flambé the rabbit pour over it:
(2 oz. brandy)
Add:
1½ cups stock or dry wine
and, in a cloth bag:
A piece of lemon rind
10 peppercorns
2 sprigs parsley
2 ribs celery with leaves
Cover the pot closely. Simmer the meat until done, 1 hour or more, or put it in a 300° oven covered for about 2 hours—but do not let it boil at any time. Ten minutes before you remove the rabbit from the pot, take out the seasoning bag and add the mushrooms and shallots. Place the rabbit on a hot serving dish. Remove the sauce from the heat and thicken with:
Beurre Manié, page 321

ABOUT SQUIRREL

Gray squirrels are the preferred ones; red squirrels are small and quite gamey in flavor. There are, proverbially, many ways to skin a squirrel, but some hunters claim the following one is the quickest and cleanest. It needs a sharp knife.

♦ To skin, cut the tail bone through from beneath, but take care not to cut through the skin of the tail. Hold the tail as shown on the left and then cut the skin the width of the back, as shown in the dotted lines. Turn the squirrel over on its back and step on the base of the tail. Hold the hind legs in one hand and pull steadily and slowly, as shown in the center sketch, until the skin has worked itself over the front legs and head. While holding the squirrel in the same position, pull the re-

maining skin from the hind legs. Proceed then as for Rabbit, page 452, cutting off the head and the feet and removing the internal organs, plus two small glands found in the small of the back and under each foreleg, between the ribs and the shoulders.

Stuff and roast squirrels as for Pigeons, page 475, barding them, or use them in Brunswick Stew, page 470, or prepare as for Braised Chicken, page 467. Season the gravy with:

Walnut catsup

and serve with:

Polenta, page 177

OPOSSUM

If possible, trap 'possum and feed it on milk and cereals for 10 days before killing. Clean, but do not skin. Treat as for pig by immersing the unskinned animal in water just below the boiling point. Test frequently by plucking at the hair. When it slips out readily, remove the possum from the water and scrape. While scraping repeatedly, pour cool water over the surface of the animal. Remove small red glands in small of back and under each foreleg between the shoulder and rib. Parboil, page 132, 1 hour. Roast as for pork, page 407. Serve with:

Turnip greens

BEAR

Remove all fat from bear meat at once, as it turns rancid very quickly.

If marinated at least 24 hours in an oil-based marinade, all bear, except black bear, is edible. Cook, after marination, as for any recipe for Beef Pot Roast or Stew, pages 412-420. Bear cub will need about 2½ hours cooking; for an older animal, allow 3½ to 4 hours. Bear, like pork, can carry trichinosis, so be sure the meat is always well cooked through.

RACCOON

Skin, clean and soak overnight:

1 raccoon

in:

Salt water

Scrape off all fat inside and out. Blanch, page 132, for 45 minutes. Add:

2 tablespoons baking soda

and continue to cook uncovered for 5 minutes. Drain and wash in warm water. Put in cold water and bring to a boil. ♦ Reduce heat and simmer 15 minutes. Preheat oven to 350°. Stuff the raccoon with:

Bread Dressing, page 456

Bake covered, about 45 minutes ♦ uncover and bake 15 minutes longer before serving.

MUSKRAT

2 Servings

Skin and remove all fat from hams of:

6 muskrats

Poach, page 129, for 45 minutes. Sauté until golden:

½ cup minced onions

in:

2 tablespoons butter

Add the drained, dried muskrat hams and cook until brown. Serve with:

Creamed Celery, page 271

WOODCHUCK

Dress woodchuck as for rabbit, but watch for and remove 7 to 9 small sacs or kernels in the small of the back and under the forearm. Soak overnight in salted water. Drain and wipe dry. Cook by any recipe for rabbit or chicken.

BEAVER

Use young animals only.

Remove kernels in small of back and under forelegs, between rib and shoulder. Hang in the cold for several days. Poach in salted water for 1 hour. Braise as for beef, page 412, until tender.

BEAVER TAIL

Hold over open flame until rough skin blisters. Remove from heat. When cool, peel off skin. Roast over coals or simmer until tender.

PECCARY

Immediately after killing, remove the musk glands in the middle of the back. This meat needs marinating before cooking. After this, you may prepare it as in any pork recipe in the section on Pot Roasts and Stews, page 412.

WILD BOAR

If very young, prepare as for:

Suckling Pig, page 407

If older, prepare by a moist heat process for:

Pork, page 425

ABOUT VENISON

This romantic word can cover any of the edible animals taken in the chase, but we are discussing here only antlered types. A famous sportsman called venison a gift of joy to some, a matter of secret interment to others.

Today, when hunters are so aware of the need to treat their booty with care from the moment it is shot, joy can prevail. No matter what the method of handling, certain preparations are basic. Game shot in an unsuspecting moment is more tender than game that is chased and will also deteriorate less quickly. Avoid buying any trapped animals for food. Immediate and careful gutting, page 752, immediate removal of all hair near exposed flesh and prompt skinning are essential.

Some authorities recommend only a week of hanging, some as long as 4 weeks in 40° temperature in a cool, airy place, away from sun, screened against insects and protected from predators. Venison is lean and needs barding, page 384, or larding, page 383.

♦ Care must be taken, though, to remove all fat from any of these game animals themselves, as it grows rancid rapidly. ♦ Do not use it to grease pans or for sautéing or browning. The livers and heart are often eaten and should be marinated under refrigeration or soaked in salt water for 12 hours or longer. As with all game, the lushness of the season and the age of the animal contribute to the decision as to how to cook it.

Moose meat, which is relatively fat, calls for cooking like pork and can also have the same sweet and sweet-sour garnishes and sauces. Elk is more like beef than any other game. Calf elk sours rapidly. Cook it as for veal.

The choice cuts of very young deer or goat and fat old bucks can be roasted or broiled as for beef. Other cuts should be marinated, drained, dried and prepared as for any moist-processed beef, see pages 413-416.

For sauces for game, see page 327. Cabbage, turnips, chestnuts and mushrooms are often suggested as classic game accompaniments, as are brandied fruits.

SADDLE OF DEER, MOOSE OR ELK
8 Servings

Preheat oven to 550°.
Lard, page 383:
    A 6 to 7 lb. saddle of venison
Rub it with:
    A cut clove of garlic
    Butter
Place the roast, fat side up, uncovered on a rack in the oven. ♦ Reduce the heat to 350° and cook, allowing in all 20 minutes to the pound. Make:
    Pan Gravy, page 322
Serve with:
    Hot Cumberland Sauce, page 331
    Wild Rice, page 179

ROAST LEG OF VENISON
Bard the roast. Cook as for Beef Roast, page 384.

VENISON STEAKS
I. Have ready:
    ½-inch young venison steaks
Before frying, rub with:
    Garlic
To keep them crisp and brown on the outside, rare and juicy within, sauté them, page 126, in:
    1 tablespoon butter
    2 tablespoons cooking oil
5 to 6 minutes to the side. Serve with:
    Hot Cumberland Sauce, page 331
or with:
    Maître d'Hôtel Butter, page 339
or with:
    Puréed celery with croutons and
    Sauce Poivrade, page 328

II. Soak for 24 hours refrigerated:
    ¾-inch venison steaks
in:
    Lamb or Game Marinade, page 337
Drain and dry. Sauté and serve as for Venison Steaks I, above.

BRAISED VENISON
For this process, use the less tender cuts of meat either in 1 large piece or cut into small ones, but be sure to remove all fat. Place the meat in a marinade, page 337, from 12 to 48 hours in the refrigerator. Turn it from time to time. Dry it. Prepare as for Pot Roast, page 412. If you have marinated, use the marinade in the stock. Cook until tender—depending on the age of the animal.

VENISON HAMBURGER
To make this lean meat more interesting in ground form, combine:
    2 parts ground venison
with:
    1 part fresh sausage meat
Cook as for Hamburger, page 426, but allow extra time ♦ to be sure the meat is no longer pink.

VENISON MEAT LOAF
Prepare:
    Meat Loaf I, page 431
using:
    ¾ lb. ground venison
    ¼ lb. ground sausage

STUFFINGS, DRESSINGS, FARCES OR FORCEMEAT

When you get that desperate feeling that you simply must find a new species of meat—try instead combining meats or variety meats with some unusual dressing or farce. Don't save stuffings just for heavy festive meals; make them part of your daily fare.

Many foreign and old-fashioned stuffing recipes call for bread soaked in a liquid and then pressed before using. We find that most American bakery breads are already so soft in texture that soaking produces too pasty a dressing.

The quality of the crumbs is very important, so check page 501 to differentiate between fresh or dry. ◗ Never grind bread, as the stuffing will be too compact. It is important ◗ to stuff food just before cooking; ◗ to handle stuffings lightly so as not to compact them; and ◗ to allow space when stuffing, so the mixture can swell and stay light. Should there be extra dressing that does not fit the cavity of fish, fowl or roast, cook it separately in a greased baking dish.

A useful rule of thumb in judging the amount of stuffing needed is ◗ to allow ½ cup of stuffing for each pound of bird or fish.

◗ Never use raw pork in dressings. Dressings are done when they reach an internal temperature of 165° to 170°.

For stuffings for vegetables, see individual stuffed vegetable recipes and page 255.

BREAD DRESSING WITH MUSHROOMS, OYSTERS, NUTS, GIBLETS, ETC.

About 5 Cups

There is no set rule for the proportions of ingredients in bread dressing. It should be palatable, light and slightly moist, well flavored but bland. Chopped green peppers, nut meats, sautéed mushrooms and drained or slightly sautéed oysters may be added to it. Stock or oyster liquor may be substituted for milk.

Chop:
 Giblets
Melt:
 ¼ cup butter
Add and sauté for about 2 minutes:
 (2 tablespoons or more chopped onion)
and the chopped giblets. Combine these ingredients with:
 4 cups crustless day-old or slightly toasted, diced white, whole wheat or corn bread crumbs
 ¼ cup chopped parsley

 ¼ to 1 cup chopped celery
 1 teaspoon dried tarragon or basil
 ¾ teaspoon salt
 ½ teaspoon paprika
 ⅛ teaspoon nutmeg
 Milk, stock or melted butter to moisten the dressing very lightly
 (2 or 3 eggs)
You may add:
 1½ cups nut meats: Brazil, pine, pecans, walnuts
and one of the following:
 1 cup browned sausage meat
 1 cup or more sliced mushrooms, sautéed with onion
 1 cup chopped or whole drained oysters
 1 cup chopped or whole soft-shell clams
 1 cup cooked chopped shrimp

DRY DRESSING

This name is given by our cook, Sarah Brown, to a dressing she frequently makes, which is by no means dry when served. Proportions seem to be of little importance here, as the ingredients are never measured and the dressing always turns out light and good. Chopped pecans, oysters, olives, etc., may be added to it.
Make of day-old white, graham or whole wheat bread:
 Soft bread crumbs, as sketched on page 501
Combine with:
 Chopped celery
 Chopped onion
Season with:
 Salt and paprika
Partly fill chicken, quail or turkey with the dressing. Melt:
 ¾ to 1 cup butter
Pour ½ of it onto the dressing in the cavity. Fill it lightly with the remaining dressing and pour the remaining butter on it. Sew up the opening.

SHERRY BREAD DRESSING

1½ Cups

Soak for 10 minutes:
 1 cup bread crumbs
in:
 ½ cup dry sherry
Wring the wine from the bread. Stir and sauté for 3 minutes:
 ¼ cup finely chopped green pepper
 ½ cup finely chopped onion
in:
 3 tablespoons butter
Add the bread crumbs and:
 2 teaspoons chili sauce

½ cup canned or Sautéed Mushrooms,
    page 281
2 tablespoons chopped parsley

OYSTER BREAD DRESSING

2½ Cups

Enough for a 4 lb. fish or the crop of a
turkey.
Melt:
    6 tablespoons butter
Sauté in the butter until brown:
    ¼ cup chopped onion
Add:
    1 tablespoon chopped parsley
    2 cups bread crumbs
    1 cup drained whole or chopped
        oysters: ½ pint
    ¾ teaspoon salt
    ¼ teaspoon paprika
    2 tablespoons capers
    (½ cup drained chopped spinach)

BREAD DRESSING FOR FISH

2 Cups

A fine but plain, unsophisticated dressing.
Combine:
    1½ cups bread crumbs
    2 tablespoons chopped onion
    ½ cup chopped celery
    2 tablespoons chopped parsley
    1 or 2 beaten eggs
Season these ingredients well with:
    ½ teaspoon salt
    ⅛ teaspoon paprika
    ½ teaspoon dried tarragon or dill seed
    2 tablespoons capers
    (¼ teaspoon nutmeg)
Use enough:
    Milk, melted butter or soup stock
to make a loose dressing.

GREEN DRESSING FOR FISH
OR FOWL

About 1½ Cups

This has a tempting pistachio green color.
Sauté until transparent:
    2 tablespoons chopped shallots
in:
    2 tablespoons butter
Cool slightly. Place this in a blender and
⅃ blend to a paste with:
    1 egg
    ½ cup tender celery with leaves
    ½ cup parsley tops
    ¼ cup water cress tops
    ½ cup crumbled crustless bread
    ½ teaspoon salt
    ⅛ teaspoon dried basil
Blend in with a fork:
    ½ cup pulled crustless bread crumbs,
        page 501
    ¼ cup pistachio nuts or sliced
        water chestnuts

SAUSAGE DRESSING

About 2½ Cups

Heat and stir in a skillet:
    ½ cup sausage meat
Drain off the surplus fat. Add:

½ cup chopped celery
2 cups cracker crumbs
¼ teaspoon minced onion
¼ teaspoon salt
⅛ teaspoon paprika
(½ cup chopped tart apples)
Moisten the dressing with:
    ½ cup stock

CHESTNUT DRESSING FOR GAME

About 4 Cups

Rice:
    2½ cups cooked chestnuts, page 272
Combine them with:
    ½ cup melted butter
    1 teaspoon salt
    ⅛ teaspoon pepper
    ¼ cup cream
    1 cup dry bread or cracker crumbs
    2 tablespoons chopped parsley
    ½ cup chopped celery
    (1 tablespoon grated onion or
        ¼ cup seedless raisins)
You may add, but remember this will in-
crease the amount:
    ½ cup liver sausage, ¼ cup chopped
        Chipolata sausage or 2 cups raw
        or creamed oysters

ONION DRESSING

About 4 Cups

Prepare:
    2 cups chopped onions
Drop them in:
    4 cups boiling salted water
Simmer for 10 minutes. Drain. Mix **the**
onions and:
    3 cups dry bread crumbs
    1 beaten egg
    ½ cup melted butter
    ¾ teaspoon salt
    ⅛ teaspoon paprika
    ½ teaspoon poultry seasoning
    (1 cup chopped tart apple or ½ cup
        sliced olives)
Moisten the mixture slightly with:
    Stock

FENNEL DRESSING

About 1 Cup

Brown:
    1 cup bread crumbs
in:
    1 tablespoon butter
    1 teaspoon Meat Glaze, page 492
Cut into julienned strips:
    1 carrot
    1 white base of leek
    2 stalks celery
Add the above to the butter mixture. Add:
    2 drops garlic juice
and simmer until coated. Add:
    A sprig of chopped fresh fennel
    1 small pinch thyme and bay leaf
    ¼ teaspoon salt
Mix with the crumbs:
    Freshly ground pepper

APPLE AND PRUNE DRESSING
About 4½ Cups

Combine lightly:
    3 cups diced crustless bread
    ½ cup melted butter or drippings
    1 cup cubed apples
    ¾ cup chopped cooked prunes
    ⅓ cup chopped nut meats
    1 teaspoon salt
    ½ teaspoon paprika
    1 tablespoon lemon juice

APPLE AND ONION DRESSING
About 12 Cups

Place in boiling water for 5 minutes:
    1 cup raisins
Drain well. Add them to:
    7 cups soft bread crumbs
Melt:
    ¾ cup butter
Sauté in it for 3 minutes:
    1 cup chopped onion
    1 chopped clove garlic
    1 cup chopped celery
Add these ingredients to the bread crumbs with:
    3 cups tart diced apples
    ¼ cup finely chopped parsley
    1½ teaspoons salt
    ¼ teaspoon paprika

HAM DRESSING FOR TURKEY
About 7 Cups

Combine:
    1 to 1½ cups ground cooked ham
    4 cups soft bread crumbs, page 501
    1 cup crushed pineapple
    1 cup plumped white raisins
    1 cup walnuts
    ¼ to ½ cup honey

LIVER DRESSING
About 4 Cups

Chop:
    ½ lb. calf or baby beef liver
Sauté it lightly in:
    1½ tablespoons butter
    (1 tablespoon grated onion)
Combine these ingredients with:
    2 cups soft bread crumbs
    ¾ cup chopped nut meats
    2 beaten eggs
    ½ cup rich milk or cream and stock
    1 teaspoon salt
    ½ teaspoon paprika
    1½ tablespoons mixed minced chives
        and parsley
    1 teaspoon chopped fresh tarragon
    ½ teaspoon lemon juice
    (2 tablespoons dry sherry)

RICE DRESSING
About 5 Cups

Mince:
    6 slices bacon
Sauté lightly for 5 minutes with:
    3 tablespoons chopped onion
Pour off all but 2 tablespoons of the fat.
Combine the contents of the skillet with:

    4 cups cooked rice
    1 cup dry bread crumbs, page 501
    1 cup chopped celery
    ¾ teaspoon salt
    ¼ teaspoon pepper
    ⅛ teaspoon sage or nutmeg
    ½ cup milk
    ½ cup cream

WILD RICE DRESSING FOR GAME
About 3 Cups

Chop:
    Giblets
Bring to the boiling point:
    4 cups water, stock or tomato juice
    1 teaspoon salt
Drop the giblets into the water and simmer for about 15 minutes. Remove from the water, bring it to a rolling boil and stir into it:
    1 cup wild rice, page 179
♦ Simmer until nearly tender, about 30 minutes. Melt in a skillet:
    ¼ cup butter
Sauté in it for about 3 minutes:
    2 tablespoons chopped shallots
    1 tablespoon chopped green pepper
    ¼ cup chopped celery
Add the hot drained rice and the chopped giblets. You may also use one or two of the following ingredients, but remember the quantity of dressing will be increased:
    1 cup sautéed mushrooms
    ½ cup chopped ripe or green olives
    ¼ cup tomato paste
    ½ cup chopped nuts
    ½ cup sliced water chestnuts

DRESSING FOR CORNISH HEN OR PIGEON

Soak for 10 minutes:
    ½ cup white raisins
in:
    ¼ cup cognac
Sauté them in:
    6 tablespoons butter
Add:
    ¼ cup chopped shallots
Combine with the above and toss lightly:
    ½ teaspoon salt
    1½ cups Boiled Rice, page 178
    ¼ cup chopped pistachio nuts

CHICKEN FARCE OR FORCEMEAT
Enough for 3 Six-Pound Chickens

A gala stuffing for boned chicken, squabs or galantines.
Grind 3 times:
    About 3½ lbs. raw chicken meat
    3 cups mushrooms
Add to this mixture:
    2 cups pistachio nuts
    1⅓ cups dry sherry
    ¼ cup sliced truffles
    1 teaspoon grated onion
    8 or 9 slightly beaten eggs
    1⅓ cups butter, cut in small dice
    1½ tablespoons salt
    ¼ teaspoon freshly ground pepper

STUFFINGS, DRESSINGS, FARCES OR FORCEMEAT

459

Grating of fresh nutmeg
Moisten until just softened:
2 cups soft bread crumbs
in:
1½ to 2 cups milk
Add the bread crumbs to this mixture with:
¼ cup cognac, brandy, Madeira or
lemon juice

SEAFOOD DRESSING
For filling fish or for use in Vegetable
Cases, page 255.
Add to:
1 cup flaked crab meat, drained
oysters or mussels
2 slightly beaten eggs
Melt:
2 tablespoons butter
Sauté in it:
½ cup chopped onion
¾ cup chopped celery
2 slices minced bacon
1 cup fresh bread crumbs
Combine with the seafood.
Correct the seasoning
Add:
(1 teaspoon Worcestershire sauce,
1 tablespoon dry sherry, ⅛ teaspoon
ginger or ½ teaspoon grated lemon
rind)

TANGERINE OR PINEAPPLE
RICE DRESSING

2 Cups

Try this for chicken and squab.
Combine:
6 ribs pascal celery, leaves and
stems cut up
¼ cup chopped parsley
1 cup dry cooked rice, lightly
sautéed in chicken fat or butter
Sections and julienned strips of
1 tangerine and its rind
or 1 cup drained crushed pineapple
⅓ cup lightly sautéed shallots
⅓ cup lightly sautéed mushrooms
(⅓ cup pine nuts)

APRICOT OR PRUNE DRESSING
About 5 Cups

Cut into strips:
1½ cups cooked apricots or
seeded prunes
Combine with:
4 cups dry bread crumbs or
3 cups Boiled Rice, page 178
¼ cup melted butter
½ teaspoon salt
⅛ teaspoon pepper
½ cup chopped green pepper or celery
Moisten lightly with:
Stock or apricot water

POTATO DRESSING
About 6 Cups

Beat:
2 eggs

Add:
2 cups milk
and pour over:
4 cups soft bread crumbs
Fold in:
1½ cups freshly mashed potatoes
Sauté until golden:
½ cup finely chopped onion
½ cup finely chopped celery
in:
¼ cup butter
Add:
2 tablespoons chopped parsley
Combine with the potato mixture.

SWEET POTATO AND SAUSAGE
STUFFING
About 7 Cups

Sufficient for a 10 lb. turkey.
Prepare:
4 cups Mashed Sweet Potatoes,
page 298
Sauté until light brown:
½ lb. sausage meat: 1 cup
Break it up with a fork. Remove it from
the pan. Add to the pan and sauté for 3
minutes:
3 tablespoons chopped onion
1 cup chopped celery
Add the sausage meat, the sweet potatoes
and:
2 cups dry bread crumbs
(3 tablespoons chopped parsley)
Correct the seasoning
Mix these ingredients well.

SWEET POTATO AND APPLE
DRESSING
About 5 Cups

Prepare:
Sweet Potatoes and Apples, page 299
replacing the apple water with light or
dark stock.

APPLE DRESSING
About 4 Cups

Peel and slice:
6 cups tart cooking apples
Combine them with:
1 cup currants or raisins
(2 tablespoons lemon juice)
You may steam the currants or raisins in 2
tablespoons of water in the top of a double boiler for 15 minutes before combining with the apples.

SAUERKRAUT DRESSING FOR GAME
Mix:
1 quart chopped drained sauerkraut
with:
1 clove garlic
¼ cup chopped onion
1 tart peeled and chopped apple
(2 tablespoons brown sugar)
(¼ cup dried currants)
(1 cup chopped water chestnuts)
(⅛ teaspoon thyme)
Correct the seasoning

POULTRY AND GAME BIRDS

The chicken is a world-citizen; duck and geese cosmopolites. Along with a number of the game birds which migrate from continent to continent, they are international favorites. And each nation has learned to cook them in a manner distinctively its own. The worldly-wise cook will not be content with chicken and dumplings, roast turkey or quail on toast. But he will welcome into the kitchen some of the specialties—chicken cacciatore, duck bigarade, turkey mole, pheasant smitane—all of which have enlivened a global cuisine.

The principles of cooking poultry and game birds are just sufficiently different to warrant separate treatment; wild fowl having its own peculiarities in handling before cooking. There is the length of hanging time and the method of determining age— the results of which, in turn, establish the specific method of cooking. ♦ Wild fowl also demands extra fat during the cooking process. Preliminaries are identical. Bleeding the bird, plucking, singeing, drawing, removing tendons, trussing, stuffing, cutting it up—even boning, if you need this information—these steps are alike for all fowl, wild or domestic, as described later.

Whether you shoot your bird, catch it or buy it, you will always have to assess its quality and potential, sizing it up for the application of those cooking techniques which will be most individually suitable and rewarding. ♦ See, for example, under the dry heat processes, page 122, ways to cook young birds. Consult the moist heat processes, page 127, for those of questionable age or cook them in milk or marinate to tenderize.

ABOUT POULTRY

Poultry cooks and tastes best if used within 8 to 24 hours after slaughter. Cut-up poultry is more perishable than whole birds and turkey more perishable than chicken. All poultry is difficult to keep well in home refrigerators and, if you have to hold it more than a day or two, cook it and reheat it in a sauce before serving. Should you have bought chicken in airtight wrappings, loosen the wrapping before refrigerating.

For amounts of bird to allow per serving, see individual recipes, but if a large number of people are to be fed, turkey meat is the least expensive and turkey breast yields the greatest amount of protein per pound— duck, the least. The net amount of edible meat, minus fat or skin, is about 46% for turkeys, 41% for chicken and 22% for duckling.

Although a federal inspection stamp for poultry is authorized, its use is voluntary and applies only to already slaughtered birds in interstate commerce. It is well worth looking for, as its presence insures certain sanitary and grading standards.

Young chickens of either sex are called broilers if they weigh about 2½ lbs. and fryers if they weigh 2½ to 3½ lbs. Roasters also of either sex, are under 8 months old and weigh 3½ to 5 lbs. and are very good for rotisseries or for use in Suprêmes, page 471. Capons, or castrated males, weigh 6 to 8 lbs. "Fowl" is a broadly polite "nom de plume" for hens aged 10 months or more and "stag" and "cock" for males that are too old to roast, but are well-flavored adjuncts for the stock pot.

♦ To size up a chicken, look for moist skin, soft legs and feet, bright eyes, a red comb, a wing tip that yields readily pressed back and, most importantly ♦ flexible breastbone. If the tip of the bone bends easily, the bird is young; if it stiff, the bird is past its prime. For prepackaged chicken, the last test is the only one applicable. ♦ Beware of skin which is dry, hard, purplish, broken, bruised or scaly or that has long hairs sprouting from it.

On any bird that is frozen, watch for brownish areas called freezer burn, which indicate dehydration or long and improper storage. ♦ Commercially frozen birds may have been watered before freezing and the loss of this water on thawing may make them more expensive and less flavorful than those freshly killed.

In some households, arguments rage every Thanksgiving as to whether a cock or a hen turkey is to grace the board. The butcher might settle most of these disputes since he invariably charges more for the latter.

ABOUT PLUCKING AND SINGEING POULTRY

Poultry is usually plucked and drawn when purchased. Buy dry-picked poultry whenever possible. If it is not plucked, do so at once—except for those game birds which must hang and are easier to pluck later. It is much easier to pluck and draw a bird that is thoroughly chilled. ♦ To pluck, pick the feathers from a bird. Remove all pin feathers—use a pair

weezers or grasp each pin feather be-
ween forefinger and the tip of a knife,
nen pull.

After removing the coarser feathers, if
nose remaining are downy or small, you
nay use the paraffin method. Make up
mixture of ⅜ lb. melted paraffin and
quarts boiling water. Brush enough of
nis mixture over the bird to cover. Allow
to harden. Pull against the paraffined
ating and it will carry the feathers with

TO SINGE A BIRD

old it by the legs and singe the pin
athers over a gas flame or a candle. Turn
, so that all parts of the skin are exposed
the heat. ◗ But do not singe a bird that
to be frozen until you are just ready to
e it. The heat of singeing breaks down
e fat and hastens rancidity.

BOUT PREPARING AN UNDRAWN
IRD FOR SAUTÉ OR FRICASSEE

rst remove the wings and legs as shown
low and on left at the top of the next
ge. Then be careful in making the diago-
l incision—shown in the center illustra-
n, below, by a dotted line—not to cut so
eply as to pierce the innards. Now reach
with the palm down and loosen the en-
ils at the top of the cavity. Place the
rd on its back as on the right and crack
e backbone by bending it sharply. Cut
ound the vent and remove the entrails.
scard the lungs and kidneys and save the
lets. Remove the oil sac, as described
page 463.

BOUT PREPARING GIBLETS

Among the entrails of a fowl the most
uable are the giblets, the heart, the
er and the gizzard. Remove veins, ar-
ies, thin membrane and blood from
und the heart and discard them. Cut
green sac or gall bladder away from
liver very carefully. Is is better to leave
small piece of liver attached to the sac
n to cut the sac so close to the liver as to
puncturing it, for the bitterness of its
d will ruin whatever it touches. Discard

the gall bladder. Cut away any portion of
the liver which may be discolored. ◗ If
the liver of a fryer is yellow, it should very
definitely be discarded. However, it may
be normal to find a yellow liver in a stewer.
Sever the intestines from the gizzard and
remove membrane and fat from it. Then
cut a shallow slit along the indented curve
of the gizzard, being careful not to cut so
deeply as to pierce the lining of the inner
sac. Push against the outside of the opened
gizzard with the thumbs to force out the
sac. Discard it. Wash and dry giblets.
Keep them well refrigerated and use or
cook them as soon as possible. See Variety
Meats, page 451, for the many ways to use
giblets as meat and for stuffing, as well as
in Gravies and Sauces, page 322.

ABOUT CUTTING UP A
DRAWN BIRD

If the bird has been drawn, hold it up by
a wing, letting its weight tug against the
skin at the wing joint, see below. Clip
through the skin, flesh and joint, severing
the wing from the body. Use the same
method to sever the second wing. For
easier eating, you may want to transform
the wings into mock legs. Just cut off the
wing tips and straighten the two remaining
joints with the hands. You may have to
cut through the skin to do this. Pull them
into a straight line to look like a small
double leg. Silly, but the wings seem to
taste better this way.

To cut off the legs, press them outward
and down. If the bird is young the joint
will break easily under this pressure. You
will have to make a longer gash into the
skin of the legs and continue the cut until
it nearly meets in the back. Now cut the
body apart in two pieces, separating the
breast from the back. Cut, as sketched
—below—along the dotted line. With a
young chicken, it is possible to make a
gash toward the back on either side of the
opening previously used to eviscerate the
chicken and to pry the body apart until the
back cracks, as shown on the right. Leave
the breast in 1 piece or cut it into from
2 to 4 pieces.

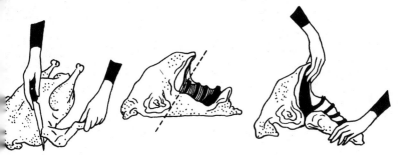

♦ TO REMOVE TENDONS

In large domestic fowl and in game birds the leg tendons are apt to be tough and should be removed. Most butchers use a clever gadget that breaks the foot, holds the carcass securely and draws the tendons as the foot separates from the body. Amateurs have a somewhat harder time. It is easier to get the tendons out if the feet have not been cut off. Cut through the skin 1½ inches above the knee joint. Be careful not to cut the tendons. Lay the fowl down at the edge of a table or board, with the cut in the skin occurring just on the board and the rest of the leg projecting beyond it. Press the foot and ankle down, sharply, to snap the bone at the knee joint. Pull steadily. The tendons should come away with the foot and lower leg bone. If they do not, remove them by forcing a skewer under each and pulling them out one by one, as shown above.

ABOUT BONING FOWL

Chicken breasts are easy to bone either in a butterfly double or in singles. The two singles break down into a large upper and small lower fillet and are sometimes separated for quicker cooking. It is almost impossible to bone a bird that is already dressed and to restuff it to look like its original self. This is due to the careless way in which the cavity opening and neck are usually cut. A dressed fowl can, however, be made into a Galatine, page 436, but be sure to ♦ choose a bird in which the cavity opening is as small as possible.

In these instructions, we are assuming that the bird you are boning is not dressed. The procedure for boning a dressed one is very similar, except that you must provide protection against possible leakage from the entrails. Singe the bird, page 460. Cut off the feet and the first two joints of the wings. Cut off the head, so that the neck is as long as possible and at once catch and bind the two tubes that come from the craw, so that nothing from it can leak out. During the entire boning job—and it is not too difficult once you

have tried it—♦ be careful not to pier the skin except for the initial slits. A through the cooking period, the skin a as protection, encasement and insulatio
♦ Always keep the tip of the kn toward the skeleton and stay close to t bone at all times. When all the bor are out, the result, when held up, shou look like a small romper with wing a leg sleeves pulled into the lining.

Begin the boning by placing the b breast down on the board. Make an : cision the entire length of the spi through both skin and flesh. Using a sharp-pointed boning knife, follow as cl to the frame as you can cut, pushing skin and flesh back as you cut. Work t skin of the neck down, so you can get neck bone to extend way beyond it. Ch the neck off short, protecting the skin a being careful ♦ not to cut through the cr tubes. Work first toward the ball-ai socket joint of the shoulder, cutting free and boning the shoulder blade. P the wing bone through from the insi bringing the skin with it. Bone the m from the wing and reserve it. Then str for the ball-and-socket joint of the leg a pull the bone through. Reserve the me After you have freed and reserved be wings and legs, continue to work the m free, first from one side of the body, th from the other, until the center front the breast-bone is reached. ♦ Here gr care is needed to free the skin with piercing it, as it is very thin at this po You should now be able to get the wh skeleton out with its contents all in piece. Leave the severing of the open into the intestine to the last. When skeleton is removed, wash the skin flesh in cold running water and pat wit towel ♦ until it is very dry. For a farce boned chicken, see page 458.

ABOUT PREPARING AN UNDRAWI BIRD FOR ROASTING

Cut off the head, so that the neck is as l as possible and at once catch hold of bind the 2 tubes attached to the craw

event leakage. Draw down the neck
in. Cut or twist off the neck, close to
e body ♦ being careful not to tear or
t through the tubes or the neck skin.
e skin should then be loose enough to
ow you to reach in at the base of the
ck and draw out the bound tubes and the
p.

Now make an incision through the skin
low the breastbone, large enough to
mit the hand, as sketched above. Insert
e hand, palm down, into the cavity be-
een the organs and the breast bone.
el for the gizzard, which is firm and
ndish and pull it out steadily. It will
ng most of the other entrails with it.
ep giblets for gravies or stuffings. Re-
ve the kidneys in the hollows near the
e of the backbone and the spongy red
gs to either side of the spine between
ribs. Explore carefully to ensure the
noval of every bit of the viscera from the
ity, as well as surplus fat, as it may be
strong in flavor. Turn the chicken
r and cut out the oil sac at the base of
tail, as shown on the right, by making
small oyster-shaped scoop above the
rt-shaped area called the croupion or—
the irreverent—the pope's nose.

Do not soak the bird in water at any
e. Wipe it well with a damp cloth after
ving. Should it be necessary to wash
bird, hold it briefly under running
er to cleanse the inside and ♦ dry it
l with a cloth.

ABOUT STUFFING AND TRUSSING A BIRD

Always wait to stuff a bird until just before
roasting. This may not be convenient, but
it is much the safest procedure. Contamination is frequent in prestuffed fowl, for even
when the dressing is refrigerated, the cold
may not fully penetrate it.

Fill the bird only three-fourths full,
as the dressing will expand. Stuff it
loosely, as sketched below, left. Your
task will be easier if you place the bird
in a large pan. The crop cavity may be
stuffed, too. You may also loosen the
breast skin with a spoon and fill out the
breast between the skin and the flesh.
Close the openings with small skewers
and a crisscrossed string. Or use a spiral
skewer as shown in the center drawing,
or sew them with the old-fashioned needle
and thread. Fasten the legs so they will
be close to the body by tying the ends of
the drumsticks together, as shown in the
center. Tie a piece of string around the
skin of the neck. Leave two long ends.
Turn the wings back, as shown on the
right, and pass the string around them
and secure it.

ABOUT ROASTING CHICKEN, CAPON, CORNISH HEN OR TURKEY

You may want to salt both the outside
and inside of poultry before roasting. We

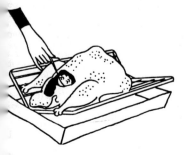

prefer to salt, if at all, after the browning
and never salt the interior. If the bird
is lean, rub it well with melted unsalted
shortening. Place it on a greased rack
♦ uncovered, in a roasting pan, breast
side up with the oven preheated to 450°.
Reduce the heat immediately to 350°,
baste frequently with pan drippings or
additional fat and cook until tender. Some
people like to use an even, slow heat
throughout the cooking period, placing
the bird in a preheated 325° oven and
not basting at all. This method has gained
popularity because it is carefree and because it was, until recently, reputed to
entail less meat shrinkage. It has now
been conclusively proved that even-heat
roasting does not reduce shrinkage. And
we are quite convinced, on the basis of
the old reliable taste-test, that the flavor of
meat sealed at the onset of roasting by
high heat is markedly superior.

♦ In timing meat, remember that many
factors are involved: the age of the bird
and its fat content, whether it was frozen
or not and, of course, its size. If it is
a large bird, the total cooking time re-
quired will be longer, but it will require
less time per pound than a smaller one.
♦ Have fowl at 70° before putting it in
the oven. If using a thermometer, insert
it between the thigh and the body of the
bird, taking care that the tip is not in
contact with the bone. Cook to an in-
ternal temperature of 190°. If not using
a thermometer, allow about 20 minutes to
the pound for birds up to 6 pounds. For
larger birds, allow about 15 minutes per
pound. In either case, add about five
minutes to the pound if the bird you are
cooking is stuffed. Other popular tests
for doneness are to prick the skin of the
thigh to see if the juice runs clear or to
jiggle the drumstick to see if the hip
joint is loose. This latter response, we
find, usually means that the bird is not
done but overdone. As a matter of fact,
in cooking any bird, you are faced with
a real and built-in problem. Putting it
simply, the flesh of a fowl is of two quite
different kinds: the tender breast meat
and the tougher, relatively fatty, legs. The
breasts are usually just right—as the
French say, "à point"—an appreciable time
before the legs have reached doneness. To
correct this imbalance, especially in cooking
larger birds, cover the breast after the first
hour of cooking with a cloth that has been
dipped in melted unsalted shortening.

There are several ways to glaze a bird
toward the end of cooking. You may re-
move the cloth and dust the bird with flour
or coat it with a thin roux during the last
half hour or so of cooking. When the flour
or roux sets, baste frequently with pan
drippings. If the flavor is compatible with
your dressing, or if the bird is unstuffed,
you may baste by brushing it with a com-

bination of peach or apricot preserves c
currant jelly mixed with melted butter.

ABOUT ROASTING DUCK OR GOOS

Pluck, singe, draw and truss, as describe
on page 460. Since these birds are fa
it is wise, especially with mature duck
and geese, to ♦ preroast them for about 1
minutes before stuffing. We often pref
to prepare a separate stuffing in a bake
so that the dressing will not be overpower
by the flavor and slickness of the fat. Bu
whether these birds are pre-roasted or n
♦ they must be pricked frequently, if light
all over to allow excess fat to escape.
they are not stuffed, you can place a cor
and peeled apple, a carrot, an onion, cele
stalks or a potato in the body cavity
attract off-flavors. Discard these vegetab
before serving. You may also hasten t
cooking with the old Chinese trick of pla
ing several heated metal forks in the cav
to intensify the heat at that point. Aft
preroasting in a 400° preheated oven
after placing the bird in a 450° preheat
oven, proceed as for chicken, allowi
about 20 minutes to the pound.

ABOUT ROASTING FOWL IN FOIL

Today, "roasting" fowl in aluminum f
has become fashionable. But calling t
process roasting is a misnomer, for t
roasting can only go on under ventilati
The foil, which causes steam to form a
entraps it, gives the bird a stewed tas
It also insulates against heat and when y
cook in it you will need a hotter oven.
further caution: if you remove the
during the last half hour or so of cook
in an attempt at browning, you will sim
dry out the meat.

ABOUT CARVING FOWL

If the bird is to be carved at table ♦ be s
the heated platter is large enough
garnish it lightly with parsley or watercr
There is a subtle art to carving, whic
not easily mastered. But a sharp, lo
bladed knife and a two-tined fork v
a guard are helpful for the amateur.
Place the bird, breast side up, o
platter. Insert the fork firmly into the k
joint, as sketched on page 465. This
act as a lever to pull the leg away f
the body of the bird. Slice the thigh f
away from the body until the ball-
socket hip joint is exposed. A twisting m
ment with the knife will disengage
tendons if the fork holds the tension ag
the knee. Have an extra platter clos
hand, on which to place the leg. Cut
joint between the thigh and drumstick
shown. Repeat the above, cutting off
other leg. Begin to arrange the piece
the extra platter, so they will look attra

when it is passed. If a large bird is being carved, some slices of meat may be cut from the thigh and the drumstick at this time. Proceed to remove the wings in a similar manner and, if the bird is large, divide the wings at the major joint. To slice the breast, begin at the area nearest the neck and slice thinly across the grain—the entire length of the breast. If the bird is very large, such as a turkey, carve only one side, unless more is needed at the first serving. This way, the meat can be kept from drying out.

In carving a duck, you will find the leg joint is more difficult to sever because it is attached much farther under the bird and is somewhat recessed at the joint. Here, as in general, for the inexperienced carver or the impatient one, poultry shears are an inspired addition to his weaponry.

ROAST CHICKEN

6 Servings

Preheat oven to 450°.

Draw, singe, stuff and truss, pages 460-463:

A 4 to 5 lb. chicken or capon

Use for the stuffing ½ the recipe for:

Rice Dressing, page 458, Bread Dressing with Oysters, Nuts and Giblets, page 456, or Chestnut Dressing, page 457

or make:

2 cups Dry Dressing, page 456

replacing the onion with:

½ cup chopped leeks—white part only

and using:

French bread

Put the bird on a rack, uncovered, in the oven and ♦ reduce the heat at once to 350°. Roast about 20 minutes per pound. Serve with gravy, page 322.

ROAST STUFFED TURKEY

12 Servings

Preheat oven to 450°.

Draw, singe, stuff and truss, pages 460-463.

A 10 to 16 lb. turkey

5 cups of one of the following stuffings should fill a 10 lb. bird:

Dry Dressing, page 456
Potato Dressing, page 459, or ½ the recipe for Apple Onion Dressing, page 458

Or you may want to use two kinds of dressing, a richer one like:

Sausage or Oyster Dressing

in the crop and:

Celery or Bread Dressing

in the cavity. Put the bird on a rack, uncovered, in the oven and ♦ reduce the heat at once to 350°, allowing about 20 minutes to the pound for an unstuffed bird and 25 minutes for a stuffed one. Baste frequently or after first half hour cover the bird with a cloth soaked in melted butter. Baste frequently with pan drippings. Remove the cloth the last half hour of roasting so the bird may brown. If using a smaller turkey allow 20 to 25 minutes per lb. For a bird weighing 18 to 25 lbs., reduce the oven to 300° and allow 13 to 15 minutes per lb. Make:

Pan Gravy, page 322

adding:

Sautéed Mushrooms, page 281

or flavoring it with the finely chopped giblets if they were not used in the stuffing.

CHICKEN AND TURKEY BAKED IN FOIL

Preheat oven to 450°.

If you don't have time to baste, an accepted way of cooking halves or parts of chicken or turkey is in a wrap of aluminum foil. But before roasting see Foil Cooking, page 131. Season it well, and add a little butter and fresh herbs, such as tarragon or rosemary. Or use one of the barbecue sauces on page 332.

Cook a 5 lb. stuffed chicken about 2½ to 3 hours; parts or halves about 45 minutes.

BROILED SPRING CHICKEN
Allow ¾ Pound per Person
Preheat broiler.
Clean and cut into halves:
    Broilers
Rub them on both sides with:
    Butter
Place them in a pan, skin side down. The skin side will brown quicker than the under side. Broil the chickens until brown, about 15 to 20 minutes, turning them occasionally. There are so many good basting sauces for broilers. We suggest that, during the cooking, you baste occasionally for excellent flavor with:
    2 tablespoons butter to 1 tablespoon lemon juice
    A grind of fresh pepper
    (Fresh or dry herbs)
Or, for an accent on beautiful color:
    2 tablespoons butter
    ¼ teaspoon paprika
Allow the above amounts for each ½ broiler. Or when the broilers are ready, flambe them, page 127, with:
    1 oz. warmed brandy
for each broiler.
Or make:
    A thickened Pan Gravy, page 322, using tarragon, or an unthickened one—deglazing with dry white wine

STUFFED BROILER
A convenient party dish, as all but the final heating may be done in advance. Broil each:
    ½ broiler, as above
until ¾ done. Remove from heat and cool. Stuff each broiler cavity with:
    ½ cup of any stuffing, page 456
Preheat oven to 350°.
Place the stuffed broilers on a baking tray and brush top of stuffing with:
    Melted butter
Bake for 15 to 20 minutes or until both broiler and stuffing are heated through.

BROILED TURKEY
Prepare for cooking:
    Turkeys weighing from 3 to 4 lbs.
Cut them into 4 pieces. Prepare as for:
    Broiled Chicken, above
allowing about 45 minutes cooking time.

▤ BARBECUED CHICKEN
♦ Please read About Outdoor Cooking, page 136. Prepare:
    Broiled Chicken, above
placing the broiler 5 inches from the heat. Cook in all about 30 minutes, turning often and brushing the birds the last 10 minutes with:
    A Barbecue Sauce, page 332
If preparing outdoors, place on a grill, cavity side down, for 15 minutes at moderate heat before turning and cooking until tender, about 10 minutes more.

OVEN-FRIED CHICKEN
I.   2 Servings
Preheat oven to 350°.
Disjoint:
    A broiler
Wipe dry. Dredge it in:
    Seasoned flour
Heat to the point of fragrance in a heavy skillet:
    ¼ cup butter
Sauté the chicken lightly. Remove from the skillet to a rack in a baking pan. Baste with the skillet pan drippings. Let it bake until tender, about 30 to 35 minutes, basting with added fat if necessary and turning occasionally.

II.   2 Servings
Preheat oven to 400°.
This is a simpler but not quite as tasty a version as I.
Disjoint:
    A broiler
Use neck, wing tips for Stock, page 490. Wipe the remaining pieces with a damp cloth and ♦ dry carefully. In a shallow 9 x 12 baking pan, melt in the preheated oven:
    ½ cup butter
Dredge the broiler in:
    Seasoned flour
Remove the butter from the oven when melted and hot. Place the chicken in it ♦ skin side down. Baste the upper surface with melted butter from the pan. Put the uncovered pan back in the preheated oven and bake the chicken 20 to 30 minutes. Turn it skin side up. Put it back in the oven. ♦ Reduce the heat to 350° and bake until tender, about 30 to 35 minutes. ♦ Do not overcook or the chicken will be dry. While baking, baste the chicken several times with the drippings. You may also wish to remove the white meat portions and keep them warm, uncovered, while you continue to cook the dark meat slightly longer. Serve at once. For gravy and other suggestions, see page 322.

PAN-FRIED OR SAUTEED CHICKEN
Allow ¾ Pound per Person
Please read About Sautéing, page 126. Do not attempt to saute chicken in this way unless it is young and tender. Clean and cut into pieces:
    Young chickens
Dredge them lightly with:
    (Seasoned flour or corn meal)
Melt in a skillet:
    A mixture of butter and oil
allowing for each half chicken 2 or more tablespoons of fat. When the fat has reached the point of fragrance, add the chicken. Cook and turn it in the hot fat until brown. Reduce the heat and continue cooking the chicken, turning frequently until done, from 20 to 30 minutes, according to size. ♦ Cook

nly until tender, as further cooking will
dry and toughen the meat. Remove the
chicken from the pan and make:
Pan Gravy, page 322
Add:
Cream or stock
Correct the seasoning
Serve at once, garnished with:
Parsley

CHICKEN IN BATTER
4 Servings

Preheat deep fryer to 350°.
Please read About Deep-Fat Frying,
pages 124-126.
Some cooks prepare this dish with raw
chicken, as in the recipe. Others prefer to
use a partially cooked fowl. Cut into pieces:
A young 3 lb. roasting chicken
Dip into:
Fritter Batter for Meat, page 221
Place the dipped pieces on a rack and let
them dry for 15 to 30 minutes. Immerse
them in the hot fat and cook for 15 to 17
minutes. Drain on paper towels. Serve hot
or cold.

I.
Allow ¾ Pound per Person

Prepare:
A young 3 lb. roasting chicken
using the recipe for:
Chicken Stew, below
Remove the meat from the liquid. Cool
thoroughly. Dry well.
Preheat deep fryer to 375°.
Dip the chicken into:
Fritter Batter for Meat, page 221
and cook in deep fat until golden. Serve
at once.

CHICKEN OR TURKEY STEW OR
FRICASSEE
5 Servings

Clean and cut into pieces:
A 5 lb. stewing chicken
Place the chicken in a stewing pan and
bring to the boiling point with:
3 cups water
1 sliced carrot
2 ribs celery with leaves
1 small sliced onion
Simmer the chicken about 15 minutes and
remove scum. Continue to ♦ simmer uncovered until the chicken is tender, 2 hours
or more. ♦ Do not boil at any time. At the
end of the first hour of cooking, add:
3 or 4 peppercorns
Remove the chicken and strain the stock.
If a very concentrated gravy is desired,
boil the stock before thickening until it is
reduced to 1½ cups. Thicken it with:
Flour, see Gravy, page 322
Pour the gravy over the chicken. Garnish
with:
Parsley
Serve it with:
Noodles, page 188, Dumplings,
page 191 or Boiled Rice, page 178

II. This can be a stew like Blanquette de
Veau, page 419, cooking the meat for 45
minutes.

III.
4 to 5 Servings
Have ready about:
1 dozen mushrooms
1 dozen small onions
cooked à Blanc, page 493, until tender
Cut into pieces:
A 5 lb. stewing chicken
reserving the neck and back for stock. Dust
the meat with:
Flour
Melt in a heavy pan:
2 tablespoons butter
When the butter reaches the point of fragrance, add the floured chicken. Cook long
enough so the flour crusts but does not
color. Add just enough to cover:
Water or chicken stock
An onion stuck with 3 cloves
1 teaspoon salt
Bring the liquid to a boil. ♦ Reduce the
heat at once. ♦ Simmer, uncovered, for
about 45 minutes. Remove the meat and
the clove-studded onion from the liquid.
Discard the onion. Keep the meat warm.
Melt in the top of a double boiler:
3 tablespoons butter
Add:
3 tablespoons all-purpose flour
Make a sauce by adding to above roux
the liquid from the meat. Simmer, stirring
about 5 minutes. Have everything else
ready to serve, because the sauce does not
hold well once the eggs are added. Add
♦ off the heat:
3 beaten egg yolks
¾ cup cream
Place the sauce ♦ over—not in—hot water,
stirring until the eggs thicken. Add the
mushrooms and onions. Place the chicken
on a hot platter, inside a:
Rice Ring, page 180
Pour the garnished sauce over the meat.
You may decorate the platter with small
bunches of:
Cooked carrots
Parsley
so arranged as to look like fresh carrots with
tops.

BRAISED BROILERS
Allow ¾ Pound per Person
If you like your chicken falling from the
bone, this is your recipe.
Preheat oven to 350°.
Clean and cut into quarters:
Young chickens
Heat in a skillet:
Butter
Add the chickens and sauté them until
brown. Place in a baking dish. Pour over
them, to the depth of 1 inch:
½ cup boiling Chicken Stock, page 490,
or milk

Before covering the dish, add:
  (1 teaspoon sautéed chopped onions)
  (1 teaspoon honey)
for each piece of chicken and for the pot
a:
  (Tiny pinch of rosemary)
Bake ♦ covered, about 40 minutes. When
tender, remove them from the dish.
Make:
  Pan Gravy, page 322
Add to the stock, if required:
  Chicken Stock, page 490
  Cream
  Salt and pepper

MARYLAND CHICKEN
                                              4 to 5 Servings
Cut into pieces for serving:
  A young frying chicken, about
  3½ lbs.
Bread it by dipping each piece in:
  Milk
and rolling it in:
  Flour
Let dry for 1 hour. Heat in a heavy skillet:
  ½ to 1 inch fat, a combination of
  cooking oils or bacon drippings
Heat the fat until it reaches the point of
fragrance. Add the chicken. Brown it on
all sides.
Preheat oven to 375°.
Place the browned chicken in a fresh pan
and bake, covered, until steamed through,
about ½ hour. This Border dish is usually
served with a cream gravy made from the
drippings, that is, some of the fat thickened
with:
  Flour
to which milk is added, see Pan Gravy,
page 322. You may further enrich the
gravy with:
  (Egg Yolks, page 320)
Serve with:
  Ham and Corn Fritters,
  page 222

SMOTHERED CHICKEN
                                              6 to 7 Servings
Preheat oven to 350°.
Prepare for cooking:
  A 4 lb. roasting chicken
Disjoint it. Place the chicken in a paper
bag with:
  ¼ cup Seasoned Flour, page 502
Close the bag and shake vigorously.
Brown the chicken in:
  ¼ cup olive or salad oil
Place it in a casserole. Cook in the fat for
10 minutes:
  1 small sliced onion
  1 sliced clove garlic
  3 or 4 chopped celery stalks
  1 medium-sized carrot
Put the vegetables in the casserole. Pour
over the mixture:
  1½ cups hot chicken stock
Bake ♦ covered, for about 1½ hours or un-

til tender. Add to the dish, 5 minute**s**
before it is done:
  (1 cup sliced sautéed mushrooms)
  (12 stuffed sliced olives)

CHICKEN PAPRIKA
                                              3 Serving**s**
Cut up as for frying:
  A young chicken: about 2½ lbs.
Melt in a heavy pot:
  1½ tablespoons butter
  1½ tablespoons cooking oil
Add and simmer until golden:
  1 cup chopped onions
  2 teaspoons to 2 tablespoons mild
  paprika
Add:
  ½ teaspoon salt
  2 cups well-seasoned stock
As soon as these ingredients have reache**d**
boiling point, add the chicken. ♦ Simme**r**
it, covered, until tender, about 1 hour. Sti**r**
  1 teaspoon flour
into:
  1 cup cultured sour cream
Stir it slowly into the pot. Heat the chick**-**
en 5 minutes longer but ♦ do not boil. Serv**e**
at once. Good with noodles or rice.

CHICKEN BRAISED IN WINE OR
COQ AU VIN
We are often asked why this recipe turn**s**
out a rich medium brown rather than th**e**
very dark brown sometimes served in res**-**
taurants. Abroad, in country places whe**re**
chickens are locally butchered, the blood **is**
often kept and added to the gravy at th**e**
last minutes as a thickener, see page 32**?**
After this addition, it is not allowed to bo**il**.
Here in America, this effect is often im**i**-
tated by adding caramel coloring. Recip**e**
I is best with a youngish chicken. If yo**u**
have an old one, use II below.

I.
                                              4 Servin**gs**
Disjoint:
  A broiler or roasting chicken
Use the back and neck for the stock po**t**
Melt:
  3 tablespoons butter or olive oil
Add and brown lightly:
  ¼ lb. minced salt pork
  ¾ cup chopped mild onions or
  ½ cup pearl onions
  1 sliced carrot
  3 minced shallots
  1 peeled clove garlic
Push the vegetables aside. Brown th**e**
chicken in the fat. Add and stir:
  2 tablespoons flour
  2 tablespoons minced parsley
  1 tablespoon fresh chervil or marjoram
  ½ bay leaf
  ½ teaspoon thyme
  1 teaspoon salt
  ⅛ teaspoon freshly ground pepper
  (1 tablespoon brandy)
Stir in:

1½ cups dry red wine or sherry
Simmer the chicken over low heat until
done, about 1 hour. Keep it covered. Add
for the last 5 minutes of cooking:
 ½ lb. sliced mushrooms
Skim off excess fat.
 Correct the seasoning
Serve the chicken on a hot platter, the
sauce and vegetables poured over it.

II. To tenderize an old chicken before
braising, place it in ♦ a closely lidded
heavy casserole on a piece of bacon rind
or a few strips of bacon. Put the casserole
in a 250° oven for about 45 minutes or
until the flesh of the bird becomes white
and has a pleasant aroma. The chicken is
then ready to use for braising, as in I above.

CHICKEN TARRAGON WITH WINE
4 Servings
Disjoint:
 2 broilers
Marinate the pieces for about 1 hour in:
 ¼ cup fresh or 2 tablespoons dried
  tarragon leaves
 4 finely minced shallots
 1 cup dry white wine
Preheat broiler.
Broil the chicken for about 20 minutes or
until tender.
Baste it with:
 Melted butter
and the strained marinade. Save some of
the marinade to deglaze the broiler pan.
 Correct the seasoning
and serve the chicken on a hot platter with
the drippings poured over it.

HUNTER'S CHICKEN, CHICKEN CACCIATORE OR CHASSEUR
4 Servings
Hunters always seem to have tomatoes and
mushrooms handy. Cut into individual
pieces:
 A 4 lb. chicken
Dredge with:
 2 to 3 tablespoons flour
Sauté until golden brown in:
 ¼ cup olive oil
with:
 2 tablespoons chopped shallots
  (1 minced clove garlic)
Add:
 ¼ cup Italian tomato paste
 ½ cup dry white wine
 1 teaspoon salt
 ¼ teaspoon white pepper
 ¾ cup chicken stock
 ½ bay leaf
 ⅛ teaspoon thyme
 ⅛ teaspoon sweet marjoram
 ½ to 1 cup sliced mushrooms
  (2 tablespoons brandy or ¼ cup
  Muscatel)
Simmer the chicken ♦ covered, for 1 hour
or until tender. Serve with:
 Boiled Spaghetti

CHICKEN MARENGO
8 Servings
A good buffet casserole which profits by a
day's aging, refrigerated.
Cut into quarters:
 2 frying chickens
Sauté until delicately colored:
 1 thinly sliced onion
in:
 ½ cup olive oil
then remove. Add the chicken pieces and
brown on all sides. Add:
 ½ cup dry white wine
 2 crushed cloves garlic
 ½ teaspoon thyme
 1 bay leaf
  Sprigs of parsley
 1 cup chicken stock
 2 cups Italian style tomatoes
  Correct the seasoning
Cover the pot and simmer for about 1 hour,
until tender. When meat is done, remove it
to a platter. Strain the sauce and reduce
it for about 5 minutes. Now sauté:
 16 to 20 small white onions
 1 lb. sliced mushrooms
in:
 ¼ cup butter
  Juice of 1 lemon
Arrange chicken quarters, mushrooms,
onions and:
 1 cup pitted black olives
in a deep earthenware casserole. Sprinkle
over all:
 1 jigger cognac
Add the sauce and reheat in a 350° oven.
Garnish with:
 Chopped parsley
Serve with:
 Rice

SPANISH CHICKEN
4 Servings
Preheat oven to 350°.
Also see Paella, page 183.
Cut into pieces:
 A 4 lb. frying chicken
Dredge them with:
 Seasoned Flour, page 502
Heat in a skillet:
 ¼ cup olive oil
Brown the chicken in it. Place in a casserole. Sauté in the oil in the skillet:
 ¼ cup chopped onion
 3 tablespoons chopped green pepper
 1 minced clove garlic
Add:
 ½ cup chopped carrots
 ½ cup chopped celery
 1 cup chopped, peeled, seeded
  tomatoes
 ¾ cup tomato juice
Pour these ingredients over the chicken in
the casserole. Bake ♦ covered, for about
1 hour or until tender. Add, if needed:
 Boiling stock
Five minutes before the chicken is done,
add:

¾ cup Sautéed Mushrooms, page 281
⅓ cup sliced stuffed olives
Make:
    Pan Gravy, page 322

FRENCH CASSEROLE CHICKEN
                       5 Servings
Whenever we see one of our contemporaries
trying to regain her youthful allure with
gaudy sartorial trappings, we think of a
dish we found in a collection of college
alumnae recipes, called: "Suprême of Old
Hen." We all know that "Suprême," in
chef's parlance simply means a breast of
fowl. But, in this case, it really lives up
to its billing and makes such a good dish
out of a poorish bird that the old girl is still
an acceptable morsel.
Prepare for cooking and disjoint:
    A 5 lb. fowl
Sear the pieces in:
    ¼ cup hot butter
Add:
    ¼ cup dry white wine
Remove the chicken from the pot. Place in
the pot:
    2 pared, cored, sliced tart apples
    6 chopped celery ribs with leaves
    1 minced or grated onion
    3 sprigs parsley
    ½ teaspoon salt
    ¼ teaspoon paprika
Cover and cook these ingredients gently
until tender. Stir in:
    2½ tablespoons flour
    2 cups Stock, page 490
Cook and stir the sauce until it boils. Add
the chicken. Cover and simmer until it is
tender, 1 hour or more. Remove the chick-
en to a hot ovenproof serving dish. Strain
the sauce. Warm over hot water and add to
the strained sauce:
    ⅓ cup sweet or cultured sour cream
    Correct the seasoning
Add:
    1 tablespoon fresh tarragon or basil
Pour the sauce over the chicken. Sprinkle
it generously with:
    Parmesan cheese
Place it under a broiler until the cheese is
melted.

BRUNSWICK STEW
                       8 Servings
Disjoint for cooking:
    A 5 lb. chicken
Sauté it slowly until light brown in:
    ¼ cup butter or drippings
Remove from the pan. Brown in the fat:
    ½ cup chopped onions
Place in a large stewing pan the chicken,
onions and:
    1½ to 2 cups peeled, seeded, quartered
        tomatoes
    3 cups fresh lima beans
    1 cup boiling water
    A few grains cayenne
    (2 cloves)

▶ Simmer these ingredients, covered, until
the chicken is nearly tender. Add:
    3 cups corn, cut from the cob
Simmer the chicken and vegetable mixture,
covered, until tender. The chicken meat
may be removed from the bones.
    Correct the seasoning
Add:
    2 teaspoons Worcestershire sauce
Stir in:
    (1 cup toasted bread crumbs)

CHICKEN KIEV
                       8 Servings
Preheat deep fryer to 325°.
Bone, skin, page 462, cut in halves and
pound, page 383, to a ¼-inch thickness:
    4 chicken breasts
Form into 8 balls:
    ½ lb. butter
Roll butter balls lightly in a mixture of:
    2 tablespoons chopped chives
    2 tablespoons chopped parsley
    (1 minced clove garlic)
    ½ teaspoon salt
    ¼ teaspoon white pepper
Place one of the seasoned butter balls in
the center of each half breast and roll so
that the butter is completely enclosed.
Secure with a toothpick, if necessary. Dust
with:
    Flour
Brush with:
    Beaten egg
Roll in:
    Dry bread crumbs
Fry in deep fat, page 124, until golden
brown, about 5 to 7 minutes.

BRANDIED CHICKEN BREASTS
                       4 Servings
Remove the breasts from:
    4 young chickens
Skin, bone and divide into halves, and rub
with:
    Brandy
Let them stand about 10 minutes. Season
with:
    Salt, pepper and marjoram
Heat to the point of fragrance:
    6 tablespoons sweet butter
Sauté the fillets over medium heat, 6 to 8
minutes on each side. Remove to a heated
ovenproof platter and keep warm. To the
remaining butter in the pan, add:
    ½ cup dry sherry
Simmer over ▶ low heat until the liquid is
reduced to half. Add, stirring constantly:
    2 cups cream
beaten with:
    4 egg yolks
Season with:
    Salt, pepper and nutmeg
Stir and cook until slightly thickened. Pour
the sauce over the chicken breasts. Sprinkle
with:
    Grated Swiss cheese

mixed with equal parts of:
Fine buttered crumbs
Glaze under the broiler.

BREAST OF CHICKEN COCKAIGNE
Allow a Single Breast per Serving
This delicate recipe does not work with frozen chicken. Cook up a flavorful stock, page 490, from the skin and bones of the chicken you are using. Skin, bone, divide in halves:

Chicken breasts

When ready to cook, dust the chicken breasts, which should be 70°, lightly with:

Flour

For each breast, heat to the point of fragrance, in a heavy skillet:

½ tablespoon butter
½ tablespoon cooking oil

Put the floured pieces of chicken in the hot oil. Shake the pan constantly so the flour crusts but does not color. Cover and poach in the butter over very low heat, turning occasionally, for 10 to 15 minutes, depending on the thickness of the meat. Remove from heat and allow to stand covered for about 10 minutes more. This rather unorthodox procedure makes breasts puff up, so the meat is both tender and moist. Remove from the pan and keep warm. Make a gravy from the pan drippings and the stock made from the bones and skins.

CHICKEN SUPRÊME PAPILLOTE
Preheat oven to 400°.
Prepare:

Breast of Chicken Cockaigne

allowing it to cook until ½ done. Place it on a parchment heart for Papillote, page 132. Before folding, place:

1 tablespoon Colbert Butter, page 339

on each ½ breast. Seal the paper and bake on a baking sheet for about 15 minutes. Serve with:

Pilaf, page 183

STUFFED CHICKEN BREASTS
Individual Serving
These are quickly prepared in a chafing dish or electric skillet.
Have ready:

A boned, skinned breast of chicken

beaten with a cleaver until very thin. Heat to the point of fragrance:

1½ to 2 tablespoons butter

Quickly move the chicken about in this hot fat until it is no longer pink, about 2 to 3 minutes in all. Fold this thin piece over once to hold:

1 thin slice Virginia ham
1 very thin small piece Swiss cheese

Remove the chicken from the pan and keep it warm. Sauté with pan drippings:

1 tablespoon finely minced shallots
3 mushroom caps

When mushrooms have cooked for about 3 minutes, add:

¼ cup dry white wine
2 tablespoons freshly chopped, peeled, seeded tomato

Simmer about 3 minutes again. Add to this sauce:

2 tablespoons cream

Heat the chicken breasts in the sauce slowly, but ◆ do not let them boil. Turn them once or twice. When heated through, about 3 minutes, add:

1 tablespoon chopped parsley
Correct the seasoning

Serve at once, over:

Saffron rice or fine buttered noodles

CHICKEN BREASTS IN QUANTITY FOR CREAMING OR SALAD
This recipe is particularly useful in preparing large quantities of chicken meat for such dishes as Chicken à la King, page 235, or Chicken Pot Pies, page 225. Many knowledgeable cooks consider poaching an ideal approach, but we should like to suggest this method which we find more flavorful. After the chicken is baked, save the pan juices and make a stock of the skins and bones. Combine these two defatted by-products in making sauce if the chicken is to be served hot or in an aspic. Or use the juices and defatted stock for broth or other cooking if the chicken is served as salad.
Preheat oven to 300°.
Place on a rack in a large shallow pan, skin side up:

Chicken breasts

Brush them, allowing for each whole breast:

1½ tablespoons butter

Bake for about 1 hour. When slightly cooled, remove the skins and bone the breasts. Cover and refrigerate the meat until ready to use.

STUFFED CHICKEN LEGS
Allow 1 or 2 Legs per Person
I. Preheat oven to 350°.
Remove bone and tendons, page 462, from:

Large chicken legs

Stuff the cavities with:

Bread or other dressing, page 456

Close the opening with poultry pins. Brown the legs lightly in:

Butter or other fat

to which you may add:

A slice of onion

Place the stuffed legs in a casserole. Cover the bottom of the dish with:

⅓ inch boiling Chicken Stock, page 490

Bake the meat, covered, until tender, about 45 minutes. Make:

Pan Gravy, page 322

II. Bone:
    4 chicken legs
Replace the bone with:
    4 pineapple spears
Dredge the stuffed legs in:
    A Bound Breading, page 502
Melt in a skillet, to the point of fragrance:
    2 tablespoons butter
    2 tablespoons cooking oil
Sauté the chicken legs, uncovered, until golden brown. Cover them with:
    ½ cup shredded fresh coconut
Cover the skillet and ♦ simmer the chicken until tender. Meanwhile, make up a mixture of:
    ½ cup pineapple sirup
    ½ cup chicken stock
    2 slices fresh gingerroot
    1 to 2 teaspoons cornstarch
and cook until the cornstarch is clear. Pour this sauce over the chicken and heat through again. Serve with:
    Rice and Orange and Avocado Salad

BONED CHICKEN

See About Boning Fowl, page 462.
This recipe, which we have enjoyed on many holiday occasions with Clara Kupferschmid, is one she has brought close to perfection over the years. Choose a very fresh, dry-picked, undressed:
    6 lb. chicken
Be sure the skin is intact. Bone it, page 462. Allow for filling ⅓ of the recipe for:
    Chicken Farce, page 458
Before stuffing the chicken, tie it off securely at the neck, wing ends and legs. Sew shut the vent under the tail. Be sure not to pack the farce or fill the skin too tightly or it may burst during the cooking as the stuffing swells. In filling, pretend you are a taxidermist or a frustrated sculptor and try to shape the stuffing so that, when you have sewed the seam down the back, the bird will resemble its former self. Preheat oven to 450°.
Bard, page 384, the chicken with:
    ⅛ inch thick salt pork
If you do not like a salt pork flavor, brush the bird generously all over with:
    Clarified Butter, page 338
Allow for this and for subsequent basting, about ½ lb. butter. Prick the chicken all over with a darning needle and repeat this operation after every basting. Place the bird on a rack in a pan in the hot oven and ♦ reduce the heat at once to 350°. If the chicken was not barded, baste it at 10 minute intervals after 40 minutes of cooking and continue until it is done, about 2 hours in all. If the bird was barded with salt pork, remove the barding about 20 minutes before the end of the cooking time in order to give the bird a better color. Boned stuffed chickens may be served hot, but are unusually delicious when chilled for at least 24 hours to allow the seasonings to develop.
Slice very thin with hot serrated knife when serving.

COUNTRY CAPTAIN OR EAST INDIA CHICKEN CURRY
                                  4 Servings
This dish has become a favorite in America, although it probably got its name not from the sea-captain who brought the recipe back to our shores, but from the Indian officer who first made him acquainted with it. So says Cecily Brownstone, a great friend; and this is her time-tested formula. For still another Oriental chicken curry, see Rijsttafel, page 183.
Preheat oven to 350°.
Cut into 10 pieces:
    A fryer
Coat them with:
    Seasoned Flour, page 502
Brown the chicken in:
    ¼ cup butter
Remove, drain and place in a casserole.
♦ Simmer gently in the pan drippings until golden:
    ¼ cup finely diced onions
    ½ cup finely diced green pepper
    1 clove minced garlic
    1½ teaspoons curry powder
    ½ teaspoon thyme
Add:
    2 cups stewed tomatoes
and ♦ simmer until the pan is deglazed. Pour this sauce over the chicken and bake ♦ uncovered, for about 30 minutes or until the chicken is tender. During the last 5 minutes of cooking, add:
    3 tablespoons currants
Serve with:
    Steamed Rice
garnished with:
    Toasted slivered almonds

CHICKEN OR TURKEY À LA CAMPAGNE
                            10 to 12 Servings
Roast, uncovered, at 350° for 2 hours:
    A 5-lb. chicken
Remove meat from bones. Use bones, skin and any vegetable parings in your stock pot. Sauté, page 281:
    1 lb. small button mushrooms
Have ready:
    1 cup cooked green peas
    (3 cups canned artichoke hearts)
Prepare à la Parisienne, page 251:
    1 cup each cooked carrots and white turnips
Arrange these ingredients in a 3-quart casserole, alternating layers of chicken and vegetables until all are used, with chicken on the top layer. Make the sauce by putting into a saucepan:
    ½ cup melted butter

Add and stir until smooth over low heat about:

½ cup flour

Continue to stir over low heat and add:

2 cups strong chicken stock
1 cup dry white wine
½ cup dry sherry
1 cup cream
½ cup chopped parsley

Season to taste with:

Salt
Monosodium glutamate
Freshly ground white pepper

Continue to cook over low heat for 10 minutes. Pour the sauce over the food in the casserole. Shake it well, so the sauce penetrates all layers. You may cover the top with:

Au Gratin, page 342

and heat for about 30 to 40 minutes. If you ✳ freeze this mixture, cool uncovered before freezing. To reheat, remove from freezer 3 hours in advance. Bake, uncovered, at 350° for 1 to 1¼ hours.

TURKEY CASSEROLE MOLE

This Mexican recipe combines the native peppers and chocolate with a native bird. ◗ Please read About Deep-Fat Frying, pages 124-126.

Preheat deep fryer to 370°.

Cut up:

A 12 to 14 lb. turkey

Dip the pieces first in:

Milk

then in:

Flour

and put them on a rack to dry. Prepare:

6 Chimayo peppers
6 broad peppers
3 chili peppers

If the chilies are dry, drop them into hot water for about 10 minutes before removing seeds and veins. Deep-fat fry all 3 kinds of peppers for about 5 minutes. Drain and reserve them.

Preheat oven to 325°.

When the turkey pieces have dried about 15 minutes, slide them gently into the 370° pepper-flavored fat and deep fry them for about 5 minutes. Drain the pieces and put them in a large casserole. Cover them with:

Turkey or game stock

◗ Cover the casserole and bake the turkey about 1 hour. Toast in a dry pan, over gentle heat:

1 tablespoon sesame seeds
½ cup pine nuts
½ cup blanched almonds

Grind together with the browned peppers:

2 tortillas

Cook:

3 minced cloves garlic

n

2 tablespoons oil

Add:

2 cups peeled, seeded tomatoes
1 bay leaf
½ teaspoon coriander
3 cloves
1 teaspoon cinnamon

Combine the above ingredients with the nuts and pepper mixture and ◗ simmer for 15 minutes. Put this thick sauce with about 2 cups of turkey stock over the cut up turkey and simmer, covered, for about 2½ hours more. This dish may be made a day or two before serving, but its most characteristic ingredient is reserved for the very last. Just before serving, add:

1 to 2 oz. grated chocolate

mixing it well into the heated sauce.

ROAST DOMESTIC DUCK

3 Servings

Most duck on the American market is not descended from the wild native variety, but from a type bred in China where, of course, this bird is held in high esteem. As duck has both a heavy frame and a high fat content, allow 1⅓ to 1½ lbs. per serving.

Preheat oven to 450°.

Pick, clean and singe, pages 460-461, if necessary:

A 5 to 6 lb. duckling

Rub it with:

(Garlic)

Place it on a rack in a roasting pan. Stuff with:

Celery stalks and sliced onions or a
quartered apple, which you remove
before serving or with an apple
stuffing, page 459

Put the bird in the oven and ◗ reduce the heat at once to 350°. Cook until tender, allowing about 20 minutes to the lb. Make:

Pan Gravy, page 322

Serve with:

Polenta, page 177

or, if the duck has not been stuffed, with:

Crushed pineapple, Orange Sauce
for Duck, page 326, Sauce Rouennaise,
page 474, or any other suitable sauce

APRICOT HONEY GLAZED DUCK

Serves 2 to 3

Preheat oven to 450°.

For those who like sweet with meat.

Prepare and roast as for Roast Duck:

3½ to 4 lb. domestic duck

Remove from oven just before done.

Make a thick glaze to pour over the duck. Combine and mix well:

1 cup apricot preserves
½ cup clover honey
1 tablespoon brandy
1 tablespoon cointreau or other
orange-flavored liqueur

Coat the duck with this glaze and return to the oven for 10 to 15 minutes until the glaze caramelizes.

DUCKLING ROUENNAISE
Unless you choke your duck, pluck the down on its breast immediately afterward and cook it within 24 hours, you cannot lay claim to having produced an authentic Rouen duck. The first two steps assure the dark red flesh and the special flavor of this dish. If, as is likely, duck-strangling will bring you into local disrepute, you may waive the sturdy peasant preliminaries and serve a modified version, garnished with quotation marks.
Clean:
    A duckling
reserving the liver. Free it from the gall. Tuck the liver into the body cavity. Use a spit or rotisserie to roast the duck only 20 to 22 minutes in all. Only the breast and legs, if tender, are reserved and kept warm. The rest of the carcass is pressed, see About Salmi, page 477.
Meanwhile melt:
    2 tablespoons butter
When the fat reaches the point of fragrance, add and simmer:
    1 finely minced onion
    ¾ cup Burgundy
When the duckling is done, remove and crush the liver and add to the reduced wine mixture. Poach it gently in the wine with the drippings from the pressed carcass. Add several tablespoons of:
    (Pâté de Foie, page 432)
    Correct the seasoning
Slice the breast lengthwise into about 20 thin strips and put them in a chafing dish. Should you want to serve the legs, they must at this point be removed and grilled, as they are too raw without further cooking. We prefer to utilize them later in some other dish, so the breast can be served "à point."
♦ Cover the sliced meat quickly with the hot liver sauce, and serve ♦ immediately from the chafing dish at table.

ROAST DUCK BIGARADE
This famous recipe depends for its flavor on the Seville or bitter orange, known also as "bigarade."
Prepare:
    Roast Duck, page 473
When it is done, remove it from the roasting pan and keep warm. Degrease the pan juices and deglaze the pan, as described in Orange Sauce for Duck or Goose, page 326, omitting the lemon juice. The curaçao is optional.

★ ROAST GOSLING OR GOOSE
                                                      6 Servings
Economy-minded farmers raise geese because it takes only about ⅓ as much cereal feed to fatten them as it does for other fowl. Economy-minded housewives know that they get more protein value from turkey, page 460. There is, of course, the ad-

vantage of having goose liver, which is superior, page 432. Preroasting of goose or pricking to release fat is imperative, page 464. Unless goose is under ten months old, it is apt to be tough. Braise rather than roast any bird you suspect of being over this age limit.
Preheat oven to 450°.
Prepare for cooking, page 462:
    An 8 lb. gosling or a 12 to 14 lb.
    goose
Fill the cavities with:
    Apple, Prune, Chestnut or other
    dressing, page 456
    (Sauerkraut made with wine)
Allow 1 cup dressing to each pound of bird. Place the goose on a rack in an uncovered pan, allowing 25 minutes to the pound. ♦ Reduce the heat at once to 350° and pour off the fat as it accumulates.   Make:
    Pan Gravy, page 322
Season it with:
    Ginger and pearl onions
Or serve with:
    Prunes in Wine, page 120, Gooseberry
    Preserves, page 776, Red Cabbage,
    page 268, Curried Fruit, or
    Chestnut Purée, page 272, and
    Cucumber Salad, page 85

BRAISED PARTS OF GOOSE OR GAENSEKLEIN
Rub with garlic:
    Goose back, neck, gizzard, wings
    and heart
Let them stand for several hours. Place in a heavy pot. Add:
    Mirepoix, page 541
Half cover with boiling water. Simmer ♦ closely covered, until nearly tender, about 1½ hours.
    Correct the seasoning
and add:
    (A pinch of ginger)
Cover and simmer the meat until tender about ½ hour longer. Remove from the pot. Strain the stock, removing the grease. Make:
    Pan Gravy, page 322
Pour it over the meat. Serve with:
    Apples Stuffed with Sauerkraut
Also good with:
    Chopped parsley
    Dumplings and applesauce

POTTED GOOSE OR CONFIT D'OIE
Draw, pluck, singe, page 461, and cut up for fricassee:
    A 10 lb. goose
Cut off, reserve and refrigerate the heavy fat. Salt the pieces of goose well on all sides. Place in an earthenware crock and weight with a nonresinous hardwood board. Cover and leave in a cool, dry place 6 to 8 days.
When ready to cook, place the refrigerated fat in the bottom of a large heavy pan

Put on top of it:
>   A Bouquet Garni, page 541
Wipe the salt from the meat and put the
pieces on the fat layer. ♦ Simmer slowly
for about 2 to 4 hours. ♦ Be sure, as the
fat melts, that there is enough to cover the
meat completely. If not, add, as needed:
>   Lard
Use at once or store in a cool place, again,
making sure that the meat is ♦ well covered
with the fat. This dish will keep for months
and can be served cold or reheated in the
fat. If hot, a good accompaniment is:
>   Franconia Potatoes, page 293
which are cooked in the goose fat. Or use
in:
>   Cassoulet, page 423

GUINEA FOWL, ROAST PIGEONS, SQUABS OR CORNISH HENS
>   Allow 1 Small Bird Per Person
Preheat oven to 450°.
Pick and draw:
>   Small guinea fowl, pigeons, squabs
>   or Cornish hens
It is best to coat them with a Roux, page
319. They may be stuffed with:
>   Cooked Wild Rice, page 179, or
>   Bread Dressing, etc., pages 456-459
or:
>   A Fruit Dressing, page 459
Bard, page 384, or brush with:
>   Melted butter
Dredge with flour. Place the birds, uncovered, in the oven. ♦ Reduce the heat
at once to 350° and roast until tender,
45 minutes or more if stuffed, about 30
if not. They may be basted while cooking.
If barded, remove the bacon and allow to
brown. Make:
>   Pan Gravy, page 322, with
>   mushrooms
or serve with:
>   Bar le Duc Jam, page 776

BREASTS OF GUINEA HEN
>   Allow 1 Breast per Person
Preheat oven to 425°.
Bard, page 384, each:
>   Breast of guinea hen
Put in oven and ♦ reduce the heat at once
to 350°. Baste the breasts frequently. Cook
them for about 45 minutes or until they are
tender. Serve "sous cloche," or under a
glass bell, with:
>   Colbert Butter, page 339

POTTED PIGEONS OR SQUABS
>   6 Servings
Preheat oven to 350°.
Cut into pieces or leave whole:
>   4 large pigeons or 6 squabs
Dredge them with:
>   Seasoned Flour, page 502

Melt:
>   ¼ cup butter
Sauté the birds slowly in the butter until
they are just seared. Place them in a casserole. Add to the fat in the pan:
>   ¼ cup chopped onion
>   1 diced carrot
>   ¼ cup chopped celery
Stir these ingredients for about 3 minutes.
Add:
>   1 cup boiling chicken stock or water
Pour this over the birds. Cover them
closely. Roast them until they are tender,
about 45 to 60 minutes. You may add for
the last ½ hour:
>   1 cup sliced mushrooms
Do not permit the birds to become dry.
If they do, add more stock or water. Make:
>   Pan Gravy, page 322
to which you may add:
>   Cultured sour or sweet cream
>   (Chopped olives)
Serve the squabs in a border of:
>   Rice
Sprinkle them with:
>   Chopped parsley or chives

BROILED PIGEONS OR SQUABS
Preheat broiler.
Pick, then split down the back and remove
entrails from:
>   Squabs
Flatten them. You may cut out the back
bone with shears. Put them on a greased
broiler, skin side up. Brush well with:
>   Melted butter
Place the birds 4 inches from the heat.
Broil from 15 to 30 minutes, turning once.
Season when you turn them with:
>   Salt and paprika
Serve on:
>   Buttered toast
Pour the drippings over them. Good with:
>   Chopped parsley
>   Cranberry jelly
>   Crusty Spoon Bread, page 579

ABOUT WILD BIRDS

The opening of the season for grouse—
that very British bird which dwells in and
feeds on heather—stirs up a degree of
knowledgeable excitement equalled only by
a vendange in the Côte d'Or. All over
Southern Europe, each autumn, small birds,
spicy with berries, are netted by the hundreds. And along the shores of Chesapeake
Bay, the canvasback duck—which in October feeds on the wild celery of the shore-
line—is preferred above all others.
We lived for years under one of the
major flyways of the world and looked forward to the days when the males in our
family sought out the bird-blinds in the
surrounding marshes and rich fields. On

their return, dinner parties were held in profusion. The children usually clamored for the plump little quail, leaving the rare, well-hung ducks to their more sophisticated elders.

To a large extent, proper care, immediately after shooting, determines the ultimate excellence of flavor in wild birds. While the bird is still warm, the neck is split and the carcass bled. To keep the blood for use in sauces, see page 321. Check the neck for any undigested food and remove.

Some birds—snipe, woodcock and plover —are cooked with the trail still inside, see page 480. Quail and a few other smaller birds should be plucked, drawn and cooked within 24 hours of killing. But do not pluck or draw any wild fowl until you are ready to cook it, since the added surface exposure of the carcass to air will induce spoilage before the necessary tenderization can be accomplished.

To tenderize and improve flavor, it is necessary to hang many wild birds, specifically partridge, prairie fowl, ducks and plover, grouse and hazel hen—unless they are to be roasted. How long to hang depends first on age. Old birds can be held longer than young ones. A second consideration is the weather. In muggy periods ripening is accelerated. The third—and perhaps the most important—is personal preference. Some hunters go to extremes, holding a bird until the legs stiffen, even until head and body part company. A more moderate and acceptable state of maturity is reached when the feathers just above the tail can be drawn out easily or when a slight bluish green tinge appears on the thin skin of the abdomen. However long birds are to be hung ♦ suspend them, undrawn, by the feet ♦ in a cool, dry, airy place. If the weather is very warm, dust the feathers with charcoal. In any season, the birds should be protected with cheesecloth or screening.

♦ Dry pluck all fowl. Remember that this is easier to do if the bird is chilled. Scalding or soaking preparatory to plucking breaks down the fatty tissues in the skin too rapidly if they are subsequently to be held for even a short time or are to be frozen. ♦ To pluck, see page 460.

Before cooking, look the birds over carefully and remove any shot with a pointed utensil. Cut out meat that has discolored near the shot or any dog-damaged areas. Remove the oil sac, page 463. After plucking, wild fowl should never be washed before cooking, merely wiped with a damp cloth. Safe exceptions are fish-feeding ducks which, if they must be used, should be parblanched for ½ hour before cooking.

♦ Singe all fowl just before cooking, including those which have been frozen. ♦ All game should be at 70° before timing for cooking. The interior of the bird may first be salted or rinsed with 2 tablespoons of brandy or sherry. Should it be necessary to counteract a too gamey taste, we suggest cooking with sauerkraut or using a marinade. Never try to soak out the taste with water. If the bird is to be cooked unstuffed, the placement in it of an apple, an onion, a carrot, parsley, a few celery stalks or some juniper berries helps attract off-flavors. These fillers are, of course, discarded before serving.

♦ Age determines how wild fowl shall be cooked. To judge age refer to the individual recipes. If you are at all doubtful that a bird is young or prime, do not hesitate ♦ to use a moist heat method of cooking, page 127. Very old birds are fit only for the stock or soup pot or for making hash, forcemeat and sauces.

On many occasions only the breasts of wild fowl are served, as the legs are often tough and full of tendons. If you use the legs, remove the tendons, see page 462. Otherwise, simmer the legs with the wings, necks and giblets for game stock. This is most useful, for in no cooking is less gravy naturally produced as in that of game. Therefore, it is doubly important to increase the stock of the game you are cooking, in order to bring up the flavor of a sauce or aspic. If game stock is not available, veal is the most sympathetic substitute.

Before roasting or marinating wild fowl, break down the breast bone by a blow with the flat side of a cleaver. This not only makes carving easier, but reduces the amount of marinade needed. To prepare a wild fowl for broiling, split the back and spread the breasts flat, using poultry shears for small birds.

Whether roasted or broiled, wild birds are, without exception, leaner than domestic varieties and should usually be barded, page 384. Sometimes a flour and butter paste is used to coat them before the barding is applied. The barding may be removed halfway through the cooking process but, if so, basting with butter or pan drippings should continue until the bird is taken from the heat. If a paste has not been applied you may, after the removal of the barding, want to dust the bird with flour to hasten its browning.

♦ Most light-fleshed wild fowl is cooked well done and most dark fowl is cooked "vert-cuit" or "saignant," that is roasted brown on the outside under high heat, but still rare and running with juice and blood within. With these differences in mind, you can cook most wild fowl by the recipes suggested for chicken, pages 465 to 472, but suggestions are given in individual game recipes for those combinations which are classic with game.

Let us also recommend, as sympathetic accompaniments, a dressing of chestnuts or wild rice; a salad of chicory or cress; a dish of gooseberry or quince conserve; a sour cream or wine sauce—not too powerfully seasoned.

If you have more game than you can use immediately, you may consider freezing, page 766, or smoking, page 756. ♦ To cook smoked game, parsteam it, page 756, a few minutes to remove excess salt. Then cook as for ham.

ABOUT SALMI OF WILD BIRDS

A true salmi has two major characteristics. The meat is roasted—barely so, if the game is dark. And the meat from the breasts and from the legs, if they are choice, is sliced and put to one side and kept warm. Preparation is concluded at table, much as in Duck Rouennaise, page 474, where the skin and the chopped carcass are pressed in a duck press. The pressed juices are combined with the flambéed livers, the sauce reduced with a Mirepoix and then strained. Reinforce the sauce by a Demiglaze Sauce, page 326, or Sauce Espagnole, page 326, based on the same kind of game as that being served. If the game is a water-bird, the skin may be too oily to use. Salmis may also be enriched with mushrooms or truffles. The meat is just heated through at table in a chafing dish with this very rich sauce, given a swirl of butter, page 321, and served at once.

Obviously, a classic salmi, fully accoutered, is only for the skilled cook whose husband is a Nimrod and has presented her with more than a single bird. If she is less well endowed, she will have to base her sauce on the backs, wings and necks of the bird that is being presented and eke out her Espagnole Sauce with veal stock. Needless to say, the dish is rarely presented in its original form. And the salmis that appear on menus are usually made from reheated meat, with sauces which have been previously confected. They can still be delicious, especially if care is taken ♦ not to boil the sauce and thereby toughen the meat. Another simpler way to serve precooked game is to make up a mixture similar to Pheasant in Game Sauce, page 478, which lends itself even to ✳ freezing.

MARINATED WILD BIRDS

Serves 2

♦ Please read About Wild Birds, page 475. Clean and disjoint a:

Pheasant, partridge or grouse

Place in a casserole and cover with a marinade of:

1 small quartered onion
1 small bay leaf
1 clove garlic
2 cups port wine
1½ teaspoons salt
½ teaspoon pepper

Be sure the wine covers the pieces. Let stand in the refrigerator for 3 days. Remove the bird from the marinade, dry with a towel. Save the marinade.
Preheat oven to 375°.
Put:

2 tablespoons butter

in a casserole. Brown and roast the pieces for about 45 minutes, turning several times. Strain the marinade and pour it over the pieces. Return to the oven for another 30 minutes or until tender. Take the pieces from the casserole. Keep warm. Reduce the sauce and:

Correct the seasoning

Serve with:

Wild rice or noodles

ABOUT WILD DUCKS

Flavor depends so much on the way ducks have been feeding. The shallow water types may have been feeding in nearby grain fields and may be very succulent. These include mallard, black duck, pintail, baldpate, gadwall and teal. The deepwater or sea ducks thrive on aquatic vegetation. They include canvasback, redhead, the golden eyes, scaup and ring neck. The mergansers or fish eaters should be used only in emergencies.

Wild ducks are usually not stuffed, but their insides may be greased to help retain juices. If too gamey, they may be rubbed with ginger or lemon. Also celery, grapes or sliced apple in the cavity help minimize a too pronounced taste. Discard before serving.

Cooking times vary with types. They may be as long as 20 minutes for canvasback or just 12 minutes for teal.

ROAST WILD DUCK

4 Servings

To draw, pluck, singe and truss ♦ please read About Wild Birds, page 475. This method seems to be the hunter's ideal. The juices are red and flow freely when the duck is carved.
Preheat oven to 500°.
Prepare:

2 wild ducks

Have them at room temperature. Dry them thoroughly inside and out. Rub the insides with:

Butter

Fill the cavities loosely with:

A few skinned onions or peeled, cored and chopped apples or drained sauerkraut

Bard, page 384. Place the ducks on a rack in a roasting pan. ♦ Reduce heat to 350° and roast, uncovered, for 18 to 20 minutes. Degrease the drippings, and add:

Wine and stock

Reduce, then remove from heat and add:

Cultured sour cream

Reheat, but ♦ do not boil. Serve at once with:

Braised Celery, page 271

■ BROILED OR BARBECUED WILD DUCK

Preheat broiler.
A good way to cook wild duck and an easy fashion of serving it is to split it down the back, clean it well and wipe until dry. Rub with:

(Garlic)

Spread with:

Unsalted butter

Season with:

Paprika

Broil about 4 inches under the broiler or 4 inches above charcoal. Baste frequently with:

An unsalted fat or oil and wine

Cook until tender. Remove to a hot platter.

Correct the seasoning

Make a sauce with the drippings, page 322. Serve with:

Poached Oranges or Kumquats, page 116

Fried hominy is a well-known accompaniment to wild ducks. So are grilled sweet potatoes or apples stuffed with sweet potatoes.

BRAISED WILD DUCK

➧ To draw, pluck, singe and truss:

A wild duck

please read About Wild Birds, page 475. Melt in a heavy casserole:

4 tablespoons butter

When it reaches the point of fragrance, put in the duck and brown on all sides. Add, when browned:

1 leek—white part only or 6 button onions
4 tender turnips
1 Bouquet Garni, page 541

➧ Simmer, covered, 25 to 35 minutes or until the duck is tender. Degrease the drippings and garnish the casserole with:

Cooked tender green peas

Serve at once.

ABOUT PHEASANT

➧ Please read About Wild Birds, page 475. We hope your pheasant is young, with a flexible breast bone, grey legs and a pointed, large terminal feather in its wings. If it is a cock, it should have rounded, not sharp or long, spurs. Then you may roast or broil it even without hanging. Barding is advisable.

Otherwise, to give it both flavor and tenderness, about a 3 day hanging period is advised, during which the color of the breast will change somewhat and there will be a slight odor.

An old bird should be barded and either braised or used in a moist heat recipe, see page 127.

ROAST PHEASANT

3 Servings

Preheat oven to 400°.
➧ Please read About Wild Birds, page 475, and About Pheasant, above.
Bard, page 384:

A young pheasant

You may stuff it with:

A Chestnut and Sausage Dressing

Place in oven. ➧ Reduce heat at once to 350°. Cook about 25 minutes to the lb. or until tender. If unstuffed, serve with:

Fried Croutons, page 342, Bread Sauce, page 325, Currant Jelly and Braised Celery or Rice Pilaf, page 183, and Gooseberry Preserves, page 779

or, classically, with:

Sauce Smitane, page 325

BRAISED PHEASANT

This recipe comes from a hunting fan:
➧ Please read About Wild Birds, page 475, and About Pheasant, above.
Preheat oven to 400°.
Prepare:

A pheasant

Pound:

A thin slice salt pork

Separate the skin from the breast flesh of the pheasant and insert the salt pork. Place in the body cavity the pheasant liver and:

A small peeled tangerine

Lace the opening tightly. Truss the pheasant. Melt in a heavy pan:

¼ cup lard

Brown the pheasant, turning it and basting until it is golden all over. Place in a casserole. Add and turn in the fat:

12 sliced mushroom caps

Pour these over the pheasant. Melt in a saucepan:

¼ cup butter

Stir in, cook, but do not permit to brown:

3 shallots or 1 small minced onion
2 teaspoons flour

Stir in gradually:

¼ to ⅓ cup Marsala or Madeira
½ teaspoon salt and freshly ground pepper

Pour this into the casserole.
Our correspondent adds a sprig of fresh fennel and 2 crushed juniper berries.
➧ Cover the casserole and bake the pheasant for about ½ hour. Serve it from the casserole with:

Fried hominy and currant jelly
A green salad

✱ PHEASANT IN GAME SAUCE

10 to 12 Servings

Preheat oven to 400°.
Prepare for roasting:

5 or 6 pheasants

Bard, page 384, with:

Bacon or salt pork

Fill the cavity, if you wish to reduce the game taste, with:

Apple or onion slices

Discard them after birds are roasted. Roast at 400° for 20 minutes. Remove meat from bones. Keep the meat in as large pieces as possible. Cook for 2 hours or until reduced about ⅓, a stock made from the bones, skins, drippings and barding, using:

**2 large chopped onions
2 cloves garlic
2 bay leaves
1 tablespoon black peppercorns
1 teaspoon thyme
1 small pinch rosemary
1 cup chopped parsley
(6 juniper berries)
¼ lb. ham trimmings
1 quart dry red wine
2 quarts water or chicken stock
Stems from 2 lbs. mushrooms
3 fresh tomatoes**

Strain the stock and add it to:

¾ cup Cream Sauce, page 322

Add to this sauce:

**Caps of 2 lbs. mushrooms
¾ cup red wine**

Simmer about 25 minutes.

Correct the seasoning

Reduce by ⅓, strain and add:

¼ cup cognac

Simmer another 10 minutes. Arrange meat in 3-quart casserole. You may put it on a bed of:

(Cooked wild rice)

Pour sauce over it. To serve, reheat, uncovered, in a 350° oven, 45 to 55 minutes. If frozen, thaw and bring to room temperature before reheating.

PHEASANT SMITANE

3 Servings

Bard, page 384:

A 3½ to 4 pound pheasant

with:

Sliced salt pork or bacon

Brown the pheasant in:

Butter

in a heavy pan. Then place in a deep casserole with the drippings. Cover tightly and let simmer over low heat until tender, about 45 minutes. Add:

**4 cups diced tart apples
2 tablespoons cognac or Calvados
2 cups cultured sour cream
Correct the seasoning**

and cook over low heat until the apples are tender. ♦ Do not boil. Serve with:

Wild Rice, page 179

ABOUT PARTRIDGE

Beware of an old bird, which must be braised or marinated, even if it is hung to the maximum of seven days. You will recognize an old bird in its feathers—by a conspicuous red ring on the eye circle, its yellow beak, its dark legs and, in a restaurant, by the French term "perdrix." For, by some strange convention, old partridges —regardless of sex—are ungraciously designated as female. If a partridge is under six months old, it still has its pointed first-

flight feather and, on the menu, is gallantly referred to as perdreau or male—sex discrimination again actually being ignored. The red-legged French partridges are larger and not considered as delicate as the English. There is some confusion in America about the very name of partridge. No true partridge is native, but the name is given in the north to the ruffed grouse and in the south to quail.

If the bird is fresh, it has a rigid vent. ♦ A true partridge can be cooked by any recipe for chicken if larded; or, if barded, as for pheasant. But, if it is old, a longer cooking period may be necessary. It may be served in a Salmi, page 477, as for duck. Some people like it braised with Sauerkraut, page 269, allowing 2 lbs. of the sauerkraut to three 3 lb. birds. Add the sauerkraut the last ½ hour of cooking. Others shudder at so strongly flavored an accompaniment. A more delicate one is Braised Endive, page 278—and stuff it before cooking with marrow. Or wrap the partridge in grape leaves, simmer it in wine and stock for 35 minutes. Then roast it in a 350° oven for 25 minutes. Allow 1 lb. per person. Make Pan Gravy, page 322, and serve the partridge with Boiled New Potatoes, page 290, and water cress.

GROUSE, PTARMIGAN OR PRAIRIE CHICKEN

Allow 1 lb. per Person

Preheat oven to 300°.

Young grouse which feeds on the tender shoots of the heather is one of the more coveted of all game. To test for youth, hold the bird aloft by the lower mandible. If this breaks, failing to support the weight of the bird, you have a young specimen. Roast or broil if young. Braise if old. The same treatments apply to Canadian Grouse or Black Game, also known as Black Grouse or Coq de Bruyère. Resinous in flavor, this is not quite as good as true grouse. However, it is cooked in the same way.

Prepare for cooking as you would a chicken:

Young grouse

You may lard the breast, page 383, with thin strips of:

Salt pork

or bard it, page 384. You may stuff it with:

A small apple, a skinned onion or ribs of celery

Grouse is served rare, to a pale pink tone. Allow about 30 to 45 minutes cooking in all. Baste it frequently with:

Melted butter or drippings

Remove the bacon. Brush the bird with:

Butter

Dredge it lightly with:

Flour

Place it in a hot 500° oven, until brown. Make:

Pan Gravy, page 322

Serve with:
> Rowanberries or Cranberry Sauce

BROILED GROUSE
The bird must be young, see above. Bard,
page 384, and broil only the:
> Breast of young grouse

Prepare it by splitting down the back and
flattening the breast without separating it.
Brush with:
> Cooking oil

Broil about 7 minutes to each side, heating the bony side first. It is classic to serve
it with:
> Bread Sauce, page 325, or
> Sauce Périgueux, page 327

WILD GOOSE AND WILD TURKEY
> 1 lb. per Person

If you talk to someone who has eaten only
an old goose—and they do live to a great
old age—he will claim it is abominable.
Indeed, these birds are worth bothering
with only if they are less than a year old.
Hang from 24 hours to a week and cook
with moist heat, page 127, whether the
goose is old or young. Weights fluctuate,
depending on variety and age, from about
4 to 9 lbs.
♦ To draw, pluck, singe and truss, see
pages 460-463.
For young goose and wild turkey proceed
as for turkey, page 465, or cut as for fricassee, page 461:
> A 5 to 6 lb. wild goose

In a heavy casserole heat to the point of
fragrance:
> ¼ cup butter
> 1½ cups small, white, whole onions

Add:
> ¼ lb. finely diced salt pork

and continue to cook until onions are
golden. Lift out onions and pork and discard. In the remaining fat, brown the cut
up bird. Add:
> Juice of ½ lemon
> ½ teaspoon allspice
> (A few slivers gingerroot)

♦ Simmer, covered, about 30 minutes. Stir
if necessary. Add:
> 2 cups dry red wine

♦ Simmer, covered, at least 45 minutes
longer or until tender. Thicken the pan
gravy slightly with:
> Toasted dry bread crumbs

Serve with:
> Noodles
> Spiced apricots or crabapples

POTTED WILD FOWL
> Allow 1 lb. per Person

A good way to preserve any extra wild
fowl.
♦ Please read about Wild Goose, above.
Draw, pluck, singe and cut for fricassee:
> A young wild goose or other
> wild fowl

Prepare as for:
> Potted Goose, page 474

Serve either hot or cold.

HAZEL HEN
> Allow 1 lb. per Person

Since this bird is quite resinous, it is best
to poach it first in milk for 15 minutes.
Bone and grill for about 12 minutes in all.

ABOUT SMALL GAME BIRDS
Birds here discussed are of many kinds:
ortolans, figpeckers, coot, doves, woodcock,
snipe, rails, curlew, plover, quail, larks,
reed birds, thrush, moorhen and gallinule.
They are bracketed on the basis of similar
treatment and the fact that they are served
one or more to a person. ♦ Small birds are
usually used as fresh as possible, although
they remain edible as long as the legs are
flexible. Quail, which is about the largest
discussed here, should not be hung longer
than 24 hours. ♦ All small birds should be
dry plucked. In fact, some, like snipe,
plover, ring dove and woodcock may be
cooked undrawn, although the eyes and
crop are discarded before roasting. To use
the entrails after cooking, sieve or chop
the intestines and flambé them, page 127,
briefly, in cognac. Mix with pan drippings
and spread on a crouton or over the bird
as a glaze before serving. Or, if you draw
the bird before cooking, reserve the intestines, chop them, sauté them briefly in
butter, then proceed as above.
  Small birds should be barded, page 384,
or you may wrap them first in fig or grape
leaves. All these birds lend themselves to
roasting and skewering or broiling from
3 to 10 minutes. Blackbirds and crows, if
eaten as a matter of necessity, must be
parblanched first, page 132.
  All these small birds produce very little
pan dripping. Pour what there is on a
Crouton, page 342, or a piece of crisp
scrapple. Or combine the drippings with a
Demiglaze Sauce and wine or lemon, page
326, with Smitane Sauce or Sauce Veneur
or use any recipe for braised chicken—allowing in the timing for difference in size.
Any peculiarities or classic combinations
are listed in individual recipes.

ROASTED SMALL GAME BIRDS
♦ Please read About Small Birds, above.
Preheat oven to 450°.
Bard, page 384:
> 6 small birds

It is not necessary to stuff them, although
a few peeled grapes or bits of celery or
parsley may be tucked inside and discarded
later. Place in the pan:
> 1 tablespoon butter

Bake the birds for about 5 minutes ♦ reduce
the heat to 350° and bake them from 5 to
15 minutes longer, according to their size

Quail—unstuffed	10 to 15 minutes
—stuffed	15 to 18 minutes
Woodcock	8 to 10 minutes

BROILED SMALL GAME BIRDS
Preheat broiler.
Bard, page 384:
6 small game birds
Place them on a broiler. Cook them from
12 to 20 minutes, according to size. Turn
frequently. The barding may be removed
toward the end of the cooking period and
the birds browned briefly by further broiling. Add the juice of:
1 lemon
to:
Stock or wine
if there is an insufficient amount of drippings.
Correct the seasoning
Serve the birds on:
Fried toasts
Pour the gravy over them. Garnish them
with:
Parsley
Permit the sauce to soak into the toast.

BRAISED SMALL GAME BIRDS
♦ Please read About Small Game Birds.
Preheat oven to 350°.
Prepare for cooking:
6 birds
Melt in a saucepan:
2 tablespoons butter
Add and sauté for 1 minute:
A Mirepoix, page 541
Add the birds and sauté them until they
are lightly browned. Add:
½ cup boiling stock or wine
Cover the birds with a poaching paper,
page 129, and bake them for 15 to 20 min-
utes. Make:
Pan Gravy, page 322
Add to the gravy:
(2 tablespoons lemon juice or cultured
sour cream or brandy)
Serve on:
Croutons, page 342
garnished with:
Parsley

⊟ SKEWERED SMALL BIRDS
♦ Please read About Small Game Birds.
Wrap in buttered grape or fig leaves:
Small birds
and then bard in very thin slices of:
Salt pork
Roast skewered over coals 10 to 15 minutes.
To finish for serving, you may remove the
barding, roll the birds in bread crumbs,

baste with drippings and heat in a moderate oven 5 minutes longer.

DOVE OR WOOD PIGEONS
1 to 2 Servings

♦ Please read About Small Game Birds.
A dark meat with a fine flavor. The brain
may be mixed with the meat. To prepare
these parts, see page 480. Unless the birds
are very young, prepare as for:
Braised Small Game Birds, this page
Serve the sauce garnished with:
Almond stuffed olives
or with a compote of:
Red Sour Cherries, page 107

QUAIL
1 per Person

Sometimes called partridge in our deep
South. ♦ Please read About Small Game
Birds. This bird has a delicious white
meat. If the fat of the bird is hard rather
than firm before cooking, the flesh will be
tough and must be prepared by a moist
heat method. If the bird is young, roast
or broil.
♦ Never overcook. Serve with:
Quince preserves and curried rice
or water cress and lemon wedges
or serve with:
Sauce Smitane, page 325, and
green grapes or a baked pear, the
core stuffed with a pimiento
If you have broiled the quail, brush it with:
(Anchovy Butter, page 339)

SNIPE OR WOODCOCK
Allow 1 to 2 Birds per Person

Known in France as bécassine and bécasse,
respectively, these birds are highly prized
by some epicures, in the fall, when they are
fat and meaty. But de Pomiane claims that
it takes man's snobbishness to elevate to
one of life's great moments the woodcock
flambé, with its long beak, meager body
and prominent eyes. He claims that even
dogs scorn this status symbol and that the
entrail-soaked crouton alone deserves attention.
♦ Please read About Small Game Birds.
Prepare and cook as for:
Small Game Birds, page 480
or use the recipe for Grouse, page 479. You
may use the trail, see page 480. Skin the
head, but leave it on. Remove the eyes
and crop. Bring the long, curved beak
down to pierce and hold the legs in place.
Bard, page 384, and roast 10 to 15 minutes.

KNOW YOUR INGREDIENTS

Oddly enough, many of the very basic cooking materials—those that go into ninety-nine out of a hundred recipes—are so familiar, or rather so constantly used, that their characteristics are taken for granted even by experienced cooks. And this is to say that, by beginners, their peculiarities are often simply ignored. Yet success in cooking largely depends on one's becoming fully aware of how grass roots ingredients react. Here and now we put them all—from butter to weather—under the enlarging glass and point out just what it is that they contribute to the cooking process. With the knowledge gained in this chapter and the chapter on Heat, plus the information keyed by symbol and reference into our recipes at the point of use, we assure you a continuous and steady development from would-be to sure-fire cook.

ABOUT MILKS AND CREAMS

"Drink your milk" is an admonition less and less frequently heard in this generation. Many of our children lazily and almost automatically pour "down the hatch" considerably in excess of the 1½ to 2 pints they need every day, instead of mustering enough energy to chew other equally nourishing foods, as they should. Beware, incidentally, of assuming that chocolate milk is the nutritional equivalent of whole milk, see page 30.

Most adults, including the middle-aged and their seniors, are well aware of the value of milk in their diet and manage to ingest their daily pint, if not as a drink, in soups, sauces or puddings. Sometimes they may prefer to substitute with cheeses. But if they do, they must be sure to get adequate B vitamins in the rest of their diet; for in cheese-making more B vitamins are lost in the whey than can be subsequently recreated in the final product.

Milk is as perishable as it is valuable and everything possible should be done ◗ to keep it constantly refrigerated at about 40° ◗ to protect it from sunlight, which robs it quickly of vitamin B content and ◗ not to hold milks of any type longer than three days before using. Milks vary in color, even when the animals from which they are taken have all been pastured in the same fields, on the same fodder. The milk of Jersey cows will be yellower than that of Holsteins and Holstein milk, in turn, yellower than the almost white milks of ewes and goats. Yellow coloring reveals the presence of a provitamin A factor called carotene, which some individuals can convert better than others into vitamin A—itself almost colorless. ◗ In this book the word milk means pasteurized fluid, whole milk unless otherwise specified. Such milk contains about 87% water, 4% fat, 3% protein, 5% carbohydrate and 1% ash, which includes its minerals and vitamins.

PASTEURIZATION OF MILK AND CREAM

Milks sold in interstate commerce must be law be pasteurized and most communities have enacted the same regulation for milk sold within their limits. Some people oppose pasteurization because of certain changes that occur in the milk as a result, such as losses of vitamin C and enzymatic changes affecting fermentation. But pasteurization, a mild, carefully controlled heating process, effectively halts many dreaded milk-borne diseases that the sanitary handling and certification of raw milk —no matter how scrupulously carried out —cannot achieve. Raw milk or cream may be pasteurized at home in one of the three following ways. The first two require the use of a dairy thermometer and all demand a ◗ quick cooling of the processing water or processing pan, so that the milk does not take on a "cooked" taste.

I. This is the preferred method. Arrange empty, sterile, glass, heatproof jars on rack, in a deep kettle. Allow an inch or two of headroom when you pour the raw milk or cream into the jars. Fill the kettle with water until it comes above the fill line of the milk in the jars. ◗ Put the thermometer in one of the jars. ◗ Heat the water and, when the thermometer registers 160°, hold the heat at that temperature for 15 to 30 minutes. ◗ Cool the water rapidly to between 50° and 40°. ◗ Refrigerate, covered, at once.

II. This method is more apt to leave a cooked taste, as the heat is harder to control than in I. Heat milk or cream slowly over direct heat to ◗ 143° and keep there for 30 minutes. Plunge the pan at once into ice water and reduce the heat to between 50° and 40°. ◗ Refrigerate, covered, at once, in sterile jars.

III. This method should be used only in emergencies, as the milk flavor is definitely altered. Place the milk to a one-inch depth in a wide pan and bring it quickly to rolling boil, stirring constantly. ◗ As soon as the boiling reaches its full peak, reduce the heat by plunging the pan into ice water. When the bottom of the pan is cool enough to touch, ◗ refrigerate the milk once in covered sterile jars.

If any pasteurized milk develops an "off" or bitter flavor, it has been held too long after processing. Unpleasant flavor may also appear in milk when cows eat wild garlic or other strongly scented herbage. "Cowy" or cardboardy tastes are also due to improper feeding and a fishy taste may be the result of processing in the presence of copper.

SWEET MILK

Milk is sold in many forms, some with added vitamins—especially D—to make its calcium and phosphorus more available to the body. Much milk is "standardized," which simply means that it comes from a milk pool covering a wide area and has cream or skim milk added to make it conform to the prevailing legally required balance between these two elements. If milk is marked as follows, it has a definite composition.

WHOLE MILK

This is a fresh, fluid milk containing 4% butterfat. The fat accounts for a cream line that forms above the milk when the fat particles rise. The cream is plainly evident if the milk has been left undisturbed for some time.

HOMOGENIZED MILK

Also a fresh, fluid milk, this has the same percentage of fat as whole milk. However, it has no cream line, as during preparation the fat particles are broken up so finely that they remain uniformly dispersed throughout. Its finer curd is more easily digested than that of whole milk. Processors appreciate homogenization because it allows them to mix older and newer milks without the tell-tale evidence of curdling which tends to characterize milks beginning to stale.

Fresh homogenized milk produces a different texture in cooking than does whole milk. Sauces are stiffer and fat separation greater. Cornstarch puddings are more granular and soups, gravies, cooked cereals, scalloped potatoes and custards tend to curdle. This texture change is not present, however, when homogenized milks are evaporated.

SKIM MILK

This has all the protein and mineral value of whole milk but, because the fat is removed, only half its caloric value. It is also deprived of the valuable fat-soluble vitamins A, D, E and K.

EVAPORATED MILK

This is whole milk which is freed of half its moisture content and canned. It can be reconstituted by adding ½ cup water to the same quantity of evaporated milk and used to replace 1 cup fresh whole milk in any recipes except those calling for junket. Because it can be preserved during times of excess production, it is sometimes less expensive than whole milk. It has a slightly caramelized taste, due to the processing. The cans, which come in 6 oz. and 14½ oz. sizes, should be reversed every few weeks in storage to keep solids from settling. Do not hold condensed milk over 6 months before using. Once opened, the milk should be stored and treated as fresh milk. To make it flow easily from the can, punch two holes near the rim at opposite sides of the top.

SWEETENED CONDENSED MILK

This process was used as early as Civil War days. It is milk in which the water content has been reduced about 60%. The 15-oz. can contains the equivalent of 2½ cups milk and 8 tablespoons sugar. It, too, settles during storage. The can should be reversed about every 2 weeks and not held longer than 6 months before using. Once opened, the can should be refrigerated. Because of the high sugar content, the milk will keep somewhat longer than regular condensed milk after opening.

DRY MILK SOLIDS

These are pasteurized milk particles, air dried to eliminate all but about 5% moisture. They come in both whole and skim milk form and should be free of any rancid, tallowy, scorched or soapy odors or flavors. Milk solids should always be stored in a lightproof, airtight container, in a cool place. Once opened, it is best to refrigerate the package.

◗ To reconstitute whole dry milk solids or skim milk solids, use 3 to 4 tablespoons of powdered milk to 1 cup water. Or follow the instructions on the package. This quantity will equal 1 cup fresh milk. For the best flavor, reconstitute at least 2 hours in advance of use. Dry milk solids are useful in enriching the diet, but need special handling. They scorch easily, requiring a lower temperature in baking meat loaves or similar mixtures to which dry milk solids have been added. To avoid scorching gravies and sauces made with dry milk, use a double boiler or very low heat. Do not add more than 3 tablespoons of milk solids to each cup of liquid in preparing sauces. To avoid lumping, mix the milk solids first with the flour and then with the melted fat, off the heat, and then add the warm, but not hot, liquid gradually.

In cooked cereals, add 3 tablespoons dry milk solids to each ½ cup of the dry cereal—before cooking—then use the same amount of water or milk called for in the regular recipe.

For cocoas, custards and puddings, add 3 tablespoons of dry milk solids for each cup of liquid.

In baking, mix dry milk solids with the flour ingredients, see Cornell Triple Rich Formula, page 556, but be careful never to add more than ¼ cup of milk solids for each cup of flour or the result will be too dense a crumb.

SWEET CREAMS

Cream is that fatty part of whole milk which rises to the surface on standing. The longer the milk stands, the richer—up to a point—it gets. There are few dishes which do not improve with a slight addition of cream, if it is properly incorporated.

The following terms are used throughout this book:

HALF-AND-HALF

This is 12% cream and often suggested as a drink in fattening diets.

CREAM

Cream is just "cream," without further qualification. It has between 18% and 20% butterfat and reaches this stage after about 12 hours of standing. It is sometimes referred to as Coffee or Cereal Cream.

WHIPPING CREAM

This is skimmed from milk after 24 hours standing. It has between 32% and 40% butterfat. When containing 32%, it is referred to as Light Cream and when 40%, Heavy Cream.

WHIPPED CREAM

This is whipping cream, at least a day old, which is expanded from 1 cup to 2 cups by the incorporation of air. To get the right texture, the bowl, beaters and cream should all be chilled in a refrigerator at least 2 hours before whipping, so that the milk fat stays firm during whipping rather than becoming oily from the friction involved. In warm weather beat over ice, see illustration, page 193. If the cream is warmer than 45°, it will, on beating, quickly turn to butter. ◗ Never overwhip. We like our cream whipped just to the point where it falls in large globs and soft peaks, but still carries a gloss. This is a state almost comparable to the ◗ stiff, but not dry, of Beaten Egg White, see page 515. It is posible to use it in this desirable delicate state only if it is prepared the last split second before serving.

If whipped cream is to be used decoratively, bring it to the point where the cream molecules are about to become buttery. Should the cream really threaten to turn into butter, whip in 2 or more tablespoons of "top" or evaporated milk or

cream and continue to beat. Cream at th stage may also be forced through a past tube for decorating. ◗ To freeze sm decorative garnishes, shape them on fo Freeze them uncovered on the foil, wr when firm and return to the freezer f future use.

◗ To beat cream with an electric beat turn to medium high speed until t chilled cream begins to thicken, then low the speed and watch like a hawk. Do n try to whip cream in a blender. If whipp cream is to be held for 24 hours or so, sometimes is suggested that a small amou of gelatin be incorporated for stiffenin but we have never found this technique be an advantage. It does help, if the crea is to be flavored, to mix in a small quanti of confectioners' sugar, as the cornstar in the sugar forms a stabilizer. For inte esting ways to flavor whipped creams, s page 645.

CREME CHANTILLY

This is the French equivalent of o Sweetened Whipped Creams, page 645. Unsweetened, it is called "Fleurette."

WHIPPED CREAM SUBSTITUTES

First, let us say there are really no ve satisfactory substitutes for whipped crea but the following makeshifts are som times used. It is often wise to add vanil 1 teaspoon per cup, or one of the oth flavors suggested in Sweetened Whipp Creams, page 645, to mask both the i ferior flavor and texture of these subs tutes.

I. If you allow 20% cream to stand frigerated for 48 hours and skim it, ◗ skimmed portion will sometimes—not ways—whip. Handle as for whipp cream, above.

II. Soak:
    1 or 1½ teaspoons gelatin
depending on heaviness of cream desir in:
    2 tablespoons cold water or fruit juice
When it is clear, dissolve it well in:
    ½ cup scalded 20% cream
Add:
    1 cup 20% cream
    1 tablespoon powdered sugar
Refrigerate. Stir from time to time. D ing the early part of the 4 to 6 ho needed to chill properly, add:
    ½ teaspoon vanilla
Then beat as for whipped cream, about to 7 minutes.

III. Chill for 12 hours:
    1 can evaporated milk
For each 13-oz. can, add:
    1 teaspoon lemon juice
Whip until stiff.

MILK AND CREAM SUBSTITUTIONS

Sometimes it is convenient to substitute milk for cream. But, if the substitution is made for baking, a different texture will result—unless the fat content of the cream is compensated for. ◖ To substitute for 1 cup 20% cream, use ⅞ cup milk and 3 tablespoons butter. To substitute for 1 cup 40% cream, use ¾ cup milk and ⅓ cup butter. This substitution, of course, will not whip.

SWEET AND SOUR MILK SUBSTITUTIONS

If recipes for baking specify sour or buttermilk when you have only sweet milk on hand, you may then proceed as follows: interchange sweet milk and baking powder with sour milk and soda. ◖ Use the same amount of liquid as is called for in the recipe. ◖ To sour the sweet milk, have the milk at 70°. Place in the bottom of a measuring cup:

   1 tablespoon lemon juice or distilled
   white vinegar

Then fill the cup with:

   Fresh sweet milk or the equivalent
   amount of reconstituted evaporated
   or dried whole milk solids

Stir and let the mixture stand about 10 minutes to clabber. It should have the consistency of cultured buttermilk or yogurt. ◖ If the leaven is baking powder or soda, be sure that it is added to the dry, not the liquid, ingredients. Make the following adjustments: for every teaspoon baking powder indicated in the recipe, use ¼ teaspoon baking soda plus ½ cup sour milk or ¼ teaspoon baking soda and ½ teaspoon vinegar or lemon juice plus ½ cup sweet milk.

SOUR AND FERMENTED MILKS
AND CREAMS

The long life of the Arabs, Bulgars and other Eastern peoples is often attributed to their diet of fermented milks. The friendly bacteria in these milks settle in the intestines where they break down the sugar in the lactic acid and where some, like yogurt and koumis, are reported to manufacture B vitamins. Soured milks and creams also play an important part in cooking. The presence of lactic acid gives them all a tenderer curd and this, in turn, makes for a tenderer crumb in baking and a smoother texture in sauces. In sauces, too, they contribute a slightly acid flavor which is highly prized.

Milks and creams may be allowed to sour naturally, but yogurt and some other similar varieties are processed by means of specially introduced bacterial cultures. When pasteurized dairy products are used, they never sour naturally and must always be cultured to do so. In this book, for reasons of safety, we recommend only sour milks and creams that have been pasteurized and cultured. In cooking ◖ be sure to add these milks and creams at the very last and off the heat or over very low heat, or they will curdle. And in breadmaking, don't scald, just heat until warm.

Should a recipe—like the classic Smitane Sauce, page 325—call for the addition of sour cream or milk at the start of the cooking process, be sure to use naturally soured dairy products, and no other, to prevent curdling. ◖ In either case, after adding the sour milk ingredient, the mixture should never be allowed to boil. In any sour cream recipes, use salt sparingly, as salting also tends to cause curdling.

BUTTERMILK

Originally this was the residue from the butter churn. Today it is usually made from pasteurized skim milk. A culture is added to develop flavor and to produce a heavier consistency than the skim milk from which it is made. Buttermilk differs nutritionally from skim milk mainly in its greater amount of lactic acid. As its protein precipitate is in the form of a fine curd, it is also more quickly digested than skim milk. Commercial buttermilk frequently has added cream or butter particles. Try making buttermilk yourself:

Combine:

   1 quart 70° to 80° skim milk
   ½ cup 70° cultured buttermilk
   ⅛ teaspoon salt

Stir well and cover. Let stand at 70° until clabbered. Stir until smooth. Refrigerate before serving. Store as for fresh milk.

SOUR MILK

This is whole or skim milk that is allowed to sour naturally. It is good only if it is made from unpasteurized or unscalded milk. Pasteurized or scalded milk will not sour, but simply spoil. In this book, therefore, recipes which formerly called for sour milk now call for buttermilk.

YOGURT

If you have ever eaten good, naturally flavored yogurt, you will try, as we have, to make it. We hope these directions will spare you some of our exasperating failures. Eastern yogurts are made with milk reduced by about ⅓. Our commercial yogurts have the same value as the milk from which they are made. This is also true of the yogurt you can make yourself.

Like yeast, the activator in yogurt is a living organism sensitive to temperatures. Test the milk with a thermometer for consistent results. Use milk from skim to half-and-half richness. Yogurt has the added idiosyncrasy that it doesn't care to be jostled while growing, so place all your equipment where you can leave it undisturbed for 8 hours. However, there are electric devices which can produce yogurt in 3 hours. If you use one of these, follow the directions carefully. Failure may result if milk or utensils are not absolutely clean.

We make yogurt regularly without the use of any heat other than that retained in the milk—using either an insulated cooler or the "snug nest" described next.

For this very satisfactory contraption, you will need a lidded vessel like a deep-well liner. Acquire enough inch-thick foam rubber and plastic wrapping or bags to cover the foam rubber—thus insuring a sanitary, well-insulated lining for your pan. Cut the foam rubber into 3 pieces. Make one round to fit the bottom, one overlapping, long, narrow piece for the side wall and a small round that will fit snugly into the top of the side wall. This smaller disk will be held in place between the top of the cups and the lid. Fit into this insulated space any heat-resistant cups or jars that fit your vessel. Also have ready a piece of foil to go between the cups and the top pad.

For the first batch, you will need a starter. Buy a jar of yogurt, get a small quantity from a friend or buy a package of yogurt culture from a health store. If you use the culture, heat a pint of milk to 180°. Cool it to 110°. Stir into this milk very thoroughly a package of the culture. Do not allow the milk to register less than 106° when it is in the jars. Then place them in the insulated equipment. Cover the jars at once and check in 7 to 8 hours to see if the contents have reached a thick, custardy consistency. Then check every half hour. Refrigerate when ready. Reserve from this first batch a small quantity to use for the second batch. Preferably, this should be not older than 5 days when used as a starter. The yogurt will keep for about 6 to 7 days.

When you are ready to start the second batch, have the equipment where you will be able to leave it for the next 8 hours. Measure the contents of your jars or cups. Heat that amount of milk. Bring it to 180° and pour it directly into the clean jars that are in place, except for the foil closures. Cool the jars until the milk reaches between 109° and 106°. When this state has been reached, it is important to work quickly. Take one tablespoon of milk from each pint. Add to the combined amount, for each tablespoon, ½ teaspoon of starter yogurt. Distribute the yogurt and milk mixture evenly into the bottles, stirring it in gently. Cover the jars with foil, pad and lid. Let it set 7 to 8 hours.

You may wonder why so little starter is used and think that a little more will produce a better result. It won't. The bacillus, if crowded, gives a sour, watery prod-

uct. But if the culture has sufficient Lebensraum, it will be rich, mild and creamy. If the yogurt should not have thickened in 8 hours, you may start all over again and have success by reheating the same yogurt slowly to 180°, cooling to 109°-106° and adding a fresh starter. Should you not succeed, it may be due to too great heat in the mixing so that you have killed the culture; it may be that your culture was a poor one or that there were antibiotics in the milk. Always remember ♦ don't eat every drop of your most recent batch. Keep those few teaspoons to form the starter for the next one.

CULTURED SOUR CREAM

The mention of sour cream may bring from the uninitiated a disdainful sniff and a vision of a yellowed mass of decomposed solids swimming on a bluish whey. But the seasoned cook responds to the term with delight, for she sees the culinary possibilities of this smooth semiplastic and rolls her tongue in anticipation of its promise. Many uses for sour cream are suggested in this book and if your dairy does not carry it, try making it yourself.

Place in a quart glass jar:

1 cup pasteurized 20% cream

♦ The cream must be at least this heavy and may be heavier—the heavier the better for the texture of the end product. Add:

5 teaspoons cultured buttermilk

The commercial type which is 1% acid and has carefully controlled bacteria is suggested rather than the less acid and less controlled home product. Cover the jar and shake these ingredients vigorously. Stir in:

1 cup pasteurized 20% cream

Cover the jar and allow this mixture to stand at about 75° to 80° for 24 hours. The sour cream may then be used at once, although storage under refrigeration for another 24 hours makes a finer product.

It is possible to "stretch" sour cream. Use half a jar and fill with 20% cream.

DEVONSHIRE OR CLOTTED CREAM

One of those regional specialties we always wish we could make locally. If you have a cow, you might try! In winter, let fresh cream stand 12 hours; in summer, about 6 hours, in a heatproof dish. Put the cream on to heat—or on the back of a peat or well-insulated iron coal stove—the slower the heat the better. It must never boil, as this will coagulate the albumen and ruin everything. When small rings or undulations form on the surface, the cream is sufficiently scalded. Remove at once from heat and store in a cold place for 12 hours. Then skim the thick, clotted cream and serve it very cold, as a garnish for berries.

CREME FRAICHE

This is served in France with fruits. It is actually a crème aigre, a naturally matured, slightly sour-flavored raw cream. ♦ To substitute 1 cup crème fraîche for 1 cup whipped cream, stir into:

1 cup raw 30% cream
1 teaspoon commercial buttermilk

Heat to 85°. Let stand at a temperature between 60° to 85° until it has thickened. Stir gently and refrigerate until ready to use.

SOUR CREAM SUBSTITUTE

A low-calorie substitute to be used only in uncooked dressings or for garnish.
I. ⅃ Mix for 2 or 3 seconds in a blender:

1 tablespoon lime or lemon juice
⅓ cup buttermilk
1 cup smooth cottage cheese

II. Mix:

1 cup 70° evaporated milk

with:

1 tablespoon vinegar

Allow it to stand until it clabbers and thickens.

SCALDING MILK

In this day of pasteurized milk, scalding is employed more often to hasten or improve a food process than to destroy bacteria. If, as a cook, you happen to talk to a food chemist about "scalding" milk, you may find yourself in an argument. To him, scalding will be that point at which milk begins to come up in a light froth, just as it boils, around 212°. To cooks, as high a temperature as this means scorched pots and frazzled tempers. In practice, we rely on the age-old visual test for scalding and, in this book, milk is scalded ♦ when tiny bubbles form around the edge of the pan and the milk reaches about 180°. Heating may be either over direct heat or in the top of a double boiler ♦ over—not in—hot water. Before heating milk for scalding, it is a help to rinse out the pan with cold water. To scald milk for bread, see page 553; for custards, page 684.

VEGETABLE MILKS

These are all valuable nutritionally, but not comparable to animal milks, as their protein is of lower biologic value, page 2.

SOY BEAN MILK

This milk—which can be substituted cup for cup in any recipe calling for regular milk—also gives a taste and cooking reaction very similar to cow's milk in finished recipes. Though very different nutritionally from cow's milk and with a basic lack of iodine, it is, however, commonly used for feeding babies in the Orient.

I. Soak, well covered in water for 12 hours:

1½ lbs. dried soy beans

Drain the beans. Put them through a food grinder, pouring on them while grinding a slow, steady stream of:

Water

Continue pouring the water until the entire mixture reaches 1 gallon. Heat this mixture until it is disagreeable to hold a finger in it, 131°. Put the mixture in a cloth bag and allow it to drip. Heat the drippings in a double boiler for 45 minutes, stirring frequently. Sweeten with dextrose or honey to taste. Add enough water to make in all 5 quarts.

II. Mix gradually, so as to avoid lumping:

1 quart soy bean flour
4 cups water

Strain this mixture in a cloth bag. Heat the drippings for 15 minutes in a double boiler, stirring frequently. Cool and keep the milk under refrigeration.

NUT AND COCONUT MILKS

Almond and walnut milks have long been known to Europe's peasants and our own Indians used hickory nuts and pecans. These rather fragilely-flavored milks, as well as coconut milk, are a great delicacy in sauces and puddings. ♦ They are as perishable as cow's milk and should be stored the same way, page 482. To use them, see About Coconut Milk and Cream, page 523, a staple wherever these beautiful palms grow.

As nuts vary in weight, look up the measurement equivalent to almonds and blanch the nuts, if necessary. Then substitute accordingly in the following recipe. These milks are often used to substitute for milk in desserts, with sugar added. If using for sauces other than dessert sauces, you may use stock as your liquid base.

ALMOND MILK

I. Blanch:

⅔ cup almonds
(2 or 3 bitter almonds)

Drain and discard the liquid. Cool the nuts. Pound them in a mortar with:

¼ cup sugar
(1 tablespoon orange water)

If necessary, add from time to time a tablespoon or so ice water to keep the nuts from becoming oily. When this mixture is quite smooth, stir in:

2 cups cold water

Stir well. Cover and refrigerate about 2 hours. Strain the liquid through a cloth-lined sieve and refrigerate until ready to use.

II. ⅃ For an American hurry-up version that will shock the painstaking French, use the above ingredients, but blend with:

2 tablespoons water

(2 tablespoons orange water)
Add the water gradually. Strain through a
cloth-lined sieve. Refrigerate.

ABOUT STOCKS AND STOCK
SUBSTITUTES

Antique dealers may respond hopefully to
dusty bits in attics, but true cooks palpitate
over even more curious oddments: mushroom and tomato skins, fowl carcasses,
tender celery leaves, knucklebones, fish
heads and chicken feet. These are just a
few of the treasures for the stock pot—
that magic source from which comes the
telling character of the cuisine. The juices
made and saved from meat and vegetable
cookery are so important that in France
they are called bases or "fonds." You will
note in the recipes for gravies, aspics,
soups or sauces the insistent call for stocks.
While these need not always be heavily
reduced ones ♦ do experiment by tasting
the wonderful difference when these liquids replace water. ♦ When stocks are
specified in long-cooking recipes, they are
always meat stocks, as vegetable and fish
stocks deteriorate in flavor under prolonged cooking.

You will want to store separately and
use very sparingly certain strongly flavored
waters, like cabbage, carrot, turnip and
bean or those from starchy vegetables, if
the stock is to be a clear one. You may
look askance at the liquids in which modern hams and tongues have been cooked
because of the many chemicals now used
in curing. You will, of course, never want
to use the cooking water from an "old"
ham. And you will certainly reserve any
light-fleshed fish and shell-fish residues for
use in fish dishes exclusively. Fish and
vegetable stocks with vegetable oils are
important in "au maigre" cooking, as con-
trasted with "au gras" or meat and meat-
fat based cooking. But, whether you are
a purist who uses only beef-based stock
with beef, or chicken with chicken or
whether you experiment with less classic
combinations, for both nutrient values and
taste dividends ♦ do save and make stocks.

STOCK-MAKING

While we beg you to utilize the kitchen
oddments described under Household
Stock, page 490, we become daily more
aware that the neat packaged meats and
vegetables most of us get at the supermar-
ket give us an increasing minimum of
trimmings. The rabbits, old pheasants and
hens that make for such picturesque reading in ancient stock recipes—fairly thrust-
ing the hunter and farmer laden with
earthy bounty straight into the kitchen—
have given way to a well-picked-over turkey carcass and a specially purchased soup
bunch. But even these are worthwhile.
♦ Stock-making is an exception to almost
every other kind of cooking. Instead of

calling for things young and tender ♦ remember that meat from aged animals and
mature vegetables will be most flavorsome.
Remember, too, that instead of making
every effort to keep juices within the materials you are cooking, you want to extract
and trap every vestige of flavor from
them—in liquid form. So ♦ soaking in cold
water and starting to cook in cold water—both of which methods draw juices—
are the first steps to your goal; but have
the ingredients to be cooked and the water
at the same temperature at the onset of
cooking. ♦ Bones are disjointed or crushed;
meat is trimmed of excess fat and cut up;
and vegetables, after cleaning, may even
be ⅄ blended.

♦ In making dark stocks, browning a
portion of the meat or roasting it until
brown, but not scorched, will add flavor.
♦ For a strong meat stock, allow only 2
cups of water to every cup of lean meat
and bone. They may be used in about
equal weights. When this much meat is
used, only a very few vegetables are
needed to give flavor to the soup.

Bones, especially marrow bones and
ones with gelatinous extractives, play a
very important role in stock. But, if a too
large proportion of them is used, the stock
becomes gluey and is reserved for use in
gravies and sauces. Raw and cooked bones
should not be mixed if a clear stock is desired. Nor, for clear stock, should any
starchy or very greasy foods be added to
the stock pot. Starchy foods also tend to
make the stock sour rapidly.

Before you put the browned meat and
the cooking herbs in the pot, discard any
fat that may have been extracted. The
factor that retains the flavor of the extracted juices most is ♦ to have a steady
low heat for the simmering of the brew.
You may laugh at the following primitive
suggestion. But it is our answer to the
thinness of modern pots and the passing of
that precious source of household heat,
"the back of the stove," now seldom found

in modern equipment. ♦ If you do not have an asbestos pad to produce an evenly transmitted heat, get two or three bricks—depending on the size of your pot. Put them on your burner, set at low heat and place your soup pot on them, as shown in the sketch. You need then have no worries about boiling over or about disturbing the steady, long, simmering rhythm. Or, for a similar effect, use a double boiler. When choosing a heavy stock pot, avoid aluminum, as it will affect the clarity of the stock.

As the stock heats, quite a heavy scum rises to the surface. ♦ If a clear soup is wanted, it is imperative to skim this foamy albuminous material before the first half hour of cooking. After the last skimming, wipe the edge of the stock pot at the level of the soup. Some nutritionists advise against skimming stocks to be used for brown sauces.

♦ Simmer the stock ♦ partially covered, with the lid at an angle, until you are sure you have extracted all the goodness from the ingredients—over 2 hours and at least 12 if bones are used. To keep the stock clear, drain it, not by pouring, but by ladling. Or use a stock pot with a spigot. Then strain it through 2 layers of cheesecloth that have been wrung out in water. Cool it ♦ uncovered. Store it ♦ tightly covered and refrigerate. The grease will rise in a solid mass which is also a protective coating. Do not remove this until you are ready to reheat the stock for serving or use. For more about this coating, see About Drippings, page 511.

Stocks keep 3 to 4 days refrigerated. The best practice is to bring them to a boil at the end of this period and cool before re-storing. It is also good practice to boil them if adding other pot liquors to them.

SEASONINGS FOR STOCKS AND SOUPS

These all-important ingredients should be ♦ added sparingly in the initial cooking of soups and stocks and the seasoning should be corrected just before the soup is served.

♦ Never salt heavily at the beginning of stock-making. The great reduction both in original cooking and in subsequent cooking —if the stock is used as an ingredient— makes it almost impossible to judge the amount you will need. And a little extra salt can so easily ruin your results. ♦ If stocks are stored, the salt and seasoning are apt to intensify and ♦ if any wine is used in dishes made from stock, the salt flavor will be increased.

♦ The discreet use of either fresh or dried herbs and spices is imperative. Use whole spices like peppercorns, allspice, coriander and celery seeds and bay leaf—but not too many. Add mace, paprika and cayenne in the stingiest pinches. Be sure to use a Bouquet Garni, page 541, and for a quick soup, try a Chiffonade, page 173.

An onion stuck with two or three cloves is de rigueur and, if available, add one or two leeks. Monosodium glutamate is a great help when the flavor of the stock is thin. For further details, see Seasonings, page 538.

CLARIFYING STOCK

If you have followed the directions in Stock-making carefully, your product should be clear enough for most uses. But for extra-sparkling aspic, jellied consommé, or chaud-froid you may wish to clarify stock in one of 2 ways. Both are designed to remove cloudiness; but the second method also strengthens flavor. ♦ Be sure the stock to be clarified has been well degreased; and never let it boil.

For the first method, allow to each quart of broth 1 slightly beaten egg white and 1 crumpled shell. If the stock to be clarified has not been fully cooled and is still lukewarm, also add a few ice cubes for each quart. Stir the eggs and ice into the soup well. Bring the soup very, very slowly ♦ without stirring, just to a simmer. As the soup heats, the egg brings to the top a heavy, crusty foam, over an inch thick. Do not skim this, but push it very gently away from one side of the pan. Through this small opening, you can watch the movement of the simmering—to make sure no true boiling takes place. Continue simmering 10 to 15 minutes. Move the pot carefully from the heat source and let it stand 10 minutes to 1 hour. Wring out a cloth in hot water and suspend it, like a jelly bag, above a large pan. Again push the scummy crust to one side and ladle the soup carefully so it drains through the cloth. Cool it ♦ uncovered. Store it ♦ covered tightly and refrigerate.

The second method of clarification produces a double-strength stock for consommé. Add to each quart of degreased stock ⅛ to ¼ lb. of lean ground beef, 1 egg white and crumpled shell and to the pot several uncooked fowl carcasses; and, if the stock is beef, fresh tomato skins. Some cooks also use a few vegetables. Beat these additions into the stock. Then ♦ very slowly, bring the pot just to a simmer.

Should the stock have boiled at any time during the process just described, the clarification is ruined. It will be necessary to start over again, proceeding as follows. After what should have been the simmering period in the second method, remove the pot from the heat and skim it. Allow the stock to cool to about 70°. Again add an egg white and a crumpled eggshell for each quart of stock. Then continue as for the first method above. Allow the simmer to last up to 2 hours. Then remove the pot from the heat source and let it rest an hour or more. Ladle and strain it, as previously

described. Cool it ♦ uncovered. Store it
♦ tightly covered and refrigerated.

BROWN STOCK
I.   **About 2 Quarts**
♦ Please read About Stocks, page 488.
Cut in pieces and brown in a 350° oven:
    6 lbs. shin and marrow bones
Place them in a large stock pot with:
    4 quarts water
    8 black peppercorns
    6 whole cloves
    1 bay leaf
    1 teaspoon thyme
    3 sprigs parsley
    1 large diced carrot
    3 diced stalks celery
    1 cup drained canned or fresh tomatoes
    1 medium diced onion
    1 small, white, diced turnip
Bring to boil. ♦ Reduce heat and simmer,
uncovered, for 2½ to 3 hours or until reduced by half. Strain stock. Cool uncovered and refrigerate.

II.   **About 3½ Cups**
While Brown Stock I is more strongly fla-
vored and clearer, do not scorn stocks
made from cooked meats and bones.
♦ Please read About Stocks, page 488.
Cut the meat from the bone. To:
    2 cups cooked meat and bones
Add, in a heavy stock pot:
    4 or 5 cups water
    ¼ teaspoon salt
    1 cup chopped vegetables: carrots,
      turnips, celery, parsley, etc.
    1 small onion
    1 cup tomatoes
    ½ teaspoon sugar
    2 peppercorns
    ¼ teaspoon celery salt
Bring the soup just to the boiling point,
turn down the heat and ♦ simmer, uncovered, for 1½ hours. Strain the soup, chill
it. For quick chilling, place it in a tall,
narrow container set in cold water. Remove the fat and reheat the soup.
    Correct the seasoning

VEAL OR LIGHT STOCK
                                          About 2 Quarts
♦ Please read About Stocks, page 488.
Blanch II, page 132:
    4 lbs. veal knuckles or 3 lbs. veal
      knuckles and 1 lb. beef
Drain and discard water and add meat
and bones to:
    4 quarts cold water
    8 white peppercorns
    1 bay leaf
    1 teaspoon thyme
    6 whole cloves
    6 parsley stems
    1 medium diced onion

    3 stalks diced celery
    1 medium diced carrot
Bring to a boil. ♦ Reduce heat at once to
a simmer and cook 2½ to 3 hours or until
reduced by half. Strain stock and ♦ cool
uncovered.

✪ QUICK STOCK
                                          4 to 6 Servings
Wash and cut into 1-inch cubes:
    2 lbs. lean beef: soup meat
Brown it slowly in the pressure cooker in:
    2 tablespoons melted fat
Drain off the fat. Add:
    1 quart boiling water
    A cracked soup bone
    1 medium sliced onion
    1 diced carrot
    4 diced stalks celery with tender leaves
    ½ bay leaf
    2 peppercorns
    ½ teaspoon salt
♦ Do not have the pressure cooker more
than ½ full. Adjust the cover and cook at
15 pounds pressure for 30 minutes. Reduce
pressure instantly. Strain. Cool ♦ uncovered.
    Correct the seasoning

✪ QUICK HOUSEHOLD STOCK
A careful selection of refrigerator oddments can often produce enough valid ingredients to make up a flavorful stock to
use as a reinforcer for soups—canned,
dried and frozen—and in gravies and
sauces. If cooked and uncooked meats are
combined, a darker, cloudier stock results.
Put in a pressure cooker:
    1 cup nonfat meat, bone and
      vegetables, cooked and uncooked
    1 to 1½ cups water
Use the smaller amount of water if you
are short on meat. For vegetables to in-
include, see Vegetables for Soup, page 491.
Do not fill the pressure cooker more than
½ full. If raw meat and bone are included,
add:
    (2 tablespoons vinegar)
Cook them first 10 minutes at 15 lbs. pressure. Add the other food and cook 10 to
15 minutes longer.
    Correct the seasoning

CHICKEN OR LIGHT STOCK
I.   **About 2 Quarts**
♦ Please read About Soup Stocks, page
488.
Blanch II, page 132:
    4 lbs. chicken backs, necks, wings
      and feet
Drain, discard water and bring the chicken
slowly to a boil in:
    4 quarts cold water
with:
    8 white peppercorns
    1 bay leaf

1 teaspoon thyme
6 whole cloves
6 parsley stems
1 medium diced onion
3 diced stalks celery
1 medium diced carrot

♦ Reduce the heat at once and simmer 2½ to 3 hours or until reduced by half. Strain stock. ♦ Cool uncovered and refrigerate until ready to use.

II.   From Chicken Feet
This stock gives a jellied, not too flavorful, but economical base. Cover with boiling water:

Chicken feet

Blanch them for about 3 minutes. Drain. Strip away the skin and discard. Chop off the nails. Place the feet in a pan and cover with:

Cold water

Add:

Vegetables

as suggested under Fowl Stock I. Simmer for about 1½ hours or use a ☼ pressure cooker. Strain and cool.

FOWL, RABBIT OR GAME STOCK
I.   About 9 or 10 Cups
Put in a heavy pot:

4 or 5 lbs. fowl or rabbit
3 quarts cold water
5 celery ribs with leaves
½ bay leaf
½ cup chopped onion
½ cup chopped carrots
6 sprigs parsley

Simmer the stock for 2½ hours, uncovered. Strain it. Chill it. It will solidify and make a good aspic or jellied soup. Degrease it before serving.

II.   1½ to 2½ Pints
The housewife frequently meets up with the leavings of a party bird from which a good stock can be made. Try this simpler soup when you have left over cooked chicken, duck or turkey. Break into small pieces:

1 cooked chicken, duck or turkey
    carcass

Add and simmer ♦ partially covered, for about 1½ hours in:

4 to 6 cups water

The amount of liquid will depend on the size or number of carcasses you use. Add also to the pot:

1 cup chopped celery with tender
    leaves
1 large sliced onion
½ cup chopped carrot
    Lettuce leaves
½ bay leaf
3 or 4 peppercorns
    Parsley
    A Bouquet Garni, page 541

Strain and chill it. Degrease before serving.

FUMET OR FISH STOCK
This is most useful for cooking "au maigre," on those days when religious observance calls for meatless meals. Combine the fumet with vegetables and cream as a base for soup or use it in sauces or aspics. It will keep for several days, covered, in the refrigerator, or for several weeks frozen.
Melt in a pan:

3 tablespoons butter

Add and cook gently about 5 minutes:

½ cup chopped onions or shallots
¼ cup chopped carrot
½ cup chopped celery

Then add:

6 white peppercorns
3 or 4 cloves
½ cup white wine or 2 tablespoons
    vinegar
2 cups cold water
    A Bouquet Garni, page 541
    A twist of lemon rind
1 to 1½ lbs. washed fish bones, heads,
    tails, skins and trimmings

The fish heads are particularly flavorful, but ♦ avoid strong-flavored fish trimmings like mackerel, skate or mullet. Use salmon only for salmon sauce. Shells from crab, shrimp and lobster are delicious additions, but these are usually cooked with bay leaf, thyme and wine rather than with vinegar. Heat until the liquid begins to ♦ simmer and continue cooking, uncovered, over rather brisk heat, not longer than 20 to 30 minutes—or a bitter flavor may develop. Add, at the last minute:

Any extra oyster or clam juices

Strain the stock and use in soups or sauces. To clarify fish fumet for aspic, proceed as for the quick method of beef stock clarification, page 489.

VEGETABLES FOR STOCK AND SOUP

In vegetable stock for soup, your goal is to draw all the flavor out of the vegetable, see Vegetable Stock, page 492. To prepare, use about 1½ to 2 times as much water as vegetable. Prepare vegetables for soup as you would for eating—wash, scrape or pare, as needed, and remove bruised or bad portions. Onions are the exception, as the skins may be left on to give color to the soup.

♦ For quicker cooking and greater extraction, you may ⅄ blend the vegetables before cooking. If the cooking liquid tastes palatable, keep it for judicious use with other full-bodied sauces or gravies.

It is very important to taste the vegetable liquors you reserve. They vary tremendously, depending on the age of the vegetable and whether the leaves are dark outer ones or light inner ones. Green celery tops, for instance, can become bitter through long cooking in a stock, while the tender yellowish leaves do not. Often, too, celery is so heavily sprayed with chemicals that the outer leaves and tops taste strongly enough of these absorbed flavors to carry over into foods. Nutritionists recommend the outer leaves of vegetables because of their greater vitamin content. Eat these raw in salads, where the bitterness is not accented as it is in soups.

Also balance the amounts and kinds of vegetables to other stock flavors. The cooking liquors from white turnips, cabbage, cauliflower, broccoli and potatoes, used with discretion, may be a real asset to a borsch and a real calamity in chicken broth. We find pea pods and water from peas, except in pea soups, a deadening influence. Carrots and parsnips tend to sweeten the pot too much. Tomatoes, unless just the skins are used, can make a consommé too acid and yet be just the touch you want in a vegetable soup or a sauce. Some vegetable juices like those from leeks, water cress and asparagus seem ever welcome. ♦ Use any of these liquids, whether from fresh, canned or frozen vegetables, if you taste good.

You may also purée leftover cooked vegetables as thickeners for soup.

There are several ways to bring up the flavor of soup vegetables. One is to sauté them gently in butter, see Brunoise, page 146. The other is to cook them in meat stocks.

Unlike the above ♦ when you add vegetables to soup as a garnish, the trick is not to soften them to the point where their cells break down and they release their juices, but to keep them full of flavor. However, if the vegetables you are using as a garnish are strong like peppers or onions, blanch them first.

VEGETABLE STOCK
About 1 Quart

To add color to this stock made from raw vegetables, begin by caramelizing, page 508:

    1 teaspoon sugar
in a heavy pot or sauté:
    ½ cup finely chopped onion
in:
    2 tablespoons fat
Add:
    A dash of white pepper
    A dash of cayenne
    ½ teaspoon salt
    A Bouquet Garni, page 541
    ¼ cup each carrots, turnips, parsnips
    2 cups diced celery ribs and yellow leaves
    (1 cup shredded lettuce)
    (Mushroom or tomato skins)
Add enough to cover:
    Cold water
Bring to a boil ♦ cover partially and simmer about 1½ hours or until the vegeta-

bles are very tender. Strain and chill. Degrease before using, if necessary.

❂ PRESSURE COOKED STOCKS AND SOUPS

While these are not as delicate in flavor as stocks cooked at lower temperatures, they are not to be scorned.

♦ Allow one quart of liquid to about 2 lbs. of meat in a 4-quart pressure cooker. ♦ Season very lightly. You may prefer to almost finish cooking the meat, about 30 minutes at 15 lbs. pressure. Then reduce the pressure and add the vegetables. If there is a mixture, you will have to judge the time it will take to release their juices. Add about 3 minutes to the time given in individual recipes for pressure cooked vegetables. Strain the stock.

If you want to make a vegetable soup, strain and degrease the stock before adding the vegetables. Then cook them in the soup for the same length of time you would normally cook them as indicated in individual recipes.

ABOUT GLAZES

Glazes are meat stocks cooked down very slowly until they solidify. These overpoweringly strong stocks from meat and fowl are our first choice when we have the patience to make them. Ideally, properly cooked food should produce its own glaze but these results have all but vanished in most kitchens, as they prove both expensive and time consuming. Even meat glazes made by reducing stocks to a glutinous consistency are now the exception in home kitchens—but what a convenience and delight they are when skillfully used. They ✳ freeze very well, too.

♦ To make a glaze, or glace, reduce brown stock to the point where it evenly coats a spoon when inserted into it. ♦ Use glazes discreetly, as their strength can easily over-balance a sauce or gravy.

STOCK REINFORCERS

I. BEEF JUICE

This is another rich stock item. To make this, see Beef Tea, page 147.

II. CANNED BOUILLON AND CONSOMMÉ

These are both a great help. You may prefer the bouillon—which is less sweet than the consommé.

III. CANNED, FROZEN AND DRIED SOUPS

Alone or when combined with household stocks, these can produce very sophisticated results. Suggestions for their use appear in detail under Soups, Sauces, Aspics and Gravies. Bouillon cubes and beef extracts, each diluted in ½ cup boiling liquid are also useful.

IV. MILK AND CREAM

When diluted with stock and even the following seasoned water, milk and cream precede the use of plain water every time.

V. SEASONED WATER

Boil briskly for about 10 minutes:
> **2 cups water**

to which you have added:
> **1 teaspoon monosodium glutamate**
> **1 peppercorn**
> **½ teaspoon soy sauce or salt**

ABOUT COURT BOUILLON

Court bouillons are seasoned liquids which, as their name implies, are cooked only a short time. Their composition varies. They may simply be Acidulated Water, page 494, acidulated water reinforced with braised or fresh vegetables, or even a hot marinade with oil.

They are not actual broths or stocks in themselves but, rather, prototypes that may develop into them. Sometimes they are used only as a blanching or cooking medium. Then they are discarded, as in the cooking of vegetables where their purpose is to retain color or leech out undesirable flavors. Sometimes they are used as a liquid in which to store the food processed in them, as in Vegetables à la Grecque, page 255. Or they may be used as a hot marinade in which fish is soaked before cooking. And, sometimes, as in the cooking of delicately flavored fish, they become—after the fish is drained from them—a Fumet or Fish Stock, page 491.

COURT BOUILLON FOR FISH

Use this for any fish which is to be poached or "boiled." See also Truite au Bleu or Blue Trout, page 362.

Trim and clean:
> **3 lbs. fish**

and rub with:
> **Lemon juice**

Meanwhile, in a large pan, bring to a boil:
> **2 quarts water**

Add:
> **½ bay leaf**
> **¼ cup chopped carrot**
> **½ cup chopped celery**
> **1 small onion stuck with 2 cloves**
> **½ cup vinegar or 1 cup dry white wine**
> **1 teaspoon salt**
> **(Parsley or a Bouquet Garni, page 541)**

When the mixture is boiling, plunge the fish in and ♦ at once, reduce the heat so the court bouillon simmers. Simmer the fish ♦ uncovered, until tender. Drain and serve. You may keep and use this court bouillon for several days for poaching other fish, but it is not used in soups, sauces and gravies, as is a fumet or fish stock, see above.

COURT BOUILLON BLANC

For use in retaining good color in variety meats and vegetables.

I. Allow to every:
> **1 quart boiling water**
> **2 tablespoons lemon juice**

Blend until smooth and add to the above:
> **2 tablespoons water**
> **1 tablespoon flour**
> **(3 tablespoons chopped suet)**

Add:
> **(An onion stuck with cloves, celery, carrot or leek)**

II. Or add the vegetables to a mixture of boiling:
> **½ seasoned water**
> **½ milk**

Reduce to a simmer at once. The milk may curdle slightly, but this will not affect the food adversely.

ABOUT WATER

One of our family jokes involved an 1890 debutante cousin from Indianapolis who, when asked where her home town got its water, replied: "Out of a faucet." Many of us have come to assume that there is a kind of nationwide standardization in tap water. As long as it runs pure, plentiful, hot and cold and reasonably pleasant to the taste, we no more bother our heads with its further analysis than did our pretty Victorian cousin. Yet both its purity and its composition are of considerable importance in the kitchen.

In this book, when the word ♦ water appears in the recipes, we assume it has a 60°-80° temperature. ♦ If hotter or colder water is needed, it is specified.

♦ Soft water is best for most cooking processes, although very soft water will make yeast doughs soggy and sticky. ♦ Hard water and some artificially softened waters affect flavor. They may toughen legumes and fruits and shrivel pickles. They markedly alter the color of vegetables in the cabbage family and turn onions, cauliflower, potatoes and rice yellow. If your water is hard, cooking these vegetables à blanc is a superior method of preparation. Hard water retards fermentation of yeast, although it strengthens the gluten in flour. Alkaline waters, however, have a solvent effect on gluten, as well as diminishing its gas-retaining properties—and the size of the loaf.

Water hardness is due to various combinations of salts and there are a number of ways by which it may be reduced. Passing hard water through a tank containing counteractive chemicals may be helpful, but most of these systems principally exchange sodium for calcium compounds and are more effective for water used in dish washing than in cooking. If the salts happen to consist of bicarbonates of calcium and magnesium, simply boiling the water for 20 or 30 minutes will cause them to precipitate. But if the water originally held in solution large amounts of sulphates, boiling it will increase hardness, rather than reduce it—because the sulphates are concentrated by evaporation. Certain types of hard water must be avoided by people who are on low sodium-free or salt-free diets.

Sodium chloride, or common salt, often occurs in inland, as well as ocean waters. Should you be interested in finding out what type of water you have, call your local waterworks or health department, if you live in a town, or your county agent, if you live in the country.

Most old recipes recommend long soaking of food in water. But we know that fruits, salad greens and vegetables should be washed as quickly and briefly as possible. Soaking leaches out their water soluble vitamins. ♦ And, because of this leaching action, it is a good plan to utilize all soaking and cooking waters, unless they have bitter or off-flavors.

Occasionally recipes indicate ♦ water by weight, in which case use 1 tablespoon for ½ oz., 2 cups for 1 lb.

▲ The boiling temperature of water at sea level—212°—is increased in direct proportion to the number of particles dissolved in it. The amount of salt added in cooking is not enough to change the normal sea level boiling point. With the addition of sugar, however, the boiling point is lowered appreciably, see Jellies, page 774. For boiling at high altitudes, see page 122.

ACIDULATED WATER
I. To 1 quart water, add 1 tablespoon vinegar.

II. To 1 quart water, add 2 tablespoons vinegar or 3 tablespoons lemon juice (1 teaspoon salt).

III. To 1 quart water, add ½ cup wine. Sometimes brines, page 525, are stipulated.

WATER PURIFICATION

In using or storing water, be sure of two things: that the source from which you get it is uncontaminated and that the vessels you store it in are sterile. The color of water has nothing to do with its purity. As disease germs are more often derived from animal than from vegetable matter, a brown swamp water may be purer than a blue lake water. ♦ Should water have been exposed to radioactive fallout, do not use it. Water from wells and springs, if protected from surface contamination, should be safe from this hazard. For water storage in shelters, use nonbreakable glass or plastic bottles that are surrounded by and separated from each other by excelsior or packing. Inspect the stored water periodically and replace any that is

cloudy. Allow for each person, for drinking, a minimum of 7 gallons for each 2 week period and for personal cleanliness, another 7 gallons.

If you are in doubt as to the purity of water, treat it in one of the following ways:
I. Boil water vigorously 3 minutes. Boiled water tastes flat, but can be improved in flavor if aerated by pouring it a number of times from one clean vessel to another.

II. Use water purification tablets in the dosage recommended on the label.

III. Add to ♦ clear water, allowing 8 drops per gallon, any household bleach solution that contains hypochlorite in 5.25% solution. The label should give you this information. ♦ If the water is cloudy, increase to 16 drops per gallon. ♦ In either case, stir and allow the water to stand 30 minutes after adding the hypochlorite. ♦ The water should have a distinct chlorine taste and odor. This is a sign of safety and, if you do not detect it by smell, add another dose of the hypochlorite and wait 15 minutes. If the odor is still not present, the hypochlorite may have weakened through age and the water is not safe for storage.

IV. ♦ Add to clear water, allowing 12 drops per gallon, 2% tincture of iodine. Stir thoroughly before storing. ♦ To cloudy water, allow 24 drops for each gallon. Stir thoroughly before storing. This method is not recommended for persons with thyroid disturbances.

ABOUT WINE AND SPIRITS FOR COOKING

There is no doubt that the occasional addition of wine—or of spirits and cordials—gives food a welcome new dimension. If yours is a wine-drinking household, you have probably always enjoyed cooking with "the butts." If wine is a stranger to your table, you may be hesitant about breaking open a new bottle for experimentation. When you do decide to take the plunge ♦ remember that the wine you choose need not be a very old or expensive one, but that it should be good enough, at least, to be drunk with relish for its own sake.

What kind of wine to use? The specific answer depends on the kind of food used with it, as listed later. Start your purchasing with a dry white and a full-bodied red. Try Bonne Femme Sauce for fish, page 351, a wine pot roast, an orange fruit soup and before you know it you will have developed a palate and a palette, and be well on your way to some strikingly colorful effects in a new medium.

In general, however, keep wine away from very tart or very piquantly seasoned foods, unless you are using it as a Marinade, page 336, or to mask an off-flavor. Incidentally, ♦ be sure that the dish in which you marinate is glazed or made of glass, stainless steel or enamel.

How much wine to use? ♦ Never add so much as to overbalance or drown out the characteristic flavor of the food itself. ♦ Count the wine as a part of any given sum total of liquid ingredients, not as an extra. A recipe for pot roast with wine may call for the addition of as much as a cup per pound. When you use it here, be sure it is warmed before adding. In meat or fowl recipes calling for both wine and salt pork, watch for too great saltiness. Correct the seasoning at the end of cooking.

Brandy, sherry and whiskey combat graininess and fishiness of flavor. In general, 2 tablespoons of heavy wine—such as sherry, Madeira or port—will equal in flavoring strength about ½ cup of dry red or white wine. In aspics, replace part of every cup of other liquid indicated with 1 to 1½ tablespoons fortified wine or 2 to 2½ tablespoons ordinary wine. You may wish to reduce wine as a means of increasing its flavoring power and to avoid overdilution in sauce-making. If so, remember that 1 cup of wine will reduce to about ¼ cup in 10 minutes of cooking.

When to add wine? This question is a hotly disputed one. If a wine sauce is heated, it not only loses its alcoholic content but, if cooked too long, its flavor. Add wine to a sauce only during those periods when the dish can be covered, whether marinating, cooking, storing or chilling. While you may boil wine to reduce it ♦ never raise the heat to above a simmer when cooking food in wine. We feel that if you aim at mellow penetration or at tenderizing, the time to add wine is at the onset of cooking. ♦ To avoid curdling or separation, wine should always be added beforehand in any recipes which include milk, cream, eggs or butter. It should then be reduced slightly and the other ingredients mentioned added in turn, off the heat. If the dish cannot be served at once, it may be kept warm in a double boiler ♦ over—not in—hot water. To achieve a pronounced wine flavor, swirl reduced wine into the food at the very end of the cooking process, after it has been removed from the heat. In aspics, wine should be added after the gelatin is dissolved. One of our favorite practices is to add wine to a pan in which meat has been cooking, deglazing, page 321, the pan juices and so building up a pleasant substitute for roux-based gravy.

Spirits, liqueurs and cordials are most frequently used in flavoring desserts. Whiskey is becoming increasingly popular but, except for desserts, do not use bourbon, as it is too sweet. One of the more spectacular wine-cooking techniques is flambéeing

—sometimes at midpoint in preparation and sometimes as a final flourish in the dining room. To flambée fruits and other foods, see page 127. ♦ Flambéing is sure-fire only if the liquor to be ignited is previously warmed as well as the food.

Exceptions not only prove the rule—they sometimes improve it. We list below certain time-tested combinations in wine-cookery; but we encourage defiance and initiative.

For Soups: Cream sherry or semisweet white wines.

For Fish, Poultry and Eggs: Dry white wines.

For Red Meat: Dry red wine or rosé.

For Pork, Veal, Lamb or Game: Red or white wine or rosé.

For Aspics and Wine Jellies: Any type—but red wines tend to lose their color. Brandy compliments an aspic of game.

For Sauces: Dry or semisweet Bordeaux or Burgundy, champagne, riesling, vermouth, see individual sauce recipes.

For Desserts: Sweet sherry, port, Madeira, Tokay, muscatel, rum, liqueurs, cordials.

Beer and cider, as well as wine, have virtues in cooking, especially if the beer is flat and the cider hard, as their fermentative qualities help tenderize meats, doughs and batters. You will find them indicated where their use is appropriate in a number of the recipes.

ABOUT VINEGAR

Whether a vinegar is sharp, rich or mellow makes a tremendous difference in cooking. ♦ All vinegars are corrosive—so be sure to mix pickled, vinaigretted or marinated foods in glass, enamel or stainless vessels. Keep away from copper, zinc, galvanized or iron ware.

Vinegars divide roughly into the following types:

DISTILLED WHITE VINEGAR

This is based on chemicals usually with a 40% acetic acid count or grain. It is used in pickling when the pickle must remain light in color.

CIDER AND MALT-BASED VINEGARS

These are full-bodied and usually run between 50% to 60% acetic acid.

WINE VINEGARS

Made from both red and white wines, these are the blandest. They have about a 50% acetic acid content.

We have often admired the lovely light quality of dressings based on Italian wine vinegar. A friend told us his secret lies in fermenting a homemade, unpasteurized red wine, but not allowing it to reach the point of bitterness. If you don't want to bother with this process, a substitute is to dilute sharp vinegars with red or white wine. Wine vinegars "mother," forming a strange, wispy residue at the base of the bottle. As they are of uncertain strengths, they are not recommended for pickling. Should you plan making spiced vinegars in quantity for gifts, please profit by our experience and mix in small batches.

HERB VINEGARS

These can be made with any of the above vinegars. Use individual herbs like tarragon or burnet or develop your favorite herb combinations—allowing not more than 3 tablespoons fresh herb leaves per quart of vinegar. If garlic is used, crush it and leave it in the jar only 24 hours. The reason for not overloading the vinegar is that its preservative strength may not be great enough to hold more vegetable matter. After 4 weeks of steeping, filter the vinegar, rebottle it in sterilized containers and keep tightly corked.

FRESH HERB VINEGAR

Combine:
    1 gallon cider or white wine vinegar
    2 dozen peppercorns
    1 dozen sliced shallots
    ¾ cup tarragon
    8 sprigs rosemary
    8 sprigs thyme
    4 branches winter savory
    1 sprig chervil
    1 well-cleaned, unpeeled, sliced
      celeriac root
    ½ cup parsley
    1 sliced parsley root
Bottle these ingredients. After 2 weeks, strain the vinegar through cheesecloth. Place in sterile bottles and cork tightly.

SPICED VINEGAR

An excellent, if deceptive, mixture. It tastes like a delicious blend of herbs, but it is flavored with spices whole or ground. If ground spices are used, filter the vinegar before using it. Combine, stir and heat slowly until just under the boiling point:
    ¼ cup whole cloves
    ¼ cup allspice
    2 tablespoons mace
    3 tablespoons celery seed
    ¼ cup mustard seed
    6 tablespoons whole black pepper
    3 tablespoons turmeric
    ¼ cup white ginger root
    1½ gallons cider vinegar
    2 cups sugar
Place these ingredients in jugs or fruit jars. Slice and add for 24 hours:
    4 or more cloves garlic
Cork the jugs or screw down the jar lids tightly. The vinegar is ready for use in 3 weeks. Combine it with oil for French Dressing, page 311.

GARLIC VINEGAR

Heat to the boiling point:
    1 cup vinegar

Cut into halves and add for 24 hours:
    4 cloves garlic
When the vinegar is cold, place it in a closed jar. After 2 weeks, strain it. Use it in dressings or sauces.

QUICK HERB VINEGAR
About 1 Cup

Combine:
    1 cup well-flavored vinegar: wine
      or cider
    1 teaspoon dried crushed herbs:
      basil, tarragon, etc.
You may use this at once with salad oil. You may add ½ clove of garlic and fish it out later. Shortly before serving, add:
    2 tablespoons chopped parsley
    1 tablespoon chopped chives

TARRAGON OR BURNET VINEGAR
About 2 Cups

Wash, then dry well:
    1½ tablespoons fresh tarragon or
      burnet leaves
Crush them to bruise them slightly. Add them to:
    2 cups warmed vinegar
    2 whole cloves
    1 skinned halved clove garlic
Place these ingredients in a covered jar. After 24 hours, remove the garlic. After 2 weeks, strain and bottle the vinegar. This makes a strong infusion that may be diluted later with more vinegar.

RED RASPBERRY VINEGAR

Put in a large glazed or stainless steel bowl:
    6 quarts red raspberries
Cover them with:
    1 quart wine vinegar
Let stand in a cool place for about 20 hours. Then strain. Measure the liquid into an enamel or stainless steel pan and add an equal quantity of:
    Sugar
Bring to a boil and ♦ simmer 10 minutes. Cool and store in tightly lidded sterile jars.

CHILI VINEGAR

You can make a really hot French dressing with this. See also Chilis Preserved in Sherry, page 785.
Steep:
    1 oz. chilis
in:
    1 pint vinegar
for 10 days. Shake daily. Then strain and bottle.

ABOUT WHEAT FLOURS AND GRAINS

In our miraculously mechanical but standardized economy, the average housewife, oddly enough, finds at hand only two kinds of white flour, both the result of highly milled or "patent" processing. They must meet rigid government specifications and, when manufactured, contain not more than 15% moisture. But they often acquire more in careless storage. Or they dry out in high altitudes or during the winter months. These varying moistures affect the way flours "handle." So some recipes for breads and pastries may read "2½ to 2¾ cups flour." If they do ♦ add the smaller amount of flour first and enough of, or even more than, the remaining flour until the dough begins to clean the sides of the bowl. Don't add more than is needed for good handling. These two easily available flours, called "all-purpose" and "cake," are used as their names imply. ♦ The single word "flour" in our recipes always means wheat flour.

ALL-PURPOSE FLOUR

This is a blend of hard and soft wheat flours. The presence of more and tougher gluten in the hard wheat constituent results in a rather elastic and porous product. Some of the flours sold in our South as all-purpose are closer to cake flour in texture. If using them with yeast, give them only one rising period—to not quite double the volume—and then let the dough rise to normal, using the finger test sketched on page 555. ♦ You may substitute for 1 cup of all-purpose flour 1⅛ cups of cake flour.

CAKE FLOUR

This is made of soft wheats and their delicate, less expansive gluten bakes to a crumblier texture. Although you will not get the same result—you may, in emergencies ♦ substitute ⅞ cup of all-purpose flour for 1 cup cake flour.

BREAD FLOUR

Although not easily come by, this type is highly desirable, as its high gluten content allows the absorption of more moisture than either of the above. The elasticity from its higher gluten content also allows it to expand and still hold the gas liberated by the yeast. This flour feels almost granular or gritty when rubbed between the fingers.

PRESIFTED FLOURS

These are ground to a point of pulverization and whether resifted or not give a different texture to baking. Some of them also have a larger percentage of hard durum wheat and, although the manufacturers may suggest them to replace cake flour, the greater gluten content may tend to toughen cakes. If you use them, be sure to use 1 tablespoon less per cup than our recipes call for. ♦ We suggest resifting.

BROWNED FLOUR

This has many uses. It adds both color and flavor to sauces, but browning it de-

stroys part of its thickening power. Heat all-purpose flour in a very slow oven 200° to 250° in a very heavy pan. Shake the pan periodically so the flour browns evenly. To substitute, use 1½ tablespoons browned flour for every tablespoon all-purpose flour.

PASTRY FLOUR

Finely milled, soft, low-gluten flour—often available in the South, where it is used for quick breads and pastries.

SELF-RISING FLOUR AND PHOSPHATED FLOURS

These contain the right amounts of leavens and salt for baking. Many people do not like to use them because during delays in merchandising or storing the leavens are apt to lose their potency. If used in pastry, these flours give a spongy texture and are advised only for crusts where a low fat content is the objective and the fat in the recipe has been reduced. They are not recommended for making bread.

SEMOLINA

This is a creamy-colored, granular, protein-rich durum wheat flour used commercially for all types of pasta. It is not your fault if homemade pastas and noodles fail to hold their shape no matter how carefully you have prepared and cooked them. The trouble lies in the lower gluten content of all-purpose flour on which housewives usually have to depend.

FARINA

This is also a creamy-colored, granular, protein-rich meal made from hard—but not durum—wheat.

ENRICHED FLOUR

We have become so accustomed to our highly bleached white flours that we forget that earlier cooks knew only whole-kernel flours. These were not the so-called whole wheat of our commercial world, but the whole grain, which includes the germ. Even the fine manchet flour of tradition contained some germ. But flours in general use today completely lack it. As Dr. A. J. Carlson, a leading investigator on foods and nutrition, says so graphically, "When rats and gray squirrels are given corn in abundance, they eat the germ and leave the rest. People leave the germ and eat the rest." This nutritious and tasty entity, the germ, is removed in modern milling because flours made with it are both harder to mill and to keep. After the removal of the outer coats and germ, our flours may be "enriched," but the term is misleading. ♦ Enriched flour contains only four of the many ingredients known to have been removed from it in milling.

WHOLE-GRAIN OR GRAHAM FLOUR

These, and some commercial whole wheats, retain their original vitamins, mineral salts, fats and other still unknown components—whether coarsely or finely milled. Scientists are aware of about twenty of these substances, even if they have so far failed to isolate them all or to produce them synthetically.

Most grains are similar, in their structure, to the wheat kernel sketched in cross-section. The outer bran layers contain,

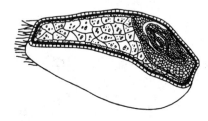

with the germ—indicated by the darker swirl on the right—most vitamins and minerals. The germ, which is only 2% of the entire kernel, contains the highest grade protein and all of the fat. The endosperm indicated on the left is largely starch with some protein—different from, but complementary to, the protein of the germ. But the outer coating and the germ—small compared with the whole kernel in this enlarged drawing—are of unchallenged importance in content and irreplaceable in flavor.

♦ You may substitute 1 cup of very finely milled whole-grain flour, sometimes called whole-kernel or graham flour, for 1 cup of all-purpose flour. For coarsely ground whole-grain flour, substitute 1 cup for ⅞ cup of all-purpose flour. This is stirred lightly rather than sifted before measuring.

Yeast breads from whole wheat flours do not have to be kneaded. They can be mixed and allowed to rise just once in the pan. If kneading is omitted, the texture will be coarse.

BRAN FLOUR

This flour often gives a dry result unless you soften the bran by allowing the wet bread mixture, minus the yeast or baking powder, to stand for eight hours or so. Bran flours are usually mixed with some all-purpose flour.

CRACKED WHEAT

This is cut rather than ground. It gives up little of its starch as a binder. Therefore, it must be mixed with some all-purpose flour in baking.

GLUTEN FLOUR

This is a starch-free flour made by washing the starch from high protein wheat flour. The residue is then dried and ground. See Gluten Bread, page 561.
♦ For 1 cup all-purpose flour, substitute 13 tablespoons gluten flour.

Gluten is found in its most complete form in wheat. Scientists think—but they do not know—that 2 substances, glutenin and gliadin, occurring separately in the wheat, interact to form gluten. Gluten can never develop except in the presence of moisture or when the grain is agitated—as in kneading. ♦ To prepare gluten from gluten flour, knead into a stiff dough:

    4 cups whole-grain or unbleached flour
    1½ to 3 cups lukewarm water

Roll it into a ball and submerge it in water for 2 hours. Then, still keeping the dough ball under water, work the starch out of it by kneading. At intervals, pour off the starchy water. Replace the water you pour off and continue to knead, repeating this operation until the water is almost clear. The gluten is then ready to cook. ♦ Form the starch-free dough into a loaf and cut it into ½-inch slices. Put in a 3-quart pan for which you have a tight lid:

    ¼ cup vegetable oil

You may flavor the gluten at this point by sautéeing until clear and golden:

    1 medium-sized finely sliced onion

Put the gluten slices in the pan; cover with:

    Boiling water

Simmer, closely covered, for 1 hour and drain. Store refrigerated and closely covered. Gluten can then be further cooked by dipping in egg and potato or rice flour and browning it slowly in an oiled pan. Or cover with undiluted tomato, mushroom or celery soup and heat in a preheated 350° oven for about 20 minutes or until it is hot all the way through.

WHEAT-GERM FLOUR

This may be ♦ substituted by using ⅓ cup of powdered wheat germ and ⅔ cup of all-purpose flour for 1 cup of all-purpose flour. Be sure that the wheat germ, either powdered or whole, is very slightly toasted before combining it with the dough.

ABOUT NON-WHEAT FLOURS

Some of the following non-wheat flours can be used alone. But in any bread recipe that fails to call for wheat flour—at least in part—you must expect a marked difference in texture, as wheat gluten has an elastic quality which is unique. This protein gluten factor in wheat is activated when the flour is both moistened and handled, at which time the gluten is said to "develop." The flour is then able to absorb as much as 200 times its weight in moisture.

In describing non-wheat flours, some of which are richer in over-all protein content than wheat, we give the closest substitutions we have been able to find but, if possible ♦ we advise using at least 1 cup wheat flour for every 2 cups other flour, or a very heavy dough results. For increased protein content, we suggest the use of Cornell Triple Rich Formula, page 556. ♦ Coarse flours need not be sifted before measuring. They do need more leavening than wheat types. ♦ Allow 2½ teaspoons baking powder for every cup of flour.

CORN FLOUR OR CORNSTARCH

Corn flour in its starchy, rather than its granular, form is a very valuable thickener. The new waxy starches made from certain varieties of corn are revolutionizing frozen sauces and fillings by their great stabilizing powers, but ♦ are not to be used in baking. For thickening ♦ substitute 1 tablespoon waxy corn flour for 2 tablespoons all-purpose flour. For non-waxy cornstarch ♦ substitute 1½ teaspoons cornstarch for 1 tablespoon all-purpose flour.

There is nothing more discouraging than the lumps any cornstarch can form or the raw taste it produces if it is badly handled or insufficiently cooked. Here are the things we have learned that help us to handle it more easily.

♦ Use a double boiler.

Avoid lumping, in recipes calling for sugar, by mixing cornstarch, sugar and salt together just before adding it gradually to the ♦ cold liquid.

In recipes without sugar, make a paste of 1 tablespoon of cornstarch to 1 cup of the liquid called for in the recipe. Introduce this paste gradually into the ♦ hot, but not boiling, liquid.

Cornstarch, along with tapioca and arrowroot, is recommended for thickening very acid fruits because it does not lose its thickening power as quickly as does flour in the presence of acid. But if it is ♦ overcooked, it loses its thickening power very quickly, regardless of the presence of acid. These facts account for the endless letters we get on pie fillings. In the extra special care cooks lavish on fillings, they are apt to overcook or ♦ overbeat them after cooking. Be very careful to check the cooking stages described later on.

Other causes for breakdown of thickening may come from too high a percentage of sugar in the recipe and, strangely, even from using too much cornstarch.

Also, tests have shown that ♦ the material from which the double boiler is made has a direct effect on the thickening quality and the success of unmolding cornstarch puddings. Aluminum, stainless steel and enamel are superior—in that order—to heatproof glass or heavy crockery.

But to get on with the cooking. Once the cornstarch is properly added to the liquid, either dispersed in sugar or in a cold paste, it goes through 2 main cooking periods, 3 if eggs are added. To keep the temperature right for the timing given here, use an aluminum, enamel or stainless steel pan. Fill the base of the double boiler so that the water just dampens the bottom of the liner. ♦ Bring the water to a bubbling boil before starting the timing. During the first period of about 8 to 12 minutes ♦ constant, gentle stirring is necessary to blend the mixture free from lumps and to hold the starch particles in suspension until gelatinization takes place and the mixture thickens. In this time, it should have reached at least 185°, a temperature which is essential for proper unmolding.

Then follows the second period of about 10 minutes when the mixture is ♦ covered and cooked undisturbed to complete gelatinization. Maintain the 185° temperature.

A third period, of about 2 minutes, follows the addition of the eggs. This adding procedure is just like any other when eggs or egg yolks meet hot liquid. The eggs are well beaten first. A portion of the hot mixture is added to the eggs very gradually. This is returned to the original mass, which has temporarily ♦ been removed from the heat. ♦ The stirring is less constant and extremely gentle during the next 2 minutes. The pudding should thicken much more in cooling. Have ready molds, rinsed out in cold water. Stir the mixture very gently into them—releasing heat which would condense and thin the mixture. Cool for about 30 minutes at room temperature and 1 to 2 hours refrigerated—for successful unmolding of individual molds. Larger molds will take 6 to 12 hours.

Cornstarch can be used in combination as a wheat flour allergy substitute, see page 501.

CORN MEAL

When water-ground, corn meal not only retains the germ but has a superior flavor. Yellow corn meal has more vitamin A potential than white corn meal, but there is little difference in their nutritional or baking properties. Corn breads vary from all-corn Dodgers made without a riser, see page 579, to moist and tender corn and wheat bread prepared with yeast, see page 561. To avoid graininess in corn breads, mix corn meal and the liquid in the recipe, bring to a boil and cool before mixing with the other ingredients.

RICE FLOUR

This makes a close but delicately textured cake in recipes heavy in egg. To avoid graininess, see Corn Meal, above. ♦ Substitute ⅞ cup rice flour for 1 cup all-purpose flour. But be sure, in baking, not to choose a waxy type of rice flour, also known as "sweet flour." Instead, use these waxy rice flours in making sauces. They have remarkable stabilizing powers which prevent the separation of frozen gravies and sauces when reheated. They are also much less apt to lump.

RYE FLOUR

When used in most of the rye breads we buy, this flour is usually combined with a large proportion of wheat flour. This is because the rye flour gluten factor provides stickiness, but lacks elasticity. Breads made largely with rye flour are moist and compact and usually call for a Sour Dough Leavener, see page 504. ♦ Substitute 1¼ cups rye flour for 1 cup all-purpose flour.

RYE MEAL

This is simply coarsely ground whole-rye flour. ♦ Substitute 1 cup rye meal for 1 cup all-purpose flour. See Rye Flour, above.

SOY FLOUR

This flour has both a high protein and a high fat content. However, some soy flour is made of beans from which the fat has been largely expressed. It may be made from either raw or very lightly toasted beans. Because of the fat, it is not mixed with the dry ingredients but is creamed with the shortening or blended with the liquids. It is usually substituted ♦ 2 tablespoons of soy flour plus ⅞ cup of all-purpose flour for 1 cup of all-purpose flour. But it may constitute, if you like the flavor, up to 20% of the weight of the flour in the recipe. Soy flour causes heavy browning of the crust, so reduce baking temperatures about 25°.

POTATO FLOUR

Chiefly used in soups, gravies, breads and cakes, in combination with other flours or alone in Sponge Cakes, page 621. To avoid lumping, blend it with sugar before mixing—or cream it with the shortening before adding a liquid. In bread recipes, it gives a moist slow-staling loaf. ♦ To substitute as a thickener, use 1½ teaspoons potato flour for 1 tablespoon all-purpose flour or, in baking, ⅝ cup potato flour for 1 cup all-purpose flour.

TAPIOCA AND SAGO

These are similar in their uses. Tapioca is processed from the Brazilian cassava root and sago from certain Indian palms. Sago and the so-called pearl tapioca must both be soaked for at least 1 hour before using. Soak ¼ cup of the pearls in ½ cup water which should be completely absorbed. If it isn't, the pearls are too old to use. Should you have already embarked on mixing the recipe, you can substitute rice in equal parts for pearl tapioca. ♦ To sub-

stitute so-called minute or granular for pearl tapioca, allow 1½ tablespoons of this finer form for 4 tablespoons of the soaked pearl.

TAPIOCA FLOUR

Like the Waxy Rice and Corn Flours, page 499, these are popular for sauces and fruit fillings that are to be frozen. These sauces reconstitute without breaking down and becoming watery, as flour-thickened sauces may do during frozen storage.
♦ To use in freezing, substitute 1 tablespoon tapioca flour for 2½ tablespoons all-purpose flour to 1 cup liquid. ♦ In non-frozen sauces, substitute 1½ teaspoons tapioca flour for 1 tablespoon all-purpose flour.

Tapioca flour is popular for making very clear glazes. Cook the tapioca and fruit juice or water only to the boiling point.
♦ Beware of overcooking, as it will become stringy.
♦ Never boil. When the first bubbles begin to break through the surface, remove the pan from the heat at once. The mixture will still look thin and milky. After standing 2 or 3 minutes, stir. Wait 2 or 3 minutes longer and stir again. If the recipe calls for butter, stir it in at this time. After 10 minutes more of undisturbed cooling, the glaze should be thick enough to apply to the food you are glazing.

ARROWROOT FLOUR OR STARCH

This is another popular base for cream sauces and clear and delicate glazes. It cooks by the same method as cornstarch but ♦ substitutes in the amount of 1 tablespoon arrowroot to 2½ tablespoons flour for every cup of liquid. If arrowroot glaze is to be used on cold acid fruits—to ensure an attractive consistency—dissolve 1½ teaspoons gelatin in 1 tablespoon cold water and add it to the hot glaze. Spoon the cooled, thickened glaze over the chilled fruit and keep cold until you serve it.

BARLEY FLOUR

♦ To substitute, use ½ cup barley flour for each cup of all-purpose flour.

COTTON SEED FLOUR

This flour is high in protein and may be used in baking to increase protein content.
♦ Substitute 2 tablespoons cottonseed flour plus ⅞ cup all-purpose flour for 1 cup all-purpose flour.

PEANUT FLOUR

High in protein, this flour may be ♦ substituted up to 2 tablespoons plus ⅞ cup all-purpose flour for 1 cup all-purpose flour.

OAT FLOUR AND OATMEAL

These are ground to different consistencies to combine with wheat flours up to ⅓.

Oatmeal is better in baking if soaked in boiling water with the shortening and cooled before the yeast or other leaven is added.

ROLLED OATS

These are separate flakes that respond to steaming. They are popular for adding flavor to cookies. ♦ Substitute 1⅓ cups rolled oats flakes for 1 cup all-purpose flour—combining, in breads, with wheat flours, only up to ⅓ the total.

BEAN FLOUR

♦ Substitute 4 to 5 cups bean flour for 1 cup all-purpose flour.

NUT MEAL

These finely ground dry nuts are used as a flour substitute in many Torten, see page 637.

CAROB FLOUR

This is milled into a powder from the pod of tamarind or St. John's bread. In sponge cakes, it can be used just like all-purpose wheat flour—provided the baking heat does not exceed 300°. It is more frequently used in baking to add flavor. ♦ To substitute, allow ⅛ to ¼ cup carob powder plus ⅞ to ¾ cup flour for every cup of flour. Do not bake in an oven higher than 300°, as carob powder scorches easily.

WHEAT FLOUR ALLERGY SUBSTITUTE

This can be kept on hand for use in gravies and some quick breads, pancakes and biscuits. Sift together, 6 times, ½ cup cornstarch with any of the following: ½ cup rye flour, potato flour or rice flour. If you use this combination for baking, you will need 2 teaspoons baking powder for each cup of the flour mixture. If using cornstarch or rice flour, be sure to avoid the waxy types in baking.

COOKED CEREAL

This may be ♦ substituted 1 cup cooked cereal for ¼ cup flour. But you must also cut the fluid in the recipe by 1 cup for each cup of cooked cereal used. To mix, stir the cooked cereal into the remaining fluid before combining with the other ingredients.

ABOUT CRUMBS

Be sure, in reading recipes, to note what kind of bread crumbs are called for. The results are very different, depending on whether they are dry, browned or fresh.

Finely crushed cracker crumbs, cornflakes or corn or potato chips are sometimes used in place of bread crumbs.

DRY CRUMBS

These are made from dry bread, zwieback or cake. If these materials are not sufficiently dry, crisp them, on a baking sheet in a 250° oven, before making the crumbs. Do not let the crumbs color. If only a few are being made, grind them in a rotary hand grater, or as sketched on page 521, or in a ⅄ blender. If making them in large quantities, put them through a meat grinder with a medium chopping blade. Tie a bag tightly over the mouth of the grinder to catch them all.

♦ Measure dry bread crumbs as you would sugar, page 543. Store dry bread crumbs in a cool, dry place, not too tightly lidded, or they may mold.

BROWNED BREAD CRUMBS

♦ To prepare these, use dry bread crumbs, as described. Allow for each cup dry bread crumbs ½ teaspoon salt and brown them slowly in ⅓ cup butter. Use at once.

SOFT BREAD CRUMBS

♦ To prepare these, use two- to four-day-old bread. You may crumb it ♦ very lightly with your fingers. But a safer way to retain the light texture desired in such crumbs is to pull the bread apart with a fork—using a gingerly motion, as sketched. Do not crush the bread with the hand that is holding it.

♦ To measure soft bread crumbs, pile them lightly into a cup. Do not pack them down. Use at once. Sometimes the recipe calls for soaking these fresh crumbs in water, milk or stock and pressing the moisture out before using.

ABOUT FLOURING, BREADING AND CRUMBING FOODS

When dredging food with flour or crumbs or with a more elaborately bound coating, the main thing to remember is this: you want a thin, even and unbroken covering that will adhere. The food should be about 75° and should be ◆ dry. If the food is floury to begin with or has a thickened sauce—like croquettes—the flouring may be omitted. But for fish fillets, shrimp, meat, anything with a moist surface, first a wiping and then a flouring is essential.

◆ To prepare a simple breading, have ready finely sifted crumbs, flour or cornmeal. Cornmeal gives the firmest coating. If the food is not fragile, simply put a small quantity of the seasoned coating material in a paper or plastic bag with the object you want to cover. Shake vigor-

ously. You will find this method gives a very even, quick and economical coating. Or prepare:

SEASONED FLOURING OR BREADING

I. Mix:
>1 cup all-purpose flour, finely sifted dry bread crumbs or finely crushed corn flakes
>1 teaspoon salt
>¼ teaspoon pepper or ½ teaspoon paprika
>(⅛ teaspoon ginger or nutmeg)

II. Mix:
>1 cup finely sifted dry bread crumbs or crushed corn flakes or crackers
>3 tablespoons grated Parmesan cheese
>½ teaspoon dried herbs: savory, chervil, chives, basil or tarragon or ¹⁄₁₆ teaspoon rosemary

III. To prepare a more adhesive bound breading—or coating à l'anglaise—requiring egg or milk, begin by wiping the food dry. Then dip the dry food into a shallow bowl of seasoned flour. Have ready, aside from the flour, two other bowls. In the first bowl, put a mixture of slightly beaten egg, diluted with 2 teaspoons to a tablespoon of water or milk for each egg used. You may also add 2 teaspoons oil for each egg. Stir these ingredients together with 10 or 12 mild strokes. Do not let the egg get bubbly, as this makes the coating uneven.

In the other bowl, have ready sifted, seasoned dry bread crumbs. Allow about ¾ cup crumbs for every diluted egg. This amount will coat about 8 croquettes.

As each piece of food is floured, toss it lightly from one palm to the other, patting it gently all over and encouraging any excess flour to fall off, as sketched on the left, below. Then slide the flour-coated food through the egg mixture, making sure the entire surface is contacted, as shown at center. Allow any excess moisture to drip off. Then place the food in the crumb-lined bowl. See that the crumbs adhere evenly to the shallow sides of the food as well as to its larger surfaces. If you see any vacant places sprinkle a few crumbs on them. Again discourage by patting any excess crumbs which might fall off and brown too rapidly—thus discoloring the frying fat. Handle the food very gently, so that the coating will not be cracked. ◆ Place it on a rack to dry for about 20 minutes before frying. ◆ Do not chill this food before frying, as this will tend to make it absorb an undue amount of fat.

ABOUT LEAVENS

We are all so accustomed to light breads and cakes that we seldom question the part that leavens play in the results.

Where does this rising power lie? First, the steam converted from the moisture, in any baking, may account for ⅓ to ⅘ of the expansion of the dough. The greater amount is characteristic of popovers and cakes which are rich in egg white. So, to

encourage the generation of this easily lost asset ♦ preheat your oven.

We usually think of leavens resulting from Baking Powders, page 504, sour milk and soda, page 505, and yeast—all of which expand with the steam to form a gas as a major force. But we tend to forget the importance of the mechanical incorporation of air from which the rest of the rising power comes. To give a boost to the chemical reactions, be sure you know how to cream fat and sugar, page 616; how to fold and mix batters, page 617; how to beat eggs, page 515; and, especially, be sure to know how to beat the whites to that state called "stiff, but not dry," page 515.

ABOUT YEAST

Yeasts are living organisms with 3,200 billion cells to the pound—and not one is exactly alike. They feed on sugars and produce alcohol and carbon dioxide—the "riser" we are after. But you may prefer, as we do, to accept a Mexican attitude toward yeast doughs. They call them almas, or souls, because they seem so spirited.

When flour is mixed with water to form a dough which is kept covered—and in a warm place—the wild yeast coming from the air and in the flour will start working and form a sour dough. There are enzymes in the flour to convert the wheat starch into sugar, on which the yeast feeds, making alcohol and carbon dioxide. Organic acids and other fragrant compounds are also created to give the sour effect. Sour doughs, discussed later, are examples of this primitive bacterial method. They are so primitive that they are recorded in Egyptian history of 4000 B.C. This leavened bread has been called the first "convenience" food—as its yeast content gives it excellent keeping quality.

But with fine strains of yeasts available, it seems foolish to try so chancy a method. In case of necessity, this sour dough can still be made. ♦ Two cups of this foamy mixture are substituted for 1 cake of compressed yeast. A really well-developed sour dough may give bread an appealing tasty flavor. But the kind of uncontrolled starter you get from wild yeast in the air may well give you both poor rising power and disagreeable off-flavors—unless some commercial yeast is also used. For the more sophisticated taste that a sour dough gives, see page 560—and for a modern version of this method.

Yeast, just because it is a living organism, is dependent on definite temperature ranges. It begins to activate at about 50° ♦ and is at its best between 78° and 82°. It begins to die around 120° and is useless for baking after 143°. These temperatures and the amount of food available limit its life span. Therefore, its force can be easily computed. One-half an ounce raises 4 cups of flour in about 1½ to 2 hours. One ounce raises 28 cups of flour in about 7 hours. For speedier raising, an excess of yeast is often added. But this is not necessary and often affects flavor and gives a porous texture. Small quantities of sugar also speed yeast activity, but too much will inhibit it. You may have noticed that it takes very sweet doughs longer to rise. As salt also inhibits yeast, never use salted water for dissolving yeast. In very hot weather, after the yeast is dissolved and added to the flour, salt may be added in small quantities to control too rapid fermentation.

Yeast dough is allowed to rise and fall a number of times during dough-making to improve the texture, but if allowed to over-expand it can use up its energy. In this case, there is little rising power left for the baking period when it is most needed.

For different methods to incorporate yeast in doughs, read about sponge doughs and the direct method, page 553. The liquids added to yeast, either alone or in combination, are: water, which brings out the wheat flavor and makes a crisp crust, or skim milk which not only adds to the nutritive value but also gives a softer crumb. The fat in whole and homogenized milk tends to coat the yeast and prevent its proper softening. Potato water may also be used, but it hastens the action of the yeast and gives a somewhat coarser, moister texture to dough. Both milk and potato water increase the keeping quality of bread somewhat.

To produce the best yeast bread, the dough must be given time to rise slowly—the entire process taking about 4 to 5 hours before baking. If you use 1 cake of yeast to 1½ cups of liquid and if the temperature is right, you can count about 2 hours or more for the first rising; 1 or more for the second; and 1 hour in the pans. You may increase the yeast content in any recipe and reduce your rising time considerably. Some successful quick recipes are given, but if you are going to the effort of using yeast, you might as well work for the superlative result which comes from the slower process.

COMPRESSED YEAST

We like to use this moist cake weighing ⅔ oz. But it must be kept refrigerated. Although compressed yeast comes in larger sizes, when 1 cake is specified in this book it means the ⅔ oz. size. If bought fresh, it will keep about 2 weeks. In a freezer, it will keep for 2 months. When at its best it is a light grayish tan in color. It crumbles readily, breaks with a clean edge and smells pleasantly aromatic. When old, it becomes brownish in color. To test for freshness, cream a small quantity of yeast with an equal amount of sugar. It should become liquid at once. You may let crumbled, compressed yeast dissolve in warm water or warm pasteurized skim milk at about 80° for about 5 minutes before combining with other ingredients, as called for in the recipes.

DRY YEAST

This comes in granular form and is liked by many persons for its better keeping qualities. It comes dated and, if kept in a cool place, will hold for several months—and somewhat longer in a refrigerator. It needs greater heat and more moisture to activate it than compressed yeast. ♦ Use more water to dissolve it but ♦ decrease by that amount the liquid called for in the recipe and ♦ heat the dissolving water to between 105° and 115°. To dissolve it best, sprinkle the powdered yeast on the surface of the water.
♦ To substitute dry granular yeast for compressed yeast, use 2 teaspoons dry yeast granules to a ⅔ oz. cake of compressed yeast.

DEBITTERED BREWERS' YEAST

Another form of dry yeast—but one without leavening power—which adds nutritive value to foods. It may be added to breads in the proportion of 1 to 3 teaspoons to 1 cup of flour, without affecting flavor or texture adversely. See Cornell Triple-Rich Formula, page 556.

ABOUT SOUR DOUGH

This term brings to mind at once the hard-bitten pioneer whose sharing of the bread "starter" was a true act of friendship. Of course, the best French breads and many other famous doughs are also based on flour and water mixtures fermented in various ways to trap natural yeast. In kitchens where yeast baking has been going on for centuries, these organisms are plentiful and success is quickly assured. But in an uninitiated streamlined kitchen, we recommend beginning a sour dough with a commercial yeast, especially in winter.

Remember, the sour dough starter is just as fragile as the yeast and must be cosseted along. After you have made your starter, you can continue to use it for about 3 days at room temperature without reworking it and for about a week if it is refrigerated. But never allow it to freeze. And never add more at one time for each cup of sour dough than 1 cup 85° water and 1 cup sifted flour, then beat them until smooth. Let this rise for 3 hours. In about 2 days, but no sooner, you can increase the sour dough in the same way if you like. If possible, refrigerate until ready to use again. When reusing a refrigerated sour dough, let it stand for about 1 hour before mixing the bread.

Expect the sour dough to have an odor very like salt rising bread. Should it develop any abnomal coloration discard it. To avoid spoilage, wash the starter crock about once a week with a detergent and warm water. Rinse and dry carefully before returning the starter to the crock. Try these suggestions if you are adventurous, persistent and leisurely. To use a sour dough, see page 560 and opposite column.

SOUR DOUGH

To make a sour dough more or less from scratch, sift into a ♦ large crockery jar—as the mixture will bubble up:

    4 cups flour
    2 teaspoons salt
    2 tablespoons sugar

Add:

    3 to 4 cups potato water

See Salt Rising Bread II for a good method of fermenting or let stand loosely covered at from 89° to 100° for about 2 days.

ABOUT BAKING POWDERS
AND BAKING SODA

When confronted with the questions growing out of the use of various baking powders now on the market, the puzzled layman is apt to sigh for the good old days, when this product was rather haphazardly mixed at home. ♦ Just in case you run out of baking powder, mix—for every cup of flour in the recipe—2 teaspoons of cream of tartar, 1 teaspoon of bicarbonate of soda and add ½ teaspoon salt. But don't try to store this mixture. ♦ Its keeping qualities will be poor. Commercial baking powders contain small amounts of such materials as starch, to prevent absorption of moisture from the air—a cause of loss of leavening power. Today's products are packed in airtight cans which also keep your powder dry. If you doubt its effectiveness ♦ test any baking powder by mixing 1 teaspoon of baking powder with ⅓ cup of hot water. Use the baking powder only if it bubbles enthusiastically.

There are three major kinds of baking powders and you will find the ♦ type carefully specified on the label. In all of them there must be an acid and an alkaline material reacting with one another in the presence of moisture to form a gas—carbon dioxide—which takes the form of tiny bubbles in the dough or batter. In baking, these quickly expand the batter which is set by the heat to make a light textured crumb.

TARTRATE BAKING POWDERS

In these, the soda is combined with tartaric acid or a combination of cream of tartar and tartaric acid. They are the quickest in reaction time, giving off carbon dioxide the moment they are combined with liquid. Therefore, if you are using this kind, be sure ♦ to mix the batter quickly and ♦ have the oven preheated so too much gas does not escape from the dough before the cells can become heat-hardened in their expanded form. Especially ♦ avoid using tartrate powder for doughs and batters that are to be stored in the refrigerator or frozen before baking.

▲ Because of the decrease in barometric pressure at high altitudes, the carbon dioxide gas expands more quickly and thus has greater leavening action. For this reason, the amount of baking powder should be decreased if you are using a recipe designed for low altitudes. You may select recipes designed especially for high altitudes, if you wish; see pages 648 to 650.

PHOSPHATE BAKING POWDERS

These use calcium acid phosphate or sodium acid phosphate as the acid ingredient. They are somewhat slower in reaction but give up the greater part of their carbon dioxide in the cold dough, the remainder being released when the mixture is baked.

S.A.S. BAKING POWDERS

These use sodium aluminum sulfate and calcium acid phosphate as the acid ingredients. They, too, start work in the cold dough but the great rising impact does not begin until the dough contacts the heat from the hot oven. They are often referred to as ♦ combination, or double-acting, baking powders and are the baking powders we specify consistently in this book.

BICARBONATE OF SODA, OR BAKING SODA

This is often used in place of baking powder in recipes involving sour milk or some acid factor like molasses, honey or spice. This combination gives one of the very tenderest crumbs. For more details about soda and sour milk and cream reactions, see page 485. The reaction of the soda with the acid is essentially the same as that which takes place when the two ingredients in baking powder meet moisture. Some recipes with these acid ingredients may call for both baking powder and baking soda. If they do, use about ½ teaspoon baking soda and ½ teaspoon baking powder for each 2 cups flour. The small amount of soda is desirable for neutralizing the acid ingredients in the recipe, while the main leavening action is left to the baking powder.

The amounts of baking powder per cup of flour suggested above are for low altitudes.

▲ In high altitudes baking soda is decreased as for baking power where the symbol appears above; but, in recipes using sour milk where its neutralizing power is needed, never beyond ½ teaspoon for every cup of sour milk or cream called for in the recipe.

ABOUT SOLID SUGARS

Most of our cooking is done with sugars made from beets or from cane. Both are so similar in their cooking reactions and their taste that only the label gives us the clue to their source. But the various grinds of solid sugars affect not only their comparative volumes but their sweetening powers as well. Liquid sweeteners, again, according to type, react very differently in cooking combinations. Whichever type you use—more is needed to sweeten iced dishes or drinks.

For a quick survey of relative volumes and weights, see page 545. ♦ In substituting liquid for dry sweeteners, a moisture adjustment must be made, especially in baking, as described later. Sugar sirups are easily made and have many uses. See Sirups for Canning, page 749; Sirups for Beverages, page 36; Sirups for Freezing, page 761; Sirups for Fruits, page 106; and Caramel for flavoring and coloring, page 508.

Among other things, sugars, like fats, give tenderness to doughs. In small amounts, with yeast, they hasten its working. However, too much sugar at this early juncture will inhibit yeast activity. Sugar in bread, rolls and muffins will also yield a golden brown crust. Small pinches added to some vegetables bring up their flavor.

Like flours, sugars are not always interchangeable — measure for measure — as their weights and sweetening powers vary greatly. For a quick comparison of sugar weights and volumes, see page 545. Many baking recipes call for the sifting of sugar before measuring. In America, where we are spoiled in having free-flowing, unlumpy granulated and powdered sugars, this initial sifting before measuring is usually ignored. But it is important to measure these and other sugars by filling the measuring cup with a scoop or spoon to overflowing. Be careful not to shake down the contents to even it. Then level off the top with a knife, as shown on page 543.

GRANULATED SUGAR

♦ In this book when the word sugar appears, the recipe calls for granulated sugar —beet or cane. As we buy it in America, it can be used for almost every purpose, even for meringues. The English granulated is too coarse for this and their castor sugar, closer to our powdered, is used instead. ♦ One pound of granulated sugar equals approximately 2 cups.

POWDERED SUGAR

This is a finer grind of granulated. It is
sometimes called superfine or berry sugar,
as it dissolves rapidly when put over fruits.
It is also used in cold drinks. The term
"powdered" is actually a misnomer, this
grind being still coarse enough so that the
individual crystals are easily discernible.
Do not confuse it with confectioners' sugar,
which is actually powdery in texture. ◗ It
substitutes cup for cup with granulated
sugar.

CONFECTIONERS' SUGAR

In its finest form—10X—this sugar might,
at a quick glance, be mistaken for cake
flour. Confectioners' sugar is approximately the European or English icing
sugar. In order to lessen lumping, it comes
with a small quantity of cornstarch added.
Should it lump, sieve it. Measure confectioners' sugar as you would flour, page 544.
Since the cornstarch tends to give so-called
"uncooked" icings a raw flavor, it is wise,
before spreading this kind of mixture, to
let it heat for about 10 minutes ◗ over hot
water, see page 677. The dense texture of
confectioners' sugar also gives a different
crumb to cakes in which it is used. ◗ Do
not try to substitute it for granulated sugar
in baking. However, in other uses, substitute 1¾ cups confectioners' for 1 cup granulated.

BROWN OR BARBADOES SUGAR

This is a less refined and moister beet or
cane sugar which comes light or dark—
the latter more strongly flavored. As both
types harden and lump easily, keep them
in tightly covered containers. Should the
sugar have become lumpy, sprinkle it very
lightly with a few drops of water and heat
in a low oven for a few moments. ◗ In
this book the term brown sugar means the
light form. If a stronger flavor is wanted,
the term dark brown sugar appears. ◗ To
substitute either of the brown sugars for
granulated sugar, use 1 cup firmly packed
brown sugar for each cup granulated sugar.
To measure brown sugar, see page 543.

RAW SUGAR

This unrefined residue after removal of
molasses from cane juice has a coarse,
squarish, beige-toned crystal. It is closest
in character to yellow or brownish De-
merara sugar—often called for in English
recipes.

LUMP SUGARS

These are granulated sugars molded or cut
into convenient rectangular sizes for use in
hot drinks. Rock Candy Crystals, page
735, make an interesting stand-in for lump
sugar and, when separated, a sparkling
garnish or iced cakes.

CRYSTALLIZED SUGAR

See Rock Candy, page 735.

MAPLE SUGAR

This is treasured for its distinctively strong,
sweet taste but, because of its high cost,
is often reserved just for flavoring. As it
dissolves slowly, grate or sliver it before
combining it with other ingredients. ◗ In
substituting, allow about ½ cup for each
cup of granulated sugar.

ABOUT LIQUID SUGARS

There are a number of factors to contend
with in substituting liquid for solid sweeteners. For one thing, their sweetening
powers vary greatly. For another, their
greater moisture content has to be taken
into account and those that have an acid
factor need neutralizing by the addition of
baking soda. So if you plan substituting,
read further to see just how to proceed.
To measure liquid sugars, you may want
to grease your measuring container first.
Then pour these sticky substances into the
measure, or spoon just to the level mark.
Scrape out all the contents. ◗ Never dip
the spoon into the honey or molasses container, for the added amount clinging to
the bottom and sides may make your
dough too sweet or too liquid.

CORN SIRUP

This comes in a light and dark form. ◗ In
this book the term corn sirup applies to
the light type. The stronger-tasting dark
is specified, if needed. ◗ For the same
amount of sweetening power, you have to
substitute 2 cups corn sirup for 1 cup
sugar. However, for best results ◗ never
use corn sirup in cooking to replace more
than ½ the amount of sugar called for in
a recipe. In baking, you are taking a
chance in substituting corn sirup in this
proportion. But, if you have to, for each
2 cups of sugar in the recipe reduce the
liquid called for—other than sirup—by ¼
cup. For example: suppose you are baking a cake that calls for 2 cups of sugar.
"Maximum sirup tolerance" here would be
1 cup sugar, 2 cups sirup. And for each 2
cups of sugar originally called for, you
would reduce the other liquid ingredients
by ¼ cup.

HONEY

This is an extremely variable ingredient.
Old German cooks often refused to use it
until it had aged for about a year. Variations in honey today are due in part to
adulterants, usually the physically harmless addition of glucose—a type of sugar
sirup sweeter than sugar itself. Explore
the many wonderful flavors in comb and

liquid form: thyme from Hymettus, tupelo from Florida or orange blossom from California—all as memorable as good vintages. Honey is often stored covered at room temperature and, if it becomes crystallized, it can easily be reliquefied by setting the jar in a pan of very hot water. Do not heat it over 160°, as this affects the flavor adversely.

In puddings, custards and pie fillings ♦ it is often suggested that honey replace sugar, cup for cup. As honey has almost twice the sweetness of sugar, this will greatly alter flavor. Honey added to cake, cookies and bread doughs gives them remarkable keeping qualities as well as a chewy texture and a browner color. Also, in guarding flavor, see that the honey is not a very dark variety, as dark honey is often disagreeably strong.

Warm the honey or add it to the other liquids called for to make mixing more uniform. ♦ In baking breads and rolls, substitute 1 cup honey for 1 cup sugar. ♦ In baking cakes and cookies, use ⅞ cup honey for 1 cup sugar—but reduce the liquid called for in the recipe by 3 tablespoons for each cup of honey substituted.

Unless sour milk or cream is called for in the recipe, add a mere pinch—from ¹⁄₁₂ to ⅛ teaspoon—baking soda to neutralize the acidity of the honey. Usually, because of its acid content, too great browning results if honey is substituted for more than ⅓ the sugar called for in the recipe. But if it is extremely acid, add ¼ to ½ teaspoon baking soda for every cup of honey substituted. If honey is substituted in jams, jellies or candies, a higher degree of heat is used in cooking. In candies, more persistent beating is needed and careful storage against absorption of atmospheric moisture.

MAPLE SIRUP

If so labeled, maple sirup must contain a minimum of 35% maple sap by government regulation. When properly processed so as neither to ferment or crystallize, one quart should weigh 2¾ pounds. The best grades are light in color. It is often stored covered at room temperature. But mold growth is inhibited if, after opening the sirup container, it is stored in the refrigerator. Should the sirup crystallize, set the jar in hot water and the sirup will quickly become liquid and smooth again. Products labeled "maple flavored"—while not as rich in flavor—may be used just as you use maple sirup.

♦ To substitute for sugar in cooking, generally use only ¾ cup maple sirup to each cup of sugar. ♦ To substitute maple sirup for sugar in baking, use these same proportions, but reduce the other liquid called for in the recipe by about 3 tablespoons for every cup of sirup substituted.

One pint maple sirup has the same sweetening power as 1 pound maple sugar.

MOLASSES

There are 3 major types of molasses. 1. Unsulphured molasses is made from the juice of sunripened cane which has grown from 12 to 15 months. It is a deliberately manufactured product. 2. Sulphured molasses is a by-product of sugar making. Sulphur fumes are used in the making of sugar—hence the presence of sulphur in the molasses. 3. Blackstrap molasses is a waste product. It is the result of a third boiling—with more sugar crystals extracted; and is unpalatable.

Molasses is best in sweetening power if it replaces no more than ½ the amount of sugar called for in the recipe. But in baking it is sometimes ♦ substituted—1 cup molasses for every cup of sugar. Add ½ teaspoon soda for each cup added, and omit the baking powder called for in the recipe, or only use a small amount. Make sure also to reduce the other liquid in the recipe by ¼ cup for each cup of molasses used.

CANE SIRUP

This is substituted like Molasses, above.

TREACLE OR GOLDEN SIRUP

This is milder in flavor and used only where specified as it does not substitute properly for molasses.

SORGHUM

This has a thinner, sourer flavor than cane molasses. Use the same substitutions as called for under Molasses.

I. CARAMELIZED SUGAR FOR GLAZES

A marvelous flavoring which can be made in several ways. While its caramel flavor is strong, its sweetening power is reduced by about one-half.

For hard glazes, heat in any ♦ very heavy, nonferrous pan, over ♦ very low heat, 1 cup granulated sugar. For a **Croquant**, or brown nougat, add 1 tablespoon water. Stir constantly with a long handled spoon for 8 to 10 minutes until the sugar is melted and straw-colored. Remove the pan from the heat. ♦ Add ¼ cup very hot water—very slowly and carefully—for a quick addition might cause explosive action. This safeguard against the spurting of the hot liquid will also help make the sirup smooth. To make the sirup heavier, return the pan to low heat for another 8 to 10 minutes, continuing to stir, until the sugar mixture is the color of maple sirup. Toward the end of this process, to avoid cooking it too dark, you may remove the pan from the heat and let the caramelization reach a bubbling state from the stored heat of the pan. Store the sirup covered on a shelf for future use. The sirup hardens on standing but, if stored in a heatproof jar, is easily remelted by heating the jar gently in hot water. Should it burn, use it for coloring, see below.

II. CARAMELIZED SUGAR FOR COLORING

Melt in a ◗ very heavy nonferrous pan, over low heat, 1 cup sugar. Stir constantly until it is burned black to smoky. ◗ Remove from the heat and be sure to let it cool. Then, as in caramelizing above, ◗ add, almost drop by drop, 1 cup hot water. ◗ Quick addition of water to intensely hot sugar which is well over 300° can be explosive in effect and very dangerous. After the water is added, stir over low heat until the burnt sugar becomes a thin dark liquid.

If stored covered on a shelf, it will keep indefinitely. This can be used to replace the more highly seasoned commercial gravy colorings. The intense heat under which it is processed destroys all sweetening power.

SYNTHETIC SWEETENERS

There is some reason to question the systemic effect of all non-caloric sweeteners. Any substitutes should be used on doctor's orders only and, when cooked or used in baking, should follow manufacturer's directions. The saccharin types should not be cooked, as they produce a bitter flavor. Cyclamates are more suitable for cooking and baking, as they retain their sweetness when heated and, with some cooked foods, their sweetening power actually increases. Cyclamate substitutes do not give the same texture in baking as do true sugars and therefore should be used only in recipes specially developed for them. For amounts to be used in substitutions, please see pages 551 and 552.

ABOUT SEASONED SUGARS

Keep these on hand for quick flavoring.

CINNAMON SUGAR

Mix 1 cup sugar with every 2 tablespoons cinnamon. Use for toast, coffee cake and yogurt toppings.

CITRUS FRUIT FLAVORED SUGARS

Extremely useful in custards and desserts. Prepare Citrus Zest, page 540. Allow 1 to 2 tablespoons zest for every cup of sugar. Store covered in a cool place.

VANILLA SUGAR

Make this by keeping a whole vanilla bean closed up in a canister of sugar. Or you can crush it with a few tablespoons of sugar before adding it to the sugar you are storing. Then, you may strain the sugar before using and replace it with new sugar until the bean loses its flavoring power.

ABOUT FATS IN COOKING

Nothing reveals the quality of a cuisine as unmistakably as the fat on which it is based. Bacon arouses memories of our South, olive oil evokes Mediterranean cooking and sweet butter will bring forth memories of fine meals in many places. Not only flavors but food textures change with the use of different fats whose materials are as individual as their tastes. ◗ Most of the recipes in this book call for sweet butter. Sometimes amounts vary in a single recipe. In such instances, the lesser amount will give you a palatable result, while the larger quantity may produce a superlative one.

Authorities grant that 20% to 30% of our dietary intake should come from fats. But our present per capita consumption is closer to 40%, representing 8% to 18% of all household money spent! Few of us realize that, like an iceberg, the larger part of the fat we eat is invisible. Who would guess that ripe olives and avocado are about ¼ fat, that egg yolk, cheese, peanut butter, chocolate and the average hamburger contain about ⅓ fat and that Bologna sausage and pecans can be almost ¾ fat! For more about the dietary and calorie role of fats, see pages 1 and 2.

Let's take a bird's eye view of fat versatility in cooking. Fats, when used with discretion and skill, have the power to force flavor in foods, to envelop gluten strands and "shorten" them into more tender structure. Fats also form the emulsifying agent in gravies and mayonnaise and can act as a preservative in coating some foods like Stocks, page 489, and Terrines, page 435. And butter gives the most beautiful browning in breads and pastries.

Fats for cooking, of course, include both solid fats and liquid oils. ◗ Fats are solid at about 70°. ◗ Oils remain liquid at these temperatures although they may become solidified when refrigerated. It is fashionable today to scorn fats for their weight-inducing power and to fear certain "saturated" fats for their alleged cholesterol-inducing tendencies, page 2. ◗ Examples of highly saturated fats are butter and the hydrogenated fats. ◗ Other fats, like vegetable and nut oils, are polyunsaturated.

MEASURING FATS

Bulk butter and solid shortenings are most easily measured by the displacement method. ◗ To measure fats, see illustration, page 545.

ABOUT BUTTER

All butter is made from fresh or soured cream and by law must have a fat content of 80%. The remaining 20% is largely water with some milk solids. Small amounts of salt are sometimes added for flavor or for preservative action. Without the addition of color, most butter would be very pale rather than the warm "butter yellow" to which we are accustomed.

The word "creamery" which sometimes appears on both sweet and salt butter packages is a hangover from the days when cream went to a place called a creamery to be processed. The word now carries no standard or type significance—it's just meant to be reassuring!

◗ All butter should be stored in the refrigerator and kept covered to prevent absorption of other food flavors. Two weeks is considered the maximum storage time for refrigerated butter. For longer storage, it may be frozen, see page 767.

◗ One pound of butter equals 2 cups.
◗ To substitute butter for other fats, see page 549; for seasoned butters, see page 338; for nut butters, see pages 57 and 521.

SWEET BUTTER

The word butter, as used in this book, means first grade butter made from sweet cream with no added salt. Without this preservative factor, its keeping qualities are less than those of salt butter. Its delicate flavor is especially treasured for table use and for preparing certain baked foods, see About Cakes, page 622.

SALT BUTTER

This may be made from sweet or soured cream. It too is very desirable and keeps longer than the sweet.

PROCESSED BUTTER

Often sold in bulk, this is made by rechurning less desirable butter with fresh milk to remove unwanted odors or flavors.

EXPANDED BUTTER

For dieters and frugal housewives, this is a favorite spread. Soak ¼ cup gelatin in 1 pint milk until dissolved and heat over hot water. Put 1 pound butter cut in pieces in a dish over hot water. Whip the gelatin mixture into the butter gradually. Add salt to taste. Should milk bubbles appear, continue beating until they go away. Pour the butter into molds and chill well before serving.

For Clarified or Drawn Butter, see page 338.

HOW TO MAKE SWEET BUTTER

Butter is just as good as the cream from which it is made. Clean whole milk is kept cool and covered during separation, which takes about 24 hours by gravity. Skim the cream, pasteurize it, page 482, stirring frequently to deter "skin" formation. Cool the cream at once to 50° or less and keep about 55° all during the butter-making period. Start to churn after 3 to 24 hours of chilling. Most of us have inadvertently turned small quantities of cream into butter in an electric beater or ⅃ blender. We may even have imitated churning by flipping a jar of cream rhythmically in a figure 8 motion. For larger quantities, use a churn and keep the cream between 55° and 60°. A higher temperature will produce a greasy consistency—a lower one, a brittle, tallowy one. A gallon of cream should yield about 3 lbs. of butter.

Using at least 30% cream, fill a sterile churn ⅓ to ½ full. Depending upon the quantity you are churning, the butter should "make" within 15 to 40 minutes. We used to visit a neighbor while she churned and were amazed at how much slower the process was in threatening or stormy weather. The cream usually stays foamy during the first half of churning. Afterwhile it will look like cornmeal mush. At this point, proceed cautiously. It then grows to corn kernel size. Now, stop churning. Drain off and measure the buttermilk. Wash the butter twice, with as much 50° to 70° pure water as you have buttermilk.

If you salt the butter, use ⅔ to 1 tablespoon salt to 1 pound butter, folding the salt into the butter with a wet paddle. Mold it in a form or fashion it into rolls, using a damp cloth. Wrap it in parchment or foil.

If you wonder why the lovely, pale, delicately fragrant, waxy curl on your Paris breakfast tray is so good, here is one reason. The Brittany cows are fed and milked so the butter-making can be coordinated with the first possible transportation to Paris, where it is served at once. So use butter promptly. ✻ Freeze butter not more than 6 months at 0° temperature. If no refrigeration is available, butter is best wrapped and kept in brine, page 525, in a cool place.

ABOUT VEGETABLE SHORTENINGS

These have an oil base like soybean, corn, cottonseed or peanut, which is refined and deodorized. Frequently they are ◗ hydrogenated. This process of hydrogenation changes the form of the free fatty acids of oils, although it improves their keeping qualities—as the hydrogen binds the oxygen. It also makes them more acceptable for baking, as during the processing air is incorporated and plasticity is given to the solid fat. These solid fats and the shortenings based on them are bland and practically indistinguishable one from the other in taste or in use.

Some oil-based shortenings may further have animal or dairy fats blended with them during the processing. If color is added to any of these products, it is so stated on the label. They may also have minute additions of emulsifiers, mono and diglyceride fats, which give to cakes and other baked foods greater volume and a softer, spongier texture.

◆ Vegetable shortening may be stored covered in a tin at 70° over long periods.

◆ To substitute solid shortening for butter, replace measure for measure as the water in the butter compensates for the air in the shortening. ◆ But, if substituting weight for weight, use 15% to 20% less shortening than butter.

ABOUT MARGARINES

Margarines, like butter, must, by law, contain 80% fat—the rest being water, milk solids and salt. Almost all margarines are enriched also with added vitamins and color, to try to make them equate butter. Margarines today are usually emulsions of milk and refined vegetable oils, although some have added animal or dairy fats. Read the label for this information.

◆ Margarines, because of their similar moisture content, may be substituted for butter, weight for weight or measure for measure. They produce textures somewhat different from butter in both cooking and baking and lack the desirable butter flavor. They are perishable and must be kept covered, under refrigeration.

ABOUT OILS

Vegetable oils are pressed from various common seeds and fruits. Among these are corn, cottonseed, olive, soybean, sesame, safflower, sunflower. There are also such nut oils as peanut, walnut, hickory and beechnut, which are best for salads, as they break down under high heat.

After pressing, the oils are refined, bleached and deodorized so thoroughly that, except for olive, the end products are rarely distinguishable one from the other by flavor or odor, or in use.

Most oils for salad are further treated to remove cloudiness at refrigerator temperatures. Oils should not be held too long at 70° even if tightly closed and in dark bottles. Most of them remain in a liquid state under refrigeration. Olive oil, which becomes semisolid when refrigerated, should be allowed to stand at 70° to return to a liquid condition before using.

Olive oils are like wines in the way their flavors are affected by the soils in which they are grown. Greek, Spanish, Italian—try them all to find your favorite. It is so much cheaper to buy by the gallon but, as olive oil is susceptible to rancidity—especially the cold press type—when exposed to light and air, decant it into smaller containers. Use one and keep the other resealed bottles in a cool, dark place. For further discussion of their value in the diet, see page 2.

As oils are 100% fat, they ◆ must be reduced by about 20% when substituted for butter, either by weight or by measure. However, there are additional complications when substituting them for solid fats, especially in baking, see page 634. So in this book ◆ when oil is used in recipes, it is specifically indicated and the proper amounts are given.

ABOUT LARD

Lard, which is fat rendered from pork, is a softer, oilier fat than butter, margarine or the other solid shortenings. Due to its more crystalline structure, it cuts into flour to create flakier textures in biscuits and crusts, although this same crystalline character handicaps it for cake baking. This is less true for those lards which have been hydrogenated, refined and emulsified. Ordinary lards are offered in bulk or package form.

◆ All lards should be stored in covered containers in a cool place, preferably the refrigerator. ◆ To substitute lard for butter in cooking, use about 20% to 25% less lard.

LEAF LARD

Whether bought or home-rendered, this is a definitely superior type. It comes from the layered fat around the kidneys, rather than from trimmings and incidental fatty areas.

ABOUT POULTRY FATS

Fats from chicken, turkeys, ducks and geese, whether home or commercially rendered, are highly regarded for dietary reasons. When rendered from the leaf or cavity fat, they are firm, bland and light in color. From sources such as skimmed broth and other cooking, they are likely to be soft, grainy and darker in color. ◆ Store them covered in the refrigerator.

◆ To substitute, use ¾ cup clarified poultry fat to 1 cup butter.

ABOUT PORK FAT

This is used both in its fresh and salted form. Salt pork, which comes from the flank, is used to line Pâtés, page 433, for

Lardoons, page 383, and for Larding, page 383. It may also be sautéed in butter to use as a garnish for sweetbreads.

♦ To remove excess salt from salt pork Blanch II, page 132, for about 2 minutes. Fresh pork fat, especially the kidney fat, is used as an ingredient in farces, sausages and in pâté mixtures.

ABOUT DRIPPINGS

These are fats which are rendered in the process of cooking fat meats. They are all desirable in reinforcing the flavors of the meats from which they come when making gravies, although lamb and mutton should be used with great discretion. Bacon and pork fats are often stored separately for use in corn breads and meat pie crusts and for flavoring other dishes where salt pork may be called for. Other fats may be mixed together for storage.

♦ To substitute drippings for butter, use 15% to 20% less drippings.

♦ All these fats should be clarified before storage in the refrigerator, to improve their keeping qualities. The natural desire to keep a container handy at the back of the stove to receive and reuse these drippings needs to be curbed. Exposed to varying degrees of warmth, these are subject to quick spoilage.

ABOUT RENDERING FATS

Trying out solid fats such as chicken, duck, suet tallow and lard improves the keeping quality by removing all connective tissue, possible impurities and moisture. Dice the fat and heat it slowly in a heavy pan with a small quantity of water. You may speed up this process by pressing the fat with the back of a slotted spoon or a potato masher. When the fat is liquid and still fairly warm, strain it through cheesecloth and store it ♦ refrigerated. The browned connective tissues in the strainer—known as "cracklings"—may be kept for flavoring.

ABOUT CLARIFYING FATS

To clarify fats that have been used in frying and to rid them of burned food particles and other impurities ♦ heat them slowly. You may add to the fat during this heating 4 to 5 slices of potato per cup of fat to help absorb unwanted flavors. When the potato is quite brown, strain the fat while still warm through cheesecloth. ♦ Store refrigerated.

ABOUT REMOVING EXCESS SALT FROM FATS

To remove excess salt from bacon or salt pork, parblanch it before use for larding, page 132, or in delicate braises and ragouts. Put it in a heavy pan. Cover it with ♦ cold water. Bring the water slowly to a boil and ♦ simmer uncovered for 3 to 10 minutes. Allow the longer time if the dice are as big as 1 x 1 x ½ inches.

To remove salt from cooking butter, heat it slowly and avoid coloring it. Skim it. Allow it to cool in the pan and remove the fat cake. Any sediment and moisture should be in the bottom of the pan. Butter so treated is used in a number of ways, especially to seal off potted meats and in cooking where a slower browning is wanted, as in boned chicken.

ABOUT CHEESES

The ways of cheese-making are ancient and the results are not only chancy but extraordinarily varied—so varied that even to list their names is a geographical impossibility. Man makes cheese from many milks—goat, ass, ewe, camel and water buffalo, as well as the more reassuring cow. Natural cheeses can substitute nutritionally for meat, milk or eggs, see page 2, since they retain large amounts of the protein and casein. Soft cheeses, described later, are richer in water-soluble vitamins than hard cheeses—although they are poorer in calcium. Except for pot and cottage types, all cheeses are heavy in fat, from at least 20 to 30 per cent.

Someone has said that while you cannot make a good cheese from poor milk, you can very easily make a poor cheese from good milk. The high fat and protein content demands gentle heats—usually not over 110°—during the making of cheese and always below boiling point when cooking with it later. Moreover any cooking period—even the heating of a cheese sauce under a broiler—should be as brief as possible to avoid separation or toughening, see page 2.

Some cheeses originate when milk comes in contact with the curdling enzymes from the stomachs of unweaned animals or from certain plants. This enzymatic material is rennet, often used in making puddings, although ♦ as compounded for this latter purpose it does not always have enough strength to act as a cheese-starter. Acid-curd cheeses form when bacteria in the lactic acid turn milk into curds and whey. ♦ Only raw, unheated milk will respond to the acid-curd method.

Originally, if the cheese bore a place name, that was its source. Now many molds and starters have been transplanted and you may find your Roquefort coming from South America instead of France, your Emmenthaler from Austria rather than Switzerland. Some of these transplants are delicious, some doubtful. Reserve judgment on "named" cheeses until you have tasted them as produced at their point of origin.

Let us stress again the marked individuality of cheeses within the same type and of the same provenance. In the first place ♦ natural cheeses are seasonal. Often the best milk is available in April or August. The flavor will depend not only on the soils of the fields on which the cattle are fed but also on the season and the aging.

If cheese is your hobby and it's "named" cheeses you are after, rather than give you elaborate charts which may prove meaningless, we suggest you find a good cheese broker who has the latest market knowledge. The other thing to do—which is rewarding—is to find sources of good cheese native to your region. Many cheese makers take great pride in their products and you may be pleasantly surprised as to what your locale may produce.

For Dessert Cheeses, see page 707, for cheese combinations for hors d'oeuvre, see Index, and for cheese entrées, see Luncheon Dishes, page 242.

For Processed Cheese, see below.

All natural cheeses, no matter how they may vary in individual character, are divided into three basic types: soft, semi-hard and hard.

SOFT CHEESES

This type is the most easily made in the home and a few recipes are given later. They retain from 45% to 85% moisture and are highly perishable, lasting only 3 or 4 days. They must ♦ be kept under refrigeration and, for complete safety, should derive from pasteurized milk. The curds can be frozen before washing and stored for a month or two. Soft cheeses may be unripened, mold-ripened or bacteria-ripened.

Typical unripened soft cheeses are cottage, farmers, pot, Neufchâtel, Primost, Petit Gervais, ricotta and bakers' cheese, which is high in rennet and very dry. Some unripened soft cheeses may be enriched with cream after forming, like creamed cottage cheeses, or may be brine-held, like the Greek variety called feta.

Mold-ripened soft cheeses are such types as Camembert, Brie, Pont L'Évêque and Livarot.

Soft cheeses may also be bacteria-ripened, such as Limburger, Liederkranz and hand cheese; and those we might designate as "near-cheeses," like Cultured Sour Cream, page 486, and Yogurt, page 485. Except for these last two and for cottage cheese and ricotta, soft cheeses are not generally used in cooking. When they are, the heat must be of a very mild character. They cook best in Cheese Cakes, page 611, Lasagne, page 190, and Blini, page 214.

SEMI-HARD CHEESES

These are also ♦ poor for cooking, as they become gummy. If aged, they retain about 45% moisture. Their aging is as tricky as their manufacture. If aged 60 to 90 days, the milk need not be pasteurized. We feel that these so-called natural cheeses

from raw milk are far superior in flavor to the processed cheeses which are made of pasturized milk. Semi-hard types include mold-ripened crumbly cheeses like Gorgonzola, bleu, Stilton; and bacteria-ripened cheeses like Muenster, brick, Port du Salut, Bel Paese, Fontina, Gammelost, Gouda and Jack.

HARD CHEESES

After aging, these cheeses retain about 30% moisture. They are ♦ superlative for cooking. And they are made from raw milk and are all bacteria-ripened—for a longer or shorter period. Appitost, nokkelost and Kuminnost need 2 to 3 months; American, apple, asiago, cheddar, Edam, gjetost, Gruyère, provolone, sapsago, Sbrinz and Swiss need 3 to 12 months; and Cheshire, Parmesan, Reggiano, Romano and Sardo need 12 to 16.

In cooking with cheeses that are very hard ♦ grate just before using. Try combinations in cooking like grated Parmesan with Romano or Gruyère, cantal or caccio cavallo with cheddar.

TO STORE HARD CHEESES

To store a wheel or a large piece of cheese after cutting, butter the cut edges before wrapping in foil and refrigerating the rest.

ABOUT PROCESSED CHEESES

We can only echo Clifton Fadiman when he declares that processed cheeses represent the triumph of technology over conscience.

Processed cheeses are pasteurized blends of green new cheese, one or more aged cheeses, emulsifiers and water—which may run from 1% to 40% higher than in natural cheeses. If sold as so-called "cheese-food," they may legally contain up to 44% water or milk; if labelled "cheese-spread," up to 60% water, gums and gelatins. In fact, some "cheese-spreads" have no cheese in them at all, but are based on cheese-curds.

Processed cheeses are a convenience to a desensitized housewife—to say nothing of a profit-minded manufacturer. They have remarkable keeping qualities as they stand up sturdily to almost indefinite refrigeration. But here their interest ends. If you are willing to condone the gummy texture and the insipid taste of processed cheeses, you are still advised to read the list of ingredients on the package. Otherwise, you may find yourself paying an exorbitant price for some highly synthetic and commonplace materials.

ABOUT MAKING UNRIPENED SOFT CHEESES

Time was when milk was allowed to rest in a warm place until clabbered, when the curds and whey were separated by draining until the curds were firm to the touch. They were then refrigerated for several hours, after which they could be beaten with additional cream until smooth to make a cottage or Schmierkaese.

Commercial creamed cottage cheeses must by law have a 4% fat content.

For safety reasons, the recipes which follow are given for ◖ pasteurized milk. But, because the milk is pasteurized, ◖ Cultured Buttermilk, page 485, or Rennet, page 695, must be added to all the recipes to activate the curd. In making these cheeses use stainless steel, enamel or crockery vessels. Have ready: a dairy thermometer, a long wooden spoon, a large pan, a rack and a muslin sack or Chinese cap strainer, page 170, for dripping the cheese.

Also useful, if you make these soft cheeses often, is a curd cutter made of a stainless wire looped into an elongated "U" with the arms about 2 inches apart, and deep enough to fit the pan in which you develop the curd. Make up the recipes as described. When the curd is ready, cut through it with your curd cutter, lengthwise and crosswise of the pan. Then cut through in depth at 2-inch intervals to form cheese curd cubes. Process as described in the recipe. When the curds are ready, you may add additional cream. ◖ Store these cheeses refrigerated. Do not keep more than 4 or 5 days. To serve these unripened cheeses, see:

> Cottage Dessert Cheese, page 708
> Coeur à la Crème, page 708

or serve with:

> Chopped chives, burnet, basil or
> tarragon, chopped olives

or use as a base for hors d'oeuvre and dips and to fill tomato cases.

COTTAGE CHEESE

About 1½ Pounds

This cheese goes by many other names: **clabber, pot, Dutch, farmer's, Schmier-kaese** and **bakers'**. The latter is very, very dry.

◖ Please read About Making Unripened Soft Cheeses, page 512.

Have at 70° to 72°:

> 1 gallon pasteurized fresh skim milk

If whole milk is used, the cream is lost in the whey. Stir in:

> ½ cup fresh cultured Buttermilk,
> page 485

Leave this mixture in an oven 70° to 75° temperature until clabbered, about 12 to 14 hours. Cube the curd, as described previously. Let rest for 10 minutes. Add:

> 2 quarts 98° to 100° water

Set the pan on a rack in a larger pan of water and heat until the curd reaches 98° to 100°. Hold at this temperature ◖ not higher or the curd will toughen, for about 30 minutes to 1 hour, stirring gently every 5 minutes. Do not break the curd. As the

whey is forced out, the curds will settle. ◖ To test for doneness, squeeze them. They should break clean between the fingers and, when pressed, should not leave a semifluid milky residue. Pour the curds and whey ◖ gently into a scalded sack or Chinese cap strainer. Rough handling can cause as much as a 20% loss in bulk. Rinse the curds with:

> (Cold water)

to minimize the acid flavor. Let drain in a cool place until whey ceases to drip; but the surface of the cheese should not become dry-looking. The cheese may then be combined with:

> (Whipping cream)

To serve or store, see About Making Unripened Soft Cheeses, page 512.

NEUFCHÂTEL

About 1½ Pounds

◖ Please read About Unripened Soft Cheeses, page 512.

Combine:

> 1 gal. fresh pasteurized whole milk
> ½ cup fresh cultured Buttermilk,
> page 485

Dissolve in:

> ¼ cup cold water
> ¼ to ½ household rennet tablet

and mix with the milk, which should be at 85°. ◖ Stir gently for 10 minutes and begin to watch for any thickening. ◖ Stop stirring the moment you sense the thickening. Put the filled bowl you are using in a larger one of warm water and maintain the milk at 80° to 85° until whey covers the surface and the curds break clean from the sides of the bowl when it is tipped. Cut into 1-inch curds, as described previously. Now put the curds and whey into a colander and, when nearly drained, press out any remaining whey. Reserve and chill the whey until you can skim off the butter, like cream, and work the cream back into the curds. When the cheese is firm, add:

> 1½ teaspoons salt
> (Additional seasoning)
> (Cream)

To serve or store, see About Unripened Soft Cheeses, page 512.

RICH CREAM CHEESE

About 1½ Pounds

◖ Please read About Making Unripened Soft Cheeses, page 512.

Proceed as for:

> Neufchâtel, above

using:

> 3½ quarts fresh pasteurized milk
> 1 to 1½ pints whipping cream
> ½ cup cultured buttermilk
> ¼ to ½ rennet tablet

dissolved in:

> ¼ cup cold water

Save and chill the whey until you can skim off the butter and work the butter back into the cheese.

> Correct the seasoning

ABOUT EGGS

Nothing stimulates the practiced cook's imagination like an egg.

Eggs can transform cake doughs by providing a structural framework for leaven, thicken custards and make them smooth, tenderize timbales and produce fine-grained ice creams. They bind gravies and mayonnaise; clarify or enrich soups; glaze rolls; insulate pie doughs against sogginess; create glorious meringues and soufflés; and make ideal luncheon and emergency fare.

Because fresh eggs do all these things better than old eggs and because there is no comparison in taste and texture between the two ◗ always buy the very best quality you can find. It doesn't matter if their yolks are light or dark or if their shells are white or brown—as long as the shells are not shiny. While there is no test, except tasting, for good flavor ◗ the relative freshness of eggs may be determined by placing them in a large bowl of cold water. The ones that float are not usable. Unshelled onto a plate ◗ a truly fresh egg has a yolk that domes up and stays up, and a thick and translucent white.

Strange as it may seem, after stressing the purchase of fresh eggs, we now tack on an amendment. ◗ Do not use eggs fresher than three days for hard-cooking, beating and baking. If you do, hard-cooked eggs will turn greenish and become difficult to peel and cakes may fail to rise properly because the eggs will not have been beaten to the proper volume.

◗ Never use a doubtful egg, one that is cracked or one that has any odor or discoloration. Fertile eggs have a small dark fleck which is easily removed with the tip of a knife if the egg is to be used in a light-colored sauce or confection.

Eggs should really be bought and measured by weight, but tradition is against this sensible approach. ◗ We assume in this book that you are using 2-ounce eggs. These are known in the trade as "large." They should carry a Grade A stamp as well as the date of grading. If in doubt about size, weigh or measure them. The yolk of a 2-ounce egg is just about 1 tablespoon plus a teaspoon; the white, about 2 tablespoons. For more equivalents, see pages 549 and 550. To realize how great a difference egg-size has on volume, notice below that two large eggs give you about half a cup, but it takes three medium

eggs to fill that same half-cup. If you substitute the same number of larger or smaller eggs for the 2-ounce variety, you may be disappointed in the results—especially in baking. When you decrease a recipe and want to use only part of an egg, beat the egg slightly and measure about 1½ tablespoons for half an egg and about 1 tablespoon for one-third.

To substitute eggs of other fowl, from lark to ostrich—which, by the way, will serve 18 for brunch—allow 2 ounces for each hen's egg called for in the recipe. Don't expect the same texture or flavor. Be very sure of freshness in using off-beat eggs. This is especially important in duck eggs. When aging, they often carry dangerous bacteria, which can be destroyed by boiling the eggs for 10 minutes or by baking them in a cake for not less than 1 hour.

ABOUT COOKING EGGS

It is possible, on a hot summer day, "they" say, to fry an egg on the sidewalk. We do not recommend this particular extravagance; we mention it to remind you that eggs cook quickly over any kind of heat—beginning to thicken at 144°.

Sometimes, even when their cooking has been carried on over hot water, the stored heat of the pan will cause eggs to curdle. Be doubly careful then ◗ with all egg dishes, not to use excessive heat and not to prolong the cooking period. Should you suspect you have done either of these things, dump the egg mixture at once into a cold dish and beat vigorously or add a tablespoon of chilled cream. You may in this way save the dish from curdling.

Only prior precautions, however, will produce smooth baked custard dishes. For, once the protein of the egg has shrunk, it can no longer hold moisture in suspension and the results are bound to be watery. If you are combining eggs with a hot mixture, add a small quantity of it to the beaten eggs first. This conditions eggs before their addition to the remaining mixture. Often, at this point in egg cookery—if you are preparing a soufflé base or thickening soup or sauces with yolks—there is enough stored heat in the pan to do the necessary cooking.

If you are going to cook an egg yolk and sugar mixture, beat the eggs, add the sugar and continue to beat until the mix-

ture runs in a broad ribbon from the side of the spoon. When this condition is reached, the eggs will cook without graining.

Now, armed with 2 more secrets, you can expect real magic from the rich, complete and tasty protein that is so tidily packed inside an egg shell. For more details about the nutritive value of eggs, see page 2. In baking and in making omelets or scrambled eggs, remember that eggs will give better texture and volume if they are at about 75° when you start to use them. Also remember that egg yolk is almost ⅓ fat and that, as eggs cool in a pudding or sauce, you can count on some slight thickening action.

ABOUT BEATING EGGS

◆ To beat whole eggs to their greatest volume, have them at about 75°. Beat whole eggs and yolks vigorously—unless otherwise directed in the recipe—until they are light in color and texture, before adding them to batters and doughs.

For some recipes, whole eggs and yolks profit by as much as 5 minutes or more of beating in the electric mixer and will increase up to six times their original volume.

To describe the beating of egg whites is almost as cheeky as advising how to lead a happy life. But, because the success of a dish may rest entirely on this operation, we go into it in some detail. To get the greatest volume ◆ see that the egg whites are at about 75° and properly separated. We have already referred to the bride who couldn't boil an egg. But there are plenty of housewives who can't even break one. Here's how. Have 3 bowls ready, as sketched. Holding an egg in one hand, tap the center of the side of the egg lightly, yet sharply, on the edge of one of the bowls—making an even, crosswise break. Then take the egg in both hands with the break on the upper side. Hold it over the center of a small bowl and tip it so that the wider end is down. Hold the

edges of the break with the thumbs. Widen the break by pulling the edges apart until the egg shell is broken into halves. As you do this, some of the egg white flows into the bowl underneath. The yolk and the rest of the egg white will remain in the lower half of the shell. Now pour the remaining egg back and forth from one half-shell to the other, letting some more of the white flow into the bowl each time until you have only the yolk left. During this shifting process, you will be able to tell quickly, with each egg in turn, if there is any discoloration or off-odor. This way, you can discard it before it is put with the yolks on the left or with the whites in the large bowl on the right.

Should the yolk shatter during breaking, you can try to remove particles from the white by inserting the corner of a paper towel moistened in cold water and making the yolk adhere to it. Should you fail to clear the yolk entirely from the white, keep that egg for another use, because the slightest fat from the yolk will lessen the volume of the beaten whites and perceptibly change the texture.

◆ Choose a large deep bowl in which to beat, shaped as sketched on the right, below. Be sure it is not aluminum, which will grey the eggs, or plastic, which frequently has a chemical that deters volume-development. The French dote on copper. But if cream of tartar is used—as it so frequently is—to give a more stable and tender foam, the acid which is present will turn the eggs greenish. Not to mention what the eggs in turn may do to you.

In recipes for meringues and in some cakes, a portion of the sugar, about 1 teaspoon per egg, is beaten into the egg whites when they are foamy. Although this reduces volume slightly and means a longer beating period, it does give a much more upstanding foam.

The lightness of the beating stroke, plus the thinness of the wire whisk used, also makes an appreciable difference in building up the air capacity of egg-white cells. ◆ Choose as a beater a many thin-wired long whisk, as shown. ◆ Be sure that both

the bowl and the beater are absolutely free from grease. To clean them, use a detergent or a combination of lemon juice and vinegar. Rinse and dry carefully.

If you are going to use the whites in baking, have the oven preheated. Start beating only when all other ingredients are mixed and ready. Be prepared to give about 300 strokes in 2 minutes to beat 2 egg whites. You can expect 2½ to 4 times the volume you start with. Begin slowly and lightly with a very relaxed wrist motion and beat steadily until the egg whites lose their yellowish translucency. They will become foamy. Then increase the beating tempo gradually. Beat without stopping ◗ until the whites are both airy and glossy and stand in peaks that are firm, but still soft and elastic, see page 515.

From start to finish, there should be no stopping until that state is reached that is best described as ◗ stiff, but not dry. Another test for readiness is the rate of flow when the bowl is tipped. Some cooks use the inverted bowl test in which the whites cling dramatically to the bottom of the upside-down bowl. Usually, when this is possible, the eggs have been beaten a trifle too long and are as a consequence too dry. Although they may have greater volume, their cells will not stretch to capacity, when baked, without breaking down.

Folding in egg whites should always be a manual operation rather than a mechanical one, since it is essential again to retain as much air in the whites as possible.

◗ Work both quickly and gently. Add the lighter mixture to the heavier one. Then combine the two substances with two separate movements. Various special tools, like wire "incorporators" and spatulas, have been suggested for this process, but nothing can compare for efficiency with the human hand. First use a sharp, clean action, as though cutting a cake. Then, with a lifting motion, envelop the whites by bringing the heavier substance up from the bottom of the bowl. Repeat these slicing and lifting motions alternately, turning the bowl as you work.

ABOUT STORING EGGS

The storage of eggs is not difficult if you follow a few simple rules. ◗ To store eggs in the shell, wipe but do not wash them until ready to use. When taken from the nest, eggs are covered with a soluble film which protects the porous shell against bacterial entry. ◗ If there is no special storage area for them, place eggs still in their carton in the refrigerator. ◗ Raw eggs in the shell and foods containing raw eggs—like mayonnaise and custards in which the eggs are only slightly cooked—should be kept under refrigeration, 33° to 37°, and away from strong-smelling foods, as they absorb odors easily.

To store egg whites in the refrigerator,

cover them closely and do not keep them longer than 4 days. ◗ Use them only in recipes that call for cooking. To store unbroken egg yolks, cover them first with water, which you then drain off before using. Cover the storage dish before refrigerating. Yolks may be stored uncooked up to 4 days or for a few days longer if poached in water until firm. They should only be used in recipes that call for cooking. Sieve the poached eggs with a pinch of salt. Use in sauces or as a garnish for vegetables. To use extra whites or yolks, see page 552.

Before we leave this subject, we pull out of our hat a conjurer's trick. Should you have any doubts about which eggs in your refrigerator are hard-boiled and which are not, a quick test is to twirl them on their pointed ends. The hard-boiled eggs will spin like a top; the others will simply topple over.

Dried eggs are a convenience when fresh eggs are not available, but they are not an economy. Because of bacterial dangers, they must always be used in recipes that call for cooking, unless a large percentage of acid is indicated. Packaged dried eggs should be stored at 70° and, if opened, should be refrigerated at about 45°. To reconstitute the equivalent of 12 fresh eggs, sift 6 oz. dried egg powder over 1⅞ cups water. Whip until smooth. To substitute for 1 egg, use 2½ tablespoons sifted dry egg powder to 2½ tablespoons water. Beat until smooth. Use either of these mixtures within five minutes after combining. You may prefer to add the egg powder to the dry ingredient and the water to the rest of the liquid called for in the recipe.

✳ To use frozen eggs, see page 767.

Preserve eggs at home only if you have no alternative. The commonest method is immersion in waterglass or sodium silicate. If possible, use nonfertile eggs that are at least 12 hours old. Do not pack too many layers on top of each other, as the weight might crack those below. Eggs so kept are not good for boiling, as the shells become too fragile—nor do the whites beat well for meringues, soufflés, etc.

To preserve 10 dozen eggs, pour 9 quarts of boiling water into a 5 gallon sterile crock. Add 1 quart waterglass, stir thoroughly and add the eggs. The water glass should cover the eggs 2 inches above the top egg. Cover crock and store in a cool place no longer than 6 months.

And a hint about washing egg-soiled dishes. Start with cold water, which releases rather than glues on the protein. Rub sulphur off stained silver with salt if polish is not handy.

ABOUT GELATIN

Gelatin is sympathetic to almost all food ◗ except fresh or frozen pineapple which contains a substance that inhibits jelling. Cooked pineapple presents no problem.

Gelatin is full of tricks. It can turn liquids into solids to produce gala dessert and salad molds. It makes sophisticated chaud-froid and ingenuous marshmallows. It also makes a show case for leftovers and keeps delicate meats and fish in prime condition for buffet service. Chopped and used as a garnish or cut into fancy shapes, clear gelatins add sparkle to a dish that is dull in color.

♦ Gelatin dishes must, of course, be refrigerated until ready to use. And, in buffets, they are best presented on chilled trays or platters set over crushed ice.

While gelatin must be kept cold, it should ♦ never be frozen unless the fat content is very high—as in certain ice creams. Gelatin also gives a smoother texture to frozen desserts, jellies and cold soups. It thickens cold sauces and glazes, page 341, and in sponge and whipped desserts it doubles the volume.

Gelatin's power to displace moisture is due to its "bloom," or strength. In household gelatins, this is rated at 150 and means that 1 tablespoon can turn about 2 cups of liquid into a solid. Gelatin often comes ready to use in granules, but the most delicate fish and meat aspics are made with stocks reduced from bones, skin and fish heads. It also comes in sheets. For equivalents, see page 550.

To get the most nourishment out of gelatin, which is not a complete protein, see page 2. To get the most allure ♦ never use too much. The result is rubbery and unpleasant. The finished gelatin should be quivery—not rigid—when jostled.

Unless a recipe is exceedingly acid, 1 tablespoon of gelatin to 2 cups of liquid should produce a consistency firm enough to unmold after 2 hours of chilling—if the gelatin is a clear one. But it must get 4 hours of chilling if the gelatin has fruits, vegetables or nuts added to it. Also allow proportionately more jelling time for large, as opposed to individual, molds. If you prefer a less firm texture, use 1 tablespoon of gelatin to 2¼ to 2½ cups liquid. These gelatins will not mold but are delightful when served in cups or in coupes.

In our high-speed age, we are told how quickly gelatins can be made by soaking them and then dissolving them in a small quantity of hot liquid, replacing the rest of the required liquid with the proper amount of ice. If you are in a hurry and are making a gelatin which calls for 1 cup water and 1 cup stock or fruit juice, you can prepare it by dissolving the gelatin as usual—boiling your cup of stock or fruit juice and then stirring about 8 large or 10 small ice cubes into the hot liquid to cool it. Stir the cubes constantly 2 to 3 minutes. Remove the unmelted ones. Let the mixture stand 3 to 5 minutes. Incorporate the fruit or other solids called for, and mold.

For an even faster gelatin with frozen fruit, see Blender Fruit Whip, page 697.

In recent years, various other gelatin-mixing methods have been advocated, but we still get the best results using either one of the following:

I. Sprinkle 1 tablespoon of gelatin granules over the surface of ¼ cup cold water and let it soak for about 3 minutes until it has absorbed the moisture and is translucent. ♦ Do not disturb it during this period. Have ready at the boiling point 1¾ to 2 cups stock, fruit juice, milk, wine or water. Combine it with the soaked gelatin and stir until dissolved.

II. If you do not want to subject the liquid in the recipe to high heat or reduce its flavor and vitamin content, use a double boiler and sprinkle 1 tablespoon gelatin over ¼ cup cold water. Dissolve this mixture ♦ over—not in—hot water. Add to the dissolved gelatin 1¾ to 2 cups 75° liquid and stir well. If you are making up your own sweet gelatin recipe, dissolve the sugar in the liquid before measuring and adjust the amount of gelatin needed because the liquefaction of the sugar must be counteracted. If you are ♦ doubling a gelatin recipe that originally called for 2 cups of liquid, use only 3¾ cups in the doubled recipe. For further discussion of this precaution, see page 546.

You may allow the dissolved gelatin to cool at room temperature, over a bowl of cracked ice or in the refrigerator—but not in the freezer, as a gummy look is apt to develop and the surface cracks miserably. It is interesting that gelatins which are slow to jell are also slow to break down when they are removed from the refrigerator, but any gelatin will begin to weep if exposed too long to high temperatures.

♦ For basic gelatin aspic recipes, see pages 95 through 104. For Gelatin Desserts, see pages 693-698.

♦ To make an aspic glaze for hors d'oeuvre or sandwiches ♦ be sure you have the food to be glazed and the tools you are working with well chilled. Apply a thin, even coat of aspic which has begun to jell. Chill. Repeat, if needed, with a second layer and chill again.

ABOUT MAKING FANCY GELATIN MOLDS

Have ready well-drained and chilled foods before starting to make fancy designs in gelatin. Allow about 1¼ cups of solids for each cup of aspic. Just as the aspic thickens to about the consistency of uncooked egg white, put a small amount in a chilled mold or dish with sloping sides, which has been rinsed in cold water. Sometimes oiling a mold is recommended, but with clear gelatins a blurred surface results. Roll and tip the mold in such a way that a thin layer of gelatin coats its inside surface. Refrigerate the mold to set the gelatin.

Now impale bits of food on a skewer or toothpick. Dip them one by one into the gelatin and place them just where you want them on the hardened layer in the mold, to form the design. When the decorations for one layer are in place, fill the spaces between with more aspic. Return the mold to the refrigerator until this has set and proceed with this method until it is filled.

When using a fish-shaped or other fancy mold, accent the lines of the design with slivers of egg white, cucumber or peppers, if for a salad; with citron, cherries, crystallized rinds or fruits, if for a dessert.

An easier way to make layered molds is to choose nuts, fruits and vegetables of different weights and porosity. Put them in a very slightly jelled mixture and let them find their own levels. The floaters are apple cubes, banana slices, fresh grapefruit sections or pear slices, fresh strawberry halves, broken nut meats and marshmallows. The sinkers are fresh orange slices, fresh grapes, cooked prunes and the following canned fruits: apricots, Royal Ann cherries, peaches, pears, pineapple, plums and raspberries. If you are making gelatins to serve in champagne coupes, you can decorate the tops with grape halves. Even though they are technically sinkers, you can wait until the gelatin is almost set and hold each grape for just a second until it makes enough contact not to turn wrong side up.

Another way to make fancy molds is to combine layers of clear and whipped or sponge gelatins, as described next. To make gelatin whips, it is essential ♦ to use a cold bowl or put a bowl over ice and be sure the gelatin has been chilled to a consistency slightly thicker than unbeaten egg white.

♦ If the gelatin is not firm enough when

you start to beat it, it will revert to a clear gelatin in setting.

Use an electric mixer, a rotary beater or a ⅃ blender. To make sponges, follow these directions, but before beginning to beat ♦ add to the chilled gelatin the cold unbeaten egg whites. Beat until the mixture is very stiff.

Mousses and Bavarians are based on gelatinized custards and frequently have both beaten egg white and cream folded in before final chilling. In these desserts, the additions of egg and cream are made when the gelatin mixture mounds slightly if dropped from a spoon. They are then chilled until firm.

♦ To prepare molds for clear gelatins, rinse them well in cold water, as shown at the left below. After filling an undecorated mold, run a knife through the mixture to release any air bubbles that might be trapped in it. Then refrigerate until ready to unmold.

♦ To unmold aspics or gelatin puddings, have ready a chilled plate large enough to allow for a garnish. You may moisten the dish slightly. This will prevent the gelatin from sticking, and enable you to center the mold more easily. You may first use a thin knife at several points on the edge to release the vacuum. Then reverse the mold onto the plate. If necessary, place a warm damp cloth over the mold for a few seconds, as shown. If the food is still not released, shake the mold lightly, bracing it against the serving dish. Some people dip the mold into hot water for just a second. We find this risky with delicate gelatins, as the water must not go above 115°.

ABOUT NUTS

Whether they are seeds—like pecans and walnuts; fruits—like lichees; or tubers—like peanuts, nuts have concentrated protein and fats. Except for Chestnuts, page 520, they contain very little starch. But it is for their essential oils, which carry the flavor, that we treasure them so much.

And the textural contrast they bring always makes them welcome. The reason they are so often listed as an optional ingredient in our recipes is merely because the recipes will carry without them—and with so much less cost and calorie value. Except for green almonds and pickled green walnuts, nuts are nearly all eaten when ripe.

ENGLISH AND AMERICAN WALNUTS AND PECANS

These are perhaps the most familiar and most easily available types. The latter are probably the heaviest in fat of all our natives, sometimes as much as ¾ of their bulk.

HICKORIES AND BUTTERNUTS

Rich natives, like pecans, and they never need blanching.

FILBERTS OR HAZELNUTS

Varieties less rich than the above and almost identical in their sophisticated flavor. Filberts are the more subtle European versions of our native hazelnuts.

ALMONDS

These have comparatively little fat and come in two varieties, sweet and bitter. ♦ When mentioned in this book, they are the dry sweet form, which you find not only ground in Torten, page 637, Marzipan, page 729, and Almond Paste, page 729, but slivered in Amandine, page 350. The dry sweet almond may also be eaten, while green and soft, with cheese and wine.

ALMOND PASTE

This must be kept cool when you work with it—so the oil does not separate out. Should you buy, rather than make, almond paste—see that it is marked "genuine." If it has a slightly bitter taste, it may be crushed apricot, peach or plum seed.

ORGEAT SIRUP

An almond emulsion used to flavor drinks and sweets. Blanch and pound into a paste:

   1 lb. almonds
   10 bitter almonds

Squeeze out the oil. Mix the remaining powder with enough:

   Water

to make a paste. Let it rest for 24 hours in a cool place. Dissolve in:

   1½ cups water
   2 teaspoons tartaric acid

and add this mixture to the paste. Filter **and** add to the resulting liquid:

   2¼ cups sugar
   (2 tablespoons orange water)

Stir until dissolved and store refrigerated.

BITTER ALMONDS

An altogether different type with a strangely bitter taste—an accent desirable in ♦ very small quantities for flavoring. Use as in Almond Milk, page 487, and Orgeat, opposite.

ALMOND OIL

An extract made from bitter almonds is often called for in European recipes. But it is dangerous to use it to excess and in America it is available only on prescription.

BRAZIL NUTS

The more delicate types do not ship well and we must rely on a rather coarse, tough variety that does. To slice these large kernels, cover the shelled nuts with cold water and bring slowly to a boil. Simmer 5 minutes. Drain. Slice lengthwise or make curls with a vegetable slicer. You may toast the slices at 350° for about 12 minutes.

MACADAMIA NUTS AND CASHEWS

These are also popular. Cashews have an edible, fleshy fruit covering which can be eaten raw, but ♦ the nuts must always be roasted carefully to destroy a poison they contain. Make cashew butter as for Peanut Butter, described later.

PISTACHIO NUTS

Although maddeningly small, these are delicious, loved for their color and often used in farces or pâtés.

PINE OR INDIAN NUTS

Known also as Piñon in Spain or Pignola in Italy—where the variety is richer. These are good in Dolmas, page 431, and in Pesto, page 539.

BEECHNUTS

A real treat—but just try to beat the squirrels to this harvest.

PUMPKIN, SQUASH, MELON AND SUNFLOWER SEEDS

All of these are flavorful and nutritionally valuable. ♦ To roast the tiny nutlike seeds, see page 521.

PEANUTS

If you enjoy the flavor, peanuts are nutritionally valuable and are used in Nut Loaves, Nutburgers, Peanut Brittle, **page** 736, Cookies, page 658, and of course, Peanut Butter, see the recipe on page 521. These underground legumes—also called groundnuts or in their larger form, goobers —are high in valuable proteins. If the heart is left in, they make a real and economical contribution to the diet. The small

Spanish types will grow in the northern states. All peanuts are best eaten right after roasting, before they get limp. If roasting them in the shell at home, keep the oven at 300° and roast 30 to 45 minutes—or 20 to 30 minutes if shelled. Turn them constantly to avoid scorching. Check for doneness by removing skins. The inner skins, heavy in thiamin, are pleasantly flavored. But little is gained by home roasting, as a steam process used commercially for peanuts in the shell gives superior results.

CHESTNUTS: MARRONS AND OTHER VARIETIES

These need long and loving care—just like navy beans, which are often substituted for them in frugal European kitchens. One of our more knowing friends insists you cannot tell the difference when a strong lacing of coffee, chocolate or almond paste is used in the dessert. Chestnuts are frequently used as stuffing for fowl and traditionally combined with Brussels sprouts and red cabbage. Do not confuse the chestnuts in these recipes with the ones you find under ornamental allées or with those crisp Chinese water chestnuts we usually know only in canned form.

♦ To shell chestnuts, make two crosscut gashes on their flat side with a sharp pointed knife. Sometimes the shell will come off when you do this, but the inner skin will protect the kernel. Place the nuts in a pan over a quick heat, dropping oil or butter over them—1 teaspoon to 1 pound of nuts. Shake them until they are coated, then place them in a moderate oven until the shells and inner brown skins can be removed easily.

Or cover chestnuts with boiling water and simmer them 15 to 25 minutes. Drain them and remove the shells and skins. The meats should be sufficiently tender to be put through a purée strainer. If not, cover them with boiling water and cook them until tender.

For use as a vegetable, see page 272; as Marrons Glacés, page 743; or in desserts, page 694. Chestnuts are available fresh, canned in sirup and dried.

♦ To reconstitute dried chestnuts, soak in water to cover overnight. Rinse and pick over. Simmer in a deep pan covered with about 3 inches of water until they are tender and puffed up. Substitute them for cooked fresh chestnuts, cup for cup.

The Portuguese and Chinese are not as sweet as the Italian. The American chestnut is represented, since the blight, only by smaller types like the chinquapin.

Allow about 1½ lbs. in the shell for 1 lb. shelled. 35 to 40 whole large-type chestnuts make about 2½ cups peeled. The brown inside skin is bitter and must be peeled off while still warm.

ROASTED CHESTNUTS
Preheat oven to 425°.
Prick the skins of:
  Chestnuts
with a fork before putting them in the oven for 15 to 20 minutes or they may explode. More hazardous, but more fun, is to roast the chestnuts on a cold winter's evening, at the edge of an open fire. A childhood game was for each of us to cheer our own chestnut on to pop first.

SKEWERED CHESTNUTS
Prepare by boiling in:
  Milk
  Boiled Chestnuts I, page 272
Omit the vinegar. When the chestnuts are cooked until soft enough to penetrate with a fork, roll them in a mixture of:
  Au Gratin III, page 342
Place on a greased baking dish and run under the hot broiler for a few moments. Dust with:
  Chopped parsley
Serve at once on picks.

WATER CHESTNUTS

There are 2 types—both of which are crispy and delicious. In one type, the shell grows together into a horn at one end. The other is bulbous. Use water chestnuts in Hors D'oeuvre, page 71, Vegetables, page 309, and Salads, page 82.

LICHEE NUTS

Really, these are a soft, firm, sweet, spicy fruit, protected by a most exquisite fragile shell, as shown on page 110. Serve 3 to 5 nuts on green leaves or as a garnish on a fruit bowl for dessert. They are also available canned in sirup, but the flavor is not as hauntingly aromatic.

ABOUT STORING AND PREPARING NUTS

The best way to store nuts is to keep them in their shells. This protects them from light, heat, moisture and exposure to air—factors which tend to cause rancidity in the shelled product. The difference in the keeping time for shelled pecans, for instance, may range from 2 months at about 70° to as long as 2 years in a freezer. So if nuts are already shelled, store them tightly covered in a cool, dark, dry place or in a freezer. Some nuts, like pecans and Brazil nuts, are more easily shelled if boiling water is poured over them and they are allowed to stand for 15 to 20 minutes

To open coconuts, see page 523.
♦ For yield of kernels from nuts in the shell, see page 551. Be sure to discard any

kernels that are shrivelled or dry, as they may prove bitter or rancid.

TO BLANCH NUTS

In addition to the tough outer shell, nuts have a thin inner lining or skin. Just before using, try one of the following methods:

I. Pour boiling water over the shelled nuts. For large quantities, you may have to let them stand for about 1 minute at the most ♦ the briefer the length of time the better. Drain. You may pour cold water over them to arrest further heating. Redrain. Pinch or rub off the skins.

II. For peanuts, filberts and pistachio nuts, you may prefer to roast at 350° for 10 to 20 minutes and then rub off the skins.

TO ROAST AND TOAST NUTS

This both crisps them and brings up the flavor. Unless otherwise specified, place them blanched or unblanched in a 300° oven and turn frequently to avoid scorching. ♦ To avoid loss of flavor and toughening, do not overtoast.

Recipes for deep fat, roasting shelled, roasting in the shell, oven-roasted, spiced and seasoned nuts: see pages 65, 66, 736, and 737.

TO PREPARE NUTS FOR SALTING

♦ Coat a bowl with egg white, butter or olive oil, add the nuts and shake them until they are coated. Spread the nuts on cookie tins and heat in a 250° oven. If you salt before cooking, allow not more than ½ teaspoon salt to one cup of nuts. Roast about 10 to 15 minutes, stirring frequently to achieve even browning. A more rapid way is to heat in a heavy iron skillet 2 tablespoons oil for every cup of nuts. Stir constantly for about 3 minutes. Drain on absorbent paper. Salt and serve.

TO CHOP NUTS

If rather large pieces are needed, simply break nuts like pecans and walnuts with the fingers. For finer pieces, use a knife or a chopping bowl and chopper. ♦ It is easier if the nuts are moist and warm and if the knife is a sharp French one, page 251. Group the nuts in a circle with a diameter of about the length of the blade. Grasp the knife on top in both hands as you would a bar at both hilt and blade ends. Chop briskly with a rocking motion beginning at the knife point, rocking from point to hilt and gradually working the knife back in a semi-circle from the pointed end.

Almonds may be chopped in a ⅄ blender. Process only ½ cup at a time for 30 seconds at highest speed.

TO GRIND NUTS

♦ Use a special type of grinder—one that shreds or grates them sharply to keep them dry, rather than a type that will crush them and release their oils. Do small quantities in a rotary grinder, as sketched. Light, dry, fluffy particles result, which can be substituted for flour in Nut Torten, page 637.

Sometimes, however, for butters and pastes, a meat grinder or a ⅄ blender is used. We do not otherwise recommend a blender for grinding nuts, as it tends to make the nuts too oily—except for almonds.

Peanut butter is so popular that it has overshadowed the use of other nut butters. Try grinding almonds, pecans or walnuts into butter. These are so rich they need no additional oil. Use for every cup of nuts ⅓ teaspoon salt.

⅄ PEANUT BUTTER

Smooth and delicious as commercial peanut butters may be, they are often made without the germ of the nut. This valuable portion—as in grains—contains minerals, vitamins and proteins and is literally fed to the birds. The commercial objection to the germ is twofold: 1. That the flavor of the butter is made somewhat bitter, 2. that, as with whole grains, the heat of processing and the heat in storage may cause the finished product to grow rancid. If you are smart, make your own full-bodied peanut butter in an electric blender.
Use:

> **Fresh roasted or salted peanuts**

It is wise to start with a bland oil:

> **Safflower or vegetable oil**

Allow 1½ to 3 tablespoons to 1 cup peanuts. If nuts are unsalted, add salt to taste:

> **About ½ teaspoon salt per cup**

ABOUT DRIED FRUITS

The high caloric and nutritive values of dried fruits can be readily grasped if you realize that it takes 5½ lbs. of fresh apricots to yield 1 lb. when dried. A few dried fruits as a garnish or as a dessert go a long way. When fruits are dried without cooking, their subsequent contact with the air—as well as the enzymatic activity which takes place within them—tends to darken the pulp. A sulphur dioxide solution is often used to lessen darkening.

Dates, figs, apples, peaches, prunes, plums, apricots, currants and raisins are among the most used dried fruits. They must all be ▸ stored tightly covered in a cool, dark place. Under most household shelf conditions, they are likely to deteriorate in a matter of months. This is especially true of raisins. All varieties must be watched for insect infestation that develops in them with age.

Raisins divide into two major types: seedless, those which grow without seeds; and seeded, which have had the seeds removed. As their flavors are quite different, it is wise to use the types called for in the recipes—without interchanging. White raisins, often called muscats, are specially treated to retain their lovely color. Currants and raisins both profit, unless they are very fresh, by plumping, especially when used in short-cooking recipes. This can be done by soaking them in the liquid in which they are to be cooked—such as the liquid called for in cakes—for 10 to 15 minutes before use. Raisins and currants may also be plumped by washing briefly, draining, spreading on a flat pan and then heating, closely covered, in a 350° oven until they puff up and are no longer much wrinkled.

Small fruits are often messy to cut or chop. Flour them, if they are very sticky ▸ using for this purpose, when baking, a portion of the flour called for in the batter. Don't use additional flour, as it will make the dough too heavy. They may also be more easily cut if the scissors or knife-blade is heated. Handle the knife as for chopping nuts. But, if you are chopping in quantity, you may want to use a meat grinder instead. ▸ Heat the grinder very thoroughly in boiling water before feeding in the fruit.

Candied and preserved fruits are sometimes substituted for dried fruits. If candied fruits are used, allow for their extra sugar content. With preserved fruits, compensate for both sugar and liquid.

ABOUT CHOCOLATE AND COCOA

Both these delights come from the evergreen trees of the genus Theobroma, "Food of the Gods." Up to the moment when the chocolate liquor is extracted from the nibs, or hulled beans, and molded into solid cakes, the manufacture of chocolate and cocoa is identical. At this point, part of the "butter" is removed from some of the cakes, which become cocoa, and added to others which, in turn, become the bitter chocolate we know as cooking chocolate.

Cocoa butter is remarkable for the fact that, under normal storage conditions, it will keep for years without becoming rancid. There are many pharmaceutical demands for it and, in inferior chocolate, it is sometimes replaced by other fat.

Ideal storage temperature for chocolate is 78°. The bloom that turns chocolate greyish after it has been stored at high temperatures is harmless—merely the fat content coming to the surface.

The best sweet chocolate is made by combining the melted bitter cake with 35% cocoa butter, finely milled sugar and such additions as vanilla and milk—depending on the type of chocolate desired. In this book, when the magic word ▸ chocolate appears all alone in recipes, it means bitter cooking chocolate. An entire square equals 1 ounce. Two-thirds cup of semi-sweet chocolate is 6 ounces by weight—or 10⅔ tablespoons by volume. But in any semisweet chocolate, you have about 60% bitter chocolate and 40% sugar. German's chocolate, which is conditioned against heat, refers not to the country but to a very canny person of that name, who early realized there was a greater profit if the sugar was already added to the chocolate when it was sold.

Should you want to substitute semi-sweet for bitter, make the adjustment in the recipe using less sugar, more chocolate and a dash of vanilla.

▸ For exact substitution and equivalents of chocolate and cocoa, see page 549. In some quick-cooking recipes, this substitution may not be successful, as the sugar doesn't crystallize properly with the chocolate. If semi-sweet chocolate stiffens when melted—in sauces, for instance—add a small amount of butter and stir well until smooth. ▸ Substituting cocoa for chocolate in sauces can be adjusted more easily than in baking. Just add 1 tablespoon butter to 3 tablespoons cocoa for each ounce of chocolate. But ▸ in baking it is wiser to choose recipes written either for cocoa or for chocolate, as the cocoa has a flourlike quality that must be compensated for—or the cake will become too doughy.

▸ All chocolate scorches easily, so melt it over hot water. If you don't like to clean the pot, float the chocolate on a small foil "boat" and discard the foil after use. Place wrapped squares, folded edges up, in the top of a double boiler ▸ over, not in, hot water for 10 to 12 minutes. Cool chocolate to about 80° before adding it to cake, cookie or pudding mixtures.

▸ To grate chocolate, chill it and try shaving it or grating it in a rotary grinder, see page 521. If you grate it, have a big bowl ready to receive it—or you may be annoyed by its flighty dynamism. In cakes and cookies, soda is often used to give chocolate a ruddy tone. A few drops of vinegar serve the same purpose.

▸ To make chocolate curls for decorating

parfaits or cream pies, hold a wrapped square of unsweetened chocolate in the hand to warm it slightly. Unwrap and shave chocolate with long thin strokes, using a vegetable peeler or a small, sharp knife.

◗ For chocolate as a seasoning, see Mole, page 473.

Cocoa is pulverized from the dry cocoa cakes which, after processing, still contain from 10% fat for regular cocoa up to 22% to 24% fat for breakfast cocoa. The so-called Dutch type maintains the heavier fat content and the small quantity of alkali introduced during the processing produces a slightly different flavor. Instant cocoa, which contains usually 80% sugar, is pre-cooked and has an emulsifier added—to make it dissolve well in either a hot or cold liquid. For details about cocoa and chocolate as beverages, see page 30. For Dipping Chocolate, see page 731.

ABOUT COCONUTS

If you live in coconut country, you know the delight of using the flower sap as well as the green and the mature fruit of this graceful palm. In cooking, you may sub-titute its "milk," "cream" and "butter" for dairy products. However, be aware that this exchange is not an equal one nutri-tionally—because the coconut is much lower in protein. ◗ Coconut milk and cream are very sensitive to high heat. For this reason, they are added to hot sauces at the last minute or are cooked over hot water. They are especially treasured in preparing curries and delicate fish and fruit dishes.

The first thing to do with a coconut, of course, is to get at it. Lacking power tools, you drop the large fruit onto a rocklike substance. If it doesn't crack open enough so that the husk pulls away, use your trusty axe. Out comes a fiber-covered nut. Shake it. A sloshing noise means that the nut is fresh and that you can count on some milk. If the husked coconut is green, the top can be lopped off with a large, heavy knife or a machete. The liquid within is clear and the greenish jellylike pulp makes ideal food for small children and invalids. To open the harder shell of the mature nut, you may pierce the three shiny black dots which form a monkey face at the peak. Use a skewer or sharp, sturdy knife-point. Allow the liquid to drain. Reserve it. More about this milky substance, which is quite different from the coconut milk and cream extracted from coconut meat, follows. Tap the nut briskly all over with a hammer. It usually splits lengthwise, and these halves can be used as containers for serving hot or cold food. See illustrations, page 524.

You may also open the shell with heat, but then the shell is useless for serving hot food. To do so, place the un-drained husked coconut in a preheated 325° oven for 15 to 20 minutes. ◗ Do not overcook, as this destroys the flavor. Remove from the oven and cool until the nut can be handled. Wrap it in a heavy cloth to prevent any pieces from flying off. Then crack it with hammer taps. ◗ Have a bowl ready to catch the milky liquid—remembering that this liquid should be constantly under refrigeration and used within 24 hours. Coconut cream, very rich in fat, is made from the grated, mature, white stiff meat of the nut. The grating is sometimes done while the meat is still in the shell, see illustration. Or you may leave the thin

brown skin on and use it to protect the fingers as you hand-grate. If the skin is removed, cut the meat into small chunks and chop in the ⅃ blender.

In the East Indies, they heat the grated coconut meat in its own natural milk ◗ just to the boiling point, then remove it from the heat and cool. In the West Indies, they pour boiling water over grated coco-nut and add the natural "milk"—allowing in all about 1 pint liquid for a medium coconut. In either case, when the mixture has cooled, the coconut is drained through two thicknesses of cheesecloth and the meat, retained in the cloth, is squeezed and kneaded until dry. The drained liquid is allowed to set. When the "cream" rises, it is skimmed off and refrigerated.

Another way to extract milk from the coconut meat is to crack the outer casing and shell, but not to remove the brown rind that adheres to the white meat—unless the recipe so states. Wash, drain, grate or ⅃ blend the pulp. Add ¼ cup hot wa-ter. Then strain and measure. If more milk is needed than results, add more hot water, reblend and strain again.

Coconut "butter"—though vegetable in origin—contains completely saturated fatty acids. It is made from chilled coconut "cream"—also very rich in fat—by churn-ing with a rotary beater or in a ⅃ blender. When the solid mass rises, force any ex-cess water out of it with the back of a spoon. To utilize the coconut that remains,

make **polvo de amor,** a garnish for breakfast foods and desserts, by simply browning it slowly in a heavy pan over low heat. Use about 2 tablespoons of sugar to 1 cup of coconut and cook until golden brown. To toast grated coconut, spread it thinly on a baking sheet and heat for about 10 minutes in a preheated 325° oven. Stir frequently. For a dessert or a spread made from grated coconut, see Coconut Dulcie, page 713.

The meat of the coconut is grated for many uses. You may grate it fresh, see sketch, page 523. You may buy it dry-shredded and use it as it comes. Or you may soak it for 6 hours refrigerated in milk to cover, and drain it before use. This gives it about the same moisture content as the canned, shredded or flaked types—for which it may be substituted.

◗ To substitute coconut, pack the measures and use 1⅓ cups flaked to 1 cup grated. Shown on page 523 is a grater given us by an Indian friend, which simplifies the preparation of coconut for cakes and garnishes.

Coconut shells can make interesting food and drink containers. For a bowl, saw the upper third off the shell. For a rack to hold this round-bottomed shell upright, cut about ½ off the smaller piece as sketched on the left, above. For serving salads, cut the shell lengthwise. The shells can also be used to heat and serve sauced foods. Cut off the top ⅓ to serve as a lid. The food may be heated in a 350° oven by placing the lidded nutshell in a small custard cup or on an inverted canning jar lid in a pan of hot water. Baste the shell about every 10 minutes. Then you may simply fill the shell with very hot food. The cup may form a base when you serve; or you may fold a napkin or ti leaf for support, as sketched, center and right.

ABOUT SALTS

Salt has many powers. The interplay of salt and water is essential to life itself. The maintenance of a proper salt balance is vital to the system and no attempts to cut down on or delete salt from the diet should be made without advice from a physician. ◗ Salt's powers of preservation made possible our ancestors' survival in the waters, wastes and wilderness through which they forged the world's great trade routes. While its use in preserving food has become much less important with the advance of refrigeration it is surprising how much we still depend on it: in food processing of various kinds; in the curing of meats; in the brining and pickling of vegetables; in freezing ice cream; even, now and then, for heating oysters and baking potatoes.

In food preservation, the action of salt is twofold. It draws out moisture by osmosis, thus discouraging the microorganisms which are always more active in moist than in dry food. Afterwards, the brine formed by the salt and moisture in combination further prevents or retards the growth of surface microorganisms. In Sauerkraut, page 787, and Salt-Rising Bread, page 558, the more salt-tolerant friendly bacteria survive to give the food its characteristic quality, while the ones that cause spoilage are destroyed.

◗ Salting of present day meats is, in most cases—except for "old hams"—too mild to allow them to be held safely without refrigeration. To cook salted meats see page 409; to remove excess salt from bacon and salt pork, see page 511, from anchovies, page 539. ◗ The power of salt to heighten the flavor of other foods is its greatest culinary asset. This is true even in candy-making, when a pinch of salt often brings out a confection's characteristic best, and with uncooked food, as when sprinkled on citrus fruits.

Its reaction on cooked food is, otherwise, several-sided. It tends to dehydrate when added to water in which vegetables are cooked, and firms them. It draws the moisture from meats and fish in cooking processes. And it tends to deter the absorption of water by cereals, although it helps retain the shape of the grain. It toughens eggs. And it must be used cautiously in bread-making, as too much inhibits the growth of yeast and adversely affects gluten formation. For the effects of salt water on cooking, see page 494.

These diverse properties of salt have provoked arguments, from time to time, as to just when this very important ingredient should be added when cooking food. It must, of course, be used very sparingly, if at all, at the start of any cooking in which liquids will be greatly evaporated—such as the making of soups, stocks and sauces. But small quantities of salt, added early to soups and stews, will help in clarification

It is obviously good practice to sear grilled, broiled or roasted meat before adding salt, to retain juices and flavor—unless the meat is floured or breaded, page 501. And since it is almost impossible to get rid of salt in cooked foods—although occasionally a touch of sugar will make them more palatable—the amount must be calculated with care.

We know, from long experience, that the flavor-enhancing power of salt is most effective if it is added during, not after, cooking. Our best judgment is, in general, to add it judiciously toward the end of the process and to correct the seasoning just before serving. Don't taste with the tip of the tongue only, but with the middle and sides as well, where the greatest response to salt-stimulus lies.

Salt occurs within foods in varying amounts, animal sources having a higher salt content than vegetable. Sea fish, especially shellfish, are heavier in salt than fresh water types. Of course, pickled, cured or corned meats and sausages, broths, catsups and extracts, brine-processed frozen fish, sardines, herrings and anchovies, as well as canned soups, fish and meats—all are high in salt. Do watch your salting arm when dealing with any of the foods mentioned above, and in cooking beets, carrots, celery, chard, kale, spinach, dandelion greens, endive and corn—all of which are twice as naturally salty as most vegetables. And be cautious with dates, coconut and molasses.

Various kinds of salt are mentioned in this book. When the word salt is used without qualification, it means ♦ cooking or table salt.

♦ For amount of salt to use in seasoning, see page 539.

COOKING OR TABLE SALT

This is a finely ground free-flowing type, about 40% sodium chloride—to which dehydrators are frequently added.

IODIZED SALT

This is recommended for certain areas where the water and soils are lacking in this essential trace element, page 3. ♦ To keep these fine-crystal salts free-flowing, put a few grains of rice in the salt cellars.

COARSE OR KOSHER SALT

This is squarish-grained sea salt, with a natural iodine and other minerals, very flavorful when used in cooking. It is often served sprinkled over meats, after carving and just before serving, so that it does not have time to melt completely. It is also sprinkled over rolls, pretzels and bread before baking, as a sparkling garnish.

BRINE

Brine is a solution of salt and water—preferably soft water. Its purpose is to draw the natural sugars and moisture from foods and form lactic acids which protect them against spoilage bacteria. A 10% brine, about the strongest used in food processing, is made by dissolving 1½ cups salt in 1 gallon of liquid or allowing 6 tablespoons salt to a quart of liquid. A 10% brine is usually strong enough to discourage even such destructive bacteria as botulinus. But after brining, as more liquid continues to be drawn from fruits and vegetables, the brine may be weakened. ♦ A rule of thumb to test for 10% brine is that it will float a 2 oz. egg. Allow about 2 gallons of 10% brine plus enough food to fill a 4 gallon jar.

PICKLING OR DAIRY SALT

A pure salt that is free from additives which might cloud the pickle liquid. Granulated and flake forms of salt may be substituted pound for pound. But, if measuring by volume, use for every cup granulated salt about 1½ cups flake salt.

ROCK SALT

A nonedible, unrefined variety which is used in the freezing of ice cream—also as a base for baking potatoes or heating oysters.

VEGETABLE SALTS

These are sodium chloride with added vegetable extracts—such as celery and onion. If you use them cut down on the amount of salt called for in the recipes.

SEASONED SALTS

These are usually a compound of vegetable salts, spices and monosodium glutamate. In using flavoring salts, be sure not to add regular cooking salt before tasting.

I.
    10 tablespoons salt
     3 tablespoons pepper
     5 tablespoons white pepper
     2 tablespoons red pepper
     1 teaspoon each nutmeg, cloves, cinnamon, bay, sage, marjoram, rosemary

II.
     4 tablespoons salt
     1 tablespoon sugar
     1 tablespoon monosodium glutamate
     1 tablespoon paprika
     1 teaspoon mace, celery salt, nutmeg, curry, garlic powder, onion powder, mustard

HERB SALTS

I. Blend in a mortar for 3 or 4 minutes:
     1 cup non-iodized salt
     1½ cups pounded fresh herbs

Spread the mixture on a heatproof tray to dry.

II. You may also preserve some herbs by salting them down green in a covered crock, alternating ½-inch layers of salt with ½-inch layers of herbs. Begin and end with slightly heavier salt layers. After a few weeks, the salt will take on the flavor of the herbs you have chosen to combine and will be ready for use. The herbs which remain green may also be used.

MONOSODIUM GLUTAMATE

A concentrated form of sodium which is usually extracted from grains or beets. It is also present in bean curd and soy sauce. Long known as the magic powder of the East, where tons and tons of it are consumed annually, it is being used increasingly in this country—especially in commercially processed foods—because of its power to intensify some flavors. It seems to have no effect on eggs or sweets. It may modify the acidity of tomatoes, the earthiness of potatoes and the rawness of onions and eggplant. It acts as a blender for mixed spices used in meat and fish cookery. Monosodium glutamate is the ingredient that causes for some devotees of Chinese food the allergic reaction known as Chinese restaurant syndrome.

While it accentuates the saltiness of some foods, just as wine does, it lessens the saltiness of others. ♦ We, personally detect a certain deadening similarity in foods when we use monosodium glutamate. And we prefer, if a meat or vegetable is prime, to let its own choice character shine.through unassisted.

SOUR SALT

A citric acid which is sometimes used to replace a lemon flavoring or to avoid discoloration in fruits or canned foods.

SMOKED SALTS

Hickory or other scented smokes have been purified of tars and are chemically bound to these salts by an electrical charge.

SMOKY SALT MIXTURE

    1 teaspoon smoked salt
    ½ cup catsup
    ¼ cup olive oil
    2 tablespoons mustard

SALT SUBSTITUTES

These are chlorides in which sodium is replaced by calcium, potassium or ammonium. They should be used only on the advice of a physician.

ABOUT SPICES

Long before the first New England farm wife bought a wooden nutmeg, spice traders have known ways to camouflage their wares. We are lucky today that both government agencies and trade associations work hard to develop and maintain high standards in these relatively costly and still most important condiments.

Pepper, like salt, because of its preservative qualities, has been at times worth its weight in gold. And we are acquainted with a treasured bay leaf that on festive occasions—all during the last war—made the rounds of ten or fifteen beleaguered English households.

Perhaps our interest in spices is the greater because of our descent from a sailing family, not in New England but in the old Hansa town of Lübeck, where ships with their cargoes of Kolonialwaren anchored at the wharves on the Trave. And the spices were stored in the mowlike corbie-stepped warehouses hard by—above the merchants' living quarters.

Spices, indeed, bring all the world together. Like wines and cheeses, their individuality is intense and their identification with places a vivid one. We associate the best bay leaves with Turkey; the best real cinnamon with Ceylon; the best red hot peppers with Louisiana. And there have been lively controversies over the relative merits of Spanish and Hungarian paprika, of Mexican and Malagasy vanilla bean.

Since spices are used in such small quantities, we recommend that you purchase from impeccable sources. We also suggest that ♦ if you are using ground spices they be replenished at least within the year, as they tend in this form to lose strength rapidly. Be sure to date you jars when you clean and fill them. Store spices in tightly covered nonabsorbent containers and in as dark and cool an area as your kitchen provides. But have them handy! Their discriminating use will pique many a dish from obscurity to memorableness.

In cooking, put whole spices in a cloth or a stainless metal tea ball—so you can remove them more readily when the dish is done. ♦ Do not overboil spices, in particular caraway, as they become bitter. And do not use high heat for paprika or curry, for they scorch easily. Some spices are available as distilled essences, and these clear additives are valuable in light Fruit Butters, page 777, or Pickles, page 78. Their flavor does not last as long as that of whole spices cooked with the food. ✻ Frozen spiced foods do not hold up well when stored for any length of time. And in ♦ quantity cooking, if you are enlarg ing household recipes, spice to taste rather than to measure.

We have tried throughout this book to vary our recipes with appropriate seasoning which combines spices and herbs. We have suggested amounts which are pleasurable for the average person. Spice tolerances vary tremendously with individuals and you may wish to use more or less of the quantities we have indicated. For a further discussion of spice combinations, see Seasonings, page 538. The following comments describe various spices and their uses.

ALLSPICE

In this book, pimiento, the name for true peppers of the Capsicum family, see page 536, is reserved for them. And pimento, a probably perverted spelling, is kept for allspice only. Within its single small reddish-brown berry lies a mixture of cinnamon, clove, nutmeg and juniper berry flavors. And this is why the French sometimes call allspice "quatre épices." They also use this term for a blend of spices. Use allspice from soup to nuts, alone or in a combination with other spices.

THE CARDAMONS

Powder the plump seeds of Elettaria cardamomum only as needed, for otherwise the aromatic loss is great. Use as for cinnamon and cloves, alone or in combination. Delicious in coffee. The smaller type —amamum cardamomum—is used whole in barbecue, basting sauces and pickles.

THE CINNAMONS

True cinnamon—Cinnamomum zeylanicum—is the bark of a tree that flourishes in Ceylon and along the Malabar Coast. It is extremely mild whether rolled in a tight quill or stick or in powdered form. Most of the so-called cinnamon on the market is really cassia—Cinnamomum cassia. This is a similar bark that is not quilled, but formed as though a short scroll were rolled from both ends and left with its center portion flat. It has slightly bitter overtones compared to the warm, sweet, aromatic true cinnamon. The best forms of cassia come from Saigon. Use the stick form of either of these spices in hot chocolate, mulled wine, fruit compotes and pickles. We need hardly suggest trying cinnamon on toast, dustings on cookie tops or incorporating it into desserts and baked items. But maybe its use, in small quantities, in meats and seafoods is new to you.

THE CLOVES

This spicy, dried, rich red, unopened bud of the clove tree—Caryophyllus aromaticus—contains so much oil that you can squeeze it out with a fingernail. Because its flavor is so strong, the heads of the cloves are sometimes removed so the seasoning will be milder. These milder portions are often used in the powdered form. Always remove any whole cloves used in cooking before serving. Oil of clove is available for use in light-colored foods, but watch out for its terrific pungency. The best cloves come from Madagascar and Zanzibar. Use in curries, stewed fruits, marmalades and chutneys, pickles, marinades and, in small quantities, with onions and meats; also of course, with ham, as well as in spiced baked stews. An onion stuck with 3 or 4 cloves is a classic addition to stocks and stews.

CURRY

We think of curry, which is really a highly seasoned sauce, mainly as a powder sitting on the shelf ready to be added when foods need a lift. But curry powders are best when the spices are freshly ground or incorporated into a paste with onion, garlic, fruits and vegetables as commonplace as apples and carrots and as exotic as tamarind and pomegranate.

The curry, either in powder or paste form, has its flavor developed in olive oil, or ghee, a clarified butter. The paste is then cooked in a low oven over a period of several hours before the final stage of preparation with the main food. Curries should be specially blended for each kind of dish: a dry one for coating meat; a sour one for marinated meats; and other mixtures in between for chicken or mutton, rice, beans, vegetables and fish. They range in strength from the fiercely hot curries of Madras to the mild ones of Indonesia. The mixtures below give you an idea of the variety and extent of curry bases. Amounts to use per portion are a matter of tolerance. Choose beer or a tart limeade as a beverage with curried foods. While making up the dish, use plenty of fresh garlic and onion and, if possible, fresh coconut milk, page 523.

I.

> 1 oz. each ginger, coriander and
>   cardamon
> ¼ oz. cayenne
> 3 oz. turmeric

II.

> 2 oz. each of the seeds of coriander,
>   turmeric, fenugreek, black pepper
> 2½ oz. cumin seed
> 1½ oz. each poppy and cardamon seeds
> ½ oz. mustard seed
> ½ oz. dry ginger
> 2 oz. dry chilis
> 1 oz. cinnamon

III.

> 1 oz. each turmeric, coriander
>   and cumin

½ oz. dry ginger and peppercorns
¼ oz. dried hot peppers and fennel seed
⅛ oz. each mustard, poppy seeds,
    cloves and mace

GINGER

The root of a bold perennial, Zingiber of-
ficinale—with the most heavenly scented
lily—must be harvested at just the right
moment to avoid being fibrous and having
a bitter after-taste. Whole fresh or green
ginger should be smooth-skinned and even
in color and must be kept dry or it will
sprout and be useless for flavoring. It
tastes best sliced thin, unpeeled and
sautéed in oil to extract the flavor. When
fresh it can also be mashed. When dry it
may be cut into ½-inch cubes and steeped
for several hours in marinades or in cold
water, after which the liquid can be used
as seasoning. Peeled or thinly sliced ginger
can be added to stews or rubbed over duck
or fish, as you would garlic. It will do
much to remove "fishy" flavors. Boiled and
then preserved in sirup, it is known, in this
milder form, as Canton ginger. This is
delicious in desserts, chopped fine and used
with or without its sauce. And it is worth
trying with bananas and even tomatoes,
squash, onions and sweet potatoes. Ginger
is also candied and, in a pinch, can in this
form be washed of its sugar and substituted
for fresh ginger. When ground, we all
know the value of ginger for flavoring
baked items. Equivalent flavoring strengths
of the above forms are: ½ teaspoon ground
equals 1 to 2 thinly sliced preserved, equals
2 tablespoons sirup.

NUTMEG AND MACE

These flavors are so closely allied because
they come from the same tough-husked
fruit of Myristica fragrans. It is sun- or
charcoal-dried and, when opened, has a
lacy integument which is used whole in
cooking fruits or desserts or ground into
mace for seasoning. The hard, inner kernel is the nutmeg. Use it sparingly but
often and, for its full flavor, grind it fresh
from a handy nutmeg grinder that merely
needs a twist—like a pepper mill. Try it
not only in baked items but in spinach,
with veal, on French toast—and always
with eggnog.

THE WHITE AND BLACK PEPPERS

Both these peppers come from the berry of
Piper nigrum. There is some difference in
flavor, the white being slightly more aromatic, but their use is almost interchangeable.
    The white is made from the fully ripe
berry from which the dark outer shell is
buffed before the berry is ground. White
pepper flavor holds up better in sausages
and canned meats. This form is also used
in all light-colored foods or sauces.

Black pepper is processed from the
green, underripe, whole dried berries, and
then cured. They are used in poivrade
dishes, crushed—rather than ground—so
the oils are not dispersed. And they are
added the last few minutes before the sauce
is strained. But pepper, which can be used
in any food except sweets—and even here
there is the further exception of Pfeffer
nuesse, page 657—is best freshly ground
It is not only a remarkable preservative
but manages to strengthen food flavor
without masking them as much as other
spices do.
    Unless otherwise specified, the word
pepper in this book means black pepper.

POPPY SEED

This seed comes from Papaver phoeas
different from the opium poppy. The most
desirable is grown in Holland and colored
a slate blue. The seed is best when roasted
or steamed and crushed before use in
cooking—so its full flavor is released. If it
is one of your favorite flavors, it is worth
getting a special hand-mill for grinding it
Use it in baked items and try it on noodles

TURMERIC

This Indian rhizome—Curcuma longa—is
bitterish, and its rather acrid fugitive fra
grance warms the mouth, so it must be
used with discretion. Its golden color gives
the underlying tone to curry powders and
to certain pickles. In small quantities, it
is used as a food coloring, often replacing
saffron for this purpose.

VANILLA BEAN AND EXTRACT

Vanilla bean, before being marketed, is
fermented and cured for 6 months. Vanilla
extract is prepared by macerating the
beans in a 35% alcohol solution. To retain its greatest flavor, add it only when
food is cooling. Try 2 parts vanilla to 1
part almond flavoring—a great Viennese
favorite. Or try keeping vanilla beans in
brandy and using the flavored brandy as
seasoning. ◗ Beware of synthetic vanilla
whose cheap flavor is instantly detected
and which ruin any dish that is frozen
This tawdry quality is characteristic also
of nonalcoholic liqueur seasonings.

MOCHA

This name is given to dishes flavored with
a lightly roasted coffee bean. We include
it here, for coffee can often be used profit-
ably as a spice, especially when combined
with chocolate.

OTHER SWEET EXTRACTS AND FLAVORINGS

There are a number of other extracts, all
of which should be used sparingly, such
lemon and almond. Derivatives of almon

re: orgeat, page 519, and falernum, a
syrup of lime, almond and spices dominated
by ginger; grenadine, made from the juice
of pomegranates, and rose and orange waters which are both sweetened distillations.
We do not recommend nonalcoholic liqueur flavorings.

ABOUT HERBS

Confucius, a wise man, refused to eat anything not in season. Everyone who has
tasted the difference between food served
with fresh rather than dried herbs knows
how wise he was. Few herbs can be
bought in a fresh state at market, but the
most important ones can be easily grown
in a small sunny plot. We know, for we
have grown and used all the culinaries in
this section. Therefore, we beg you to
exercise your green thumb at least on
those whose evanescent oils deteriorate or
almost disappear in drying. Chervil, borage, burnet and summer savory suffer the
greatest losses. And those mainstays—
chives, tarragon, parsley and basil—can
ever in their dry form begin to approach
the quality of their fresh counterparts.
Even the flavor of sage when fresh can be
so delicate as to be almost unrecognizable.

ABOUT GROWING AND DRYING
HERBS

As long ago as the 17th century, the
herbalist Parkinson in his "Paradisi in
Sole," stressed the importance of proper
drainage in herb-growing. We, too, have
discovered that good drainage, whether
secured by boxing or simply by the selection of terraced ground, is the very first
consideration in beginning an herb garden.
We know, also, that some of the most
pungent and aromatic herbs flourish in the
seemingly impoverished soil of the Mediterranean area.

We do find that we can grow the various thymes, pot marjoram and winter savories in a dry rock garden, treat them
with neglect and reap them for twenty
years. But we also find, with our hot sum-
mers and variable winters, that sage and
perennial culinaries, at least, are more apt

to hold over in well-enriched garden soil.

A third factor, in raising practically all
herbs well, is sun. Most varieties, including those which are most popular, require
plenty of it. Exceptions are specifically
mentioned later. In designing an herb
garden, we like to define its pattern with
some precision. The plants themselves,
with their contrasting shapes and their
tendency to sprawl, seem to need regi-
mentation. To maintain year-round attrac-
tiveness we plant evergreen perennials alternating with deciduous types.

A 15-inch to 2-foot unit area for each of
most culinaries is more than enough to
supply household demands. Sometimes, if
we want only a single specimen—for instance, a sage or a lavender—we keep it
pruned to a central shrub and use the
edges around it for smaller plants. Sometimes we repeat a color accent—like the
gray of sage or lavender—to unify the
whole complex of squares.

If you haven't room for a more extended
layout, try setting out a few pots of an-
nuals on your patio. Some of the evergreen perennials will weather the winter
in a strawberry jar. To prepare the jar for
herbs, fill it with a mixture of ⅓ rich fria-
ble soil and ⅔ sand. Try the thymes, sweet
marjoram, burnet and chervil on the shady
side. You can dwarf fennel, borage and
sage by root confinement. Replace the
coarse marjorams with dittany of Crete,
coarse mints with Requienii.

Pots can be used, too, for growing herbs
indoors in sunny windows. We have had
moderate success with rosemary, sweet
marjoram, the basils, dittany of Crete,
lemon verbena and scented geranium. All
of these were from late summer cuttings,
and dill and bronze fennel from seed.
Tarragon dug after cold weather dormancy
and potted up indoors showed six inches
of green within ten days. A small potted
sweet bay is both decorative and useful.
◗ But most house plant herbs deteriorate
in flavor, just as do hothouse tomatoes.

Many herbs are characterized by quite
inconspicuous bloom; so if you clip constantly for fresh or dried culinary use you
may never allow the plants to reach the

blossoming stage. For ♦ most herbs are harvested—unless noted in the individual descriptions—just before their flowers form. At this time, when they are budding up, the leaves are at their most aromatic. Pick early in the day, as soon as the dew has dried off the leaves. Wash if necessary and dry the leaves without bruising.

It should not be necessary to note that herbs, which are remarkably free from insect pests, should be grown where they are not subject to sprays or the attention of dogs. You may tie them together and hang them, when dry, in small bunches. The location always traditionally recommended is a cool, airy attic. Since such spaces are becoming scarce, a shady breezeway will do. And lacking a breezeway, room-drying is preferable to oven-drying, for even when the oven is preheated as low as 200° and shut off the moment the herbs are inserted, their flavor is weakened. For thick-leaved varieties, the oven process may have to be repeated several times until the herbs are bone-dry.

♦ To test for dryness before packaging, put a few sprigs or leaves in a tightly stoppered glass jar and watch for condensation, mold development or discoloration. This is important, especially with basil. However you dry herbs ♦ store them in tightly covered, preferably lightproof, jars —in a dark, cool place. Should they show insect activity, discard them. You may want to strip leaves from the stems before drying or freezing herbs. ♦ Dried herbs retain their flavor best if pulverized just before using.

♦ To substitute dried herbs for fresh use ⅓ teaspoon powdered or ½ teaspoon crushed for every tablespoon fresh chopped herbs. ♦ To reconstitute dried herbs and develop their flavors, soak them in some liquid you can incorporate in the recipe— water, stock, milk, lemon juice, wine, olive oil or vinegar—for ten minutes to one hour before using. Or, simmer them in hot butter. For cooking, place nonpowdered dry herbs in a cloth bag, or a stainless metal tea ball for easy removal. For blends, see pages 540 and 541.

You may freeze herbs. If so, use them before defrosting. They are too limp for garnishes, but have much the same seasoning strength as fresh herbs. We find that some herbs, like chives, get slimy when frozen. ♦ To freeze, parblanch, page 132, for ten seconds, plunge into ice water for one minute, dry between towels. Put them up individually in recipe-sized packets for seasoning a salad dressing or a batch of stew or freeze with mixed bouquets garnis for soups and sauces. You may also preserve herbs by salting them down in covered crocks, alternating ½-inch layers of salt and ½-inch layers of herbs. Herbs and savory salt will have stabilized within two weeks.

ABOUT USING HERBS

Handy as it might seem, we have refrained from giving an herb chart, because some herbs are overpowering and it is so difficult to indicate in a general way the amounts to use. Suitable quantities of herbs are listed in the individual recipes. Below we set down detailed characteristics of culinary herbs. Let us add that the delicately flavored types should be placed in sauces and soups only toward the end of preparation and left just long enough to lose their volatile oils. And once again, while we advocate a constant use of herbs, don't use too many kinds at once or too much of any one kind.

To familiarize yourself with herb flavors, some "lazy day," when you feel experimental, blend ½ pound mild cheddar cheese with 2 tablespoons sour cream and 2 tablespoons vodka. Divide the mixture into small portions and add herbs and herb combinations. Label the cheese samples as you mix them. Let them rest for about an hour to develop flavor. Then have a testing party with your husband, your wife or a friend.

ANGELICA

This slightly licorice-flavored plant can be candied, page 743, for use in desserts, as a decorative garnish. Its seeds are used in pastry.

THE ANISES

These have strangely subtle licorice over tones. Try the seeds for your family in Anise Cookies, page 656; the oil as a flavoring in sponge cake; or the Chinese star anise in watermelon-rind pickle. To release the full flavor of the seeds, crush them between towels with a rolling pin.

BEE BALM

Use the lemony leaves for tisane or as garnish in fruit punch or fruit soup.

THE BASILS

Not without reason called l'herbe royale, these versatile herbs have a great affinity for tomatoes, fish and egg dishes, but are good in almost all savory dishes. They darken quickly after cutting. Serve them as they do in Italy—where basil is very popular—in a bouquet of sprigs set in small vase of water. Be sure to try Pesto, page 539, with spaghetti.

THE BAYS

Always use these leaves, fresh or dry, with discretion—only ⅓ of a fresh leaf or ⅙ of a dry leaf in a quart of stew—and only a pinch if in powdered form. But do use them, not only in stuffings but in stocks, sauces, marinades, in the cooking of vegables and meats and in a Bouquet Garni, age 541. Do not confuse the edible bay, Laurus nobilis, with the cherry laurel, Prunus laurocerasus, of our gardens—as the cherry laurel leaf is poisonous.

BORAGE

This herb is only good fresh—as its flavor vanishes as it dries. Use the leaves wherever you want a cucumber flavor in fish sauces or white aspics. It is traditional in some fruit punches and the choice blue starlike blooms are beautiful floated in punches and lemonades or used in food garnishes. Young borage can be cooked like spinach, page 300.

BURNET

Sometimes called salad burnet, this herb has a haunting cucumberish flavor. It does not dry well but, as it keeps green all winter long, it can be picked at any time. Pick the center leaves, as the older ones are bitter. Use the leaves or soak the seeds in vinegar and use in salads.

Poterium sanguisorba, a hardy perennial growing to 2 feet, is almost fernlike in habit. It comes very quickly and easily from seed in any well-drained soil, in sun.

CAMOMILE

This is famous as a Tisane, page 30, and a small quantity is occasionally put into beef stock. Sometimes the fresh leaves are used, but it is the center of the flower only that is most prized. The petals of this tiny daisy are removed after the flower is dried.

THE CAPERS AND CAPERLIKE BUDS AND SEEDS

When picked, these bulletlike buds of the caper bush taste like tiny sharp gherkins. Use them in Tartare Sauce, page 316, with fish and wherever you wish a piquant note.

Also used as inadequate substitutes for true capers are the so-called English caper, more loosely budded, less pungent blossom; also, pickled immature or mature nasturtium seeds and buds of marsh marigold. Similar in use are: Chinese fermented black beans, or toushi, which are available in cans; and the pickled green seeds of martynia—an annual growing to 2½ feet—easy and a pleasure to grow, with dramatic flowers, leaves and a horned pod.

CARAWAY

Use the leaves of this herb sparingly in soups and stews. The seeds, similar to cumin in flavor, are classic additions to rye breads, cheeses, stews, marinades, cabbage, sauerkraut, turnips. And they are the basic flavoring of kümmel. If added to borsch or other soups, put them in a bag for the last 30 minutes of cooking only, as protracted heating makes them bitter. Crush them before adding to vegetables or salads, to release their flavor.

THE CELERIES

The tender leaves of Apium graveolens, the celery you grow or buy, can be used fresh or dried in almost all foods. Celery salt is a powdered form of it combined with salt. But the seeds sold for flavoring are not those of the plant we grow, but those of a wild celery. These seeds, either whole or ground, have a powerful flavor and must be used sparingly: whole in stocks, and court bouillon, in pickles and salads; or in ground form in salad dressings, seafoods or vegetables.

CHERVIL

One of the famous "fines herbes," this is more delicate and ferny than parsley. The leaf is used with chicken, veal, omelets, green salad and spinach—as a garnish, of course—and always in the making of a Béarnise, page 329, or Vinaigrette Sauce, page 311. It is one of the herbs it pays to grow—for when dried it is practically without flavor.

Pluches de cerfeuille are sprigs of fresh or fresh blanched chervil often specified in stocks and stews.

CORIANDER

Many of us know this flavor from childhood as the seed in the heart of a "jaw breaker," in gingerbread, apple pie or as an ingredient of curry. But few of us know the fresh leaves of this plant as Chinese parsley, as the Cilantro of the Caribbean, the Kothamille of Mexico or the Dhuma of India where its somewhat foetid odor and taste are much treasured. Use leaves only—no stems—and do not chop. Float the leaves in pea or chicken soups and in stews, place them on top of roasts or use them in a court bouillon for clams.

CUMIN

This flavor is classic in cheese, sauerkraut and unleavened bread. It is also used whole in marinades, chilis and tomato sauces. One of the principal ingredients of curry, it is even incorporated in baked items and eggs as well as in beans, rice dishes and Enchiladas, page 226.

DILL

Both seed and leaf of this feathery, pungent and slightly bitter plant are used in sour cream, fish, bean, cucumber and cabbage dishes as well as in potato salad— or on new potatoes. If using dill butter sauce, do not brown the butter. The seed is also good in vinegar.

THE FENNELS

The leaves of both common and Florence fennel can be used interchangeably where a slightly vigorous flavor is wanted. But it is only the white, bulbous-stalked finocchio that is used as a vegetable, page 278— either raw or cooked as for celery.

In flavoring, both the leaves and seeds are used—as for dill—especially for fat fish and in lentils, rice and potatoes. The seeds are often used in apple pies. Fish is sometimes cooked over fennel twigs. But in sauces—as with dill—do not let the leaves cook long enough to wilt, unless they have been previously blanched. The leaves do not retain flavor in drying.

FENUGREEK

This has the same odor as celery but a bitterer flavor. Popular as a Tisane, page 30, it is also used in many African dishes and constitutes one of the main ingredients of curries and the base for artificial maple flavor.

FILE

Filé powder is a necessary ingredient of creole gumbos.

Any concoction of sassafras needs very careful handling and should be added to a hot dish ◗ off the heat, and never be allowed to boil—as then it strings most miserably. It leaves a pleasantly lasting astringent quality in the mouth.

To make filé, gather the very young leaves of Sassafras variifolium. Dry and powder in a mortar—adding dried okra, allspice, coriander and sage, if you wish. Store tightly lidded. The bark is used for Tisane, page 30.

GERANIUM

The many-flavored geranium leaves—rose, nutmeg, lemon, apple—are used in pound cake, jellies, compotes or merely as floaters in fingerbowls.

Try a lemon-scented leaf in custard or an apple-flavored one in baked apples.

HOREHOUND

The woolly leaves of this plant are made into an extract which is combined with sugar into confections.

HORSERADISH

Along with coriander, nettle, horehound and lettuce, horseradish is one of the five bitter herbs of the Passover. It is overpowering and it does get bitter if held more than 3 months. If you do not have fresh roots to grate into lemon juice or vinegar, it is best to reconstitute the ground dried root about 30 minutes before serving. Just soak 1 tablespoon of dried horseradish in 2 tablespoons of water and add ½ cup of heavy cream. The flavor of the dried reconstituted root, however, is strong and not nearly as desirable as the fresh.

It is also prized for use in fatty meat and cocktail sauces, in potato salad and for use with cold meats and fish.

HYSSOP

The leaves of this minty, spicy, somewhat bitter herb are used with salads and fruits; the dried flowers in soups.

JUNIPER BERRIES

Three to 6 per serving are prized for seasoning game, bean dishes and certain alcoholic drinks like gin. In fact, ½ teaspoon of these berries soaked for a long time in a marinade—or cooked long in a stew—gives a seasoning equivalent of ⅓ cup gin.

LAVENDER

The leaves and flowers of this highly aromatic plant give a bitter pungency to salads. We prefer to use it as a sachet rather than as a seasoner. But its grayness lends a lovely accent to the herb garden.

LEMON VERBENA

This, like lavender, in our opinion is better reserved for sachets or closets than for food; although it is often used as a lemon substitute for drinks.

LOVAGE

The leaves of this bold herb whose stems can be candied like Angelica, page 743, or blanched and eaten like celery, are often used as a celery substitute with stews and tongue. The seeds are sometimes pickled like capers.

THE MARJORAMS

These, whether called sweet, pot, orégano orégano dulce or wild, are all very pungent. While similar in their uses, they are not quite the same in their growth habits. Use them in sausages, stews, tomato dishes; with lamb, pork, chicken and goose; with omelets, eggs, pizzas, and cream cheeses; with all of the cabbage family and with other vegetables such as green beans; in minestrone and mock turtle soups; and, of course, don't fail to try them fresh and finely chopped for salads.

There is great horticultural confusion in regard to the oréganos of commerce and seeds ordered under the name oreganum vary enormously.

THE MINTS

We all know peppermint and spearmint. But there are many other mints worth trying.

ing, like the curly varieties and apple, orange and pineapple. These are less penetrating but equally refreshing. Use any of them in fruit cups, cole slaw, peas, zucchini, lamb, veal, cream cheeses; in chocolate combinations, teas and of course in jellies and juleps. These leaves, fresh or candied, see page 743, make attractive garnishes. If using fresh leaves, ¼ to ½ teaspoon—crushed just before using—is enough per serving. But, if using this flavoring in the form of oil, a drop is often too much—so go easy.

All of the following grow rampant in any soil, sun or partial shade, dry or moist: Mentha viridis, perhaps the most peppery of all; Mentha piperita, the peppermint we know best; Mentha spicata or spearmint; and the woolly apple mint—frosted in appearance and fine for a drink garnish.

All the mints are perennial and easily raised from root divisions. They should be in areas confined by metal or rock edgings to keep them from invading less sturdy neighbors in the herb garden. Keep them pruned to have bushy tops for beverage garnishes. If your growing area is confined, try Mentha Requienii or Corsican mint—a tiny-leaved plant, as discreet as a moss.

And, incidentally, field mice hate mint odor and will stay away from any food near which it is scattered.

MARIGOLD

The dried centers of this garden flower are sometimes used as a color substitute for saffron and the young leaves can be used in salads. The petals are used only when the recipe calls for cooking, as in stews.

THE MUSTARDS

Mustard fanciers will argue the merits of a mild champagne-based, or poupon Dijon, or a Louisiana mix—against the sharp English or the fiery Jamaican or Chinese. There are many ways to prepare mustards from mustard powder, which is the dry residue left after the oil is expressed from the seed. But the freshness of the mix is an important factor. For the flavor changes rapidly once moisture is added and, especially, once a bottle is opened after mixing. Try keeping it fresh by putting a slice of lemon on top of it before closing the lid. The lemon needs renewal about once a week. The ground seed varies from white to yellow to brown. The white or English seed is very scarce and superb; the brown, the next best. Commercial mustards with their blends of flour and spices—often heavy in turmeric to color them—may be based on water, wine or vinegar. If you want to mix your own, allow 2 to 3 tablespoons liquid to ¼ cup dry mustard. More details about preparing mustard follow.

Mustard can be added advantageously in small quantities to cheese, seasoned flour, chicken or pot roasts and to sauces, hot or cold. It is classic served with cold meats and for use in pickles—both ground and as seed. Prepared mustard has about ⅓ to ½ the strength of dry mustard.

There are two basic ways to prepare mustards. ◆ Hot mustards are based on cold liquids—water, vinegar or flat beer. Add 2 to 3 tablespoons liquid to about ¼ cup dry mustard. If it is too hot, tone it with a little olive or cooking oil, garlic, tarragon leaves and a pinch of sugar.

◆ Suave mustards can be made in one of the following ways by using boiling water or herb-vinegar. The heat inhibits the reaction of two of the more violently pungent mustard elements, myrosin and sinigrin. But the vapors in processing the following formula are a secret weapon against the common ailment—sinus. We have tried valiantly throughout the spice and herb sections to refrain from mentioning herbal remedies. Allow us this one Dioscoridian lapse in **Double-Purpose Mustard.**

I. This recipe involves bringing water to a rolling boil. It is then poured 3 times over about 2 ounces of dry mustard and worked as follows. Use a heatproof glass or enamel dish. Pour enough boiling water over the mustard to make a paste. Cover the paste completely with boiling water. Let it stand until it no longer steams—15 to 30 minutes. While it is cooling, use a rubber scraper to churn the mustard around, down from the sides and across the top. All of this under water. Let settle slightly and drain off water. Cover the mustard with boiling water. Let stand 10 minutes. Drain. Cover the mustard again with boiling water. Let stand 5 minutes. Drain. Add 2 teaspoons sugar and ¼ to ½ teaspoon salt. If you want a bright mustard, add ¼ teaspoon turmeric, vinegar and other spices to your taste. Put mustard in a jar. Let cool uncovered 1 to 2 hours. Then cap tightly. Keep at room temperature. Do not refrigerate.

II. This is much easier to do, but without as great "curative" effects. Put in a heatproof glass double boiler top about 2 ounces of dry mustard. Pour water which has been brought to a rolling boil over it to cover. Place over ◆ not in, rapidly boiling water for 15 minutes. Before covering see that the mustard has been stirred into a paste but is still covered with the hot liquid. Drain any excess water. Cool and store as described above.

NASTURTIUM

Flowers, seeds and leaves are all used as flavorings. The leaves and lovely orange and yellow flowers are fine in salads and the pickled pods often replace capers. These pods are best picked just as soon as the blossom drops, and prepared at once. To preserve nasturtium pods, see page 785.

ABOUT ONIONS IN SEASONING

Never since our first encounter with the host of alliums in a bulb catalogue have these lilies lost their allure for us as food or flower—from the tiniest chive to the enormous Schuberti with its choicest florets held captive within a flowered cage. This is a plea not only to use a variety of onions in your cooking, but to grow the perennial ones so you will always have them on hand. We have tried to indicate their use in individual recipes. To cook onions as vegetables, see page 284. Nothing can add such subtlety to a dish, yet none is more abused than in the cooking than onions. And when we say onions, we mean any of these culinaries we list later.

Use onion bulbs fresh or dry; the green tops of onions or leeks in making soups and court bouillon; and don't forget that ◗ a touch of onion freshly added to canned vegetables and soups often disguises the "canned" taste and varies the expected one.

◗ High heat and a too long cooking period bring out the worst features. ◗ If you scorch onions, they will be bitter. ◗ Yet onions must be cooked long enough to get rid of any rawness. If you want them to taste mild in soups, like Potage St. Germain, page 154, or in delicate stews, the flavor of the dish can be improved with less onion odor during the cooking if you follow this procedure. ◗ Parblanch the onions for 15 minutes, if they are 1 inch in size, before adding them to the soup or stew. If you want them ◗ mild in sautéing, cook them only until translucent—tender, but not flabby. If you want them ◗ penetrating, sauté until golden. If you want them ◗ all-pervasive, brown them very slowly, as for an onion soup, see page 148, or a Lyonnaise. To give color and flavor to a Petite Marmite, see page 147.

To shorten cooking time, onions are frequently chopped and minced fine. There are a number of ways to make this process less tearful. Pare them while holding them under running water, or use a special onion chopper that is enclosed in glass. Mincing is easier and safer if you first slice a flat base for your operations and use a sharp French knife, see page 250. Or when you haven't time to sauté an onion properly, but do not want a raw taste in cold dishes, hot sauces or dressings, use ◗ onion juice. Ream a cut onion on a lemon juicer or scrape the cut center of the onion with the edge of a spoon.

◗ To get rid of onion traces, rub your hands with salt, vinegar or lemon juice. Eat raw parsley, or see page 60 for the most perfect raw onion canapé. Or moisten pots, sprinkle them generously with salt, let stand and rinse with very hot water to rid them of onion taste.

We jokingly refer to onions in health, page 284, but the use of onions for the bacteria-destroying power of their vapor was demonstrated on a large scale in World War II. However, this antibacterial action was present only when the onion was freshly cut. This power disappeared within 10 minutes. Onions deteriorate rapidly once the outer skin is removed and ◗ should not be stored for reuse after cutting.

◗ All onions are of easy culture. They prefer sandy, moist, rich earth, sun and shallow planting. The dry ones should all be sun dried a few days after being dug up. You may braid the tops so the bulbs can be hung in clusters for even airing during storage. If the tops are cut, do not cut too close to the neck of the bulb. Store all onions in a cool, dark, dry, well-ventilated place. Below are descriptions of onion types most used in cooking.

CHIVES—ALLIUM SCHOENOPRASUM

An 8- to 10-inch variety and a slightly larger one called **Sibericum** are hardy. They are shown blooming in the center sketch, page 536, and are used widely in white cheeses, green sauces and with eggs. Cut and add them to hot and cold food just before serving. ◗ Do not put chives in a cottage cheese or any uncooked dish you plan storing even as long as overnight, as they get unpleasantly strong. To keep the plants looking well, cut a few of the thin tubular leaves low rather than bobbing the top which will brown where cut. Remember that, like all bulbs, chives rely for plant renewal strength on the leaves—so don't cut any one plant too often, 3 or 4 times a season. The leaves are tenderer after each cutting. Also keep the blooms picked low so the tougher stem does not get mixed with the leaves when you use them and so you are not bothered with seeding. About 3 to 6 small bulbs set in the fall will make a good cluster by the following summer.

GARLIC CHIVES—ALLIUM TUBEROSUM

This coarser, flat-leaved, 14-inch-high perennial has a charming starry white bloom cluster which can be used sparingly as a garnish. Only the leaves are eaten—also sparingly. Use and cultivate as for chives.

GARLIC, AIL OR ORIENTAL GARLIC—
ALLIUM SATIVUM

This is perhaps the most controversial addition to food. We couldn't live without it and we think we have learned to use it discreetly. For our guests have sometime been obviously relishing and unaware eating food with garlic in it—while inveighing loudly against it. If you are fond of it ◗ you have to keep a check on the amounts used—for tolerance to it may grow apace to the discomfort of your friends. Use the very young leaves, but the bulb second on the left, page 536, in

...e treasure. Note the "cloves" that make
...p the bulb sketched with it to the right
... the lower left hand corner. ◗ In this
...ook, when we say 1 clove garlic, it is as-
...med that the clove is peeled of its husk.
...earn to rest slivers of garlic clove on
...eat before cooking it; to put a clove of
...arlic on a skewer, cook it in a sauce or
...ew and remove it before serving; to rub
...salad bowl lightly with a cut clove; or to
...ake Chapons, page 79. Drop a peeled
...love into French Dressing 24 hours be-
...ore serving or put a small squeeze in a
...uce. This is easy to do with a garlic
...ress, a handy kitchen utensil. Should you
...ot own a press, you may use the back of
... spoon against a small bowl or a mortar
...nd pestle to crush garlic with salt. The
...lt softens the bulb almost at once, but if
...ou drop a whole clove into a liquid for
...easoning ◗ be sure to strain it out before
...erving. ◗ Never allow garlic to brown.
...lways use fresh garlic. Powdered and salt
...rms tend to have rancid overtones. ◗ To
...lanch garlic, drop the unpeeled cloves
...to boiling water. Cook for 2 minutes.
...rain, peel and simmer slowly in butter
...r about 15 minutes. Add this, minced, to
...e dish for flavoring sauces. True garlic
...ulbs are not hardy. Bulbs planted in
...arch should be ready for lifting in late
...uly or in August, if the season is a wet
...ne. Be sure to sun-dry the cloves until
...ey are white.

...OPPING GARLIC, GIANT GARLIC, OR ...OCHAMBOLE—ALLIUM SORODOPRASUM

...his hardy plant has a beautiful glaucous
...eaf and an entrancing pointed bud—
...ketched—first, upper left, page 536—car-
...ied on a furled stem. Its unwinding is a
...ource of great pleasure to watch. The
...dible bulbs that bunch at the top are
...ndistinguishable in taste and form from
...he tender Oriental garlic shown below it.

...HALLOTS—ALLIUM ASCALONICUM

...his bulb, queen of the sauce onions, is
...ot hardy but well worth growing. It is
...hown fourth on the left, below the chives.
...hallot flavor is perhaps closer to garlic
...han to onions, and although it has a much
...reater delicacy, it must still be used with
...iscretion. Shallots are indispensable in
...ercy Butter, page 339, where they should
...e minced simultaneously with the herbs;
...nd they taste especially good in wine
...ookery. In sautéing them, mince fine so
...s not to subject them to too much heat.
...Never let them brown, as they become
...itter. ◗ Substitute 3 to 4 shallots for 1
...edium-sized onion.
...Shallot sets should be put in, barely cov-
...red, in the early spring. They should be
...arvested by late June when the leaves are
...o longer upright—caving in at the neck—
...ut not yet turning in color. Allow them

to dry off on the ground for several days
and then braid the leaves so the shallots
can be hung in strands in a dry place for
use as wanted.

BUNCHING, TOPPING OR TREE ONIONS— ALLIUM CATAWISSA

These are a good substitute for a medium-
sharp onion and, unlike dry onions purchased in markets, are perennial. They
have a fibrous root system, and the onions
develop early in the season at the top of
the blooming stock. In fact, some even
begin to sprout there too, see second sketch
on top row, page 536—and, in turn, produce more onions at the top of the second
sprout, the same season. The nonsprout-
ing bulblets can be kept for planting the
following August or the next spring. The
original plants may also be separated.
There is really no excuse for not trying
anything that easy. These are the American version of the Egyptian topping onion
—Cepa viviparum—which, being tender,
is more troublesome, even if it has an additional usable bulb at the base.

LEEKS, THE BELOVED FRENCH POIREAU— ALLIUM PORRUM

King of the soup onions. These biennials
grow their first year—as sketched, second
from the right, page 536, with an elongated
root and with closely interlaced foliage.
They are often hilled to keep them white.
This practice traps grit unless the leeks are
grown with a paper collar. Be sure to rid
them of this grit by washing well. They are
choice the first year. When you buy leeks,
if they show a tough, hollow stem—from
which the glorious silver-green bloom was
cut from the center of the foliage—and a
more bulbous form at the base as sketched,
upper right, the leek is in its second year
and will prove too tough to eat. However,
the green portion can be utilized in soups
and seasonings. Leeks lend themselves to
braising.

DRY ONIONS—ALLIUM CEPA

Shown in a group on the lower right, page
536. These are biennials, the major onions
of commerce. They vary greatly in flavor,
skin color and shape. On the whole, American cepa varieties are smaller, have stronger
flavors and keep better than foreign cepa
types. Mild in cooking are the big, yellow
or white Bermudas. Even more so are the
flat Spanish reds, which are a favorite raw
garnish on hamburgers and salads. They
mush somewhat in cooking, so if you want
a mild red cooker, try the rounder, more
elongated Italian redskins. Pearl onions,
including the kind you find in the bottom
of your Gibson cocktail, are cluster sow-
ings of cepa varieties. Cepa types, if
planted in sets in February, are harvested
in July when the browning leaves have
died down.

SCALLIONS—ALLIUM CEPA OR ALLIUM FISTULUM

These are either the thinnings of Allium cepa plantings or special onions like fistulum which do not form a bulb. They are shown illustrated in the center, above, to the right of the chives. The leaf is good as a soup flavoring, the white flesh with about 4 inches of leaf is often braised as for Celery or Leeks, page 271, and they are eaten raw by self-assertive people.

WILD LEEKS, RAMPS OR THE BROAD-LEAVED WOOD ALLIUM—ALLIUM TRICOCCUM

Around these bulbs many folk festivals revolve. These and the strong field garlic —Allium vineale—in your lawn are not recommended by us although we frequently see them praised by others.

This is true also of ◗ onion substitutes, which we scorn, but if you care to try them, use ¼ teaspoon garlic powder for 1 small clove of garlic or ¾ teaspoon onion powder for 1 small onion. Cut down on the salt in the recipe, though.

THE PARSLEYS

These plants—root, stem and leaves—have a high protein-carrying factor. They are flavorful in themselves but also valuable as an agent for blending the flavors of other herbs, and have the power to destroy the scent of garlic and onion, see page 534. There is practically no salad, meat, or soup in which they cannot be used. But they should be handled with discretion, particularly the root of the soup, or Hamburg-type, parsley. These roots are sometimes cooked as for Parsnip, see page 287.

There are at least 37 varieties of curly parsley, varying in strength. In mincing or deep-fat frying, remove the florets from the more strongly scented stems. The stems are used in white stocks and sauce for their strength of flavor and because they do not color them as does the lea Petroselinum hortense and its curled varie ties—crispum—are the parsleys seen mos frequently in the markets. This biennia grows to about 1 foot in rich loamy so and sun.

To grow from seed, soak in water t cover about 24 hours. The uncurled typ or Italian is better for fall use, as its leave shed the snow and stay green longe Carum petroselinum, the coarser-growin heavier-rooted biennial, grows to 3 fee Soak seeds as above.

THE RED AND GREEN PEPPERS

These plants of the Capsicum family a heavy in vitamin A and C values and als are said to have a bacteria-deterrent qua ity. Native to the Americas, they are widel grown in Europe and very different fro the white and black peppers which com from the Orient, see page 528. The caps cums all have this in common: that th ◗ seeds and membranes are irritating an should always be removed if you use the fresh. The condiments from these drie peppers are made both with and withou the seeds. ◗ To skin fresh peppers, plac them in a 350° oven until the skin slightly scorched, when it is easily remove or blanch them for a moment in deep fa at 375°.

The sweet or broad bell peppers, varie C. grossum, are the ones frequently mi named "mangoes" in the market. Thes 4- to 5-inch peppers, both green and, their more ripened state, red, are used fc stuffing and diced for flavoring. Also this general type belong the bonnet or C tetragonna peppers from which paprik are ground. The mild Hungarian typ are seeded and deprived of their stalks b fore grinding. Paprika is sensitive to he and should be added toward the end of the cooking period. When added to broiled food to color, it browns when scorched. Buy in small quantities, as paprika develops insect life in storage.

The longer peppers, variety C. longum, which include most of the chili peppers and cayenne, come in many colors, from chartreuse green to yellow to red. There are hundreds of crosses and in the endless regional recipes for chili or mole powder, as many as 6 or 8 varieties of capsicum will be indicated with names like anchos, pasillo, chipotle.

Cayenne, which comes from C. annuum L., is often adulterated or replaced in commerce by C. fructescens, a small, red, dried tree berry, or C. croton annuum, known also as bird peppers. ♦ Cayenne is so very hot, it should be used only in the smallest pinches. Very hot too are the red clustered C. fasciculatum varieties, with fruit over 6 inches long, for which the seeds are supposed to have come from Tabasco in Mexico. Grown in Southern Louisiana, they constitute the base for hot pepper sauces which are often matured 2 to 3 years. Red pepper, not as hot as cayenne, is ground from this type.

♦ To prepare dried chili peppers for use in sauces, soak 6 dry chilis in 1 cup water and simmer until tender for about 20 minutes. Drain and reserve the water. When chilis are cool, split them, remove and discard seeds. Scrape the pulp from the skin and add it to the reserved water. For other Capsicum recipes see Chili Powder, page 540, Chili Vinegar, page 496, and Cherry Peppers, page 785. ♦ For decorating with pimientos, see Truffle Garnish, page 283.

ROSEMARY

The stiff resinous leaves of this sub-shrub are extremely pungent and must be handled with caution. In marinades, for which this flavoring is popular, allow about ⅛ to ¼ teaspoon fresh for 4 servings. Use the lightly crushed leaves sparsely with lamb, duck, partridge, rabbit, capon and veal; and on peas, spinach and pizza.

RUE

This perennial herb is sometimes suggested as a flavoring for fruit cups. As many people are allergic to its irritant qualities which produce symptoms comparable to poison ivy ♦ we do not recommend its use.

SAFFRON

The golden orange stigmas of the autumn crocus are used to both color and flavor cakes, breads, and dressings and are classic in Risottos, page 183, and Bouillabaisse, page 163. Even a ♦ small amount of saffron has an overpoweringly medicinal quality, so use only as directed in the recipes. If using mainly for color, just ¼ teaspoon to 2 tablespoons hot water will suffice for 5 to 6 cups of flour. Use only about ¼ to ⅓ teaspoon in 2 tablespoons hot water or white wine to season 6 to 8 servings of a sauce.

THE SAGES

Sage and Clary Sage leaves should both be used sparingly for seasoning. Sage is perhaps the best known and loved of all American seasonings for fatty meat like pork and sausages; and for duck, goose and rabbit. It is also used in cheeses and chowders. There is no comparison between the flavor of the freshly chopped tender leaves and the dried ones which lose much of their volatile oil. Dry carefully, as the leaves are thick and mould easily. Fresh clary sage is used in omelets and fritters.

THE SAVORIES

Winter savory is a rather resinous perennial evergreen sub-shrub whose leaves are useful in stews, stuffings and meat loaves. The leaves of the annual summer savory are much more delicately flavored and have many more uses. It is classic in green beans and green bean salad; in horseradish sauce and lentil soup; and even in deviled eggs. It is also used with fat fish, roast pork, potatoes, tomatoes and French dressing.

SESAME SEED OR BENNE

This is a favorite topping for breads, cookies and vegetables. Its nutty flavor tastes strongest when the seeds are lightly toasted for about 20 minutes in a 350° oven and stirred frequently. Crushed, it is made into an oily paste, called tehina when mixed with chick peas. Crushed sesame and peas also form the base for Halvah. Sesame oil from the seeds is desirable in salads.

THE SORRELS

The elongated leaves of these plants are rather high in oxalic acid and are used to flavor soups or sauces or to combine with other vegetables, rather than to serve alone. The somewhat acid purée is good as a garnish for goose or pork. The leaves may be pounded in a mortar with sugar and vinegar to make a tart sauce.

SWEET WOODRUFF OR WALDMEISTER

The beautiful dark green starlike whorled fresh leaves of this plant are floated in Maibowle, page 49, or other cold punches, but should not be left in longer than about ½ hour.

SWEET CICELY

The green seeds and fresh leaves of this soft, ferny plant may be used as a garnish in salads and cold vegetables. Use dry seeds in cakes, candies and liqueurs.

TARRAGON

Called "estragon" by the French, this herb when fresh is one of the luxuries of cooking. The flavor, chemically identical to anise, is pretty well lost in drying. Also in drying, the leaf vein stiffens and does not resoften when cooked. So, if the dry leaf is used, it must be carefully strained out before the food is served. To avoid straining and to retain flavor better than by drying, we hold tarragon in vinegar and remove the leaves as needed. Do not crowd the vinegar bottle, allowing about 3 tablespoons of leaves to 1 quart mild vinegar. This gives enough acid to keep the leaves from spoilage. Always keep them well immersed. If you do dry and store tarragon, watch it for insect activity. The fresh leaves are often blanched for decorations, see page 132. Although tarragon is too pungent to be cooked in soups it is good added to practically everything else: eggs, mushrooms, tomatoes, sweetbreads, tartar and mustard sauces, fish or chicken. And in a Béarnaise sauce it is essential. True tarragon can be propagated only by division.

THE THYMES

There are so many of these charming plants and their flavors so varied that a collection of them makes a garden in itself. The narrow-leaved French with its upright habit and grey-green balsamic leaves and the glistening, small-bushed, strongly-scented lemon variety are the thymes most commonly found in commerce. Caraway-scented thyme or Herba Barona is traditional with a baron of beef. Thymes may also be used sparingly on mutton, veal, pork and rabbit; with creole and gumbo dishes; in brown sauces; with pickled beets and tomatoes; with fat fish, stews, stuffings and most vegetables; and are always found in stocks.

ABOUT SEASONINGS

"Correct the seasoning"—how that time-tested direction stimulates the born cook! We have spoken of herbs and spices and of how they can complement and compliment food. Now we would like to discuss herb and spice blends. By the traditional combinations of both we may give to a dish its finishing touch.

Because the sense of taste reacts most frankly to seasonings, it may be well to reveal for a moment just how it does so. The anatomy of taste is the tongue; and it acknowledges and differentiates between only four basic sensations. The top of the tongue detects sweet and sour; the sides salt and acid; the back bitter. When we taste things, they pass so quickly over these areas that usually a quick sequence of tastes results, like an arpeggio or chord. When we were young, lollipops were their sweetest. This not without reason, because senses dull with age and our taste buds were more impressionable to sweets when we too were unopened blossoms. When we were young, we were told not only to gulp our medicines fast—to get them over that bitter-sensitive back band—but were often given them iced to reduce their impact. By the same token, as adults, we hold chilled wine in our mouth until it has had a chance to warm up and release its flavor. Similarly, also, the ice cream we freeze, to taste normally sweet must be sugared more than warm foods.

Sweet, sour, bitter and salt are only the foundations of taste. Upon them we build a far more complex and subtle structure and its charm is due rather to the olfactory organs than to those which lie in the mouth. If you don't believe us, try tasting food while holding your breath and notice that flavor at its fullest and most characteristic is only realized when the breath is expelled through the nostrils. Prolonged drinking before and smoking during a meal tend to desensitize the passages along which food is appreciated. The prudent hostess will do her tactful best to discourage both but, failing, will season her dishes a little more.

There is an interplay between types of seasoning. Salt, for example, can make sugar less cloying and tone down acidity. Sugar, as a corollary, or vinegar, sometime modifies saltiness; and monosodium gluta-mate—though it loses its magic over starches and eggs—heightens the taste of commonplace foods. The use of ginger, brandy or sherry lessens "gaminess" in fish and wild fowl; while salt, pepper and parsley seem to act as catalysts for other flavors.

The history of seasonings is an ironic one. Back in medieval days the spice routes to the Orient were fiercely contended for so that the poorly preserved food of Europe could be rendered palatable enough to eat. Today many foods in our Western world are so successfully and uniformly preserved that seasonings must be used to make them interesting enough to eat.

First and best, of course, even before seasoning, are the built-in flavors—from food grown in rich soils or from animals which have been nourished on flavor-inducing vegetation. Examples are: the famous sea-marsh-grazed lamb of France, the heather-dieted grouse of Scotland, our own southern peach-fed pigs or northern game birds—after they have taken their fill of juniper and lingonberries.

Next come the flavors accentuated by heat: the glazes on browned meats; the essential roasting of coffee and cocoa beans; the toasting of nuts, seeds and breads; the highly treasured "ozmazome"—

as the gourmet calls it—which results from rich broths, as well as the blending of flavors achieved generally through slow cooking.

Then there are the flavors induced by fermentation and bacterial activity, as in wines and cheeses; those created by distillation in extracts and liqueurs; and those brought about by smoking, see page 754. Intensification of flavor in foods can be purely mechanical, too. The cracking and softening of seeds—like those of poppy, anise, coriander and caraway—releases their essential oils. This is also true of the mincing of herbs, the crushing of spices in a mortar, the puréeing of pods to remove their more fibrous portions. And include marinating, also, as an integral flavoring process in which the acids of wine, milk, lemon or vinegar react chemically with food.

♦ When adding seasoning, the greatest care must be used to enhance the natural or previously acquired flavor of the food at hand. The role of the seasoner is the role of the impresario, not the actor: to bring out the best in his material, not to stifle it with florid, strident off-key delivery or to smother it with heavy trappings.

A good many of our adult preferences in seasoning go back to family tradition. Some, more imperatively, may stem from oversensitivity to certain types of condiment. Today we are becoming increasingly appreciative of a broader range—the more exotic seasonings like Indian curry, Mexican chili, Italian pesto—some of which are distinctly an acquired taste.

An observation to seasoners on bland diets—it is worth asking your doctor if he agrees with some recent research which tends to show that while cloves, mustard seed and peppers—black, white and chili—should be avoided, the following condiments are nonirritating to the intestinal mucosa: mustard in powdered form, cinnamon, allspice, mace, thyme, sage, paprika, caraway, bay, onion, nutmeg, curry powder, garlic, peppermint, vanilla bean, vanilla and almond extract.

What quantities of seasoning to use, of course, is a question which can only be resolved by sound judgment and successive sampling. Good taste, like charity, began at home—more specifically in the kitchen. And while it was spread about to things like furniture, music and etiquette, it still applies with all its original pertinency to the flavoring of food.

Here are, for what they are worth, a few rules of thumb. Allow 1 teaspoon salt to each of the following: 1 quart soup, 4 cups flour, 1 lb. meat, 2 cups of the liquid in which cereals are cooked. Substitute ⅓ to ½ dried herbs or ¼ teaspoon powdered herbs for 1 tablespoon fresh herbs. Allow ½ teaspoon dried herbs to 2 cups flour.

♦ In using wine, soy sauce or vegetable-flavored salts for seasoning, be sure to taste before adding regular salt. And, in seasoning sauces to which unseasoned or mildly seasoned solids are added, be sure to retaste after adding the food. Above all, perhaps ♦ heat seasoned food with great care, since certain spices like cayenne, paprika and curry blends scorch easily, and others, if overheated, became bitter.

Keep scissors handy to add bits of flavorful foods, see below.

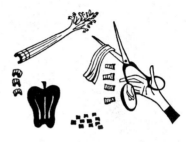

ANCHOVIES AS SEASONING

The uses of anchovies for seasoning are really a trick to know about. For, if discreetly added to food, they can bring a piquancy the source of which is most difficult to trace. About ⅛ of an anchovy to a cup of sauce will turn the trick, or ⅛ of a teaspoon of anchovy paste. The paste is both less strong in flavor and apt to be saltier than the whole anchovies, which may be treated in several ways:

I. For a salad, soak anchovies in cold water or milk for about ½ to 1 hour. Drain and dry on paper towels before using.

II. For a sauce, soak them in warm water 5 to 10 minutes. Drain before using. Anchovies are sometimes used to season meats as lardoons, see page 383.

ANCHOVY PESTO
Crush together:
    1 anchovy fillet
    2 tablespoons grated Parmesan cheese
Combine with:
    Equal parts of butter

BASIL PESTO
This uncooked seasoning can be used on pasta, about 2 tablespoons to a portion, with equal parts of butter; or 1 tablespoon to a dish of minestrone or on a baked potato. It can be made in advance and stored in a cool place. Run a film of olive oil over the top before covering, and store refrigerated.
Pound in a mortar about:
    1½ cups fresh basil leaves
Parsley may be substituted but, of course, the flavor is very different.
    2 cloves garlic
    ¼ cup pine nuts
Add, until it forms a thick purée:

**About ¾ cup thinly grated
Sardinia or Parmesan chese**

When the mixture is really thick, add very slowly, stirring constantly:

About ¾ cup olive oil

until of the consistency of creamed butter.

CHIFFONADE OF FRESH HERBS

One of our very favorite ways to disguise canned soup combinations is to gather a bouquet of tender fresh herbs. These we mince or blend, if we are in a hurry, right in with the soup; except for chives, which we mince separately to keep them from being too pervasive.

CHILI

Chili blends may be based on a combination as varied as cumin, coriander, orégano, black pepper, clove seeds and sweet and hot peppers, or may be made up quickly from a combination of:

**3 tablespoons paprika
⅛ teaspoon cayenne
1 tablespoon turmeric**

But, no matter how simple or how complex the mix, use with it plenty of:

Garlic

CITRUS ZESTS AND JUICES

What better name than "zest" could be found for the gratings of the colorful outer coatings of lemons, oranges, tangerines and limes—those always available, valuable, yet somehow not fully appreciated ingredients! Zest is the very quality they add to baked items, stuffings, sauces, soups, meats and desserts. Laziness—or perhaps unawareness—may be the only reason that deprives the cook of this magic wand for transforming commonplace or heavy combinations. Zests must, however, be used with a light touch. If you keep an easily cleaned hand grater hanging near the stove, you will be amazed at the subtlety you can add quickly to your seasoning.

Use only the colored portions of the skin, as the white beneath is bitter. These rinds are more intense in flavor than juice because of their heavy oil concentration. Fold them into icings, for instance, when the major beating is over, so as not to disturb the texture. Another way to get this oily residue for flavor is to grate the rinds coarsely, place them in a piece of cheesecloth and wring the oils onto sugar. Let stand about 15 minutes before using.

And enough can never be said in favor of the frequent use of small quantities of citrus juices—especially in salt-free diets where these flavors serve as cover up for lack of salt. Use them as a substitute for vinegar wherever delicacy is wanted. Lemons and limes can be juiced quickly by holding the cut side against the palm and allowing a tablespoon or so of juice to run into a sauce. If properly held, the seeds will be trapped. Although we give equivalents for dried zest and extracts ♦ it

is only the fresh rind and juice of these citrus fruits that we feel hold the really magic seasoning power. Approximate substitutions are: 1 teaspoon dried zest = 1 teaspoon freshly grated zest = ½ teaspoon extract = 2 tablespoons fresh juice = 2 teaspoons grated candied peel. ♦ To get the greatest amount of juice out of citrus fruit, roll the whole fruit—gently but firmly pressing it with the palm while rolling—before cutting for juicing.

In buying citrus, choose yellow-colored lemons. If tinged with green, they are not properly "cured." In choosing limes, the dark green ones are usually stronger in acid and preferable to the yellow types. And, if they are available, don't neglect the use of Seville or bitter oranges. These give their name to such famously flavored dishes as Duck Bigarade, page 474, and are very distinctive as beverage flavoring. ♦ Keep on hand seasoned sugars, page 508. ♦ To make citrus peels for fruit sauces, take off just the colored portion of the peel with a potato peeler. Blanch for 3 minutes to a limp stage. Wash in cold water. Shred and resimmer with the sauce.

DUXELLES

A delicious seasoning, used in meat and fish cookery or added to sauces and gravies. It is sometimes strained out before serving. Use also in stuffings. Whenever a mushroom flavor is wanted, duxelles can be added. Allow 2 tablespoons added to 1 cup chicken sauce. A convenient way of using up mushroom stems and storing or preserving them.

Chop very fine:

½ lb. mushrooms

Squeeze in a cloth, twisting to extract as much moisture as possible. Cook until golden:

¼ cup chopped onion or 2 tablespoons chopped shallots

in:

**2 tablespoons butter
3 tablespoons olive oil**

Add the mushrooms and:

**¼ teaspoon grated nutmeg
Correct the seasoning**

Sauté on high heat until the mushroom moisture is absorbed. Keep duxelles in a covered jar, refrigerated, until ready to use.

FINES HERBES

This classic phrase connotes a delicate blend of fresh herbs suitable for savory sauces and soups, and all cheese and non sweet egg dishes. Fines herbes are usually equal parts of parsley, tarragon, chives and chervil—although some other milder herb may creep in. Their charm lies in their freshness and the quality they achieve when minced together with a sharp knife and added the last minute to the food being cooked, so their essential oils are not lost.

BOUQUETS GARNIS OR FAGGOTS

Nothing helps a soup or stock as much as one of the combinations below. They are best made of fresh materials. To make removal easier, the smaller ingredients can be bound inside an informal tube made from the overlapping celery stalks and tightly tied with white string.

I. Bunch together:

    3 or 4 sprigs parsley or chervil
    ⅛ to ½ bay leaf
    2 sprigs fresh thyme
    (1 leek, white portion only)
    (2 cloves)

Place them inside:

    Several celery stalks

and bind tightly with a white string.

II. Tie in a bunch:

    3 sprigs chervil
    3 sprigs parsley
    ½ bay leaf
    2 sprigs fresh thyme

III. If you cannot get fresh materials, wrap your freshly dried herbs still on the stem or coarsely crumbled but not powdered in 4-inch squares of cheese cloth. Tie them into bags and store them in a tightly covered container, see sketch, page 529. ♦ Cook them not longer than 25 to 30 minutes, during the last part of the cooking period.

Allow for 12 bags:

    2 tablespoons dried parsley
    1 tablespoon each thyme and marjoram
    2 bay leaves
    2 tablespoons dried celery

FOUR SPICES OR SPICE PARISIENNE

Also called Quatre Épices. This is a mixture which is such a favorite for sweets and meats.
Mix:

    1 teaspoon each clove, nutmeg
        and ginger
    1 tablespoon cinnamon

MIREPOIX AND MATIGNON

About ⅔ Cup

These vegetable blends, made just before using, are alike in ingredients and use—but differ in size. They can cover or be used as a base for cooking roasts of meat and fowl or shellfish and are essential to Sauce Espagnole, page 326. If minced, the term is **Matignon**. For mirepoix, dice the ingredients. For Lenten dishes, omit the ham or salt pork.
Dice:

    1 carrot
    1 onion
    1 celery heart: the inner ribs

Add:

    ½ crushed bay leaf
    1 sprig thyme
    (1 tablespoon minced raw ham
        or bacon)

These may be used raw as a base under meat or, if for a seasoning, on top of it. Simmer the above in:

    1 tablespoon butter

until the vegetables are soft. Deglaze the pan with:

    Madeira

MUSHROOMS AS SEASONING

This family, as seasoning, contributes some of the most coveted of all flavors. ♦ Never discard stems nor, particularly, the skins—for it is here that the greatest amount of seasoning lies. Even the scrapings of their rarefied cousins, truffles, are sold at a good price and can be cooked with gelatin to form pungent garnishes for cold foods, see page 283. To bring more flavor into canned mushrooms, sauté them in butter. Consider also for seasoning—powdered mushrooms. And for a classic mushroom seasoning, see Duxelles, page 540.

Agaricus campestris, the variety most commonly in our markets, is strengthened in flavor as it withers but must be kept free of moisture in drying, so as not to mold.

♦ To dry mushrooms for storage, select fresh, firm specimens. You may wash them and dry them on paper towels or simply place them on a screen or thread them on a string to sun-dry them. When thoroughly dry, put them in sterile, tightly sealed glass jars. Keep from all moisture until ready to reconstitute for use. Wash briefly in 3 waters then soak them 1 to 3 hours in 70° water. The soaking-water may be used in stocks.

For mushroom types and a discussion of the dangers of collecting, see page 280. Mushroom spores are often sold in brick form for basement culture, but unless conditions are ideal and temperatures constantly between 50° and 60° experience has shown it is cheaper and safer to buy your mushrooms at market.

DRIED MUSHROOMS

Wash in 3 waters and then soak in boiling water 15 minutes:

    ½ lb. dried mushrooms

Drain, bring them quickly to a boil and cook over high heat for 10 minutes in:

    3 cups cold water
    3 teaspoons soya sauce
    1 teaspoon salt
    (2 teaspoons sugar)

Reduce heat and simmer 50 minutes. Keep these refrigerated to use in Chinese recipes.

GREMOLATA

A mixture of seasonings for sauces and pan gravies.

Mix:

    2 tablespoons parsley
    1 clove minced garlic
    ½ teaspoon lemon rind

Sprinkle this mixture on hot dishes. Continue to process the food over very low heat, covered, for 5 minutes, so it can absorb the flavor.

SALT PORK, BACON AND HAM AS SEASONING

These give an interesting fillip to many bland foods. Bacon and salt pork are often blanched, page 132, to remove excess salt. Although they may be used interchangeably, the flavors are quite distinct.

SEASONED LARD

This yellow lard is called **Soffrito** in the Caribbean, but this same term in Italy is applied to Mirepoix, page 541. It gets its color from the annatto seed—a coloring often used here to accentuate the yellow in pale butter. It is made in advance of use and stored refrigerated. Wash, drain and melt ♦ uncovered over slow heat in a heavy pan, stirring occasionally:

    1 lb. salt pork

Remove from heat and strain into another heavy pan.
Wash and drain:

    ¼ lb. annatto seeds

Add them to the strained melted lard and heat slowly for about 5 minutes. Strain the colored lard into a large heavy kettle.
Grind and add:

    1 lb. cured ham
    1 lb. cored and seeded green peppers
    ¼ lb. seeded sweet chili peppers
    1 lb. peeled onions
    6 peeled cloves garlic

Mash in a mortar and add:

    15 coriander leaves
    1 tablespoon fresh orégano

Cook these ingredients over low heat, stirring frequently, for about 30 minutes more. After the mixture has cooled, store ♦ covered and refrigerated.

TOMATOES AS SEASONING

The tomato weaves its way into innumerable dishes—whether fresh, canned, cooked, puréed; as paste or catsup, and even as soup. To get the flavor without too much moisture, fresh tomatoes should be cut at the stem end and squeezed to release extra moisture and seeds and then be peeled before using. Canned and cooked ones are best drained, then strained so thoroughly that the tasty pulpy part is forced through the sieve leaving only the skin to discard. In substituting purées, pastes and catsups, be sure to compensate for moisture differences and allow for the variations in strength of flavor.

ABOUT COMMERCIAL SAUCES

Ali Bab—in his great "Gastronomie Pratique"—refers to soy, Worcestershire, catsups, tabascos and other such commercial condiments as "sauces violentes" which mask out all other flavors. We find them useful as occasional accents, much too powerful to use unmodified; and we indicate suitable quantities as components in various sauces.

SOY SAUCE

This is made from fermenting soybeans, roasted wheat and salt. It contains glutamic acid, see monosodium glutamate, page 526. Never add it to a light-colored dish which needs more cooking, as the soy will darken the dish. Add after removing from heat or serve separately.

WORCESTERSHIRE SAUCE

This sauce is claimed as original by the English. Its roots are said to be Roman and, not unlike their **Garum**, has a base of anchovy.

TABASCO SAUCE

This is made from hot tabasco peppers. ♦ Go easy—a few drops may be too much. Use in soups, cocktail sauce, piquant sauces.

ABOUT COLOR IN FOOD

Don't, we urge you, be a culinary lily-gilder! Resist the impulse to add color to food from little bottles or by the use of chemicals like soda. Instead, determine, in general, to maintain whatever color is inherent in the food itself and to heighten it by skillful cooking and effective contrast.

First steps begin with the selection of fresh, well-grown foods, properly washed, dried and trimmed, then prepared according to the "pointers" in our individual recipes. ♦ Choose utensils made of materials suitable to the foods cooked in them, page 141. If you have done so and are still unhappy with the results, check the kind of water you are using, page 493. ♦ Never overcook foods: nothing so irrevocably dulls the kitchen palette.

Here are some further ways to keep foods colorful. While the color of soups and sauces is built into them by the way their stocks are made, see page 490, it will be least affected if they are scummed while heating and cooked uncovered. Meats, if light, maintain better color if scummed. If dark, their color will be improved by browning; by greasing during roasting or broiling; by glazing or flambéing. Fish and light meat grills profit in color by a prior dusting of paprika.

Cook variety meats—or vegetables and fruits that discolor on exposure to air—in slightly acidulated water, or à blanc, page 494. But first sprinkle the cut surfaces of such foods with a little lemon juice. Vent stews by the use of poaching paper, page 129. And keep in mind that color in all foods is enhanced if they are not held hot and covered after cooking.

Breads and pastries develop beautiful crust color not only through the use of fat in their doughs, but by the discreet addition of saffron or safflower. And color may also be improved just before baking by butter-brushing, page 682, egg-glazing, page 682, or sugar-coating. Foods served in light sauces may be gratinéed, page 342, or glazed, page 340. And sauces may be glamorized with herb chiffonades; tomato or red pepper; lobster coral, page 373; Lobster Butter, page 339; egg yolks, saffron, meat glaze, mushrooms and browned flour.

If you are faced with really listless-looking vegetables, a green coloring additive may be very quickly made up in a blender—use spinach, parsley or water-cress mixed with a small quantity of stock. And if you are tempted to disregard our earlier advice and go in for artificial color—watch out for greens and reds. Dilute yellows and just plain avoid blue.

As to color combinations and color contrasts, no one can lay down hard and fast rules, except to say that they need not be spectacular. Even so simple a combination as light and dark lettuces in a salad—or an accent of cress—will make for substantially greater interest. The occasional use of edible garnishes—suggestions for which are scattered throughout this book, see pages 38, 83, 169—will be helpful. Do consider, too, the total background: dishes and colorful tableware, table surface, linens and decor are all part and parcel of satisfactory and colorful food presentation.

ABOUT WEATHER

Weather—moist, dry, hot or cold—plays an important part in cooking. When its role is decisive, it is so noted in individual recipes. Let's review just a few instances. Since flours and cereals tend to dry out in winter, our indications for rice and flour amounts, pages 497 and 178, are more variable than we would like to have them. Damp weather will greatly affect sugars after food is cooked—as in meringues and during candy-making, page 726. Cold and heat have a tremendous effect on the creaming of butter and sugars and on success with Puff Paste, page 593, Anise Wafers, page 656, or the rising of bread, page 555. Threatening weather will even delay the "making" of butter, page 509, and Mayonnaise, page 314. In storing foods, note if they are to be kept tightly lidded. It is evident that Mark Twain was wrong when he complained that nobody did anything about the weather. The circumspect cook takes account of its vagaries and acts accordingly.

ABOUT MEASURING

♦ All recipes in this book are based on standard U.S. containers: the 8 oz. cup and a tablespoon that takes exactly 16 level fillings to fill that cup level. We suggest that you test for size the tablespoon you select for this purpose—because those on sale do not invariably meet standard requirements.

All our recipes, in turn, are based on level measurements, hedgers like "heaping" or "scant" having been weeded out of our instructions years ago. Until you are experienced, we strongly urge you to make a fetish of the level standard measure.

To prove how very much careful measurement affects quantity, conduct this simple experiment. Dip the standard spoon into flour or baking powder and then level its contents. Don't shake. But, as recommended, use a knife, as shown second on the left below. Then scoop up a heaping spoonful of the same ingredients without leveling. You will find that lighter materials, if casually taken, often triple or quadruple the amounts indicated in the recipes. Ten to one the cook who prides herself on

using nothing but her intuition as a guide to quantity is the same "old hand" who, for years, has used the same bowls, cups and spoons, the same stove, even the same brands of staples and who, in addition, gets more than her share of lucky breaks. Like as not, too, she doesn't mind variations in her product.

◗ Accuracy in measuring basic ingredients is especially necessary when making bread, pie and cake and in using recipes which include gelatin.

Most cake recipes call for sugar to be sifted before measuring. We confess that, instead, we sometimes short-cut by spooning our granulated sugar lightly into a measuring cup and then level it off, as sketched second on the left, page 543.

◗ For dry ingredients, use a cup which measures 1 cup even—with a flush rim for leveling. Put brown or powdered sugar, if lumpy, through a sieve, using a spoon.

◗ But, in measuring, brown sugar is always packed firmly into a measuring cup. See the sketch second from the right on

page 543. And then unmold it as shown next, sandcastle-wise.

◗ No short-cuts should be adopted if the recipe requires the sifting of flour. If they are, the outcome is chancy, to say the least. In fact, frequent sifting after measurement will improve the texture of all cakes. ◗ Sifting salt, leavens and spices with the flour insures even distribution.

It is particularly important that flour is not packed in measuring. ◗ In baking, sifting-before-measuring is essential. There is a very easy way to do this neatly and quickly. Keep two 12-inch squares of stiff paper, foil or plastic on hand. Sift the flour on to the first square, as shown bottom left. Rest your sifter on the second. Pick up the first sheet and curve it into a slide from which the flour can funnel itself into the measuring cup, which should be a dry measure shape, center. For very accurate measuring, cups designed for ¼, ⅓ and ½, as shown underneath are also desirable. When the measure is filled, take a knife and level the flour by running it across the top of the cup; see sugar, sketched, page 543. ◗ Never try to level the flour contents by shaking the cup, as this just repacks the sifted flour. Now you are ready to resift the flour with the other dry ingredients. Between siftings, move the sifter to the empty sheet and funnel the dry ingredients of the other sheet into the sifter top, the same way you did in measuring the flour in the center illustration.

Forgive us if we have said this repeatedly before, but always remember the important fact that ◗ flour can vary over 20% in its ability to absorb moisture, depending on the type of wheat from which it is milled, its processing and the amount of moisture absorbed during storage. For this reason, even the most accurate measurement may sometimes not produce unqualified success and adjustments must be made, on a purely experimental basis. See details on flour and flour substitutes, page 496.

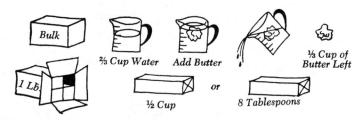

Bulk

1 Lb.

⅔ Cup Water   Add Butter   ⅓ Cup of Butter Left

½ Cup   or   8 Tablespoons

♦ We suggest measuring bulk fats by the displacement method. If you want ⅓ cup fat, fill the measuring cup ⅔ full of water. Put in fat until the water reaches the 1 cup calibration mark. Drain the cup of water. The amount of fat remaining in the container will then, of course, equal ⅓ cup. One pound of butter or butter substitute equals 2 cups and, when the pound is wrapped in quarters, each stick equals 8 tablespoons or ½ cup. See sketch above.

Some people prefer to use the sets of measuring cups especially for oils. These hold respectively ¼, ⅓, ½ and 1 whole cup. But, if you use them, push the solid shortening down well into the bottom of these measures or a considerable space may be left, which will make your measurement inaccurate.

The measurement of what we might call side-ingredients, such as flavorings and spices, is important too, but here much depends on individual taste, to say nothing of the age of the spices, and amounts may vary considerably without risking failure.

ABOUT SUBSTITUTIONS AND EQUIVALENTS

You're a new cook and you run out of granulated sugar. Don't think that this doesn't happen to old cooks too! So you just substitute confectioners' sugar. And when the cake is not as sweet as it should be and the texture is horrid you wonder what happened.

Good recipes and the reasonable use of standard measures allow you to cook well without knowing that it takes about 2 cups of sugar or butter to make a pound, but that you will need about 4 cups of flour for that same pound. This you discover fast enough if you leave the United States, for almost everyone else cooks by weight, not volume.

Let's look at a few lucky volume-weight relationships that for the moment protect you, as a new cook, from the menace of that old dragon Mathematics—and his allies, Physics, Chemistry and Semantics. Here are some of our victorious, if homely, weapons, tested in many a battle with these old tricksters.

By weight, if not quite by volume, 2 tablespoons butter equal 2 tablespoons butter, melted. But try to incorporate this positive knowledge in a cake and utter failure results. See About Butter and Shortening Cakes, page 622, and About Cakes with Melted Butter or Oil, page 634.

By weight, if not by volume, 1 cup 32% whipping cream equals 1 cup 32% cream, whipped. By volume, 1 cup 32% whipping cream equals about 2 cups 32% cream, whipped.

♦ If the recipe calls for whipped cream rather than for whipping cream, you need the solider, drier texture that results from whipping.

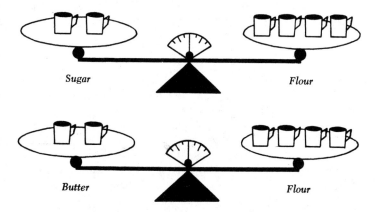

Sugar   Flour

Butter   Flour

Let's take a closer look at sugars.

1 cup granulated = 8 oz.
1 cup confectioners' = 4½ oz.
1 cup brown = 6 oz.
1 cup molasses, honey or corn sirup = 12 oz.

These are only differences in weight. But you have to reckon with changes in sweetening power, in texture and—in the case of molasses and honey—with liquids that also have an acid factor. And don't forget about taste, that most important element of all.

If any of the foregoing ingredients are called for in a recipe, it is written to take care of inequalities. But if you are substituting in emergencies, say, sugar for molasses, please read About Molasses first. Some substitutions work fairly well, others only under special circumstances. ♦ But never expect to get the same results from a friend's recipe if she uses one kind of shortening and you use another. Your product may be better or worse than hers, but it won't be the same.

Before leaving you to delve in the tables which follow, like English standard measures versus those of the United States or the complexities of the metric system, we would like to introduce our ♦ multiply-and-conquer principle for fractions.

You are preparing only ⅓ of a given recipe. The recipe calls for ⅓ cup of flour. Well, ⅓ cup of flour equals 5⅓ tablespoons. 1 tablespoon equals 3 teaspoons. So 5⅓ tablespoons equals 16 teaspoons and, finally, 16 teaspoons divided by 3—you are working for ⅓ of the recipe, remember?—give you 5⅓ teaspoons. Now maybe you can get this result by leaving out some of these steps, but we can't.

Here is another tried and true kitchen formula—one for proportions. You want to make your grandmother's fruit cake that has a yield of 11 pounds. You'd like only 3 pounds. The recipe calls for 10 cups of flour. How much flour should you use for 3 pounds of cake? Make yourself a formula in simple proportion: 11 lbs. of cake is to 3 lbs. of cake as 10 cups of flour is to ? or X cups of flour: i.e. 11:3 = 10:X. Multiply the end factors—11 x X—and the inside factors—3 x 10—to get 11X = 30. Divide 30 by 11 to find that X = 2$\frac{8}{11}$ or approximately 2¾ cups. If you are in any doubt that $\frac{8}{11}$ is close to ¾, divide 8 by 11, finding the decimal closest to the standard measure. It is worth going through the same reducing process for the other basic ingredients such as egg, liquid and fruit—so the cake will hold together. Approximate the spices. But one more caution in changing recipes. ♦ Don't increase or enlarge recipes by dividing or multiplying by any number larger than 4—purists recommend 2. This sounds and is mysterious. But the fact remains that recipes are just not indefinitely expandable or shrinkable.

TABLES OF EQUIVALENTS AND CONVERSIONS

It is most unfortunate that in United States' measuring systems the same word may have two meanings. For instance, an ounce may mean $\frac{1}{16}$ of a pound or $\frac{1}{16}$ of a pint; but the former is strictly a weight measure and the latter a volume measure. Except in the case of water, milk or other ingredients of the same "density," a fluid ounce and an ounce of weight are two completely different quantities. A little thought will make clear that a "fluid ounce"—volume measure—of gold, for instance, will be much, much heavier—in terms of weight—than a "fluid ounce"—volume measure—of feathers! ♦ So always read recipes carefully to determine which kind of ounce you are dealing with.

UNITED STATES MEASUREMENTS

All these equivalents are based on United States "fluid" measure. In this book, this measure is used not only for liquids such as water and milk, but also for materials such as flour, sugar and shortening, since the volume measure for these is customary in the United States.

LIQUID MEASURE VOLUME EQUIVALENTS

A few grains	= Less than ⅛ teaspoon
60 drops	= 1 teaspoon
1 teaspoon	= ⅓ tablespoon
1 tablespoon	= 3 teaspoons
2 tablespoons	= 1 fluid ounce
4 tablespoons	= ¼ cup
5⅓ tablespoons	= ⅓ cup
8 tablespoons	= ½ cup
16 tablespoons	= 1 cup or 8 ounces
8 tablespoons	= 1 tea cup or 4 ounces
¼ cup	= 4 tablespoons
⅜ cup	= ¼ cup plus 2 tablespoons
⅝ cup	= ½ cup plus 2 tablespoons
⅞ cup	= ¾ cup plus 2 tablespoons
1 cup	= ½ pint or 8 fluid ounces
2 cups	= 1 pint
1 gill, liquid	= ½ cup or 4 fluid ounces
1 pint, liquid	= 4 gills or 16 fluid ounces
1 quart, liquid	= 2 pints
1 gallon, liquid	= 4 quarts

DRY MEASURE VOLUME EQUIVALENTS

Be careful not to confuse dry measure pints and quarts with liquid measure pints and quarts. The former are about ⅙ larger than the latter. Dry measure is used for raw fruits and vegetables, when dealing with fairly large quantities.

1 quart	= 2 pints
8 quarts	= 1 peck
4 pecks	= 1 bushel

WEIGHT OR AVOIRDUPOIS EQUIVALENTS

1 ounce	= 16 drams
1 pound	= 16 ounces
1 kilo	= 2.20 pounds

COMPARATIVE U.S. AND BRITISH MEASUREMENTS

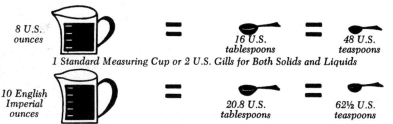

8 U.S. ounces = 16 U.S. tablespoons = 48 U.S. teaspoons

1 Standard Measuring Cup or 2 U.S. Gills for Both Solids and Liquids

10 English Imperial ounces = 20.8 U.S. tablespoons = 62½ U.S. teaspoons

1 English Breakfast-Cup or 2 Imperial Gills for Both Solids and Liquids

♦ Although many British or "Imperial" units of measurement have the same names as United States units, not all are identical. In general ♦ weights are equivalent, but volumes are not. The most important difference for the cook, and one we were slow to realize until we had had consistent failures using English recipes with American measures, is shown graphically above, and in chart form below.

LIQUID MEASURE VOLUME EQUIVALENTS

1¼ U.S. teaspoons	= 1 English teaspoon
1¼ U.S. tablespoons	= 1 English tablespoon
1 U.S. gill	= ⅚ English teacup
2 U.S. gills	= ⅚ English breakfast-cup
1 U.S. cup	= ⅚ English breakfast-cup
1 U.S. gill	= ⅚ English—Imperial—gill
1 U.S. pint	= ⅚ English—Imperial—pint
1 U.S. quart	= ⅚ English—Imperial—quart
1 U.S. gallon	= ⅚ English—Imperial—gallon

DRY MEASURE VOLUME EQUIVALENTS

1 U.S. pint	= 1 English pint
1 U.S. quart	= 1 English quart
1 U.S. peck	= 1 English peck
1 U.S. bushel	= 1 English bushel

WEIGHT EQUIVALENTS

1 U.S. ounce	= 1 English ounce
1 U.S. pound	= 1 English pound

METRIC DRY MEASURE VOLUME EQUIVALENTS

1 U.S. pint	= .551 liters
1 U.S. quart	= 1.101 liters
1 U.S. peck	= 8.81 liters
1 U.S. bushel	= 35.24 liters

LIQUID MEASURE VOLUME EQUIVALENTS

1 U.S. teaspoon	= 5 milliliters
1 U.S. tablespoon	= 15 milliliters
1 U.S. cup	= ¼ liter, approx.
1 U.S. gill	= .118 liters
1 U.S. pint	= .4732 liters
1 U.S. quart	= .9463 liters
1 U.S. gallon	= 3.785 liters

WEIGHT EQUIVALENTS IN GRAMS

1 U.S. ounce	= approximately 30 grams
1 U.S. pound	= approximately 454 grams
1 teaspoon cornstarch	= 3 grams
½ cup, less 1 tablespoon butter—7 tablespoons	= approximately 100 grams
¾ cup, less 1 tablespoon of all-purpose flour—11 tablespoons ...	= approximately 100 grams
½ cup, less 1 tablespoon sugar—7 tablespoons or 21 teaspoons ..	= approximately 100 grams
2 oz. egg	= approximately 60 grams
1 microgram	= 0.001 milligram
1 milligram	= 1000 micrograms
1 gram	= 1000 milligrams

LINEAR MEASURES

1 centimeter	= 0.394 inches

1 inch	= 2.54 centimeters
1 meter	= 39.37 inches

APPROXIMATE TEMPERATURE CONVERSIONS

	FAHRENHEIT	CENTIGRADE
Coldest area of freezer	—10°	—23°
Freezer	0°	—17°
Water freezes	32°	0°
Water simmers	115°	46°
Water scalds	130°	54°
Water boils—at sea level	212°	100°
Soft Ball	234°-238°	112°-114°
Firm Ball	240°-242°	115°-116°
Hard Ball	248°-250°	120°-121°
Slow Oven	268°	131°
Moderate Oven	350°	177°
Deep Fat	375°-400°	190°-204°
Hot Oven	450°-500°	232°-260°
Broil	550°	288°

◗ To convert Fahrenheit into Centigrade, subtract 32, multiply by 5, divide by 9. To convert Centigrade into Fahrenheit go into reverse. Multiply by 9, divide by 5, add 32.

$$100°C \times 9 = 900°$$
$$900° \div 5 = 180°$$
$$180° + 32 = 212°$$

CAN SIZES	WEIGHT	APPROXIMATE CUPS
8 oz.	8 oz.	1
Picnic	10½ to 12 oz.	1¼
12 oz. vacuum	12 oz.	1½
No. 300	14 to 16 oz.	1¾
No. 303	16 to 17 oz.	2
No. 2	1 lb. 4 oz. or 1 pint 2 fl. oz.	2½
No. 2½	1 lb. 13 oz.	3½
Baby Foods	3½ to 8 oz.	
Condensed Milk	15 oz.	1⅓
Evaporated Milk	6 and 14½ oz.	⅔-1⅔

AVERAGE FROZEN FOOD PACKAGES

Vegetables	9 to 16 oz.
Fruits	10 to 16 oz.
Canned Frozen Fruits	13½ to 16 oz.
Frozen Juice Concentrates	6 oz.

EQUIVALENTS AND SUBSTITUTIONS FOR COMMON FOODS

Almonds
Unblanched, Whole	1 cup	6 oz.
Unblanched, Ground	2⅔ cups	1 lb.
Unblanched, Slivered	5⅔ cups	1 lb.
Blanched, Whole	1 cup	5⅓ oz.
Ammonium Carbonate	1 teaspoon ground	1 teaspoon Baking Powder

Apples—see approximate
yield fruits, page 749	3½ to 4 lbs. raw	1 lb. dried
Apples	3 cups pared, sliced	1 lb. unpared
Apples	1 cup pared, sliced	4 oz.
Apricots, dried	3 cups	1 lb.
Apricots, cooked, drained	3 cups	1 lb.

Arrowroot—see Flour
Baking Powder
Rising Equivalent	1 teaspoon	⅓ teaspoon baking soda plus ½ tsp. cream of tartar
	1 teaspoon	¼ teaspoon baking soda plus ½ cup buttermilk or yogurt
Double Acting, SAS	1 teaspoon	1½ tsps. phosphate or tartrate
Bacon	1 lb. rendered	1 to 1½ cups grease
Bananas	3 to 4 medium-sized	1 lb.
		2 cups mashed
Beans, Kidney, dry	1½ cups = 1 lb.	9 cups cooked

Beans, Lima, dry	2⅓ cups = 1 lb.	6 cups cooked
Beans, navy, dry	2⅓ cups = 1 lb.	6 cups cooked
Bread Crumbs, dry	⅓ cup	1 slice
soft	¾ cup	1 slice
Butter		
1 stick	8 tablespoons	½ cup
4 sticks	2 cups	1 lb.
Butter	1 cup	1 cup margarine
Butter	1 cup	⅘ cup bacon fat, clarified
Butter	1 cup	¾ cup chicken fat, clarified
Butter	1 cup	⅞ cup cottonseed, corn, nut oil, solid or liquid
Butter	1 cup	⅞ cup lard
Butter	1 cup	⅘ to ⅞ cup drippings
Butter	8 oz.	7.3 oz. hydrogenated fats

You may note there is a weight difference between butter and hydrogenated fats, but in cooking use cup for cup.

Buttermilk	1 cup	1 cup yogurt
Cabbage	½ lb. minced	3 cups packed
Cane Sirup, see About Sugars, page 507		
Castor or fine granulated	1 cup	1 cup granulated
Cheese, dry	4 cups	1 lb.
Cheese, freshly grated	5 cups	1 lb.
Cheese, cottage	1 cup	½ lb.
Cheese, cream	6 tablespoons	3 oz.
Cherries, candied	3 cups	1 lb.
Chestnuts	1 lb. shelled	1½ lbs. in shell
Chicken	2 cups cooked, diced	3½ lb. drawn chicken
Chocolate	1 square	3 tablespoons cocoa, plus 1 tablespoon fat
Chocolate	1 square	1 oz.
Chocolate	1 square	4 tablespoons, grated
Chocolate	1 oz., plus 4 teaspoons sugar	1⅔ oz. semi-sweet chocolate
Cocoa	4 cups	1 lb.
Cocoa	3 tablespoons cocoa, 1 tablespoon fat	1 oz. chocolate
Coconut, fine grated	3½ oz.	1 cup
Coconut, flaked	3½ oz.	1⅓ cups
Coconut	1 tablespoon dried, chopped	1½ tablespoons fresh
Coconut	5 cups shredded	1 lb.
Coconut Milk	1 cup	1 cup milk
Coconut Cream	1 cup	1 cup cream, see page 523
Coffee	40 cups	1 lb.
Coffee, Instant	25 servings	2 oz. jar
Cornmeal	3 cups	1 lb.
Cornmeal	1 cup uncooked	4 cups cooked
Cornstarch, see Flour		
Cracker Crumbs	¾ cup	1 cup bread crumbs
Cream, Sour—see About Cream, page 485	1 cup	3 tablespoons butter, plus ⅞ cup sour milk
Cream, Sour, Cultured—see About Cream, page 485	1 cup	⅓ cup butter, plus ¾ cup sour milk
Cream, Coffee, at least 20%	1 cup	3 tablespoons butter, plus ¾ cup milk
Cream, 40%	1 cup	⅓ cup butter, plus ¾ cup milk
Cream, Whipping, at least 32%	1 cup	2 to 2½ cups whipped
Dates	2½ cups pitted	1 lb.
Eggs, Hen, large, whole	5—2 oz.	About 1 cup
medium	6	About 1 cup
small	7	About 1 cup
Eggs, Whites, large	8—2 oz.	About 1 cup
medium	10-11	About 1 cup
small	11-12	About 1 cup

Eggs, Yolks		
large	12—2 oz.	About 1 cup
medium	13-14	About 1 cup
small	15-16	About 1 cup
Eggs, dried	2½ tablespoons sifted and beaten with 2½ tablespoons water	1 whole egg
Eggs, Bantam	1	⅔ oz.
Eggs, Duck	1	3 oz.
Eggs, Goose	1	8 to 10 oz.
Figs	2⅔ cups chopped	1 lb.
Flour, All-Purpose	1 cup sifted	1 cup, plus 2 tablespoons cake flour
Cake	1 cup sifted	⅞ cup sifted all-purpose— 1 cup less 2 tablespoons
Bread	4 cups	1 lb.
Cake	4¾ cups	1 lb.
White	4 cups or 1 lb.	3½ cups cracked wheat
White	1 cup	2 tablespoons farina
		½ cup barley flour
		1 cup corn meal
		½ to ⅝ cup potato flour
		⅞ cup rice flour
		1½ cups rye flour
		1½ cups ground rolled oats— bake more slowly
		1³⁄₁₆ cup gluten flour
Graham, Whole Grain or Whole Wheat	3¾ to 4 cups finely milled	1 lb.

♦ Be sure to read About Flours, page 496.

Flours

For Thickening	1 tablespoon flour	1½ teaspoons cornstarch, potato starch, rice starch, arrowstarch or 2 teaspoons quick-cooking tapioca
	1 tablespoon flour	1 tablespoon waxy rice flour
	1 tablespoon flour	1 tablespoon waxy corn flour
	½ tablespoon flour	1 tablespoon browned flour
Garlic	⅛ teaspoon powder	1 small clove
Gelatin	¼ oz. envelope	1 tablespoon
Gelatin for 1 qt. liquid	1 oz.	6 medium sheets—4½ x 6
Ginger	1 tablespoon candied, washed of sugar or 1 tablespoon raw	⅛ teaspoon powdered ginger
Gum Tragacanth	¼ oz.	1 tablespoon
Herbs	⅓ to ½ teaspoon dried	1 tablespoon fresh
Honey, see About Sugars, page 506		
Horseradish	1 tablespoon fresh	2 tablespoons bottled
Horseradish	6 tablespoons dried	6 oz. bottled
Lemon	1	2 to 3 tablespoons juice, 2 teaspoons rind
Lemon	1 teaspoon juice	½ teaspoon vinegar
Lime	1	1½ to 2 tablespoons juice
Macaroni	4 cups dry	1 lb.
Macaroni	1 cup uncooked	2 to 2¼ cups cooked
Maple Sirup, see About Sugars, page 507		
Maple Sugar, grated and packed	1 tablespoon	1 tablespoon white granulated
Maple Sugar	1 gallon	11 lbs.
Maple Sugar	½ cup	1 cup maple sirup

♦ For sweetening power, and use in recipes, see page 506.

Meat

Beef, cooked	3 cups minced	1 lb.
Beef, uncooked	2 cups ground	1 lb.
Milk	1 cup	½ cup evaporated, plus ½ cup water
Milk	1 cup	4 tablespoons powdered milk, plus 1 cup water
Milk	1 cup	1 cup soy or almond milk
Milk	1 cup	1 cup fruit juice or 1 cup potato water in baking
Milk	1 cup	1 cup water, plus 1½ teaspoons butter
Milk		
To Sour	1 cup sweet	Add 1 tablespoon vinegar or lemon juice to 1 cup minus 1 tablespoon lukewarm milk. Let stand 5 minutes
Milk, whole	1 qt.	1 qt. skim milk, plus 3 tablespoons cream
Milk, whole dry solids	1 lb.	3½ cups
Milk, dry, nonfat solids	1 lb.	4 cups
Milk, whole	1 cup	3 to 4 tablespoons dry whole milk solids, plus 1 cup water
Milk, skim	1 cup	3 to 4 tablespoons dry nonfat milk solids
Molasses, see About Sugars, page 507		
Mushrooms	3 oz. dried	1 lb. fresh
Mushrooms	6 oz. canned	1 lb. fresh
Mushrooms	½ lb. sliced raw	2½ cups raw
Noodles	1 cup uncooked	1¾ cups cooked
Nuts	½ lb. kernels, a little less for heavier nuts and a little more for lighter ones	1 lb. in shell
Oatmeal	2⅔ cups	1 lb.
Oil	2 cups	1 lb. fat
Onions, see About Onions, page 536		
Orange	1 medium	6 to 8 tablespoons juice
Orange Rind	1 medium	2 to 3 tablespoons rind
Peanuts	1 lb. in the shell	2¼ quarts
	1 lb. shelled	2¼ cups
Peas, dry	2½ cups	1 lb.
Peas, cooked	5½ cups	1 lb.
Peas, split	2 cups—1 lb.	5 cups cooked
Pecans	3½ cups	1 lb.
	2½ lbs. in the shell	1 lb. shelled
Pomegranate	1 average	½ cup pulpy seeds
Potatoes	1 lb. raw unpeeled ...	2 cups mashed
Prunes, raw	2¼ cups pitted	1 lb.
Prunes, cooked, drained	2 cups	1 lb.
Raisins		
Seeded Whole	3¼ cups	1 lb.
Seedless Whole	2¾ cups	1 lb.
Rennet	1 tablet	1 tablespoon liquid rennet
Rice		
Long Grain	2½ cups uncooked	1 lb.
Cooked	2½ cups uncooked	8 cups
Rolled Oats	4¾ cups	1 lb.
Saccharin	¼ grain	1 teaspoon sugar
Salt	1 cup	12 ounces
Sorghum Molasses, see About Sugars, page 507		
Sugar Sirups, see pages 36, 106, 506, 749 and 761.		
Sugar, in baking	1 cup	1 cup molasses, plus ¼ to ½ teaspoon soda. Omit baking powder

Sugar, in baking	1 cup	½ cup maple sirup and ¼ cup corn sirup. Lessen liquid by 2 tablespoons
Sugar, granulated	2 cups	1 lb.
Sugar, brown, packed	2¼ cups	1 lb.
Sugar, brown, packed	1 cup	1 cup granulated sugar
Sugar, powdered	1 cup	1 cup granulated sugar
Sugar, confectioners, packed ..	3½ cups	1 lb.
Sugar, confectioners, packed ..	1¾ cups	1 cup granulated sugar
Sweetener—noncaloric solution	⅛ teaspoon	1 teaspoon sugar
Tapioca	1½ to 2 tablespoons quick-cooking	4 tablespoons pearl, soaked
Tapioca	2 teaspoons	1 tablespoon flour
Tea	125 cups	1 lb.
Water	2 cups	1 lb.
Walnuts	3½ cups	1 lb.
Yeast, fresh	1 package	⅗ oz. or 2 tablespoons
Yeast, dry	1 package	Reconstitute in 2 tablespoons water 1¾ tablespoons dry yeast. Decrease liquid in recipe by 2 tablespoons
Yogurt	1 cup	1 cup buttermilk

ABOUT LEFT-OVERS

The minister's bride set her luncheon casserole down with a flourish, and waited for grace. "It seems to me," murmured her husband, "that I have blessed a good deal of this material before."

Left-overs can, of course, stand for simple repetition; but they can also stimulate a cook's ingenuity. For our part, we feel positively blessed when we have a tidy store of them garnered away in the refrigerator. So often they give a needed fillip to a dish we are making from scratch. Sometimes they combine to make a vegetable soufflé or to dress up an omelet. And how often they turn a can of soup into a real delicacy!

One secret we have learned is to limit the number of left-over ingredients we are working with so that they retain some semblance of identity. If there is too much of a mish-mash, the flavors simply cancel out —as well as the appetite.

Another secret is to watch left-overs for color Freshen them up by presenting them with the more positive accents of tomatoes or bright greens; or with a color-contrasting sauce.

Still another secret is to be careful that you create some contrast in texture. When left-over mixtures are soft, contrast can be achieved by adding minced celery or peppers, nuts, water chestnuts, crisp bacon or freshly minced herbs.

Consult the Index under the category you wish to utilize or try one of the following suggestions:

See About Uses for Ready-Baked and Left-over Breads, Cakes and Crackers, page 586; also About Crumbs, page 501 and Bread Dressing, page 456.

For uses of cooked cereals and pastas, see Cooked Cereal Muffins, page 582, or Garnishes for Soups, pages 171 and 17⁹ Also see Croquettes, page 218, and Griddl Cakes, page 215, or Calas, page 721-722.

See About Stocks, page 490, and Abou Soups, page 144, for uses of bones, and fc meat, fowl, fish and vegetable trimming

For cooked meat, fish and vegetable lef overs, see Brunch, Lunch and Suppe Dishes, page 223, mousses, soufflés, tin bales, meat pies, About Cases for Foo page 223, and Stuffed Vegetables, pag 255. See also About Economical Use c Large Cuts of Meat, pages 389 and 398.

For cooked potatoes, see the Index; us in Shepherd's Pie, page 234.

Use left-over gravies and savory sauce with vegetables, pastas, meats, and he sandwiches.

For cheese, see Soufflés, Timbales, Sauce and Au Gratin, page 342.

For uses for egg yolks, see Spong Cakes, page 621, Yolk Cookies, page 66. yolk cakes, salad dressings, custards; an use poached yolks in sauces or riced as garnish.

For uses for egg whites, see Angel an White Cakes, pages 619 and 623, me ringues of all kinds, fruit whips hot an cold, page 697, dessert soufflés, page 68⁹ Icings, page 673, insulation for pie crust and for breading, page 589, and Eggs in Nest, page 201.

For citrus peels, see Candies, page 74⁹ and Zests, page 540.

For uses for sour or buttermilk, se About Sour and Fermented Milks, pag 485.

For fruit juices, see fruit drinks or gela tins. Use as the liquid in cakes and cu tards, for meat basting, for sauces or fru salad dressings.

For uses for left-over coffee, see coffe and mocha desserts and dessert sauces.

YEAST AND QUICK BREADS
AND COFFEE CAKES

here was a time when the word from hich "lady" sprang meant a "loaf-neader." To our own and our families' istinct profit—and with little effort—we ousewives can become "ladies" again. egin, if you like, with a loaf of whole 'heat, which requires neither sifting nor neading, and go on from there to more unning triumphs. Brioche, biscuit, corn one, scones—the very names conjure up ultures that produced breads as charac-ristic as their makers. Will our culture e judged by the pallid commercial bread af in general use today? What a heritage or our children!

BOUT YEAST BREAD MAKING

you have never made real bread, behold ne of the great dramas of the kitchen. very ingredient is a character. As a pro-ucer-director, assemble your cast. Yeast the prima donna. Her volatile tempera-nent is capable of exploitation only ithin given limits of heat—and does she sent a drafty dressing room! For more timate details, see page 503. Wheat flour the hero. He has a certain secret mething that makes his personality elas-c and gives convincing body to his per-rmance. Rice, rye, corn—no other flour n touch him for texture; but he is willing share the stage with others—if they give m the limelight. For differences in ours, see page 497. Water, milk or other quid ingredients are the intriguers. Any ne of them lends steam to the show, see age 502. As for salt and sugar, they make sential but brief entrances. Too much of ther inhibits the range of the other actors. at you can enlist or leave. Use him to dow your performance with more tender d more lasting appeal. There are quite few extras too, which you can ring in to ve depth and variety, see page 556.

As director you also control the pace. Be ick and casual in batter bread. But the ore emphatic your rhythm in kneaded ugh, the finer your crumb. Success de-nds greatly on the relation of tempera-re to timing. Watch your prima donna, ast. She has just so much energy to ve. Don't keep her dangling in her big oments. If you are new at producing, ve her her head in a simple part like 'hole Grain Bread or No-Knead Light olls, that call for neither working nor aping. Gain her confidence before you unge her into the longer, more classic le of White Bread. Now, knowing our

actors and their quality, "the play's the thing." Let's look into the types, the mix-ing and the baking of bread.

Batters are the simplest of all doughs. For baking powder batters, see page 574. Yeast, if used, is dissolved first and added to the other liquids. Batter yeast breads call for stirring and beating. They are usually allowed to rise only once, so put them to rise in the pan in which you in-tend to bake them. Small unbroken bub-bles will appear all over the surface when the dough has risen sufficiently.

Sponge breads were favorites in days when yeast strains were poorly controlled. Today they are often made with dry yeast. To mix sponge breads, dissolve the yeast in a larger than usual amount of wa-ter, to which a portion of the flour is added. When this batter has fermented—and it takes sometimes as long as one hour —it becomes foamy and spongy, as the name of the product implies. The sponge is then added to the rest of the ingredients. Sponge doughs make a lighter textured, coarser grained loaf or roll than straight dough, the complete mixing of which is described next. In all bread types, butter and eggs, if called for, additional salt and sugar and the remaining flour are then mixed into the dough with the yeast mix-ture.

ABOUT MIXING BREAD DOUGH

♦ To prepare the yeast for the straight dough method, dissolve it, if compressed, in liquid at 85°. If the yeast is in dry powdered form, it will need liquid be-tween 110° and 115°. Formerly milk was always scalded to kill bacteria. Now, with pasteurized milk, air-dried milk solids and canned milk, this operation is no longer needed. However, scalding does save time in dissolving the sugar and melting the fat.

Small quantities of sugar and salt help activate the yeast. But ♦ do not use more of either than called for. If the yeast is active, you should be conscious of its working within a few minutes, and it should dissolve in about 10 minutes with-out stirring. ♦ To mix a kneaded bread, start stirring the flour into the dissolved yeast mixture with a spoon. Mix in half the required flour, gradually, and beat about one minute. Then, as the rest of the flour is added, mix by hand. When the dough begins to leave the sides of the bowl, turn it out onto a lightly floured board or pastry cloth.

♦ To flour a board lightly, allow about 1 tablespoon flour for each cup of flour in the recipe. Use even less if you want a very light dough.

ABOUT KNEADING, PROOFING, SHAPING AND BAKING BREAD

Flours vary in moisture content, see page 497, and only experience can tell you exactly how much to add at this point. Hence, some variations in flour amounts are indicated in the recipes. ♦ Cover the dough with a cloth and let it rest 10 to 15 minutes. Now the kneading begins. When the dough is first turned out on the board it is slightly sticky, as can be seen on the left, above. Then, as the gluten develops in the wheat flour through continued kneading, the dough becomes smooth and elastic. The first kneading of about 10 minutes must be thorough, but ♦ the pressure exerted on the dough should be neither heavy nor rough.

♦ To knead, fold the dough over toward you. Then press it with the heel of the hand, as shown above, give it a slight turn, fold it and press it again. Repeat this process rhythmically until the dough becomes smooth, elastic and satiny. Air blisters will appear just under the surface coating. The dough at this point should no longer stick to the board or cloth. Next, grease a large bowl evenly, put the dough in it and then turn it over ♦ so that the entire surface will be lightly greased. ♦ Cover the bowl with a damp cloth that has been well wrung out. Set the dough to rise. This process and the covering step after sepa-

rating the bread into loaf sizes are show graphically to emphasize the importance c these so-called "proofing" periods. Durin this resting time, a smooth film develop over the surface of the dough and make it much easier to handle.

Yeast dough should rise at a temperatur of about 75° to 80°. If the room is col you may place the dough in the bowl on rack ♦ over a pan of warm water. The firs time it rises it should double in bulk, if th loaf is to have a moist crumb. Should th dough rise to more than double its bulk, will fall back in the bowl. Do not perm this to happen unless the recipe calls fo it, as it may result in a coarse, dry bread To make sure that dough has risen suffi ciently press it well with the fingertip: When it has doubled in bulk, usually i about 2 hours ♦ the imprint of the finger tips will remain in the dough, as shown i the center below. ♦ Now punch dow the dough with a balled hand, as illu: trated on the right. Work the edges to th center and turn the bottom to the top.

▲ Yeast bread dough rises more rapidl at high altitudes and may become over proofed if it is not watched carefully an allowed to rise only until doubled in bulk

Now you will be ready for the secon kneading. ♦ Note that it is not called fo if soft flour is used. Its purpose is to giv a finer grain. It lasts only a few minute and may be done in the bowl. Then pe: mit the covered dough to rise again, if in dicated, until it has a second time ♦ almos but not quite, doubled in bulk.

Now you are ready to prepare for shar ing the loaves. Pinch the dough into th

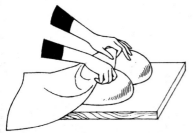

umber of pieces called for in the recipe.
hape them lightly into mounds. Place the
ieces on a board ♦ cover them with a
loth and allow them to rest for 10 min-
tes.

Meanwhile get your pans ready. Glass
nd enamel pans require a lower tempera-
are than darkened tin or dull aluminum
nes. Any of these will give you a well-
rowned crust. To form the loaf, throw
own onto the board one of the pieces of
ough which have been resting. You may
se a rolling pin or your palm to press it
venly before forming. Professional bakers
rm it first into a circle and fold the
urved segments toward the center to make
teir rectangle before shaping the loaf.
ou may be content to roll yours as shown,
sing the heel of your hand to fasten one
ıop to the next as you roll. Then with
our stiffened hands at either end of the
ıll, compress the short ends and seal the
ıaf as shown below on the left, folding
ınder any excess as you slide the dough
ıto the pan. Practice first by baking some
ıall loaves. But no matter what the size
it is important that the finished dough
ontact the short ends of the pan to help
ıpport the dough as it rises. When the
ıaf is in the pan, you may grease its top
ghtly.

Cover the pan with a damp cloth. The
ough will eventually fill out to the corners
f the pan. While it is rising—to almost,
ut not quite, double in bulk—preheat
our oven. When ready to bake, the loaf
ill be symmetrical and ♦ will allow a
ight impression to remain when you press

it lightly with your fingers. To bake, see
directions in the recipes.

ABOUT TESTING, COOLING AND STORING BREAD

♦ To test for doneness, notice if the loaf
has shrunk from the sides of the pan. Another test is to tap the bottom of the pan
to release the loaf. Then tap the bottom of
the loaf and if a hollow sound emerges,
the bread is done. Otherwise, return the
loaf to the pan and bake a few minutes
longer. When the bread has finished baking, remove it at once from the pan and
place it on a wire rack to cool. ♦ Keep it
away from drafts, which cause shrinkage.

People have passions for different kinds
of crust. ♦ The choice of pan will affect
the crust. Glass, darkened tin and dull
aluminum will all give a thick one. Vienna
breads, hard rolls and rye breads sometimes are baked on a greased sheet sprinkled with corn meal, which prevents these
low-fat breads from sticking. Milk, either
used in the recipe or brushed on at the end
of the baking period, gives a good all-over
brown color. Cream or butter may also be
brushed on for color, then the bread is returned to the oven for about 5 to 10 minutes. Setting a pan of warm water in the
bottom of the oven during baking will
harden crusts—also brushing them, when
partially baked, with salted water. Allow
1 teaspoon salt to ½ cup water.

For a glazed crust, you may brush the
top toward the end of baking with an egg

glaze, page 682. To keep the crust soft,
brush the crust with butter after the bread
is out of the pan, then cover it with a damp
cloth. ◗ Permit the bread to cool completely before wrapping, storing or freezing. Bread is best stored in covered tins in
which there are a few pinhole-size openings for ventilation. It is sterile as it comes
from the oven, but if not cooled sufficiently
before wrapping, condensation may cause
rapid molding. Most breads can be
✳ frozen, page 769, but dry out rapidly
after thawing.

ADDITIONS TO YEAST DOUGHS
Raisins, dates, prunes, citron, nuts, slightly
sautéed onions, wheat germ, milk solids
and brewers' yeast, page 504, often called
improvers, are added to yeast doughs for
flavor and increased nutritional values.
With the exception of milk solids and yeast,
they are not added to the dough until it is
ready to set for the last rising. See Cornell
Triple-Rich Flour Formula, below. Unless gluten flour is substituted for some of
the regular flour, improvers are never used
in greater quantity than up to about ¼ the
weight of the flour called for in the recipe.
Some of the flour called for can be used to
dust the fruits, which tend to stick together.
Dusting helps disperse them more evenly
throughout the dough.

CORNELL TRIPLE-RICH
FLOUR FORMULA
Especially among low-income and institu-
tionalized groups, commercial bread is still
the staff of life. How weak a staff in most
instances can be seen on page 497. Work
accomplished under Dr. Clive McCay at
Cornell has done much to raise this standard for large segments of the population by
the addition of supplements in their natural
forms to unbleached, synthetically enriched bread flours.
Use this Cornell Triple-Rich Formula,
which follows, in your favorite bread,
cookie, muffin or cake recipe, as described.
When you measure the flour in the directions, put in the bottom of each cup of
flour called for:
  1 tablespoon soya flour
  1 tablespoon dry milk solids
  1 teaspoon wheat germ
Then fill the cup with sifted unbleached
enriched flour.

WHITE BREAD
                        Two 5 x 9-Inch Loaves
This is an even-grained, all-purpose bread
which stales slowly and cuts well for sandwiches.
◗ Have all ingredients at about 75°. Scald:
  1 cup milk
Add:
  1 cup hot water
  1 to 1½ tablespoons shortening or lard
  1 to 1½ tablespoons butter
  2 tablespoons sugar

  2½ teaspoons salt
In a separate large bowl, crumble:
  1 cake compressed yeast
and soak about 10 minutes or until dissolved, in:
  ¼ cup 85° water
When the milk mixture has cooled to 85°,
add it to the dissolved yeast. Sift before
measuring:
  6½ cups all-purpose flour
◗ To mix, beat, knead, shape and proof
follow the arrow symbols and illustrations
on pages 553 and 554, allowing the bread
to rise once in the bowl and once in the
pan.
Preheat oven to 450°.
To achieve the kind of crust you like, see
page 555. Bake the bread in greased tins
for 10 minutes. Reduce heat to 350° and
bake for about 30 minutes longer. Test for
doneness, page 566. Remove loaves
once from pans and cool on a rack before
storing.

WHITE BREAD PLUS
                        Three 5 x 9-Inch Loaves
"Plus" for flavor, keeping quality and nutrition.
◗ Have ingredients at about 75°. Dissolve
  1 cake compressed yeast
  1 tablespoon sugar
in:
  ½ cup 85° water
Permit to stand in a warm place for about
10 minutes. Beat in:
  1 beaten egg
  ½ cup melted lard or shortening
  2 cups lukewarm water
  1½ teaspoons salt
  ¼ cup sugar
Sift:
  8 cups all-purpose flour
◗ To mix, beat, knead, shape and proof
follow the arrow symbols and the illustrations on pages 553 and 554, allowing the
bread to rise once in the mixing bowl and
once in the baking pan. To bake, place
loaves in a cold oven. Turn the heat to
400°. After 15 minutes, reduce heat to
375° and bake 25 minutes longer. Test
for doneness, page 555. Remove the loaves
at once from the pans and cool on a rack
before storing.

RAISIN, PRUNE OR NUT BREAD
Add to any unflavored bread doughs:
  1 cup drained, cooked, chopped
    prunes or 1 cup washed, well-drained
    seeded raisins or 1 cup nuts
Sprinkle the above with:
  1 tablespoon flour
Add them to the dough just before the last
rising.

CHEESE BREAD
                        Two 5 x 9-Inch Loaves
◗ Have all ingredients at about 75°. Scald:
  1½ cups milk

Add to it and cool to about 85°:

⅛ cup sugar
¼ cup butter
1 tablespoon salt

In a large bowl, dissolve for 10 minutes:

2 cakes compressed yeast

in:

½ cup 85° water

Stir in the cooled milk mixture. Add and beat until smooth:

1 well-beaten egg
1½ cups grated sharp cheddar cheese

Beat in well:

3 cups sifted all-purpose flour

Add, and then continue beating and stirring until the dough begins to leave the sides of the bowl, another, more or less:

3 cups sifted all-purpose flour

♦ To knead the dough and shape the loaves, follow the illustrations and arrow symbols on pages 554 and 555. Brush the loaves with:

(Melted butter)

Allow to rise in the pans, covered, until doubled in bulk. Bake in a preheated 375° oven about 30 minutes. To test for doneness, to cool and to store, see page 555.

BRIOCHE LOAF COCKAIGNE

This light egg loaf has a feathery, tender crumb. While very similar to a true brioche, page 566, it is very much easier to make. Serve it right out of the oven, if possible. Use an angel cake server, page 620, or 2 forks held back to back, leaving a pulled surface rather than a cut surface.
♦ Have all ingredients at about 75°. Dissolve and let stand for 10 minutes:

2 cakes compressed yeast

in:

3 tablespoons warm milk: 80° to 85°

Beat well:

3 tablespoons sugar
3 eggs

Add:

½ cup soft butter
2 cups sifted all-purpose flour
½ teaspoon salt

Add the yeast mixture to the batter. Beat well for 3 minutes. Place in a greased bread pan or a 9-inch tube pan. Permit to rise in a warm place, until doubled in bulk, about 2 to 2½ hours. Bake in a preheated 450° oven for about 15 to 20 minutes. Test for doneness as for cake, page 555.

FRENCH BREAD

To an American who travels in France, the commonest of tourist sights at the noon hour is what looks like "tout le monde" coming from the baker, afoot or a-cycle, with a couple or three long loaves of French bread, naked and gloriously unashamed, strapped on behind. French cookbooks ignore French bread, and French housewives leave the making of this characteristic loaf to the commercial baker. Why? Because he alone has the tradi-

tional wood-fired stone hearth with its evenly reflected heat, and the skilled hand with sour dough—both of which are necessary to produce it. We regard French bread as uniquely delicious and consider the closely approximate substitute recipe given below as rather more than well worth following. It was contributed some years ago by Mr. Julian Street.

2 Long Loaves

Scald:

½ cup milk

Add to it:

1 cup boiling water

While this liquid cools to 85°, dissolve:

1 cake compressed yeast

in:

¼ cup 85° water

After the yeast rests 10 minutes, add it to the milk mixture with:

1½ tablespoons melted shortening
1 tablespoon sugar

Measure into a large mixing bowl:

4 cups sifted all-purpose flour
2 teaspoons salt
2 teaspoons sugar

Make a hole in the center of these ingredients. Pour in the liquid mixture. Stir thoroughly, but do not knead. The dough will be soft. Cover with a damp cloth and set in a warm place to rise, allowing about 2 hours for it. Break down the dough. Place on a lightly floured board and pat into 2 equal oblongs. Form each into a French loaf by rolling the dough toward you, as sketched below. Continue rolling, pressing outward with the hands and tapering the dough toward the ends until a

long, thin form is achieved. Place the 2 loaves on a greased baking sheet, cut diagonal, ¼-inch deep slits across the tops with sharp-pointed scissors to form customary indentations. Set in warm place to rise to ♦ somewhat less than double in bulk.
Preheat oven to 400°.
On bottom of oven, place a pie tin filled with ½ inch boiling water. Bake the bread for 15 minutes, then reduce the heat to 350° and bake about 30 minutes longer. About 5 minutes before the bread is fin-

ished, brush the loaves with a glazing mixture of:

1 beaten egg white
1 tablespoon cold water

We once received a letter from a gentleman in Junction City, Kansas, which began: "My wife is too old to cook and I am too old to do anything else." It seems that he was an enthusiastic baker of French bread, but he complained that his loaves turned out too flat. We suggested that he try shaping them in the following manner: Make a long oblong of the dough, fold over one edge to the center, repeat the operation for the second edge and taper the ends slightly. The bottom of the loaf may be pressed on a board which has been dusted with corn meal and the loaf then placed on a large greased sheet for baking.

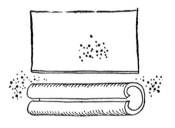

This correspondent made several batches of bread and then wrote again: "Your plan works fine in shaping the loaves and I am also using ¼ cup less water. This makes the loaves come up a better shape, although it makes the dough harder to mix thoroughly. I think, however, the bread is just as good, and my French son-in-law says it is the best French bread he has eaten outside of France."

BREAD STICKS OR GRISSINI
Prepare:

French Bread, page 557

Roll into an oblong about ¼ inch thick, one dimension of which is about 8 inches. Cut into strips 2 inches wide and 8 inches long. Roll them to form sticks. Place on a greased baking sheet and brush with:

Egg Wash, page 682

Sprinkle with:

Coarse salt
(Caraway, sesame or dill seeds)

Allow to rise until not quite doubled in bulk. Bake in a preheated 400° oven for about 15 minutes. Try serving the sticks warm.

SALT-RISING BREAD
This unusually good formula, which has provoked the most dramatic correspondence, relies for its riser on the fermentation of a bacterium in corn meal or potato which is salt-tolerant. ♦ The corn meal must be water-ground. Since water-ground corn meal is not always available, we give also a potato-based recipe. ♦ Do not attempt this bread in damp, cold weather unless the house is heated, and protect the batter well from drafts.
♦ Have all ingredients at about 75°.

I. Corn Meal Salt-Rising Bread
Three 5 x 9-Inch Loaves

Measure:

½ cup coarse, white ♦ water-ground corn meal

Scald and pour over the corn meal:

1 cup milk

Permit it to stand in a warm place until it ferments, about 24 hours. By then it should be light and have a number of small cracks over the surface. If it isn't light in texture, it is useless to proceed, as the bread will not rise properly. Scald:

3 cups milk

Pour it over:

1 tablespoon salt
1 tablespoon sugar
5 tablespoons lard

Stir in:

3½ cups sifted all-purpose flour

Stir in the corn mixture. Place the bowl containing these ingredients in a pan of lukewarm water for about 2 hours, until bubbles work up from the bottom. Keep water warm this length of time. Stir in:

5 cups sifted all-purpose flour

Knead in until smooth, but not stiff:

2½ cups sifted all-purpose flour

Place dough in 3 greased 5 x 9-inch pans, cover and let rise until it has doubled in bulk. ♦ Watch it, for if it gets too high, it may sour. Preheat the oven to 400° and bake the dough for 10 minutes. Reduce the heat to 350° and bake 25 to 30 minutes more. To test for doneness, to cool and to store, see page 555.

II. Potato Salt-Rising Bread
Three 5 x 9-Inch Loaves

A fan, trapped by her grandchild's measles, sent us a treatise on lessening the fantastic odors of "salt-rising." She says, "Use non-mealy, 2½-inch-diameter, new red-skinned potatoes for the starter. Place them in a stainless steel bowl. Set bowl in water in

an electric dutch oven with heat maintained at about 115° to 120°. Perfect results are produced in 15 hours with only a mild odor—like that of good Italian cheese." As we lived for some years in an apartment with a salt-rising bread addict and shared the endless variety of smells she produced, we would settle any day for a mild cheese aroma. If you do not own the electric equipment suggested, use the same principle as described above in a reliable contraption we devised for making yogurt, described on page 485.
Pare, then cut into thin slices:

    2½ cups new non-mealy potatoes
Sprinkle over them:
    1 tablespoon salt
    2 tablespoons water-ground corn meal
Add and stir until salt is dissolved:
    4 cups boiling water
Permit the potato mixture to stand, covered with a cloth for 15 hours. Now squeeze out the potatoes. Discard them. Drain the liquid into a bowl and add, stirring until very well blended:
    1 teaspoon soda
    1½ teaspoons salt
    5 cups sifted all-purpose flour
Beat and beat "until the arm rebels." Set the sponge in a warm place to rise until light. Bubbles should come to the surface and the sponge should increase its volume by about ⅓. This will take about 1½ hours.
Scald:
    1 cup milk
    1 teaspoon sugar
When lukewarm, add:
    1½ tablespoons butter
Add this mixture to the potato sponge with:
    6 cups all-purpose flour
Knead dough for about 10 minutes before shaping into 3 loaves. Place in greased pans. Permit to rise, covered, until ♦ light and not quite double in bulk. Bake in a preheated 350° oven for about 1 hour.

WHOLE-GRAIN BREAD
Two 5 x 9-Inch Loaves
♦ Please read About Whole-Grain Flour, page 498.
Sift before measuring:
    2¼ cups all-purpose flour
Crumble:
    1 to 2 cakes compressed yeast
into:
    ¼ to ½ cup 85° water
Stir in:
    1 tablespoon sugar
Let stand about 10 minutes until foamy. Combine in mixing bowl:
    2 cups scalded milk
    2 tablespoons melted shortening
    2 tablespoons sugar
    1 tablespoon salt
When lukewarm, stir in the yeast mixture. Stir in and beat well:
    3¾ cups whole-grain flour

Stir in enough of the all-purpose flour to make a soft dough. Knead while working in more flour until dough is pliable but not sticky.
Allow the dough to rise once in the mixing bowl and once in the baking pans.
Preheat oven to 400°.
Bake at 400° for 10 minutes, then in a 375° oven for about 25 to 30 minutes longer.

WHOLE GRAIN BREAD PLUS
Three 5 x 9-Inch Loaves
One of the best breads we know.
Prepare the yeast as for White Bread Plus, page 556. Then use the following ingredients. You will note there is less fat and more liquid adjustment required with the use of the whole-grain flour.
♦ Have all ingredients at about 75°.
Beat together:
    1 beaten egg
    ¼ cup melted butter
    2½ cups lukewarm water
    1½ teaspoons salt
    ½ cup sugar
Add, without sifting, a mixture of:
    4 cups whole-grain flour
    4 cups all-purpose flour
♦ To mix, beat, knead, shape and proof, follow the arrow symbols and illustrations, pages 554 and 555, allowing the dough to rise once in the mixing bowl and once in the baking pan. Bake as for White Bread Plus, page 556.

WHOLE-GRAIN BREAD COCKAIGNE
Two 4 x 8-Inch Loaves
♦ Have ingredients at about 75°.
Dissolve and soak for about 10 minutes:
    ½ to 1 cake compressed yeast
    1 tablespoon brown sugar
in:
    ¼ cup 85° water
The larger quantity of yeast makes the rising more rapid and is not enough extra to taste in the finished product. Measure and combine:
    6 cups whole-grain flour
    ½ cup dry milk solids
Combine:
    2 cups 85° water
    1 tablespoon salt
    1 to 3 tablespoons melted bacon fat
    4 to 6 tablespoons dark molasses
    or honey
Combine the yeast and water mixtures gradually. Beat in the flour. Knead briefly, adding flour if necessary. Allow the dough to rise once in the mixing bowl and once in the baking pans. Bake in a 350° oven for 45 minutes. To test for doneness, to cool and to store, see page 555.

CRACKED-WHEAT BREAD
Two 5 x 9-Inch Loaves
This quick recipe contributed by a fan

makes a coarse, heavy bread which is delicious with cheese.

♦ Have all ingredients at about 75°.

Dissolve:

    2 cakes compressed yeast

in:

    ¾ cup 85° water

Permit to stand about 10 minutes. Mix with:

    3 tablespoons melted shortening
    3 tablespoons sugar
    6 cups sifted all-purpose flour
    3 cups cooked, lukewarm cracked wheat
    1 tablespoon salt

Knead and allow to rise once in bowl and once in greased pans. Bake in a preheated 400° oven for about 1 hour. To test for doneness, to cool and to store, see page 555.

SWEDISH RYE BREAD

                          2 Loaves

A moist aromatic loaf that keeps well.

♦ Have all ingredients at about 75°.

In a large bowl, crumble:

    2 cakes compressed yeast

into:

    1½ cups 85° water

Let rest 10 minutes and stir until dissolved. Add:

    ¼ cup molasses
    ⅓ cup sugar
    1 tablespoon salt
    2 tablespoons grated orange rind
    1 tablespoon fennel seed
    1 tablespoon anise seed

Stir in:

    2½ cups sifted, finely milled rye flour
    2 tablespoons softened butter

Beat all these ingredients together until smooth. Add:

    2½ to 3 cups sifted all-purpose flour

If the dough is soft to handle, use the larger amount of flour. ♦ To knead, follow the arrows and illustrations, pages 554 and 555. Allow the dough to rise once in the bowl and once on the baking sheet. To shape, form into two slightly flattened ovals on a greased baking sheet dusted with corn meal. Cover with a damp cloth and let rise until almost double in bulk, about 1 hour. Make four ¼-inch-deep diagonal slashes in the top of the loaves. Bake in a preheated 375° oven for 30 to 35 minutes. To test for doneness, to cool and to store, see page 555.

ALL-RYE FLOUR BREAD

               2 Rather Flat Loaves

Rye flour lacks the gluten of wheat, so a loaf made of all rye has a dense, heavy texture, similar to that of pumpernickel.

♦ Have all ingredients at about 75°.

Dissolve and soak for about 10 minutes:

    1 cake compressed yeast

in:

    ½ cup 85° water

Scald:

    2 cups milk

As it cools, add:

    2 tablespoons butter
    1 tablespoon sugar
    2 teaspoons salt

When it reaches about 85°, add the yeast mixture and stir in:

    2 cups rye flour

Let this sponge rise for about 1 hour. Then add slowly, while stirring:

    3 cups rye flour

Let rise for about 2 hours. Sprinkle a board with:

    1 cup rye flour

Knead the dough into it for 10 minutes. Divide into 2 parts. Put on a well-greased baking sheet, grease the tops of the loaves, cover and allow to rise for about 2 hours more. Bake in a preheated 350° oven for about 1 hour. To test for doneness, to cool and to store, see page 555.

SOUR DOUGH RYE BREAD

           2 Round or 2 Long Loaves

The best-flavored rye breads call for sour doughs, page 504. In this recipe, the sour dough is used more for its flavor than for its rising power. Today, when controlled strains of yeast are easily available, we suggest, in households where baking is not done daily, that the sour dough be remade for each baking. We love this recipe which comes from Merna Lazier who has, among many other successful projects, run a bakery of her own. She says: "You may object to the number of stages in this process, but I must say that old-time bakers who were proud of their rye bread really nursed it along—so there must be a reason." For this recipe, on one day you make a sour dough, using ½ cake of yeast. The following day, you make two sponges, using the other ½ cake of yeast.

The first day, prepare the sour dough. Mix in a bowl and work together lightly:

    ½ cup rye flour
    ¼ cup water
    ½ cake compressed yeast

Cover this sour dough tightly so it will not dry out and keep it in a warm place at about 80° for 24 hours. Then work into it:

    ¾ cup water
    1 cup rye flour

The sour dough should be ready to use after it has fermented, covered, 4 hours longer.

I. To prepare Sponge I, mix with the sour dough until a smooth but firm dough is obtained:

    1¾ cups rye flour
    ⅔ of ½ cake compressed yeast

Allow this sponge to ferment, covered with a damp cloth at an 80° temperature until it drops. This means it will expand to its fullest and fall back on itself.

II. To prepare Sponge II, add to Sponge I:

1¾ cups rye flour
1¾ cups all-purpose flour
Remaining ⅓ of ½ cake compressed yeast
1 cup water

The sponge should be of a consistency similar to that of Sponge I. Allow to ferment until it drops. Then add:

1 cup water
1 tablespoon salt
1¾ cups all-purpose flour
1 tablespoon caraway seed

Let the mixture rest, covered, for about 15 to 20 minutes. Turn the dough out onto a floured board and knead with:

1¾ to 2 cups all-purpose flour

until you have a stiff dough—one that will not flatten or spread. Divide it, shape it into 2 long or 2 round loaves. ♦ Place them on a greased pan and allow to rise, but not double in bulk. Too much rising will result in a flat loaf.
Preheat oven to 425°.
Place a flat pan, filled about ¼ full of water, in the oven. Bake the loaves for about 1 hour. You may have to replenish the water, but remove the pan after 20 minutes. As soon as the bread is done, spread it with:

Melted butter

or, if you wish a glazed crust, spread it with:

Salted water—1 teaspoon salt to ½ cup water

Cool loaves on a rack, away from drafts.

CORN-MEAL OR ANADAMA BREAD
One 5 x 9-Inch Loaf

♦ Have all ingredients at about 75°.
Scald:

1¼ cups milk

Combine 1 cup of this hot milk in a large bowl with:

½ cup yellow corn meal
2 tablespoons sugar or ¼ cup molasses
2½ teaspoons salt
2 tablespoons shortening

When the remaining ¼ cup of milk cools to about 85°, dissolve in it for 10 minutes:

1 cake compressed yeast

Meanwhile sift, then measure:

3½ to 4 cups all-purpose flour

Combine yeast and milk mixtures. Stir in enough of the sifted flour to make a dough that will knead well. Knead for 10 minutes. Place dough in a greased bowl, covered, in a warm place, about 80°, until it has ♦ almost doubled in bulk, about 1 hour. Punch down and shape in greased pan. Allow to rise until almost doubled in bulk. Bake in a preheated 375° oven for about 40 minutes. To test for doneness, to cool and to store, see page 555.

STEEL-CUT OAT BREAD
One 5 x 9-Inch Loaf

♦ Have all ingredients at about 75°.
Measure into a mixing bowl:

1 cup steel-cut oats
¼ cup dark molasses
1 tablespoon softened shortening
¾ teaspoon salt

Pour over these:

2 cups ♦ boiling water

Stir in:

2 cups sifted all-purpose flour

While this is cooling, crumble and dissolve:

1 cake yeast

in:

¼ cup 85° water

After soaking for 10 minutes add the yeast mixture to the oats mixture. Work in:

2 cups sifted all-purpose flour

You may incorporate:

(1 cup broken pecan meats)

♦ To knead, shape and proof, follow the arrow symbols and the illustrations on pages 554 and 555, allowing the dough to rise once in the greased mixing bowl and once in the greased baking pan. Bake in a preheated 375° oven for about 40 minutes. To test for doneness, to cool and to store, see page 555.

GLUTEN BREAD
Two 5 x 9-Inch Loaves

♦ Have all ingredients at about 75°.
Combine:

3 cups 85° water
1 crumbled cake compressed yeast

After 10 minutes, when the yeast is dissolved, beat in:

2 cups gluten flour

Permit this sponge to rise in a warm place until light and foamy. Combine, beat and then stir into the sponge:

1 beaten egg
2 tablespoons melted shortening
½ teaspoon salt
(2 tablespoons sugar)

Stir in:

About 4 cups gluten flour

Use only enough flour to make a dough that will knead well. Knead and then shape into 2 loaves. Allow to rise until double in bulk. Bake in a preheated 350° oven for about 1 hour. To test for doneness, to cool and to store, see page 555.

HEALTH BREAD
Two 5 x 9-Inch Loaves

For nutritious additions to use in your other baking, see Cornell Triple-Rich Flour Formula, page 556.
♦ Have all ingredients at about 75°.
Crumble and dissolve for about 10 minutes:

2 cakes compressed yeast

in:

¼ cup 85° water

Scald:

2 cups milk

And pour it over:
    1 cup rolled oats
Add:
    2 teaspoons salt
    ¼ cup cooking oil
    ½ cup brown sugar
Cool this mixture to 85° and add the dissolved yeast, plus:
    1 or 2 slightly beaten eggs
    ¼ to ½ cup wheat germ
    1 cup soy flour
    2 cups whole-wheat or rye flour
    3 to 4 cups sifted, unbleached,
      all-purpose flour.
◗ To knead, shape and proof, follow the arrow symbols and illustrations on pages 554 and 555, allowing the dough to rise once in the mixing bowl and once in the baking pan. Bake in a preheated 350° oven for about 1 hour. To test for doneness, to cool and to store, see page 555.

BREAD PRETZELS

4 Dozen 6-Inch Sticks or
Twelve 6-Inch Pretzels

Let stand for 1 hour:
    1¼ cups 85° water
    1 cake compressed yeast
    ½ teaspoon sugar
Mix with:
    4½ cups flour
Knead for about 7 or 8 minutes. Let the dough rise ◗ covered, in a greased bowl until double in bulk. Form into sticks or pretzels. Place on a greased sheet. Apply a thin:
    Egg Wash, page 682
Sprinkle lavishly with:
    Coarse salt
Allow the pretzels to rise until not quite double in bulk. Bake in a preheated oven at 475° for about 10 mintues. To cool and store, see page 555.

ABOUT YEAST ROLLS

There is little difference in bread and roll making, so if you are a novice ◗ please read About Yeast Bread Making, page 553. The visual appeal of delicately formed, crusty or glazed rolls is a stimulant to the appetite. For varied shaping suggestions, see the illustrations in this chapter.

Professional cooks weigh the dough to keep the rolls uniform in size for good appearance and even baking. If you do not use muffin pans, place the dough at regular intervals over the entire baking sheet.

You may use additions to bread dough and coffee cake, page 556, to vary the flavor. Sprinkle the tops with poppy, celery, fennel, caraway, or lightly toasted sesame seeds, depending on the rest of your menu.

To bake, follow the individual recipes. ◗ Remove the rolls at once from the pan to a cooling rack. ◗ To reheat, sprinkle them lightly with water and heat, covered, in a 400° oven or in the top of a double boiler. Sometimes, the suggestion is made that the rolls be put in a dampened paper bag and heated until the bag dries. We find, however, that some types of bags can transmit a disagreeable flavor.

NO-KNEAD LIGHT ROLLS

Eighteen 2-Inch Rolls

These are the rolls we remember as light as a feather and served in a special, soft linen napkin. Although they require no kneading, they are best chilled from 2 to 12 hours. They are not true refrigerator rolls since this recipe is not heavy enough in sugar to retard the rising action, and all the dough should be baked after the 2- to 12-hour period.
◗ Have all ingredients at about 75°.
Dissolve for 10 minutes:
    1 cake compressed yeast
in:
    ¼ cup 85° water
Place in a separate bowl:
    ¼ cup butter or shortening
    1¼ teaspoons salt
    2 tablespoons sugar
Pour over these ingredients and stir until they are dissolved:
    1 cup boiling water
When they reach 85°, add the yeast. Beat in:
    1 egg
Stir in and beat until blended:
    About 2¾ cups sifted all-purpose
    flour, to make a soft dough
Place the dough in a large greased bowl, then turn it over, so it is lightly greased on top. Cover with foil and chill from 2 to 12 hours—or, you may place it in a greased bowl, covered with a damp cloth, until it doubles in bulk. Punch it down. Shape the rolls to fill about ⅓ of greased muffin tins. Permit them to rise until about double in bulk. Bake in a preheated 425° oven for about 15 to 18 minutes. Cool at once.

CLOVER LEAF ROLLS

Twenty-Four 2-Inch Rolls

◗ Have all ingredients at about 75°.
Cream:
    1 tablespoon lard
    1 tablespoon butter
    1½ tablespoons sugar
Add and beat well:
    1 cup scalded milk
Dissolve for about 10 minutes:
    1 cake compressed yeast
in:
    ¼ cup 85° water
Add these ingredients to the milk mixture. Sift before measuring and add:
    1½ cups all-purpose flour
Beat well. Cover with a cloth and permit to rise until double in bulk. Sift before measuring:
    1½ cups all-purpose flour
Add it to the batter with:
    1¼ teaspoons salt

Beat well. Place the dough in a greased bowl and turn it, so that it is lightly greased all over. Cover with a cloth and permit to rise until about double in bulk. Now, fill greased muffin tins about ⅓ full with 3 small balls, as sketched below. Brush the tops with:

> Melted butter

Permit the rolls to rise, covered, in a warm

place until about double in bulk. Bake in a preheated 425° oven for about 15 to 18 minutes. Remove at once from pans.

PARKER HOUSE ROLLS
About Thirty 2-Inch Rolls

♦ Have all ingredients at about 75°.
Scald:

> 1 cup milk

Add and stir until dissolved:

> 1 tablespoon sugar
> 2 tablespoons butter
> ¾ teaspoon salt

When these ingredients are at 85°, add:

> ½ cake compressed yeast

dissolved for 10 minutes in:

> 2 tablespoons 85° water

Beat in:

> (1 egg)

Sift before measuring and add:

> 2⅔ cups all-purpose flour

Stir in part of the flour, knead in the rest. Use only enough flour to form a dough that can be handled easily. Place in a greased bowl. Brush the top with:

> Melted butter

Cover and let rise in a warm place until doubled in bulk. Roll the dough and cut into rounds with a floured biscuit cutter. Dip the handle of a knife in flour and use it to make a deep crease across the middle of each roll. Fold the rolls over and press the edges together lightly. Place rolls in rows on a greased pan. Permit to rise in a warm place until light, only about 35 minutes. Bake in a preheated 425° oven for about 20 minutes. Remove at once from pans.

PALM LEAF ROLLS
About 4 Dozen Leaves

Sweet enough for a dessert. Serve with coffee and fruit.
♦ Have all ingredients at about 75°.

Crumble and dissolve for 10 minutes:

> 1 cake compressed yeast

in:

> ¼ cup 85° water

Sift:

> 3 cups all-purpose flour
> 1½ teaspoons salt

Cut in, until reduced to the size of peas:

> ½ cup butter

Blend and add:

> 2 beaten eggs
> 1 cup cultured sour cream
> 1 teaspoon vanilla

and the dissolved yeast. Cover and chill for about 2 hours or more. When ready to bake, sprinkle a board with:

> ½ cup vanilla sugar, see page 508

or a mixture of:

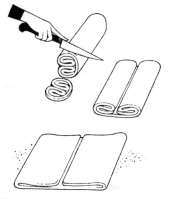

> ½ cup sugar
> 1 teaspoon cinnamon

Roll ½ the dough into a 6 x 18 x ¼-inch strip. Fold as sketched on the left below, bringing the short ends to within about ¾ inch of each other. Repeat this folding as shown in the right foreground and again as shown in the rear. Slice into ¼-inch-thick "palms." Repeat this process with the other half of the dough, first sprinkling the board with the sugar mixture. Fold and cut as directed above. Put palms on an ungreased baking sheet. Allow to rise about 20 minutes. Bake in a preheated 375° oven until golden brown, about 15 minutes.

BUTTERMILK ROLLS OR FAN TANS
About 24 Rolls

Rolls prepared in this way need not be buttered. Fine for a serve-yourself party.
♦ Have all ingredients at about 75°.
Sift before measuring:

> 4 cups all-purpose flour

Heat:

> 2 cups buttermilk

Cool to about 85°. Dissolve for 10 minutes:

> 1 cake compressed yeast

in ⅓ cup of the lukewarm buttermilk. Add

to the remaining buttermilk, with:
    ¼ teaspoon soda
    2 teaspoons salt
    ¼ cup sugar
Beat well, then stir in gradually half the
flour. Add:
    2 tablespoons melted butter
and the rest of the flour. Place dough in a
greased bowl and turn it, so it is lightly
greased all over. Cover with a moist cloth
and permit to rise until more than double
in bulk. Knead lightly for 1 minute. Separate into 2 parts. Roll each part into a
square, about ⅛ inch thick. Brush the
dough with melted butter. Cut into strips
1½ inches wide. Stack them. There
should be from 6 to 8 layers of strips
stacked. Cut off pieces about 1½ inches
wide, with a string, as shown below.
Place them in buttered muffin tins, with
the cut edges up. Permit to rise in a warm
place until doubled in size. Bake in a preheated 425° oven from 15 to 20 minutes
until well browned.

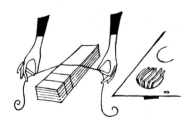

SOUR CREAM ROLLS
OR KOLATCHEN
                    About Thirty-Six 2-Inch Rolls
◗ Have all ingredients at about 75°.
Beat until creamy:
    6 tablespoons butter
    Grated rind of 1 lemon
    2 tablespoons sugar
Beat in well:
    4 beaten eggs
    1 cup cultured sour cream
Dissolve for 10 minutes:
    1 cake compressed yeast
in:
    2 tablespoons 85° water
Beat this into the egg mixture. Measure:
    3 cups sifted all-purpose flour
Resift with:
    ½ teaspoon salt
    1 teaspoon soda
Beat these ingredients into the egg mix-
ture. Fill greased muffin tins ½ full. Cover
the dough and let it rise in a warm place
85° until doubled in bulk. Brush the tops
with:
    1 slightly beaten egg white
Decorate them with:
    Chopped nut meats
Bake the rolls in a preheated 375° oven for
about 15 to 20 minutes.

Dust before serving with:
    Confectioners' sugar

OVERNIGHT ROLLS
                                About 48 Rolls
◗ Have all ingredients at about 75°.
Combine:
    1 crumbled cake compressed yeast
    2 teaspoons sugar
Permit these ingredients to stand until dis-
solved, about 10 minutes. Scald:
    1 cup milk
Add and stir until melted:
    7 tablespoons lard
Cool. Combine and beat well:
    7 tablespoons sugar
    3 beaten eggs
    1 teaspoon salt
Stir in the milk mixture and cool to 85°.
Stir in the yeast mixture and:
    4½ cups sifted all-purpose flour
Beat the dough about 5 minutes. Place in
a foil-covered bowl in the refrigerator
overnight. Take out just before baking.
Divide dough into 3 parts. Roll each part
into a circle about 9 inches in diameter.

Cut each circle into 16 wedge-shaped
pieces. Before they are rolled further,
brush with:
    Melted butter
and dust with:
    Sugar and cinnamon
or fill with:
    Coffee Cake Filling, page 573
Roll each piece by beginning at the wide
end. Stretch the end a bit as you start to
roll it. Brush with:
    Egg Wash, page 682
Permit rolls to rise until double in bulk.
Bake for 15 to 18 minutes on a greased
sheet in a preheated 425° oven. Take care.
They burn easily.

FILLED PINWHEEL ROLLS
Follow the recipe for:
    Overnight Rolls, above
Prepare the dough and let rise until dou-
bled in bulk. Roll to ¼-inch thickness.
Cut into 4-inch squares. Spread the
squares generously with:
    Butter
    Sugar and cinnamon
Place in the center of each square:
    6 or more raisins or 2 teaspoons
    apricot jam

Cut diagonally into the dough from each corner to within ½ inch of the center. Fold the points toward the center. Place pin-

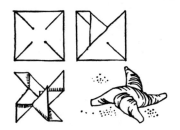

wheels on a greased pan. Let them rise slightly. Bake in a preheated 425° oven for about 18 minutes.

CHEESE ROLLS
Prepare:
    Cheese Bread, page 556
Shape and bake as for:
    Overnight Rolls, page 564

✳ VERSATILE ROLLS
        About 5 Dozen Rolls
You may make these excellent rolls in advance and reheat them before serving. Wrap and keep them in a refrigerator 2 weeks or in a freezer 3 months. As they call for neither eggs nor shortening, they appeal to the allergic and the dieter.
◗ Have all ingredients at about 75°.
Scald:
    2 cups milk
Add:
    5 teaspoons salt
    ¼ cup sugar
Cool this mixture to 85°. Dissolve for 10 minutes:
    2 cakes compressed yeast
in:
    1 cup 85° water
Combine above ingredients and mix until smooth. Add gradually:
    8 to 10 cups all-purpose flour
Knead the dough well and let it rise, covered, until almost double in bulk. Shape the dough as you prefer. Permit rolls to rise in covered pans until almost double in bulk. Bake for about 40 minutes in a preheated 275° oven. If storing, leave them in the pans to cool for 20 minutes. When they reach room temperature, wrap them well. To serve, reheat until brown on a greased baking sheet about 10 minutes in a 400° oven.

BUTTERMILK POTATO ROLLS
       About 46 Clover Leaf Rolls
◗ Have all ingredients at about 75°.
Prepare:
    ¾ cup freshly cooked, riced potatoes
While still hot, mix with:
    ½ cup butter

Heat:
    2 cups buttermilk
Cool to about 85°. Crumble into about ½ cup of the buttermilk:
    1 cake compressed yeast
    2 tablespoons sugar
    1 teaspoon salt
and rest it for 10 minutes. Add the remaining buttermilk and mix with the potatoes. Beat until light and add:
    2 eggs
Sift before measuring:
    7½ cups all-purpose flour
Stir in 6 cups of the flour. Knead in the rest. Place the dough in a greased bowl and turn it, so that it is greased lightly on all sides. Cover with a damp cloth and let rise until double in bulk. Punch down. Shape as for Clover Leaf Rolls, page 562. Glaze tops with:
    (Egg Wash, page 682)
Sprinkle with:
    (Poppy seeds)
Bake in a preheated 425° oven for 15 to 18 minutes. Remove at once from pans.

CINNAMON BUNS OR SNAILS
Prepare:
    Stollen, page 571, or Scandinavian
    Pastry, page 572, or Overnight
    Rolls, page 564
When the dough has doubled in bulk, roll it on a floured board to the thickness of ¼ inch. Spread generously with:
    Melted butter
Sprinkle with:
    Cinnamon
    Brown sugar
Add, if desired:
    Chopped nut meats
    Seedless raisins
    Chopped citron
    Grated lemon rind

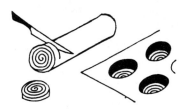

Roll the dough like a jelly roll, page 642. Cut into 1-inch slices. Rub muffin tins generously with:
    Butter
Sprinkle well with:
    Brown sugar
    (Chopped nut meats)
Place each slice of roll firmly on bottom of a muffin tin. Permit to rise in a warm place for ½ hour. Bake in a preheated 350° oven for about ½ hour.

CARAMEL BUNS OR SCHNECKEN
Prepare one of the doughs in:
Cinnamon Snails, above
♦ Be sure to use in the filling:
**Grated lemon rind
Raisins
Pecans**
Roll as for Jelly Roll, page 642. Cut into
1½-inch slices, as shown on page 565. Fill
bottom of each muffin tin with a mixture of:
**1 teaspoon melted butter
1 teaspoon warmed honey**
Cover with:
**2 teaspoons brown sugar
A few chopped or whole pecans**
Lay the slices of dough over sugar mixture.
Bake in a preheated 350° oven for about
20 minutes. Watch closely for signs of
scorching.

WHOLE-GRAIN ROLLS
About 40 Rolls
Prepare:
Whole-Grain Bread Plus, page 559
Shape dough into rolls after the second ris-
ing. Butter the tops. Sprinkle with:
(**Coarse salt, chopped nuts or
sesame seeds**)
Bake in a preheated 400° oven for 15 to
20 minutes.

RYE ROLLS
About 36 Rolls
Prepare:
Swedish Rye Bread, page 560
Shape rolls after the first rising. Sprinkle
tops with:
Coarse salt
For the crust of your choice, see About
Cooling Bread, page 555. Bake in a pre-
heated 375° oven about 20 minutes. Re-
move from pans at once and cool on a rack.

OAT-MOLASSES ROLLS
Prepare:
Steel-Cut Oats Bread, page 561
After the first rising, butter your fingers
and pinch off pieces large enough to fill
greased muffin tins about ⅓ full. Permit
the dough to rise until about double in
bulk. Bake in a preheated 375° oven for
about 18 minutes.

BRIOCHE
About 15 Brioches
Our recipes for French bread, due to a
number of special circumstances, are close
approximations. So, for similar reasons, is
our recipe for another superb French specialty—the brioche. But we are proud of
them all. The method for making brioche
is more complicated to describe than to
carry out. It involves good timing between the rising of a small amount of
floating yeast paste, or starter, and the
working of the rest of the dough. Please
read about this process before plunging in.

Have ready:
6 tablespoons butter, creamed at 85°
Sift and then measure:
2 cups all-purpose flour
Make a well, see page 594, with about ¼
of this flour and crumble into it:
1 cake compressed yeast at 75°
♦ Be sure to use this much. A high yeast
and butter content distinguishes this
dough. Mix the flour and crumbled yeast
with:
2 tablespoons 85° water
Gradually work the flour into a paste.
When it becomes a small soft ball, snip a
cross in the top with scissors and then
drop it into a 2-quart pan, filled with water at 85°. ♦ The ball will sink to the bottom of the pan, so be sure it is not over a
burner, where additional heat might kill
the yeast. As the yeast develops, the ball
of dough, or starter, rises to the surface
and doubles in size in about 7 to 8 minutes
—if the water temperature is right. If the
water chills too much, add hotter water to
bring the temperature back to 85°. ♦ When
the starter has doubled in bulk, it must be
removed from the water. Should this state
be reached before you are ready to use it,
drain and cover it. Meanwhile, once you
have dropped the starter in the water,
shape into another well the remaining
flour, mixed with:
**1 tablespoon sugar
1 teaspoon salt**
Break into the center of it:
2 eggs, room temperature
Mix them in by drawing the flour from the
sides of the well gradually. Also work in:
2 to 3 tablespoons milk
until the ingredients form a sticky but co-
hesive mass which you continue to work as
follows. Use only one hand. Do not try to
release it from the dough. Just keep picking up as much as will adhere and throw
it back hard onto the board with a turn of
the wrist, gathering more from the board
each time. ♦ This rough throwing process
develops the gluten and is repeated about
fifty times. By then the dough should be
glistening and smooth and your fingers will
have become free. At this point, work the
butter into the paste. When it is all absorbed, scoop the floating starter out of the
water by spreading wide the fingers of one
hand and ♦ drain the starter for a moment
on a dry towel. Work the starter into the
smooth paste, which will remain shining
and of about the consistency of whipped
cream. ♦ Now, get the paste ready to chill
for at least 1 hour. Gather up as much as
you can, releasing the rest of the dough
from the board with a spatula. Put it into
a greased or floured bowl and chill, covered. Have ready the classic, fluted and
flaring brioche forms—or muffin tins.
When the dough has chilled, knead it with
floured hands. It should be firm enough
not to require a floured board. Now for

each brioche, make 2 balls—about 2 tablespoons of dough for one, 1 tablespoon for the other. The first ball is placed in the base of a tin. The smaller ball will form the characteristic topknot of this bread.

Mold it into a pear-shaped form. Cut a small gash in center of the large ball, then 3 more shallow gashes radiating out from the center. Now, insert the point of the "pear," so it is seated firmly. The brioches are then permitted to rise until almost doubled in bulk—under good conditions for about 15 to 20 minutes. Glaze them with Egg Wash, see page 682 ♦ but be sure it does not slip into the crack and bind the topknot to the base, as it would keep the topknot from rising properly.
Preheat oven to 450°.
Bake the brioches about 10 minutes or until the egg-washed portions are a lovely brown. Should the topknots brown too rapidly, cover them loosely with a piece of foil. They should have puffed when baked to the proportionate size shown in the illustration. Serve at once or release from the tins and cool on a rack. Reheat before serving.

BRIOCHE AU CHOCOLAT

A favorite French after-school treat.
Prepare:
> **Brioche, above, or Scandinavian Pastry, page 572**

Cut in 2-inch squares. Roll in each square a pencil-shaped piece of:
> **Semi-sweet chocolate: about ¼ oz.**

Bake as directed for Scandinavian Pastries, page 572.

FRENCH CRESCENTS OR CROISSANTS

About 18 Crescents

Rich, somewhat troublesome, but unequaled by any other form of roll.
Have all ingredients at about 75°.
Scald:
> **⅞ cup milk**

Stir into it, until melted and dissolved:
> **1 tablespoon lard**
> **1½ tablespoons sugar**
> **¾ teaspoon salt**

Cool until lukewarm. Add:
> **1 cake yeast**

dissolved in:
> **⅛ cup 85° water**

Stir in or knead in to make a soft dough about:
> **2½ cups sifted all-purpose flour**

Knead the dough on a lightly floured surface until smooth and elastic. Place it in a greased bowl and turn it so all sides are lightly greased. Cover with a damp cloth. Permit to rise until doubled in bulk, about 1½ hours. Cover the dough with a lid and place in the refrigerator until thoroughly chilled, at least 20 minutes. Then roll it out into an oblong ¼ inch thick. Now beat until creamy:
> **1 cup butter**

Dot ⅔ of the surface of the dough with ¼ cup of the butter. Fold the undotted third over the center third. Then, fold the doubled portion over the remaining third of the butter-dotted portion. The dough is now in 3 layers, see Puff Paste, page 593. Swing the layered dough a ¼ turn—or, as in bridge, bring East to South. Roll it again into an oblong ¼ inch thick. Again, dot ⅔ of the surface with ¼ of the butter. Fold the undotted third over the center dotted third. Then fold the doubled portion over the remaining dotted third as before. Swing the dough a quarter turn. Roll and fold it twice more, dotting each time with ¼ cup butter. Cover and chill the dough for at least 2 hours. Then, roll it again on a slightly floured surface to the thickness of ¼ inch. Cut off any folded edges which might keep the dough from expanding. Cut the dough into 3-inch squares. Cut the squares on the bias. Roll the triangular pieces beginning with the wide side and stretching it slightly as you roll. Shape the rolls into crescents, as sketched below. Place them on a baking

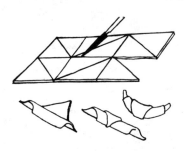

sheet. Chill them at once for ½ hour. Never allow them a final rising, as they will not be crisp if you do.
Preheat oven to 400°.
Bake the crescents for 10 minutes, then reduce the heat to 350° and bake them until they are done—about 10 to 15 minutes longer.

ENGLISH OR RAISED MUFFINS
About Twenty 3-Inch Muffins
These are heavenly when eaten fresh and
do not taste at all like "store-bought" ones,
but begin to resemble them the second
day. They may be baked with or without
muffin rings. The classic size is about 4
inches. We make our own rings from small
unlacquered fish cans and deviled meat
cans. The tops and bottoms are removed
and the rims are thoroughly scrubbed.
English muffins are always baked on a
greased griddle.
♦ Have all ingredients at about 75°.
Combine in a mixing bowl:
    1 cup hot water
    ½ cup scalded milk
    2 teaspoons sugar
    1 teaspoon salt
Dissolve for 10 minutes:
    1 cake compressed yeast
in:
    2 tablespoons 85° water
Combine the two mixtures. Sift before
measuring:
    4 cups all-purpose flour
Beat 2 cups flour gradually into the milk
mixture. Cover the bowl with a damp
cloth. Permit the sponge to rise in a warm
place, 85°, for about 1½ hours or ♦ until
it collapses back into the bowl. Beat in:
    3 tablespoons softened butter
Beat or knead in the remaining flour. Let
the dough rise again until doubled in bulk.
You may put it in greased rings for the
final rising, filling them ½ full. If not using rings, place the dough on a lightly
floured board. Pat or press it until about
¾ inch thick. Cut it into rounds about 3
inches in diameter. Let them stand until

the dough has doubled in bulk. Cook until light brown on a fairly hot, well-buttered griddle. Turn them once while cooking, using a pancake turner. Cool them
slightly on a rack. To separate the muffins
before the traditional toasting, take 2 forks
back to back and pry them open horizontally. Butter generously and toast. The
uneven browning gives them great charm.
Serve with:
    Marmalade or
    (Poached egg)

CRUMPETS
Crumpets are essentially similar to English
muffins, except that muffin rings must be

used when preparing them, see illustration
on this page, as the batter is more liquid.
Follow the recipe for English Muffins, using in all:
    2⅔ cups milk

FILLED SWEET CRESCENTS
About 28 Crescents
Prepare the dough for:
    Refrigerator Potato Rolls, page 569,
    or Scandinavian Pastry, page 572
Use for each crescent:
    2 teaspoons nut or fruit filling,
    page 573
If using the refrigerator dough, roll out to
¼-inch thickness before chilling and cut
into 3-inch squares. If using the Scandinavian dough, shape it after chilling. Cut
the squares diagonally. Shape as shown,
page 567. Begin the roll with the wide
edge of the triangle. Curve the rolls into
crescents. Place on a greased sheet. Let
them rise until double in bulk. Brush
lightly with:
    Egg Wash, page 682
Bake in a preheated 375° oven for about
18 to 20 minutes. Cool on a rack or serve
hot.

ORANGE TEA ROLLS
These must be served the same day they
are baked.
Prepare:
    Refrigerator Potato Rolls, page 569
Shape them into bite-size rolls. In the
center of each roll, embed:
    A section of fresh orange
which has been rolled in:
    Brown sugar
Bake in a preheated 400° oven 8 to 10
minutes. Before reheating, glaze with
a mixture of equal parts of:
    Sugar, water and Cointreau

HARD OR VIENNA ROLLS
Twelve 3-Inch Rolls
♦ Have all ingredients at about 75°.
Sift:
    4 cups all-purpose flour
Crumble and dissolve for 10 minutes:
    1 cake compressed yeast
in:
    ¼ cup 85° water
Combine:
    1 cup water
    1 tablespoon sugar
    1 teaspoon salt
    2 tablespoons melted shortening
and the dissolved yeast mixture. Fold in
thoroughly, but lightly:
    2 stiffly beaten egg whites
Add enough of the sifted flour to make a
soft dough. To knead and proof, see page
554. Allow the dough to rise twice. After
the second rising, punch down and knead
for about 1 minute, then let rest, covered,
for about 10 minutes before shaping into
12 oblong pieces. Place them about 3

inches apart on a greased baking sheet. ♦ To insure a hard crust, have in the oven a 9 x 13-inch pan, filled with ½ inch boiling water. Bake at once in a preheated 450° oven for about 20 minutes or until golden brown.

ABOUT REFRIGERATOR DOUGHS

By "refrigerator," we mean just that—these are not freezer doughs. If it's a freezer product you're after, by all means ♦ bake before freezing for the best results. We find the following recipes somewhat limited in use as ♦ the milk-based ones can be kept chilled only three days and the water-based ones five days. Yeast action is slowed by the cold, but it does continue, so both more fat and more sugar are needed in refrigerator doughs than in other kinds to keep the yeast potent during the storage period. We find that kneading before storage helps to retain rising power.

The advantage of this type of dough, of course, is that you can bake some at once and keep the rest for later. To store for chilling, you must ♦ keep the dough from drying out. Store in a greased plastic bag large enough to allow for expansion, or place the balled dough in a greased bowl, turn it so the entire surface is evenly coated, cover it closely with wax paper or foil and weight it down with a plate.

After removal from refrigeration, always ♦ rest the dough, covered, for 30 minutes before shaping it. Then ♦ punch it down to let the gases escape before further handling. After shaping or filling, see About Yeast Rolls, page 562. Be sure the dough at least doubles in bulk. Allow ample time for rising because of the chilled condition of the dough. To bake, see individual recipes.

NO-KNEAD REFRIGERATOR ROLLS
Eighteen 2½-Inch Rolls
♦ Have all ingredients at about 75°.
Sift before measuring:
> 3½ cups all-purpose flour

Scald:
> 1 cup milk

Stir in, until dissolved:
> 6 tablespoons shortening or butter
> 6 tablespoons sugar
> 1 to 1½ teaspoons salt

Cool to 85°. Place in a measuring cup:
> 1 cake compressed yeast

Dissolve it in:
> ½ cup 85° water

Allow it to rest for 10 minutes, then beat in:
> 1 egg

Add these ingredients to the milk mixture. Beat in ½ the flour. Beat the dough for 2 minutes. Add the remaining flour and beat the dough until it blisters. To store for chilling, to shape and to prepare for baking, see About Refrigerator Doughs, above. Bake in a preheated 425° oven for about 15 minutes.

REFRIGERATOR POTATO ROLLS
About Forty 2-Inch Rolls
♦ Have all ingredients at about 75°.
Prepare:
> 1 cup freshly cooked and riced potatoes

Dissolve for about 10 minutes:
> 1 cake compressed yeast

in:
> ½ cup 85° water

Place in a separate bowl:
> ½ cup lard or shortening

Scald and pour over it:
> 1 cup milk

Stir until the lard is melted. When the mixture reaches about 85°, add the dissolved yeast and the riced potatoes. Add:
> 3 beaten eggs
> ¾ cup sugar
> 2 teaspoons salt

Beat well. Sift before measuring:
> 5 cups all-purpose flour

Add 4 cups of the flour and beat the batter thoroughly. Stir in the remaining flour or toss the dough on a board and knead the flour in. To store for chilling, to shape and to prepare for baking, see About Refrigerator Doughs, this page. Bake the rolls in a preheated 425° oven for about 15 minutes.

REFRIGERATOR WHOLE-GRAIN ROLLS
About Twenty 2-Inch Rolls
♦ Have all ingredients at about 75°.
Dissolve for about 10 minutes:
> ½ to 1 cake compressed yeast

in:
> 1 cup 85° water

Beat until creamy:
> ¼ cup shortening
> 6 tablespoons sugar

Stir in the yeast mixture. Sift before measuring:
> 1¾ cups all-purpose flour

Mix in:
> 1¼ teaspoons salt
> 1½ cups whole-grain flour

Stir the flour mixture gradually into the yeast mixture. Beat until well blended. To store for chilling, to shape and to prepare for baking, see About Refrigerator Doughs, this page. Bake in a preheated 425° oven for about 15 minutes.

REFRIGERATOR BRAN ROLLS
About Forty-Eight 2-Inch Rolls
♦ Have all ingredients at about 75°.
Combine:
> 1 cup shortening
> ¾ cup sugar
> 1½ to 2 teaspoons salt

Pour over these ingredients and stir until the shortening is melted:
> 1 cup boiling water

Add:
> 1 cup bran or bran cereal

In a separate bowl, dissolve for about 10 minutes:

2 cakes compressed yeast

in:

1 cup 85° water

When the first mixture reaches about 85°, add to it:

2 well-beaten eggs

and the dissolved yeast. Sift before measuring and add:

6 cups all-purpose flour

Beat the batter well. To store for chilling, to shape and to prepare for baking, see About Refrigerator Doughs, page 569. Bake in a preheated 425° oven for about 15 minutes.

WHITE, WHOLE-GRAIN, GRAHAM OR RYE BREAD STICKS

Pinch off small pieces of:

Bread Dough, page 556, or

Refrigerator Roll Dough, page 569

that has risen once. This may be done with buttered hands. Roll into sticks. Brush with:

Melted butter or 1 beaten egg

Place the sticks on a buttered sheet. Sprinkle them with a choice of:

(Coarse salt)

(Poppy seed)

(Fresh celery seed)

(Chopped nut meats)

(Caraway seed)

Permit to rise until doubled in bulk. Bake in a 425° oven until brown and crisp.

ABOUT YEAST COFFEE CAKES

Remember when you are baking bread and rolls that many of these doughs can be made into very acceptable coffee cake and sweet rolls. Try some with the special fillings suggested at the end of this section. For a comparatively effortless but delicious result, bake the No-Knead Coffee Cake, below. If you have a little time on your hands, don't fail to try the Scandinavian varieties.

NO-KNEAD YEAST COFFEE CAKE OR PANETTONE

Two 9-Inch Tube Pans

Baked in 1 lb. greased coffee cans and attractively packaged, this cake makes wonderful gifts.

◗ Have all ingredients at about 75°.

Dissolve for about 10 minutes:

2 cakes compressed yeast

in:

1 cup 85° water

Sift and stir in:

1 cup all-purpose flour

Cover this sponge and permit it to rise in a warm place until it has doubled in bulk. Sift:

½ cup sugar

Beat until soft:

½ cup butter

Add the sugar gradually. Blend these ingredients until they are light and creamy. Beat in, one at a time:

2 to 3 eggs

Add:

1 teaspoon salt

2 teaspoons grated lemon rind

Beat in the sponge. Sift and beat in gradually:

3½ cups all-purpose flour

Beat the dough for 5 minutes more. Add:

(⅛ cup chopped citron)

(¼ cup white raisins or chopped candied pineapple)

(1 cup broken nut meats)

Cover the bowl with a cloth and permit the dough to rise for about 2 hours or until it has almost doubled in bulk. Place it in greased tube pans and let it rise for about ½ hour. Brush the tops with:

Melted butter

If you have added no fruit or nut meats to the batter, you may combine:

½ cup blanched, shredded almonds

¼ cup sugar

Sprinkle this mixture on the dough.

Preheat oven to 350°.

Bake in either the tubes or the greased pans for about ½ hour. If you have omitted the top dressing of almonds and sugar, you may, after the cake has baked and cooled, spread on it:

Milk or Lemon Glaze, page 682

★ KNEADED COFFEE CAKE FOR FILLED BRAIDS, RINGS OR VANOCKA

Prepare:

Buttermilk Potato Roll Dough, page 565, or White Bread Plus, page 556

adding an additional:

¼ cup sugar

To give these breads an interesting color, use the tiniest smidgen of:

Saffron, page 537

Consider beforehand whether to make a wreath, to roll like a jelly roll, to shape a filled roll as shown under Scandinavian Coffee Cake, page 572, or to braid. One of the most famous Christmas breads is Vanocka—the finished loaf is supposed to resemble the Christ Child in swaddling clothes. To shape Vanocka or the filled cake sketched above, see the next page.

To make **Vanocka,** divide the dough into
9 parts. First, braid a 4 plait strip, then a
3 plait, last, a 2 plait. Use the widest for
a base and center the 3 plaits on it. Then
top with the centered 2 plait. A way to
braid a filled coffee cake so the filling is
well protected is shown on page 570. Make
a rectangle about 9 x 12 inches and ¼ inch
thick. Put the filling down the center
lengthwise, cut the outer thirds diagonally
into 2 inch strips and lace them as shown,
folding the ends inside.

★ STOLLEN OR CHRISTMAS LOAF
2 Loaves

♦ Have all ingredients at about 75°.
Sift before measuring:

6 to 8 cups all-purpose flour

Crumble:

1½ to 2 cakes compressed yeast

in:

1½ cups 85° water or scalded,
cooled milk

for about 10 minutes, until dissolved. Add
1 cup of the sifted flour. Permit this
sponge to rise in a warm place until doubled in bulk. Sprinkle a little of the sifted
flour over:

½ lb. raisins
½ lb. blanched chopped almonds
(½ cup chopped candied fruits)

Sift:

¾ cup sugar

Beat until soft:

1½ cups butter

Add the sifted sugar gradually. Blend until light and creamy. Beat in, one at a
time:

3 eggs

Add:

¾ teaspoon salt
¾ teaspoon grated lemon rind
(2 tablespoons brandy or rum)

Add the fruit and nuts. Add the sponge
and the remaining flour and knead the
dough until smooth and elastic. Permit it
to rise until almost doubles in bulk. Toss
it onto a floured board. Divide it into 2
loaves and place them in greased pans.
Brush the tops with:

Melted butter

Let the loaves rise, covered, until they
again almost double in bulk.
Preheat oven to 350°.
Bake the loaves for about 45 minutes.
When cool, brush them with:

Milk or Lemon Glaze, page 682

BUNDKUCHEN OR KUGELHOPF

A true Kugelhopf is baked in a fluted tube
pan. It is the traditional Name Day cake
—not your birthday, but the birthday of
the saint for whom you were named. This
recipe also makes a good Baba or Savarin,
page 640.
♦ Have all ingredients at about 75°.
Sift before measuring:

4 cups all-purpose flour

Scald:

1 cup milk

When cooled to about 85°, pour it over:

3 cakes crumbled compressed yeast

After the yeast has dissolved, beat in 1
cup of the sifted flour and set the sponge
to rise in a warm place until about double
in bulk. Sift:

¾ cup sugar

Beat until soft:

1 cup butter

Add the sifted sugar gradually. Blend
these ingredients until very light and
creamy. Beat in, one at a time:

5 eggs

Beat in:

1 teaspoon salt

Add the sponge, the remaining flour and:

½ teaspoon grated lemon rind
1 cup seedless raisins

Beat the batter well until smooth and elastic. Spread in the bottom of a greased 9-
inch tube pan:

⅛ cup blanched almonds

Place the dough on top of them and per-
mit it to rise until almost double in bulk.
Preheat oven to 350°.
Bake the cake from 50 to 60 minutes.
When cool, sprinkle the top with:

Confectioners' sugar

FRUIT-TOPPED YEAST COFFEE CAKE
Four 8-Inch Cakes

For other versions of Galette, see page 592.
Prepare:

White Bread Plus Dough, page 556

adding an additional:

¼ cup sugar

After the last rising, pat the dough out thin
in the greased pans, perforate it and allow
it to relax. Then make a rim by pinching
the top edges all around. Brush the surface
with:

Melted butter

or apply an:

Egg Wash, page 682

Although the egg wash always tends to
toughen, it does prevent sogginess. Now
cover the entire surface of the cake closely
with rows of:

Fruit—cored, sliced apples, peaches,
seeded cherries or plums

Cover the fruit with:

Streusel, page 682, or cinnamon
and sugar

♦ Allow the fruit-covered dough to rise
only half as high as usual for bread.
Preheat oven to 385°.
Bake for about 25 minutes. ♦ If using an
electric oven, see page 140. When the
cake cools somewhat, you may cover it
with:

Apricot Glaze, page 683

For a simpler, quicker and, we think, quite
delicious solution, simply bake:

Fresh Fruit Cake Cockaigne,
page 606

SCANDINAVIAN COFFEE CAKE
OR PASTRY

Two 9-Inch Rings

Call them Danish, Swedish or Norwegian, these light confections fall between rich coffee cakes and rich pastries. The method of folding and rolling the dough, similar to that used in Croissants, page 567, accounts for the characteristic flakiness of the superbly light crumb. The basic dough can be used for the ring shown below. Fillings and toppings are usually rich in nuts, with cardamon and saffron frequent in the flavoring.

◖ Have all ingredients at about 75°.
Beat well:

   2 eggs

Add:

   ¾ cup 85° water

Dissolve in this mixture:

   1 cake compressed yeast

Let all these ingredients rest refrigerated for about 15 minutes. Meanwhile blend with a pastry blender or by hand, until smooth:

   4 cups sifted all-purpose flour
   1 teaspoon salt
   2 tablespoons sugar
   ½ cup butter
   10 crushed cardamon seeds or
   1½ teaspoons powdered cardamon

Make a ring of the blended flour prepared in the step above. Now pour the chilled yeast mixture into the center and work it gradually into the dry ingredients. Knead until smooth for about 2 minutes. Form the dough into a ball and rest it, covered, for about 20 minutes in the refrigerator. Roll out the dough ◖ lightly into an oblong about ⅜ inch thick. Beat until creamy:

   1⅛ to 1½ cups butter

Dot the dough over ⅔ of its surface with ¼ of the butter. Fold the undotted third over the center third. Then fold the doubled portion over the remaining third of the butter-dotted portion. The dough is now in 3 layers, see Puff Paste, page 593. Swing the layered dough a ¼ turn or, as in bridge, bring East to South. Roll it ◖ lightly again into an oblong about ⅜ inch thick. Again dot ⅔ of the surface with ¼ of the butter. Fold the undotted third over the center dotted third. Then fold the doubled portion over the remaining butter-dotted third as before. Swing the dough a quarter turn. Roll and fold it twice more, dotting each time with ¼ of the butter. Cover and chill the dough for at least 2 hours. Then roll it again on a slightly floured surface, to the thickness of ⅜ inch. Cut off any folded edges that might keep the dough from expanding. To shape the ring as shown below, roll it first into an oblong, about 29 x 11 inches. Fill it with any rich filling for coffee cake, page 573. It is not necessary to shape the roll on a cloth but you may need to use a spatula or pancake turner to help lift it if the dough should stick to the lightly floured board. Bring the two ends of the roll together using a little water for glue to make them hold. Place the ring on a greased baking sheet. With floured scissors held perpendicularly to the roll, cut bias gashes about 1 to 2 inches apart into the outer edges of the ring, to within one inch of the inner circle. As you cut, you may turn each partially cut slice flat onto the tin. Sometimes the slices are cut very narrow and one slice is turned toward the outer rim, the other twisted and turned toward the inner rim, as shown on the right. Wash the top areas with:

   Egg Wash, page 682

being careful not to cover the cut portions as the glaze may harden later too rapidly in baking and inhibit further rising of the dough. Cover the cut ring with a damp cloth and allow to rise for about 25 minutes, until the mass has doubled in bulk.
Preheat the oven to 400° for a ring, to 375° for filled rolls or croissants.
Bake a ring about 25 minutes. Bake rolls for about 15 minutes. If a Fruit Glaze, page 683, is to be applied, allow the pastry to cool and apply the glaze warm. For other glazes, see page 682.

ABOUT SEASONINGS, FILLINGS AND TOPPINGS FOR COFFEE CAKE

Housewives often wonder why their coffee cakes and fillings seem insipid in flavor and in color when compared with some of the more sophisticated commercial products. First of all, a slight touch of yellow coloring often used in commercial coffee cakes lends them a more convincing "eggy" look. Often too, for gusto, bakers add to their crumb mixtures crushed macaroons, almond paste, rolled cake crumbs, and finely ground nuts—especially hazelnuts. Sometimes they use pecans, walnuts, almonds and, occasionally, brazil nuts. Considerably less effective—and not usually recommended—are finely chopped peanuts, coconut and cashews.

Home bakers may also add distinction to pastry fillings with a small quantity of lemon juice, grated lemon rind, dried currants, a bit of finely chopped citron; or, for piquancy, they can avoid more solid fillings altogether and substitute a thin layer of jam or marmalade. Fillings are added to doughs during the final shaping and last rising. A 9-inch ring needs a cup or a little more of filling, individual rolls about 2 teaspoons. For various toppings and glazes, see pages 681-683.

NUT FILLINGS FOR COFFEE CAKES
I.   For One 9-Inch Ring
If made with almonds, this is known as Edelweiss.
Cream:
   ½ cup confectioners' sugar
   ¼ to ½ cup butter
Stir in:
   ½ teaspoon vanilla or 1 teaspoon
      grated lemon rind
   ½ cup blanched shredded or ground
      almonds or other nuts
   (1 egg)

II.   For One 9-Inch Ring
Combine:
   ½ cup ground hazelnuts or other nuts
   ½ cup sugar
   2 teaspoons cinnamon
   ½ teaspoon vanilla
   2 tablespoons finely chopped citron
      or orange peel
Beat well and add:
   1 egg
Thin these ingredients with:
   Milk
until they are of the right consistency to spread over the dough.

III.   For One 9-Inch Ring
Chop:
   ¼ cup each blanched almonds, citron
      and raisins
Melt:
   ¼ cup butter or ⅛ cup butter and
   ⅛ cup cultured sour cream

After rolling the dough, spread it with the melted butter and the chopped ingredients.
Sprinkle with:
   (Sugar)
   (Cinnamon)

IV.   For Three 9-Inch Rings
If you buy canned almond paste to use in coffee cake fillings, mix:
   10 oz. almond paste
   1 cup sugar
   2 egg whites
Work it in a bowl placed over ice to keep it cool, so the oil in the almonds is not released.

CRUMB FRUIT FILLING
For One 9-Inch Ring
Mix well:
   ¾ cup crushed macaroons
   3 tablespoons melted butter
   2 tablespoons sugar
   ½ cup raisins or chopped dates,
      cooked prunes or grated coconut
   (¼ cup chopped nuts)

APPLE COFFEE CAKE FILLING
For Two 9-Inch Rings
Combine and boil for 4 minutes:
   2½ cups pared and chopped apples
   1 cup brown sugar
   ⅓ cup butter
   1 cup raisins
   ½ teaspoon cinnamon
   ½ teaspoon salt
Cool slightly and spread over dough.

PRUNE OR APRICOT FILLING
FOR COFFEE CAKE AND ROLLS
For One 9-Inch Ring
Combine:
   ½ cup sweetened puréed prunes
      or apricots
   2 to 4 tablespoons butter
   2 teaspoons orange or lemon rind
   (¼ cup nuts or coconut)

DATE OR FIG FILLING
FOR COFFEE CAKE
For One 9-Inch Ring
Melt and simmer about 2 minutes:
   ¼ cup butter
   ⅛ cup brown sugar
Remove from heat and stir in:
   ¾ cup chopped dates or figs
   ¼ cup almond paste
   ½ teaspoon cinnamon
      A grating of fresh nutmeg
Cool slightly before using.

POPPY SEED FILLING COCKAIGNE
For One 9-Inch Ring
This filling is for that special occasion.
Grind or crush in a mortar:
   ½ cup poppy seeds
Put the poppy seeds in the top of a double boiler and bring to a boil with:
   ¼ cup milk

Remove pan from the heat and add:

⅓ cup brown sugar
2 tablespoons butter

Put the pan ♦ over—not in—hot water and add:

2 egg yolks

Heat until the mixture thickens, stirring constantly. When it has cooled slightly, add:

⅛ cup almond paste or ½ cup
    ground almonds
(3 tablespoons citron)
(2 teaspoons lemon juice)
(1 teaspoon vanilla)

Cool and have ready to add to strudel or use for coffee cake.

POPPY SEED OR MOHN FILLING
I.   For Two 9-Inch Rings
Mix together well:

¾ cup ground poppy seeds
¼ cup sugar
¼ cup raisins
½ cup sour cream
⅛ teaspoon cinnamon
1 teaspoon grated lemon rind

II.   For Four 9-Inch Rings
Grind or mash between towels with a wooden mallet:

2 cups poppy seeds

Mix in:

1 egg
⅓ cup honey
1 tablespoon lemon juice
¼ cup chopped nuts

III.   For One 9-Inch Ring
Grind or mash between towels with a wooden mallet:

¼ cup poppy seeds

Place in a bowl and add:

About 2 tablespoons milk

just enough to make this mixture feel buttery between your fingers. Then add:

2 tablespoons melted butter
2 tablespoons dry cake crumbs
1 teaspoon cinnamon
1 teaspoon grated lemon rind

POT-CHEESE OR RICOTTA FILLING
For One 9-Inch Coffee Cake Ring
Put through a ricer or a strainer:

1½ cups pot or Ricotta cheese

Mix well with:

¼ cup sugar
1 slightly beaten egg yolk
¼ to ½ cup raisins
2 teaspoons lemon rind

Beat until ♦ stiff, but not dry, and fold in:

1 egg white

ABOUT QUICK TEA BREADS AND COFFEE CAKES

These sweet breads are delightful but, with the exception of nut and fruit breads, should be served immediately after baking as they wither young. If you want breads that keep and reheat well, see recipes for yeast breads and yeast coffee cakes.

Nut and fruit breads are attractive baked in 6 oz. fruit juice cans so that they slice prettily for tea. If you use cans, do not fill them more than ¾ full to allow for expansion of the dough. Quick nut and fruit breads slice better if, after baking, they are wrapped in foil and refrigerated for about 12 hours.

▲ When baking quick breads at high altitudes, reduce the baking powder or soda in the recipe by ¼. ♦ But do not decrease the soda beyond ½ teaspoon for each cup of sour milk or cream used.

QUICK NUT OR DATE BREAD
A 9 x 5-Inch Loaf
Preheat oven to 350°.
♦ Have all ingredients at about 75°.
Sift into a bowl:

2 cups all-purpose flour
⅓ cup white or ½ cup brown sugar
2 teaspoons double-acting
    baking powder
1 teaspoon salt

Melt and cool slightly:

2 tablespoons butter

Beat until light:

1 egg

Beat with the egg:

1 cup milk

Add the melted butter. Beat the liquid ingredients into the sifted ones until well mixed. Fold in:

¾ cup broken nut meats or part dates
    and part nut meats

Place the dough in a greased bread pan and bake for about 40 minutes.

QUICK SALLY LUNN
A 9 x 13-Inch Pan
A light bread. For an even lighter one, try Brioche Loaf Cockaigne, page 557, or Brioche, page 566.
Preheat oven to 425°.
♦ Have all ingredients at about 75°.
Sift before measuring:

2 cups all-purpose flour

Resift with:

2¼ teaspoons double-acting
    baking powder
¾ teaspoon salt

Combine and cream well:

½ cup shortening
½ cup sugar

Beat in, one at a time:

3 eggs

Add the sifted ingredients to the batter in about 3 parts, alternately with:

1 cup milk

Stir the batter lightly ♦ until the ingredients are just blended. Bake in a greased pan for about 30 minutes. Break the bread into squares. Serve hot.

QUICK PRUNE, APRICOT OR CRANBERRY BREAD

A 9 x 5-Inch Loaf

Preheat oven to 350°.
♦ Have all ingredients at about 75°.
Sift before measuring:
   1½ cups all-purpose flour
Resift with:
   ½ teaspoon salt
   1 teaspoon soda
Add:
   1½ cups whole-grain flour
Cream:
   ¼ cup shortening
with:
   ½ cup sugar
Beat in:
   1 egg
Add:
   ¾ cup unsweetened, cooked, mashed
      prune, apricot or cranberry pulp
   ¼ cup prune, apricot or cranberry juice
Add the sifted ingredients alternately to
the butter mixture with:
   1 cup buttermilk
Stir the batter ♦ with a few swift strokes,
until just blended. Fold in:
   1 cup broken nut meats
   Grated rind of 1 orange
Place the dough in a greased loaf pan.
Bake the bread for about 1¼ hours. Let it
cool in the pan.

QUICK ORANGE BREAD

Two 8½ x 4½-Inch Loaves

This is an economical, easily made tea
bread. If you want a quick treat, break it
apart and eat it while hot, with or without
lots of good butter. If you intend it for
sandwiches bake it in cans, see About
Quick Tea Breads, page 574. You'll find
it easier to slice on the second day.
Preheat oven to 350°.
♦ Have all ingredients at about 75°.
I. Sift, then measure:
   3 cups all-purpose flour
Resift it into a large bowl with:
   3 teaspoons double-acting
      baking powder
Combine and add:
   1 tablespoon grated orange rind
   ½ to ¾ cup sugar
For a more cakelike result, use the larger
amount of sugar. Combine and beat:
   1 egg
   ¼ cup orange juice
   1¼ cups milk
   2 tablespoons melted shortening
You may add:
   1 cup chopped or broken nut meats
Pour the liquid mixture into the bowl.
Combine all ingredients with a few swift
strokes. Stir lightly until barely blended.
Bake the bread in two greased loaf pans
for about 50 minutes or until done.

II.   Two 8½ x 4½-Inch Loaves
        or 3 Round Cans That Hold 1¾ Cups

Fill the cans only ¾ full. Parboil 3 times,
for 10 minutes each time:
   Rind of 3 navel oranges
Then cut them into strips, as for marmalade, and cook them with:
   1 cup water
   ½ cup sugar
until almost dry. Cool.
Preheat oven to 350°.
Cream:
   1 cup sugar
   3 tablespoons butter
Add:
   1 beaten egg
Sift together:
   3 cups sifted all-purpose flour
   3 teaspoons double-acting
      baking powder
   1 teaspoon salt
and add it alternately to the creamed ingredients with:
   1 cup milk
until the mixture is smooth. Fold in the
orange rinds and bake for about 1 hour in
greased pans or cans.

QUICK BANANA BREAD

An 8½ x 4½-Inch Loaf

Preheat oven to 350°.
♦ Have all ingredients at about 75°.
Sift before measuring:
   1¾ cups all-purpose flour
Resift with:
   2¼ teaspoons double acting
      baking powder
   ½ teaspoon salt
Blend until creamy:
   ⅓ cup shortening
   ⅔ cup sugar
   ¾ teaspoon grated lemon rind
Beat in:
   1 to 2 beaten eggs
   1-1¼ cups ripe banana pulp
Add the sifted ingredients in about 3 parts
to the sugar mixture. Beat the batter after
each addition until smooth. Fold in:
   (½ cup broken nut meats)
   (¼ cup finely chopped apricots)
Place the batter in a greased bread pan.
Bake the bread for about 1 hour or until
done. Cool before slicing.

QUICK BANANA WHEAT-GERM BREAD

Prepare:
   Banana Bread, above
Use in all:
   1½ cups all-purpose flour
Add:
   ¼ cup wheat germ

QUICK IRISH SODA BREAD

A 9 x 5-Inch Loaf

Preheat oven to 375°.
♦ Have all ingredients at about 75°.
Sift together in a large bowl:
   2 cups sifted all-purpose flour
   ¾ teaspoon baking soda
   ½ teaspoon salt

1 tablespoon sugar

Cut into the flour mixture with a pastry blender, until of the consistency of coarse corn meal:

6 tablespoons chilled shortening

Stir in:

½ to 1 cup raisins
1 tablespoon caraway seeds

Add gradually:

½ to ⅔ cup buttermilk

The mixture should not be dry   Knead briefly and shape into a round loaf or a 9 x 5-inch one. Put the dough in a greased bread pan. Cut a bold cross on top, letting it go over the sides so the bread will not crack in baking. Brush the top with:

Milk

Bake for 40 to 50 minutes. To test for doneness, see page 555.

To bake ▤ outdoors, see Skillet Bread, page 578.

QUICK SWEET WHOLE-WHEAT BREAD

A 9 x 5-Inch Loaf

A "homely" coarse sweet bread, good served with fruit salads and cottage cheese.

Preheat oven to 375°.

◗ Have all ingredients at about 75°.

Mix:

2½ cups whole-wheat flour
½ teaspoon cinnamon
¼ teaspoon salt
1 teaspoon soda

Combine:

1 beaten egg
½ cup molasses
¼ cup brown sugar
¼ cup sesame, peanut or safflower oil
1 teaspoon grated lemon
or orange peel

Add the egg mixture, alternately with:

⅔ cup yogurt

to the dry ingredients. Pour into a buttered pan and bake for about 50 minutes.

QUICK BRAN BREAD WITH MOLASSES

Two 8½ x 4½-Inch Loaves

Preheat oven to 375°.

◗ Have all ingredients at about 75°.

Combine:

2 cups bran
2 cups whole-grain flour
2 teaspoons double-acting
baking powder
1 teaspoon salt
1 teaspoon soda

Combine and beat:

1 egg
1¾ cups sour milk or buttermilk
½ cup molasses or ¾ cup packed
brown sugar

Beat in the dry ingredients. You may add:

1 cup raisins, figs or nut meats

Place the batter in 2 greased pans. Bake for 1 hour or more.

QUICK BRAN DATE BREAD OR MUFFINS

Two 8½ x 4½-Inch Loaves

Preheat oven to 350°.

◗ Have all ingredients at about 75°.

Prepare:

2 cups chopped dates

Pour over them:

2 cups boiling water

In a separate bowl, beat until light:

2 eggs

Add slowly, beating constantly:

¾ cup brown sugar or
½ cup molasses

When these ingredients are creamy, sift in:

1 cup whole-grain flour
2 teaspoons double-acting
baking powder
1 teaspoon soda

Add ½ the date mixture and:

1 cup whole-grain flour
2 cups bran
1 teaspoon vanilla

Add the remaining date mixture and:

1 cup or less chopped nut meats

Place the dough in a lightly greased loaf pan or greased muffin tins. Bake for about 1 hour.

ALMOND BRAN BREAD

A 9 x 5-Inch Loaf

This makes a one-inch-high loaf.

Preheat oven to 325°.

◗ Have all ingredients at about 75°.

Beat until light:

2 egg yolks

Cream with:

2 tablespoons butter

Grind in a nut grinder and mix in:

1 cup finely ground blanched almonds
1 teaspoon double-acting
baking powder

Fold in:

2 tablespoons bran
2 stiffly beaten egg whites

Pour batter into greased bread loaf pan and bake for about 25 minutes.

BAKED BROWN BREAD

Two 8½ x 4½-Inch Loaves

Preheat oven to 350°.

◗ Have all ingredients at about 75°.

Sift before measuring:

2 cups graham flour
1 cup all-purpose flour

Resift with:

2 tablespoons sugar
¾ teaspoon salt
1 teaspoon soda

Stir in:

1 cup buttermilk
1 cup dark molasses

You may add:

1 cup broken nut meats and/or raisins

Combine all ingredients well and bake in two greased pans or fill buttered cans ¾ full and bake about 1 hour.

BOSTON STEAMED BROWN BREAD
Two 1-Pound Loaves or
Two 1-Quart Pudding Molds
◆ Have all ingredients at about 75°.
Combine:

1 cup yellow water-ground corn meal
1 cup rye flour
1 cup graham flour
2 teaspoons soda
1 teaspoon salt

Combine in a separate bowl:

2 cups buttermilk
¾ cup molasses
1 cup chopped raisins

Add the liquid to the dry ingredients. Pour the batter into 2 buttered one-quart pudding molds or fill buttered cans about ¾ full. Butter the lids before closing molds and tie the lids or tape them on, so rising bread does not break the seal. ◆ Steam 3 hours in one inch water if not using a pressure cooker. ❷ Otherwise, add 2 cups hot water to the pressure cooker. Adjust cover. Steam over low heat for 15 minutes without pressure, that is, with the valve open. Then cook for 30 minutes at 15 pounds pressure. Reduce heat instantly. To cut without crumbling, use a tough string and slice with a sawing motion.

QUICK COFFEE CAKE
A 9 x 9-Inch Pan
Preheat oven to 375°.
◆ Have all ingredients at about 75°.
Sift before measuring:

1½ cups all-purpose flour

Resift with:

¼ teaspoon salt
2 teaspoons double-acting
baking powder

Sift:

¼ to ½ cup sugar

Cream until soft:

¼ cup butter

Add the sugar gradually and cream these ingredients until light. Beat in:

1 egg
⅔ cup milk

Add the sifted ingredients to the butter mixture. Add:

(¾ teaspoon grated lemon rind or
½ teaspoon vanilla)

Stir the batter until smooth. Spread in a greased pan and bake for about 25 minutes. Cover with a Streusel, page 681.

QUICK KUGELHOPF
A 7-Inch Tube Pan
Preheat oven to 350°.
◆ Have all ingredients at about 75°.
Sift before measuring:

3½ cups all-purpose flour

Resift with:

3 teaspoons double-acting
baking powder
½ teaspoon salt

Cream until soft:

1 cup butter

Add gradually:

1 cup sifted sugar

Cream until very light. Beat in, one at a time:

5 eggs

Add the sifted ingredients to the butter mixture in 3 parts, alternately with thirds of:

1 cup milk

Stir the batter until smooth after each addition. Add:

1 cup seedless raisins
1 teaspoon grated lemon rind
1 teaspoon vanilla

Bake the cake in a greased tube pan for about 45 to 50 minutes. When cool, sprinkle with:

Confectioners' sugar

QUICK SOUR CREAM COFFEE CAKE
A 9 x 9-Inch Pan
Made on a muffin principle, this cake is wonderfully good and easy.
Preheat oven to 350°.
◆ Have all ingredients at about 75°.
Sift before measuring:

1½ cups all-purpose flour

Resift with:

1 cup sugar
2 teaspoons double-acting
baking powder
½ teaspoon soda
¼ teaspoon salt

Combine and beat well:

1 cup cultured sour cream
2 eggs

Add the sifted ingredients to the cream mixture. Beat until smooth. Spread in a lightly greased pan. Sprinkle with:

Streusel, page 681

Bake for about 20 minutes.

QUICK, RICH, MOIST COFFEE CAKE
A 9 x 13-Inch Pan
Preheat oven to 350°.
◆ Have all ingredients at about 75°.
Sift together:

2 cups all-purpose flour
¾ cup sugar
2 teaspoons double-acting
baking powder
½ teaspoon salt

Cut in:

½ cup butter

Break into a measuring cup:

1 egg

Fill with:

Milk

enough to make 1 cup. Beat and add to the dry ingredients with:

1 teaspoon vanilla

Pour batter into a greased pan and cover with:

Honey Bee Glaze, page 682

Bake about 25 minutes.

QUICK SPICE COFFEE CAKE WITH OIL

An 8 x 8 x 2½-Inch Pan
Preheat oven to 350°.
◗ Have all ingredients at about 75°.
Combine in a mixing bowl:

2 cups sifted all-purpose flour
⅔ cup sugar
¾ teaspoon each baking powder
   and soda
½ teaspoon salt
½ teaspoon freshly grated nutmeg
1 teaspoon cinnamon

Combine in another bowl and mix well:

½ cup vegetable oil
1 beaten egg
½ cup buttermilk or yogurt
⅓ cup corn sirup: light or dark
¾ cup raisins

Pour this into the flour mixture, stirring rapidly until blended. All the lumps need not have vanished. Pour into a greased pan and cover the top with:

Topping for Coffee Cake I, page 573

Bake the cake about 35 minutes or until done.

EGGLESS, ALL RYE, HONEY CAKE COCKAIGNE

One 4½ x 8-Inch Loaf
Like a soft, deliciously spiced **Lebkuchen**, this confection keeps for weeks. It also toasts well for tea. Age it three days or more in a plastic bag or tin box before eating.
Preheat oven to 350°.
◗ Have all ingredients at about 75°.
Heat in the top of a double boiler until small bubbles appear through the mixture:

⅓ cup honey
¾ cup water
½ cup sugar

Remove from the heat and beat into the following mixture:

2 cups very finely milled rye flour
½ teaspoon soda
2 teaspoons double-acting
   baking powder
1 tablespoon cinnamon
½ teaspoon each cloves and allspice
⅛ teaspoon cardamon

Beat 10 minutes in an electric beater. When thoroughly amalgamated, beat in:

¼ cup pecans or blanched
   shredded almonds
1 tablespoon grated orange rind
¼ to ½ cup finely chopped citron

Place a pan of water on the bottom shelf of the oven. Bake the cake for about 1 hour.

SKILLET OR GRIDDLE BREADS
Prepare:

Irish Soda Bread, page 575, or
Skillet Corn Bread, below

Either one of these simple doughs will make acceptable, even good skillet bread on an open fire ▤ especially over charcoal. But our results on these heats did not com-

pare in quality with those obtained when the same recipes were oven-baked. Bake them covered. If you prefer **Irish Farls**, cut the bread in triangular wedges, about 1 inch thick and bake them on a griddle heated to about 370° and lightly rubbed with oil. Allow about 10 minutes for one side, turn and allow 10 minutes more.

ABOUT CORN BREADS

Anyone who grew up on Southern corn breads hankers for a rich brown crust and a light but slightly gritty bite. We can assure you that without water-ground corn meal and a heavy, hot pan, your end product will be pale and lifeless. For a very crisp crust, grease the pan well and heat it by itself first in a 425° oven. Whether you bake as muffins, sticks or bread, you may vary the corn and wheat proportion within a 2 cup limit to your own taste. We like 1¼ cups corn meal to ¾ cup all-purpose flour.

▲ When baking corn breads at high altitudes, reduce the baking powder or soda by ¼. ◗ But do not reduce soda beyond ½ teaspoon for each cup of sour milk or cream used.

CORN BREAD, MUFFINS OR STICKS

A 9 x 9-Inch Pan, or
About Fifteen 2-Inch Muffins
Preheat oven to 425°.
◗ Have all ingredients at about 75°.
Grease the pan with butter, oil or bacon drippings. Place it in the oven until sizzling hot. Sift together:

¾ cup sifted all-purpose flour
2½ teaspoons double-acting
   baking powder
1 to 2 tablespoons sugar
¾ teaspoon salt

Add:

1¼ cups yellow or white water-ground
   corn meal

Beat in a separate bowl:

1 egg

Beat into it:

2 to 3 tablespoons melted butter
   or drippings
1 cup milk

Pour the liquid into the dry ingredients. Combine with a few rapid strokes. Place the batter in the hot pan. Bake for about 25 minutes.

SKILLET CORN BREAD
Follow the rule for:

Corn Bread above

▤ Cook it in a 10-inch covered skillet for about ½ hour or until done. You may add to the dough about:

¼ to ½ cup cooked ham or bacon bits

BUTTERMILK CRACKLING CORN BREAD

A 9 x 9-Inch Pan or
Twenty 2-Inch Muffins

Preheat oven to 425°.
◗ Have all ingredients at about 75°
Sift, then measure:
   1 cup all-purpose flour
Resift with:
   ½ teaspoon soda
   1½ teaspoons double-acting
      baking powder
   1 tablespoon sugar
   1 teaspoon salt
Add:
   ¾ cup yellow water-ground corn meal
Combine and beat:
   1 cup buttermilk
   2 eggs
   3 to 4 tablespoons melted butter
      or bacon fat
Stir the liquid into the dry ingredients
with a few swift strokes. You may add:
   ¼ cup salt pork cracklings
Pour the batter into a preheated greased
pan and bake the bread for about ½ hour.

CORN ZEPHYRS COCKAIGNE
About Twenty 2-Inch Puffs

In our endless search for the best recipe of
its type, we welcomed the offer of a Southern acquaintance to send us the Zephyr
recipe she was raving about. It arrived,
and was word for word our own favorite
Zephyr recipe in "The Joy." We consider
this the highest of compliments. These
puffs are delicate and delicious with a salad
course or luncheon dish.
◗ Have all ingredients at about 75°.
Combine:
   1 cup white water-ground corn meal
   1 tablespoon lard
Scald these ingredients by pouring over
them:
   4 cups boiling water
Add:
   1 teaspoon salt
Cook the corn meal in a double boiler for
30 minutes, stirring frequently. Before
cooling it, butter the top slightly to keep it
from crusting. Cool. Preheat oven to 350°.
Whip until stiff:
   4 egg whites
Fold them lightly into the corn meal mixture. Drop the batter from a teaspoon
onto a greased baking sheet. Bake for
about ½ hour.

GOLDEN CORN PUFFS
About Twenty 2-Inch Puffs

Preheat oven to 425°.
◗ Have all ingredients at about 75°.
Pour:
   2¼ cups boiling water
over:
   1 cup yellow water-ground corn meal
Add:
   1 tablespoon sugar
   1 teaspoon salt
   2 tablespoons butter
Cook and stir over low heat until you obtain a thick mush. Cool. Beat in:

   2 beaten egg yolks
Beat until stiff, then fold in:
   2 egg whites
Drop the batter from a teaspoon onto a
hot buttered pan. Bake the puffs for about
20 minutes.

CORN MEAL CRACKLES
About 20

Preheat oven to 350°.
Combine and stir well:
   1 cup yellow corn meal
   ½ cup sifted all-purpose flour
   ¼ teaspoon salt
   ¼ teaspoon soda
   ⅛ teaspoon paprika
   2 tablespoons bacon fat, oil or
      other shortening
   ⅓ cup milk
Knead the dough for about 10 minutes.
Roll it into 1-inch balls, flatten them well
by rolling them or slapping them between
the palms of your hands, Mexican-tortilla
fashion. They should be paper thin. Bake
on an ungreased sheet for about 15 minutes. While hot, brush with:
   1 tablespoon butter
Sprinkle with:
   Salt
Cool on a rack.

CORN DODGERS
About 24

Preheat oven to 400°.
Combine:
   1 cup water-ground corn meal
   1 teaspoon salt
   1½ teaspoons sugar
   1 to 2 tablespoons butter or
      bacon drippings
Pour over the dry ingredients and stir:
   1 cup boiling water
Beat in:
   (1 beaten egg)
Beat until blended. Drop the batter from
a spoon onto a greased sheet or dip your
hand in cold water, fill it with batter and
reverse the hand, releasing the batter
"splat" on the sheet. The hand method
was learned from our Sarah, who, as a
child, helped her father make dodgers at
the Kentucky Derby. Bake for about 20
minutes.

CRUSTY OR SOFT-CENTER
SPOON BREAD
4 Servings

Preheat oven to 375°.
Combine, then sift:
   ½ cup yellow corn meal
   ¼ cup all-purpose flour
   1 tablespoon sugar
   ¾ teaspoon salt
   1 teaspoon double-acting
      baking powder
Stir in:
   1 beaten egg
   1 cup milk

Beat until well blended. Melt in an 8 x 8-inch baking dish:

    2 tablespoons butter

Pour in the batter. Pour over the top:

    ½ cup milk

Place in the oven. Bake for 45 minutes or more, until good and crusty.

CORN OR RICE SPOON BREAD
                6 Servings

In Italy, bits of cooked ham and cooked seafood are added to the batter, which is baked until very crisp.

Preheat oven to 325°.

Combine in the order given, then stir until blended:

    1 cup boiled rice or boiled corn meal
    ¼ cup corn meal
    2 cups buttermilk
    ½ teaspoon soda
    1 teaspoon salt
    2 beaten eggs
    2 tablespoons melted fat or butter

Place the batter in a greased ovenproof dish. Bake for about 1 hour. This is good with a meat course or served as a main dish with:

    Mushroom Sauce, page 327, or
    Tomatoes Provençale, page 305

HUSH PUPPIES
    About Twelve 2½-Inch Puppies

Fishermen cooked these finger-shaped concoctions at their fish fries. Rumor has it that they threw the fatty bits as a sop to the dogs with the exclamation, "Hush, puppy!" Maybe this is still the best use for them.

Mix together:

    1 cup water-ground corn meal
    ½ teaspoon double-acting
      baking powder
    ½ teaspoon salt
    2 tablespoons minced onion

Beat together:

    1 egg
    ¼ cup milk

Combine with dry ingredients and form into finger-shaped patties. Deep fry, see page 124, at 370° until golden brown. Drain on absorbent paper and serve at once.

ABOUT MUFFINS

Muffin batters are easily made. ♦ To mix, add the beaten liquid ingredients to the sifted, combined dry ones in a few swift strokes. ♦ The mixing is held to an abso-lute minimum, a light stirring of from 10 to 20 seconds, which will leave some lumps. Ignore them. The dough should not be mixed to the point of pouring, rib-bonlike, from the spoon, but should break in coarse globs. If the batter has been beaten too long, the gluten in the flour will develop and toughen the dough. The grain of the muffin will be coarse and full of tunnels, as shown in the drawing on the right.

Good muffins should be straight-sided and slightly rounded on top, as shown on the left. The grain of the muffin is not fine but uniform and the crumb is moist. The center drawings show, first the weary muf-fin peak caused by oven heat that is too slow. The next drawing shows the cracked, wobbly-peaked, unsymmetrical form caused by oven heat that is too high.

To bake, fill well-greased tins about ⅔ full. Should the dough not fill every muf-fin cup, put a few tablespoons of water in the empty forms, both to protect the pans and to keep the rest of the muffins moist. Unless a different indication is given in the individual recipe ♦ bake at once in a pre-heated 400° oven for 20 to 25 minutes. ♦ If muffins remain in the tins a few mo-ments after leaving the oven, they will be easier to remove. They are really best eaten at once. If you must reheat them, enclose them loosely in foil and heat about 5 minutes in a preheated 450° oven.

ADDITIONS TO MUFFINS

Muffins may be enriched by these addi-tions, but have them all ready and beat them in so that the total beating time agrees exactly with the one described above.

I.
      ¼ to ½ cup nuts, riced apricots,
        prunes, dates, figs, alone or
        in combination
      ½ cup mashed ripe bananas or
        chopped apples
      ½ cup very well drained crushed
        pineapple
      6 to 8 slices cooked, crumbled bacon

II.
      2 tablespoons milk solids, replacing
        2 tablespoons flour

III.
      2 teaspoons brewer's yeast

MUFFINS
About 2 Dozen 2-Inch Muffins
Preheat oven to 400°.
◖ Have all ingredients at about 75°.
Sift before measuring:
   2 cups cake flour or 1¾ cups
      all-purpose flour
Resift with:
   ¾ teaspoon salt
   ¼ cup sugar
   2 teaspoons double-acting
      baking powder
Beat in a separate bowl:
   2 eggs
Combine and add:
   2 to 4 tablespoons melted butter
   ¾ cup milk
◖ To mix and bake, see About Muffins,
page 580.

SOUR CREAM MUFFINS
About 2 Dozen 2-Inch Muffins
Preheat oven to 400°.
◖ Have all ingredients at about 75°.
Sift before measuring:
   2 cups cake flour or 1¾ cups
      all-purpose flour
Resift with:
   1 teaspoon double-acting
      baking powder
   ½ teaspoon salt
   2 tablespoons sugar
   ½ teaspoon soda
Measure:
   1 cup cultured sour cream
Combine with:
   1 beaten egg
◖ To mix and bake, see About Muffins,
page 580.

BUTTERMILK MUFFINS
Prepare:
   Sour Cream Muffins, above
Substitute for the sour cream:
   1 cup buttermilk
Add to the milk:
   3 tablespoons melted butter

WHOLE-GRAIN MUFFINS
Twenty 2-Inch Muffins
Preheat oven to 400°.
◖ Have all ingredients at about 75°.
Combine:
   ⅔ cup sifted all-purpose flour
   1⅛ cups whole-grain flour
   2 tablespoons molasses
   1 teaspoon salt
   2 teaspoons double-acting
      baking powder
   (¼ cup chopped dates or raisins)
You may omit the all-purpose flour and
use instead 1½ cups whole-grain flour.
Beat in a separate bowl:
   (1 egg)
Beat in:
   1 cup milk
   2 to 3 teaspoons melted butter
◖ To mix and bake, see About Muffins,
page 580.

EGGLESS GRAHAM MUFFINS
Twenty 2-Inch Muffins
Preheat oven to 400°.
◖ Have all ingredients at about 75°.
Sift before measuring:
   1 cup all-purpose flour
Resift with:
   ¼ cup sugar
   ½ teaspoon salt
   1 teaspoon soda
   ¾ teaspoon double-acting
      baking powder
Add:
   1½ cups graham flour
In a separate bowl beat:
   (2 eggs)
The eggs are optional. They add richness
and flavor, but the muffins are crisp and
good without them. Add and beat in:
   3 tablespoons melted butter
   1½ cups buttermilk or yogurt
Combine the liquid and the dry ingredients with a few swift strokes. ◖ To mix
and bake, see About Muffins, page 580.

BRAN MUFFINS
About Twenty-Two 2-Inch Muffins
These muffins are rather hefty. Served
with cheese, they make excellent picnic
companions.
Preheat oven to 350°.
◖ Have all ingredients at about 75°.
Combine and stir well:
   2 cups all-purpose or whole-grain flour
   1½ cups bran
   2 tablespoons sugar
   ¼ teaspoon salt
   1¼ teaspoons soda
   (1 to 2 tablespoons grated orange rind)
Beat:
   2 cups buttermilk
   1 beaten egg
   ½ cup molasses
   2 to 4 tablespoons melted butter
Combine the dry and the liquid ingredients
with a few swift strokes. Fold in, before
the dry ingredients are entirely moist:
   1 cup nut meats or nut meats and
      raisins combined
   (½ cup mashed bananas)
Bake about 25 minutes.

RICE FLOUR MUFFINS
About Two Dozen 2-Inch Muffins
As these muffins need special handling,
please read ◖ About Rice Flour, page 499,
and About Muffins, page 580.
Preheat oven to 450°.
◖ Have all ingredients at about 75°.
Measure into a bowl:
   1 cup rice flour
   ½ teaspoon salt
   2 teaspoons double-acting
      baking powder
   (1 to 2 tablespoons sugar)
Melt:
   2 tablespoons shortening
and, when slightly cooled, add it to:

1 well-beaten egg
1 cup milk

Mix the dry ingredients well and then with a few light strokes combine with the liquid mixture. About 10 strokes are all that is necessary. The muffins are less crumbly if you add to them, before the dry ingredients are completely moistened:

⅛ cup raisins or 2 tablespoons orange
   or pineapple marmalade

If you omit the marmalade, omit the sugar. Bake 12 to 15 minutes and serve at once.

COOKED-CEREAL MUFFINS
About Thirty 2-Inch Muffins

A good way of utilizing leftover cereals or rice.
Preheat oven to 400°.
Beat:

2 egg yolks

Add:

1 cup cooked rice, oatmeal or
   cornmeal
1¼ cups milk
2 tablespoons melted butter

Sift before measuring:

1½ cups all-purpose flour

Resift with:

1 tablespoon sugar
½ teaspoon salt
2 teaspoons double-acting
   baking powder

Beat until stiff:

2 egg whites

Combine the liquid and the dry ingredients with a few swift strokes, then fold in the egg whites. To bake, see About Muffins, page 580.

CHEESE MUFFINS
About Thirty-Two 2-Inch Muffins

Preheat oven to 350°.
♦ Have all ingredients at about 75°.
Sift before measuring:

2 cups cake flour or 1¾ cups
   all-purpose flour

Resift with:

3 teaspoons double-acting
   baking powder
1 tablespoon sugar
½ teaspoon salt

Stir into the sifted ingredients, until all the particles of cheese have been separated:

¼ to ½ cup grated American cheese

Combine and beat well:

1 egg
1 cup milk
3 tablespoons melted butter

♦ To mix and bake, see About Muffins, page 580.

BLUEBERRY OR CRANBERRY MUFFINS
About Thirty 2-Inch Muffins

Preheat oven to 400°.

♦ Have all ingredients at about 75°.
Prepare:

Muffins, page 581

Use in all:

⅛ cup sugar
¼ cup melted butter

Fold into the batter, before the dry ingredients are completely moist:

1 cup fresh blueberries, 1 cup canned,
   well-drained blueberries, lightly
   floured or 1 cup chopped cranberries
(1 teaspoon grated orange or
   lemon rind)

♦ To mix and bake, see About Muffins, page 580.

POPOVERS
About 9 Popovers

Everyone enthusiastically gives us a favorite popover recipe and is equally enthusiastic, but contradictory, about baking advice. We prefer a preheated 450° oven. Popovers, like soufflés, need bottom heat only, so be sure ♦ if your oven is the type that supplies top heat when set on Bake, to remove the upper heating element. Have ready buttered deep muffin or popover tins. If you use highly glazed deep custard cups, grease them lightly and—depending on what you are serving with the popovers—dust the cups with sugar, flour or grated Parmesan cheese. This will give the egg something to cling to. ♦ Have all ingredients at about 75°.
Beat just until smooth:

1 cup milk
1 tablespoon melted butter
1 cup all-purpose flour
¼ teaspoon salt

Add, one at a time, but ♦ do not overbeat:

2 eggs

The batter should be no heavier than whipping cream. Fill the buttered deep bakers ¾ full. Don't overload—too much batter in the pans will give a muffinlike texture. ♦ Bake at once. After 15 minutes, lower the heat ♦ without peeping, to 350° and bake about 20 minutes longer. To test for doneness, remove a popover to be sure the side walls are firm. If not cooked long enough, the popovers will collapse. You may want to insert a sharp paring knife gently into the other popovers to allow the steam to escape, after baking.

WHOLE-GRAIN POPOVERS

Prepare:

Popovers, above

Substitute for the flour:

⅔ cup fine whole-grain flour
⅓ cup all-purpose flour

CHEESE POPOVERS

Preheat oven to 450°.
Prepare:

Popovers, above

Grate into a separate bowl:

½ cup sharp cheddar or
   Parmesan cheese

Add:

**⅛ teaspoon paprika
A few grains cayenne**

Pour 1 scant tablespoon of batter into each cup and cover it with a few teaspoons of cheese and another tablespoon of batter. To bake, see Popovers, page 582.

ABOUT HOT BISCUITS

Now, as in pioneer times, biscuits are popular for the speed with which they can be made. A light hand in kneading gives the treasured flaky result. The amount of liquid called for in the recipe determines if the biscuit is a rolled or dropped type. ♦ Use shortening and liquids at a temperature of about 70°. The solid shortening, preferably part lard, is ♦ cut into the dry ingredients with a pastry blender or 2 knives, until the mixture is of the consistency of coarse corn meal. Make a well in the center of these ingredients. ♦ Pour all the milk or milk and water in, at once. Stir cautiously until there is no danger of spilling, then stir vigorously until the dough is fairly free from the sides of the bowl. The time for stirring should be a scant ½ minute. Turn the dough onto a lightly floured board. ♦ Knead the dough gently and quickly for another scant ½ minute—just long enough so the dough is neither knobby nor sticky and until the riser is well distributed. If it isn't, or if soda is used in excess, tiny brown spots will show on the surface of the baked biscuits. Roll the dough with a lightly floured rolling pin or pat it gently with the palm of the hand until it has the desired thickness—about ¼ inch is right for a plain biscuit, ½ inch or less for a tea biscuit and 1 inch or more for shortcake. Cut the dough in typical rounds, with a biscuit cutter that has been lightly dipped in flour. Do not twist the cutter.

There are many ways to shape biscuit dough. For easy filled biscuits, pat 2 thin squares of dough. Put a filling on the first. Cover with the second. Glaze the top with milk. Cut into smaller squares. For a breakfast ring, see Quick Drop Biscuits, page 583. Make for the children Biscuit Easter Bunnies, page 585. You may also place small rounds of dough on top of a casserole, cut dough in sticks for hors l'oeuvre or fill as for Pin Wheels, page 565. Use a spatula to place these on an ungreased baking sheet.

For a brown finish, brush the tops of the biscuits with milk or butter. Place biscuits 1 inch apart if you like them crusty all over, close together if not. Bake in a ♦ 450° preheated oven for about 12 to 15 minutes, depending on their thickness. To reheat, see page 562.

▲ At high altitude, baking powder biscuits should require no adjustment of leavening.

ADDITIONS TO BISCUITS

Biscuit flavors are easily varied to suit the menu. Dust them, before baking, with:

Cinnamon and sugar

or, just before they are finished, with:

Grated Parmesan and paprika

Or, press into the top center:

1 lump sugar

soaked in:

Orange juice

Or incorporate into the dough:

**2 tablespoons finely chopped parsley or chives or 2 teaspoons finely chopped fresh sage or ⅓ cup Roquefort or cheddar cheese
3 to 6 slices cooked, crumbled bacon or 3 tablespoons chopped cooked ham or 4 tablespoons sautéed chopped onions**

Prepare them like rissoles, placing between the layers either of the following:

**1 cup fresh, sugared strawberries, raspberries or blueberries
¼ cup nuts, dates or figs
½ cup raisins or currants
1 cup cooked, ground and seasoned meat, poultry, sausage or ham**

ROLLED BISCUITS
About Twenty-Four 1½-Inch Biscuits

♦ Please read About Hot Biscuits, this page.
Preheat oven to 450°.
Sift before measuring:

2 cups cake flour or 1¾ cups all-purpose or whole-wheat flour

Resift the cake flour, or mix the whole wheat flour in a bowl with:

**1 teaspoon salt
2½ teaspoons double-acting baking powder**

Add:

2 to 6 tablespoons chilled butter or shortening or a combination of both

Cut solid shortening into dry ingredients with a pastry blender until the mixture is of the consistency of coarse corn meal. Make a well in the center of these ingredients. Add, all at once:

⅔ to ¾ cup milk

Stir until the dough is fairly free from the sides of the bowl. The time for stirring should be a scant ½ minute. Turn the dough onto a lightly floured board. Knead gently and quickly for a scant ½ minute, making about 8 to 10 folds. Roll with a lightly floured rolling pin, until the dough has the desired thickness. Cut with a biscuit cutter dipped in a very little flour. ♦ Cut straight down with the cutter and be careful not to twist it. Brush the tops of the biscuits with:

(Milk or melted butter)

Place on an ungreased baking sheet. **Bake** until done—12 to 15 minutes.

QUICK DROP BISCUITS

No kneading or rolling is necessary in these recipes. The biscuits are very palatable but less shapely, unless you drop them into muffin tins. For a good breakfast ring, bake the Drop Biscuit I, below, at 400° for about 25 minutes. Form the dough into 12 balls, roll them in melted butter. Bake them in a 7-inch ring mold, into the bottom of which you have poured Caramel Roll Topping, page 682.

I. Preheat oven to 450°.
Prepare:
    Rolled Biscuits, page 583
using in all:
    1 cup milk
♦ Stir the dough for 1 scant minute. Drop onto an ungreased sheet and bake 12 to 15 minutes or until lightly browned.

II.   About Twenty-Four 1½-Inch Biscuits
If, for some reason, you must use oil, it is preferable to flavor the biscuit highly. See Additions to Biscuits, page 583.
Preheat oven to 475°.
Sift into a bowl:
    2 cups sifted all-purpose flour
    3 teaspoons double-acting
      baking powder
    1 teaspoon salt
Pour over the top, all at once, without mixing:
    ⅓ cup cooking oil
    ⅔ cup milk
Stir with a fork until the mixture leaves the sides of the bowl readily and can be formed into a ball. It may now be dropped from a spoon onto an ungreased sheet. Bake for about 10 to 12 minutes.

BISCUIT STICKS
Prepare any recipe for:
    Rolled biscuit dough
Cut it into sticks ½ inch thick, ½ inch wide, 3 inches long. Brush the sticks with:
    Melted butter
Bake them and stack them log-cabin fashion.

BUTTERMILK BISCUITS
             About Twenty-Four 1½-Inch Biscuits
This recipe, because of the sour milk and soda, has a very tender dough. ♦ To mix, please read About Hot Biscuits, page 583.
Preheat oven to 450°.
Sift before measuring:
    2 cups cake flour or 1¾ cups
      all-purpose flour
    1 teaspoon salt
    2 teaspoons double-acting
      baking powder
    1 teaspoon sugar
    ½ teaspoon soda
Cut in:
    ¼ cup lard or 5 tablespoons butter
Add, as directed:
    ⅔ to ¾ cup buttermilk
After lightly mixing, turn the dough onto a floured board. Knead it lightly for ½ minute. Pat the dough to the thickness of ¼

inch. Cut with a biscuit cutter. Bake from 10 to 12 minutes.

WHIPPED CREAM BISCUITS
             About Eighteen 2-Inch Biscuits
Preheat oven to 450°.
Sift before measuring:
    2 cups all-purpose flour
Resift with:
    2¼ teaspoons double-acting
      baking powder
    ¾ teaspoon salt
Whip until stiff:
    1 cup whipping cream
Fold lightly into the flour mixture, using a fork. Turn the dough onto a floured board. Knead it lightly for ½ minute. Pat to the thickness of ¼ inch. Cut with a biscuit cutter. Bake from 10 to 12 minutes.

FLUFFY BISCUITS OR
SHORTCAKE DOUGH
             About Twenty-Four 1½-Inch Biscuits
For other shortcakes, see Index. ♦ To mix, see About Hot Biscuits, page 583.
Preheat oven to 450°.
Sift before measuring:
    2 cups cake flour or 1¾ cups
      all-purpose flour
Resift with:
    2½ teaspoons double-acting
      baking powder
    1¼ teaspoons salt
    1 tablespoon sugar
Cut in, as directed:
    ⅛ to ¼ cup butter
Add:
    ¾ cup milk or cream
Stir lightly into the flour mixture, using a fork. Turn dough onto a floured board. Knead lightly for ½ minute. Pat to the thickness of ¼ inch. Cut with a biscuit cutter. Bake for 10 to 12 minutes.

PINEAPPLE BISCUITS
Preheat oven to 450°.
Prepare:
    Fluffy Biscuits, above
Use part rich milk and part:
    Canned pineapple juice
Dent the top of each biscuit. Fill the depression with:
    Drained, canned, crushed pineapple
Sprinkle lightly with:
    Confectioners' sugar
Bake for 15 or 20 minutes.

PINWHEEL BISCUITS
Use this same form also for other fillings such as meat or cheese.
Preheat oven to 450°.
Prepare any:
    Rolled biscuit dough
Roll it to the thickness of ½ inch. Spread the surface with:
    ¼ cup soft butter
    ¾ cup brown sugar
    (Chopped nuts)
    (Chopped raisins)

Roll the dough like a jelly roll, but rather loosely. Cut into 1-inch slices. Lift them carefully with a pancake turner onto a lightly greased cookie sheet. Bake about 12 minutes.

BISCUIT EASTER BUNNIES

Preheat oven to 425°.

Prepare:

Fluffy Biscuits, page 584

Pat or roll out the dough to the thickness of ½ inch. Cut it out with 3 sizes of cutters: 1—large, about 3 inches; 2—½ as large, and 3—¼ as large. Assemble your bunnies as sketched below. Use the large biscuit for the body, the second one for the head and roll the third one into a ball for the tail. Flatten some of the second-size biscuits slightly and shape them into ovals for the ears. Place the bunnies on a greased sheet. Bake for about 15 minutes or until done.

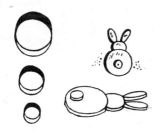

GRIDDLE BISCUITS

Prepare:

Biscuit Dough, page 583

Bake the biscuits on a hot, lightly greased griddle, 1 inch apart. Brown them on one side for about 5 to 7 minutes, turn and brown them on the other side for the same amount of time.

BEATEN BISCUITS

About Forty-Four 1½-Inch Biscuits

Preheat oven to 325°.

To win interminable gratitude, serve this classic accompaniment to Virginia hams to any homesick Southerner. The following lines by Howard Weeden in "Bandanna Ballads" sum up in a nutshell the art of making biscuits:

"Of course I'll gladly give de rule
  I meks beat biscuit by,
Dough I ain't sure dat you will mek
  Dat bread de same as I.

" 'Case cookin's like religion is—
Some's 'lected an' some ain't,
An' rules don't no more mek a cook
  Den sermons mek a saint."

Sift 3 times:

1 tablespoon sugar
4 cups all-purpose flour

1 teaspoon salt
(1 teaspoon double-acting
  baking powder)

Cut into the flour, with a pastry blender or 2 knives:

¼ cup chilled leaf lard

When ingredients are of the consistency of corn meal, add to make a stiff dough:

Equal parts of chilled milk and
  ice water, approximately 1 cup in all

Beat the dough with a mallet until it is well blistered or put it 10 times through the coarse chopper of a meat grinder. Fold it over frequently. This is a long process, requiring ½ hour or more.

Miss Weeden's verse goes on to say:

"Two hundred licks is what I gives
  For home-folks, never fewer,
An' if I'm 'specting company in,
  I gives five hundred sure!"

If you make these often, it might be worth investing in a biscuit machine, available from a bakers' supply company. When the dough is smooth and glossy, roll it to the thickness of ½ inch and cut it with a floured biscuit cutter. Spread the tops with:

Melted butter

Pierce through the biscuits with a fork. Bake for about 30 minutes.

SHIP'S BISCUITS

About Twenty-Four 1½-Inch Biscuits

These are really a simpler version of Beaten Biscuits, above. The longer they are folded and beaten, the better the results, so let the children have a fling with these.

Preheat oven to 325°.

Mix:

2 cups all-purpose flour
½ teaspoon salt

Work in, with the finger tips:

1 teaspoon shortening

Stir in to make a very stiff dough:

About ½ cup water

Beat this dough to a ½ inch thinness with a mallet. Fold it into 6 layers. Beat it thin again and refold 5 or 6 times until the dough is very elastic. Before cutting with a floured biscuit cutter, roll to ½ inch again. Bake for about 30 minutes and store tightly covered.

SWEET POTATO BISCUIT

About Twenty-Four 1½-Inch Biscuits

Preheat oven to 450°.

Into:

¾ cup cooked mashed sweet potatoes

beat:

¼ cup melted butter

Stir in:

⅔ cup milk

Sift, then measure:

1¼ cups all-purpose flour

Resift with:

    4 teaspoons double-acting
      baking powder
    1 tablespoon sugar
    1 teaspoon salt
Stir the sifted ingredients into the sweet
potato mixture. Turn the dough out on a
floured board and toss it lightly until
smooth on the outside. Roll or pat it to
the thickness of ½ inch and cut with a
floured biscuit cutter. Bake on a greased
pan for about 15 minutes.

SCONES

About 12 Scones

These are richer than ordinary biscuit be-
cause of the addition of cream and eggs.
Fine with a light luncheon.
Preheat oven to 450°.
Sift:

    2 cups sifted cake flour or 1¾ cups
      sifted all-purpose flour
    2¼ teaspoons double-acting
      baking powder
    1 tablespoon sugar
    ½ teaspoon salt

Cut into these ingredients, until the butter
is of the size of a small pea, using a pastry
blender or 2 knives:

    ¼ cup butter

Beat in a separate bowl:

    2 eggs

Reserve 2 tablespoons of this mixture. Add
to the remainder and beat:

    ⅓ cup cream

Make a well in the dry ingredients. Pour
the liquid into it. Combine with a few
swift strokes. Handle the dough as little
as possible. Place it on a lightly floured
board. Pat until ¾ inch thick. Cut with a
knife into diamond shapes or Biscuit
Sticks, page 584. Brush with the reserved
egg and sprinkle with:

    Salt or sugar

Bake for about 15 minutes.

ABOUT USES FOR READY-BAKED AND LEFTOVER BREADS, CAKES AND CRACKERS

An involuntary feeling of guilt sweeps over
everyone who wastes food, especially the
bread that so often accumulates. There
are many ways to convert these bits and
pieces into attractive assets.

A bread surplus can be put to many
good uses—so don't throw a piece away!
It can be used for Melba Toast, page 587,
Bread Pudding, page 700, Bread Sauce,
page 325; and it can become a thickener
for soups and gravies—see Panada, below.

Many recipes in "The Joy" call for dry
bread, cracker or cake crumbs. In fact, dry
cake crumbs are so prized that commercial
bakeries make sheets of cake solely for this
purpose.

In recipes, we always specify ◖ dry,
page 501, or ◖ soft, page 501, bread
crumbs. Even the way they are measured

is different. So, in puddings, timbales,
stuffings and au gratin foods, be sure to
use what is called for ◖ because the kind
of bread crumbs added makes a tremendous
difference in the texture of the finished
product.

ABOUT PANADAS

These are thickeners made of leftover
breads or based on flour, potato and rice.
If used as thickeners, see Quenelles, page
193, and Farces, page 456, or Thickeners
for Soups, page 145; as a soup, see page
155; as a sauce, see page 325.

TOASTED BUTTERED BREAD LOAF OR GARLIC BREAD

Preheat oven to 350°.
Cut into very thin slices:

    A medium-size loaf of bread or
      French bread

Do not slice it all the way through; leave
the bottom crust undisturbed. Spread the
bread with:

    ½ cup melted butter

The butter may be flavored with garlic
and/or your favorite herb. You may also
crush 2 cloves of garlic with a little salt
until smooth. Spread a little on each slice.
Follow up with melted butter, as shown
below. Separate the slices slightly, so that
the butter will be evenly distributed. Cover
the loaf with a piece of foil. Place it in

the oven until the bread is light brown,
for about 20 minutes. Remove from the
oven, place on a platter and permit the
guests to serve themselves.

CINNAMON LOAF

Slice a loaf of:

    French or Vienna bread

and spread it, as illustrated above, with
the following mixture, baking 8 minutes:

    ⅓ cup melted butter
    ⅓ cup sugar
    2 teaspoons cinnamon
    A grating of nutmeg
    ¼ teaspoon grated lemon peel

CINNAMON TOAST OR STICKS

Remove the crusts from bread. Spread
the tops of:

    Thin bread slices

or spread all 4 sides of:

¾-inch bread sticks
with a mixture of:
   3 tablespoons softened butter
   5 tablespoons confectioners' or light
      brown sugar
   1 to 1½ teaspoons cinnamon or a
      combination of 1 teaspoon cinnamon
      and freshly grated nutmeg
You may sprinkle the bread sticks with:
      (Rum)
Place the slices or strips in a 400° oven for
about 8 minutes. Be sure to toast the
sticks on all sides. You may also place
them under a broiler to crisp them. Applesauce is a good complement to this dish.

FRENCH TOAST
Beat slightly:
   4 eggs
Add:
   ½ teaspoon salt
   1 cup milk
Flavor with:
   (½ teaspoon vanilla or
      1 tablespoon rum)
Dip into this mixture:
   8 slices bread
The bread may be cut in rounds with a
doughnut cutter. Brown the bread on each
side on a well-buttered hot griddle. Serve
hot, sprinkled with:
      Sugar
      Cinnamon
Garnish the cooked rounds with:
      Bright red jelly
or serve with pie cherries, sweetened,
lightly thickened and flavored with lemon,
with applesauce flavored with cinnamon
and cloves or with maple sirup.

MELBA TOAST
Cut into the thinnest possible slices:
      White or other bread
Remove crusts. Place bread in an oven
that is at about 250°. Leave it in until it
becomes crisp and a light golden brown
and until all the moisture is withdrawn.

HONEY BUTTER TOAST
Prepare:
      Honey Butter, page 714
Spread it on a slice of bread. Cover it with
another slice. Cut the bread into 1-inch
strips. Toast the strips on both sides under
a broiler. Serve sprinkled with:
      Cinnamon

ORANGE TOAST
Good with tea.
Combine:
      Grated rind of 1 orange
      ¼ cup orange juice
      ½ cup sugar
Cut:
      6 slices of bread
Remove the crusts and toast the bread.
Spread it, while hot, with:

      Butter
Cover it with the orange mixture. Put the
toast in the oven or under a broiler, just
long enough to brown the tops lightly.

ZWIEBACK OR TWICE-BAKED
BREAD
Bake:
      White Bread Plus, page 556
using in all 2 eggs. Replace the 2 cups of
water with 2 cups of milk. The finished
loaf should be just half as high as a normal
slice of bread, so bake in six, rather than
in three, pans. Maybe this shape was
evolved to suit baby mouths, for no one
enjoys this confection more than the very,
very young. When the bread is cool, cut it
in ½-inch slices and toast as for Melba
Toast. You may want to glaze it before
toasting with:
      Lemon Topping for Cookies or Bars,
         page 682
In the slow heat of the oven, this turns a
golden brown.

BIRTHDAY BREAD HORSE
As our children have always demanded a
piece of their birthday cake for breakfast,
we concocted a bread horse to be supple-
mented later in the day by the candle-
lighted birthday cake of richer content.
This also makes a good Christmas or
Fourth of July breakfast decoration.
You will need a well-rounded loaf of
bread—a log-shaped cinnamon roll is fine
—an oval bun or roll, about 2½ x 3½
inches, 2 braided rolls about 1 x 3½ inches,
5 peppermint candy sticks 1 x 8 inches, 2
raisins, 2 almonds and a piece of cherry or
a redhot. Use the loaf for the body. Mount
it on 4 of the candy sticks. Break off about
⅓ or less of the fifth candy stick. Use it
for the neck. Stick it into one end of the
loaf at an angle. Put the oval roll on the
other end for the head. Use the braided
rolls for the mane and tail, the raisins for
eyes, the almonds for ears and the piece of
cherry for the lips. Bed the horse on
leaves or grass. Add ribbon bridle, if you
care to.

PIES, PASTES AND FILLED PASTRIES

At home and abroad, Americans boast about pie. It has apparently always been so. Way back in the clipper era, sailors brought home, not only heart-shaped boxes crusted over with tiny rare shells, but the pie-jaggers they had carved to while away the doldrum days in outre-mer. These implements of bone, often furnished with as many as three wheels, but marvelously precise all the same, sped the fancy cutting of lattice in many a New England cottage. Whatever the nation, skill in pastry making has been regarded as a worldwide passport to matrimony. In Hungarian villages, for example, no girl was considered eligible until her strudel dough had become so translucent that her beloved could read the newspaper through it.

Let's consider what makes for success, whether your objective be pie, strudel, puff paste, Muerbeteig or poppadums:

♦ Have all ingredients, to begin with, at about 70°.

♦ Handle your dough lightly, for two reasons: to incorporate as much air as possible and to inhibit the development of gluten. The aim here is a flaky and tender crust.

♦ Avoid too much flour, which toughens pastry.

♦ Avoid too much liquid, which makes it soggy.

▲ In making pies at high altitudes, you may find the greater evaporation will mean that you have better results if you add a trifle more liquid.

♦ Avoid too much shortening, which makes doughs greasy and crumbly.

♦ Chilling pastry dough after mixing tenderizes it, keeps it from shrinking during baking and makes it easier to handle. We recommend refrigerating it, covered, for 12 hours or more. Be sure to remove the dough from the refrigerator at least one hour before shaping, otherwise you will be obliged to over-handle it. Pinch off just enough dough for one pie shell. Press it into the approximate shape needed. Roll

as lightly and as little as possible, usin the directions in the illustration belov Pie dough will hold for a week or more the refrigerator.

♦ Choose non-shiny pie pans for goo browning.

♦ Always start the baking in a very h oven, preheated to the temperature inc cated. The contrast between the coolne of the dough and the heat of the ove causes rapid air expansion and contribut to the desired lightness of texture. Ever one has a favorite recipe for pie doug But our own basic one made with lard v find especially satisfactory. Many p doughs ✱ freeze well. ♦ It is better shape them before freezing. See Froze Baked Pie, page 770, Frozen Unbaked Pi page 770.

ABOUT BASIC PIE DOUGH

For a one-crust, 9-inch pie, use ½ t recipe below. For a double-crust, 9-inc or a single-crust pie with a generous la tice, use the following:
Sift, then measure:
2 cups all-purpose flour
Resift it with:
1 teaspoon salt
Measure and combine:
⅓ cup 70° leaf lard or shortening
¼ cup chilled butter
or use in all ⅔ cup shortening. Cut ½ the shortening into the flour mixture wi a pastry blender, see below, or work it lightly with the tips of your fingers until has the grain of cornmeal. Cut the remai ing half coarsely into the dough until it pea size. Sprinkle the dough with:
5 tablespoons water
♦ Blend the water lightly into the doug You may lift the ingredients with a for allowing the moisture to spread. If neede add ♦ just enough water to hold ingred ents together. When you can gather t dough up into a tidy ball, as shown belov stop handling it.

ABOUT ROLLING PIE DOUGH

♦ To make 2 pie shells, divide the dough evenly before rolling it. To make a double crust pie, divide the dough into 2 slightly uneven parts, keeping the smaller one for the top. ♦ A pastry cloth and roller stocking are highly recommended. They practically do away with sticking and require the use of very little additional flour. Rolling the dough between 2 sheets of foil or wax paper, although more difficult, also avoids adding unwanted flour. When ready, remove the top paper, reverse the crust into pan and then remove the other paper.

If you use neither of the above methods, flour the rolling surface and the rolling pin lightly. As to the roller, whether it's a French broomstick-type or a bottle, the important thing is how you use it. ♦ Roll the dough from the center out. Lift the roller. Do not push it to and fro, stretching the dough. Roll the dough to at least ⅛-inch thickness or less. Should it have a few tears, patch them carefully rather than trying to reroll.

ABOUT CUTTING AND FORMING PIE DOUGH

♦ To cut pie dough, allow a piece about inches larger than the pan dimensions, as shown above, to take care of inevitable shrinkage. It is fun to cut fancy edges with a pastry wheel.

♦ To form the crust, have ready a 9-inch pie pan. It's a poor pie crust that requires a greased pan, but buttering will help brown the bottom of the crust. Loosen the pastry from the board, fold it in half, lift

it, lay the fold across the center of the pan and unfold it; or, after rolling it around the rolling pin, unroll it onto the pan. See above, where this method is being used to form a top crust.

Ease the dough into the pan loosely, but firm it in place so that no air will be left between dough and pan to form blisters in baking. You may cut a small square of dough, form it into a ball, dip it in flour and use it to press the dough down and shape it against the pan. Trim off the excess with a knife, using an easy slashing motion against the edge of the pan; or use scissors. Trimmings can be given to the children for play dough or baked up into bits for hors d'oeuvre or small pastries.

ABOUT FILLED PIES

♦ For filled pies, use a deep pie pan with a wide channeled rim to catch any juices. For a one-crust pie, make a fluted edge with the dough that laps over, or build up a rim with a strip of pastry. Full it on. Use a fork to press it down or pinch it with the thumb and forefinger, as shown below on the left. This edge is important, as it will help to hold the juices in the pie. Do not prick the lower crust. If the filling for the pie is to be juicy, first brush the bottom crust lightly with the white of an egg, melted butter or a solution of gum arabic. Any of these will keep the crust from becoming soggy. Putting the filling in very hot helps, too.

There are many attractive ways to make the lattice. You may cut plain ½-inch strips with a knife or pink them with a jagger. Or you may roll, then twist ½-

inch rope-like pieces and weave any of these together or place them crisscross.

To weave, place ½ the strips from left to right over the pie about ¾ inch apart. Fold back every other strip half-way, as shown on page 589, at right. Place a strip across the unfolded strips from front to back. Unfold the strips. Fold back the alternates. Place the next strip ¾ inch from the last. Continue until ½ the pie is latticed. Then, repeat the process, beginning on the other side of the center line.

When the whole pie is latticed, attach the strips to the pie edge loosely to allow for shrinkage. Moisten the ends slightly to make them stick. Cut them off before crimping the pie.

For a solid top crust, cut the rolled ⅛-inch-thick dough 1 inch larger than the pan. To allow the steam to escape, prick it with a fork in several places, double it over and gash it along the fold or make fancy patterns with whatever cutting tool you like. Place the top crust on the pie. Full in the surplus dough and press it down around the edges with a fork. Or you may tuck it under the lower crust and press it around the edge with a fork, or cut the lower crust ½ inch larger than the upper crust and fold it over like a hem. ♦ Allow 4 cups of filling for a 9-inch pie and 3 cups for a 7-inch pie. If you prefer, after sealing the edges by pressing with a fork, you may make a vent with a one-inch hollow tube of dough—3 inches high—only partially sunk into a hole in the center of the upper crust. Support it with a round border of fulled on dough which will hide any discoloration from juices bubbling over when you cut the vent down to the decorative support after the baking. Should any juice spill over onto the oven, sprinkle it with salt to prevent smoke and smell.

Be sure to thicken acid fruits with tapioca, cornstarch or arrowroot as suggested in the recipes, because the acidity of the fruit may neutralize the thickening power of the flour.

ABOUT UNFILLED PIE SHELLS

♦ If the pie shell is to be baked unfilled, ♦ prick the dough generously with a fork after you have placed it in the pie pan, or weight the bottom of the shell with dry rice, beans, or, as they do in France, with small clean round pebbles. This keeps it from heaving and baking unevenly. Remove the beans or pebbles a few minutes before the oven period is over. To cut a round for a prebaked top crust, prick it and bake it on a baking sheet.

When making individual pies, use an inverted muffin tin or, for deeper shells, inverted custard cups. Cut the rounds of dough 4½ or 5½ inches in diameter and fit them over the cups or, with the help of foil as a support, create your own fancy

shapes—fluted cups, simple tricornes, long barquettes. You may even make your tarts into baskets by forming handles with strips of dough molded over inverted custard cups. When baked, sink the handles into the filling just before serving. ♦ Prick shells before baking. When you fill baked shells, spoon the filling in carefully.

To protect a baked crust from overbrowning when heating a filling in it, put the pie, still in its pan, into an extra pan to keep it from too much heat.

♦ To glaze pie crust, choose one of the many glazes which add either flavor or color to your pie, see pages 681-683—but they also tend to toughen crusts.

♦ Baking time will vary according to the material of which the pan is made. If it is ovenproof glass or enamelware, cut the baking time indicated by ⅕ to ¼. When tins are used, those that are perforated, have lost their shininess or have a base of screen material are helpful for producing a well-browned crust.

♦ It is essential that the oven be preheated to the temperatures indicated in the recipes. For meringue pies, please turn to pages 599, 681. For baking filled pies, note directions in each recipe. Unbaked shells, whether for individual or big pies, are baked in a preheated oven 450° for about 12 minutes or until lightly browned.

FLOUR PASTE PIE CRUST
A 9-Inch Double-Crust

Preheat oven to 450°.
Sift, then measure:

2 cups all-purpose flour

Resift it into a bowl with:

1 teaspoon salt

Measure ⅓ cupful of this mixture and place it in a small bowl or cup. Stir into it, to form a smooth paste:

¼ cup water

Cut into the flour mixture in the first bowl with a pastry blender, until the grain in it is the size of small peas:

⅔ cup 70° shortening

Stir the flour paste into the dough. Work it with your hand until it is well incorporated and the dough forms a ball.

QUICK AND EASY PIE CRUST
I.   A 9-Inch Single Crust

Preheat oven to 425°.
Sift, then measure:

1½ cups all-purpose flour

Resift it into a bowl with:

½ teaspoon salt

With a pastry blender, work in:

½ cup 70° shortening

until the grain in the mixture is pea size. Stir in, 1 tablespoon at a time:

3 tablespoons water

until the mixture holds together when you gather it into a ball. Pat it evenly into the pie pan. For details on lining a pan, see page 589. Bake 12 to 15 minutes. Cool before filling.

II. Two 9-Inch Pie Shells or 8 Tarts

Preheat oven to 425°.
The oil gives this a somewhat mealy rather than a flaky texture.
Sift into a pie pan:

    2 cups sifted all-purpose flour
    1¼ teaspoons salt

Mix in a cup until creamy:

    ⅔ cup cooking oil
    3 tablespoons cold milk

Pour the mixture over the flour all at once. Stir these ingredients lightly with a fork until blended. Form them into a crust, right in the pan, by patting out the dough with your fingers. Bake 12 to 15 minutes. Cool before filling.

HOT-WATER PIE CRUST
A 9-Inch Double-Crust

Hot water crust is apt to be mealy rather than flaky.
Preheat oven to 450°.
Place in a bowl:

    ¾ cup 70° lard

Pour over it:

    6 tablespoons boiling water

Beat these ingredients until they are cold and creamy. If there is time, chill them. Sift before measuring:

    2 cups cake flour

Resift with:

    ½ teaspoon any baking powder
    1 teaspoon salt

Combine the liquid and the sifted ingredients and stir until they form a smooth ball. Cover the dough and chill until firm. Roll or form and bake 8 to 10 minutes.

WHEATLESS PIE CRUST
A 9-Inch Single-Crust

Sift 6 times:

    ½ cup cornstarch
    ½ cup finely milled rye flour

The repeated sifting is very important.
Work as for pastry and add:

    ½ cup fine dry cottage cheese
    ½ cup 70° butter
    ½ teaspoon salt

Chill the dough from 2 to 12 hours. To roll, form and bake, see the illustrations on page 589.

PÂTE BRISÉE
A 9-Inch Pie Shell

This short French pie dough has a remarkable way of withstanding a moist filling. The recipe can be doubled or tripled and stored refrigerated for a week or more before baking.
Allow:

    ½ cup butter plus 2 tablespoons lard

to reach 70°. Rub it very lightly into:

    2 cups sifted all-purpose flour
    ½ teaspoon salt

This can be done best by working the flour and butter first with the fingers and then between the palms of the hands. Make a well, page 594, of the rubbed flour and butter. Pour in gradually:

    5 to 6 tablespoons water

The index finger is used to stir the liquid quickly into the flour, in a spiral fashion, beginning at the inside of the well and gradually moving to the outer edge. The dough should be soft enough to gather up into a ball but should not stick to the fingers. Allow the dough to rest refrigerated from 2 to 36 hours. Cover it with a damp, wrung-out cloth for the shorter period or a piece of foil for the longer one. The resting of the dough breaks any rubbery reactions it might develop when rolled and handled. To roll, shape and bake, see page 589.

ABOUT PASTRY FOR MEATS

For meat pies, rissoles or turnovers, use any unsweetened crust. For Meat en Croûte, see page 387; for Pâté en Croûte, page 433.

RICH EGG PIE CRUST, MUERBETEIG OR PÂTE SUCRÉE
Six 3-Inch Tart Shells

There are many versions of this paste, varying in richness and sweetness. This one makes a very tender paste for fresh fruit fillings. For a sweeter dough, use Rolled or Rich Rolled Cookie Dough, page 661. See illustration, page 594, to combine and make a well with:

    1 cup flour
    2 tablespoons sugar
    ½ teaspoon salt

Add and work with your fingers until light and creamy:

    1 egg yolk
    ½ teaspoon vanilla
    1 tablespoon lemon juice

Work into it as you would for pastry, using a pastry blender or the tips of your fingers:

    6 tablespoons softened 70° butter

until the mixture forms one blended ball and no longer adheres to your fingers. Cover it and refrigerate for at least ½ hour. Roll to ⅛-inch thickness, as for pie dough, see page 589. Line the greased tart pans with this dough. Weight down with beans or pebbles, see page 590. Bake in a 400° oven 7 to 10 minutes or until lightly browned. Unmold the pastry shells and cool on a rack. Fill with fresh fruit. Glaze with:

    Melted, cooled Currant or Apricot Glaze, page 683

Garnish with:

    (Whipped cream)

ABOUT GALETTE DOUGH

Fifty million Frenchmen can't be wrong; but it is hard to get two of them to agree on the exact formula for this classic pastry. In some regions, galette is almost like a Kuchen dough. Perhaps the most famous is Galette des Rois, served on Twelfth Night. Regardless of the type of dough used for the "King's Galette," it has a dried bean baked in it, which is expected to bring good fortune to the guest who gets the lucky slice.

Our version of galette which, we hope, will merit majority approval, is a well-pricked Rough Puff Paste, see page 596, rolled to 1-inch thickness and coated with a heavy French Egg Wash glaze, page 682. ◗ Keep the glaze on the top surface only, for if it runs over the edge it will solidify early in the baking and prevent the dough from puffing as it should.

Another version is to use a yeast coffee cake dough. After the last rising, pat it out thin and make a rim by pinching the dough edges all around. Put the fruit in the depression and cover it with a Streusel, page 682. Bake as directed for bread. You may, as the cake cools, cover it with Apricot Glaze, page 683. A simpler and, we think, delicious solution is simply to bake Apple, Peach or Plum Cake Cockaigne, page 606.

VIENNA PASTRY

Eight 3-Inch Tarts
Delicious as tart shells, turnovers or thin wafers served with soup or salad. Sift before measuring:

1 cup all-purpose flour
Resift with:

(**¼ teaspoon salt**)
Cut into these ingredients with a pastry blender:

½ cup 70° butter
4½ oz. soft cream cheese
When the ingredients are well blended, wrap the dough in foil and refrigerate for at least 12 hours. When ready to use, roll to ⅛-inch thickness, using as little additional flour as possible.
I. To use as tarts, form pastry over inverted muffin tins and bake at 450° for about 12 minutes.

II. To use as turnovers, see page 55.

III. To use as wafers, roll and cut the dough into rounds or put it directly into a cookie press without rolling. Before baking, dot with sesame or poppy seed. Bake 8 to 10 minutes at 450°.

ABOUT COOKIE AND KUCHEN CRUSTS

If a sweet or spicy crust is desired, try Rolled Cookie Doughs, page 661. For a pie-like Kuchen dough, see the very good German Cherry Pie, page 602. There are many, many forms of fruit Kuchen, see Apple, Plum or Peach Cake Cockaigne, page 606, French Apple Cake, page 607, Quick Sour Cream Coffee Cake, page 577. For less sweet versions, try fruit toppings on raised coffee cake doughs, page 570 to 572.

CHEESE-CAKE CRUST

To Line a 10-Inch Pan
This crust works well if filled before baking with dry cheese cake fillings such as Ricotta, page 612.
Have at about 70°:

½ cup butter
Work this into a crust with:

¼ teaspoon salt
2 cups flour
to mix pie dough, see page 589. Gradually add:

1½ to 2 tablespoons cognac
Chill about half an hour before rolling to line the pan. Roll about ⅛ inch thick.

SUGGESTED ADDITIONS TO CRUSTS

Vary your favorite basic pie crust by adding, before rolling, for a double crust, one of the following:

1 tablespoon poppy or caraway seed
3 tablespoons toasted sesame seed
¼ to ½ cup chopped nuts
¼ to ⅓ cup grated aged cheese
2 tablespoons confectioners' sugar
⅛ teaspoon cinnamon or nutmeg
1 teaspoon grated citrus rind
1 tablespoon sugar

ABOUT CRUMB CRUSTS

These crusts, mixed and patted into the pan, are a shortcut to pie making. To avoid overbrowning, use ◗ a shiny metal or enamel pan which will reflect heat. An easy way to form crumb crusts is to place the crumb mixture in a pie pan, distributing the crumbs fairly evenly. Now press another pie pan of the same diameter firmly into the crumbs. When the top pan is removed, presto!—a crust of even thickness underneath. Trim any excess which is forced to the top edge.

Crumb crusts need not be baked before filling ◗ but, if used unbaked, must be first chilled thoroughly or the filling will immediately disintegrate the crust. If baked before filling, they require a 300° oven for about 15 minutes. ◗ It is best to cool the empty baked shell before filling.
Fill a prebaked shell with:

A gelatin pie filling or sweetened fresh fruit
Top with:

Whipped cream
For a meringue pie, chill the unbaked shell and fill with a previously cooked and cooled:

Custard, cream or fruit filling
Cover with a Meringue, see page 591. Bake in a 300° oven for about 15 minutes.

PIES, PASTES AND FILLED PASTRIES

GRAHAM CRACKER, ZWIEBACK OR GINGER SNAP CRUST
A 9-Inch Crust and Topping
Preheat oven to 350°.
Crush or grind fine, or put in a ⅃ blender until very fine:

　1½ cups crumbs of graham crackers,
　　zwieback, or Ginger Snaps, page 501

Stir into them until well blended:

　¼ cup sifted confectioners' sugar
　6 tablespoons melted butter
　(1 teaspoon cinnamon)

Reserve ¼ to ½ of the crust. Pat the rest into the pan to the desired thickness. When the pie is filled, use the reserved crumbs as topping. To form the shell and bake, see About Crumb Crusts, page 592.

LUXURY CRUMB CRUST
For a 10-Inch Torte
Preheat oven to 350°.
Crush, blend or grind until very fine:

　1½ cups crumbs of graham crackers or
　　zwieback

Stir into them:

　6 tablespoons ground unblanched
　　almonds
　6 tablespoons sugar
　¼ cup light cream
　½ cup melted butter
　(⅛ teaspoon cinnamon)

Pat the dough into the pan. To form the shell and bake, see About Crumb Crusts, page 592.

BREAD OR CAKE CRUMB CRUST
Preheat oven to 350°.
A good way of utilizing stale bread or cake. To be successful, this crust must be fully baked before filling. Follow the rule for Graham Cracker Crust, above. Substitute for the graham cracker or zwieback crumbs:

　1½ cups toasted, sifted bread
　　or cake crumbs

If you use cake crumbs, omit sugar. To form the shell and bake, see About Crumb Crusts, page 592.

CEREAL PIE CRUST
A 9-Inch Crust
Preheat oven to 350°.
Roll or grind:

　6 cups flaked or puffed type
　　breakfast cereal

There should be 1½ cups after crushing. Combine with:

　½ cup melted butter
　¼ cup sugar—if the cereal is not
　　presweetened
　(⅛ teaspoon cinnamon)

To form the shell and bake, see About Crumb Crusts, page 592.

COOKIE CRUMB CRUST
Follow the rule for Graham Cracker or Luxury Crust, this page. Omit sugar. Sub-

stitute for graham cracker, etc., crumbs in whole or in part:

　Ginger Snaps
　Vanilla Wafers
　Chocolate Wafers

The flavor of your filling should determine which of the above cookies you use. Form the shell and bake as directed in About Crumb Crusts, page 592.

PUFF PASTE OR PÂTE FEUILLETÉE
Puff paste recipes usually start "Choose a bright, windy, chilly day . . ." We stand off unfavorable weather with an electric fan, but are careful not to train it on the work surface. If you ask, "What does a commercial bakery do about puff paste and the weather?"—the answer is: they use a highly emulsified, very impervious margarine. To become an amateur champion, keep in mind first and foremost that this most delicate and challenging of pastries must be made the way porcupines make love—that is, very, very carefully. Then shut off the telephone for an hour or two, cut yourself some paper patterns as shown on page 594 and set to work.

◗ It is best to use flour that has a high gluten content, to develop real elasticity—and this is hard to come by. We do succeed however with all-purpose flour by using the procedure we describe. To be "puffy" ◗ the paste must be chilled, well-kneaded and handled in such a way as to trap air and finally ◗ baked in a high, thoroughly preheated oven. Then the air inside the dough expands with almost explosive effect. ◗ The surface on which you work—preferably marble—the tools, the ingredients and your fingers should be chilled throughout the operation, as it is necessary to hold the fat, which is in very high proportion to the flour, in constant suspension.

◗ The paste must not absorb undue moisture, but it must never dry out. ◗ It must entirely envelop the butter. Try not to let any cracks or tears develop, as they release the air which is your only riser. If they do appear, mend them at once to keep the butter encased. With these ideas firmly in mind, try making this small quantity first. As you become experienced, double or triple the recipe. Knead:

　¼ lb. sweet butter

in ice water or under very cold running water. The butter should become soft through kneading, but in no sense soft through melting. Quite on the contrary—it must stay soft and chilled at the same time throughout the operation. The final kneading of the butter is best done on a marble slab; or the butter may be patted briskly in the hands until no water flies. Shape it into an oblong, about 4 x 6 x ¾ inches. Wrap in foil and chill for about 15 minutes. Mix:

¼ lb. all-purpose flour
which must be weighed, not measured. Make a ring, as shown below, on a chilled smooth surface with the flour, allowing about a 6-inch hollow center.

Pour into the ring gradually—meanwhile forming the flour into a ball with it—a mixture of:

2 to 2½ oz. ice water
(1 teaspoon lemon juice)
¼ teaspoon salt
Knead the dough lightly until smooth. The whole process should not take more than about 2 minutes if you are experienced. Cover the dough carefully and refrigerate it for 15 minutes or so. When you remove the butter and dough from the refrigerator, they should be of about the same consistency—chilled but not hard. Roll the dough into a very neat oblong measuring about 6 x 16 inches and less than ⅓ inch thick, as in the following sketch. At this

point, the dough is somewhat elastic and may have to be cajoled into the rectangle. Make the edges as even and thickness as constant as possible. Quickly place the chilled butter pad about 1 inch from a

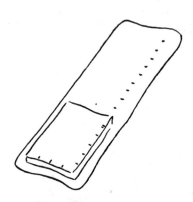

short end and sides of the dough oblong, as shown above.

Fold the rest of the dough over the butter to make a pouch with one side folded and the three others sealed. Seal the two layers firmly together on all three sides pressing with the fingers, as shown below or with the sides of your hands.

With the narrow dimension always toward you as you work, roll the dough evenly, being careful not to break the layers nor force the roller in such a way that the edges of the dough envelope become cracked. Should any opening develop, be sure to patch it at once with small piece of dough taken from the long sides. Keep the pastry 6 inches in width while rolling and extend it to about 1 inches in length, as shown, opposite.

The use of 2 paper patterns makes th

easuring very quick to judge. Fold the astry into three exact parts, see above.

ake sure that the corners match neatly. ompress it slightly with the roller. At this int, the dough should have a transparent uality. The yellow of the butter should ow through, but not break through any-here. Wrap the dough, now approxi-ately 4 x 6 x 1 inch, in foil and chill for) minutes. You have now made your first urn" and, if you need a reminder, you an professionally make one shallow finger p imprint in one corner, as shown above, efore refrigerating. You can keep track of ur turns by increasing the finger prints ter each rolling.

After the dough has chilled, remove it om the refrigerator and repeat the roll-g. ◆ Always roll with the narrow dimen-on of the dough toward you as you work. oll as before, until the dough again meas-es about 6 x 16 inches. Fold once more three equal parts. This time, make two ger tip impressions before refrigerating, vered, for 30 minutes. Repeat the turns til you have six prints in the dough. You ay store the dough for 24 hours before aking. Wrap it first in foil and then in a y towel. Refrigerate it.

If you prefer to bake the same day, rest e dough after the 6th turn for 30 min-es to 1½ hours. Then roll it to about of an inch. This paste can be cut in any shapes. ◆ Whichever you choose, be sure to cut off a narrow slice along the folded edges. The folds have the inhibit-ing character of a selvage on cloth and do not allow the dough to expand evenly and freely.

◆ Always cut puff paste with a very sharp and thin hot knife, a hot cutter or a sharp, hot pastry wheel. Do not let the knife drag, as this will distort the layering.

Since making puff paste is time-consum-ing, you will want to use every scrap. But never, after cutting, reroll the dough for the same purpose. Get your patty shells and vol-au-vent and other classic shapes, see below, from the first cutting. Make out of rerolled scraps only those related types of pastry—such as flan, barquettes, crois-sants—for which the puff requirement is less exacting.

To prepare the pan for baking any of the classic shapes, sprinkle it lightly with cold water, but ◆ be sure to see that the side that was up when cut is now down against the wet baking surface. Puff paste, if properly made and cut, should rise six to eight times the height of the rolled dough.

Before baking an unsweetened paste, you may give it a lovely color by brushing the top with a combination of egg, salt and milk, see page 682. ◆ Do not let this glaze spill over the edge, as the quick setting of the egg will have a deterrent effect on the rising. For a paste to be used with sweet-ened food, brush with a combination of sugar and milk. For a real crispy finish, glaze also with a light sugar and water sirup just as the finished product comes from the oven.

To bake ◆ have ready an oven that has been thoroughly preheated to 500° for at least 20 minutes. Bake at this temperature for 5 minutes, reduce the heat to 375° and bake for 25 to 30 minutes more, depending on the size of the pastry. If it colors too rapidly, place a piece of baker's paper or bond over it during the last stages of bak-ing. The pastry is done when very light when lifted. Should it rise unevenly, the fault may lie with uneven rolling or with the uneven heat of the oven. In hot weather, it may tend to slide to one side. Nothing can be done about this.

All puff paste recipes are best used fresh, but will keep closely covered and stored in a refrigerator for several days or frozen for a few weeks. For shapes to make with puff paste, see the illustration on the next page and some of the follow-ing recipes.

Top left shows the cutting of a Vol-au-vent, page 596. It is really a larger version of the bouchée or patty shell illustrated in its dough and baked form in the three drawings on the left.

At the top right is a Napoleon, page 596. The remaining three forms are the succes-sive development of Cream Rolls, page 596. To cut Palm Leaves, see page 563.

Do not try to make these shapes with the Rough Puff Paste below, which is placed here because it is folded and baked just like puff paste.

ROUGH OR HALF-PUFF PASTE OR PÂTE DEMI-FEUILLETÉE
Do not expect this crust to rise even half as high as does Puff Paste. It is made from the ingredients described below, but given fewer turns; or is formed from the rerolled parings of true Puff Paste, when additional handling has driven off some of the trapped air. Use this paste for barquettes or croissants. Prepare:
    Puff Paste, page 593
using in all:
    6 oz. butter
    2 oz. water
Give it only 3 to 4 turns. To cut, shape and bake, see Puff Paste, page 593.

PALM LEAVES
                        About 20 Palm Leaves
Roll:
    Puff Paste, page 593
into a 6 x 18-inch strip, ¼ inch thick. To sugar, fold and cut, see pages 594 and 595.

✳ PATTY SHELLS OR BOUCHÉES
                        Ten 4-Inch Shells
Prepare:
    Puff Paste, see above and note
    ♦ pointers
Roll the chilled paste into an oblong, 7 x 16 inches. Use a 3¼-inch hot cutter on the dough ten times. ♦ Be sure that the cutter is well within the rounded edge of the dough. Using a 2½-inch cutter and centering it in turn on each of the 3¼-inch rounds, make incisions, as shown above, about ⅔ through the dough. To chill, shape and bake the dough, see Puff Paste, page 593. As soon as the patty shells come from the oven, release the inner circles that were cut ⅔ into the shell. The first ⅓ will act as the lid when the shell is filled. The second is usually damp and is discarded. The third uncut portion forms the base of

the shell. These shells are suitable fo luncheon entrées. They can be made int much smaller sizes for hors d'oeuvre, an are then called **Petites Bouchées**, or "littl mouthfuls."

✳ VOL-AU-VENT
                        One 9-Inch She
Prepare:
    Puff Paste, page 593, and note
    ♦ pointers
Roll the chilled paste into an oblong, 9 17 inches. Use the removable bottom of a 8-inch round cake pan or make an 8-inc cardboard circle as a cutting guide. Cu two circles with a sharp, hot knife. Leav one whole. Place the cut-side down on baking sheet sprinkled with water. Cut 5-inch round out of the center of the othe circle. Place the 1½-inch rim which th cut forms also cut-side down over th whole circle and gash it diagonally alon the edge, as shown opposite. You may bak the 5-inch circle separately as a lid or cu it into petites bouchés, see above. T chill and bake, see Puff Paste, pag 593. Fill at once with creamed food an serve, or cool to serve filled with fruits.

CREAM ROLLS
                        Eight Rol
If you visit a Konditorei in Weimar, yo will find Schillerlocken or cream roll named after the long curls worn by th romantic German poet. To make then you need a special cone-shaped for known as a cornet.
Prepare:
    Puff Paste, see page 593 and note
    ♦ pointers
Roll the chilled paste into an oblon, 12½ x 9 inches. Remove the rolled edge of the paste with a very sharp hot knife pastry wheel. Cut the dough into eig 12-inch strips. Roll the strips around th cones, as shown at right, opposite. Chi the cornets, covered, for at least ½ hou Glaze the top of the strips with:
    Milk Glaze, page 682
Stand the cornets on a baking tin. T bake, see Puff Paste, page 593.

NAPOLEONS
                        About Forty 2 x 3 Inch Ba
Could the Emperor have had these i mind when he contended that "an arm marches on its stomach"?
Preheat oven to 450°.
Prepare:
    Puff Paste, page 593
Roll the chilled paste into an oblong, 24 33 inches to a thickness of ⅛ inch or les ♦ Trim all folded edges carefully to depth of ½ inch. Divide the paste int three 11 x 24-inch oblongs. Place the 3 th equal oblongs upside down on bakin sheets that have been sprinkled with co water. Prick them uniformly with a for

Bake them about 25 to 30 minutes in all, see Puff Paste, page 593. When cool, you may glaze the layer reserved for the top with 2 successive coats of:

Quick Icing I, page 677

Let the first coat dry before applying the second or dust the top layer with:

Powdered sugar

Stack the 3 layers and cut into 2 x 3-inch oblongs. Put between the layers:

Sweetened Whipped Cream, page 645 or Crème Patissière, page 646

The finished pastry is shown at the top right of the illustration on page 596.

ABOUT CREAM PUFF SHELLS, PÂTE À CHOUX OR POUF PASTE

Please cease to think of this basic, quite easy paste as something for adventurous moments only. Use it unsweetened as a base for Gnocchi, page 177; for Dauphine Potatoes, page 296; as a bland foil for fillings; as soup garnishes or as hors d'oeuvre cases. Pâte à choux, when sweetened, imparts great individuality to the presentation of food, as you can see in the sketches below. With a pastry tube you may make elegant Éclairs, page 598, Beignets, page 706, characteristic cabbagy or choux shapes for cream puffs, Swans, page 597, dainty choux paste cases or the towering pyramid, Croquembouche, page 598. If you serve éclair cases filled with ice cream or cream and covered with a sauce, they are called Profiteroles, page 598.

CREAM PUFF SHELLS
Two Dozen 3-Inch Shells
Preheat oven to 400°.

Have the eggs at room temperature. It is best to use a high-gluten flour. Sift before measuring:

1 cup high-gluten or all-purpose flour
⅛ teaspoon salt
1 tablespoon sugar, if the puffs are
    to be used with a sweet filling

Place in a heavy pan:

1 cup water or milk

⅛ cup butter

When the mixture boils, add the flour in one fell swoop and stir quickly with a wooden spoon. It looks rough at first, but suddenly becomes smooth, at which point you stir faster. In a few minutes the paste becomes dry, does not cling to the spoon or the sides of the pan and when the spoon is pressed on it lightly, it leaves a smooth imprint. ◗ Do not overcook, for then the dough will fail to puff. ◗ Remove pan from heat for about 2 minutes. It never returns to the heat and this is why, to cook properly, ◗ the eggs must be at room temperature. Add ◗ one at a time, beating vigorously after each addition:

4 to 5 eggs

Continue to beat each time until the dough no longer looks slippery. The paste is ready to bake when the last egg has been incorporated, and it has reached proper consistency when a small quantity of the dough will stand erect if scooped up on the end of the spoon. It is best to use the dough at once.

Use a spoon or a pastry bag to form the different shapes. Be sure to press the filled bag until you are rid of all the air in the tube. Allow space for expansion around shapes, as you squeeze them onto the greased pan. To form the puff or characteristic cabbagy, choux shape ◗ hold the tube close to the baking sheet. ◗ Do not move the tube. Simply let the paste bubble up around it until the desired size is reached. To form éclairs, draw the tube along for about 3 to 4 inches while pressing and always ◗ finish with a lifting reverse motion. To form small pastry cups, make one-inch globules. The small point left when you lift the bag can be pressed down with a moistened finger. Before baking, sprinkle a few drops of water over the shapes on the pan—lightly—as you would sprinkle laundry. Bake cream puff shells and éclairs in a preheated 400° oven for 10 minutes. Reduce the heat to 350° and bake for about 25 minutes longer. Do not remove them from the oven until they are quite firm to the touch. Cool the shells away from any draft before filling. For filling, cut them horizontally with a sharp knife. If there are any damp dough filaments inside, be sure to remove them. For suggested cream puff fillings, see next page.

CHOUX PASTE SWAN

Use a simple cut-off round tube, see Decorative Icings, page 675, to form the head and neck all in one piece. Squeeze hard at the inception of the movement to force a greater quantity of paste for the head and swing the tube in an arc for the neck, as shown on the tray, left. Head and neck sections are baked on a greased sheet for only 10 minutes in a 400° oven. For the rest of the swan's anatomy, use a serrated tube to form 3-inch éclairs. Cut them

lengthwise. Just before serving, fill the
bottom piece with cream. Divide the top
piece lengthwise for the wings. Imbed
them and the neck in the fluffy cream filling. The wings are braced somewhat diagonally to steady the neck. Dust the
whole swan lightly with confectioners'
sugar. Perfect for a little girl's party!

CHOCOLATE ÉCLAIRS

To form and bake the shells, see Cream
Puff Shells, page 597. Gash the shell sufficiently to get the filling in or squirt it in
with a pastry tube. Fill the shells as close
to serving time as possible with:

> Whipped cream or Custard
> Chocolate or Coffee Fillings,
> see page 646

Cover them with:

> A chocolate icing, page 679, or
> Caramel Icing, page 676

Garnish with:

> Slivered toasted almonds

PROFITEROLES

To form and bake the shells, see Cream
Puff Shells, page 597. Divide the shells
horizontally and fill as close to serving time
as possible with:

> Crème Chantilly, page 645, or
> ice cream

Cover with:

> Chocolate Sauce, page 711

or fill with:

> Whipped Cream, page 484

and serve with a strawberry sauce.

CROQUEMBOUCHE

Serves 10 to 12

This spectacular dessert is a mechanical
marvel. It needs considerable organization, for it is best when assembled as close
to serving time as possible. See illustration on preceding page. Caramelize:

> 2 cups sugar, page 507

Form on the base of a 9-inch greased pie
pan or directly on a footed cake tray a thin
caramelized layer. Keep the rest of the
caramelized sugar soft in a 250° oven.
When the thin layer has hardened, put it
on the platter on which you intend to serve
the dessert. Have ready:

> Cream puffs under 2 inches in size,
> made from Pâte à Choux, page 597

filled with:

> Whipped or flavored cream, page 645

Remove the caramel from the oven and
work quickly. Reheat the sirup slowly if
it tends to harden. ◗ Dip a portion of each
filled puff in turn, as you place it in de-
creasing circular layers on the caramel
disc. Arrange the puffs on the outer layers

so their tops form the exposed surface.
Serve by pulling apart with 2 forks.

ABOUT FILLINGS FOR CREAM PUFF SHELLS AND ÉCLAIRS

Use Sweetened Whipped Creams, page
645, Custards, page 684, Crème Patissière,
page 646, or almost any of the fillings in
Complete Dessert Cakes, page 644. ◗ Fill
as close to serving time as possible to avoid
sogginess. In any case, remember ◗ that
cream-based and particularly egg-based
fillings must be kept cool or refrigerated.
Egg fillings, if carelessly stored, are subject to bacterial activity which may be
highly toxic although they give no evidence of spoilage. For unsweetened puff
shells, see Canapés, page 55.

With a sweetened dough try one of the following:

I. For a marvelous tea-teaser, put in the
base of a puff shell a layer of:

> Whipped cream

Lightly insert with the pointed end up:

> A flawless ripe strawberry

II. Or fill the puffs with:

> Soft cream cheese
> A dab of bright jelly

STRUDEL

When the last princess slip was freshly
beribboned, our beloved Hungarian laun-
dress sometimes gave us a treat. She would
make strudel. Draping the round dining
room table with a fresh cloth, she patiently worked flour into it. Neighborhood
small fry gathered on the fringes of the
light cast by the Tiffany dome, and their
eyes would pop as she rolled the dough, no
larger than a soft ball, into a big thin circle. Then, hands lightly clenched, palms
down, working under the sheet of dough
and from the center out, she stretched it
with the flat plane of the knuckles, as
shown next page. She would play it out,
so to speak, not so much pulling it as coax-
ing it with long, even friction, moving
round and round the table as she worked.

In our household, the filling was invariably apple. But whether you make strudel
dough yourself or buy it—for it now comes
ready to use—there are endless possibilities
for "interior decoration": poppy seed,
ground meat mixtures, cheese, cherries or
just pepper worked originally into the
dough. This last makes an excellent hors
d'oeuvre pastry.

Our Janka had organized her filling well
in advance. Browned bread crumbs, lemon
rind grated into sugar, raisins, currants,
very finely sliced apples, almonds and a
small pitcher of melted butter were all set
out on a tray. These were strewn alter-

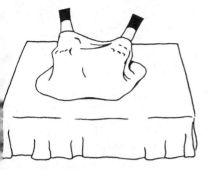

nately over the surface of the dough. Then came the forming of the roll. Using both hands, Janka picked up one side of the cloth and, while never actually touching the dough itself, tilted and nudged the cloth and the sheet this way and that until the dough rolled over on itself—jelly-roll fashion—and completely enclosed the filling. Finally, she slid the long cylinder onto a greased baking sheet and curved it into a horseshoe. From beginning to end the process had masterly craftsmanship. Would that we could give you her skill as easily as we give you her recipe. Now are you ready? Prepare the filling ingredients. Do not feel limited by these proportions or materials. See other fillings, page 573.

Mix:

    1 tablespoon cinnamon

with:

    4 to 6 tablespoons browned
        bread crumbs
    1 tablespoon lemon rind

grated into:

    1 cup sugar
    ¾ cup raisins or currants
    (½ cup shredded blanched almonds)
    6 to 8 cups finely chopped tart apples

Have ready:

    5 tablespoons melted butter

Preheat oven to 400°.
Have a cloth ready on a large table-height surface, around which you will be able to walk. Work lightly into the cloth:

    Flour

Sift onto a board:

    1½ cups all-purpose flour
    ¼ teaspoon salt

In testing, we have tried as many as 3 different commercially available flours during the same morning with amazingly different results. Part of the fame of this age-old pastry rests on the fine flours formerly available in Hungary. Add gradually, as you work the dough with your fingers:

    1 egg

beaten with:

    ⅓ to ½ cup tepid water or milk
    (2 teaspoons vinegar)

Depending on your flour, you may have to add a few tablespoons more of tepid water. Combine the ingredients quickly with your fingers and knead them on a board until the dough no longer sticks to it. You may brush the surface with melted butter. Cover the ball of dough with a warm bowl and let it rest for 20 to 30 minutes. Roll it out on the board as thin as possible. Move to the table. Begin to stretch the dough gently from the center out, trying not to tear it, as patching is difficult. If you are skillful, this should stretch to about a 2-yd. square. A heavier edge of dough or a border will develop as you work and whatever remains of this must be cut off with a knife before the filling is spread or the pastry rolled up. Use this excess dough for making patches. Before filling, brush the dough with some of the melted butter. Sprinkle over the surface the bread crumbs, sugar and lemon rind, currants, raisins, almonds and apples. Dust with:

    Cinnamon

Form the roll as described above ♦ not too tightly, as the dough will expand. Slide it onto the greased baking sheet. Brush the surface of the roll with some of the melted butter and sprinkle it lightly with water. Bake for 20 minutes at 400°, then lower the heat to 350°, brush the strudel again with the remaining butter, and bake about 10 minutes longer, until brown. Remove from oven and dust with:

    Confectioners' sugar

Cut in wide diagonal slices and serve.

ABOUT MERINGUE PASTE

There are many variations of meringue—all based on egg white and sugar. They include glamorous glacées and vacherins, served with ices or creams, including ice cream; Christmas meringue cookies, of which cinnamon stars are, perhaps deservedly, the best beloved; mountainous, fluffy pie toppings; more discreet Italian types of meringue, used over puddings and tarts; insulating meringues like those prepared for Omelette Soufflé Surprise and Baked Alaska; Swiss Meringue or Royal Glaze. Each calls for special treatment.

In this day of the electric mixer, showy meringue desserts have become effortless to make. There are several ways of confecting and baking meringues, and they have attracted vociferous partisans. You will find them described below.

Ingredients and proportions do not vary. For every 4 egg whites (from 2-oz. eggs) use ½ lb. sugar. As you know, sugars of the same weight differ tremendously in volume, see About Solid Sugars, page 505. Eggs should be at about 70° and you should open, separate and whip them when you are ready to mix the meringue. The baking is more a drying than a heating process. ♦ Use bottom heat only. A preheated 225° oven will give you a soft, crunchy meringue; a preheated 275° oven, a chewy one. A third, highly recommended baking method, if you have a very well-insulated oven, is to preheat it to 475°. Have your meringues ready to bake; pop them quickly into the 475° oven; turn off the heat immediately and forget about them for 8 hours.

If you wonder about the indestructible meringues served in public places, they are based on confectioners' sugar; the egg whites are heated over hot water as for Génoise, page 640; and the meringues dried overnight in a warming oven, not over 175°. Whichever baking procedure is chosen, the classic confectioner does not allow his meringues to color. ♦ Store meringues tightly covered, as they absorb moisture and disintegrate easily.

To form meringue paste, use a spoon and spatula or a pastry bag. Make individual kisses or rings to fill with ices, ice creams or frozen desserts for meringue glacées. Shape the paste into a large nest on a heat-resistant platter and fill it with fruits and cream for **Pinch Pie.** Bake it in spring form layers and fill them for **Schaumtorten,** or swirl the paste into flat coils, one plain and one decorated at the edges with large contiguous baroque dots, to place as a crown on the cream filling for **Vacherin Rings.** For filling suggestions and an all-in-one meringue baked with cake, see Cake Fillings, page 644, and Meringue Cream Tart, page 641.

I.　　　　　　　Twelve 3-Inch Meringues
　　　　　　　　　　　　or a 9-Inch Pie
Preheat oven to 225°.
♦ Have egg whites at about 75°. Beat until foamy in an electric mixer:

4 egg whites

Add:

1 teaspoon vanilla
(⅛ teaspoon cream of tartar)

Add, while continuing to beat, 1 teaspoon at a time:

1 cup sifted finely powdered sugar or
1 cup minus 1 tablespoon sifted sugar

When the mixture stands in stiff peaks on the beater, it is ready to be baked. ♦ Do not overbeat. To shape, see above. For a glaze, you may dust the meringues lightly with:

Granulated sugar

Cook on baking sheets covered with parchment paper for about 1 hour or longer, depending on the size. The reason for the use of paper is not to prevent sticking but to diffuse the heat. In some famous kitchens the meringues are baked on a thick board. ♦ Do not remove from the oven at once, but turn off the oven, open the door and leave them for at least 5 minutes. Cool them gradually, away from a draft. Remove them from the sheet when cool. If kisses are to be filled, crush the smooth side lightly with the thumb while

the meringues are still warm. Shortly before serving, fill the hollows with:

Sweetened and flavored whipped
cream or a frozen mixture

Place 2 filled meringues together. Serve them with:

Ice cream or whipped cream

covered with:

Sweetened crushed fruit, or
a chocolate sauce, page 711

II.　　　　　　Twelve 3-Inch Meringues
　　　　　　　　　　　or a 9-Inch Pie
Preheat oven to 225°.
♦ Have egg whites at about 75°. Sift:

1 cup very finely powdered sugar or
1 cup minus 1 tablespoon sugar

Beat until foamy:

4 egg whites

Add:

1 teaspoon vanilla
(⅛ teaspoon cream of tartar)

Add, while continuing to beat, 1 teaspoon at a time:

2 tablespoons sifted sugar

Beat this mixture until ♦ stiff but not dry, see To Beat Egg Whites, page 515. ♦ Fold in by hand, quickly and lightly, the rest of the sugar. If this is not done quickly the meringues will be soft. To bake, see Method I.

ABOUT FRUIT PIES

If you don't find the fruit combination you are looking for in our fruit pie recipes, perhaps you would like to experiment with fillings for yourself. A 9-inch fruit pie needs about 4 cups of fresh fruit or 3 cups of cooked fruit. Use about 2⅔ tablespoons quick-cooking tapioca to thicken the fruit juice. Let the fruit and tapioca stand for 15 minutes before filling the shells and baking. Correct the sweetening, then proceed as directed in berry pies. Some suggested proportions are:

½ apple and ½ pear
½ rhubarb and ½ strawberry
⅓ gooseberry and ⅔ strawberry
½ cherry and ½ rhubarb
⅓ cranberry and ⅔ apple
½ mincemeat, ¼ apple sauce and
¼ crushed pineapple
½ fresh strawberries and ½ bananas,
plus sugar and whipped cream
⅔ raspberries and ⅓ currants

Fruit pies ✷ freeze well, but ♦ do not freeze those with a custard base.

APPLE PIE
　　　　　　　　　　　　　A 9-Inch Pie
Call it "à la mode" if you garnish your pie with ice cream.
Preheat oven to 450°.
Line a 9-inch pie pan with:

Pie Crust, page 590, or Cheese
Pie Crust, page 592

Peel, core and cut into very thin pieces:

5 to 6 cups apples

Have you ever tried half apples and half green tomatoes? The result is amazingly like a very tart apple pie—with an interesting difference. If you are using dried apples, allow 1 lb. apples to 1 quart water and cook 35 to 45 minutes. Combine and sift over the apples:

    ½ to ⅔ cup white or brown sugar
    ⅛ teaspoon salt
    1 tablespoon to 1½ tablespoons
        cornstarch
    (¼ teaspoon cinnamon)
    (⅛ teaspoon nutmeg)

Only very tart apples require the larger amount of sugar. Only very juicy apples require the larger amount of cornstarch. Stir the apples gently until they are well coated. Place them in layers in the pie shell. Dot them with:

    1½ tablespoons butter

If the apples lack flavor, sprinkle them with:

    1 tablespoon lemon juice
    ½ teaspoon grated lemon rind
    (1 teaspoon vanilla)

If you are serving the pie with cheese, omit the above flavors and use:

    (1 teaspoon fennel or anise seed)

If the apples are very dry, add:

    2 tablespoons water or cream

Cover the pie with a pricked upper crust, see Pie Crust, page 589. Bake the pie in a 450° oven for 10 minutes. Reduce the heat to 350°. Bake the pie until done, from 45 minutes to 1 hour in all. For a delicious touch, sprinkle the top crust lightly with sugar and cinnamon as you put it into the oven. Some cooks brush it first with milk. The pie may be made without an upper crust. Bake in a 450° oven for 20 minutes, then sprinkle over the top:

    (1 cup grated cheese)

Run under a broiler to melt the cheese.

APPLE TARTS
                                    8 Tarts
Preheat oven to 375°.
Line eight shallow 3-inch muffin cups or individual pie pans with:
    Any Pie Crust, page 590
Fill them with:
    4 cups peeled, thinly sliced apples
Combine and pour over the fruit:
    ½ cup sugar
    2 slightly beaten eggs
    2 tablespoons melted butter
    1 tablespoon lemon juice
    1 cup cream or ½ cup evaporated
        milk and ½ cup water
    (½ teaspoon cinnamon)
    (⅛ teaspoon nutmeg)
Place on cookie sheet. Bake about 40 minutes.

PEACH PIE
                            A 9-Inch Pie
Preheat oven to 400°.

Line a pie pan with:
    Any Pie Crust, page 590
Combine and blend well:
    1 egg or 2 egg yolks
    2 tablespoons flour
    ⅔ to 1 cup granulated sugar
    (⅛ cup melted butter)
Pour this mixture over:
    Halves of canned or fresh peaches
that have been placed cut side up in the pie shell. Bake for 15 minutes at 400°, then reduce the heat to 300° and bake it about 50 minutes longer. Serve hot or, if cold, garnish with:
    (Whipped Cream)

II.   A 9-Inch Pie
Follow the recipe for:
    Apple Pie, page 600
Substitute for the apples:
    5 cups peeled, sliced peaches
Use the smaller amount of sugar.

BERRY PIE WITH FRESH FRUIT
                            A 9-Inch Pie
Use:
    Gooseberry, Currant, Blackberry,
    Raspberry, Strawberry, Blueberry,
    Huckleberry or Loganberry
Preheat oven to 450°.
Line a pie pan with:
    Any Pie Crust, page 590
Prepare by picking over and hulling:
    4 cups fresh berries
At this point we should like to raise the question of thickening for berries. Technically, each batch would require a different amount of thickener, depending on the variety of fruit, degree of ripeness, etc. For practical purposes, an often suggested formula is 4 tablespoons of flour for 4 cups of fruit. But we much prefer either of the following substitutions, the first dry, the second moist. Either add and mix:
    2⅔ tablespoons quick-cooking tapioca
to:
    ⅔ to 1 cup sugar
or mix:
    2 tablespoons cornstarch
with:
    ¼ cup water or fruit juice
until very smooth and then blend with:
    ⅔ to 1 cup sugar
Whether you use tapioca or cornstarch, let the mixture stand for 15 minutes after blending it gently into the fresh berries and before putting it into the pie shell. Season the fruit with:
    1½ tablespoons lemon juice or
    ½ teaspoon cinnamon
Dot the fruit with:
    1 to 2 tablespoons butter
Cover the pie with a top crust or with a lattice, page 589. Bake the pie in a 450° oven for 10 minutes. Reduce the heat to 350° and bake about 40 to 45 minutes.

FRESH CHERRY PIE
A 9-Inch Pie

Follow the recipe for Berry Pie with Fresh Fruit, page 601. Use fresh, pitted, sour cherries and thicken with tapioca or cornstarch. Omit the cinnamon. Add:

**2 drops almond flavoring or
2 tablespoons kirsch**

This pie may call for as much as 1⅓ cups of sugar in all. Fine made with a lattice top. Bake as for Berry Pie with Fresh Fruit, page 601.

BERRY OR CHERRY PIE WITH COOKED FRUIT
A 9-Inch Pie

Allow approximately:

**2½ cups sweetened canned or cooked
berries or cherries
1 cup fruit juice**

Proceed as directed in the above recipe for Berry Pie with Fresh Fruit, but for thickening use only:

**1½ tablespoons quick-cooking tapioca
or 1 tablespoon cornstarch**

mixed with:

2 tablespoons water

and ◗ be sure to combine as described above. You may bake the filling in the unbaked pie shell as in Berry Pie with Fresh Fruit or you may thicken the fruit juice by heating it separately with the thickener, then mix it with the fruit and put it in a baked shell to serve.

BERRY OR CHERRY PIE WITH FROZEN FRUIT
A 9-Inch Pie

Preheat oven to 450°.
Line a pie pan with:

Any Pie Crust, page 590

Mix and let stand for 15 minutes:

**2 pkgs. frozen berries or cherries—
20 oz.— defrosted enough so that
the fruit separates easily
3 tablespoons quick-cooking tapioca
½ cup sugar
⅛ teaspoon salt
2 tablespoons melted butter**

Fill the pie shell. Cover with crust or lattice and bake in a 450° oven for 10 minutes. Reduce the heat and bake at 350° for 45 minutes to 1 hour.

GERMAN CHERRY PIE
About 5 Servings—A 9-Inch Pie

The Germans who became political refugees in 1830 and 1848 brought with them to their new American home this treasured recipe for their Cherry Cake or Pie. There **are**, of course, different versions of the **same** pie. Ours is a fairly modern one, **which** may call the displeasure of old-timers down on our heads. However, even **a** German Cherry Cake or Pie recipe must **bow** to the Zeitgeist.
Drain and keep the juice from:

**2½ cups solid pitted cherries,
fresh or canned**

Pour over the cherries:

6 tablespoons sugar

Very acid cherries may require more sugar Permit to stand for about ½ hour, until the sugar is dissolved. Stir gently several times. Drain and reserve juice. Prepare:

1½ cups sifted flour

Resift it with:

**1½ teaspoons cinnamon
6 tablespoons sugar
⅛ teaspoon salt**

Cut into these ingredients with a pastry blender or 2 knives, until blended:

½ cup butter

Add to the above:

1 beaten egg

Now, wade in with your hands and work the dough until it holds together, but no longer. Chill it. Pat it into a 9-inch oven proof glass pie pan. Let it come to the upper edge of the pan. See that it is spread evenly. Crimp the dough around the edge with the tines of a fork.
◗ Preheat oven to 350°.
Measure the sirup drained from the cherries. There should be ¾ cup. Taste it Add sugar if it seems to be too sour. Reserve ¼ cup. Place the rest over low heat Stir into the ¼ cup, until smooth:

4 teaspoons cornstarch

When the rest of the juice is boiling, stir in the cornstarch mixture. Stir and cook over low heat for 2 or 3 minutes until the mixture is no longer cloudy. Add:

(¼ teaspoon almond extract)

Place the cherries in the pie shell, pour the hot juice over them and bake from 50 to 60 minutes.

SOUR CREAM CHERRY PIE
A 9-Inch Pie or 6 Tar

Preheat oven to 325°.
Follow the rule for a 9-inch pie shell of:

**Zwieback or Ginger Snap Pie Crust,
page 593**

Fill the chilled shell with the following cherry custard. Beat:

3 eggs

Add:

**¾ cup sugar
¾ cup cultured sour cream
2 cups fresh or canned
drained cherries**

Bake the pie until the custard is firm, about 1 hour. Serve it very hot or very cold.

STRAWBERRY OR RASPBERRY CREAM PIE
A 9-Inch F

Prepare any:

Any Baked Pie Shell, page 590

When cool, fill with:

Bavarian Berry Cream, page 694

GLAZED FRUIT PIE
A 9-Inch P

Prepare with a generous high rim:

Any Baked Pie Shell, page 590

PIES, PASTES AND FILLED PASTRIES

>**1 quart strawberries or red or black**
>   **raspberries**

Reserve and ↶ blend or sieve 1 cup of the
fruit. Combine and cook, stirring until
thickened over low heat for about 10 to 15
minutes:
>**¾ cup sugar**
>**2½ tablespoons cornstarch**
>**¼ teaspoon salt**
>**1 cup water**

Add the blended fruit to give color. Put
the whole berries into the pie shell, evenly
distributed. Pour the sirup over the berries, coating them thoroughly by turning
but not displacing them. Chill the pie in
the refrigerator at least 4 hours. Serve it
garnished with:
>(Whipped cream)

BLUEBERRY OR HUCKLEBERRY TART

A 9-Inch Pie

If seeds are small, it's blueberries you
have; if many and large—huckleberries.
The flavor is almost identical.

Prepare:
>**Galette, page 592, or Pie Dough,**
>   **page 588**

Place it in a pan and chill as directed.
Bake in a 450° oven for about 15 minutes.
Cover with:
>**1 quart blueberries**
>**½ cup sugar**
>(**3 tablespoons lemon juice**)

Bake the tart in a 375° oven for about 10
minutes. Cook and stir over—not in—boiling water until thick:
>**½ cup cream**
>**2 or 3 beaten egg yolks**
>**½ cup sugar**
>**⅛ teaspoon salt**

Cool the custard and pour it over the
lightly cooled tart. Cool it well. Cover
with a:
>(**Meringue, page 681**)

RHUBARB PIE

A 9-Inch Pie

Use:
>**4 cups young, unpeeled, diced**
>   **rhubarb stalks**
>**¼ cup flour**
>**1¼ to 2 cups sugar**
>**1 tablespoon butter**
>(**1 teaspoon grated orange rind**)

Follow the rule for baking Berry Pie with
Fresh Fruit, page 601.

GRAPE PIE

A 9-Inch Pie

Preheat oven to 450°.
Use:
>**4 cups blue grapes**

Slip the pulp out of the skins. Reserve the
skins. Cook the pulp until the seeds
loosen. Press through a colander to remove seeds. Combine the pulp, the skins
and:

>**¾ cup sugar**
>**1½ tablespoons lemon juice**
>**1 tablespoon grated orange rind**
>**1 tablespoon quick-cooking tapioca**

Permit these ingredients to stand for 15
minutes. Prepare:
>**Any Pie Crust, page 590**

To form the shell, see page 589. Fill the
shell with the grape mixture and form a
lattice of pastry over the top, see page 589.
Bake the pie for 10 minutes at 450°, then
lower the heat to 350° and bake for about
20 minutes more.

★ MINCEMEAT

This is enough filling for about 20 pies.
Some of our fans make this recipe for
Christmas gifts. It is best if prepared at
least 2 weeks before using.
Prepare:
>**9 quarts sliced, peeled apples**

Combine with:
>**4 lbs. lean, chopped beef or ox heart**
>**2 lbs. chopped beef suet**
>**3 lbs. sugar**
>**2 quarts cider**
>**4 lbs. seeded raisins**
>**3 lbs. currants**
>**1½ lbs. chopped citron**
>**½ lb. dried, chopped, candied**
>   **orange peel**
>**½ lb. dried, chopped, candied**
>   **lemon peel**
>   **Juice and rind of 1 lemon**
>**1 tablespoon each cinnamon,**
>   **mace, cloves**
>**1 teaspoon each salt and pepper**
>**2 whole grated nutmegs**
>**1 gallon sour cherries with juice**
>**2 lbs. broken nut meats**
>(**1 teaspoon powdered coriander seed**)

Cook these ingredients slowly for 2 hours.
Stir frequently. Seal in sterile jars. Before
serving, season with:
>**Brandy**

★ MINCE PIE

A 9-Inch Pie

Preheat oven to 450°.
Line a pie pan with:
>**Any Pie Crust, page 590**

Fill it with:
>**Mincemeat, above**

Add to the mincemeat:
>(**2 to 4 tablespoons brandy**)

Cover the pie with an upper crust. Bake at
450° for 10 minutes, then bake at 350° for
about 30 minutes.

★ MINCE PIE FLAMBÉ

A quickly assembled gala dessert.
Bake:
>**Cookies or pie crust rounds**

Heap:
>**Hot mincemeat**

in the center of an ovenproof dish. Surround it just before serving with:

Baked rounds of pie crusts
    or cookies
Have ready to pour over the mincemeat:
    ⅛ cup warmed brandy
To flambé, see page 127.

★ MOCK MINCE PIE
                                        A 9-Inch Pie
Cut into pieces:
    1½ cups seeded raisins
Pare, core and slice:
    4 medium-size tart apples or a
        combination of apples and green
        tomatoes
Combine the raisins and apples. Add:
    Grated rind of 1 orange
    Juice of 1 orange
    ½ cup cider or other fruit juice
Cover these ingredients and simmer until
the apples are very soft. Stir in until well
blended:
    ¾ cup sugar
    ½ teaspoon each cinnamon and cloves
    2 or 3 tablespoons finely crushed
        soda crackers
If the apples are dry, use the smaller
amount. This mixture will keep for several days. Shortly before using it, add:
    (1 or 2 tablespoons brandy)
Line a pie pan with:
    Any Pie Crust, page 590
Fill it with mock mincemeat. Cover with
an upper crust or with a lattice of pastry.
Bake in a 450° oven for 10 minutes and
about 20 minutes longer at 350°.

PRUNE OR APRICOT PIE
                                        A 9-Inch Pie
Preheat oven to 325°.
Prepare by any recipe:
    Any baked Pie Shell, page 590
Put stewed, unsweetened prunes or apri-
cots through a ricer. Combine:
    ¾ cup prune or apricot pulp
    ½ teaspoon grated lemon rind
    1 tablespoon lemon juice
    ½ cup sugar
Beat until stiff but not dry:
    3 egg whites
Beat in very slowly:
    ½ cup sugar
Fold the egg whites into the fruit mixture.
Fill the pie shell. Bake for about 20 min-
utes or until set.

RAISIN PIE
                                        A 9-Inch Pie
Prepare by any recipe:
    Any baked Pie Shell, page 590
Cook to the boiling point:
    1 cup seedless or seeded white raisins
    1 cup water
Add:
    ½ cup white or brown sugar
Cool ½ cup of this mixture. Stir into it
gently:
    2 tablespoons butter
    2 tablespoons all-purpose flour

Return it to the saucepan. Cook and stir
these ingredients over low heat until the
flour has thickened. Remove the pan from
the heat. Beat in:
    2 egg yolks
    1 teaspoon grated lemon rind
    3 tablespoons lemon juice
Cool the filling. Fill the pie shell. Cover
with Meringue I, page 681, and bake as
directed.

✱ LINZERTORTE
                                A 9-Inch Pie or Cake
The following is a delicious German
"company" cake or pie. It looks like an
open jam pie and, being rich, is usually
served in thin wedges. It should serve 16
Preheat oven to 400°.
Sift:
    1 cup sugar
Beat until soft:
    ½ to ⅞ cup butter
Add the sugar gradually. Blend these in-
gredients until very light and creamy
Add:
    1 teaspoon grated lemon rind
Beat in, one at a time:
    2 eggs
Stir in gradually:
    1¼ cups sifted all-purpose flour
    1 cup unblanched almonds, ground in
        a nut grinder or a ⅃ blender
    ½ teaspoon cinnamon
    ¼ teaspoon cloves
    1 tablespoon cocoa
    ¼ teaspoon salt
The old recipe reads, "Stir for one hour
but of course no high-geared American h
time for that. If the dough is very so
chill it. Pat it into an ovenproof dish
the thickness of ⅛ inch. Rechill it for
hours. Cover the bottom of the cake ge
erously with a good quality of:
    Raspberry jam, preserves or
        apple butter
Place the remaining dough in a pastry tu
and give the pie a good edge and lattice
forcing the dough through the bag. Ba
the cake in a 400° oven about 25 minut
Before serving, fill the hollows with ad
tional preserves. You may also dust the
with:
    Confectioners' sugar

BANBURY TARTS
                            About Six 4-Inch Ta
Have ready:
    Individual baked Pie Shells,
        page 590
Combine:
    1 cup seeded raisins
    1 cup sugar
    2 tablespoons cracker crumbs
    1 well-beaten egg
    Grated rind of 1 lemon
    1½ tablespoons lemon juice
    2 tablespoons butter
    ¼ cup chopped candied fruits

ook and stir these ingredients over low
eat until they begin to thicken. Remove
om the heat. Cool. Partly fill the tart
nells. Top with:
(Whipped cream)
ou may use this filling in Turnovers, page
08.

RUMB OR GRAVEL PIE
A 9-Inch Pie

'reheat oven to 325°.
Jse a:
Baked Pie Shell, page 590
or this Pennsylvania Dutch specialty.
prinkle the bottom of shell with:
(½ cup raisins)
Combine and cook in a double boiler un-
il thick:
1 cup brown sugar, mild molasses
or honey
½ cup hot water
3 beaten eggs
Cool and pour these ingredients into the
ie shell. Combine and work like pastry:
1 cup cake or cookie crumbs
⅓ cup flour
½ to 1 teaspoon cinnamon
¼ teaspoon nutmeg
⅛ teaspoon ginger
⅓ cup soft butter
Sprinkle this mixture over the filling. To
make Gravel Pie don't combine the above
ngredients. Instead, sprinkle them alternately over the pie—with the crumbs on
op. Bake for 20 to 30 minutes.

JEFFERSON DAVIS PIE
A 9-Inch Pie

Preheat oven to 325°.
Prepare:
A baked Pie Shell, page 590
Cream:
½ cup butter
2 cups packed light brown sugar
Beat in:
4 egg yolks
Mix, then add:
2 tablespoons all-purpose flour
1 teaspoon cinnamon
½ teaspoon allspice
1 teaspoon freshly grated nutmeg
Stir in:
1 cup cream
½ cup chopped dates
½ cup raisins
½ cup broken pecan meats
Fill the shell. Bake the pie until set, about
30 minutes. When cool, top with:
Meringue I, page 681
Bake as directed.

CHESS TARTS
Fill:
Baked Tart Shells, page 590
with filling for:
Jefferson Davis Pie, above
omitting the dates and spices. When cool,
cover with:
Whipped cream

PECAN PIE
A 9-Inch Pie
This pie may also be made with walnuts.
Preheat oven to 450°.
Prepare:
An unfilled Pie Shell, page 590
and bake it only partially, from 5 to 7 minutes. Allow it to cool. Reduce oven heat
to 375°. Cream:
¼ cup butter
1 cup firmly packed brown sugar
Beat in, one at a time:
3 eggs
Stir in:
½ cup light corn sirup or molasses
1 to 1½ cups broken pecans or walnuts
1 teaspoon vanilla or 1 tablespoon rum
½ teaspoon salt
Fill the shell. Bake the pie about 40 minutes or until a knife inserted in the filling
comes out clean. Serve warm or cold.

TRANSPARENT PIE
We have encountered this great Southern
favorite at all sorts of gatherings, from
fiestas to funerals. There are many variations, but we like to use our recipe for
Pecan Pie, above, omitting the pecans and
replacing the vanilla with:
A grating of nutmeg or 1 tablespoon
lemon juice
You might try adding some tart jelly for
flavor.

ABOUT PUMPKINS
When Halloween comes 'round, we welcome pumpkins as symbols of harvest and
sources of shivery fun. For holiday decorations, why not have each of the children
carve his own small pumpkin? ♦ Then
stack them into a totem pole. Use the topmost cutout as a lid, the remainder for
ears and noses. Stems make good features,
too. Choose pumpkins of varied shapes, as
shown on page 606, and encourage the
sculptors to vary their expressions.
Abroad, we find almost everywhere that
a great diversity of puddings, soups and
vegetable dishes are prepared from these
members of the squash family. Here in
America we restrict their use mostly to pie.
♦ To cook pumpkin, wash and cut it in
half, crosswise. Remove seeds and strings.
Place it in a pan, shell side up, and bake it
in a 325° oven for 1 hour or more, depending on size, until it is tender and
begins to fall apart. Scrape the pulp from
the shell and put it through a ricer or
strainer.

PUMPKIN OR SQUASH PIE
A 9-Inch Pie
Prepare:
A baked Pie Shell, page 590.
Mix in the top of a double boiler and cook
over, not in, hot water until thick:
1½ cups cooked pumpkin or squash

crunches lend themselves well to bakin
for individual servings.

COBBLERS AND DEEP-DISH PIES

A cobbler, first cousin to a deep-dish pie
involves a rich biscuit dough, page 584
and fruit. It is baked with the fruit eithe
under or over it. It is usually served wit
Hard Sauce, Sweetened Butters, or Desser
Sauces, page 709; but try a fresh hot black
berry cobbler with vanilla ice cream.
Preheat oven to 425°.
Prepare the fruit as for any fruit pie filling
♦ Have the fruit boiling hot. Have ready
    Fluffy Biscuit Dough, page 584
Use ½ the amount given. Place the dough
in a greased 8 x 8-inch pan and cover i
closely with the hot fruit or place the ho
fruit in the bottom of an 8-inch baking
dish and cover it with the dough. Dot the
fruit with:
    2 tablespoons butter
Sprinkle it with:
    (**¾ teaspoon cinnamon**)
Bake the cobbler for about ½ hour.

APPLE, PEACH OR
PLUM CAKE COCKAIGNE
              A 9 x 9 x 2½-Inch Pan
Our friend Jane Nickerson, formerly Food
Editor of the New York Times, suggests
using fresh guavas in this dish.
Preheat oven to 425°.
If the fruit used is very juicy, reduce the
liquid in the dough by at least 1 table-
spoon. Sift before measuring:
    1 cup all-purpose flour
Resift with:
    1 teaspoon double-acting
      baking powder
    ¼ teaspoon salt
    2 tablespoons sugar
Add:
    1½ to 3 tablespoons butter
Work these ingredients like pastry, page
588. Beat well in a measuring cup:
    1 egg
    ½ teaspoon vanilla
Add:
    Enough milk to make a ½-cup
    mixture
Combine with the flour and butter to make
a stiff dough. You may pat the dough into
the pan with a floured palm or spread it in
part with a spoon and then distribute it
evenly by pushing it with the fruit sections
when you place them closely in overlapping rows. Use about:
    3 to 4 cups sliced, pared apples or
      peaches or sliced, unpared plums
Sprinkle with a mixture of:
    About 1 cup sugar
    2 teaspoons cinnamon
    3 tablespoons melted butter
Bake about 25 minutes.

1½ cups undiluted evaporated milk or
   rich cream
  ½ cup brown sugar
  ¼ cup white sugar
  ½ teaspoon salt
  1 teaspoon cinnamon
  ½ teaspoon ginger
  ⅛ teaspoon cloves
  4 slightly beaten eggs
Cool slightly and add:
  (1 teaspoon vanilla or 2 tablespoons
    brandy or rum)
  (¾ cup black walnut meats)
Pour the mixture into the baked pie shell.
Serve with:
    Whipped cream

ABOUT FRUIT PASTRIES

Here we include cobblers, deep-dish pies,
fresh fruit cakes, shortcakes, upside-down
cakes, crisps and crunches. Remember
that large shortcakes, fresh fruit cakes and

FRENCH APPLE OR PEACH CAKE
A Deep 8-Inch Pie Pan
Sweet and rich.
Preheat oven to 425°.
Grease the pan or ovenproof dish and cover the bottom well with:

2 cups or more sliced apples, peaches or other fruit

Sprinkle the fruit with:

⅔ cup sugar
Cinnamon or nutmeg
Grated rind and juice of 1 lemon

Dredge with:

1 tablespoon flour

Pour over surface:

2 to 4 tablespoons melted butter

Prepare the following batter. Sift before measuring:

1 cup all-purpose flour

Resift with:

½ cup sugar
1 teaspoon any baking powder
¼ teaspoon salt

Beat and add:

2 egg yolks
1 tablespoon melted butter
¼ cup milk

Beat these ingredients with swift strokes until blended. Cover the fruit with the batter. Bake the cake for about 30 minutes. Reverse it on a platter. Cool slightly. Use the egg whites for:

(Meringue II, page 681)

SKILLET OR UPSIDE-DOWN CAKE
A 9- or 10-Inch Heavy Skillet
Vary this recipe, which conventionally calls for canned pineapple, by using canned peaches or apricots. The last two require only ½ cup sugar. Fresh fruit, peaches, cherries, apples, etc., may require more than 1 cup, according to the acidity of the fruit.
Preheat oven to 325°.
Melt in a skillet:

¼ or ½ cup butter

Add, cook gently and stir until dissolved:

1 cup packed brown sugar

Remove the pan from the heat and add:

(1 cup pecan meats)

Drain and place on the bottom of the skillet:

Slices or halves of drained canned fruit

Cover the fruit with the following batter:
Sift:

1 cup cake flour

Resift with:

1 teaspoon double-acting baking powder

Beat in a separate bowl:

4 egg yolks

Add:

1 tablespoon melted butter
1 teaspoon vanilla

Sift in a separate bowl:

1 cup sugar

Whip until ◗ stiff but not dry:

4 egg whites

Fold in the sugar, 1 tablespoon at a time, then the yolk mixture and finally the sifted flour, ¼ cup at a time. Bake the cake for about ½ hour. Serve upside down, after sprinkling the fruit with:

(Brandy or rum)

The cake may be garnished with:

Whipped cream or a dessert sauce, page 709

For individual servings, try this method: Put butter, sugar and fruit in base of custard cups, run batter given above on top of the fruit and bake until done in a 350° oven.

FRESH FRUIT CRISP OR PARADISE
6 Servings
This dessert may be baked in an ovenproof dish from which you can serve at table. Its success, when made with apples, depends upon their flavor. See About Apples, page 110.
Preheat oven to 375°.
Peel, core and slice into pie pan or dish:

4 cups tart apples

or use the same amount of:

Peaches, slightly sugared rhubarb or pitted cherries

Season with:

(2 tablespoons lemon juice or kirsch)

Work like pastry with a pastry blender or with the finger tips:

½ cup all-purpose flour
½ cup packed brown sugar
¼ cup butter
½ teaspoon salt, if butter is unsalted
(1 teaspoon cinnamon)

The mixture must be lightly worked so that it does not become oily. Spread these crumbly ingredients over the apples. Bake in a 9-inch pie pan or dish for about 30 minutes. Serve hot or cold with:

(Sweet or cultured sour cream)

QUICK CHERRY CRUNCH
A 9 x 9 x 2-Inch Pan
A well-flavored, easy cherry pastry.
Preheat oven to 350°.
Mix and let stand 15 minutes:

½ cup cherry juice
1½ tablespoons quick-cooking tapioca

Melt in a large pan:

½ cup butter

Mix with it:

1 to 1½ cups packed brown sugar
1 cup flour
1 cup quick-cooking oatmeal
¼ teaspoon each baking powder, salt and soda

Put half of this mixture in the baking pan. Scatter over it:

2 cups drained canned red cherries

and the juice and tapioca mixture. Cover the fruit with the other half of the pastry mixture. Bake about 30 to 35 minutes or until brown.

SWEET TURNOVERS OR RISSOLES

To shape these tea pastries, see Filled
Cookies, page 664.
Prepare:
> Any Pie Crust, page 590

Use for filling:
> Well-flavored apple sauce
> Preserves or jam
> Mincemeat, page 603
> Banbury Tart Filling
> Filled Cookie Filling

To cook, see Rissoles, page 55. While still
warm, dust pastries with:
> Powdered sugar

FRUIT DUMPLINGS

4 Dumplings

Prepare:
> Pie Crust, page 590, Cheese Pie
> Crust, page 592, or Biscuit Dough,
> page 584.

Chill it. Pare and core:
> 4 medium size apples or 4 peeled,
> pitted and halved peaches or apricots

If using canned fruit, drain well and sprinkle with:
> Lemon juice or rum

and use less sugar. Combine until blended:
> ¾ cup packed brown sugar
> ¼ cup soft butter
> ½ teaspoon salt
> ½ teaspoon cinnamon
> (Grated lemon rind or citron)

Fill the core hollows with this mixture or
with:
> Raspberry jam

and spread the remainder over the fruit.
Preheat oven to 450°.
Roll out the dough in a thin sheet, ⅛ inch
for pastry, ¼ inch for biscuit dough. Cut
it into 4 squares. Brush squares with the
white of an egg, to keep the dough from
becoming soggy. Place an apple on each
square. Enclose the apple entirely within
the dough. Press the edges together, using
a little water, if necessary, to make them
stick. Prick the tops of the dumplings in
several places. They may be chilled for
several hours or baked at once. Brush the
tops with milk. Bake for about 10 minutes
at 450°, reduce the heat to 350° and bake
for about 45 minutes, until the apples are
tender. Test them with a toothpick. Serve
with:
> Brown Sugar Butter Sauce, page 712

If you wish to bake the dumplings in
sauce, combine and simmer for 5 minutes:
> 1 cup water
> ½ cup sugar
> 2 tablespoons butter
> ½ teaspoon cinnamon

For enhanced flavor, if you are using apples, you may simmer the cores and peelings in 1½ cups water for 15 minutes.
Drain and use the fruit liquid in place of
the water. Pour it boiling hot over the
dumplings when they begin to color.

Dumplings that are not baked in sauce may
be served hot or cold with:
> Fluffy Hard Sauce with Rum, page
> 714, Foamy Sauce, page 714,
> Lemon Sauce, page 709, or cream

RAISED DUMPLINGS
OR DAMPFNUDELN

About 16 Dumplings

It has been fun to dig in old cookbooks for
this recipe, if only because it made us
realize that the modern method of writing
for cooks is an immense improvement over
the old. Our grandmothers had to hack
through a labyrinth, undoubtedly armed
with a ball of string, plus a rabbit's foot,
in order to arrive at their goal. This
homely old-time favorite is worth resur-
recting. Try it in its modern form. A well-
known Cincinnati hostess serves it as a
dessert at formal dinners with much success.
Dissolve:
> ½ cake compressed yeast

in:
> ½ cup scalded milk, cooled to 85°

Work in:
> 1 tablespoon sugar
> 1¼ cups sifted all-purpose flour

Permit this heavy sponge to rise, covered
with a cloth in a warm place, until light,
for about 1 hour. Cream:
> 1 tablespoon butter
> 2 tablespoons sugar
> ½ teaspoon salt

Beat in and stir until light:
> 1 whole egg

Add this to the sponge and work in about:
> ½ cup sifted all-purpose flour

or enough to stiffen, as for yeast cake.
Cover the bowl with a cloth. Permit the
dough to rise until doubled in bulk. Shape
it into about 16 biscuits. They may be
rolled out and cut. If you have time, permit them to rise again. From here on
there is a great divergence in treatment.
The old method required the use of a
Dutch oven, but a covered, deep, 10-inch
oven-proof glass baking dish is preferable,
as it enables you to watch the cooking
process. Place in it one of the hot liquids
indicated below and then the dumplings.
If they are to be served with a meat course
with lots of gravy, use ½ cup butter and
½ cup scalded milk. If they are to constitute a dessert, use 1½ cups sirup, fruit
juice, preserves or stewed fruit. ◗ Cover
the pot closely, place it in a 275° oven and
cook the dumplings for about 1½ hours. If
you have not used a glass baker, do not
lift the lid, even to peek. Old recipes add
that your sense of smell must be your
guide as to when to uncover. Do it when
the dumplings begin to give off a tempting
fragrance of finality, telling you that the
liquid has been absorbed. Test the dumplings with a straw. Remove them from
the pot and serve at once. An outstand-

ing accompaniment for this dessert is stewed blue plums or prunes. Use part of the sirup in the pot. Serve the dumplings with the remaining fruit. The plums or prunes may be stewed with part white wine and part water. In addition, it is customary to serve:

Custard Sauce, page 710, or Rich Custard, page 685

ABOUT CUSTARD PIES

How many puzzled inquiries we have answered about "Custard, my family's favorits pie"! In a recent one, our correspondent gloomily points out: "My mother thinks it's lumpy because I cook it too long. My husband thinks it gets watery because I put it in the icebox." How right, unfortunately, are both of this bride's critics! ♦ Custard and cream pies, unless eaten almost at once, must be kept well chilled. The lightly cooked eggs are especially subject to adverse bacterial activity, even though they may give no evidence of spoilage. It is Hobson's choice here: eat within 3 hours if the pie is left unrefrigerated or risk wateriness under refrigeration.

Again, pie dough needs a high heat, while the custard itself demands a low one. How to reconcile these contradictions? We find that the easiest way to satisfaction is to prebake crust and filling separately; then, just before serving, to slip the cooled filling into the cooled shell. To prebake the filling, select a pie pan of the same size as the crust. Grease well. Bake a custard in the pie pan, until just firm. Cool quickly. Before serving, slide the filling into the crust, see below. This method

takes a bit of dexterity but, after you get used to it, you will prefer it. The filling need not even be preformed but, if precooked, can be spooned carefully into the prebaked shell. If you use a topping, see page 682, no one will be the wiser. Two more important comments about fillings which are precooked, but not preformed.

♦ Always cook them over—not in—hot water. ♦ When they are thickened, beat them until they are cool to allow all steam to escape. The steam will otherwise condense and thin the filling too much. Mark Twain inelegantly wrote of a frustrated crow that it was "sweating like an ice pitcher," and this is exactly what custard filling will do, unless beaten until cool. When it is 70° or cooler, place the filling in the prebaked shell and the pie is ready to serve.

CUSTARD OR CREAM PIE
A 9-Inch Pie

Preheat oven to 450°.

The partial baking of this pie shell before filling insures a crisper undercrust. Line a pie pan with any:

Pie Crust, page 590

Build up a fluted rim. Prick the crust and bake it in a 450° oven for about 10 minutes. Reduce heat to 325°. Fill the shell with the following custard which should be ready and cool. Pull the oven rack part way out and pour the filling into the crust or remove the crust from the oven only long enough to fill it. Beat slightly:

3 eggs or 6 egg yolks

Add and stir well:

½ cup sugar
¼ teaspoon salt
2 cups milk or milk and light cream
1 teaspoon vanilla or
1 tablespoon rum

Pour these ingredients into the partly baked pie shell. Sprinkle the top with:

(¼ teaspoon nutmeg)

Bake the pie in the already reduced 325° oven for about 30 minutes or until done. See About Custard Pies, this page.

CUSTARD TARTS OR FLAN WITH FRUIT

To be assembled just before serving.
Fill:

Prebaked Tart Shells, page 590

with:

½-inch layer of Baked Custard

Top the custard with:

Strawberries or other berries, cooked drained apples, drained cherries, peaches, bananas, pineapple or coconut

Coat the fruit with Glaze for Tarts, page 683, to which you may add:

(1 tablespoon or more of brandy or rum)

Garnish with:

(Whipped cream)

CHOCOLATE-TOPPED CUSTARD PIE

Follow the recipe for:

Custard Pie, this page

Omit the nutmeg. Stir and cook in a double boiler ♦ over—not in—hot water:

1½ oz. chocolate
5 tablespoons sugar
2 beaten eggs
⅛ teaspoon salt

Cook these ingredients until slightly thickened, about 4 minutes. ◗ Beat until slightly cooled. Add:

1 tablespoon rum or ½ teaspoon
vanilla

Pour the mixture over the baked custard.

CARAMEL CUSTARD PIE

A 9-Inch Pie

Prepare:

A baked Pie Shell, page 590.

and:

Caramel Custard Pudding, page 685

Cool the pudding and fill the slightly cooled pie shell. Garnish with:

Sweetened Whipped Cream II,
page 645

CHOCOLATE PIE

A 9-Inch Pie

Prepare by any rule:

A baked Pie Shell, page 590

Scald in a double boiler or over very low heat with constant stirring:

2½ cups milk

Cut up and add:

2 oz. chocolate

In a separate bowl, mix until smooth:

⅓ cup flour

in:

¼ cup milk

Add:

¼ teaspoon salt
1 cup sugar
(⅛ teaspoon cinnamon)

Add to the mixture in double boiler. Cook and stir ◗ over, not in, hot water, for 15 minutes. Pour a small quantity over:

3 to 4 beaten egg yolks

Beat and add to mixture in double boiler. Stir and cook the custard for 3 minutes. Add:

2 tablespoons butter

Remove from heat. Beat gently until very smooth. Add:

1 teaspoon vanilla
(½ cup chopped nut meats)

Cool this mixture. Pour it into the pie shell. Cover with:

Meringue I, page 681

and bake as directed.

CHOCOLATE CREAM PIE

A 9-Inch Pie

Here are some of the many good ways to make this pie.

Prepare:

A baked Pie Shell, page 589

Fill it with ½ the recipe for:

Pots de Crème, page 687

Garnish with:

Whipped cream or French
Chocolate Mousse, page 687, or

Rum Chocolate Mousse, page 687,
or Mocha Filling, page 646

and keep chilled until ready to serve, or, follow the recipe for:

Custard Pie, page 609

Melt in the scalded milk:

2 oz. chocolate
⅔ cup sugar

◗ Cool slightly and proceed with the recipe. Cover with:

¼-inch layer whipped cream

or top with:

Meringue II, page 681

and bake as directed.

COFFEE TARTS OR PIE

Prepare:

6 baked Tart Shells or baked Pie
Crust, page 589

I. Prepare:

2 cups hot strong coffee

Combine and stir until smooth:

1 cup cream or evaporated milk
6 tablespoons sifted all-purpose flour
⅔ cup sugar
¼ teaspoon salt

Stir these ingredients into the hot coffee. Cook and stir the mixture over low heat in a double boiler over, not in, hot water, until it thickens, about 20 minutes. Pour part of it over:

2 beaten eggs or 5 egg yolks

Return this to the pan, stir and cook for 2 or 3 minutes over low heat to permit the eggs to thicken slightly. Add:

2 tablespoons butter

◗ Cool, then add:

1 teaspoon vanilla or 2 teaspoons rum

Fill tart shells or pie crust. Chill and serve topped with:

Whipped cream
Crushed Nut Brittle, page 736

II. Or use:

Coffee Marshmallow Cream,
page 698

BUTTERSCOTCH PIE

A 9-Inch Pie

Prepare by any recipe:

A baked Pie Shell, page 589

Combine in a double boiler ◗ over—not in—hot water:

1 cup brown sugar
¼ cup all-purpose flour
3 tablespoons butter
¼ teaspoon salt

Stir and cook these ingredients until blended. Add:

2¼ cups scalded milk

Beat until light:

4 egg yolks

Pour a little of the milk mixture over them. Beat well and return it to the double boiler. Stir and cook until the yolks thicken slightly. ◗ Beat custard until cool and add:

½ teaspoon vanilla

(½ cup nut meats or crushed
    Peanut Brittle, page 736)
Pour the custard into the baked pie shell.
Cover with:
    Meringue, page 681
and bake as directed or cover with:
    Whipped cream

ORANGE CREAM PIE

                                    A 9-Inch Pie
Prepare:
    A baked Pie Shell, page 590
Mix thoroughly in a double boiler over,
not in, hot water:
    ½ cup sugar or more if the orange
        juice is very tart
    ¼ cup all-purpose flour
    ⅛ teaspoon salt
Add:
    1 cup scalded milk
Cook and stir these ingredients over very
low heat until thick. Pour part of this mix-
ture over:
    3 well-beaten egg yolks
Return to pan. Add:
    ⅔ cup orange juice
    2 teaspoons grated orange rind
    1 teaspoon butter
Stir and cook the custard over very low
heat until the eggs thicken slightly. Add:
    (½ cup pecan meats)
♦ Cool the custard and pour it into the
baked pie shell. Cover with:
    Meringue I, page 681
and bake as directed.

ABOUT CHEESECAKE

No wonder pictures of starlets are called
cheesecake! We think the six following
recipes are starlets. Take your pick, but remember to ♦ watch temperatures. If the
recipe calls for baker's cheese, or curd,
procure this very dry, lean cottage cheese
or use farmer's cheese. Put it through a
sieve, as shown on page 544, or a food-mill,
or grind it. Cheesecakes are egg-based.
They need low heat and are usually left in
the turned-off oven with the door open,
after baking. Expect a slight shrinkage,
as they cool. If there is great shrinkage,
you have baked them with too high a heat.
They all profit by ♦ thorough chilling before serving, preferably 12 hours. For
storing safely, see About Custards, page
684.
    A few wine-soaked currants, finely
shaved almonds, tiny pieces of angelica or
citron are sometimes mixed with the filling
or used as topping. Shaved curled chocolate may be added as a surface garnish. To
glaze cheesecakes, see Strawberry Glaze
and Apricot Glaze, page 683.

BAKER'S CHEESE PIE OR CAKE

                                    12 Servings
This cheese pie or cake is luscious. It
should be 1½ inches or more in depth.
Bake it in a pan with a removable rim or

in an ovenproof baking dish, 9 inches wide,
2⅝ inches high.
Prepare:
    Zwieback Crust or Crumb Crust,
        page 592 and 593
Reserve ½ cup of the mixture. Line a deep
baking dish and press the crust lightly on
the bottom and against the sides. Chill
thoroughly. Fill with:
    Cheese Filling
To make filling, dissolve:
    1 cup sugar
in:
    ⅓ cup whipping cream
Add:
    2 lbs. baker's cheese: about 2 pints
    4 beaten egg yolks
    3 tablespoons flour
    1 teaspoon vanilla or 2½ tablespoons
        lemon juice and 1 teaspoon grated
        lemon rind
Whip until stiff, but not dry:
    4 egg whites
Fold them into the cheese mixture. Fill
the shell and sprinkle the reserved crumbs
over the top. Bake the pie in a 350° oven
for about 1 hour.

WHIPPED CREAM CHEESECAKE

                                    16 Servings
Double the recipe for:
    Graham Cracker Crust, page 593
Reserve 1 cup of this mixture. Press the
remainder with a spoon or the palm of the
hand on the bottom and sides of a 12-inch
spring form pan. Chill this shell thor-
oughly. Or you may line a spring mold
with galette dough, page 592.
To make the filling, sift:
    1½ cups sugar
Beat until light:
    6 eggs
Add the sugar gradually. Beat these ingredients until very light. Add:
    ⅛ teaspoon salt
    2 teaspoons grated lemon rind
    3 tablespoons lemon juice
    1 teaspoon vanilla
Whip and fold in:
    1 cup whipping cream
Blend well:
    ½ cup all-purpose flour
    3½ pints smooth cottage cheese: 2¼ lbs.
Put these ingredients through a sieve. Fold
into the egg and cream mixture. Fill the
pie shell. Sprinkle the reserved crumb
mixture over the filling. Bake in a 350°
oven for about 1 hour. Turn off the heat
and permit the pie to stand in the oven for
1 hour longer with the door open or until
cooled.

SOUR CREAM CHEESECAKE

                                    12 Servings
Line a 9-inch, 2½-inch-deep spring mold
with:
    Zwieback Crust, page 593

Chill the crust well.
Preheat oven to 375°.
Mix well, then pour into the shell:

2 well-beaten eggs
4 packages soft cream cheese: ¾ lb.
½ cup sugar
1 teaspoon lemon juice or ½ teaspoon
** vanilla**
½ teaspoon salt

Bake for about 20 minutes. Remove from
oven. Dust the top with:

Cinnamon

Let cool to room temperature. Heat oven
to 425°. Mix well and pour over the cake:

1½ cups thick cultured sour cream
2 tablespoons sugar
½ teaspoon vanilla
⅛ teaspoon salt

Bake in the oven for about 5 minutes to
glaze it. Permit it to cool, then refrigerate
from 6 to 12 hours before serving. You
may garnish with a crumb lattice topping.

GELATIN CHEESECAKE

A 10-Inch Cake

This sumptuous Torte will serve 18 persons. It is handsome and delectable and
may be made a day in advance.
Prepare:

Zwieback Crust, page 593

Reserve ¼ of the crumbs. Spread or pat
the rest in a thin layer over the bottom and
sides of a 3-inch-deep, 10-inch spring
mold. Bake the crust for about 15 minutes. Cool it. Scald in the top of a double boiler:

⅛ cup milk

with:

A vanilla bean

Beat:

4 egg yolks
¾ cup sugar
¼ teaspoon salt

Remove the vanilla bean. Add the milk
gradually to the beaten egg mixture. Heat
and stir this custard over, not in, hot water
until it thickens. Soak:

2 tablespoons gelatin

in:

½ cup water

Stir this mixture into the hot custard until
dissolved. Cool the custard. Add:

(¼ cup lemon juice)

Work with a fork until smooth:

1½ lbs. soft cream cheese

Stir into the custard until well blended.
Whip until stiff ♦ but not dry:

4 egg whites

Whip in gradually:

½ cup sugar

Fold this into the custard. Beat until stiff,
then fold in:

1 cup whipping cream

Fill the zwieback crust with the custard.
Sprinkle the reserved crumbs over the top.
Chill the Torte well in the refrigerator un-
til ready to serve.

FRUIT GELATIN CHEESECAKE

8 Servings

Prepare:

Zwieback Crust, page 593

Line a deep 10-inch dish with it. Drain
and reserve the juice of:

2½ cups canned cubed pineapple
** or apricots**

Soak:

2 tablespoons gelatin

in:

½ cup fruit juice

Beat until light:

3 egg yolks

Beat in gradually:

½ cup sugar
½ cup pineapple or apricot juice

Cook and stir these ingredients in a double
boiler ♦ over, not in, hot water, until they
thicken. Add the soaked gelatin. Stir until
it is dissolved. Cool the custard. Stir in:

1 lb. smooth cottage cheese
1 teaspoon grated lemon rind
3 tablespoons lemon juice
¼ teaspoon salt

Fold in ¾ of the pineapple cubes and:

2 cups whipped cream

Fold in:

3 stiffly beaten egg whites

Fill the pie shell. Garnish the top with the
remaining pineapple cubes. Sprinkle with:

Cinnamon

Chill the pie for at least 3 hours.

RICOTTA CHEESE PIE OR CAKE

A 10-Inch Pie

This North Italian delight is a favorite of
our friend, Jim Beard, who has generously
allowed us to include it. Cheesecake Crust
with cognac should accompany it. To prepare it, see page 592.
Preheat oven to 375°.
Have all ingredients at 75°. Combine:

1½ pounds ricotta cheese
3 tablespoons toasted pine nuts
2 tablespoons chopped blanched
** almonds**
2 tablespoons chopped citron

and dust with:

1 tablespoon flour

Beat until light and lemony in color:

4 eggs

Gradually add:

1 cup sugar
1½ teaspoons vanilla

Add the cheese mixture to the eggs until
well blended. Pour the filling into the unbaked crust and bake about 40 minutes or
until done.

LEMON MERINGUE PIE

A 9-Inch Pie

Prepare:

A baked Pie Shell, page 590

Combine in the top of a double boiler:

1 cup sugar
5 to 6 tablespoons cornstarch
⅛ teaspoon salt

Add very gradually:

2 cups water or milk

Stir and cook these ingredients ◗ over— not in—hot water for about 8 to 12 minutes or until the mixture thickens. See About Cornstarch, page 499. Cover and cook for 10 minutes more. Stir occasionally. Remove the mixture from the heat. Pour a little of it over:

3 beaten egg yolks

Beat this and return to mixture in double boiler. Cook and stir gently, still over boiling water, about 5 minutes more. Remove from heat. Beat in:

3 tablespoons butter
⅛ cup lemon juice
2 teaspoons grated lemon rind

Some people prefer the rind coarsely grated. ◗ If you want a very lemony flavor add more rind—rather than more juice. Additional acid liquid may thin the filling too much. Cool the custard by stirring very, very gently to release any steam which might condense to thin the filling. Pour it cool into the cold pie shell. Cover with:

Meringue I, page 681

and bake as directed.

LEMON OR LIME PIE COCKAIGNE
A 9-Inch Pie

Prepare:

A baked Pie Shell, page 590

Preheat oven to 325°.
Beat until very light:

4 egg yolks

Beat until soft:

½ cup butter

Add very slowly:

1 cup white or packed brown sugar

Blend these ingredients until creamy. Beat in the egg yolks and:

3 tablespoons lemon juice and
1½ teaspoons grated lemon rind

Fill the pie shell with this mixture. Bake the pie until firm, about 30 minutes. It may be cooled and:

Meringue II, page 681

may be placed on it. Bake as directed.

EGGLESS LEMON OR LIME CREAM PIE
A 9-Inch Pie

Prepare:

A baked Pie Shell, page 590

Combine:

1 can sweetened condensed milk: 15 oz.
⅛ cup lime or lemon juice
1 tablespoon grated lemon or lime rind
¼ teaspoon salt

◗ Stir until thickened. The thickening results from the reaction of the milk and citrus juice. Blend in gently:

(⅔ cup well-drained canned pineapple)

Turn the filling into the baked shell. Chill

about 3 hours. Serve garnished with:

(Whipped cream)
(Shaved sweet chocolate)

✻ FROZEN LEMON OR LIME CREAM PIE
A 4½ x 11 x 1¼-Inch Refrigerator Tray
5 to 6 Servings

If fresh cream is not available, try this recipe using:

1 cup evaporated milk

chilled for 12 hours. Otherwise use:

1 cup whipping cream

Butter the refrigerator tray well. Line it with ¾ recipe for:

Crumb Crust, page 593

reserving ¼ for a topping. Combine in the top of a double boiler ◗ over—not in—hot water and cook until it forms a custard:

6 tablespoons sugar
2 slightly beaten egg yolks
Grated rind of ½ lemon
⅛ cup lemon juice

Cool the custard. Whip until stiff, but not dry:

2 to 3 egg whites

Gradually beat in:

2 tablespoons sugar

Fold the egg whites into the custard. Whip the cream or the chilled evaporated milk and fold into it:

2 tablespoons confectioners' sugar

Fold into the custard. Place the filling lightly into the crumb-lined refrigerator tray. Top it with a sprinkling of the reserved crumb crust. Freeze until firm.

ANGEL PIE
A 10-Inch Pie

Prepare a shell of:

Meringue Paste, page 599

Butter the bottom of a deep 10-inch ovenproof dish, and cover with the meringue. Bake as directed. Let cool in the oven with the door open. Prepare the following filling in a double boiler ◗ over—not in— hot water. Beat well:

4 egg yolks

Add:

½ cup sugar

Cook until thickened, beating constantly. Add:

Juice and rind of 1 lemon

Whip:

1 cup whipping cream

Put ½ of the cream in the meringue shell, then the cooked lemon filling. Cover with the remaining cream. Chill for 24 hours.

ABOUT CHIFFON PIES

Many chiffon pies call for egg white that is not cooked—a state of affairs that is not approved by some health authorities, see page 695. Only in Frozen Lemon or Lime Cream Pie, and when the word gelatin appears in the title do our pie fillings call for uncooked egg white.

LEMON OR LIME CHIFFON PIE
A 9-Inch Pie

One version of this pie is made with Key limes. If you are a Floridian or can otherwise avail yourself of this pungent fruit, by all means try it in any of our recipes that call for lemon.

Prepare:

A baked Pie Shell, page 590

Combine in a double boiler:

⅛ to ½ cup sugar
2 tablespoons water
4 to 5 egg yolks

Cook and stir these ingredients ♦ over—not in—hot water, until thick. Add:

Grated rind of 1 lemon
3 tablespoons lemon juice

Cool the mixture.

Preheat oven to 400°.

Whip:

3 egg whites

until stiff, but not dry. Fold in:

¼ cup sugar

Fold this mixture lightly into the custard. Fill the pie shell. Brown the pie in the oven for about 10 minutes or place it under a broiler until lightly browned.

ORANGE CHIFFON PIE
A 9-Inch Pie

Use well-flavored orange juice for this pie. Indifferently flavored orange juice may be improved by the addition of 2 teaspoons of vanilla.

Prepare:

A baked Pie Shell, page 590

Cook and stir in a double boiler ♦ over—not in—hot water, until thick:

3 tablespoons all-purpose flour
3 egg yolks
2 tablespoons lemon juice
1 cup orange juice
½ teaspoon grated orange rind
¼ cup sugar

Use more sugar if the orange juice is acid. Cool these ingredients. Whip until stiff, but not dry:

3 egg whites

Fold them into the orange custard. Fill the pie shell. Brown the pie in a preheated 400° oven for about 10 minutes.

CHOCOLATE GELATIN CHIFFON PIE
A 9-Inch Pie

Prepare:

A baked Pie Shell, page 590

Soak:

1 tablespoon gelatin

in:

¼ cup cold water or strong coffee

Combine and stir until smooth:

6 tablespoons cocoa or 2 oz. melted chocolate

½ cup boiling water or strong coffee

Stir in the soaked gelatin until it is dissolved. Combine gently:

4 lightly beaten egg yolks
½ cup sugar

Combine both mixtures and chill until about to set. Add:

1 teaspoon vanilla

Beat with a wire whisk until light. Whip until ♦ stiff, but not dry:

4 egg whites

Fold them into the chocolate mixture with:

½ cup sugar

Fill the pie shell. Chill the pie to set it. Shortly before serving, cover the top with thinly sliced ripe:

(Bananas)

Spread with:

Whipped cream

RUM GELATIN CREAM PIE
A 9-Inch Pie

The headiest of them all.

Prepare:

A baked Crumb Crust, page 593, or Pie Shell, page 590

Beat until light:

6 egg yolks

Beat in gradually:

⅞ cup sugar

Soak:

1 tablespoon gelatin

in:

½ cup cold water

Place this mixture in the top of a double boiler ♦ over—not in—hot water and stir until the gelatin is dissolved. Pour it over the egg and sugar combination in a slow stream, beating constantly. Cool. Stir in:

½ cup Jamaica rum

Whip until stiff:

1 pint whipping cream: 2 cups

Fold into the egg mixture. Cool the filling, but before it begins to set pour it into the pie shell. When set, sprinkle the top with:

Grated bittersweet chocolate or toasted, grated coconut or finely shaved pistachio nuts

Chill pie to set.

BLACK BOTTOM GELATIN PIE
A Deep 9-Inch Pie

Prepare:

Baked Crumb Crust, page 593, or Pie Crust, page 590

Soak:

1 tablespoon gelatin

in:

¼ cup cold water

Scald:

2 cups rich milk

Combine:

½ cup sugar
4 teaspoons cornstarch

Beat until light:

4 egg yolks

lowly stir the scalded milk into the eggs.
tir in the sugar mixture. Cook these in-
redients over, not in, hot water, stirring
ccasionally, about 20 minutes—or until
he custard coats a spoon heavily. Take
ut 1 cup of the custard. Add to it:

1½ oz. melted chocolate

eat these ingredients until well blended
nd cool. Add:

½ teaspoon vanilla

our this custard into the pie shell. Dis-
olve the soaked gelatin in the remaining
ustard. Be sure it is hot. Let it cool, but
o not permit it to stiffen. Stir in:

1 tablespoon or more rum

eat until well blended:

3 egg whites

Add:

¼ teaspoon cream of tartar

Beat the egg whites until they are stiff,
ut not dry. Beat in gradually, a teaspoon
t a time:

¼ cup sugar

Fold the egg whites into the custard. Cover
he chocolate custard with the rum-flavored
ustard. Chill to set. Whip until stiff:

1 cup whipping cream

Add gradually:

2 tablespoons confectioners' sugar

Cover custard with the cream. Top with:

½ oz. shaved chocolate

MOCHA GELATIN CHIFFON
CREAM PIE

A 9-Inch Pie

Prepare:

A baked Pie Shell, page 590

Soak:

2 tablespoons gelatin

in:

½ cup cold water

Dissolve:

2 tablespoons cocoa

in:

2 cups hot strong coffee

and bring to a boil. Dissolve the soaked
gelatin in this mixture. Stir in:

⅛ cup sugar

Cool slightly and pour these ingredients
slowly onto:

2 to 3 well-beaten egg yolks

Cook and stir these ingredients in a double
boiler ♦ over, not in, hot water, until they
thicken. Cool the filling until about to set.
Beat with a wire whisk until fluffy. Add:

1 teaspoon vanilla

(1 tablespoon brandy)

Whip until stiff:

1 cup whipping cream

Fold in:

1 tablespoon sugar

Whip until stiff but not dry:

2 to 3 egg whites

Fold the whipped cream and beaten egg
whites into the coffee mixture. Pour filling
into pie shell. Chill pie thoroughly.

MAPLE GELATIN CHIFFON PIE

A 9-Inch Pie

Prepare:

A baked Pie Shell, page 590.

Soak:

1 tablespoon gelatin

in:

2 tablespoons cold water

Heat and stir in a double boiler:

½ cup milk

½ cup maple sirup

⅛ teaspoon salt

Pour part of this over:

2 beaten egg yolks

Return to double boiler. Stir and cook the
custard ♦ over, not in, hot water, until
thickened. Add the soaked gelatin and stir
until dissolved. Chill these ingredients until they begin to thicken. Whip until stiff:

1 cup whipping cream

Fold into ¾ of it:

⅓ cup chopped hickory nuts

1 teaspoon vanilla

Whip until stiff but not dry:

2 egg whites

Fold these and the cream and nuts into the
custard. Fill the pie shell. Garnish with
the remaining cream. Chill to set.

PUMPKIN GELATIN CHIFFON PIE

A 9-Inch Pie

Prepare:

A baked Pie Shell, page 590

Soak:

1 tablespoon gelatin

in:

¼ cup cold water

Beat slightly:

3 egg yolks

Add:

½ cup sugar

1¼ cups canned or cooked pumpkin

½ cup milk

¼ teaspoon salt

½ teaspoon each cinnamon and nutmeg

Cook and stir these ingredients over, not
in, hot water until thick. Stir in the soaked
gelatin until dissolved. Chill. Whip until
stiff but not dry:

3 egg whites

When the pumpkin mixture begins to set,
stir in:

½ cup sugar

and fold in the egg whites. Fill the pie
shell. Chill to set. Serve garnished with:

Whipped cream

CAKES, CUP CAKES, TORTEN, AND FILLED CAKES

At weddings and birthdays, a cake can become the center of interest; and this interest, happily, has been known to extend to the cook. Thirty years of fan mail prove to us that almost every woman wants to bake a perfect cake. If you are a born baker, skip our advice to the "cakelorn." Otherwise, it will be more than worth your while to learn a few simple but highly significant mixing and baking techniques.

♦ Start, of course, with high-quality materials. Never jeopardize your results with damp flour, old milk or eggs or doubtful fats. Pay attention to the ♦ measurements and proportions you use ♦ the temperature of the ingredients and ♦ the heat of your oven, page 140. Most recipes call for ingredients at room temperature. As kitchen temperatures vary, we suggest ♦ ingredients be about 75°, the ideal recommended by professional bakers. Pay attention also to ♦ the physical states you induce by stirring, creaming and folding. Our drawings and descriptions can only get you off to a flying start. The proper "look" of well-creamed butter and eggs, of batter ready for the oven—these and other critical stages in cake making you will learn to recognize most effectively through practice.

ABOUT CAKE TYPES

We divide cakes according to their leavens. If you know what makes them rise or fall, it will help you to preserve their lifting action during mixing. Angel and sponge cakes are sometimes called ♦ foam cakes, because they depend for their leavening exclusively on the expansion of the vapor trapped in their light egg-rich doughs. Egg white contains no fat, but egg yolk does. As a consequence, angel cakes are fat-free; but ♦ sponge cakes, though light in texture, contain appreciable fat by reason of their yolk-content, see page 508.

♦ Butter and shortening cakes need baking powder for proper leavening. We feel that all cakes in this category are more delicious if butter alone is used as the fatty ingredient. If you care to use, instead, one of the bland white vegetable shortenings now on the market, you will trade distinctive flavor for a measure of economy, a spongier texture and a somewhat greater volume. Whatever the fat used, "butter" cakes gain lightness if the butter ingredient, at about 70°, is creamed with the sugar as a first step. To this mixture the beaten egg yolk is added and the

combination, in turn, well beaten. Dry and liquid ingredients are then added alternately and the beaten egg whites folded in last. For quicker, but not better, result the entire egg may be beaten into the creamed mixture. See About Quick Cakes, page 635.

In commercial baking and mixes, the use of emulsifying agents not available to the housewife gives extremely fine spongy textures. In cakes made with ♦ melted butter, such as the classic Génoise, page 640, the butter is put in last. In cakes made with oils, special mixing procedures are used to allow the incorporation of air into the batter. Our cake recipes are all adjusted in method to the specific demands of the ingredients. So, for success, please follow directions as given.

All these cake types may be ✳ frozen, see page 770, but dry out rapidly after thawing.

▲ In high altitudes, reduce the baking powder or soda by ½. ♦ But do not reduce soda beyond ½ teaspoon for each cup of sour milk or cream used.

ABOUT CAKE MIXING

After reading About Leavens, page 502, look at the top of page 617. At the left, you see how to stir a batter. Begin at the center of the bowl, using a circular motion and widening the circle as the ingredients become blended. ♦ To cream, work fat at about 70° lightly with the finger tips—or use the back of a wooden spoon. Press the mixture in a gently gliding motion between the back of the spoon and the side of the bowl, in short rocking strokes, over a rather limited area shown between the arrows in the sketch. The sugar mixture should become light in color, even, smooth and creamy in texture. If it looks curdled and frothy, you have worked it too long and the oil in the butter has separated and will result in a coarsely grained cake. To beat or whip, use a long, free-swinging, lifting motion, which brings the bottom mass constantly to the top, trapping as much air as possible in the mixture, as shown on the right. A slotted spoon makes the work quicker; a wooden, rather than a metal, spoon keeps the ingredients in the best condition. Whipping is done rapidly with an increasing tempo. If you use a longer, thinner whip, such as the one shown immediately next to the bowl, you will get the best results in handling egg white. For beating cream, use a wider whisk like

the one shown to its left. In choosing a mechanical mixer, see that the beaters have many wires that are as thin as is consistent with durability.

Folding in is one of the most tactful of cake making operations: the objective is to blend thoroughly, yet not lose any of the air you have previously worked into your materials.

♦ To fold, first of all have a large enough bowl. A flat whip as shown below is usually recommended, but this tool can be maddening because it cuts through the whites and its too widely spaced wires allow the heavier substances to fall through. We commonly dispense with tools for this step and use the flat of the hand. You may begin by folding into the dough a small quantity of the whites. When thoroughly mixed, fold in the rest of the whites by scooping up some of the more solid material and covering the whites. Then, cut it in with a determined, gentle slicing motion to the base of the mixing bowl. Turn the bowl slightly with the other hand each time you repeat the folding motions. It is surprising how well and quickly blending is achieved by this simple procedure.

♦ Baking directions are given with each recipe. If you use an electric oven ♦ be

sure to remove the upper heating element before heating the oven.

♦ To test for doneness, insert a wire cake tester or a toothpick, and if it emerges perfectly clean the cake is done. It should be lightly browned and beginning to shrink from the sides of the pan. If pressed with a finger, it should at once come back into shape, except in very rich cakes and chocolate cakes which may dent slightly and still be done. When removed from the oven, the cake is cooled in the pan on a rack, for about 5 minutes, and then cooled out of the pan, on a rack, until all heat has left. For exceptions, see About Angel, page 619, Sponge, page 621, Génoise, page 640, and Fruit Cakes, page 630. For an obstinate cake, set the pan on a cloth wrung out in hot water. This often helps in removing the cake from the pan.

ABOUT CAKE PANS

If you want a thin, evenly browned crust, try using ♦ medium weight metal pans, shiny on the upper surfaces and slightly dulled beneath. If you prefer heavier, browner crusts, use glass or enamel pans or those that are dark in color—all of which absorb and hold more heat. Should

you choose from the second group, reduce the oven heat by 25°. In baking layer cakes, use pans with straight sides. Note also that too-high sides will prevent good browning. But even more important to the crumb and volume of your cake is the relation of dough to the size of the pan. All our cake recipes indicate the proper pan sizes. Cake pans are measured across the top.

The dough, for a velvety texture, should be at least 1 inch deep in the pan. If the pan is too big, the cake will not rise properly and may brown unevenly. If the pan is too small, the texture will be coarse and the batter may overflow before it sets. If it doesn't overflow, it will probably sink in cooling. Most pans are filled at least half full, but not more than ⅔. Loaf and tube pans can be filled higher. If you have no pan corresponding to the size called for in the recipe, see the chart below to find out what area is called for. Then substitute a pan size you own that has the approximate area. For instance, a recipe calls for a 9-inch round pan which has an area of approximately 64 square inches. From other tables you see that you could equally well use an 8 x 8-inch square pan, which offers also an area of 64 square inches. Should your pan be too large, you can reduce the baking area of a rectangular pan by folding a piece of foil as shown in the drawing on the right below. The dough will help to hold the divider in place on one side. Place dry beans or rice on the other, see center sketch.

♦ Note that a round 9-inch-diameter pan equals only about ¾ the area of a square 9-inch pan. This ¾ proportion holds for any round pan, the diameter of which equals the side of the square pan, as you can see illustrated below by comparing the square pan surface, left, with the area of the dotted circle.

♦ To know how much batter to mix for

oddly shaped pans or molds, first measure their contents with water. Then make up ⅔ as much dough as the amount of the water measured.

COMPARATIVE PAN SIZES

ROUND CAKE PANS

8 x 1½	...............50 sq. inches
9 x 1½	...............64 sq. inches
10 x 1½	...............79 sq. inches

RECTANGULAR CAKE PANS

7¾ x 3⅝ x 2¼	............28 sq. inches
8 x 8 x 1½	............64 sq. inches
9 x 5 x 2¾	............45 sq. inches
9 x 9 x 1½	............81 sq. inches
11 x 4½ x 2¾	............50 sq. inches
11 x 7 x 1½	............77 sq. inches
13 x 9 x 2	............117 sq. inches
15 x 10 x 2	............150 sq. inches
15½ x 10½ x 1	............160 sq. inches
16 x 5 x 4	............80 sq. inches

ABOUT CAKES IN A MIXER

Electric mixers are the greatest boon to cake bakers but, as models vary in speed and efficiency ♦ be sure to read the manual which comes with your particular appliance. The following comments can give only approximate speeds and times. So-called one-bowl cakes can be mixed in as little as 3 minutes. Butter cakes may take as long as 8 to 10 minutes. Basically, you apply the same principles that you use in hand mixing. ♦ Have all ingredients assembled. If chocolate, honey or molasses mixtures are called for, melt or heat them ♦ and cool, before using, to about 75°, which should be the approximate temperature of all your ingredients. Sift and measure the flour, sift it once again with the baking powder, the soda, the spices and the cocoa, if called for. You may then

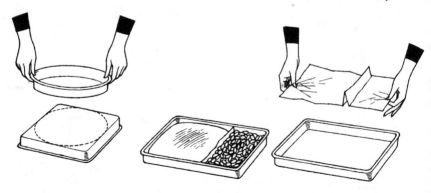

mix just as though you were working by hand or use the one-bowl method described below. ♦ The main things to observe are the beating speed and the timing of each process. We find it wise to stop the beating during the addition of most ingredients. During these breaks is the time, too, when the sides of the bowl should be scraped down with a rubber or plastic scraper, unless you have a heavy duty mixer which revolves with an off-center motion, covering every bit of the mixing area.

To mix a typical butter cake, cream the ♦ butter conditioned to 75°, until light, at low speed. Then cream it with the sugar at medium speed until the mix is of the consistency of whipped cream. If the recipe calls for whole eggs, they may be creamed from the beginning with the sugar and butter. If the eggs are separated, add the yolks at the end of about a 3 to 5 minute creaming period of the butter and sugar. The whites are added later. For descriptions of the textures that these ingredients should have, read About Butter Cakes, page 622. Then ♦ using low speed and ♦ stopping the mixing between additions, add the flour mixture in 3 parts and the milk in 2 parts. Begin and end with the flour. Mix until just smooth after each addition. The whole operation should not take more than about 2 minutes or you will have a too finely grained cake. If nuts and other lumpy substances are to be added, fold them in lightly with a fork at the end of the mixing period or briefly use the low speed on the beater. If the recipe calls for separated whites, beat them at this time in a grease-free bowl. Having an extra mixer bowl and beater is a great convenience if you bake often.

Be sure ♦ before you begin beating the egg whites that your oven has reached the right temperature and that your pans are greased. Beat the whites at medium speed for about ½ minute—until foamy. Now, the cream of tartar, if called for, is added. Then beat at high speed for another ½ minute until the whites are ♦ stiff, but not dry, see page 514. For the best results from this point on, the beater is no longer used and the beaten whites are folded in by hand, see page 617.

To mix so-called one-bowl cakes with unseparated eggs and solid fats, conditioned to 75° ♦ assemble and sift all dry ingredients needed. ♦ Have pans greased and oven preheated. Put sifted flour, baking powder, spices and cocoa, if called for, the fat and ⅔ of the liquid into the mixer bowl at once. Beat on medium speed about 2 minutes. Add the rest of the liquid. Add, unbeaten, the whole eggs, the yolks or the whites, as called for in the recipe, and beat for 2 minutes more. ♦ Scrape the bowl several times during this beating period. ♦ Overbeating will reduce the volume and give a too densely grained cake.

ABOUT PACKAGED BAKING MIXES

"Mother!" cried a little girl, "it says here in this book that you take milk and eggs and mix—but it doesn't say what kind of mix." We say it could be almost any kind of packaged mix, because those added expensive ingredients which make results taste something like the homemade article are left to the initiative of the housewife. We know that people think they save time by using mixes—just how much time is a sobering consideration—but we also know they do not save money, nor are they assured of good ingredients and best results. Use mixes, if you must, in emergencies. But consider that, under present distribution methods, the mix you buy may be as old as 2 years—if the store has a slow turnover. Remember that, in contriving the mix originally, everything has been done to use ingredients that will keep. Egg whites are used in preference to whole eggs, as the fat from the yolks may turn rancid. For the same reason, non-fat dry milk solids are preferred. Even when the natural moisture content of flour has been greatly lowered, what remains in the packaged mix can still deteriorate baking powders, flavorings and spices. Furthermore, even the most elaborate packaging is not proof, over a protracted storage period, against spoilage by moisture from without. So why not become expert at a few quick cakes and hot breads? Build up your own baking speed, control your ingredients, create really topnotch flavor and save money.

ABOUT ANGEL CAKES

Laboratory research in some types of recipes—and no cake has a larger bibliography than angel cake—has become so elaborate as to intimidate the housewife, who can rarely know the exact age of the eggs she uses or the precise blend of flour. Yet, working innocently as she must, she can still contrive a glamorous result with a little care. The main risers in angel cake are air and steam, so the egg white volume is important. See About Eggs, page 514.

♦ Have egg whites ready. They should be at least 3 days old, at about 60° to 70° and separated just before use. These are preferable to leftover egg white. Divide the beating time into 4 quarters. During the first quarter, beat whites gently ♦ until foamy. Add salt, cream of tartar and liquid flavoring. Be sure the cream of tartar has been in a closely covered container. It is added midway during the first quarter of the beating and controls both the stabilizing of the foam and the whiteness of the cake. End the first quarter of the beating with an increasing speed and gradually add, while continuing to beat at high speed, ¾ of the sugar called for in the recipe. Finely granulated fruit or berry sugar is best.

If you are using an electric mixer, this sugar addition begins in the second quarter because it guards against overbeating the whites. If you are beating by hand with a flat whip—and this gives the best results —or a rotary one, the gradual addition of sugar is made in the last half of the beating time. In either case, the remaining ¼ of the sugar is sifted with the cake flour to keep the flour well dispersed when it is folded into the egg and sugar mixture. ♦ The folding should never be done mechanically. As in all ♦ hand folding, the movement is both gentle and firm, but rapid. Avoid breaking down the cellular structure of the egg whites which have trapped air.

The pan and its preparation are integral with good results. Choose a tube pan with a removable rim. Since the dough is light, it helps to have a central tube to give it additional support while it rises. If the pan has been used for other purposes and any grease remains, the batter will not rise. Wash a suspect pan with detergent, scrubbing well to remove every trace of grease. After putting the batter in the pan, draw a thin spatula gently through the dough to destroy any large air pockets.

Endless experiments have been performed for baking angel cakes—starting with a cold oven and ending with a very hot one. But ♦ the best oven is one that is not so slow that it will dry and toughen the cake and not so hot that it will set the protein of the whites before they can expand to the fullest volume. In other words, the ideal is a moderate, preheated oven. We use 350° for about 45 minutes for the recipes given here. Place the pan on a rack, adjusted in the lower third of the oven. When the cake is done ♦ reverse the pan when you remove it from the oven, as shown in the illustration. Use an inverted funnel to rest the pan on, if the tube is not high enough to keep the cake above the surface of the table. Let the cake hang for about 1½ hours until it is thoroughly set.

Be sure to remove it from the pan before storing. Do not cut a fresh angel or sponge cake with a knife, but use a divider such as the one shown on the left or 2 forks inserted back to back to pry the cake gently apart. To make an angel cake for a roll, use ½ the recipe for a 10½ x 15½-inch pan. Grease the pan-bottom.

ANGEL CAKE

I.   **A 9-Inch Tube Pan**

Preheat oven to 350°.
Sift twice:
    1¼ to 1½ cups sugar
Sift separately before measuring:
    1 cup cake flour
Resift the flour 3 times with ½ cupful of the sifted sugar and:
    ½ teaspoon salt
Whip until foamy:
    1¼ cups egg whites: 10 to 12 egg whites
    (2 tablespoons water or 1 tablespoon
      water and 1 tablespoon lemon juice)
Add:
    1 teaspoon cream of tartar
Whip the egg whites ♦ until stiff, but not dry. Gradually whip in, about 1 tablespoon at a time, 1 cup of the sifted sugar. Fold in:
    ½ teaspoon vanilla
    ½ teaspoon almond extract
Sift about ¼ cup of the sugar and flour mixture over the batter. Fold it in gently and briefly with a rubber scraper. Continue, until all the mixture is used. Pour the batter into an ungreased tube pan. Bake about 45 minutes. To cool, see About Angel Cakes, page 619.

II.   **A 10-Inch Tube Pan**

Preheat oven to 350°.
Sift, then measure:
    1 cup cake flour
Add and resift 6 times:
    ½ cup sugar or confectioners' sugar
Combine:
    1½ cups egg whites
    2½ tablespoons cold water
    1½ teaspoons cream of tartar
    1 scant teaspoon vanilla
    1 teaspoon almond extract or
    (1 or 2 drops anise flavoring)
    ½ teaspoon salt
Beat ♦ until stiff, but not dry. Stop while the mixture is still glossy. Fold in, about 2 tablespoons at a time:
    1 cup sifted sugar
Fold in the dry ingredients lightly—a little at a time—with a rubber scraper. Fold in:
    (1 cup chopped black walnut meats or
      ¾ cup blanched, thinly sliced,
      toasted almonds)
Bake the batter in an ungreased tube pan for about 45 minutes. To cool, see About Angel Cake, page 619.

COCOA ANGEL CAKE
                     A 9-Inch Tube Pan

This is incredibly delicate.
Preheat oven to 350°.
Sift before measuring:
    ¾ cup cake flour
Resift 5 times with:

¼ cup cocoa
¼ cup sugar
Sift separately:
  1 cup sugar
Place on a large platter and whip until foamy:
  1¼ cups egg whites: 10 to 12 egg whites
Add:
  1 teaspoon cream of tartar
Whip until stiff, but not dry. Fold in the sifted sugar, 1 tablespoon at a time. Add:
  1 teaspoon vanilla
  ½ teaspoon lemon extract
Sift a small amount of the flour mixture over the batter and fold it in. Repeat this process until the flour is used up. Bake the cake in an ungreased tube pan for about 45 minutes. When cool, cover the cake with:
  White Icing, page 673, and Chocolate Coating, page 676, or with Coffee Icing, page 679

FLAVORED ANGEL CAKE
These are choice as cup cakes. See About Cup Cakes, page 632.
Add to the flour for Angel Cake:
  1 teaspoon cinnamon
  ½ teaspoon nutmeg
  ¼ teaspoon cloves
or, crush with a rolling pin:
  ⅓ cup soft peppermint sticks
Fold into the egg and flour mixture. This is good iced with Boiled White Icing, page 673, to which you may add more crushed candy for color or:
  (1 to 2 teaspoons instant coffee)

MARBLE ANGEL CAKE
Prepare:
  Angel Cake I, page 620
Prepare:
  Cocoa Angel Cake
Alternate the batters in 2 ungreased 9-inch tube pans. Bake the cake by any rule for Angel Cake.

ANGEL ALMOND CAKE
A 7-Inch Tube Pan
Preheat oven to 350°.
A fairly fat-free cake. Blanch, then grind in a nut grinder, page 518:
  1½ cups almonds
Sift:
  1½ cups confectioners' sugar
Beat until stiff:
  7 egg whites
Fold in the sugar and almonds. Bake for about 45 minutes or until done. To cool, see About Angel Cakes, page 619.

ABOUT SPONGE CAKES
In true sponge cakes, as in angel cakes, the main riser is air, plus steam, so all the suggestions for trapping air given in About Angel Cakes apply here—with this added admonition: egg yolks beat to a greater

volume if they are at about 75°. Beat the yolks until light and foamy; add the sugar gradually, while continuing to beat, until the mixture is pale in color and thick in texture. It has reached proper consistency when a sample dropped from a spoon remains raised for a moment above the rest of the batter and then rather reluctantly settles down to the level in the bowl.
  ♦ In sponge cakes, an electric or rotary beater gives a better result than a hand whip. You can beat the egg and sugar mixture mechanically as long as 7 minutes, with good results for the amounts given in the recipes here. Then stir the dry ingredients carefully in, by hand. When they are blended, use the folding technique illustrated, page 617. For pan preparation and baking, see About Angel Cakes, page 619.
  True-blue sponge cake enthusiasts scorn baking powder, but it does give added volume in the basic recipe just below. Sponges may be flavored by adding one teaspoon grated lemon or orange rind. Or these citrus rinds may be omitted in favor of 4 drops of anise oil, 1½ teaspoons vanilla, or additions as for Flavored Angel Cakes, opposite.

SPONGE CAKE
Economical, if you use the minimum number of eggs. Especially delightful, if you vary the flavors.
A 9-Inch Tube Pan
Preheat oven to 350°.
Grate, then stir:
  1 teaspoon lemon or orange rind
into:
  1 cup sifted sugar
Beat until very light:
  3 to 6 egg yolks
Beat in the sugar gradually. Beat in:
  ¼ cup boiling water or coffee
When cool, beat in:
  1 tablespoon lemon juice or
  1 teaspoon vanilla or 3 drops anise oil
Sift before measuring:
  1 cup cake flour
Resift with:
  1½ teaspoons double-acting baking powder
  ¼ teaspoon salt
Add the sifted ingredients gradually to the yolk mixture. Stir the batter until blended. Whip ♦ until stiff, but not dry:
  3 to 6 egg whites
Fold them lightly into the batter. Bake the cake about 45 minutes. To prepare the pan, bake and cool, see About Angel Cakes, page 619.

RICE OR POTATO FLOUR SPONGE CAKE
A 9-Inch Tube Pan
Because rice and potato flours have different glutens from wheat, do not expect the same cake texture.
Preheat oven to 350°.

Sift 3 times or more:
¾ cup potato or rice flour
½ cup sugar
Beat until light and creamy:
8 egg yolks
Stir them into the flour mixture. Beat
♦ until stiff, but not dry:
9 egg whites
Fold the egg whites into the yolks gently
but rapidly. Bake the cake for about 45
minutes. To prepare pan, bake and cool,
see About Angel Cakes, page 619.

SUNSHINE CAKE
A 9-Inch Tube Pan
Preheat oven to 350°.
Sift before measuring:
1 cup cake flour
Resift with:
½ teaspoon cream of tartar
Boil to the soft-ball stage at 240°, see page
726:
⅓ cup water
1¼ cups sugar
Whip ♦ until stiff, but not dry:
5 to 7 egg whites
Pour the sirup over them in a fine stream.
Beat constantly until the mixture is cool.
Add:
1 teaspoon vanilla
Beat well and fold in:
5 to 7 egg yolks
Fold in the sifted flour, 1 tablespoon at a
time. Bake the cake about 45 minutes.
To prepare pan, bake and cool, see About
Angel Cakes, page 619.

CHOCOLATE SPONGE CAKE
A 7-Inch Tube Pan
Butterless but rich in taste.
Preheat oven to 350°.
Melt:
4 oz. chocolate
in a pan with:
1 cup milk
Sift before measuring:
1¼ cups cake flour
Resift with:
½ teaspoon salt
**2½ teaspoons double-acting
baking powder**
Cool the chocolate mixture and add it to:
4 beaten egg yolks
creamed with:
2 cups sifted confectioners' sugar
1 teaspoon vanilla
Stir in the sifted flour. Beat ♦ until stiff,
but not dry:
4 egg whites
Fold the beaten whites into the chocolate
mixture. Bake about 50 minutes. To prepare pan, bake and cool, see About Angel
Cakes, page 619.

DAFFODIL CAKE
A 9-Inch Tube Pan
A yellow and white marble cake.
Preheat oven to 350°.
Sift before measuring:

1⅛ cups cake flour
Resift it twice. Sift separately:
1¼ cups sugar
Whip on a platter until frothy:
10 egg whites
Add:
½ teaspoon salt
1 teaspoon cream of tartar
Whip until they hold a point. Fold the
sifted sugar in gradually. Separate the mixture into halves. Fold into one half, a little at a time, ¾ cup of the sifted flour and:
6 beaten egg yolks
Grated rind of 1 orange
Fold into the other half, a little at a time,
½ cup of the sifted flour and:
1 teaspoon vanilla
Place the batters, a cupful or more at a
time, in the ungreased tube pan, alternating the colors. Bake about 45 minutes
or until done. To prepare pan, bake and
cool, see About Angel Cakes, page 619.

ABOUT BUTTER OR
SHORTENING CAKES

For flavor and texture, butter is our strong
preference. It is not a very novel one, for
way back when the cathedrals were white,
one of the spires at Rouen was nicknamed
The Butter Tower, having been built, re-
putedly, with money paid for indulgences
permitting the use of butter during Lent.

The butter, margarine or shortening—
but not lard, as it is best reserved for pastries, see page 588—♦ should be at about
70° when ready to cream. If much cooler,
it fails to disperse into the other ingredients to best advantage. If melted, it prevents the proper incorporation of air into
the batter. ♦ So don't try to hasten the
conditioning of shortenings with heat.

Creaming softens and lightens cake ingredients. If the weather is very hot, cream
butter and sugar in a bowl immersed in a
pan of 60° water. Add the sugar ♦ gradually, continuing to cream with a light
touch.

♦ Add beaten egg yolk gradually, or add
egg yolks unbeaten, one at a time, beating
well after each addition. ♦ The sifted dry
ingredients and the 75° liquids are added
in 3 or more alternating periods, usually
beginning with the dry ingredients. ♦ After
the addition of flour the blending should be
gentle, so as not to develop the gluten and
then continued until the flour is no longer
dry. ♦ Over-blending will cause too fine a
crumb. We suggest, for a cake made with
double-acting baking powder, about 200
strokes by hand or 2 minutes at medium
speed with an electric mixer. If you use
other baking powders, they may require
about ⅓ less beating. The whites **are**
beaten ♦ just before incorporating them **in**
the batter to a state described as "stiff, but
not dry." ♦ The whites are then simultaneously folded and cut in gently but

quickly, as shown in the illustrations, page 617. For a more stable foam, reserve ¼ of the sugar called for in the recipe and beat it in as described in Fudge Meringue Cake, page 627. ♦ Bake the cake in a preheated oven. Grease the bottoms of pans—not the sides. ♦ Use the pan sizes indicated for each recipe or adjust by consulting the Pan Size Chart, page 618.

WHITE CAKE

This recipe is amazing in that it can be multiplied by 8 and still give as good a result as when made in the smaller quantity below. See formula for Enlarging Recipes, page 546. We once saw a wedding cake made from this recipe which contained 130 eggs and was big enough to serve 400 guests. This formula is also the classic base for Lady Baltimore Cake, page 624, for which, in the Good Old Days, 5 layers were considered none too many.

I.   **Three 8-Inch Round Pans**

Preheat oven to 375°.
♦ Have all ingredients at about 75°.
♦ Sift before measuring:

   3½ cups cake flour

Resift it twice with:

   4 teaspoons double-acting
      baking powder
   ½ teaspoon salt

Sift:

   2 cups sugar

Cream well:

   1 cup butter

Add the sifted sugar gradually and continue creaming until very light. Add the flour mixture to the butter mixture in 3 parts, alternately with thirds of:

   1 cup milk

Stir the batter until smooth after each addition. Beat in:

   1 teaspoon vanilla
   (¼ teaspoon almond extract)

Whip ♦ until stiff, but not dry:

   7 or 8 egg whites

Fold them lightly into the cake batter. Bake in greased pans for about 25 minutes. Spread the cake when cool with:

   A choice of Icings, page 672

II. Children love this cake.

When baked, the recipe will fill a mold of 7-cup capacity, see below, or use two 9-inch round pans.
Preheat oven to 350°.
♦ Have all ingredients at about 75°.
Sift before measuring:

   2¼ cups cake flour

Resift with:

   2½ teaspoons double-acting
      baking powder
   ½ teaspoon salt

Cream until fluffy:

   1¼ cups sugar
   ½ cup butter

Combine:

   1 cup milk
   1 teaspoon vanilla

Add the sifted ingredients to the butter mixture in 3 parts, alternating with thirds of the liquid combination. Stir the batter until smooth after each addition. Whip ♦ until stiff, but not dry:

   4 large egg whites

Fold them lightly into the batter and bake in layers, about 25 minutes. When cool, ice with:

   Luscious Orange, page 676, or
   Quick Chocolate Icing, page 679

ABOUT TWO-PIECE CAKE MOLDS

Lambs, bunnies and Santas need firm, compact doughs.
Prepare:

   White Cake II, above, or
   One Egg Cake, page 636

Keep nuts, raisins, etc., for decorations, rather than using them in the dough itself, because these solid ingredients, while they make the cake more interesting, tend to break down the tensile strength of the dough. Ground spices, however, are a good addition. Grease the mold with unsalted fat or oil. Use a pastry brush and be rather lavish. Then dust the greased surface with flour, reversing the mold to get rid of any excess. If the mold has steam vents, fill the solid section with the dough, to just below the joint. We have baked successfully in cake molds, even when they had no steam vents, using the following directions. Move a wooden spoon gently through the dough to release any air bubbles. ♦ Be careful not to distrub the greased and floured surface of the mold. Insert wooden toothpicks upright in the snout or lengthwise into the ears where they join the head. ♦ Watch for the toothpicks, through, when you cut the cake. Put the lid on the mold, making sure it locks, and tie or wire together so the steam of the rising dough will not force the two sections apart.

To bake, put the filled mold on a cookie sheet in a 370° preheated oven for about 1 hour. Test as you would for any cake, inserting a thin metal skewer or toothpick through a steam vent. Put the cake, still in the mold, on a rack for about 15 minutes. Carefully remove the top of the mold. Before you separate the cake from the bottom, let it continue to cool for about 5 minutes more to let all steam escape and to allow the dough to firm up a little. After removing, continue to cool on a rack. ♦ Do not try to let it sit upright until it is cold. If the cake has constitutional weaknesses, reinforce it with a wooden or metal skewer before icing. Ice with:

   Boiled White Icing, page 673, or
   Seven Minute Icing, page 676, or
   Caramel Icing, page 676

If you ✻ freeze the cake before frosting it, the job is somewhat easier. Or if you are in a hurry, try a:

French Icing, page 678
Caramel icing is a good variation for a
bunny mold. Increase the recipes by ½
for a heavy coat. For woolly or angora
effects, press into the icing:
    ½ to 1 cup shredded coconut
To accentuate the features use:
    Raisins, nuts, cherries and citron
Surround your animals with seasonal flowers and ferns. If bunnies or lambs are

made for Easter, you may want to confect
cake eggs and decorate them with icings
of different colors. See Angel Cake Balls,
page 633.

ABOUT WEDDING OR
LARGE CAKES

Be sure for any big cake to ♦ choose a
recipe that enlarges successfully, see comment under White Cake I, or use a large
fruit-cake recipe. We find that, when rather shallow pans are used—not more than
2 inches deep for each layer—the cake
bakes more evenly and cuts more attractively. For any large cake, lower the oven
temperature indicated by 25°. For more
even baking, swing it around in the oven
frequently during the necessarily longer
baking period. Test for doneness as you
would with any cake, see page 617. To
ice, see Decorative Boiled Icing, page 675,
or Royal Glaze, page 678.

After the bride's first slice, whether the
wedding cake is round or rectangular, the
cutting begins at the lowest tier. To make
the cuts even in depth, run a knife perpendicularly through the bottom layer,
where it abuts the second layer. Continue
this process at each tier. Cut successive
slices until a single cylindrical central core
remains, crested by the ornate top, as
shown on the left. Remove and save this,
see page 770, or freeze it for the first anni-
versary party. Then finish slicing the central core beginning at the top.

LADY BALTIMORE CAKE
Prepare the batter for:
    White Cake I, page 623
Bake it in 3 layers. When cool, place the
following filling between the layers. Chop:
    6 figs
    ½ cup seeded raisins
    1 cup nut meats
Prepare:
    Boiled White Icing or Seven Minute
    White Icing, page 673
Reserve a generous third of this. To the
rest, add the nuts, figs and raisins. Spread
the filling between the layers and the reserved icing over the top.

COCONUT MILK CAKE
                        Two 9-Inch Round Cakes
Some years ago we gave a pet recipe to a
friend who later presented us with the one
which follows—best made with fresh coconut milk. She said that, in her family,
whenever a treasured recipe was received,
they gave an equally treasured one of their
own in return. We love this festive adopted
child.
Preheat oven to 350°.
♦ Have all ingredients at about 75°. Have
ready:
    1½ cups freshly grated coconut
♦ Sift before measuring:
    3 cups cake flour
Resift it with:
    3 teaspoons double-acting
        baking powder
    ½ teaspoon salt
Sift:
    1½ cups sugar
Cream well:
    ¾ cup butter
Add the sifted sugar gradually and continue creaming until these ingredients are
very light. Beat in:
    3 beaten egg yolks
Add the sifted flour mixture in 3 parts to
the butter mixture, alternately with:
    ¾ cup coconut milk or milk
    ½ teaspoon vanilla
Stir the batter until smooth after each ad-
dition. Then add ¾ of a cup of the grated
coconut. Whip ♦ until stiff, but not dry:

3 egg whites

Fold the egg whites gently into the batter. Bake in greased layer pans for about 25 minutes. To serve, fill between the layers with:

Currant, strawberry or raspberry jelly

Cover the cake with:

Sea Foam Icing, page 676

Coat it with the remaining ¾ cup grated coconut.

MARBLE CAKE
A 9-Inch Tube Pan

This old-fashioned cake is still a great favorite.
Preheat oven to 350°.
Prepare:

White Cake II, page 623

Before whipping the egg whites separate the batter into 2 parts. Add to ½ the batter:

1½ oz. melted, cooled chocolate
1 teaspoon cinnamon
¼ teaspoon cloves
⅛ teaspoon soda

Whip the egg whites as directed and fold ½ into the light and ½ into the dark batter. Grease a tube pan. Place large spoonfuls of batter in it, alternating light and dark dough. Bake for about 1 hour. Spread when cool with:

Boiled White Icing, page 673, or
Banana Icing, page 680

WHIPPED CREAM CAKE
Two 9-Inch Layers

Preheat oven to 350°.
◗ Have all ingredients except the whipping cream at about 75°. Sift before measuring:

2 cups cake flour

Resift twice with:

2¾ teaspoons double-acting baking powder
¾ teaspoon salt

Whip until stiff:

1 cup whipping cream

Fold into the cream:

1⅛ cups powdered sugar

and add gradually, stirring gently until smooth:

½ cup water
1½ teaspoons vanilla or almond flavoring

Whip ◗ until stiff, but not dry:

3 egg whites

Combine the cream and the egg whites. Fold the sifted ingredients into the cream mixture, about ⅓ at a time. Bake in layer pans for about 25 to 30 minutes. Fill with:

Ginger Fruit Filling, page 647

SOUR CREAM CAKE
Two 8-Inch Round Pans

Preheat oven to 375°.
◗ Have all ingredients at about 75°. Sift before measuring:

1¾ cups cake flour

Resift with:

¼ teaspoon soda
1¾ teaspoons double-acting baking powder
¼ teaspoon salt

Sift:

1 cup sugar

Cream until soft:

⅓ cup butter

Add the sugar gradually. When these ingredients are creamy, beat in:

2 beaten egg yolks
1 teaspoon vanilla

Add the sifted flour mixture to the butter mixture in 3 parts, alternating with thirds of:

⅔ cup yogurt or 1 cup cultured sour cream

Stir the batter after each addition until smooth. Whip until ◗ stiff, but not dry:

2 egg whites
¼ teaspoon salt

Fold them lightly into the batter. Bake in greased pans for about 25 minutes. When cool, spread with:

Almond, Fig or Raisin Filling, page 647

Cover with:

Boiled White Icing, page 673

GOLD LAYER CAKE
Two 8-Inch Round Layers

Preheat oven to 375°.
◗ Have all ingredients at about 75°. Sift before measuring:

2 cups cake flour

Resift with:

2 teaspoons double-acting baking powder
¼ teaspoon salt

Sift:

1 cup sugar

Cream until soft:

½ cup butter

Add the sugar ◗ gradually, creaming these ingredients until light. Beat in:

3 well-beaten egg yolks

Add:

1 teaspoon vanilla or 1 teaspoon grated lemon rind

Add the flour mixture to the butter mixture in 3 parts, with thirds of:

¾ cup milk

Stir the batter until smooth after each addition. Bake in layer pans for about 25 minutes. Spread layers, when cool, with:

A lemon icing, page 678, or
other icing

or spread between the layers:

Lemon Filling, page 646

This cake is delicious filled with a layer of good raspberry jam. Dust the top with:

Powdered sugar

FOUR-EGG CAKE
Three 9-Inch Round Pans
This is the old-time One-Two-Three-Four
Cake, slightly modernized.
Preheat oven to 350°.
Have all ingredients about 75°. Sift before
measuring:
    2⅔ cups cake flour
Resift with:
    2¼ teaspoons double-acting
        baking powder
    ½ teaspoon salt
Sift:
    2 cups sugar
Cream until soft:
    1 cup butter
Add the sugar gradually. Cream these in-
gredients until very light. Beat in, one at
a time:
    4 egg yolks
Add:
    1½ teaspoons vanilla or 1 teaspoon
        vanilla and ½ teaspoon almond
        extract
Add the flour mixture to the butter mixture
in about 3 parts, alternating with thirds of:
    1 cup milk
Stir the batter until smooth after each ad-
dition. Whip ♦ until stiff, but not dry:
    4 egg whites
Fold them lightly into the batter. Bake in
greased layer pans from 30 to 35 minutes.
Spread the layers, when cool, with:
    Pineapple or Ginger Fruit Filling,
        pages 645 and 647
Cover with:
    Whipped cream

COCONUT LOAF OR LAYER CAKE
Follow the recipe for:
    Four-Egg Cake, above
Add to the batter, before folding in the
egg whites:
    ¾ cup shredded coconut
    1½ teaspoons grated lemon rind
    ¼ teaspoon salt
Bake in a greased 8-inch tube pan for
about 1 hour.

EIGHT-YOLK CAKE
Three 9-Inch Layers
Bake it as a second cake after making
Angel Food Cake with the whites.
Preheat oven to 375°.
Have all ingredients about 75°. Sift before
measuring:
    2½ cups cake flour
Resift 3 times with:
    2⅔ teaspoons double-acting
        baking powder
    ¼ teaspoon salt
Sift:
    1¼ cups sugar
Cream until soft:
    ¾ cup butter
Add the sugar gradually. Cream these in-
gredients until very light. In a separate
bowl, beat until light and lemon colored:

    8 egg yolks
Beat them into the butter mixture. Add
the flour mixture in 3 parts, alternating
with thirds of:
    ¾ cup milk
Stir the batter after each addition. Add
and beat for 2 minutes:
    1 teaspoon vanilla
    1 teaspoon lemon juice or
        grated lemon rind
Bake in greased layer pans for about 20
minutes. Sprinkle with:
    Powdered sugar
or, when cool, spread with:
    Quick Orange Icing, page 678, or
    with one of the Seven-Minute Icings,
    page 676

POUND CAKE
**Two 9 x 5-Inch Pans or
One 10-Inch Tube Pan**
We have tried traditional pound cakes:
1 lb. butter, 1 lb. sugar, 1 lb. flour, 1 lb.
eggs—about 8 to 10—and any number of
variations. But we like this one best. It
differs from a true pound cake in that milk
is one of the components.
Preheat oven to 325°.
Have all ingredients about 75°. Sift before
measuring:
    4 cups cake flour
Resift with:
    1 teaspoon salt
    4 teaspoons double-acting
        baking powder
    (½ teaspoon mace)
Cream very well:
    1½ cups butter
Add and continue creaming until light:
    3 cups sugar
Add, one at a time, and continue beating
well after each addition:
    8 eggs
Add the flour mixture alternately with:
    1 cup milk
    2 teaspoons vanilla
    (2 tablespoons brandy or
        8 drops rose water)
♦ Stir only until thoroughly blended. Bake
in greased pans for 15 to 20 minutes, if in
layers. If baked in loaf pans, prepare them
by lining each one with parchment paper.

Let the paper project for easy removal of
the loaves and bake for 1 hour.
    ▲ In baking pound cakes at high alti-
tudes, omit any leavening called for.

SEED CAKE

A cake that reminds us of antimacassars and aspidistras.
Prepare:

Pound Cake, preceding page

Add:

2 teaspoons caraway seed
⅓ cup shaved citron
1 teaspoon grated lemon rind

LADY CAKE

A 9-Inch Tube Pan

This makes a tube or loaf cake or an excellent base for Petits Fours, see page 634. It tastes and looks a great deal like a conventional white wedding cake.

Preheat oven to 350°.

Have all ingredients about 75°. Sift before measuring:

1¾ cups cake flour

Resift twice with:

2 teaspoons any baking powder

Sift:

1 cup sugar

Cream until soft:

¾ cup butter

Add the sugar gradually, creaming these ingredients until very light. Add the flour mixture in 3 parts to the butter mixture, alternating with thirds of:

½ cup milk

Stir the batter for a few minutes after each addition. Add:

1 teaspoon almond extract
Grated rind of 1 lemon

Whip ♦ until stiff, but not dry:

3 egg whites

Fold them lightly into the cake batter. Bake in a greased tube pan for about 45 minutes. Sprinkle with:

Powdered sugar

or spread, when cool, with:

Quick Lemon Icing, page 678

CHOCOLATE CAKE

A 9 x 13-Inch Pan

Known as "Rombauer Special." A delicious light chocolate cake, always in demand.

Preheat oven to 350°.

Have ingredients at about 75°. Sift before measuring:

1¾ cups cake flour

Resift with:

3 teaspoons double-acting
baking powder
¼ teaspoon salt
(1 teaspoon cinnamon)
(¼ teaspoon cloves)
(1 cup coarsely chopped nuts)

Melt over hot water:

2 oz. chocolate

Add:

5 tablespoons boiling water

Sift:

1½ cups sugar

Beat until soft:

½ cup butter

Add the sugar gradually. Blend until very light and creamy. Beat in, one at a time:

4 egg yolks

Add the cooled chocolate mixture. Add the flour mixture in 3 parts to the butter mixture, alternating with thirds of:

½ cup milk

Stir the batter until smooth after each addition. Add:

1 teaspoon vanilla

Whip ♦ until stiff, but not dry:

4 egg whites

Fold them lightly into the cake batter. Bake in a greased pan for about ½ hour. Spread with thick:

White Icing, page 673, and Chocolate Coating, page 676, or Quick Chocolate or Peppermint Cream Filling, page 645

FUDGE LAYER CAKE

Two 8-Inch Round Layer Pans

Preheat oven to 350°.

Prepare:

Brownies, page 653

Separate eggs and fold in the stiffly beaten whites after the batter is mixed. Bake as directed. Garnish with:

Whipped cream

FUDGE MERINGUE CAKE

A 9 x 13-Inch Pan

Preheat oven to 350°.

Have all ingredients at about 75°. Sift:

2 cups cake flour

Resift with:

1 tablespoon double-acting
baking powder
¼ teaspoon salt

Melt ♦ over—not in—hot water:

4 oz. chocolate

Cream:

¼ cup butter

Add gradually; continue to cream and mix:

1½ cups sugar

Add:

3 well-beaten egg yolks
1 teaspoon vanilla

and the cooled chocolate. Then add, alternating in 3 parts with:

1 cup milk

the sifted flour. Stir well after each addition. Beat ♦ until stiff, but not dry:

3 egg whites

Fold in:

½ cup sugar

Beat to a meringue consistency before adding to batter. Bake about 35 minutes in a greased pan. When cool, ice with:

French Butter Icing, page 693

DEVIL'S FOOD CAKE COCKAIGNE

Two 9-Inch Round Layers

The best chocolate cake we know. Whether made with 2 or 4 oz. chocolate, it is wonderfully light, but rich and moist.

Preheat oven to 350°.

Prepare the following custard:

Cook and stir in a double boiler ♦ over—not in—hot water:

    2 to 4 oz. chocolate
    ½ cup milk
    1 cup light brown sugar, firmly packed
    1 egg yolk

Remove from the heat when thickened. Have other ingredients at about 75°. Sift before measuring:

    2 cups cake flour

Resift with:

    1 teaspoon soda
    ½ teaspoon salt

Sift:

    1 cup white sugar

Beat until soft:

    ½ cup butter

Add the sugar gradually. Blend until very light and creamy. Beat in, one at a time:

    2 egg yolks

Add the flour to the butter mixture in 3 parts, alternating with thirds of:

    ¼ cup water
    ½ cup milk
    1 teaspoon vanilla

Stir the batter until smooth after each addition. Stir in the chocolate custard. Whip ♦ until stiff, but not dry:

    2 egg whites

Fold them lightly into the cake batter. Bake in greased pans for about 25 minutes. Spread, when cool, with:

    Caramel Icing, page 676 or
    Chocolate Fudge Icing, page 677

★ OLD-WORLD CHOCOLATE
SPICE CAKE WITH CITRON
                    A 9-Inch Tube Pan

A tempting tube cake with a firm texture. Preheat oven to 350°.
Have all ingredients about 75°. Sift before measuring:

    2⅛ cups cake flour

Resift with:

    1½ teaspoons any baking powder
    ½ teaspoon cloves
    1 teaspoon cinnamon
    ½ teaspoon freshly grated nutmeg

Cream until soft:

    ½ cup butter

Add gradually and cream until light:

    1½ cups sugar

Beat in, one at a time:

    4 eggs

Stir in:

    4 oz. grated sweet chocolate
    ½ cup very finely shaved citron,
        candied orange or lemon peel

Stir the flour mixture into the butter mixture in about 3 parts, alternating with thirds of:

    ⅞ cup milk

Stir the batter after each addition until smooth. Most European cakes are stirred a long time. This gives them a close, sandy texture. Bake the cake in a greased tube pan or in a loaf pan for about 1 hour. Ice the cake, when cool, with:

    Chocolate Butter Icing, page 678
    or dust with:
    Powdered sugar

SPICED CHOCOLATE PRUNE CAKE
                    A 9 x 13-Inch Pan

A delightful dessert when served with whipped cream or pudding sauce.
Preheat oven to 350°.
Have all ingredients about 75°. Cook and cool:

    1 cup lightly sweetened puréed prunes

Sift before measuring:

    1½ cups cake flour

Resift with:

    1⅛ teaspoons double-acting
        baking powder
    ¼ teaspoon soda
    ¼ teaspoon salt
    (1 teaspoon cinnamon)
    (½ teaspoon cloves)

Sift:

    ¾ cup sugar

Cream until soft:

    ⅛ cup butter

Add the sugar gradually. Cream until light. Melt and add when cool:

    1 oz. chocolate

Beat well and add to the butter mixture:

    2 eggs

Add the flour mixture to the butter mixture in 3 parts, alternating with thirds of:

    ½ cup milk

Stir the batter until smooth after each addition. Add the prunes and:

    ½ teaspoon vanilla

Bake in a greased pan for about 25 minutes. Spread, when cool, with:

    French Icing, page 678

CHOCOLATE APRICOT CAKE

Follow the recipe for:

    Chocolate Prune Cake, above

Substitute for the prunes:

    1 cup cooked, lightly sweetened,
        well-drained apricots

Omit the spices. Ice, when cool, with:

    Whipped cream

or serve with:

    Foamy Sauce, page 714

VELVET SPICE CAKE

                    A 9-Inch Tube Pan

This cake has a very delicate consistency. Among spice cakes its flavor is unequaled. ♦ Be sure to bake it in a 9-inch tube pan.
Preheat oven to 350°.
Have all ingredients about 75°. Sift before measuring:

    2⅛ cups cake flour

Resift twice with:

    1½ teaspoons double-acting
        baking powder
    ½ teaspoon soda
    1 teaspoon freshly grated nutmeg
    1 teaspoon cinnamon
    ½ teaspoon cloves
    ½ teaspoon salt

Sift:

  1½ cups sugar

Cream until soft:

  ¾ cup butter

Add the sifted sugar gradually. Cream until very light. Beat in:

  3 egg yolks

Add the sifted ingredients to the butter mixture in 3 parts, alternating with thirds of:

  ⅞ cup yogurt or buttermilk

Stir the batter after each addition until smooth. Whip ♦ until stiff, but not dry:

  3 egg whites

Fold them lightly into the cake batter. Bake in a greased tube pan for 1 hour or more. Spread, when cool, with:

  Chocolate Butter Icing, page 678, or
  Boiled White Icing, page 673

BURNT-SUGAR CAKE

Two 9-Inch Round Pans

A handsome creation.

Have all ingredients about 75°. Caramelize:

  ½ cup sugar, page 507

and add ♦ very slowly:

  ½ cup boiling water

Boil the sirup until it is of the consistency of molasses. Cool it.

Preheat oven to 375°.

Sift before measuring:

  2½ cups cake flour

Resift with:

  2½ teaspoons any baking powder
  ¼ teaspoon salt

Sift:

  1½ cups sugar

Cream until soft:

  ½ cup butter

Add the sugar gradually. Cream until very light. Beat in, one at a time:

  2 egg yolks

Add the flour mixture in 3 parts to the butter mixture, alternating with thirds of:

  1 cup water

Stir the batter after each addition until smooth. Stir in:

  3 tablespoons of the caramelized sirup
  1 teaspoon vanilla

Whip ♦ until stiff, but not dry:

  2 egg whites

Fold them lightly into the cake batter. Bake in greased pans for about 25 minutes. Spread, when cool, with:

  A white icing, page 673

In making the icing, flavor it in addition to the vanilla with:

  4 teaspoons of the caramelized sirup

Place any remaining sirup in a closed jar. It will keep indefinitely.

BROWN-SUGAR SPICE CAKE

An 8½ x 4½-Inch Loaf Pan

Preheat oven to 375°.

Have all ingredients at about 75°. Sift before measuring:

  2½ cups cake flour

Resift with:

  1 teaspoon salt
  ¼ teaspoon soda
  2½ teaspoons double-acting
    baking powder
  1 teaspoon cinnamon
  ½ teaspoon cloves
  ¼ teaspoon nutmeg
  (2 teaspoons grated orange rind)

Cream until light:

  1½ cups packed brown sugar
  ½ cup butter

Beat in:

  3 egg yolks

Stir the flour mixture into the butter mixture in about 3 parts, alternating with thirds of:

  1 cup milk

Stir the batter after each addition until smooth. Have ready a greased loaf pan. Bake for about 40 minutes or until done. Cover the top of the cake with:

  French Icing, page 678

APPLESAUCE CAKE

A 9-Inch Tube Pan

Preheat oven to 350°.

Have all ingredients at about 75°. Sift before measuring:

  1¾ cups cake flour

Sift a little of the flour over:

  1 cup raisins
  1 cup currants, nut meats or dates

Resift the remainder with:

  ½ teaspoon salt
  1 teaspoon soda
  1 teaspoon cinnamon
  ½ teaspoon cloves

Sift:

  1 cup white or packed brown sugar

Cream until soft:

  ½ cup butter

Add the sugar gradually. Cream until light. Beat in:

  1 egg

Stir the flour mixture gradually into the butter mixture until the batter is smooth. Add the raisins, nut meats and:

  1 cup thick, lightly sweetened
    applesauce

Stir it into the batter. Bake in a greased tube pan for about 50 to 60 minutes. Spread, when cool, with:

  Caramel Icing, page 676

FIG SPICE CAKE

A 9-Inch Tube Pan

Have all ingredients at about 75°. Cool, drain, then cut into ¼-inch cubes and reserve the sirup:

  1 lb. dried stewed figs

There should be 2 cups of figs. Combine:

  ½ cup fig juice
  ½ cup buttermilk or yogurt

Preheat oven to 350°.

Sift before measuring:

  1½ cups cake flour

Resift with:
 1 teaspoon any baking powder
 1 teaspoon salt
 ½ teaspoon cinnamon
 ¼ teaspoon cloves
 ½ teaspoon soda
Sift before measuring:
 1 cup sugar
Cream until soft:
 ½ cup butter
Add the sugar gradually. Cream until
very light. Beat in, one at a time:
 2 eggs
Add the flour mixture to the butter mixture
in about 3 parts, alternating with thirds of
the milk and fig juice. Stir the batter after
each addition until smooth. Add the figs
and:
 1 teaspoon vanilla
 (1 cup broken nut meats or raisins)
Bake in a greased tube pan for about 50
minutes. Spread, when cool, with:
 Coffee or Mocha Icing, page 679

DATE SPICE CAKE
                          An 8½ x 4½-Inch Loaf
Preheat oven to 325°.
Have all ingredients at about 75°. Cut
into small pieces:
 1 cup dates
Pour over them:
 1 cup boiling water or coffee
Cool these ingredients. Sift before measuring:
 1½ cups cake flour
Resift with:
 1½ teaspoons double-acting
   baking powder
 ¾ teaspoon freshly grated nutmeg
 ¼ teaspoon salt
 ¼ teaspoon soda
Cream together:
 3 tablespoons butter
 1 cup sifted sugar
 1 beaten egg
Add the flour mixture to the butter mixture in about 3 parts, alternating with
thirds of the date mixture. Stir the batter
well after each addition. Fold in:
 1 cup raisins
 1 cup broken pecan meats
Bake in a greased loaf pan for about 45
minutes. Dust with:
 Powdered sugar

TUTTI FRUTTI CAKE
                          A 9-Inch Tube Pan
A well-flavored summer fruit cake.
Preheat oven to 350°.
Sift before measuring:
 2 cups and 2 tablespoons cake flour
Resift with:
 1 teaspoon each cloves, cinnamon,
   nutmeg
 1 teaspoon soda
 ½ teaspoon salt
Sift:
 1½ cups packed brown sugar

Cream until soft:
 ½ cup butter
Add the sugar gradually. Cream until
light. Beat in, one at a time:
 2 eggs
Stir the flour mixture into the butter mixture in about 3 parts, alternating with
thirds of:
 1 cup lightly drained crushed
   pineapple
Stir in:
 ½ cup each raisins and currants
 1 cup broken nut meats
Bake in a greased tube pan for about 1
hour.

BANANA CAKE
                        Two 9-Inch Round Pans
Do try this, if you like a banana flavor.
Preheat oven to 350°.
Have all ingredients at about 75°. Sift before measuring:
 2¼ cups cake flour
Resift with:
 ½ teaspoon any baking powder
 ¾ teaspoon soda
 ½ teaspoon salt
Sift:
 1½ cups sugar
Cream:
 ½ cup butter
Add the sifted sugar gradually. Cream until very light. Beat in, one at a time:
 2 eggs
Prepare:
 1 cup lightly mashed ripe bananas
Add:
 1 teaspoon vanilla
 ¼ cup yogurt or buttermilk
Add the flour mixture to the butter mixture
in about 3 parts, alternating with thirds of
the banana mixture. Stir the batter after
each addition until smooth. Bake in
greased pans for about ½ hour. When cool,
place between the layers:
 2 sliced ripe bananas
Spread the cake with:
 A white icing, page 673
If served at once, this cake is good without
icing—just sprinkled with powdered sugar
or served with whipped cream.

ABOUT FRUIT CAKES

Many people feel that these cakes improve
greatly with age. When they are well saturated with alcoholic liquors, which raise
the spirits and keep down mold, and are
buried in powdered sugar in tightly closed
tins, they have been enjoyed as long as 25
years after baking.
 Fruit cakes are fundamentally butter
cakes with just enough dough to bind the
fruit. Raisins, figs and dates can be more
easily cut if the scissors or knife used is
dipped periodically in water.
 For a 2½ lb. cake, use an 8-inch ring

mold or a 4½ x 8½-inch loaf pan, either
filled to about 2½ inches. To prepare loaf
pans, see Pound Cake, page 626. To prepare a tube pan, line the bottom with a
round of greased waxed paper or foil and
cut a straight strip for sides. Bake as long
as indicated in individual recipes.

Fruit cakes, still in the pan, are cooled
from 20 to 30 minutes on a rack. Then the
parchment or foil in which they are baked
is carefully removed and the cake rack-
cooled further until entirely free from heat.
To decorate the cakes with candied fruit
or nut meats, dip the undersides of the
decorations into a light sugar sirup before
applying them, or simply cover the cake
with a sugar sirup glaze and arrange the
trimming on it.

To store, wrap the loaves or tubes in
brandy- or wine-soaked linens. If you prefer, you may make a few fine skewer punc-
tures in the cake and pour over it very
slowly, drop by drop, ¼ to 1 cup heated,
but not boiling, brandy or wine. However
you glaze or soak the cake, wrap it in
liquor-soaked linen, then in foil. For very
long storage, bury the liquor-soaked cake
in powdered sugar. In any case, place it
in a tightly covered tin in a cool place.

▲ In baking fruit cakes at high altitude,
omit any leavening called for.

★ FRUIT CAKE COCKAIGNE
                Two 4 x 8½-Inch Loaves
Not unlike a pound cake. The fruits stay
light in color.
Preheat oven to 350°.
◗ Please review About Butter Cakes, page
622, and About Fruit Cakes, above.
◗ Have all ingredients at about 75°. Sift
before measuring:
    4 cups all-purpose flour
Reserve ½ cup. Mix it with 4 cups nuts
and fruits.
We particularly like:
    1⅛ cups pecans or hickory nuts
    1⅛ cups white raisins
    1⅛ cups seeded and chopped
        preserved kumquats
Resift the remainder of the flour with:
    1 teaspoon double-acting
        baking powder
    ½ teaspoon salt
Cream until light:
    ¾ cup butter
Then cream it with:
    2 cups sugar
Beat in, one at a time:
    5 eggs
Add:
    1 teaspoon vanilla
and continue to beat until light. Stir the
flour mixture into the egg mixture and continue beating until thoroughly mixed. Fold
in the reserved floured nuts and fruits. Bake
for about 1 hour. To prepare pans, cool,
remove and store, see About Fruit Cakes,
above.

★ CURRANT CAKE
Prepare the dough for:
    Fruit Cake Cockaigne, above
Add, instead of the suggested fruit mix-
ture:
    1 to 1½ cups currants
Bake, cool and store as for the above cake.

★ WHITE FRUIT CAKE
                Two 4 x 8½-Inch Loaves
Preheat oven to 350°.
Prepare the batter for:
    Fruit Cake Cockaigne, above
Beat in:
    1 cup chopped nut meats, preferably
        blanched, slivered almonds
    ½ cup finely sliced citron, candied
        orange or lemon peel
    1 cup white raisins
    ¼ cup chopped candied pineapple
    ¼ cup chopped candied cherries
    (½ cup finely shredded coconut)
Bake about 1 hour. To prepare pans, cool
and store, see About Fruit Cakes, above.

★ DARK FRUIT CAKE
I.   Two 4½ x 8-Inch Loaves, plus
                Two 9-Inch Tube Pans—
                    About 12 Pounds
◗ Please review About Butter Cakes, page
622, and About Fruit Cakes, above.
Preheat oven to 275°.
◗ Have all ingredients at about 75°. Sift
before measuring:
    4 cups all-purpose flour
Reserve 1 cup. Resift the remainder with:
    1 tablespoon each of cinnamon, cloves,
        allspice and nutmeg
    ½ tablespoon mace
    1½ teaspoons salt
Wash:
    2½ lbs. currants
Cut up:
    2½ lbs. raisins
    1 lb. citron
Break coarsely:
    1 lb. pecan meats
Sprinkle these ingredients well with the re-
served flour. Sift:
    1 lb. brown sugar: 2⅔ cups, packed
Cream until soft:
    1 lb. butter
Add the sugar gradually. Cream until very
light. Beat in:
    15 beaten egg yolks
Add the flour mixture to the butter mix-
ture, alternately with:
    ¼ cup bourbon whisky and ¼ cup wine
    or ½ cup thick fruit juice: prune,
        apricot or grape
Fold in the floured fruits and nuts. Beat
◗ until stiff, but not dry:
    15 egg whites
Fold them into the butter mixture. Bake a
2½ lb. cake in prepared pans, for 3 to 4
hours. Over 5 lbs., allow at least 5 hours.
Place a shallow pan filled with water in
the oven. Remove it the last hour of baking. Cool and store.

II.   Two 4½ x 8-Inch Loaves, plus
Two 8-Inch Tube Pans—
About 11 Pounds

◗ Please review About Butter Cakes, page 622, and About Fruit Cakes, page 630.
Preheat oven to 275°.
◗ Have all ingredients at about 75°. Sift before measuring:

4 cups all-purpose flour

Reserve 1 cup. Resift the remainder with:

1 teaspoon cinnamon
½ teaspoon cloves
½ teaspoon nutmeg
1 teaspoon salt, if butter is unsalted

Sprinkle the reserved flour over:

2 lbs. seedless raisins
1 lb. chopped citron
¼ lb. chopped candied orange peel and lemon peel
1 lb. chopped figs or dates
2 lbs. whole pecan meats
12 candied cherries

Sift:

2 cups sugar

Cream until soft:

2 cups butter

Add the sugar gradually. Cream until very light. Beat in:

12 beaten egg yolks

Add the flour mixture to the butter mixture ½ cupful at a time, alternately with:

½ cup grape jelly
½ cup grape juice
½ cup brandy or dry wine

Stir the floured fruits into the batter. Whip
◗ until stiff, but not dry and fold in gently:

12 egg whites
¼ teaspoon salt

To bake, see Dark Fruit Cake I, page 631. Cool and store.

III.   Two 4½ x 8 x 2½-Inch Loaves, plus
Two 8-Inch Tube Pans—
About 11 Pounds

In this recipe the fruit is preconditioned, so it does not draw moisture from the cake during or after baking.
◗ Please review About Butter Cakes, page 622, and About Fruit Cakes, page 630.
◗ Have all ingredients at about 75°. Place and cook in a heavy pot for 5 minutes, stirring constantly:

1½ cups apricot nectar
2½ cups seedless white raisins
2½ cups seedless raisins
1 cup pitted, chopped dates
1 cup diced candied pineapple
2 cups diced candied cherries
1 cup diced candied apricots

Remove from heat, cover and let stand 12 to 15 hours.
Preheat oven to 300°.
Sift before measuring:

6 cups all-purpose flour

Resift with:

2 teaspoons salt
½ teaspoon soda

2 teaspoons cinnamon
1 teaspoon each allspice and nutmeg
½ teaspoon cloves
¼ teaspoon cardamon

Cream until light:

2 cups butter
2 cups sugar

Add and beat in well:

10 beaten eggs

Add:

2 tablespoons vanilla

Stir in the sifted flour mixture. Combine the batter with the fruit sirup and fruit and:

3 cups coarsely chopped pecans

until well mixed. Pour into the loaf and tube pans and bake for 3 to 3½ hours or until the tests indicate that the cake is done. To prepare pans, see About Fruit Cakes, page 630. Cool and store.

ABOUT CUP CAKES

Nearly all cake doughs lend themselves to baking in individual portions. Bake them in muffin, madeleine or ladyfinger molds. On informal occasions, like children's parties, bake and serve in fluted paper baking cups. If the papers are set in muffin tins the cakes retain their shape better. ◗ Fill molds about ⅓ full and bake in a 375° preheated oven for 20 to 25 minutes. The baked cakes can be filled and iced. For suggested combinations, see Filled Cakes and Torten, page 639. For quick icing methods, see page 677, or garnish the cakes with nuts, diced dried fruits or a dusting of powdered sugar.

YELLOW CUP CAKES
About Two Dozen 2-Inch Cakes

Preheat oven to 375°.
See About Cup Cakes, above. Prepare:

Hurry-Up Cake, page 635, or
Lightning Cake, page 636

ONE-EGG CUP CAKES

◗ See About Cup Cakes, above.
Preheat oven to 375°.
Prepare:

One-Egg Cake, page 636

Add to the batter:

(1 cup raisins or washed, dried currants)

When cool, sprinkle the tops with:

Confectioners' sugar

SPONGE CUP CAKES
OR MARGUERITES

See About Cup Cakes, above.
Preheat oven to 375°.
Prepare:

Any sponge cake

Permit the cakes to cool in the pans, then sprinkle with:

Powdered sugar

MADELEINES
About 15 Cakes
These light-as-a-feather French tea cakes are usually baked in scalloped madeleine shells or muffin tins. Who could guess that their tender crumb results from an overdose of butter? The method of making them is just like that of Génoise.
Preheat oven to 450°.
Melt and allow to cool:
¾ cup butter
Heat in a double boiler until lukewarm:
2 eggs
1 cup sugar
Stir constantly. Remove from heat and beat until thick but light and creamy, incorporating as much air as possible. When cool, sift and add gradually:
1 cup sifted cake flour
Add the cool, melted butter and:
1 tablespoon rum
1 teaspoon vanilla or 1 teaspoon grated lemon rind
Bake for about 15 minutes.

LADYFINGERS
About 30 Small Cakes
Preheat oven to 375°.
♦ Have ingredients at about 75°. Sift before measuring:
⅛ cup cake flour
Resift it 3 times. Sift:
⅓ cup confectioners' sugar
Beat until thick and lemon colored:
1 whole egg
2 egg yolks
Whip until stiff, but not dry:
2 egg whites
Fold the sugar gradually into the egg whites. Beat the mixture until it thickens again. Fold in the egg yolk mixture and:
¼ teaspoon vanilla
Fold in the flour. Shape the dough into oblongs with a paper tube, see page 618, on ungreased paper placed in a pan; or pour it into greased ladyfinger or small muffin tins. Or you may put it through a cookie press. Bake for about 12 minutes.

CORNSTARCH PUFF CAKES
Fifteen Small Cupcakes
Preheat oven to 350°.
Have ingredients at about 75°. Cream:
½ cup butter
1 cup sifted powdered sugar
Add and beat until light:
4 well-beaten eggs
1 teaspoon vanilla
Sift before measuring:
1 cup cornstarch
Sift 3 times afterwards, with:
2 teaspoons double-acting baking powder
Combine the creamed and the sifted ingredients until blended. Fill muffin tins ½ full and bake about 15 minutes.

JAM CUP CAKES
Prepare the batter for:

Rombauer Jam Cake, page 636
Bake in greased muffin tins, at 375° for about 20 minutes.

ANGEL CUP CAKES OR BALLS
About Sixteen 2½-Inch Cup Cakes
Preheat oven to 375°.
Prepare the batter for:
Angel Cake, page 620, or Flavored Angel Cake, page 621
Place it in ungreased, deep muffin tins. Bake for about 20 minutes. When cold, split the cup cakes horizontally and fill them. See Filled Cakes and Torten, page 639. For a luxurious tea cake, ice with a rather soft icing and roll in chopped nuts or shredded chopped coconut.

LANGUE DE CHAT OR CAT'S TONGUE
About 2 Dozen
Preheat oven to 350°.
Cream:
¼ cup butter
¼ cup sugar
Beat in:
4 eggs
Fold in:
½ cup all-purpose flour
1 teaspoon vanilla
The pans for these wafers are similar in shape to ladyfinger pans. Bake about 15 minutes or until done. Serve frosted, or put a filling between two of the cakes of 3 parts chocolate icing and 1 part crushed nut brittle, to form **Maquis**.

CHOCOLATE CUP CAKES
♦ Read About Cup Cakes, page 632.
Preheat oven to 375°.
Prepare any recipe for:
Chocolate Cake, page 627
Bake for 20 to 25 minutes or until done.

CARAMEL CUP CAKES
About Twenty-Four 2-Inch Cakes
♦ Read About Cup Cakes, page 632.
Preheat oven to 375°.
Prepare:
Hurry-Up Caramel Cake, page 635
Bake in greased muffin tins for 20 to 25 minutes or until done.

SOUR MILK SPICE CUP CAKES
About Twenty 2-Inch Cakes
♦ Read About Cup Cakes, page 632.
Preheat oven to 375°.
Prepare:
Sour Cream Layer Cake, page 625
substituting for the white sugar:
Brown sugar
Add:
½ teaspoon cinnamon
¼ teaspoon cloves
Fold in:
¾ cup nut meats
Bake in greased muffin tins for about 20 minutes or until done.

COCONUT CUP CAKES
Prepare batter for:
> Coconut Loaf Cake, page 626

Bake in small greased muffin tins.

✳ PETITS FOURS
Prepare:
> Lady Cake, page 627, or Génoise,
> page 640

Pour the dough into pans, so that you may cut the cake into small cubes. You may cut the cubes in half horizontally and apply a filling, page 646. To apply Fondant, the traditional icing, see page 676, and the illustration below.

ABOUT CAKES WITH MELTED BUTTER OR OIL

If liquid fats are used in cake making, they demand special mixing processes. Génoise, page 640, and Madeleines, page 633, are examples of melted butter batters. In this book, all cakes made with cooking oil carry the word "oil" in the title. They are included not for their excellence, for they have too fine a grain, but for those who use unsaturated fats.

♦ Olive oil should never be used because its flavor is too strong. To be light in texture, oil cake recipes need a disproportionate amount of sugar. ♦ Because of the difference in mixing and the greater demand for sugar ♦ do not try to substitute oil for solid fats in other cake recipes. You may vary the recipes given for oil cakes, however, by the addition of spices, flavorings, nuts and raisins.

CHIFFON OIL CAKE
> A 10-Inch Pan or
> a 9 x 13-Inch Oblong

This cake has a very fine light texture, but requires a larger amount of sugar than a solid shortening cake. ♦ Mix it exactly as indicated.
Preheat oven to 325°.
Sift twice and put in a beater bowl:
> 2¼ cups sifted cake flour
> 1½ cups sugar
> 3 teaspoons double-acting
> baking powder

1 teaspoon salt
Beat until smooth and fold in all at once:
> ½ cup cooking oil
> 6 beaten egg yolks
> ¾ cup water
> 1 teaspoon grated lemon rind
> 2 teaspoons vanilla

Beat until foamy:
> 6 to 10 egg whites

Add:
> ½ teaspoon cream of tartar

Beat until ♦ stiff, but not dry. Fold the flour, egg and oil mixture gently into the egg whites. Do this by hand, not in the mixer, see page 515. Bake the cake in an ungreased tube pan about 1 hour and 10 minutes or in an ungreased 9 x 13-inch flat pan for about 30 to 35 minutes. Place the pan on a rack adjusted in the lower third of the oven. Reverse the tube pan to cool the cake, as shown on page 620, or set the oblong pan reversed and supported at the edges by two other pans while the cake cools. Ice with:
> Banana Icing, page 680

CHIFFON MOCHA OIL CAKE
> A 10-Inch Tube Pan or
> a 9 x 13-Inch Oblong

Mix and bake as for preceding cake.
Preheat oven to 325°.
Melt over hot water:
> 3 oz. chocolate

Sift twice and put in a beater bowl:
> 2¼ cups sifted cake flour
> 1⅜ cups sugar
> 3 teaspoons double acting
> baking powder
> 2 teaspoons instant coffee
> 1 teaspoon salt
> ¼ teaspoon cinnamon

Beat until smooth and fold in all at once:
> ½ cup cooking oil
> 6 beaten egg yolks
> ½ cup milk
> 2 teaspoons vanilla

and the cooled melted chocolate. Blend well. Beat until frothy:
> 6 to 8 egg whites

Add:
> ½ teaspoon cream of tartar

Continue to beat until the whites are ♦ stiff, but not dry. Gently fold the egg whites into the flour, egg and oil mixture. Place the batter in an ungreased tube pan or an ungreased oblong pan. Place the pan on a rack adjusted in the lower third of the oven. If in a tube pan, bake for about 1 hour and 10 minutes; if in the oblong pan, for about 35 minutes. To cool, reverse the tube pan or let the oblong pan rest reversed on two other pans. Ice with:
> Luscious Orange Icing, page 676

QUICK WHITE OIL CAKE
> Two 9-Inch Square Pans

Preheat oven to 375°.

Have all ingredients at about 75°. Sift into a mixing bowl:

2¾ cups sifted cake flour
3½ teaspoons double-acting
    baking powder
1 teaspoon salt

Mix and add:

⅔ cup cooking oil
¾ cup water
½ cup skimmed milk

Beat the two mixtures together until you have a smooth batter. Beat until foamy:

4 egg whites

Add:

¼ teaspoon cream of tartar

Continue to beat until the whites are ♦ stiff, but not dry. Continue to beat, adding gradually:

1½ cups sugar

until a meringue-like texture results. Fold the egg white mixture into the other ingredients. Bake in greased pans for 25 to 30 minutes.

QUICK SPICE OIL CAKE

Prepare:

Quick White Oil Cake, above

using in all:

2½ cups, plus 2 tablespoons cake flour
2 teaspoons cinnamon
½ teaspoon each cloves and allspice
2 teaspoons grated orange rind

Mix and bake exactly as directed in Quick White Oil Cake.

QUICK CHOCOLATE OIL CAKE

Prepare:

Quick White Oil Cake, above

using in all:

2¼ cups cake flour
⅓ cup cocoa

Beat in, at the last, in all:

1¾ cups sugar

Mix and bake exactly as directed in Quick White Oil Cake.

ABOUT QUICK CAKES

We all want a good cake in a big hurry. But let's not delude ourselves that the shortcuts listed in the Index as Quick Cakes and made with unseparated eggs are as lovely in texture as those which require separation of the eggs. Lightning Cake, especially if made with a heavy duty mixer, is amazingly moist and tender. All quick cakes, especially those calling for oil or emulsified hydrogenated fats, demand a larger proportion of sugar than cakes baked with solid shortening, and have a closer grain. ♦ Mix oil cakes just exactly as describe, page 634; and quick butter cakes as in the following recipes. Deviation spells disaster. ♦ Never try to mix just any recipe by the one-bowl method.

HURRY-UP CAKE

A 9 x 13-Inch Pan

This cake—and its variations which can be made in one bowl—speaks for itself. It can be mixed by hand or with a rotary or electric mixer. It is best as a flat cake, iced and cut into cubes. Be sure to have all ingredients at 75°.

Preheat oven to 350°.

Sift before measuring:

1¾ cups cake flour

Resift with:

1 cup sugar

Add:

½ cup soft butter
2 eggs
½ cup milk
¼ teaspoon salt
1¾ teaspoons double-acting
    baking powder
1 teaspoon vanilla

Beat vigorously with a wire whisk or a rotary beater for 2 or 3 minutes. Bake in a greased pan for about ½ hour. Spread with:

Chocolate Butter Icing, page 678, or
Quick Lemon Icing, page 678

HURRY-UP CARAMEL CAKE

Prepare:

Hurry-Up Cake, above

Substitute for the white sugar:

1 cup packed brown sugar

You may add to the batter:

¾ cup nut meats
¾ cup chopped dates

Spread the cake, when cool, with:

Caramel Icing, page 676

HURRY-UP COCOA CAKE

Prepare:

Hurry-Up Cake, above

Deduct ¼ cup cake flour.

Add:

¼ cup Dutch process cocoa

Ice the cake, when cool, with:

European Chocolate Icing, page 679

HURRY-UP SPICE CAKE

Prepare:

Hurry-Up Cake, above

Add:

1 teaspoon cinnamon
½ teaspoon cloves

When cool, dust the cake with:

Confectioners' sugar

CARAMEL CORNFLAKE RING

8 Servings

Stir, melt and cook to the soft-ball stage, at 238°:

1 cup packed brown sugar
1½ tablespoons light corn sirup
⅛ cup milk
2½ tablespoons butter

Place in a large buttered mixing bowl:

4 cups cornflakes

Stir in the hot sirup until blended. Pack the flakes in a buttered 8-inch ring mold. Cool. Invert and serve, filled with:

Sugared or stewed fruit

LIGHTNING OR WHIPPED TEA CAKE

Two 8-Inch Square or Two 8-Inch Round Pans

Prepare this cake as described, or vary it in flavor by making the substitutions as directed in any of the variations for Hurry-Up Cake, page 635.
Preheat oven to 375°.
♦ Have all ingredients at about 75°. Let soften to the consistency of mayonnaise:

½ cup butter

If you want a wonderful, thin tea cake, have ready a topping of:

½ cup powdered sugar
1 tablespoon cinnamon
¼ cup chopped pecans

and prepare the 8-inch square pans. If you want a thicker layer cake to ice, use the 8-inch round pans and omit the topping. Sift into a beater bowl:

1¾ cups cake flour
½ teaspoon salt
1 cup sugar

Add:

2 eggs
½ cup, plus 2½ teaspoons milk

and the softened butter. Using the ♦ whip attachment of your beater, whip for 1 minute at low speed. Scrape the bowl. Whip for 1½ minutes at slightly higher speed. Scrape the bowl again and fold in:

1½ teaspoons baking powder

Whip for 30 seconds on first speed. Pour the batter into 2 pans, sprinkle with the topping and bake for 20 minutes.

ONE-EGG CAKE

Two 8-Inch Round Pans

Preheat oven to 375°.
Have all ingredients at about 75°. Sift into an electric mixer bowl and mix for about 2 minutes at medium speed:

1¾ cups sifted all-purpose flour
1¼ cups sugar
2½ teaspoons double-acting
    baking powder
1 teaspoon salt
⅛ cup soft butter
¾ cup milk

Add and mix for ♦ 2 minutes more, scraping bowl constantly:

1 egg
⅛ cup milk
1 teaspoon vanilla

Pour the batter into greased pans and bake for about 25 minutes. See Quick Icings for a choice and apply when cake is cool.

GINGERBREAD

A 9 x 9 x 2-Inch Pan

Preheat oven to 350°.
Melt in a heavy pan and let cool:

½ cup butter

Beat together well:

½ cup sugar
1 beaten egg

Sift:

2½ cups sifted all-purpose flour
1½ teaspoons soda
1 teaspoon each cinnamon and ginger
½ teaspoon salt
(1 tablespoon grated orange rind)

Combine:

½ cup light molasses
½ cup honey
1 cup hot water

Add the sifted and liquid ingredients alternately to the butter mixture until blended. Bake in a greased pan about 1 hour.

WHEATLESS GINGERBREAD

A 9 x 9 x 2-Inch Pan

Unusual, yet perhaps the best of all.
Preheat oven to 325°.
Sift together 6 times:

1¼ cups rye or rice flour
1¼ cups cornstarch
2 teaspoons soda
1 teaspoon cinnamon
¼ teaspoon each cloves and ginger

Mix:

½ cup sugar
1 cup molasses
½ cup butter

with the flour mixture. Add:

1 cup boiling water

Add:

2 well-beaten eggs

Bake in a greased pan about 45 minutes.

PARKIN

An 8 x 8-Inch Pan

A not-too-sweet Guy Fawkes Day cake.
Preheat oven to 350°.
Heat ♦ over—not in—hot water, until the butter is melted:

½ cup butter
⅔ cup treacle

Mix in a bowl:

⅔ cup rolled oats
1 cup all-purpose flour
1 tablespoon sugar
½ teaspoon ginger
¼ teaspoon cloves
½ teaspoon salt
½ teaspoon soda
(1 teaspoon grated lemon rind)

Add alternately with the melted butter mixture:

⅔ cup milk

Combine until the dry ingredients are just moist. The batter will be thin. Bake in a greased pan for about 35 minutes or until the cake begins to pull from the sides of the pan.

ROMBAUER JAM CAKE

A 7-Inch Tube Pan

Preheat oven to 350°
Have all ingredients at about 75°. Sift, then measure:

1½ cups all-purpose flour

Resift with:

> 1 teaspoon double-acting
> baking powder
> ½ teaspoon soda
> ½ teaspoon cloves
> 1 teaspoon each cinnamon and nutmeg

Cream until light:

> 6 tablespoons butter
> 1 cup brown sugar

Beat in, one at a time:

> 2 eggs

Beat in:

> 3 tablespoons cultured sour cream

Stir the flour mixture into the butter mixture until barely blended. Stir in:

> 1 cup rather firm raspberry
> or blackberry jam
> (½ cup broken nut meats)

Pour the batter into a greased tube pan. Bake it for about ½ hour or until done. When cool, ice the cake with:

> Quick Brown Sugar Icing, page 679

EGGLESS, MILKLESS SPICE CAKE
A 7-Inch Tube Pan

Preheat oven to 325°.

Boil for 3 minutes:

> 1 cup water or beer
> 2 cups seeded raisins
> 1 cup brown sugar
> ⅛ cup butter or margarine
> ½ teaspoon each cinnamon and allspice
> ½ teaspoon salt
> ⅛ teaspoon nutmeg

Cool these ingredients. Sift before measuring:

> 2 cups cake flour

Resift with:

> 1 teaspoon double-acting
> baking powder
> 1 teaspoon soda

Stir the flour gradually into the other ingredients. Stir the batter until smooth. Add:

> (1 cup chopped almonds)

By the addition of 1 cup chopped dates, figs and citron, this becomes an acceptable fruit cake. Bake in a greased tube pan for 1 hour or more. Spread with:

> Caramel Icing, page 676

MYSTERY CAKE
A 9-Inch Tube Pan

This curious combination of ingredients makes a surprisingly good cake. But why shouldn't it? The deep secret is tomato, which after all is a fruit.

Preheat oven to 350°.

Have all ingredients at about 75°. Sift before measuring:

> 2 cups all-purpose flour

Resift with:

> ½ teaspoon salt
> 1 teaspoon cinnamon
> ½ teaspoon each nutmeg and cloves
> 1 teaspoon soda

Sift:

> 1 cup sugar

Cream until soft:

> 2 tablespoons butter

Add the sifted sugar gradually and cream these ingredients well. Stir the flour mixture in about 3 parts into the sugar mixture, alternating with thirds of the contents of:

> 1 can condensed tomato soup: 10½ oz.

Stir the batter until smooth after each addition. Fold in:

> 1 cup nut meats
> 1 cup raisins

Bake in a greased tube pan for about 45 minutes. Spread, when cool, with:

> Boiled White Icing, page 673

ABOUT TORTEN

So many people speak of Torten as unattainable, not realizing that mixing a Torte is just a matter of replacing the flour in certain recipes with crumbs not too finely ground, and nuts ground to a dry meal. There are 3 tricks in making Torten. 1. ♦ The nuts should never be ground in a meat grinder, which simply crushes them and brings up the oil. A small hand grinder with a sharp cutting edge like the one shown in About Nuts, page 521, will produce the light, dry, fluffy particles needed. 2. ♦ Never grease the pan sides. 3. ♦ Use a pan with a removable rim—either a spring form or a tube from which you can remove the bottom, see sketch below, because this kind of pastry is often too delicate in texture to stand much handling. Torten are good just as baked, with black coffee. But who can possibly object to a whipped cream or fruit sauce garnish?

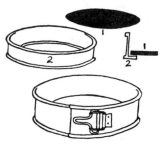

✻ ALMOND TORTE COCKAIGNE
An 8-Inch Removable-Rim Pan

The following recipe is the well-known German **Mandeltorte**. It may also be baked in a loaf or in layers. ♦ Please read About Torten, above.

Preheat oven to 350°.

Have all ingredients at about 75°. Sift:

> 1 cup sugar

Beat:

> 6 egg yolks

Add the sugar gradually and beat until very creamy. Add:

> Grated rind and juice of

1 lemon or of 1 small orange
1 teaspoon cinnamon
1 cup ground unblanched almonds
½ cup toasted white bread crumbs
(⅓ teaspoon almond extract)

Whip ♦ until stiff, but not dry:

6 egg whites

Fold them lightly into the batter. Bake for
about 40 minutes in an ungreased pan.
Permit to cool in the pan. Spread with:

Chocolate Butter Icing, page 678

or bake it in two 8-inch ungreased removable-rim layer pans. Spread between the
layers:

Lemon and Orange Custard Filling,
page 647

Spread the top with:

Sifted confectioners' sugar

or with one of the fillings suggested on
page 644. This cake is very light and consequently difficult to remove from the pan,
so be careful.

✻ PECAN TORTE

For a richer, moister cake, prepare:

Almond Torte, above

substituting pecans for the almonds. ♦ Be
sure to grind the nuts in a nut grinder.

✻ BREAD TORTE OR BROTTORTE
A 9-Inch Removable-Rim Pan

•In the following recipe for a celebrated
German confection, the ingredients differ
only slightly from those in the preceding
Mandeltorte, but the results, thanks to the
wine bath, are amazingly different.
Preheat oven to 350°.
♦ Have all ingredients at about 75°. Sift:

1 cup sugar

Beat:

6 egg yolks

Add the sugar gradually. Beat until
creamy. Combine and add:

1¼ cups dry bread crumbs
½ teaspoon double-acting
    baking powder
½ teaspoon cinnamon
2 oz. citron, cut fine
1 cup unblanched almonds, ground
    in a nut grinder
Rind and juice of 1 lemon

Whip ♦ until stiff, but not dry:

6 egg whites

Fold them lightly into the cake batter.
Bake for 1 hour or more in an ungreased
pan. Heat, but do not boil:

¾ cup dry sherry
2 tablespoons water
2 whole cloves
1 stick cinnamon
¼ cup sugar

Strain these ingredients and place the sirup
in a small pitcher. Pour it very slowly onto
the hot cake. When all the liquid has
been absorbed, cool the cake and remove
it from the pan. Spread with:

A flavored Crème Patissière, page 646

DOBOS OR DRUM TORTE

The many-tiered Hungarian chocolate-
filled torte that looks rich, is rich and en-
riches everyone who eats it.
♦ Have all ingredients at 75°. Prepare:

Génoise, page 640

Using well-greased 8-inch cake pans, bake
the cake in 9 layers, 5 to 9 minutes each.
Work rapidly. If your oven will not hold
so many layers, bake thicker ones and
slice them in two, professionally, holding
them as shown on page 645. Stack them
so that you apply the icing to the baked
rather than to the cut surfaces. When
cool, spread between the layers the following filling. Place in a double boiler:

½ cup sugar
4 eggs
1 inch vanilla bean

or omit the vanilla bean and add 1 teaspoonful of vanilla extract after the filling
has cooled. Beat until the eggs begin to
thicken. Cool the filling slightly. Cut into
pieces and dissolve:

4 oz. chocolate

in:

2 tablespoons boiling water

Keep this warm. Cream until light:

⅞ cup butter: 1¾ sticks

Add the chocolate mixture. Beat into the
egg mixture. This filling may also be
spread over the top and sides of the cake
but the true Hungarian will spread it between layers only, reserving the best looking layer for the top. Glaze this chef
d'oeuvre with:

½ cup Clear Caramel Glaze, page 683

The hard topping gives the cake its name.
Before the caramel sets, use a hot buttered
knife to cut 12 to 18 radial lines into the
top glaze, so the cake may be easily sliced.
"Rest" the cake in a chilled place for 12
hours or more before serving.

✻ HAZELNUT TORTE
A 10-Inch Removable-Rim Pan

♦ Please read About Torten, page 637.
Preheat oven to 350°.
♦ Have all ingredients at about 75°. Sift:

1 cup sugar

Beat:

12 egg yolks

Add the sugar gradually. Beat well until
ingredients are very creamy. Grind in a
nut grinder:

¼ lb. hazelnuts
¼ lb. pecans or walnuts

Add:

(2 tablespoons bread crumbs)

Whip ♦ until stiff, but not dry:

8 egg whites

Fold them lightly into the other ingredients. Bake the cake in an ungreased pan
for about 40 minutes. When cool, spread
between the layers:

Whipped cream, flavored with
vanilla or sweet sherry
Spread the cake with:
(Coffee or Caramel Icing, page 676)

CHOCOLATE WALNUT TORTE
A 9-Inch Removable-Rim Pan
♦ Please read About Torten, page 637.
♦ Have all ingredients at 75°. Sift:
⅞ cup sugar
Beat until light:
6 egg yolks
Add the sugar gradually. Beat until well
blended. Add:
½ cup finely crushed cracker crumbs
¼ cup grated chocolate
¾ cup chopped walnut meats
2 tablespoons brandy or rum
½ teaspoon double-acting
baking powder
½ teaspoon cinnamon
¼ teaspoon each cloves and nutmeg
Whip ♦ until stiff, but not dry:
6 egg whites
Fold them lightly into the cake batter.
Bake in an ungreased pan for about 1 hour.
Spread with:
Chocolate Butter Icing, page 678
or serve with:
Wine Custard, page 686

CHOCOLATE DATE TORTE
A 9-Inch Tube Pan
A richly flavored, exceedingly good cake.
Prepare:
Chocolate Sponge Cake, page 622
Sprinkle:
2 tablespoons sifted flour
over:
¾ cup chopped dates
1 tablespoon grated orange rind
(⅓ cup chopped nut meats)
Beat these ingredients into the cake batter
before folding in the egg whites. Bake as
directed. Sprinkle with:
Powdered sugar
We serve this to everybody's intense satis-
faction with:
Liqueur Cream Sauce, page 714, or
Foamy Sauce, page 714

POPPY SEED CUSTARD TORTE
Two 9-Inch Round Layer Pans
Preheat oven to 375°.
♦ Have all ingredients at 75°. Combine
and soak for 2 hours:
⅔ cup poppy seed
¾ cup milk
Beat until soft:
⅔ cup butter
Add gradually:
1½ cups sugar

Cream these ingredients until fluffy. Sift
before measuring:
2 cups cake flour
Resift with:
2½ teaspoons double-acting
baking powder
½ teaspoon salt
Combine the poppy seed milk mixture
with:
¼ cup milk
1 teaspoon vanilla
Add the sifted ingredients to the butter
mixture in about 3 parts, alternating with
the liquid ingredients. Beat the batter
after each addition until blended. Whip
♦ until stiff, but not dry, then fold in:
4 egg whites
Bake for about 20 minutes. Place between
the layers:
Crème Patissière, page 646
Serve with:
Chocolate Sauce Cockaigne, page 709
or dust with:
Powdered sugar

SACHERTORTE
A 9-Inch Removable-Rim Pan
A recipe of the famous restaurant keeper
Frau Sacher, who fed the impoverished
Austrian nobility long after they had
ceased to pay.
Preheat oven to 325°.
♦ Have all ingredients at about 75°.
Melt in a double boiler over, not in, hot
water:
5 oz. semi-sweet chocolate, not
in chip form
Cream until fluffy:
¾ cup sugar
¾ cup butter
Beat in gradually until light in color:
5 egg yolks
and add the melted cooled chocolate. Sift
and add gradually:
¾ cup all-purpose flour
Beat until stiff but not dry:
5 to 6 egg whites
Gently fold the whites into the chocolate
mixture. Bake in an ungreased pan 50
minutes to 1 hour. When cool slice the
Torte horizontally and insert a filling of:
Puréed Apricot Jam
Cover the torte with:
European Chocolate Icing, page 679
using strong coffee instead of the cream.
If you are really Viennese you put on a
great gob of "Schlag" or whipped cream.

ABOUT FILLED CAKES

In modern service, especially for buffets, a
ready-to-serve, complete dessert often replaces the separate presentation of ice
cream and cake, pudding and cake or fruit

and cake. Such combinations may take varied forms—see illustrations in this section. They may also be as rich and substantial or as light in texture and calorie content as you choose.

We have assembled in the next pages some individual recipes that we enjoy serving as complete desserts. We also suggest a number of ways that basic cakes can be combined with fillings. Read about Pinch Pies, Roll Cakes, Charlottes, Torten, Trifles, Savarins and Filled Rolled Cookies. See illustrations for making a secret filling, page 645, lining pudding molds, page 692, or turning a simple Baked Alaska into an Omelette Surprise, page 692.

If you must, buy your basic angel and sponge cakes, ice cream and ice fillings. But when you combine them, make a delicious sauce of your very own with fresh eggs or fruit and—most important of all—real vanilla, fresh spices and quality spirits. The quantities you need for flavorings are small and should be of the best, see About Spices on page 528. And all the recipes for sponge, angel cakes, Génoise, Daffodil Cake, roll cakes, nut Torten, lady-fingers and rolled cookies are suitable for mold linings. For additional fillings and combinations, see page 644.

REFRIGERATOR CAKES
Line molds, page 692, or make a secret panel cake, page 645.
Fill with:

> Bavarians or mousses
> Whipped gelatin puddings
> Pastry creams or charlotte mixtures
> Cream pie or chiffon pie fillings
> Sweetened whipped creams

Refrigerate at least 6 hours, covered, before serving. Garnish with:

> Fruits and nuts

or serve with:

> Sauce or whipped cream

Dust with:

> Toasted nuts
> Shredded coconut or Praliné,
> page 736

✳ GÉNOISE
Two 9-Inch Layers
This rich, moist Italian cake, which the French and we have borrowed, has no equal for versatility. It also keeps well and freezes well. It may be used for dessert rolls with cream fillings, see About Roll Cakes, page 642, or Baked Alaska, page 692; also with butter icings or as a foil for fruit. You may bake it as Lady-fingers, page 633, or in layers. For a very elaborate Génoise, sprinkle it after cooling with Cointreau or kirsch, fill it with Sauce Cockaigne, page 709, or cover it with whipped cream, or European Chocolate Icing, page 679. For a children's party,

bake favors in the cake, see Galette des Rois, page 592.
Preheat oven to 350°.
Melt and put aside:

> ¼ cup butter

Do not let it get cooler than about 80°. Break into a double boiler ▶ over—not in— hot water until they are lukewarm:

> 6 eggs

Add:

> ⅔ cup sugar

Beat with a rotary or electric mixer at medium speed for 7 minutes. Add:

> ⅓ cup sugar

Increase speed and beat for 2 minutes longer or until the mixture is lemony in color and stands in soft peaks. Gently add:

> 1 teaspoon vanilla

Fold in:

> 1 cup sifted cake flour

Add the melted butter with a folding motion. Pour the batter into the pans and bake about 40 minutes or until done. ▶ Turn cakes out at once onto a rack to cool.

MOHRENKOEPFE OR MOORS' HEADS
These Moors' heads, along with Individual Nut Tarts, page 665, and Macaroon Jam Tarts, page 665, were specialties of a famous St. Louis bakery, now extinct, and graced a thousand Kaffeeklatsches. While the true Mohrenkopf is baked in a special half-round mold, the full taste effect can be gained by the following method:
Cut in rounds or squares:

> Thin Génoise, above

Make a "sandwich" filling of:

> Hazelnut flavored whipped cream

Cover with:

> European Chocolate Icing, page 679
> or Chocolate Sauce Cockaigne,
> page 709

TRIFLE OR RASPBERRY RUM CAKE
A good use for dry cake. Combine it with raspberries, which are traditional. But apricot jam or other preserves, thickened pie cherries, fresh or cooked drained fruit, may be substituted.
Place in a deep dish:

> Rounds of yellow, sponge or
> layer cake, etc.

Sprinkle the cake with:

> (2 tablespoons rum or sherry)

Spread the pieces with:

> ½ cup jam or jelly or
> 1 to 2 cups sweetened fruit
> (¼ cup blanched, slivered almonds)

Prepare:

> Rich Custard, page 685

Pour the custard over the cake. Whip until stiff:

> (1 cup whipping cream)

Garnish the dish with the cream.

BABA AU RHUM OR SAVARIN
Beloved by the French, who frequently

serve it with tea. This is an American version. **Savarin** is really a larger version of Baba au Rhum. The same dough and the same sirup are used, but the dessert is baked in a ring mold with a rounded base. When it is turned out, the center is filled with fruit. If you fill it with tart red cherry compote, you need hardly be told it will have become **Savarin Montmorency!** Prepare:

> **Bundkuchen, page 571,** or
> **Brioche dough, page 566**

Place it in a greased 8-inch tube pan. Permit to rise, and bake as directed. Remove from the pan, cool and return to the pan. Prepare a sirup by boiling for 10 minutes:

> ½ cup water
> 1 cup sugar

Cool it slightly. Flavor it generously with:

> **Rum or whisky: at least ¼ cup**

Place the sirup in a small pitcher. One hour before serving the cake, pour slowly, drop by drop, onto the baba. Use as much as will be absorbed. Permit the cake to stand until ready to serve. Remove it from the pan. If it is to be a dessert, top it with:

> **Whipped cream**

You may serve individual baba cakes. Bake them in muffin tins. Soak them as directed or cut a slice from the top, hollow the cakes slightly and fill the hollows with the raspberry or apricot jam. Serve with:

> **Lemon Sauce, page 709**

or, slice the muffins in half, cover each half with a slice of fresh pineapple and currant jelly, sprinkled with confectioners' sugar and kirsch.

ORANGE-FILLED CAKE

Three 9-Inch Round Pans

Most recipes for orange cake prove to be disappointing, for upon reading them you find that they are merely sponge or butter cake with an orange filling. This one calls for orange juice in the batter plus orange filling and icing. Earrings for an elephant with no apologies!
Preheat oven to 375°.
Have all ingredients at about 75°. Sift before measuring:

> **3 cups cake flour**

Resift with:

> **¾ teaspoon salt**
> **3½ teaspoons double-acting baking powder**

Grate:

> **Rind of 1 orange**

into:

> **1½ cups sugar**

Cream this until light with:

> **¾ cup butter**

Beat in, one at a time:

> **3 eggs**

Measure:

> ½ cup orange juice
> ½ cup water
> **2 tablespoons lemon juice**

Add the flour mixture in about 3 parts to the butter mixture, alternately with the liquid. Stir the batter after each addition until smooth. Bake the cake in 3 greased layer pans for about ½ hour. When the cake is cool, spread between the layers:

> **Orange Cream Filling, page 647**

BOSTON CREAM PIE OR CAKE

Traditionally called a pie, this is really a 2-layer cake. There are many versions, but the most prevalent one today reads as follows.
Place between 2 layers of:

> **Gold Layer Cake, page 625**

a thick coating of:

> **Crème Patissière, page 646**

Leave the sides exposed, but cover the top with:

> **A chocolate icing, page 678**

CREAM MERINGUE
TART COCKAIGNE

Two 8-Inch Layer Pans

The following recipe is not at all difficult to make, yet it is an optical as well as a gastronomic treat. A cake batter and a meringue are baked at the same time.
Preheat oven to 325°.
Blanch and shred:

> **(⅓ cup almonds)**

Sift:

> **1½ cups sugar**

Beat until soft:

> **¼ cup butter**

Add ½ cup of the sifted sugar gradually. Blend until light and creamy. Beat in, one at a time:

> **4 egg yolks**

Add:

> ½ teaspoon vanilla

Sift before measuring:

> **1 cup cake flour**

Resift with:

> **1 teaspoon double-acting baking powder**
> **¼ teaspoon salt**

Add the sifted ingredients to the butter mixture, alternately with:

> **5 tablespoons cream**

Beat the batter until smooth. Spread it in 2 greased pans with 1½-inch sides. Cover it with the following meringue. Whip until stiff, but not dry:

> **4 egg whites**

Add the remaining cup sifted sugar slowly, about 1 tablespoon at a time. Beat constantly. When all the sugar has been added, continue to beat for several minutes. Fold in:

> **1 teaspoon vanilla**

Spread the meringue lightly over the cake batter in both pans. If using the almonds, stud one meringue with the blanched, shredded almonds, placing the shreds close together. Bake the layers for about 40 minutes. Remove them from the oven and permit them to cool in the pans. Shortly before serving the cake, place the unstudded layer, meringue side down, on a cake plate. Spread one of the following fillings over it, reserving ¼ cup for the top. Place the almond studded layer, meringue side up, on the cream filling and place the reserved filling in the center on top using:

> **A Cream Filling, page 644; Sauce Cockaigne, page 709, and whipped cream**

ABOUT ROLL CAKES

Any number of doughs lend themselves to rolling, see Jelly Rolls, below, Angel Cake Roll, page 643, Chocolate Cream Roll, page 643, etc. They may be baked in sheets, 10½ x 15½ x 1 inch. Simply grease the baking sheet well, pour in the batter and bake in a 375° oven for about 12 minutes. ♦ To roll, loosen the edges as soon as the cake comes from the oven. Reverse the pan onto a clean towel that has been dusted with:

> **Sifted confectioners' sugar**

Trim off any crusty edges. There are 2 ways to roll the cake. If the filling is a perishable one, roll the cake while it is still hot, with the towel, as shown in the illustration below. Place the cake, still

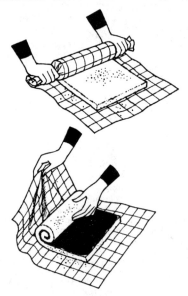

wrapped in the towel, on a rack to cool. Later, when ready to fill, unroll the cake, fill it and use the towel to roll it again, as shown in the lower sketch.
Fill with at least:

> ½ cup jelly or tart jam or 1 cup or more cream or custard filling

When the cake is rolled after filling ♦ place it on the serving plate with the seam side down.

JELLY ROLL
A 10½ x 15½ x 1-Inch Pan

This standard roll cake, or jelly roll, recipe also bakes well in two 8-inch round layer pans. To prepare pan, bake and roll, see About Roll Cakes, above.
Preheat oven to 375°.
Sift:

> ¾ cup sugar

Beat until light:

> 4 egg yolks

Add the sugar gradually. Beat until creamy. Add:

> 1 teaspoon vanilla

Sift before measuring:

> ¾ cup cake flour

Resift with:

> ¾ teaspoon double-acting baking powder
> ½ teaspoon salt

Add the flour gradually to the egg mixture. Beat the batter until smooth. Whip ♦ until stiff, but not dry:

> 4 egg whites

Fold them lightly into the cake batter with:

> ½ cup finely chopped nuts

Bake for about 13 minutes. When cold, spread with at least:

> ½ cup jelly

LEMON ROLL
Prepare:

> **Jelly Roll, above**

Substitute for the jelly:

> **Lemon Filling, page 646**

Roll and fill.

BUTTERSCOTCH SPICE ROLL
A 10½ x 15½ x 1-Inch Pan

♦ To prepare pan, see About Roll Cakes, this page.
Preheat oven to 400°.
Place in a bowl over hot water:

> 4 eggs
> ¼ teaspoon salt

Beat until the eggs are thick and lemon colored. Beat in gradually:

> ¾ cup sugar

Remove from the heat. Sift before measuring:

> ¾ cup cake flour

Resift with:

> ¾ teaspoon double-acting baking powder
> 1 teaspoon cinnamon
> ½ teaspoon cloves

Fold in the sifted ingredients and:

> 1 teaspoon vanilla

Bake the batter for about 13 minutes. To roll and fill, see About Roll Cakes, this page. A good filling is:

> **Butterscotch Filling, page 646**

ALMOND SPONGE ROLL
♦ To prepare pan and bake, see About Roll Cakes, this page.
Preheat oven to 325°.

Beat until light:

8 egg yolks

Beat in gradually:

½ cup sugar

Add:

½ cup blanched, ground almonds
Beat ♦ until stiff, but not dry:

8 egg whites

Fold in:

1 teaspoon vanilla

Fold the egg whites into the yolk mixture. Bake about 15 minutes, roll and, when cold, spread with any desired filling, see pages 645, 647.

ANGEL CAKE ROLL

Preheat oven to 350°.
Sift twice:

1¼ to 1½ cups sugar

Sift separately before measuring:

1 cup cake flour

Resift the flour 3 times with ½ cupful of the sifted sugar and:

½ teaspoon salt

Whip until foamy:

**1¼ cups egg whites: 10 to 12 egg whites
(2 tablespoons water or 1 tablespoon
water and 1 tablespoon lemon juice)**

Add:

1 teaspoon cream of tartar

Whip the egg whites ♦ until stiff, but not dry. Gradually whip in, about 1 tablespoon at a time, 1 cup of the sifted sugar. Fold in:

**½ teaspoon vanilla
½ teaspoon almond extract**

Sift about ¼ cup of the sugar and flour mixture over the batter. Fold it in gently and briefly with a rubber scraper. Continue until all the mixture is used. Pour the batter into an ungreased tube pan. Use the smaller amount of egg whites and sugar, as suggested at the end of the recipe. Make only ½ the amount if you wish to have 1 roll. Pour the batter in a shallow, 10½ x 15½-inch pan which has been greased with greased parchment paper and bake in a 300° oven for about 20 minutes. The pan is greased here in order to get the cake out intact for rolling. To roll and fill, see About Roll Cakes, page 642. Use any of the fillings suggested for the various Cake Rolls in this chapter. Raspberry or apricot jam and whipped cream are fine.

CHOCOLATE FILLED ROLL

Preheat oven to 375°.
Sift:

¾ cup sugar
Beat until light:

4 egg yolks
Add the sugar gradually. Beat until creamy. Add:

1 teaspoon vanilla
Sift before measuring:

¾ cup cake flour
Resift with:

**¾ teaspoon double-acting
baking powder**
Add the flour gradually to the egg mixture. Beat the batter until smooth. Whip ♦ until stiff, but not dry:

4 egg whites
Fold them lightly into the cake batter with:

½ cup finely chopped nuts
Bake for about 13 minutes. When cold, spread with:

**Chocolate Sauce Cockaigne,
page 711
Whipped Cream**

★ CHOCOLATE CREAM ROLL OR BÛCHE DE NOËL

For Christmas this can be made into a Yule Log by roughing up the icing and adding snowy cream details. Trim it the same way for Washington's Birthday.
Preheat oven to 325°.
Sift:

½ cup powdered sugar
Beat until light:

3 to 6 egg yolks
Add the sugar gradually and beat these ingredients until creamy. Add:

1 teaspoon vanilla
Sift and add:

2 to 6 tablespoons cocoa
If you use less than 4 tablespoons cocoa, add:

**(2 tablespoons all-purpose flour)
⅛ teaspoon salt**
Whip ♦ until stiff, but not dry:

**3 to 6 egg whites
½ teaspoon cream of tartar**
Fold lightly into the cake batter. Line a shallow 8 x 12-inch pan with heavy greased paper and spread the dough in it to the thickness of ¼ inch. Bake the cake for about 25 minutes. Let it cool in the pan for 5 minutes. To roll and fill, see About Roll Cakes, page 642. Cover with:

Chocolate Sauce, page 711

ABOUT CHARLOTTES

How dull seem the charlottes of our youth, with only a cream and a cherry, when compared with those put together in the sophisticated society we now seem to frequent!

Today's fillings include all kinds of creams and Bavarians, nuts, angelica, citron, jams, chestnuts, fruits and ices. Whether the mold is lined with ladyfin-

644   CAKES

gers, sponge or Génoise, it may still be called a charlotte. For combinations, see below.

CHARLOTTE RUSSE
6 Servings

Soak:
   ¾ tablespoon gelatin
in:
   ¼ cup cold water
Dissolve it in:
   ⅛ cup scalded milk
Beat in:
   ⅛ cup powdered sugar
Cool. Flavor with:
   2 tablespoons strong coffee
Whip until stiff:
   1 cup whipping cream
Fold it lightly into the chilled ingredients. Line a mold with:
   Ladyfingers, page 692
Pour the pudding into it. Chill thoroughly. Unmold and serve with:
   Custard Sauce, page 710, flavored with rum

CHOCOLATE CHARLOTTE
Prepare:
   French Chocolate Mousse, page 687
   or Rum Chocolate Mousse, page 687
Line a mold as described in About Dessert Molds, page 692. Fill the ladyfinger-lined mold with the mousse.

MAPLE CHARLOTTE
10 Servings

Soak:
   1 tablespoon gelatin
in:
   ¼ cup cold water
Dissolve it in:
   ¾ cup hot maple sirup
Chill until it falls in heavy sheets from a spoon. Whip until the cream holds soft peaks:
   2 cups whipping cream
Fold in with a spoon:
   (½ cup blanched, chopped almonds)
Fold in the gelatin until well blended. Line a bowl with pieces of:
   Sponge Cake, page 621
   Ladyfingers, page 633
Pour the gelatin into it. Chill until firm. Unmold and serve garnished with:
   Whipped cream

INDIVIDUAL SHORTCAKES
Prepare:
   Fluffy Biscuit Dough, page 584
Cut the dough into 3-inch rounds. Bake the biscuits, split them while they are hot and spread them with:
   Butter

Place between the biscuit halves and pour over them:
   Sugared or cooked fruit

LARGE SHORTCAKE
Prepare:
   Fluffy Biscuit dough, page 584
   Scone dough, page 586, or any of
   the plain sponge cakes, page 621
Bake it in 2 layers. Place between the layers and over them:
   Sugared or cooked fruit

✳ QUICK MOCHA FREEZER CAKE
About 10 to 12 Servings

Cut:
   Angel Cake, page 619
in 4 layers. Soften:
   ½ gallon Mocha Ice Cream, page 718
Stir in:
   3 shaved sweet chocolate and
   almond bars
Put the ice cream between the layers and cover the cake all over with it. Put into the ✳ freezer and allow to set for about an hour. Should you have made this the day before and kept it in the freezer, be sure to unfreeze ½ hour before serving.

SEMISWEET CHOCOLATE CASES
6 Servings

Melt in the top of a double boiler:
   6 squares semisweet chocolate
   1 tablespoon butter
When melted, beat thoroughly. Swirl the mixture into the insides of crinkled paper baking cups. Place cups in muffin tins and allow the chocolate to harden. To serve carefully remove the paper, and fill the chocolate cases with:
   Ice Cream or Custard, page 685

ABOUT FILLINGS
If you happen to be pressed for time or are just plain lazy, you may prefer occasionally to buy the "baked goods"—sponge, angel cakes, macaroons, ladyfingers—which make the foundation for many and varied fancy desserts. Such pastries may be mixed or matched to your preference and filled with seasonally flavored creams, pastry creams, Bavarians, mousses, zabagliones or layers of jam or jelly. Garnish these desserts with candied fruits and creams. Many pie fillings, fruit, custard and chiffon, as well as whipped gelatin puddings, also lend themselves to use with cake bases. Try a cream base, flavored with lemon, apricot, orange or pineapple, with nut Tortens. Should you choose flavored creams and the less-stable fillings such as gelatins or ice creams, add them to your cake just before serving to forestall sogginess. For the same reason be sure to choose fillings heavy in cream for freezing.

Thickened fillings, such as those having the word custard in the title, or the heavier nut and fruit fillings, can stand somewhat longer storage before serving; but do not hold them over 24 hours—especially those based on gelatin. Fillings seem to adhere better if the cakes are placed with the bottom crusts facing one another. For a charming but not rich finish, coat filled cakes with a dusting of confectioners' sugar, see page 672. Filling yields are given in cups. For approximate coverage, see Chart on page 672.

To prepare a tube cake for a secret filling, see the illustrations below. If your knife is sharp and you feel bold, you may hold a cake on the palm of your left hand and slice deftly across the cake, one inch from the top. If your knife is not sharp, we suggest you mark the cutting line with about six toothpicks as shown, then, with the cake firmly on the table and your left hand on top of it, you can easily feel if the knife is going up or down and so control an even cut. Reserve the top slice for the lid.

Then start to cut a smooth-rimmed channel in the remaining section, to receive the filling. Allow for 1-inch walls by making 2 circular, vertical incisions, to within 1 inch of the base. To remove the cake loosened by these incisions, insert your knife next diagonally, first from the top of the inside of the outer rim to the base cut of the inner rim, and continue to cut diagonally all around through the channel core. Then reverse the action and repeat the cut from the top of the inside of the inner rim to the base cut of the outer rim. These two X-like operations, performed with a saw-bladed knife, should give you 3 loose triangular sections which are easily removed. The fourth triangle protruding into the channel but still attached at the base is then cut free one inch from the base of the cake. A curved knife is a help here. The cake which formed the channel area can be used for Angel Balls, page 633, or be shredded and mixed with the filling. Ladle the filling of your choice into the channel as shown in the center. Replace the lid. Top this whole cake with whipped cream or icing. When you cut the cake, each slice will look like the cross-sections sketched on the cake-stand.

SWEETENED WHIPPED CREAM OR CRÈME CHANTILLY FILLINGS
About 3 Cups

Whip until stiff:
   1 cup whipping cream
I. Fold in:
   (1 to 3 tablespoons sifted
      confectioners' sugar)
   ½ teaspoon vanilla
You may use this way or add any one of the following:

II.
   ½ cup blanched, slivered, toasted
      almonds, walnuts, pecans or
      hazelnuts, or ¼ cup nut paste
III. or:
   ½ cup lightly toasted coconut
   1 tablespoon rum

IV. or:
   ½ cup jam or orange or ginger
      marmalade

V. or:
   ¾ cup fresh, canned or frozen fruit
      purée
   (2 tablespoons kirsch)

VI. or:
   ¾ cup fresh fruit
Reserve ¼ cup of perfect berries or fruit slices for garnish.

VII. or:
   ½ cup crushed soft peppermint
      stick candy

VIII. or:
   ⅔ cup brown sugar or ½ cup
      maple sugar
   1 teaspoon vanilla or
   ¼ teaspoon nutmeg

IX. or:
   1 teaspoon instant coffee
   ¾ cup crushed nut brittle

X. or:
   ¼ cup almond or hazelnut paste,
      page 729

Here are two other variations:
I. Prepare an angel or sponge cake shell.

Shred the removed cake. Combine it with
the whipped cream.
Then add:

> 2 cups crushed drained pineapple
> 1 cup shredded coconut
> 12 or more maraschino cherries
> (20 diced marshmallows)
> 2 teaspoons semi-sweet chocolate
> 2 teaspoons rum or Cointreau

Chill the cake for 6 hours.

II. Heat in a double boiler 2 tablespoons
of the whipped cream and:

> ¼ cup sugar
> ⅛ teaspoon salt
> 1 oz. chocolate, cut in pieces

When the sugar is dissolved and the chocolate melted, beat the filling with a wire
whisk until well blended. Cool. Blend in
the remainder of the whipped cream.

CUSTARD CREAM PASTRY FILLING
OR CRÈME PATISSIÈRE
About 2 Cups

The custardy pastry fillings below can all
be varied. Enrich them by folding in ¼ to
¾ cups of whipped cream and/or chopped
nuts, candied fruits and liqueur flavorings.

I. Vanilla custard
Scald:

> 1½ cups milk
> A vanilla bean

Blend and mix in the top of a double
boiler ♦ over—not in—hot water:

> ½ cup sugar
> ¼ cup flour
> 3 to 4 well-beaten egg yolks or
> 2 eggs and 2 yolks

Cream this mixture until light. Now remove the vanilla bean and add the scalded
milk gradually. Stir until all is well
blended. Cook, stirring constantly, until it
just reaches the boiling point. Remove
from the heat and continue to stir to release the steam and prevent crusting. Do
not fill the pastry until the mixture is cool.

II. Chocolate
Add to the milk, when scalding:

> 2 to 4 oz. semisweet chocolate

III. Coffee
Add to the milk, when scalded:

> 1 to 2 teaspoons instant coffee
> (Ground hazelnuts)

IV. Banana
Before spreading the custard, add to it:

> 2 or more thinly sliced bananas

FRANGIPANE CREAM

Prepare Crème Patissière above, but after
removing from the heat, beat in:

> 2 tablespoons butter
> ¼ cup crushed macaroons or
>   chopped blanched almonds
> 2 teaspoons chopped candied nuts

BUTTERSCOTCH FILLING
About 1½ Cups

Prepare:

> Butterscotch Pie Filling, page 610

using in all:

> 1½ cups milk

MOCHA FILLING
About 2½ Cups

Combine, cook and stir in a double boiler
♦ over—not in—hot water, until smooth:

> 2 oz. chocolate
> ⅔ cup cream
> 1⅓ cups strong coffee

Then add and stir into this mixture a
smooth paste of:

> 2 teaspoons cornstarch
> 2 tablespoons cold coffee

Stir and cook the filling for about 8 minutes. Cover and continue to cook for 10
minutes more. Meanwhile, combine and
beat:

> 4 egg yolks
> 1 egg
> ¼ teaspoon salt

Beat in gradually:

> 1¾ cups sugar

Pour some of the hot cornstarch mixture
over the egg mixture and then gradually
return it to the double boiler. Cook for 2
minutes longer, stirring gently and constantly. Remove the filling from the heat
and stir gently until cool.

RICOTTA CHOCOLATE FILLING
About 3½ Cups

Combine and beat until light and fluffy:

> 2¾ cups ricotta cheese: 1¼ lbs.
> 2 cups sugar
> 1 teaspoon vanilla
> 2 tablespoons crème de cacao

Fold in:

> 2 tablespoons shaved semisweet
>   chocolate
> 2 tablespoons chopped candied fruit

LEMON FILLING
About 1½ Cups

Mix in the top of a double boiler:

> 2½ tablespoons cornstarch
> ¾ cup sugar
> ¼ teaspoon salt

Gradually stir in:

> ½ cup water or orange juice
> 3 tablespoons lemon juice
> ½ teaspoon grated lemon rind
> 1 tablespoon butter

Cook ♦ over—not in—boiling water about
5 minutes, stirring constantly. Cover and
cook gently 10 minutes longer without
stirring. ♦ Remove from heat and stir in
gently:

> 3 slightly beaten egg yolks

Return to heat and cook for about 2 minutes longer. To cool, see About Cornstarch, page 499.

LEMON ORANGE CUSTARD FILLING
About 1½ Cups
Stir and cook in a double boiler ♦ over—
not in—hot water, until thick:
- 2½ tablespoons lemon juice
- 6 tablespoons orange juice
- ⅛ cup water
- ½ cup sugar
- 2 tablespoons flour
- ⅛ teaspoon salt
- 3 egg yolks or
  - 1 egg and 1 yolk
- (½ teaspoon grated lemon or
  - orange rind)

Cool the filling.

ORANGE CUSTARD FILLING
About 1½ Cups
Stir in the top of a double boiler ♦ over—
not in—hot water:
- ⅓ cup sugar
- 5 tablespoons all-purpose flour
- ¼ teaspoon salt

Stir in until smooth:
- 1 cup milk

Then stir in:
- ½ cup orange juice

Cook for about 10 minutes, stirring frequently. Beat slightly:
- 1 egg

Beat about ⅓ of the sauce into it. Return
it to the pan. Continue to cook and stir
for about 2 minutes or until it thickens.
Cool, then spread the filling.

CHOPPED FRUIT FILLING
About 1¾ Cups
Cook in a double boiler over—not in—hot
water:
- ¾ cup evaporated milk
- ¼ cup water
- ¾ cup sugar
- ⅛ teaspoon salt

When the sugar is dissolved, add and cook
until thick:
- ¼ cup each chopped dates, figs

Cool these ingredients and add:
- 1 teaspoon vanilla
- ½ cup chopped nut-meats

APRICOT CUSTARD FILLING
About 2 Cups
Follow the rule for:
- Lemon Orange Custard Filling,
  above

Add:
- ½ to ⅔ cup sweetened thick
  apricot pulp

ORANGE CREAM FILLING
About 2½ Cups
Soak for about 5 minutes:
- 1 teaspoon gelatin

in:
- 1 tablespoon water

Combine in a double boiler:
- 2 tablespoons each cornstarch and
  flour
- ¾ cup sugar

Add:
- ¾ cup hot water

Stir and cook these ingredients, over—not
in—hot water for 8 to 12 minutes. Stir
constantly. ♦ Cover and cook undisturbed
for 10 minutes more. Add:
- 1 tablespoon butter

Pour part of this mixture over:
- 2 egg yolks

Beat and pour back into the double boiler.
Cook and stir the custard gently, about 2
minutes, to permit the yolks to thicken.
Add the soaked gelatin. Stir until dissolved. Remove custard from heat. Add:
- Grated rind of 1 orange
- 3 tablespoons each orange and
  lemon juice

Cool the custard. Beat until stiff:
- ½ cup whipping cream

Fold it into the custard. Chill for 1 hour.
Spread between the layers of cake. Ice
with:
Luscious Orange Icing, page 676

GINGER FRUIT FILLING
About 1½ Cups
Mix well in the top of a double boiler and
cook, stirring constantly, over—not in—hot
water for about 8 to 10 minutes or ♦ until
the mixture thickens, see About Cornstarch,
page 499:
- ¼ cup sifted confectioners' sugar
- 3 tablespoons cornstarch
- ½ teaspoon salt
- 1 cup canned pineapple juice

Cover and cook about 10 minutes longer.
Remove from the heat and add:
- ½ cup mashed banana
- ½ cup canned crushed pineapple

Return to the heat for 2 minutes more,
stirring gently. Add:
- 3 tablespoons finely chopped
  drained candied ginger
- 1 teaspoon vanilla
- (¼ cup slivered, blanched almonds)

ALMOND, FIG OR RAISIN FILLING
About 1½ Cups
Blanch, sliver, then toast:
- ¾ cup almonds

Combine:
- ½ cup sugar
- 1 tablespoon grated orange rind
- ½ cup orange juice
- 2 tablespoons flour
- ½ cup water
- 1½ cups chopped or ground figs
  or seeded raisins
- ⅛ teaspoon salt

Simmer these ingredients for 5 minutes.
Stir constantly. Add the almonds and:
  ½ teaspoon vanilla

TOASTED WALNUT OR
PECAN FILLING

About ¾ Cup

Combine, stir and heat in a double boiler
♦ over—not in—hot water, until sugar is
dissolved:
  ½ cup packed brown sugar
  ¼ teaspoon salt
  2 tablespoons butter
  1 tablespoon water
Stir part of this into:
  1 slightly beaten egg yolk
Return it to the double boiler. Stir and
cook until the egg yolk is slightly thickened. Cool. Add:
  ¾ cup toasted walnuts or pecans
  ½ teaspoon vanilla

ALMOND OR HAZELNUT
CUSTARD FILLING

About 1½ Cups

Stir and heat in a double boiler ♦ over—
not in—hot water:
  1 cup sugar
  1 cup cultured sour cream
  1 tablespoon flour
Pour ⅓ of this mixture over:
  1 beaten egg
Return it to the double boiler. Stir and
cook the custard until thick. Add:
  1 cup blanched or unblanched
    shredded or ground almonds or
    ground hazelnuts, see page 521
When the custard is cool, add:
  ½ teaspoon vanilla or
  1 tablespoon liqueur

▲ ABOUT HIGH ALTITUDE BAKING

Cake doughs at high altitudes are subject
to a pixie-like variation that often defies
general rules. Read the comments and
then launch forth on your own, keeping
records at first until you know what gives
you the greatest success. On the whole,
♦ cup and layer cakes are better textured
than loaf cakes.

Up to 3000 feet, if you reduce the air in
the cakes by ♦ not overbeating eggs, you
will probably need no adjustment of the
cake formula. ♦ Also raise the baking
temperature about 25°. In elevations
higher than 3000 feet, continue to under-
beat the eggs as compared to sea level
consistency. Another way to reduce their
volume is to keep the eggs refrigerated
until almost ready to use.

At around 5000 feet, it will also help to
reduce the double-acting baking powder
by ⅛ to ¼ teaspoon for each teaspoon
called for in the recipe. Decrease sugar 1
to 2 tablespoons for each cup called for
and increase liquid 2 to 3 tablespoons for
each cup indicated. Raise the baking temperature about 25°.

At 7000 feet, decrease double-acting
baking powder by ¼ teaspoon for every
teaspoon called for. Decrease sugar by 2
to 3 tablespoons for each cup indicated
and increase liquid by 3 to 4 tablespoons
for each cup in the recipe. Raise the baking temperature about 25°.

At 10,000 feet, decrease the double-
acting baking powder by ¼ teaspoon for
every teaspoon called for in the recipe
and add an extra egg, but do not overbeat
the eggs. Decrease the sugar 2 to 3 tablespoons for each cup in the recipe. Increase
the liquid by 3 to 4 tablespoons for each
cup liquid indicated. Increase the baking
temperature about 25°.

Following are some basic high altitude
recipes from Government sources. But
should you hate to give up your own recipes from home, we also throw in as a
talisman the homely formula of a friend
who has for years had luck with it at 7000
to 8000 feet, using her old Chicago favorites. She merely uses ¾ the amount of
double-acting baking powder called for;
adds 1 additional tablespoon flour and 1
extra egg, decreases the butter by a few
tablespoons if the recipe is very rich and
increases the oven heat by about 25°.

But whatever formula you use ♦ grease
your baking pans well and dust them with
flour or line them with wax paper. For, at
high altitudes, cakes have a tendency to
stick to the pan.

▲ HIGH ALTITUDE ANGEL CAKE

10-Inch Tube Pan

This recipe is for baking at 5000 feet. If
baking at 7000 feet, add 1 tablespoon cake
flour and decrease sugar by 2 tablespoons.
If baking at 10,000 feet, add 2 tablespoons
cake flour and decrease sugar by 4 tablespoons.
♦ Please read About Angel Cakes, page
619.
Preheat oven to 375°.
Mix and sift together 3 times:
  1 cup plus 2 tablespoons sifted
    cake flour
  ½ cup sugar
Keep refrigerated until ready to use:
  1½ cups egg whites
Beat the egg whites until foamy and add:
  1½ teaspoons cream of tartar
  ½ teaspoon salt
Continue beating until egg whites are
glossy and ♦ form peaks which just barely
fall over. Fold in, with about 25 strokes:
  1 cup sugar
Beat until mixture is fluffy and meringue
like. Beat briefly while adding:
  1½ teaspoons vanilla
Add the dry ingredients about ¼ at a time
by sifting them over the egg mixture, using
about 15 folding strokes after each addition. After last addition, use about 10
more strokes to blend completely. Pour
into ungreased tube pan. Cut through batter with knife to release air bubbles. Bake

or about 40 minutes. Invert pan, as shown
on page 621, and allow cake to cool before
removing it from the pan.

▲ HIGH ALTITUDE CHOCOLATE ANGEL CAKE

Prepare:

High Altitude Angel Cake, page 648

Use in all 1 cup cake flour and add:

¼ cup cocoa
¼ cup sugar

▲ HIGH ALTITUDE SPICE ANGEL CAKE

Prepare:

High Altitude Angel Cake, page 648

Omit the vanilla and substitute by sifting
with dry ingredients:

¼ teaspoon cloves
½ teaspoon nutmeg
1 teaspoon cinnamon

▲ HIGH ALTITUDE WHITE CAKE
Two 8-Inch Round Pans

This recipe is for baking at 5000 feet. If
baking at 7500 feet, reduce baking powder
by ½ teaspoon. If baking at 10,000 feet,
reduce baking powder by 1 teaspoon.
◗ Please read About Butter or Shortening
Cakes, page 622.
Preheat oven to 375°.
Place in a mixer:

½ cup soft butter

Mix, sift together twice and then sift into
the beater bowl with the butter:

2 cups sifted cake flour
2 teaspoons double-acting baking
powder
½ teaspoon salt
1 cup sugar

Add and mix 2 minutes:

¾ cup milk
1 teaspoon vanilla

Beat until foamy:

4 egg whites

Add and beat ◗ until stiff, but not dry:

¼ cup sugar

Add this meringue to batter with:

3 tablespoons milk

and beat 1 minute. Grease the pans and
dust well with flour or line with waxed
paper, pour in the batter and bake about
35 minutes or until done.

▲ HIGH ALTITUDE FUDGE CAKE
Two 8-Inch Square Pans

This recipe is for baking at 5000 feet. If
baking at 7500 and 10,000 feet, decrease
baking powder by 1 teaspoon and if bak-
ing at 10,000, decrease sugar by ¼ cup.
◗ Please read About Butter or Shortening
Cakes, page 622.
Preheat oven to 350°.
Melt over hot water:

4 squares chocolate

Mix, sift together 3 times:

2 cups sifted cake flour
2 teaspoons double-acting
baking powder

1 teaspoon salt

Soften:

½ cup butter

Add slowly to butter and cream longer than
you would at sea level:

2¼ cups sugar

Remove from the refrigerator and separate:

3 eggs

Beat and add the yolks and the cooled
melted chocolate. Add alternately by thirds
the dry ingredients and:

1½ cups milk
2 teaspoons vanilla

After each addition of flour, beat about 25
strokes. After each addition of liquid, beat
about 75 strokes. Whip the egg whites until ◗ stiff but not dry. Fold them into the
batter. Grease pans and dust well with
flour or line with waxed paper. Pour in
the batter and bake for about 45 minutes
or until done.

▲ HIGH ALTITUDE TWO-EGG CAKE
Two 8-Inch Pans

The following high altitude recipe is for a
cake baked at 5000 feet. If baking at 7500
feet, decrease baking powder by ¼ teaspoon and add 2 tablespoons milk. If baking at 10,000 feet, decrease baking powder
by ½ teaspoon and add 2 tablespoons milk.
Preheat oven to 375°.
Mix and sift together 3 times:

2 cups sifted cake flour
1½ teaspoons double-acting
baking powder
½ teaspoon salt

Have ready at 70°:

½ cup butter

Add gradually to the butter:

1 cup sugar
1 teaspoon vanilla

Cream until light and fluffy, somewhat
longer than you would at sea level. Beat,
add to creamed mixture and mix thoroughly:

2 eggs

which were refrigerated until ready to use.
Add alternately by thirds the sifted dry
ingredients and:

¾ cup plus 1 tablespoon milk

using about fifty strokes each time the
liquid is added. Grease the layer pans,
dust them well with flour or line them
with waxed paper. Bake for about 50 minutes or until done.

▲ HIGH ALTITUDE COCOA CAKE

Prepare:

High Altitude Two-Egg Cake, above

observing the adjustments depending upon
altitude at which you are baking. Add to
the dry ingredients before the final sifting:

½ teaspoon nutmeg
¼ teaspoon cloves
1 teaspoon cinnamon

Replace ½ cup cake flour with:

½ cup cocoa

▲ HIGH ALTITUDE SPONGE CAKE
An 8-Inch Tube Pan

This recipe is for an altitude of 5000 and 7500 feet. If baking at 10,000 feet, add 5 tablespoons sifted cake flour and bake at 350°.

◗ Please read About Sponge Cakes, page 621.

Preheat oven to 350°.

Remove from the refrigerator and separate:

6 eggs

Beat the yolks slightly. Add to them:

1½ tablespoons water
1 teaspoon vanilla
½ teaspoon salt

Continue to beat while adding gradually:

½ cup sugar

Beat until thick and lemon yellow in color. Beat the egg whites until foamy and add:

½ teaspoon cream of tartar

Then add gradually to egg whites:

½ cup sugar

◗ Beat just until peaks form and fall over slightly when beater is removed from mixture. Fold yolk mixture into the beaten whites. Add one-fourth at a time, using about 15 strokes after each addition:

**1¼ cups plus 1 tablespoon sifted
      cake flour**

After last addition, mix for about 10 additional strokes. Fold in:

1½ tablespoons lemon juice
1 tablespoon grated lemon rind

Bake in an ungreased tube pan for about 50 minutes. Invert pan, as shown on page 620, and allow cake to cool completely before removing from pan.

▲ HIGH ALTITUDE GINGERBREAD
A 9 x 2½-Inch Square Pan

This recipe is for baking at 5000 feet. If baking at 7500 feet, decrease soda by ¼ teaspoon. If baking at 10,000 feet, reduce soda by ½ teaspoon, sugar by 3 tablespoons and molasses by 2 teaspoons.

Preheat oven to 350°.

Mix, sift together 3 times:

2⅓ cups sifted all-purpose flour
¾ teaspoon soda
½ teaspoon salt
¼ teaspoon cinnamon
¼ teaspoon nutmeg
¼ teaspoon allspice
1 teaspoon ginger

Beat:

½ cup soft shortening

Add gradually to shortening and cream somewhat longer than you would at sea level until light and fluffy:

½ cup sugar

Add 1 at a time and beat well after each addition:

2 eggs

Add and mix in thoroughly:

¾ cup molasses

Add the dry ingredients alternately by fourths with:

⅔ cup boiling water

Beat about 20 strokes after each addition of flour and 30 strokes after each addition of liquid. Grease the pans and flour them well or line with waxed paper, pour in the batter and bake about 50 minutes.

COOKIES AND BARS

★ ABOUT CHRISTMAS COOKIES

Christmas and cookies are inseparable. Stars, angels, bells, trees, Santas and even pretzels—the pilgrim's token—are memorialized in rich holiday confections. Why not make use of these charming cookie shapes to decorate a small table tree at Christmas? To cut molds, see Gingerbread Men, page 662. You can bake the strings for hanging right into the cookies. It irks us that such delightful sweets as Christmas cookies should be relegated to a period of a few weeks. In the hope that you will prolong the season, we have marked with this symbol ★ recipes which are generally recognized as traditional, as well as some which have become traditional with us, if for no other reason than that they can be baked in advance of a busy season.

We find that egg-white cookies, a natural by-product of Christmas baking, need special handling. Some of the meringues heavy in nuts, like Cinnamon Stars, page 670, keep well if tightly tinned. In packing mixed boxes, though, be sure to ♦ add meringue-based cookies at the last moment, for, unwrapped, they dry out quickly; and, if freshly made and stored with cookies rich in fruit, they may disintegrate. To soften hard dry cookies, put them with a piece of bread into a tightly closed container. Replace the bread every few days, for it molds easily. Another way to restore moisture is to use a dampened paper napkin, wrapped in punctured foil.

♦ Most cookie doughs freeze satisfactorily. If you have frozen baked cookies and are serving them for immediate consumption ♦ thaw them unwrapped, then heat them for a moment on a cookie sheet in a 300° oven to restore crispness. This is also a good plan for weary "bought" cookies. If you are sending cookies or cakes to out-of-towners, wrap them individually or put them into a polyethylene bag and bed them down in popcorn. Fill all the crannies of the box with the corn, until it just touches the lid.

ABOUT COOKIES

Having put the cart before the horse, we have told you how to pack and store cookies. Now let's talk about making and baking them. If you are planning a number of kinds, see that they complement each other in texture and flavor and that they use up ingredients economically. Choose shapes which will look pleasant on serving dishes. Many of these recipes call for butter as the basic fat. ♦ If you feel that, for reasons of economy, you cannot afford all butter, do try to use at least ⅓ butter. You will notice a marked superiority in flavor.

The mixing of cookies is usually quick, because, with most types, overworking the dough tends to cause toughness. Some ingredients must be well stirred together; some are creamed like cakes and, abroad, are called biscuits; others are blended like pastry. Use whatever mixing process the recipe calls for.

Electric equipment has eased the beating of tough, tight, honey and molasses doughs, the kind that often include carbonate of ammonia—a favorite leaven of commercial bakers. Baking powder may be substituted for this leaven, see page 504, but the results are somewhat different.

You may want to combine different flours. If you do so ♦ be sure to see the note on flour substitutions, page 501. To avoid flat flavors, taste the dough before cooking and correct the seasoning. ♦ Chill cookie doughs well and keep them covered until ready to bake.

To decorate cookies, dip the garnish before baking either into a simple sirup or unbeaten egg white. Then press the gar-

nish firmly onto the cookie surface. Or dust sugar onto the cookies after placing them on the sheet and press it in with a wide spatula. See also Icings and Glazes, page 672.

Would you like your cookies not only to taste better because of your choice of quality ingredients but to look as uniform in size and color as professionally made ones? Then preheat the oven to the degree indicated. Choose a flat baking sheet or use the bottom of a reversed baking pan. Treat the dough as shown illustrated on the left, page 661; or, if you prefer, cut the cookies on a board and transfer them to the reversed pan bottom. The heat can then circulate directly and evenly over the cookie tops. A pan with high sides will both deflect the heat and make the cookies hard to remove when baked. The very best aluminum sheets have permanently shiny baking surfaces and specially dulled bottoms to produce an even browning. ◆ Dark cookie sheets absorb heat and cookies may brown too much on the bottom.

Grease cookie sheets with unsalted fats, preferably sweet butter or beeswax. For delicate cookies, use a greased parchment paper or foil liner from which they peel off easily when slightly cooled. ◆ The baking sheet should always be cold when you put the cookie on it so it will not lose its shape. ◆ Always fill out a sheet, placing the cookies ◆ of even size and thickness about 1 inch apart, unless otherwise indicated. On a partially filled sheet the heat is drawn to the area where the cookies lie and the batch may burn on the bottom. If you haven't enough dough on your last baking to fill a whole baking sheet, reverse a pie pan or turn a small baking pan upside down, as shown on page 661.

◆ Always preheat the oven. The placement of the pans during baking is very important. ◆ Fill only one rack and be sure the pan or pans are disposed at least 2 inches from the oven walls. If using two smaller pans, see that they are spaced evenly one from the other.

Heat should circulate all around the pans. Should you use 2 large sheets on 2 racks, you will find that the heat circulates so that the bottoms of the cookies on the lower rack and the tops of the cookies on the upper rack brown too rapidly. Few ovens are so perfect that they will brown a large sheet evenly. During the baking process, do turn the sheet sometimes to compensate for uneven baking. Oven thermostats are also variable, so watch closely, especially when baking molasses and brown-sugar cookies, which burn easily. Even a few seconds matter. Should cookies bake too brown at the edges and still be soft in the middle, run them under a broiler—about 5 or 6 inches from the heat—until the desired color is achieved. When done ◆ take cookies from the baking sheet at once or they will continue to cook. ◆ Always cool cookies on a rack ◆ not overlapping, and store as suggested above.

Our recipes are completely tested, but the consistency of your dough may have to be modified, due to variations in the size of eggs and in the moisture content of honey, molasses and flour. To test for consistency, see About Rolled Cookies, page 661.

▲ In altitudes up to 5000 feet, simple cookies usually need no adjustment. But for cookies rich in chocolate, nuts, or dates a reduction of about ½ the baking powder or soda may be advisable. And, at very high altitudes, a slight reduction in sugar may help. ◆ But the soda should not be reduced beyond ½ teaspoon for each cup of sour milk or cream used.

If you wonder why commercial cookies are often large, the answer lies in handling and oven costs. A true sign of home baking is a small delicate cookie. However, you, too, want to save time and energy, so plan your cutting and baking patterns efficiently. To color cookies for special occasions, stir into 1 egg yolk ¼ teaspoon water. Divide the mixture into several custard cups and color each one with a few drops of different food coloring. This coloring applied with a soft brush before baking allows you to make elaborate patterns.

Successful baking depends on the preheating of the oven, as well as on the kind of baking sheet used, its size, the material of which it is made—even its temperature.

ABOUT SQUARES AND BARS

The quickest and easiest way to produce uniform small cakes is in squares and bars. Bake them in pans with at least a 1½-inch rim. ◆ Do observe pan sizes indicated in recipes, because the texture is much affected by thickness, etc. A pan smaller than indicated in the recipes will give a cakey result—not a chewy one. Too large a pan will give a dry, brittle result. If your pan is too large, divide it with a piece of foil folded as illustrated on page 618. The dough over the horizontal lap will help hold the divider in place. Most bars, unless meringue based, bake about 25 minutes in a preheated 350° oven. We suggest the use of muffin tins for individual servings with ice cream, or pie tins to make festive rounds. See Chart of comparative pan sizes, page 618.

If for immediate use, store bar cookies in the pan in which they are baked. Cover with aluminum foil. However, to prolong freshness, be sure to wrap these bars individually in foil after cooling and cutting. They are then all ready for serving, freezing or for packing lunch boxes. Different flavors, wrapped in different colored foils, or one dull side up and one shiny side up in regular foil, make an attractive dessert to pass at an informal outdoor buffet.

BROWNIES COCKAIGNE
About 30 Brownies
Almost everyone wants to make this classic
American confection. We guarantee good
results if you follow the ♦ signals. Brownies may vary greatly in richness and contain anywhere from 1½ cups of butter and
5 ounces of chocolate to 2 tablespoons of
butter and 2 ounces of chocolate for every
cup of flour. If you want them chewy and
moist, use a 9 x 13-inch pan; if cakey, use
a 9 x 9-inch pan. We love the following.
Preheat oven to 350°.
Melt in a double boiler:
  ½ cup butter
  4 oz. chocolate
♦ Cool this mixture. If you don't, your
brownies will be heavy and dry. Beat until ♦ light in color and foamy in texture:
  4 eggs ♦ at room temperature
  ¼ teaspoon salt
Add ♦ gradually and continue beating until well creamed:
  2 cups sugar
  1 teaspoon vanilla
With a few swift strokes, combine the
cooled chocolate mixture into the eggs and
sugar. ♦ Even if you normally use an electric mixer do this manually. Before the
mixture becomes uniformly colored, fold
in, again by hand:
  1 cup sifted all-purpose flour
And before the flour is uniformly colored,
stir in gently:
  1 cup pecan meats
Bake in a 9 x 13-inch pan for about 25
minutes. Cut when cool. Wrapped individually in foil, these keep well 3 or 4
days.
A good way to serve Brownies is to garnish
with whipped cream.

BUTTERSCOTCH BROWNIES
About 16 Thin 2¼-Inch Squares
An all-time favorite, easily made.
Preheat oven to 350°.
Melt in a saucepan:
  ¼ cup butter
Stir into it until dissolved:
  1 cup brown sugar
Cool these ingredients slightly. Beat in
well:
  1 egg
  1 teaspoon vanilla
Sift, then measure:
  ½ cup all-purpose flour
Resift it with:
  1 teaspoon double-acting
    baking powder
  ½ teaspoon salt
Stir these ingredients into the butter mixture. Add:
  ½ to 1 cup finely chopped nuts or
    ¾ cup grated coconut
Chopped dates and figs may be substituted
entirely or in part. Use a little of the flour
over them. Pour the batter into a greased

9 x 9-inch pan. Bake for about 20 to 25
minutes. Cut into bars when cool.

MOLASSES BARS
About Sixteen 2-Inch Squares
Preheat oven to 375°.
Sift:
  ⅓ cup powdered sugar
Beat until soft:
  6 tablespoons butter
Add the sugar gradually. Blend these ingredients until they are very light and
creamy. Beat in:
  1 egg
  ⅓ cup molasses
  ⅛ teaspoon each salt and soda
Sift before measuring:
  ⅞ cup all-purpose flour
Add the flour in 3 parts to the butter mixture. Stir in:
  1 teaspoon vanilla
Beat the batter after each addition until
smooth. Fold in:
  1 cup broken nut meats
Bake in a greased 8 x 8-inch pan, about 15
minutes. Cut the cake into bars before it
is cold. Roll them in:
  Powdered sugar

★ CHRISTMAS CHOCOLATE BARS COCKAIGNE
About 108 Bars, 1 x 2 Inches
These bars differ very much from the preceding cakes, for they are opulently flavored with chocolate. If you cannot choose
between them, better bake them both and
ice one with chocolate icing, and the other
with a white glaze.
Preheat oven to 350°.
Sift:
  2¾ cups light brown sugar: 1 lb.
Beat until light:
  6 eggs
Add the sugar gradually and beat these ingredients until well blended. Grate and
add:
  4 oz. chocolate
Combine and sift:
  3 cups all-purpose flour
  1 tablespoon cinnamon
  1½ teaspoons cloves
  ½ teaspoon allspice
  1 teaspoon each soda and salt
Add the sifted ingredients to the egg mixture, alternately with:
  ½ cup honey or molasses
Chop and add in all:
  2½ cups citron, candied lemon,
    orange, pineapple and nuts—
    preferably blanched almonds
Spread the dough with a spatula in two
9 x 13-inch greased pans. Bake about 20
minutes. When cool, ice with:
  Chocolate Butter Icing, page 678
Cut into bars.

★ GERMAN HONEY BARS
**About Three 8 x 8-Inch Cakes,
Plus One 9 x 9-Inch Cake**

Honey, like molasses, may be troublesome. Old German cooks used to insist on its being over a year old. Very good cakes are made with fresh honey, but then the amount of flour is a little hard to gauge. Carbonate of ammonia can be the leaven, if a crisper bar is desired. Substitute it for the baking powder and soda given below. Use 1 teaspoon carbonate of ammonia dissolved in 2 tablespoons warm water, rum or wine. These German Honey Bars will keep 6 months in a tightly closed tin.
Preheat oven to 350°.
Heat slightly in a large saucepan:

> 1⅓ cups honey or molasses
> ¾ cup sugar

Add and melt:

> 3 tablespoons butter

Sift and add:

> About 2 cups all-purpose flour,
> enough to make a semi-liquid dough
> 1 teaspoon baking powder
> (½ teaspoon soda)

Add:

> ½ cup blanched almonds
> ¼ cup each chopped citron and
> chopped candied orange or lemon
> peel
> ¼ teaspoon ginger
> ½ teaspoon cardamon
> 2 teaspoons cinnamon
> ⅛ teaspoon cloves

Add:

> 1½ to 2 cups more flour

The dough should be sticky to the touch. You may age the dough or pat it out at once into a ¼-inch thickness in buttered pans. If you age it, you may find it necessary to heat it slightly before working it into the pans. Bake about 25 minutes. Cut into squares and ice with:

> Lemon Glaze, page 682

★ DATE, FIG OR PRUNE BARS
About Forty-Two 2½ x 1-Inch Bars

Preheat oven to 325°.
Sift:

> 1 cup sugar

Beat until light:

> 3 eggs

Add the sugar gradually. Blend these ingredients until very light. Sift before measuring:

> ⅞ cup all-purpose flour

Resift with:

> 1 teaspoon double-acting
> baking powder
> ⅛ teaspoon salt

If spices are desired, add:

> ¼ teaspoon each cloves
> and cinnamon
> (½ teaspoon allspice)

Add the sifted ingredients to the egg mixture with:

> 1 teaspoon vanilla

Beat until ingredients are well blended. Add about:

> 2 cups chopped dates, figs or prunes
> 1 cup broken nut meats

Pour the batter into a greased and floured 9 x 13-inch pan. Bake for about 25 minutes. When cool, cut into bars, roll in:

> Confectioners' sugar

ABOUT CAKE AND COOKIE HOUSES

No matter how peculiar the medium or incongruous the scale, the instinct to build persists. We have tried and discarded many cake construction methods. Professionals use Pastillage, page 738, and Royal Glaze, thus achieving rather cold-looking but clean-cut and intricate models. We suggest two simple approaches. The first is the less nerve-racking.

I. Prepare any close-grained cake like:
> Cake for a Lamb Mold
> Chocolate Old World Spice Cake
> Eggless All Rye Honey Cake

Bake in deep loaf tins or in oblong angel-cake pans. ◆ When the cake is thoroughly cool, lay it broad-side down. Cut off a slice for chimney material—about 1 inch. Then cut the remainder into 2 pieces, ⅓ and ⅔ of the length. To roof it, cut the shorter piece diagonally so that, by putting the two triangular pieces together you form a gable as long as the house portion. Ice the whole, and then apply, in icing of contrasting color, windows, door, shingle tiles and other details. See Decorative Icings, page 673.

II. ★ Prepare slabs of:
> German Honey Cookies, page 657

Cut a paper pattern with 2 oblongs for the side walls, two gabled short walls, one of them ◆ carrying the outline of an end-wall chimney. This gives you a good solid element on which to affix later the other three chimney walls. ◆ Now, find an extra pair of hands. To assemble, mitre the edges where the walls meet and shamelessly drive toothpick "nails." ◆ Watch for these when the cake is eaten. When the walls are in place, use slabs for the roof, nailing them again with toothpicks where they touch the side walls, or fold in half an oblong of:
> Light wire screening

that projects over the long side walls and the gables to form eaves. With the help of:
> Royal Glaze, page 678

build up overlapping roof tiles and make doors and shutters of thin:
> Molasses Crisps Cockaigne, page 660

Affix these with the glaze. This icing, which dries hard and colors easily, makes a perfect cement for the various building elements and whatever decorations you want to glue onto the house.

ABOUT DROP COOKIES

Drop cookie doughs vary in texture. Some fall easily from the spoon and flatten into wafers in baking. Stiffer doughs need a push with a finger or the use of a second spoon to release them, as shown in the center below. When chilled, some of these doughs are formed into balls. These can be baked round, as shown on the left. You may, in molding these, want to dust your hands with flour or powdered sugar; or, if the cookies are a dark or chocolate dough, use cocoa for dusting. If you care to flatten the balls, as shown on the right, use a glass tumbler greased lightly on the bottom or dusted with flour, powdered sugar or cocoa, or a spatula dipped in ice water. To make uniform soft drops, use a measuring teaspoon or half teaspoon.

TORTELETTES
About Forty 1½-Inch Cookies
Preheat oven to 375°.
Prepare recipe for:
Butter Thins, page 661
Season them with:
Grated rind of ½ lemon
Shape into 1-inch balls. Flatten balls until dough is very thin. Beat slightly:
1 egg white
1 tablespoon water
Brush the cakes with this mixture. Combine:
1 cup blanched, shredded almonds or other nut meats
½ cup sugar
1 tablespoon cinnamon
¼ teaspoon nutmeg
⅛ teaspoon salt
Sprinkle the cakes with this mixture. Bake until light brown.

BUTTERLESS DROP COOKIES
Preheat oven to 325°.
Prepare:
Anise Drop Cookies, page 656
If you prefer a different flavor, omit the anise and use:
1 teaspoon grated lemon rind or
2 teaspoons grated orange rind
1 teaspoon vanilla
Do not let them stand for 12 hours—bake at once.

DROP BUTTER WAFERS
About Forty-Eight 2¼-Inch Wafers
These, when baked, automatically produce a lovely brown paper-thin rim.
Preheat oven to 375°.
Cream until light:
½ cup butter
⅓ to ½ cup sugar
Beat in:
1 egg
1 teaspoon vanilla
¼ teaspoon grated lemon rind
Add:
¾ cup sifted cake flour
(1½ tablespoons poppy seed or
1 teaspoon grated orange rind)
Drop the cookies from a teaspoon, well apart, on a greased sheet. Bake for about 7 minutes or until the rims brown.

CHOCOLATE-CHIP DROP COOKIES
About Forty-Five 2-Inch Cookies
Preheat oven to 375°.
Cream:
½ cup butter
Add gradually and beat until creamy:
½ cup brown sugar
½ cup white sugar
Beat in:
1 egg
½ teaspoon vanilla
Sift and stir in:
1 cup and 2 tablespoons sifted all-purpose flour
½ teaspoon salt
½ teaspoon soda
Stir in:
½ cup chopped nut meats
½ cup semi-sweet chocolate chips
Drop the batter from a teaspoon, well apart, on a greased cookie sheet. Bake for about 10 minutes.

SUGAR DROP COOKIES WITH OIL
About 5 Dozen Cookies
Preheat oven to 375°.
Sift together:
2½ cups all-purpose flour
1½ teaspoons double-acting baking powder
¾ teaspoon salt
1 teaspoon cinnamon or ¼ teaspoon freshly grated nutmeg

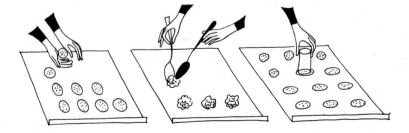

Combine:

1 cup sugar
¾ cup cooking oil

Add to this mixture and beat well after each addition:

2 eggs
1 teaspoon vanilla

Add the flour mixture all at once and beat well. Shape the dough into ½-inch balls. Dip the balls in:

Granulated sugar

or, flatten the balls as thin as you can between very lightly floured hands. To give a corrugated effect, score them in parallel lines, as shown below, with a fork dipped in flour. Sprinkle with:

Granulated sugar

Bake about 10 to 12 minutes on a lightly greased baking sheet.

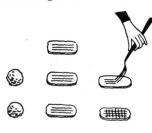

★ GINGER THINS
About Three Hundred ¾-Inch Wafers

Mme. Bu Wei, in her charming book, "How to Cook and Eat in Chinese," tells us that these little cakes, served between meals in her native country, are called "dot hearts." They should have the diameter of a quarter when baked for, if they are larger, they toughen.

Preheat oven to 325°.

Cream:

¾ cup butter
1 cup brown sugar
1 beaten egg
¼ cup molasses

Sift before measuring:

1½ cups all-purpose flour

Resift with:

¼ teaspoon salt
½ teaspoon soda
½ teaspoon each cloves, cinnamon
**   and ginger**

Combine the above ingredients and stir until smooth. Put dots of ⅛ teaspoon of dough 1 inch apart on a buttered pan and bake for 5 to 6 minutes. Cool cookie sheet on a rack. Cookies snap off if you twist the sheet slightly.

★ ANISE DROP COOKIES
About Ninety-Six 1-Inch Cookies

These professional-looking, self-glazing cookies with the charming puffed top are best made in cool weather. They do not turn out well if the humidity is over 50%.

Sift:

1 cup sugar

Beat until light:

3 eggs

Add the sugar gradually. Beat at least 3 to 5 minutes on medium speed with an electric beater, longer if beating by hand, then add:

½ teaspoon vanilla

Sift before measuring:

2 cups all-purpose flour

Resift with:

1 teaspoon double-acting
**   baking powder**

Add:

1½ tablespoons crushed anise seed

Beat the batter another 5 minutes. Drop ½ teaspoon at a time, well apart, on a cookie sheet lined with foil. The ½ teaspoon of dough should flatten to 1-inch round, but should not spread more. If it does, add a little more flour. Permit the drops to dry at room temperature for 18 hours. Bake the cakes in a preheated 325° oven, until they begin to color, about 12 minutes. When done, they will have a puffed meringue-like top on a soft cookie base.

ROCKS OR FRUIT DROP COOKIES
About Thirty 2-Inch Cookies

Preheat oven to 375°.

Sift:

¾ cup brown sugar

Beat until soft:

½ cup butter

Add the sugar gradually. Blend these ingredients until very light and creamy. Beat in, one at a time:

2 eggs

Sift before measuring:

1½ cups all-purpose flour or
**   whole grain flour**

Resift with:

½ teaspoon soda
1 teaspoon cinnamon
½ teaspoon cloves
¼ teaspoon allspice
⅛ teaspoon salt

Add the sifted ingredients in 3 parts to the butter mixture, alternately with thirds of:

¼ cup water or sherry

Beat the batter until it is smooth after each addition. Stir in:

1 cup broken nut meats
1 cup raisins, chopped dates, figs,
**   apricots or citron**

Drop the batter from a teaspoon onto a greased tin. Bake for about 12 minutes.

HERMITS
About Thirty 2-Inch Cookies

Preheat oven to 375°.

Sift:

1 cup brown sugar

Beat until soft:

½ cup butter

Add the sugar gradually. Blend these ingredients until very light and creamy

Beat in:
>   1 egg
>   ½ cup cultured sour cream, sour milk or
>   strong coffee

Sift before measuring:
>   1⅓ cups all-purpose flour

Resift with:
>   ¾ teaspoon cinnamon
>   ½ teaspoon cloves
>   ¼ teaspoon soda

If coffee has been used above, the spices are optional. Add the sifted ingredients to the butter mixture. Beat the batter until smooth. Stir in:
>   ½ cup chopped raisins
>   ¼ cup hickory or other nut meats
>   ¼ cup coconut may be added,
>   if desired

Drop batter from a teaspoon onto a greased sheet. Bake for about 15 minutes.

PFEFFERNÜSSE
About 3 Dozen 2-Inch Cookies
The classic recipe for these ball-like Peppernuts is made with a great deal of flour. In our judgment, it is both hard and uninteresting in texture. We have substituted a more subtle seasoning in a rather rich base. This version makes a flat cookie.
Preheat oven to 350°.
Cream together:
>   ½ cup butter
>   ½ cup sugar
>   2 well-beaten eggs

Sift together and add:
>   1 cup sifted all-purpose flour
>   ¼ teaspoon each salt and soda
>   ½ teaspoon each freshly ground black
>   pepper, nutmeg, cloves and allspice
>   1 teaspoon cinnamon
>   ⅛ teaspoon cardamon
>   1 to 3 drops oil of anise
>   ¼ cup ground blanched almonds
>   1½ tablespoons grated lemon peel
>   ¼ cup chopped citron

Drop the dough from a teaspoon onto a well-greased cookie sheet. Space cookies about 2 inches apart. Bake 10 to 12 minutes. Store tightly covered.

GERMAN HONEY COOKIES
About Two Hundred 2½-Inch Cookies
Cut into small pieces and combine:
>   3 oz. each of citron, candied orange
>   peel and candied lemon peel

Add:
>   1 cup chopped blanched almonds
>   1 teaspoon grated lemon rind
>   3 tablespoons cinnamon
>   1 tablespoon cloves
>   3⅓ cups confectioners' sugar

Beat until light and add:
>   6 eggs
>   ¼ cup orange juice

Bring to the boiling point and cool until lukewarm:
>   1 pint honey
>   2 tablespoons hot water

Stir this into the egg mixture with:
>   5 cups sifted all-purpose flour
>   1 tablespoon soda

Cover the dough and let it stand for 12 hours or more.
Preheat oven to 350°.
Drop the batter from a spoon, well apart, on a greased baking sheet. Bake the cakes until light brown. When cool, decorate with:
>   Lemon Glaze, page 682

or decorate before baking with:
>   Blanched almonds

CARROT DROP COOKIES
About Thirty 2½-Inch Cookies
A sophisticatedly flavored soft tea cookie with an oil base.
Preheat oven to 350°.
Beat:
>   1 egg

Add and beat well:
>   ⅓ cup cooking oil
>   ⅓ cup sugar

Measure:
>   ¾ cup all-purpose flour
>   ⅔ teaspoon double-acting
>   baking powder
>   ¼ teaspoon salt
>   1 teaspoon grated orange rind
>   ⅓ cup cooked, mashed carrots
>   (2 to 4 tablespoons white raisins
>   or citron)
>   (½ teaspoon ginger)

Drop from a teaspoon on a greased tin. Space generously. Bake 10 to 12 minutes or until cookies are golden brown.

QUICK OATMEAL COOKIES
About 3 Dozen 2-Inch Cookies
Preheat oven to 350°.
Measure:
>   ½ cup brown sugar, firmly packed
>   ½ cup granulated sugar

Cream with:
>   ½ cup butter

Combine and beat in until smooth:
>   1 egg
>   1 teaspoon vanilla
>   1 tablespoon milk

Sift together and add to the above ingredients:
>   1 cup all-purpose flour
>   ½ teaspoon soda
>   ½ teaspoon double-acting
>   baking powder
>   ½ teaspoon salt

When beaten smooth, add:
>   1 cup uncooked quick rolled oats
>   (¾ cup chocolate chips)
>   (1 teaspoon grated orange rind)

Beat the mixture well. Drop cookies 2 inches apart on well-greased cookie sheet and bake until light brown.

* OATMEAL GEMS
About Fifty 2-Inch Cookies
Preheat oven to 350°.

Cream:
  ½ cup butter
  ½ cup granulated sugar
  ½ cup light-brown sugar
Add:
  1 unbeaten egg
  ¼ teaspoon salt
  ½ teaspoon double-acting
    baking powder
  1 teaspoon vanilla
  1 cup uncooked quick rolled oats
  ¾ cup flour
  1 can flaked coconut
You may spice these with:
  (½ teaspoon cinnamon)
  (¼ teaspoon each cloves and
    freshly grated nutmeg)
Bake 8 to 10 minutes or until browned.

GLAZED OR FLOURLESS
OATMEAL WAFERS
                    About Eight Dozen 2-Inch Wafers
A pale yellow, crisp yet chewy cookie with
a shiny bottom.
Preheat oven to 350°.
Beat:
  3 whole eggs
Add gradually, beating constantly:
  2 cups sugar
Stir in:
  2 tablespoons melted butter
  ¾ teaspoon vanilla
  1 teaspoon salt
Remove beater. With a spoon, stir in:
  1 cup shredded coconut
  2 cups uncooked rolled oats
Line cookie sheet with foil. Drop by ½
teaspoons 1 inch apart into pan. Bake
about 10 minutes or until the edges are
lightly browned. Lift foil from pan, cool
until wafers can be easily removed.

ORANGE-MARMALADE DROPS
                    About Forty-Eight 2-Inch Cookies
This cookie is chewy and also pleasantly
tart in flavor.
Preheat oven to 375°.
Sift:
  ⅔ cup sugar
Beat until soft:
  ⅓ cup butter
Add the sugar gradually. Blend these ingredients until light and creamy. Beat in:
  1 whole egg
  6 tablespoons orange marmalade
Sift:
  1½ cups all-purpose flour
Resift with:
  1¼ teaspoons double-acting
    baking powder
Stir the sifted ingredients into the butter
mixture. Drop the batter from a teaspoon,
well apart, on a greased sheet. Bake the
cookies for about 8 minutes. It is difficult
to prescribe the right amount of flour, as
marmalades differ a great deal in consistency. Follow the rule, then try out 1 or 2
cookies. If they are too dry, add a little

more marmalade; if too moist, a little mor
flour and some grated lemon rind.

PEANUT BUTTER COOKIES
                    About Sixty 1½-Inch Cookie
For those who dote on peanut-butter cook
ies, try these rich and crumbly ones.
Preheat oven to 375°.
Sift:
  ½ cup brown sugar
  ½ cup granulated sugar
Beat until soft:
  ½ cup butter
Add the sugar gradually and blend thes
ingredients until creamy. Beat in:
  1 egg
  1 cup peanut butter
  ½ teaspoon salt
  ½ teaspoon soda
Sift before measuring:
  1½ cups all-purpose flour
Add the flour to the batter and:
  ½ teaspoon vanilla
Roll the dough into small balls. Place the
on a greased tin. Press them flat with
fork, as illustrated on page 656. Bake fo
about 15 minutes.

BUTTERSCOTCH NUT COOKIES
Preheat oven to 375°.
For flavor, chewiness and ease of makir
we prefer:
  Butterscotch Brownies, page 653
Should you prefer the look of a drop cook
to that of a bar, follow the recipe for th
Brownies, but add:
  2 tablespoons flour
Drop well apart on a greased cookie she
and bake for about 6 minutes.

COCONUT MERINGUE COOKIES
                    About Fifty 1½-Inch Kiss
Preheat oven to 300°.
Sift:
  1 cup sugar
Beat until stiff:
  3 egg whites
  ⅛ teaspoon salt
Add the sugar very slowly, beating co
stantly. Fold in:
  1 teaspoon vanilla
  1¼ cups shredded coconut
Drop the batter from a teaspoon onto
greased and well-floured tin. Bake
about 30 minutes.

COCONUT MACAROONS
                    About Twenty 1-Inch Cook
Preheat oven to 250°.
Use:
  ¼ lb. shredded coconut
Add:
  1 teaspoon vanilla
  ⅛ teaspoon salt
Combine these ingredients with sufficie
  Sweetened condensed milk
to make a thick paste. Roll the paste i
balls or drop it from a teaspoon o

reased tins, about 2 inches apart. These
ookies are much improved by folding into
he batter:

1 to 3 stiffly beaten egg whites

Drop the batter from a spoon. Bake until
ghtly browned. Remove from the oven
vhen the balls can be taken from the tin
vithout breaking. They may be rolled in:

Sifted confectioners' sugar

CHOCOLATE COCONUT MACAROONS

repare the preceding:

Coconut Macaroons

Heat the milk and add:

2 tablespoons cocoa or
¾ oz. chocolate

ool the mixture before adding it to the
oconut.

COCOA KISSES

About Forty 1-Inch Meringues

reheat oven to 250°.

ft:

1 cup sugar

Whip until stiff but not dry:

3 egg whites
⅛ teaspoon salt

ld gradually ½ of the sugar. Combine:

2 teaspoons water
1 teaspoon vanilla

ld the liquid, a few drops at a time, al-
rnately with the remaining sugar. Whip
nstantly. Fold in:

3 tablespoons cocoa
½-1 cup chopped pecans

rop the batter from a spoon onto a lightly
eased tin and shape into cones. Bake
til the kisses are partly dry and retain
eir shape. Remove from the pan while
t.

CHOCOLATE CRACKER KISSES

About Sixty 1-Inch Kisses

he only people who will guess these in-
edients are those who, in adolescence,
ppened to be devotees of thin chocolate
dy bars between salted soda crackers.
eheat oven to 350°.

at over hot water:

⅔ cup semi-sweet chocolate chips or
1 oz. chocolate, plus ¼ cup sugar

ol for about 5 minutes. Beat until very
f:

2 egg whites

Add:

¼ teaspoon vanilla
¼ teaspoon cream of tartar

Beat in gradually:

⅔ cup sugar

Fold in gently:

3 tablespoons crushed salted
soda crackers

and the cooled chocolate mixture. Drop
the meringue-like dough, a teaspoonful at
a time, onto a well-greased cookie sheet.
Bake about 10 to 12 minutes. Remove
from the oven when a glazed cap has
formed and puffed up over a ¼-inch platform of the dough—similar in looks, but
more peaked than that of Anise Cookies,
page 656. Store, when cool, in a tightly
closed container.

ABOUT REFRIGERATOR COOKIES

Their production proves quicker than that
of rolled cookies and they are usually more
delicate because their chilling and quick-
shaping characteristics permit a reduction
in flour content. After mixing the dough,
form it into a 2-inch-diameter roll on a
piece of foil, in which you wrap it securely. Chill the roll for 12 to 24 hours,
after which time it can be very thinly
sliced for baking. You may hasten the
chilling by placing the roll in the freezer.

An added advantage of these doughs is
that they can all be dropped before chilling if you want to make up a batch immediately. Whole nut meats may be combined with the dough or they may be used
to garnish the slices; or else, the entire
roll of dough may be rolled in chopped
nuts, so as to make a border when the
cookie is cut, as shown on the left, below.

Two sheets of differently colored dough
may be rolled together, see below. These,
when sliced, become pinwheel cookies. To
bake drop cookies, see page 655. Bake the
refrigerator cookies on a greased cookie
sheet, in a 400° oven, for 8 to 10 minutes.
Refrigerator cookies ✳ freeze well baked
or unbaked.

VANILLA REFRIGERATOR COOKIES

About Forty 2-Inch Cookies

This cookie resembles a Sand Tart, but is

less troublesome to prepare. It makes a good Filled Cookie, page 664, or rich Drop Cookie if the lesser amount of flour is used.

Sift:

    1 cup sugar

Beat until soft:

    ½ cup butter

Add the sugar gradually. Blend these ingredients until very light and creamy. Mix in:

    1 beaten egg

Add:

    1 teaspoon vanilla

    (½ teaspoon grated lemon rind
      or cinnamon)

Sift before measuring:

    1¼ to 1¾ cups all-purpose flour

Resift with:

    ¼ teaspoon salt

    1½ teaspoons double-acting
      baking powder

Stir the sifted ingredients into the butter mixture. Add:

    (½ cup nut meats)

To chill, form and bake, see About Refrigerator Cookies, page 659. Before baking, sprinkle the cookies with:

    (Sugar)

to make them sandy, or with:

    (Chopped or half nut meats)

BUTTERSCOTCH REFRIGERATOR COOKIES

Prepare:

    Vanilla Refrigerator Cookies, above

Substitute for the white sugar:

    1¼ cups firmly packed brown sugar

You may substitute for the nut meats:

    (1 cup grated coconut or
      1 teaspoon cinnamon)

CHOCOLATE REFRIGERATOR COOKIES

Prepare:

    Vanilla Refrigerator Cookies, above

Melt, then cool and mix into the dough:

    2 oz. chocolate

    (1 tablespoon brandy or rum)

To chill, form and bake, see Refrigerator Cookies, page 659.

PINWHEEL REFRIGERATOR COOKIES

Prepare:

    Vanilla Refrigerator Cookies, above

Divide the dough in half. Add to ½ the dough:

    1 oz. melted chocolate

If the dough is soft, chill until easily rolled. Then roll the white and brown dough separately into oblongs to the thickness of ⅛ inch. Place the dark dough on the light dough and roll the layers like a jelly roll. To chill, form and bake the rolled layers, see About Refrigerator Cookies, page 659.

★ MOLASSES CRISPS COCKAIGNE
About 6 Dozen 2 x 3-Inch Cookies

Heat to the boiling point over hot water:

    ½ cup dark molasses

Remove from heat, add and beat unt blended:

    ¼ cup sugar

    6 tablespoons butter

    1 tablespoon milk

    2 cups all-purpose flour

    ½ teaspoon salt

    ½ teaspoon double-acting
      baking powder

    ½ teaspoon each fresh ground nutmeg
      and cloves

    2 teaspoons cinnamon

Wrap in foil and cool until firm. To form slice very thin and, if necessary, pat thi on tin with fingers until they are tran lucent. Press into the center of each:

    ½ a pecan or blanched almond

Preheat oven to 325° and bake for 10 12 minutes on greased cookie sheets.

★ REFRIGERATOR LACE COOKIES
About Sixty 2-Inch Cookie

Stir until well blended:

    ½ cup white sugar

    ½ cup brown sugar

    ¾ to 1 cup sifted all-purpose flour

    ½ teaspoon each soda and salt

    ½ cup soft butter

    1 egg

    1 tablespoon milk

    (1½ teaspoons grated orange or
      lemon rind)

    ½ teaspoon almond or vanilla extract

Work in with the hands:

    1 cup rolled oats

To vary the flavor, you may use 1½ tab spoonfuls of molasses and 2 additional t blespoonfuls of flour. Chill, form and bak see About Refrigerator Cookies, page 659

★ JUBILEE WAFERS
About Seventy 2-Inch Wafe

Good for all those festive anniversaries, they can be confected long before the pre sure of events threatens to crowd them the calendar. Soften and mix over h water:

    ⅔ cup honey

    1 cup sugar

    ¼ cup butter

Sift together and add:

    2½ cups all-purpose flour

    1 teaspoon double-acting
      baking powder

    ¼ teaspoon each mace and cardamon

    ½ teaspoon soda

    2 teaspoons cinnamon

    ½ teaspoon cloves

Combine with all the above ingredients:

    ½ cup whisky

Add:

    1 cup blanched, grated almonds

    2 tablespoons each chopped citron,
      candied orange and lemon rind

Roll, chill, slice and bake as for Refrige tor Cookies, page 659.

ABOUT ROLLED AND MOLDED COOKIES

Aunties and grandmothers who roll cookies for and with children are scarce these days. But shaping cookies is such fun that children should be encouraged to learn to make them for themselves. Inexperienced bakers often ruin rolled cookies by using too much flour in the rolling process. To use as little extra flour as possible ♦ chill the dough at least 1 hour before rolling it and ♦ use a pastry cloth and rolling pin cover. These practically do away with sticking and require the use of very little additional flour. ♦ Remember never to use a pan with deep rims for cookie baking. Removal of the cookies from such a pan is very difficult.

♦ Use cutters that interlock, as shown above, so that dough need be handled as little as possible and baking time is economically employed. An even easier method to form fancy shapes which will not be distorted by handling is to grease the back of a baking pan. Spread dough on pan, as shown on left, above. Place cutters for maximum yield. Lift out the dough scraps between the shapes and reroll or reform them on another pan to make more cookies.

The roller cutter shown on the right speeds cookie-cutting. Two time-saving molds are an old French one of dove-tailed hearts and diamonds and a wheel cutter, also shown, which spins out the shapes with great rapidity. Amusing cutters lurk in antique shops. We wish a designer today would charm us with something contemporary. If you have a yen to do your own, take your designs to a tinsmith or make them from cardboard. See Gingerbread Men, page 662.

ROLL COOKIES
About Forty 2-Inch Cookies
This dough is remarkable for its handling quality. It can be shaped into crusts and dumpling covers, as well as cut into intricate patterns.
Cream:
  ½ cup white or brown sugar
with:
  ½ cup butter

Beat in:
  2 eggs
  2½ to 2¾ cups all-purpose flour
  2 teaspoons double-acting
    baking powder
  1 teaspoon vanilla
Chill the dough 3 to 4 hours before rolling. Preheat oven to 375°.
To roll, cut and bake, see About Rolled Cookies, above. Bake 7 to 12 minutes.

RICH ROLL COOKIES
About Sixty 2-Inch Cookies
Just what they are named, and delicious!
Cream:
  1 cup butter
  ⅔ cup sugar
Beat in:
  1 egg
Combine and add:
  2½ cups sifted all-purpose flour
  ½ teaspoon salt
  1 teaspoon vanilla
Chill dough 3 to 4 hours before rolling. Preheat oven to 350°.
Roll out and cut. See illustration and read About Rolled Cookies, above. Bake for 8 to 10 minutes or until slightly colored.

BUTTER THINS
About Twenty-Eight 2-Inch Cookies
Blend until creamy:
  6 tablespoons to ½ cup butter
  ⅛ cup sugar or ½ cup brown sugar
Beat in:
  1 egg or 2 egg yolks
  ½ teaspoon vanilla or almond extract
  ¼ teaspoon grated lemon rind or
    1 tablespoon cinnamon
  1 cup sifted all-purpose flour
  ⅛ teaspoon salt
  (2 tablespoons poppy seed)
Chill the dough for several hours.
Preheat oven to 375°.
Roll the dough on a board or shape it into 1-inch balls. Flatten between lightly floured hands or with the bottom of a tumbler. Place on a greased cookie sheet. You may decorate them with:
  Sugar, sugar and cinnamon or
    colored sugar
  ½ nut meat or a candied cherry
Bake from 10 to 12 minutes until the edges are brown.

SAND TARTS
About Eighty 1½-Inch Cookies

When touring in Normandy we met up with a famous local specialty which, curiously enough, proved to be our very own sand tarts.

Sift:

1¼ cups sugar

Beat until soft:

¾ cup butter

Add the sugar gradually. Blend these ingredients until very soft and creamy. Beat in:

1 egg
1 egg yolk
1 teaspoon vanilla
1 teaspoon grated lemon rind

Sift before measuring:

3 cups all-purpose flour

Resift with:

¼ teaspoon salt

Stir the flour gradually into the butter mixture until the ingredients are well blended. The last of the flour may have to be kneaded in by hand. Chill the dough for several hours.

Preheat oven to 400°.

Roll the dough until very thin. See page 661 for rolling cookies. Cut into rounds. Brush the tops of the cookies with:

The white of an egg

Sprinkle generously with:

Sugar

Garnish with:

(Blanched, split almonds)

Bake on greased tins for about 8 minutes. A good sand tart with a slightly different flavor may be made by following this recipe, but substituting for white sugar 1⅓ cups brown sugar.

GINGER SNAPS
About 10 Dozen 2-Inch Cookies

Like "boughten" ones in texture, but with a dreamy flavor.

Preheat oven to 325°.

Cream:

¾ cup butter

with:

2 cups sugar

Stir in:

2 well-beaten eggs
½ cup molasses
2 teaspoons vinegar

Sift and add:

3¾ cups all-purpose flour
1½ teaspoons soda
2 to 3 teaspoons ginger
½ teaspoon cinnamon
¼ teaspoon cloves

Mix ingredients until blended. Form dough into ¾-inch balls. Bake on a greased cookie sheet for about 12 minutes. As the ball melts down during baking, the cookie develops the characteristic crinkled surface. A topping to delight the children is ½ a marshmallow, cut side down, on the almost baked cookies. Return to oven about 4 minutes. When cool, ice to taste.

★ GINGERBREAD MEN
**About Eight 5-Inch Long Fat Men or
16 Thinner Ones**

Even quite young children are good at making these, if the modeling method suggested below is followed.

Preheat oven to 350°.

Blend until creamy:

¼ cup butter
½ cup white or brown sugar

Beat in:

½ cup dark molasses

Sift:

3½ cups all-purpose flour

Resift with:

1 teaspoon soda
¼ teaspoon cloves
½ teaspoon cinnamon
1 teaspoon ginger
½ teaspoon salt

Add the sifted ingredients to the butter mixture in about 3 parts, alternately with:

¼ cup water, if you roll the dough or
⅛ cup, if you model it

You may have to work in the last of the flour mixture with your hands if you are not using an electric mixer. If you are satisfied with a crude approximation, roll a ball for a head, a larger one for the body and cylinders for the arms and legs. Stick them together on a greased pan to form a **fat boy or girl**. Be sure to overlap and **press** these dough elements together carefully, so they will stay in one piece after baking. If you want something looking less like Primitive Man, roll the dough first to any thickness you like. A good way to do this is to grease the bottom of a baking sheet and to roll the dough directly onto it. Now, cut out your figures, either by using a floured cookie tin or by making a pattern of your own, as follows.

Fold a square of stiff paper or light cardboard lengthwise and cut it. Unfold it and you have a symmetrical pattern. Grease or flour one side of the pattern and place it on the rolled dough. Cut around the outlines with a sharp knife. Remove the scraps of dough between the figures, using them to make more men. Decorate before baking with small raisins, bits of candied cherry, redhots, decorettes, citron, etc., indicating features, buttons, etc. The men may receive further decorations, as described later

Bake the cookies for about 8 minutes or longer, according to their thickness. Test them for doneness by pressing the dough with your finger. If it springs back after pressing, the gingerbread cookies are ready to be cooled on a rack. Stir in a small bowl, to make a paste:

¼ cup confectioners' sugar
A few drops water

You may add:

A drop or two of vegetable coloring

Apply the icing with a toothpick or a small knife for additional garnishes—caps, hair, mustaches, belts, shoes, etc.

★ ALMOND PRETZELS OR MANDELPLAETTCHEN
About 2 Dozen 2-Inch Pretzels

Sift:

1 cup sugar

Beat until soft:

1 cup butter

Add the sugar gradually. Blend these ingredients until very light and creamy. Beat in:

1 to 2 egg yolks
2 eggs
¼ cup cultured sour cream

Sift and stir in:

2½ cups all-purpose flour

You may add:

1 teaspoon double-acting baking powder
1 teaspoon cinnamon
1 teaspoon grated lemon rind

Chill the dough for several hours until easy to handle.
Preheat oven to 375°.
Shape the dough into long thin rolls and twist these into pretzel shape. Place the pretzels on a greased tin. Brush with:

Yolk of an egg

Sprinkle the tops with:

Blanched, chopped almonds
Sugar

Bake them at once for 10 to 15 minutes. Do not let them color.

SCOTCH SHORTBREAD

Prepare:

Almond Pretzels, this page.

You may omit the egg yolk and seasoning. Use the almonds blanched and sliced as a topping with added candied citrus peel. Preheat oven to 325°.
Press dough into 4 8-inch rounds. Flute the edges and prick dough well. Bake about 20 minutes or until lightly colored. Cut into wedges while still warm.

YOLK COOKIES
About 100 Initials or Thin 1½-Inch Cookies

A great lexicographer said that an expression such as—"It's me"—was a sturdy indefensible. These cookies are our version of a sturdy indefensible. While not unusual, they use up leftover yolks. They have good tensile strength and make an excellent base for filled nut or jam tarts. We have used them as "initial" cookies for engagement parties.

Sift:

1 cup sugar

Beat until soft:

1 cup butter
½ teaspoon salt, if unsalted butter is used

Add the sugar gradually. Blend these ingredients until very light and creamy. Add:

½ teaspoon grated lemon rind
1½ tablespoons lemon juice

Beat in:

8 egg yolks

Stir in:

4 cups all-purpose flour

Chill the dough for 1 hour.
Preheat oven to 375°.
Roll the dough into sticks ¼ inch in diameter. Shape these into letters. Brush them with:

Yolk of an egg

Sprinkle them with:

Colored or white sugar

Bake them on a greased tin, 6 to 8 minutes.

★ SPRINGERLE
About 5 Dozen Cookies

This recipe produces the well-known German Anise Cakes, which are stamped with a wooden mold, shown at the upper right, page 651, or roller, into quaint little designs and figures. If you have no mold, cut the dough into ¾ x 2½-inch bars. Sift:

2 cups sugar

Beat until light:

4 eggs

Add the sugar gradually. Beat the ingredients until creamy. Sift before measuring about:

3 to 3½ cups all-purpose flour
½ teaspoon double-acting baking powder

Sprinkle a half cup flour on a pastry cloth. Turn the dough onto the cloth and knead in enough flour—about ½ cup more—to stiffen dough. Roll to the thickness of ⅓ inch and the size of your mold. Use the floured Springerle board and press it hard upon the dough to get a good imprint. If the dough is too soft, pick it up and add more flour. Separate the squares, place them on a board and permit them to dry for 12 hours, uncovered, in a cool dry place.
Preheat oven to 300°.
Grease cookie sheets and sprinkle them with:

1 tablespoon crushed anise seed

Place the cakes on them. Bake about 15 minutes or until the lower part is light yellow. To store, see page 651.

★ CHOCOLATE ALMOND SHELLS
About Sixty 1½-Inch Cookies

This batter is usually pressed into little wooden molds in the shape of a shell, but any attractive ones like individual butter molds will do. If molded, the batter must stand for 12 hours. If not molded, it may be baked after mixing.

Grind, in a nut grinder:

    ½ lb. unblanched almonds

Sift:

    1 cup sugar

Whip until stiff:

    4 egg whites
    ¼ teaspoon salt

Add the sugar gradually. Whip constantly. Fold in the ground almonds and:

    1½ teaspoons cinnamon
    ⅛ teaspoon cloves
    1 teaspoon grated lemon rind
    1 tablespoon lemon juice
    2½ oz. grated chocolate

Permit this batter to stand uncovered in a dry cool place for 12 hours.

Preheat oven to 300°.

Shape the batter into balls. Prepare shell molds by dredging them with a mixture of:

    Sugar and flour

Press the balls into the molds. Unmold them. Bake on a greased sheet for about 30 minutes.

★ SPECULATIUS
About Twenty-Eight 2 x 4-Inch Thin Cookies

A rich cookie of Danish origin, pressed with carved wooden molds into Santas and Christmas symbols.

Work as for pie dough, until the particles are like coarse corn meal:

    ⅔ cup butter
    1 cup flour

Cream:

    1 egg

with:

    ½ cup brown sugar

Add:

    ⅛ teaspoon cloves or
      1/16 teaspoon cardamom
    1 teaspoon cinnamon

Combine the egg and butter mixtures well.

Spread the dough on a 14 x 17-inch baking sheet. Let it rest chilled for 12 hours.

Preheat oven to 350°.

Stamp the figures with the floured molds. Bake about 10 minutes or until done.

COOKIE-PRESS OR SPRITZ COOKIES
About 5 Dozen Cookies

These may also be made in a pastry bag.

Sift together:

    2¼ cups all-purpose flour
    ¾ cup sugar
    ¼ teaspoon double-acting
      baking powder
    ½ teaspoon salt

Blend in, until mixture resembles coarse crumbs:

    1 cup butter

Break into a measuring cup:

    1 egg

If it does not measure ¼ cup, add water up to ¼ cup line. Stir into the crumb mixture the egg and:

    1 teaspoon vanilla

Beat well, then chill. Put dough through cookie press onto ◗ an ungreased cookie sheet. ◗ The dough should be pliable but, if it becomes too soft, re-chill it slightly. Bake for 10 to 12 minutes in a 350° oven.

ABOUT FILLED COOKIES AND FILLED BARS

The recipes which follow describe individual ways to shape and fill cookies and bars. But, first, here are simple and basic ways to shape and fill them as sketched below.

Prepare:

    Rolled or Rich Rolled Cookies, page 661; Butter Thins, page 661; Sand Tarts, page 662, or Yolk Cookies, page 663

Form a ball and make an imprint with your thumb to hold a filling as shown on the left, below. Or roll the dough thin and cut into rounds. For a turnover, use a single round of dough and less than a tablespoon of filling. Fold over and seal edges firmly by pressing them with a floured fork. A closed tart takes 2 rounds of dough. Place

a tablespoon of filling on one and cover with the other, then seal. For a see-through tart, employ the same bottom round and filling, but cut the top with a doughnut cutter and seal outer edge in the same way.

To make bars, line a 9 x 13-inch pan with ⅔ of the dough, spread one of the fillings over it, see below, and cover the filling with the remaining ⅓ of the dough. Bake at 350°, 20 to 25 minutes. Here are 3 basic fillings. For others, see Nut Bars, below, or Pecan Slices, page 666.

I. Raisin, Fig or Date Filling
Boil and stir until thick:
    1 cup chopped raisins, figs or dates
    6 tablespoons sugar
    5 tablespoons boiling water
    ½ teaspoon grated lemon rind
    2 teaspoons lemon juice
    2 teaspoons butter
    ⅛ teaspoon salt

II. Coconut Filling
Combine:
    1 slightly beaten egg
    ½ cup brown sugar
    1 tablespoon flour
    1½ cups flaked or chopped
        shredded coconut

III. ★ Drained Mincemeat, page 603

JELLY TOTS
                    About Forty-Two 1¼-Inch Cookies
You may call these Hussar Balls, Jam Cookies, Thumbprint Cookies, Deep-Well Cookies or Pits of Love—the latter borrowed from the French—but a rose by any other name, etc.
Preheat oven to 375°.
Prepare the dough for:
    Butter Thins, page 661
Use the larger amount of butter. Roll the dough into a ball. You may chill it briefly for easier handling. Pinch off pieces, to roll into 1-inch balls.

I. Roll the balls in:
    1 slightly beaten egg white
then in:
    1 cup finely chopped nut meats
For baking, follow directions under II, below.

II. Roll the balls in:
    Sugar
Place them on a lightly greased and floured sheet. Bake for 5 minutes. Depress the center of each cookie with a thimble or your thumb, as shown in sketch on opposite page. Continue baking until done, for about 8 minutes. When cool, fill the pits with:
    A preserved strawberry, a bit of jelly or jam, a candied cherry or pecan half, or a dab of icing

III. Before baking, make a depression in each ball. Fill with jam. Close over depression with dough. Bake, widely spaced, on a buttered sheet.

MACAROON JAM TARTS
                    About Fourteen 3-Inch Cakes
The star of stars.
Blend until creamy:
    2 tablespoons sugar
    ½ cup butter
Beat in:
    1 egg yolk
    ½ teaspoon grated lemon rind
    1½ tablespoons lemon juice
Stir in gradually, until well blended:
    1½ cups sifted all-purpose flour
alternately with:
    2 tablespoons cold water
Chill the dough for 12 hours.
Preheat oven to 325°.
Roll out dough to ⅛ inch. Cut into 3-inch rounds. Whip until stiff but not dry:
    3 egg whites
Beat in gradually:
    1⅓ cups sifted confectioners' sugar
    1 teaspoon vanilla
Fold in:
    ½ lb. almonds, blanched and ground
        in a nut grinder
Place mixture around the edge of each cookie, making a ¾-inch border. Use a pastry bag, a spatula or spoon, as sketched on opposite page. Bake 20 minutes or until done. When cool, fill centers with:
    Jam

INDIVIDUAL NUT TARTS
                    About 10 to 12 Tarts
Prepare and chill for 12 hours:
    **Vanilla Refrigerator Cookie Dough,
        page 659**
Preheat oven to 350°.
Pat or roll the dough until very thin. Line shallow muffin pans with it. Beat until light:
    3 egg yolks
Beat in gradually:
    1 cup sugar
    ¼ teaspoon salt
Grind in a nut grinder and add:
    1 cup blanched almonds
        or other nuts
Stir in:
    1½ tablespoons lemon juice
Fold in:
    3 stiffly beaten egg whites
Fill the lined shallow muffin tins with this mixture and bake until done, for about 20 minutes.

★ NUT BARS
                    About Forty-Eight 1 x 2-Inch Sticks
Preheat oven to 350°.
These, like the following Pecan Slices, are made on a rich, sweet pastry base. They are equally good and popular.

Cream until well blended:
  ½ cup butter
  (¼ cup sugar)
Beat in well:
  1 egg
Combine:
  1¼ cups sifted all-purpose flour
  ⅛ teaspoon salt
Add these dry ingredients in about 3 parts
to the butter mixture, blending them well.
Work in:
  (½ teaspoon vanilla)
Use your hands to pat the dough evenly in
a 9 x 12-inch pan. Bake for about 15 minutes. Beat, in a heavy saucepan:
  2¼ cups finely chopped pecans
  1 cup sugar
  1½ teaspoons cinnamon
  4 egg whites
Cook and stir this mixture over low heat.
After the sugar has dissolved, increase the
heat slightly. Stir and cook until the mixture leaves the sides of the pan, but remove it from the heat before it is dry.
Spread it over the pastry base. Bake the
cake for about 15 minutes longer. When
cool, cut into sticks.

★ PECAN OR ANGEL SLICES
                     About Forty-Eight 1 x 2-Inch Bars
Many a copy of the "Joy" has been sold on
the strength of this recipe. One fan says
her family is sure these are the cakes St.
Peter gives little children at the Gates of
Heaven, to get them over the first pangs of
homesickness. Her family has dubbed
them Angel Cookies.
Preheat oven to 350°.
Line a pan with dough, as for the preceding Nut Bars. Bake as directed. Spread
with the following mixture:
  2 beaten eggs
  1½ cups brown sugar
  ½ cup flaked coconut
  1 cup chopped pecan meats
  2 tablespoons flour
  ½ teaspoon any baking powder
  ½ teaspoon salt
  1 teaspoon vanilla

If preferred, omit the coconut and use 1½
cups nut meats instead. Bake the cake for
about 25 minutes. When cool, ice with:
  1½ cups sifted confectioners' sugar
thinned to a good spreading consistency
with:
  Lemon juice
Cut the cake into oblongs.

PLUM BOMBS
                                    About 2 Dozen Bombs
Prepare and chill well:
  Rolled Cookie Dough, page 661
Preheat oven to 350°.
Drain thoroughly and remove pits from:
  Canned plums
Stuff them with a combination of:
  Pine nuts or chopped larger nuts
  White raisins
Enclose the plums in thin wrappings of the
rolled dough. Place well apart on a greased
baking sheet and bake about 25 minutes or
until slightly colored.

FRANKFURTER OBLATEN
Prepare:
  Butter Krumkakes, page 667
Fill in, between two wafers, a thin layer
of:
  Soft flavored fondant or
  French Icing, page 678

ABOUT CURLED COOKIES

Some curled cookies are simply dropped
on a baking sheet, others require a special
iron. In either case they are very dressy
looking—whether they make a tube or
cornucopia or are just partially curled,
after being shaped over a rolling pin while
still warm. Filled ◆ just before serving,
they make a complete dessert. Use flavored whipped cream fillings, page 645, a
cake filling, page 646, or cream cheese.
Serve them as tea cakes with a contrasting
butter-cream filling. Dip the ends in:
  Ground pistachio or chocolate shot
  "gimmies"
to lend a most festive look.

SCANDINAVIAN KRUMKAKES

To make these fabulously thin wafers, you will need the inexpensive iron shown on page 666. It fits over a 7-inch surface burner, either gas or electric, and is ♦ always used over moderate heat. For each baking period the iron should be lightly rubbed at the beginning with unsalted butter; but after this initial greasing, nothing more is required. The dough needs a preliminary testing as it is quite variable, depending on the condition of the flour; so, do not add at once all the flour called for in the recipe. Test the dough for consistency by baking 1 teaspoonful first. The iron is geared to use 1 tablespoon for each wafer and the dough should spread easily over the whole surface, but should not run over when pressed down. If the batter is too thin, add more flour. Should any dough drip over, lift the iron off its frame and cut off the dough with a knife run along the edge of the iron. Cook each wafer about 2 minutes on each side or until barely colored. As soon as you remove it from the iron, roll it on a wooden spoon handle or cone form as illustrated and, when cool, fill it. You may prefer to use these cookies as round filled sandwich cookies. For suggestions for fillings, see Curled Cookies, above.

I. Butter Krumkakes
About Thirty 5-Inch Wafers

A teenage neighbor recommends an ice cream filling. We like cultured sour cream with a spot of tart jelly or a flavored whipped cream, page 645.
Beat until light:

    2 eggs
Add slowly and beat until pale yellow:
    ¾ cup sugar
Melt and add slowly:
    ½ cup butter
Stir in, until well blended:
    1¾ cups flour
    1 teaspoon vanilla
To cook, roll and fill, see Krumkakes, above.

II. Lemon Krumkakes
About Thirty 5-Inch Wafers

Cream:
    1 cup sugar
    ½ cup butter
Combine and add:
    3 beaten eggs
    ½ cup cream, whipped
    ½ teaspoon grated lemon rind
Add enough flour to make a dough that spreads easily on the iron—not more than:
    1½ cups flour
To bake, form and fill, see Krumkakes, above.

III. Almond Krumkakes
About Twelve 5-Inch Wafers

To make Fortune Cookies, see below.
Cream and beat well:
    ¼ cup butter
    ½ cup sifted confectioners' sugar
Add by degrees:
    3 unbeaten egg whites
    2 tablespoons ground almonds
    ½ cup sifted flour
    1 teaspoon vanilla
To cook, roll and fill, see Krumkakes, above.

ICE CREAM CONES
OR GAUFRETTES
7 Large or 12 Small Cones

If made on a krumkake iron, as illustrated, this dough can be rolled into delicious thin-walled cones. If made on an oblong waffled gaufrette iron, they become the typical French honeycombed wafer or gaufrette, so often served with wine or ices. Preheat the krumkake or gaufrette iron over a moderate surface burner. Melt and let cool:
    ¼ cup butter
Beat until very stiff:
    2 egg whites
Fold in gradually:
    ¾ cup sifted confectioners' sugar
    ⅛ teaspoon salt
    ¼ teaspoon vanilla
Fold in:
    ½ cup sifted all-purpose flour
Add the cooled butter, folding it in gently. Put 1 tablespoon of this batter into the preheated iron. After about 1½ minutes, turn the iron and bake on the other side until a pale golden beige in color. Remove and use flat or curl the wafer into a cone. When cool, fill and serve.

ALMOND CURLS OR
FORTUNE COOKIES
About 5 Dozen Cookies

Preheat oven to 350°.
If you want to make these cookies, or Almond Krumkakes, into fortune favors for a party, have your remarks printed on thin papers, 3 x ¾ to 1 inch in size. After the cookies are curled, insert a slip in each, letting part of the paper project. Pinch the ends of the roll closed while the cookie is still warm. Combine and mix, until sugar is dissolved:
    ¾ cup unbeaten egg whites: 5 to 6
    1⅔ cups sugar
    ¼ teaspoon salt
Stir in separately and beat until well blended:
    1 cup melted butter
    1 cup all-purpose flour
    ¾ cup finely chopped blanched
        almonds
    ½ teaspoon vanilla or 1 tablespoon
        lemon juice
Drop the dough in tablespoonfuls, well apart, onto an ungreased baking sheet.

Bake about 10 minutes or until the edges are a golden brown. Mold cookie over a wooden spoon handle. See illustration, page 666, and Curled Caramel Cookies, below.

BRANDY SNAPS
About Twenty 3½-Inch Cookies
Preheat oven to 300°.
Stir over low heat:
    ½ cup butter
    ½ cup sugar or ¼ cup sugar plus ¼ cup
        grated, packed maple sugar
    ⅛ cup dark molasses
    ¼ teaspoon ginger
    ½ teaspoon each cinnamon and
        grated lemon or orange rind
Remove from heat and add:
    1 cup all-purpose flour
    2 teaspoons brandy
Roll into ¾ inch balls.
Bake on an ungreased sheet, for about 12 minutes. Remove cookies from pan, after a minute or so, with a spatula. Roll over a spoon handle, see sketch, page 666. Store in a tightly covered tin.

MAPLE CURLS
About Fifteen 3-Inch Curls
Preheat oven to 350°.
Bring to a hard boil for about ½ minute:
    ½ cup maple sirup or maple
        blended sirup
    ¼ cup butter
Remove from heat and add:
    ½ cup sifted flour
    ¼ teaspoon salt
Stir this in well. When blended, drop the dough onto a greased cookie sheet, 1 table-spoonful at a time, 3 inches apart. Bake from 9 to 12 minutes or until the cookie colors to the shade of maple sugar. Remove pan from oven. When slightly cool, remove cookies with a spatula, roll as shown on page 666, and cool on a rack.

CURLED CARAMEL COOKIES
About 24 Cornucopias
Preheat oven to 400°.
Cream well:
    ¼ cup butter
    ½ cup brown sugar
Beat in:
    1 egg
When well blended, beat in:
    ½ teaspoon vanilla
    ⅛ teaspoon salt
    3 tablespoons all-purpose flour
Stir in:
    ¼ cup ground or minced nut meats
Black walnuts or hazelnuts are excellent. Drop the batter from a teaspoon, well apart, on a greased sheet—about 6 to a sheet. Flatten the cookies with the back of a spoon. Bake for 8 or 9 minutes. Cool slightly and remove from pan with a small pancake turner. Then roll the cookies over a wooden spoon handle or a rolling pin, or roll them with your hands. If they cool too

quickly to manipulate, return them ♦ for a minute to the oven.

CURLED NUT WAFERS
About 20 Wafers
Preheat oven to 375°.
Sift:
    ⅔ cup sugar
Beat until soft:
    2 tablespoons butter
    2 tablespoons shortening
Add the sugar gradually. Blend these ingredients until very light and creamy. Beat in:
    1 egg
    2 tablespoons milk
    ½ teaspoon vanilla
    ¼ teaspoon almond extract
Sift before measuring:
    1⅓ cups all-purpose flour
Resift with:
    1 teaspoon double-acting
        baking powder
    ½ teaspoon salt
Add the sifted ingredients to the butter mixture. Beat batter until smooth. Grease a cookie sheet. Spread the batter evenly, to the thickness of ⅛-inch, over the pan with a spatula. Sprinkle dough with:
    ½ cup chopped nut meats
Bake for about 12 minutes. Cut the cake into ¾ by 4-inch strips. Shape the strips while hot over a rolling pin. If the strips become too brittle before they are shaped, return them to the oven until they become pliable again.

ABOUT NUT COOKIES

The first six recipes, all delicious, may read as though they are much alike, yet they differ greatly when baked. They have in common a brown sugar and egg base ♦ so don't try to bake them in hot humid weather. In such weather, choose, instead, Pecan Puffs or Florentines. To prepare nuts, please read About Nuts, page 518.

Most of these cookies are fragile. But if made small and baked on a beeswaxed sheet or a foil pan liner they are easy to remove intact. ♦ Should they harden on the pan, return the baking sheet for a moment to the oven before trying to remove them.

PECAN DROP COOKIES
About Fifty 1½-Inch Wafers
Preheat oven to 325°.
See About Nut Cookies, above. Grind in a nut grinder:
    1 cup pecan meats
Put through a sieve:
    1⅓ cups firmly packed brown sugar
Whip until stiff but not dry:
    3 egg whites
Add the sugar very slowly, beating constantly. Fold in the ground pecans and:
    1 teaspoon vanilla

Drop the batter from a teaspoon, well apart, onto a greased and floured tin. Bake for about 15 minutes.

NUT WAFERS
About 30 Cookies
At Williamsburg this cookie is served with Greengage Ice Cream.
Preheat oven to 325°.
See About Nut Cookies, page 668. Work:
(1 tablespoon flour)
into:
1 cup brown sugar
Beat until stiff, then fold in:
1 egg white
Fold in:
¾ teaspoon vanilla
1⅛ cups coarsely chopped pecans or hickory nuts
Drop the batter from a teaspoon onto a greased and floured cookie sheet. Bake about 15 minutes or until done.

PECAN OR BENNE WAFERS
About Fifty 2½-Inch Wafers
Preheat oven to 375°.
See About Nut Cookies, page 668. Whip until light:
2 eggs
Add gradually:
1⅓ cups firmly packed brown sugar
Beat these ingredients until they are well blended. Add:
5 tablespoons all-purpose flour
⅛ teaspoon salt
⅛ teaspoon double-acting baking powder
1 teaspoon vanilla
Beat the batter until smooth, then add:
1 cup broken nut meats or
½ cup toasted benné seeds
Grease and flour baking sheets. Drop the batter on them, well apart, from a teaspoon. Bake for about 8 minutes. Remove from sheets while still warm.

MOLASSES NUT WAFERS
About Fifty 2½-Inch Wafers
Preheat oven to 375°.
See About Nut Cookies, page 668.
Sift:
1 cup dark brown sugar
Whip until light:
2 eggs
Add the sugar gradually. Beat these ingredients until well blended. Add:
1 tablespoon dark molasses
¼ teaspoon double-acting baking powder
6 tablespoons all-purpose flour
⅛ teaspoon salt
Beat the batter until smooth. Stir in:
1 cup chopped black or English walnuts, hazelnuts or mixed nut meats
Drop the batter, well apart, from a teaspoon onto a well greased sheet. Bake for about 8 minutes.

★ HAZELNUT WAFERS
About Sixty 1½-Inch Cookies
Preheat oven to 325°.
This dough, when cut in 2½ x 4-inch oblongs and baked on fish-food-like wafers from bakers' suppliers, is much like the one used for Nürnberger Lebkuchen. See About Nut Cookies, page 668.
Grind in a nut grinder:
1 lb. hazelnut meats
Sift:
2¾ cups brown sugar
Whip until stiff:
6 egg whites
⅛ teaspoon salt
Add the sugar gradually. Whip constantly. Add:
1 teaspoon vanilla
Fold in the ground nuts. Shape the batter lightly into 1-inch balls. Roll them in:
Granulated sugar
Bake on a greased tin until light brown, about 15 minutes.

★ FLOURLESS NUT BALLS
About Thirty-Six 1¼-Inch Balls
Preheat oven to 325°.
See About Nut Cookies, page 668.
Grind in a nut grinder:
1½ cups almonds or pecans
Combine in a pan with:
1 cup brown sugar
1 egg white
1½ teaspoons butter
Stir these ingredients over very low heat until well blended. Cool the mixture. Shape the dough into small balls or roll it out and cut it into shapes. If the dough is hard to handle, use a little confectioners' sugar. Place the cookies on a very well greased sheet. Bake for 30 to 40 minutes. Leave on the sheet until cool. Ice with:
Lemon Glaze, page 682, or
Chocolate Icing, page 679

PECAN PUFFS
About Forty 1½-Inch Balls
Rich and devastating.
Preheat oven to 300°.
Beat until soft:
½ cup butter
Add and blend until creamy:
2 tablespoons sugar
Add:
1 teaspoon vanilla
Measure, then grind in a nut grinder:
1 cup pecan meats
Sift before measuring:
1 cup cake flour
Stir the pecans and the flour into the butter mixture. Roll the dough into small balls. Place balls on a greased baking sheet and bake for about 30 minutes. Roll while hot in:
Confectioners' sugar
To glaze, put the sheet back into the oven for a minute. Cool and serve.

★ FLORENTINES
30 Very Thin 3-Inch Cookies
A great European favorite—really choice.
Preheat oven to 350°.
Stir well:

    ½ cup whipping cream
    3 tablespoons sugar

If you can get a heavier cream, use it.
Stir in:

    ⅛ cup blanched, slivered almonds
    ¼ lb. preserved diced orange peel
    ¼ cup all-purpose flour

Spread a cookie sheet with unsalted shortening, flour it lightly. Drop the batter on
it from a teaspoon, well apart. Bake the
cookies until golden brown, from 10 to 15
minutes. They burn easily—so watch
them. When cool, spread the bottoms of
the cookies with:

    4 oz. melted semi-sweet chocolate

Use a spatula or impale a cookie on a fork
and dip it into the chocolate. Dry on wax
paper, bottoms up. Used without the
chocolate, the dough makes a delicious
"lace" cookie.

LEAF WAFERS
These thin crisp wafers add distinction to
a cookie tray when, like Florentines, they
are dipped on one side in icing, chocolate
or glaze. You may roll the dough very
thin on a greased cookie sheet and cut the
leaves around a pattern. Then remove the
excess dough between the leaves. However, there are metal stencils which make
all this easier. Put the stencil on the
greased sheet. Spread dough over the leaf
opening with a spatula. Remove excess
dough and lift the stencil. Bake at 375°
for about 10 minutes. Remove from the
pan at once to prevent sticking.

I. Black Walnut Leaves
About 60 Thin Leaves
Preheat oven to 375°.
Cream together:

    ¼ cup butter
    1 cup brown sugar

Add and mix well:

    1 beaten egg
    ½ teaspoon each baking soda and
        cream of tartar
    ¼ teaspoon salt
    1¾ cups cake flour

Stir in:

    ½ cup very finely chopped
        black walnuts

To form, bake and ice, see above.

II. Almond Leaves
About 50 Thin Leaves
Preheat oven to 375°.
Cut into thin slices:

    ½ lb. almond paste: 1 cup

Knead in gradually and work until the
mixture is very smooth:

    2 egg whites
    1 tablespoon water

Stir in and beat well:

    ¾ cup sifted confectioners' sugar
    ¼ cup cake flour

To form, bake and ice, see above.

RUM DROPS, UNCOOKED
About Forty-Five 1-Inch Balls
Fine served with tea or with lemon ice.
Place in a mixing bowl:

    2 cups finely sifted crumbs of toasted
        sponge cake, zwieback or graham
        crackers

Add:

    2 tablespoons cocoa
    1 cup sifted powdered sugar
    ⅛ teaspoon salt
    1 cup finely chopped nut meats

Combine:

    1½ tablespoons honey or sirup
    ¼ cup rum or brandy

Add the liquid ingredients slowly to the
crumb mixture. Use your hands in order
to tell by the "feel" when the consistency
is right. When the ingredients will hold
together, stop adding liquid. Roll the mixture into 1-inch balls. Roll them in:

    Powdered or granulated sugar

Set the drops aside in a tin box for at least
12 hours to ripen.

★ ALMOND MERINGUE RINGS
About 36 Rings
Decorative in Christmas boxes, but add
them at the last minute as they do not
keep well.
Preheat oven to 300°.
Blanch:

    ¼ lb. almonds

Cut them lengthwise into thin shreds.
Toast lightly. Whip until stiff but not dry:

    2 egg whites

Add gradually, beating constantly:

    1 cup sifted confectioners' sugar

Our old recipe says "stir" for ½ hour, but
of course you won't do that, so whip until
you are tired or use an electric beater.
Fold in the almonds and:

    1 teaspoon vanilla

Shape the batter into rings on a greased
tin. Bake until the rings just begin to
color.

★ CINNAMON STARS
About Forty-Five 1½-Inch Stars
Deservedly one of the most popular Christ-
mas cakes, also one of the most decorative.
See About Nut Cookies, page 668.
Preheat oven to 300°.
Sift:

    2 cups confectioners' sugar

Whip until stiff but not dry:

    5 egg whites
    ⅛ teaspoon salt

Add the sugar gradually. Whip these ingredients well. Add:

    2 teaspoons cinnamon
    1 teaspoon grated lemon rind

Whip constantly. Reserve ⅓ of the mixture. Fold into the remainder:

1 lb. ground unblanched almonds

Dust a board or pastry canvas lightly with confectioners' sugar. Pat the dough to the thickness of ⅓ inch. It is too delicate to roll. If it tends to stick, dust your palms with confectioners' sugar. Cut the cakes with a star or other cutter or simply mold them into small mounds. Glaze the tops with the reserved mixture. Bake on a greased sheet for about 20 minutes.

★ NUT AND DATE COOKIES
Two 9 x 13-Inch Pans

Not a German classic, but very like Basler Leckerle in flavor.
See About Nut Cookies, page 668.
Preheat oven to 350°.
Grind in a nut grinder:

1 cup nut meats
1 cup seeded dates

Sift:

1 cup sugar

Whip until stiff but not dry:

2 egg whites
⅛ teaspoon salt

Add the sugar gradually. Whip constantly. Fold in:

1 tablespoon cream

Sift before measuring:

1 cup all-purpose flour

Resift with:

1 teaspoon double-acting
baking powder

Fold in the sifted ingredients, the nuts and the dates. It may be necessary to combine them with the hands. Grease and flour a baking sheet. Place the batter on it and pat it down to the thickness of ¼ inch. If the batter is sticky, dip the palms of the hands in confectioners' sugar. Bake for about 10 minutes. Spread while hot with:

Lemon Glaze, page 682

Cut while hot into bars or squares.

MACAROONS
About Thirty 2-Inch Macaroons

Work with the hands, until well blended:

1 cup Almond Paste, page 729: ½ lb.
⅞ cup sugar

Work in:

3 egg whites
½ teaspoon vanilla

Sift, then add and blend in:

⅓ cup powdered sugar
2 tablespoons cake flour
⅛ teaspoon salt

Force the dough through a pastry bag, well apart, onto parchment paper or the shiny surface of foil. Let cookies stand covered for 2 hours or more. Glaze with:

(Gum Arabic solution, see Glazed
Mint Leaves, page 741)

Preheat oven to 300°.
Bake for about 25 minutes. When cool, store tightly closed.

TEA WAFERS
About 300 Paper-Thin Wafers

Sometimes when a recipe looks as innocuous as this one, it's hard to believe the result can be so outstanding. These tender, crisp squares are literally paper thin.
◗ They must be placed, as soon as cool, in a tightly covered tin. They keep several weeks this way, but we have a hard time hiding them successfully enough to prove it.
Preheat oven to 325°.
Cream:

½ cup butter

Sift, then measure and beat in:

1 cup confectioners' sugar

Beat until smooth. Add:

1 teaspoon vanilla

Sift, then measure:

1¾ cups all-purpose flour

Resift and add to the creamed mixture, alternately with:

½ cup milk

Beat until creamy. Butter a cookie sheet lightly. Chill the sheet. With a spatula, spread some of the mixture over it as thinly and evenly as possible, no more than ¹⁄₁₆ inch thick. You may sprinkle the batter with:

Chopped nut meats or cinnamon
and sugar or grated lemon rind

It is well to press them down a bit so that they will stick. Take a sharp knife and mark off the batter in 1½-inch squares. Bake about 8 to 10 minutes or until light brown. When done, take from oven and, while still hot, quickly cut through the marked squares. Slip a knife under to remove from sheet. The cakes grow crisp and break easily as soon as they cool, so you have to work fast.

ICINGS, TOPPINGS AND GLAZES

Icing some cakes is like gilding lilies. If a cake is sweet and rich enough by itself, there is no need to gold-plate or gold-fill it. But we always make sure that the filling adds contrast in texture and color—and subtlety in flavoring. Many cakes need no icing but are made more attractive with a mere dusting of confectioners' sugar, as

shown here and described in the variation on page 681. Try Old World Chocolate Spice, Sponge, Poppy Seed Custard and Pound Cakes this way.

For easy handling of an iced cake, try this method: lay several strips of sturdy paper on working area. Place cake on top so that ends of paper project on opposite sides. After cake has been iced, lift it by the strip ends onto the serving platter. Now, pull out strips or tear off ends.

ABOUT ICING YIELDS

Yields on icing and filling recipes are given in cups, so you can mix or match your choice in sizes. For Comparative Pan Sizes and Areas, see page 618. We consider the following list a sufficient coverage:

> **For the top and sides of one 9-inch round layer cake, use ¾ cup.**
> **For the tops and sides of two 9-inch round layers, use 1½ cups.**
> **For the tops and sides of three 9-inch round layers, use 2¼ cups.**
> **For the top and sides of a 9½ x 5½ x 3-inch loaf pan, use 1 to 1½ cups.**
> **For a 16 x 5 x 4-inch loaf pan, use 2 to 2½ cups.**
> **For 16 large or 24 small cup-cake tops, use 1 to 1¼ cups.**
> **For glazing a 10 x 15-inch sheet, use 1⅛ cups.**
> **For filling a 10 x 15-inch roll, use 2 cups.**

ABOUT BOILED ICINGS

Just as in candy making, success with boiled icing depends on favorable weather

and the recognition of certain stages in preparing sugar sirup. If the icing is too soft or too hard take the corrective steps suggested below. ♦ Never ruin a good cake with a doubtful icing. ▲ In high altitudes it helps to add to the sugar ⅛ teaspoon glycerin and to allow a longer cooking period.

For boiled icings ♦ the cake must be cooled before the icing is applied. If the cake is uneven, you may want to trim it slightly. In some cases, icing will adhere better and apply more evenly if you reverse the cake bottom-side up. Should the layers tend to slip, skewer them together until the icing starts to set. If you are doing a complicated decorative icing, a stand or turntable is a great help.

If you are at all disclined to make a boiled icing, turn to the many good, foolproof, quick icings, page 677, and to the fillings which can double for soft icings, page 644.

Boiled white icings are based upon a principle known as Italian Meringue—the cooking of egg whites by beating into them ♦ gradually, a hot but not boiling sirup.

♦ Have all utensils absolutely free of grease, and eggs at room temperature. Separate the whites ♦ keeping them absolutely free of yolk and put them in a large bowl. You may start with unbeaten, frothy, or stiffly whipped whites. ♦ Have available a stabilizer: lemon juice, vinegar, cream of tartar or light corn sirup; and also a small quantity of boiling water—in case the icing tends to harden prematurely.

Cook the sirup to 238° to 240°. It will have gone through a coarse thread stage and, when dropped from the edge of a spoon, will pull out into thickish threads. When the thick thread develops a hairlike appendage that curls back on itself, remove the sirup from the heat. Hold the very hot, but not bubbling, sirup above the bowl and let it drop in a slow and gradual thin stream onto the whites as you beat them. In an electric mixer, this is no trick. If you are beating by hand, you may have to steady your bowl by placing it on a folded wet towel.

As the egg whites become cooked by the hot sirup, the beating increases the volume of the icing. By the time all the sirup is poured, you should have a creamy mass, ready for spreading. At this point, add any of the stabilizers—a few drops of lemon juice or vinegar, a pinch of cream of tartar or a teaspoon or two of light corn sirup. These substances help to keep the icing

rom sugaring and becoming gritty. Then
beat in the flavoring of your choice. When
the icing begins to harden at the edges of
the bowl it should be ready to put on the
cake. ◗ Do not scrape the bowl.

If the sirup has not been boiled long
enough and the icing is somewhat runny,
beat it in strong sunlight. If this doesn't
do the trick, place the icing in the top of
double boiler or in a heatproof bowl
over—not in—hot water, until it reaches
the right consistency for spreading. If the
sirup has been overcooked and the icing
tends to harden too soon, a teaspoon or
two of boiling water or a few drops of
lemon juice will restore it. If raisins, nut
meats, zest or other ingredients are to be
added to the icing, wait until the last moment to incorporate them. They contain
oil or acid which will thin the icing.

BOILED WHITE ICING
About 2 Cups
Stir until the sugar is dissolved and bring
to a boil:

    2 cups sugar
    1 cup water

Cover and cook for about 3 minutes, until the steam has washed down any crystals
which may have formed on the sides of the
pan. ◗ Uncover and cook to 238° to 240°.
At that temperature the sirup will spin a
very thin thread on the end of coarser
thread. This final thread will almost disappear, like a self-consuming spider web.
Whip until frothy:

    2 egg whites
    ⅛ teaspoon salt

Add the sirup in a thin stream, whipping
eggs constantly. When these ingredients
are all combined, add:

    (⅛ teaspoon cream of tartar or a few
        drops lemon juice)
    1 teaspoon vanilla

WHITE-MOUNTAIN ICING
About 1¾ Cups
You need an electric mixer for this recipe.
Stir until the sugar is dissolved, then cook
covered until the sirup boils rapidly:

    1 tablespoon white corn sirup
    1 cup sugar
    ⅓ cup water

Beat for about 2 minutes in a small bowl
at high speed:

    1 egg white

Add 3 tablespoons of the boiling sirup.
Let the mixer continue to beat. Meanwhile ◗ cover the remaining sirup and cook
covered about 3 minutes, until the steam
has washed down from the sides of the
pan any crystals which may have formed.
Uncover and cook until the sirup reaches
238° to 240°. Pour the remaining sirup
gradually into the egg mixture, while continuing to beat at high speed. While still
beating, add:

    1 teaspoon vanilla

Now, beat the icing until it is ready to be
spread—4 to 6 minutes.

RAISIN OR NUT ICING
Chop:

    1 cup seeded raisins or ½ cup
        raisins and ½ cup nuts

Add them at the last minute to:

    Boiled White Icing, this page

or, sprinkle raisins and nuts on the cake,
and spread the icing over them.

COCONUT ICING
Coconut enthusiasts would tell you to add
as much shredded or grated fresh or dried
coconut as the icing will hold. One good
way to do this is to press the coconut into
the icing lightly. Or, as illustrated below,

while the icing is still soft you can hold the
cake firmly on the palm of one hand, fill
the palm of the other hand with grated
coconut and cup it to the curve of the
cake, to let it adhere to the icing. Have a
bowl underneath to catch excess coconut,
which can be re-used.
To prepare fresh coconut, see page 523.

ABOUT DECORATIVE ICINGS
There are several types of pastry bags
available in stores. They are made of canvas or plastic. And there is also a rigid
metal "bag" on the market. If you choose
canvas, be sure to use it with the ragged
fabric seam outside. Several metal tips,
with cutouts for making different patterns,
are included in pastry bag kits. The most
useful tips have a rose, star or round cut-
out.

Here's how to make your own decorating bag: Using heavy bond or bakery paper, cut an oblong about 11 x 15 inches.
Fold the oblong diagonally as shown on
the left, page 674. Keep the folded edge
away from you. Make an imaginary line
from the folded edge to the center of the
left-hand point, as indicated in sketch. Roll
the paper from right side into a cornucopia
with a tight point, until you reach the
imaginary line. If the point is tight at the
bottom, the bag will not give way later

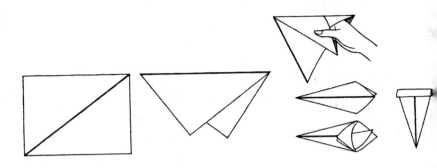

when pressure is applied. Keeping the point firm, continue to roll the remaining paper to form a cornucopia. Turn it with the seam toward you. The seam should lie in a direct line with the point of one of the highest peaks of the bag, so that, by folding the peaks outward and toward you, you stabilize the shape of the cornucopia and the seam. This is shown by the two horizontal bags illustrated. If you could see through the lower one, you would find the hollow cone ready to receive the icing. The upright bag at the end shows the final fold at the top after the bag is filled and closed—with the peaks folded inward. However, before filling, the point must be cut. Press the tip of the paper bag flat and cut off the end. If you plan to use the metal tips from your pastry bag kit, be sure the opening is large enough for the tip to fit, but not so large that the tip will slip through under pressure. If you plan on using the paper point to make its own designs, make three paper cornucopias. Cut one straight across to make a small round opening; clip the others with a single and a double notch, to achieve the star and rose cutouts. These three cuts will make all of the patterns shown in the drawings on page 675, depending upon the angle at which the bags are held and the amount of pressure you give them. You can control the scale of the decoration by the size of the cut.

Now, for the actual decorating. You have a choice of two fine icings—Royal Glaze, page 678, or Decorative Icing, page 673. The Decorative Icing is tastier to eat, but less versatile in handling and does not keep as well as the Glaze. Apply a smooth base coat of either icing to the cake. ♦ Use a spatula dipped in tepid water for a glossy finish. ♦ Allow the base coat to dry. If using several colors for decoration, divide the icing into small bowls and tint with: Vegetable Paste or Liquid Vegetable Coloring. ♦ Keep the bowls covered with a damp cloth. Fill the bag, but never more than to ½ or ⅔ of its capacity. For colors needed in small quantities, make the bags

half size. Use a small spatula to push the icing well down into the point of the bag.

Now, still holding the seam toward you, start to close the bag by pressing the top edges together and roll them inward—until the seam is locked tightly by the roll.

Before beginning any trimming, press the bag to equalize the icing in it and force any unwanted air toward the tip so no bubbles will later destroy the evenness of your decorations. If the bag becomes soft through use or has been unsatisfactorily made, cut a generous piece off the point and press the icing directly into a new bag.

Practice making and filling bags. Then apply the icing on an inverted cake pan. The icing can be scraped off repeatedly and re-used. Make patterns like old-fashioned Spencerian-writing doodles until you have achieved some ease. ♦ Experiment with the feel of the bag, until you can sustain the pressure evenly for linear effects and with a varying force in the formation of borders, petals and leaves. With the bag in your right hand, you may work with as much freedom as in drawing.

Now you are ready to make the designs. It is a great help if the cake can be on a turntable or lazy susan. In any case, when working on the sides, try to have the cake just above elbow level as you work. The responsibility for pressure and movement, as we said before ♦ lies in the right hand. ♦ The left is used only for steadying, see next page. As shown in the drawing, grasp the bag lightly but firmly in the palm of the hand ♦ with the thumb resting on top, leaving the fingers free to press the bag, as the hand and wrist turn to form the designs.

Sometimes, the bag rests in the scissor-like crotch of the first two fingers. At other times it acts as a mere guide, as shown in the second to last figure at the top of the page. As the icing diminishes, refold the bag at the top so that the icing is pushed down to the bottom.

First shown at the bottom, next page, are forms executed from a bag with simply crosscut at the tip—making a small round

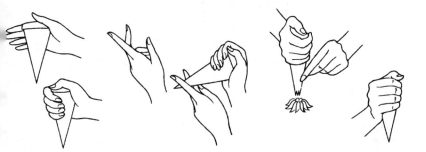

ening. The second group was achieved
th a notch—like a "V;" and the elab-
te composite-type flower needed a dou-
 notch—like a "W." The decoration on
 cake involves the use of all three types
 cuts.

As in any work of art, the concept must
minate the technique. Make a sketch
t of what you would like to do, or have
ır goal clearly in mind. The patterns
own below are conventional ones; try
em—and then develop your own style.
e remember a cake that Alexander Cal-
r did for a mutual friend—complete
th mobile and showing a clarity of line
characteristic of his talent.

It is a great temptation when decorating
kes to overload them. Try out some
mmetrical compositions. Partially bind
 top and sides of the cake with gar-
ıds, heavy in relief but light in values,
1 remember to leave plenty of undeco-
ed space to set them off. At first, you
ıy make some of the more complicated
signs separately on a piece of wax paper
1 let them dry before applying them to
 cake. Use Royal Glaze as an adhesive.

CORATIVE ICING OR
VICE-COOKED ICING

About 1¾ Cups

is is a fine recipe for decorative icing.
will keep without hardening for a long
ıe if closely covered with waxed paper.

Stir until the sugar is dissolved, then boil
without stirring:

    1 cup sugar
    ½ cup water

Meanwhile, whip until stiff but not dry:

    2 egg whites
    ⅛ teaspoon salt

Sift and add very slowly, whipping constantly:

    3 tablespoons sugar

When the sirup begins to fall in heavy
drops from a spoon, add a small quantity
of it to the eggs and sugar; continue beating. Repeat this process, adding the sirup
to the eggs in 4 or 5 parts. If these additions are properly timed, the last of the
sirup will have reached the thread stage.
Beat the icing constantly. Have a pan
ready, partly filled with water. Place it
over heat. The bowl in which the icing is
being made should fit closely into this pan,
so that the bowl will be over—but not in—
the water. When the water in the pan
begins to boil, add to the icing:

    ¼ teaspoon icing powder: equal parts
       of baking powder and tartaric acid

Continue to beat the icing until it sticks to
the sides and the bottom of the bowl and
holds a point. Remove from heat. Place
as much as is required for the decoration,
usually about ⅓, in a small bowl. Cover it
closely with waxed paper. To the remainder, add:

    1 teaspoon or more hot water

to thin it to the right consistency to be spread. Beat it well and spread it on the cake. To decorate, see About Decorative Icings, page 673.

CHOCOLATE COATING OVER BOILED WHITE ICING
About 2¼ Cups
The supreme touch to something that is already good in itself.
Melt:
2 oz. chocolate
Cool and spread with a broad knife or spatula over:
Boiled White Icing, page 673, or
Seven-Minute White Icing, below
This may be done as soon as the white icing is set. Allow several hours for the coating to harden. In summer or moist weather, add to the chocolate before spreading it:
(¼ teaspoon melted paraffin)
This coating is always thin when applied, and hardens more rapidly if refrigerated.
♦ It is not recommended for use in damp hot weather. Transfer the cake to a fresh plate before serving.

SEVEN-MINUTE WHITE ICING
About 2 Cups
A very fluffy, delightful icing, that never fails. Place in the top of a double boiler and beat until thoroughly blended:
2 unbeaten egg whites
1½ cups sugar
5 tablespoons cold water
¼ teaspoon cream of tartar
(1½ teaspoons light corn sirup)
Place these ingredients ♦ over rapidly boil-ing water. Beat them constantly with a rotary beater or with a wire whisk for 7 minutes. Remove icing from heat. Add:
1 teaspoon vanilla
Continue beating until the icing is the right consistency to be spread. You may add to it, at this point:
½ cup chopped nut meats or grated coconut or 1 stick crushed peppermint candy

SEVEN-MINUTE LEMON ICING
Prepare:
Seven-Minute White Icing, above
Use only:
3 tablespoons water
Add:
2 tablespoons lemon juice
¼ teaspoon grated lemon rind

SEVEN-MINUTE ORANGE ICING
About 1½ Cups
Place in the top of a double boiler and beat until thoroughly blended:
1½ cups sugar
2 egg whites
1 tablespoon lemon juice
½ teaspoon orange rind

¼ cup orange juice
Follow the rule for Seven-Minute Whi Icing, this page.

SEVEN-MINUTE SEA-FOAM ICING
Cook:
Seven-Minute White Icing, this page
for 8 minutes. Fold in:
4 teaspoons caramelized sugar I, page 507
Don't forget the vanilla.

FONDANT ICING
About 2 Cu
This is the classic icing for Petits Fours a is tricky to apply evenly.
Prepare:
Basic Fondant, page 727
Just before you are ready to use it, he the fondant ♦ over—not in—boiling wate beating it constantly until it melts. Th add any desired flavoring or colorir Spread at once, as this icing tends to gla over rapidly and then needs reheating. I the icing drip across, from one narr edge of the cake to the other, as shown page 634. Reheat and re-use any icing th falls onto the sheet below. If you have on a very few cakes to frost, place them one a time on a slotted pancake turner or spo held over the pot and ice them individ ally.

LUSCIOUS ORANGE ICING
About 1½ Cu
This icing becomes firm on the outside a remains soft inside.
Stir over heat until dissolved:
1 cup granulated sugar
1 tablespoon white corn sirup
⅛ teaspoon cream of tartar
½ cup water
♦ Cover and cook for about 3 minutes until the steam has washed down any cr tals which may have formed on the sid of the pan. ♦ Uncover and cook to 23 to 240° without stirring. Pour the sirup a slow stream, over:
2 beaten egg whites
Beat for 10 minutes. Add:
¼ cup powdered sugar
1 teaspoon grated orange rind
1 tablespoon orange juice or
¾ teaspoon vanilla
Beat the icing until it is of the right co sistency to be spread.

CARAMEL ICING
About 1½ Cu
Stir until the sugar is dissolved:
2 cups brown sugar
1 cup cream or ½ cup butter
plus ½ cup milk
♦ Cover and cook for about 3 minutes until the steam has washed down any cr tals which may have formed on the sid of the pan. ♦ Uncover and cook witho stirring to 238° to 240°. Add:
3 tablespoons butter

Remove the icing from the heat and cool to 110°. Add:

    1 teaspoon vanilla

Beat the icing until it is thick and creamy. If it becomes too heavy, thin it with a little:

    Cream

until it is of the right consistency to be spread.

Top with:

    (Chopped nuts)

MAPLE SUGAR ICING
About 1½ Cups

Combine and cook, stirring frequently until the mixture reaches a boil:

    2 cups maple sugar
    1 cup cream

Then ♦ cover and cook about 3 minutes or until the steam has washed down any crystals which may have formed on the sides of the pan. ♦ Uncover and cook to 234°. Remove the icing from the heat. Cool to 110°. Beat well until creamy. Fold in:

    ½ cup chopped nut meats, preferably
      butternut meats or slivered
      toasted almonds

CHOCOLATE MARSHMALLOW ICING
About 2 Cups

Stir until the sugar is dissolved:

    1½ cups sugar
    1½ cups water

Then ♦ cover and cook for about 3 minutes or until the steam washes down any crystals which may have formed on the sides of the pan. ♦ Uncover and cook without stirring to 238° to 240°. Remove from the heat and add:

    2 oz. grated chocolate
    1 dozen large marshmallows, cut into
      eighths and steamed until soft

Permit these ingredients to stand until the mixture no longer bubbles. Add:

    ⅛ teaspoon cream of tartar

Whip until stiff but not dry:

    2 egg whites
    ⅛ teaspoon salt

Pour the sirup over the egg whites in a thin stream. Whip constantly, until the icing is of the right consistency to be spread.

CHOCOLATE-FUDGE ICING
About 2 Cups

See:

    Fudge Cockaigne, page 730

Use in all:

    1 cup milk

Beat until the icing is of the right consistency to be spread.

BROWN-SUGAR
MARSHMALLOW ICING
About 1½ Cups

Cut into small cubes:

    12 large marshmallows

Stir over low heat until dissolved:

    2 cups brown sugar
    ½ cup milk

♦ Cover the sirup for about 3 minutes or until the steam has washed down any crystals which may have formed on the sides of the pan. ♦ Uncover and cook without stirring to 238°. Remove from the heat, add the marshmallows and:

    ¼ cup butter

When these ingredients are melted and the icing reaches 110°, beat until it is of a good consistency to be spread. If too heavy, thin with a little:

    Cream

Pour the cream a few drops at a time. Add:

    (½ cup chopped nut meats)

ABOUT QUICK ICINGS

Most quick icings, unless heavy in butter, are best spread on warm cakes. ♦ Those which have eggs in them, if not consumed the day they are made, should be refrigerated. Recipes calling for confectioners' sugar are tastier when ♦ allowed to stand over—not in—hot water for 10 to 15 minutes, to cancel out the raw taste of the cornstarch filler. If you don't mind that taste, you can mix these icings more quickly in a ⅃ blender. ♦ Any delicate flavoring should be added after the icing leaves the heat. A glossy finish can be achieved by dipping your spatula frequently in hot water while icing the cake.

QUICK WHITE ICING
I.
About 1 Cup

Sift:

    2 cups confectioners' sugar

Beat until soft:

    3 tablespoons butter or hot
      whipping cream

Add the sugar gradually. Blend these ingredients until creamy. Add:

    ¼ teaspoon salt
    2 teaspoons vanilla or 2 tablespoons
      dry sherry, rum, coffee, etc.

If the icing is too thin, add:

    Confectioners' sugar

If too thick, add:

    A little cream

See About Quick Icings, above.

II.
About ¾ Cup

Melt and stir in a skillet until golden brown:

    6 tablespoons butter

Blend in gradually:

    1½ cups confectioners' sugar

Add 1 tablespoon at a time, until the icing is of a good consistency to be spread:

    Hot water

Flavor with:

    1 teaspoon vanilla

ROYAL GLAZE, SWISS MERINGUE OR QUICK DECORATIVE ICING
About 2 Cups

This icing will become very hard. To avoid a naturally grayish tone that develops during preparation, add to portions that you want to keep white a slight amount of blue vegetable coloring. Do not use blue in any icing that you plan to color yellow, orange or any other pale, warm tint.
Sift:
> 3½ cups confectioners' sugar

Beat until stiff, but not dry:
> 2 egg whites

Gradually, add the sifted sugar and:
> Juice of a lemon
> 1 to 2 drops glycerin

until it is of a good consistency to be spread. Cover with a damp cloth until ready to use.
To apply as piping or for decorative effects, see About Decorative Icing, page 675. Should you want the icing stiffer, add a little more sifted sugar. To make it softer, thin it ♦ very, very gradually with lemon juice, more egg white or water.

LEMON TOPPING FOR COOKIES OR BARS
About 1½ Cups

Whip until stiff but not dry:
> 2 egg whites
> ⅛ teaspoon salt

Sift and add gradually about:
> 2 to 2½ cups confectioners' sugar
> Grated rind and juice of 1 lemon

QUICK LEMON ICING
About 1 Cup

A very subtle flavor may be obtained by grating the rind of an orange or lemon coarsely, wrapping it in a piece of cheesecloth and wringing the citrus oils onto the sugar before it is blended. Stir the oils into the sugar, and allow it to stand for 15 minutes or more.
Blend well:
> 2 cups confectioners' sugar
> ¼ cup soft butter

Beat in:
> 1 or more teaspoons cream

If you have not treated the sugar as suggested above, add:
> Grated rind and juice of 1 lemon or
> 3 tablespoons liqueur such as apricot or crème de cacao

THREE-MINUTE ICING
Use this soft icing as a substitute for whipped cream or meringue.
Beat until blended, then place in a double boiler over boiling water:
> 2 egg whites
> ½ cup sugar
> ⅛ teaspoon salt
> 2 tablespoons cold water

Beat these ingredients for 3 minutes, or until stiff, with a wire whisk. Remove the icing from the heat. Add:
> 1 teaspoon vanilla or almond extract

Beat the icing well. Spread it over jellied fruit, pies or tarts, cakes, etc., that have been cooled.♦ Top it with:
> Chopped nut meats or coconut

FRENCH ICING
About 1½ Cups

Sift:
> 2 cups confectioners' sugar

Beat until soft:
> ¼ cup butter

Add the sugar gradually. Blend these ingredients until creamy. Beat in:
> 1 egg
> 1 teaspoon vanilla

See About Quick Icings, page 677.

CREAM CHEESE ICING
About ¾ Cup

Sift:
> ¾ cup confectioners' sugar

Work until soft and fluffy:
> 3 oz. cream cheese
> 1½ tablespoons cream or milk

Beat in the sugar gradually. Add:
> 1½ teaspoons grated lemon or orange rind

or:
> 1 teaspoon vanilla and
> ½ teaspoon cinnamon

or:
> A good dash liqueur, lemon or orange juice and grated rind

If you want a pink icing, blend in:
> 1 tablespoon chopped maraschino cherries

QUICK ORANGE ICING
About 1 Cup

Place in the top of a double boiler:
> 2 cups sifted confectioners' sugar
> 1 tablespoon melted butter
> 1 tablespoon grated orange rind
> ¼ cup orange juice or 3 tablespoons orange juice and 1 tablespoon lemon juice

Place these ingredients ♦ over—not in—hot water for 10 minutes. Beat the icing until cool and of a good consistency to be spread. See About Quick Icings, page 677.

BUTTERSCOTCH ICING
About 1¼ Cups

Combine, stir and heat in a double boiler until smooth:
> ¼ cup butter
> ½ cup brown sugar
> ⅛ teaspoon salt
> ⅓ cup rich or evaporated milk

Cool this slightly. Beat in, to make of a good consistency to be spread:
> 2 cups, more or less, of confectioners' sugar

You may add:
> ½ teaspoon vanilla or 1 teaspoon rum
> ½ cup chopped nut meats

CHOCOLATE BUTTER ICING
About 1½ Cups

This icing can be used for decorating.

elt over very low heat:
    2 to 3 oz. chocolate
Melt in it:
    2 teaspoons to 3 tablespoons butter
Remove these ingredients from the heat
and add:
    **¼ cup hot water, cream or coffee, or
        an egg**
    ⅛ teaspoon salt
Add gradually about:
    2 cups sifted confectioners' sugar
    1 teaspoon vanilla
You may not need quite all the sugar.

QUICK BROWN-SUGAR ICING
About ¾ Cup
A quick, but rather coarse icing.
Combine, stir and cook slowly to the boil-
ing point:
    1½ cups brown sugar
    5 tablespoons cream
    2 teaspoons butter
    ⅛ teaspoon salt
Remove from the heat. Cool slightly, add:
    ½ teaspoon vanilla
Beat the icing until it can be spread.
You may add:
    ½ cup chopped nut meats

CHOCOLATE CREAM CHEESE ICING
About 2 Cups
Melt:
    3 oz. chocolate
Soften:
    3 oz. cream cheese
in:
    ¼ cup milk
Add gradually:
    4 cups confectioners' sugar
    ½ teaspoon salt
Combine this mixture with the melted
chocolate and beat until smooth and ready
to be spread.

EUROPEAN CHOCOLATE ICING
About ⅔ Cup
A homesick letter from an American bride
made us realize that familiar tastes abroad
have as foreign an accent as English words
do when spoken by other nationals. Where
to get bitter chocolate for icing, to make
it taste as she thought it should? Chef
James Gregory made her feel almost at
home with this semi-sweet solution.
Melt in a double boiler ♦ over—not in—
hot water:
    1 tablespoon butter
    4 oz. semi-sweet chocolate
When melted, add and beat well:
    6 tablespoons whipping cream
Sift and add, until the desired sweetness is
reached and the icing is smooth, about
    1½ cups confectioners' sugar
    1 teaspoon vanilla
Spread while warm.

EASY CHOCOLATE ICING
About 1¾ Cups
Melt in a double boiler ♦ over—not in—

hot water:
    3 oz. chocolate
    2 tablespoons butter
Combine in a blender or mixer with:
    2¾ cups sifted confectioners' sugar
    ½ teaspoon salt
    1 teaspoon vanilla
    6 tablespoons light cream
Combine with the butter and chocolate
mixture in the double boiler and heat for
10 minutes to destroy the uncooked taste
of the cornstarch in the confectioners'
sugar. Add:
    1 teaspoon vanilla
If stiff, blend in:
    1 tablespoon cream
before spreading.

QUICK CHOCOLATE ICING
Melt over hot water:
        **Sweet chocolate bars or
        chocolate peppermints**
Cool slightly, then spread the icing. If the
chocolate seems stiff, beat in a little:
        Cream
and to perfect the flavor, add:
        Vanilla

COFFEE OR MOCHA ICING
About 1¼ Cups
Sift:
    1⅔ cups confectioners' sugar
    1 to 2 tablespoons cocoa
Beat until soft:
    ¼ to ½ cup butter
Add the sugar gradually. Blend these in-
gredients until creamy. Add:
    ⅛ teaspoon salt
    3 tablespoons strong, hot coffee
Beat for 2 minutes.
When the icing is cool, add:
    1 teaspoon vanilla or rum
Permit it to stand for 5 minutes. Beat well
and spread.

QUICK MAPLE ICING
About 1 Cup
Sift:
    2 cups confectioners' sugar
Add and blend:
    1 tablespoon butter
    ¼ teaspoon salt
    ½ teaspoon vanilla
Beat in, to make of a good consistency to
be spread:
        Maple sirup
        (½ cup toasted coconut)

QUICK HONEY
PEANUT-BUTTER ICING
This appeals mainly to the small fry.
Combine and bring to a boil:
    2 tablespoons shortening
    2 tablespoons butter
    ¼ cup honey
Remove from heat and add:
    ½ cup coarsely ground peanuts
Stir until well blended. Spread on a warm

cake. Toast it very lightly under a broiler at medium heat. Watch it carefully.

APRICOT OR PINEAPPLE ICING
About 1 Cup
This is a soft icing. Stir until smooth:
    ½ cup sweetened, cooked dried
        apricot pulp or partly drained
        pineapple, crushed
with:
    1½-2 cups sifted confectioners' sugar
Beat in:
    1-3 tablespoons soft butter
    ½ tablespoon lemon juice
Add more confectioners' sugar, if needed.

PINEAPPLE ICING
About 1½ Cups
Sift:
    2 cups confectioners' sugar
Beat until soft:
    ¼ cup butter
Add the sugar gradually. Blend until creamy. Beat in:
    1 teaspoon lemon juice
    ⅛ teaspoon salt
    ½ teaspoon vanilla
    ½ cup chopped, drained pineapple
Permit to stand for 5 minutes. Beat the icing until creamy. Add more sugar, if necessary.

BANANA ICING
About 1 Cup
Put soft bananas through a ricer, until you have:
    ½ cup banana pulp
Sift:
    2 cups confectioners' sugar
Stir the sugar into the pulp until smooth. Beat in:
    ⅛ teaspoon salt
    1 teaspoon lemon juice
    ½ teaspoon vanilla
Add more confectioners' sugar, if needed.

BAKED ICING
Glaze for an 8 x 8-Inch Cake
This icing is baked at the same time as the cake. Use it on a thin cake only, one that will require 25 minutes of baking or less—such as spice, ginger or coffee cake.
Preheat oven to 375°.
Sift:
    ½ cup brown sugar
Whip until stiff but not dry:
    1 egg white
    ⅛ teaspoon salt
Fold in the sugar or beat it in slowly. Spread the icing on the cake. Sprinkle it with:
    ¼ cup broken nut meats
For an exciting new taste, fold in:
    (2 tablespoons cocoa)
Bake the cake as indicated in the recipe.

BROILED ICING
For an 8 x 8-inch Ca
Combine and spread on a cake, coffee ca or cookies, while they are warm, a mixtu of:
    3 tablespoons melted butter
    ⅔ cup brown sugar
    1 to 2 tablespoons cream
    ⅛ teaspoon salt
    ½ cup shredded coconut
        or other nut meats
Place the cake 3 inches below a broil with the heat turned low. Broil the ici until it bubbles all over the surface, b see that it does not burn.

QUICK-DIPPING ICINGS
Dip tops and sides of small cakes in icin see illustration, page 681, then right the on a cake rack to drip. Catch the dri pings on a pan and use them to ice oth cakes.

I.   **About 1½ Cu**
Stir over heat, then boil for 1 minute:
    1 cup sugar
    ½ cup butter
    ½ cup milk
Cool slightly. Add:
    1¼ cups sifted confectioners' sugar
    ½ teaspoon salt
    ½ teaspoon vanilla
        A few drops of vegetable coloring
    (¼ teaspoon almond flavor)

II.   **About 1½ Cu**
Place over hot water and stir until smoot
    3 oz. cut-up chocolate
    3 tablespoons butter
Pour:
    5 tablespoons scalding hot milk
over:
    2 cups sifted confectioners' sugar
    ¼ teaspoon salt
When dissolved, add the chocolate mix ture and:
    1 teaspoon vanilla
Beat until of the right consistency to b dipped or spread.

ABOUT ICING SMALL CAKES AND COOKIES

Here are a number of ways to ice and ga nish small cakes quickly. Some are show sketched. **I.** Place on a hot cup cake small piece of semi-sweet or sweet choc late. Spread it as it melts. **II.** Just befor removing cookies from the oven, put o each one a mint-flavored chocolate cand wafer and return the cookie sheet to th oven until the wafer melts. **III.** To ice cu cakes or leaf cookies, dip them rapidly i a dipping icing. Swirl the cakes as show The cookies are most easily iced if impale on a skewer. **IV.** For cup cakes, sift confec tioners' sugar over them through a strainer page 681.

QUICK LACE TOPPING

A good, quick decorative effect can be gained on any cake with a slightly rough top, see sketch, page 672. Place a paper doily or monogrammed cut paper pattern on top of the cake and fill the interstices with sugar. Be sure that the sugar, confectioners' or colored, is dusted lavishly over the doily and filters down into all the voids. Lift the doily or pattern off gingerly, with a straight upward motion, and you will find a clearly marked lacy design on your cake top. Shake into a bowl any surplus sugar left on the pattern. Reserve it for future use. You may also follow this principle in applying finely grated semisweet chocolate on an iced cake.

HARD-SAUCE TOPPING

Soften slightly, then apply a thin layer of brandied:

Hard sauce, page 714

to any cooled cake or coffee cake.

ABOUT MERINGUE TOPPINGS

Pie and pudding meringues are delicate affairs that ♦ are best made and added to pastry shortly before serving. Since meringue is beaten constantly until the moment to spread it, have the ♦ oven preheated to between 325° and 350°. Lower heat will dry the meringue. Higher heat will cause egg protein to shrink or shrivel. The two toppings below differ greatly in volume, texture and method. The first is cooked on the pie or dessert itself. The second is cooked separately and beaten until cool before applying; it may or may not be browned later. As volume in the egg white is essential, please follow these suggestions: ♦ Have the utensils absolutely free of grease, with ♦ egg whites at about 75° and ♦ without a trace of yolk. Add sugar, as specified in each recipe. Excess sugar, beaten into the meringue, will cause it to be gummy and to "bead" out. If you prefer a topping sweeter than these for which the recipe is given, you may glaze the surface, after the meringue is in place, by sprinkling it with additional sugar. This also makes the meringue easier to cut cleanly when serving. You may also top it with a sprinkling of coconut or slivered almonds before baking.

Meringue toppings for small tarts may be baked on foil and slipped onto a cooked or fresh pie filling just before serving. For a large pie, spread it lightly from the edges toward the center of the pie. ♦ Should it not adhere well to the edges at all points, it will pull away during the baking. ♦ To avoid shrinkage, cool meringues in a warm place, away from drafts.

MERINGUE TOPPING

I.   **For a 9-Inch Pie**

Preheat oven to 325° to 350°.

Whip until they are frothy:

2 egg whites

Add:

¼ teaspoon cream of tartar

Whip them until they are ♦ stiff, but not dry; until they stand in peaks that lean over slightly when the beater is removed. Beat in, ½ teaspoon at a time:

3 tablespoons sugar or
4 tablespoons powdered sugar

♦ Do not overbeat. Beat in:

½ teaspoon vanilla

Bake 10 to 15 minutes, depending on the thickness of the meringue.

II.   **About 1¼ Cups**

This classic Italian meringue does not require baking, because the egg whites are already cooked by the hot sirup. You may want to brown it lightly in a 350° oven. This is not as stiff a meringue as the preceding one.

Heat in a heavy pan and stir until dissolved:

½ cup water
¼ teaspoon cream of tartar
1 cup sugar

When the sirup is boiling ♦ cover and cook for about 3 minutes or until the steam has washed down any crystals which may have formed on the sides of the pan. ♦ Uncover and cook to 238° to 240°. Pour the sirup ♦ very gradually onto:

3 well-beaten egg whites

beating constantly, until this frosting meringue is cool and ready to be spread on the pie filling or pudding.

TOPPINGS OR STREUSEL FOR COFFEE CAKES, PIES AND SWEET ROLLS, APPLIED BEFORE BAKING

I. Streusel   **For an 8 x 8-Inch Cake**

Prepare:

Any Coffee Cake Dough, pages 570-572

After spreading it with butter, combine:

2 tablespoons all-purpose flour
2 tablespoons butter
5 tablespoons sugar

Blend these ingredients until they crumble. Add:

½ teaspoon cinnamon

Sprinkle the crumbs over the cake and bake as directed.
Add:

(¼ to ½ cup chopped nuts)

II. Streusel

For 9-Inch Pie

Frequently called Danish or Swedish and much like the topping for Apple Paradise. This is a crumb topping usually served in place of a top crust on apple or tart fruit pie, but which does well for coffee cakes. Melt:

6 tablespoons butter

Stir in and brown lightly:

1 cup fine dry cake crumbs
¾ teaspoon cinnamon

III. Honey Glaze

For a 9 x 13-Inch Cake

Cream:

½ cup sugar
¼ cup butter

Blend in:

1 unbeaten egg white

Add:

¼ cup honey
½ cup crushed nut meats
½ teaspoon cardamon

Spread these ingredients on coffee cakes that are ready to be baked.

IV. Honey-Bee Glaze

For Two 9-Inch Square Cakes

Stir and bring to the boiling point over low heat:

½ cup sugar
¼ cup milk
¼ cup butter
¼ cup honey
½ cup crushed nut meats

Spread these ingredients on coffee cakes that are ready to be baked.

V. Caramel-Roll Topping

Enough for 6 Rolls

This heavy topping is put in the bottom of the pan and when the cake or rolls are reversed it becomes the topping.
Melt:

¼ cup butter

Stir in until dissolved:

½ cup sugar
3 tablespoons packed brown sugar
1 to 2 teaspoons cinnamon
½ teaspoon chopped lemon rind
3 tablespoons chopped nuts

Add:

(2 tablespoons finely chopped citron)

GLAZES APPLIED BEFORE OR DURING BAKING

I. To give color to yeast dough or pastry brush with:

Milk or butter or a combination of milk and sugar

II. French Egg Wash or Dorure

To give color and gloss to yeast dough or pastry, brush with:

1 egg yolk diluted with
1 to 2 tablespoons water or milk

III. To sparkle a glaze, sprinkle before baking with:

Granulated sugar

IV. For a clear glaze, just before the pastry has finished baking, whisk with brush dipped in:

¼ cup sugar

dissolved in:

¼ cup water or hot strong coffee
(½ teaspoon cinnamon)

and return to oven.

V. To give yeast dough or pastry a glow and flavor, brush with sweetened fruit juice and lemon rind.

VI. To gloss and harden crust of yeast dough, brush with a cornstarch and water glaze, several times during the baking.

VII. Broiled Icing, page 680.

VIII. Baked Icing, page 680.

GLAZES APPLIED AFTER BAKING

Just after these glazes are applied, decorate with:

Whole or half nuts, cherries, pineapple bits and citron

When it dries, the glaze will hold the decorations in place on cakes and sweet breads.

I. Milk Glaze

This can be used as a substitute on small cakes similar to petits fours, which are classically iced with fondant.
Sift:

½ cup confectioners' sugar

Add:

2 teaspoons hot milk
¼ teaspoon vanilla

II. ★ Lemon Glaze

About ½ Cup

No heating is necessary. Spread it right on the warm cakes or Christmas cookies. It is of a fine consistency for imbedding decorative nuts and fruits. Enough glaze to cover four 8 x 8-inch cakes.
Mix or ⅄ blend:

1¼ cups confectioners' sugar

with:

¼ cup lemon, orange or lime juice

1 teaspoon vanilla
Mix until smooth.

III. ↗ Blender-Whipped Cheese Topping
About ⅓ Cup
Soften:
    3 oz. cream cheese
with:
    1 tablespoon cream
    ½ teaspoon vanilla
Blend in and cream well:
    3 tablespoons confectioners' sugar

IV. Liqueur Glaze
About ⅔ Cup
Combine and mix well:
    2 cups sifted confectioners' sugar
    3 tablespoons liqueur
    2 tablespoons melted butter
Spread over cake or cookies.

V. Glaze for Breads
To make a crisp crust, brush with water
immediately when taken from oven.

VI. Glaze for Puff Paste
For a crisp crust, brush with a light sugar
sirup immediately when taken from oven.

GLAZES FOR FRUIT PIES, TARTS AND COFFEE CAKES
I. Apricot Glaze
For already baked pastries, the following
recipe is easy to use:
    Sweetened, cooked dried apricot
    pulp or preserves or melted currant,
    quince or apple jelly
However, we like to have on hand the
glaze below, which keeps well if refriger-
ated.
Prepare:
    3 cups strained apricots,
    peaches or raspberries
Cook until the sugar is dissolved with:
    1 cup sugar
    1 cup light corn sirup
While the mixture is still warm, glaze the
cooled pastry.

II. Fruit Glaze
Sufficient for Glazing 3 Cups of Berries or Fruit
Boil to the jelly stage, page 774, then
strain these ingredients:
    ¼ cup water
    1 cup sugar
    1 cup cleaned fruit
    2 medium-sized chopped apples
    A little red vegetable coloring
    (1 tablespoon butter)
The butter will keep the glaze supple.
Cool. When the jelly is about to set, pour

it or spread it over the fruit to be glazed.

III. Strawberry Glaze
Sufficient for a 9-Inch Pie Shell or Six 2½-Inch Tarts
Hull and crush:
    3 cups strawberries
Strain them first through a ricer, then
through a fine sieve. Add to the juice:
    ⅓ cup sugar
    1 tablespoon lemon juice
    1 tablespoon cornstarch
    A little red vegetable coloring
Cook and stir these ingredients over low
heat until thick and transparent. Cool.
Spread over the fruit to be glazed.

IV. Thickened Fruit Glaze
Glaze may also be made of canned fruit
sirups or jellies. Boil the sirup until thick.
To each ½ cup, add:
    1 teaspoon cornstarch or arrowroot
blended with:
    1 tablespoon sugar
The cornstarch will give a smooth glaze,
the arrowroot a more transparent and
stickier one.

CLEAR CARAMEL GLAZE
About 1 Cup
This brittle topping is used on many European cakes, especially the famous Dobos
or Drum Torte, page 638.
Place in a large, heavy skillet over low
heat:
    1 cup sugar
Cook and stir with a wooden spoon, using
the same kind of gentle motion you use for
scrambling eggs. ◆ Keep agitating the pan
as this scorches very easily. When the
sugar bubbles, remove the pan from the
heat. The glaze should be clear and light
brown and smooth and have reached a
temperature of about 310°. Spread it at
once with a hot spatula. ◆ If you work
quickly enough, you may score it in patterns for easier cutting later. Use a knife
dipped in cold water.

FRESH FLOWERS FOR CAKES
Cake decorations can be made from flowers, if you are sure they were ◆ not
sprayed. Place on the cake just before it is
served. Choose delicately colored open-
petaled flowers like hollyhocks. Remove
the stamens. Cut off all but ¾ inch of the
stem. Arrange the flowers on an iced cake.
Place a small candle in the center of each
one. A hemerocallis wreath is good for
daytime decorations, but closes at night.
Field daisies and African daisies hold up
well. ◆ Beware of flowers like lilies of the
valley or Star of Bethlehem, which have
poisonous properties.

DESSERTS

A family we know had a cook who always urged the children to eat sparingly of the main course, so as to leave a little room for the "hereafter." Desserts can indeed be heavenly. They also give the hostess a chance to build a focal point for a buffet, produce a startling soufflé, or confect an attractively garnished individual plate. See also Filled Cakes, page 639, and Torten that serve as complete desserts, page 637.

ABOUT CUSTARDS

Custard puddings, sauces and fillings accompany the seven ages of man in sickness and in health. Rarely anywhere, however, are these delicacies prepared in ways that enhance their simple charm. To do so, remember some simple precautions. ♦ When pasteurized milk is used in making custards, it is not necessary to scald it; but scalding does shorten the cooking time. If scalded, cool the milk enough afterward to keep the eggs, when added, from curdling. For a baked custard, simply whip the ingredients together well, pour them into custard cups, set them on a rack or on a folded towel in a pan in which you have poured an inch of hot but not boiling water. Bake them at low heat, around 325°, for about 20 to 30 minutes. If you have used homogenized milk, allow about 10 minutes longer. To test for doneness, insert a knife ♦ near the edge of the cup. ♦ If the blade comes out clean, the custard will be solid all the way through when cooled. There is sufficient stored heat in the cups to finish the cooking process. Remove the custards from the pan and cool on a rack. ♦ However, should you test the custard at the center and find it as well done as at the edge, set the custard cups in ice water at once to arrest further cooking.

For softer top-of-the-stove custards and sauces, use a double boiler, cooking ♦ over —not in—hot water. Too high heat will toughen and shrink the albumen in the eggs and keep it from holding the liquid in suspension as it should. Beat the eggs well. Add about ¼ of a cup of the hot liquid to them and then slowly add the rest of it, stirring constantly. Cook until the custard is thick enough to coat a spoon. Remove pan from heat. Strain. Then continue stirring to release steam. If the steam is allowed to condense it may make the custard watery. If you suspect that the custard has become too hot, turn it into a chilled dish and whisk it quickly or put it in the blender at high speed to cool it rapidly. ♦ Always store custards or custard-based dishes like pies and éclairs in a very cool or refrigerated place as they are highly susceptible to bacterial activity although they may give no evidence of spoilage.

CUSTARD
About 2½ Cups
♦ This artless confection, often referred to as "boiled" custard, is badly nicknamed as it must not be permitted to boil at any time. ♦ Very slow cooking will help deter curdling.
Beat slightly:
   3 or 4 egg yolks
Add:
   ¼ cup sugar
   ⅛ teaspoon salt
Scald and stir in slowly in a double boiler:
   2 cups milk
Place the custard ♦ over—not in—hot water. Stir it constantly until it begins to thicken. Cool. Add:
   1 teaspoon vanilla, rum or dry sherry,
      or a little grated lemon rind
Chill thoroughly. This is not as firm as baked custard because stirring disturbs the thickening. It is really more like a custard sauce.

⅄ BAKED OR CUP CUSTARD
5 Servings
Preheat oven to 300° to 325°.
   Delicious as is, but better as a summer brunch served over unsweetened dry cereal with fresh berries, or as a company dessert molded over cored pear halves, fresh or stewed, sprinkled with rum, the centers filled with a stewed pitted prune dusted in cinnamon. If you want to unmold the custard, use the larger quantity of egg.
Blend together:
   2 cups pasteurized milk
   ¼ to ½ cup sugar or ⅓ cup honey
   ⅛ teaspoon salt
Should the milk be unpasteurized, be sure to see About Custards, above. Add and beat well:
   2 to 3 beaten whole eggs or 4 egg yolks
The greater the proportion of yolk, the tenderer the custard will be. You may even use 2 egg whites to 1 yolk for a quite stiff custard.
Add:
   ½ to 1 teaspoon vanilla
   (⅛ teaspoon nutmeg)
When this is all well beaten, pour it into a baker or into individual custard cups. Place the molds in a pan of water in the oven for an hour or more. To test, see About Custards. Chill and serve with:
   Caramel Sirup, page 738, fruit
   juice, or
   Maple Sirup Sauce, page 712

⅄ COFFEE CHOCOLATE CUSTARD
4 Servings

A sophisticated dessert easily made in a blender.

Put in blender:

    ½ to 1 oz. finely cut-up chocolate

Pour over it:

    1 cup strong, hot coffee

Add:

    1 cup milk
    4 to 6 tablespoons sugar
    ⅛ teaspoon salt
    2 whole eggs or 3 egg yolks

Blend this mixture. To bake, see About Custards, page 684.

CARAMELIZED CUSTARD, SPANISH CREAM OR CRÈME CARAMEL
4 to 5 Servings

Caramelize I:

    ½ cup sugar, page 507

Place it in a 7-inch ring mold or custard cups. Turn the mold to permit the caramel to spread evenly, then push the coating with a wooden spoon until the entire base of the dish is covered. At this point the sirup should be, and should remain, thick if you have caramelized the sugar properly.

Use the recipe for:

    Cup Custard, page 684

Bake as directed. Invert it when cold onto a platter. To be sure the caramel comes out intact, dip the mold to the depth of the caramel quickly in hot water, as you would in releasing a gelatin. Now the center may be filled with:

    Whipped cream

Sprinkle the top with:

    Shredded toasted almonds or
    crushed nut brittle

CARAMEL CUSTARD

Prepare:

    Cup Custard, page 684

omitting the sugar. Mix with it:

    ½ cup Caramelized Sugar I, page 507

To bake, see About Custards, page 684.

RICH CUSTARD
6 Servings

Mix in the top of a double boiler:

    ¾ cup sugar
    2 tablespoons cornstarch
    ⅛ teaspoon salt

Gradually stir in:

    2 cups milk and cream, mixed

Cook covered ♦ over hot water for 8 minutes without stirring. Uncover and cook for about 10 minutes more. Add:

    4 well-beaten egg yolks
    2 tablespoons butter

Cook and stir these ingredients over hot water for 2 minutes longer. Cool, stirring occasionally to release steam, then add:

    1½ teaspoons vanilla

Fold in:

    1 cup whipped cream

Chill the custard. It will have the consistency of a heavy whipped cream. It is divine with:

    Dampfnudeln, page 608, or
    Drained Tutti Frutti, page 780

FLOATING ISLAND
I.
4 Servings

This is the delicate French dessert called **Oeufs à la Neige** or **Eggs in Snow.**

Whip until stiff:

    3 egg whites

Beat in gradually:

    ¼ cup sugar

Scald:

    2 cups milk

Drop the meringue mixture from a tablespoon in rounds onto the milk. Poach them gently without letting the milk boil, for about 4 minutes, turning them once. Lift them out carefully with a skimmer onto a towel. Use the milk to make:

    Custard, page 684

Cool the custard. Place the meringues on top. Chill before serving.

II.
4 Servings

This American dessert is a great favorite—our children call it "eating clouds."

Preheat oven to 500°.

Prepare:

    Custard, page 684

Flavor it with:

    Lemon rind

Pour it in a baking dish.

Whip until stiff:

    3 egg whites

Add very slowly, whipping constantly:

    3 tablespoons sugar
    ½ teaspoon vanilla or a few drops
    almond extract

Heap the egg whites on the custard. Place the custard dish in a pan of ice water and put the whole into the hot oven just long enough to brown the tips of the meringue.

CRÈME BRULÉE
6 Servings

A rich French custard—famous for its hard, caramelized sugar glaze.

Heat in a double boiler until hot:

    2 cups whipping or even heavier cream

Pour it slowly over:

    4 well-beaten eggs

Beat constantly while pouring. Return the mixture to the double boiler. Stir in:

    (2 tablespoons sugar)

Heat until the eggs thicken and the custard coats a spoon heavily. Place the mixture in a greased baking dish or custard cups. Some people insist this custard should be made and chilled the day before it is caramelized. In any case, chill it well. **Cover** the custard with:

¼- to ⅛-inch layer of lump-free
light-brown sugar or maple sugar

Place the custard cups or dish in a shallow
pan. If the custard has been chilled for
12 hours, put it in a cold oven. Turn the
heat to 250° and heat until the sugar is
caramelized. If the custard has been
chilled a shorter time, put the dish in a
shallow pan. Surround it with ice. Place
it under a hot broiler just long enough to
let the sugar form a crust. Keep the oven
door open and regularly rotate the dish to
even the heating. While the sugar caramelizes, watch carefully as it may scorch.
Serve at once. A delicate garnish is:

A compote of greengage plums
and apricots

BRULÉE CRUSTS

This is an assembly job, rather than a
welded one. Making the brulée crusts
separately relieves tension and assures a
professional look. Cut a piece of aluminum
foil the exact size of the dish in which you
want to serve the brulée.
Grease the foil on one side with:

Butter

Pat onto the buttered side in a firm, lacy
disk pattern about ¼-inch thick:

Brown sugar

Put the sugar-covered foil on a cookie
sheet. ◗ At this point the operation needs
your entire attention. Put the cookie sheet
under broiler heat until the sugar is caramelized or glazed. Remove it from the
oven and reverse the foil, with sugar disks,
onto a cake rack to cool. When slightly
cooled, the sugar topping should peel off
the foil like a large praline. You may repeat this process and freeze a quantity of
these large or small disks. Place them on
the custard just the moment before serving, so they do not disintegrate.

FRUIT JUICE CUSTARD

So rich a dessert, this should serve 4.
Mix:

4 beaten egg yolks
⅔ cup sugar
1 cup fruit juice

We like a combination of canned pineapple and fresh orange juice. Bake as directed for Cup Custard, page 684.

ZABAGLIONE OR SABAYON
6 Servings

Very similar to Weinschaum, below, but
somewhat sweeter. It is served as sauce,
dessert or beverage. Marsala is the classic
wine, but Madeira or sherry are also
used. If for a sauce, you might even try a
good dry white wine and a little Cointreau.
For Sabayon Sauce, which can be made in
advance and held, see page 710. Beat until very light:

8 egg yolks
1 cup confectioners' sugar

Place these ingredients in the top of a
double boiler ◗ over—not in—boiling water. ◗ Do not permit the water to touch
the bottom of the double boiler top. Beat
the custard constantly with a wire beater.
When foamy, add gradually:

½ cup dry Marsala, Madeira or sherry

Continue to beat the custard until it doubles in bulk and begins to thicken. Remove
it from the heat. Sometimes the egg
whites are omitted. If you want a fluffier
result, whip until stiff:

8 egg whites

Fold in the custard. Serve the Zabaglione
at once in sherbet glasses.

WINE CUSTARD OR WEINSCHAUM
6 Servings

Place in the top of a double boiler ◗ over
—not into—boiling water:

2 cups dry white wine
½ cup water

Add:

4 unbeaten eggs
½ cup sugar

Beat these ingredients vigorously with a
wire whisk. Cook the custard until it
thickens. Beat it constantly. Serve it hot
or cold.

ORANGE CUSTARD WITH
MERINGUE
6 Servings

Preheat oven to 325°.
Grate the rind of:

2 oranges

into:

⅛ cup sugar

Peel:

6 oranges

Separate the sections and remove the membrane, see page 115. Place sections in a
baking dish. Scald:

3 cups milk

Pour over:

3 beaten egg yolks

Beat these ingredients until well blended.
Combine the sugar with:

2 tablespoons cornstarch
¼ teaspoon salt

Stir this mixture into the custard. Cook
and stir in a double boiler until thick, for
about 7 minutes. Cool. Pour over the
oranges. Top the custard with a Meringue,
page 681. Bake for about 15 minutes.
Serve chilled.

ABOUT SPONGE CUSTARDS

From a fan came a drawing of an elaborate
mold and the question, "Can you tell me
how my great-aunt used to make a dessert
that had a spongy bottom and a clear quivery top?" Her objective must have been a
sponge custard baked and unmolded. This

batter holds together when put into the baker, but magically separates while cooking. If you serve it in the baker, the sponge will form a decorative top. If you prefer a meringue-like quality rather than a spongy one, reserve ¼ cup sugar to beat slowly into the stiff egg whites before folding them into the egg-yolk mixture.

PINEAPPLE SPONGE CUSTARD
4 Servings

Please read About Sponge Custards, above. Preheat oven to 350°.
Combine and stir in the order given:

    5 tablespoons sugar
    3 tablespoons all-purpose flour
    ½ cup pineapple sirup
    1 teaspoon grated lemon rind
    2 tablespoons lemon juice
    2 or 3 beaten egg yolks
    ½ cup milk
    1½ tablespoons melted butter

Whip until stiff, then fold in:

    2 or 3 egg whites

Place in the bottom of a 7-inch baking dish or in four 3½-inch individual ones:

    1¼ to 1½ cups coarsely cut
        drained pineapple

Pour the custard mixture over the fruit. Place the dishes in a pan in 1 inch of hot water. Bake the custard for about 1 hour for the dish and 45 minutes for the cups. Serve hot or cold.

ORANGE OR LEMON SPONGE CUSTARD
4 to 6 Servings

Preheat oven to 350°.
Please read About Sponge Custards, page 686.
Cream:

    ¾ cup sugar
    1½ tablespoons butter
    1 tablespoon grated orange rind or
        2 teaspoons lemon rind

Add and beat well:

    2 or 3 egg yolks

Stir in:

    3 tablespoons all-purpose flour

alternately with:

    ⅛ cup orange juice, or
    ¼ cup lemon juice
    1 cup milk

Beat until stiff ♦ but not dry:

    2 or 3 egg whites

Fold them into the yolk mixture. Place the batter in buttered custard cups, or in a 7-inch ovenproof dish, set in a pan filled with 1 inch of hot water. Bake for about 45 minutes for the cups and about 1 hour for the baking dish, or until set. Serve hot or ice cold with:

    (Thick cream or Raspberry Sauce)

CHOCOLATE CUSTARD OR POTS-DE-CRÈME

Some custard recipes are perfect for use in added antique pots-de-crème. Although the classic procedure is baking, the consistency is easier to control by this top-of-the-stove method.

I.   **6 Servings**

Combine and cook over very low heat:

    2 cups milk or cream or half milk
        and half cream
    5 to 8 oz. grated, best quality
        sweet chocolate
    (2 tablespoons sugar)

Cook and stir these ingredients until they are blended and the milk is scalded. Remove from heat. Beat into them:

    6 lightly-beaten egg yolks
    1 teaspoon vanilla or grated rind
        of 1 orange

Strain the custard. Pour into custard cups. Chill well.

II. Pots-de-Crème Café

            4 Servings

Cook and serve as above, using:

    ½ cup heavy cream
    ½ cup sugar
    1 tablespoon instant coffee
    6 egg yolks
    1 tablespoon brandy

RUM CHOCOLATE MOUSSE
8 to 10 Servings

A phenomenally smooth, rich dessert that is quickly assembled. A specialty of our friend Chef Pierre Adrian.
Cook over very low heat until dissolved but not colored brown:

    ¼ cup sugar
    2 to 4 tablespoons rum

Melt in a double boiler:

    ¼ lb. semi-sweet or sweet chocolate

When the chocolate is melted, stir in:

    2 to 3 tablespoons whipping cream

Add the sirup to the melted chocolate and stir until smooth. When the mixture is cool but not chilled, fold into it:

    2 stiffly beaten egg whites

and then fold this combination very gently into:

    2 cups whipped cream

Chill in sherbet glasses at least 2 hours before serving.

FRENCH CHOCOLATE MOUSSE
6 Servings

Stir and scald in a saucepan over low heat:

    2 cups milk
    ¼ cup sugar
    3 oz. grated sweet chocolate

Pour part of these ingredients over:

    4 beaten egg yolks

Return the sauce to the pan. Stir the custard constantly over low heat until it thickens. Strain it. Cool by placing the pan in cold water. In a separate bowl, whip until stiff:

    ¾ cup heavy cream

Add:

1 teaspoon vanilla

Fold the cold custard into the whipped cream mixture until it is well blended. Fill custard cups with the pudding. Chill thoroughly before serving.

CHESTNUT MOUND OR MONT BLANC

6 Servings

Boil in water for 8 minutes:

2 lbs. chestnuts

Remove shells. Cook the hulled nuts until mealy in a double boiler over hot water in:

1 quart milk

Drain, discard milk, then cook in a sugar sirup made of:

1 cup water
1 cup sugar

until the sirup is reduced. Add:

(¼ cup almond paste)

When partially cool, add:

1 teaspoon vanilla or 2 or more
   tablespoons brandy, curaçao, etc.

Put chestnuts through a ricer. Let them fall lightly onto a large plate into a mound. If necessary to touch them, try to do so very lightly, so that they will not be mashed. Whip until stiff:

1 cup whipping cream

Fold in:

1 teaspoon vanilla
2 tablespoons sifted confectioners' sugar

Place the cream on the mound and let it overflow onto the sides. Chill well before serving. You may cover the top of the cream with a grating of:

Sweet chocolate

And then, as our dear old French friend would have said, "I'd be so pleased, I would not thank the King to be my uncle."

CORNSTARCH CUSTARD PUDDING OR BLANCMANGE

8 Servings

To be really good, this pudding needs loving care. For success, see About Cornstarch, page 499.

Mix in the top of a double boiler:

½ cup sugar
6 tablespoons cornstarch
¼ teaspoon salt

Gradually, add while stirring well:

4 cups milk

Place the mixture ◆ over boiling water and stir constantly for 8 to 12 minutes, when it should have begun to thicken. Cover and continue to cook for about 10 minutes more. Stir 1 cup of this thickened mixture, slowly, into:

2 well-beaten eggs

Return it to the milk mixture and continue to cook for 2 minutes, stirring constantly. Do not overcook. The pudding will thicken more as it cools. Remove from heat, and when slightly cooled by gentle stirring, add:

1 teaspoon vanilla

To mold, see About Cornstarch, page 499.

CARAMEL CUSTARD CORNSTARCH PUDDING

8 Servings

◆ Please read About Cornstarch, page 499.

Heat slightly in the top of a double boiler over direct heat:

3 cups milk

Caramelize I:

1 cup sugar, page 507

Put it gradually into the warm milk and heat to the boiling point. Make a thin paste by stirring and pouring gradually over:

3 to 4 tablespoons cornstarch
1 cup cold milk

When this is smooth, combine the two mixtures by pouring the hot one ◆ gradually into the cold one, and stirring until smooth again. Place the top of the double boiler ◆ over boiling water and stir constantly for 10 minutes until the mixture begins to thicken. Cover and continue to cook for 10 minutes more. Mix 1 cup of this thickened mixture slowly into:

2 well-beaten eggs

Return to the rest and continue to cook for 2 minutes, stirring constantly. Then remove pudding from heat. Stir gently until slightly cooled, then add:

1 teaspoon vanilla

To mold, see About Cornstarch, page 499.

CHOCOLATE CORNSTARCH PUDDING

4 Servings

◆ Please read About Cornstarch, page 499.

Melt in a double boiler:

1 oz. chocolate

Stir in slowly:

½ cup sugar
1¾ cups milk
⅛ teaspoon salt

Heat these ingredients to the boiling point. Dissolve:

3 tablespoons cornstarch

in:

¼ cup milk

Stir the cornstarch slowly into the hot milk mixture. Cook over boiling water for 10 minutes, stirring constantly. Cover and cook for 10 to 12 minutes more until you can no longer taste the cornstarch. Cool by stirring very gently. When slightly cool add:

1 teaspoon vanilla

To mold, see About Cornstarch, page 499.

Serve with:

Cream

FRIED CREAM OR CRÈME FRITE

◆ Please read About Cornstarch, page 499.

Place in the top of a double boiler:

1 vanilla bean
1 cinnamon stick
1½ cups milk

Bring to a boil over direct heat and the cool slightly. Mix in a bowl until smooth

¼ cup sugar

1 tablespoon flour
¼ cup cornstarch
½ cup milk

Remove vanilla bean and cinnamon stick from the slightly cooled milk and stir the smooth cornstarch mixture into the milk. ♦ Cook over hot water until it begins to thicken—about 10 minutes. Pour some of this mixture over:

3 beaten egg yolks

Return the egg mixture to pan and cook ♦ stirring gently for about 3 minutes more. Beat in:

1 tablespoon butter
¼ teaspoon salt

Pour the thickened cream into a 9 x 9 inch buttered pan. Cool. Cut into diamonds or squares, about 1½-inches long. Beat:

1 egg

Dust cream with:

Finely crushed bread or cake crumbs

Dip the pieces of cream in the egg, then again in the crumbs. Fry in deep fat, heated to 370°. Drain and roll in:

Powdered vanilla sugar

Serve at once sprinkled with:

Rum

or with:

Fruit Sauces, page 709

ABOUT DESSERT SOUFFLES

If you have never made sweet soufflés before, ♦ please read the directions for making and baking them on page 203. ♦ To prepare a dish for sweet soufflé, use a straight-sided ovenproof baker. Butter it and dust the inside with powdered sugar.

Some fruit and nut soufflés are very close in texture to omelets and whips, having no binding sauce. For such soufflés, the proper beating of the egg whites and the right baking temperatures are more important than ever. If the egg whites are under- or over-beaten or the baking heat too high, they have the look and texture of an old leather belt. If mixed and baked with care, these same ingredients produce a delicacy and strength that remind us of dandelion seed puffs just before they blow. Some soufflés are made on a cream-puff or choux-paste base. See Apricot Omelette Soufflé, page 692.

If you decide to add liqueurs as a flavoring, allow an extra egg yolk for every 2 tablespoons of liqueur. Otherwise, the mixture will be thinned too much.

To glaze a soufflé, dust it 2 or 3 minutes before it is to come from the oven with powdered sugar. The soufflé should have doubled in height and be firm before the glaze is applied. Watch it closely with the oven door partially open. The glaçage will remain fairly shiny when the soufflé is served.

Cold soufflés are based on gelatins and resemble mousses or Bavarians, see page 693. They are frequently heightened by preparing a collar or band of paper tied around the outside of the dish in which the soufflé is to be served, and extending a few inches above it. Remove the collar just before serving. We have never found a collar to be an asset in making a hot soufflé.

Note carefully the size of the baker indicated as this affects the lightness and volume of the result. A 7-inch baker should serve 3 to 4; a 10-inch baker 8 to 10.

VANILLA SOUFFLE
A 9-Inch Soufflé Dish

♦ Please read About Dessert Soufflés, above, to prepare a soufflé baker.

This soufflé has a versatile wardrobe and many aliases. You may add a very few drops of oil of anise or a few marrons glacés; or you may replace the sugar with ⅓ to ½ cup of sirup from preserved ginger; also, add about ¼ cup very finely chopped candied fruits that have been soaked in Danziger Goldwasser or kirsch. In the latter guise, it is called **Soufflé Rothschild.**
Sift before measuring:

½ cup all-purpose flour

Resift with:

¼ cup sugar
¼ teaspoon salt

Stir in until smooth:

½ cup cold milk

Scald:

2 cups milk

with:

A vanilla bean

Remove the bean and stir in the flour mixture with a wire whisk. Cook and stir these ingredients over low heat until they thicken. Remove from the heat. Stir in:

¼ cup butter
4 to 5 beaten egg yolks

You may add:

(¾ cup chopped nut meats)

Cool the batter.
Preheat oven to 350°.
Whip until ♦ stiff, but not dry:

5 egg whites

Fold them lightly into the batter. Bake soufflé for about 25 minutes. Serve with:

A fruit sauce
Maple Sirup Sauce, page 712, or
Rum Sauce, page 710

SOUFFLÉ GRAND MARNIER
An 8-Inch Soufflé Dish

Preheat oven to 400°.
♦ Please read About Dessert Soufflés, this page, to prepare a soufflé baker.
Beat in a double boiler over hot water:

8 lightly beaten egg yolks
⅔ cup sugar

Continue to beat until the mixture forms a broad ribbon as it runs from a lifted spoon. Add:

½ cup Grand Marnier liqueur

To arrest the cooking, transfer the mixture to a bowl and beat it over ice until cooled. Beat until foamy:

  10 egg whites

Add:

  ¼ teaspoon cream of tartar

Continue to beat until ♦ stiff, but not dry. Fold the egg yolk mixture into the whites, see illustration, page 617. Mound the mixture in a soufflé dish. Bake 12 to 15 minutes and serve at once.

PINEAPPLE SOUFFLÉ
A 7-Inch Soufflé Dish

Preheat oven to 325°.
♦ Please read About Dessert Soufflés, page 689, to prepare a soufflé baker.
Melt over low heat:

  3 tablespoons butter

Stir in:

  3 tablespoons flour

When blended, stir in:

  1 cup crushed, drained pineapple

When thick and smooth, stir in:

  ⅔ cup dry, crushed macaroons
  3 egg yolks

Permit the yolks to thicken slightly. Cool the mixture.
Beat until ♦ stiff, but not dry:

  3 to 4 egg whites

Beat in gradually:

  2 tablespoons sugar
  ½ teaspoon vanilla

Fold this into the soufflé mixture. Bake in a soufflé dish for about 30 minutes.

CHOCOLATE SOUFFLÉ
A 9-Inch Soufflé Dish

♦ Please read About Dessert Soufflés, page 689, to prepare a soufflé baker.
Melt:

  2 tablespoons butter

Stir in until blended:

  1 tablespoon all-purpose flour

In a separate saucepan, heat but do not boil:

  1 cup milk
  1 oz. chocolate, cut in pieces
  ⅓ cup sugar

Add the hot milk mixture to the flour mixture, stirring constantly until well blended. Beat until light:

  3 egg yolks

Beat part of the sauce into the yolks, then add the yolk mixture to the rest of the sauce and stir the custard over very low heat to permit the yolks to thicken slightly. Cool the custard well.
Preheat oven to 350°.
Add:

  1 teaspoon vanilla

Whip until ♦ stiff, but not dry:

  3 egg whites

Fold them lightly into the cooled chocolate mixture. Bake in a soufflé dish set in a pan of hot water for about 20 minutes or until

firm. Serve at once with:

  Cream, Vanilla Sauce, page 713
  Foamy Sauce, page 714, or
  Weinschaum Sauce, page 710

LEMON SOUFFLÉ
An 8-Inch Soufflé Dish

♦ Please read About Dessert Soufflés to prepare a soufflé baker, on page 689.
Preheat oven to 350°.
Sift:

  ¾ cup sugar

Beat until very light:

  5 egg yolks

Add the sugar gradually. Beat constantly until the eggs are creamy. Add:

  1 teaspoon grated lemon rind
  ¼ cup lemon juice
  (½ cup chopped nut meats)

Whip until stiff but not dry:

  5 egg whites

Fold them lightly into the yolk mixture. Bake the soufflé in a dish set in a pan of ♦ hot, but not boiling, water, for about 35 minutes, or until it is firm. Serve at once with:

  Cream

FRESH FRUIT SOUFFLÉ
A 7-Inch Soufflé Baker

♦ Please read About Dessert Soufflés to prepare a soufflé baker, on page 689.
Preheat oven to 350°.
Prepare, by peeling and mashing, ripe fruits to make:

  1 cup sweetened fruit pulp: fresh
  apricots, nectarines, peaches, plums
  or raspberries

Add:

  1½ tablespoons lemon juice
  4 beaten egg yolks
  ⅛ teaspoon salt
  (1 tablespoon grated orange rind)

Beat until ♦ stiff, but not dry, and fold in:

  4 egg whites

Bake the mixture in a pan of ♦ hot, but not boiling, water for about 30 minutes. Serve hot with:

  Cream

PRUNE OR APRICOT SOUFFLÉ OR WHIP
A 9-Inch Soufflé Baker

♦ Please read About Dessert Soufflés to prepare a soufflé baker, on page 689.
Preheat oven to 350°.
Have ready:

  1 cup sweetened, thick dried prune or
  apricot purée

Whip until ♦ stiff, but not dry:

  5 egg whites

Add:

  ¼ teaspoon cream of tartar

Fold in the prune or apricot pulp and:

  (½ cup broken nut meats)
  (1 teaspoon grated lemon rind)

Place the soufflé in a baking dish set in a pan of hot water. Bake for about 1 hour or until firm. Serve hot with:

> Cream or Custard Sauce, page 710

HAZELNUT SOUFFLÉ
An 8-Inch Soufflé Baker

◗ Please read About Dessert Soufflés to prepare a soufflé baker, on page 689.
Preheat oven to 350°.
Put through a nut grinder:

> ¾ cup hazelnuts

Heat to just below the boiling point and pour over the nuts:

> 1 cup milk

Beat until light:

> 3 egg yolks

Beat in gradually:

> 3 tablespoons sugar
> 3 tablespoons flour
> ⅛ teaspoon salt

Stir a small quantity of the hot mixture into the eggs and then return this combination to the rest of the hot mixture. Stir and cook these ingredients over low heat to permit the yolks to thicken slightly. Stir in:

> 3 tablespoons butter

Cool. Beat in:

> ½ teaspoon vanilla or
> 1 tablespoon rum

Beat until ◗ stiff, but not dry:

> 3 egg whites

Fold them into the cooled custard. Bake for about 30 minutes. Serve hot with:

> 1 cup whipped cream

flavored with:

> Caramel or coffee

NUT SOUFFLÉ
A 12-Inch Soufflé Baker

◗ Please read About Dessert Soufflés to prepare a soufflé baker, on page 689.
Preheat oven to 350°.
Sift:

> 1 cup confectioners' sugar

Beat until very light:

> 8 egg yolks

Add the sugar gradually. Beat constantly until the yolks are creamy. Fold in:

> 2 teaspoons grated lemon rind or
> 1 teaspoon vanilla
> ½ lb. blanched ground almonds or
> walnuts

Whip until stiff but not dry:

> 8 egg whites

Fold them lightly into the yolk mixture. Place the batter in the baking dish, set in a pan of ◗ hot, but not boiling, water. Bake until firm, about 45 minutes.
Serve with:

> Sabayon Sauce, page 710, or
> Fruit Sauce, page 709

SOUR CREAM APPLE CAKE COCKAIGNE
A 12 x 17-Inch Pan or
Ten 4-Inch Round Bakers

We had this, our great-grandmother's specialty, once served to us in a pie crust, as a renowned confection of Lyons. We feel the pie shell makes an attractive container. However, the crust does not greatly improve the flavor.
Preheat oven to 325°.
Pare, core, and slice:

> 5 to 6 cups tart apples

Melt in a large, heavy skillet:

> ¼ cup butter

Add the apples and cook them uncovered over medium heat, stirring them often until they are tender. Do not let them brown. Combine and pour over the apples:

> ½ cup cultured sour cream
> Grated rind and juice of 1 lemon
> 1 cup sugar, scant unless apples
> are very tart
> 2 tablespoons all-purpose flour
> 8 egg yolks
> (½ cup blanched shredded almonds)

Stir these ingredients over low heat until they thicken. Cool the mixture. Whip until ◗ stiff, but not dry:

> 8 egg whites

Fold them lightly into the apple mixture. Spread the soufflé to a thickness of 1 inch in a large pan or ovenproof dish. Sprinkle the top with a mixture of:

> ¼ cup sugar
> 2 tablespoons cinnamon
> ¼ cup dry bread crumbs
> ¼ cup blanched shredded almonds

Bake for about 45 minutes or until firm. The cake may be served hot, but it is best very cold, covered with:

> Whipped cream, flavored with
> vanilla or with Angelica Parfait,
> page 721

OMELETTE AUX CONFITURES
2 Servings

Prepare as for a French Omelette, page 198, using:

> 2 egg yolks

Beat them until light. Beat in gradually:

> ¼ cup confectioners' sugar

Add:

> ½ teaspoon vanilla or a grating of
> orange or lemon rind

Whip until stiff, ◗ but not dry:

> 4 egg whites

Fold them lightly into the yolk mixture. Melt in a skillet:

> 2 tablespoons butter

When the butter is very hot, pour in the omelet mixture. To cook and fold, see page 617. When done, sprinkle with:

> Confectioners' sugar

Serve with:

> Preserves or jelly

or fold the omelet and spread with:

Applesauce, prune or apricot pulp, drained canned fruit or sugared berries

BAKED ALASKA, NORWEGIAN OMELET OR OMELETTE SOUFFLÉ SURPRISE

12 Servings

This tour de force speaks several languages and always seems gala. It needs last minute preparation to be "à point"—the meringue glazed and delicately colored, the ice cream firm, the cake not soggy—in other words, "Just right!" There are either individual, see below, or large pans, and also oven-proof dishes made especially for this dessert. You may even build a "cake case" on an oval heatproof dish.
Preheat broiler.
Line the dish with a ½-inch layer of:
      Génoise, see page 640, or sponge
      or angel cake
Three-day-old cake is suggested, so it will absorb any liquid from the ice cream. Sprinkle it lightly with:
      (Brandy)
Have ready:
      ¾-inch strips of Génoise, sponge
      or angel cake to cover the ice
      cream later
Make a meringue as follows. Beat:
      4 egg yolks
Beat in:
      ¼ cup sugar
      ½ teaspoon grated lemon rind
Whip until stiff ♦ but not dry, and fold in:
      6 egg whites
Or use instead a triple portion of Meringue I or II, see page 681. Quickly form on the cake base an oval mound made of:
      1½ quarts ice cream
♦ softened just enough so you can shape it. Cover this melon-mold shape with the cut strips of cake. Cover it at once with the meringue, so the cake surface is entirely coated to at least a ¾-inch thickness. Bring the meringue right down to the dish sur-

face. You may use some of the meringue **in a** pastry bag to pipe on fluted edges and **patterns** and you may accent the patterns with:
      (Candied fruit)

Run this meringue-covered confection under a 500° broiler—not more than 3 minutes—to brown. Watch it very closely! Serve at once.
You may like to try out this baked meringue covering by using orange cups as a base to hold the ice cream. Bring the meringue well down over the edge of the orange cup.

APRICOT OMELETTE SOUFFLÉ

6 Servings
Two 9-Inch, Round Pans with
Removable Rims

Preheat oven to 325°.
Blend together in the top of a double boiler and heat ♦ over—not in—hot water, until the mass leaves the sides of the pan:
      ¼ cup butter
      1 cup flour
      1 tablespoon sugar
      1¼ cups cream
      ¾ cup milk
Cool the mixture and add one at a time, beating after each addition:
      6 egg yolks
      1 teaspoon vanilla
Beat until stiff ♦ but not dry and fold in:
      6 egg whites
Pour the omelette mixture into the pans and bake 25 to 30 minutes. While baking, heat in the top of a double boiler:
      1½ cups apricot jam
Have ready a heated serving dish, on which to reverse one of the omelet layers. Cover it lightly with the jam. Reverse the second layer over it. Cover second layer with jam and serve at once with:
      (Whipped cream)

ABOUT DESSERT MOLDS

Almost any bowl that splays out is suitable for a pudding mold. Be sure the slanted sides allow molded ingredients to slide out easily when the mold is inverted. For straight-sided desserts, use spring forms, see page 518. One of the favorite shapes for Bavarians is the melon mold.
   To prepare the mold, rinse it out with cold water. Oil is sometimes used to coat the mold, but may leave an unpleasant finish, especially on clear gelatins.
   Dessert molds are often cake-lined. To make a pudding mold from a cake itself, see description below and illustration on page 693. If the mold is deep and the pudding or cake surface very tender, always use the paper lining as a safety measure. Cut as shown on the left, page 693. The simplest cake linings are made with thin sheets of Génoise—see page 640—or large areas cut from Jelly Rolls—see page 642—while they are still flat, before filling. Shown on the right is a mold lined with filled jelly roll slices. Macaroons and cookies can also be used in this pattern. In the center, you see ladyfingers, either whole or split, forming the mold. If they are split, be sure to put the curved sides

against the form. To make an even top, slice each section to a point by cutting it diagonally, as shown, and placing it with the pointed end toward the middle, until the base is filled. You may want to cut a small round for the very center.

If the ladyfingers are barely moistened with a liqueur or a fruit juice after placing, they will soften enough to fill any crevices. If moistened too much, they will disintegrate.

For fillings in such molds, see suggestions on page 644. Whatever fillings you choose, be sure to ♦ refrigerate them, preferably 12 hours before unmolding. Garnish the molded food with flavored creams, sauces or fruit and serve at once.

ABOUT CARAMEL-COATED MOLDS

I. Sprinkle a mold with:

>Sugar

Heat it in a slow—250° to 300°—oven or over low heat until the sugar is brown and bubbling. This is a simple method to be used if only the top of the custard or pudding is to be caramelized when the mold is reversed.

II. Spread the mold with:

>Caramelized Sugar I, page 507

before the sirup hardens. If necessary, spread the caramel around with a wooden spoon to coat the sides. Then reverse the mold before filling, to let the caramel harden.

ABOUT BAVARIAN CREAMS

You can count on finding eggs as ingredients in a classic Bavarian. In an hors d'oeuvre, the term can mean a Hollandaise base for a fish purée. For desserts, the eggs are usually combined with gelatin and cream. ♦ If Bavarian puddings are to be unmolded, chill them 12 hours or more. If served in sherbet glasses, chill 4 hours. If very heavy in egg and cream content, they may be frozen for a few days. Bavarians are often called "Cold Soufflés."

CABINET PUDDING OR BAVARIAN DE LUXE

>**10 Servings**

Whose Cabinet? Cabinet de Diplomate. Where else could you find anything so rich and suave? The classic Cabinet Pudding is baked. We prefer this one, a variation developed by our friend Chef James Gregory.

Heat in a double boiler until lukewarm, about 85°:

>5 whole eggs

Beat at medium speed for 7 minutes; then beat in:

>¼ cup sugar

until a mayonnaise consistency is reached. Beat in an additional:

>¼ cup sugar

♦ but do not overbeat. The eggs should stand in soft peaks. Dissolve over hot water:

>1½ tablespoons gelatin
>¼ cup cold water

Fold the gelatin very gently into the egg mixture. Chill the mixture, while you beat over a bowl of ice until stiff:

>2 cups whipping cream

♦ Do not overbeat the cream. Let it still have a glistening finish when you combine it with the egg mixture. Dribble onto it:

>2 teaspoons vanilla or
>1 tablespoon kirsch or Grand Marnier

You may fold into it:

>⅓ cup preserved ginger or
>½ cup sliced candied kumquats

Chill this mixture until it is like heavy cream. Line a mold with:

>Ladyfingers, see above

Build a pattern of rum or lemon sprinkled fruits and berries in layers with ladyfinger crumbs and the Bavarian mixture. Repeat these layers until the mold is complete, with ladyfingers on top. ♦ Refrigerate about 12 hours before unmolding.

CHOCOLATE OR COFFEE BAVARIAN

Add to any of the Bavarians calling for scalded milk, page 694:

>2 oz. melted sweet chocolate and/or
>2 teaspoons instant coffee

NESSELRODE PUDDING
Prepare:
Cabinet Pudding, page 693
You may use the fruits or not, as you like.
Fold into it, after putting through a ricer:
**2 cups slightly sweetened
Chestnut Purée, page 272
5 oz. crumbled Glazed Chestnuts,
page 743**
Serve it garnished with:
Crème Chantilly, see page 645

BAVARIAN BERRY CREAM
8 Servings
Crush:
**1 quart hulled strawberries
or raspberries**
Add:
1 cup sugar
Permit them to stand ½ hour. Soak:
2 teaspoons gelatin
in:
3 tablespoons water
Dissolve it in:
3 tablespoons boiling water
Stir this into the berries. You may add:
1 tablespoon lemon juice
Cool the gelatin. When it is about to set,
fold in lightly:
2 cups whipped cream
Pour the cream into a wet mold. ♦ Chill
for 12 hours if you plan to unmold it.
Serve with:
Strawberry or Fruit Glaze, page 683

HAZELNUT BAVARIAN CREAM
8 Servings
Soak:
1 tablespoon gelatin
in:
2 tablespoons cold water
Scald:
½ cup milk
Beat together:
**¼ cup sugar
4 egg yolks
⅛ teaspoon salt**
Combine the milk with the egg mixture
♦ by pouring first a little of the hot milk
over the mixture and adding the rest gradually. Stir ♦ over—not in—hot water until
the ingredients begin to thicken. Stir in
the soaked gelatin until dissolved. Grind
and add:
¾ cup hazelnuts
Add:
1 teaspoon vanilla
Chill these ingredients until they are about
to set. Whip until stiff:
2 cups whipping cream
Fold into the other ingredients. Place the
pudding in the dish from which it is to be
served—or in a wet mold. Chill thoroughly, if you plan to unmold it—12 hours
or more. Serve with:
Raspberry juice

CARAMEL OR MAPLE
BAVARIAN CREAM
8 Servings
Soak:
1 tablespoon gelatin
in:
¼ cup water
Prepare:
**¾ cup Caramelized Sugar I, see
page 507, or ½ cup maple sirup**
When the sugar is slightly cooled, put it or
the maple sirup in the top of a double
boiler with:
**1 cup hot milk
¼ cup sugar
¼ teaspoon salt**
Stir over hot water until these ingredients
are dissolved. Pour part of this over:
3 beaten egg yolks
Return the sweetened yolks to the double
boiler. Stir and cook the mixture over hot
water until it coats a spoon heavily. Stir
in the soaked gelatin until it is dissolved.
Cool the custard. Add:
**1 teaspoon vanilla or
1 tablespoon rum**
Fold in:
1 cup whipped cream
Place the bavarian in a wet mold. Chill at
least 12 hours or more before serving—if
you plan to unmold it.

EGGLESS BAVARIAN CREAM
8 Servings
Not classic but pleasant, and will lend itself to all the variations in the previous
recipes.
Soak:
1 tablespoon gelatin
in:
2 tablespoons cold water
Scald:
1½ cups milk
If a richer pudding is preferred, use instead ½ cup milk and 1 cup whipped
cream. Add:
**⅛ to ½ cup sugar
¼ teaspoon salt**
Stir the gelatin into this mixture until dissolved. Chill. As it thickens, flavor with:
**1½ teaspoons vanilla
(¼ teaspoon almond extract)**
Whip it with a wire whisk until fluffy.
Beat until stiff:
1 cup whipping cream
Fold into gelatin mixture. Place pudding
in a wet mold. If desired, alternate the
pudding mixture with:
**6 broken macaroons or ladyfingers
soaked in rum or dry sherry and
½ cup ground nut meats, preferably
almonds**
♦ Chill the pudding, at least 12 hours or
more if you plan to unmold it. Serve with:
**Whole or crushed berries or stewed
fruit and whipped cream**

RENNET PUDDING OR JUNKET

4 Servings

This favorite English dish is made of milk, coagulated with extract from the lining of unweaned calves' stomachs. It has a consistency much like that of a tender blanc-mange. Dioscorides said that rennet had the power to join things that were dispersed and to disperse things that come together. No chemist these days dares match such a claim!

Put into a bowl in which it will be served:

2 cups milk

warmed to exactly 98°. Add:

2 teaspoons sugar

Stir in:

2 teaspoons essence of rennet or
1 teaspoon prepared rennet
(2 teaspoons brandy)

Let the pudding stand about 1½ hours until it coagulates. Sprinkle with:

Cinnamon or nutmeg

Serve cold.

MOLDED PINEAPPLE CREAM

4 Servings

Soak:

1 tablespoon gelatin

in:

¼ cup cold water

Combine and stir constantly over very low heat until slightly thickened:

2 egg yolks
½ cup sugar
2 cups unsweetened pineapple juice
⅛ teaspoon salt

Add the soaked gelatin. Stir until dissolved. Pour half of this mixture into a wet mold. Chill it. Chill the remaining gelatin until it begins to set. Then fold into it:

1 cup whipped cream

Fill the mold. Chill until firm.

ABOUT GELATIN PUDDINGS

These desserts vary greatly in texture. ♦ For details about handling gelatin, see About Gelatin, page 516. Easiest to prepare are the clear jellies, to which you may add fruit and nuts. If you add puréed fruits, you lose clarity at once and the dessert bears some similarity to a mousse. When gelatins are allowed to set partially and are then beaten or combined with egg whites, they are known as **whips, sponges** or **snows.** Whipped gelatins double in volume—snows and sponges, which include egg white, may triple. Sometimes, a clear and a spongy gelatin are combined in layers in a single mold.

For very rich gelatin puddings, see Bavarians, page 693. For both Bavarians and clear fruit gelatins, you may line the mold with macaroons. Sprinkle them lightly with fruit juice, rum or cordial before adding the pudding or gelatin.

A word of caution: gelatin puddings with uncooked egg whites are often served to children or invalids over protracted periods of time. Since it has been discovered recently that biotin deficiency is occasionally induced by over-proportionate quantities of raw egg white, we suggest varying such diets. Substitute instead some of the puddings we describe, in which the egg whites are cooked like meringues.

To get a snow or whip texture, begin as for clear gelatin. Chill to a sirupy consistency. ♦ Work in a cold bowl or over ice. ♦ If the gelatin is not sufficiently chilled before whipping or adding the egg white, it may revert to a clear jelly. Gelatins without cream or eggs ♦ must be refrigerated, but cannot be frozen. Bavarians, mousses and ice creams made in the refrigerator tray and place in the freezing unit have a gelatin base as a stabilizer. The use of gelatin in these puddings prevents the formation of coarse crystals and produces a lovely smooth texture. ♦ Do not deep freeze this type of pudding longer than four or five days.

LEMON GELATIN

4 Servings

Soak:

1 tablespoon gelatin

in:

¼ cup cold water

Dissolve it in:

1½ cups boiling water

Add and stir until dissolved:

¾ cup sugar
¼ teaspoon salt

Add:

½ cup lemon juice
(1 teaspoon grated lemon rind)

Pour the jelly into a wet mold. ♦ Chill for 4 hours or more. Serve with:

Cream or Custard Sauce, see
page 710

ORANGE GELATIN

4 Servings

Soak:

1 tablespoon gelatin

in:

¼ cup cold water

Dissolve it in:

½ cup boiling water

Add and stir until dissolved:

½ cup sugar
¼ teaspoon salt

Add:

6 tablespoons lemon juice
1½ cups orange juice
(1½ teaspoons grated orange rind)

Pour jelly into a wet mold. Chill 4 hours or more. Unmold and serve with:

Cream or Custard Sauce, see
page 710

FRUIT MOLDED INTO LEMON OR ORANGE GELATIN
Prepare:

Lemon or Orange Gelatin

◗ Chill it until nearly set. It will fall in sheets from a spoon. Combine it with well-drained:

Cooked or raw fruit

Add:

(Nut meats)

(Marshmallows cut into quarters)

◗ Do not use more than 2 cupfuls of solids in all. ◗ Fresh pineapple must be poached before it is added to any gelatin mixture. Pour jelly into a wet mold and ◗ chill for 4 hours or more before serving.

PINEAPPLE GELATIN

8 Servings

◗ Note that fresh pineapple must be poached before being added to any gelatin. Soak:

2 tablespoons gelatin

in:

1 cup cold water

Dissolve it in:

1½ cups boiling pineapple juice

Add:

1 cup boiling water

Add and stir until dissolved:

¾ cup sugar

⅛ teaspoon salt

◗ Chill the gelatin until it is about to set—it will fall in sheets from a spoon. Add:

2½ cups canned, shredded, drained pineapple

3 tablespoons lemon juice

Pour the jelly into a wet mold. ◗ Chill for 4 hours or more. Unmold and serve with:

Cream or Custard Sauce, see page 710

FRUIT-JUICE GELATIN

4 Servings

Soak:

1 tablespoon gelatin

in:

¼ cup cold water

Dissolve it in:

¾ cup boiling water

Add:

1 cup sweetened fruit juice: prune, apricot, peach or cooked pineapple

(2 tablespoons lemon juice)

and if not sweet enough, add:

Sugar

When gelatin is ◗ about to set, it will fall in sheets from the spoon. Add:

Drained diced fruit

Pour jelly into a wet mold and chill for 4 hours or more before serving.

QUICK FRUIT GELATIN

4 Servings

Dissolve:

1 package fruit flavored gelatin

in:

1 cup boiling water

Chill rapidly by adding any but pineapple:

1 can frozen fruit juice: 6 oz.

Pour jelly into sherbet glasses. Chill further until firm.

WINE GELATIN

8 Servings

Soak:

2 tablespoons gelatin

in:

¼ cup cold water

Dissolve it in:

¾ cup boiling water

The proportions of water, fruit juice and wine may be varied. If the wine is not strong, use less water to dissolve the gelatin and increase the amount of wine accordingly. This makes a soft jelly of a very good consistency, suitable for serving in sherbet glasses or from a bowl. If a stiff jelly is desired for molds, increase the gelatin to 3 tablespoons.
Stir in until dissolved:

½ cup or more sugar

It is difficult to give an accurate sugar measurement. One-half cup is sufficient if both the oranges and the wine are sweet. Taste the combined ingredients and stir in additional sugar if needed.
Cool these ingredients. Add:

1¾ cups orange juice

6 tablespoons lemon juice

1 cup well-flavored wine

If this mixture is not a good color, add:

A little red vegetable coloring

Pour the jelly into sherbet glasses. Chill until firm. Serve with:

Cream, whipped cream or Custard Sauce, page 710

MOCHA GELATIN

4 Servings

The subtle flavor of this gelatin comes from coffee combined with a sirup from canned fruit. Dress it up if you want with nuts or cream, but we like it served simply with a light custard sauce.
Soak:

1 tablespoon gelatin

in:

¼ cup cold water

Dissolve it in:

1 cup very hot double-strength coffee

Add:

¾ cup canned fruit sirup

(¼ cup sugar)

You may use single or mixed flavors—peach, pear, apricot, pineapple, etc. If you use a mold, be sure to moisten it before filling. ◗ Chill 4 hours or more. Unmold and serve with:

Custard Sauce, page 710

BLANCMANGE

8 Servings

Blancmange, in America, is often a cornstarch pudding, see page 688, but the true French type is made with almond milk and gelatin.

To prepare almond milk, pound in a mortar:

    ½ lb. blanched almonds
    (3 or 4 bitter almonds blanched)

adding gradually:

    ¼ cup water
    ½ cup milk

Make an effort to extract as much flavor as possible from the almonds and then strain the liquid through a cloth. Soak:

    1 tablespoon gelatin

in:

    ¼ cup water

Heat until scalded:

    1 cup cream
    ½ cup sugar

Dissolve the gelatin in the hot cream mixture. Stir in the almond milk. Add:

    1 tablespoon kirsch or orgeat sirup

♦ Chill it for about 4 hours. Serve the pudding in sherbet cups with:

    Fresh or stewed fruit

PERSIAN CREAM

                           6 Servings

Soak:

    1 tablespoon gelatin

in:

    ¼ cup cold milk

Scald:

    1½ cups milk

Dissolve the gelatin in it. Beat:

    2 egg yolks
    ⅓ cup sugar

Beat a little of the hot milk into the yolks, then return to saucepan. Cook and stir these ingredients over ♦ very low heat until they begin to thicken. Cool. Add:

    1 teaspoon vanilla or rum

Whip until stiff but not dry:

    2 egg whites

Fold them lightly into the gelatin mixture. Chill for 4 hours or more. Serve very cold with:

    Crushed fruit or fruit sauce

FRUIT WHIPS

                     6 to 8 Servings

♦ Please read About Gelatin Puddings, on page 695. Oranges, raspberries, peaches, strawberries, apricots, prunes, etc.—raw or cooked—may be used alone or in combination. ♦ If fresh pineapple is preferred, it must be poached before being added to any gelatin mixture. Stir:

    1 teaspoon grated lemon rind

into:

    ⅞ cup sugar

Soak, according to the juiciness of the fruit:

    2½ teaspoons to 1 tablespoon gelatin

in:

    ¼ cup cold water

Dissolve it in:

    ¼ cup boiling water

Stir in the sugar until dissolved.

Add:

    3 tablespoons lemon juice
    1 cup crushed or riced fruit

If a single kind of fruit is used, add:

    1 teaspoon vanilla

Place the pan holding these ingredients in ice water. When they are chilled ♦ to a sirupy consistency, whip them with an egg beater until frothy. Whip until stiff:

    4 egg whites

Whip these ingredients into the gelatin mixture until the jelly holds its shape. Pour it into a wet mold. ♦ Chill 4 hours or more. Serve with:

    Cream or Custard Sauce, see
    page 710

⅄ BLENDER FRUIT WHIP

                           4 Servings

Cut into 16 pieces:

    A 10 oz. package frozen fruit

Put into an electric blender:

    1 tablespoon gelatin
    2 tablespoons lemon juice
    ½ cup boiling water

Cover and blend for 40 seconds. Add:

    2 unbeaten egg whites

Cover and blend 10 seconds. Continuing to blend, uncover the container and drop in, a few at a time, the pieces of still frozen fruit until they are all mixed in. Pour into a wet mold and chill 4 hours or more.

MARSHMALLOW PUDDING

                     6 to 8 Servings

Sift:

    1 cup sugar

Soak:

    1½ tablespoons gelatin

in:

    ½ cup cold water

Dissolve it in:

    ½ cup boiling water

Cool these ingredients. Whip until stiff:

    4 egg whites

Add the gelatin to the egg whites in a slow stream. Whip the pudding constantly. Add the sugar, ½ cupful at a time. Whip well after each addition. Whip in:

    1 teaspoon vanilla

Continue to whip until the pudding thickens. ♦ Chill 4 hours or more. Serve with:

    Custard Sauce, see page 710

Flavor the custard when it is cold with:

    Cointreau

or serve the pudding with:

    Crushed sweetened fruit

★ PINEAPPLE SNOW

                           8 Servings

A pretty Christmas pudding. Soak:

    1 tablespoon gelatin

in:

    ¼ cup cold water

Heat:

2 cups canned crushed pineapple
◗ If fresh pineapple is used, be sure it is poached before adding it to the gelatin mixture. Stir in:

1 cup sugar
⅛ teaspoon salt
When these ingredients are boiling, add the soaked gelatin. Remove pan from heat and stir in the gelatin until dissolved. ◗ Chill jelly until it is about to set. Whip until stiff:

2 cups whipping cream
Add:

½ teaspoon vanilla
Fold in the pineapple. Place pudding in a wet mold. Chill 4 hours or longer. Unmold and serve with:

(Maraschino cherries)

EGGLESS FRUIT WHIP

2 Servings
An easy dessert, if canned puréed baby fruits are used.
Soak:

1 teaspoon gelatin
in:

⅛ to ½ cup fruit juice
Dissolve over hot water. Add the contents of:

1 small jar puréed apricots, prunes, applesauce or peaches, etc.
3 tablespoons sugar
½ teaspoon vanilla
◗ Chill these ingredients until they reach a sirupy consistency. Whip in a chilled bowl until the gelatin has doubled in bulk. Chill for at least 4 hours before serving with:

Cream

COFFEE MARSHMALLOW CREAM

6 Servings
Melt in the top of a double boiler, over boiling water:

1 lb. diced marshmallows
in:

1 cup double-strength coffee
Stir and cook these ingredients until the marshmallows are dissolved. Chill the mixture until it is about to set. Fold in:

2 cups whipped cream
Place the jelly in a wet ring mold. Chill at least 4 hours. Invert and cover the top of the cream with:

Slivered toasted Brazil nuts or crushed nut brittle

INDIAN PUDDING

8 Servings
This dish is sometimes made with apples. In that case, add 2 cups thinly sliced apples and use, in all, 2 cups milk.
Preheat oven to 325°.
Boil in the top of a double boiler over direct heat:

4 cups milk
Stir in:

⅓ cup corn meal
Place these ingredients over boiling water. Cook them for about 15 minutes. Stir into them and cook for about 5 minutes:

¾ cup dark molasses
Remove from heat. Stir in:

¼ cup butter
1 teaspoon salt
1 teaspoon ginger
3 tablespoons sugar
(1 well-beaten egg)
(½ cup raisins)
(½ teaspoon cinnamon)
Pour the batter into a well-greased baking dish. To have a soft center, pour over the top:

(1 cup milk)
Bake the pudding from 1½ to 2 hours. Serve pudding hot with:

Hard Sauce, see page 714, or cream
It is a barbarous New England custom to serve it with:

Vanilla Ice Cream, see page 717

FARINA PUDDING

6 Servings
Try this for a finicky breakfaster.
Boil:

2 cups milk
¼ cup sugar
Add:

½ cup farina
Stir and cook the farina over low heat until thick. Add and stir until melted:

1 tablespoon butter
Remove pan from heat. Beat in, one at a time:

2 egg yolks
Cool. Add:

1 teaspoon vanilla
(½ teaspoon grated lemon rind)
Place on a platter and whip until stiff, but not dry:

(2 egg whites)
Fold into the farina mixture. If used as a dessert, serve the pudding cold with:

Cream, tart fruit juice, stewed fruit, crushed sweetened berries or Hot Wine Sauce, page 711, using claret.

MILK-RICE RINGS

6 Servings
This dessert is frequently served in Europe, where rice puddings are highly appreciated. Steam covered in the top of a double boiler for about 1 hour:

¾ cup rice
3 cups milk
¾ teaspoon salt
When the rice is tender, cool slightly and add:

1½ tablespoons butter
2 teaspoons vanilla or 1 teaspoon
vanilla and 1 teaspoon lemon
rind, grated
2 teaspoons sugar

Pack the rice into buttered individual ring molds. Chill. Turn out onto plates. Fill the centers with:

Stewed or canned fruit, crushed
sweetened berries or Jelly Sauce,
page 710, using quinces

or serve with:

Caramel Sauce, see page 713, or
with cinnamon and sugar

RICE PUDDING

6 to 8 Servings

Preheat oven to 325°
Have ready:
2 cups cooked rice, see page 178
Combine, beat well and add:
1⅛ cups milk
⅛ teaspoon salt
4 to 6 tablespoons sugar or
½ cup brown sugar
1 tablespoon soft butter
1 teaspoon vanilla
2 to 4 eggs
Add:
½ teaspoon grated lemon rind
1 teaspoon lemon juice
(⅛ cup raisins or dates)
Combine these ingredients lightly with a fork. Grease a baking dish. Cover the bottom and sides with:
(Cake or cookie crumbs)
Put rice in dish and cover top with more crumbs. Bake the pudding until set—about 50 minutes. Serve hot or cold with:
Cream, Fruit Sauce, see page
709, fruit juice or Hot Wine
Sauce, see page 711

RICE AND FRUIT CREAM

5 Servings

Combine:
1 cup cooked rice
1 cup drained apricots, pineapple, etc.
Whip until stiff:
½ cup whipping cream
Fold in the rice mixture. Add:
12 diced marshmallows
Place the cream in individual dishes. Chill thoroughly. You may top it with:
Crushed nut brittle

RICE PUDDING WITH
WHIPPED CREAM

10 Servings

Boil, see page 178:
⅓ cup rice: about 1 cup cooked rice
Drain off any excess liquid. Soak for 5 minutes:
2 teaspoons gelatin

in:
¼ cup cold water
Dissolve over heat. Add to the rice. Stir in:
6 tablespoons sugar
(½ cup blanched, shredded almonds)
Chill. Whip until stiff:
2 cups whipping cream
Fold into the cream:
2 teaspoons vanilla
Fold the cream into rice. Place in a wet mold. Chill 4 hours or more. Unmold and serve very cold with:
Cold Currant Jelly Sauce, see page
710, or Hot Butterscotch Sauce,
see page 712

QUICK TAPIOCA CUSTARD

4 Servings

For a fluffy pudding, separate the eggs and add one stiffly beaten white after the tapioca cools.
Combine and stir in a double boiler:
3 tablespoons quick-cooking tapioca
½ cup sugar
¼ teaspoon salt
1 or 2 beaten eggs
2 cups milk
Cook these ingredients without stirring ♦ over rapidly boiling water for 7 minutes. Stir and cook them 5 minutes longer. Remove from steam. The tapioca thickens as it cools. Fold in gradually:
½ teaspoon vanilla or 1 teaspoon
grated orange or lemon rind
Chill. Serve with:
Cream, fresh berries, crushed or
canned fruit or
Chocolate Sauce, page 711
Additions may be made to this recipe. In that case, the eggs may be omitted. Suggestions:
¼ cup or more coconut or
toasted almonds
½ cup or more chopped dates
½ crushed banana and
½ diced banana
1 cup sliced, drained, cooked apples
½ cup fruit, soaked in wine or liqueur
If the eggs are omitted, serve with:
Custard Sauce, page 710

BUTTERSCOTCH TAPIOCA CUSTARD

4 Servings

Follow the preceding rule for:
Quick Tapioca Custard
but omit the sugar. Melt:♦
2 tablespoons butter
Stir in until it melts and bubbles:
⅓ cup packed brown sugar
Add this mixture to the cooked tapioca.

CRUSHED-FRUIT
TAPIOCA PUDDING

8 Servings

This may be made with pineapple, prunes, berries, etc. It is eggless.

Boil in the top of a double boiler over direct heat:

2 cups water

Combine and stir in gradually:

⅓ cup quick-cooking tapioca
½ cup sugar
¼ teaspoon salt

When these ingredients are boiling, place them ➧ over—not in—rapidly boiling water. Cook and stir them for about 5 minutes. Remove from heat. Cool slightly. Fold in:

2½ cups canned crushed pineapple or 2 cups cooked prune or apricot pulp or 2 cups crushed sweetened berries
2 tablespoons lemon juice

Chill. This may be served in sherbet glasses with:

Whipped cream, plain cream or custard sauce

PEARL-TAPIOCA PUDDING

8 Servings

Soak overnight, refrigerated:

1 cup pearl tapioca

in:

1 cup milk

Add these ingredients to:

3 cups milk

and cook them for 3 hours in a double boiler ➧ over—not in—hot water. Cool. Preheat oven to 325°

Beat and add:

5 egg yolks
Grated rind of 1 lemon
Juice of ½ lemon
¾ cup sugar

Beat until stiff, but not dry:

5 egg whites

Line a baking dish with a layer of the tapioca mixture, a layer of the egg whites, another layer of tapioca and end with the egg whites on top. Bake for about 15 minutes. Serve hot or cold, with or without a sauce such as:

Hot Fruit Sauce, see page 709

BREAD PUDDING WITH MERINGUE

6 Servings

Preheat oven to 350°.

Cut bread into slices and trim away crusts. It should be measured lightly, not packed. Soak for 15 minutes:

3 to 5 cups diced fresh bread or 3⅓ cups stale bread, or stale cake

in:

3 cups warm milk or 2 cups milk and 1 cup fruit juice
¼ teaspoon salt

Combine and beat well:

3 egg yolks
⅓ to ½ cup sugar
1 teaspoon vanilla
(½ teaspoon nutmeg)

Add:

Grated rind and juice of ½ lemon
(¼ cup raisins, dates or nut meats or ½ cup crushed, drained pineapple, or ¼ cup orange marmalade)

Pour these ingredients over the soaked bread. Stir them lightly with a fork until well blended. If preferred, the meringue may be dispensed with and the stiffly beaten egg whites may be folded in at this time. Bake the pudding in a baking dish set in a pan of hot water for about ¾ hour. Cool pudding. Cover with:

Meringue I, see page 681

Bake in a 300° oven until the meringue is set, for about 15 minutes. Serve hot with:

Hard Sauce, page 714, Fruit Hard Sauce, page 714, or cream, fruit juice or dabs of tart jelly

BROWN BETTY

5 Servings

Who would ever think that this simple old favorite could turn into a sophisticated tea dish?

Preheat oven to 350°.

Combine:

1 cup dry bread or graham cracker crumbs
¼ cup melted butter

Line the bottom of a baking dish with ⅓ of the crumb mixture. Prepare:

2½ cups peeled, diced or sliced apples or peaches, cherries or cranberries

Sift:

¾ cup packed brown sugar
1 teaspoon cinnamon
¼ teaspoon each nutmeg and cloves
½ teaspoon salt

Add:

1 teaspoon grated lemon rind
(1 teaspoon vanilla)

Place ½ of the apples in the dish. Cover the layer with ½ of the sugar mixture. Sprinkle with:

1 tablespoon lemon juice

Add:

2 tablespoons water

Cover the apples with ⅓ of the crumb mixture and:

(¼ cup raisins or currants)

Add the remaining apples and sprinkle them as before with the sugar mixture and:

2 tablespoons lemon juice
2 tablespoons water
(¼ cup raisins or currants)

Place the last ⅓ of the crumb mixture on top. Cover the dish and bake for about 40 minutes, until the apples are nearly tender. Remove cover, increase heat to 400° and permit pudding to brown for about 15 minutes. Serve hot with:

Hard Sauce, see page 714, or cream or Lemon Sauce, see page 709

PRUNE OR APRICOT BETTY

Follow the preceding recipe for:
Brown Betty
Use only:
2 tablespoons sugar
Substitute for the apples:
1½ cups stewed, drained, sweetened prunes or apricots
Substitute for the lemon juice and water:
¾ cup prune or apricot juice

BAKED PINEAPPLE BETTY

4 Servings

This may be made in advance. It is equally good served hot or very cold.
Preheat oven to 325°.
Cream until light:
½ cup butter
¾ cup sugar
Beat in:
5 egg yolks
¼ cup dry bread crumbs
1 cup crushed, drained pineapple
1 tablespoon lemon juice
Whip until stiff, then fold in:
3 egg whites
Place the mixture in a baking dish. Cover with a meringue, see page 681, and bake it, set in a pan of hot water, for about 30 minutes. Serve with:
Cream or whipped cream

★ BAKED FIG PUDDING

14 Servings

Preheat oven to 325°.
Beat until soft:
½ cup butter
Add and beat until fluffy:
2 eggs
1 cup molasses
Add:
2 cups finely chopped figs
½ teaspoon grated lemon rind
1 cup buttermilk
(½ cup broken black walnut meats)
Sift before measuring:
2½ cups all-purpose flour
Resift with:
½ teaspoon soda
2 teaspoons baking powder
1 teaspoon salt
1 teaspoon cinnamon
½ teaspoon nutmeg
One teaspoon ginger may be substituted for the cinnamon and nutmeg. Stir the sifted ingredients into the pudding mixture. Bake in a greased 9-inch tube pan for about 1 hour. Serve hot with:
Brown Sugar Hard Sauce, see page 714, Sabayon Sauce, page 710, or Hot Wine Sauce, see page 711

★ BAKED DATE RING OR CHRISTMAS WREATH

6 Servings

You may bake this in a ring mold. When cold, unmold it onto a platter, cover it well with whipped cream and stud it with maraschino cherries. Surround it with holly leaves. Although very effective this way, it tastes just as good baked in a shallow pan, cut into squares and served with Foamy Sauce.
Preheat oven to 350°.
Prepare:
1 cup pitted minced dates
1 cup chopped nut meats
Combine these ingredients with:
½ cup white or brown sugar
1 tablespoon flour
1 teaspoon baking powder
2 beaten egg yolks
1 teaspoon vanilla
Fold in:
2 stiffly beaten egg whites
Bake the pudding in a well-greased 9-inch ring mold for about ½ hour. You may sprinkle over it, while hot, ¼ cup Madeira or sherry or 3 tablespoons brandy or rum. Permit it to cool in the pan.
Whip until stiff:
1 cup heavy cream
Fold in:
2 tablespoons powdered sugar
1 teaspoon vanilla
Garnish the ring as suggested above.

★ BAKED PLUM PUDDING

10 Servings

Not for Jack Horner's legendary thumb, but a rewarding confection just the same.
Preheat oven to 375°.
Beat until soft:
½ cup butter
Add gradually:
1 cup sugar
Blend these ingredients until creamy. Beat in, one at a time:
6 eggs
Combine:
1 cup raisins, currants and pecans
Sprinkle lightly with:
Flour
Add these ingredients to the butter mixture. Combine:
2 cups bread crumbs
2 teaspoons cinnamon
½ teaspoon cloves
½ teaspoon allspice
Stir these ingredients into the butter mixture. Bake in a greased pan or baking dish for about ½ hour. Serve with:
Hard Sauce, see page 714, Lemon Sauce, see page 709, or Hot Wine Sauce, see page 711

COTTAGE PUDDING

6 Servings

Preheat oven to 400°.
Follow the recipe for:
One Egg Cake, see page 636
For a new fillip, line a greased 8 x 8-inch pan with:

1 cup heated marmalade

Pour the batter over the marmalade. Marmalade or none, bake the pudding for about 25 minutes. Serve cut into squares with:

> Crushed fruit, stewed fruit, Fluffy Orange Sauce, Raisin Sauce, see page 710, Coffee Sauce, see 713, Wine Sauce, see page 711, or Hot Brown Sugar Sauce, see page 712

PANCAKE AND WAFFLE DESSERTS

Serve:

> Pancakes or waffles

spread with:

> Thick cultured sour cream
> Strawberry or other preserves

or serve with:

> Crushed sweetened berries or fruit or with Sauce Cockaigne, see page 709

CHOCOLATE FEATHER PUDDING

8 Servings

Perhaps this should be placed among the steamed puddings, but they are more troublesome and this one might be neglected in such surroundings. It is an inexpensive and delightful dessert.

Preheat oven to 350°.

Sift:

> 1 cup sugar

Beat until light:

> 1 egg

Stir in sugar, gradually. When these ingredients are well blended, stir in:

> 1 cup milk or coffee
> 1 tablespoon melted butter
> 1½ oz. melted chocolate

Sift:

> 1½ cups all-purpose flour

Resift with:

> ¼ teaspoon salt
> 1½ teaspoon double-acting baking powder

Stir these ingredients into the egg mixture. Add:

> ½ teaspoon vanilla

Place the batter in well-greased deep custard cups—about ⅔ full. Cover with foil. Steam in the oven, by setting cups in a pan of hot water, for about ½ hour; or place pan over low heat on top of stove for same length of time. Remove foil and serve pudding at once with:

> Vanilla Sauce, see page 713, flavored with rum

SWEET-POTATO PUDDING

6 Servings

Preheat oven to 350°.

Combine and beat well:

> 2 cups cooked, mashed sweet potatoes
> 1 cup sugar
> ½ cup melted butter
> 6 beaten egg yolks
> 1½ teaspoons grated lemon rind

1 cup orange juice
¼ teaspoon nutmeg or
2 tablespoons rum

Fold in:

> 2 stiffly beaten egg whites

Bake pudding in a greased baking dish for about 1 hour. The top may be sprinkled before baking with:

> Sliced citron
> Broken nut meats

After the pudding is baked and cooled, it may also be topped with a Meringue, see page 681, made with the remaining egg whites. Bake in a 325° oven for about 15 minutes.

PERSIMMON PUDDING

8 Servings

This can be made with the small native Diospyros virginiana or with the large Japanese Diospyrokaki. Use the greater amount of flour for the Japanese fruit, as it is very juicy. The native fruits give a waxy, but not tough, consistency to the pudding.

Preheat oven to 325°.

Put through a colander:

> Persimmons

There should be about 2 cups of pulp.

Beat in:

> 3 eggs
> 1¼ cups sugar
> 1 to 1½ cups all-purpose flour
> 1 teaspoon any baking powder
> 1 teaspoon soda
> ½ teaspoon salt
> ½ cup melted butter
> 2½ cups rich milk
> 2 teaspoons cinnamon
> 1 teaspoon ginger
> ½ teaspoon freshly grated nutmeg

One cupful raisins or nut meats may be added to the batter. Bake the pudding in a greased 9 x 9-inch baking dish until firm—about 1 hour. Serve with:

> Cream or Hard Sauce, page 714

ABOUT STEAMED PUDDINGS

To steam pudding mixtures in a steamer use pudding molds or cans with tightly fitting lids—like baking powder tins. First grease insides of molds well, then sprinkle with sugar. Containers should be ◆ only ⅔ full. Place molds on a trivet in a heavy kettle over 1 inch of boiling water. Cover kettle closely. Use high heat at first, then as the steam begins to escape, low heat for rest of cooking.

◆ To steam pudding mixtures in ⦿ pressure cooker, use tightly-lidded molds or cans as described above and ◆ fill only ⅔ full. Place them on a rack in the bottom of the cooker—allowing space both between the molds and the walls of cooker. Add boiling water ◆ until it is halfway up the sides of the molds.

If the steaming period in a regular steamer is supposed to be 30 minutes, steam with vent off for 5 minutes, then pressure cook at 15 pounds for 10 minutes. If steaming for 45 minutes to 1½ hours is called for, steam without closing the vent for 25 minutes, then pressure cook at 15 pounds pressure for 25 minutes. If steaming for 2 to 4 hours is called for, steam without closing the vent for 30 minutes, then pressure cook at 15 pounds pressure for 50 minutes. ◗ After steaming, reduce the heat at once. True steamed puddings need complete circulation of steam, so do not expect good results if you use a greased double boiler. Always ◗ before unmolding, take the lid from the mold and allow the pudding to rest long enough to let excess steam escape. The pudding will be less apt to crack in unmolding.

▲ In high altitudes, reduce the leavening by ½ the required amount.

STEAMED BROWN PUDDING
14 Servings
Combine and blend well:
    1 cup packed light-brown sugar
    ½ cup shortening
Add:
    1 cup milk
    1 cup molasses
    1 cup dry bread crumbs
    2 beaten eggs
    2 cups chopped seeded raisins
Sift before measuring:
    2 cups all-purpose flour
Resift with:
    2 teaspoons double-acting baking
      powder
    ½ teaspoon soda
    1 teaspoon cinnamon
    ½ teaspoon each ginger, cloves and
      grated nutmeg
Add sifted ingredients to the molasses mixture. Pour batter into a well-greased pudding mold. Steam for 1½ hours. To steam or ✿ pressure cook and unmold, see About Steamed Puddings, page 702. Serve hot with:
      Hard Sauce, page 714, or Foamy
      Sauce, see page 714

★ STEAMED FRUIT SUET PUDDING
12 Servings
Less cooking is needed here, as the thickener is bread crumbs. See About Steamed Puddings, page 702.
Beat until soft:
    1 cup beef suet: ½ lb.
Add gradually:
    1 cup sugar
When these ingredients are well blended, beat in:
    3 egg yolks
Stir in:
    1 cup milk
    3 tablespoons brandy

Put through a grinder and add:
    1 lb. figs or dates or 2 cups peeled
      sliced apples
    (1 cup chopped pecans or walnuts)
Grate and add:
    2 teaspoons orange rind
    1 teaspoon freshly ground nutmeg or
      ginger
Combine and add:
    1½ cups dry bread crumbs
    2 teaspoons any baking powder
Whip until stiff, then fold in:
    3 egg whites
Pour the ingredients into a greased mold. Steam slowly for 4 hours. To steam or ✿ pressure cook and unmold, see About Steamed Puddings, page 702. Serve with:
      Hot Sabayon Sauce, page 710, or
      Hot Wine Sauce, see page 711
Flavor the sauce with:
    (2 teaspoons or more brandy)

★ STEAMED DATE PUDDING
8 Servings
Not so rich as Steamed Fruit Suet Pudding, but equally good.
Sift:
    1 cup brown sugar
Beat until soft:
    ¼ cup butter
Add the sugar gradually. Blend these ingredients until they are creamy. Beat in:
    1 egg
    ½ teaspoon vanilla
Sift before measuring:
    1¼ cups all-purpose flour
Resift with:
    2⅔ teaspoons double-acting baking
      powder
    ½ teaspoon salt
Add sifted ingredients to butter mixture in 3 parts, alternately with thirds of:
    1 cup milk
Beat batter until smooth after each addition. Fold in:
    1 cup chopped dates
    1 cup broken nut meats
Pour into a greased pudding mold. Cover closely. Steam for 2 hours. To steam or ✿ pressure cook and unmold, see About Steamed Puddings, page 702. Serve hot with:
      Foamy Sauce, page 714, or
      Fluffy Hard Sauce, page 714

STEAMED CHOCOLATE PUDDING
6 Servings
This is richer than Chocolate Feather Pudding, which may also be steamed in a mold.
Beat until light:
    6 egg yolks
Beat in gradually:
    1 cup sugar
Stir in:
    ¾ cup grated chocolate
    2 tablespoons finely crushed crackers
      or toasted bread crumbs

1 teaspoon any baking powder
1 teaspoon vanilla
½ teaspoon cinnamon
(½ cup grated nut meats)
Beat until stiff but not dry:
    6 egg whites
Fold them lightly into the batter. Pour
into a greased pudding mold. Steam for
1½ hours. To steam or ❂ pressure cook
and unmold, see About Steamed Puddings,
page 702. Serve with:
    Hard Sauce or cream

STEAMED CARAMEL PUDDING
                                    6 Servings
Try this as a company pudding.
Melt in a heavy skillet:
    ⅓ cup sugar
When it is light brown stir in ♦ very
slowly:
    ¾ cup hot milk
Cool this sirup. Beat until soft:
    2 tablespoons butter
Beat in one at a time:
    5 egg yolks
Add the sirup and:
    1 teaspoon vanilla
    1½ tablespoons all-purpose flour
    1 cup ground, unblanched almonds
Beat batter until smooth. Place on a
platter and whip ♦ until stiff, but not dry:
    5 egg whites
Fold them lightly into the batter. Pour
into a greased pudding mold sprinkled
with:
    Sugar
Cover closely. Steam for 1 hour. To steam
or ❂ pressure cook and unmold, see About
Steamed Puddings, page 702. Serve hot
with:
    Whipped cream or Sauce Cockaigne,
    see page 709

STEAMED APPLE MOLASSES PUDDING
                                    6 Servings
Cream until fluffy:
    ¼ cup butter
    ½ cup packed brown sugar
Beat in:
    1 egg
    ½ cup molasses
    1 tablespoon grated orange rind
Measure:
    1½ cups sifted all-purpose flour
Resift with:
    ½ teaspoon soda
    1 teaspoon double-acting baking
    powder
    1 teaspoon each ginger, cinnamon
Add these ingredients to the butter mix-
ture, alternately with:
    ½ cup buttermilk
Stir in:
    1 cup chopped apples
Place the pudding in a greased mold.
Steam it for 1½ hours. To steam or

❂ pressure cook and unmold, see About
Steamed Puddings, page 702. Serve with:
    Lemon Sauce, see page 709, or
    Hard Sauce, see page 714

★ STEAMED PLUM PUDDING
                                    24 Servings
A truly festive Christmas dish that needs
patience in the making. ♦ The slow six-
hour cooking is necessary, so that all the
suet melts before the flour particles burst.
If the pudding cooks too fast and the flour
grains burst before the fat melts, the pudding will be close and hard.
Sift:
    1 cup all-purpose flour
Prepare and dredge lightly with part of the
flour:
    1 lb. chopped suet: 2 cups
    1 lb. seeded raisins
    1 lb. washed dried currants
    ½ lb. chopped citron
Resift the remaining flour with:
    1 grated nutmeg
    1 tablespoon cinnamon
    ½ tablespoon mace
    1 teaspoon salt
    6 tablespoons sugar or
    ½ cup brown sugar
Combine the dredged and the sifted in-
gredients.
Add:
    7 egg yolks
    ¼ cup cream
    ½ cup brandy or sherry
    3 cups grated bread crumbs,
    white or rye
The latter helps make the pudding light.
Place on a platter and whip until stiff:
    7 egg whites
Fold them lightly into the raisin mixture.
Pour the batter into a greased, covered gal-
lon mold and steam for 6 hours. To steam
or ❂ pressure cook and unmold, see About
Steamed Puddings, page 702. Serve with:
    Hot Sweet Wine Sauce or Hard
    Sauce, page 714

UNCOOKED DATE LOAF
                                    12 Servings
Crush:
    ½ lb. graham crackers
Remove pits and cut into pieces:
    1 lb. dates: 2 cups
Cut into pieces:
    ½ lb. marshmallows
Chop fine:
    1 cup pecan meats
Whip until stiff:
    1 cup whipping cream
Fold in:
    1 teaspoon vanilla
Combine ½ the cracker crumbs with the
dates, marshmallows, nuts and whipped
cream. Shape into a roll. Roll it in the
remaining cracker crumbs. Chill for 12
hours. Serve, cut into slices, with:
    Cream or whipped cream

ABOUT DOUGHNUTS

For tender doughnuts ♦ have all ingredients at about 75°, so the dough can be mixed quickly. This prevents the development of gluten in the flour, which would tend to toughen the batter. Keep the mix just firm enough to be easy to handle. Chill the dough slightly to shape it, before cutting, so that the board won't have to be too heavily floured. Roll or pat the dough to about a ½-inch thickness. ♦ Cut with a well-floured double cutter, or 2 sizes of biscuit cutters. ♦ If you allow the dough to dry 10 or 12 minutes on a very lightly floured board or absorbent paper, you will find that the doughnuts will absorb less fat while frying. The richer and sweeter the dough, the more fat they absorb. ♦ To cook doughnuts, please read About Deep Fat Frying, pages 124-126. Bring the fat to 375° unless otherwise stated. Then, one at a time ♦ slide the doughnuts into the fat at the side of the kettle. They will keep their shapes well if you transfer them to the fat with a pancake turner which has already been dipped into the kettle.

Each doughnut takes about 3 minutes to cook. ♦ Never crowd the frying kettle. You can develop a machine-like precision by adding one doughnut at a time to the kettle, at about 15-second intervals for the first six doughnuts. Turn each as soon as brown on one side. It will usually rise at this point. When done, remove with a fork or tongs and place on absorbent paper to drain. Replace it immediately with an uncooked one to keep the fat at an even temperature. When the doughnuts cool, dust them with powdered, spiced or flavored sugar. For an easy method, use a paper bag. Or glaze them with Milk or Lemon Glaze, see page 682.

▲ Yeast-based doughnuts require no adjustment for high altitudes. For quick leavened doughnuts, reduce the baking powder or soda by ¼. ♦ But do not reduce soda beyond ½ teaspoon for each cup of sour milk or cream used.

SWEET MILK DOUGHNUTS
About 36 Doughnuts
♦ Please read About Doughnuts, above.
Preheat deep fryer to 370°.
Beat:

    2 eggs

Add slowly, beating constantly:

    1 cup sugar

Stir in:

    1 cup milk
    4 or 5 tablespoons melted shortening

Sift before measuring:

    4 cups all-purpose flour

Resift with:

    4 teaspoons double-acting baking
      powder

    ¼ teaspoon cinnamon or 1 teaspoon
      grated lemon rind
    ½ teaspoon salt
    (¼ teaspoon nutmeg)

Mix moist and dry ingredients. To fry, see About Deep Fat Frying, pages 124-126.

SOUR CREAM DOUGHNUTS
About 36 Doughnuts
♦ Please read About Doughnuts, above.
Preheat deep fryer to 370°.
Beat well:

    3 eggs

Add slowly, beating constantly:

    1¼ cups sugar

Stir in:

    1 cup cultured sour cream

Sift before measuring:

    4 cups all-purpose flour

Resift with:

    1 teaspoon soda
    2 teaspoons double-acting baking
      powder
    ¼ teaspoon cinnamon or
    ½ teaspoon nutmeg
    ½ teaspoon salt

Stir the sifted ingredients and the egg mixture until they are blended. To fry, see About Deep Fat Frying, pages 124-126.

YEAST POTATO DOUGHNUTS
About 48 Doughnuts
Preheat deep fat fryer to 375°.
Prepare:

    Buttermilk Potato Roll, page 565

When ready to shape, pat into ½-inch thickness. Cut into rings or into strips ½ x 3½ inches. Twist the strips gently. You may bring the ends together to form twisted wreaths. Allow the twists to rise ♦ uncovered for about 30 minutes. Meanwhile, please read ♦ About Deep Fat Frying, pages 124-126. To cook, see About Doughnuts, above.

QUICK POTATO DOUGHNUTS
About 36 Doughnuts
Preheat deep fat fryer to 370°.
♦ Please read About Doughnuts, above.
Prepare:

    1 cup freshly riced potatoes

Beat well:

    2 eggs

Add very slowly, beating constantly:

    ⅔ cup sugar

Stir in the potatoes and:

    1 cup buttermilk
    2 tablespoons melted butter

Sift before measuring:

    4 cups all-purpose flour

Resift with:

    2 teaspoons double-acting baking
      powder
    1 teaspoon baking soda
    ⅔ teaspoon salt
    ¼ teaspoon nutmeg or
    ¼ teaspoon cinnamon

Stir in the sifted ingredients and the potato mixture until they are blended. Add enough of the sifted flour to form a soft dough. Chill the dough until it is easy to handle. ♦ To fry, see About Deep Fat Frying, pages 124-126.

DOUGHNUT VARIATIONS
I. Molasses Doughnuts
Prepare Sour Cream Doughnuts, page 705.
Replace ¼ cup sugar with:

> ½ cup molasses

Add:

> 1½ teaspoons ginger

II. Berlin or Jelly Doughnuts
Prepare Yeast Potato Doughnuts, page 705.
Cut the dough into 2½-inch rounds instead of rings. Place on one round:

> 1 heaping teaspoon jelly or
> preserves

Brush the edges of the round with:

> Egg white

Cap it with another round. Press the edges together. Repeat the process. After allowing the doughnuts to rise, fry them as directed in About Doughnuts, see page 705.

III. Orange Doughnuts
Prepare any of the recipes for Doughnuts.
Substitute:

> The grated rind of 1 orange and
> ¼ cup orange juice

for ¼ cup of the milk.

IV. Chocolate Doughnuts
Prepare any one of the recipes for Doughnuts, adding 5 tablespoons flour.
Melt:

> 1½ oz. chocolate

Add it to the melted shortening. Stir in:

> 1½ teaspoons vanilla

V. Pecan or Date Doughnuts
Prepare any recipe for Doughnuts. Add:

> ½ cup broken nut meats or
> ½ cup pitted diced dates

VI. Drop Doughnuts
While devoid of the characteristic hole, these are lighter in texture.
Prepare any recipe for doughnuts, using ¼ to ½ cup less flour. Slide a tablespoon of dough at a time into the hot fat.

ABOUT CRULLERS AND BEIGNETS

To be good, these must be delicate in flavor, therefore the frying fat must be impeccable. If you fry in a usual bland cooking oil, heat it between 365° to 370° and cook the batter until almost golden. If you use butter or part butter, start frying with the fat at 330° and let the heat rise, over about a 7 minute period, to 360°. ♦ Be sure to bring the heat of the fat down to 330° again between cookings. Drain . on absorbent paper. Beignets may be served

hot with a sauce or cold, either dusted with:

> Powdered sugar

or frosted with:

> Milk or Lemon Glaze, see page 682

Very similar to beignets are Rosettes, see page 203, and some fritters, page 220.

BEIGNETS OR FRENCH FRITTERS
I.   4 to 6 Servings
These are as light as air.
Heat deep fat to 370°.
Combine in a saucepan and boil and stir over low heat for about 5 minutes:

> 6 tablespoons water
> 1 tablespoon butter
> 6 tablespoons all-purpose flour

Remove the pan from the heat. Beat in one at a time:

> 4 eggs

Beat the batter for about 3 minutes after each addition. Add:

> 1 teaspoon vanilla

Drop the batter from a teaspoon into deep hot fat. Cook until golden. Drain. Dust with:

> Confectioners' sugar

Serve at once with:

> Lemon Sauce, see page 709

Or fill with:

> Gooseberry Conserve

II. Heat deep fat to 370°.
Prepare dough for:

> Cream Puff Shells, see page 597

Add:

> (½ teaspoon grated lemon or
> orange rind)

but instead of baking, drop in deep fat, a teaspoon of dough at a time. As soon as they are cooked enough on one side, they will automatically turn themselves over. Remove when brown on both sides. Drain and sprinkle with:

> Powdered sugar

Serve with:

> Vanilla or Apricot Sauce, see
> page 713

CRULLERS
This recipe makes a lot—hard to gauge the exact amount!
♦ Please read About Crullers, this page.
Heat deep fat to 370°.
Sift:

> ⅔ cup sugar

Beat until light:

> 4 eggs

Add the sugar gradually, blending until the mixture is creamy. Add:

> ¾ teaspoon grated lemon rind
> ⅓ cup melted shortening
> ⅓ cup milk

Sift before measuring:

> 3½ cups all-purpose flour

Resift with:

½ teaspoon cream of tartar
½ teaspoon soda
¼ teaspoon salt

Stir the sifted ingredients into the egg mixture. Roll the dough to the thickness of ¼ inch. Cut it into strips of about ½ x 2½ inches with a pie jagger. To make a fancier shape, twist the strips slightly into several convolutions. To cook, read About Deep Fat Frying, on pages 124-126.

RICE CRULLERS OR CALAS
4 to 5 Servings

Prepare:

1 cup cooked rice

Mix and add to it:

3 beaten eggs
½ cup sugar
½ teaspoon vanilla
½ teaspoon nutmeg or grated
lemon rind
2¼ teaspoons double-acting
baking powder
6 tablespoons all-purpose flour

◗ Please read About Deep Fat Frying, pages 124-126, and bring the fat to 365°. Drop the batter into the fat from a teaspoon. Fry the calas until they are golden brown—about 7 minutes. Drain on absorbent paper. Sprinkle with:

Confectioners' sugar

Serve with:

Tart jelly

RAISED CALAS

These are the famous breakfast delicacies which are hawked on the New Orleans streets in the early morning.

Mash:

¾ cup cooked rice

Dissolve in:

½ cup water at 85°
½ cake compressed yeast

Mix these ingredients together and let stand covered overnight. In the morning, add:

3 well-beaten eggs
⅛ cup sugar
½ teaspoon salt
¼ cup all-purpose flour
¼ teaspoon nutmeg

Let the mixture rise covered for about 15 minutes. Preheat deep fryer to 365°. Drop the batter into the fat from a teaspoon. Fry until golden brown, about 10 minutes, and drain on absorbent paper. Serve the calas hot, dusted with:

Powdered sugar

ABOUT DESSERT CHEESES

Although in some climates certain types of cheese are cellared for years, like wines, the American housewife, with no comparable storage facilities, is hard put to it to keep cheeses "à point." Cheeses are constantly changing, do not freeze well, refrigerate only on a short-term basis, and if served properly, almost have to be brought to their peak of ripeness in small lots and used at once. There are special cheese-keepers which have platforms elevated above a vinegar base, and a cloche cover. Another device for short-term preservation is to wrap cheeses in cloths which have been wrung out in vinegar. Sometimes storing cheese in covered glass or enameled containers helps. Other expedients include refrigeration and the separate wrapping of each variety of cheese. The most drastic methods—at which true turophiles wince—are to buy canned cheese, or to pot natural cheese in crocks, with a sufficient addition of wine, brandy or kirsch to arrest enzymatic action. If you are interested generally in cheese types, methods of ripening and how to use cheeses in cooking, please read About Cheese, page 511.

Dessert cheeses may be served after the roast, with the same red wine that has accompanied that course, or after the salad. They may also be served following the sweet or with a suitable dessert fruit such as apples, pears, grapes, cherries, plums or melons. Cheeses should always be served at a temperature of about 70°. Some types which are best when "coulant" or runny, should be removed from refrigeration 3 to 6 hours before serving.

Usually some pats of sweet butter are added to the cheese-board. Toast, crackers, pumpernickel, crusty French bread, page 560, or Sour Rye, page 557, follow the cheese on a separate tray. Salted, toasted or freshly shelled nuts, roasted chestnuts, celery or fennel make pleasant accessories. Try mixing mild cheeses with the more highly ripened, aromatic or smoked ones.

Above all, remember that cheeses have their own seasons. And choose varieties that are in season. Below are listed some favorite dessert cheeses.

Soft types include uncrusted, unripened cheeses like Petit Gervais and Petit Suisse, Ricotta and Coulommiers; as well as those which are ripened and have soft edible crusts, such as Brie, Camembert, Liederkranz and Poona.

Among the semihards are the famous "fromages persillés," or mold-ripened blue-greens, in which the mold patterns the cream-colored bases in traceries resembling parsley. The interior mold, which contribute to the characteristic flavor, must be distinguished from green mold on the exterior of the cheese, which may be harmless but should be removed.

The famous blues include Stilton, Gorgonzola, Bleu, Dorset Vinney and Roquefort. Other well-known semihard dessert cheeses are Muenster, Port du Salut, Bel Paese and Gammelost.

Hard types, from which come the very best cheeses for cooking, afford many choice ones for dessert: cheddar, Gruyère, Provolone, Gjetost, Emmentaler, Cheshire and Edam, to name a few.

DESSERT CHEESE MIX
Many people like to mix sweet butter with the stronger cheeses in serving them for dessert. The combinations are legion. This one is a favorite of our friend, Helmut Ripperger, who likes to prepare it at the table. However, sometimes these mixtures are made in advance, formed into a large ball, and rolled in toasted bread crumbs.
♦ Have ingredients at room temperature.
Mix:

2 parts Roquefort cheese
1 part sweet butter
Add enough:
Armagnac or your favorite brandy
to make a soft spreadable paste. Serve with:
Toasted crackers

POTTED CHEESE
About ¾ Cup
If you would like to make up a combination of cheeses to keep, try one based on a mixture of:

4 oz. cheese
2 oz. butter
3 tablespoons port, sherry or brandy
Correct the seasoning with:
Pepper or cayenne
(Mace)

COEUR À LA CRÈME OR FRENCH CHEESE CREAM
6 Servings
When the fruit is prime, this very simple dessert is as good as any elaborate concoction we know or use.

Beat until soft:
1 lb. rich firm cream cheese
2 tablespoons cream
⅛ teaspoon salt
Have ready:
1 cup cultured sour cream or
1 cup whipped cream
Fold the cheese into the cream. Place these ingredients in a wet mold, in individual molds or in the traditional heart-shaped wicker basket, lined with moistened

cheesecloth. Chill the cheese thoroughly. Unmold it. Serve with:
Fresh unhulled strawberries, raspberries or other fresh fruit, or
Cherry Sauce, see page 709

YOGURT, COTTAGE OR CREAM CHEESE DESSERT
Sweeten:
Yogurt, cottage or cream cheese
with:
Sugar
Vanilla
Sprinkle the top with:
Cinnamon
Serve the mixture very cold with:
Stewed cherries, crushed strawberries, apricots or peaches

BAR-LE-DUC
About 1 Cup
A pleasant summer dish. Serve it with toasted crackers.
Stir to a smooth paste:
¾ cup firm cream cheese
1 or 2 tablespoons cream
Fold in:
2 tablespoons Bar-le-Duc Preserves, page 776
Refrigerate to firm the dessert, but serve at about 70°.

LIPTAUER CHEESE
About 2 Cups
If you can't buy the real thing, try this savory cheese made by mixing together, until well blended:

½ lb. dry cottage cheese
½ lb. soft butter
½ teaspoon paprika
½ teaspoon caraway seed
1 teaspoon chopped capers
½ teaspoon anchovy paste
½ teaspoon mild prepared mustard
1 tablespoon chopped chives
Serve within 6 hours of mixing, as the taste of the chives may grow strong.

ABOUT SAVORIES

Traditionally English, savories are a course presented before the fruit or after the sweet to cut the sugar taste before the port is served. They function like an hors d'oeuvre —see page 63—although they are slightly larger in size. See Oysters or Chicken Livers in Bacon; also Sardine, Caviar and Roe Croûtes or Pancakes, Tomato Tart, Deviled or Curried Seafish Tarts or Toasted Cheese Balls. If you are serving wine, choose cheese straws or cheese-and-cracker combinations rather than the fishy savories.

To most Americans savories seem curious desserts. Of course, ours must also seem strange to the English—for, to them, the word "dessert" signifies fruit. Their term for our cold desserts is "sweets," and they call our hot ones "puddings."

DESSERT SAUCES

With pudding sauces, "the object all sublime" is to "let the punishment fit the crime." In fact, unless the sauce can complement the dessert, omit it. Should the pudding be tart, tone it down with a bland sauce; if it is bland, use a sauce to which a tablespoon of liqueur imparts the final sprightly touch. Sauces based on sugar are usually very simple to confect. They have distinct branches similar to those of their unsweetened counterparts. The main things to remember are ♦ don't overbeat cream bases or cream garnishes ♦ do cook egg sauces over—not in—hot water. ♦ Be sure that sauces thickened with flour and cornstarch are free from lumps and cook them thoroughly to avoid any raw taste. See Flour Paste, page 320, and Cornstarch, page 320. ♦ In preparing heavy sirups, do not let them turn to sugar, see page 726.

LEMON, ORANGE OR LIME SAUCE
About 1 Cup
A lovely, translucent sauce.
Combine and stir in a double boiler ♦ over —not in—hot water until thickened:
    ¼ to ½ cup sugar
    1 tablespoon cornstarch
    1 cup water
Remove sauce from heat. Stir in:
    2 to 3 tablespoons butter
    ½ teaspoon grated lemon or orange rind
    1½ tablespoons lemon or lime juice or
    3 tablespoons orange juice
    ⅛ teaspoon salt

FRUIT SAUCE
About 1½ Cups
Combine, stir and heat to the boiling point, in the top of a double boiler:
    1 cup unsweetened fruit juice
    ½ to ¾ cup sugar
Mix, add and cook ♦ over—not in—hot water, until thick and clear:
    1 tablespoon cornstarch or
    2 tablespoons flour
Remove sauce from heat. Stir in:
    2 teaspoons lemon juice
    (2 tablespoons butter)
Cool. You may add:
    (1 cup crushed, shredded fruit, fresh or stewed)
Flavor with:
    Sherry or other wine or liqueur
Serve hot or cold.

CHERRY SAUCE
About 2½ Cups
Drain well:
    2 cups canned cherries, red or Bing
Add to the cherry sirup and simmer for about 10 minutes in the top of a double boiler over direct heat:
    ¼ cup sugar

¼ cup corn sirup
    1 stick cinnamon: 2 inches
    1 tablespoon lemon juice
Remove the cinnamon. Mix:
    2 teaspoons cornstarch
    1 tablespoon cold water
Stir this mixture into the hot cherry juice. Cook ♦ over—not in—hot water and stir until it thickens. Add the cherries. Serve hot or cold.

CHERRY JUBILEE SAUCE
About 1¼ Cups
This sauce always involves the use of liqueurs. If you do not wish to ignite the brandy, you may soak the cherries in it, well ahead of time. Otherwise, be sure that the fruit is at room temperature. Other preserved fruits may be substituted for the cherries.
Heat well:
    1 cup preserved, pitted Bing or other cherries
Add:
    ¼ cup slightly warmed brandy
Set the brandy on fire. When the flame has died down, add:
    2 tablespoons kirsch
You may serve the sauce hot, on:
    Vanilla ice cream

MELBA SAUCE
About 1¾ Cups
Combine and bring to the boiling point in the top of a double boiler over direct heat:
    ½ cup currant jelly
    1 cup sieved raspberries
Mix and add:
    1 teaspoon cornstarch
    ⅛ teaspoon salt
    ½ cup sugar
Cook ♦ over—not in—hot water, until thick and clear. Chill before using.

⅃ QUICK AMBROSIA SAUCE
About 1¾ Cups
Mix:
    ¾ cup puréed apricots
    ¾ cup puréed peaches
Add:
    ¼ cup orange juice
    1 teaspoon grated lemon rind
    2 tablespoons rum or sloe gin

SAUCE COCKAIGNE
About 8 Cups
Good with custards, glazed bananas, cottage pudding and waffles, by itself or combined with whipped cream. One of its distinct advantages is the availability of its ingredients at any and all seasons.
Cook gently, in a wide-bottomed, covered pan, until the fruit is pulpy and disinte-

grates easily when stirred with a wire whisk:

2 cups dried apricots
1¼ cups water
Add:
1½ cups sugar
Stir until dissolved. Add:
5 cups canned crushed pineapple
Bring the mixture to a boil. Pour into jars and cover. Keep under refrigeration.

RAISIN SAUCE
About 1⅔ Cups
Boil for 15 minutes:
1½ cups water
⅓ cup seeded raisins
¼ cup sugar
⅛ teaspoon salt
Melt:
2 tablespoons butter
Stir in, until blended:
1 teaspoon flour
Add the hot sauce slowly. Stir and cook until it boils. Mix in:
A grating of nutmeg or lemon rind
Serve over:
Steamed puddings, page 702

JELLY SAUCE
About ¾ Cup
Expressly for steamed and cornstarch puddings.
Dilute over hot water in double boiler:
¾ cup currant or other jelly
Thin with:
¼ cup boiling water or wine
Serve hot or cold. This sauce may be thickened. To do this, melt:
1 tablespoon butter
Blend in:
1 tablespoon flour
Add the jelly mixture. Stir over low heat until it thickens. You may spice it with:
1 teaspoon cinnamon
⅛ teaspoon ground cloves
⅛ teaspoon grated lemon rind

JAM SAUCE
About ¾ Cup
Combine in a small saucepan:
¼ cup raspberry, damson, gooseberry, grape or peach jam
(2 tablespoons sugar)
½ cup water
Stir and boil these ingredients for 2 minutes. Remove from heat and add:
1 teaspoon kirsch or ¼ teaspoon almond extract
Serve hot or cold. Use on:
Bread, farina and other cereal puddings, page 698

CUSTARD SAUCE
Prepare:
Custard, page 684
You may add:
(½ cup slivered almonds)

QUICK FRUIT CUSTARD SAUCE
About 3 Cups

Cream:
¼ cup butter
Add gradually and beat until fluffy:
1 cup sugar
Beat in, one at a time:
2 eggs
(One or two extra eggs will add richness)
Beat in slowly and thoroughly:
1 cup scalded milk
1 teaspoon vanilla
1 teaspoon nutmeg
Fold in:
(1 cup crushed berries, sliced peaches, etc.)

CLASSIC SABAYON SAUCE
About 3 Cups
Prepare:
Zabaglione or Sabayon, page 686
You may omit the egg white if you prefer a richer and denser texture. If you do, use in all:
1 cup wine

HOT SABAYON SAUCE
About 2 Cups
Excellent with beignets and fruit cake. Marsala is traditional in Italian recipes. We find that it gives the sauce a rather dull color and prefer to use, instead, a sweet white wine—after the French fashion. This mixture should be creamy rather than fluffy. For a fluffy sauce, see the following recipe.
Stir constantly until thick in the top of a double boiler ♦ over—not in—hot water:
6 egg yolks
⅓ cup sugar
1 cup white wine or ½ cup water and ½ cup Cointreau or Grand Marnier

COLD SABAYON SAUCE
About 1¼ Cups
The advantage of this sauce over the classic version is that it will keep under refrigeration. Use it over fresh fruits. Combine, beat and heat in the top of a double boiler ♦ over—not in—hot water:
4 egg yolks
¾ cup sugar
¾ cup dry sherry or other dry wine
Beat with a whisk until very thick. Set the double boiler top in a pan of cracked ice and continue to beat the sauce until cold. Add:
(¼ cup lightly whipped cream)

WEINSCHAUM SAUCE
Prepare:
Wine Custard or Weinschaum, page 686

RUM SAUCE
About 2½ Cups
Beat:
2 egg yolks
Add and beat until dissolved:
1 cup sifted confectioners' sugar
Add slowly:

6 tablespoons rum
Beat these ingredients until well blended.
Whip until stiff:
    1 cup whipping cream
Fold in:
    1 teaspoon vanilla
Fold the egg mixture into the cream.

RED WINE SAUCE

About 2 Cups

Boil for 5 minutes:
    1 cup sugar
    ½ cup water
Cool and add to the sirup:
    ¼ cup claret or other red wine
    ½ teaspoon grated lemon rind

HOT WINE OR
PLUM PUDDING SAUCE

About 1½ Cups

Cream:
    ½ cup butter
    1 cup sugar
Beat and add:
    1 or 2 eggs
Stir in:
    ¾ cup dry sherry, Tokay or Madeira
    1 teaspoon grated lemon rind
    (¼ teaspoon nutmeg)
Shortly before serving, beat the sauce over
hot water in a double boiler. Heat thor-
oughly.

CRÈME-DE-MENTHE
OR LIQUEUR SAUCE

Allow, for each serving, about:
    1½ tablespoons crème de menthe
      or other liqueur
Pour it over:
    Ice cream, ices or lightly
      sugared fruits
Garnish with:
    A few maraschino cherries

NESSELRODE SAUCE

About 4 cups

Combine and stir well:
    ¾ cup chopped maraschino cherries
    ⅛ cup chopped citron or orange peel
Add:
    1 cup orange marmalade
    ½ cup coarsely chopped,
      candied ginger
    2 tablespoons maraschino juice
    1 cup cooked, chopped chestnuts,
      page 272
    ½ cup or more rum, to make the sauce
      of a good consistency
Place in jars and seal. Ripen for 2 weeks.

CIDER SAUCE

About 2 Cups

Melt over low heat:
    1 tablespoon butter
Stir in, until blended:
    ¾ tablespoon flour
Add:
    1½ cups cider
Add, if needed:

(Sugar)
    (1 teaspoon cinnamon)
    (¼ teaspoon cloves)
Stir and boil these ingredients for about 2
minutes. Serve hot or cold on a bland
pudding.

CHOCOLATE SAUCE COCKAIGNE

About 2 Cups

Dreamy on vanilla, coffee or chocolate ice
cream.
Melt in the top of a double boiler ♦ over—
not in—hot water:
    3 oz. chocolate
Combine, then stir into the chocolate:
    1 well-beaten egg
    ¾ cup evaporated milk
    1 cup sugar
Cook for about 20 minutes. Remove from
heat and beat with a rotary beater for 1
minute or until well blended. Stir in:
    1 teaspoon vanilla
Cool sauce before using. If tightly covered and placed in the refrigerator, it will
keep for several days.

⅄ BLENDER CHOCOLATE SAUCE

About 1 Cup

Fine for ice cream, puddings, soft frosting
or flavoring for milk. Put into an electric
blender:
    2 squares chopped chocolate
    ½ cup sugar
    6 tablespoons warm milk, cream,
      coffee or sherry
    ½ teaspoon vanilla or rum
    ⅛ teaspoon salt
Blend until smooth.

CHOCOLATE SAUCE

About 1 Cup

Stir until dissolved, then cook, without
stirring, to the sirup stage, about 5 minutes:
    ½ cup to 1 cup water
    ½ cup sugar
Melt in the sirup:
    1 to 2 oz. chocolate
Cool. Add:
    1 teaspoon vanilla
If the sirup is too thick, thin it to the right
consistency with:
    Cream, dry sherry or brandy
Serve hot. If made in advance, keep hot
in a double boiler.

HOT FUDGE SAUCE

About 1 Cup

The grand kind that, when cooked for the
longer period and served hot, grows hard
on ice cream and enraptures children.
Melt in a double boiler ♦ over—not in—
hot water:
    2 oz. unsweetened chocolate
Add and melt:
    1 tablespoon butter
Stir and blend well, then add:
    ⅛ cup boiling water
Stir well and add:
    1 cup sugar
    2 tablespoons corn sirup

Permit the sauce to boil readily, but not too furiously, over direct heat. Do not stir. If you wish an ordinary sauce, boil it for 5 minutes. If you wish a hot sauce that will harden over ice cream, boil it for about 8 minutes. Add just before serving:

 1 teaspoon vanilla or 2 teaspoons rum

When cold, this sauce is very thick. It may be reheated over boiling water.

CHOCOLATE CUSTARD SAUCE
About 2¼ Cups

Heat in a double boiler ♦ over—not in— hot water, until melted:

 2 oz. chopped chocolate
 2 cups milk

Beat well:

 4 egg yolks
 ¾ cup sugar
 ⅛ teaspoon salt

Beat the hot mixture gradually into the yolks. Return to double boiler for 5 minutes and cook gently, stirring constantly. Cool. Add:

 1 teaspoon vanilla

Serve, hot or cold, over:

   Filled cream puffs, puddings
   or ice cream

CHOCOLATE NUT-BRITTLE SAUCE
8 Servings

Melt in a double boiler ♦ over—not in— hot water:

 3 oz. sweet chocolate

Add:

 1¼ cups crushed nut brittle

Stir in slowly:

 ½ cup boiling water

Heat until the candy is melted. Cool slightly. Before serving, add:

 1 tablespoon brandy

Serve over:

   Ice cream

MOCHA SAUCE
About 1½ Cups

Bring to a boil and cook over moderate heat for about 3 minutes, stirring occasionally:

 ½ cup cocoa
 ⅛ teaspoon salt
 1 cup dark corn sirup
 ¼ cup sugar or 16 average-sized
   marshmallows
 ¼ cup water
 1 teaspoon instant coffee

Swirl in:

 2 tablespoons butter

When slightly cool, stir in:

 ½ teaspoon vanilla

Serve hot or cold.

CHOCOLATE MINT SAUCE
6 Servings

Melt in a double boiler ♦ over—not in— hot water:

 10 large chocolate peppermint creams

Add:

 3 tablespoons cream

Stir well.

CHOCOLATE CARAMEL SAUCE
About 1 Cup

Melt over low heat:

 4 oz. semi-sweet chocolate

Stir in and cook until sauce is thick:

 1 cup packed brown sugar
 ½ cup cream
 1 tablespoon butter

Cool slightly and add:

 1 teaspoon vanilla

MAPLE SIRUP SAUCE
About ¾ Cup

Heat, but do not boil:

 ½ cup maple sirup

Add:

 ½ teaspoon grated lemon peel
 ¼ teaspoon freshly grated nutmeg or
   ⅛ teaspoon ginger or cloves
 (2 to 3 tablespoons nut meats)

Chill and serve cold. If you serve it hot, swirl in:

 1 to 2 tablespoons butter

MAPLE SUGAR SAUCE
About 2 Cups

Stir over low heat until dissolved, then boil, without stirring, to a thin sirup:

 1 lb. maple sugar
 ½ cup evaporated milk

Add:

 ¼ cup corn sirup
 ½ teaspoon vanilla
 ½ cup shredded nut meats

BUTTERSCOTCH SAUCE
About ¾ Cup

Boil to the consistency of heavy sirup:

 ⅓ cup white corn sirup
 ⅝ cup packed light-brown sugar
 2 tablespoons butter
 ⅛ teaspoon salt

Cool these ingredients. Add:

 ⅓ cup evaporated milk or cream

Serve the sauce hot or cold. It may be reheated in a double boiler.

HOT BROWN-SUGAR SAUCE
About 1½ Cups

Cook for 5 minutes, stirring occasionally:

 1 cup brown sugar
 ½ cup water

Pour the sirup in a fine stream over:

 1 beaten egg

Beat constantly. Cook and stir in double boiler ♦ over—not in—hot water for 2 minutes.

Add:

 3 tablespoons dry sherry
 ⅛ teaspoon salt

Serve hot.

BROWN-SUGAR BUTTER SAUCE
About 1 Cup

Fine with hot puddings or waffles.

Cream in a small saucepan:

 ¼ cup butter
 1 cup closely packed brown sugar

Add gradually:

 1 cup warm thin cream

Stir over low heat until it boils. Remove
from heat. Add:
    ¼ cup bourbon or brandy
Beat with an egg beater until smooth.
Add and mix in:
    (⅛ cup chopped nuts)

BROWN-SUGAR CREAM SAUCE
About 1½ Cups

Place in a double boiler ♦ over—not in—
hot water:
    3 beaten egg yolks
    ¾ cup cream
    ¾ teaspoon salt
    ½ cup brown sugar
Stir and cook until thick and creamy.
Add a little at a time, stirring constantly:
    3 tablespoons butter
    1½ tablespoons lemon juice

BROWN-SUGAR ORANGE SAUCE
About 1 Cup

Good for filling coffee cakes or poured over
pancakes and waffles.
Combine in a saucepan:
    ¾ cup brown sugar
    ¼ cup butter
    ½ cup orange juice
Stir constantly and heat for 3 minutes,
then cool.

CARAMEL SAUCE
About 1 Cup

Prepare and cool, so as not to curdle the
cream:
    ½ cup Caramel Sirup, page 738
Add:
    1 cup cream or strong coffee
    1 teaspoon vanilla
    ⅛ teaspoon salt
If you use coffee, swirl in:
    2 tablespoons butter
You may keep the sauce hot over hot
water.

CARAMEL CREAM SAUCE
About 1½ Cups

Combine and stir in a double boiler ♦ over
—not in—hot water, until melted:
    ½ lb. Caramels, page 732
    1 cup whipping cream or
      evaporated milk

COFFEE SAUCE
About 1½ Cups

Beat:
    2 eggs
Beat into them, very slowly:
    ½ cup strong boiling coffee
Add:
    ¼ cup sugar
    ⅛ teaspoon salt
Cook ♦ over—not in—hot water and stir
the sauce in the top of a double boiler un-
til it coats a spoon. Chill.
Shortly before serving, fold in:
    ½ cup whipped cream
    (¼ cup chopped candied ginger)

HONEY SAUCE
About 1 Cup

Combine and stir well:
    ¼ cup hot water
    ½ cup honey
    ¼ cup chopped nut meats
    ¼ cup minced candied orange or lemon
      peel or candied ginger
Chill.

HONEY MINT SAUCE
About ¾ Cup

Recommended for fruit compotes.
Combine:
    ½ cup orange juice
    2 tablespoons lemon juice
    2 tablespoons honey
    ⅛ cup finely chopped fresh mint

VANILLA SAUCE
About 1 Cup

Prepare:
    Lemon, Orange or Lime Sauce,
    page 709
Use the smaller amount of sugar and substitute for the lemon juice:
    1 inch of vanilla bean, page 528 or
    1 to 2 teaspoons vanilla or
    1 tablespoon rum

MARSHMALLOW SAUCE
About 2 Cups

Stir over low heat until the sugar is dissolved:
    ¾ cup sugar
    1 tablespoon light corn sirup
    ¼ cup milk
Bring to a boil, then simmer gently for
about 5 minutes. Dissolve in top of double boiler by stirring ♦ over—not in—hot
water:
    ½ lb. marshmallows, page 730
    2 tablespoons water
Pour the sirup over the dissolved marshmallows, beating well.
Add:
    1 teaspoon vanilla
Serve the sauce hot or cold. It may be reheated in a double boiler. Beat well before serving.

COCONUT DULCIE
About 4½ Cups

Good by itself over fruit puddings, or
combined as a sauce with purées of tart
fruit such as guava and currant.
Boil to the thick sirup stage:
    4 cups water
    3 cups sugar
Add:
    1 freshly grated coconut, page 523
Cook slowly for about 25 minutes until the
mixture is translucent. Pour into sterile
jars and seal.

SWEETENED BUTTERS
I.   **About ¼ Cup**

Cream, then chill:
    3 tablespoons butter
    ½ cup sifted confectioners' sugar
    ¾ teaspoon cinnamon

II. Honey Butter
About ½ Cup

This is delicious on waffles or toast.
Beat well:

 ¼ cup honey
 2 tablespoons soft butter
 2 tablespoons whipping cream

III. See Henri's Butter Sauce, page 213.

HARD SAUCE
About 1 Cup

The basic ingredients of hard sauce are
always the same, although proportions and
flavoring may vary. In this recipe, the
larger amount of butter is preferable. An
attractive way to serve hard sauce on cold
cake or pudding is to chill it and mold it
with a small fancy cutter—or to put it
through an individual butter mold.
Sift:

 1 cup powdered sugar

Beat until soft:

 2 to 5 tablespoons butter

Add the sugar gradually. Beat these ingredients until they are well blended. Add:

 ⅛ teaspoon salt
 1 teaspoon vanilla or 1 tablespoon
   coffee, rum, whisky, brandy,
   lemon juice, etc.

Beat in:

 (1 egg or ¼ cup cream)

When the sauce is very smooth, chill thoroughly.

SPICY HARD SAUCE
About 1 Cup

Prepare:

 Hard Sauce, above

Beat into it:

 ½ teaspoon cinnamon
 ¼ teaspoon cloves
 1 teaspoon vanilla
 ½ teaspoon lemon juice
 ⅛ teaspoon salt
   (Liqueur, to taste)

Chill.

BROWN-SUGAR HARD SAUCE
About 1¾ Cups

Sift:

 1½ cups brown sugar

Beat until soft:

 ½ cup butter

Add the sugar gradually. Beat these ingredients until well blended. Beat in
slowly:

 ⅓ cup cream

Beat in, drop by drop:

 2 tablespoons dry wine or
 1 teaspoon vanilla

Chill well. Add for garnish:

 (¼ cup chopped nuts)

FRUIT HARD SAUCE
About 1¾ Cups

Sift:

 1 cup confectioners' sugar

Beat until soft:

 ⅓ cup butter

Add the sugar gradually. Beat well

blended. Beat in:

 ¼ cup cream
 ⅔ cup crushed strawberries,
   raspberries, apricots or bananas

Chill thoroughly.

FLUFFY HARD SAUCE
About 1½ Cups

Sift:

 1 cup sugar

Beat until soft:

 1 tablespoon butter

Add the sugar gradually and:

 1 tablespoon cream

Beat until well blended. Whip until stiff:

 3 egg whites

Fold them into the sugar mixture. Add:

 2 tablespoons cream
 1 teaspoon or more vanilla, rum or port

Beat the sauce well. Pile it in a dish. Chill
thoroughly.

FOAMY SAUCE
About 2 Cups

Sift:

 1 cup powdered sugar

Beat until soft:

 ⅓ to ½ cup butter

Add the sugar slowly. Beat until well
blended. Beat in:

 1 egg yolk
 1 teaspoon vanilla or
 2 tablespoons wine

Place the sauce in a double boiler ♦ over—
not in—hot water. Beat and cook until the
yolk has thickened slightly. Whip until
stiff:

 1 egg white

Fold it lightly into the sauce. Serve hot or
cold.

LIQUEUR CREAM SAUCE
About 1½ Cups

So zestful that it will glorify the plainest
cottage pudding, cake or gingerbread. Less
extravagant, too, than it sounds—only a
small amount being needed.
Beat until soft in the top of a double
boiler ♦ over—not in—hot water:

 ⅓ cup butter

Add gradually and beat until creamy:

 1 cup sifted confectioners' sugar

Beat in slowly:

 3 tablespoons brandy or other liqueur

Beat in, one at a time:

 2 egg yolks

Add:

 ½ cup cream

Cook until slightly thickened.

SOUR CREAM SAUCE
About 1½ Cups

Use as dressing for berries, or combine
berries with it and serve over cake or fruit
gelatin.
Combine:

 1 cup cultured sour cream
 ½ cup packed brown sugar
 (1 cup berries)
 (½ teaspoon vanilla)

ICE CREAMS, ICES AND
FROZEN DESSERTS

ABOUT CHURNED ICE CREAMS AND ICES

Nowadays, with plentiful ice and electric churning, few people recall the shared excitement of the era when making ice cream was a rarely scheduled event. Then the iceman brought to the back door, on special order, a handsome 2-foot-square cube of cold crystal and everyone in the family took a turn at the crank. The critical question among us children was, of course, who might lick the dasher. A century or so ago the novelist Stendhal knew only hand-churned ice cream and, when he first tasted it, exclaimed, "What a pity this isn't a sin!"

Hand-churning is still tops for perfectionists, for no power-driven machine has yet been invented that can achieve a comparable texture. Even French Pot, the very best commercial method for making ice cream, calls for finishing by hand.

Ice creams are based on ◆ carefully cooked ◆ well-chilled sirups and heavy custards, added to ◆ unwhipped cream. ◆ No form of vanilla flavoring can surpass that of vanilla sugar or of the bean itself, steeped in a hot sirup. If sweetened frozen fruits are incorporated into the cream mixture instead of fresh fruits, be sure to adjust sugar content accordingly.

◆ Make up mixtures for churn-frozen ice creams the day before you freeze, to increase yield and to produce a smoother-textured cream. ◆ In churn-freezing ice creams and ices, fill the container only ¾ full to permit expansion. ◆ To pack the freezer, allow 3 to 6 quarts of chipped or cracked ice to 1 cup of coarse rock salt. Pack about ⅓ of the freezer with ice and add layers of salt and ice around the container until the freezer is full. Allow the pack to stand about 3 minutes before you start turning. Turn slowly at first, about 40 revolutions a minute, until a slight pull is felt. Then triple speed for 5 or 6 minutes. If any additions, such as finely cut candied or fresh fruits or nuts are to be made, do so at this point. Then repack and taper off the churning to about 80 revolutions a minute for a few minutes more. The cream should be ready in 10 to 20 minutes, depending on the quantity.

If the ice cream or ice is to be used at once, it should be frozen harder than if you plan to serve it later. Should the interval be 2 hours or more, packing will firm it. ◆ To pack, pour off the salt water in the freezer and wipe off the lid. Remove the dasher carefully, making sure that no salt or water gets into the cream container. Scrape the cream down from the sides of the container. Place a cork in the lid and replace the lid. Repack the container in the freezer with additional ice and salt, using the same proportions as before. Cover the freezer with newspapers, a piece of carpet or other heavy material.

The cream should be smooth when served. If it proves granular, you used too much salt in the packing mixture, over-filled the inner container with the ice cream mixture or turned too rapidly. ✱ If you are making a large quantity with the idea of storing some in the deep-freeze, package in sizes you plan on serving. Should ice cream be allowed to melt even slightly and is then refrozen, it loses in volume and even more in good texture.

GARNISHES AND ADDITIONS TO ICE CREAM MIXTURES

Add to ice cream, when it is in a partially frozen state, allowing the following amounts per quart:

    1 cup toasted chopped nuts
    1 cup crushed nut brittle
    ⅓ cup preserved ginger and 1 table-
        spoon of the sirup
    1 cup crushed chocolate molasses chips
    1 cup crushed macaroons plus
        2 tablespoons sherry or liqueur
    ½ cup Polvo de Amor, page 523

For fruit additions, see Fruit Ice Creams, page 716.

To garnish ice cream, add just before serving:

    Chopped nuts or shredded coconut
    Candied violets
    Chopped candied citrus peel or
    other candied fruits
    Crystallized angelica, cut in tiny
    fancy shapes
    Decorettes
    Shaved or chopped sweet or bitter
    chocolate
    Marzipan fruits or rosettes

SNOW ICE CREAM

This is the ancestor of all frozen delights and a favorite winter scoop for small fry. Arrange attractively in a chilled bowl, trying not to compact it:

    Fresh, clean snow

Pour over it:

    Sweetened fruit juice

or a mixture of:

    Cream
    Sugar
    Vanilla

VANILLA ICE CREAM   I
About 9 Servings

Warm over low heat, but do not boil:
  1 cup cream
Stir in, until dissolved:
  ¾ cup sugar
  ⅛ teaspoon salt
Chill. Add:
  3 cups cream
  1½ teaspoons vanilla
To churn-freeze the ice cream, see page
715. Serve with:
  **Tutti Frutti, page 780, Cherries
  Jubilee, page 709, or a liqueur**

DELMONICO ICE CREAM
OR CRÈME GLACÉE
                              About 9 servings
Scald over low heat, but do not boil:
  1½ cups milk
Stir in, until dissolved:
  ¾ cup sugar
  ⅛ teaspoon salt
Pour the milk slowly over:
  2 or 3 beaten egg yolks
Beat these ingredients until well blended.
Stir and cook in a double boiler ♦ over—
but not in—hot water, until thick and
smooth. Chill. Add and fold into the custard:
  1 tablespoon vanilla
  1 cup whipping cream
  1 cup cream
To churn-freeze the ice cream, see page
715. Serve with:
  Crushed Nut Brittle, page 736

CARAMEL ICE CREAM
Prepare:
  **Vanilla or Delmonico Ice Cream,
  above**
Add:
  **2 to 4 tablespoons Caramelized Sugar I,
  page 507**
To churn-freeze and serve, see page 715.
Garnish with:
  Chopped pecans or toasted almonds

PEPPERMINT-STICK ICE CREAM
                              About 12 Servings
Grind or crush:
  ½ lb. peppermint-stick candy
Soak for 12 hours in:
  2 cups milk
Add:
  1 cup cream
  1 cup whipping cream
To churn-freeze and serve, see page 715.
Serve with:
  **Shaved Sweet Chocolate, page 522,
  or Chocolate Sauce Cockaigne,
  page 711**

CHOCOLATE ICE CREAM
                              About 8 Servings
Dissolve in the top of a double boiler ♦
over—not in—hot water:
  2 oz. chocolate
in:
  2 cups milk
Stir in:
  1 cup sugar

  ⅛ teaspoon salt
Remove from the heat. Beat with a wire
whisk until cool and fluffy. Add:
  1½ teaspoons vanilla
  1 cup whipping cream
  1 cup cream
Fold the cream into the chocolate mixture.
To churn-freeze the ice cream, see page
715. You may serve it in:
  (Meringues, page 600)
with:
  (Chocolate Sauce, page 711)

COFFEE ICE CREAM
                              About 9 Servings
Scald over low heat, but do not boil:
  2½ cups milk
Stir in, until dissolved:
  1½ cups sugar
Pour the milk slowly over:
  2 beaten eggs
Beat until well blended. Stir and cook in a
double boiler ♦ over—not in—hot water,
until thick and smooth. Chill. Add:
  ½ cup strong cold coffee
  ½ teaspoon salt
  1 cup whipping cream
When almost frozen, add:
  1 teaspoon vanilla
  3 tablespoons rum
To churn-freeze and serve, see page 715.
Garnish with:
  Shaved chocolate

★ PISTACHIO ICE CREAM
                              About 9 Servings
A pretty Christmas dessert served in a
meringue tart garnished with whipped
cream and cherries.
Shell:
  4 oz. pistachio nuts
Blanch them, page 521. Pound them in a
mortar with:
  A few drops rose water
Add to them:
  ¼ cup sugar
  ¼ cup cream
  1 teaspoon vanilla
  ½ teaspoon almond extract
  A little green coloring
Stir these ingredients until the sugar is dissolved. Heat, but do not boil:
  1 cup cream
Add and stir until dissolved:
  ¾ cup sugar
  ⅛ teaspoon salt
Chill these ingredients. Add the pistachio
mixture and:
  2 cups whipping cream
  1 cup cream
To churn-freeze and serve, see page 715.

FRUIT ICE CREAMS
                              About 9 Servings
Delicious fruit creams can be made using:
  **2 to 2½ cups sweetened puréed or
  finely sliced fruit—greengage plums,
  mangoes, peaches, apricots or
  bananas**

Add:

> ¼ teaspoon salt
> Lemon juice to taste
> 2 to 3 cups whipping cream
> 1 cup cream

To churn-freeze the cream, see page 715.

APRICOT OR PEACH ICE CREAM
About 9 Servings

Pare, slice and mash:

> 4 lbs. ripe peaches or apricots

Stir in:

> ½ to ¾ cup sugar
> ⅛ teaspoon salt

Cover the peaches or apricots closely and permit them to stand in the refrigerator until the sugar is dissolved. Combine:

> 1 teaspoon vanilla
> ½ cup sugar
> 2 cups cream
> 2 cups whipping cream

Partly churn-freeze these ingredients, see page 715. When they are half-frozen, add the fruit mixture and finish freezing.

ORANGE ICE CREAM
About 9 Servings

Heat but do not boil:

> 1½ cups cream

Stir in, until dissolved:

> 1½ cups sugar

Chill. Add:

> 1½ cups whipping cream

Churn-freeze the cream, see page 715, until it has a slushy consistency. Add:

> 3 tablespoons lemon juice
> 1¼ cups orange juice

Finish freezing. Serve with:

> Polvo de Amor, page 523

STRAWBERRY OR RASPBERRY ICE CREAM
About 9 Servings

Hull:

> 1 quart berries

Sieve them. Stir into the pulpy juice:

> ⅞ cup sugar

Chill thoroughly. Combine with:

> 2 cups cream
> 2 cups whipping cream

To churn-freeze, see page 715.

ABOUT STILL-FROZEN ICE CREAMS, ICES, BOMBES, MOUSSES AND PARFAITS

In our family, a richly loaded bombe, even more than a churned ice cream, betokened festivity—the burst of glory which topped off a party dinner. These fancy molds were reserved for winter festivities and we always hoped that they would be buried in the snow. Finding them again was such a lark.

Then, as now, these still-frozen desserts ◊ needed an emulsifying agent—eggs, cornstarch, gelatin or corn sirup—to keep large crystals from forming during the freezing process. Classic French recipes specify at least 8 eggs to a cup of sugar sirup to obtain the requisite smoothness.

Here are some good combinations:

> Strawberry ice outside, Delmonico with strawberries in kirsch inside
> Raspberries and pistachios
> Coffee and vanilla praliné
> Coffee and banana mousse
> Chocolate and angelica
> Vanilla, orange and chocolate

◊ To still-freeze creams and ices ◊ whip the cream only to the point where it stands in soft peaks. Any further beating will make the dessert disagreeably buttery. The cream and any solids such as nuts and candied fruits are incorporated when the rest of the mixture is partially frozen, and liqueurs are added almost at the end of the freezing period.

Descriptions of the many desserts that can be made in the ✳ freezer or in the freezing compartment of the refrigerator will follow. When the mixtures are in the mold, rest them in the deep freeze on other packages, not directly on the evaporator shelves. They may be made the day before you plan to use them but do not keep well much longer than this. ◊ Remove them from the freezer about ½ hour before use, leaving them in the mold until ready to serve. Then garnish with meringues, fruits, sauces or cakes. ◊ To make ornamental bombes, put the cream into tall, fancy or melon molds or in the special ones from which they took their playfully sinister name.

Churn-frozen ices or ice creams may form a single or double outside coating. They are applied as a rather thin layer to the inside surface of the mold, each layer being, in turn, individually frozen, see Gelatin Molds, page 517. The softer, still-frozen bombe, mousse or Bavarian mixtures are then filled into the center and the mold covered before placement in the freezer. To pack in refrigerator trays, cover with foil. ◊ In the absence of a freezer, set the well-covered mold in a bed of cracked ice. Allow from 2 to 4 parts of ice to 1 of salt and use a bucket or a pail that will ensure complete coverage—about 3 inches on top, bottom and sides. Chill the cream from 4 to 6 hours. Serve parfaits in narrow and tall-stemmed glasses or place in layers between preserved fruits, ice creams and sauces, topped with whipped cream and a maraschino cherry.

VANILLA ICE CREAM II
About 9 Servings

Soak:

> 2 teaspoons gelatin

in:

> ¼ cup cold water

Scald in a double boiler:

> ¾ cup milk

with:

> 1 vanilla bean

Stir into it, until dissolved:

> ¾ cup sugar
> ⅛ teaspoon salt

Stir in the soaked gelatin. Cool and place this mixture in refrigerator trays until thoroughly chilled. Whip with a wire whisk until thickened, but not stiff:

3 cups whipping cream

Fold into the chilled and beaten gelatin mixture. ◗ Still-freeze the cream in a mold, or in a foil-covered refrigerator tray, see above. Serve with:

Chocolate Mint Sauce, page 712, or
Maple Sugar Sauce, page 712

or cover with:

Shredded coconut
Chocolate sauce

An attractive way to serve vanilla ice cream in summer is to place balls of cream in the center of a large platter and surround them with mounds of red raspberries, black raspberries and fresh pineapple sticks, using green leaves as a garnish. You may also use any of the additions suggested in Vanilla Ice Cream I, page 715.

VANILLA ICE CREAM WITH EGG YOLKS

6 Servings

Beat:

2 egg yolks

Beat in until well blended:

½ cup confectioners' sugar
¼ cup cream

Cook and stir in a double boiler ◗ over—not in—hot water, until slightly thickened. Chill. Add:

1 teaspoon vanilla or 1 tablespoon
or more dry sherry

◗ Whip until thickened, but not stiff:

1 cup whipping cream

In a separate bowl, whip until stiff ◗ but not dry:

2 egg whites

Fold the cream and the egg whites into the custard. ◗ Still-freeze the ice cream in a mold, page 717, or in foil-covered refrigerator trays, page 717. Serve with:

Jelly Sauce, page 710

FROZEN EGGNOG

Prepare:

Delmonico Ice Cream, page 716, or
Vanilla Ice Cream with Egg Yolks

When almost frozen, make a funnel-shaped hole in the center. Place in it:

Several tablespoons rum, brandy
or whisky

Stir the liquor into the ice cream. Let the mixture continue to freeze.

VANILLA ICE CREAM WITH EVAPORATED MILK

4 Servings

Start to make this the day before you need it. During the process of evaporating milk, a caramel overtone develops, which plays hob with the delicate flavor of vanilla. We prefer to accentuate the caramel by adding:

2 to 4 tablespoons or more Caramel
Sirup, page 738

Or you may transform the caramel flavor with:

1 to 2 teaspoons instant coffee

To prepare the ice cream, stir over heat, but do not boil:

⅓ to ½ cup sugar
¼ cup cream

Chill. Add:

1½ teaspoons vanilla

Prepare for whipping by the recipe on page 484:

1¼ cups evaporated milk

Whip. Combine lightly with the sugar mixture. To still-freeze and serve, see page 717.

BISCUIT TORTONI OR MACAROON BOMBE

4 Servings

Combine:

¾ cup crushed macaroons
¾ cup cream
¼ cup sifted confectioners' sugar
A few grains salt

Permit these ingredients to stand for 1 hour. ◗ Whip until thickened, but not stiff:

1 cup whipping cream

Fold in the macaroon mixture and:

1 teaspoon vanilla

Place in paper muffin cups set in a refrigerator tray. To still-freeze, see page 717. Either before freezing or when partly frozen, decorate tops with:

Maraschino cherries
Unsalted toasted almonds
Crystallized angelica, etc.

MOCHA ICE CREAM

8 Servings

In spite of an almost lifelong prejudice against marshmallows, we give the next 2 recipes a more than grudging approval. Melt in a double boiler ◗ over—not in—hot water:

18 average-size marshmallows: ¼ lb.
½ lb. semi-sweet chocolate

Cool slightly and stir in:

2 cups whipping cream
¾ cup strong coffee

Pour this mixture gradually over:

4 well-beaten egg yolks

◗ Be sure that the mixture is not so hot as to curdle the eggs. To still-freeze and serve, see page 717.

CHOCOLATE ICE CREAM WITH EVAPORATED MILK

4 Servings

Chill until ice-cold:

1 cup evaporated milk

Combine:

6 tablespoons cocoa or 1½ oz.
melted chocolate
6 tablespoons sugar
¼ teaspoon salt

Stir in gradually:

½ cup evaporated milk
½ cup water

Stir and cook these ingredients in a double boiler ♦ over—not in—hot water, until smooth. Add and stir until melted:

18 average-size marshmallows: ¼ lb.

Cool this mixture. Whip the chilled milk until stiff, then fold it in. To still-freeze the ice cream in a mold, see page 717, or in foil-covered refrigerator trays, page 717.

GREENGAGE PLUM ICE CREAM
12 Servings

Drain:

3½ cups canned greengage plums

Put them through a ricer. There should be about 1½ cups of pulp. Soak:

1½ teaspoons gelatin

in:

¼ cup cold water

Heat to the boiling point:

2 cups milk
¾ to 1 cup sugar
⅛ teaspoon salt

Dissolve the gelatin in the hot milk. Cool, then add the plum pulp and:

2 tablespoons lemon juice

Chill the mixture until slushy. Add when whipped, until thickened but not stiff:

2 cups whipping cream

Still-freeze the ice cream in a mold, see page 717, or in foil-covered trays, page 717.

DELMONICO BOMBE
About 15 Servings

Soak:

1½ teaspoons gelatin

in:

¼ cup cold water

Stir and bring to the boiling point:

2 cups milk
1½ cups sugar

Dissolve the gelatin in the hot milk. Pour part of this mixture over:

2 beaten egg yolks

Beat until blended. Stir and cook in a double boiler ♦ over—not in—hot water, until the eggs thicken slightly. Cool the custard. Add:

1 teaspoon vanilla

Chill until about to set. ♦ Whip until thickened, but not stiff:

4 cups whipping cream

In a separate bowl whip until ♦ stiff, but not dry:

2 egg whites

Fold the cream and the egg whites lightly into the custard. Have ready:

18 macaroons

Sprinkle them with:

Cointreau or kirsch

Spread them with:

Tart jelly

Place alternate layers of cream and macaroons in a mold or in refrigerator trays. To still-freeze the ice cream, see page 717.

CHOCOLATE BOMBE
About 10 Servings

Soak:

1½ teaspoons gelatin

in:

1 cup cold water

Stir and bring to the boiling point:

1 cup milk
1½ cups sugar
2 tablespoons cocoa

Dissolve the gelatin in the mixture. Cool. Add:

1 teaspoon vanilla

Chill until about to set. ♦ Whip until thickened, but not stiff:

2 cups whipping cream

Fold lightly into the gelatin mixture. To still-freeze the bombe in a mold or in foil-covered refrigerator trays, see page 717.

STRAWBERRY OR RASPBERRY BOMBE

Prepare:

Bavarian Berry Cream, page 694

using in all:

1½ cups sugar

To still-freeze the ice cream, see page 717.

BUTTER PECAN ICE CREAM
About 6 Servings

Boil for 2 minutes:

1 cup packed light brown sugar
½ cup water
⅛ teaspoon salt

Beat:

2 eggs

Beat in the sirup slowly. Cook in a double boiler ♦ over—not in—hot water, stirring constantly until slightly thickened. Add:

2 tablespoons butter

Cool, then add:

1 cup milk
1 teaspoon vanilla extract
1 tablespoon sherry

Beat until ♦ thickened, but not stiff:

1 cup whipping cream

Fold it into the egg mixture. To still-freeze, see page 717. When partially frozen, fold in:

½ cup broken toasted pecan meats

If the nuts are salted, a very special piquancy results.

FRUIT BUTTERMILK ICE CREAM
About 5 Servings

This is a low-fat dish and quite acceptable. Combine:

1 cup sweetened fruit purée: apricot, peach or strawberry

with:

3 tablespoons lemon juice
⅛ teaspoon salt
1½ cups buttermilk

To still-freeze, see page 717.

PERSIMMON ICE CREAM
About 6 Servings

A California creation.

Put through a ricer:
4 ripe Japanese persimmons
Add:
2 tablespoons sugar
6 tablespoons lemon juice
◗ Whip until thickened, but not stiff:
2 cups whipping cream
Still-freeze in a mold, page 717, or in foil-covered refrigerator trays, page 717.

FRUIT MOUSSE

About 9 Servings

Prepare:
2 cups crushed fruit—peaches,
apricots, bananas, strawberries or
black raspberries
Stir in:
⅛ teaspoon salt
¾ to 1 cup confectioners' sugar
Soak:
1½ teaspoons gelatin
in:
2 tablespoons cold water
Dissolve it in:
¼ cup boiling water
Chill and add:
2 tablespoons lemon juice
Stir into the fruit mixture. ◗ Whip until thickened, but not stiff:
2 cups whipping cream
Fold into the fruit and gelatin mixture. Still-freeze in a mold, page 717, or in foil-covered refrigerator trays, page 717.

APRICOT MOUSSE WITH
EVAPORATED MILK

About 6 Servings

Surprisingly good—the fruit flavor being decided enough to disguise the evaporated milk taste.
Prepare for whipping, page 484:
1¼ cups evaporated milk
Put through a ricer or blend:
¾ cup cooked sweetened drained
dried apricots
We do not like to substitute the canned ones, as the flavor is not strong enough.
Soak:
1 teaspoon gelatin
in:
2 tablespoons cold juice
Dissolve it in:
2 tablespoons hot juice
Add the gelatin to the apricot purée. Chill until about to set. Whip the chilled evaporated milk and add to it:
½ teaspoon vanilla
⅛ teaspoon salt
Fold lightly into gelatin mixture. To still-freeze in foil-covered refrigerator trays, see page 717.

COFFEE PARFAIT

About 6 Servings

Combine:
2 tablespoons cornstarch
⅔ cup sugar
⅛ teaspoon salt
Stir into this:

2 tablespoons milk
Beat, then add:
2 egg yolks
1 cup strong coffee
Stir and cook this custard in a double boiler ◗ over—not in—hot water, until it thickens. Chill. ◗ Whip until thickened, but not stiff and fold in:
1½ cups whipping cream
To still-freeze in foil-covered refrigerator trays, see page 717. Serve in tall glasses, topped with:
Whipped cream
(Grated chocolate)

TUTTI FRUTTI PARFAIT

About 6 Servings

Cover and soak:
1 cup chopped candied fruit
in a combination of:
Brandy, rum, liqueur and sirup from
canned stewed fruit
Drain well. Reserve liquid for flavoring puddings. Soak:
1 teaspoon gelatin
in:
2 tablespoons water
Dissolve it over hot water. Boil to the thread stage, page 726:
½ cup water
½ cup sugar
Beat ◗ until stiff, but not dry:
2 egg whites
Pour the sirup over the egg whites in a fine stream, beating constantly. Add the dissolved gelatin and continue beating until mixture thickens somewhat. Beat in drained fruit. ◗ Whip until thickened, but not stiff:
1 cup whipping cream
1 teaspoon vanilla
Fold into fruit and egg mixture. Still-freeze in a mold, page 717, or in foil-covered refrigerator trays, page 717. Serve topped with:
Whipped cream
Candied cherries

CARAMEL PARFAIT

About 9 Servings

Soak:
1½ teaspoons gelatin
in:
½ cup cold water
Prepare:
¾ cup warm Caramelized Sugar I,
page 507
Beat:
2 egg yolks
Beat in slowly:
½ cup sugar
Beat these ingredients until well blended. Add the caramel mixture. Stir in a double boiler ◗ over—not in—hot water, until the custard coats a spoon. Stir in the soaked gelatin. Cool. Add:
2 teaspoons vanilla
Chill until about to set. ◗ Whip until thickened, but not stiff:

2 cups whipping cream
old lightly into the custard. Still-freeze
1 a mold, page 717, or in foil-covered re-
rigerator trays, page 717. Garnish with:
Toasted slivered almonds

UTTERSCOTCH PARFAIT
About 6 Servings
tir and melt in a saucepan over low heat,
hen boil for 1 minute:
⅔ cup packed brown sugar
2 tablespoons butter
⅛ teaspoon salt
dd:
½ cup water
ook the butterscotch until smooth and
rupy. Beat:
4 egg yolks
dd the cooled sirup slowly, beating con-
antly. Cook and stir in a double boiler
over—not in—hot water, until light and
uffy. Chill. ♦ Whip until thickened, but
ot stiff:
1 cup whipping cream
dd:
2 teaspoons vanilla
old into egg mixture. Still-freeze in a
iold, page 717, or in foil-covered re-
rigerator trays, page 717.

IAPLE PARFAIT
About 9 Servings
ook and stir ♦ over—not in—hot water
ntil thick:
6 egg yolks
¾ cup maple sirup
⅛ teaspoon salt
Vhen the custard coats a spoon, remove it
om the heat. Pour into a bowl and beat
ith a wire whisk until cool. ♦ Whip until
iickened, but not stiff:
2 cups whipping cream
old it lightly into the custard. When par-
ally frozen, add:
(½ cup crushed Nut Brittle, page 736)
till-freeze in a mold, page 717, or in foil-
overed refrigerator trays, page 717.

ASPBERRY PARFAIT
About 9 Servings
rush and strain through 2 thicknesses of
ieesecloth:
1 quart raspberries
oil to the thread stage, page 726:
¾ cup water
1 cup sugar
Vhip until stiff ♦ but not dry:
3 egg whites
ur the sirup over them in a slow stream.
Vhip constantly until cool. Fold in
ushed berries. In a separate bowl ♦ whip
itil thickened, but not stiff:
2 cups whipping cream
old lightly into other ingredients. Still-
eeze in a mold, page 717, or in foil-
overed refrigerator trays, page 717.

NGELICA PARFAIT
About 12 Servings

Try combining layers of angelica, chocolate and lime.
Boil to the thread stage, page 726:
1½ cups sugar
½ cup water
Whip ♦ until stiff, but not dry:
2 egg whites
Pour sirup over them in a slow stream.
Whip constantly. When cool, add:
1 teaspoon vanilla or 1 tablespoon or
more Cointreau
♦ Whip until thickened, but not stiff:
3 cups whipping cream
Fold lightly into egg mixture. Still-freeze
in a mold, page 717, or in foil-covered refrigerator trays, page 717. Serve with:
Raspberry Juice, or
Chocolate Sauce, page 711

ABOUT ICES AND SHERBETS

Ices and glaces are made simply of fruit
juice, sugar and water. Sherbets have
variants, like Italian Graniti and French
Sorbets. These may add egg white, milk or
cream and are generally less sweet confections. Sherbets may be appropriately
served with the meat course, as well as for
dessert. Both are best when churn-frozen.
Some types may be still-frozen without the
addition of gelatin or egg white, but their
texture is considerably lighter and less
flinty when these modifying ingredients
are included.

Freezing diminishes flavoring and sweetening, so sugar your base accordingly.
♦ However, if ices are too sweet they will
not freeze: be sure there is never more
than 1 part sugar to 4 parts liquid. Stir in
any liqueurs after the ices have frozen.

♦ To churn-freeze ices and sherbets, follow the directions for processing ice
creams, page 715. Like ice creams, they
can be molded, after freezing, into attractive shapes. Pack a mold in salted ice for
3 hours. Remove the ice or sherbet from
it about 5 minutes before serving.

♦ To still-freeze ices and sherbets, put
them in a covered mold or a refrigerator
tray covered with foil and place them in
the freezer. While they are still slushy,
they should be stirred or beaten from front
to back in the tray to reduce the size of
the crystals. Repeated beating at ½ hour
intervals will give them the consistency of
a coarse churn-frozen water ice. Remove
them from freezer to refrigerator about 20
minutes before serving. Ices and sherbets
are especially delectable when served in
fruit shells—fancy-cut and hollowed-out
lemons, tangerines, oranges, cantaloupes,
even apples—garnished with leaves. See
also Frozen Orange Surprise, page 723.

Of course, meringues topped with
whipped cream are containers as wonderful as crystal coupe or frappé goblets. Ices
and sherbets lend themselves particularly to combinations with fruits—fresh,
poached, preserved and candied; to chest-

nut garnishes with touches of liqueur; and
if you are really professional, to veils of
spun sugar.

FRUIT ICE
About 10 Servings

♦ Be careful not to use more than 1 part
sugar for every 4 parts liquid, as too much
sugar prevents freezing.
Use:
    1 cup any fruit purée
Add to taste:
    (Lemon juice)
Combine with:
    4 cups water
To churn-freeze, see page 715. If adding:
    (Liqueur)
♦ have the ice almost completely churned
before you do so, as the high alcoholic
content tends to prevent the freezing.

LEMON AND ORANGE ICE
About 9 Servings

Combine and stir:
    2 teaspoons grated orange rind
    2 cups sugar
Stir in and boil for 5 minutes:
    4 cups water
    ¼ teaspoon salt
Chill. Add:
    2 cups orange juice
    ¼ cup lemon juice
To churn-freeze, see page 715. Top each
serving with:
    1 teaspoon rum or orange marmalade

RASPBERRY OR
STRAWBERRY ICE   I
About 10 Servings

This method makes delicious linings for
bombes. The still-frozen method combines well with angelica or Biscuit Tor-
toni, page 718. Try either ice served in
green apple cups, the cut parts of which
you have sprinkled with lemon juice to
prevent browning.
Cook until soft:
    2 quarts strawberries or raspberries
Strain the juice through 2 thicknesses of
cheesecloth. There should be about 2 cups
of thick juice. Combine, stir until the
sugar is dissolved, then boil for 3 minutes:
    4 cups water
    2 cups sugar
Chill. Add the thick berry juice and:
    1 tablespoon lemon juice
To churn-freeze, see page 715.

PEACH ICE
About 12 Servings

Combine:
    2 cups peach pulp: fresh peaches,
        peeled and riced
    6 tablespoons lemon juice
    ¾ cup orange juice
Boil for 5 minutes:
    3 cups water
    1 cup sugar

Chill. Combine with the fruit pulp an
juices. To churn-freeze, see page 715
Top each serving with:
    1 teaspoon cassis or Melba Sauce,
        page 709

APRICOT ICE
About 9 Servings

Put through a ricer or a sieve:
    3½ cups drained canned apricots
Add:
    2¼ cups orange juice
    6 tablespoons lemon juice
Stir in until dissolved:
    1 cup sugar
To churn-freeze, see page 715.

PINEAPPLE ICE
About 9 Servings

Boil for 5 minutes:
    1 cup sugar
    4 cups water
Chill the sirup and add:
    1 cup canned crushed pineapple
    6 tablespoons lemon juice
To churn-freeze, see page 715. Garnis
with:
    Mint leaves

LEMON MILK SHERBET
About 9 Servings

Dissolve:
    1⅛ cups sugar
in:
    7 tablespoons lemon juice
Stir these ingredients slowly into:
    3½ cups milk or milk and cream
If the milk curdles, it will not affect tex
ture after freezing. To churn-freeze, se
page 715.

ORANGE MILK SHERBET
About 10 Servings

Combine and stir:
    1½ teaspoons grated orange rind
    1½ cups sugar
Dissolve the sugar mixture in:
    ¼ cup lemon juice
    1½ cups orange juice
    (1½ riced bananas)
Stir these ingredients gradually into:
    4 cups very cold milk
If the milk curdles slightly, it will not a
fect the texture after the sherbet is frozen
To churn-freeze, see page 715.

PINEAPPLE MILK SHERBET
About 10 Servings

Combine and stir:
    1 cup unsweetened pineapple juice
    1 teaspoon grated lemon rind
    ¼ cup lemon juice
    1 cup sugar
    ⅛ teaspoon salt
Stir these ingredients slowly into:
    4 cups chilled milk
To churn-freeze, see page 715.

FROZEN ORANGE OR LEMON SURPRISE

This dessert can be made well in advance. If it is removed from the freezer and set in place just before the guests are served— and if the meal is not a long one—it may even be used as a centerpiece or table decoration. Choose:

Navel oranges or heavy-skinned lemons

Cut a fancy opening near the top, which later serves as a lid. Hollow out the pulp. Use it for juice or for making fruit ice or sherbet. Refill the orange with:

Fruit ice or sherbet

or a combination of:

Fruit ice
Ice cream
Partially frozen raspberries, peaches, strawberries
A touch of liqueur

Serve on fresh green leaves, garnished with a leaf on top of the lid. A note of warning: ♦ match bottoms and tops of fruit shells before you start filling. Also have all ingredients ready for filling and work fast, so that no undue melting takes place. Wrap fruits individually in foil and deep-freeze immediately, until ready to serve. Depending upon the temperature of the room, allow about ½ hour or more to defrost.

LEMON ICE
About 9 Servings

Grate:
2 teaspoons lemon rind
into:
2 cups sugar
Add, stir over heat until sugar is dissolved, then boil for 5 minutes:
4 cups water or tea
¼ teaspoon salt
Chill. Add:
¾ cup lemon juice
To churn or still-freeze, see page 715 or 717. Serve in a mound or ring with:
Fruit or canned fruit used in some attractive combination, flavored with curaçao, Cointreau or rum

RASPBERRY OR STRAWBERRY ICE II
About 4 Servings

Strain:
1 quart strawberries or raspberries
Soak:
1 teaspoon gelatin
in:
1 tablespoon cold water
Boil for 3 minutes:
1 cup water or ½ cup water and ½ cup pineapple juice
¾ to 1 cup sugar
Add:
1 to 2 tablespoons lemon juice
Dissolve the gelatin in the hot sirup. Chill. Combine juice with sirup. To still-freeze, see page 717.

LEMON SHERBET
About 5 Servings

Soak:
2 teaspoons gelatin
in:
¼ cup cold water
Boil for 10 minutes:
2¼ cups water
¾ cup sugar
Dissolve gelatin in hot sirup. Chill. Grate:
1 teaspoon lemon rind
Add to it:
¾ cup lemon juice
Add these ingredients to the sirup. Fold into this chilled mixture:
2 stiffly beaten egg whites
To still-freeze, see page 717. Serve topped with:

(Finely chopped candied orange or lemon rind)

ORANGE SHERBET
About 5 Servings

Soak:
2 teaspoons gelatin
in:
¼ cup cold water
Boil for 10 minutes:
1 cup water
⅔ to ¾ cup sugar, as needed
Dissolve gelatin in hot sirup. Cool. Add to it:
1 teaspoon grated lemon rind
1 teaspoon grated orange rind
1½ cups orange juice
⅛ cup lemon juice
Beat ♦ until stiff, but not dry and add:
2 egg whites
To still-freeze, see page 717. Garnish with:
Fresh pineapple slices

LIME SHERBET
About 6 Servings

Boil for 10 minutes:
⅔ cup sugar
1¾ cups water
Stir in:
1¼ teaspoons gelatin
dissolved in:
¼ cup cold water
Cool slightly. Add:
½ cup lime juice
2 drops green coloring
Beat until ♦ stiff, but not dry and add:
2 egg whites
To still-freeze, see page 717. Serve in:
Lemon shells
Garnish with:
Green leaves

GRAPEFRUIT SHERBET
About 4 Servings

Soak:
2 teaspoons gelatin

in:
½ cup cold water
Boil for 10 minutes:
1 cup sugar
1 cup water
Dissolve the gelatin in the hot sirup. Chill.
Add to it:
¼ cup lemon juice
2 cups fresh grapefruit juice
⅛ cup orange juice
¼ teaspoon salt
Beat until ◖ stiff, but not dry and add:
2 egg whites
To still-freeze, see page 717. Serve in:
Grapefruit shells

RASPBERRY OR STRAWBERRY SHERBET
About 5 Servings
Soak:
2 teaspoons gelatin
in:
¼ cup cold water
Press through a sieve or a ricer:
1 quart fresh berries
Add to them:
¼ cup lemon juice
Boil for 10 minutes:
1¾ cups water
¾ cup sugar
Dissolve the gelatin in the hot sirup. Cool
and add berries. Chill. Beat until ◖ stiff,
but not dry and add:
2 egg whites
To still-freeze, see page 717.

BANANA PINEAPPLE SHERBET
About 8 Servings
Combine and stir until dissolved:
1½ cups crushed pineapple
¾ cup confectioners' sugar
Add:
**1½ cups banana pulp: about 3 large
bananas**
½ cup orange juice
6 tablespoons lemon juice
Place in refrigerator trays. Freeze until
nearly firm. ◖ Beat until stiff, but not dry:
2 egg whites
Add fruit mixture gradually. Beat sherbet
until light and fluffy. Return to trays. To
still-freeze, see page 717.

★ CRANBERRY SHERBET
About 8 Servings
Boil until soft:
1 quart cranberries
1¾ cups water
Strain the juice and put berries through a
sieve. Add to them and boil for 5 minutes:
1¾ cups sugar
1 cup water
Soak:
2 teaspoons gelatin
in:
¼ cup cold water
Dissolve the gelatin in the hot juice. Chill.
Beat until ◖ stiff, but not dry and add:

2 egg whites
To still-freeze, see page 717. Serve in:
Orange cups

MINT SHERBET OR ICE
About 9 Servings
A refreshing alternate for the mint jelly
which traditionally accompanies lamb.
Prepare:
Any orange or lemon ice or sherbet
After the sirup reaches the boiling point,
pour it over:
½ cup fresh chopped mint leaves
Steep briefly, drain out the mint leaves
and add dissolved gelatin, if necessary.

WINE SHERBET
About 8 Servings
A dry sherbet—good served after roasted
meat or as a garnish for a fruit compote.
Soak:
1 tablespoon gelatin
in:
¼ cup cold water
Boil for 10 minutes:
1 cup water
¾ cup sugar
Dissolve gelatin in hot sirup. Chill. Add:
2 cups dry white wine
1 cup unstrained lime juice
1 tablespoon crème de menthe
Beat until ◖ stiff, but not dry and fold into
this chilled mixture:
1 egg white
Serve garnished with:
Fruit
or in:
Lemon cups

CHAMPAGNE SHERBET
About 8 Servings
Stir until dissolved and boil for about 5
minutes until thick:
1¼ cups sugar
1 cup water
Cool. Stir in:
1½ cups champagne
3 tablespoons lemon juice
Churn-freeze, page 715, until almost set.
Fold in:
Meringue I, page 681
When ready to serve, pour over each portion:
2 tablespoons champagne

FRUIT MILK SHERBET
Any of the milk sherbets may be frozen
as for Lemon Ice, page 723, but they
are somewhat lighter and less granular
if prepared with gelatin.
Prepare:
**Any of the lemon, orange, pineapple
or banana sherbets**
Soak:
2 teaspoons gelatin
in:
2 tablespoons cold water
Dissolve over heat. Add to the other ingredients. Add:

3½ cups milk or milk and cream
Stir well. Place in foil-covered trays in refrigerator. To still-freeze, see page 717.

PINEAPPLE BUTTERMILK SHERBET
About 6 Servings
Combine:
  2 cups buttermilk
  ½ cup sugar
  1 cup crushed pineapple
Freeze these ingredients until they have a
slushy consistency. Place them in a chilled
bowl. Add:
  1 slightly beaten egg white
  1½ teaspoons vanilla
Beat until light and fluffy. Replace in foil-
covered refrigerator trays. To still-freeze,
see page 717.

ORANGE ICE ANGELICA
About 6 Servings
Prepare:
  2 cups orange juice
Add:
  ⅛ cup sugar
Dissolve over hot water:
  1 teaspoon gelatin
in:
  ¼ cup cold water
Add the gelatin to the orange juice.

♦ Whip until thickened, but not stiff:
  2 cups whipping cream
Fold into it:
  1 teaspoon vanilla
  1 tablespoon or more powdered sugar
  (½ cup broken nut meats)
Place orange juice mixture in bottom of a
mold or tray. Pile the cream on top. Still-
freeze in a mold, page 717, or foil-covered
refrigerator trays, page 717.

FROZEN SUCKERS
Fourteen 1½-inch Suckers
Quickly made from canned baby fruits.
When these mixtures are partially frozen
in a compartmented ice tray or in individual paper cups, insert a looped para-
fined string or a paper spoon into each
unit to form a handle. Then freeze until
hard.
I. Mix and stir well:
  2 cups sweetened puréed fruit
  1 cup orange juice
  2 tablespoons sugar
Freeze as described above.

II. Mix and freeze, as described above:
  ¾ cup orange or grape juice
  1 cup yogurt
  ½ teaspoon vanilla
  (1 tablespoon lemon juice)

CANDIES AND CONFECTIONS

The fudge pot is responsible for the beginnings of many a good cook. So be tolerant when, some rainy day, your children take an interest in the sweeter side of kitchen life. Weather and altitude play important roles for confectioners, young and old. On humid days, candy requires longer cooking and ingredients must be brought to a heat at least 2 degrees higher than they do on dry ones. In fact, dry, cool weather is a necessary condition for certain types of confections, such as those made with honey, hard candies, glazes, divinities, fondant and nougats.

To avoid a mess ♦ always choose a pan with about four times as great a volume as that of the ingredients used, so that the candy will not boil over. ♦ To keep from burning the candy see that the pan has a heavy bottom. ♦ To keep from burning yourself, use a long wooden spoon that will not heat up during the prolonged cooking period.

ABOUT SUGARING IN CANDIES

When we were inexperienced, we were constantly baffled by the tendency of smooth, promising candy sirups to turn with lightning speed into grainy masses. We did not realize that one clue to our failure was stirring down the sugar crystals which formed on the sides of the pan into crystals of quite different structure in the candy mass.

Here are other tips to prevent sugaring in making candy: ♦ If the recipe calls for butter—and remember, always use unsalted butter—you may grease the sides of the pan before putting in the other ingredients. Here is a method we have used with never-failing success. ♦ Bring the liquid—whether milk or water—to a boil. ♦ Remove pan from heat and add the required sugar ♦ stirring until it is dissolved. For the addition of other ingredients see individual recipes. ♦ Return the pan to heat, cover it long enough for the candy to boil and to develop enough steam to wash down crystals from the walls of the pan. This is a matter of 2 or 3 minutes only. ♦ Now, uncover the pan to allow for evaporation. ♦ Do not stir after uncovering, but continue cooking until the mixture has reached the desired temperature. Use ♦ medium heat if the liquid is milk ♦ greater heat if the liquid is water. When you test for temperature, be sure to use an absolutely clean spoon or thermometer; the reason being, again, to avoid introducing extraneous sugar crystals. Should the candy start to sugar, add a small quantity of water and begin over again.

Those who make candy frequently will do well to provide themselves for the finishing step with a marble slab of generous proportions. For candies which require rapid cooling, this kind of material absorbs heat quickly and evenly, but not so rapidly as to affect crystallization adversely. The next best thing is a heavy stoneware platter. Both surfaces should be buttered in advance, except for fondant.

ABOUT CANDY THERMOMETER TEMPERATURES

As successful candy making depends largely on the temperatures at which different crystallizations of sugar occur ♦ an accurate professional candy thermometer, properly used, is invaluable. To test your thermometer for accuracy, heat it—in water, gradually to avoid breakage—and keep it in boiling water for 10 minutes. It should register 212°. If there is any variation, add or subtract the number of degrees necessary to make its reading conform to a standard scale.

When actually using the thermometer, warm it as for testing before inserting it into the candy. Place it near the center of the pan and do not let the bulb touch the bottom. Heat rises slowly to 220°, then takes a spurt—so watch carefully. ♦ For true accuracy, read at eye level, which of course means some gymnastics on your part. Have a spoon ready when you remove the thermometer to catch any sirup drops that might fall back into the pan. Clean the thermometer after each use by letting it stand in warm water.

If you have no thermometer, practice can make you expert in recognizing the subtle differences in color, bubbling and threading that correspond to the basic temperatures. Always remove the pot from the heat while testing so as not to overcook, as a few extra degrees can bring the candy up into the next stage of crystallization.

THREAD—230° to 234°

Drop a small quantity of sirup into ice water. This is a coarse-thread stage.

SOFT BALL—234° to 240°

Drop a small quantity of sirup into ice water. It forms a ball which does not disintegrate but flattens out of its own accord when picked up with the fingers.

FIRM BALL—244° to 248°

Drop a small quantity of sirup into ice water. The ball will hold its shape and will not flatten unless pressed with the fingers.

HARD BALL—250° to 266°

Drop a small quantity of sirup into ice water. The ball will hold its shape but is still pliable.

SOFT CRACK—270° to 290°

Drop a small quantity of sirup into ice water. It will separate into hard threads, which, when removed from the water, will bend and not be brittle.

HARD CRACK—300° to 310°

Drop a small quantity of sirup into ice water. The sirup will separate into threads that are hard and brittle.

CARAMELIZED SUGAR—310° to 338°

Between these temperatures sirup turns dark golden, but will turn black at 350°.

▲ For candy making at high altitudes, adjust for temperatures as follows: If soft ball at 236° at sea level is called for: test for soft ball at 226° at 3000 feet, 223° at 5000 feet and 220° at 7000 feet.
◆ Do not jostle the pan when removing it from heat or during the cooling period.
◆ The candy should never be beaten until it has cooled to at least 110°. There are two ways of cooling. If you are the impatient type, place the pot gently—the minute you take it from the heat—into a pan of ice-cold water and allow it to remain until you can touch the bottom without discomfort. The other way is to pour the candy onto a marble slab or a buttered heavy platter. If it is taffy, caramel or brittle, hold the pouring edge of the pan away from you and only a few inches above the slab to avoid spattering. With these candies, too, let the mix run out of the pan of its own accord. ◆ Do not scrape the dregs out of the pan. The reason is to avoid sugaring. There is a difference in crystallization rate between the free flowing portion and the other, near the bottom of the pan, which was exposed to greater heat. If you have neglected to use butter to grease the sides of the pan, you may drop it onto the surface of the hot candy and beat it in after the candy reaches 110°.

These are general principles. For particulars, follow the individual recipes carefully. If you substitute honey in part for sugar, remember that honey needs a higher degree of heat and longer beating. Frequently, because honey attracts atmospheric moisture, the candies become sticky.

In gauging the yields for the following recipes, we have not counted in nuts, fruits and other additions where such additions are optional.

ABOUT CANDY WRAPPINGS

For that professional look, wrap candies in attractive foils or buy, at small cost, fancy fluted foil cups into which you can pour directly. Delight the children with lollipop cords or let them package hard candies between a double strip of self-adhesive plastic, which you cut into squares after inserting the candy.

ABOUT FONDANT AND CENTERS

One of the charms of fondant is that a batch can be made and ripened and then used at will over a period of weeks, with varying flavors, colors and shapes to suit the occasion. Basic Fondant also lends itself to variations during cooking. You may replace the water in the recipe with strong coffee or you may use half white and half brown sugar or you may use half white and half maple sugar. But in case you don't want to make up a large batch of Basic Fondant, read the alternate processes given after the basic recipe—or use recipes carrying the word "center" in the title.

BASIC FONDANT
About 1¼ Pounds

Bring to a boil in a large, heavy pan:
    1 cup water
Remove from heat and stir in until dissolved:
    3 cups sugar
Return to heat and have ready:
    ⅙ teaspoon cream of tartar
More will make the fondant harder to work later. ◆ Just as the sirup comes up to a boil, add the cream of tartar to the mixture by tapping it from the spoon on the edge of the pan. Be ready to stir, as it will tend to make the sirup boil over. ◆ Cover until the steam can wash down the sides of the pan. ◆ Cook this mixture uncovered, without stirring, until it reaches 238° to 240°. Remove pan gently from heat. Pour sirup onto a wet marble slab or platter. ◆ Do not scrape pan. ◆ Let the sirup cool thoroughly.

Work it with a candy scraper or a wooden spoon by lifting and folding always from edges to center. When the sirup loses its translucency and begins to become opaque and creamy, knead it well with the hands. Dust them with confectioners' sugar if necessary.

Even experts sometimes cook fondant too hard to knead it. If you have done so, add two-thirds of a cup of water. Melt the mixture very slowly in the top of a double boiler ◆ over—not in—hot water, stirring constantly until the boiling point is reached again. Then proceed by covering, letting the steam wash down the sides of the pan and cooking again to 238° to 240°.

After kneading fondant, put it in a tightly covered container. Allow it to remain in a cool place for from 24 hours to a week or more.

To prepare fondant for shaping, put it in a double boiler ◆ over—not in—hot water. Heat it slowly, with the water at 170° to 180°, until you can shape it, then put it on a slab.

If you want to color the fondant, make a depression in the mass and pour in a few drops of food coloring. Gash it in several places but not all the way through to the slab—allowing the color to spread into the candy. Continue chopping and folding to complete the spreading process. Flavoring can be worked in the same way. At this time, you may also incorporate chopped or whole nuts, candied fruits, ginger, coconut or jam. Allow equal portions of these additions to the amount of fondant. Correct to the proper consistency with confectioners' sugar if necessary.

Form fondant by rolling it into one-half inch rods then cut into round or oval pieces. You are now ready to dip them in:

Chocolate Coating, see page 730

◆ Be sure to have centers at room temperature to keep chocolate from developing gray streaks.

SOFT CENTER FONDANT
About 1 Pound

This is the type of fondant often used around a candied cherry in a chocolate coating. It is not allowed to ripen but must be molded and dipped at once. After dipping, the egg white causes it to become liquid inside its coating.

Bring to a boil in a large, heavy pan:

2 cups sugar
1 cup water
¼ teaspoon glycerin
1 tablespoon light corn sirup

Stir these ingredients until the sugar is thoroughly dissolved. Place the pan over low heat. ◆ When the mixture begins to boil, cover it, so that the steam will wash down any crystals that may have formed on the sides of the pan. Cook the sirup for about 3 minutes. ◆ Uncover and continue cooking sirup without stirring until it reaches the soft-ball stage, 238° to 240°. Remove it gently from heat. Pour onto a wet slab or platter. Cool sirup to 110°. Spread over it with a spatula:

1 well-beaten egg white

To work, flavor, form and dip, see Basic Fondant, above. These processes must be done as quickly as possible.

UNCOOKED FONDANT
About 1½ Pounds

Tempting, opulent-looking—not for reducers. This candy is the specialty of a very clever hostess, whose parties seem incomplete without it. Her son calls them "knockout drops" because he once indulged in 13 and suffered the consequences. This candy must be kept refrigerated.

Beat until soft:

½ cup butter

Add very slowly and cream until very light:

1 lb. sifted confectioners' sugar

Add:

¼ cup whipping cream
1 scant teaspoon vanilla

Work the fondant well with the hands and shape it into 1-inch balls. To roll the balls use about:

¼ lb. sifted confectioners' sugar

Raisins, nut meats or a bit of candied fruit may be rolled into the center of the balls. Place balls on foil in the refrigerator, covered, until they are hard. To dip, see Chocolate Coating, page 730.

When coating has hardened, store balls in a covered container in refrigerator until ready to serve.

CARAMEL FONDANT
About 1¼ Pounds

Heat in a large, heavy pan:

½ cup milk

Remove from heat and stir in until dissolved:

1½ cups sugar
¼ cup butter

Return to heat and bring very slowly to a boil. Meanwhile, caramelize—see page 507—in a heavy skillet:

½ cup sugar

When the sugar and butter mixture boils, stir in the caramelized sugar very slowly. Boil, then ◆ cover about 3 minutes until any crystals on the sides of the pan have been washed down by the steam. Cook candy to soft-ball stage, 238°, without stirring. Cool candy to 110°. Beat it until creamy. Pour it into a pan and mark it into squares or form candy into small balls. Place between them:

Nut meats

or dip them in:

Chocolate Coating, see page 730

NEWPORT CREAMS OR CENTERS
About 1½ Pounds

Much like an opera cream in texture.
Bring to a boil in a large, heavy pan, stirring until the sugar is dissolved:

⅔ cup light corn sirup
2 cups brown sugar
6 tablespoons hot water

◆ Cover about 3 minutes until any crystals on the sides of the pan have been washed down by the steam. ◆ Uncover and cook, without stirring, to the thread stage, 234°. Whip until stiff:

1 egg white
A few grains of salt

Pour sirup slowly into the egg white, whipping constantly. Add:

1 teaspoon vanilla
1¼ cups nut meats

When you can no longer stir the candy flatten it out on a buttered tin. When it is cold, cut it into squares.

OPERA CREAMS OR CENTERS
About 1¼ Pounds

Bring to a boil in a large, heavy pan, stirring until the sugar is dissolved:

2 cups sugar
¾ cup whipping cream
1 cup milk
2 tablespoons light corn sirup
⅛ teaspoon salt

♦ Cover and cook about 3 minutes until the steam has washed down any crystals on the sides of the pan. ♦ Uncover and cook over low heat to 238°. Remove from heat. Cool to 110°. Add:

1 teaspoon vanilla

Beat the mixture until it is creamy. Pour it into special candy rubber-sheet molds or a buttered pan. When cold, cut into squares. Place in an airtight container. This candy improves if aged at least 24 hours. When it has ripened, you may dip it in a:

Chocolate Coating, see page 730

MAPLE CREAM CANDY

About 1 Pound

Who would ever suspect that this delicious confection was just plain maple sirup in a more solid form?

Boil over very low heat without stirring:

2 cups maple sirup

until it reaches the late thread stage, 233°. Allow this reduced sirup to cool to 110°, about 1 hour, without stirring. Add:

(1 teaspoon vanilla)

Beat until it becomes light in color and fluffy in texture and is hard enough to hold its shape for patties or in molds. This candy dries out on exposure to air, so box tightly as soon as cool.

PEPPERMINT CREAM WAFERS

About 1¼ Pounds

Stir over low heat in a large, heavy pan until the sugar is dissolved:

2 cups sugar
¼ cup light corn sirup
¼ cup milk
¼ teaspoon cream of tartar

Cook and stir these ingredients slowly until they boil. ♦ Cover for about 3 minutes until any crystals on the sides of the pan have been washed down by the steam. Uncover and cook without stirring to the soft-ball stage, 238°. Remove from heat. Cool slightly. Beat until creamy. Flavor with:

8 to 12 drops oil of peppermint

Tint lightly with vegetable coloring if desired. Drop the mixture from a teaspoon onto foil to form patties in the size you want. These and the preceding wafers are delightful decorated or initialed for teas. See About Decorative Icings, page 673.

★ ALMOND OR FILBERT PASTE

About 2 Pounds

In some parts of Europe this almond confection is traditional at Christmas time. It is molded into fancy shapes or into flat cakes that are pie-shaped and elaborately decorated. A thin wedge is served to visitors, together with a glass of dessert wine. You may also prepare filberts this way for cake fillings.

Blanch, see page 521:

1 lb. almonds or filberts

Grind them. All our other recipes for grinding almonds read: "Put through a nut grinder." This is the only recipe that says: "Put them through a meat grinder." This time you want the nuts to be oily. Use the finest blade and grind the nuts at least 4 times. If you use a ⅃ blender, use the orange juice or kirsch called for to start the blending action. Cook to the end of the soft-ball stage, 240°, in a large heavy pan:

2 cups sugar
1 cup water

Add the ground nuts and:

6 to 8 tablespoons orange juice or kirsch
(A few drops rosewater)

Rosewater is the traditional flavoring. Stir these ingredients until they are thoroughly blended and creamy. Permit them to cool until you can knead them. There are 2 things that make kneading easier: put confectioners' sugar on your hands or cover the paste and permit it to rest for about 12 hours. Flatten it on a hard surface dusted with confectioners' sugar, then mold it into any desired shape. Pack in a closely covered tin or jar. Ripen from 6 to 8 days.

★ MARZIPAN OR MARCHPANE

About ½ Pound

The Arabs brought this confection to Europe; and at various times since, in tribute to its preciousness, the word which describes it has meant "a sitting king," "a little box," "a stamped coin."

Marzipan cake and dessert decorations made in advance are useful to have on hand, and those by the first method can be ✳ frozen for future use.

I. Whip until fluffy:

1 egg white

Work in gradually:

1 cup Almond Paste, see recipe above.

Add:

1½ cups sifted confectioners' sugar

Use more if necessary to make a paste that is easy to handle. Should it become too thick, work in drop by drop:

Lemon juice

Should it become too oily, work it in a dish over ice. In either case, knead the paste. Mold it into any desired shape. Small fruit shapes are great favorites. If you wish to color it, use a pastry brush with a little diluted vegetable coloring. Glaze the "fruits" with a solution of:

Gum arabic, see page 741

Also, you may roll the paste in:

Equal parts of cocoa and
powdered sugar

or use it as a center for dipping. Wrap each piece separately in foil. Store in a cool place.

II. Use:
   **Equal parts of almond paste
   and fondant**
Knead, mold and color as above.

MARSHMALLOWS

About 1¾ Pounds
This recipe requires the use of an electric mixer. Results are also much improved if you can get, at a professional outlet, gelatin of 250 bloom—a more concentrated form than that sold to the housewife.
Put in the mixer bowl and let stand for 1 hour:
   **3 tablespoons gelatin
   ½ cup cold water**
Then in about ½ hour start to prepare a sirup. Place in a heavy pan over low heat and stir until dissolved:
   **2 cups sugar
   ¾ cup light corn sirup
   ½ cup water
   ¼ teaspoon salt**
When the mixture starts to boil ♦ cover it for about 3 minutes to allow any crystals which have formed to be washed down from the sides of the pan.
Continue to cook ♦ uncovered and unstirred over high heat until the thermometer reaches 240° to 244°. Overcooking will make marshmallows tough. Remove from heat and pour slowly over the gelatin, beating constantly. After all the sirup is added, continue to beat for about 15 minutes. When the mixture is thick but still **warm** add:
   2 tablespoons vanilla
Put the mixture into an 8 x 12 inch pan that has been lightly dusted with cornstarch. When it has dried for 12 hours remove it from the pan, cut it into squares with scissors dusted with cornstarch and store the fully dusted pieces in a closed tin.

CHOCOLATE COATING

For a long time our attempts to dip candies attractively were not an unqualified success. We finally sought the advice of Larry Blumenthal, whose family has been "in chocolate" for generations. He finds our procedure solid, but warns us that when you heat chocolate and cool it to dipping temperature, you have "tempered" it, and that its reactions from this point on are somewhat unpredictable. In the candy trade, dipping is turned over to a "handcoater," who uses no specially processed chocolate, although he may thicken his mix adroitly by adding at just the right moment a few drops of water at 65° to 70°—but who, through long practice, develops a "knack."
   ♦ Choose crisp dry weather for dipping.
   ♦ Work in a room where the temperature is 60° to 70° and where there are no drafts.
Grate about:

   **1 lb. chocolate, sweet, bitter,
   bittersweet or milk**
Melt it very, very slowly in the top of a 1½ quart double boiler ♦ over—not in—hot water. ♦ Stir the chocolate until its temperature reaches 130°. If you do not stir constantly at temperatures over 100°, the cocoa butter will separate out. Remove from the heat and cool to about 88°. Heat water to 90° in the bottom of the double boiler. Place chocolate in the upper part of the double boiler.
Before dipping into chocolate be sure the candy centers or fillings are at room temperature. Otherwise, the chocolate may streak with gray. Immerse the centers one at a time in the chocolate—maintaining its temperature. Lift them out with a fork or a candy-dipping fork onto a ¼-inch wire rack, above a pan or tray—to catch chocolate drippings, which may be re-melted and re-used. There is always surplus on the dipping fork—this is lifted directly above the candy to make designs which identify the various fillings.

FUDGE COCKAIGNE

About 1¼ Pounds
Bring to a boil in a large heavy pan:
   1 cup, minus 1 tablespoon, rich milk
Remove from heat and stir in until dissolved:
   **2 cups sugar
   ⅛ teaspoon salt
   2 oz. grated chocolate**
♦ Bring to a boil and cook covered 2 to 3 minutes until the steam washes down from the sides of the pan any crystals which may have formed. ♦ Uncover, reduce heat and cook without stirring to soft-ball stage, 238°. When nearing 238°, there is a fine overall bubbling with, simultaneously, a coarser pattern, as though the fine bubbled areas were being pulled down for quilting into the coarser ones. Remove from heat without jostling or stirring ♦ Cool the candy to 110°. You may hasten this process by placing the hot pan in a larger pan of cold water until the bottom of the pan has cooled. Add:
   2 to 4 tablespoons butter
Beat fudge partially. Add:
   1 teaspoon vanilla
Then beat until it begins to lose its sheen. At this point the drip from the spoon when you flip it over, holds its shape against the bottom of the spoon. Quickly add:
   ½ to 1 cup broken nut meats
Pour the fudge into a buttered pan. Cut into squares before it hardens. To use fudge for centers, beat until thick, knead and shape.

COCOA FUDGE OR CENTERS

About 1½ Pounds
We find that when made with dry milk solids this candy has an unusually interesting texture for centers. We like to cut

...t into caramel-size cubes for dipping. If you prefer to make it with fresh milk use the same liquid proportions but mix and cook as for Fudge Cockaigne, see page 730. Melt in a large, heavy skillet over medium heat:

    ¼ cup butter

Add:

    1½ cups boiling water

Mix and stir into the hot mixture:

    3 cups sugar
    ⅔ cup cocoa
    ⅛ teaspoon cream of tartar

♦ Continue to stir until the mixture boils. Cover about 3 minutes to allow steam to wash down any crystals that may have formed on sides of pan. ♦ Uncover, lower heat and cook slowly ♦ without stirring to the soft-ball stage, 236°. Do not stir after removing candy from heat. When the mixture has cooled to 110° add:

    6 tablespoons whole or skim milk solids
    1 teaspoon vanilla

Beat until creamy. Pour into an 8 x 8-inch buttered pan or, when it becomes firm, knead it into 1-inch balls. If it seems too stiff to knead, cover with a damp cloth for about an hour.

COFFEE FUDGE
About 1 Pound
Bring to a boil in a large, heavy pan:

    1 cup strong coffee

Remove from heat and stir in until dissolved:

    2 cups sugar
    1 tablespoon cream
    1 tablespoon butter
    ⅛ teaspoon salt
    ¼ teaspoon cream of tartar

Cook these ingredients quickly, stirring them constantly until they boil. ♦ Cover and cook for about 3 minutes until the steam washes down any crystals which may

have formed on the sides of the pan. ♦ Uncover and cook over moderate heat to 238°. Remove from heat. Cool to 110°. Add:

    ½ teaspoon almond extract or
    ½ teaspoon cinnamon

Beat until the mixture begins to harden. Add:

    1 cup broken pecan or hickory nuts

Pour onto a buttered surface. Permit the candy to cool and harden before cutting into squares.

COCONUT FUDGE OR CENTERS
About 1¼ Pounds
Combine in a deep saucepan:

    1½ cups sugar
    ½ cup corn sirup
    ½ cup top milk
    ¼ cup molasses
    (1 tablespoon vinegar)
    ⅛ teaspoon salt

Stir these ingredients over medium heat until the sugar is dissolved. Bring to a boil and ♦ cook covered for about 3 minutes until the steam has washed down from the sides of the pan any crystals which may have formed. ♦ Uncover and cook slowly to the soft-ball stage—238° —without stirring. Remove from heat and stir in:

    1¼ cups moist shredded coconut
    3 tablespoons butter

Pour candy onto a buttered platter. When cool enough to handle, shape into small balls or centers. Place them on foil to dry.

DIVINITY
About 1½ Pounds
Pick a dry day. This candy does not keep well. If you use the brown sugar and vinegar, you may prefer to call this Sea Foam. Bring to room temperature:

    2 egg whites

Bring to a boil in a heavy pan:

    ½ cup water
    ½ cup light corn sirup

Dissolve in it:

    2 cups sugar or brown sugar
    (1 tablespoon vinegar)

When boiling ♦ cover pan and cook about 3 minutes until the steam has washed down any crystals that may have formed on the sides of the pan. ♦ Remove lid and cook over moderate heat, without stirring, to the hard-ball stage, 254°. While sirup is cooking, beat egg whites in a large bowl until they just hold their shape. When the sirup is ready, pour it slowly over the egg whites in a steady thin stream, whipping slowly at the same time. Toward the end, add the sirup more quickly and whip faster. ♦ Do not scrape pan. After all sirup has been added, put in:

    1 cup broken nut meats
    (1 cup raisins)

As a variation try omitting nuts and raisins

and add:

(1 cup crushed peppermint candy)

Beat until candy can be dropped onto a buttered surface into patties which hold their shape.

CARAMEL CREAM DIVINITY
About 2 Pounds

A smooth, rich candy which keeps better than divinity. Bring to a boil in a large, heavy pan:

2 cups cream

♦ Remove from heat and stir in:

3 cups sugar

1 cup white corn sirup

Return to heat and cook slowly. When the candy boils ♦ cover and cook for about 3 minutes until the steam washes down any crystals which may have formed on the sides of the pan. ♦ Uncover and cook slowly, without stirring, to the soft-ball stage, 238°. Remove sirup from heat. Cool to 110°. Beat until very stiff. Beat in:

1 cup pecan meats

Pour the candy into a buttered pan. Cut it when cool.

NOUGAT
About 1¼ Pounds

Southern France and Italy are famous for luscious nougats with distinctive flavors due to regional honey variations. So, why is there no honey in our recipe? For the answer, see About Honey, page 506. Pick a dry day. This is a 2-part process and an electric mixer is almost imperative.

First, cook in a 2-quart heavy saucepan:

6 tablespoons sugar

1 tablespoon water

¼ cup light corn sirup

Blend over low heat and stir until boiling. ♦ Cover and cook for about 3 minutes until the steam has washed down any crystals which may have formed on the sides of the pan. Cook ♦ uncovered over medium heat, without stirring, to the soft-ball stage, 238°. Remove pan from heat and let stand while you beat in a mixer until very stiff:

¼ cup egg whites

Add the hot sirup gradually to the whites, continuing to beat for at least five minutes until the mass thickens.

Blend in a heavy 1-quart pan and stir over low heat until it boils:

1 cup light corn sirup

1 cup sugar

Stop stirring ♦ cover again for 3 minutes, then uncover and boil rapidly, without stirring, to 285°. Remove from heat and let stand until sirup stops bubbling. Now pour the second mixture into the first and beat until well combined. Beat in:

2 tablespoons butter cut
in small chunks

Add:

1 cup blanched almonds

½ cup blanched pistachio nuts

(⅓ cup chopped candied cherries)

Pour into an 8 x 8-inch buttered pan dusted with confectioners' sugar or lined with baker's wafer paper. Let set in a cool place 12 hours. If hard to get out of pan, release sides with a knife. Then hold bottom of pan briefly over heat and reverse the block onto a board for slicing.

VANILLA CREAM CARAMELS
About 2½ Pounds

Dissolve over low heat in a large, heavy pan, stirring until the mixture boils:

2 cups sugar

2 cups dark corn sirup

1 cup butter

1 cup cream

Cook over moderate heat, stirring constantly, to 240°. Remove from heat and add very gradually:

1 cup cream

Return to heat and cook to 244° to 246°. Pour the mixture at once, without stirring, into a buttered pan. When firm, about 3 hours later, invert the candy onto a wooden board and cut into squares with a thin bladed knife. Use a light sawing motion.

MAPLE CARAMELS
About 1½ Pounds

Stir in a large, heavy pan over quick heat until the sugar is dissolved:

2 cups brown sugar

1½ cups maple sirup

½ cup cream

Stir and cook these ingredients slowly to the firm-ball stage, 242°. Add:

1 tablespoon butter

Pour candy onto buttered tin. Cut into squares as it hardens. Nuts may be added to the candy just before removing it from the heat or they may be sprinkled on the buttered tin before pouring the candy. When cool, about 3 hours later, invert onto a board and cut into squares.

CHOCOLATE CARAMELS
About 1½ Pounds

Stir over quick heat until the sugar is dissolved:

3 cups sugar

1 cup light corn sirup

1 cup milk

1½ tablespoons butter

Cut into small pieces and stir in:

3 oz. chocolate

Stir and boil these ingredients slowly to the firm-ball stage, 248°. Add:

1 teaspoon vanilla

Pour candy into lightly buttered tin. When firm—about 3 hours later, invert onto a board and cut into ¾-inch squares.

CHOCOLATE CREAM CARAMELS
About 1 Pound

Stir over quick heat until the sugar is dissolved:

1 cup sugar

¾ cup light corn sirup
3 oz. chocolate
¼ teaspoon salt
½ cup cream

Over moderate heat bring the ingredients to the soft-ball stage, 238°. Stir constantly. Add:

½ cup cream

Cook candy until it again reaches the soft-ball stage, 238°. Add:

½ cup cream

Cook the candy until it reaches the firm-ball stage, 248°. Remove candy from heat and pour into an 8 x 4-inch buttered pan. Do not scrape can. When candy is firm, about 3 hours later, invert onto a board and cut into squares.

FILLED CARAMELS

Prepare:

Chocolate Cream Caramels, above

Pour the candy into two 4 x 8-inch buttered pans. When it holds its shape, remove the two layers from pans. Slice a ¼-inch layer of:

Basic Fondant, page 727

Place it over the surface of one layer. Cover it with the other layer. Cut the caramels in ½- or ¾-inch squares, using a sharp knife and a sawing action. Wrap individually.

OLD-FASHIONED BUTTERSCOTCH
About 1 Pound

Place in a heavy pan, large enough to allow for foaming:

2 cups brown sugar
¼ cup molasses
½ cup butter
2 tablespoons water
2 tablespoons vinegar

Stir these ingredients over quick heat until the sugar is dissolved. Boil quickly—stirring frequently—to the hard-crack stage, 300°. Drop candy from a teaspoon onto a buttered slab or foil to form patties.

BUTTERSCOTCH
About 1¾ Pounds

Stir in a large, heavy saucepan until dissolved:

2 cups sugar
⅔ cup dark corn sirup
¼ cup water
¼ cup cream

Cook these ingredients to just below the hard-ball stage—260°—then stir constantly until they almost reach the hard-crack stage, 288°. Pour candy into a buttered pan. When cool and almost set, mark into squares or bars. When cold, cut or break apart.

COFFEE DROPS
About 1¼ Pounds

Use same ingredients as in above recipe for Butterscotch, but cook to 295°. Have ready an essence made of:

6 to 8 tablespoons coffee
⅔ cup water
1 tablespoon vinegar

Simmer slowly until about three tablespoons or less of liquid remain. Drain from the grounds and add:

½ teaspoon glycerin

Remove sirup from heat. Sprinkle coffee essence over the surface. Stir it in very gently. Drop sirup into ¾-inch patties from the edge of a spoon onto a buttered surface. When cool, wrap individually and store in a tightly covered container.

ABOUT TAFFIES

If you have a hankering to re-create an old-time "candy pull," be sure you have a reasonably stout pair of arms or an adolescent in the family who wants to convert from a puny weakling to a strong man. This way, taffy pulling is fun and seems easy. However, should you lack these advantages and wish to pull taffy often, you will find that a candy hook is well worth the investment.

When the sirup has cooked to the indicated temperature ♦ pour it slowly onto a buttered slab. ♦ Hold the pouring edge of the pan away from you and only a few inches above the slab, so you won't be spattered with the dangerously hot sirup. Allow the sirup to cool briefly. ♦ This is the moment to flavor the taffy. Because of the great heat, use flavoring essences based on essential oils. See flavoring of Hard Candies, page 735. Sprinkle these over the surface of the hot sirup. Go easy, as they are very strong. If chocolate is to be added, grate it on the buttered slab before pouring. Nuts, fruits and coconut can be worked in during the pulling process.

Begin to work the sirup up into a central mass, turning it and working it with a candy scraper until it is cool enough to handle with your oiled fingertips. ♦ Take care in picking up the mass. It may have cooled on the surface and still be hot enough to burn as you press down into it. Taffy cooked to 270° should be pulled near a source of heat. When you can gather it up, start pulling it with your fingertips, allowing a spread of about 18 inches between your hands. Then fold it back on itself. Repeat this motion rhythmically. As the mass changes from a somewhat sticky, side-whiskered affair to a glistening crystal ribbon—see illustration page 734—start twisting, while folding and pulling. ♦ Pull until the ridges on the twist begin to hold their shape, see center illustration, next page.

The candy will have become opaque, firm and elastic but will still retain its satiny finish. Depending on proper cooking, the weather and your skill, this pulling process may last from five to twenty minutes.

♦ Have ready a surface dusted with con-

fectioners' sugar or cornstarch. Then form the candy into a ball in your hands and press it into a narrow point at the fingertip end. Grasping the narrow point in one hand, pull it away from the rest of the ball into a long rope about one-inch thick. Let the rope fall out onto the dusted board like a snake. Cut it into the size you prefer with well-buttered shears. Let it cool. If you do not want to wrap separately, put it in a tightly covered tin, dusting and all. Some taffies, especially those heavy in cream, will, of their own accord, turn from a pulled chewy consistency to a creamy one. This happens sometimes a few minutes after cutting, sometimes as long as 12 hours later. After creaming takes place, be sure to wrap the taffies in foil and store them in a closed tin. They dry out readily on exposure to air.

VANILLA TAFFY
About ½ Pound

If you allow this candy to become creamy, it rivals the very rich Cream Pull Candy, next page. Combine and stir over slow heat until the sugar is dissolved:

1¼ cups sugar
¼ cup water
2 tablespoons mild vinegar
1½ teaspoons butter

Cook these ingredients quickly, without stirring, to just between the very-hard-ball and the light-crack stages, 268°-270°. Add:

½ teaspoon vanilla or other flavoring

Pour candy on buttered platter or marble slab and let cool until a dent can be made in it when pressed with a finger. Gather it into a lump and pull it with fingertips until light and porous, see page 733. Pull any desired flavoring or coloring into the candy. Roll it into long thin strips and cut into 1-inch pieces. Place candy in a tightly covered tin if you wish it to become creamy.

MOLASSES TAFFY
About 1 Pound

Stir over quick heat until the sugar is dissolved and stir until boiling:

1 cup molasses
2 teaspoons vinegar

1 cup sugar
⅛ teaspoon salt

♦ Cover pan and, without stirring, cool sirup rather quickly to just below the firm ball stage, 240°. Add, by dropping in small pieces:

2 tablespoons butter

Boil sirup slowly—just past the very-hard ball stage, 270°. Holding the pouring edge of the pan away from you and a few inches above the slab allow sirup to spread over slab. ♦ Do not scrape pan. Sprinkle surface of taffy with:

4 drops oil of peppermint

To work, pull and form, see About Taffies, page 733. To make chips, pull in long very thin strips. For coating with:

Chocolate, see page 730

PULLED MINTS
About 1 Pound

Like the old-fashioned cushion ones we used to buy in tins. Combine in a large heavy pan and stir until it again reaches boil:

1 cup boiling water
2 cups sugar
¼ teaspoon cream of tartar

♦ Cook covered about 3 minutes until the sides of the pan are washed free of crystals. ♦ Uncover and cook without stirring to hard-ball stage, 262°. Remove from heat and pour onto buttered marble slab. Sprinkle:

A few drops oil of peppermint

To work, pull, form and cream, see About Taffies, page 733.

SALT WATER TAFFY
About 1½ Pound

Combine and stir over low heat until sugar is dissolved:

2 cups sugar
1½ cups water
1 cup light corn sirup
1½ teaspoons salt
2 teaspoons glycerin

Cook the sirup without stirring to the hard-ball stage, 265°. Remove it from the heat. Add:

2 tablespoons butter

Holding the pouring edge of the pan away

from you, and a few inches above the oiled slab, allow the sirup to spread. ♦ Do not scrape pan. To work, pull, flavor and form, see About Taffies, page 733.

CREAM PULL CANDY
About 1½ Pounds

Do not try this in damp, hot weather. Combine in a heavy saucepan and stir over low heat until dissolved and boiling:

3 cups sugar
1 cup boiling water
⅛ teaspoon soda
½ teaspoon salt

♦ Cover about 3 minutes until steam has washed crystals from sides of the pan. ♦ Uncover and cook without stirring to 236°. ♦ Reduce heat—but not below 225° —while adding gradually:

1 cup cream
(¼ cup butter cut in small bits)

Cook over moderate heat ♦ without stirring, to 257° and pour sirup at once over buttered marble slab. Hold the pouring edge away from you, and a few inches above the slab. Allow sirup to spread over the slab. ♦ Do not scrape pot. To work, pull, flavor, form and cream, see About Taffies, page 733.

HARD CANDY OR LOLLIPOPS
About 1½ Pounds

Bring to a boil in a large, heavy pan:

1 cup water

Remove from heat. Add and stir until dissolved:

2 cups sugar
¾ cup light corn sirup
1 tablespoon butter

Return to heat. When boiling ♦ cover for about 3 minutes so the steam can wash down any crystals on the sides of the pan. ♦ Uncover and cook at high heat without stirring until the thermometer reaches 310°. Prepare a slab or molds by brushing them well with butter or oil. If you are going to make lollipops, have stiffened lollipop cords on the oiled slab ready to receive patties. Remove candy mixture to low heat and add:

A few drops coloring matter

Choose a vegetable color suitable to the flavor you have decided to use. An alcohol-based flavor like vanilla will evaporate in the intense heat. So be sure to use a flavor based, instead, on essential oils. For the above recipe, for instance, we suggest one of the following:

¼ teaspoon, or less, oil of peppermint or
1 teaspoon, or less, oil of orange,
    lime or wintergreen
¼ teaspoon or less oil of cassia
    or cinnamon
⅛ teaspoon oil of anise

ROCK CANDY

Broken into small pieces and piled in an open bowl, this makes a sophisticated-looking sugar substitute for coffee. Small clumps clustered on ⅛-inch dowels make attractive swizzle sticks for drinks. Whether the candy be on sticks or on strings, the process of making it is a fascinating experiment in crystallization. Produce it, first, on a very small scale by letting a supersaturated heated sirup cool undisturbed in a test tube into which you have previously sunk a weighted string. Make it on a larger scale by punching holes at the top edge of a thin 8-inch square pan and lacing about seven strings from one side to the other. Place the laced pan in a deeper pan to catch excess sirup. Dissolve:

2½ cups sugar

in:

1 cup water

and cook without stirring to 247°-252°. Pour sirup into pie pan. It should reach a level about ¾ of an inch above the strings. Cover the surface with a piece of foil. Watch and wait. It sometimes takes a week to crystallize. Lift the laced pan out. Cut the strings and dislodge the rock candy. Rinse quickly in cold water, and put on racks in a very low oven to dry.

HOREHOUND CANDY
About 2½ Pounds

Make an infusion of:

6 cups boiling water
1 quart loosely packed horehound
    leaves and stems

Steep for 5 minutes. To 2 quarts of this bitter dark brew, add:

4 cups sugar
1¼ cups dark cane sirup
1 tablespoon butter

Cook these ingredients until they reach the hard-crack stage, 300° to 310°. Skim off any scum. Pour into a 15 x 10 x 1-inch pan and score into pieces before it sets. Allow to cool.

NUT CRUNCH
About 2 Pounds

Sliver large, dense nuts like almonds and Brazil nuts. Others can be left whole. You may add them at once to the mixture if you like a roasted quality in the nut. If not, spread them on a buttered slab or pan and pour the sirup over them after cooking. Heat in a large, heavy skillet:

1 cup sugar
1 cup butter
3 tablespoons water

Cook rapidly and stir constantly for about 10 minutes or until the mixture reaches 295°. Add:

1 to 1½ cups nuts

Turn the candy quickly onto the buttered slab. Form into a shape about 1-foot square. When almost cool, brush with:

¼ lb. melted semi-sweet chocolate

Before the chocolate hardens, dust with:

¼ cup finely chopped nuts
Break into pieces when cold.

ENGLISH TOFFEE
About 1½ Pounds

Combine in a large, heavy saucepan and
stir over quick heat until the sugar is dissolved:

    1¾ cups sugar
    ⅛ teaspoon cream of tartar
    1 cup cream

Stir and boil these ingredients for about 3
minutes. Add:

    ½ cup butter

Cook and stir the sirup until it is light
colored and thick to the soft-crack stage,
285°-290°. Remove from heat. Add:

    1 teaspoon vanilla or 1 tablespoon rum

Pour candy onto a buttered pan. When
cool, cut into squares. To cover it with
semi-sweet chocolate and nuts, see Nut
Crunch, page 735.

ABOUT PENUCHE AND PRALINES

The taste of these candies is very similar.
Penuche is often cut in squares, like fudge,
while pralines are usually made into 3- to
4-inch patties. Why so large, we wonder?
We prefer small sugared nuggets made by
separating the nuts as the sugar begins to
harden. They are best when freshly made
with nuts of finest quality. Sometimes
raisins or coconut are added. Pralines do
not keep well unless wrapped in foil and
stored in tightly covered containers.

PENUCHE AND PRALINES
About 1 Pound

I. Dissolve in a large, heavy pan and stir
constantly until boiling:

    3 cups brown sugar
    ¼ teaspoon salt
    1 cup milk or cream

♦ Cover and cook about 3 minutes until
the steam has washed down any crystals
from the sides of the pan. ♦ Uncover and
cook slowly, without stirring, to the soft-
ball stage, 238°. Remove candy from heat
and add:

    1 to 2 tablespoons butter

Cool to 110°. Beat until smooth and
creamy. Add:

    1 teaspoon vanilla
    1 cup nut meats

In summer try adding instead:

    (½ cup grated fresh pineapple)
    (1 teaspoon lemon juice)

Drop candy from a spoon onto a buttered
surface.

II.   **About 2 Pounds**

Dissolve in a large, heavy pan over low
heat until boiling:

    1½ cups sugar
    ⅔ cup brown sugar
    ⅔ cup water
    ⅝ teaspoon vinegar
    ⅛ teaspoon salt

♦ Cover and cook for about 3 minutes to
allow the steam to wash down any crystals
from the sides of the pan. ♦ Uncover and
cook to the soft-ball stage, 236°. Remove
pan from heat and add:

    2 to 3 tablespoons butter

♦ Cool candy to 110°. Beat until it begins
to lose its gloss and thickens. Quickly
stir in:

    2 cups pecans

Drop candy in patties from a spoon onto a
buttered platter. When hardened, wrap
them individually in foil.

PEANUT OR NUT BRITTLE
About 2 Pounds

Have ready a pair of clean white cotton
gloves. It is best to use raw nuts and cook
them in the sirup. Should only roasted
nuts be available, add them after the sirup
is cooked. In this case the candy is best if
aged 24 hours. If the nuts are salted, rub
them between paper towels and omit salt
from the recipe. This recipe makes a
tender clear brittle. For a porous one,
combine ¼ teaspoon cream of tartar with
the sugar, and sprinkle ½ teaspoon of soda
all over the hot sirup just before pouring.
Bring to a boil in a large, heavy pan:

    1 cup water

♦ Remove from heat and stir in until dissolved:

    2 cups sugar

Then add and stir in:

    1 cup corn sirup
    2 cups raw Spanish peanuts, pecans,
        Brazil nuts or some other nut
        combination
    1 teaspoon salt

Stir occasionally to keep any exposed nuts
submerged, so they cook thoroughly and
the candy does not burn. Cook to 295°.
Remove from heat. Stir in lightly:

    1 to 2 tablespoons butter
    ¼ teaspoon baking soda

Pour onto a well-buttered slab at once,
scraping out bottom of pan. Spread mixture rapidly with a spatula. At this point
don the cotton gloves. Loosen the mass
from slab with a scraper, reverse it and
discarding the scraper, stretch and pull the
brittle so thin that you can see through it.
When cool, crack into eating-size pieces
and store in a tightly covered tin.

NUT BRITTLE, GLAZED NUTS
AND PRALINÉ FOR GARNISH
I.   **About ½ Pound**

This clear candy when ground or crushed
is called praliné. Delicious over ice cream
or when added to icings and dessert sauces.
Melt in a skillet over low heat:

    1 cup sugar

Stir constantly. When the sirup is light
brown, 310°, stir in until well coated:

1 cup toasted almonds or hazelnuts
or toasted benné seeds
Pour the candy onto a buttered platter. When it is cool crack into pieces.

II. For another sirup to use over nuts, see:
Glazed Fresh Fruits, pages 741-743.

ALMOND CREAMS
Blanch and toast lightly:
Almonds or hazelnuts
Cover them first with:
Basic Fondant, page 727, or
Uncooked Fondant, page 728
Then dip them at once in:
Chocolate Coating, page 730
Place them on a wire rack to dry.

SPICED CARAMEL NUTS
Have ready:
Toasted, blanched almonds, hazelnuts
or pecans, see page 521
Prepare:
Chocolate Cream Caramels, page 732
Add to the dissolved ingredients:
1 teaspoon cinnamon
When the candy has cooked to 248°, remove it from heat and spread to a ¼-inch thickness on a marble slab. Score the candy in 1-inch squares. Place a whole toasted nut on each square. Before candy hardens, enclose each nut in its candy square, shaping it to the nut.

SUGARED OR BURNT ALMONDS
About 2 Pounds
Cook over slow heat, stirring constantly:
2 cups sugar
½ cup water
1 teaspoon or more cinnamon
Boil the sirup rapidly. When it is clear and falls in heavy drops from a spoon, add:
1 lb. unblanched almonds,
hazelnuts or peanuts
Stir the nuts until they are well coated. Remove candy from heat and stir on a marble slab until nuts are dry. Sift them to remove the superfluous sugar. Add a very little water to the sifted sugar, a few drops of red vegetable coloring and as much additional cinnamon as is desired. Boil sirup until it is clear, then add the nuts and stir them until they are well coated. Drain and dry.

SPICED NUTS
About ¼ Pound
Preheat oven to 250°.
Sift into a shallow pan:
½ cup sugar
¼ cup cornstarch
⅛ teaspoon salt
1½ teaspoons cinnamon
½ teaspoon allspice
⅛ teaspoon each ginger and nutmeg
Combine and beat slightly:

1 egg white
2 tablespoons cold water
Dip in this mixture:
¼ lb. nut meats
Drop them one at a time in the sifted ingredients. Roll them about lightly. Keep nut meats separated. Place them on a cookie sheet. Bake for about 1½ hours. Remove from the oven and shake off excess sugar. Store tightly covered.

CHOCOLATE TRUFFLES
About ⅓ Pound
Not a hot weather dish—it is definitely a brisk weather confection.
Coarsely grate:
3 oz. chocolate
Melt it with:
¼ cup butter
Add:
2 tablespoons cream
Gradually stir in until lump free:
7 tablespoons sifted confectioners' sugar
2 tablespoons grated hazelnuts
Let the mixture stand covered in a cool place 12 to 24 hours. Make individual balls by rolling a small teaspoonful of the mixture in the palm of the hand. This friction and warmth will cause chocolate to melt slightly, so that final coating will adhere. Roll balls in:
Cinnamon-flavored cocoa or
Chocolate pastilles or shots
This covering will stick to them very satisfactorily. Keep refrigerated, but remove 2 hours before serving for best flavor.

★ BOURBON BALLS
About ⅛ Pound
Sift together:
2 tablespoons cocoa
1 cup powdered sugar
Combine and stir in:
¼ cup bourbon whisky
2 tablespoons light corn sirup
Add and mix thoroughly:
2½ cups crushed vanilla wafers
1 cup broken pecans
Roll mixture into small balls. Dredge in:
½ cup powdered sugar

HEAVENLY HASH CANDY
About 1¼ Pounds
Surely, at least, a child's idea of heavenly!
Dice:
12 marshmallows
Chop:
1 cup nut meats
Boil water in bottom of a double boiler. Turn off heat. Place in top:
1 lb. milk chocolate
Stir occasionally. Line a tray with waxed paper. Pour in ½ the chocolate when melted. Cover with marshmallows and nut meats. Pour rest of chocolate over this. Cool and break candy into pieces.

CHOCOLATE CLUSTERS
About ¾ Pound
Melt over hot water:

½ lb. semi-sweet chocolate

Stir in slowly:

¾ cup sweetened condensed milk

When well blended, add:

1 cup nut meats or unsweetened
ready-to-eat cereal, sesame seed
or wheat germ

Drop candy from a teaspoon onto foil.

PEANUT BUTTER FUDGE
OR CENTERS
About 2 Pounds
Mix and stir until blended:

1 cup peanut butter

1 cup corn sirup

1¼ cups nonfat milk solids

1¼ cups sifted confectioners' sugar

Mix, then knead. Form into balls.

ABOUT POPCORN

One-half cup corn equals about 1 quart when popped. If popcorn has the right moisture content, you will hear it in a minute—popping gently. It will be completely fluffy and ready in another minute. If it does not respond in this way, put it in a closed jar with 2 tablespoons of water, shake well and let stand for several days. For best results, never overload popper. Wire ones, used over coals, will process about ¼-cup popcorn at a time. A heavy lidded, or electric, skillet or a 4-quart pressure pan will pop ½-cup corn at a time. With an electric popper, follow the manufacturer's directions. Unless you are using an open popper, add to the preheated pan for each cooking:

1 tablespoon peanut or corn oil

♦ Cook over high heat. ♦ Keep pan moving constantly. When corn stops popping, discard all imperfect kernels. For each 4 cups of hot popcorn, sprinkle with:

¼ to ½ teaspoon salt

2 tablespoons or more melted butter
or grated cheese

CANDIED POPCORN

Besides making a tasty confection, candied popcorn lends itself well to large, but mostly inedible, decorations. For a smaller decoration, use a well-oiled or buttered fancy two-piece cake mold, such as a lamb or rabbit form, ramming the corn tightly into all the nooks and crannies after you have coated it with sirup. If you want to color popcorn, use plenty of coloring matter to counteract the whiteness of the base over which it is spread.

To prepare popcorn for shaping, have ready in a large bowl:

6 cups popped corn

Prepare any of the sirups below. When the sirup has been taken from the heat, pour it over the popped corn. Stir corn gently with a wooden spoon until well

coated. Then, when you are sure the corn is cool enough to handle with lightly buttered fingers, press it into balls or lollipops as illustrated above.

WHITE SUGAR SIRUP
Stir until the sugar is dissolved:

⅔ cup sugar

½ cup water

2½ tablespoons white corn sirup

⅛ teaspoon salt

⅛ teaspoon vinegar

Bring to a boil. ♦ Cook covered for about 3 minutes until steam washes down sides of pan. ♦ Uncover and cook, without stirring, nearly to the hard-crack stage, 290°.

MOLASSES SIRUP
Melt:

1 tablespoon butter

Add:

½ cup molasses

¼ cup sugar

Stir these ingredients until sugar is dissolved. Bring to a boil. ♦ Cover and cook for about 3 minutes until the steam has washed down the sides of the pan. ♦ Uncover and cook without stirring, nearly to the hard-crack stage, 290°

CARAMEL SIRUP
Melt:

1½ tablespoons butter

Add:

1½ cups brown sugar

6 tablespoons water

Stir these ingredients until sugar is dissolved. Bring to a boil. ♦ Cover and cook for about 3 minutes until the steam has washed down the sides of the pan. ♦ Uncover and cook without stirring to the soft-ball stage, 238°.

PASTILLAGE OR GUM PASTE
About 3 Cups
This is a favorite mixture for decorations, especially on wedding cakes, and makes lovely molded leaves and flowers. The shapes are separately formed and held together later with Quick Decorative Icing, see page 678. Gum paste can be rolled out like pie crust, but never roll more at a time than you plan to shape immediately because it dries rapidly and becomes cracked and grainy.

Dissolve in the top of a double boiler:

1 tablespoon gelatin
½ cup water
1 teaspoon cream of tartar
1 tablespoon powdered gum tragacanth

To keep paste white, add:

1 or 2 drops blue coloring

If you want different colors, work them later into separate portions of the paste as you knead it. Knead the above mixture as you would pastry into:

4 cups confectioners' sugar

Store it in a bowl covered with a damp cloth and let it rest at least one-half hour. When you are ready to use the gum paste, dust a board, a roller and your hands with cornstarch. Roll as much paste as you will immediately use to the desired thickness. Cut into shapes. Large flat ones are allowed to dry on the cornstarch-covered board for at least 24 hours. Cover tops also with cornstarch. Petals, leaves, etc., are shaped and stored in cornstarch or cornmeal until dry and ready to assemble.

TURKISH FRUIT PASTE, TURKISH DELIGHT, OR RAHAT LOUKOUM
About 1½ Pounds

Called "Peace Candy" in Turkey, this sweet is served with coffee to friends who drop in for a visit. It calls for simultaneous cooking and stirring in 2 pans. Have everything ready before you turn on the heat.

Put in a very heavy 2-quart pan:

2 tablespoons water
¾ cup liquid fruit pectin

Stir in:

½ teaspoon baking soda

The soda will cause foaming. Do not be alarmed. Put in another pan:

1 cup light corn sirup
¾ cup sugar

Put both pans on high heat. Stir alternately from 3 to 5 minutes or until foaming has ceased in the pectin pot and boiling is active in the other. Then, still stirring the corn sirup mixture, gradually and steadily pour the pectin mixture into it. Continue stirring and boiling and add during the next minute:

¼ cup any jelly: apple, currant,
    raspberry, peach or quince

Remove from heat and stir in:

1 tablespoon lemon juice
(1 teaspoon grated lemon rind)
(½ cup broken pistachio or other
    nut meats)

If the color of the jelly is not a pleasant one, add:

A few drops of vegetable coloring

Pour the mixture into an 8 x 8-inch pan. Let stand at room temperature for about 3 hours. When it is very firm, cut in shapes or squares. Dust well with confectioners' or powdered sugar or cornstarch. If you plan packaging these candies, let them stand sugared 12 hours or more on a rack. Re-dust on all sides and pack.

MEXICAN ORANGE DROPS
About 2 Pounds

Heat in the top of a double boiler:

1 cup evaporated milk

Melt in a deep saucepan:

1 cup sugar

When the sugar is a rich brown, stir in slowly:

¼ cup boiling water or orange juice

Add the hot milk. Stir in until dissolved:

2 cups sugar
¼ teaspoon salt

♦ Bring to a boil and cook covered for 3 minutes until the steam washes down any crystals on the sides of the pan. ♦ Cook uncovered over low heat, without stirring, to the soft-ball stage, 238°. Add:

Grated rind of 2 oranges

Cool these ingredients. Beat until creamy. Stir in:

1 cup nut meats

Drop the candy from a spoon onto foil.

GINGER CANDY OR CENTERS
About 1¾ Pounds

Bring to a boil in a large, heavy pan:

¾ cup milk

♦ Remove from heat. Add and stir until dissolved and cook until boiling:

2 cups white sugar
1 cup brown sugar
2 tablespoons white corn sirup

♦ Cover and cook for about 3 minutes until the steam washes down any crystals which may have formed on the sides of the pan. ♦ Uncover and cook to 238°. Remove from heat and drop on surface of sirup:

2 tablespoons butter

Cool to 110°. Beat until it begins to thicken. Add:

1 teaspoon vanilla
¼ lb. finely chopped ginger

If preserved ginger is used, drain it well. If candied ginger is preferred, wash the sugar from it in the milk, then dry ginger in paper towels and chop it.
Pour candy onto a buttered platter. Cut into squares before it hardens. These candy squares may be dipped in:

Chocolate Coating, page 730

HAWAIIAN CANDY OR CENTERS
About 1 Pound

A fine combination—the tart flavor of pineapple with the spicy taste of ginger.
Bring to a boil in a large, heavy pan:

1 cup cream

♦ Remove from heat and stir until dissolved:

½ cup brown sugar
1 cup sugar
½ cup crushed drained pineapple

Stir constantly until these ingredients boil. ♦ Cover and cook for about 3 minutes until the steam washes down any crystals which may have formed on the sides of the pan.

♦ Uncover and cook over low heat, stirring only if necessary, to the soft-ball stage, 238°. Remove from heat and add:

    1 tablespoon butter
    1 teaspoon preserved ginger
    ½ cup broken pecan meats
    1 teaspoon vanilla

Cool to 110°. Beat until creamy. Pour into a shallow buttered pan. Cut into squares before it is cold.

★ CANDY FRUIT ROLL OR CENTERS

About 5 Pounds

Bring to a boil in a large, heavy pan:

    1 cup cream
    ¼ cup water

♦ Remove from heat and stir in until dissolved:

    5 cups light brown sugar
    ¾ cup light corn sirup
    1 tablespoon butter
    ¼ teaspoon salt

Bring these ingredients slowly to a boil, stirring constantly. ♦ Cover and boil about 3 minutes until the steam has washed down any crystals which may have formed on the sides of the pan. ♦ Uncover and cook without stirring to the soft-ball stage, 238° Remove from heat and add:

    1 lb. blanched shredded almonds
    ¼ lb. chopped figs
    1 lb. seeded chopped raisins

Cool to 110°. Beat mixture until it begins to cream. Shape into a roll. Cover with foil. Roll in, when almost firm:

    (Melted semi-sweet chocolate)

When the candy is cold and firm, cut into slices and roll in:

    (Finely chopped nuts)

★ PERSIAN BALLS OR CENTERS

Some or all of the fruit ingredients may be used. Put through the coarsest cutter of a meat grinder:

    ½ lb. pitted dates
    1 lb. dried figs with stems cut off
    1 lb. seeded raisins
    1 lb. pecan meats
    ½ lb. crystallized ginger or candied orange peel

If the mixture is very stiff, add:

    1 or 2 tablespoonfuls lemon juice

Shape these ingredients into balls or centers for dipping or make a roll to be sliced. Roll in:

    Confectioners' sugar

Then wrap in foil.

★ DATE ROLL OR CENTERS

Boil to the soft-ball stage, 238°:

    3 cups sugar
    1 cup evaporated milk

Stir in:

    1 cup chopped dates
    1 cup chopped nut meats

When cool enough to handle, form these ingredients into a roll with buttered hands. Wrap the roll in foil. Chill and slice later.

★ STUFFED DRIED FRUITS

Steam over hot water in a covered colander for 10 to 20 minutes:

    1 lb. apricots, prunes, dates or figs

Stuff fruits as soon as cool with one or two of the following:

    Fondant, see page 727
    Hard Sauce, see page 714
    Nut meats
    Candied pineapple
    Candied ginger
    Marshmallows, etc.

I. After steaming, the fruits may be rolled in:

    Granulated or powdered sugar or grated coconut

II. Or, you may coat the fruits in a meringue glaze. Preheat oven to 250°. Beat until stiff:

    2 egg whites

Add gradually, beating steadily:

    ½ cup sugar
    ½ teaspoon vanilla

Place the stuffed fruits on a fork. Dip them in the egg mixture until well coated. Place on a wire rack with a baking sheet underneath. Sprinkle tops with:

    Grated coconut

Bake for about ½ hour.

★ APRICOT ORANGE BALLS

About 2 Pounds

Placed in Christmas cookie boxes, these confections keep the tougher cookies from drying out. Use best quality, slightly soft, dried apricots. Steam any that are too dried out. Grind twice in a meat grinder using the finest knife:

    1 lb. apricots
    1 whole seedless orange or 5 seeded finely ground preserved kumquats

You may also grind with them a choice of:

    (¼ lb. candied lemon rind)
    (¼ lb. candied citron)
    (½ cup shredded coconut)
    (½ cup nut meats)

Shape into balls or patties. Dust in:

    Granulated sugar

Store closely covered.

★ APRICOT OR PEACH LEATHER

About 2 Pounds

An old-time Southeast Seaboard favorite. Cover with:

    1 cup boiling water

and soak for 12 hours in a glass dish:

    1 lb. dried apricots or ¾ lb. dried apricots and ¼ lb. dried peaches

If tenderized fruit is used, omit soaking. Grind fruit with finest blade. Mix in:

    (2 teaspoons grated lemon rind)

Sprinkle on a board:

    Powdered sugar

You will need about 2 cups sugar in all Start rolling a small quantity of the fruit pulp with a rolling pin. Sprinkle powdered sugar on the surface if the mass sticks. Continue to roll and to add sugar, as necessary, until you have a very thin sheet resembling leather in texture. This amount should make about a 12 x 16-inch sheet, $\frac{1}{16}$-inch thick. Cut it into 1¼ x 2-inch strips and roll the powdered strips very tightly. Store closely covered.

ABOUT CANDIED, CRYSTALLIZED OR GLAZED FRUITS, LEAVES AND BLOSSOMS

There are a number of different methods suggested in the following recipes and the "keeping" qualities of the product vary. Some fruits and leaves are glazed for temporary decorative effects, which involve a ♦ superficially applied covering of sirup or egg and sugar. Unless used on very thin leaves and blossoms, they will hold for only a day. If the leaves or blossoms are thin and are stored ♦ after thorough drying, in a tightly covered container, they will keep for several months.

The other methods described call for ♦ sugar penetration as well as glazing, and the fruits will keep for about 3 months. Different sirup weights and different time intervals of drying are suggested, but the principles in these recipes demanding sugar penetration remain the same.

There is a third hot sirup method for blossoms, especially the imported violets, Viola odorata, which is much like the sirup for Candied Kumquats, page 742. Our native violets are too tender to use.

♦ In every operation keep the fruit or other material covered with the sirup to avoid any hardening or discoloration. To begin with, the fruit is dropped into a thin sirup, which can penetrate the skins and cells. Then the sirup is reduced or replaced with a heavier one. This also penetrates, after the thin sirup has opened the way, and finally sugars out or dries into a crystal coating.

GLAZED FRESH FRUITS

Enough to Cover About 1 Cup of Solids
The beauty of these sparkling confections depends on sparkling weather and last minute preparation. They must be eaten the very day they are prepared. Use only fresh fruits that are in prime and perfect condition. If you are covering a large quantity of fruit, divide it into several batches for successive sirup cooking. All fruit must be at room temperature and very dry. Orange sections must be dried for at least 6 hours in advance. Work very quickly to keep the sirup effective. Stir in a heavy saucepan, over low heat, until dissolved:

> 1 cup sugar
> ½ to ¾ cup boiling water

$\frac{1}{16}$ teaspoon cream of tartar

Bring sirup to the boiling point. Cover and cook without stirring for about 3 minutes. The sirup should reach the hard-crack stage, 300°. Remove pan from heat and place over hot water. Dip fruits or nuts a few at a time and remove them with a fork. Place them on a wire rack until the coating hardens. Should sirup in the pan harden, reheat it over hot water and repeat the dipping. If reheated more than once, the sirup is apt to burn.

EGG-GLAZED BLOSSOMS, LEAVES OR FRUITS

For an alternate method, which stores better, see Glazed Mint Leaves, below.
Pick while still dewy:

> Borage and violet blossoms, rose petals, mint leaves, johnny jump-ups, grapes

Allow them to dry on paper towels. Stir:

> 1 egg white

Causing as little foam as possible, beat in:

> 1 to 2 teaspoons cold water

Hold the leaf or flower in your fingers and paint this mixture over it with a very soft brush. Dust the sticky leaf or flower thoroughly with:

> Granulated sugar

Let sugar fall into a bowl beneath for reuse. Put blossom on a screening rack to dry. When dry, store in a tightly-closed container.

GLAZED MINT LEAVES

Have ready the following solution.
Dissolve and cook over low heat until clear:

> 1 cup sugar
> ½ cup water

Cool the sirup slightly, before blending in thoroughly:

> 4 teaspoons powdered acacia

This mixture is called **gum arabic.**
♦ Refrigerate it until chilled, before using. The mint leaves should be freshly picked and kept cold, so as not to wilt. Prepare by carefully stripping from the main stem individual leaves, with their small stems attached. Wash and dry thoroughly. Put on a napkin over ice. Dip each leaf in the gum arabic and sugar solution. Run your forefinger and thumb gently over each leaf to make a smooth, thin coating. ♦ Be sure every bit of leaf is covered, for any uncoated area will turn brown later. Place leaves carefully on a rack. Turn with a spatula after 12 hours. When the coated leaves become thoroughly dry, store them in tightly-covered containers.

CANDIED APPLES

I. Cook the sirup used for:

> Glazed Fresh Fruits, above

Add:

> A few drops of red vegetable coloring

After cooking glaze, keep it in a double boiler ♦ over—not in—hot water. Now, work quickly. Dip in:

Apples on skewers

Place them on a well-buttered surface or on a metal flower holder to harden, see sketch below.

II. Wash, dry and stick a skewer in the stem end of:

5 medium-sized apples

Place in the top of a double boiler:

1 lb. caramels
2 tablespoons water

Heat and stir these ingredients until they melt into a smooth coating. Dip the skewered apples into the sauce, twirling them until completely coated. Dry as above. They will harden in a few minutes, if refrigerated.

GLAZED PINEAPPLE

Drain and reserve juice from:

3½ cups sliced canned pineapple

Dry slices with a cloth or paper towel. Add to the juice:

2 cups sugar
⅛ cup light corn sirup

Stir and bring these ingredients to a boil in a large, heavy pan. Add the fruit, but do not crowd it. Simmer until the fruit is transparent. Lift pineapple from sirup. Drain it on racks until thoroughly dry. Place between waxed paper and store tightly covered.

★ CANDIED CITRUS PEEL

This is good eaten as candy, or it can be grated for zest in cakes and desserts. A moist peel.
Grate fruit slightly to release oil from cells. Cut into thin strips and place in a heavy pan:

2 cups grapefruit, orange, lime
or lemon peel

Cover it with:

1½ cups cold water

Bring slowly to the boiling point. Simmer 10 minutes or longer if you do not like a very bitter taste. Drain. Repeat this process 3 to 5 times in all, draining well each

time. For each cup of peel make a sirup of:

¼ cup water
½ cup sugar

Add peel and boil until all sirup is absorbed and the peel is transparent. Roll it in:

Powdered sugar

Spread on racks to dry. When ♦ thoroughly dry, dip in:

Chocolate Coating, see page 730

II. This quicker process makes a softer peel, which does not keep as well as the one prepared according to the first method. Cut into strips:

Grapefruit or orange peel

Soak for 24 hours in:

Salt water to cover

Use 1 tablespoon salt to 4 cups water. Drain peel. Rinse and soak for 20 minutes in fresh water. Drain, cover with fresh water and boil for 20 minutes. Drain again. Measure in equal parts with the peel:

Sugar

Cook the peel. Add a very little water—only if necessary—until it has absorbed the sugar. Shake the pot as the sirup diminishes, so that the peel does not burn. ♦ Dry thoroughly and store tightly covered.

★ CANDIED OR PRESERVED KUMQUATS OR CALAMONDINS

These miniature oranges should first be washed well in warm soapy water. Then cover with fresh water and boil 15 minutes:

1 lb. kumquats or calamondins

Drain well and repeat twice. Make a sirup of:

1½ cups sugar
4 cups water

Boil for 5 minutes. Place drained kumquats in hot sirup and bring sirup to 238° or let boil gently until the kumquats are transparent. To plump up the fruit, cover pan just before heat is turned off and allow fruit to remain covered in hot sirup for about half an hour. At this point, you have Preserved Kumquats or Calamondins. Pack in sterile jars. Serve as a meat garnish or with desserts. If you chop them, be sure to slit them to take out the seeds.
To candy the kumquats, drain from the sirup. Prick a hole in the stem end. Bring to a boil a heavier sirup of:

1 part water to
1 part sugar
(⅛ teaspoon cream of tartar for every quart of liquid)

Reboil the kumquats for 30 minutes. Remove them from heat but allow them to stand in the sirup 24 hours. Bring them to a boil again. Cook for 30 minutes more. Drain, dry on a rack and roll in:

(Granulated sugar)

★ GLAZED CHESTNUTS OR MARRONS GLACÉS

Prepare:
Chestnuts II, see page 272
Soak overnight, covered with cold water, to which you have added:
Juice of 1 lemon
Next morning, drain and drop into boiling:
Water or milk
Simmer until tender but firm. Drain chestnuts and discard water or milk. For every cup of nuts, make a sirup by cooking to 238°:

1 cup sugar
1 cup water
¼ teaspoon cream of tartar

Drop nuts into boiling sirup and simmer for about ten minutes. Remove from heat and let stand, covered, for 24 hours. Drain nuts, reserving sirup. While preparing the sauce, put nuts in a 250° oven to dry. Reduce the sirup until it is very thick. Place nuts in jars. Add to each jar:

1 to 2 tablespoons cognac

Fill jars with the heavy sirup and seal. To candy the nuts they must be dried not once but three times, dipping them between dryings in the reduced sirup. After the final drying roll them in
Granulated sugar
Store in tightly-covered tins.

CANDIED CRANBERRIES

Because of their innate keeping qualities cranberries can be candied by a rather simple method. They will remain good during about 3 months' storage if kept covered. Stir until dissolved and bring to a boil:

2½ cups sugar
1½ cups water

Have ready in a heat-resistant bowl:

1 quart cranberries

Pour the boiling sirup over the berries. Put the bowl in a steamer for 45 minutes. Remove and cool without stirring. Leave in a warm, dry room for 3 to 4 days. Stir at intervals. When the sirup reaches a jelly-like consistency, remove berries and let them dry 3 days longer—out of the sirup. Turn them for uniform drying. When the fruit can be handled easily, store in a tightly covered container. Use the berries

on toothpicks to stud a ham or for other garnishing.

FRUIT PASTE

You find this delicacy in Italy, Spain, the American tropics, and in Germany where it bears the quaint name of Quittenbrod or Würste because quince is a favorite flavor. The trick is to reduce, until they are stiff, equal parts of:

Fruit pulp—guava, quince, apricot, etc.
Sugar

◗ The real trick, of course, is to find the patience and time to watch this mixture so it won't scorch. When stiff, spread the mixture to a ½-inch thickness in pans that have been dipped in cold water. Cut into squares and dry on racks in a cool place, turning once a day for 3 to 4 days. Dust the squares with:
Granulated sugar
Or, stuff the stiff pulp without drying into cellophane sausage casings. Before pouring or stuffing, you may add at the last minute:
Ground cinnamon, cloves, citron or almonds
Slices or squares look attractive when served on a green leaf.

CANDIED OR CRYSTALLIZED ROOTS AND STALKS

About 1 Pound

Wash:
2 cups angelica roots and young stalks or cleaned scraped acorus calamus roots

Place them in a crock. Pour over to cover:
⅛ cup salt
2 cups boiling water

Cover crock and let the angelica soak for 24 hours. Drain, peel and wash in cold water. Cook to 238°:
2 cups sugar
2 cups water

Add the cleaned angelica roots and stems. Cook for 20 minutes. Drain the angelica, but reserve sirup. Put the angelica on a wire rack in a cool, dark place for 4 days. Then bring the sirup and roots to 238° and cook 20 minutes or until the sirup candies the roots. Drain on a rack until ◗ thoroughly dry. Store tightly covered.

THE FOODS WE KEEP

This section divides into those foods we freeze, can, salt, smoke and preserve. It also includes those items with both long and short keeping-tolerance that we buy at rather frequent intervals and store briefly. On the whole we take greater care with the former, perhaps because of the effort we personally put into processing them.

Most purchased staples come under state and local laws; and any that are in interstate commerce are covered by Federal Food and Drug legislation. A special and recent subject of federal concern is additives—those extra substances which are present in food as a result of the manufacturers' determination to boost nutritive content or of special conditions growing out of processing, packaging or storage. Some additives are time-honored, like seasonings and salts. Some provide enrichment, such as vitamins. Some are chemicals which improve flavor, color, consistency and keeping quality. An entirely different kind of additive is the unintentional or accidental kind—the one which results from improper processing, contamination, imperfect sealing, careless storage. In this area, again, there is a whole series of federal rulings.

A change in the nature of legal concepts during the past few years now puts the burden of proof for the safety of additives on the manufacturer and thus provides more immediate and positive protection for the consumer. It is the business of each and every one of us to support further legislation controlling amounts and kinds of food additives—so that we may be sure they will not increase beyond human tolerance. ◗ Read the labels and carefully note both contents and weight of all the packaged or preserved food you buy.

For most of us, the responsibility for keeping food in good condition starts as we roll our baskets past the checker. And what a lot we push! In one week, one normally well-fed American uses a minimum of 3½ quarts of milk, ½ pound of fat, 4½ pounds of meat, poultry, fish, cheese, beans or nuts, 3 pounds of cereals and ½ pound of sugar. Add fruits and vegetables and multiply by 52, then by the number of persons in your family. If there are four of you, the total will stand at something like a ton and a half a year. This is an impressive investment in hard currency: an item, in fact, amply huge to warrant protecting your market purchases to the very best of your ability.

But all of us are guilty on occasion of picking up Junior at the swimming and tennis club after shopping and getting involved in some friendly gossip—while the lettuces back in the car wilt down and the frozen foods begin disastrously to thaw. Remember that heat and moisture encourage spoilage, bacteria, insect-infestation and mold. And sunlight may destroy vitamin content, as in milk; or cause flavor deterioration, as in spices.

Many molds need no light and thrive on acids; some may only occur on the surface but give off gases which may adversely affect the rest of the food. ◗ Store most foods in a cool, dark, dry place, preferably with a constant temperature around 70°; or, if indicated, refrigerate. Throughout this book, we have listed ideal storage suggestions with individual types of food, but following is a quick rundown on storage standards and the keeping life of typical larder items. ◗ Any stockpiled food should be kept on a rotating system. Place the new food at the back of the shelves and use the older purchases from the front for the day to day needs of the household. Although we know canned foods may not spoil for years, flavor and nutritive qualities, as the months roll by, are progressively lessened.

Once again we urge you to ◗ use a preponderance of fresh foods whenever possible. Build your menus around government "best buys" on produce that appear regularly in the newspapers. These items are apt to be both reasonable in price and fresh, because they are seasonal. After buying, store them as suggested later and cook them carefully, following the "pointers" ◗ so as to assure topmost nutritive and taste value.

ABOUT LONG TERM STORAGE

You may store in an area that ◗ stays around 70°:

◗ For about 2 years: Salt, sugar, whole pepper.

◗ For about 18 months: Canned meat, poultry and vegetables—except tomatoes and sauerkraut—alone or mixed with cereal products. Canned fruit—except citrus fruit and juices and berries. Dried legumes, if stored in metal.

◗ For about 12 months: Canned fish, hydrogenated fats and oils, flour, ready-to-eat dry cereals stored in metal, uncooked cereal in original container, canned nuts, instant puddings, instant dry cream and bouillon products, soda and baking powder.

◗ For about 6 months: Evaporated milk, nonfat dry whole milk in metal containers, condensed meat and beef soups, dried fruit in metal container, canned citrus fruit and juices, canned berries. To store water, see page 494.

If temperatures are lower than 70° but still above freezing, the permissible storage period for most of these items is longer.

STAPLES FOR THE AVERAGE FAMILY
Beverages: coffee, tea
Bacon
Cereals: breakfast foods, rice, macaroni, spaghetti, noodles, farina, corn meal, tapioca
Cottage and other cheeses
Chocolate, cocoa
Coconut
Butter, lard, cooking oil or other shortening
Flour: whole-grain, all-purpose, cake flour
Sugar: granulated, confectioners', brown, loaf, maple
Bread, crackers
Fruits: fresh, dried, canned
Fruit and vegetable juices: canned, frozen
Potatoes: white, sweet
Onions, garlic, shallots, chives
Sirups: corn, molasses, maple
Mayonnaise and French dressing
Salad oils, vinegars
Milk, cream, eggs
Milk solids, evaporated and condensed milk
Canned meats, fish
Beef, chicken and vegetable cubes
Nuts
Vegetables: fresh, canned, frozen
Honey, preserves, marmalade, jellies
Soups: frozen, canned, dried
Raisins, currants
Peanut butter
Debittered brewers' yeast
Worcestershire and hot pepper sauce
Gelatin: flavored, unflavored
Catsup, chili sauce, horseradish
Flavorings: vanilla, almond, etc.
Baking powder, baking soda
Cornstarch
Ground and stick cinnamon
Ground and whole cloves
Ground ginger
Allspice
Whole nutmeg
Bay leaves
Salt
Celery seed
Celery salt
Dry and prepared mustard
Black and white peppercorns
Paprika, cayenne

Curry powder
Garlic and onion salt
Chili powder
Dried herbs: tarragon, basil, savory, sage, etc. See Herbs, page 529
Monosodium glutamate

KITCHEN HINTS
Glasses, to wash: Glasses may be safely washed in very hot water if slipped in edgewise. For hard water use a low sudsing detergent rather than soap.

Glasses or pitchers with milk residue: Rinse with cold water, then warm water.

Refrigerator: Wash inside with a mixture of 1 tablespoon powdered borax to 1 quart water.

Bread Box: To deter mold, wash with a mixture of 2 tablespoons vinegar to 1 quart water.

Pots and Pans: Lime deposits may be removed by boiling vinegar in the pan.

Food Chopper: To fasten securely, place a potholder under the foot before tightening the screw.

Mixing Bowls: To keep steady when mixing or whipping, place on a wet folded cloth.

Broken Glass: To remove small slivers from a rug, press sticky tape against it. To remove from a smooth surface, use wet paper tissues.

STAIN REMOVAL
Gum, Adhesive Tape, etc.: Lemon juice will remove it from hands and clothes. It will also remove ink, fruit and other stains.

Wax or Paraffin: Scrape cloth to remove hardened wax. Place blotting paper under the cloth and press with warm iron. Cool and sponge with cleaning fluid.

Chocolate and Cocoa: For washable material, use soap and hot water. Otherwise, scrape off and apply cleaning fluid.

Coffee: Boiling water poured from a height of 2 feet is good for fresh stains.

Fruit: Boiling water as for coffee stains, or try bleaching in sun after moistening with lemon juice and salt.

For other stains, we recommend the Home and Garden Bulletin No. 62 of the U. S. Department of Agriculture, Washington, D.C.

CANNING, SALTING
AND SMOKING

It is a thrill to possess shelves well stocked with home-canned food. In fact, you will find their inspection—often surreptitious—and the pleasure of serving the fruits of your labor comparable only to a clear conscience or a very becoming hat.

In fact, you must carry a clear conscience right with you through the processing itself, making absolutely sure that the food you keep is safe to eat. Great care must be exercised in the canning of all foods to avoid spoilage. Even greater care is required in the canning of non-acid foods—see page 751—to prevent the development of *Clostridium botulinum*, a germ so deadly that "1 oz. could theoretically kill 100 million people." The spores of botulinus may resist 212°, or boiling temperature, even after several hours of processing, and produce a fatal toxin in the canned product. Botulinus poisoning may be present even if no odor, gas, color changes or softness in food texture indicate its presence.

Whether or not your suspicions are aroused, ◗ do not test home-canned, nonacid food by tasting it out of the container. Instead, follow the recommendations of all reputable authorities, and cook home-canned vegetables, meat and fish—without exception—for 15 minutes in boiling liquid, uncovered, stirring frequently before serving. By this means—high heat in the presence of air—botulinus toxin is positively destroyed.

Don't let the botulinus bogey haunt you when you use commercially canned foods, for in the last thirty years botulism cases reported from commercial sources have been extremely rare.

◗ For maximum nutritional value only the freshest and best food should be canned. Inspect it with an eagle eye, discarding all blemished or rotted portions and washing or scrubbing the selected remainder to remove spray, soil or insects. Produce which is imperfect before processing may spoil the rest of the food in its container afterwards, producing color changes and encouraging the formation of mold or gases. Obviously if, as a result of careless preliminary handling, your jars, when opened, show these evidences of spoilage, their contents should be discarded at once.

◗ Good organization and proper equipment simplify canning and give you, with a minimum of effort, gay-looking shelves of glistening, jewel-like jars, filled with canned fruits and vegetables, all labeled and dated and ready to use.

Seasonal heat and heat from the stove inevitably accompany canning. Hot fluids in hot jars and heavy pans have to be handled carefully. ◗ Have a funnel, plenty of dry pot-holders, strong tongs or a jar lifter, and paraffin at hand.

ABOUT CANNING PROCESSES

◗ Remember that all nonacid vegetables and all meats and fish must be pressure-processed. ◗ The boiling-water bath is not recommended for any nonacid foods. ◗ Oven canning is not recommended under any circumstances. The open-kettle method has been abandoned by officialdom but is still used by some housewives for acid fruits. Work quickly on those steps in the canning process which involve the exposure of the food to air. To can specific foods, see alphabetical listings in this chapter.

In canning, follow these general steps. ◗ Line up your equipment and read below about the type you are using. If the lids call for separate rubbers, test the rubbers even though they may be newly purchased. Unused left-over rubbers may deteriorate from one canning season to another. ◗ To test rubbers, bend them into small pleats. If they crack, discard them. Or stretch them to see if they will return to their original shape. If not, they are worthless. ◗ Should you be using a pressure canner—see illustration, page 748—make sure that the jars are the type which can stand 240° or more of heat. ◗ In any case, check all jars against chipping, cracking or other defects. Next, check the closures between the jars and lids. If using screw types, first place them on sound jars without a rubber. Screw them tight. They are usable if it is impossible to insert a thin penknife blade or a thumbnail between the jar and the lid. Unscrew them. Put the rubbers in place and fill the jars with water. Screw down the lids. Invert the jars. If there is no seepage, the jars and lids are safe to use. This test may also be applied to the clamp or wire-bail type of closure.

Lids are of two main types—those which need separate rubbers and adjustment both before and after processing, and those which have an attached rubber and are adjusted once before processing and then close automatically by vacuum when cooling. The vacuum type is sketched first on the left. Lids with attached rubbers should never be sterilized. Merely pour boiling water over them.

◆ Unless you are pressure canning, other jars and lids shown with separate rubbers should be sterilized for 15 minutes in boiling water. The rubbers should be washed in soap and hot water, well rinsed, and then placed in a pan. Cover them with boiling water and leave them there until ready to use.

The first three types sketched above fit on the regular grooved-top canning jars, whether of pint, quart or half-gallon size. The zinc- and glass-disk tops, shown second and third above, are placed on the rubber ring, screwed clockwise as tight as possible, and then turned counterclockwise ¼ inch.

The jar with the all-glass lid shown next has a wire-bail or clamp closure. While processing, the longer wire rests in the groove of the lid. The shorter wire is not snapped down in its final position until after processing. ◆ The slight openings provided by all these adjustments are temporary. They allow excess air to be forced out of the jars during processing, and thus avoid possible explosion.

ABOUT PREPARING FOOD FOR CANNING

◆ To prepare food for canning, wash, clean, pare and cut up food just as you would if planning to cook it for immediate use. ◆ Remember that vitamins escape quickly, so prepare only small batches of food, about 1 quart at a time. The size in which pieces are cut may depend on convenience in packing. When making sirups for fruit, allow about 1 cup of sirup for each quart of fruit, see page 749.

◆ To blanch or precook foods for canning, put large fruits and all vegetables in a wire basket and immerse them, about 1 quart at a time, in boiling liquid for 5 minutes, counting from the time the water begins to boil again after immersion. Then dip them up and down quickly in cold water 2 or 3 times to reduce the heat quickly. This will keep the food shapely and make handling easier. Blanching shrinks food and drives out air so that produce may be packed more closely. Its most important role, however, is to arrest some undesirable kinds of enzymatic action.

Berries, soft fruits and tomatoes may be canned without blanching. ◆ The liquid in which the foods were precooked or steamed should be used to fill the jars, thus saving valuable minerals. Meat may be partially cooked (about two-thirds done) by simmering or roasting. For more details about meat, see page 753.

◆ To steam foods for canning, use a steam basket or a cheesecloth bag. Steam only a small quantity at a time. ◆ Do not crowd the food, as the steam must penetrate all of it. Use a kettle with a tightly fitting lid. Have in the kettle several inches of boiling water. Suspend the steam basket or bag over it and close the lid tightly. Steam food the length of time given in individual recipes for fruit or vegetables.

ABOUT PACKING JARS

◆ In canning, pack containers firmly, but not so tightly that the material is crushed. ◆ Pack fruits and vegetables to within ½ inch of jar-tops, with the exception of Lima beans, dried beans, peas and corn, which swell considerably more than other vegetables. ◆ These and meats canned under pressure should be packed to within 1 inch of jar tops, and the jars filled with boiling water to within ½ inch of the top. You may add salt to meats and vegetables at the rate of 1 teaspoon per quart.

Fill jars of fruit with sugar sirup to within ½ inch of top. For sugar sirup formulas, see page 749. ◆ Before putting on lids, make sure that any air which may be trapped in the liquid is expelled. Run a long thin spatula down between the inside of the jar and the produce, changing the position of the contents enough to release the trapped air as shown on page 748. Then carefully wipe the top of the jar.

◆ When jars are packed, it is always wisest to follow the manufacturer's directions in adjusting the lids. If the type of lid you are using requires a separate rubber, be sure it is wet.

ABOUT PRESSURE CANNING

♦ Pressure canning or cooking is the only method recommended for nonacid fruits and vegetables. ♦ A pressure canner or cooker is in any case a necessity for those who plan to do a lot of canning. Detailed directions for the use of such appliances are furnished by the manufacturer and should be followed carefully—especially the checking of pressure gauges. ♦ Be sure also to exhaust the air from the canner for at least 10 minutes so that no cold spots develop and cause the food to be under-processed. ♦ If using a small steam pressure saucepan, keep the heat constantly at 10 pounds pressure, and be sure to add 20 minutes to the processing time. For vegetable pressure canning, see page 751.

▲ If canning at high altitudes in a pressure canner ♦ add ½ pound to the pressure gauge for each additional 1000 feet. For instance, if processing requires 5 pounds pressure at sea level, use 7 pounds at 4000 feet, 9 pounds at 7500 feet; if 15 pounds at sea level, use 17 pounds at 4000 feet, 19 pounds at 7500 feet.

ABOUT CANNING IN A BOILING WATER BATH

♦ The boiling-water bath process is used only for acid fruits and brined vegetables. A regular hot-water canner or a clean wash boiler or lard can may be used if it has a tight-fitting lid.

An important utensil in canning is a rack for the bottom of the boiler to keep the jars from cracking when they come in contact with heat. A wire rack may be bought for this purpose, or one may be made of coarse wire mesh at home. Have ready a holder for lifting jars out of boiling water. Fill the boiler with water to about jar height. When the water is boiling, lower the jars into the boiler. ♦ The jars must not touch one another or the sides of the container. Leave a 2-inch space between them. ♦ The jars should rest on the rack. Add more boiling water to cover them at least 1 inch above the tops. Continue to add boiling water as the water in the boiler evaporates. Process the required length of time for the particu-

lar food chosen—see pages 749-751—counting from the time the water begins to boil after the jars have been added.

▲ Canning at high altitudes in a boiling-water bath ♦ requires a 1-minute increase in processing time for every 1000 feet above sea level if the total time is 20 minutes or less, and 2 minutes per 1000 feet if the total time is more than 20 minutes.

♦ To remove the jars from the boiling water, use tongs or a jar lifter as soon as the time is up. ♦ Do not lift the jars by the lids. ♦ Place the jars on wood, a paper pad, or a cloth surface, allowing several inches between them. See that there is no draft on the hot jars, as sudden cooling may cause the glass to crack.

ABOUT SEALING AND LABELING JARS

♦ Seal all jars according to manufacturer's directions. With the types of lids described above, the rubber-attached metal lid is self-sealing and should not be touched. The zinc screw type and the glass-disk and metal-ring lid should be turned clockwise as far as possible. Be sure to screw lids with a slow, steady turn, so as not to displace the rubbers. The shorter wire on the bail or clamp type should be snapped down into place. ♦ Whatever type you use, be sure to leave the jars upright and undisturbed for 12 hours. With the first and third lids from the left on page 747, you may remove the metal ring, for when the jar is cold the thin top should be tight enough to hold by itself. While the jars are still hot after sealing, you may see active bubbling going on. If it ceases as the contents cool, it was merely continued boiling due to the lowered boiling point produced by the vacuum in the jar.

♦ Test-seal the metal tops by tapping the lids lightly with a metal spoon or knife. A ringing note indicates a safe seal. If the contents touch the inner side of the lid, the sound may be dull but not hollow. ♦ If the note is both dull and hollow, reprocessing with a new lid is in order. Or, if you prefer, use the food right away.

♦ Label and store the jars in a cool dark place. Storage temperatures between 45° and 60° maintain good color and are generally suitable for all properly heat-processed foods.

ABOUT FRUIT CANNING

♦ Choose fresh, firm fruit that is not overripe. Imperfect fruit may be used, but it must be carefully gone over and all blemishes removed. Wash the fruit. Prepare as for table use. If it is to be pared, it may be dipped in boiling water until the skins loosen, and then dipped for a moment in cold water. It is best to process a small quantity—about a quart of fruit at a time.

♦ To keep fruit from discoloring until you can pack it, mist it over with lemon juice or ascorbic acid solution, see page 762, or one of the following solutions, as you would sprinkle clothes. Allow to 1 quart water 3 tablespoons lemon juice or ½ teaspoon dissolved ascorbic acid crystals.

APPROXIMATE YIELD OF TYPICAL FRUITS

FRUIT	POUNDS PER QUART	QUARTS PER BUSHEL
Apples	2½	28
Berries	1⅓	24
Cherries	1⅓	20
Peaches	2¼	21
Pears	2¼	30
Plums	2	28
Tomatoes	3	18

ABOUT SIRUPS FOR CANNING

Sirup for canned fruit varies in consistency, depending upon the fruit or the use to which it will be put. The following formulas will help you decide on the most appropriate blend of sugar and water. ♦ For choicest results make the sirup from the water in which the fruit was cooked or cook some of the cut-up fruits and use the liquid as your sirup base instead of water. Allow ¾ to 1 cup sirup for each quart jar.

THIN SIRUP
About 2¼ cups
One cupful sugar to 2 cupfuls water. Stir well before heating and bring slowly to a boil, 236°. Use for naturally sweet fruits and to approximate the quality of fresh fruits.

MEDIUM SIRUP
About 2¾ cups
1½ cupfuls sugar to 2 cupfuls water. Prepare as for thin sirup. Good for canning fruits that are not highly acid.

HEAVY SIRUP
About 1¼ cups
Use 1 cupful sugar to 1 cupful water. ♦ Dissolve and boil very carefully to prevent crystallization and scorching. Use for very sour fruits like rhubarb; also suitable for dessert use. If too heavy a sirup is used the fruit may rise to the top of the jar during processing.

SYNTHETIC SWEETENER
Use a sodium cyclamate base type: 1 tablespoon or 24 tablets to each cup boiling water. Sour cherries require 2 tablespoons or 48 tablets; large fruits like pears, applesauce and berries, 2 teaspoons or 16 tablets. Do not use this substitution constantly without a doctor's consent.

ABOUT PROCESSING NON-ACID FRUITS

Use a pressure canner. Place jars as described on page 748. Vent canner for 10 minutes. Process fruits 5 minutes at 5 lbs. pressure.

ABOUT PROCESSING ACID FRUITS

The following directions are for quart jars processed in a boiling-water bath. Start counting time when the water surrounding the lidded jars reaches a fast boil. Reduce the processing time by 10% if pint jars are used, by 25% for tomatoes. Increase the processing time by 15 minutes for half-gallon jars. ♦ Do not use iron, copper, aluminum or tin pans in fruit processing, as these may produce discoloration. ♦ See that all jars and lids are sterile.

APPLES
Select firm, sound, tart varieties. Wash, pare and core; cut into quarters or halves. Drop into discoloration solution, see page 762. Drain. Boil 1 minute in thin or medium sirup. Pack in jars, cover with boiling sirup and process 20 minutes in boiling-water bath. Apples may also be baked, packed, covered with boiling sirup and processed 15 minutes in a boiling-water bath.

APPLESAUCE
Prepare applesauce, pack boiling hot. Process at once for 10 minutes in a boiling-water bath. To prevent darkening at top of jar, add at the last moment before sealing 1 teaspoon lemon juice.

APRICOTS
Select ripe, firm fruit. Blanch to remove skins. Pack wholes or halves into jars and cover with boiling medium sirup; process 25 minutes in a boiling-water bath.

BERRIES
Pick over, wash if gritty, stem, pack closely in jars, fill with boiling medium sirup and process 15 minutes in a boiling-water bath. For strawberries, the following more com-

plicated procedure will yield plump, bright-colored fruit. Wash if gritty, then hull. Add 1 cup sugar to each quart prepared berries, placing in alternate layers in shallow pans, and let stand 2 hours. Simmer them for 5 minutes in their own juice. Fill jars full and add boiling thin sirup if additional liquid is needed. Process at once 15 minutes in a boiling-water bath.

CHERRIES

Wash and stem. Can whole or pitted. To seed, use a cherry pitter or the rounded end of a paper clip. If not seeded, prick with a pin. Use heavy sirup for sour cherries; medium sirup for sweet. Pack, cover with boiling sirup and process at once 15 minutes in a boiling-water bath.

CRANBERRIES

Wash and stem. Boil 3 minutes in heavy sirup. Cover with boiling sirup. Process 3 minutes in a boiling-water bath.

CURRANTS

Same as for berries, above.

GRAPES

Use only sound, firm grapes. Wash and stem. Bring to a boil in medium sirup. Cover with boiling sirup. Process 20 minutes in a boiling-water bath.

GRAPE JUICE

Wash sound, ripe grapes. Cover with boiling water and heat slowly to simmering. ♦ Do not boil. Cook slowly until fruit is very soft, then strain through a bag. Let stand 24 hours refrigerated. Strain again. Add ½ cup sugar to each quart juice. Reheat to simmering and pour into hot sterile jars. Seal and process for 20 minutes in a water bath held at 180°.

OTHER FRUIT JUICES

Select sound, ripe fruit, crush and heat slowly to simmering point. Strain through several layers of cheesecloth. Heat again and simmer for 10 minutes. ♦ Do not boil, as it ruins the flavor. Pour into clean hot jars, seal, and process in a water bath held at 180° for 20 minutes. Do not allow water to boil.

Juices from uncooked fruit may be pressed out in a cider press and heated to lukewarm before being poured into jars and processed as above. Peach, cherry, apple juice and cider canned this way are less likely to taste flat. The addition of sugar to tart fruit juices before canning is more satisfactory than sweetening after canning. One cup sugar to 1 gallon juice is a moderate proportion.

PEACHES

Use firm, ripe fruit. Scald to remove skins.

Halve peaches. Pack in jars, cover with boiling medium sirup and process at once for 20 minutes in a boiling-water bath.

PEARS

Pare, core, halve, quarter or slice. Drain. Boil gently about 5 minutes in medium sirup. Pack into jars, cover with boiling sirup, process for 20 minutes in a boiling-water bath. Hard pears are best if cooked in water only until nearly tender. The sugar is then added in the same proportions as for a medium sirup and the whole brought to a boil. Pack into jars, cover with boiling medium sirup and process at once for 20 minutes in a boiling-water bath.

PINEAPPLE

Slice, pare, core, remove eyes. Shred or cut in cubes. Pack, cover with boiling thin or medium sirup, depending on sweetness of fruit. Process at once for 20 minutes in a boiling-water bath.

PINEAPPLE JUICE

Discarded eyes, cores and skins of fresh fruit can be used in making pineapple juice. Cover with cold water. Cook slowly in covered kettle from 30 to 40 minutes. Strain through a jelly bag. Measure juice, heat. For each cup of juice add ⅛ cup sugar. Boil rapidly 10 minutes and process for 5 minutes in boiling-water bath. Juice may also be extracted from pineapple by putting the pared fruit through the fine blade of a food chopper with a large bowl beneath to catch the liquid.

PLUMS

Use moderately ripe fruit. Wash and prick skins. Pack firmly, but do not crush, into jars. Cover with boiling sirup, thin for sweet plums, medium for tart varieties. Process at once for 25 minutes in a boiling-water bath.

PUREES AND PASTES

Use ripe, soft, unblemished fruit. Simmer until it can be forced through a fine strainer or food mill. You may want to reduce the liquid by further cooking. You may add sugar to taste, unless you are puréeing tomatoes. Reheat the purée, fill the jars, seal and process for 20 minutes in a boiling-water bath.

QUINCES

"Preserved," notes an herbalist, optimistically, in 1562, "they do mightily prevail against drunkenness."
Use well-ripened fruit. Pare, cut into convenient-size pieces and boil gently in a medium or heavy sirup about 1½ minutes.

Or, for easier handling, wipe the fuzz from the quince, cut out the stem and blossom ends and cook the fruit gently in several inches of water, covered, for 20 minutes. Drain the water for use in the canning sirup. Pare or simply cut the fruit from the core unpared. Pack into jars, cover with boiling sirup, and process at once for 60 minutes in a boiling-water bath.

RHUBARB
Wash stalks and cut into ½-inch pieces. Pack, cover with boiling heavy sirup, process at once for 10 minutes in hot-water bath.

TOMATOES
Use firm, fresh tomatoes, scald 1 minute and then dip 1 minute in cold water to remove skins. Cut out cores. Leave whole, halve, or quarter. Pack closely in jars, fill with boiling water or tomato juice. Process at once for 45 minutes in a boiling-water bath.

TOMATO JUICE
Use soft but perfect tomatoes. Wash, remove stem ends and cores. Chop or cut into small pieces. Heat in a covered kettle until the juice flows freely. Put through a fine sieve. Pack hot into jars to within ½ inch of top. Process in a boiling-water bath for 10 minutes. Flavor just before serving.

APPROXIMATE YIELD OF TYPICAL VEGETABLES

RAW VEGETABLE	POUNDS PER QUART	QUARTS PER BUSHEL
Beans, Lima in the pod	2	7
Beans, snap	1¾	17
Beets	2¾	18
Carrots	2¾	18
Corn cut off cob	7 ears	8
Greens	2	7
Okra	2	17
Peas in the pod	2	6
Squash, summer	2	18
Sweet potatoes	2½	20

Tomatoes, see Fruits, above.

ABOUT VEGETABLE PRESSURE CANNING

♦ Pressure canning is the only process recommended for vegetables. Vegetables must be very carefully and quickly washed, through several waters if necessary or under running water, to remove all soil. Prepare only one pressure canner load at a time and work quickly.

Great care must be exercised in the canning of nonacid foods to prevent the development of *Clostridium botulinus*, a deadly germ which may be present even though no odor or color changes indicate its presence. The U.S. Government warns that all nonacid home-canned vegetables should be boiled in an open pan for 15 minutes before tasting or serving. They should be stirred frequently during cooking.

The Department of Agriculture does not recommend home canning the following vegetables:

cabbage, except sauerkraut
cauliflower
celery
cucumbers
baked beans
eggplant
lettuce
onions
parsnips
turnips
vegetable mixtures

The following directions are for 1-quart glass jars, unless otherwise specified, processed in a steam pressure canner at 10 pounds pressure.

ARTICHOKES
Wash well, precook 5 minutes in brine of ¾ cup vinegar or lemon juice and 3 tablespoons salt to 1 gallon water. Pack in hot jars. Fill brine to ½ inch of top. Process 25 minutes at 10 pounds pressure.

ASPARAGUS
Wash, remove loose scales and tough ends. Grade for uniformity. Place upright in wire basket. Hold in boiling water which reaches just below tips for 3 minutes. Or cut in 1-inch lengths and boil 2 to 3 minutes. Pack and fill jars with boiling water. Process 40 minutes at 10 pounds pressure.

BEANS, GREEN, SNAP OR WAX
Wash, remove strings and tips. Break into small pieces. Precook 5 minutes. Reserve water. Pack and fill jars with boiling reserved water. Process 40 minutes at 10 pounds pressure.

BEANS, FRESH LIMA
Sort and grade for size and age. Boil young beans 5 minutes, older beans 10 minutes. Pack loosely, allowing 1 inch head space. Cover with boiling water. Process 55 minutes at 10 pounds pressure.

BEETS
Boil for 15 minutes small whole beets with 1 inch stem and all the root. Trim off roots and stems. Slip off skins. Pack in jars. Add boiling water. Process 45 minutes at 10 pounds pressure.

CARROTS
Sort and grade for uniformity. Wash and scrape. Boil 5 minutes. Reserve water. Slice or pack whole. Fill jars with boiling reserved water. Process 45 minutes at 10 pounds pressure.

CORN, WHOLE-KERNEL

Use tender, freshly gathered corn. Cut from cob. Do not scrape cobs. To each quart of corn add only 1 pint boiling water. Heat to boiling. Pack at once, adding no more water. Process for 75 minutes at 10 pounds pressure.

CORN, CREAM-STYLE

Pack in pints only. Cut off the tops of kernels, scrape cobs with back of knife or corn scraper—see page 273—to remove all pulp. Add half as much boiling water as corn, by weight. Heat to boiling. Pack at once. Process pints for 75 minutes at 15 pounds pressure.

GREENS

Use fresh, tender greens. Wash thoroughly, discard any decayed leaves and tough stems. Steam about 8 minutes, or until wilted. Pack quickly and loosely. Fill jars with boiling water. Process for 1¾ hours at 10 pounds pressure.

HOMINY

Pack loosely, boiling hot. Leave 1½ inches head space. Cover with boiling liquid. Process at once for 60 minutes at 10 pounds pressure.

MUSHROOMS

Wash well. Peel if wilted or old. Drop into hot water with 1 tablespoon vinegar or white wine per quart. Cover and precook 3 to 4 minutes. Drain. Pack hot, covering with freshly boiled water. Process 40 minutes at 10 pounds pressure.

OKRA

Use tender pods only. Wash and remove caps without cutting into pod. Cover with boiling water and bring to a boil. Pack hot. Cover with boiling liquid. Process 40 minutes at 10 pounds pressure.

PEAS

Pack only in pint jars because they overcook and become mushy if packed in quarts. Shell, sort for size. Cover with boiling water, boil 5 minutes. Pack loosely into jars. Cover with boiling cooking liquid to within 1 inch of top of jars. Process 45 minutes at 10 pounds pressure.

PUMPKIN AND SQUASH

Peel and cut into 1-inch cubes. Add enough water to prevent sticking. Cook or steam until tender. Mash and pack hot in jars. Process 90 minutes at 10 pounds pressure.

SWEET POTATOES

Wash well. Boil about 15 minutes or until skins will slip off easily. Skin and cut into pieces. Pack hot. Cover with fresh boiling water. Process 1 hour and 50 minutes at 10 pounds pressure.

TOMATOES

See directions under Fruits, page 751.

ABOUT MEAT, POULTRY, GAME AND FISH PRESSURE CANNING

Methods for canning fish are not given in this book because the various recommended processes are controversial. Government bulletins call for long processing and, in addition, before the food is served, for prolonged cooking of home-canned fish and sea food. This causes great loss of flavor and food value. ◗ The freezing of fish is recommended as an alternative for better retention of both qualities, see page 767. But the canning of meats, poultry and game in homes can be both a safe and economical procedure and a much more convenient one than the old-fashioned method of preserving by salting and smoking, although again not nearly so satisfactory as freezing, see page 756. The Government warns that all home-canned meats should be boiled in an open pan for 10 minutes before tasting or eating.

For safe serving of home-canned meat products, process all these nonacid foods in a pressure canner. ◗ Make sure that the temperature reaches at least 240°.

ABOUT PREPARING GAME

The hunter must almost of necessity learn to clean, cut and store his meat, since most states forbid the use of packing plants or butcher shops for this purpose. Quick cooling, scrupulous cleaning and careful preservation greatly enhance that deliciously and legitimately gamey flavor which derives from the fruit, the seeds, the berries or the grasses on which the animal has fed. All too often, gaminess is just the unpleasantly exaggerated result of improper care and manipulation before cooking.

Immediately after the kill, the animal must be bled. If it is a bird or small mammal, place it in a funnel that has an opening wide enough so that the head can hang through. For details about handling birds, see About Wild Birds, page 475. Behead the animal or cut the jugular vein at the base of the neck, slightly to the left of center. Have a bowl ready underneath to keep the blood, which you may want to use later for blood sausage—see page 438 —or as a thickener for gravies, see page 321. To store see page 321.

If the animal is large, place it on a slope with its head at the lowest point. Cut the vein as described above and make sure the blood is flowing freely. Should the animal have been shot in a vital organ, the blood may not be released through the neck but inwardly. It will then be necessary to gut the carcass as quickly and as cleanly as possible to avoid taint from the bullet-ruptured organs.

Whatever procedure you use ♦ clean and cool the meat as rapidly as possible. Leaving the animal with its head lower than the body, you may cut off the feet, pierce the legs and turn it on its back. Tie a rope or wire to each leg and attach them to a shrub or tree nearby, so that, when you split the breast bone and cut all the way down the center, the animal will be steadied. You may prefer to brace the animal by putting rocks or logs on either side of it.

A good way to start the center cut is to slit the skin for about three or four inches at the breast bone. Insert your free hand and press the inner organs down out of the way as you continue to cut. In doing this ♦ being very careful, of course, not to pierce the intestines, turn the blade of the knife upward and rip the skin all the way to the vent.

Continue to press downward with your free hand as you go. When the long slit is made, roll the skin back about three or four inches on either side of the cut, keeping the loose hairs away from the flesh. Cut the breast bone and pull the ribs apart. Cut all the organs loose for removal after tying off both the colon and the bladder, which are removed through the anal cavity. The colon will need a double tie before removal. To make it, grasp the colon near the center and squeeze it, clearing a four- or five-inch section as well as possible. Tie it tightly at each end of the cleared area. Then cut between the ties so none of the feces can contaminate the meat. With deer, the musk sacs will have pulled off with the skin.

Work if possible in such a way that after removal of the internal organs you will merely have to wipe the cavity with a dry cloth. If internal bleeding has taken place, however, and fluids from the organs have touched the flesh, scrape or cut the flesh as clean as possible and wipe the areas with salted water. Dry carefully. If the weather is warm, dust the entire cavity with black pepper or powdered charcoal.

To shorten the cooling time of large animals, prop the cavity open with sticks. Separate the heart and liver from the entrails, being careful not to pierce the gall. Don't be surprised, incidentally, if you do not find the gall in deer. They have none.

Use the edible variety of meats at once in camp cooking. Skin furry animals as quickly as possible. Over large areas the skin can be pulled free rather than cut. ♦ Allow no hairs to remain on the meat. Scrape and wash thoroughly any bullet-pierced areas. Keep the meat as cool as possible.

Before canning or freezing soak meat for 24 hours in water to remove all traces of blood. Any blood allowed to remain in the meat may produce "fishy" off-flavors. After killing, meats, game and poultry should be well bled and cooled to below 40°, preferably for 24 hours, before can-ning. Beef is better if allowed to age for a week or 10 days at 34° to 38°. Large game animals are prepared and processed like beef; small game, like poultry. Copper or iron utensils may produce discoloration. Meat should not be left in galvanized utensils for more than ½ hour, or it may take up harmful quantities of zinc.

♦ Spices should be used sparingly in this type of preservation, and vegetables omitted altogether. White pepper retains a better flavor than black pepper in meat products. If you like, you may place 1 teaspoon salt in each empty quart container. It flavors, but does not help to preserve the meat.

ABOUT PRECOOKING, PACKING AND PROCESSING MEATS FOR CANNING

To bake, preheat oven to 350°. Cut the meat into pieces about 1 pound each. Place in uncovered pans in the oven. Roast until the red or pink color of the meat has almost disappeared at the center, about 20 to 40 minutes. Cut the meat into pieces small enough to fit the jars. Pack closely while still hot into hot, sterile jars, at least 2 pieces to a pint jar. Skim fat from drippings. Add enough boiling water or broth to them to cover the meat, leaving ½ inch head space. Remove air bubbles, see page 748.

To stew, cut meat in uniform pieces about 1 pound each, drop in boiling water and simmer 12 to 20 minutes or until the raw color has disappeared at center. Cut meat into smaller serving pieces, salt, pack closely, cover with the boiling broth. ♦ To remove air bubbles, see page 748.

Frying is the least desirable method of precooking. It makes the surface of the meat hard and dry and often gives an undesirable flavor to the finished product.

♦ Meat that is not covered with liquid will discolor and lose some flavor in storage. Depending on the shape of the pieces, 1 to 1½ pounds of meat will fill a pint jar and still remain submerged. ♦ Pint jars are preferable to larger containers, as the heat penetrates more readily to the center of the container.

✪ Most meat is processed at 10 pounds pressure. Process for the length of time given below. ▲ For high altitude processing, see page 748.

ROASTS AND STEAKS

Remove all large bones, gristle and excess fat, leaving just enough fat for flavor. Precook in oven or hot water except for pork, which has a better flavor when precooked in an oven. Pack hot and cover with the boiling liquid in which the meats were cooked. Process pints for 75 minutes, quarts for 90 minutes, in a pressure cooker at 10 pounds pressure.

GROUND BEEF

Be sure the meat is fresh and is kept clean and cold. Grind lean meat, using plate with ⅛-inch holes. Form into flat cakes that can be packed without breaking. Precook in moderate oven 350° until medium done. Pack hot. Skim fat from drippings. Cover cakes with drippings and boiling water. Leave 1-inch head space. Process for same length of time as for roasts or steaks, above.

MEAT FOR STEWS OR HASH

Use less tender cuts and small pieces. Cut meat into 1 inch cubes. Add boiling water to cover. Simmer until raw color is gone. Pack hot. Cover with boiling broth. Process pints for 75 minutes, quarts for 90 minutes in pressure canner at 10 pounds.

LIVER

Wash, remove veins and membranes, slice or cut as desired. Drop into boiling salted water, simmer about 5 minutes. Pack. Cover with boiling water. Process as for stews, above.

HEART

Wash, remove thick connective tissue. Precook by stewing, as above. Pack, salt and add boiling broth to cover. Process as for stews, above.

TONGUE

Wash, place in boiling water and simmer about 45 minutes or until skin can be removed. Skin, slice or cut into pieces. Reheat to simmering in broth. Pack. Add broth to cover. Process as for stews, above.

SOUP STOCK AND BROTH

Crack or saw bones. Simmer them in salted water until the meat is tender. Strain stock to remove bones. Skim off excess fat. Meat may be returned to stock. Reheat to boiling and pour into jars. Process pints for 20 minutes, quarts for 25 minutes at 10 pounds pressure.

SAUSAGE

Make country-style sausage—page 437— according to your favorite recipe, but omit sage. One-fourth beef may be used. Form into flat cakes. Brown in moderate oven, 350°, or on top of stove in heavy skillet over moderate heat, pouring off fat as it accumulates. Pack hot. Cover with boiling pan gravy and water. Leave 1-inch head space. Process as for stews, above.

POULTRY AND SMALL GAME

Chickens should be dressed, cut as for frying and cooled at 40° or lower for at least 8 hours—preferably 24—before canning. Mature chickens yield a more flavorful canned product than do younger ones, though either may be used.

Trim off all lumps of fat. Separate the meat into 3 piles—the meaty pieces, the bony pieces and the giblets. The giblets discolor the meat and are best canned alone.

To precook the chicken, first prepare a broth by simmering the bony pieces until tender. Add broth to meaty pieces and simmer until medium done. Skim fat from broth. Pack meaty pieces with or without bone and add boiling broth to cover, leaving 1-inch head space. Work out air bubbles, see page 748. Remove meat from bone, cut in uniform pieces and can, covered with boiling broth. Process pints for 65 minutes, quarts for 75 minutes at 10 pounds pressure.

It is desirable to can livers separately, gizzards and hearts together. Cover giblets with boiling chicken broth or water. Cover and cook until medium done. Pack hot. Cover with boiling broth. Leave 1-inch head space. Work out air bubbles, see page 748. Process pints for 75 minutes at 10 pounds pressure.

ABOUT SMOKING AND BRINING HAM

Somebody has defined eternity as a ham and two people. But one may while away the time more than tolerably if he remembers to serve the choicer parts of a ham first; then to slice, chop and grind the rest for emergency storage in the refrigerator where—if covered—it will remain in good condition up to three weeks. For other suggestions, see Economical Use of Large Cuts of Meat, pages 389 and 398.

The distinctive flavor of a ham depends on what the animal has been fed: corn, acorns, peanuts, peaches or table scraps. We have always been incensed that there is no universal legislation which could reduce the incidence of trichinosis to a minimum by requiring that refuse fed to hogs be presteamed. Since it is not, it is imperative for you to be sure that the hams you buy are processed long enough and at a high enough temperature to kill the dangerous trichina parasite. The internal heat should reach at least 140°. ♦ Smoking, page 135, alone, will not suffice. But any ham marked with the round purple U.S. Inspection stamp should be safe to eat; although even if marked "fully cooked" it will probably need ♦ further cooking, for palatability, up to 160° to 180°.

There are two chief ways to salt hams: brining and dry-curing. When hams are soaked in brine or, in the more modern technique, when brine is forced through the arterial system under pressure, temperatures must be very carefully controlled.

Neither type of brining is recommended for the amateur. The arterial method, plus steam-smoking, gives us the commercially processed ham usually encountered in the meat market. So prepared, it needs neither soaking nor simmering before baking. Dry-cured hams include "old hams" like Smithfield, Virginia, Kentucky and Dijon—the last being imported from France. Very salty, they need 12 hours of soaking, as well as long simmering, before they are ready to bake with their final garnish. Two especially interesting foreign varieties of aged hams are Westphalian and the Italian Prosciutto. The Italian porkers during their happy lifetime are fed on a diet of chestnuts and the ones native to Parma get whey from the local cheese. The Westphalians thrive on sugar-beet mash. With their succulent translucence, they are very close in texture to smoked salmon. Both are painstakingly aged. Unlike the "old" hams previously mentioned, they are ready to eat without further preparation or cooking.

Dry-cured hams are more tolerant of fluctuating temperatures under processing than those treated with brine. And, while they are less salty than brined, they will still profit by a six-hour soaking before cooking. Ideally, the curing and storing of hams should take place in a 36° to 40° temperature. Even considering the somewhat inconveniently higher temperatures in which most of us are obliged to work, we still recommend dry-curing rather than brining in home-processing. This way is more certain to win the race between salt-penetration and bacterial growth.

◗ To dry-cure ham, allow the meat to cool as naturally and rapidly as possible after butchering. Spread the pieces out on racks, never allowing them to overlap. Sprinkle them at once ◗ very lightly with salt. Do not blanket them at this time with the salt, as this would retard cooling. When cool, rub them repeatedly with the following salt mixture, being sure to cover the entire surface well in the process. Then pack them in salt. Allow for every 10 lbs. of ham a mixture of:

1 cup salt
¼ cup sugar
2 teaspoons saltpeter

with:

(2 bay leaves)
(2 coriander seeds)
(3 cloves)
(6 peppercorns)

which you have crushed in a mortar.

The salt and pepper are preservatives, the sugar adds flavor and the saltpeter will help the meat hold a good color. To secure effective salt-penetration, allow three days for each pound of meat per piece. Boned hams and small pieces will of course cure more rapidly. If the temperature should go below 36° at any time, be sure to add an equal length of time to the curing period, as salt-penetration is slowed to a standstill in freezing temperatures.

Salting takes perseverance, but smoking takes skill. For directions to build a smoke oven and fuel it, see page 135. Our farm neighbors always leave a piece of skin on the meat they smoke. This is because the weight of the meat will not tear it in hanging where a loop of wire or string goes through it. The hams must be hung so they do not touch each other at any point, for they will not "take" the smoke where they do. Dry-curing requires longer smoking than brining. For this reason, allow at least 36 hours to drive out any excess moisture. Try not to let the temperature rise over 120° at any time.

When the hams are cool, wrap them in a densely woven cloth and bury them in wooden boxes in the cooled ashes which have been retrieved from the smoking-fire. The ashes will deter moisture and insects and add an increasingly good smoked flavor to your hams. Sometimes, in carving even professionally cured ham, an odor is detectable as you get near the bone. This means that the ham was insufficiently smoked. If a rainbow iridescence appears on sliced ham, it is merely due to light refraction on the fat film. Ham should be served warm or cool, but never chilled. Many people freeze ham, page 766. We find it retains good flavor for only a relatively short time—especially if it has been brined arterially and reprocessed with tenderizing enzymes.

SALT OR PICKLED PORK

◗ Please read About Pickling Ingredients and Equipment, page 781.
Cut into pieces 6 inches square:

Fat back or other thin pieces of
fat pork

Rub each square well all over with:

Pickling salt

Pack the salted pork tightly in a clean crock and let stand 12 hours. For each 25 lbs. of meat, mix and cool the following brine:

2½ lbs. salt
½ oz. saltpeter
4 quarts boiling water

Pour the ◗ cooled brine over the meat to cover. Store the pork ◗ weighted and covered at 35° to 38° temperature until ready to use.

HARD SAUSAGE

After smoking, hang in a cool dry place, about 1 to 2 months, to cure.
Have ready:

2½ lbs. peeled potatoes

Cook 12 minutes, drain, cool overnight covered. Grind three times:

2½ lbs. of top round of beef
2½ lbs. lean pork
2½ lbs. small-diced pork fat

Mix with:
> **2 tablespoons salt**
> **1 teaspoon saltpeter**
> **2 teaspoons coarsely ground pepper**

Grind the cooked potatoes once and add to the meat. Work together until well mixed. Put into sausage casing and smoke, page 135.

ABOUT SMOKING FOWL

If birds are to be smoked for preservation, they must be brined as for ham. If the smoke flavor is your aim and you plan using them just as you would fresh fowl, roast them, page 464, for ¾ the normal cooking time. Then smoke at 140° from 6 to 8 hours. This smoking period will both flavor and finish the cooking.

To smoke wild birds, cut off meat in strips, dust with salt and pepper. Smoke as for ham, page 754.

♦ To cook smoked birds, steam for a few minutes to remove excess salt. Then cook as for ham, page 409.

ABOUT SMOKING OR KIPPERING FISH

For fish suitable for smoking, see page 344. Prepare a Smoke Oven, page 135. Use a nonresinous wood or sawdust. The smoking period and temperatures will depend on the length of time you want to preserve the fish. To keep them 2 weeks under refrigeration, smoke at least 24 hours. If they are to be kept longer than 2 weeks, use method II, or a 5-day or longer smoke period—longer if the weather is not clear and dry. Or use a Chinese Smoke Oven, page 136.

I. For small whole fish, we suggest a dry salting, cold smoke method. The best temperature is 70° to 80°. Be sure it does not go above 90°. It is easier to handle small fish with the heads on. Either split them for cleaning or make a small incision just under the gills and pull them out as well as the viscera with the thumb and forefinger. Prepare a brine of:
> **1 gallon water**
> **1 cup salt**

Immerse the thoroughly cleaned fish for 30 minutes. Drain, rinse in fresh ♦ cold water. Drain again to remove all excess moisture. Have ready a wooden box lined with a ½-inch layer of pickling salt and a tub or large pan filled with enough fine-grained salt in which to dip the fish, allowing them to pick up as much of it as will cling to

them. Pack the fish in single layers in the salt-lined box, with layers of salt between the layers of fish. Leave it in 6 hours if split, 12 hours if whole. Remove from salt, rinse and arrange fish on grill or rods just as they will hang or be racked in the barrel. ♦ Be sure not to crowd them so the smoke can circulate freely. Hang them first in a shady spot for about 3 hours until a shiny casing forms over their surface. Place them without disturbing this surface in the preheated smoke can, as indicated previously—depending on the time you plan keeping the fish before use.

II. For smoking large salt water fish fillets, try this hot smoke method. Fillet the fish, but do not remove the skin. Cut into 3- to 4-inch chunks. Wash carefully to remove all blood and viscera. Let chunks stand refrigerated 14 to 18 hours in a brine made of:
> **1⅛ cups granular pickling salt to**
> **each gallon of water**

Rinse well. Place on racks, skin side down, leaving a space between pieces so smoke can circulate well. Place rack in preheated Smoke Oven, page 135. Smoke with a non-resinous wood 3 to 4 hours. During this period never let the smoke get over 90°. Then raise heat to 165° to 170° for 45 to 50 minutes. This both cooks the fish and gives it a lovely golden brownish sheen. Cool fish. Refrigerated, they will keep 3 to 5 weeks. For a longer period, pressure can, page 748, at 10 lbs, in sterile ½-pint jars, 60 minutes for boned fish, 90 minutes if the bones are still left in.

ABOUT PREPARING ROE FOR CAVIAR

Remove from very fresh fish, as soon as possible:
> **Roe**

Tear the egg masses into small-size pieces. Work them through a ¼-inch or finer screen to free the eggs from the membrane. Place them for 15 to 20 minutes in a cold water brine made of:
> **1⅛ cups granular pickling salt, page 525,**
> **to every quart of cold water**

If you use a salinometer, the reading should be 28.3. There should be twice as much brine as roe in volume. Remove from liquid and drain thoroughly by allowing to drip through a strainer for about 1 hour. Keep refrigerated during this operation. Place in an airtight nonmetal container and store at 34° for 1 to 2 months. Remove, drain and repack, storing at 0° Fahrenheit until ready to use.

FREEZING

We are indebted to an Arctic explorer for the following Eskimo recipe for a frozen dinner: "Kill and eviscerate a medium-sized walrus. Net several flocks of small migrating birds and remove only one small wing feather from each wing. Store birds whole in interior of walrus. Sew up walrus and freeze. Then two years or so later, find the cache if you can, notify clan of a feast, partially thaw walrus. Slice and serve." Simplicity itself.

Simple, too, are the mechanics of home freezing, a comparatively easy method of food preservation which has been advertised as all things to all cooks. The result is that some frozen food enthusiasts toss any type of food into the poor freezer and expect fabulous results. Yes, some foods can be preserved by freezing more successfully than in any other way, but quality produce comes out only if quality produce goes in. There are other important factors, too. Suitable foods must be chosen and given ♦ quick and careful preparation. They must be sealed in ♦ moisture-vapor-proof wrappings and kept at ♦ constant zero or lower temperatures during storage. Then, of course, they must be properly thawed and cooked.

In spite of necessary precautions, meats, fish, poultry, fruits and precooked foods are quite easy to freeze. Vegetables, because of the necessity of blanching, require both more time and care. But even so, freezing takes a third to a half the amount of time and labor as compared with canning. And the yields per bushel of produce are about the same, see pages 749-751.

ABOUT THE FREEZER AND ITS CONTENTS

The economics of keeping a well-stocked freezer presents what we have heard called a "mooty" point. Unless you are a strong-willed planner and dispenser, it may lead to extravagance. Faced with an emergency, it is a great temptation to use that choice cut of meat reserved for company, and children love to draw on the seemingly unlimited freezer resources of ice cream and desserts. ♦ It is often only by sharp-eyed husbanding of supplies and by raising your own meat and vegetables that the satisfactions as well as the cash savings from a freezer are realized. ♦ You may also profit, as a quick-witted trader, when markets are glutted with raw vegetables and fruits or meat and poultry specials. But avoid bargain frozen foods that have been stored a long time—for they will not have a full complement of vitamins and flavors.

In any case, the freezer is not meant for miserly hoarding but ♦ should be managed on an over-all, continuously shifting plan —a seasonal plan—geared to your family's food needs and preferences. But keep the freezer stocked with favorites, so the family will continue to ask: "What's thawing?"

Space estimates differ, depending on family appetites, but a minimum allowance of 3 cubic feet per person is average if you schedule a turnover every six months.

ABOUT FILLING THE FREEZER

♦ Neither overload your freezer ♦ nor add, at one time, more than 2 to 3 lbs. for each cubic foot of freezer space, during any 24 hour period. Either procedure will cause damage to the food you are storing. ♦ Until the new packages are frozen, keep them against the freezer plates or the walls of the freezer, unless the manufacturer directs otherwise. ♦ Exceptions are sandwiches and baked items, which attract moisture to themselves if placed there. These items should be put upon other frozen packages away from the walls. When you finally use these frozen treasures ♦ allow enough time for proper thawing and cooking.

ABOUT DEFROSTING THE FREEZER

Your freezer operates most economically if it is located in an area where the temperature is between 50° to 70°. It is hard to specify just how often a freezer will need defrosting. The number of times it is opened, the state of loading, and how carefully food is wrapped all affect the build-up of condensation. ♦ Defrost whenever there is ½ inch of frost on the plates or sides. If frost has not solidified into ice, scraping is a good method. ♦ Turn off the current first, though. Remove all food from the freezer and refrigerate it immediately. Pans of hot water are sometimes used, but must be elevated on racks so that they are not in direct contact with freezer walls or plates. No matter how often you have to defrost ♦ be sure to clean up any spillage when it occurs and ♦ to wipe out your freezer at least once a year with a cloth that has been dipped in a solution of 1 tablespoon baking soda to 1 quart of lukewarm water. ♦ Dry the freezer well, either with a cloth or a hair dryer. ♦ Be sure the lining is thoroughly dry before you turn the current on again. It is wise to let the freezer run for one-half hour before returning food to it.

ABOUT POWER BREAKS

The seriousness of a power break should not be underestimated because a 25° rise in temperature over a 24-hour period is ruinous to nutritive values. So, if a prolonged break is indicated call your local dealer or ice cream company for a source of dry ice. This ice has a temperature of 110° below zero F. A 50 lb. cake, if placed in the freezer soon after the electricity fails, will prevent thawing for 2 or 3 days. ◗ Handle dry ice with heavy gloves. Do not attempt to chip or cut it, as a stray chip might cause injury. If you use dry ice in the freezer, do not lock the box or fasten the clamp. However, actual thawing, if the ◗ freezer is kept closed, is not likely to occur in even 4- to 6-cubic-foot freezers within the first 15 to 20 hours. After 48 hours, the temperature will just reach 40° to 45°—the normal refrigerator range. Food that still retains ice crystals can be refrozen, but meats, poultry and fish registering more than 50° must be cooked and used at once.

ABOUT TYPES OF FOOD SUITABLE FOR FREEZING

If you have rushed to this chapter to learn what discoveries in home freezing we have made since the last edition of "The Joy," we must report that the methods previously described are still the recommended ones—and will be until major changes in principle are introduced into household freezing equipment.

It is true that you will find a host of new ready-cooked frozen items in the shops. Among them are potatoes and other watery foods processed with recently developed machinery which removes harmful excess moisture. But such freeze-dry vacuum-processing is beyond the scope of the home-freezing equipment presently available. And, although its proponents claim much for it, the foods it preserves cannot be regarded as equal in flavor to those freshly prepared. There are on the market, however, several ◗ waxy corn and rice flours which do help in stabilizing frozen sauces, see pages 500 and 499.

Beware of using the freezer for certain types of processing. ◗ Freezing, for example, will ruin gelatins. In yeast and some other refrigerator doughs, the leavening action that should continue to take place is often stopped by the lower temperature of the freezer. ◗ In general, most cooked foods can be frozen, but some do not justify the amount of preparation required. Always balance original preparation time against the time it takes to prepare properly for freezing, and omit quick broils, quick-cooking pastas or quick sautés. Freezing techniques, as described later, have settled down into a practice as reliable as canning. But keep in mind that the storage life of frozen food is not in the least comparable.

This principle bears repetition. ◗ The retention of nutritional values and flavors depends on the speed with which food can be processed after harvesting, the favorable temperatures at which it is held until frozen and the manner in which it is thawed. Work quickly with small quantities of fruits and vegetables and keep the rest chilled in the refrigerator.

ABOUT QUALITY

Whatever quantity you freeze, the quality of the food you use is of first importance. ◗ Quality cannot be created in the freezing process itself. It is sometimes lost even though well-fed animals, and fruits and vegetables from rich soils are used. For example, the keeping qualities of varieties of the same fruit or vegetable differ. Elberta peaches grown in New York are considered tops for freezing, but Elberta peaches grown in Virginia are often reported poor for that purpose.

Time and conditions of harvest or slaughter are also factors to reckon with. ◗ Crops are prime when they have sun just before maturing. Undue rain before harvest may cause the entire pack to be mediocre. Crops such as ◗ early apples, the first asparagus, etc., keep their flavor best.

Because new discoveries are being made constantly, it is wise, if you are barging into freezing in a big way, to ◗ consult your county agricultural agent about the best varieties of fruits and vegetables to grow and to buy from your neighborhood. Watch government bulletins and state experimental station publications, too, for these agencies continue to make discoveries in the science of home-freezing.

◗ The retention of nutritional values and flavors depends on the speed with which food can be processed after cropping. From then on ◗ it must be kept at such favorable temperatures that microbial and enzymatic activities are held to a minimum, see page 744. Should they have begun before freezing, the freezing process will not destroy the resultant contamination, but only arrest it temporarily. Therefore ◗ you are courting danger to allow perishable frozen foods to thaw for any length of time before cooking. Modern once-a-week marketing is feasible if the transfer of food packages from commercial compartment to home-freezer is effected with all speed. Remember ◗ once thawed —do not refreeze.

◗ Any frozen foods stored in the ice cube compartment of the refrigerator should be used within 1 week, as the temperature range in this section is between 10° and 25° in most refrigerators, not the required 0° or minus of a freezer. ◗ Permitting the temperature of frozen food to rise to 25° or 30° for even 1 day does more damage to its eating quality and nutritional value than holding it at zero for a year.

ABOUT WRAPPING, PACKAGING AND SEALING

After selecting quality food, decide how to package it. ♦ Excess air within the frozen food package is a real enemy. Choose only those wrappings which will insure an absolutely moisture-proof and vapor-proof seal, both to protect the food from drying out and to keep odors from penetrating into the freezer and causing off-flavors in other food. Air left in the containers dries out the food during the inevitable temperature variations of storage, drawing moisture from the food itself to form a frost in the package—a frost made from the juices and seasoned with the flavors of the food itself. ♦ So, try always to exclude as much air as possible from the package.

♦ Liquid foods must be stored in leak-proof containers and enough space allowed for the expansion of the liquid during the freezing process. Allow ½ inch in pint and ¾ inch in quart cartons. If you use glass, allow 1 inch for a pint and 1½ inches for a quart container. Always choose vapor- and moisture-proof containers of convenient size and shape. ♦ Cubical containers conserve a good deal more storage space than cylindrical ones of the same dimensions.

Meats and irregularly formed foods are wrapped in aluminum foil or special laminated papers. ♦ The foil, which should have a weight of .0015 or thicker, needs no sealing, but profits from an overwrap of stockingnet which helps to hold the wrapping close to the food and also protects against tearing of the foil. For economy, old nylon stockings may be used in place of stockingnet.

Plastics and papers vary in quality and it is often difficult to judge their efficiency. They need careful sealing with tapes adapted to low temperatures. Some may be sealed with heat. A special iron is available for heat sealing, although a not-too-hot curling or pressing iron will do.

♦ All sheet wrappings should be applied with a lock-seal or drugstore wrap shown below or, where size demands, with the costlier butcher wrap shown on page 760. To make the drugstore or lockseal wrap, place the food in the center of a piece of paper large enough so that when the ends are brought together they can be folded into an interlocking seam, as shown on the left. Make the seam and draw the paper down against the food to enclose it tightly, as shown in the center. Reverse the package, so that the seam lies on the table. Now turn the package, so that the closed ends are at right angles to your body. Pleat-fold the end farthest from you and make an extra fold in the end, before pressing the folded end against the package. Spin the package around, so that the doubly folded end can be braced against your body, as shown on the right. Now very carefully force any excess air from the package. Then fold the remaining open end. Seal the package with ♦ a tape that is adapted to low temperature.

To make the butcher wrap, the food is placed on a large square of paper on the diagonal. One corner is brought over it generously, as shown on the left, on page 760. The adjoining corners are then folded over, as shown in the center, and the entire package folded over in turn, as shown on the right. This wrap requires great care if excess air is to be excluded from the package and the food kept flat. ♦ Easiest to handle are polyethylene bags made of a plastic which can be heat-sealed, but it is equally good practice and simpler to twist them tightly into a goose neck and secure them closely with a rubber band. These bags remain pliable even at zero temperature, need no overwrap and can be re-used. Pliofilm bags may also be reused if handled carefully, but an overwrap of stockingnet is advisable.

Some frugal housewives keep their old butter and ice cream cartons and line them with pliofilm bags, but such cartons must be considered as merely protective overwraps for a moisture- and vapor-proof liner. Plastic boxes and heavily waxed cartons are good for liquids, but watch for a tight seal. Both may be used again. Before reusing, wash the wax cartons with a detergent and cold water to keep the wax

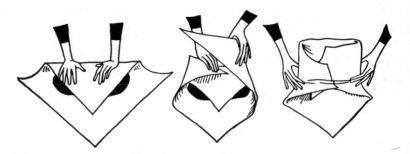

firm. ◆ Aluminum foil cartons particularly are satisfactory for foods that can be served with a mere reheating. Be extremely careful to seal them tightly. They are also satisfactory for rapid chilling before storage and can go from freezer to oven without further handling or loss of contents.

If packing vegetables in cartons, size them carefully. A device such as the one shown on the right below can be made out of a wooden box. Adjusted to your carton size, it is a great aid for quick, close packing. ◆ Should several servings of meat, cookies or other small items be combined in 1 package, they separate more easily when 2 thicknesses of moistureproof paper are placed between each 2 units, as shown on the left below, or when they are slid into folded foil, as shown in the center below, before the outside wrapping is put on. ◆ In packaging your foods, wrap in convenient serving or meal-size quantities. Holding over or recooking thawed leftovers is not advisable. Since good results depend so much on the speed with which the fresh foods are prepared and put into the freezer, it is wise to have all filling, wrapping and labeling equipment ready at hand. Use proper funnels for filling cartons, to keep liner edges dry for a perfect seal. Rectangular ones can be bought or they can be made by removing both ends from tin cans and compressing the lower end to fit the cartons.

ABOUT LABELING AND DATING

Soft wax or china marking pencils or marking pens do well for cartons. Labels may be slipped between stockingnet and other wrappings or under transparent wrap. Small, tough different-colored tags with strings attached are helpful for quick identification of stored opaque packages. ◆ Keep a master record of dates of freezing, as well as poundage on meats and of portions of other foods. ◆ The labeling and dating of the packages themselves, needless to say, is essential. While many foods keep satisfactorily for months, there are some exceptions, which are noted in detail later ◆ such as fat meats, poultry, prepared doughs and precooked foods. ◆ You may find our storage-limit recommendations short compared to others, but we believe you also prefer optimum standards for food flavor and texture to merely edible ones. Whatever you are processing, remember to start with quality food, have it properly prepared, well cooled, wrapped and labeled before storing it.

ABOUT FREEZING, THAWING AND COOKING RAW FOODS

Certain changes take place in frozen foods during storage that call for distinctive handling before and during cooking. A tendency to mushiness in vegetables and dryness in meat and fish can be lessened by proper thawing and heating.

Always thaw frozen foods in their original containers. When time allows, it is preferable to thaw them on a refrigerator shelf, with the exception of unbaked doughs, page 769. Thawing food, still

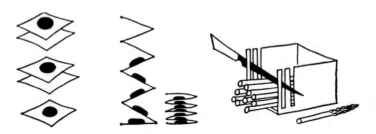

packaged, at room temperature, takes about half as long and, if the package is put before a fan, about one third as long as the refrigerator method. For emergencies, if the package is absolutely waterproof, it may be immersed in cool—not warm—water. This procedure should be adopted only when you are pressed for time, as the result is poor with fragile foods or those with high water content—like melons. Use all frozen items as soon as possible after thawing, for growth of bacteria can occur rapidly in thawed foods left at room temperature ◗ especially pot pies, TV dinners and foods containing gravies, sauces and stuffings. Rapid use after thawing is especially important with blanched products whose oxygen-resisting enzymes have been destroyed and whose further exposure to air and heat causes rapid adverse changes in quality and nutritional value. Speed in serving helps prevent these disappointing changes.

ABOUT FREEZING AND THAWING FRUITS

Choose almost any firm, sound, uniformly sun-ripened fruit. Exceptions are pears, which seldom freeze well, but do somewhat better if ripened off the tree, and bananas, which had better be kept out of the freezer. It is not essential to use sugar in freezing fruit, but it is often preferable, see below. Freshly grated, unsweetened coconut may be frozen by adding one part sugar to eight parts coconut. Mix it with its own milk, page 523, before freezing. Leftover packaged coconut may also be frozen and used as needed.

ABOUT AMOUNTS OF SUGAR FOR FREEZING FRUITS

◗ To sugar fruit, place it on a shallow tray. ◗ Just before you are ready to pack, sift the sugar over it until evenly coated. The longer you allow the fruit to stand mixed with the sugar before freezing, the more juice it will draw. When the fruit is coated, pack it gently into suitable cartons, allowing space for expansion. Seal, label and freeze.

Use 1 pound sugar to the pounds of fruit indicated below

*5 lbs. apples
  4 to 5 lbs. blackberries
*4 lbs. blueberries
*3 to 5 lbs. sour cherries
  3 lbs. currants
  4 to 5 lbs. dewberries
  3 to 4 lbs. gooseberries
*3 lbs. peaches, sliced
  3 lbs. pineapple

*3 to 4 lbs. plums
  4 lbs. raspberries, whole or crushed
  4 to 5 lbs. rhubarb, diced
†4 lbs. strawberries, whole or crushed

*Mix ½ teaspoon dry ascorbic acid crystals with every 5 lbs. of dry sugar.
**Steam-blanch, page 764, ½ to 1 minute to keep skins tender. Shake well to coat with sugar to keep them from clumping.
†After washing, prick whole strawberries with fork to release excess air before combining with sugar.

No sugar is required for these fruits.

*Apples
*Apples, sliced
**Blueberries
  Cranberries
  Currants
*Figs
  Gooseberries
  Loganberries
  Melons
  Pineapple
*Plums
  Prunes
  Rhubarb
  Raspberries
  Youngberries

*Immerse briefly in a solution of 3 tablespoons lemon juice or ¼ teaspoon ascorbic acid to 1 quart water, then drain dry on paper toweling.
**Steam-blanch, page 764, ½ to 1 minute to keep skins tender.

ABOUT SIRUP FOR FREEZING FRUIT

◗ These sirups may be made several days in advance and stored in the refrigerator, so as to be well chilled when combined with the fruit.

For light or 40% sirup, use 1¾ cups sugar to 1 pint water
For medium or 50% sirup, use 2½ cups sugar to 1 pint water
A heavier sirup is not recommended

Some people prefer to combine sugar with corn sirup. If this combination is desired, never use more than ⅓ cup corn sirup to ⅔ cup sugar. Any of these sirups may be made by merely dissolving the sugar and corn sirup in water, but it is preferable to boil the mixture until the sugar is dissolved. Chill well before using.
◗ Use enough sirup to cover the fruit well. When using sirup with small or sliced fruits or berries, allow about 1½ cups of fruit and ⅓ to ½ cup of sirup for a pint container. Halved fruits require about 1½ cups of fruit and ¾ to 1 cup of sirup to a pint container.
If the fruit tends to rise above the sirup, crush a piece of moisture-proof paper lightly and put it on top to keep the fruit

submerged until the expansion of freezing makes the sirup fill the carton. Leave the paper in the carton.

In the list below, the L stands for light sirup; the M stands for a medium one. For relative amounts or fruit and sirup, see page 761.

*‡L Apples
*L-M Apricots, peeled or unpeeled
  L Blackberries
  L Blueberries
  L-M Boysenberries
*M Cherries, sweet
  M Dewberries
*L-M Figs
  L Grapefruit
  L Guavas, pulp and rind
  L Grapes
  L-M Loganberries
*L Nectarines
  L Oranges, sections
*L Peaches
*L Pears
  L-M Pineapple
  L-M Papaya, ½-inch cubes
  L-M Pomegranate
*L-M Plums
  L-M Prunes
  L-M Raspberries, whole or crushed
  L-M Strawberries
  L-M Youngberries

*Use lemon juice or ascorbic acid opposite.
‡Blanch 1½ minutes in sirup.

ABOUT FREEZING SMALL FRUITS

People who grow their own berries may freeze them successfully without washing —provided they have not been treated with toxic spray. It is safer to wash berries which are not home grown. Fragile fruits like berries or cherries should be washed twice in cold or ice water to clean and firm them. Drain fruit well, then spread it out on several thicknesses of paper toweling and cover it lightly with additional toweling to absorb as much surface moisture as possible. To avoid crushing or bruising the fruit, use very gentle movements. After the fruit is picked over and hulled or stemmed, it is ready for packaging with or without the addition of sugar. For different methods of preparation, see page 761. Blueberry skins remain tender if the fruit is blanched, page 764, before sugar is added. Since, during cooking and cooling, the waxy bloom on blueberries becomes somewhat adhesive, shake the container now and then to avoid clumps. If whole strawberries are to be packaged without sugar, prick them with a fork to release the air. Unsweetened raspberries

may be frozen by placing them unwrapped, in a single layer, on trays in the freezer until solidly frozen. Then they can be packaged closely, sealed and stored. They may be wrapped and frozen in small packages for garnishes, but should be used for this purpose ♦ while still frozen, otherwise they will "weep."

Some fruits keep better packed in dry sugar or in Sirup, page 761. The dry method of sweetening is preferable, as the addition of water tends to weaken the flavor of the fruit. Sugar just before packaging and freeze as soon as possible, so the sugar will not draw juices from the fruit. It is sometimes suggested that fruits and berries be served only partially thawed and while still slightly icy, so they do not "weep." While this is a practical approach for garnishes, we so dislike biting into a glassy texture that we suggest ♦ frozen berries be fully thawed and used for sauces and flavorings, where their taste is superb and their "weeping" not a liability. Thaw fruits on a refrigerator shelf.

ABOUT FREEZING LARGE FRUITS

Sort them carefully. Remove pits, cores and stems and pare when necessary. Treat fruits that tend to discolor before freezing and during thawing, such as apples, peaches, apricots, pears, with one of the following **Discoloration Solutions:**

I. Do not slice fruit into a bowl, but drop it, prepared, directly into a solution of 3 tablespoons lemon juice or 2 tablespoons of vinegar to 1 quart of water, or ¼ teaspoon ascorbic acid crystals or 1 crushed tablet dissolved in 1 quart water. One quart of either of these mixtures is enough for about 4 quarts of fruit. Drain the fruit well before adding it to the sirup. It is advisable to Blanch, page 764, sliced apples and other light-colored fruits.

II. Drop the prepared fruit directly into the sirup in which it is to be frozen, adding 1½ teaspoons lemon juice or ¼ teaspoon of the ascorbic acid to each 2 cups of sirup. To distribute the acid evenly, dissolve ¼ teaspoon of the ascorbic acid crystals or powder in 1 teaspoon of water. Do this in a small bottle and shake the contents until dissolved before adding it to each 2 cups sirup. Add the lemon juice or acid to the sirup shortly before putting in the fruits. If those which tend to discolor are packed in combinations which include citrus fruits, the lemon juice or acid may be omitted.

ABOUT FREEZING PURÉES

Some fruits, such as plums, prunes, avocados, papayas, mangoes, persimmons and melons, keep better in uncooked purée form. Bananas should not be frozen. Applesauce is one of the most delicious o cooked frozen purées, especially if made with early apples. All may, if necessary, be packaged without sugar, but when packaging with sugar allow about 1 cup of it per pound of fruit.

ABOUT FREEZING FRUIT JUICES

Juices such as apple, raspberry, plum, cherry and grape, as well as fruit ciders, freeze very well. For each gallon of cherry or apple juice, add ½ teaspoon ascorbic acid or 2 teaspoons lemon juice. Peaches for pressing can be steamed to 150° to keep color clear without tasting cooked. Cherries, plums, prunes and grapes have a better flavor if slightly cooked, as some of their characteristic flavor is extracted from the skin. Raspberries are best if the whole berries are mixed with one pound of sugar to each 10 pounds of fruit and frozen. Extract the juice when ready to use. In freezing citrus juices, it is difficult to retain their vitamin content without an elaborate vacuum process. Fruit for jelly and jam may be frozen unsugared and the juice extracted later without any cooking. To make the jelly, proceed as usual, see page 774. Fruit sauces or cobbler fillings made from seedy berries, especially blackberries, are smoother if the frozen berries are broken apart and put unthawed through a meat grinder. Use a fine blade.

ABOUT FREEZING RAW VEGETABLES

Vegetables such as peas, asparagus, green beans, lima beans, broccoli and corn, take well to freezing. If the produce was garden-fresh and properly processed, its taste, when served, is hardly distinguishable from that of fresh vegetables. Kale, New Zealand spinach, white potatoes and salad materials—tomatoes, cucumbers and onions—are distinct failures. Certain other vegetables, such as sweet potatoes, the squashes, celery and cabbage are eligible for freezing only when precooked. The processing list on pages 765 and 764 includes some vegetables which, under normal circumstances, are more successfully kept by canning or root storage.

ABOUT BLANCHING VEGETABLES

Enzymes continue to be active in vegetables even after harvesting and, unless arrested, will bring about changes which lead to nutritional loss and off-flavors. Therefore, blanching is imperative before freezing, as it lessens such activity. There are 2 methods of blanching: boiling and steaming. Both may be used more or less interchangeably, although steam-blanching takes 30 seconds to 1 minute longer. Exceptions are the blanching of leafy vegetables, which must be boiled if the heat is to penetrate quickly, and watery vegetables like squashes and cut sweet corn, which lose flavor badly through leaching and must be steamed. Since blanching is not meant to be a cooking process, but merely a preparatory one, it should be carefully timed to avoid textural and nutritional breakdowns. Removal of excess moisture after blanching, and proper chilling before packaging, are two extremely important steps.

Choose young, tender vegetables. The starchy ones, such as peas, corn and lima beans, are best when slightly immature. If not prepared and frozen at once, vegetables should be kept fresh by remaining chilled between harvesting and processing. Prepare them quickly, as for regular cooking. In order to blanch them evenly and pack them efficiently, sort the vegetables for size. Several handy devices for sizing and cutting are available and a corn scraper, page 273, is a great asset for preparing corn cream-style. Better food values and flavor are retained if vegetables are not shredded or frenched.

♦ To blanch by boiling, allow 6 to 10 quarts of boiling water to 1 pound of vegetables. The larger amount of liquid is preferable, as boiling resumes more rapidly after the vegetables are added and tends to leach them less. Put 1 pound of vegetables in a wire basket. Submerge them completely in the boiling water and wait until it again reaches a boil. Begin to time the blanching, see next page. Shake the wire basket several times during this period to allow even penetration of heat. When finished, lift vegetables from boiling water and put at once into a pan of ice water. Chill until the vegetables are cool to the center. Remove, drain and package.

♦ To steam-blanch, bring 6 quarts of water to an active boil in a kettle. Put the vegetables, not more than a pound at a time, in a wire basket and suspend them above the water. Cover the kettle. When the steam starts to escape under the lid, begin to time for blanching. Shake the basket several times during this period to make sure that all the vegetables are uniformly exposed to the steam. Whether you have used the boiling or steam method, when the time is up, remove the vegetables from the heat at once. Since the blanching process is not meant to cook them, but merely to halt the enzymatic action, they must be chilled at once to stop further softening of the tissues by heat. If your tap water is 60° or less, hold the vegetables under it. If not, immerse them in ice water or chill them over it, as directed in the chart. Drain the vegetables well and spread them on several thicknesses of paper toweling. Also cover them with paper toweling to absorb as much of the surface moisture as possible before

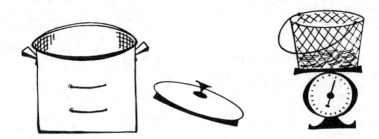

packaging. Except for greens like spinach, which should have a ½ inch head space, the containers should be closely and completely filled, but not stuffed. Some vegetables keep best as purées. If frozen vegetables toughen consistently, the water used ♦ may be too hard for good results.

ABOUT BLANCHING EQUIPMENT

Whether you parboil or parsteam, the equipment consists preferably of a special blanching kettle with a tight-fitting lid and a wire basket. In either case, handle no more than 1 pound of produce at a time.

BLANCHING CHART FOR VEGETABLES
Showing preferred method

Vegetable	Minutes to parboil	Minutes to parsteam	Minutes to chill in ice water
†Artichoke, whole	8 to 10		12 to 15
Asparagus, medium size	3 to 12		3 to 5
Bamboo Shoots	7 to 13		3
Beans, French		2	5
Beans, Lima	1½		3
Beans, Shell	1¾		3
Beans, Green	2		5
Beans, Soy and Broad	4, in pod		Cool, shell and pack
°Bean Sprouts	4 to 6		Cool over, not in, cold water
Beans, Wax	2		5
Beet Greens	2		5
Beets, small	Until tender		Cool over, not in, cold water
Broccoli, split		3 to 5	4 to 5
Brussels Sprouts	4 to 6		8 to 12
°Cabbage, leaf or shredded	Until tender	3 to 4	Cool over, not in, cold water
Carrots, scrubbed	3		5
Cauliflower, florets		3	4
°Celery, diced	Until tender		Cool over, not in, cold water
Chard	2		5
Chayote, diced	2		5
°Chinese Cabbage, shredded	1½		Cool over, not in, cold water
Collards	2		5
Corn, cream-style, white or yellow	3 to 5 off the cob 8 on cob		Cool over, not in, cold water 15
Corn, medium size, cut, yellow			15 on cob, then cut off for packing

Corn on Cob, page 273
Corn, scraped for pudding, page 274

BLANCHING CHART FOR VEGETABLES Cont.

Vegetable	Minutes to parboil	Minutes to parsteam	Minutes to chill in ice water
*Dasheen	2½		5
†Eggplant, 1½-inch slices	4		‡4 in ascorbic acid solution
*Kale	4 to 6		4 to 5
Kohlrabi, diced		1¾	5
*Mushrooms, medium, whole	3½		5
*Mustard Greens	Until tender		Cool over, not in, cold water
Okra, medium, whole	2		5
Parsnips		3	5
Peas, Black-eyed	2		5
Peas, Green		1⅛ to 3¾	2 to 5
Peppers	2		2 to 5
*Potatoes, Sweet, purée	Until tender		Cool over, not in, cold water Add 1 teaspoon ascorbic acid to every quart potatoes
*Pumpkin, purée	Until tender		Cool over, not in, cold water
Rutabaga	2		5
Spinach	2½		3
*Squash, Winter, purée	Until tender		Cool over, not in, cold water
Turnip Greens	2½		4
Turnips, sliced, peeled		1½	5
Vegetables, mixed	Blanch separately, as directed above; combine after chilling		

*Cook before freezing
†Add 1 teaspoon ascorbic acid to each quart of water used in blanching
‡Ascorbic acid solution—2 teaspoons acid to 2 pints of ice water

ABOUT THAWING AND COOKING FROZEN VEGETABLES

Most frozen vegetables, because of previous blanching and a tenderizing process induced by temperature changes during storage, cook in from one-third to one-half the time that fresh vegetables require, see page 252. Uncooked frozen vegetables may be substituted in recipes calling for fresh vegetables, but shorten their cooking time. Example: add them to stews for the last minutes of cooking. As with fresh vegetables, it is imperative, if flavor and food values are to be retained, not to overcook them, especially if you use a pressure pan, see page 128.

The question of thawing or not thawing before cooking vegetables is a controversial one. If you do thaw, cooking must follow immediately, otherwise adverse changes take place. To unfreeze a 12- to 16-ounce package of vegetables, allow about 6 hours in the refrigerator, 3 at room temperature or 1 before a fan. Broccoli and spinach profit by partial thawing and corn on the cob should always be completely thawed. It is delicious if buttered and rewrapped in the aluminum foil in which it was frozen, then baked at 400° for 20 minutes. Frozen corn on the cob may also be prepared first by pressure cooking without previous thawing for 1 minute at 15 lbs. pressure, cutting off kernels, adding salt and butter and heating in an ovenproof dish under moderate broiler heat for 2 minutes. Do not thaw frozen mushrooms before cooking as they will become pulpy.

When cooking unthawed vegetables, break them apart into 4 or 5 pieces before removing from the carton to allow the heat to penetrate rapidly and evenly. To cook them, use the smallest possible amount of boiling water—¼ cup is enough for most vegetables. However, lima beans take almost a cup and soybeans and cauliflower about ½ cup. They should be covered ♦ at once with a lid. Once the boiling has begun again ♦ simmer the vegetables until tender. They will take from one-third to one-half the time required for fresh vegetables. As the addition of water is ruinous to the flavor of some frozen vegetables, steaming or pressure cooking on a rack over hot water, double boiler cooking or baking, is recommended. This is especially true for corn cut from the cob, or squash.

ABOUT FREEZING MEATS

Meats, both domestic and game, should be slaughtered, chilled and aged as for canning, page 752. Then they should be divided into meal-size quantities for packaging, see page 759. ♦ The reheating of once-thawed and cooked meats does not make for very tasty, nutritious or safe eating. Serve such leftovers cold or heat them immediately in a hot sauce.

The same advice as for all frozen produce applies to the choice of meats: watch quality. Storage at low temperatures does not induce enough change to make tough meats tender. If you usually buy quality cuts over the counter, make sure you can trust a new source which sells in quantity.

Beef, lamb and mutton must be properly aged in a chill-room before being frozen, but not too long, see below. ♦ Pork and poultry should be frozen as soon as they cool, after slaughtering, to forestall the tendency of the fat to turn rancid.

Although some frozen meats may be held over a year, it is a questionable economic or gastronomic procedure. Hold corn-fed beef, lamb and mutton a year if necessary; pork, veal and young chicken no more than 8 to 9 months; old chickens, turkeys and variety meats 3 to 4 months. Game storage depends, in part, on the type of game and, in part, on the laws of your state, which may limit holding time. For large game, see directions for meat above. For birds, see directions for poultry below. ♦ Ground and sliced meats do not keep as well as solid cuts. ♦ Do not hold meat loaves over 3 months, as the seasonings deteriorate. Salted or fat meats, such as fresh sausage, should never be held longer than a month, as the salt tends to make the fats rancid. Smoked meats, like bacon and ham, will keep 2 to 4 months, but ♦ extra precautions should be taken in wrapping smoked meats ♦ to keep the odor from penetrating other foods. Bones, which add flavor to meats during cooking, take up considerable locker space and may also cause wrappings to tear. Even though removal of bones requires both skill and time, it is worth it. Cook bones, thus removed, with meat trimmings to make a concentrated stock, see page 488. This is valuable for soups, gravies ♦ or for packaging precooked meats, page 753. Freeze stock in ice-cube-sized trays, remove and wrap for storage. These concentrates make quick gravy or soup.

ABOUT THAWING AND COOKING FROZEN MEATS

Frozen meats may be cooked thawed or unthawed. ♦ But partial or complete thawing helps retain juiciness in thick cuts. Thin cuts and patties may toughen if left frozen and ♦ variety meats or meats prepared by breading or dredging must be completely thawed. ♦ Always defrost in the original wrappings and, when possible, on a refrigerator shelf. Allow 5 hours for each pound of thick cuts, less for thinner ones. Defrosting wrapped meat at room temperature takes about half as long as the refrigerator method and about a third as long when put before a fan. ♦ Cooking unthawed large cuts of meat takes one and a half times as long as fresh ones. Small, thin cuts take one and a quarter times as long. ♦ Thawed cuts are cooked as for fresh ones. ♦ In any roasting process, use only the slow method, see page 386. A meat thermometer is a reassuring aid, see page 387.

ABOUT FREEZING AND THAWING POULTRY

Uncooked broilers, fryers and roasting chickens are most desirable for freezing. For stewers, see About Freezing and Thawing Precooked Foods, page 767. If you raise your own, starve the chickens for 24 hours before slaughtering, but give them plenty of water. Then bleed them well. Clean and dress, pages 461 and 460, immediately. Be careful not to tear or bruise the flesh. Chill not longer than 2 hours. ♦ Do not age them, unless you are fortunate enough to have wild duck or pheasant, which should be aged 2 or 3 days. For details, see directions listed under recipes for each kind of wild fowl. Remove excess cavity fat. ♦ Wrap giblets separately in moisture-proof wrappings and store in the cavity. Wrap and seal ♦ being careful to expel as much air as possible from the package. One helpful method is to put the bird in a freezer bag and plunge it quickly into a deep pan of cold water—keeping the top of the bag above the surface of the water. Twist the top and fasten.

When preparing several birds, storage space is saved if chickens are halved or disjointed before packaging. Freeze halves, breasts, thighs and drumsticks separately and wrap with double moisture-proof paper between them or store in cartons. Cook the backbones, wings and necks, remove the meat and freeze in the chicken broth. Store young chickens no longer than 9 months, older ones 3 to 4 months. Keep ducks and turkeys 6 to 9 months. A slight discoloration of the bones may occur during storage. It is harmless.

◖ It is not advisable to freeze stuffed poultry, as frequently the stuffing does not freeze fast enough to avoid spoilage. Freeze the stuffing separately.

Poultry is always best when thawed before cooking, unless used for fricassee, see page 467. The usual method is to thaw in the original wrappings and allow 2 hours per pound on the refrigerator shelf, 1 hour per pound, wrapped, at room temperature, 20 minutes per pound if the package is placed before a fan. Cook immediately after thawing. Although we do not recommend it ◖ unthawed fowl needs about one and one-half the time to cook that nonfrozen fowl requires. ◖ Treat thawed fowl like nonfrozen fowl.

ABOUT FREEZING, THAWING AND COOKING FISH

Fish, shellfish and frog legs freeze most successfully when cleaned and frozen immediately. If this is impractical, keep fish under refrigeration from catching to freezing, but in no case over 24 hours. Fish weighing 2 pounds or less, minus viscera, head, tails and fins, are frozen whole. For fish weighing 2 to 4 pounds, filleting is advised, page 345. Larger fish are usually cut into steaks, page 346. Separate fillets or steaks with a double thickness of waterproof paper, page 760.

Fish heavy in fat, like salmon, should be used within 2 months. Lobster and crab freeze best if cooked first as for the table, but without salt. Shrimp, minus head, are best frozen uncooked, as they toughen if frozen after cooking. In fact, most shellfish are apt to toughen, cooked or uncooked, if held over 2 months. Types like lobster and shrimp may be closely dry-packed. Oysters, clams and scallops should be shelled. The liquor is saved. Scallops may be washed after shelling, but not the other shellfish. Package all of these in their own liquor to cover and freeze. Hold no longer than 6 months.

Fish and shellfish are often packed commercially in an ice glaze to seal from oxygen. This is a good method, but hard to do at home.

Slowly thawed fish loses less juice and is more delicate when cooked than fish quickly thawed. Thaw fish in the original wrappings and allow about 8 hours per pound if placed on a refrigerator shelf, 4 hours per pound wrapped and at room temperature, 2½ hours per pound if the package is put before a fan. Lobster takes slightly more, scallops, oysters, shellfish and uncooked shrimp slightly less time than given above. Shrimp need not be thawed before cooking, unless it is to be deep-fat fried.

Unthawed fish must be cooked both longer and at much lower temperatures than fresh fish—usually about one and one-quarter times as long.

ABOUT FREEZING AND THAWING EGGS

Eggs must be removed from the shell before freezing. For short periods, shelled eggs may be frozen individually in an ice-cube tray, then packaged and stored. Usually, yolks and whites are stored separately. The whites are simply packaged in vapor-proof, small recipe-sized containers, perhaps in the exact amount for your favorite angel cake. Whole eggs or yolks should be stabilized or they become pasty and hard to mix after freezing. Stabilization is accomplished as follows: If yolks are to be used for unsweetened food, add 2 teaspoons of salt to each pint. If for desserts, add 2 tablespoons of sugar, honey or corn sirup to each pint. You will, of course, do well to label the yolks accordingly. To use ◖ thaw in the refrigerator for 8 to 10 hours; at room temperature for 4 to 5 hours.

If you prefer to package whole eggs, stir in with them 2 tablespoons of sugar or corn sirup or 1 teaspoon of salt to each pint. In packaging, allow a small head space for expansion during freezing. Thaw all eggs before using in recipes. To reconstitute a whole egg from your separately packed whites and yolks, allow 1 tablespoon of yolk and 2 tablespoons of white.

ABOUT FREEZING BUTTER, CREAM AND MILK

Unsalted butter stores well, but if salt is added, 3 months should be the limit of storage. ◖ Cream, whether in butter or stored separately, should be pasteurized first, page 482. When thawed, the uses for thick cream are limited mainly to whipping or making frozen desserts. Its oil rises on contact with coffee and the texture is not good for cereals. If making ice cream or frozen desserts for the freezer, choose a recipe which calls for heating the cream first. ◖ If milk is frozen, pasteurize first, page 482, and allow 2 inches for expansion in freezing. To use ◖ thaw butter about 3 hours on a refrigerator shelf and milk or cream about 2 hours at room temperature.

ABOUT FREEZING CHEESES

Cheeses of the hard or cheddar type may be stored for 6 months. Cream cheese, but not creamed cottage cheese, may be stored for 2 weeks. Dry cottage cheese can be frozen only before the curds are washed free of whey, see page 513. It is then washed after thawing, and drained. To thaw, rest cheese for about 3 hours on a refrigerator shelf.

ABOUT FREEZING AND THAWING PRECOOKED FOODS

The precooked frozen meal, for better or

for worse, is a reality. The following suggestions present increments for labor saving. Bake several pies, cakes or batches of bread at one session and store the extras; or double a casserole recipe and store half. Prepare school lunches in advance. We urge you, though, to read about the kinds of products really suitable for freezing, page 758, about quality, page 758, and to remember ♦ to cool the cooked dishes you plan to freeze through and through before you pack them. If you do not cool them sufficiently, the outside edges may freeze hard and the interior may not cool quickly enough to prevent spoilage. ♦ Also, do not try to freeze too much at one time, for overloading your freezer raises the temperature to the detriment of your already-stored frozen foods. Be just as careful with packaging cooked foods, page 759, as with raw ones. Do not hold them too long before using and in reheating be sure to thaw properly or reheat slowly.

Perhaps the most important thing to consider in precooking frozen foods is not to overcook foods that are to be reheated later. ♦ Also, watch seasonings carefully. Baffling changes take place. Onion and salt tend to vanish, as do herb flavorings, even the indomitable sage. Garlic and clove grow stronger and curry acquires a musty flavor. Do not use synthetic flavorings of any kind, including substitutes for true vanilla.

Sauces have their own peculiar reactions. Avoid freezing all sauces based on egg. Sauces heavy in fat have a tendency to separate on reheating, but often recombine with stirring, while those with much milk or cheese tend to curdle. Thickened sauces may need thinning. The best thickeners so far available for frozen sauces are waxy corn and waxy rice flours. Use them in the same amounts as you would all-purpose flour or use half the waxy type and half all-purpose.

ABOUT FREEZING CANAPÉS AND SANDWICHES

Canapés and sandwiches should not be stored longer than a few weeks. Make them up quickly to keep the bread from drying out. For mass production methods, see page 53. Be sure to spread all bread well and to make the fillings rather heavy in fats, so that the bread will not become saturated. Or you may prefer to prepare and freeze sandwich spreads for use later with fresh bread. As a corollary, bread for canapés can be cut into fancy shapes, frozen and then thawed slightly just before spreading. ♦ In choosing recipes for fillings, avoid mayonnaise and boiled salad dressings, hard-cooked egg whites, jellies and all crisp salad materials. Garnishes like cress, parsley, tomato and cucumber cannot be frozen, so add these the last moment before serving. Ground meats,

fish, butter, cream and cheddar-type cheese, sieved egg yolk, peanut butter, nut meats, dried fruits and olives are all suitable for freezing.

You may freeze canapés on trays first or wrap them carefully and then freeze them. In either case, keep the different kinds separated from one another and away from the interior walls of the freezer, as this contact makes the bread soggy. Canapés and sandwiches should always be thawed in the wrappings. They take from 1 to 2 hours to thaw on a refrigerator shelf and from 15 to 45 minutes at room temperature—depending on size.

ABOUT FREEZING SOUPS

To freeze soups, prepare them as for regular use. Chill them rapidly over ice water. Store in any containers suitable for liquids, page 759, allowing head space of ½ inch in pint and 1 inch in quart containers. Concentrated meat or fish stock, the stock simmered until reduced to one-half or one-third its original quantity, see Soup Stock, page 491, are the most space-saving soups to store. Freeze them first in ice-cube trays for additions to gravy and sauces. If a soup or chowder calls for potato, it is preferable to add freshly cooked potato just before serving. If you do freeze the potato, undercook it. Fish and meat stock thawed and combined in a ⅃ blender with fresh vegetables make delicate soups in short order. To serve frozen soups, bring them to a boil in a saucepan, unless they are thick or on a cream base, when a double boiler is necessary. For cold soups, thaw until liquid and serve while still chilled.

ABOUT FREEZING MAIN DISHES

Main dishes of the creamed type, stews, casseroles, meat pies, rissoles, croquettes and spaghetti sauces are among the most convenient of precooked foods for freezing. Fried foods almost without exception tend to rancidity, toughness and dryness when frozen. There is no time saving in freezing such starchy foods as macaroni, noodles, rice. And potatoes should not be frozen.

Prepare main dishes as usual—following your favorite recipes. But, in all instances, undercook the vegetables involved. Chill precooked foods rapidly over ice water and package closely and carefully, see page 759, before freezing.

Reheat stews and creamed dishes in a double boiler or in the oven at 350° in a heatproof dish that has been placed in hot water. Stir as little as possible. Allow 1½ times as long as normal to heat a frozen casserole at the usual temperature. Put frozen meat pies into a 350°-375° oven until brown.

Thaw croquettes or ♦ any breaded food that is to be sautéed or deep fried ♦ uncovered, at room temperature, so moisture does not form. If the food is already fried, thaw ♦ uncovered, at room temperature and bake in a 400° oven. Oven-prepared meats, fish and fowl hold much better than fried ones, which tend to rancidity.

Stewed meats keep best in heavy sauces. If they are to be used for salads, freeze them in clear concentrated stock.

Chill rapidly to room temperature. Cut in meal-sized portions; package closely and freeze. Hold no longer than 3 months. Thaw in original wrappings on a refrigerator shelf, allowing about as much time as for uncooked meats. Reheat in a double boiler or in the oven, in a pan of hot water at 350°.

ABOUT FREEZING VEGETABLE DISHES

A number of vegetables such as squash, boiled and candied sweet potatoes and creamed celery are best cooked before freezing and good to have on hand. See Chart, page 764, for these and other suggestions. All such vegetables may be heated in a double boiler or in a 400° oven without thawing.

Corn Pudding, page 274, was once a seasonal treat but is now available in frozen form at any time. Prepare the pudding as for immediate use. Put it into aluminum cartons, heat it in a moderate oven at 325° for 10 minutes. Cool over cold water. Cover, seal when thoroughly cool and freeze at once. To serve, heat in a 250° oven for about 1 hour until brown. If you plan keeping the corn longer than 4 months, merely scrape it, heat, chill and seal it as above. Then when ready to serve it, thaw in a 250° oven until soft, add butter, cream and salt and continue to heat the pudding until brown. For an attractive way to serve corn on the cob, see page 273.

ABOUT FREEZING SALAD INGREDIENTS

The materials that the word salad brings to mind—fresh crisp greens, tomatoes, cucumbers and aspics—are impossible to freeze, but some of the foods traditionally served with them freeze well and will shorten salad preparation time. For instance, frozen precooked meats and fish—whole, diced or sliced and covered with concentrated stocks—are welcome ingredients for a salad. Precooked green beans, evenly sized and unsliced, may be packaged, frozen and later coated with French dressing. And almost any fruit mixture, excluding bananas and pears, may be frozen for use in fruit salads later.

ABOUT FREEZING UNBAKED PASTRY AND DOUGHS

♦ Doughs, batters and unbaked pastry on the whole respond less favorably to freezing than do the finished products. ♦ We do not recommend the freezing of cake doughs and batters. For one thing, the spices and condiments used in their preparation have a disconcerting tendency to "zero out" during the freezing process. For another, all leavens are highly variable under frozen storage, particularly those incorporated in the moister kinds of dough.

Unbaked yeast bread dough is most acceptable when frozen and stored for only a week or ten days. It is made up in the usual way, see page 553, kneaded and allowed to rise once until double in bulk, then kneaded again and shaped before packaging into loaves not more than 2 inches thick. Thin loaves, of course, will thaw with much greater rapidity than thick ones. Frozen bread dough is a notable exception to the rule that frozen foods are best when slowly thawed. Place the dough in a 250° oven for 45 minutes, then bake it as usual, cool and serve. "Serve soon" would be a timelier suggestion, because thawed and baked bread dough dries out very rapidly. Partially baked breads in the brown-and-serve category may be put into the oven without thawing.

Unbaked dough for yeast rolls should not be held frozen for more than one week. Follow the procedure for frozen dough, above. Grease all roll surfaces; freeze them 2 to 4 hours on trays. Set them away from interior walls of the freezer and package them within 24 hours after freezing, or wrap them before freezing, separating the rolls with sheets of moisture-vapor-proof material. To serve, remove the rolls from the package, cover them with a cloth, put them in a warm place to rise until doubled in bulk, 2 to 4 hours, and bake as usual.

Unbaked biscuits may also be frozen on trays or packaged before freezing. They, too, rise well and thaw quickly if rolled thin. Thaw them wrapped at room temperature for 1 hour and bake as usual. Pastries heavy in fat, like pies, tarts, filled rings and rich cookies, whether frozen baked or unbaked, come through zero storage rather well; but whenever possible, it is good practice to store all but the cookies in the same containers in which they will ultimately be baked. If you want to cut cookies before freezing, put them on trays until hard. Then package for freezing. But if you want to cut them after freezing, make a roll of the dough and wrap it in moisture-vapor-proof material in batch sizes and seal. These uncooked cookie doughs keep about 2 months. Bake cookies in a 350°-375° oven for 10 to 12 minutes.

ABOUT FREEZING BAKED PASTRY, CAKES, COOKIES AND DOUGHS

Doughs previously baked are quicker and easier to freeze than the corresponding raw material and, generally speaking, yield more satisfactory results. Careful packaging for either category is imperative. ◗ Always plan to unfreeze just the amount of baked articles needed, for they dry out rapidly after thawing.

Precooked pastries heavy in fats are the most successful "freezers" of all. Their storage limit is about 3 months. Baked yeast bread and rolls have the longest storage potential—6 months or more—but they do begin to lose flavor after eight weeks. Bake all of these varieties in the usual way and, before packaging, let them cool for 3 hours, page 553. If bread is to be used for toast, it is not necessary to thaw it. Otherwise thaw it wrapped, at room temperature, for 1 hour before serving. Should you freeze "boughten" bread, leave it in its original wrapper and slip it into a plastic bag or wrap it in foil as well.

◗ Baked cakes will keep 3 to 4 months unfrosted, but only 2 months if frosted. Filled cakes tend to sogginess and any filling with an egg base is to be avoided. Actually, it is a better policy to wait and add fillings just before serving. Spice cake should not be stored over 6 weeks, as the flavors change in the freezing process. Use a minimum of spices and omit cloves. If frosted cakes are frozen, use icings with a confectioners' sugar and butter base. Brown sugar icings and those containing egg whites or sirups tend to crystallize and freeze poorly. Boiled frosting becomes sticky on thawing. Do not wrap any iced cakes until the icing has been well firmed by chilling, unwrapped, in the freezer. Place waxed paper over iced portions before putting on the outer wrap. Seal. Protect cakes with an extra carton to avoid crushing. Thaw cakes, unwrapped, in a covered cake dish at room temperature for 2 hours before serving.

◗ When cookies are baked before freezing, they will keep about 3 months. Bake as usual, cool and package closely, separating each cookie with moisture-vapor-proof material. To avoid breakage, store in an extra carton after wrapping. Let the cookies thaw wrapped in the refrigerator. ◗ Freshen them with a quick run in a 350° oven.

ABOUT FREEZING UNBAKED PIES

Use foil pans or pans in which you are willing to store the pies so they can be frozen and then baked in the same container. You will get better results with frozen pie crust if it has ◗ a high shortening content. Pie crust may be frozen ready for rolling or be rolled and cut ready to be put in the pan, but ◗ unrolled dough must be handled while it is still chilled so it will remain tender. Freeze shells to be filled later, unwrapped in the pan, then remove and stack them in a box before wrapping or store them wrapped in disposable foil pans. In making complete pies for freezing, brush the inside of the bottom crust with shortening to keep it from becoming soggy. After filling, wipe the top crust also with shortening. Never use water, egg or milk for these glazes.

The best pie fillings for freezing are fresh fruits or mincemeat and their storage limit is 4 to 6 months. Use pumpkin pie within 6 weeks for the best flavor. Fruits, like peaches and apricots, which darken on exposure to air, should be treated with ascorbic acid, page 761, or scalded in sirup, page 761, 2 minutes. Cool before using. The fillings for unbaked pies should have about 1½ times more cornstarch or tapioca than usual or, if possible, use waxy starches, page 500 and 499. ◗ Never freeze a cream or custard pie.

Allow at least 1 pint of filling for an 8-inch pie. ◗ Freeze the pie before wrapping if the filling is a wobbly one. Then package closely. Seal and protect against weight of other objects in the freezer until frozen hard.

Bake uncooked pies unthawed in a 450° preheated oven 15 to 20 minutes on the lowest shelf. Reduce heat to 375° until done, about 1 hour in all.

ABOUT FREEZING BAKED PIES

Use foil pans or containers you are willing to store, so the ◗ pie can be cooked, stored and reheated in the same pan.

Use a high proportion of shortening in the crust. After lining the pan with the crust, brush the inside with melted shortening to keep it from becoming soggy when filled and, after the pie is covered, wipe the top also with shortening. ◗ Never use water, egg or milk for these glazes.

◗ Unfilled baked pie shells are one of the most convenient of all frozen items for filling quickly before serving with creamed foods or fruits. Freeze them unwrapped in the pan, then remove and stack them in a box before wrapping or store them wrapped in disposable foil pans. If you are freezing any precooked fillings with starch, be sure to ◗ cook them very thoroughly and, if possible, use waxy starches, page 499 and 500.

The best pie fillings for freezing are fresh fruit and mincemeat. Store 4 to 6 months. Use pumpkin pie within 6 weeks for best flavor. Fruits like peaches or apricots which darken on exposure to air should be treated with ascorbic acid, page 761, or scalded in sirup, page 761, for 2 minutes. Cool before using. Allow about 1 pint of filling for an 8-inch pie. Freeze wobbly fillings before packaging or be very careful to keep them level during packaging and freezing. Package pies closely, seal carefully and protect with carton or tin against the weight of other objects in the freezer.

Thaw a baked pie at room temperature for 8 hours if it is to be served cold. If it is to be served hot, place it unthawed in a 400° preheated oven for 30 to 50 minutes, depending on size.

♦ Never freeze a cream or custard pie. Chiffon pies can be frozen in a baked shell if, before freezing, the filling has at least ½ cup of whipping cream incorporated into it. ♦ Defrost unwrapped at room temperature for 1 to 2 hours. Garnish with whipped cream before serving, if preferred.

ABOUT FREEZING DESSERTS

The same principles apply to desserts made in zero storage cabinets as to those which are still-frozen in refrigerators. Whipped cream, whipped egg white or a gelatin base are necessary to prevent the formation of undesirable graininess or crystals. If these stabilizing ingredients are not used, the dessert mixture must be beaten several times during the freezing to break

up these crystals. ♦ Such desserts should be used shortly after being frozen and not stored for any length of time.

Churned ice cream is best for freezing when the recipes call for beating the cream. A final beating and refreezing may be necessary if these creams have been stored longer than 3 weeks. For safety, do not store in the freezer longer than 3 months. Remove all frozen desserts from storage 10 to 15 minutes before serving.

Fruit and steam puddings may be made, baked, cooled and then frozen. These may be kept in the freezer for as long as one year. Thaw at room temperature for 6 hours, then steam to heat them through.

ABOUT FREEZING DRIED FRUITS, NUTS AND JELLIES

Dried fruits and nut meats can be successfully frozen whole, chopped or ground. Wrap them in convenient quantities, taking the usual precautions to exclude air from the packages. Jellies and jams, especially raspberry and strawberry, retain that fresh taste and clear color they have just after preserving, for many months.

JELLIES, JAMS, PRESERVES
AND MARMALADES

Have you ever tried to raise money for your church or club at a food stand? It's the homemade breads and old-fashioned cooked-down jellies that get snapped up first, for neither of these is likely to be duplicated commercially. With jams, jellies and preserves, flavor is largely a matter of sugar percentage. ‣ The less sugar you use, the greater the impact of the fruit flavor. It has been proved that ‣ cane and beet sugars produce equally good jellies. Only the amount of sugar, not the type, is important here. ‣ But if honey is substituted, there is a distinct flavor change, delicious if the honey is a good one. ‣ Jellies or jams made with honey must be cooked longer than those based on sugar. If you try preparing jellies with artificial sweeteners, see warning, page 508, use only the cyclamate type, and follow the processor's directions for jelly making. The texture of jellies made with synthetic sweeteners is quite different from that of those prepared with either honey or sugar. ‣ Cooked-down jellies, the type we recommend, in which the juice is extracted by the open kettle method, usually contain about 60% fruit and 40% sugar. The open kettle method is not so apt to destroy the natural pectins in the fruit.

‣ Commercial jellies according to law must have at least 45% fruit and 55% sugar. The juice is extracted by pressure cooking, and although as much as ¼ more juice can be extracted than in the open kettle method, the natural pectins in the fruit are destroyed by the higher heats and must be replaced. ‣ These added pectins demand a greater percentage of sugar to fruit in order to make the fruit juices jell. In fact, pectin manufacturers suggest for homemade jellies a proportion as high as 60% sugar to 40% juice if commercial pectins are used. They point out, of course, the advantage of greater yield, because with the use of commercial pectins there is little loss of liquid. Only a minute or two of cooking is necessary after the sugar is added. ‣ No recipes for the use of commercial pectins are given here, for, whether this substance comes in liquid or powdered form, the processor always gives specific recommendations.

Although it is both more time-consuming and expensive ‣ we prefer to stick to the old-fashioned jelly-making traditions described below, combining, where necessary, fruits rich and low in pectin but keeping a basic relationship of about 60%

fruit to 40% sugar in jellies, jams, fruit butters and conserves.

Just what is the difference between these categories? Jelly has great clarity. Two cooking processes are involved. First, the juice alone is extracted from the fruit. Only that portion, thin and clear enough to drip through a cloth, is cooked with sugar until ‣ firm enough to hold its shape, but never stiff and never gummy. ‣ Jams, butters and pastes are purées of increasing density. ‣ Preserves, marmalades and conserves are bits of fruit cooked to a translucent state in a heavy sirup. These and the jams, all of which need only one cooking, take patience and ‣ careful stirring, so that they reduce without any taint of scorching. For these thicker types, some oven and double-boiler techniques are suggested in the recipes.

Let us come back to the importance of pectins in all jelly and jam making. ‣ With high-pectin fruits, such as apples, crabapples, quinces, red currants, gooseberries, plums, and cranberries, you need have no worries about jelling. If you should get a sirupy jelly with any of these fruits, either you have used too much sugar or did not cook the juice long enough after the sugar was added.

Low-pectin fruits, such as strawberries, blueberries, peaches, apricots, cherries, figs, pears, raspberries, blackberries, grapes and pineapples, or plants, such as rhubarb, have to be combined either with one of the high-pectin fruits above—or, of course, with commercial pectins.

‣ To determine if fruit juice contains a sufficient amount of pectin to jell, put 1 tablespoon of the cooled fruit juice in a glass. Add the same quantity of grain alcohol and shake gently. The effect of the alcohol is to bring the pectin together in a jelly. If a large quantity of pectin is present, it will appear in a single mass or clot when poured from the glass. This indicates that equal quantities of sugar and juice should be used. If the pectin does not slip from the glass in a mass, less sugar will be required. If the pectin collects in 2 or 3 masses, use ⅔ or ¾ as much sugar as juice. If it collects in several small particles, you may use ½ as much sugar as juice, unless the fruit is very tart. ‣ Get your equipment ready before you begin to cook the jelly or jam. If you are making jelly, have a bag ready for straining the juice, see page 774 in About Jelly Making. ‣ Have ready, too, sterilized jelly glasses. To do this, fill glasses or jars ¾ full of water and place them, well apart, in a shallow pan partly filled with water. Simmer the glasses 15 or 20 minutes. Keep hot until ready to fill. If the lids are placed lightly upon the glasses, they will be sterilized at the same time.

In jelly or jam making ♦ use a heavy enamel or stainless-steel pan in preference to aluminum, copper or iron, which may discolor the product and even prove dangerous. ♦ Again, to retain flavor, unless fruit is very acid, when sugar can be used cup for cup with fruit ♦ we recommend ¾ cup sugar to 1 cup fruit or juice. Preheat the sugar while the juice comes to a boil by spreading it in baking pans and just warming it in very low oven heat. ♦ Be sure the jars are sterile and seal tightly at once after filling to avoid spoilage. ♦ In making up jellies and jams, the best flavor results if you work in small quantities. ♦ Prepare not more than 6 cups of fruit or juice at a time, preferably only about 4 cups. ♦ If the fruit is one that discolors easily, see remedy under About Fruit Canning, page 762. ✻ Jellies and jams may be frozen to advantage, see page 771, but do not keep them in the refrigerator, as they may "weep." ♦ Keep them in a cool, dark, dry place. If stored in over 70° temperature, deterioration may be rapid.

ABOUT MAKING JAM

Jam is the easiest type to make—and the most economical—as it needs only one cooking step and utilizes the fruit pulp. Measure the fruit. In putting it into the pan, crush the lower layers to provide moisture until more is drawn from the fruit by heat; or, if necessary, add about ½ cup of water. ♦ Simmer the fruit until it is soft before adding the warmed sugar. ♦ Stir until the sugar is well dissolved. ♦ Bring to a boil and continue to stir, making sure no sticking occurs. ♦ Reduce the heat and cook until the mixture thickens. To keep the heat diffused, you may even want to use an asbestos pad. Sometimes it takes as long as half an hour for jam to thicken.

ABOUT MAKING PRESERVES AND CONSERVES

These, like jams, need only one cooking and can be made by several methods. The fruit can be placed in a crock or stainless steel pan in layers with equal parts of sugar, ending with the sugar layer on top, and allowed to rest covered for 24 hours. It is then brought slowly to a boil and is ♦ simmered until the fruit is clear. Or, the fruit can be placed with a very small quantity of water in a heavy stainless or enamel pan with sugar. Allow ¾ to ½ cup sugar per cup of fruit, depending on the sweetness of the fruit. The sugar and fruit are then brought slowly to a boil and ♦ simmered until the fruit is translucent. In either case, should the sirup not be thick enough, the fruit may be drained, put into sterile jars and kept hot while the sirup is simmered to the desired thickness. It is then poured over the fruit. Seal and store in a dark cool place.

ABOUT MAKING JUICE FOR JELLY

♦ To prepare juice for jelly by the open kettle method, wash the fruit well and drain. To accent flavor ♦ add water only if you must. Prick or crush the fruit that forms the bottom layer in the preserving kettle. Less juicy fruits, such as apples and pears, require relatively large amounts of water. Add it to the kettle until you can see it through the top layer of fruit, but ♦ never use enough so that the fruit floats. Cook over low heat until more moisture is drawn from the fruit and then increase the heat to moderate. Cook ♦ uncovered until the fruit is soft and has begun to lose its color. ♦ Have ready a jelly bag. This should be made of a material similar to flannel or of several thicknesses of cheesecloth. If well enough sewn, the bag may eventually be suspended, if not, it can be held in a strainer. Wet the bag and wring it out before you pour the jelly into it, as a dry bag can absorb a lot of the precious juice. If you want a sparklingly clear and well-flavored jelly ♦ do not squeeze the bag. Squeezing not only muddies the jelly, but may leave a bitter and unpleasant taste. After using the bag, rinse it in boiling water.

♦ Never prepare juice in a pressure cooker unless you are willing to forego prime flavor and are willing to use added commercial pectins. ♦ The higher heat destroys the natural pectin in the fruit. This method of juice extraction will, however, yield about ⅓ to ¼ more juice than the open kettle method. Wash and drain the fruit. ♦ Never fill the pressure cooker more than ⅓ full, as the vent may clog with pulp. Add the necessary amount of water, using manufacturer's directions and remembering that the less water used, the more concentrated the flavor. ♦ Adjust the cover and bring the pressure up to 15 lbs. ♦ Remove at once from the heat and let the pressure recede of its own accord. Strain the juice through a jelly bag ♦ without squeezing and proceed to make jelly as described below.

If not utilized at once ♦ the fruit juices, whether cooked by the open kettle method or by pressure, will keep for about 6 months and can be made into jelly at your convenience. ✻ You may freeze it, page 771, or you may reheat the strained juice, pour it boiling hot into sterilized jars, page 747, cover with screw tops and cook in a

hot water bath, page 748, at 185° for at least 20 minutes. ◆ Seal the jars completely and keep them ◆ stored in a cool dark place.

ABOUT MAKING JELLY

Measure the strained fruit juice and put it into ◆ a large enamel or stainless steel pan. Simmer the juice about 5 minutes. ◆ Skim off any froth that forms. ◆ Measure and add the warmed sugar. ◆ Stir until the sugar is dissolved. To guard the pectins, the color and the flavor ◆ keep the heat at simmer. Because of the addition of the sugar, the boiling point of the mixture will have been raised and the jelly will seem to be boiling at this heat. Keep the heat at a simmer and stop stirring.

Cook it just long enough to bring it to the point of jelling. ◆ Begin to test the juice 10 minutes after the sugar has been added. Place a small amount of jelly in a spoon, cool it slightly and let it drop back into the pan from the side of the spoon.

As the sirup thickens, 2 large drops will form along the edge of the spoon, 1 on either side. ◆ When these 2 drops come together and fall as a single drop, as shown at the right above, the "sheeting stage," 220° to 222°, has been reached. This makes a firm jelly. For a somewhat softer jelly or sirup for preserves, cook the sirup only until it falls in 2 heavy drops from the spoon, as shown at left above. The jelly is then ready to be taken from the heat. The required time for cooking will range from 8 to 30 minutes, depending upon the kind of fruit, the amount of sugar and the amount of juice in each pan.

Shortly before you are ready to use the jars, take them from the hot water, empty them and reverse them onto a cake cooler. Pour the jelly into them when they are ◆ still hot, but dry. Fill to within ¼ inch of the top. Cover the jars with paraffin, unless you use the jelly glasses described opposite. ◆ Melt paraffin over very low heat or over hot water. If the paraffin becomes very hot, it is apt to pull away from the sides of the jelly glass. Pour it from a small pitcher, so that it covers the jelly with a very thin coating. To make it easy to remove, you may, on the second day, place a string across the top, allowing it to project somewhat beyond the edge of the glass. Cover the jelly again with a thin film of paraffin, tilting the glass to permit it to cover every bit of the surface. The second coating should not be

more than ³⁄₁₆ inch thick. A heavier coating is apt to pull away from the sides of the glass. ◆ If the jelly you are covering has ◆ an added pectin base, the paraffin should be applied while the jelly is still hot, because added pectin jellies are not cooked as long as the others and therefore may tend to mold more rapidly unless they are quickly covered.

◆ With cooked-down jellies and preserves, let the jelly cool to the point of setting before covering with a coating of melted paraffin ⅛ to ³⁄₁₆ inches thick. If you allow jellies to remain unsealed for any length of time, you may find that they may mold later, even under the paraffin. If you use a pint or a half-pint all-purpose canning jar with a two-piece metal screw-top lid, shown first in the illustration on page 747, you will need no paraffin. Pour jelly immediately into hot jars to the top; wipe the rims. Place a clean, hot metal lid so that the sealing compound is next to the jar. Screw the metal band on firmly. ◆ Cool on a metal rack or folded dry cloth; then ◆ store in a cool, dry place. ◆ Do not remove the metal screw band until ready to use.

CURRANT JELLY

◆ Please read About Making Jelly, this page.
Wash:

Red, white or black currants
Drain and place in a stainless-steel kettle. It is not necessary to stem currants, and they may be cooked with or without water. If water is used, allow about ¼ as much water as fruit. If no water is used, crush the bottom layer of currants and pile the rest on top of them. Cook the currants first over low heat for about 5 minutes, then over moderate heat until soft and colorless. Drain through a jelly bag, page 773. Allow to each cup of juice:

¾ to 1 cup sugar
Cook only 4 cups of juice at a time.

CURRANT AND RASPBERRY JELLY

◆ Please read About Making Jelly, this page.
Prepare currants, as for Currant Jelly, above.
Crush:

Raspberries
Add from 1 to 1⅓ cups raspberries for every cup of currants. Cook the fruit until the currants are soft and colorless. Strain the fruit through a jelly bag, page

773. Allow to each cup of juice:
    ¾ to 1 cup sugar
Cook only 4 cups of juice at a time.

BLACK RASPBERRY AND GOOSEBERRY JELLY
◗ Please read About Making Jelly, page 774.
Wash and drain fruit. Place in a saucepan and stew until soft:
    4 quarts black raspberries
    ¼ cup water
Place in a separate saucepan and stew until soft:
    2 quarts gooseberries or about 2 cups sliced green apples with peel and core
    ½ cup water
Combine the fruits and strain through a jelly bag, page 773. Allow to each cup c juice:
    ¾ to 1 cup sugar
Cook only 4 cups of juice at a time.

APPLE, CRABAPPLE OR QUINCE JELLY
Good in itself, especially if made with tart fruit. Apples, crabapples or quinces are also extremely useful in combination with fruits whose pectin content is low, such as blueberries, blackberries, raspberries and grapes, whether fresh or frozen. In apples, the greatest amount of pectin lies close to the skin. Apple peelings and cores can be cooked up and strained through a jelly bag for addition to low-pectin juices.
◗ Please read About Making Jelly, page 774.
Wipe, quarter and remove stems and blossom ends from:
    Tart apples, crabapples or quinces
Place in a saucepan. Add water until it can be seen through the top layer of fruit. Cook ◗ uncovered, until fruit is soft. Put the juice through a jelly bag, page 773. Allow to each cup of juice:
    ¾ to 1 cup sugar
Cook only 4 cups at a time.

HERB AND SCENTED JELLIES
◗ Please read About Making Jelly, page 774.
Prepare:
    Apple or Crabapple Jelly, above
After testing for jelling and before removing the jelly from the heat, bruise the leaves and tie a bunch of one of the following ◗ fresh, unsprayed herbs:
    Mint, basil, tarragon, thyme, lemon verbena or rose geranium
Hold the stem ends and pass the leaves through the jelly repeatedly until the desired strength of flavoring is reached. Add a small amount of:
    (Vegetable coloring)

PARADISE JELLY
◗ Please read About Making Jelly, page 774.
Wash and cut into quarters:
    3 quarts apples
Peel and cut into quarters:
    3 pints quinces
Remove seeds. Place the apples in a pan with:
    1 quart cranberries
Barely cover with water. Boil until soft. Follow the same procedure with the quinces. Strain the juices of all the fruits through a jelly bag. Allow to each cup of juice:
    1 cup sugar
Cook only 4 cups at a time.

GRAPE JELLY
◗ Please read About Making Jelly, page 773.
Wash:
    Slightly underripe Concord or wild grapes
They are preferable to ripe or overripe grapes because of their tart flavor and higher pectin content. Remove stems. Place fruit in a kettle with a small quantity of water—about ½ cup of water to 4 cups of grapes. Add:
    1 quartered apple
If you wish to spice the jelly, add at this time:
    ⅓ cup vinegar
    1 inch stick cinnamon
    ½ teaspoon whole cloves without heads
Boil grapes until soft and beginning to lose color. Strain through a jelly bag. Allow to each cup of juice:
    ¾ to 1 cup sugar
Cook only 4 cups at a time.

WATERLESS GRAPE OR BERRY JELLY
◗ Please read About Making Jelly, page 774.
Try this recipe when slightly underripe fruits are available. It is superlative when it works, but everything depends on the condition of the fruit.
Wash:
    Concord grapes or berries
Mash them in a large pot. Cook until soft. Strain the juice. Measure it. Bring juice to a rolling boil. Remove from heat. Add 1½ times more:
    Sugar
than you have juice. Stir it over heat until dissolved. Pour the jelly into sterilized glasses and seal. ◗ Should the liquid not jell, nothing but time is lost. Allow 1 apple and ¼ cup water to every 4 cups original fruit used. Cook the apple and water until the apple is soft. Strain off the juice, add it to the unjelled jelly, and recook as for any other jelly.

GUAVA JELLY

♦ Please read About Making Jelly, page 774.

Wash and cut in quarters:

Slightly underripe guavas

Cover with water and boil, then ♦ simmer for about ½ hour. Put the juice through a jelly bag, page 773, but do not press, as the juice will become bitter. Allow to each cup of juice:

1 cup sugar

Bring again to a boil and add for each cup of juice:

1 teaspoon lime juice

Cook only 4 cups at a time.

PLUM JELLY

Goose plums make delicious jelly or jam.
♦ Please read About Making Jelly, page 774.

Wash:

Small red plums

Place in a saucepan. Add water until it can be seen through the top layer. Boil plums until soft. Put the pulp through a jelly bag. Allow to each cup of juice:

¾ to 1 cup sugar

Boil only 4 cups at a time.

RED RED STRAWBERRY JAM

♦ Please read About Making Jam, page 773.

Wash, dry well and stem:

1 quart ♦ perfect strawberries

Put them in a 10-inch ♦ very heavy cooking pot, cutting into a few of the berries to release a little juice. Cover with:

4 cups sugar

Stir the mixture ♦ very gently with a wooden spoon ♦ over low heat until it has "juiced up." Then raise the heat to moderate and stop stirring. When the whole is a bubbling mass, set your timer for exactly 15 minutes (17, if the berries are very ripe). From this point do not disturb. You may take a wooden spoon and streak it slowly through the bottom to make sure there is no sticking. When the timer rings, tilt the pot. You should see in the liquid at the bottom a tendency to set. Slide the pot off the heat. Allow berries to cool ♦ uncovered. Sprinkle surface with:

(Juice of ½ lemon)

When cool, stir the berries lightly and place in sterile jars.

BAR-LE-DUC PRESERVES

For use with Bar-Le-Duc, page 708.

Wash and stem:

Red or white currants

If you are a classicist, pierce the bottom of each berry and force the seeds through the opening. For 1 cup of currants, cook to the soft-ball stage, 238°:

1½ cups sugar
½ cup honey
1¼ cups water

Drop the berries into the boiling sirup.

Bring the sirup up to the boiling stage again and cook for 1 minute. Pour into sterilized glasses and seal.

BLUEBERRY JAM

If blueberries are picked early in the day and are only half ripe, at the red instead of blue stage, the result is a jam far more flavorful than usual—almost like the one made with Scandinavian lingonberries.
♦ Please read About Making Jam, page 773.

Pick over, wash and measure:

Blueberries

Put in a heavy stainless-steel pan. Crush the bottom layer. Add:

(½ cup water)

Cook over moderate heat ♦ simmering until almost tender. Add, for each cup of blueberries:

¾ to 1 cup heated sugar

Stir and cook over low heat until a small amount dropped on a plate will stay in place. Place in hot sterilized jars.

SPICED PEAR JAM
WITH PINEAPPLE

About 2 Quarts

♦ Please read About Making Jam, page 773.

As it is hard to gauge the acidity of the pear used, taste the jam as it cooks. Add sugar or lemon juice, as needed. Peel and core:

3 lbs. firm cooking pears

Wash well:

1 seeded orange
1 seeded lemon

Put the fruit through a grinder, using a coarse blade. Save the juices. Add to the pulp with:

1 cup crushed pineapple
4 to 5 cups sugar
3 or 4 whole cloves
About 6 inches of stick cinnamon
1 one-inch piece ginger

Stir the mixture while heating it. Boil for about 30 minutes. Pour into hot sterilized glasses.

RASPBERRY, BLACKBERRY,
LOGANBERRY OR ELDERBERRY JAM

♦ Please read About Making Jam, page 773.

Crushing a few berries, combine:

4 cups raspberries, blackberries, elderberries or loganberries

with:

3 cups sugar

If the berries are tart, use a scant cup of sugar to 1 cup of fruit. Stir and cook over low heat until the sugar is dissolved ♦ Simmer and stir frequently from the bottom, to keep them from sticking. Cool until a small amount dropped on a plate will stay in place. Pack while hot in hot sterilized jars.

FIVE-FRUITS JAM COCKAIGNE

On the whole, we like food to retain its natural flavor. Our sympathy goes out to the cowboy movie actor who is reported to have said, after his first formal dinner: "I et for two hours and I didn't recognize anything I et, except an olive." However, this jam is both mysterious and delicious.

♦ Please read About Making Jam, page 773.

Hull and place in kettle, in layers:

Strawberries

pound for pound with:

Sugar

End with a layer of sugar on top. Allow this mixture to stand, covered, for 12 hours. Now bring strawberries quickly to the boiling point and ♦ simmer with as little stirring as possible until the juice thickens, about 15 minutes. As strawberries usually appear a little in advance of the other fruits, these preserves may be placed in sterilized and sealed fruit jars and set aside until the other 4 fruits are available. Stem and seed:

Cherries

Stem:

Currants

Pick over:

Raspberries

Stem and head:

Gooseberries

The first 4 fruits are best used in equal proportions, but gooseberries have so much character that it is well to use a somewhat smaller amount, or their flavor will predominate. Bring the fruits separately or together to the boiling point. Add to each cup of fruit and juice:

¾ cup sugar

♦ Simmer the jam until thick, about 30 minutes. Combine with the strawberry preserves which have been reheated to the boiling point.

QUICK APRICOT PINEAPPLE JAM

Prepare Sauce Cockaigne, page 709.
Keep under refrigeration.

ROSE-HIP JAM

Wait to collect the hips until after the first frost. Do not use any which have been sprayed with poison insecticides.

♦ Please read About Making Jam, page 773.

Place in a heavy stainless-steel pan and ♦ simmer until fruit is tender. Allow:

1 cup water

to:

1 lb. rose hips

Rub through a fine sieve. Weigh the pulp. Allow, to each pound of pulp:

1 lb. heated sugar

♦ Simmer until thick.

APPLE BUTTER

About 5 Pints

Use Jonathan, Winesap or other well-flavored apples for good results.

Wash, remove the stems and quarter:

4 lbs. apples

Cook slowly until soft in:

2 cups water, cider or cider vinegar

Put fruit through a fine strainer. Add to each cup of pulp:

½ cup brown sugar

Add:

1 teaspoon cinnamon
½ teaspoon cloves
¼ teaspoon allspice
(Grated lemon rind and juice)

Cook the fruit butter over low heat, stirring constantly until the sugar is dissolved. Continue to cook, stirring frequently until the mixture sheets from a spoon. You can also place a small quantity on a plate. When no rim of liquid separates around the edge of the butter, it is done. Pour into hot sterilized jars. To store, see page 774.

BAKED APPLE BUTTER

About 6½ Cups

A more convenient method than the above, as stirring is not necessary.

Wash and remove cores from:

12 lbs. apples: Jonathan or Winesap

Cut them into quarters. Nearly cover with water. Cook gently for about 1½ hours. Put the pulp through a fine strainer. Measure it. Allow to each cup of pulp:

½ cup sugar

Add:

Grated rind and juice of 2 lemons
3 teaspoons cinnamon
1½ teaspoons cloves
½ teaspoon allspice

Bring these ingredients to the boiling point. Chill. Stir into them:

1 cup port, claret or dry white wine

Place about ¾ of the purée in a large heat-proof crock. Keep the rest in reserve. Put the crock in a cold oven. Set oven at 300°. Permit the apple butter to bake until it thickens. As the purée shrinks, fill the crock with reserved apple butter. When the butter is thick, but still moist, put into sterile jars. To store, see page 774.

PEACH OR APRICOT BUTTER

About 5 Pints

Wash, peel, pit and crush:

4 lbs. peaches or apricots

Cook very slowly in their own juice until soft. Stir. Put the fruit through a fine strainer. Add to each cupful of pulp:

½ to ⅔ cup sugar

Add:

2 teaspoons cinnamon
1 teaspoon cloves
½ teaspoon allspice
(Grated lemon rind and juice)

Cook and store as for Apple Butter, this page.

DAMSON PLUM BUTTER

Wash, peel and quarter:

Damson plums

Put them in a heat-proof crock, in a pan
of boiling water, over direct heat. Cover
the whole container and cook until the
fruit is soft enough to purée. To each cup
purée allow:
  1 cup sugar
Place in a heavy pan and ♦ stir over low
heat at least 45 minutes or until the fruit
butter is quite stiff. To store, see page 774.

SUNSHINE STRAWBERRY PRESERVES
Like the recipe for Waterless Jelly, page
775, this method is risky, but well worth
taking the chance if it succeeds.
Arrange in a large kettle:
  2 layers of washed, hulled,
    perfect strawberries
Sprinkle the layers with an equal amount
of:
  Sugar
Permit to stand for ½ hour. Heat over low
heat until boiling, then ♦ simmer for 15
minutes. Pour the berries onto platters.
Cover loosely with glass or plastic dome,
out of the reach of insects. Permit the
berries to stand in the sun for 2 or 3
days, until the juice forms a jelly. Turn
the berries very gently twice daily. These
preserves need not be reheated. Place in
hot sterilized glasses and seal.

STRAWBERRY AND PINEAPPLE PRESERVES
♦ Please read About Making Preserves,
page 773.
Combine:
  1 quart hulled berries
  4 cups sugar
  1 cup canned pineapple
    Rind and juice of ½ lemon
♦ Simmer these ingredients for about 20
minutes. Stir frequently. When thickened,
place in sterile jars.

STRAWBERRY AND RHUBARB PRESERVES
♦ Please read About Making Preserves,
page 773.
Cut into small pieces:
  1 quart rhubarb
Sprinkle over it:
  8 cups sugar
Permit these ingredients to stand for 12
hours. Bring quickly to the boiling point.
Wipe and hull:
  2 quarts strawberries
Add to the rhubarb. ♦ Simmer the preserves until thick, about 15 minutes.

CHERRY PRESERVES
♦ Please read About Making Preserves,
page 773.
If cherries are very sweet, ¾ pound sugar
will suffice.
Wash, stem, seed and place in pot, in
layers:
  Cherries
pound for pound with:

  Sugar
End with a layer of sugar on top. Allow
the cherries to stand covered for 8 to 10
hours. Then bring this mixture slowly to a
boil, stirring frequently. ♦ Simmer until
tender—about 20 minutes. If the juice
seems too thin, skim off the cherries and
place them in sterile jars. Simmer juice
until it thickens, then pour over cherries.

PEACH OR APRICOT PRESERVES
♦ Please read About Making Preserves,
page 773.
Use firm, slightly underripe, well-flavored
fruit.
Peel and cut into lengthwise slices:
  Peaches or apricots
The fruit may be dipped briefly in boiling
water to facilitate the removal of skins.
Reserve the stones. Crack some of them
and remove the kernels. Measure the fruit.
Allow to each cup:
  ¾ cup sugar
  2 tablespoons water
  1½ teaspoons lemon juice
Stir this sirup and cook it for 5 minutes.
Add the fruit. (If preferred, omit the water and just pour the sugar over the
peaches and permit them to stand for 2
hours before preserving them.) ♦ Simmer
until transparent. Place in glasses or jars.
If the fruit is juicy and the sirup too abundant, place the peaches in jars and reduce
the sirup until thick. Pour over peaches.
Add to each glass 1 or more peach or apricot kernels. This is optional, but they give
the preserves a distinctive flavor. Add to
the sirup:
    (Lemon juice—about 2 teaspoons to
      every cup of fruit)

DAMSON, ITALIAN PLUM OR GREENGAGE PRESERVES
♦ Please read About Making Preserves,
page 773.
Wash, cut into halves and remove the
seeds from:
  Damsons, Italian plums or
    greengages
Stir into the plums an equal amount of:
  Sugar
The sugar may be moistened with a very
little water or the fruit and sugar may be
permitted to stand for 12 hours before
cooking. Bring the preserves to a boil,
then ♦ simmer until the sirup is heavy.
Add:
    (2 minced seeded unpeeled oranges)
    (½ lb. walnut meats)

QUINCE PRESERVES
♦ Please read About Making Preserves,
page 773.
Scrub:
  Quinces
Slice them into eighths. Core and seed.
Pare and put the peelings in a pan with
just enough water to cover. To each quart
of liquid, add:

1 sliced seeded lemon
1 sliced seeded orange

♦ Simmer this mixture until the peelings are soft. Strain, reserving the liquid. Now weigh and add the quince slices. Weigh same quantity:

Warmed sugar

Bring quince slices to a boil and add the sugar. Bring to a boil again. Then ♦ simmer until the fruit is tender. Drain off the sirup and reduce it until heavy. Place the fruit in sterile jars. Cover with the reduced sirup and seal.

HARVEST PRESERVES

♦ Please read About Making Preserves, page 773.

Pare, core, seed and quarter equal parts of:

Tart apples
Pears
Plums

Prepare as for Quince Preserves, above.

TOMATO PRESERVES

♦ Please read About Making Preserves, page 773.

Scald and skin:

1 lb. tomatoes

Yellow tomatoes may be used with especially fine results. Cover tomatoes with:

An equal amount of sugar

Permit to stand for 12 hours. Drain the juice. Boil until the sirup falls from a spoon in heavy drops. Add the tomatoes and:

Grated rind and juice of 1 lemon or
2 thinly sliced seeded lemons
2 oz. gingerroot or preserved ginger or
4-inch stick cinnamon

Cook the preserves until thick.

FIG PRESERVES

About 1 Quart

♦ Please read About Making Preserves, page 773.

Wash and combine:

1 lb. finely cut unpeeled rhubarb
¼ lb. chopped stemmed figs
3 tablespoons lemon juice

Cover with:

1 lb. sugar

Let stand 24 hours in a cool place. Bring to a boil in a heavy stainless-steel pan and ♦ simmer until thickened.

GOOSEBERRY PRESERVES

♦ Please read About Making Preserves, page 773.

These, being tart, are good with a meat course, soft cream cheese or a sweet cake. Wash:

1 quart gooseberries

Remove stems and blossom ends. Place in a heavy saucepan. Add:

¼ cup water

Place over quick heat. Stir. When boiling, add:

3 to 4 cups sugar

♦ Simmer preserves until the berries are clear and the juice thick, about 15 minutes.

KUMQUAT OR CALAMONDIN PRESERVES

About 3 Pints

♦ Please read About Making Preserves, page 773.

Weigh the fruit. This recipe is for 3 lbs. Separate pulp from skins. Cover skins with:

Cold water

Cook until tender. If you do not like the bitter taste, drain several times during this process and replace with fresh water. When tender, slice fine or grind the skins. Meanwhile, cover the pulp with:

3 cups water

and simmer for 30 minutes. Strain the pulp and add to the juice:

3 cups water

Discard the pulp. Allow to each cup juice:

¾ cup heated sugar

Heat the juice and ♦ stir in the sugar until dissolved. Add the cut-up skins and cook until sirup jells.

ORANGE MARMALADE

About 8 Jelly Glasses

Fully ripe oranges may still have a greenish peel, especially in the spring, but this has nothing to do with their minimum sugar content, which the government checks before oranges are shipped for sale. Scrub well, cut into quarters and remove the seeds from:

2 large Valencia oranges
2 large or 3 small lemons

Soak the fruit for 24 hours in:

11 cups water

Remove fruit. Cut into very small shreds. Return to the water in which it was soaked. Boil for 1 hour. Add:

8 cups sugar

Boil the marmalade until the juice forms a jelly when tested, see page 774. To store, see page 774.

ORANGE, LEMON AND GRAPEFRUIT MARMALADE

About 18 Jelly Glasses

Scrub, cut in halves, remove the seeds and slice into very small pieces:

1 grapefruit
3 oranges
3 lemons

Measure the fruit and juice and add 3 times the amount of water. Soak for 12 hours. ♦ Simmer for about 20 minutes. Let stand again for 12 hours. For every cup of fruit and juice, add:

¾ cup sugar

Cook these ingredients in small quantities, about 4 to 6 cups at a time, until they form a jelly when tested, see page 774. To store, see page 774.

LIME MARMALADE
About 3 Jelly Glasses
Cut the thin outer rind from:
   6 small limes or 2 Persian limes
   3 lemons
Prepare and store as for the above Orange,
Lemon and Grapefruit Marmalade.

TAMARIND MARMALADE
Wash:
   1 quart tamarinds
Cover with:
   1½ cups water
♦ Simmer until soft. Put through sieve to
remove fibers and seeds. Heat the pulp
and allow for each cup:
   1 cup heated sugar
♦ Simmer, stirring constantly until the mixture thickens. To store, see page 774.

BLUE PLUM CONSERVE
About 20 Jelly Glasses
Peel and chop:
   The thin yellow rind of 2 oranges
   and 1 lemon
Add:
   The juice and seeded, chopped pulp
   of 3 oranges and 1 lemon
   1¼ lbs. ground seeded raisins
   9 cups sugar
Seed and add:
   5 lbs. blue plums
   4 pared, cubed peaches
Cook the conserve slowly until fairly thick.
Stir frequently. Add:
   ½ lb. broken walnut meats
♦ Simmer the conserve 10 minutes longer.
To store, see page 774.

BLACK CHERRY CONSERVE
About 8 Jelly Glasses
Cut into very thin slices:
   2 seeded oranges
Barely cover with water. Cook until very
tender. Stem, seed and add:
   1 quart black cherries
Add:
   6 tablespoons lemon juice
   3½ cups sugar
   ¾ teaspoon cinnamon
   (6 cloves)
♦ Simmer the conserve until thick and
clear. To store, see page 774.

SPICED RHUBARB CONSERVE
About 8 Jelly Glasses
Cut into very thin slices:
   1 seeded orange
   1 seeded lemon
Tie in a small bag:
   1 oz. gingerroot
   ¼ lb. cinnamon candy: redhots
   1 blade mace
   2 whole cloves
Add the spices to the fruit with:
   ½ cup water
   ¼ cup vinegar
♦ Simmer these ingredients until the fruit
is tender. Add and cook, until the conserve is thick:
   1½ cups strawberry rhubarb
   3 cups sugar
   (¼ cup white raisins)
To store, see page 774.

TUTTI FRUTTI COCKAIGNE OR BRANDIED FRUIT
A sort of liquid hope-chest, the contents
of which may be served with a meat course
or over puddings and ice cream. Be sure
that during its preparation ♦ your container is big enough to hold all the ingredients you plan putting into it and,
just as important, that ♦ you can store it
in a consistently cool place, not above 45°,
to prevent runaway fermentation. Place in
a sterile stoneware crock with a closely
fitting lid:
   1 quart brandy
Add, as they come into season, five of the
following varieties of fruit—perfect fruit
only:
   1 quart strawberries
   1 quart seeded cherries
   1 quart raspberries
   1 quart currants
   1 quart gooseberries
   1 quart peeled sliced apricots
   1 quart peeled sliced peaches
   1 quart peeled sliced pineapple
Avoid apples, as too hard; bananas and
pears, as too mushy; blackberries, as too
seedy; and seeded grapes, unless skinned, as
their skins become tough. With each addition of fruit, add the same amount of:
   Sugar
Stir the tutti frutti every day until the last
of the fruit has been added, securing the
lid well after each time. The mixture will
keep indefinitely.

PICKLES AND RELISHES

Peter Piper proved a pretty pampered pepper picker. Less privileged persons—such as you and we—are expected to pick produce unpickled and process it promptly ourselves. Pickling can be accomplished in several ways, some of them lengthy, but none of them difficult. Granted that a considerable number of vitamins and minerals leach away into liquid residue during the pickling process, it remains a piquant and important method of food preservation.

ABOUT PICKLING EQUIPMENT

♦ Because of the acid factor involved in pickle making, be sure your equipment for brining is stoneware, pottery or glass, and that your pickling kettles are stainless steel or enamel. For stirring use long-handled spoons and, for transferring the pickles, a stainless, enamel-covered or slotted wooden spoon or glass cup. Pack pickles in perfect sterile glass jars with glass lids, page 747. All equipment should be absolutely clean and grease-free.

ABOUT PICKLING INGREDIENTS

For best results it is ♦ imperative that vegetables and fruits for pickling are in prime condition and were harvested no longer than 24 hours in advance. If cucumbers have been held longer, they tend to become hollow during processing.

Black-spined varieties are the usual choice for cucumber pickles. They may be slightly underripe but must be ♦ unblemished. ♦ Scrub them well to remove any dirt which might spark bacterial activity later, and trim to retain ⅛ to ¼ inch of stem.

If using garlic as a seasoning, blanch it 2 minutes before adding it to other ingredients, or remove it from the jar before sealing. ♦ Water used should be soft, page 493. If you are in a hard water area, try to get distilled water, or trap some rainwater. If the water contains iron or sulphur compounds, the pickles will become dark.

♦ Use only pickling or dairy salt, free from additives which might deter processing, see About Salt, page 525.

♦ Vinegar should test 5% to 6% acetic acid. Distilled white vinegar gives the lightest color. Cider-based malt and herb-flavored vinegars, although they yield a richer flavor, will darken pickles. You may want to make up and have ready to use one of the spice vinegars, page 496. Homemade wine vinegars of uncertain strength should not be used, as the vinegar will "mother," page 496.

Since spices vary so greatly in strength, page 526, the amounts given are only approximate. Taste before bottling and correct the seasoning. ♦ Spices should be both fresh and whole. Ground spices darken the pickle, old spices impart a dusty flavor. Tie spices in a cloth bag for easy removal. If left in, they may cloud the liquid. Distillates, like the oils of cinnamon and of clove, are available at drug stores. They give a clearer pickle than steeped condiments, but the flavor is not so lasting.

♦ To make pickles crisp, use grape or cherry leaves during brining. Or, in short-brine pickling, after the brining period, soak the pickles for 2 hours in enough of the following lime water solution to cover. Allow:

1 tablespoon calcium oxide

to:

1 quart soft water, page 493

Stir well, and after stirring allow the solution to settle. Use only the clear portion of the liquid to cover the pickles. After the 2 hour soaking, drain and cover with the hot pickling liquid as directed. Alum is not recommended for crisping, as just a trifle too much may make the pickles bitter.

ABOUT SHORT-BRINE PICKLING

Most homemade pickles are of the less exacting short-brined type. They are soaked in a salt solution only 24 hours or so. This brining period is sufficiently long to draw out moisture, ♦ but not long enough to induce the fermentation needed for adequate keeping. An essential further step, after draining off the brine, is to pour over the produce a hot vinegar solution which penetrates the softened vegetable tissue and so preserves it.

Although in the short-brine process, the hot vinegar also tends to firm the produce, it is advisable, for greater crispness, to add to the jars a few fresh grape or cherry leaves, or to use the lime water process described above. Firmness in pickled produce contributes both to its keeping and its eating qualities.

In the short-brine process, unless lime water is used, the produce is packed as soon as the brine is drained off, and just before the addition of the vinegar. Pack closely in sterile jars—the type which have glass lids. Heat the vinegar solution to the boiling point, and fill the jars full to the top. Wipe the rims, adjust and seal the lids and process in a boiling water bath for 15 minutes, page 748. By this time the interior of the jars should have reached 180°, enough to inhibit destructive enzymes. Sometimes, even if this final precautionary treatment has been used, further fermentation takes place which shows up in the form of small bubbles or leakage from the container.

Keep an eye on your pickles after you have stored them away, and if you detect evidences of fermentation make up a fresh boiling pickling solution. Wipe the jars clean, refill them to overflowing again with boiling vinegar solution, and reprocess for 15 minutes in a boiling water bath. The flavor of almost all pickled produce is improved if it is stored for 6 weeks before using.

YELLOW CUCUMBER PICKLES
About 14 Quarts
◗ Please read About Pickling Equipment and Ingredients, page 781.

These large, luscious, firm, clear slices are served very cold with meat. Pare, cut into strips of about 1½ x 2½ x ¾ inches, and seed:

    1 bushel large yellow cucumbers

Soak the strips for 12 hours in a:

    10% Brine, page 525

Drain well. Sterilize 14 one quart jars, page 747. Place in each one:

    A slice of peeled horseradish: 1½ by ⅓ by ⅛ inches
    A ½ inch piece long hot red pepper
    4 sprigs dill blossom with seeds
    1 tablespoon white mustard seed
    2 white peppercorns

Combine:

    3 cups water
    1 cup sugar
    1½ gallons white distilled vinegar

Cook about 3 cupfuls at a time, enough to cover the bottom of a large saucepan to the depth of about ½ inch. Keep several pans going to hasten the process. Immerse in the ◗ boiling vinegar sufficient cucumber strips to cover the bottom of the pan. Let them come to the boiling point. Remove them at once to the jars. Do not cook the strips longer, as it will soften them. When a jar is filled with cucumber strips cover them with boiling vinegar. Seal the jars. Process in a boiling bath, page 748, for 15 minutes. Permit the pickles to ripen for at least 6 weeks before serving.

SWEET-SOUR YELLOW CUCUMBER PICKLES OR SENFGURKEN
About 9 Quarts
◗ Please read About Pickling Equipment and Ingredients, page 781.

Peel, cut into strips about 1½ x 2½ x ¾ inches, and seed:

    12 large yellow cucumbers

Soak them for 12 hours in:

    10% Brine, page 525

Drain. Have ready 8 or 10 sterilized quart jars, page 747. Prepare the following mixture:

    1 gallon pickling vinegar, page 495
    8 cups sugar
    ¼ cup mustard seed

Place in a cloth bag and add:

    ¾ cup whole mixed spices

◗ Boil about 5 cupfuls of the mixture at a time, enough to cover the bottom of a large stainless steel or enamel pan to a depth of about ½ inch. Place bag of spices in pan. Immerse in the boiling vinegar sufficient strips to cover the pan bottom. Bring vinegar to boiling point. Remove strips at once. Place them in jars. Fill jars with boiling vinegar mixture. Seal and process for 15 minutes in a boiling water bath, page 748.

SWEET-SOUR SPICED CUCUMBER PICKLES
About 12 Quarts
◗ Please read About Pickling Equipment and Ingredients, page 781.

These are wonderfully good. Scrub:

    20 lbs. very small cucumbers

Soak for 24 hours in brine made of:

    1 cup coarse salt
    3 quarts water: 12 cups

Remove from brine and add boiling water to cover. Drain quickly in a colander and pack closely while hot in sterilized jars, page 747. Cover at once with the following vinegar mixture, ◗ just at boiling point:

    1 gallon cider vinegar
    11 cups sugar
    2 oz. whole mixed spices
    1 oz. stick cinnamon
    1 teaspoon cloves
    4 tablespoons lime water

Seal jars at once. Process for 15 minutes in boiling water bath, page 748.

BREAD AND BUTTER PICKLES
About 6 Quarts
◗ Please read About Pickling Equipment and Ingredients, page 781.

Wash well:

    1 gallon medium-sized cucumbers: 4 quarts

Parblanch for 2 minutes, see page 132, and add:

    6 to 12 large onions or 3 cups or more small white ones
    2 green or red peppers with seeds and membrane removed

Proportions for this recipe may vary, as onion fanciers use the larger amount, and even more, of their beloved vegetable. Cut the unpared cucumbers and the peeled onions into the thinnest slices possible. Remove seeds and fibrous membranes from peppers. Shred or chop them. Place vegetables in a bowl. Pour over them:

    ½ cup coarse salt

Place in refrigerator for 12 hours with weighted lid over them. Drain vegetables. Rinse in cold water. Drain again thoroughly. A cloth bag is frequently used to let all the moisture drip from them. Prepare the following sirup:

    5 cups mild cider vinegar
    5 cups white or brown sugar
    1½ teaspoons turmeric or allspice

2 tablespoons mustard seed
1½ teaspoons celery seed
½ teaspoon ground cloves or 1 inch
    stick cinnamon

Bring these ingredients ♦ just to the boiling point. Add vegetables gradually with very little stirring. Heat to the scalding point but do not let them boil. Place pickles in hot sterile jars. Seal jars and process in boiling water bath, page 748, for 15 minutes.

SACCHARIN PICKLES
4 Quarts

♦ Please read About Pickling Equipment and Ingredients, page 781.
Scrub, dry and pack in sterile jars:
    16 cups small cucumbers

Mix but ♦ do not heat:
    1 teaspoon saccharin
    3 tablespoons mixed spices
    1 tablespoon powdered alum
    1 gallon cider vinegar
    2 tablespoons dry mustard
    ¾ cup salt

Pour this mixture over pickles and seal and store in a dark place.

MUSTARD PICKLE OR CHOW CHOW
About 6 Quarts

♦ Please read About Pickling Equipment and Ingredients, page 781.
    This formula meets with such enthusiastic approval that we are often tempted to abandon all other mixed pickle recipes.
Slice, unpeeled if tender:
    1 quart or more green cucumbers

Cover for 12 hours with:
    10% Brine, page 525

Drain well. Slice to make 4 quarts, including cucumbers, but keep all the vegetables separate:
    Green vegetables: green tomatoes,
    snap or wax beans, etc.

If the vegetables are not very young, parblanch them, page 132. Pour over the vegetables to cover:
    Boiling salted water: 1 teaspoon salt
    to 1 quart water

and bring to the boiling point. Drain well. Peel and slice:
    2 dozen small onions

Break into florets:
    1 large cauliflower

Slice:
    2 dozen or more small pickled gherkins

Keep them separate. Pour boiling salted water over them. Bring to the boiling point. Drain well. Combine all vegetables. Prepare the following mustard sauce in an enamel pan.
Combine and stir until smooth:
    1½ cups flour
    6 tablespoons dry mustard
    1½ tablespoons turmeric
    2 cups mild cider vinegar

Bring ♦ just to the boiling point:
    2 quarts malt cider vinegar
    2½ cups sugar

3 tablespoons celery seed

Slowly add the flour mixture, stirring constantly. When the sauce is smooth and boiling combine it with the drained vegetables. Add if needed:
    Salt

Place pickles in sterile jars and seal. Process in boiling water bath, page 748, for 15 minutes.

CURRY SAUCE PICKLE
About 8 Quarts

♦ Please read About Pickling Equipment and Ingredients, page 781.
Peel and chop fine:
    12 large green cucumbers
    6 large onions
    2 sweet red peppers

Sprinkle these ingredients with:
    ¼ cup coarse salt

Let stand refrigerated for 3 hours. Drain, rinse, and drain again. Peel and stew until soft:
    12 large tomatoes

Combine vegetables and tomatoes. Tie in a bag, add to the above, and ♦ simmer for 30 minutes:
    4 teaspoons curry powder
    2 teaspoons celery seed
    2 tablespoons brown sugar
    2 cups cider vinegar

Remove bag and pack pickles into jars, seal and process for 15 minutes in boiling water bath, page 748.

PICCALILLI
Approximately 5 Quarts

♦ Please read About Pickling Equipment and Ingredients, page 781.
Remove core and seeds and cut into very thin slices or dice:
    4 quarts small green cucumbers

Seed, remove membrane and slice:
    4 medium-sized green peppers

Skin, parblanch for 2 minutes, page 132, and slice:
    4 medium-sized onions

Place these ingredients for 12 hours in:
    10% Brine, page 525

Drain well. Bring ♦ just to the boiling point:
    1 quart cider vinegar
    4½ cups sugar

Place in a bag and add:
    2½ tablespoons whole mixed spices
    ½ tablespoon celery seed
    ½ tablespoon mustard seed

Add the drained vegetables. Bring to the boiling point. Remove spices. Place pickles in sterile jars, seal and process for 15 minutes in boiling water bath, page 748.

GREEN TOMATO PICKLE
OR RELISH
About 6 Quarts

♦ Please read About Pickling Equipment and Ingredients, page 781.
Wash and cut into thin slices:
    1 peck green tomatoes

Peel, cut into thin slices and add:
   12 large onions
Sprinkle with:
   1 cup coarse salt
Let mixture stand for 12 hours. Wash in clear water and drain. Heat to the boiling point:
   3 quarts cider vinegar
Seed, remove membranes and add:
   12 green peppers, sliced thin
   6 sweet diced red peppers
Add:
   12 minced cloves garlic
   4 lbs. brown sugar
Add the tomatoes and onions. Tie in a cloth bag and add:
   2 tablespoons dry mustard
   2 tablespoons whole cloves
   2 sticks cinnamon
   2 tablespoons powdered ginger
   1 tablespoon salt
   1 tablespoon celery seed
♦ Simmer until tomatoes are transparent, about 1 hour. Stir frequently. Place pickles in sterile jars and seal. A fan writes that he puts the finished product in his ϒ blender for a second or two to make his favorite relish.

TART CORN RELISH
                                            About 6 Pints
♦ Please read About Pickling Equipment and Ingredients, page 781.
Cut the kernels from:
   18 ears corn
Or, if you should want to make this in winter, use canned or frozen kernel corn.
Put through a food grinder:
   1 head green cabbage
   8 white onions
   **6 green peppers, seeds
      and membranes removed**
   6 small hot red peppers
Combine these ingredients with the corn and:
   2 teaspoons celery seed
   2 teaspoons mustard seed
   2 quarts vinegar
   ¼ cup salt
   2 cups sugar
   (1 cup flour)
   (⅓ cup minced pimiento)
Bring ♦ just to the boiling point and simmer the relish for 35 minutes. Place in sterile jars, seal, and process for 15 minutes in boiling water bath, page 748.

PICKLED ONIONS
♦ Please read About Pickling Equipment and Ingredients, page 781.
Cover with water:
   Small white onions
Add:
   **1 tablespoon coarse salt
      to every quart water**
Let the onions soak for 2 hours. Remove outer skins. Soak onions for 48 hours in:
   10% Brine to cover, page 525
Drain well. Bring ♦ just to the boiling point:

White vinegar
To each gallon vinegar add:
   1 cup sugar
Add onions and ♦ simmer for 3 minutes. Place at once in sterile jars. Cover with the vinegar. Add to each quart jar:
   ½ inch long red hot pepper pod
   ⅛ bay leaf
   (3 cloves without heads)
Seal and process for 30 minutes in boiling water bath, page 748.

CHILI SAUCE
                                            About 4 Quarts
♦ Please read About Pickling Equipment and Ingredients, page 781.
Wash, peel and quarter:
   1 peck tomatoes: 8 quarts
Put through a food grinder:
   **6 green peppers with membranes
      and seeds removed**
   1 tablespoon dried hot pepper pods
   6 large skinned white onions
Add the tomatoes and:
   2 cups brown sugar
   3 cups cider vinegar
   3 tablespoons coarse salt
   1 tablespoon black pepper
   1 tablespoon allspice
   1 teaspoon ground cloves
   **1 teaspoon each ginger,
      cinnamon, nutmeg and celery seed**
   (2 tablespoons dry mustard)
♦ Simmer these ingredients slowly until thick, about 3 hours. Stir frequently to prevent scorching. Add salt if needed. Put sauce in ♦ small sterile jars. Seal tightly and store in cool, dark place.

TOMATO CATSUP
                                            About 5 Quarts
This condiment originated in Malaya, and its name derives from the native word for "taste." No other as familiar an American food seems to have so many variations in spelling.
♦ Please read About Pickling Equipment and Ingredients, page 781.
Wash and cut into pieces:
   1 peck tomatoes: 8 quarts
Add:
   8 medium-sized sliced onions
   **2 long red peppers without seeds
      or membranes**
♦ Simmer these ingredients until soft. Rub through a food mill. Add:
   ¾ cup brown sugar
Tie in a bag and add:
   **1 tablespoon each whole allspice,
      cloves, mace, celery seed
      and peppercorns**
   2 inches stick cinnamon
   ½ teaspoon dry mustard
   ½ clove garlic
   1½ bay leaves
The spices may be varied. Boil these ingredients quickly, stirring often. ♦ Continue to stir until the quantity is reduced to ½. Remove the spice bag. Add:

2 cups cider vinegar
    (Cayenne and coarse salt)
♦ Simmer the catsup for 10 minutes longer. Pour at once into sterile bottles. Cork bottles and seal with sealing wax.

PICKLED HORSERADISH
Wash well in hot water:
    Horseradish roots
Scrape off the skin. Have ready in a glass or stainless steel bowl a combination of:
    2 cups vinegar
    1 teaspoon salt
Grate or mince the scraped roots and pack into sterile jars. Cover well with the vinegar mixture. Seal and store in a cool place.

PICKLED NASTURTIUM PODS
♦ Please read About Pickling Equipment and Ingredients, page 781.
Use these as a variation for capers.
After the blossoms fall, pick off the miniature:
    Nasturtium seed pods
For 3 days, changing daily, soak them covered with:
    10% Brine, page 525
Drain and drop them into boiling:
    Pickling vinegar, page 495
Store covered in sterile jars in a cool place.

CHILIS PRESERVED IN SHERRY
Make up this combination and use either the chilis or the sherry for flavoring. The mixture will keep for years if sherry or peppers are replenished as needed.
Wash well:
    Long thin red chili peppers
Pack tightly into sterile jars. Cover with:
    Dry sherry
Store covered in a cool dark place.

PICKLED WATERMELON RIND
                        About 5 Quarts
Good used in fruit cakes, if drained.
♦ Please read About Pickling Equipment and Ingredients, page 781.
Cut before peeling and remove the green skin and pink flesh from:
    Rind of 1 large watermelon:
    about 5 quarts
Dice the rind in 1 inch cubes. Parblanch it, page 132, until it can be pierced with a fork, ♦ but do not overcook. Drain. Make and bring ♦ just to a boil a sirup of:
    7 cups sugar
    2 cups vinegar
    ¼ teaspoon oil of cloves
    ½ teaspoon oil of cinnamon
When just boiling, pour it over the rind, making sure the rind is covered. Let stand overnight. Remove rind. Reboil sirup and pour over rind. Let stand overnight as before. On the third morning pack the rind in sterile jars. Boil sirup again and pour over rind to overflowing. Seal and store in a cool place. The flavor of this pickle may be varied by placing in each jar:

    (A star anise)
    (1 to 2 teaspoons chopped preserved ginger or Candied Lemon Peel, page 742)

PICKLED DUTCH CHERRIES
♦ Please read About Pickling Equipment and Ingredients, page 781. During processing this method needs an even temperature under 80°.
Stem, seed and put in a heavy crock:
    Sour cherries
Cover with:
    Distilled white vinegar
Let stand 24 hours. Drain. Measure cherries and have ready an equal amount of:
    Sugar
Arrange in the crock alternate layers of cherries and sugar. Let stand 1 week, covered and weighted. ♦ Stir well daily. Ladle into sterile jars and process in boiling water bath, page 748, for 15 minutes. Store well covered in a cool dark place.

PEACH OR MANGO CHUTNEY
                        6 or 7 Quarts
♦ Please read About Pickling Equipment and Ingredients, page 781.
Rub the fuzz from, wash, pit and dice:
    30 firm peaches
or use a combination of:
    15 peeled tropical mangoes and
    8 medium papayas
Mix with:
    3 tablespoons chopped preserved ginger
    ¾ cup chopped citron
    ¼ cup chopped candied lemon peel or
    ½ cup chopped preserved kumquats
Tie in a bag the following whole spices:
    2 cinnamon sticks
    30 whole cloves
    ¾ teaspoon coriander seeds
Make a sirup of:
    6 cups sugar
    4 cups cider vinegar
When the sirup ♦ just boils add the chopped fresh and candied fruits and the spice bag. Simmer for 5 minutes. Remove spice bag. Put mixture into sterile jars, seal and process for 15 minutes in boiling water bath, page 748.

INDIAN RELISH
                        About 4 Quarts
♦ Please read About Pickling Equipment and Ingredients, page 781. Put through a food chopper or chop until very fine:
    12 green tomatoes
    12 peeled cored tart apples
    3 peeled onions
Boil:
    5 cups vinegar
    5 cups sugar
    1 teaspoon red pepper
    3 teaspoons ginger
    1 teaspoon turmeric
    1 teaspoon salt
Add the chopped ingredients. ♦ Simmer for ½ hour. Pack the relish in sterile jars.

Seal and process for 15 minutes in boiling water bath, page 748.

APPLE OR GREEN TOMATO CHUTNEY

I.   **About 1½ Quarts**
♦ Please read About Pickling Equipment and Ingredients, page 781.
♦ Simmer until the fruit is tender:
    1 seeded chopped lemon
    1 skinned chopped clove garlic
    5 cups firm peeled chopped apples
        or green tomatoes
    2¼ cups brown sugar
    1½ cups seeded raisins
    3 oz. chopped crystallized ginger,
        or ¾ cup fresh ginger root
    1½ teaspoons salt
    ¼ teaspoon cayenne
    2 cups cider vinegar
    (2 chopped red peppers, seeds
        and membranes removed)
Put the chutney in sterile jars and seal them.

II.   **About 1½ Quarts**
Similar to the preceding recipe--but with onions and tomatoes added.
Combine, and ♦ simmer slowly for 3 hours:
    2 cups chopped seeded raisins
    2 cups chopped slightly underripe
        green apples
    1 cup minced onions
    ¼ cup coarse salt
    6 medium-sized ripe, skinned,
        quartered tomatoes
    3½ cups brown sugar
    1 pint cider vinegar
    4 oz. white mustard seed
    2 oz. preserved ginger
    3 chili peppers
Place in sterile jars, seal and store in a cool dark place.

SPICED PEARS
                                        About 3 Pints
♦ Please read About Pickling Equipment and Ingredients, page 781.
    If you are using Bartlett or similar soft pears, choose rather underripe fruit, and prepare as for Brandied Peaches, below. If you are using Kiefer, Seckel or other hard pears, prepare as follows:
Wash, peel and core:
    3 lbs. pears
Cook them ♦ covered until they begin to soften in:
    1½ cups boiling water
Tie in a cloth bag:
    6 cinnamon sticks, 3 inches long
    2 tablespoons whole cloves
    2 teaspoons whole ginger
and ♦ simmer for 5 minutes with:
    2 cups sugar
    1 cup pickling vinegar, page 495
Add the partially tenderized pears and the liquid in which they were cooking. Simmer with vinegar sirup for 3 minutes. Re-

move and discard spice bag. Pack fruit into sterile jars and cover with the sirup. Seal jars and process in boiling water bath for 15 minutes, page 748. Store in a cool dark place.

BRANDIED PEACHES
Select ripe, firm:
    Peaches
Weigh them. Rub away fuzz with a coarse towel.
Make a thick sirup of equal parts of:
    Sugar and water—allow 1 cup
    sugar and 1 cup water for every
    lb. of fruit
♦ Simmer the peaches in the sirup for 5 minutes. Drain and place in sterile jars, page 747. Pour over each jar:
    2 to 4 tablespoons brandy
Pour the sirup over the fruit, filling the jars. Seal and process in boiling water bath for 15 minutes, page 748. Store in a cool dark place 3 months before using.
For other liqueur-flavored fruits, see page 108.

ABOUT LONG-BRINE AND SOUR PICKLING

If produce is soaked for a long enough period at proper temperatures, a mere brine will suffice to preserve it. The salt solution draws from the vegetables soaked in it both moisture and certain natural sugars and these combine to form an acid bath which "cures" the produce, making it friendly to beneficial ferments and strong enough to resist the organisms that cause spoilage in food. Pickles subjected simply to the long-brine process and held at 86° from 2 to 6 weeks, turn, after appropriate seasoning, into "dill" types: "kosher" and non-kosher, see below. They may be de- salted and further processed in a vinegar solution at 126° for 12 hours to make sour pickles and then in a sugar solution to be- come sweet-sours.
    To learn the details for these long and exacting processes, read "Making Fer- mented Pickles," in the U.S.D.A. Farmer Bulletin, 1438.

DILL OR KOSHER DILL PICKLES
                                        About 7 Pints
This dill pickle-making procedure differs from that for long-brined pickles. The brine is weaker and the curing more rapid but the pickles do not keep as well, espe- cially if home-processed. We suggest using a heated brine. Garlic, like all members the onion family, is very susceptible to bac- terial activity, so be sure to remove the garlic cloves before sealing the jars. Wash thoroughly and cut in half lengthwise:
    4 lbs. cucumbers
Combine and heat to the boiling point:
    3 cups white vinegar
    3 cups water
    ⅓ cup salt

f you want **Kosher Dills,** add:
  12 peeled sliced garlic cloves
/hen the boiling point is reached ♦ re-
nove the garlic cloves. Pack the cucum-
ers into hot sterile jars. Add to each jar:
  2 tablespoons dill seeds
  3 peppercorns
ill the jars to within ½ inch of the top
ith the hot pickling liquid. Immediately
ljust lids. Be sure to use a glass-disked
p, see page 747. Seal and process in
>iling water bath for 10 minutes, see
ige 748.

BOUT BRINING VEGETABLES

sufficient salt is used to brine vege-
bles, no fermentation occurs, and no fur-
er processing is necessary. But in brining
getables the United States Government
commends, without exception, a final
ocessing for 30 minutes in a boiling wa-
r bath, page 748.
Before tasting or eating non-acid brined
getables, follow the same precautions as
r non-acid canned vegetables. ♦ Boil un-
vered for 15 minutes. Stir frequently dur-
g this period.

UERKRAUT

lease read About Pickling Equipment
d Ingredients, page 781.
2 gallon crock holds about 15 pounds of
ut. Choose sound, mature heads of:
    Cabbage
e:
  1 lb. salt for 40 lbs. cabbage or 2
    teaspoons salt for 1 lb. cabbage
move outside leaves, quarter heads, and
out cores. Slice the cabbage fine into
inch shreds and mix with salt. Pack

firmly in stone crocks to within 2 inches of
top. Cover with clean cloth and a plate, or
any board except pine. Place a weight on
the plate—heavy enough to make the brine
come up to the cover and wet the cloth.
When fermentation begins remove the
scum daily and place a clean cloth over
the cabbage. Wash the board daily, too.
The best quality kraut is made at a temperature below 60°, requiring at least a
month of fermentation. It may be cured in
less time at higher temperatures, but the
kraut will not be as good. If sauerkraut
turns tan, too much juice has been lost in
the fermenting process. When fermentation has ceased, store the kraut in a cool
place after sealing by either of the following methods:
Simply pour a layer of hot paraffin over
the surface of the crock; or, for greater
effectiveness, ♦ heat kraut to simmering
temperature, about 180°; pack firmly in
hot jars; add sufficient kraut juice or a
weak brine, 2 tablespoonfuls salt for 1
quart water, to cover, leaving ½ inch head
space; and process in boiling water bath,
page 748, 25 minutes for pints, 30 minutes
for quarts. ♦ Cook the sauerkraut, uncovered, 15 minutes before serving, page
746.

ABOUT DRY-SALTING VEGETABLES

Pack in a crock:
    Mushrooms, beans, herbs
    or other vegetables
in very thin layers well separated between
½ inch layers of:
    Rock salt
Cover the crock tightly and store in a cool
dark place. ♦ Cook the vegetables uncovered 15 minutes before serving.

INDEX

"Knowledge," said Dr. Johnson, "is of two kinds. We know a subject as our own, or we know where we can find information on it." Below we put into your hands the second kind of knowledge—a kitchen-door key which will help to open up the first.

If you want information on a certain food you will find that the initial listing is often an "About": giving characteristics, peculiarities of handling, tests for doneness, storage needs and serving quantities. The titles which follow usually indicate how that particular food may be cooked: Sweetbreads, braised, or Fish, broiled.

In using the Index look for a noun rather than an adjective: Torte, almond, not Almond Torte; unless the modifying term is a foreign one, in which case it will be listed and lead you to an explanation. Foreign terms are frequently translated in an alternate title, thus: Pickled Fish or Escabèche, revealing a process; or, as in Senegalese or Chicken Curry Soup, showing the ingredients mainly responsible for the term. Or the recipe itself will clear your doubts—for "à la mode" used with a savory food like beef will describe a stew, whereas with a sweet one, like pie or cake, it will indicate the expected scoop of ice cream. Since cooking terms, both foreign and domestic, are dealt with at the point of use, as described above, we have dispensed with a separate glossary.

Remember, too, that the book as a whole divides into three sections: The Foods We Eat, The Foods We Heat and the Foods We Keep, with Know Your Ingredients at the center of things. And that many "convenience" recipes are grouped under Lunch, Brunch and Supper Dishes. Within chapters, too, initial text or recipes often cover basic methods of preparation, and are followed, as in Fruits, Fish and Vegetables by alphabetical listings of varieties—from Apples to Rhubarb, Carp to Whale, Artichokes to Water Chestnuts. Under Meats you will find in the Index general comments and processes, with further references to Beef, Veal, Lamb, Pork, Ham, Ground and Variety Meats and Game. In this chapter a further differentiation is made between those cuts cooked by dry heat—often a quick process—and those cooked by moist heat which, to be effective, are always slower. Note, too, that in the listings below, illustrations can be found immediately by looking up the boldface numerals.

As you familiarize yourself with the "Joy" you will need the Index less and less and will become, in Dr. Johnson's fullest sense, a know-it-all. Meanwhile, happy hunting!

℗